THE ANCHOR BIBLE REFERENCE LIBRARY

A MARGINAL JEW

RETHINKING

THE HISTORICAL JESUS

VOLUME THREE

COMPANIONS AND COMPETITORS

JOHN P. MEIER

ABRL

Doubleday

NEW YORK   LONDON   TORONTO   SYDNEY   AUCKLAND

THE ANCHOR BIBLE REFERENCE LIBRARY

PUBLISHED BY DOUBLEDAY
a division of Random House, Inc.
1540 Broadway, New York, New York 10036

The Anchor Bible Reference Library, Doubleday, and the portrayal
of an anchor with the letters ABRL are trademarks of
Doubleday, a division of Random House, Inc.

LIBRARY OF CONGRESS CATALOGING-IN-PUBLICATION DATA
Meier, John P.
A marginal jew : rethinking the historical Jesus /
John P. Meier.—1st ed.
v. [1–2–3] ; maps ; 24 cm.—(The Anchor Bible
reference library)
Includes bibliographical references and index.
Contents: v. 1. The roots of the problem and the person—
v. 2. Mentor, message, and miracles—
v. 3. Companions and competitors.
1. Jesus Christ—Historicity.   2. Jesus Christ—Jewishness.
I. Title.   II. Series
BT303.2 .M465   1991
232.9—dc20   91-10538
ISBN 0–385–49663–4 (v.3)

Imprimatur—New York, May 17, 2001—The Most Rev. Robert A. Brucato, V.J.

IN MEMORIAM

ELIZABETH O'REILLY MEIER
RAYMOND EDWARD BROWN
JOHN JOSEPH O'CONNOR

בלע המות לנצח
Isaiah 25:8

Contents

Acknowledgments

In this third volume of *A Marginal Jew,* thanks must go first of all to the patient readers who have waited so long for this third installment of the series. Right after them must come the various doctors and surgeons who have seen me through a number of serious illnesses and operations that were a major reason why the appearance of this volume has been so long delayed. To the doctors who arranged and performed major surgery on my back I owe a special debt of gratitude. That I can sit at my computer and type these words in comfort is all their doing.

As with the first two volumes, a word of thanks is likewise due to my academic colleagues, whose number has happily multiplied because of my move from the Catholic University of America in Washington, DC, to the University of Notre Dame in Indiana—the move being another reason for the delay in completing this volume. Among my friends at Catholic University, I owe special thanks to Professors Christopher T. Begg, Joseph A. Fitzmyer, John P. Galvin, Francis T. Gignac, David W. Johnson, William P. Loewe, and Frank J. Matera. Among my new colleagues at Notre Dame, who have been most welcoming and helpful to a refugee from the Northeast Corridor, special thanks are due Professors David E. Aune, Joseph Blenkinsopp, John C. Cavadini, Lawrence S. Cunningham, Josephine M. Ford, Mary Catherine Hilkert, Robert A. Krieg, Blake Leyerle, Hindy Najman, Jerome H. Neyrey, Thomas F. O'Meara, Hugh R. Page, Michael A. Signer, Gregory E. Sterling, Robert E. Sullivan, Eugene C. Ulrich, and James C. VanderKam. To them must be added all the administrators, librarians, and research assistants who have selflessly and sometimes anonymously aided my work. Among my former students and research assistants, I would like to thank in particular Michael Anderson, David G. George, Sejin Park, and Eric C. Stewart.

I have also profited a great deal from the publications and at times the personal advice of the large number of academics writing in the field of Jesus research. Among the many who could be named, I would like to single out

Professors Dale C. Allison, James D. G. Dunn, Bart D. Ehrman, Paula Fredriksen, Daniel J. Harrington, Elizabeth A. Johnson, E. P. Sanders, Jacques Schlosser, and N. T. Wright. In the year 2000, I had the privilege of exchanging views with Professors Dunn, Harrington, Johnson, and Sanders during a colloquium held by the Sea of Galilee in Israel.

As with the first two volumes, I have profited immensely from the writings and advice of distinguished Jewish scholars, especially Professors Shaye J. D. Cohen, Louis H. Feldman, and Jacob Neusner, in addition to my two Jewish colleagues on the Theology Faculty of Notre Dame, Professors Najman and Signer. Needless to say, my thanks must not be construed as a claim that these or any other scholars named above necessarily agree with my views. I must take final responsibility for the positions adopted here, as well as for any errors of fact or interpretation.

As always, I owe a special debt of gratitude to the general editor of the Anchor Bible Reference Library, Professor David Noel Freedman, whose tireless editorial eye has prevented me from committing any number of embarrassing errors. Among the editors at Doubleday, I wish to recognize especially Mark Fretz and Andrew Corbin. For their quiet but important personal support, I must thank Mr. and Mrs. Robert McQuie.

Grateful acknowledgment is given for the reprint of the substance of the material originally presented in the following journals: "The Circle of the Twelve: Did It Exist during Jesus' Public Ministry?" *JBL* 116 (1997) 635–72; "The Debate on the Resurrection of the Dead: An Incident from the Ministry of the Historical Jesus?" *JSNT* 77 (2000) 3–24; "The Historical Jesus and the Historical Samaritans: What Can Be Said?" *Bib* 81 (2000) 202–32; "The Historical Jesus and the Historical Herodians," *JBL* 119 (2000) 740–46.

A
MARGINAL
JEW

VOLUME THREE

JESUS THE JEW IN HIS RELATIONS TO OTHER JEWS

I. THE FOCUS OF VOLUME THREE: JESUS THE JEW IN HIS RELATIONSHIPS TO OTHER JEWISH INDIVIDUALS AND GROUPS

The patient readers of the first two volumes of *A Marginal Jew* embarked upon a carefully mapped-out journey from preliminary and general questions about the historical Jesus to more particular and concrete conclusions about this enigmatic Jew.[1] With unperturbed pace they moved from an initial survey of method and sources, through the beginnings of Jesus' life and ministry, to major sayings and actions of his public career. After Volume One of *A Marginal Jew* had sketched the background, chronology, and early years of Jesus, Volume Two focused on key sayings and deeds of Jesus: his proclamation of the kingdom of God, both future and present, and his performance of startling deeds that he and his disciples considered miracles. This focus on Jesus' message and miracles was an intense but narrow one. With the one exception of Jesus' mentor, John the Baptist, Volume Two aimed the spotlight squarely at Jesus himself, Jesus alone, Jesus reflected in his most typical message and most astonishing actions.

This preliminary narrow focus in Volume Two was a necessary step, since the very meaning of the central symbol "kingdom of God" is disputed, and since Jesus' supposed miracles are the most controversial of all his deeds. But now it is time to widen the circle of light around Jesus. No human being is

1

adequately understood if he or she is considered in isolation from other human beings. A human being becomes fully human only by entering into dynamic relationships of friendship and love, enmity and hate, control, subordination, and collaboration with other humans.[2]

If this be true of human beings in general, it is all the more true of a charismatic religious leader whose very status and impact are determined by his social relationships. It is especially true of a particular 1st-century Jew named Jesus of Nazareth, whose adult life is largely defined in terms of his relationships to other individuals and groups in Palestine.[3] The adult Jesus first comes into view as he joins a particular eschatological group marked by baptism and repentance, a group led by a strange individual called John the Baptist.

Drawing some disciples from this group, Jesus soon struck out on his own with a new message of God's imminent yet present kingdom, a message addressed to all Israel. Moving from town to town in an itinerant ministry, Jesus attracted inner and outer circles of followers from among his fellow Jews. He convinced at least some people that he had healed their illnesses and expelled their demons. He engaged in religious disputes with other devout Jews, and he presumed to teach his coreligionists how to observe the Mosaic Law properly. Within his own circle he taught his disciples special prayer forms, observances, and beliefs that marked them off as an identifiable group within 1st-century Palestinian Judaism.

His ministry was also striking in that it attracted an unusual following from among women of both high and low social status and included convivial fellowship with such social and religious "low-life" as toll-collectors and "sinners." Still, not all of Jesus' contacts were so happy. In the end, his more negative relationships proved deadly. The priestly aristocracy in Jerusalem, headed by Caiaphas, decided he was dangerous; and Pontius Pilate, the Roman prefect, decided he was dangerous enough to crucify.

The point of this thumbnail sketch of Jesus' public ministry is to underline a simple truth. To tell the story of Jesus is to tell the story of his various relationships: his relation to individuals like Peter or Judas, to groups of followers like the disciples or the Twelve, and to Jewish movements like the Pharisees or the Sadducees. It is this defining web of relationships that we will examine in Volume Three, a web of relationships that all too often has been neglected in recent work on the historical Jesus. Perhaps Americans love a story about a solitary hero struggling against the evil forces of society. Or perhaps the American media simply cannot handle all the complexities of the historical Jesus. Or perhaps the popular American religious spirit does not like a historical Jesus who creates embryonic structures like the circle of the Twelve. Whatever the reason, the full range of Jesus' relationships with Jewish groups and individuals has not been a central concern of the type of Jesus research lionized in recent years by the American media. Volume Three seeks to correct the imbalance.

Moreover, Volume Three's emphasis on Jesus' relationships is inextricably interwoven with a second key emphasis, likewise neglected in some recent works on the historical Jesus: the essentially Jewish nature of these relationships. Strange to say, in recent years, a number of authors engaged in the Third Quest for the historical Jesus have been noteworthy for their lack of focus on the Jewishness of Jesus and his relationships with other Jews. This is extremely odd, considering the origins of the Third Quest in the 1970s and 1980s. When the Third Quest was launched, one of the main characteristics that distinguished it from the First Quest of 19th-century German Protestantism and the Second (existentialist) Quest of the students of Rudolf Bultmann in the 1950s and 1960s was its determination to take the Jewishness of Jesus with utter seriousness and to situate him squarely within Palestinian Judaism at the turn of the era. Both Geza Vermes in England and E. P. Sanders in North America trumpeted this new emphasis with the titles of their books. Indeed, Vermes' trilogy sounds—quite rightly—like a Jewish anvil chorus: *Jesus the Jew, Jesus and the World of Judaism,* and *The Religion of Jesus the Jew.*[4] For his part, E. P. Sanders summarized his entire program with the succinct phrase *Jesus and Judaism,* while James H. Charlesworth offered the friendly amendment of *Jesus within Judaism.*[5]

Such was the promise of the Third Quest at its beginnings. It has continued to be honored by some scholars, such as Dale C. Allison, Bart D. Ehrman, Paula Fredriksen, and Bruce Chilton on this side of the Atlantic and Jürgen Becker, N. T. Wright, and Jacques Schlosser on the other.[6] Yet, especially among certain authors now or formerly connected with the Jesus Seminar, emphasis on the Jewishness of Jesus is hardly a central concern. Whether one looks at the more serious works of writers like John Dominic Crossan and Burton L. Mack or the sensationalistic popular works of authors like Robert W. Funk, one finds Jesus the Cynic philosopher or Jesus the generic Mediterranean peasant or Jesus the social revolutionary or Jesus the religious iconoclast largely overshadowing if not obliterating the specific 1st-century Palestinian Jew named Jesus.[7] To be sure, words like "Jew" and "Jewish" often adorn titles or subtitles of such works, and politically correct comments are made about the importance of Jesus' Jewishness. But in most of these books, one searches in vain for detailed treatments of the various religious movements competing for influence in 1st-century Palestine (e.g., the Pharisees, Sadducees, and Essenes) and of the ways in which Jesus the Jew interacted with or reacted to them as he debated questions of Jewish practice and belief. One sees, then, why the double concern of Volume Three—the varied relationships that defined Jesus and the essentially Jewish nature of these relationships—needs a thorough airing.[8]

II. A ROAD MAP FOR THE JOURNEY THROUGH VOLUME THREE

The first two volumes of *A Marginal Jew* sought to lay the groundwork for this pivotal examination of Jesus the Jew and his Jewish relationships. Part Two of Volume One, "The Roots of the Person" (1. 205–433), offered a preliminary and inevitably rough sketch of Jesus' immediate familial relations as well as the linguistic, cultural, and political context in which he grew up in lower Galilee in the early years of the 1st century A.D. Volume Two brought the question of relationships into the public ministry by focusing on (1) Jesus' relationship to his mentor, John the Baptist (2. 19–233), (2) his relationship to all Israel as he presented himself to it as the eschatological prophet proclaiming the imminent-yet-present kingdom of God (2. 237–506), and (3) his relationship to a great Jewish symbol, the miracle-working prophet Elijah, on which he seemed quite consciously to have patterned a good part of his ministry (2. 509–1038).

Still, despite these initial intimations of relationships that help define Jesus, most of the first two volumes remained focused on Jesus himself: *his* familial and cultural origins, *his* core message of the kingdom, *his* startling deeds, which both he and his followers interpreted as miracles. Only at the end of these two volumes, after a preliminary rough portrait of this particular 1st-century Jew has been sketched,[9] can we now begin to widen the spotlight to include the Jewish individuals and groups that were interacting with him as he traveled about Galilee and Judea proclaiming his message of the kingdom and engaging in faith-healing. As the spotlight widens, many interrelated questions emerge: Who traveled with Jesus on these journeys? Did they do so simply of their own volition or at his bidding? Did his traveling companions constantly come and go, or was there some relatively stable group of core adherents such as the Twelve? Were all his adherents as itinerant as he was, or were there stay-at-home adherents who formed something of a support system for the itinerant Jesus and for those who followed him literally rather than figuratively? Did Jesus the eschatological prophet interact publicly with other major Jewish groups in Palestine, notably the Pharisees, Sadducees, and Essenes? Or was he interested in forming a relatively closed, sectarian group, in some ways not unlike Qumran? If there was public interaction with other groups, where did it take place—Galilee, Jerusalem, or both venues? Were the exchanges mostly positive or negative in tone?

These are the types—though not a complete list—of questions that Volume Three will seek to answer in order to make "Jesus the Jew" something more than a politically correct slogan. The varied and complicated Jewish relationships defining Jesus will help put flesh and blood on the somewhat skeletal figure sketched in the first two volumes. To provide order—hopefully, not an entirely arbitrary order—to the complicated tangle of Jesus' relationships, I have chosen to divide Volume Three into two parts: (1) Jesus' relationships with his Jewish followers of various types and (2) Jesus' relationships with the competing Jewish groups or movements in the Palestine of his day.[10]

Part One, which treats Jesus' relationships, conflictual as well as amicable, with his various types of "followers" (a problematic category in itself), arranges the swirling and no doubt overlapping clusters of followers into three concentric circles: (1) the outer circle of the crowds that followed Jesus in a physical sense (Chapter 24),[11] (2) the middle circle of the disciples whom Jesus called to follow him in both a physical and a spiritual sense (Chapter 25), and (3) the inner circle of the Twelve, specifically chosen by Jesus to symbolize his mission to the twelve tribes of Israel and to share in his mission to all Israel (Chapter 26). Fortunately for us, a few members of the Twelve, notably James and John, the sons of Zebedee, and Simon Peter, had memorable personal encounters with their leader. Hence we can give greater precision and depth to the portrait of Jesus by focusing on his relationships with some key individuals in his entourage (Chapter 27). Through all this, it is important to remember—and I will stress the point more than once—that this neat pattern of three concentric circles is a useful academic model, not without a basis in reality, but hardly reflecting what was surely a more fluid and complicated situation. As shall be noted in the treatment of the disciples, certain groups like the stay-at-home supporters, who did not give up family and employment, and the female followers do not fit comfortably into this tripartite construct.

Part Two of this volume explores the other side of Jesus' relationships. Obviously, no great historical figure, especially the leader of a group or movement within a larger society, can be adequately understood simply by examining those who followed or agreed with him or her. Competitors, opponents, or debating partners of the leader are just as—if not more—important for a full portrait. Hence Part Two considers major Jewish groups or movements that competed for influence or power (political, religious, or both) among Palestinian Jews in the early 1st century A.D. Religious as well as political influence was a highly contested commodity in 1st-century Jewish Palestine. The very fact that Jesus sought to persuade his fellow Jews to accept his message and follow his lead inevitably put him into competition with other religious and/or political groups. This holds true whether Jesus personally engaged in controversy with members of these groups (as seems to be the case with the Pharisees and the Sadducees) or competed for adherents from a physical as well as an ideological distance (as was probably the case with the Qumranites).

No doubt most prominent among Jesus' competitors were the Pharisees, if for no other reason than that they, like Jesus, were active among the common people and frequently won their respect if not their wholehearted compliance. Because of their special position among the common people, the Pharisees were to prove vital for the survival and future shape of Judaism. The great problem here is that the exact origins, nature, beliefs, and practices of the Pharisees are a hotly contested area among scholars today, Jew and Gentile alike. Hence to treat the problem of the *historical* Jesus in his relation to the *historical* Pharisees demands a lengthy disquisition into the practices and beliefs of the Pharisees. This quest for the historical Pharisee takes up a good deal of Chapter 28, which also faces the further complication that the Pharisees may have been inserted secondarily into dispute stories in which the antagonists of Jesus were originally anonymous.

But at least there is a fair amount of Gospel material about the Pharisees. Much sparser is the presence of the Sadducees in the Gospels. This stands to reason, since the rich, aristocratic Sadducees, to a great degree of priestly stock and concentrated in Jerusalem, were not actively competing for esteem and influence among the common people in the same way the Pharisees were. Hence they would not have interacted with Jesus as frequently as the Pharisees did. More problematic still is the fact that, having left no self-description or literature of their own, the Sadducees have been fated to be described only by their opponents. Yet, despite their shadowy nature and their rare appearances in the New Testament, something can be said about their interaction with Jesus, thanks to the curious dispute over the general resurrection of the dead preserved in Mark 12:18–27 parr. (Chapter 29). Insofar as many chief priests were probably Sadducean in their sympathies, the group will return, though under a different rubric, when we come to Jesus' arrest and execution in Volume Four.

Once we get past the Pharisees and the Sadducees, things become more confusing still, for we are left with a number of marginal groups of Israelites (Chapter 30). In some cases, any direct interaction between these groups and

Jesus is either highly questionable or quite limited. Here in Chapter 30—by way of a "mop-up" operation—I include the hotly debated question of the Essenes in general and Qumranites in particular, as well as a potpourri of groups whose relationship to the historical Jesus turns out to be slight or nonexistent: Samaritans, scribes, Herodians, and Zealots.

With these scattered groups we complete our survey of the various clusters of Jews who either did interact or may have interacted with Jesus during his public ministry. It is sobering to realize that often we are left with generalizations about generic groups. Personal ongoing relationships with named individuals like Simon Peter, James and John, or Mary Magdalene are few and far between—and are found almost entirely on the side of followers rather than competitors and opponents. Not until we reach the end of Jesus' career are we able to name individual opponents who both interact with Jesus and are known from sources outside the New Testament: Annas, Caiaphas, and Pilate.

As we go through this survey of various Jewish groups at the time of Jesus, we should remember that probably the vast majority of ordinary Jews in Palestine belonged to no one of the groups described above. The majority of Palestinian Jews were happy to practice the basics of their religion: circumcision, Sabbath observance, food laws, and pilgrimage to the Jerusalem temple (when possible) for the great feasts, which were celebrated according to the commonly—but not universally—accepted religious calendar inculcated by the priestly aristocracy. Whatever their personal feelings toward an Annas or a Caiaphas, they looked to the high priest presiding in Jerusalem as the divinely constituted leader and representative of their nation, just as they looked to the temple he controlled as the concrete center of their religion. As for esoteric disputes over the fine details of legal observance, they had neither the leisure, the learning, nor probably the interest that fired the zeal of competing religious groups.

Together with such nonsectarian groups as the Pharisees and the Sadducees,[12] these ordinary observant Jews made up what various scholars call "mainstream" or "common" Judaism in 1st-century Palestine (and also in the Diaspora).[13] This concept of mainstream Judaism should not be confused with the erroneous idea that there was some monolithic "normative" or "orthodox" Judaism at the time. Judaism even within Palestine was remarkably varied in belief and practice. Placing both the Pharisees and the Sadducees in this "mainstream" Judaism is meant to underline that point. Both groups as well as the mass of ordinary Jews belonged to a broad if not easily defined mainstream that held to the basic practices and beliefs of the Jewish religion, e.g., monotheism, God's choice of Israel as his special people, God's gift of the Mosaic Law, circumcision, Sabbath, and the food laws. Mainstream Judaism looked to the Jerusalem temple as its cultic center and the priestly aristocracy as its religious leaders, and (despite many internal disputes) it did not formally break away from this center and this leadership in favor of some sectarian movement—as did, for instance, Qumran. It was this mainstream Judaism of Palestine that Jesus the Jew addressed, wooed, and warned. Indeed, it was from this mainstream Judaism that Jesus emerged, and it was in relation to this Judaism that Jesus defined his special role.

If Jesus arose from and defined himself vis-à-vis mainstream Judaism, in what sense, then, should or could he be considered "a marginal Jew"? Regrettably, and contrary to my express intention as laid out in Volume One,[14] some critics have taken the phrase "a marginal Jew" to be my set definition of Jesus rather than my refusal to give a set definition. As I stressed when I introduced the phrase in Volume One, "a marginal Jew" is meant to imitate the riddle-speech of Jesus himself (just think of Jesus' use of Son of Man). Far from presenting a Cartesian clear and distinct idea of Jesus, "a marginal Jew" is intended to open up a set of questions. Indeed, sociologists themselves use "marginal" in a number of different ways.[15] The first and most important meaning I give the term as applied to Jesus underlines the simple fact that, as far as Jewish and pagan literature in the century after Jesus' death was concerned, Jesus was at most a "blip" on the radar screen. The person who was to become the religious center of European civilization started out so far on the periphery as to be barely visible. That paradox, if nothing else, is what the label "marginal" is meant to underline for the reader.

Other meanings, however, need to be probed further. In some of his teachings and practices, from rejection of voluntary fasting and divorce to symbolic warnings of the temple's destruction, Jesus seemed intent on marginalizing himself, at least from the center of power in Jerusalem, if not from more pious Jews as well. In the end, Caiaphas and Pilate marginalized him with the shameful death of crucifixion. What must be stressed in these and other possible meanings of "marginal" is that in no way is the term intended to deny, attenuate, or call into question the essential Jewishness of Jesus. To take a rough analogy: in one sense, the Qumranites had been pushed to the margins, socially and politically, by the rulers in Jerusalem; in another sense, the Qumranites had willfully marginalized themselves vis-à-vis what they saw as an apostate Israel. Yet no one would question the intense and profound Jewish nature of the Qumran community. As we shall see, Jesus was quite a different type of Jew from the average Qumranite. Yet both persons embodied in starkly different ways the paradox of an individual who was intensely Jewish and yet was marginalized by or from the institutionalized centers of Jewish power. We will be exploring aspects of this paradox in this present volume, but a final balance sheet must await the end of the story in Volume Four.

III. A REMINDER ABOUT THE RULES OF THE ROAD

The methodology governing *A Marginal Jew* was laid out in Part One of Volume One (pp. 1–201) and summarized at the beginning of Volume Two (pp. 4–6). But even the voracious minds that digested the 1,482 pages (!) of text and notes in the first two volumes might welcome a brief reminder of the goal of this work and the method by which we move toward that goal.

The goal of this work is a reasonably reliable sketch of the historical Jesus. No sooner is that deceptively simple statement made than a warning must be added: the "historical Jesus" is not to be naively identified with the total reality of Jesus of Nazareth, i.e., all that Jesus thought, said, did, and experienced during his lifetime, or even just during his public ministry. The totality of Jesus' life, or even simply a reasonably complete account of his life, is impossible to reconstruct today, given the vast gap in time and the sparse sources available.[16]

In contrast to the "real Jesus," the "historical Jesus" is that Jesus whom we can recover or reconstruct by using the scientific tools of modern historical research. The "historical Jesus" is thus a scientific construct, a theoretical abstraction of modern scholars that coincides only partially with the real Jesus of Nazareth, the Jew who actually lived and worked in Palestine in the 1st century A.D.

If the historical Jesus is not the real Jesus, neither is he the "theological Jesus" investigated by theologians according to their own proper methods and criteria. In other words, the quest for the historical Jesus must be carefully distinguished from christology, i.e., systematic theological reflection on Jesus Christ as the object of Christian faith. To illustrate what a *historical* as distinct from a *theological* investigation of Jesus must involve, I have proposed the fantasy of the "unpapal conclave": a Catholic, a Protestant, a Jew, and an agnostic—all honest historians cognizant of 1st-century religious movements—are locked up in the bowels of the Harvard Divinity School library, put on a spartan diet, and not allowed to emerge until they have hammered out a consensus document on Jesus of Nazareth.

An essential requirement of this document would be that it be based on purely historical sources and arguments. Its conclusions would have to be open to verification by any and all sincere persons using the means of modern historical research. No doubt, such a consensus document would suffer from a narrow focus, a fragmentary vision, perhaps even some distortions. It certainly would not claim to present a complete, let alone ultimate and definitive, interpretation of Jesus, his work, and his intentions.[17] Nevertheless, at least it would provide an academically respectable common ground and starting point for dialogue among people of various faiths or no faith.

To give one concrete example of what this would involve: the unpapal conclave—or just about any quester for the historical Jesus—could agree that Jesus "was crucified under Pontius Pilate and suffered death." Although these words happen to be those of the so-called Nicene-Constantinopolitan Creed of the Catholic Church, drawn up at the second ecumenical council (Constantinople I, in A.D. 381), they are nevertheless, when taken in isolation, a sober statement of historical fact. They are affirmed or intimated by Josephus and Tacitus as well as by many various streams of New Testament traditions. One does not have to be a believer to affirm this short narrative of events. What the unpapal conclave—or any historian operating *simply as a historian*—could not affirm is a slightly longer form of the quotation from the same creed: namely, that Jesus *"for us human beings and for our salvation* descended from heaven . . . , was crucified under Pontius Pilate *for our sake,* [and] suffered [death]."[18] The "for us human beings," "for our salvation," and "for our sake" are all expressions of Christian faith and christology, affirming the saving effect of Jesus' life and death. Unlike the plain affirmation of Jesus' crucifixion and death under Pontius Pilate, this longer statement is not in principle open to empirical investigation and verification by any neutral observer. Hence it is not a statement that falls under the purview of or that can be affirmed by questers for the historical Jesus in their capacity as historians—though some questers, if they are Christians, will believe on other grounds that the statement is true.[19]

To move from definitions to sources: as Volume One showed, there are very few sources for knowledge of the historical Jesus beyond the four canonical Gospels. Paul and Josephus offer little more than tidbits. Claims that later apocryphal Gospels and the Nag Hammadi material supply independent and reliable historical information about Jesus are largely fantasy.[20] In the end, the historian is left with the difficult task of sifting through the four Gospels for historical tradition. The task is difficult indeed, for these documents are all products of Christian churches in the second half of the 1st century A.D. Written some forty to seventy years after Jesus' death, they are shot through with Christian faith in Jesus as the risen Lord of the church. Hence, only a careful examination of the Gospel material in the light of the criteria of historicity (i.e., rules for judging what is historical) can hope to yield reliable results.

In the quest for the historical Jesus, five criteria have proved especially useful:

(1) The criterion of *embarrassment* pinpoints Gospel material that would hardly have been invented by the early church, since such material created embarrassment or theological difficulties for the church even during the NT period (e.g., the baptism of Jesus by John). To take an example that we shall see in Volume Three: the criterion of embarrassment argues that various unchaperoned women did in fact travel with the celibate Jesus and his male disciples on various preaching tours in Galilee.

(2) The criterion of *discontinuity* focuses on words or deeds of Jesus that cannot be derived either from the Judaism(s) of Jesus' time or from the early church (e.g., Jesus' rejection of voluntary fasting). To take an example from Volume Three: in Mark 12:26, in the dispute with the Sadducees over belief in the general resurrection of the dead, Jesus' curious appeal to Exod 3:6 ("I am the God of Abraham, and the God of Isaac, and the God of Jacob") is discontinuous vis-à-vis both rabbinic and early Christian arguments in favor of the resurrection.

(3) The criterion of *multiple attestation* focuses on sayings or deeds of Jesus witnessed in more than one independent literary source (e.g., Mark, Q, Paul, or John) and/or more than one literary form or genre (e.g., sayings of Jesus about the cost of discipleship plus narratives about his peremptory call of various disciples). For example, that Jesus forbade divorce is supported by the independent witness of Mark, Q, and Paul. That Jesus was reputed in his own lifetime to have given sight to the blind is supported by a saying in Q and by narratives in both Mark and John. To take an example from Volume Three: that Jesus had a disciple named Simon who also received the second name or nickname *Kēpāʾ* (= Cephas, Peter, "the Rock") is attested by Mark, John, special Matthean tradition, special Lucan tradition, and Paul in Galatians and 1 Corinthians.

(4) The criterion of *coherence* is brought into play only after a certain amount of historical material has been isolated by other criteria. The criterion of coherence holds that sayings and deeds of Jesus that fit in well with the preliminary "data base" established by the other criteria have a good chance of being historical. To take an example from Volume Three: Jesus' creation of an inner circle of twelve disciples, symbolizing the twelve patriarchs and/or tribes of Israel, coheres with Jesus' view of himself as the eschatological, Elijah-like prophet sent to regather all Israel in the last days.

(5) Instead of judging individual sayings or deeds of Jesus, the criterion of *Jesus' rejection and execution* looks at the larger pattern of Jesus' ministry and asks what words and deeds fit in with and explain his trial and crucifixion. A Jesus whose words and deeds did not threaten or alienate people, es-

pecially powerful people, is not the historical Jesus. To take an example from Volume Three: Jesus' ability to draw large, enthusiastic crowds, especially when on pilgrimage to Jerusalem for the great feasts like Passover, helps explain why Caiaphas and Pilate would have increasingly considered him a dangerous figure who was best eliminated before he posed a major threat to public order.

Various secondary criteria may also be invoked, but usually only as "back-up" or confirmation for the primary criteria. These secondary (some would say dubious) criteria include traces of the Aramaic language in the sayings of Jesus and echoes of the early 1st-century Palestinian environment in which Jesus lived. Still weaker as criteria (some would say useless) are the vivid and concrete nature of a narrative and the supposed general tendencies of the Synoptic tradition as it develops.

Given the difficulty involved in articulating and applying these criteria, it is not surprising that some scholars brush aside the whole question of method and criteria. They prefer to "muddle through." [21] Yet every scholar engaged in the quest for the historical Jesus is de facto operating with some method and criteria, however inchoate and unexamined. The danger in "muddling through" is that one easily begins to draw from the data the conclusions one wants rather than the conclusions the data warrant. The importance of criteria applied methodically to the data is that they can force the quester to draw conclusions he or she has not foreseen and perhaps does not desire.

For instance, it was the weight of evidence rather than personal desire that constrained me to judge that the famous "You are Peter" text of Matt 16:18–19 represents post-Easter tradition and not words of the historical Jesus spoken during his public ministry. By the same token, the weight of evidence led me to affirm the basic historicity of Jesus' argument with the Sadducees over the resurrection of the dead, even though originally I had doubted the historical nature of this particular dispute story. In sum, my own experience throughout the writing of these three volumes has convinced me that, while methodology and criteria may be tiresome topics, they are vital in keeping the critic from seeing in the data whatever he or she has already decided to see. The rules of the road are never exciting, but they keep us moving in the right direction. It is now time for us to move in the direction of Jesus' relationships with his Jewish followers and his Jewish competitors.

NOTES TO THE INTRODUCTION

¹ John P. Meier, *A Marginal Jew. Rethinking the Historical Jesus. Volume One: The Roots of the Problem and the Person* (Anchor Bible Reference Library; New York: Doubleday, 1991); *A Marginal Jew. Rethinking the Historical Jesus. Volume Two: Mentor, Message, and Miracles* (Anchor Bible Reference Library; New York: Doubleday, 1994).

² This insight is hardly unique to the quest for the historical Jesus. It is a commonplace, for instance, in phenomenology; see, e.g., Edith Stein, *On the Problem of Empathy* (Washington, DC: ICS, 1989; German original, 1917) 88, 116. Stein builds on the work of Max Scheler, *The Nature of Sympathy* (New Haven: Yale University, 1954; 5th ed. of the German original, 1948).

³ This point has often been made by Ben Witherington III in his various books. See, e.g., *The Christology of Jesus* (Minneapolis: Fortress, 1990) 24–25; *The Jesus Quest* (Downers Grove, IL: InterVarsity, 1995) 35–36. For one way of defining terms like "group" and "movement" from a sociological perspective, see Anthony J. Saldarini, *Pharisees, Scribes and Sadducees in Palestinian Society. A Sociological Approach* (Wilmington, DE: Glazier, 1988) 309–14. Granted the limited and fragmentary nature of our sources, terms like "group" and "movement," as applied to the followers of Jesus, must inevitably remain vague. For the perennial problem of how to define "sect," see n. 12 below.

⁴ *Jesus the Jew* (Philadelphia: Fortress, 1973); *Jesus and the World of Judaism* (Philadelphia: Fortress, 1983); *The Religion of Jesus the Jew* (Minneapolis: Fortress, 1993). The present author finds some comfort in the fact that the volumes appeared at ten-year intervals.

⁵ E. P. Sanders, *Jesus and Judaism* (Philadelphia: Fortress, 1985). Many of the insights of his massive study *Judaism. Practice & Belief 63 BCE–66 CE* (London: SCM; Philadelphia: Trinity, 1992) have been incorporated into his more popular presentation, *The Historical Figure of Jesus* (London: Penguin, 1993). James H. Charlesworth's basic overview, *Jesus within Judaism* (Anchor Bible Reference Library; New York: Doubleday, 1988), has been supplemented by many other books written or edited by him. Collections of essays edited by him include *Jews and Christians. Exploring the Past, Present, and Future* (New York: Crossroad, 1990) and *Jesus' Jewishness* (New York: Crossroad, 1991).

⁶ Dale C. Allison, *Jesus of Nazareth Millenarian Prophet* (Minneapolis: Fortress, 1998); Bart D. Ehrman, *Jesus Apocalyptic Prophet of the New Millennium* (Oxford: Oxford University, 1999); Paula Fredriksen, *Jesus of Nazareth, King of the Jews* (New York: Knopf, 1999); Bruce Chilton, *Rabbi Jesus* (New York: Doubleday, 2000); Jürgen Becker, *Jesus of Nazareth* (Berlin/New York: de Gruyter, 1998); N. T. Wright, *Jesus and the Victory of God* (Minneapolis: Fortress, 1996); Jacques

Schlosser, *Jésus de Nazareth* (Paris: Noesis, 1999). Needless to say, these authors differ widely among themselves when it comes to understanding *what kind of Jew* Jesus was. On the debate about what sort of Jew Jesus was, see the observations of Mark Allan Powell, *Jesus as a Figure in History* (Louisville: Westminster/John Knox, 1998) 169–72; Powell's book provides a useful overview of the positions of some major scholars engaged in the Third Quest. A briefer overview is offered by Craig A. Evans, "The Third Quest of the Historical Jesus: A Bibliographical Essay," *Christian Scholar's Review* 28 (1999) 532–43; see also the methodological reflections of Joel B. Green, "In Quest of the Historical: Jesus, the Gospels, and Historicisms Old and New," ibid., 544–60.

[7] See, among the many volumes that have flowed from present or former members of the Jesus Seminar, the following representative works: John Dominic Crossan, *The Historical Jesus. The Life of a Mediterranean Jewish Peasant* (San Francisco: Harper, 1991); idem, *Jesus. A Revolutionary Biography* (San Francisco: Harper, 1994); Burton L. Mack, *A Myth of Innocence* (Philadelphia: Fortress, 1988); Robert W. Funk, *Honest to Jesus* (San Francisco: Harper, 1998); Robert W. Funk et al., *The Five Gospels* (New York: Macmillan, 1993).

[8] Perhaps one can surmise from a certain rule of inverse proportion why both Jesus' specific Jewishness and his specific relationships to other individual Jews and Jewish groups have been neglected in some recent works: to the extent that this double focus is ignored, Jesus becomes a convenient ideological stick figure, sociological model, Jungian archetype, or mere cipher onto which any desired program or agenda can be projected. My primary interest in this question is, as always in this book, historical, not theological. For brief reflections on some of the theological ramifications of the Jewishness of Jesus, see my article, "The Present State of the 'Third Quest' for the Historical Jesus: Loss and Gain," *Bib* 80 (1999) 459–87.

[9] See the brief sketch at the end of *A Marginal Jew,* 2. 1039–49.

[10] As we shall see, at times this generic rubric has to be stretched. For instance, to what degree or in what sense the 1st-century Samaritans could be considered "Jewish" is still debated among experts today. See my treatment of the Samaritans in Chapter 30.

[11] The reader is reminded that the chapters are numbered consecutively throughout the whole series of *A Marginal Jew,* starting with Volume One. The advantage of this approach is that, for example, Chapter 2 can refer to only one chapter in the entire work, not to different chapters in different volumes.

[12] In this context I understand "sectarian" along the lines of the definition suggested by Shaye J. D. Cohen (*From the Maccabees to the Mishnah* [Library of Early Christianity 7; Philadelphia: Westminster, 1987] 125): "A small, organized group that separates itself from a larger religious body and asserts that it alone embodies the

ideals of the larger group because it alone understands God's will." Neither the Pharisees nor, a fortiori, the Sadducees separated themselves bodily from the mainstream Judaism that located its spiritual center in the Jerusalem temple. The Qumranites did.

[13] On the concept of "common Judaism," see Sanders, *Judaism. Practice & Belief,* 47–303. I incline to this view rather than to that of Roland Deines, who seeks to rehabilitate the phrase "normative Judaism" in the sense that the pre-70 Pharisees were recognized by ordinary Palestinian Jews to embody normative Judaism; see his *Die Pharisäer* (WUNT 101; Tübingen: Mohr [Siebeck], 1997) 534–55. On the position of Deines, see my review essay, "The Quest for the Historical Pharisee," *CBQ* 61 (1999) 713–22.

[14] The reader must pardon me for repeating here what I thought was clearly stated on pp. 6–9 of Volume One. The fact that some critics have misunderstood or garbled my position forces me to exegete the obvious.

[15] See, e.g., Janice E. Perlman, *The Myth of Marginality* (Berkeley/Los Angeles/London: University of California, 1976).

[16] For an understanding of the "real Jesus" that moves in the theological and christological rather than the historical realm, see Luke Timothy Johnson, *The Real Jesus* (San Francisco: Harper, 1996); cf. his *Living Jesus* (San Francisco: Harper, 1999). For example, on p. 142 of *The Real Jesus,* Johnson states that "the 'real Jesus' for Christian faith is the resurrected Jesus. . . ." I have no problem with such a definition when one is operating in the realm of faith and theology; see, e.g., *A Marginal Jew,* 1. 197. But, as I point out in that passage, there is another sense of "real," proper to modern historical investigation (cf. *A Marginal Jew,* 1. 21–24), which Johnson seems unwilling to affirm in the special case of Jesus of Nazareth.

[17] Not unlike the formatting of hard disks in computers, which allows various levels of formatting, the writing of history and biography, while always interpretive to some degree, allows various levels of interpretation. The very gathering of data and the passing of judgment as to their historicity involve a certain "low level" of interpretation. Beyond that unavoidable low level, *A Marginal Jew* attempts as much as possible to let any overarching interpretation of Jesus and his work emerge gradually and naturally out of the convergence of the data judged historical. In particular, *A Marginal Jew* does not intend to impose on the data any predetermined interpretive grid, be it political, economic, or sociological. Such grids can be useful at a later stage of interpretation, but in the quest for the historical Jesus they neither generate data concerning Jesus nor solve the problem of the data's historicity. To be sure, *A Marginal Jew* works with presuppositions, but they are the general presuppositions of historiography.

[18] The key phrases (including the words affirming the soteriological effect of Jesus' death) are in Greek *ton di'hēmas tous anthrōpous kai dia tēn hēmeteran sōtērian*

katelthonta ek tōn ouranōn . . . staurōthenta te hyper hēmōn epi Pontiou Pilatou kai pathonta. . . . A slightly expanded version of this creed is regularly used at Sunday Mass in Roman Catholic churches.

[19] For recent debates on the relation of the historical Jesus to Christian faith and christology, see the overview by William P. Loewe, "From the Humanity of Christ to the Historical Jesus," *TS* 61 (2000) 314–31.

[20] The arguments supporting this position are given in *A Marginal Jew*, 1. 112–66.

[21] Geza Vermes proclaims his disdain for "methodology" and his preference for "muddling through" in *The Religion of Jesus the Jew* (Minneapolis: Fortress, 1993) 7. The problem is, though, that any scholarly investigation that is not totally erratic operates by certain rules, whether or not they are acknowledged, labeled, and thought through. The danger of not thinking through one's method and criteria becomes evident almost immediately in Vermes' work. (1) He implicitly works with the criterion of multiple attestation of sources, but does not use the criterion properly. For example, to show that Jesus was observant of the cultic law, Vermes (p. 18) states that "all three Synoptic Gospels report that after curing a leper, he [Jesus] enjoined him to appear before a priest for examination"; Mark 1:44 is cited as evidence. Yet, in the judgment of most commentators, the Matthean and Lucan versions of the story are simply their theological adaptations of the Marcan story. There is, then, only one independent source attesting to the historical event. The Matthean and Lucan parallels certainly attest to what Matthew and Luke thought about Jesus, but they supply no independent evidence as to the historicity of the event. (Even if one preferred the view that Mark depended on Matthew, there would still be only one independent source.) (2) Vermes also uses something like a combination of the criteria of embarrassment and discontinuity (p. 17). However, when using such a criterion, one must be very careful in appealing to rabbinic material. Unfortunately, Vermes is disconcertingly free and easy in using not only the Mishna (redacted ca. A.D. 200) but also the Tosefta, the various midrashim and targums, and even the Jerusalem Talmud (redacted in the first half of 5th century) and the Babylonian Talmud (redacted in the first half of the 6th century, achieving its final form in the 8th century). The problem of using rabbinic material to understand Judaism(s) in the early 1st century A.D., a problem highlighted by the works of Jacob Neusner in particular, is not taken seriously (pp. 7–10). In contrast, see the careful weighing of the question—though hardly with agreement on all sides—in E. P. Sanders, *Jewish Law from Jesus to the Mishna. Five Studies* (London: SCM; Philadelphia: Trinity, 1990); idem, *Judaism. Practice & Belief*; Craig A. Evans, "Mishna and Messiah 'In Context': Some Comments on Jacob Neusner's Proposals," *JBL* 112 (1993) 267–89; and, in reply to Sanders and Evans, Jacob Neusner, "Mr. Sanders' Pharisees and Mine," *SJT* 44 (1991) 73–95; idem, "The Mishna in Philosophical Context and Out of Canonical Bounds," *JBL* 112 (1993) 291–304.

PART ONE

JESUS THE JEW AND HIS JEWISH FOLLOWERS

CHAPTER 24

JESUS IN RELATION TO HIS FOLLOWERS

The Crowds

I. INTRODUCTION: FINDING THE PROPER LABEL

No sooner do we turn to the task of trying to describe the various relation-ships of the people around Jesus than we run into a problem of terminology. We must deal with very different groups, from committed disciples through mildly sympathetic audiences to merely curious crowds. What umbrella term can we use to refer to all of these people? Almost automatically we tend to speak vaguely of the "followers" of Jesus, however strong or tenuous that "following" may be.

We should realize, though, that the noun "followers," used as an umbrella term, is a label we bring to the Gospel texts rather than one we find there. To be sure, the Gospels freely use the verb "to follow" *(akoloutheō)* when de-scribing various individuals and groups around Jesus. But the Gospels never use the corresponding noun "follower" *(akolouthos)*.[1] Nor is the use of the participial form of the verb "to follow" *(ho akolouthōn)* a frequent substi-tute for the noun "follower."[2] John 8:12 is a rare case of the participle used in that way: "The one following me shall not walk in darkness but shall have the light of life."

The purely metaphorical use we see in John 8:12 is also relatively rare in the Gospels.[3] More commonly, the verb "to follow" is used in the Gospels of those who in one way or another literally, physically, follow Jesus. In the case of a curious, miracle-seeking crowd, the following may be little more than physical. Indeed, the evangelists seem to imply at times that such following is equivalent to pseudo-discipleship (e.g., John 6:2,26,66). A similar ironic sense may be detected when Peter follows Jesus to the high priest's palace after the arrest in Gethsemane (Mark 14:54 parr.), only to wind up denying him. Nevertheless, in the case of people specifically called "disciples," especially the particular group called the Twelve, the physical act of following usually expresses an inner adherence to the person and message of Jesus. In brief, then: at various points in the Gospels, the verb "to follow" may connote mere physical motion (e.g., Mark 14:13; John 11:31),[4] physical movement toward Jesus that is equivalent to pseudo-discipleship (e.g., Mark 14:54), physical motion expressing inner adherence to Jesus (e.g., Mark 1:18; 2:14; Matt 8:19,22; John 1:43), and in relatively rare cases (e.g., John 8:12) inner adherence without any physical motion.

In light of these different meanings of the verb in the Gospels,[5] I think it reasonable for us to select the noun "follower" as an umbrella term to cover all the various relationships to Jesus that we will explore in this chapter and the three following. At least we can claim that our use of "followers" reflects the general contours of NT usage. Simply as a matter of fact, in the NT, the verb "to follow" *(akoloutheō)* (1) is relatively rare outside the Gospels (only 11 out of 90 instances),[6] (2) refers in the Gospels almost exclusively to Jesus as the one followed, and (3) covers a spectrum of attitudes among those following him. Hence, while "followers" is *our* generic label—and not the evangelists'—it does have a basis in NT texts.

In what order should we investigate the various types of "following" in the Gospels? One might think at first of starting with the closest circle of committed followers and then moving outward to the less committed. After all, the intent of Part One of this volume is to widen the circle around Jesus. Nevertheless, in this chapter and the three subsequent chapters, it might be wiser to reverse the procedure: i.e., to start with the outermost circle of followers and work inward. In other words, we shall begin with the vague "crowds" found at times around Jesus (Chapter 24), then move closer to examine his "disciples" (Chapter 25) in the intermediate or middle circle, and finally, within the circle of disciples, focus upon the inner circle of the Twelve, first as a group (Chapter 26) and then as individuals (Chapter 27).

The reason for this procedure is that, by moving from the outer to the inner circle of followers, we will be able to progress in orderly fashion from more general to more specific statements. Certain assertions that can be made about any followers, however superficial these followers may have been, would hold true a fortiori of the committed, many of whom may have started out just as members of the crowd. In addition, our procedure has just a slight chance of reflecting the actual evolution of Jesus' followers. It is conceivable that Jesus first attracted various occasional crowds, from which he began to draw more stable disciples, from whom in turn he finally selected a fairly permanent group of twelve followers.

Yet, while this scenario enjoys a certain verisimilitude, we must admit that Mark and John, while disagreeing with each other, both argue against this reconstruction. While differing on the details, both Mark 1:16–20 and John 1:35–51 indicate that Jesus first drew to himself at least a few key disciples, notably Peter and Andrew, before he began to attract large crowds.[7] Be that as it may, our movement from crowds through disciples to the Twelve at least has the methodological advantage of moving slowly from the less detailed to the more detailed.

In brief, then, in moving from one group to another, we imagine the followers of Jesus in terms of concentric circles: the "crowds" form the outer circle, the "disciples" the intermediate or middle circle, and the "Twelve" the inner circle. As we shall see, though, the boundaries between these various groups were hardly set in stone, and not everyone fit neatly into one or the other group. For example, certain committed adherents of Jesus, while generously supporting his movement with hospitality or money, did not follow him around Galilee. Accordingly, they do not appear to have been classified as "disciples" by the Gospels, even though they formed a kind of "support group" for the middle circle. Thus, with the exception of the Twelve, the borders between these groups were probably quite fluid. In particular, movement from the intermediate to the outer circle or from the outer circle to indifference or even hostility would have been both easy and informal since the choice lay entirely with the individuals who found themselves no longer attracted to Jesus. For instance, people who once offered Jesus hospitality or money could cease to do so without any notable repercussions, since their support was entirely voluntary. The Twelve would have been the one group that was fairly fixed because of the set number of members, the special commitment that was required, and the initiative that lay entirely with Jesus.

We begin, then, in this chapter with the outer circle, the amorphous crowds.

II. THE OUTER CIRCLE: THE CROWDS

The outer circle of Jesus' followers, usually labeled "the crowds" (ochloi) by the Gospels,[8] would have been the largest and least stable of the groups following Jesus. But did such crowds exist? Did Jesus actually attract large numbers of people as an audience during his ministry? Or are the crowds simply a stage prop of the evangelists, introduced as both a literary chorus and religious propaganda to stress Jesus' popularity and success? To be sure, no critic would deny that the crowds in the Gospels serve the literary and theological agendas of the evangelists. Being faceless and anonymous, the crowds are convenient empty vessels to be filled with the evangelists' ideas.[9] But do the crowds also reflect, to some extent, historical reality during the ministry of Jesus?

Both the criterion of multiple attestation of sources and forms and the criterion of Jesus' execution argue for the historicity of the claim that Jesus attracted large crowds. As for multiple attestation, not only do all four Gospels frequently affirm the existence of crowds listening to Jesus or seeking miracles from him, the crowds are also mentioned in various Gospel sources and in various Gospel forms. In these various sources, the crowds are often designated by the Greek word *ochlos* (plural: *ochloi*),[10] but other words such as *plēthos* ("multitude," "throng"), *polloi* ("many people"), and *pantes* ("all") are also used.[11] To focus simply on *ochlos* ("crowd"): Mark and John, independent of each other, use *ochlos* 38 times and 20 times, respectively, with both Matthew and Luke adding instances of their own. The vast majority of all these texts use "crowds" to designate the large, undifferentiated mass of people around Jesus. Only rarely is *ochlos* used for smaller, more specific groups.[12]

There is no need to treat in detail all the narratives from different sources that mention a crowd around Jesus. One clear example will suffice. That the presence of the crowds in certain stories goes back to pre-Gospel traditions is obvious from some of the material that Mark and John have in common, notably the story of the feeding of the five thousand. The substance of the story demands the presence of a large group, and in fact both Mark and John, independently of each other, speak of the "crowd(s)" that followed Jesus prior to the feeding. Naturally, the number "five thousand" must be taken with more than a grain of salt, as must many numbers in ancient biblical or Greco-Roman sources. The fact that Mark knew an alternate version of the story that mentioned four thousand instead of five thousand only confirms our caution. Still, as we saw in Volume Two, behind the stories of the feeding of the five thousand or the four thousand probably stands some remarkable symbolic meal that Jesus held with a large group of followers near the Sea of Galilee.[13]

Alongside the many narratives that mention crowds, various sayings in the Gospels affirm or presuppose a large crowd around Jesus. In a few cases, the saying is on the lips of the disciples, not Jesus. To take one example: the woman with the hemorrhage is able to touch Jesus' garment without being seen because of the large crowd surging around him.[14] When Jesus asks who touched him, the disciples naturally but not very reverently object (Mark 5:31): "You see the crowd pressing upon you, and [yet] you say, 'Who touched me'?" Interestingly, in the Marcan version of the story, Jesus keeps looking around to see who touched him, but cannot identify the person, presumably because of the size of the crowd (v 32). In the end, the woman comes forward to confess what she has done (v 33).

At other times the words of Jesus himself bespeak or presuppose a crowd around him. At the beginning of the story of the feeding of the four thousand, Jesus says (Mark 8:2): "I feel compassion for the crowd because it has stayed with me for three days." In the Q tradition (Matt 11:20–24 ‖ Luke 10:12–15), Jesus excoriates various towns that witnessed his miracles and yet refused to accept his message: "Woe to you Chorazin, woe to you Bethsaida . . . and you Capernaum. . . ." The woes presuppose that Jesus' miracles and call to repentance were aimed at these cities as a whole. His complaint makes little sense unless at least some of his miracles and preaching took place before fairly large audiences.

The Q document contains roughly three occurrences of the word *ochlos*.[15] Since Q is basically a collection of sayings, one is surprised to discover that two mentions of the crowds are found in the narrative framework of Q rather than in the sayings of Jesus. When Jesus exorcises a mute demoniac, the Q tradition states: "The mute spoke, and the crowds marveled" (Matt 9:33 ‖ Luke 11:14; cf. Matt 12:23).[16] In the second "Baptist block" in Q, after the envoys of John the Baptist leave Jesus, we are told that "Jesus began to speak to the crowds" about the Baptist (Matt 11:7 ‖ Luke 7:24).[17]

Besides Mark, John, and Q, crowds also appear in material peculiar to either Matthew or Luke (e.g., Matt 7:28; Luke 11:27), though controlling the data is more difficult in the case of special M or L tradition. Moreover, one must admit that it would have been quite natural for the evangelists to introduce crowds either at the beginning of some of Jesus' sayings to specify his audience or at the end of some of his miracles to provide an approving chorus. In fact, we need only compare parallel verses of Mark and Matthew to verify that some of the occurrences of the noun "crowds" are redactional.[18] Hence I do not claim that every mention of crowds in the four Gospels—or even in the examples presented above—is necessarily historical. Nonetheless, the presence of crowds in all the Gospel sources (Mark, John, Q, M, and L) as well as in both narrative and saying traditions more than satisfies the criterion of multiple attestation. There are sufficient grounds for asserting that Jesus regularly attracted crowds.

The Gospels, however, do not supply the only evidence for this conclusion. Fortunately, we have here a rare case where multiple attestation extends beyond the Gospels to Josephus. In his brief mention of Jesus' ministry in *Ant.* 18.3.3 §63, Josephus states that Jesus "gained a following both among many Jews and among many of Greek origin." As we saw in Volume One, the reference to "many of Greek origin" is most likely a typical example of anachronism in Greco-Roman historians: Josephus, publishing *The Jewish Antiquities* ca. A.D. 93–94, reads the success of the Gentile mission at the end of the 1st century back into the life of Jesus.[19] However, precisely because by the end of the 1st century the tide was running against any great success by Christians in their attempt to win over "many Jews," the reference to Jesus' success in attracting many Jews is less likely to be mere anachronism—and, indeed, it coincides with what the Gospels portray.[20]

The argument from multiple attestation is bolstered by the argument from coherence with Jesus' death. One of the surest things we know about Jesus is that he was crucified just outside Jerusalem by the Roman prefect Pontius Pilate ca. A.D. 30, most probably on the charge of claiming to be "King of the Jews." How a Jewish preacher, prophet, and healer from Galilee wound up being executed by Romans in Jerusalem because he supposedly claimed to be a king is one of the greatest puzzles that the quest for the historical Jesus must face.[21] But one point is fairly clear. Jesus' crucifixion is much easier to understand if he attracted large, enthusiastic crowds and much more difficult to understand if he was largely ignored by the populace and failed to gain any wide following.

As a matter of fact, various Gospel sources mention that the Jerusalem temple authorities were apprehensive of Jesus' hold on the populace (e.g., Mark 12:12; 14:2; John 11:45-54; Luke 23:5). Some of these formulations may reflect the redactional concerns of the evangelists, but we have something of a parallel phenomenon in Josephus' account of John the Baptist's ministry and death (*Ant.* 18.5.2 §116–119). As we saw in Volume Two, Josephus seems to distinguish between an original, smaller group of devout Jews who were attracted to the Baptist early on and a larger "second wave" of ordinary Jews who began to flock to John and hang on his every word.[22] Fearing that John's influence on this large, enthusiastic audience could lead to revolt, the ever-suspicious Herod Antipas decided to do away with John by a preemptive strike before a real crisis arose. In Josephus' account, then, it is paradoxically the Baptist's success that does him in; the large crowds he draws attract the unhealthy—and finally deadly—attention of the political ruler. In this as in other matters, the Baptist may have been the unwitting forerunner of Jesus.

According to Josephus, neither the Baptist nor Jesus had a monopoly on the dangerous activity of attracting large crowds of enthusiastic followers. In his accounts of the years leading up to the First Jewish War (A.D. 66–70), Josephus mentions various popular religious leaders or "sign prophets," such as Theudas and "the Egyptian false prophet," who provoked military intervention from the Roman authorities. These "sign prophets" seem to have called down Rome's wrath on their heads at least partly because of the large crowds of followers they attracted.[23] Jesus fit into this larger pattern at least to the extent that there probably was some connection between his ability to attract enthusiastic crowds and his violent end.

Indeed, Josephus' brief account of Jesus could be read as intimating a connection between Jesus' success in attracting crowds and his execution—though Josephus does not make the point explicit, as he does in his treatment of the Baptist. Strictly speaking, in the so-called *Testimonium Flavianum* Josephus gives no reason for Jesus' crucifixion. Yet, granted Josephus' way of describing the fates of both the Baptist and the various "sign prophets," it may be significant that Jesus' ability to attract many people is the last thing Josephus says about Jesus before he abruptly begins (with a bare "and" [*kai*]) the sentence mentioning Jesus' crucifixion. To be sure, this is mere inference. At the very least, though, this reading-between-the-lines of the *Testimonium Flavianum* fits in with all the other indicators pointing to a nexus between Jesus' attracting crowds and Jesus' being crucified.

If this be true, then at least one popular presentation of the course of Jesus' ministry must be questioned. All too often it is taken for granted that Jesus' Galilean ministry had a joyous beginning and a disastrous end. According to this scenario, initially the Galilean populace received his message positively. Then, at some critical turning point, this "Galilean spring" came to an abrupt end, many turned away from him, and Jesus began to sense the possibility of his rejection and violent death.[24]

There are a number of problems with this scenario. First, because the succession of events in the public ministry, as presented in each Gospel, is largely the creation of the respective evangelist, we cannot reconstruct an exact "before and after" in the years of the ministry. We simply do not know the order of most of the events between Jesus' baptism and his final days in Jerusalem.[25] The scenario of the "Galilean spring," which demands this kind of detailed knowledge, is the product of an arbitrary harmonization of bits and pieces from a number of Gospels, thus creating a story witnessed by no one Gospel.

Second, the idea of a critical turning point in the Galilean ministry, after which many former followers abandon Jesus, largely results from treating the climax of the Bread of Life Discourse in John's Gospel (chap. 6) as though it were a videotaped replay of historical events.[26] John 6:66 tells us that the response of many to Jesus' Bread of Life Discourse was negative: "From that time onward many of his disciples turned back [i.e., departed from Jesus' company] and no longer walked with him [i.e., accompanied him as disciples]."[27] As Raymond E. Brown and other Johannine commentators have pointed out, we probably have in this verse a reflection not of events in Jesus' lifetime but rather of a conflict involving the Johannine community later in the 1st century.[28] The conflict may have involved a schism within the Johannine community when most of the community left the Jewish synagogue while some Jewish Christians stayed behind. Or possibly the conflict involved a later schism, when certain Christians with gnosticizing tendencies withdrew from the Johannine community, at least partly because of a dispute over the eucharist. A third possibility, favored by Brown, is that John 6:66 reflects the conflict between the Johannine community and Jewish Christians whose faith in Christ and/or the eucharist was deemed inadequate.

In any case, granted that the Bread of Life Discourse (John 6:35–58) is a parade example of the Fourth Evangelist's high christology of preexistence and incarnation, and granted that the discourse ends with the most graphically realistic expression of eucharistic theology in the NT (6:53–58: eating the flesh and drinking the blood of the Son of Man), one cannot take the disciples' reaction described in v 66 to be a historical report of the attitude of certain Galilean Jews toward Jesus the Jew ca. A.D. 30. And once John 6:66 is excluded, no other text in the four Gospels points directly to a major defection by disciples in Galilee at a critical turning point in Jesus' ministry.

Indeed, far from suggesting that there was a large-scale desertion of Jesus by former followers sometime during the Galilean ministry, all the data we have reviewed so far would seem to point in the opposite direction. If we accept the fact that all the Gospel sources plus Josephus indicate that Jesus attracted large crowds during his ministry of A.D. 28–30, and if we further accept the likelihood of a connection between this "fatal attraction" and the decision of the authorities to execute Jesus in A.D. 30, the evidence would suggest that Jesus' power to attract crowds must still have been fairly strong toward the end of his ministry. Why a would-be leader who had turned out to be a flop with the populace would have attracted Rome's fatal attention only some time after his influence had waned is difficult to explain.

While I admit that this argument is an indirect one, I think the more probable scenario is that Jesus not only attracted large crowds for a good part of his ministry but also continued to do so up until his arrest.[29] To be sure, one can make only generalizations here: any itinerant preacher will have his successes and his failures with various audiences. But if I were to hazard any guess in the matter—and it can be only a guess—it would be that Jesus' influence was continuing to grow as he undertook his final journey to Jerusalem. Large and enthusiastic crowds in Jerusalem during a feast were a special cause of concern to the authorities, and not without reason. Hence Caiaphas and Pilate—not unlike Antipas dealing with the Baptist—decided at a certain point that it would be unwise to wait until a crisis developed. Once again a preemptive strike solved the problem, or so it seemed.

Admittedly, as with the quest for the historical Jesus so with the quest for the historical crowds, the results are distressingly vague and meager. All the Gospel sources plus Josephus justify our speaking of the large crowds Jesus attracted, but how large is large? Not only do the crowds remain faceless and anonymous, they also remain uncounted. Variations in numbers, variations between Galilee and Judea, variations in social status, variations in the crowds' estimation of Jesus—all these are lacking. This is the constant problem of trying to apply the social sciences to Jesus research. So much of what the social sciences draw upon—statistics, on-site fieldwork, one-on-one in-depth interviews—is absent from the biblical record. Abstract models from the social sciences will not supply concrete data that are otherwise lacking.

To be sure, one can venture some carefully couched generalizations. No doubt the vast majority of the faceless crowds were poor, but since the vast majority of people in 1st-century Palestine could be classified as poor in one sense or another, that does not get us very far. Even in Palestine there were varying degrees of poverty and social insecurity.[30] More to the point, when individuals emerge from the amorphous crowds to interact with Jesus (and therefore gain some personality on the narrative level), we do not find people who are uniformly poor.[31] If for the moment we may take the Gospel narratives at face value, we find Jesus interacting with or granting favors to Levi, a toll collector at Capernaum (Mark 2:13–15); a woman with a hemorrhage who had possessed some wealth but who had spent it all on "many doctors" (Mark 5:25–34); Jairus, the ruler of the synagogue who lives in a multiroom house (Mark 5:21–43); a centurion or royal official in the employ of Herod Antipas (Matt 8:5–13 par.; John 4:46–54); Zacchaeus, the rich toll collector in Jericho (Luke 19:1–10); a woman who is able to buy and then "waste" ointment worth about the annual wages of a day laborer ("more than 300 denarii," Mark 14:3-9 parr.); the anonymous Jerusalem householder who hosts Jesus and his disciples at the Last Supper (Mark 14:12–26 parr.); and the various householders who play host to Jesus and presumably his disciples at festive meals (indicated by the "reclining at table") during the public ministry.

Needless to say, this impression of Jesus hobnobbing with the well-off is more than balanced by the many narratives recounting Jesus' aid extended to lepers (Mark 1:40–45 parr.; Luke 17:11–19), demoniacs (Mark 5:1–20 parr.; 9:14–29 parr.), blind beggars (Mark 10:46–52 parr.; John 9:1–41), and many other poor and afflicted people pushed to the margins of society. I do not dispute for a moment that the majority of the outer circle of followers, the "crowds," were for the most part poor. But we should remember that the Gospel picture is not monochrome. Since the data are both sparse and variegated, sweeping and undifferentiated generalizations are to be avoided. Jesus did concentrate on the "poor" (with all the various meanings that word had in 1st-century Palestine), but he did not do so in the narrow, partisan spirit attributed to him by some streams of liberation theology.

One further generalization can be made about the Gospel portrait of the "crowds": the Gospels do not as a rule equate the crowds with "sinners." This holds true whether we understand "sinners" in terms of Jews who had for all practical purposes apostatized and lived like Gentiles or—in a questionable shift of meaning—whether we understand "sinners" simply to be Jews who did not study the Law zealously and practice it punctiliously. In the Gospels, the "sinners" *(hamartōloi)* are a separate group, sometimes yoked with the toll collectors *(telōnai)*, but never equated with the crowds in general. In my opinion, the "sinners" most likely represent those Jews who rejected the commandments of the God of Israel or in practice adopted Gentile ways—something that is not predicated of the crowds.[32] The crowds in the Gospels are not accused of ignoring or breaking the Mosaic Law or the traditions of the elders. Such accusations are made instead against Jesus and/or his disciples (e.g., Mark 2:23–28; 3:1–6; 7:1–13).[33]

Just as one should not equate the "crowds" in the Gospels with "sinners," so one should not equate them with the group that the Mishna (written down ca. A.D. 200) and later rabbinic literature label "the people of the land" *('ammê-hā'āreṣ)*. In the Mishna, "the people of the land" are ordinary Jews who do not know or at least do not practice the Mosaic Law with the exactitude that the rabbinic authorities desire, especially with respect to purity laws and tithing.[34] As a rule, the Gospels do not describe the "crowds" in such a way that one would identify them with "the people of the land" in this special rabbinic sense found in the Mishna and later literature.

A possible exception to this rule is found in the scornful remark of the Pharisees in John 7:49: "But this crowd that does not know the Law is accursed." Many commentators on John explain the "crowd" in this passage by referring to rabbinic statements about "the people of the land," [35] but one must be wary of identifying these two groups for three reasons:

1. The reference in John 7:49 is not to the common people in general but specifically to the crowd of pilgrims in Jerusalem for the feast of Tabernacles.

2. The disputes among this supposedly "accursed" crowd at the feast do not concern correct interpretation and observance of the rules of purity and tithing in the Mosaic Law but rather the correct interpretation of the person of Jesus, as understood in the light of Scripture. In the context of John 7:40–52, the Pharisees, who reject Jesus' claims, are annoyed that the crowd is fascinated by him and that at least some in the crowd are willing to entertain the notion that Jesus is a prophet or even the Messiah. Such disputes and disagreements over the Messiah do not fit the profile of "the people of the land" in the Mishna. Nothing in John 7 connects the disagreement over Jesus with his teaching on purity laws (notably lacking in John at any rate).

3. We should recognize that here in John 7, as elsewhere in the Fourth Gospel, the crowd acts as a sounding board for the christological revelation of Jesus. Hence it would be unwise to equate this "crowd," a literary and theological mouthpiece created by John, with either the historical crowd that followed the historical Jesus or "the people of the land" mentioned in rabbinic literature. At best, in John 7 we may be overhearing a debate between ordinary Jews and their leaders in the synagogue around the time that John's community broke with Judaism, i.e., in the latter decades of the 1st century A.D. In the whole debate over "the people of the land" in the Gospels or in the ministry of the historical Jesus, it is well to remember the simple fact that the canonical Gospels never use the phrase "the people of the land." Moreover, the few passages in the nonbiblical material from Qumran that use the phrase do not employ it in the special rabbinic sense we find in the Mishna. [36]

In the end, then, we are left with a few basic affirmations about the "crowds" in connection with the historical Jesus: Jesus' ministry of preaching and healing attracted large crowds; this ability to attract crowds seems to have lasted until his final days; paradoxically, his success probably contributed to his arrest and execution by the nervous authorities. Yet, while the crowds following Jesus may have been enthusiastic at times, enthusiasm did not often translate into deep, enduring commitment. Complaints by Jesus himself about "this generation" (e.g., Mark 8:12,38; 9:19; Matt 11:16 par.; 12:38–42 par.) and the unrepentant cities of Galilee (Matt 11:20-24 par.), critical remarks by the evangelists, and the relative failure of Jesus' followers after his death to win over the majority of Palestinian Jews to their new movement all argue that most people in the crowds never crossed the invisible line separating curious or sympathetic audiences from deeply committed adherents (either itinerant disciples or sedentary supporters).

Perhaps the crowds' interest in Jesus and his religious movement was somewhat analogous to the relationship many ordinary Jews had to the Pharisaic movement around the time of Jesus. Ordinary Palestinian Jews may have respected, given a sympathetic ear to, and even been partially influenced by the zealous religious movement of reform and renewal launched by the Pharisees. But that did not mean that they would have joined the movement as full members. It may have been such sympathy-at-a-distance that allowed the Jerusalem church of the first Christian generation to survive amid spasmodic bouts of persecution until the First Jewish War. In the end, as with Jesus so with the original Jerusalem church, it was not the Jewish common people but the Romans, along with certain Jewish leaders, who struck the final, mortal blow.

Of necessity, our observations about the outer circle, the amorphous crowds, have been general and vague. Things become more specific, but much more complicated, as we move to the intermediate or middle circle of the disciples.

NOTES TO CHAPTER 24

[1] Strictly speaking, *akolouthos* is an adjective meaning "following." However, in the masculine it is used in ancient Greek mostly as a substantive, "follower." Interestingly, *akolouthos* never occurs in the NT; the same is true of the abstract nouns for "following," *akolouthēsis* and *akolouthia*. For the religious sense of *akolouthos* in a Jewish-Hellenistic work, see *Ep. Arist.* 240; a critical Greek text with an English translation may be found in Moses Hadas (ed.), *Aristeas to Philocrates (Letter of Aristeas)* (Jewish Apocryphal Literature; New York: Ktav, 1973) 194–95.

[2] The participial form of the verb *akoloutheō* ("to follow") is not all that common in the Gospels to begin with. When it is used, it is not usually employed as a substantive. It most often refers to some individual or group that happens to be following Jesus physically at a given moment in the narrative (e.g., Matt 8:10 par.; Mark 10:32; 11:9).

[3] This is somewhat surprising when one considers that *akoloutheō* was already known as a metaphor for intellectual, moral, or religious "following" in classical sec-

ular Greek. This usage continued in Koine Greek, notably in popular moral philosophy. On this see Gerhard Kittel, *"akoloutheō,"* TDNT 1 (1964) 210–16, esp. 210. One wonders whether the use of *akoloutheō* for following Jesus in the Gospels is somehow connected with the fact that Jesus seems to have consciously patterned himself after the model of the itinerant, miracle-working prophet of northern Israel, Elijah (on this see *A Marginal Jew,* 2. 1041–44). When Elisha is called to follow Elijah in 1 Kgs 19:20, Elisha's promise to follow is expressed with the Hebrew construction *wĕʾēlkâ ʾaḥărêkā* ("and I will come after you"). While *akoloutheō* is not the most common verb used in the LXX to translate this Hebrew construction, it is used here in 3 Kgdms 19:20 (the LXX designation for this passage): *kai akolouthēsō opisō sou.* This construction is rare in the LXX in the sense of eagerly following a human being who is a positively evaluated religious figure. Interestingly, when Josephus recounts the episode in *Ant.* 8.13.7 §354, he uses the simple dative with the verb *(ēkolouthēsan Ēlią).* This is more proper in Greek than the use of the verb with the preposition *opisō* ("after"), which instead reflects the Hebrew construction. The construction with the simple dative is the one regularly found in the Gospels; for rare exceptions see Mark 8:34 (a disputed reading); Matt 10:38.

[4] It is hardly surprising that in the Gospels the rare cases of *akoloutheō* as mere physical motion do not involve movement toward Jesus. In Mark 14:13 par., two of the disciples are ordered by Jesus to follow a man carrying a water jar. In Matt 9:19, we have the special case of Jesus following someone, namely, a ruler who has asked Jesus to raise his dead daughter to life. In John 11:31, the Jews follow Mary, the sister of Lazarus, as she leaves her house to come to Jesus. In John 20:6, Peter follows the beloved disciple to the empty tomb.

[5] For a schematic outline of the various uses of *akoloutheō* in the NT, with relevant passages listed, see Anselm Schulz, *Nachfolgen und Nachahmen* (SANT 6; Munich: Kösel, 1962) 195–96. For a somewhat different interpretation of the data, which claims that, within the Synoptic tradition, the use of *akoloutheō* is not restricted to the relationship of the original disciples to the historical Jesus, but instead is applicable to all Christians, see Heinrich Zimmermann, "Christus nachfolgen. Eine Studie zu den Nachfolge-Worten der synoptischen Evangelien," *TGl* 53 (1963) 241-55.

[6] The verb *akoloutheō* occurs 25x in Matthew, 18x in Mark, 17x in Luke, and 19x in John; in almost all cases Jesus is the one who is followed (for rare exceptions see Mark 14:13; Matt 9:19; John 11:31). The instances of *akoloutheō* outside the Gospels are Acts 12:8,9; 13:43; 21:36; 1 Cor 10:4; Rev 6:8; 14:4,8,9,13; 19:14. None of these eleven instances refers to Jesus during his public ministry. Rev 14:4; 19:14 refer to the exalted, heavenly Christ (the Lamb, the Word of God). The almost total absence of *akoloutheō* in the epistles of the NT is striking; the one case, 1 Cor 10:4, refers to the rock that followed the Israelites in the desert. Acts 12:8,9 refer to Peter following an angel out of prison, while 21:36 refers to a hostile crowd following Paul out of the Jerusalem temple and crying out for his death. Only Acts 13:43 has an echo of the usage in the Gospels: after the meeting of the synagogue at Pisidian Antioch

breaks up, "many of the Jews and of the devout proselytes followed Paul and Bar-nabas." As for compounds of *akoloutheō* in the NT: none of the three occurrences of *exakoloutheō* in 2 Peter (1:16; 2:2; 2:15) refers to Jesus. The same is true of *parakoloutheō* in Mark 16:17; Luke 1:3; 1 Tim 4:6; 2 Tim 3:10; and of *epakoloutheō* in Mark 16:20; 1 Tim 5:10,24; 1 Pet 2:21. First Pet 2:21 alone comes close to Gospel usage when it exhorts Christians to follow *(epakolouthēsēte)* in the footsteps of Christ, who suffered for them.

[7] In saying this, I am well aware that both Mark 1:16–20 and John 1:35–51 are contoured by Mark and John to fit the literary structures and theological programs of their respective Gospels. Granted that fact and the vast differences in the details of the two narratives, it is perhaps all the more striking that the two evangelists agree (multiple attestation of sources) that Jesus attracted to himself a few prominent disciples before he started attracting large crowds and that among these key disciples were Peter and Andrew.

[8] The stock translation "crowd" for the Greek *ochlos* seems justified in almost all of the passages where the word appears in the four Gospels. As we shall see below, the description of the crowd(s) varies from context to context, but the vague translation "crowd" fits nicely the vagueness of the evangelists. One specific nuance of the generic "crowd" in certain Gospel passages is worth noting: "the populace" or "the common people" as distinct from or opposed to the rulers (e.g., Mark 11:18). Quite naturally, this meaning occurs especially in scenes laid in Jerusalem. Two other meanings of *ochlos* are barely possible in a few passages: "rabble," "mob" (e.g., in the contemptuous reference in John 7:49) and "military troops" (e.g., in the arrest scene in Gethsemane in Mark 14:43 parr.). The meaning "annoyance" or "trouble" is not represented in the NT.

[9] The redactional use each evangelist makes of the crowds for his literary and theological purposes is not our concern here. Suffice it to say that Mark makes a firm distinction early on (4:10–12) between (1) the insiders (those "around Jesus with the Twelve," a group that perhaps includes those members of the crowd who have been drawn closer to Jesus to ask further questions), to whom is given the mystery of the kingdom of heaven, and (2) the outsiders (including for the most part the large crowd of 4:1, most of whom are not drawn closer to Jesus to ask further questions), for whom everything takes place in riddles so that they may not see or understand. In Mark, however, as the story progresses, a process of reversal emerges whereby some apparent outsiders become insiders and the privileged insiders are in danger of becoming outsiders. While Matthew keeps and strengthens the basic Marcan distinction between crowds and disciples (Matt 13:10–17: the disciples do see and understand), Matthew presents the crowds as oscillating in their opinion of Jesus during the public ministry, only to coalesce fatally with the Jerusalem authorities to become "all the people" *(pas ho laos)* at Jesus' trial before Pilate (27:25). While likewise keeping Mark's distinction between the disciples and the crowds (Luke 8:9–10, cf. 8:4), Luke, who often interchanges *ochlos* with the religiously colored *laos* ("people"), tends to

present the crowds as at least somewhat sympathetic toward Jesus (note even at the execution of Jesus in Luke 23:48). The same tone of sympathy characterizes the populace in the early days of the Jerusalem church in Acts (e.g., 2:47; 5:13). For Luke, the crowd listens to Jesus and the apostles and in principle is open to conversion; it is a pool of potential disciples. But in its present state (especially during the great journey narrative of Luke 9:51–19:27), the crowd is ambivalent, lacking in understanding, and unrepentant. In general, the Gospel of John does not pay as much attention to the crowd as do the Synoptics. Only in John 6:2–24 do we hear an echo of the Synoptic presentation of the crowd following Jesus around Galilee. Apart from chap. 6, the word *ochlos* is prominent only in chap. 7, which relates Jesus' disputes during the feast of Tabernacles, and in chap. 12, which relates Jesus' final interaction with the populace before his passion. The Johannine crowd sometimes acts as a sounding board for Jesus as he develops his teaching in his discourses. On the whole, the Johannine crowd is befuddled and divided over Jesus. Attracted by his signs and teaching and not hostile in the way the Jerusalem authorities are, it nevertheless lacks true understanding of Jesus' origins "from above," "from the Father." Hence it applies inadequate religious titles and categories to Jesus and so does not come to what the evangelist considers genuine faith in Jesus. Nevertheless, it is striking that John, unlike the Synoptics, never makes the *ochlos* one of the actors in the drama of the Passion Narrative; the *ochlos* disappears after chap. 12. In sum, despite all their redactional differences, the four evangelists usually preserve a basic distinction between the ambivalent crowds and the committed disciples (as well as Jesus' sedentary supporters). On the use of *ochlos* in the Gospels in general, see Rudolf Meyer and Peter Katz, "*ochlos*," *TDNT* 5 (1967) 582–90. For Mark, see Theodore J. Weeden, *Mark—Traditions in Conflict* (Philadelphia: Fortress, 1971); Werner H. Kelber, *Mark's Story of Jesus* (Philadelphia: Fortress, 1979); Joel Marcus, *The Mystery of the Kingdom of God* (SBLDS 90; Atlanta: Scholars, 1986) 89–96. For Matthew, see Jack Dean Kingsbury, "The Verb *Akolouthein* ("To Follow") as an Index of Matthew's View of His Community," *JBL* 97 (1978) 56–73; Michael J. Wilkins, *The Concept of Disciple in Matthew's Gospel* (NovTSup 59; Leiden: Brill, 1988) 137–41. For Luke, see Heinz Schürmann, *Das Lukasevangelium* (HTKNT 3; Freiburg/Basel/Vienna: Herder, 1969) 1. 266–67, 278, 311–12; Robert C. Tannehill, *The Narrative Unity of Luke-Acts. A Literary Interpretation. Volume 1: The Gospel according to Luke* (Foundations and Facets; Philadelphia: Fortress, 1986) 143–66; Jack Dean Kingsbury, *Conflict in Luke. Jesus, Authorities, Disciples* (Minneapolis: Fortress, 1991) 28–31; Frank Matera, "Jesus' Journey to Jerusalem (Luke 9.51–19.46): A Conflict with Israel," *JSNT* 51 (1993) 57–77. For John, see Rudolf Schnackenburg, *Das Johannesevangelium. II. Teil* (HTKNT 4/2; Freiburg/Basel/Vienna: Herder, 1971) 17, 199, 218–24, 488; R. Alan Culpepper, *Anatomy of the Fourth Gospel* (NT Foundations and Facets; Philadelphia: Fortress, 1983) 131–32; Martin Meiser, *Die Reaktion des Volkes auf Jesus* (BZNW 96; Berlin: de Gruyter, 1998).

[10] The Synoptic Gospels use both the singular and the plural of *ochlos;* there is no discernible difference in meaning. For instance, Mark almost always uses the singular, while Matthew often employs the plural. A clear sign that we are dealing with

merely stylistic tendencies is the fact that in a given story Matthew will change Mark's singular to the plural with no change in sense; see, e.g., Mark 15:11 and Matt 27:20. Luke, like Matthew, oscillates freely between the singular and the plural. John, like Mark, almost always uses the singular. Indeed, John 7:12 is the only place where the plural may occur, and even that reading is disputed.

[11] The four Gospels use various forms of *polys, polloi* ("much," "many") either as substantives or as adjectives modifying nouns like *ochlos* and *plēthos*. In contrast, only Luke uses *plēthos* with any frequency: 8 times in the Gospel, 16 times in Acts. Both Mark and John use it twice, Matthew not at all. The masculine plural *pantes* ("all") has understandably a wide and vague range and often has nothing to do with crowds. In contexts where crowds are mentioned, *pantes* can modify *ochloi* directly (e.g., Matt 12:23), or it can stand alone to designate the whole crowd (e.g., Matt 14:20; 21:26: "We fear the crowd, for all consider John a prophet"). At times it designates a more specific group within the crowd: e.g., Matt 14:35: "they brought him all the sick. . . ." At times the singular form *pas* modifies *ochlos* directly (e.g., Luke 13:17). These varied uses of *polys, polloi, pas,* and *pantes* have the natural effect of creating the impression of huge crowds.

[12] Among the rare cases of smaller, more specific crowds we may certainly include the crowd of mourners creating an uproar at the house of the ruler whose daughter has died (Matt 9:23). Interestingly, Mark has no *ochlos* here, while Luke speaks vaguely of "all" *(pantes)*. Another possible case is the *ochlos* (Matthew: *ochlos polys*) that comes to arrest Jesus in Gethsemane (Mark 14:43 ‖ Matt 26:47 ‖ Luke 22:47). The meaning of *ochlos* in this passage may be "troops." Yet the fact that Matt 26:55 has Jesus addressing these "crowds" and complaining that, when he was seated daily in the temple teaching, they did not seize him leaves open the possibility of a more general understanding of *ochlos* in Matt 26:47: crowds in general or temple police? In any case, in the view of Raymond E. Brown (*The Death of the Messiah* [Anchor Bible Reference Library; 2 vols.; New York: Doubleday, 1994] 1. 247), "rabble" or "mob" would be an overinterpretation. According to Brown (p. 248), "Luke's account, which has a crowd consisting in part of Temple captains, forms a bridge between Mark/Matthew's account of a crowd and John's account which has no crowd but soldiers and police-like attendants."

[13] Meier, *A Marginal Jew,* 2. 950–67.

[14] On the story of the woman with the hemorrhage, see *A Marginal Jew,* 2. 708–10.

[15] For statistics and dubious cases (where the special material of Luke may actually come from Q), see John S. Kloppenborg, *Q Parallels* (Foundations and Facets; Sonoma, CA: Polebridge, 1988) 227.

[16] On this material, see *A Marginal Jew,* 2. 656–57.

[17] On this material, see ibid., 2. 137–42.

[18] A prime candidate would be Matthew 7:28 ("and the crowds were astonished at his teaching"), which seems to be Matthew's redactional reworking of Mark 1:22 ("and they were astonished at his teaching"), where the wording of the Greek is exactly the same except for Matthew's "the crowds" *(hoi ochloi)*. "Crowds" does not appear at all in Mark 1:21–28 (the exorcism of the demoniac in the Capernaum synagogue), though Mark 1:27 does say that "all [*pantes*] were amazed."

[19] *A Marginal Jew,* 1. 64–65.

[20] It should be noted, though, that Josephus' global statement that Jesus "won over" or "gained a following among" *(epēgageto)* many Jews may encompass two "circles" of followers that I am distinguishing: the crowds and the disciples. Some might wish to call upon Tacitus as well *(Annals* 15.44) to support the idea that Jesus had a large following during his public ministry. One might infer this idea from the way Tacitus quickly moves from the topic of the Christians executed by Nero back to the execution of Christ by Pontius Pilate and then forward again to the (ostensibly continued) existence of the Christian movement. After mentioning Jesus' death, Tacitus immediately comments: "Suppressed for the moment [i.e., by the execution of Jesus], the deadly superstition broke out again [*rursum*], not only in Judea, the land which originated this evil, but also in the city of Rome, where all sorts of horrendous and shameful practices from every part of the world converge and are fervently cultivated." Since by "deadly superstition" Tacitus means the Christian movement, and since he considers it to have been only momentarily suppressed by the execution of Jesus, the natural inference is that Tacitus thought of the movement as already existing during Jesus' lifetime. While all this is true, one must allow for the possibility that we have here an example of naive retrojection of a later state of affairs into an earlier period—a not unknown tendency among Greco-Roman historians.

[21] This point was raised briefly in *A Marginal Jew,* 2. 625–28; needless to say, it must be examined more fully later on. On the precise point at issue here, see Craig A. Evans, "From Public Ministry to the Passion: Can a Link Be Found between the (Galilean) Life and the (Judean) Death of Jesus?" in his *Jesus & His Contemporaries. Comparative Studies* (AGJU 25; Leiden: Brill, 1995) 301–18.

[22] *A Marginal Jew,* 2. 56–62.

[23] On Theudas see *Ant.* 20.5.1 §97–99 (cf. the garbled reference in Acts 5:36); on "the Egyptian false prophet" see *J.W.* 2.13.5 §261–263 (cf. *Ant.* 20.8.6 §169–172; Acts 21:38). On this point see Evans, "From Public Ministry to the Passion," 317–18. Josephus says that Theudas persuaded large numbers of the general populace *(ton pleiston ochlon)* to follow him to the Jordan; "he deceived many [*pollous*]." In *The Jewish War,* Josephus claims that "the Egyptian false prophet" attracted about 30,000 followers, while Acts 21:38 speaks of only 4,000. In *The Jewish Antiquities* (and similarly in *The Jewish War*), Josephus prefaces his account of the Egyptian with a general reference to impostors who persuaded the crowd *(ton ochlon)* to follow

them into the desert; many *(polloi)* suffered punishment for their lack of sense. One notices how, in these accounts, Josephus tends to use the same vocabulary for the common people as do the Gospels: *ochlos, polloi,* and *plēthos.* At least part of the overall pattern suggested by Josephus can be seen in the cases of the Baptist and Jesus as well: a prophetic figure who draws large crowds attracts the unhealthy attention of the civil authorities too. E. P. Sanders *(Jesus and Judaism,* 294–306), however, notes an important difference: the Romans felt it necessary to kill or capture large numbers of the followers of Theudas and the Egyptian. The civil authorities felt no such need in the cases of the Baptist and Jesus. It sufficed to kill the leader. Some probable conclusions may be drawn from this observation: (1) neither the Baptist nor Jesus had an overt political agenda that aimed at changing the government by force; (2) neither organized large crowds for political action or demonstrations; and (3) neither led large crowds (possibly armed with weapons) on a march that challenged the political and military establishment.

[24] The germ of this idea may be espied already in Ernest Renan's *Life of Jesus* (New York: Brentano's, 1863). The early days in Galilee are celebrated by Renan as a happy utopia or paradise (see pp. 114–57). A darker tone intrudes when Jesus makes his first attempt to spread his message in Jerusalem (pp. 158–69). But Renan's overall view of the development of Jesus' views is more complicated than a simple Galilean spring followed by rejection by crowds and desertion by disciples. For a mocking critique of Renan's reconstruction, see Albert Schweitzer, *Geschichte der Leben-Jesu-Forschung* (2 vols.; Siebenstern-Taschenbuch 77/78 and 79/80; Munich/Hamburg: Siebenstern, 1966, originally 1906) 207–18. For a more sympathetic evaluation, see E. A. Scheffler, "Ernest Renan's Jesus: An Appraisal," *Neot* 33 (1999) 179–99. A more developed form of the idea that the "crisis" in John 6 may reflect historical tradition can be found in C. H. Dodd, *Historical Tradition in the Fourth Gospel* (Cambridge: Cambridge University, 1963) 222: "If John's account is to be taken seriously, we can see a reason why . . . this particular part of the Ministry [i.e., the events in John 6] impressed its sequence of events on the memory of the followers of Jesus: it was a crisis and a turning point. The vast assembly [at the feeding of the five thousand] . . . represented a high point in his popularity. But this popularity took a disastrous turn . . . the result was widespread defection." See also M.-J. Lagrange, *Evangile selon saint Jean* (EBib; 5th ed.; Paris: Gabalda, 1936) 186. An alternate explanation of why Jesus terminated a Galilean ministry that had begun so well is the two-part one suggested by Xavier Léon-Dufour (*Les évangiles et l'histoire de Jésus* [Paris: Seuil, 1963] 365–67): (1) the danger posed by Herod Antipas and (2) the misunderstanding of the crowd, which dreamed of an earthly, temporal Messiah. One must ask whether this scenario does not arise from an imaginative weaving together of various Synoptic texts with John 6. In my opinion, Günther Bornkamm (*Jesus of Nazareth* [New York: Harper & Row, 1960] 153) rightly rejects the idea of a "Galilean spring." The attempt of Franz Mussner ("Gab es eine 'galiläische Krise'?" *Orientierung an Jesus* [Josef Schmid Festschrift; ed. Paul Hoffmann et al.; Freiburg/Basel/Vienna: Herder, 1973] 238–52) to salvage a Galilean spring or crisis draws too weighty a conclusion from the mere fact that Jesus' ministry included both the offer of salvation and the re-

jection of that offer; Mussner also takes too much of the redactional ordering of the Synoptists as historical.

[25] This point is emphasized in *A Marginal Jew,* 1. 406–9.

[26] It is surprising to see a careful historian like Michael Grant (*Jesus. An Historian's Review of the Gospels* [New York: Scribner's, 1977] 128) take John 6:66 as a reliable account of the failure of Jesus' mission in Galilee. As elsewhere in his book, Grant does not ask enough critical questions about the sayings and narratives on which he relies. Here in particular there is an uncritical harmonizing of John with the Synoptics and a presumption about the order of events in the ministry that would be hard to verify. Despite the title of Grant's chapter 7 ("Failure in Galilee," pp. 111–33), it is by no means certain that we can point to a particular time in Jesus' ministry when the Galilean mission was felt to have "failed," after which (or: because of which) Jesus launched a fatal challenge in Jerusalem. If one talks about the "failure" of Jesus' ministry, one should understand the word in terms of his address to all Israel and his failure to have all Israel respond to his message with the total commitment he wanted—hence, for instance, the woes spoken against Chorazin, Bethsaida, and Capernaum (Matt 11:20–24 par.). But we have no proof that this type of failure was any more prominent in Galilee than in Judea or that the ministry in Galilee "failed" at some particular critical juncture. The ultimate "failure" of a shameful death on the cross occurred in Judea, not Galilee.

[27] In John 6:66 the initial phrase *ek toutou* ("from this") is ambiguous: either "from that time onward" (temporal sense) or "because of this," i.e., "because of what Jesus had said" (causal sense). Since "from that time onward" refers to the time when Jesus delivered the Bread of Life Discourse, the basic thrust of the sentence remains the same with either interpretation. Raymond E. Brown (*The Gospel According to John* [AB 29 and 29A; Garden City, NY: Doubleday, 1966, 1970] 1. 297) suggests the possibility of a deeper theological sense: "because of this" could refer to v 65, where Jesus tells the rebellious disciples: "Because of this [*dia touto*] I told you that no one can come to me [i.e., believe in me and so be a true disciple] unless it has been given to him from the Father."

[28] Raymond E. Brown, *The Community of the Beloved Disciple* (New York/Ramsey, NJ/Toronto: Paulist, 1979) 73–74. (In his earlier work, *The Gospel According to John,* 1. 300–301, Brown seemed more disposed to see behind John 6:66 some historical event in the ministry of Jesus.) Also in favor of seeing a reference to problems in the Johannine community are Barnabas Lindars, *The Gospel of John* (NCB; Grand Rapids: Eerdmans; London: Marshall, Morgan & Scott, 1972) 270–71; Robert Kysar, *John* (Augsburg Commentary; Minneapolis: Augsburg, 1986) 112.

[29] While he tends to confuse historical, literary, and theological questions, Ulrich Hedinger ("Jesus und die Volksmenge," *TZ* 32 [1976] 201–6) is correct in stressing

that there is no reason to think that the positive relationship between Jesus and the crowds was a mere episode in the public ministry.

[30] See the observations in *A Marginal Jew*, 1. 278–85.

[31] For the sake of completeness, I include in the list in the main text both those who probably were not committed adherents to the Jesus movement when they approached Jesus (e.g., Zacchaeus, the centurion from Capernaum) and those who probably were (e.g., the woman who anointed Jesus' head before his arrest). Thus, members of both the outer circle and the intermediate circle of followers are represented in the list.

[32] This is the understanding of "sinners" defended by E. P. Sanders; for the discussion of his views as compared with those of Joachim Jeremias and James D. G. Dunn, see Meier, *A Marginal Jew*, 2. 149, 211–12.

[33] Even in Luke 13:14, where the ruler of the synagogue berates "the crowd" about proper observance of the Sabbath, he is really directing his criticism at Jesus *via* the crowd. In the immediately preceding context, Jesus, not the crowd, has supposedly broken the Sabbath by healing a crippled woman.

[34] On this, see Sanders, *Jesus and Judaism*, 176–82. For a full study see Aharon Oppenheimer, *The ʿAm Ha-Aretz: A Study in the Social History of the Jewish People in the Hellenistic-Roman Period* (ALGHJ 8; Leiden: Brill, 1977). The rabbinic sense of the phrase should not be confused with earlier (and varied) meanings of the phrase found in the OT; for the latter, see A. H. J. Grunneweg, "ʿam hāʾāreṣ—A Semantic Revolution," *ZAW* 59 (1983) 437–40. Perhaps one of the earliest documented occurrences of the rabbinic sense of ʿam hāʾāreṣ is in a saying attributed to Hillel (at least in the present context in the Mishna) in *m. ʾAbot* 2:5 (or 2:6 in some editions): "No ignorant person ["is" or "can be" must be supplied] pious" (wĕ lōʾ ʿam hāʾāreṣ ḥāsîd). In the context, the ʿam hāʾāreṣ is mentioned along with people who are uneducated, shy, hot-tempered, or overly involved in business, while not being "pious" (ḥāsîd) is mentioned along with not fearing sin, not being able to learn or teach [Torah], and not growing wise. Thus, in this saying, while a person who belongs to "the people of the land" lacks the proper moral or intellectual disposition (or perhaps simply the leisure) to study and practice the Law zealously, he is not branded as an apostate or as someone who in effect has rejected the Mosaic Law.

[35] See, e.g., Brown, *The Gospel According to John*, 1. 325; Schnackenburg, *Das Johannesevangelium. II. Teil*, 221–22.

[36] Nowhere in the four Gospels do we find a Greek phrase such as *ho laos* [or: *hoi laoi*] *tēs gēs* or *to ethnos* [or: *ta ethnē*] *tēs gēs* that would translate exactly the Hebrew ʿam [or: ʿammê] hāʾāreṣ. Contrast in this regard, e.g., 2 Kgs 11:14, where the ʿam hāʾāreṣ of the MT is translated as *ho laos tēs gēs* in the LXX (4 Kgdms 11:14); and

Neh 10:31–32, where the *'ammê hā'āreṣ* of the MT is twice translated as *tois laois* [or: *hoi laoi] tēs gēs* in the LXX (2 Esdr 20:31–32). While statements about the Qumran material must be made with caution, since we must await detailed scholarly examination of all the fragments, it seems that the few nonbiblical texts from Qumran that use *'am hā'āreṣ, 'am hā'ărāṣôt,* or *'ammê hā'ărāṣôt* do not employ the term in the special rabbinic sense that we begin to find in the Mishna. See 1 QH 4:26; 1QM 10:9; 4Q *381* 69.1; 4QVisSam 2.5; texts may be checked in James H. Charlesworth, *Graphic Concordance to the Dead Sea Scrolls* (Tübingen: Mohr [Siebeck]; Louisville: Westminster/John Knox, 1991). Interestingly, Josephus never uses *ho laos* [or: *hoi laoi] tēs gēs* in his works; see Karl H. Rengstorf, *A Complete Concordance to Flavius Josephus* (4 vols.; Leiden: Brill, 1973–1983) 3. 13–15. In sum, then, if neither the NT nor Josephus uses "the people of the land" at all, and if the few occurrences of the phrase in the nonbiblical Qumran material do not reflect the special rabbinic usage, it is questionable whether Jesus research should use the rabbinic phrase "people of the land" as an interpretive tool for understanding Jesus' ministry in the early 1st century A.D. See further on this point Claude G. Montefiore (*The Synoptic Gospels* [2 vols.; 2d ed.; New York: Ktav, 1968] 1. cvii–cx, cxxxiii–cxxxiv) and the comments on his views by Roland Deines, *Die Pharisäer* (WUNT 101; Tübingen: Mohr [Siebeck], 1997) 367–39.

CHAPTER 25

JESUS IN RELATION TO
HIS FOLLOWERS

The Disciples

From the outer circle of the crowds we move now to the middle circle of the disciples, which is problematic in its own way.[1] On the one hand, the word "disciples" has certain definite characteristics that are spelled out in the Gospels; at least certain people we know by name (e.g., Peter, Levi, Philip, and Nathanael) undoubtedly belonged to the disciples of Jesus. On the other hand, the precise boundaries of discipleship are not entirely clear. Some women, e.g., Mary Magdalene, seem to meet the requirements for discipleship; yet no individual woman is explicitly called a disciple by the Gospels. Other people, e.g., Martha and Mary, may lack one or another requirement for discipleship in the strict sense; yet their deep commitment to Jesus is beyond question. Being a disciple is not as straightforward a matter as might first appear. We cannot simply say that "disciple" means "student" or "pupil" and be done with it. We need to move carefully step by step through our survey on the nature and extent of discipleship.

First of all, we must establish the historical existence of a group of disciples around Jesus. That is to say, we must show that some sort of band called "disciples"—whatever the precise requirements for membership—was not just a creation of the early church. Second, we must ask the more troublesome question of who precisely qualified as a disciple of Jesus. In other words, what were the major characteristics of or requirements for discipleship? Third, we must grapple with one particular unclear and disputed case, i.e., the women followers of Jesus, especially those named by the evangelists. Fourth, we must examine those supporters of Jesus, both male and female, who apparently did not leave home or family to follow Jesus physically, but who accepted his message and supported his movement, especially by hospitality.

I. DID THE HISTORICAL JESUS HAVE DISCIPLES?

Fortunately, we need not spend a great deal of time on the question of whether Jesus in fact had disciples during his lifetime, since the historicity of some such group is rarely if ever denied. Indeed, simply the frequent occurrence of the word "disciple" in all four Gospels would make such a denial suspect. The presence of the word "disciple" (*mathētēs* in the singular, *mathētai* in the plural) is massive in each Gospel: 72 times in Matthew, 46 times in Mark, 37 times in Luke, and 78 times in John. In contrast, with the exception of Acts (28 times, but never in reference to the disciples during Jesus' ministry), the word is absent from the rest of the NT.[2] Apart from a relatively small number of references to the disciples of the Pharisees, of the Baptist, and of Moses, the word "disciples" in the Gospels refers solely to the disciples of Jesus.[3]

If we may judge from the total absence of the word "disciple" in Paul's epistles, the other epistles in the NT, the Epistle to the Hebrews (really, a homily), and the Book of Revelation, "disciples" was not the ordinary way Christians of the first or second Christian generation spoke to or about one other. Hence the term "disciples" in the Gospels is not to be explained as an anachronistic retrojection of the early church's way of speaking of its members into the time of Jesus' public ministry.

But what of the obvious exception, the Acts of the Apostles? I think it likely that Luke's desire to create links between the time of Jesus and the time of the church led him to take over the term "disciples" from Gospel tradition and apply it to members of the early church. In this way he could emphasize continuity between the two periods.[4] It is perhaps telling that, with one exception, "disciple" in Acts always occurs in Luke's narration, not in the words of any of the characters in the story.[5] To be sure, it is possible that in his terminology Luke is echoing the usage of his particular church. But, judged in the light of the rest of the NT documents outside the Gospels, this usage would have been quite isolated.

In sum, an argument for the historicity of a group of disciples around Jesus during his lifetime can be mounted from the criterion of discontinuity: "disciple" was not the ordinary way in which most early Christians spoke of themselves or to one another. This judgment is supported by the total absence or rare occurrence of the word "disciple" in most of the earliest Christian writings outside the NT.[6]

The absence of the word "disciple" from the NT apart from the Gospels and Acts becomes all the more intriguing when we notice that *mathētēs* is likewise absent from the entire LXX, including both proto- and deutero-canonical (apocryphal) books.[7] This absence reflects in turn the virtual absence of the Hebrew word *talmîd* ("student," "disciple") from the books of the Jewish Scriptures written in Hebrew and Aramaic, the sole exception being 1 Chron 25:8, where the word refers to an apprentice musician. There is a fascinating symmetry here. The Greek OT lacks the key word *(mathētēs)* used in the 1st century A.D. to designate the disciples of Jesus, just as the Jewish Scriptures written in Hebrew and Aramaic all but lack the key word *(talmîd)* used at least from the 2d century A.D. onwards as the technical term to designate the disciples of the rabbis.

This absence grows even stranger when we notice that *talmîd* is also absent from the nonbiblical writings discovered at Qumran. When one considers the large amount of scribal activity and study of the Scriptures at Qumran, the total absence of what would soon become the technical term for a student of Torah among the rabbis is remarkable. Stranger still, this absence on the Hebrew and Aramaic side of the ledger at Qumran is once again matched by an absence on the Greek side of the ledger in the pseudepigrapha. According to Michael J. Wilkins, the OT pseudepigrapha that are found in Greek manuscripts and that can be reasonably considered "intertestamental" (for our purposes, dating roughly from the 2d century B.C. to the middle of the 1st century A.D.) do not contain the word *mathētēs*.[8]

It is only when we come to Philo of Alexandria (ca. 25 B.C.–A.D. 50) that we meet a known Jewish author writing in Greek who uses *mathētēs* in his works. Our joy of discovery is immediately tempered when we learn that in the massive output of Philo, which fills 12 volumes in the Loeb Classical Library, there are only 14 occurrences of the noun "disciple." While Philo does use the word at times in the general sense of a learner or one receiving instruction from a teacher, he typically uses *mathētēs* within the context of his mystical views about the "perfect" person who is directly taught by God.[9] This usage is the most typical and frequent way in which *mathētēs* is employed by Philo. It fits into Philo's own brand of gnosticizing mysticism, reflecting the influence of middle Platonism and perhaps Hellenistic mystery religions. Thus, the infrequent and special use of "disciple" by Philo still leaves us without real parallels to the disciples of Jesus in the Gospels.

One might hope for more help from Josephus (ca. A.D. 37–after 100). After all, Josephus was born in Palestine not long after Jesus was crucified; and, at least later in life, Josephus claimed that he had been a Pharisee from early adulthood onwards. However, the number of occurrences of "disciple" in Josephus' writings is almost as disappointing as was the case with Philo. Despite Josephus' extensive literary production, which takes up 10 volumes in the Loeb Classical Library, *mathētēs* occurs only 15 times in his works. The occurrences are scattered throughout *The Jewish Antiquities* and *Against Apion*. Significantly, these works were written about A.D. 93–94 and A.D. 100–105 respectively, some 60 to 70 years after the death of Jesus.

The 15 occurrences of "disciple" in Josephus have a wide range of meanings. Sometimes the word has the general sense of one who learns from another's example (*Ant.* 1.11.3 §200). More importantly, Josephus uses *mathētēs* when describing various OT figures as standing in a master-disciple relationship. Thus, Joshua is called the disciple of Moses (*Ant.* 6.5.4 §84), Elisha the disciple of Elijah (*Ant.* 8.13.7 §354), and Baruch the disciple of Jeremiah (*Ant.* 10.9.1 §158). Since the LXX never uses *mathētēs* of these people, Josephus is indicating how he interprets these biblical heroes in the milieu of Hellenistic Judaism at the end of the 1st century A.D. In *Against Apion*, Josephus uses "disciple" three times, in typically Greek fashion, to describe persons or groups who follow the philosophical teachings of some other person or group that is notably distant from the learners in time and space (*Ag. Ap.* 1.2 §14; 1.22 §176; 2.41 §295).

Of special interest to us are the cases where Josephus applies the term "disciple" to Elisha's relationship to the prophet Elijah or to the relationship that various subordinates had to Elisha after he succeeded Elijah. In *Ant.* 8.13.7 §354 (cf. *Ant.* 9.2.2 §28; 9.3.1 §33), Josephus narrates how Elisha "followed" (*ēkolouthēsen*) the prophet Elijah and so became his "disciple and servant" *(mathētēs kai diakonos)*. Even more evocative of a "school" situation is Josephus' picture of the prophet Elisha sitting in his house with his disciples (*Ant.* 9.2.4 §68) or sending a disciple on a mission (*Ant.* 9.6.1 §106). The corresponding biblical passages speak instead of "elders" and "one of the sons of the prophets" respectively (2 Kgs 6:32; 9:1). Here Josephus may be rereading biblical passages in the light of the Pharisaic and nascent rabbinic movements with their schools—a phenomenon that in turn reflects Hellenistic cultural influence.

Closer to Josephus' own time is the Hasmonean ruler John Hyrcanus, who, according to Josephus, was a *mathētēs* of the Pharisees (*Ant.* 13.10.5 §289). In context, the passage probably means that Hyrcanus flattered the Pharisees by insisting how much he was influenced by their teachings. His lifestyle indicates that he was not a full-fledged member of the Pharisaic movement. The stricter sense of a true disciple of a Pharisaic teacher is found in *Ant.* 15.1.1 §3, where we hear of the Pharisee Pollion and his disciple Samaias, both early supporters of Herod the Great. Later on, Josephus indicates that both of them have constant followers (*syndiatribontōn, Ant.* 15.10.4 §370). Here the Greek idea of a master-disciple relationship within a philosophical school has clearly sunk roots in a Jewish Palestinian setting— at least as that setting is portrayed to us by the elderly Josephus writing in Rome at the end of the 1st century A.D.

It is telling that the closest 1st-century Jewish parallel we can find to the Gospels' use of *mathētēs* for the disciples of Jesus comes from the writings of Josephus, an educated Jew from Palestine who became immersed in Greco-Roman culture while asserting (at least later in life) that he was a Pharisee. It may well be that the disciples of the Pharisaic movement in the 1st centuries B.C. and A.D., the disciples of Jesus in the 1st century A.D., and the disciples of the rabbis in subsequent centuries all reflect in varying ways the influence of Hellenistic culture, which had long since penetrated Palestine.[10] In these various master-disciple relationships sprouting up in Palestine we may see a cross-fertilization between OT and Jewish traditions on the one hand and Greco-Roman school traditions on the other.

Yet it remains significant that, to find in Jewish literature a use of *mathētēs* fairly close to that of the Gospel tradition, we have to reach forward to Josephus' writings at the end of the 1st century A.D. Prior to the lifetime of the historical Jesus, there is no Jewish author we can point to who speaks of disciples who are at least in some ways similar to the disciples Jesus gathers around himself. In fact, apart from Philo—who hails from Egypt, not Palestine—prior to Jesus no Jewish author speaks of disciples, period. From this surprisingly widespread absence of the term "disciple" in the Jewish religious literature of Palestine prior to the time of Jesus—as well as in the NT apart from the Gospels and Acts—one can perhaps construct a limited type of argument from discontinuity. It would appear that the massive use of *mathētēs* for the disciples of Jesus in the four Gospels is *neither* a projection of a usage found in the OT (MT or LXX), intertestamental literature, or Qumran, *nor* a retrojection of a designation for Christian believers commonly used in the 1st century A.D.[11] It may well be that, during the public ministry, either Jesus himself or his immediate followers selected the word "disciple" (in Aramaic, *talmîdā'*), which was not yet a technical term in the later rabbinic sense. The word was chosen to designate the unusual type of relationship that existed between the Elijah-like prophet and teacher (a "rabbi," also in a nontechnical sense) and those he had called to follow him literally. In adopting this (at least for Jewish Palestine) relatively recent terminology for a specific movement, Jesus and his disciples may reflect the Hellenistic milieu that had come to influence Palestine from the days of

Alexander the Great onwards. But for Jesus, a more immediate influence and model would have been supplied by the Baptist and his group of disciples, to which Jesus may have for a while belonged.[12]

Fortunately, the criterion of discontinuity does not supply the sole argument for the historicity of Jesus' disciples. The presence of disciples around Jesus during his public ministry is also supported by the criterion of multiple attestation of sources and forms. As biblical scholars commonly agree, a key component of being a disciple in the Gospels is receiving a specific call from Jesus to follow him.[13] If, then, we count either those passages where people around Jesus are explicitly named "disciples" or those passages where Jesus specifically calls people to follow him, we have references to the disciples of Jesus in every Gospel source. Mark narrates the call of the first four disciples (Peter, Andrew, James, and John) in 1:16–20 and the call of Levi the toll collector in 2:14. Throughout the whole of his narrative, Mark mentions disciples in the company of Jesus (to give only some examples: 2:15–16; 3:7; 5:31; 6:35; 7:2; 8:1; 9:14; 10:23–24; 11:1; 12:43; 13:1; 14:12–16,32). In the sayings tradition of Mark, Jesus enunciates the stringent cost of following him in a committed fashion (8:34).

The Q tradition has two clear occurrences of the word "disciple," though the second occurrence refers to the disciples of the Baptist. In the first passage, Jesus utters what may be a proverb; but, in its present context, he seems to refer it to his own disciples: "A disciple is not above his teacher" (Matt 10:24 ‖ Luke 6:40; cf. John 13:16). The second reference is to the disciples of the Baptist, whom John sends to Jesus (Matt 11:2 ‖ Luke 7:18–19).[14] The Q tradition also contains various sayings of Jesus exhorting his audience to display their loyalty to him in public despite opposition and danger (e.g., Matt 10:26–36 ‖ Luke 12:2–9,51–53). Such sayings make sense only if addressed to committed followers. "Disciple" also occurs in the special traditions of Matthew and Luke, though here it is difficult to know when we are encountering redactional creations of the evangelists. It is fairly clear that at least some cases are redactional (e.g., Matt 10:42; Luke 14:33).[15]

John's Gospel has more occurrences of "disciple" than any other book in the NT, with the word appearing in both narratives and sayings. No doubt, the Fourth Gospel contains many passages where the word "disciple" is a redactional contribution of the evangelist. Yet some Johannine narratives that mention the disciples of Jesus have independent Synoptic parallels that also refer to the disciples (e.g., in the multiplication of loaves: cf. Mark 6:32–44; 8:1–10; John 6:1–15; at the arrest in Gethsemane: cf. Mark 14:32; John 18:1–2). Hence, at least in such passages, the presence of the disciples is not purely a redactional creation of the Fourth Evangelist.

While not using the word "disciple" to describe Jesus' followers, Josephus basically supports the Gospels' picture in his thumbnail sketch of Jesus (*Ant.* 18.3.3 §63–64). Josephus states that Jesus gained a following (*epēgageto*) both among many Jews and among many of Greek origin. More to the point, Josephus states that, after the crucifixion of Jesus by Pilate, "those who had loved him [i.e., Jesus] previously [*to prōton*] did not cease to do so. . . ." Thus, Josephus depicts a group of dedicated followers who were so devoted to Jesus during his ministry that they did not desert his cause even after his shameful death. Though the word "disciple" is not employed, these people obviously encompass the disciples portrayed in the Gospels. The argument from multiple attestation thus includes not only all the Gospel sources but also Josephus.[16]

Finally, one can mount a type of argument from coherence, though a somewhat indirect one. Mark, Q, special Lucan tradition, John, and Josephus all indicate that John the Baptist had disciples (see Mark 2:18; 6:29; Matt 11:2 par.; Luke 11:1; John 1:35–37; 3:23,25; 4:1; *Ant.* 18.5.2 §117–18; cf. Acts 19:1–7). Now, as we saw in Volume Two, Jesus, by the very fact that he submitted to John's baptism, became in that limited sense a disciple of John.[17] The baptism of Jesus by John plus the Fourth Gospel's depiction of Jesus circulating among the disciples of the Baptist (John 1:35–44) make it likely that Jesus remained for a time in the circle of John's immediate disciples. I also argued in Volume Two that the Fourth Gospel is probably correct when it presents Jesus as imitating John's practice of baptism when Jesus began his own independent ministry (John 3:22–25; 4:1).[18] In short, Jesus' adherence to John, expressed in having himself baptized, Jesus' sojourn among the Baptist's disciples, and Jesus' imitation of John's baptizing ministry in his own ministry all cohere perfectly with Jesus' imitation of another of John's practices: having disciples around him. We are not surprised, therefore, to hear from the Fourth Gospel that some of Jesus' prominent disciples (notably Andrew and Peter) were drawn from the circle of the Baptist's disciples (John 1:35–42).

One might also approach the criterion of coherence from a somewhat different direction. Practically no one would deny that, in one way or another, the historical Jesus functioned during his ministry as both Jewish prophet and Jewish teacher. Indications for both activities are abundant in various Gospel sources.[19] It is almost inconceivable that a 1st-century Palestinian Jew could have functioned for any length of time as prophet-and-teacher combined without having some disciples who heard and absorbed his prophecies and/or teachings. All this simply states the obvious: prophesying and teaching are exercises in social communication. A prophet or teacher who had absolutely no receptive audience would have a slim chance of even being remembered as a prophet or teacher by subsequent history—to say nothing of having a significant impact on that history. Having disciples simply jibes with Jesus' job description in 1st-century Jewish Palestine.

In brief, then, arguments from discontinuity, multiple attestation of sources and forms, and coherence all support a point that is pivotal for understanding the historical Jesus as well as early Christianity: Jesus gathered around himself a group of committed disciples, some of whom were also prominent in the early church.

II. WHO QUALIFIED AS A DISCIPLE OF JESUS?

As we try to sketch the disciples of Jesus, we must remember that, at the turn of the era in the Mediterranean world, the phenomenon of discipleship did not exist in a historical vacuum as a monopoly of Jesus. Throughout the Greco-Roman period, various philosophical and religious figures gathered around themselves people who might be labeled as followers, adherents, students, or disciples. These receptive audiences imbibed and cultivated their leaders' teachings, thus beginning the formation of various intellectual or religious traditions that were then handed down from generation to generation. R. Alan Culpepper has investigated this "school" phenomenon among such disparate Hellenistic groups as the Pythagoreans, the Platonists, the Aristotelians, the Epicureans, the Stoics, the "school at Qumran," the "house of Hillel," the "school" of Philo, the disciples of Jesus, and the "school" that stands behind the tradition in the Fourth Gospel.[20]

Clearly, "school" is being used here in a very wide sense—as it must be, since the teacher-disciple relationship was a very elastic one in the ancient Mediterranean world.[21] Not only the socioeconomic, political, and intellectual conditions of a particular society but also the personal genius and impact of the great founding teacher molded the "school" into specific contours. Just as it would be shoddy apologetics to try to cordon off Jesus' disciples from the larger "school" phenomenon in the Greco-Roman world, so it would be facile harmonization to ignore the distinguishing characteristics of the disciples gathered around the historical Jesus. As a religious figure within the Greco-Roman period, Jesus not surprisingly bore some resemblances to other philosophical or religious teachers of his time, notably in his desire to assemble followers or students around him. Hence, while Jesus' resemblance to wandering Cynic philosophers has been greatly overemphasized, one should not deny all similarities to philosophers in the broad Cynic-Stoic stream, mixed as it sometimes was with Pythagorean traits.[22]

Even more obvious is the resemblance to the later Jewish rabbis and their disciples. Here, however, the use of written sources reflecting the more developed stages of mishnaic and talmudic Judaism (sources ranging from A.D. 200 to 500) poses special problems. To be sure, as Shaye Cohen rightly observes, the disciples of the rabbis of the 2d century A.D. shared many characteristics with the disciples of Jesus. The rabbinic disciples, like those of Jesus, were constantly with their master. "They would live, eat, sleep, and travel with him. . . . There was little privacy for either party in this relationship. . . . In effect, joining a disciple circle was like joining a new family (cf. Mark 3:32–35; 10:29–31)." [23]

At the same time, Cohen, with his keen critical sense, puts his finger on the vital difference: "Jesus was not only a teacher . . . he was also a prophet and healer, and the traditions about him clearly derive in part from the biblical record about Elijah and his disciple Elisha. In contrast, the rabbis of the second century did not claim to be holy men or miracle workers. . . . " [24] Indeed, in Volume Two of A Marginal Jew, I argued that the preaching and teaching of Jesus must be understood within the larger framework of Jesus the eschatological prophet and miracle worker, who consciously presented himself to Israel in the likeness of Elijah. It fits perfectly with this deliberately chosen image that Jesus should peremptorily call disciples to follow him—disciples who would not only imbibe his teaching but also share his ministry of proclaiming the kingdom of God and healing the sick. Among the OT prophets, only Elijah is presented as (1) an itinerant miracle-working prophet, active in northern Israel, who (2) issues a peremptory call to another individual (Elisha) to leave home, family, and ordinary work in order to follow, serve, and ultimately succeed Elijah in the ministry of prophet. [25]

In fact, more than any other OT text, the story of Elijah's call of Elisha echoes in the call stories of the Gospel—as, I would maintain, they echoed in the actions of the historical Jesus calling his disciples. In 1 Kgs 19:19–21, Elijah finds Elisha engaged in his ordinary work and symbolically summons him to service by casting his mantle over him. Elisha asks permission to bid his parents farewell, promising "and I will come after you" (wĕʾēlĕkâ ʾaḥărêkā in the MT, kai akolouthe_so opiso_ sou in the LXX). Elijah grants permission. Elisha slaughters the oxen with which he was plowing, uses their yokes for kindling wood, and offers a feast to his comrades—thus burning his bridges behind him. Then "he went after Elijah and served him" (wayyēlek ʾaḥărê ʾēliyyāhû wayšārĕtēhû in the MT, kai eporeuthē opiso_ Ēliou kai eleitourgei autō in the LXX). The elements of (1) the prophet's sudden, peremptory call to an ordinary individual engaged in ordinary work, (2) a call that means breaking ties with one's family and livelihood, and (3) a call that involves literal following and service to the prophet all return in the Gospel stories of Jesus calling his disciples. More importantly, I will argue below that these elements go back to the historical Jesus.

Thus, it is against this OT background of Elijah calling Elisha that I understand the specific nature of the disciples of Jesus.[26] But it is one thing to state my view of the disciples, with a brief argument from coherence. It is another thing to establish my view with a detailed examination of the NT evidence. As we now probe various Gospel traditions about Jesus' disciples, we will apply the usual criteria of historicity to establish which characteristics of the disciples, as presented in the Gospels, actually go back to the call and demands of the historical Jesus. By doing this, I will be "fleshing out" the basic traits that would have qualified someone to be considered a *disciple* of Jesus, as distinct from a curious follower in the crowds or even a committed adherent of the Jesus movement who did not, however, follow Jesus physically around Galilee.

What, then, are the distinguishing traits that defined a person as a disciple of Jesus in the strict sense? As we begin our quest for an adequate definition, we need to remind ourselves that the religious rhetoric of modern Christianity often leads us to use the word "disciple" quite loosely. The drive to be relevant pushes pulpit oratory and theological musings to employ the word "disciple" in as many meanings or in as broad a sense as possible. In this regard, present-day writers might appeal to Luke as their patron saint, since, in his Acts of the Apostles, he was the first to extend the term to cover the Christians of his own day as well as the original disciples of Jesus. The Gospels, however—including Luke's—are not so generous. With a few exceptions, their usage is restricted to those who actually followed Jesus during his public ministry.

But did everyone who followed Jesus, even with commitment and devotion, automatically qualify as a disciple? It would appear not—at least if one restricts oneself, with wooden literalism, to occurrences of the word *mathētēs* in the Gospels. But should one take such a narrow approach? Up until now, we have been relying on a vague, intuitive sense of what it meant to be a disciple of Jesus. Perhaps some might prefer to stick with their intuition. They would simply take for granted that, since the basic meaning of *mathētēs* is "learner" or "student," a disciple of Jesus was anyone who listened to and learned the teachings of rabbi Jesus as one of his students.

But the Gospels' picture of Jesus' disciples is not so simple. Hence the present task: to try to clarify what being a disciple of the historical Jesus meant during his public ministry in Palestine ca. A.D. 28–30. One way to approach this problem is to ask a question that is deceptively simple: What common traits of discipleship are supported by multiple attestation (and, at times, other criteria) in the various streams of the Gospel tradition?

A. The Initiative of Jesus in Calling

One striking trait, found in a number of different Gospel sources, is that Jesus seizes the initiative in calling people to follow him.[27] Three clear examples are given by the Marcan tradition: the call of the first four disciples (Peter, Andrew, James, and John) in Mark 1:16–20; the call of Levi the toll collector in 2:14; and the (unsuccessful) call of the rich man in Mark 10:17–22. In each case, Jesus issues a peremptory call to follow him, a call addressed to people who have not taken the initiative of asking to follow him.[28]

The Q tradition also depicts Jesus calling persons to follow him. Q places special emphasis on the imperious nature of Jesus' command, a command that brooks no opposition or delay, no matter what the circumstances. In Matt 8:21–22 ‖ Luke 9:59–60, a candidate for discipleship asks Jesus' permission first to bury his (presumably recently deceased) father before accepting Jesus' call to follow him. Jesus refuses permission with shocking brusqueness: "Let the dead bury their dead." This demand to ignore a basic obligation of piety to a dead parent, an obligation acknowledged by all Jews, never appears again in the NT and is never presented as an obligation incumbent on Christians in the rest of early Christian literature. It is shockingly discontinuous from the fundamental morality that both Jews and Christians held dear.[29] Indeed, it is discontinuous from the basic sensibilities of the ancient Mediterranean world in general.

A special Lucan tradition makes the same point (Luke 9:61–62).[30] When someone asks Jesus' permission to bid his family farewell, Jesus replies sharply, "No one putting his hand to the plow and looking back is fit for the kingdom of God." Although the point is already clear in the call stories of Mark, the peremptory authority of Jesus to call people out of their ordinary lives to follow him is emphasized even more in Q and L.

The Fourth Gospel's presentation of the first contact of Jesus with his future disciples is different from Mark's, but significant for that very reason. In John 1:35–42, the Baptist directs two of his disciples to Jesus, who proceeds to encourage their initial curiosity. When the two disciples ask Jesus, "Rabbi, where do you dwell?" he replies laconically, "Come and see." Jesus' initial invitation to these two disciples then spreads by a sort of spiritual chain reaction. Andrew, one of the original two, brings his brother Simon Peter to Jesus. Philip, who, in the literary structure of chap. 1 of John's Gospel, seems to be the other original disciple,[31] cajoles Nathanael into coming to meet Jesus. Granted this redactional presentation, so filled with Johannine theology and so different from the Synoptics', it is all the more striking that, when the Johannine Jesus decides to leave the entourage of the Baptist and the environs of the Jordan to go into Galilee (John 1:43), he finds Philip and says to him in true Synoptic fashion: "Follow me [*akolouthei moi*]." For all the Johannine differences, the basic elements of Jesus' initiative and his peremptory command that people follow him in a literal, physical way appear as surely in John 1 as in Mark or Q.

Thus, Mark, Q, L, and John give us more than adequate multiple attestation of a basic element of discipleship: becoming a disciple of Jesus arises from Jesus' seizing the initiative by issuing an imperious command to follow. In all these various streams of tradition, a striking constant is the vocabulary of "following" or "coming [or: going] after" Jesus. In the case of the Q logion (Luke 9:60 par.), the criterion of discontinuity also supported this basic element.

The instrinsic connection between being called to follow and becoming a member of a group of disciples is reinforced by both Mark and John in their redactional arrangement of the opening events of Jesus' ministry. In the initial pericopes of Mark's story, the word "disciple" never appears. Instead, we hear of Jesus calling various individuals to follow him: first, Peter and Andrew (1:16–18), then James and John (1:19–20), and finally Levi (2:14). Only after Mark has presented Jesus calling a number of people to follow him does the evangelist then introduce the term "disciple" into his narrative (in 2:15, right after the call of Levi): ". . . and many toll collectors and sinners were reclining at table with Jesus *and his disciples;* for they [i.e., the disciples] were many and they followed him." [32]

For all the differences in the way John's Gospel presents the beginnings of Jesus' ministry, we nevertheless find the same basic pattern that is displayed in Mark. Chapter 1 of the Fourth Gospel speaks only of the two "disciples" of the Baptist (1:35,37), never of the "disciples" of Jesus. Only after Jesus has gathered a number of followers around himself—followers who then literally follow him from the lower Jordan into Galilee—does the Fourth Gospel speak of disciples of Jesus (2:2): "Jesus *and his disciples* were also invited to the wedding feast [at Cana]." As in Mark so in John: only after Jesus has taken the initiative in calling a number of individuals to follow him, and only after they in fact follow, do the evangelists speak of the disciples around Jesus. Discipleship thus arises from a particular social interaction: the decision and command of Jesus to call certain people to follow him and their obedience in answering his call. As presented in the Gospels, discipleship involves not just an individualistic relation of a single pupil to his teacher but the formation of a group around the teacher who has called the group into existence.

Interestingly, despite all the ways in which the two later Synoptists diverge from Mark in narrating the beginnings of Jesus' ministry, both Matthew and Luke present the same basic pattern: first Jesus' call to certain individuals to follow him (Matt 4:18–22; Luke 5:1–11), then the first mention of "his [Jesus'] disciples" (Matt 5:1; Luke 5:30). To be sure, in all four Gospels we are dealing with the redactional ordering of the material by the evangelists. Nevertheless, it is significant that Mark and John, independently of each other, and Matthew and Luke, despite their many modifications of Mark, all adhere to the basic idea that Jesus' initiative in calling someone to be his disciple was an indispensable condition for counting that person as a disciple of Jesus and as a member of the group of disciples. Thus, what is indicated in the microcosm of individual Gospel stories and sayings is confirmed by the macrocosm of the Gospels as a whole. That Jesus' authoritative call was constitutive of discipleship—discipleship understood precisely as a group phenomenon—was apparently deeply ingrained in the early Christian tradition. One finds no rival or alternate interpretation of what made a person a disciple of Jesus.

One must be careful about making sweeping claims that Jesus' habit of taking the initiative in calling disciples to follow him in a literal sense was unique to Jesus among Jewish teachers in 1st-century Palestine. The truth of the matter is that we are poorly informed about how other Jewish teachers in Palestine gathered pupils in the early 1st century A.D. As I pointed out in Volume One, descriptions of education in Jewish Palestine around the turn of the era are largely derived from later rabbinic material.[33] Moreover, it is not always clear whether the later rabbis are giving sober sociological descriptions of how education is carried out or rather exhortations inculcating an ideal.

With this caveat, it is permissible to state that Jesus' mode of acquiring disciples does seem to have been unusual, if not unique, in the Palestinian Judaism of his time. If we look back to the time of Ben Sira (ca. 190 B.C.), we see a wise man and scribe who invites persons interested in acquiring wisdom (probably from aristocratic or affluent families) to enter his school in Jerusalem (Sir 51:23).[34] There is no imperious order commanding specific individuals to come, and the invitation does not involve following an itinerant charismatic prophet in his journeys around Galilee, Judea, and beyond. Ben Sira seems to operate a school snugly ensconced in Jerusalem.

In our search for Jewish groups or individuals that we can compare with the disciples of Jesus, we run into special difficulty when we come to the time of Jesus. In the early to middle 1st century A.D., it is not easy to name, examine, and describe individual Jews who entered into master-disciple relationships. Two cases that throw some light on our quest are (1) the group of disciples around John the Baptist (e.g., Andrew and Philip) and (2) the young Josephus engaged in his quest for a spiritual guide. For all the differences between these two cases, there is one common characteristic: individuals sought out a religious leader or guru; the guru did not peremptorily call individuals to follow him as disciples.

Admittedly, our evidence is quite slight in the case of the Baptist. But, as far as we can tell from the way in which the Baptist is described in both the four Gospels and Josephus' *Jewish Antiquities,* the Baptist, unlike Jesus, did not directly "call" individuals to be his disciples and demand that they live for a lengthy period of time in a circle around him. Rather, the Baptist's main concern was to direct a call to all Israel to repent and share in his baptism. The vast majority of those baptized seemed to have returned to their homes. A few stayed around John for some time; but, if we may judge by the general picture presented in John 1:35–51, they left John's circle whenever they chose. However, we must admit that, in the case of the Baptist, we are dealing largely with an argument from silence. No source indicates that the Baptist took the initiative in calling certain individuals to be more or less permanent disciples in his entourage, but this hardly proves that he did not.

Thanks to his autobiography (*Life,* 2 §11–12), we are better informed about Josephus' mode of discipleship. When he was about 16 years old (ca. A.D. 53–54), Josephus *decided* on his own *(eboulēthēn)* to gain some experience of the major religious movements found in the Palestinian Judaism of his day: the Pharisees, the Sadducees, and the Essenes. In addition to trying each religious movement in turn, he also heard of a solitary Jewish ascetic named Bannus, who practiced ritual ablutions in the wilderness. Apparently on his own initiative, Josephus became a zealous follower *(zēlōtēs)* of Bannus and lived with him for three years. In the end, Josephus returned to Jerusalem at the age of 19 and began to live as a Pharisee—or so he claims in his *Life.*[35]

Whatever the truth of this autobiographical narrative, which no doubt is meant to present him in the best light as a person sincerely questing for spiritual guidance, Josephus takes for granted that *he* is the one who seeks out various religious guides or teachers; they do not call him to follow them. Moreover, Josephus does not convey the sense that, having tried out a particular group or person, he is under any great pressure to stay with that group or person. We are worlds away from the peremptory call initiated by Jesus, a call obliging the chosen candidate to follow him and stay with him.[36]

If we look ahead to the relationship of the later rabbis to their disciples, we

find that the usual procedure was for a would-be student to seek out an esteemed rabbi to teach him Torah.[37] It was not customary for a rabbi to confront someone he did not personally know and command in peremptory
fashion that the individual become his disciple by following him.[38] In contrast, Jesus' initiative in summoning a person to discipleship is a necessary
condition for becoming his disciple. A dedicated adherent's sincere desire to
follow Jesus is not of itself sufficient. This is dramatized perfectly at the end
of the exorcism of the Gerasene demoniac (Mark 5:18–20 ‖ Luke 8:38–39),
when the former demoniac begs Jesus for permission to stay with him as
Jesus leaves the territory of the Gerasenes. Jesus does not permit him to follow him, but rather tells him to go home and report to his family what has
happened. The former demoniac thus becomes a symbol of a whole group of
people we shall have to examine in Section IV of this chapter: devoted adherents of Jesus who do not qualify as "disciples" in the strict sense because
Jesus does not call them to follow him literally.

B. Following Jesus Physically and Therefore Leaving One's Home

We come to the second striking trait of discipleship in the Gospels, a trait already alluded to in the treatment of the first trait. Whether we look at Mark,
John, or Q, "following" Jesus was not simply a metaphor for absorbing and
practicing his teachings. Jesus called individuals to follow him literally, physically, as he undertook various preaching tours of Galilee, Judea, and surrounding areas. The traditions in Mark, Q, and L mentioned above agree on
an obvious consequence of becoming part of this peripatetic entourage: following Jesus as his disciple meant leaving behind one's home, parents, and
livelihood. One could not follow Jesus simply by staying at home and studying his teachings or by going to his schoolhouse and attending his lectures à
la Ben Sira. The very idea that becoming a pupil meant leaving family ties
and property for the sake of an itinerant ministry would be contrary to the
ethos of Ben Sira, who drilled into his students the duties of a son to his father and mother and who recommended the wise enjoyment of one's wealth
(e.g., Sir 3:1–16; 7:27–28; 14:11–16; 31:8–11).

The same would hold true of the later rabbis. In later rabbinic literature,
one hears of students "following" or "walking behind" their rabbi, but not
in the sense applied to Jesus' disciples in the Gospels. When rabbinic literature speaks of the disciple "following" (literally, "going after") his teacher,
the phrase is used simply of the respectful distance the disciple would observe
as he walked behind his master—just as a servant might walk before the

rabbi in his entourage.[39] The phrase does not serve as dense symbol, signifying a break in ties with home and family in order to follow an itinerant preacher and share his fate on various journeys around the whole of Palestine.[40] In rabbinic literature, while the language of "following" a teacher does occur, it does not function as a key theological concept.

Jesus' peremptory call to follow was open-ended not only geographically but also temporally. It did not set any time limit on the obligation to follow him. There was no course of studies, the completion of which would release a disciple from constant attendance upon Jesus. Becoming a disciple of Jesus was not a temporary appointment, after which the disciple could hope to be promoted to equality with Jesus as a younger colleague. This contrasts notably with the normal relationship of a rabbinic student vis-à-vis his teacher. The whole point of a rabbinic disciple attaching himself to a noted teacher was to learn the rabbi's wise and reliable interpretation of the Torah, communicated not only by the master's verbal instruction (carefully repeated and memorized) but also by his daily conduct (observed by living in a shared household). Ordinarily, this life of discipleship was meant to be a transitional stage. When the student completed his period of instruction in the Torah, he was free to leave his former master and undertake his own career as a rabbi.[41] The aim of this education was "to enable the student to make free and independent decisions in matters of religious law."[42] In rabbinic literature, ordination marks the transition.[43]

In contrast, as Luke 9:59–62 intimates, Jesus called disciples not primarily to learn Torah but to experience and proclaim the kingdom of God—activities that apparently bound the disciple to Jesus and his message for an unspecified future. To turn back from that call—or, equivalently, to turn back from following Jesus—was to show oneself unfit for the kingdom. Once a disciple answered the call, he was, in the eyes of Jesus, no longer free to "drop out." Not surprisingly, one hears an undertone of sharp judgment latent in Mark's laconic report of Jesus' arrest in Gethsemane: "And leaving him [Jesus], they [the disciples] all fled" (Mark 14:50 par.). Leaving Jesus— even, or especially, in the face of danger—was tantamount to desertion. This point brings us to a third notable aspect of the discipleship to which Jesus called certain chosen individuals.

C. RISKING DANGER AND HOSTILITY

The immediate costs of following Jesus physically were obvious: one left home, family, and employment. But, above and beyond this, Jesus apparently warned his disciples that hostility and danger might await them in the future, just as it might await him. Particularly as the ministry of Jesus was drawing to its tragic climax, it would have been only natural for Jesus to have warned his closest followers of possible hardships to come. While we have no way of placing most of the sayings of Jesus in particular periods of his public ministry, it may well be that his sayings on "the cost of discipleship" come mostly if not entirely from the final days of his career, as the storm clouds of conflict with the Jerusalem authorities were gathering and darkening.[44]

Fortunately, when we ask whether the historical Jesus actually taught his followers that discipleship comes at the high price of hostility and suffering, we have more than general surmise on which to rely. Abundant multiple attestation of sources argues that Jesus did in fact warn his disciples of the fierce and possibly fatal cost of following him.

1. Saving or Losing One's Life

One particular type of aphorism, in which Jesus contrasts saving and losing one's life, enjoys a rare form of triple attestation (Mark, Q, and John). As Taylor remarks, "Few sayings of Jesus are so well attested as this."[45] Indeed, if we count all the parallels, it occurs in the four Gospels six times.

I should emphasize from the beginning that, in what follows, my argument will not depend upon establishing the exact wording of *the* primitive form of this aphorism or of any of the sayings to be examined. Jesus may well have uttered aphorisms about the cost of discipleship at various times in various ways with various words.[46] I will offer some suggestions about what some primitive *forms* of this saying may have looked like. But the main point of what follows is that multiple attestation establishes the core content of what the historical Jesus taught about the cost of commitment to him. Since I am interested in the "core content" witnessed by all the variant forms of the aphorism, I will place in brackets those words in a particular form of the aphorism that may be secondary additions by the evangelist or the Christian tradition he inherited.

(a) In the Marcan tradition (Mark 8:35 parr.), Jesus' warning to his disciples is placed strategically after Peter's confession of faith in Jesus as the Messiah (8:27–30) and Jesus' first prediction of the passion and his rebuke to Peter for not accepting that prediction (8:31–33). Jesus proceeds to utter a series of aphorisms and prophecies about the costs and rewards of discipleship (8:34–9:1). Each logion in this series has its own form and tradition history, and the logia were probably collected secondarily either by Mark or more likely by a pre-Marcan bearer of the tradition.

Within this collection of sayings on discipleship, Mark 8:35 has the form of a paradoxical aphorism *(māšāl)*, the paradox being underlined by both antithetic parallelism and chiasm:[47] "For whoever wishes to save *(sōsai)* his life will lose *(apolesei)* it; but whoever loses *(apolesei)* his life [for the sake of myself and the gospel] will save *(sōsei)* it." Matthew 16:25 and Luke 9:24 repeat this Marcan form of the saying with only slight variations in wording. Significant, though, is the one place where Matthew and Luke agree against Mark: both omit "and the gospel." Adding to the puzzle, some early Greek manuscripts of Mark omit "myself and" in 8:35 while keeping "for the sake of the gospel."[48]

It may be that both later evangelists and later scribes felt that the double reference ("for the sake of myself and the gospel") overloaded the second half of a two-part aphorism constructed on the basis of antithetic parallelism. Their esthetic sense was on target: the awkwardness and lack of balance in Mark 8:35 probably point to a secondary addition, especially since Mark loves to say the same thing twice, the second phrase making the first one more precise ("Marcan duality").[49] The phrase "and the gospel" looks particularly suspicious, since (1) "gospel" is a key theological term of Mark, (2) the absolute use of "gospel" without any modifier is unique to Mark among the four Gospels, and (3) a number of occurrences of "gospel" clearly stem from Mark's redactional activity (e.g., Mark 1:1,14,15).[50] It is hardly by accident that "for the sake of myself and the gospel" occurs in two different Marcan statements on the cost of discipleship, Mark 8:35 and 10:29. Most likely, then, at least the phrase "and the gospel" does not belong to the earliest form of the saying.

I would suggest that even "for the sake of myself" may be an addition, though perhaps a pre-Marcan one.[51] It, too, lacks any corresponding phrase in the first half of the aphorism and so upsets the balance of the two-part saying. Granted, one must allow for the possibility that Jesus purposely upset the rhetorical balance to emphasize the "extra" factor in the second half of his aphorism. However, in view of the absence of any such qualification in the forms of the aphorism found in Luke 17:33 (Q) and John 12:25, I think it likely that the earliest form of Mark 8:35 was: "Whoever wishes to save his life will lose it; whoever loses his life will save it."[52]

Besides the use of antithetic parallelism and chiasm together in a tight unit, the saying may reflect a Semitic background in the ambiguous use of *psychē,* which I have translated "life." If, as many commentators think, the Greek noun *psychē* reflects here the Aramaic noun *nĕpaš, psychē* might be translated alternatively as the reflexive pronoun "himself": "Whoever wishes to save himself will lose himself; whoever loses himself will save himself." The problem here is that no one English word captures the wide-ranging sense of the Aramaic *něpaš* or the equivalent Hebrew *nepeš*. The Hebrew noun *nepeš* expresses a holistic concept: the concrete existence or life of the individual person, both in all its physical and psychological power and in all its vulnerability to suffering and death. Scholars like Gerhard Dautzenberg stress that this is the meaning of the noun *psychē* in both halves of Mark 8:35 parr.; therefore, one must not evaporate the sense of the noun *psychē* into either "soul" or "earthly life" versus "heavenly life."[53] Jesus is speaking of saving or losing one's whole life or existence, not of "saving one's soul."

Some commentators have suggested that behind this aphorism may lie an observation from Israel's wisdom tradition, an observation that was focused exclusively on this earthly life. Such a saying would have noted the paradox that trying desperately to hold on to one's life may cause one to lose it, while being willing to risk one's life courageously (for example, in battle)[54] may lead to the preservation of one's life. Obviously, within the eschatological proclamation of Jesus, the aphorism's thrust is stretched far beyond such worldly wisdom. As a reward for risking one's life in the present, Mark 8:35 parr. clearly points to life in the future kingdom of God. In this respect, the saying is a miniature example of wisdom being fused with prophecy to create apocalyptic: those who cling at all costs to this present life will lose it at the final judgment, while those willing to sacrifice their present lives to follow Jesus wholeheartedly will receive a fuller, lasting form of life at the final judgment.[55] The antithetic parallelism and chiasm of the aphorism thus enshrine Jesus' proclamation of the reversal of all human values and conditions, such as we find in the beatitudes.

(b) A divergent form of the logion is found in both Luke and Matthew and probably stems from the Q tradition. The Lucan form (17:33) reads: "Whoever seeks to preserve *(peripoiēsasthai)* his life will lose *(apolesei)* it, but whoever loses *(apolesei)* it will preserve *(zōogonēsei)* it." The Matthean form (10:39) reads: "The one who finds *(heurōn)* his life will lose *(apolesei)* it, and the one who loses *(apolesas)* his life [for my sake] will find *(heurēsei)* it."

Do these two variant forms of the aphorism really come from Q, or are they simply creative rewritings of Mark 8:35? A few authors argue for the latter alternative.[56] However, despite the great similarity of these two sayings to Mark 8:35 parr., most critics hold that Luke 17:33 ‖ Matt 10:39 represent a separate Q form of the aphorism. Three reasons argue for this view: (1) Luke tends to avoid doublets (i.e., two forms of the same saying or story). Hence it is unlikely that he would have gone out of his way to rewrite Mark 8:35, which he has already reproduced almost word for word at Luke 9:24, and then place the rewritten form later in his Gospel, at Luke 17:33.[57] (2) If Luke 17:33 ‖ Matt 10:39 were the results of both Luke and Matthew rewriting Mark 8:35 independently of each other and placing it in other discourses of their respective Gospels, we would have to suppose that Luke and Matthew just happened to hit upon the same curious way of treating this particular logion; such coincidence strains credulity. (3) Although Matthew and Luke place this saying in different contexts, both of them, independently of each other, locate it in a context of Q material. Matthew places it toward the end of his missionary discourse (10:5–42), while Luke places it toward the end of the eschatological discourse (17:22–37), which he locates near the conclusion of his great journey-to-Jerusalem narrative. Once again, without a Q form of the saying, the coincidence in editorial activity is striking. In short, derivation from Q is a much more likely hypothesis than the rewriting of Mark 8:35 by both Matthew and Luke working independently of each other.[58]

Luke 17:33 is remarkably close *not* to the final redactional form of Mark 8:35 *but rather* to what seems to have been the pre-Marcan form of the aphorism: "Whoever wishes to save his life will lose it; whoever loses his life will save it." The similarity is all the more striking when we realize that differences in vocabulary between the Marcan and Lucan formulations could reflect alternate Greek translations of the same Aramaic words.[59]

For example, the Marcan "whoever *wishes* to *save* his life" corresponds to the Lucan "whoever *seeks* to *preserve* his life." Behind the verbs "wishes" (the Marcan *thelē*) and "seeks" (the Lucan *zētēsē*) may lie either the Aramaic verb *ṣĕbēh* ("wish," "will," "desire") or the verb *bĕʾâ* ("seek," "request"). Behind the verbs "save" (the Marcan *sōsai*) and "preserve" (the Lucan *peripoiēsasthai* and *zōogonēsei*) may lie either the Aramaic verb *šêzib* ("save," "rescue") or the hapʿel form of the verb *ḥăyâ* ("to live," in hapʿel "to keep alive," "to restore to life," "to rescue").

The first half of the aphorism ends the same way in both Mark and Luke: "shall lose *(apolesei)* it"—indeed, some form of the verb "to lose" is present in all the various forms of the saying. The Greek verb for "lose" (or: "destroy") may represent the hapʿel of the Aramaic verb *ʾăbad* (in peʿal "to perish," "be lost," in hapʿel "to destroy"). The same may be said of the opening of the second half of the aphorism ("but he who loses his life"), although Luke does not repeat the object "life," perhaps because the mechanical repetition demanded by strict Semitic parallelism seemed wearisome to his refined Greek tastes.

In the conclusion of the second half of the aphorism, Mark has "shall save *(sōsei)* it," while Luke has "shall preserve *(zōogonēsei)* it." Once again, we may have alternate translations of the underlying Aramaic saying. Since the repetition of the verb "to save" probably reflects the parallelism of the Aramaic saying, *šēzib* and the hap‘el form of *ḥăyâ*, which were the likely candidates for the Aramaic background in the first half of the saying, are the most plausible candidates here as well. Luke—or his version of the Q tradition— may have sought to avoid the tiresome repetition of the Semitic parallelism by employing two different verbs *(peripoiēsasthai* and *zōogonēsei)* for the same idea ("preserve").[60] Whether at least one of these two Greek verbs stood in the Q version of the saying Luke inherited is difficult to judge.[61]

The Matthean form of the Q saying is likewise quite similar to the primitive pre-Marcan form of the saying, with the exception of the additional phrase "for the sake of myself" in Matt 10:39. As we have already seen, this phrase, which disturbs the neat parallelism and is missing in both a Lucan and a Johannine form of the saying, is probably an addition to the earliest form.

Other differences between Matt 10:39 and the primitive pre-Marcan logion are mainly stylistic and may well flow from Matthew's redaction. Instead of the introductory indefinite relative clause with a conditional sense ("whoever," *ho an* in the Greek), which we find in Mark and Luke, Matthew employs attributive participles used as substantives: *ho heurōn* ("he who finds") and *ho apolesas* ("he who loses"). This use of participles may be due to Matthean redaction. If the participles had been present in the Q form of the saying, it is difficult to see why Luke, who favors participial constructions, substituted relative clauses ("whoever"). Granted, one might argue that, in choosing relative clauses, Luke was simply following Mark 8:35. But then one must explain why Luke on the one hand made 17:33 so different from Mark 8:35 in vocabulary when on the other hand he supposedly changed his Q source to make it match Mark in syntactical structure.[62] On the whole, it seems more likely that the participial construction comes from Matthew. Admittedly, the matter is not entirely clear, since the Johannine form of the aphorism (John 12:25) likewise employs attributive participles used as substantives: *ho philōn* ("he who loves") and *ho misōn* ("he who hates").

A stronger candidate for Matthean redaction is the substitution of the verb "to find" *(heuriskō* in Matthew) for the verb "to save" or "to preserve" (expressed by various verbs in Mark, Luke, and John). According to Ulrich Luz, the verb "to find" belongs to the list of words preferred by Matthew;[63] hence it is not surprising that he would use it redactionally here. Moreover, Luke uses "to find" almost twice as often as Matthew (45 times to 27 times, plus 35 times in Acts). With Luke's fondness for the verb "to find," why would he not have kept this verb in 17:33 if it had stood in Q? It would have satisfied his desire for stylistic variation vis-à-vis Luke 9:24 ∥ Mark 8:35.

Another argument in favor of "find" being redactional in Matt 10:39 is that we have one case where Matthew certainly substituted "find" for "save"—namely, in Matthew's redaction of Mark 8:35 in Matt 16:25 (the instruction on discipleship following the first prediction of the passion). While Matthew faithfully repeats most of Mark 8:35 in Matt 16:25 (including the verb "save" in the first half of the aphorism), he suddenly substitutes "find" for "save" at the end of the aphorism. Apparently he does the same thing—but more consistently—in both halves of Matt 10:39. As already indicated, the influence of Matt 16:25 (and ultimately Mark 8:35) on Matt 10:39 is also seen in Matthew's addition of "for the sake of myself" *(heneken emou),* which comes via Matt 16:25 from Mark 8:35.

All in all, I think the peculiarities of Matt 10:39 are attributable to Matthean redaction, and so Luke 17:33 is probably closer to the primitive Q version of the aphorism.[64] The Q logion, in turn, most likely ran quite similar to if not the same as the pre-Marcan saying: "Whoever wishes [or: seeks] to save [or: preserve] his life will lose [or: destroy] it; whoever loses his life will save it." One possible Aramaic retroversion of this primitive saying found in both Mark and Q would be:

man dî yiṣbē[65] *lĕšēzābā' napšēh*	Whoever seeks to save his life
yĕhôbĕdinnah	will lose it;
wĕman dî yĕhôbēd napšēh	and whoever loses his life
yĕšēzĕbinnah[66]	will save it.

One must remember, however, that it is doubtful whether we can speak of one "original" form of the saying. Jesus may well have affirmed this teaching in different words at different times. We must leave open the possibility that some of the variant forms of the saying in Greek go back to variant forms of the saying in Aramaic. The matter is complicated by a still further variant of the saying found in John.

(c) This third independent variant of the saying occurs in John 12:25, as Jesus is delivering his final words to the Jerusalem crowd before the passion: "The one who loves *(philōn)* his life loses *(apollyei)* it, and the one who hates *(misōn)* his life [in this world] will keep *(phylaxei)* it [unto life everlasting]."

In the first two volumes of *A Marginal Jew,* I have taken the majority position that the tradition of John's Gospel is independent of the Synoptics', and once again this position seems verified when we examine John 12:25. While exhibiting scattered similarities to various Synoptic forms of the saying, John 12:25 copies none of them and has many characteristics proper to itself.[67] The only words it shares with the Synoptic forms is "his life" *(tēn psychēn autou),* "it" *(autēn,* referring to "his life"), and (in a way) "lose." However, for the verb "lose," the Greek verb *apollyō* is used (in the present tense) instead of its more common variant *apollymi;* the latter is employed (in the future tense) in all the Synoptic forms.[68] John shares these few words with *all* the other forms; the similarities cannot be used to argue for his dependence on any particular Synoptic passage. Actually, when one stops to think about it, it is hard to imagine how John 12:25 could be recognized as a parallel to Mark 8:35 parr. without at least these few words.

In contrast, the rest of the key words and phrases in John 12:25 ("love," "hate," "in this world," "unto life everlasting," "will keep") John shares with *none* of the other forms of the logion; these words are all unique to John's form.[69] John's grammatical structure of attributive participles used as substantives parallels the structure of Matt 10:39, and both forms of the saying connect their two halves with "and" rather than "but" (a possible echo of a Semitic substratum). However, the fairly sleek structure of Matt 10:39 is not reflected in John. The second half of the Johannine aphorism is weighed down with what looks like two Johannine additions, placed back to back and employing typically Johannine theological terms: "in this world" and "unto life everlasting." [70] In this overloading of the second half of the aphorism with characteristic theological terms, John 12:25 is vaguely similar to Mark 8:35.

A deeper structural difference lies in the fact that while John 12:25 displays antithetic parallelism as do the Synoptics, John 12:25 does not also employ the chiastic structure found in the Synoptics. Whatever their vocabulary, all the Synoptic forms invert the order of their main verbs in a crisscross pattern. In other words, they make what are the subordinate and main verbs of the first half of the aphorism the main and subordinate verbs of the second half of the aphorism: save/lose // lose/save (Mark 8:35 parr.); preserve/lose // lose/preserve (Luke 17:33); find/lose // lose/find (Matt 10:39). Instead, John 12:25 has the pattern of love/lose // hate/keep. The basic antithesis is kept, but the verbs are not interchanged in chiastic fashion.

When we consider (1) the massive differences in both vocabulary and structure between John and the Synoptics, (2) the minimal similarities that do not connect John's version strongly with any one Synoptic version, and (3) the completely different narrative context of the logion in John, the only plausible judgment is that John's version is independent of any or all of the Synoptic forms of the saying.[71]

Without the apparent Johannine additions, John 12:25 supplies a simple two-part aphorism, similar to but not the same as the one I suggested as the source of both the Marcan and Q forms: "He who loves his life will lose [or: destroy] it,[72] and he who hates his life will keep [or: preserve] it." To be sure, the strong opposition between "love" and "hate" is well attested in Greco-Roman literature; but it fits especially well into Johannine dualism. In this saying, it could also be an echo of a typical Semitic locution, which expresses preference and choice in stark, absolute terms of loving and hating (cf. Luke 14:26 ‖ Matt 10:37).[73] A possible Aramaic form of this saying would run like this:

man dî rāḥēm napšēh	The one who loves his life
yĕḥôbĕdinnah	will lose it,
wĕman dî śānēʾ napšēh	and the one who hates his life
yiṭṭērinnah	will keep it.

Thus, I would suggest that there were at least two basic forms of this saying circulating in Aramaic: the Mark-Q version and the Johannine version. In addition, I cannot exclude the possibility that peculiarities of other variants (e.g., Matt 10:39)—which I would prefer to explain by redactional activity—may also reflect a distinct Aramaic form going back to the public ministry of Jesus.

To sum up: especially if we leave aside the words I have bracketed as possible Christian additions—additions that in any event disturb the tight parallelism at the core of the aphorism—we are left with a number of variants of a single proverb *(māšāl)*. The proverb comments on the paradoxical relationship between the action of preserving or losing one's life and the results of such an action, results that are the exact opposite of what one would expect if one judged by superficial human standards. The terse proverb has a basic two-part antithetical structure, each part in turn expressing an antithesis as well: save/lose // lose/save—or, alternately, preserve/lose // lose/preserve—or alternately, find/lose // lose/find—or alternately, love/lose // hate/preserve. All the forms aim at one basic message: a disciple who clings selfishly or cowardly to this present life as the ultimate good will lose the ultimate good of true life in the kingdom of God, while a disciple who voluntarily risks (or actually suffers) the loss of this present life will save/preserve/find true life in the kingdom. While the saying may well include the prospect of suffering death as the price of being a disciple of Jesus, the focus is wider. Placed within the context of Jesus' eschatological message, which we explored in Volume Two, the saying tells the disciple that discipleship means a surrender of one's old life, with all its ties, securities, and expectations, if one is to find or preserve the new form of life made possible by the coming of God's kingdom.

Such a pithy, paradoxical proverb that is attested in variant forms in Mark, Q, and John has a very good chance of going back to the historical Jesus. Rarely are the aphorisms of Jesus attested by this kind of striking

Mark-Q-John "overlap." Moreover, in this case the criterion of coherence supports multiple attestation, since Jesus' preaching (e.g., in the beatitudes, aphoristic sayings, and parables) often promised a paradoxical reversal of values and judgments on the last day.[74]

2. Denying Oneself and Taking up One's Cross

Another saying of Jesus that graphically inculcates the cost of discipleship is found in both Mark 8:34 and Q (Matt 10:38 ‖ Luke 14:27).[75]

(a) Mark 8:34 reads: "If anyone wishes to follow after me *(opisō mou akolouthein),* let him deny himself and take up *(aratō)* his cross and follow me *(akoloutheitō moi).*"[76]

The structure of the saying exhibits a clever use of *inclusio* ("end as you begin") and chiasm (a crisscross A-B-B'-A' pattern).[77] The beginning and end of the saying mention the goal that the would-be disciple intends: following Jesus. The apparent redundancy of the verb "follow" is actually purposeful, leading from initial intention ("if any one *wishes* to follow after me") to achievement of goal ("follow me").[78] Sandwiched between the two references to following are the two means or ways one arrives at the goal.

First, one must "deny oneself," "totally disavow one's own interests" *(aparnēsasthō heauton),* in other words, say "no" to oneself and one's ego as the ultimate norm and goal of one's life.[79] Purposely intensifying the negative idea of this first means, Jesus adds the shocking and repulsive image of a condemned naked criminal being forced to take up the horizontal beam of his own cross and carry it to the place of execution (where the upright beam was permanently fixed). No more horrific and disgusting symbol of having to bid farewell to one's whole life (including one's property and means of support), to one's whole past (with all of one's family ties), and to one's whole future (with all its plans and projects), could be imagined by a 1st-century Palestinian Jew, who was all too familiar with this type of execution. The complete loss of control over one's life (indeed, even over one's bodily functions in public) was made all the more terrifying by the shame and mockery that accompanied this slow and painful death.[80]

Jesus often used shocking symbols to drive home his message (e.g., Matt 19:12: "Those who make themselves eunuchs for the kingdom of heaven"; Mark 14:22: "Take, this is my body"),[81] but no symbol could be more shocking than this. The point is clear: those who think they want to follow Jesus as disciples must count the costs beforehand with cold sobriety;[82] there is no easy road to discipleship. To follow Jesus is to say no to oneself as the center of one's existence ("deny himself") with such radical severity that this commitment could be equated with the most ghastly and humiliating of deaths ("take up his cross"). Only when one appreciates the full force of these two "means" to discipleship, sandwiched between the two occurrences of the verb "follow," does one feel the shock of the second and climactic mention of following, now expressed as a peremptory command: "If anyone wishes to follow me [i.e., become my disciple], let him first say no to his whole life and [metaphorically] lug his cross to his shameful public execution, and [thus, by going through this death to his whole former life] let him follow me [as my disciple]."[83]

Both the shocking imagery and the multiple attestation of sources (see below on the Q form) argue for Jesus as the source of the saying. In addition, the wording of the logion is not what we would naturally expect from a post-Easter Christian formulation. Nothing explicit is said in the logion about following a Jesus who is likewise bearing a cross; indeed, the would-be disciple is called to take up "his" (i.e., the disciple's) cross, not Jesus' cross.[84] While not impossible in a saying invented on the far side of Good Friday, this way of putting things is at least curious if one holds Mark 8:34 to be a totally Christian creation. The disturbing metaphor of bearing one's own cross to one's execution should not be pressed beyond its rhetorical purpose within the sentence into some sort of historical reminiscence of Jesus' execution or into a detailed allegory of how one is to follow Jesus.[85]

Despite the arguments from multiple attestation and characteristically shocking metaphors, some might want to disqualify Mark 8:34 parr. on the grounds that it must be a Christian creation because it uses the symbol of the cross, the Christian symbol *par excellence*. But that is to give 1st-century Christians a monopoly on an instrument of torture and death that was all too freely bestowed on non-Roman inhabitants of the outlying provinces of the empire. Before and after Jesus, Palestine was studded with crosses, some put up by native rulers in addition to those planted by the Roman overlords. As a matter of fact, Jesus was not the only 1st- or 2d-century teacher in the Roman empire to use the cross as a graphic symbol of the suffering that is sure to befall upright persons without any provocation on their part. In his *Diatribes* (*Discourses*, 2.2.20), the Stoic philosopher Epictetus (ca. A.D. 55–135) remarks to *his students:* "If you wish to be crucified *(staurothēnai)*, wait, and the cross *(ho stauros)* will come."[86] In the Greco-Roman world, part of the humiliation of being crucified was that it was all too common a punishment for marginal people: e.g., slaves, robbers, rebels, and subject peoples in general when they disturbed the peace. Hence it would naturally come to the mind of such socially marginal people as Jesus and Epictetus as a gripping and all-too-realistic symbol of suffering and death. As we have seen, Mark 8:34 parr. coheres perfectly with Jesus' penchant for graphic, shocking language that would imprint itself on his disciples' minds.[87]

(b) Besides repeating the Marcan form of the saying (Matt 16:24 ∥ Luke

9:23) with slight variations, Matthew and Luke also preserve a Q form of the logion, though the two evangelists differ somewhat in wording.[88] Matthew 10:38 reads: "Whoever does not take *(lambanei)* his cross and follow after me *(akolouthei opisō mou)* is not worthy of me." Luke 14:27 has the same basic structure but partly different vocabulary: "Whoever does not carry *(bastazei)* his own cross and come after me *(erchetai opisō mou)* cannot be my disciple."

As usual, scholars disagree on the question of which formulation reflects Q better. When we remember that ultimately we are asking about what Jesus may have said, a great deal of the debate is moot. "Follow after me" and "come after me" would be represented by one and the same clause in Aramaic: "whoever goes [or: comes] after me." Similarly, "take" and "carry" might be translation variants of the same Aramaic verb. The major difference between Matthew and Luke lies at the end of the saying. The phrase "is not worthy of me" serves as a connecting refrain in the composition of Matt 10:37–38: "He who loves father or mother more than me *is not worthy of me,* and he who loves son or daughter more than me *is not worthy of me,* and he who does not take his cross and follow after me *is not worthy of me."* The refrain of "is not worthy of me" thus seems to be a structuring device employed by Matthew or by a collector of the M tradition before him. The Gospel of Matthew uses the adjective "worthy" more than any other single book in the NT, and seven out of the nine occurrences in Matthew are concentrated in the missionary discourse of chap. 10. Hence the Lucan "cannot be my disciple" has a better chance of reflecting Q. The Q saying would therefore have read more or less as follows: "Whoever does not take [or: carry] his cross and come after [i.e., follow] me cannot be my disciple." [89]

Nevertheless, as with the variant forms of Mark 8:35 parr., it makes little difference which version or hypothetical primitive form of the Q saying is judged more original. Similarly, the debate over whether the Marcan or the Q form is more primitive may be beside the point if Jesus spoke this dire warning at various times in various ways.[90] Indeed, it seems difficult, from a structural point of view, to reduce Mark 8:34 to the parallel Q formulation, or vice versa. Mark 8:34 is positively formulated, with a positive condition (protasis) followed by three positive commands (apodosis). The Q parallel is negatively formulated in both the opening relative clause (protasis: "whoever does not . . .") and in the concluding statement (apodosis: "cannot be . . ."). Whether Mark reformulated an earlier form of a negative saying in a positive way, or whether the Q tradition did the opposite, is neither verifiable nor terribly important. The significant point is that we have another Mark-Q overlap. Thus, once again, multiple attestation of sources shows that Jesus warned his disciples about the utter seriousness of following him and the dire consequences they might face.

3. Facing Hostility from One's Family

Not all the suffering and opposition of which Jesus spoke would come from outsiders or rulers. A very practical part of the cross that Jesus promised his disciples was strife with their family and relatives, strife occasioned by their literal following of Jesus around Palestine. In the Mediterranean world, both ancient and modern, the large-scale government is usually the enemy, the necessary evil to be kept at bay. What one trusts, relies upon, and contributes to willingly is one's extended family, the primary safety net in peasant society. Ancient Mediterranean society was largely a society of "dyadic personality," where one's identity was formed and maintained in relation to other individuals in one's social unit—the usual unit being the extended family.[91] To bid farewell for an indefinite period to the bonds of emotional and financial support, to spurn the only "opinion group" whose opinion daily affected one's life, to take the shameful path of deserting one's family and work in an honor-shame society—all this was no easy choice for the ordinary Jewish peasant of Galilee or Judea, male or (especially) female. A priori, therefore, one might expect that Jesus would speak to his followers about this down-to-earth cost of discipleship. As a matter of fact, there is multiple attestation—once again, in both Mark and Q—that Jesus spoke to his disciples about the domestic cost of following him.

(a) In Mark 10:28–30 parr., Peter is presented as not-so-subtly pointing out to Jesus the price that he and other disciples have paid: "Behold, we have left all things and followed you." Jesus replies not with a denial of his disruptive impact but with a promise of a compensating reward (Mark 10:29–30 ‖ Matt 19:29 ‖ Luke 18:29–30): "Amen I say to you, there is no one who has left house or brothers or sisters or mother or father or children or fields [for my sake and the sake of the gospel] who will not receive a hundredfold. . . . "[92] Some Christian commentators go out of their way to emphasize that Jesus is enunciating neither a guarantee of a reward nor the precise conditions to be met for receiving eternal life.[93] One senses in these interpretive comments a particular concern of Christian theology that Jesus the Jew may not have shared.

(b) A similar saying in Q hammers home the special, shocking price of discipleship, namely, turning one's back on one's family (Matt 10:37 ‖ Luke 14:26)—though in this case verbal agreements between Matthew and Luke are not as great as in some of the other Q passages we have studied. Both Matthew and Luke seem to have rewritten the traditional Q saying, but

Matthew's redactional hand is the heavier of the two.[94] Matthew 10:37 reads: "He who loves father or mother more than me is not worthy of me, and he who loves son or daughter more than me is not worthy of me." In contrast, Luke 14:26 reads: "If anyone comes to me and does not hate his father and mother and [his] wife and children and brothers and sisters—yes, even his very life [*psychēn*]—he cannot be my disciple."

A good deal of Matthew's version reflects his typical vocabulary, and he has changed the more primitive, Semitic-sounding, and shocking vocabulary of hating one's family into the less disturbing description of loving one person more than another. We have already seen how Matthew uses the refrain "is not worthy of me" to tie together vv 37 + 38. The one element of Matthew's version that may reflect the primitive Q form is the tight two-part parallelism typical of a *māšāl* spoken by Jesus. In contrast, Luke's more lengthy and diffuse formulation, with its list of relatives, may stem from Mark 10:29 (via the Lucan parallel, 18:29).

As in John 12:25, the language of "hating" (in this case, the members of one's family) is typical of the shocking speech of Jesus as he emphasizes the cost of discipleship. The precise rhetorical thrust of this brutal language is clarified by the cases where the Gospels present various members of a single family as devoted followers of Jesus (e.g., Luke 10:38–42; John 12:1–8, to be treated below). In contrast to such united obedience to Jesus, "hating" refers in this logion to the necessity of preferring Jesus unreservedly when one's family opposes the commitment of discipleship or makes rival claims on the would-be disciple. We are reminded of the dutiful candidates for discipleship who wanted to bury a dead father or say farewell to their family before they followed Jesus (Luke 9:59–62). Jesus' imperious command to follow posed a grave challenge to a traditional society where reverence for one's parents— even after one attained one's majority—was a sacred obligation enshrined in the Ten Commandments. The temple authorities in Jerusalem were probably not alone in thinking this strange itinerant prophet not only alienating but also dangerous. Willy-nilly, Jesus' call to discipleship would probably occasion fierce division in certain Palestinian families.

Indeed, a Q saying presents Jesus making just such a prediction (Matt 10:34–36 ‖ Luke 12:51–53). While it is difficult to reconstruct the primitive Q form of this logion, the basic thrust of the saying is clear.[95] Jesus' disciples are not to think that he has come to bring peace on earth (or perhaps: peace to the land of Israel) but rather a sword of division: son against father, daughter against mother, daughter-in-law against mother-in-law (the daughter-in-law being obliged to move into the house of the parents of her husband and become part of their family). Thus, the closest types of social bonds, the ties every Palestinian Jew would depend on when all else failed, are the very bonds that Jesus has come to loose. While this Q saying does not have a Marcan parallel, it coheres tightly with all the other sayings we have seen on the cost of discipleship, especially Luke 14:26 par. In a larger sense, it coheres with the prophetic and especially apocalyptic traditions of Israel, which saw the loosening of loyalty in family units as a prime sign of the tribulations of the last days, tribulations often symbolized by a sword.[96]

(c) Alongside the argument from multiple attestation of sources, the criterion of coherence also comes into play in a different and remarkably personal way. As various Gospel sources show, when Jesus demanded of his disciples that they leave their homes and thus risk incurring their families' wrath, he was simply asking them to replicate his own experience. While Mark 3:20–35 is, in its present form, a Marcan composition, the various component parts that Mark has put together indicate that in the first Christian generation there was a tradition that the family of Jesus did not believe in his mission during his public ministry.[97] In Mark 3:31–35 in particular, the mother and brothers of Jesus come to see Jesus only to be rebuffed. When Jesus is informed of their presence, he coolly leaves them waiting outside the house where he is teaching. He proclaims that the attentive crowd sitting around him is his true family: "Behold my mother and my brothers. For whoever does the will of God is my brother and sister and mother." Mark himself makes this scene even more negative in his redactional introduction (3:21), where he depicts the family of Jesus *(hoi par' autou)* setting out to seize him because they think he has gone mad.[98]

This unsettling idea of a rift in Jesus' own family is supported by the criterion of multiple attestation, since a similar negative view is given by the Fourth Evangelist in John 7:5. After the brothers of Jesus insincerely urge him to "showcase" his ministry in Jerusalem, the evangelist sadly turns to the reader in a typical aside and remarks: "For not even his brothers believed in him [Jesus]."[99] In contrast to the mother of Jesus, who, though presented in an ambiguous light in the wedding feast at Cana (2:1–12), is brought back in a positive light at the cross (19:25–27), Jesus' brothers disappear from the Gospel after 7:1–10.[100] Instead, on the cross the dying Jesus implicitly designates the beloved disciple as his true brother as he commits his mother to the beloved disciple's care—for, in a spiritual sense, he has no other brother to care for his mother. To be sure, we are dealing here with Johannine theology. But behind that theology lies a basic, blithely assumed idea: the brothers of Jesus did not believe in him during his public ministry. Quite independently of John, Mark represents the same position.

Besides multiple attestation of sources, one might also appeal, in a certain limited sense, to the criterion of embarrassment insofar as both Matthew and Luke tend to soften Mark's harsh presentation of Jesus' family. The positive portrayal of Jesus' mother in the infancy narratives of Matthew and Luke no doubt influences the presentation of Jesus' family in the public ministry of the two Gospels. Indeed, in Luke's infancy narrative, Mary the mother of Jesus is portrayed with traits suggestive of an ideal disciple.[101]

All the more striking, then, is the stray logion preserved in Luke 11:27–28. When a woman in the crowd cries out: "Happy the womb that bore you and the breasts that you sucked!" Jesus responds: "Rather, happy are those who hear the word of God and keep it." When understood within the overall two-volume work of Luke, this saying represents not a rejection of Jesus' mother but rather a proper appraisal of her. Her true happiness consists not in a merely physical connection to Jesus as his mother but rather in her role as one who hears and obeys the word of God.

This positive portrait of Mary is inculcated in the infancy narrative (especially the scenes of annunciation and visitation, Luke 1:26–56; cf. 2:19,51) and is extended through the public ministry (Luke 8:19–21) to her presence in the early church as it awaits the coming of the Spirit at Pentecost (Acts 1:14—pointedly along with Jesus' brothers). The harsh light of Mark's depiction of Jesus' family is thus softened, if not extinguished. Still, one must ask what the meaning of Luke 11:27–28 was in the oral tradition before it enjoyed the softening buffer of Luke's redactional theology. Almost inevitably, the tone of Jesus' exchange with the woman, when it circulated as a stray nugget in the oral tradition, would have been somewhat brusquer and thus closer to the tone of the statements about Jesus' family that we have examined in Mark and John.[102]

The criterion of embarrassment might be invoked in a different sense insofar as what Mark—and later John—says about Jesus' family may have been embarrassing, if not deeply offensive, to a good part of the early church. Despite his apparent opposition to Jesus during the latter's public ministry, James, the brother of Jesus, claimed to have seen the risen Jesus after the latter's death (1 Cor 15:7). James quickly became a leading member of the Jerusalem church (Gal 1:18–19), in fact, one of its "pillars" along with Peter and John (Gal 2:9). Indeed, after Peter left Jerusalem, James seems to have taken on a role similar to that of a tribal patriarch or a later Christian bishop (Gal 2:12; Acts 15:13–21; 21:17–18). Being the most prominent member of the Jerusalem church, James suffered martyrdom at the hands of the high priest Ananus the Younger in A.D. 62, as Josephus tells us in *Ant.* 20.9.1 §200.[103]

Since Mark wrote his Gospel ca. A.D. 70, it is difficult to believe that he went out of his way to make up a slanderous lie about James, who was well known as the decades-long leader of the Jerusalem church and who had recently suffered martyrdom there for the new faith. Even if Mark—for whatever reason—were to engage in such falsehood, how could he hope that Christians in general would accept such a newly minted lie about a revered leader and martyr, "the brother of the Lord" (as even Paul respectfully refers to him in Gal 1:19), a person known to various Christians still living at the time Mark wrote his Gospel? The much more likely explanation is that the tradition of the unbelief of James and the other brothers of Jesus during the public ministry was factual and was widely known to be so in the early church.

It is amazing, though, that Mark and John would have enshrined such an embarrassing tradition in their Gospels. Perhaps for these evangelists the tradition of the brothers' unbelief functioned in a way similar to the story of Peter's triple denial of Jesus: namely, as a source of hope for Christians who had denied their faith in the face of persecution. The evangelists' homily would be implied but obvious: even the great leaders failed Jesus, but they were forgiven and brought to Easter faith. Latter-day sinners can hope for the same mercy.[104]

Still, it hardly seems likely that, merely for the sake of homiletics, Mark and John—independently of each other—would have gone so far as to manufacture the story of the unbelief of Jesus' brothers if their depictions had no basis in fact. We can appreciate, then, that the warnings that the historical Jesus addressed to his disciples about suffering the loss of family ties may have reflected his own sad experience. An intriguing corollary thus arises: early Christians did not create out of whole cloth the idea that Jesus' path foreshadowed that of his disciples. To his chagrin, Jesus had noticed the pattern already.

One can begin to understand why, despite the fact that Jesus' committed followers were called his "disciples" (*mathētai*, literally, "learners"), the verb "to follow" *(akoloutheō)* describes their activity in the Gospels much more than the verb "to learn" *(manthanō)*. They were called literally to leave home and family to follow Jesus on his journeys, to share and be formed by Jesus' own prophetic ministry of proclaiming the kingdom, with all its consequent dangers, and not simply to learn or memorize certain doctrinal, legal, or ethical statements.[105] To be sure, rabbinical students shared their master's life, imitated his conduct, and memorized his words. But this did not involve imitating a prophetic and healing ministry in an eschatological context. Moreover, apart from special times of crisis (e.g., the execution of Rabbi Aqiba during the Bar Kochba revolt), exposure to fierce suffering or rejection by one's family and friends was not usually seen as part of the "job description" of the rabbinic student.[106]

We are now in a position to draw together some conclusions about the key sayings of Jesus on discipleship. From the criteria of multiple attestation, discontinuity, embarrassment, and coherence we are able to piece together a rough sketch of what it meant to be a historical disciple of the historical Jesus:[107] (1) Jesus seized the initiative in deciding who would be his disciples. He confronted certain individuals with his imperious command to follow him, a command that brooked no opposition or delay. (2) Hence, in using the term "following," Jesus intended not some pious metaphor but literal, physical following on his preaching tours around Palestine. Accordingly, those who accepted his command to follow had to leave behind home, family, and other comfortable ties. (3) On top of these hardships, Jesus warned his disciples that they might face other sufferings: hostility and even deadly opposition, including opposition from one's own alienated family.

In short, Jesus made a radical demand on his disciples: they had to be absolutely committed to him and his mission. After reviewing the other major "schools" of the Greco-Roman period and comparing them with Jesus' "school," Culpepper concludes that Jesus' "absolute demand as a condition of discipleship is unique in ancient scholastic traditions; in no other tradition is the demand for commitment raised to a comparable level." [108]

Yet Culpepper notes a certain paradox in the "school" of Jesus, built on such fierce demands. Often a group living a radical ethos around a charismatic leader will have stringent borders, marking it off from those living a less radical life. In the ancient world, such borders were often clearest at the common meals that a special religious or philosophical group would hold. Such meals represented intimate fellowship and shared life; as such, they were often closed to outsiders. Such was the case, apparently, with the Pharisees around the time of Jesus. Both at meals and in daily life, Qumran pushed the separation required by the rules of Jewish purity to the extreme, creating a sectarian community on the northwest shore of the Dead Sea.

All the more startling, therefore, is a characteristic practice of Jesus and his disciples (together with his sedentary supporters): namely, holding open table-fellowship with outsiders, even the disreputable toll collectors and sinners. It is here that Culpepper sees another striking difference from other ancient schools, a number of which also enjoyed common meals, but only within the group.[109] In contrast, acceptance of Jesus and his message were the only borders that marked off the whole group of his adherents, made up of both itinerant disciples and stay-at-home supporters.

We see, then, an interesting configuration: (1) Jesus' disciples are marked by obedience to his peremptory call, denial of self, and exposure to hostility and danger; these three traits constitute the radical, stringent life of Jesus' disciples. (2) Yet this radical group, marked by these three traits, is taught to be radically open to others, even to those "outside the pale." These, then, are the basic characteristics required to qualify as a disciple of Jesus during his public ministry. We know the names of some Jews who did qualify: well-known persons like Peter and Andrew, James and John, as well as more shadowy figures like Levi and Nathanael.[110] No doubt there were many others whose names are lost to us. Now, however, we must turn to some followers of Jesus whose names have not been lost to us—for example, Mary Magdalene, Joanna, and Susanna—but whose status as disciples, if not lost to us, is at least ambiguous.

III. THE UNCLEAR BOUNDARIES OF DISCIPLESHIP: WERE THE WOMEN FOLLOWERS OF JESUS DISCIPLES?

In our reconstruction of the historical situation of Jesus' public ministry, should the designation "disciples of Jesus" be restricted to those 1st-century Palestinian Jews who fully met the stringent requirements listed above? To put the question more pointedly from our contemporary viewpoint: because only males are specifically depicted as summoned to discipleship by Jesus and because only males are specifically called "disciples" in the Gospels,[111] should modern historians likewise restrict the term to males when describing the historical conditions of Jesus' ministry? Naturally, no one would object if modern writers engaged in homiletics or hermeneutics should stretch the term "disciple" to include all present-day believers. But if we are intent on a sober historical reconstruction of the 1st-century situation, scholarly integrity would seem to demand that we follow the usage of our sources. Do our sources favor or undermine the view that the committed female followers of Jesus were considered disciples during the public ministry?

Two points should be stressed before we start our investigation of women as disciples: (1) We are involved here only in the narrow question of the historical situation of Jesus in relation to his devoted female followers during his public ministry (ca. A.D. 28–30). We are not probing the larger question of the varied conditions of women in the Christian churches of the 1st century A.D. or the even larger question of what, if any, relevance such historical investigation may have for the status and role of women in the church today. (2) Once we define the narrow focus of this quest for the historical women around the historical Jesus, we must admit immediately that the data available for this quest are extremely sparse, and little can be said even with fair probability. Problems in the recent debate over women in the ministry of Jesus and in the modern church often stem from pressing the few references beyond what they can tell us. This over-exegeting of the texts available is often fueled in turn by a desire to answer larger questions of relevance, questions that we do not treat here because they never entered the minds of the evangelists.

Granted these restrictions, what can be affirmed with fair probability about the existence or nature of women disciples around the historical Jesus? To begin with, were there such women followers? And if women did follow Jesus in a literal, physical sense, were they called or considered "disciples" during Jesus' lifetime? These questions, simple though they may seem, are surprisingly difficult to answer. To be sure, when various Gospel passages speak in general of groups of "disciples" with Jesus, without specifying further the composition of the group, it is legitimate to point out that the masculine plural noun *hoi mathētai* may be understood inclusively, since at least some plural masculine nouns in Greek were so understood (e.g., the masculine plural *hoi goneis* for "parents"). Contrary to the contemporary tendency of American English usage, the masculine plural in Greek is open to an inclusive interpretation if the context does not indicate otherwise. Hence, the grammatical form *hoi mathētai* could refer to female as well as male disciples. An argument can be mounted that Luke in particular understands the plural this way, though he never plainly and directly uses the plural *mathētai* simply of a group of women.[112]

But, if Luke does consider the women to be disciples, we are left wondering why the singular form of the noun *mathētēs* or the equivalent feminine form *mathētria* is never applied specifically to a woman follower in Luke or, for that matter, in any of the other three canonical Gospels. Should we infer instead from this omission that the androcentric evangelists, influenced by the patriarchal culture of their time, consciously or unconsciously excluded women from the category of "disciples," despite the fact that some women in the Gospels seem to qualify for the role? If one wished to champion this position, one could argue that well-known historical tradition from the earliest days of Christianity forced the evangelists, against their own theological agendas, to depict certain women acting like disciples, even though the evangelists denied these women the label "disciples."

At a certain point, though, the only proper response to hypotheses and generalizations is the examination of specific texts. Clearly, certain passages in the Gospels, especially when taken together, seem to portray women followers of Jesus as equivalently disciples:[113]

(1) Immediately after the narration of Jesus' death and the events that ac-

company it, Mark recounts: "Now there were also women, looking on from a distance, among whom were Mary from Magdala, Mary the mother of James the Younger and Joses, and Salome, who, when he [i.e., Jesus] was in Galilee, followed him and served him, and many other [women] who had come up with him to Jerusalem [for the feast of Passover]" (15:40–41).[114] Matthew 27:55–56 repeats Mark's picture with a few redactional changes. Luke 23:49 diverges more in that he mentions the women globally, but gives no names at this point in the narrative (cf. the global reference at the burial of Jesus in Luke 23:55). Luke, who dislikes doublets, can afford to pass over the names here since he has already given a list of prominent women followers during the Galilean ministry (8:2–3).

The pivotal role of the women at the cross is revealed in the subsequent Marcan narrative, where at least some of them, notably Mary Magdalene, witness both the burial of Jesus (Mark 15:47 parr.) and the finding of the empty tomb (Mark 16:1–8 parr.). What is especially surprising about the mention of these women at the cross is that they appear so suddenly in Mark's Gospel, without any real preparation in the previous narrative (contrast Luke 8:1–3).[115]

(2) The presence of the women at the crucifixion of Jesus is supported by multiple attestation of sources. Independent of the Synoptic list, John likewise mentions women at the cross, although, because of the story of Jesus commending his mother to the care of the beloved disciple, he refers to them before the narration of Jesus' death.[116] The list of the women differs in part from the Synoptics': "Now there stood by the cross of Jesus his mother and the sister of his mother, Mary the [wife] of Clopas and Mary Magdalene" (19:25). Our concern here is not with the discrepancies in the names of the women in the four Gospels, but rather with the basic consistency amid all the differences of two independent traditions: both the Synoptics and John place certain women followers at Jesus' crucifixion and at the finding of the empty tomb.[117] Common to all the lists is Mary Magdalene.

(3) During his narrative of the Galilean ministry, Luke fills in the background of at least some of the women present at the crucifixion in one long, rambling sentence (8:1–3): "He [Jesus] was traveling from one city or village to another, proclaiming and telling the good news of the kingdom of God, and the Twelve [were traveling] with him, and also some women who had been healed of evil spirits and illnesses, Mary (called the Magdalene), out of whom seven demons had come, and Joanna, the wife of Chuza, the steward of Herod, and Susanna, and many other [women], who provided for them [or: served them, ministered to them] out of their own means [or: possessions, money]." [118]

As we saw in Volume Two of A Marginal Jew, the criteria of embarrassment and coherence suggest that the reference to the cure of Mary Magdalene actually goes back to an exorcism Jesus performed during his public ministry.[119] Moreover, while Luke 8:1–3 in its present form is a composition of Luke, written in his typical style, the list of women in vv 2–3 cannot be derived simply from Mark's lists of the women at the cross, the burial, or the finding of the empty tomb (Mark 15:40–41,47; 16:1 parr.).[120] Only Mary Magdalene is common to both the Marcan and the Lucan lists. Susanna appears nowhere else, and Joanna is mentioned again only at the empty tomb in Luke 24:10. Hence the list in 8:2–3 is hardly a perfect vehicle of Luke's redactional program (1:2) to have the eyewitnesses of the public ministry function as the ministers of the word in the early church (a function that none of the women in 8:2–3 is depicted as fulfilling in Acts).[121] In addition, granted Luke's desire to present Christianity as a "respectable" religion that does not threaten the Roman order, it hardly seems likely that he would have created the potentially shocking picture of women, some married, traveling around Galilee with Jesus and his twelve male disciples without benefit of husbands. Nor is it likely that the picture in 8:1–3 was created by Luke simply to have a parallel in his Gospel to the various women in Acts who act as patrons or hostesses for apostles and missionaries. In Acts, Luke—understandably, in view of his apologetic purposes—does not shock the reader's sensibilities by portraying unchaperoned women traveling around with Peter or Paul.

Hence, Luke's picture in 8:1–3 of unchaperoned women sharing the preaching tours of a celibate male teacher is discontinuous with both the Judaism of the time and with what Luke presents—and with what we know—of the first-generation Christian mission.[122] It seems that Luke, whatever his redactional purposes, preserves a valuable historical memory in 8:1–3: certain devoted women followers accompanied Jesus on his journeys around Galilee and finally up to Jerusalem and actually supported him and his entourage with their own money, food, or property.[123] If Luke is accurate on this last point, we are reminded that, while Jesus addressed himself especially to the poor (who constituted the vast majority of the population anyway), he did not address himself solely to the poor.[124] Moreover, while the women in 8:1–3 left house and family to follow Jesus, they apparently did not feel obliged to divest themselves immediately of all their money and property. If they had done so, they could hardly have "continued to provide" (diēkonoun, imperfect tense) for Jesus and the Twelve "out of" (ek) their money and property.[125] One wonders whether some of the male disciples (e.g., Simon Peter) had made similar arrangements.

(4) Thus, multiple attestation of sources (Mark, John, and Luke's special L

source) supports the existence of devoted female followers. More specifically, the Gospels present us with a picture of women traveling with Jesus, supporting and serving Jesus out of their own means, and standing by Jesus at his crucifixion when most if not all of his male disciples deserted him—and what should qualify for discipleship if not such steadfast service and loyalty to Jesus even unto the cross?

Nonetheless, we are faced with the fact that the word "disciple" is never applied to any of these women or to the whole group of women followers when they are mentioned apart from male followers. Why so? Some might claim that well-known historical tradition forced the male-chauvinist evangelists, contrary to their own theological agendas, to mention the women, even though they stubbornly refused to call them disciples. Still, it is passing strange that the androcentric evangelists should both go out of their way to depict these women as equivalent or superior to the male disciples and yet, at the same time, deny them the title "disciples." If the evangelists were so intent on suppressing the designation, why did they not also suppress the narratives that practically cry out for the designation? Some scholars try to resolve the paradox by claiming that the evangelists do not call the women followers "disciples" because they restrict that term to the Twelve. But a careful inspection of the evangelists' usage shows that there is no such iron-clad restriction.[126] Two other considerations may be of more help in explaining this apparently self-contradictory portrait of the women followers.

First, it may be that the evangelists are somewhat inhibited by the lack of specific call stories narrating how Jesus summoned particular individual women to follow him. That Jesus did call certain women to follow him in the literal, physical sense is never stated in the Gospels. Yet, even apart from Jesus' custom of issuing explicit calls to potential male disciples, it seems hardly likely that Palestinian-Jewish women could have undertaken the unusual, not to say scandalous, step of following Jesus and his male disciples around Galilee for a good amount of time without Jesus' summons beforehand or at least his clear assent after the fact.

The striking case of Mary Magdalene, whom Jesus freed from torment by an exorcism, may suggest that at times the women who were cured by Jesus saw their cures as equivalent to being called to follow Jesus, an interpretation Jesus accepted. Something of a rough parallel may be seen in the story of Jesus' cure of the blind Bartimaeus (Mark 10:46–52), where not any explicit call on the part of Jesus but the simple fact of the cure leads Bartimaeus to follow Jesus "on the road [of discipleship]."[127] Something similar may have happened in the case of Mary Magdalene, but admittedly this is just surmise.

In any event, the fact of the matter is that some women did follow Jesus for

a considerable length of time during his Galilean ministry and his last journey to Jerusalem. Such devoted, long-term following is inexplicable without
Jesus' initiative or at least his active acceptance of and cooperation with
the women who sought to follow him. Nevertheless, for whatever reason—
androcentric bias or just the chance fluctuations of oral tradition—the evangelists apparently possessed no call stories about women in the traditions
they inherited. This may have influenced them not to apply the title "disciple" to the women followers (just as it is not applied to Bartimaeus) since one
of the main components of discipleship—a component verified in the case of
a number of male disciples—was ostensibly missing.

A second consideration that may help explain why the women followers
are not called disciples rests upon a simple philological point, seen within the
larger truth of the constraints of history. Every speaker, writer, and thinker,
however imaginative or innovative, is hemmed in by the constraints of his or
her time and place, and in particular the constraints of his or her language. If
a teacher or writer wishes not to engage in playful inner conversation with
himself or herself but rather to communicate with and convince society at
large, then the commonly accepted concepts and words of this society must
be used, however creatively—or else no communication will take place. As
prophet and teacher, Jesus obviously wished to communicate with and convince his followers and Israel at large. Hence he too was subject to the same
sort of historical constraints as any other teacher.[128]

To be sure, there was a great deal about Jesus that was innovative. The
itinerant Jesus and his band of disciples constituted a relatively new phenomenon within the Jewish-Palestinian tradition of teacher-student relationships, a phenomenon that reflected to some degree Jesus' experience in the
circle of the Baptist's disciples. The very use of the word "disciple" for the
committed itinerant followers of Jesus was probably a fairly new application
of a word that is scarcely witnessed in the Jewish Scriptures or pseudepigrapha before the time of Jesus.[129]

Granted all this newness, it is perhaps expecting too much that a new form
of the word "disciple" would also have been coined during the two or so
years of Jesus' ministry. At the time of Jesus—and likewise during the rabbinic period—the words "disciple" and "disciples" existed in Hebrew and
Aramaic only in masculine forms: *talmîd* and *talmîdîm* in Hebrew; *talmîdāʾ*
and *talmîdayyāʾ* (determined states) in Aramaic. Hence the problem: during
his public ministry, Jesus indeed had committed women followers, but there
was literally no feminine noun that could be used to describe them; there was
no noun that said "female disciple(s)."

One is reminded here of the danger of doing either history or theology simply through word-studies. New realities emerge on the historical scene before there are new words to describe them, and sometimes the time-lag between new reality and new coinage is lengthy. Hence, the lack of any feminine form for the Greek noun *mathētēs* ("disciple") in our four Gospels may be due at least in part to the tenacity and conservative nature of the Gospel tradition. During the public ministry, Jesus and his disciples never used a special word for female disciples in Aramaic—for the simple reason that none existed—and so the Greek Gospels that flow from that tradition used no such word either.

It is probably not by accident that Luke, the evangelist most interested in women,[130] is the only NT author to use the feminine form *mathētria* ("female disciple"), a relatively rare formation of Koine Greek. Quite tellingly, though, he uses it not in his Gospel, where his statements about Mary Magdalene and other female followers almost demand it, but rather in Acts 9:36 to describe Tabitha, a devout Christian woman in the early church. Apparently, Luke did not feel authorized to introduce the feminine form into the relatively fixed Gospel tradition, while he did feel free to do so in his new kind of composition, the Acts of the Apostles, where he was not so tightly constrained by a normative tradition and the usage of previous Christian documents (e.g., Mark and Q). As a matter of fact, the noun *mathētria* is not used of a female disciple who had followed Jesus during his ministry until we get to the 2d-century apocryphal *Gospel of Peter,* where in 12:50 it is applied, not surprisingly, to Mary Magdalene, a perennial favorite of apocryphal and gnostic literature.[131] But even in the *Gospel of Peter* (as far as we can tell), it is used only in the narrative of the appearance of the risen Jesus to Magdalene on Easter Sunday morning—hence, outside the public ministry.[132]

We are left, then, with something of a paradox. Did the historical Jesus have women disciples? In name, no; in reality—putting aside the question of an implicit as opposed to an explicit call—yes. Certainly the reality rather than the label would have been what caught most people's attention. The sight of a group of women—apparently, at least in some cases, without benefit of husbands accompanying them—traveling around the Galilean countryside with an unmarried male who exorcised, healed, and taught them as he taught his male disciples could not help but raise pious eyebrows and provoke impious comments. As it was, Jesus was stigmatized by his critics as a bon vivant, a glutton and drunkard, a friend of toll collectors and sinners (Matt 11:19 par.), a demoniac or mad man (Mark 3:20–30 parr.; John 8:48). A traveling entourage of husbandless female supporters, some of whom were former demoniacs who were now giving Jesus money or food, would only

have heightened the suspicion and scandal Jesus already faced in a traditional peasant society. Yet, scandal or no scandal, Jesus allowed them to follow and serve him. Whatever the problems of vocabulary, the most probable
conclusion is that Jesus viewed and treated these women as disciples.

IV. THE UNCLEAR BOUNDARIES OF DISCIPLESHIP:
SUPPORTERS OF JESUS WHO DID NOT LEAVE THEIR HOMES

In addition to the male disciples who left home, family, and occupation to
follow Jesus physically, the Gospels present a number of male adherents to
the Jesus movement who supported Jesus by offering food and lodging when
he visited their city or town. Zacchaeus in Luke 19:1–10, Lazarus in John
12:1–2, the anonymous host of the Last Supper in Mark 14:13–15, and possibly Simon the leper in Mark 14:3 come to mind—giving us, by the way,
multiple attestation of sources. In exactly the same way—once again we find
a parallel between male and female adherents—we find in the Gospels depictions of committed women who, instead of joining Jesus' itinerant ministry,
show their loyalty to him by supporting him with their hospitality. These
women are not called disciples, but in this case neither are the male adherents, since all of them, male and female alike, lack the conditions (peremptory call from Jesus to follow, abandonment of home and family, exposure to
danger and hostility as one journeyed through Israel) necessary for being
considered disciples. Not all committed adherents were committed disciples,
and this held true for women as well as for men.

There is an odd sort of multiple attestation of sources (Luke and John) for
the existence of these women adherents who were not disciples. The memorable picture of Martha and Mary as Jesus' hostesses is presented in very different contexts in Luke 10:38–42 (where Jesus has just recently begun his
journey from Galilee up to Jerusalem) and John 11:1–45 + 12:1–8 (where
Mary and Martha are sisters of Lazarus and reside in a house in Bethany,
near Jerusalem). Whatever the historical reality, both Luke and John use
Mary and/or Martha to depict certain ideals of Christian faith that are to be
imitated.[133]

In Luke 10:38–42, Mary, precisely because she refuses to be distracted by
any mundane activity like preparing a meal, precisely because she chooses instead to sit (like a good disciple)[134] at the feet of Jesus, listening to his word,
is praised for having chosen the one necessary "portion."[135] Like Mary
the mother of Jesus, Mary the sister of Martha represents for Luke one of
the ideals of discipleship: listening to and treasuring the word of God (cf.
Luke 2:19,51; 11:27–28).

In John 11:27, it is Martha, not Simon Peter (cf. 6:69), who voices the high christology of the evangelist himself: "Yes, Lord, I have come to believe that you are the Messiah, the Son of God, who is to come into the world" (notice the last clause, emphasizing preexistence and incarnation, and the similar statement of faith by the evangelist in 20:31; cf. Matt 16:16). Moreover, in John 12:1–8, Mary performs a lavish act of love by anointing Jesus' feet at a banquet, an act Jesus interprets as pointing forward to his burial. Understandably, then, the Fourth Evangelist places Mary and Martha right alongside Lazarus as the objects of Jesus' love (11:5). Even if Martha and Mary—along with other male and female followers who support Jesus by giving him hospitality—do not qualify as "disciples" in the strict Gospel sense, they obviously occupy a special place of intimacy that far transcends the outer circle of the merely curious, itinerant crowd. At least certain things they say or do belong to the ideal portrait of a disciple. To be sure, the stories as we have them now in the Gospels are very much formed by the theological visions of Luke and John. But the multiple attestation of these two evangelists—to say nothing of the practical logistics of supporting the itinerant ministry of Jesus and his disciples[136]—argues for the existence of devoted men and women who offered Jesus food, lodging, and other forms of support when he came to their cities or towns on his preaching tours.

Another consideration bolsters this conclusion. In Volume Two of *A Marginal Jew,* we saw at length how Jesus qualified in the eyes of his adherents not only as a prophet but also as a miracle worker.[137] Whatever the explanation, a fair number of people claimed that they had been healed or exorcised by Jesus. It only stands to reason that, after their recovery, these people, along with their families and friends, would have become supporters of Jesus, offering him shelter, food, and money when he passed through their area. To be sure, this is a commonsense conclusion that probably held true in general, though not necessarily in every case. John's portrait of Mary and Martha, the sisters of Lazarus (John 12:1–8), certainly exemplifies the faith and gratitude we would expect from the families of those who benefitted from Jesus' miracles. At the same time, the obtuse paralytic in John 5:1–15 and the nine thoughtless lepers in Luke 17:11–19—all of whom show crass ingratitude toward Jesus after their healings—remind us that, while our commonsense conclusion may hold true in general, not everyone has common sense. Still, it remains likely that many of those who received Jesus' healing power, as well as their families and friends, became sedentary supporters of the Nazarene in the scattered towns and villages of Galilee and Judea.[138]

We come, then, to the end of our survey of the second or middle circle around Jesus, made up primarily of committed disciples: i.e., those called by

Jesus to follow him literally and physically, who consequently had to leave behind families, possessions, and livelihood, and who thus were left vulnerable to misunderstanding, hostility, and attacks even by their own families, as was the prophet-teacher they followed. Both male and female disciples (in fact if not in name) followed Jesus, apparently with equal access to his teaching and healing, but not, as things turned out, with equal fidelity and tenacity, and not with equal labels. We have also seen that there were certain "auxiliaries" or "support groups" (dare one say "third orders" or "fifth columns"?) associated with this middle circle. These supporters were committed adherents who did not "take the plunge" of complete discipleship— or who were not summoned or allowed by Jesus to do so—but who showed their devotion and loyalty to Jesus by offering him hospitality.

The picture of smaller circles within a larger circle begins to crystallize. Within the outer circle of "the crowds," that is to say, within the larger group of all those who followed Jesus physically at least for a while, there is the middle circle of "the disciples," a special subset created by the conscious initiative of Jesus, a subset supported, as Jesus was, by hospitable adherents who did not leave home and family.[139] In similar fashion, Jesus took the initiative to create a still smaller subset, an inner circle within the group of these committed, itinerant disciples. The new, smaller subset was strictly limited to twelve men, whose names are recorded by the Synoptics and Acts. It is to this third or inner circle of followers, the Twelve, that we must now turn our attention, for they played a pivotal role in the conduct, conclusion, and continuation of Jesus' ministry. Jesus' conscious choice of precisely twelve Israelite men as an inner circle not only dramatized his understanding of his mission to Israel, it also proved fateful for that mission and fatal to himself.

NOTES TO CHAPTER 25

[1] For initial orientation and further bibliography on the word and concept "disciple," see Theobald Süss, "Nachfolge Jesu," *TLZ* 78 (1953) 129–40; Eduard Schweizer, *Lordship and Discipleship* (SBT 28; Naperville, IL: Allenson, 1960); Schulz, *Nachfolgen und Nachahmen;* Pierson Parker, "Disciple," *IDB,* 1. 845; Nils A. Dahl, *Das Volk Gottes. Eine Untersuchung zum Kirchenbewusstsein des Urchristentums* (2d ed.; Darmstadt: Wissenschaftliche Buchgesellschaft, 1963) 158–74; Kittel, *"akoloutheō,* etc.," 210–16; Karl Heinrich Rengstorf, *"didaskō, didaskalos,* etc.," *TDNT* 2 (1964) 135–65; idem, *"manthanō,* etc.," *TDNT* 4 (1967) 390–461; Hans Dieter Betz, *Nachfolge und Nachahmung Jesu Christi im Neuen Testament* (BHT 37; Tübingen: Mohr [Siebeck], 1967) 13–43; Ferdinand Hahn, "Die Nachfolge Jesu in vorösterlicher Zeit," *Die Anfänge der Kirche im Neuen Testament* (ed. Paul Rieger; Göttingen: Vandenhoeck & Ruprecht, 1967) 7–36; Martin Hengel,

Nachfolge und Charisma (BZNW 34; Berlin: de Gruyter, 1968) = *The Charismatic Leader and His Followers* (New York: Crossroad, 1981); Eduard Lohse, *"rabbi, rabbouni," TDNT* 6 (1968) 961–65; Robert P. Meye, *Jesus and the Twelve. Discipleship and Revelation in Mark's Gospel* (Grand Rapids: Eerdmans, 1968); Heinz Schürmann, "Der Jüngerkreis Jesu als Zeichen für Israel (und als Urbild des kirchlichen Rätestandes)," *Ursprung und Gestalt* (Kommentare und Beiträge zum Alten und Neuen Testament; Düsseldorf: Patmos, 1970) 45–60; Ulrich Luz, "Discipleship," *IDBSup* (1976) 232–33; Ernest Best, "The Role of the Disciples in Mark," *NTS* 23 (1976–77) 377–401; Rainer Riesner, *Jesus als Lehrer* (WUNT 2/7; Tübingen: Mohr [Siebeck], 1981) 408–98; Fernando F. Segovia, "Introduction: Call and Discipleship," in Fernando F. Segovia (ed.), *Discipleship in the New Testament* (Philadelphia: Fortress, 1985) 1–23; Claude Coulot, *Jésus et le disciple* (EBib n.s. 8; Paris: Gabalda, 1987); Michael J. Wilkins, *The Concept of Disciple in Matthew's Gospel as Reflected in the Use of the Term* Mathētēs (NovTSup 59; Leiden: Brill, 1988); C. Clifton Black, *The Disciples According to Mark. Markan Redaction in Current Debate* (JSNTSup 27; Sheffield: JSOT, 1989); Christopher D. Marshall, *Faith As a Theme in Mark's Narrative* (SNTSMS 64; Cambridge: Cambridge University, 1989); Ben Witherington III, *The Christology of Jesus,* 118–43; Joachim Gnilka, *Jesus von Nazaret. Botschaft und Geschichte* (HTKNT Supplementband 3; Freiburg/Basel/Vienna: Herder, 1990) 166–93; Hans Weder, "Disciple, Discipleship," *The Anchor Bible Dictionary* (ed. David Noel Freedman; 6 vols.; New York: Doubleday, 1992) 2. 207–10; James D. G. Dunn, *Jesus' Call to Discipleship* (Cambridge: Cambridge University, 1992); Stephen C. Barton, *Discipleship and Family Ties in Mark and Matthew* (SNTSMS 80; Cambridge: Cambridge University, 1994); Whitney Taylor Shiner, *Follow Me! Disciples in Markan Rhetoric* (SBLDS 145; Atlanta: Scholars, 1995); Christoph Heil, "Was ist 'Nachfolge Jesu'?" *BK* 54 (1999) 80–84. One should note that the articles by Kittel and Rengstorf in the *TDNT,* while useful for purely philological data, are governed by a theological interpretation that is hostile to later rabbinic and Christian developments. Wilkins' *The Concept of Disciple* is a better guide to the OT, Jewish, and Greco-Roman material.

[2] Proportionate to the total wordage of a given book, *mathētēs* is found in descending order of frequency in John, Mark, Matthew, Luke, and Acts. These statistics come from my own count; the "bottom line" is a total number of 261 occurrences of *mathētēs* in the NT. However, various reference works give slightly differing counts. Robert Morgenthaler, for instance, counts 262 occurrences because he identifies 73 cases in Matthew; see his *Statistik des neutestamentlichen Wortschatzes* (Zurich/Frankfurt: Gotthelf, 1958) 118. The reason for the differing counts is that Matthew in particular has a number of text-critical variants in the passages where *mathētēs* appears: e.g., 8:21,25; 20:17; 26:20. Still, the overall impression created by the large number of occurrences in the Gospels is not altered by these minor variations. To these statistics one may add (1) the sole occurrence in the NT of *symmathētēs* ("fellow disciples") in John 11:16 (Thomas the Twin speaking to his fellow disciples); and (2) the sole occurrence in the NT of *mathētria,* "female disciple," used of a Christian woman named Tabitha in Acts 9:36.

[3] For disciples of the Pharisees, see Mark 2:18 ‖ Luke 5:33; Matt 22:16; for disciples of the Baptist, see Mark 2:18 *(bis)* parr.; Mark 6:29 par.; Matt 11:2 ‖ Luke 7:18 *(bis);* Luke 11:1 (also, by implication, Acts 19:1); John 3:25; for disciples of Moses, see John 9:28 (the only occurrence in the NT). In Acts 9:25 we have the unique case of "his disciples" referring to the disciples of Paul; on the text-critical problem, see Gerhard Schneider, *Die Apostelgeschichte* (HTKNT 5; Freiburg/Basel/Vienna: Herder, 1980, 1982) 2. 32, 37.

[4] See on this point I. Howard Marshall, *Luke: Historian and Theologian* (Grand Rapids: Zondervan, 1971) 193. This peculiar Lucan usage in Acts might be explained at least in part by suggesting that Luke took it over from some of the sources he drew upon for Acts; so, e.g., Rengstorf, *"manthanō,* etc.," 442–43. But such an explanation is of little value as long as there is no consensus on the existence, nature, and extent of the sources Luke employed in writing Acts; see, e.g., Jacques Dupont, *The Sources of the Acts* (New York: Herder and Herder, 1964) 166; Schneider, *Die Apostelgeschichte,* 1. 82–103. On the various ways in which Luke creates continuity between the narrative of his Gospel and that of Acts, notably by emphasizing parallel figures and events, see Robert F. O'Toole, *The Unity of Luke's Theology. An Analysis of Luke-Acts* (Good News Studies 9; Wilmington, DE: Glazier, 1984) 62–94; cf. Charles H. Talbert, *Literary Patterns, Theological Themes, and the Genre of Luke-Acts* (SBLMS 20; Missoula, MT: Scholars, 1974); Luke Timothy Johnson, "Luke-Acts, Book of," *The Anchor Bible Dictionary,* 4. 403–20, esp. 409–10.

[5] The one exception is in the speech of Peter at the "Council of Jerusalem" in Acts 15:10. Most critics would agree that Peter's speech, at least in its precise wording, is a redactional creation of Luke; see, e.g., Martin Dibelius, "Das Apostelkonzil," *Aufsätze zur Apostelgeschichte* (FRLANT 60; 5th ed.; Göttingen: Vandenhoeck & Ruprecht, 1968) 85–86; Ernst Haenchen, *Die Apostelgeschichte* (MeyerK 3; Göttingen: Vandenhoeck & Ruprecht, 1968) 386–87, 398–400; Hans Conzelmann, *Acts of the Apostles* (Hermeneia; Philadelphia: Fortress, 1987, German original 1972) 116–17. Most likely Luke himself is responsible for having Peter refer to the Gentile Christians as "disciples" and for having him proclaim the same doctrine of salvation by grace, not by law, that Paul enunciates in Acts 13:38–39. As Schneider points out (*Die Apostelgeschichte,* 2. 181), the view of the law expressed in Acts 15:10 belongs neither to 1st-century Judaism nor to Paul, but rather reflects the viewpoint of a Christian for whom the separation from Judaism is already past history.

[6] I refer here to the noncanonical Christian works called the "Apostolic Fathers," which range from the late 1st century to the early or middle 2d century. What is most striking is the complete absence of the noun *mathētēs* in a large number of the Apostolic Fathers: *1 Clement* (ca. A.D. 96), *2 Clement* (ca. 150), *The Epistle of Barnabas* (ca. 130–138), *The Epistle of Polycarp to the Philippians* (ca. 110–130, depending on one's view of the unity or composite nature of the letter), *The Shepherd of Hermas* (ca. 140–150), and *The Didache* (ca. 100–150). In the rest of the Apostolic Fathers (Ignatius of Antioch, Papias, *The Martyrdom of Polycarp*) there are only twelve au-

thentic cases; for a list of occurrences, see Edgar J. Goodspeed, *Index Patristicus* (Peabody, MA: Hendrickson, 1993, originally 1907) 135. The Apostolic Father who uses *mathētēs* the most—indeed, he has nine out of the twelve occurrences—is Ignatius in his letters (written somewhere between A.D. 108 and 117). Most of the examples in Ignatius reflect his particular situation of imminent martyrdom. For Ignatius, the true disciple is the martyr; Ignatius, as he writes his letters, is only on the way to that status (Ephesians 1:2; Romans 4:2; 5:3; *Trallians* 5:2; *Magnesians* 9:1; and probably Ignatius' letter to Polycarp 7:1). Once, while speaking of death and resurrection, he refers to the OT prophets as spiritual disciples of Jesus Christ (*Magnesians* 9:2). In two cases, Ignatius uses *mathētēs* in a sense close to that of the Acts of the Apostles, i.e., Christians in general in the church (so in Ignatius' letter to Polycarp 2:1 and in *Magnesians* 10:1). Intriguingly, Ignatius never uses *mathētēs* of the disciples of Jesus during the public ministry. It is only when we come to Papias of Hierapolis in his *Interpretation of the Sayings of the Lord* (written ca. A.D. 130, fragments of which are preserved in Eusebius' *Ecclesiastical History*) that we find two references to "the disciples of the Lord" in a context where figures such as Andrew, Peter, Philip, Thomas, James, John, and Matthew are named (*Ecclesiastical History,* 3.39 §4). The fragments show that Papias knew the Gospels of Mark and Matthew; hence his use of *mathētai* for the disciples of Jesus probably reflects his knowledge and use of these Gospels. *The Martyrdom of Polycarp* 17:3 (written ca. A.D. 156) reflects the Ignatian usage of describing martyrs as *mathētai;* 17:3 also contains the only occurrence in the Apostolic Fathers of "fellow disciple" *(symmathētēs).* (Two other occurrences of *mathētēs* in *The Martyrdom of Polycarp* are found in later postscripts to the work.) While *The Epistle to Diognetus* is sometimes listed among the Apostolic Fathers, it probably dates from the late 2d or early 3d century and properly ranks among the Apologists; it contains four examples of *mathētēs* (once of the author, once of those becoming Christians, and twice of the original disciples of Jesus). In sum, most of the Apostolic Fathers never use *mathētēs*. Ignatius, who accounts for the vast majority of occurrences, uses it mostly of martyrs, rarely of contemporary Christians in general, and never of the original disciples of Jesus. All this supports my contention that "disciple" was not a widespread self-designation of Christians in the early church, a self-designation that was then secondarily retrojected onto the original followers of Jesus.

⁷ The three passages where *mathētēs* appears in the Codex Alexandrinus of the LXX (Jer 13:21; 20:11; 26:9 [= MT 46:9]) are all clearly cases of mistranslation, scribal errors in copying, or possibly even Christian influence; see Rengstorf, *"manthanō, etc.,"* 426.

⁸ Wilkins, *The Concept of Disciple,* 97.

⁹ For the treatment of *mathētēs* in Philo and Josephus, I am especially indebted to the work of Wilkins, *The Concept of Disciple,* 100–104, 111–16. To give some examples of Philo's usage: at times, *mathētēs* is used in a general sense of a learner (e.g., of a child vis-à-vis its parents in *Special Laws* 2.39 §227). The word *mathētēs* is used

in an ordinary school context of one who receives instruction from teachers (*Special Laws* 4.26 §140). As he formulates a hierarchy of learning, Philo uses "disciple" of a more advanced learner, a person situated above ordinary people but below the perfect. Such a person is suited to teach others who seek wisdom (*The Worse Attacks the Better* 19 §63–66). The highest type of disciple, though, is the one who has left behind human instruction. Being perfect, such a person is taught directly by God himself (*The Sacrifices of Abel and Cain* 2 §7).

[10] The classic work on this point is Martin Hengel, *Judaism and Hellenism. Studies in Their Encounter in Palestine during the Early Hellenistic Period* (2 vols.; Minneapolis: Fortress, 1974); see also his *The 'Hellenization' of Judaea in the First Century after Christ* (London: SCM; Philadelphia: Trinity, 1989). Hengel's valid insights can be and at times have been overdone. For healthy warnings against exaggerating the Hellenization of Jewish Palestine around the turn of the era, see Ben Witherington III, *Jesus the Sage. The Pilgrimage of Wisdom* (Minneapolis: Fortress, 1994) 118–23; and much more strongly, Louis H. Feldman, "Hengel's *Judaism and Hellenism* in Retrospect," *JBL* 96 (1977) 371–82; idem, *Jew and Gentile in the Ancient World. Attitudes and Interactions from Alexander to Justinian* (Princeton: Princeton University, 1993) esp. 3–44.

[11] Joseph A. Fitzmyer (*Luke the Theologian. Aspects of His Teaching* [New York/Mahwah, NJ: Paulist, 1989] 118–21) points to the abundant attestation of "disciple" in the Gospels and Acts over against its almost complete absence from the Hebrew Scriptures, the LXX, and Qumran. He suggests (p. 121) that " 'discipleship' in a religious sense may have emerged as a Christian phenomenon." The tractate *Sanhedrin* in the Babylonian Talmud mentions five "disciples" of Jesus by name: Mattai, Naqai, Nester, Buni, and Todah (*b. Sanh.* 43a). (They have been identified with various disciples named in the NT; Joseph Klausner [*Jesus of Nazareth* (New York: Macmillan, 1925, Hebrew original 1922) 28–30] favors Matthew, Luke, Andrew, John, and Thaddeus.) Actually, this talmudic text comprises two distinct passages: the first passage simply names the five disciples, while the second narrates a comic story about their being sentenced one after another to death. In his *Jesus of Nazareth* (pp. 28–30), Klausner gives good reasons for doubting the historical accuracy of the two passages ("baraitas") involved. The text in *Sanhedrin* seems to result from a garbling of information in the NT mixed together with a macabre narrative that puns on the names of the five disciples as they are sentenced to death. Most likely we have here a Jewish polemical response to certain Christian traditions. While the Talmud therefore does not supply us with another independent source for the argument from multiple attestation, the wording of the passages in *b. Sanh.* 43a at least confirms the supposition that the natural Hebrew equivalent of the Greek *mathētai* (at least when applied to Jesus' disciples) was *talmîdîm,* since that is the word used in the talmudic text. The suggestion of T. W. Manson (*The Teaching of Jesus* [2d ed.; Cambridge: Cambridge University, 1935] 237–40) that *mathētēs* in the Gospels represents not the Aramaic *talmîdāʾ* ("disciple," "student") but the Aramaic *šĕwilyāʾ* ("apprentice") has not received general acceptance among scholars. The suggestion is based on (1) a tenuous

theory about mistranslation of Aramaic words into Greek and on (2) the supposition that Jesus consciously chose a word that stood in opposition to rabbinic schools with their *talmîdîm*. The problem here is that Manson presupposes what is probably not true: that there was a fixed system of rabbinic schools at the time of Jesus, with *talmîd* serving as a technical term for a rabbinic student in such a school. On all this, see Wilkins, *The Concept of Disciple*, 94–95.

[12] "Disciples" of the Baptist enjoy multiple attestation of sources: Mark (2:18 parr. [*bis*]; Mark 6:29 par.), Q (Matt 11:2 ‖ Luke 7:18 [*bis*]), L (Luke 11:1; also by implication Acts 19:1–4), and John (3:25). The only hesitation arises from the possibility that pervasive Christian thought-modes and vocabulary have affected the presentation of the followers of the Baptist in the Gospels. One notes that Josephus' description of John's followers does not use the vocabulary of *mathētēs* (*Ant.* 18.5.2 §116–19).

[13] This point will be established at length in Section II, "Who Qualified as a Disciple of Jesus?" For now it is accepted as a commonplace of NT research.

[14] John Kloppenborg suggests that "disciple" may have occurred in a few other Q passages that are preserved in either Matthew or Luke but not in both; see his *Q Parallels* (Foundations and Facets; Sonoma, CA: Polebridge, 1988) 224. I prefer to cite only the two occurrences that are clearly Q material. As an aside, I might note the danger of affirming or denying a group's historical existence during the public ministry of Jesus solely on the basis of abundant or poor attestation in the Q document. Hardly anyone denies the existence of disciples around Jesus, yet they are poorly attested in Q. One should remember this when one comes to the question of the historical existence of the Twelve.

[15] To treat the question of Matt 10:42, we must go back to Mark 9:41, which reads: "For whoever gives you a cup of water to drink in [the] name [*en onomati*] that you are of Christ [*hoti Christou este*, i.e., on the grounds that you belong to Christ], Amen I say to you that he will certainly not lose his reward." The phrase "because you are of Christ" seems a roundabout way of saying "because you are a Christian." If that is the case, the precise Marcan wording of the saying does not go back to the historical Jesus, whatever one thinks of the substance of the logion. On this see Rudolf Pesch, *Das Markusevangelium* (HTKNT 2; 2 vols.; Freiburg/Basel/Vienna: Herder, 1976, 1977) 2. 111–12; Morna D. Hooker, *The Gospel According to Saint Mark* (Black NT Commentary; Peabody, MA: Hendrickson, 1991) 231; against later Christian influence is Gundry, *Mark*, 511–12, 522–23. While the matter is not entirely clear, it seems that Matt 10:42 is dependent on Mark 9:41, to which Matthew makes a number of typically Matthean alterations, including the insertion of his beloved word "disciple": "And whoever gives one of these little ones just a cup of cold water to drink in [the] name of a disciple [*eis onoma mathētou*, i.e., on the grounds that he is a disciple], Amen I say to you, he will certainly not lose his reward." If one grants that Matthew is dependent on a Marcan saying that already shows some Christian influ-

ence, and if one grants that Matthew has a liking for "disciple" vocabulary (*mathētēs* occurs 72 times in his Gospel, as opposed to 46 times in Mark and 37 times in Luke), then it becomes highly questionable to attribute the Matthean form of the logion, with its mention of "disciple," to the historical Jesus. On the Matthean redaction of Mark 9:41, see Robert H. Gundry, *Matthew. A Commentary on His Literary and Theological Art* (Grand Rapids: Eerdmans, 1982) 202–3. Gundry points out that Matthew has probably adjusted the wording of the Marcan logion to fit in with the two previous sayings on reward in Matt 10:41, with their refrain of "in the name of a prophet . . . in the name of a just man."

An example of a "disciple" saying unique to Luke is 14:33: "So, then, everyone of you who does not bid farewell to all of his possessions cannot be my disciple." While the matter is difficult to judge because of the lack of a parallel, it seems likely that this verse is a redactional creation. In typically Lucan manner, it serves as the logical and rhetorical conclusion ("So, then . . .") to the preceding double parable (14:28–32) and to the whole mini-discourse of 14:25–32 (picking up the refrain of vv 26 + 27: ". . . cannot be my disciple"). Moreover, v 33 hammers home Luke's emphasis on the need to renounce all possessions (see, e.g., 5:11; 12:33; 18:22); on this redactional concern, see Luke Timothy Johnson, *The Literary Function of Possessions in Luke-Acts* (SBLDS 39; Missoula, MT: Scholars, 1977). In view of all this, Joseph A. Fitzmyer (*The Gospel According to Luke* [AB 28 and 28A; Garden City, NY: Doubleday, 1981, 1985] 2. 1061) judges 14:33 redactional.

[16] Perhaps the text of Josephus points as well to a different sort of argument for the existence of the disciples during Jesus' ministry, an argument that flows from what in fact happened after that ministry. The reason we have Gospels from which we can construct arguments about the historical Jesus is that some of Jesus' followers continued what they understood to be his mission and in time became leaders in the early church. Without this phenomenon of a stable group of disciples providing some continuity, the quest for the historical Jesus would not be a feasible project.

[17] *A Marginal Jew,* 2. 116–30.

[18] Ibid., 2. 119–29.

[19] A good deal of Volume Two of *A Marginal Jew* was spent substantiating the portrait of Jesus as a miracle-working eschatological prophet in the mold of Elijah; for a summary of the presentation, see *A Marginal Jew,* 2. 1041–47. There is abundant multiple attestation of Jesus' activity as a teacher: (1) blocks of teaching material are preserved in all the streams of the Gospel tradition: Mark, Q, M, L, and John; (2) likewise, Jesus is described or addressed as a teacher (*didaskalos*) or rabbi in all the streams of the Gospel tradition as well as in Josephus (*Ant.* 18.3.3. §63: *didaskalos anthrōpōn tōn hēdonē talēthē dechomenōn,* "a teacher of people who receive the truth with pleasure"); (3) the verb "to teach" (*didaskō*) is used to describe Jesus' activity in Mark, M, L, John, and possibly Q. As one might expect, the noun "teaching" (*didachē*) is used with reference to Jesus in all four Gospels. That Jesus functioned as

a teacher is so obvious that there is no need to belabor the point. The surprising element is not that Jesus was a teacher but that he combined the role of teacher with other roles not commonly associated with a Palestinian Jewish teacher in the early 1st century A.D.: eschatological prophet and miracle worker. For treatments of Jesus as teacher, see Riesner, *Jesus als Lehrer;* Vernon K. Robbins, *Jesus the Teacher. A Socio-Rhetorical Interpretation of Mark* (Philadelphia: Fortress, 1984); Samuel Byrskog, *Jesus the Only Teacher. Didactic Authority and Transmission in Ancient Israel, Ancient Judaism and the Matthean Community* (ConBNT 24; Stockholm: Almqvist & Wiksell, 1994). In view of all this, it is astounding to read Rengstorf's claim (*"manthanō,* etc.," 453) that "recollection of Jesus as a teacher seems to have been quite secondary." Here Rengstorf is driven by his theological program to deny any "principle of tradition" in the activity of Jesus and the first Christian generation. Rengstorf views the principle of tradition as foreign to Jesus because it is "Greek or Rabbinic," and hence something that is to be evaluated negatively.

[20] R. Alan Culpepper, *The Johannine School* (SBLDS 26; Missoula, MT: Scholars, 1975). His position contrasts strikingly with that of Rengstorf (*"manthanō,* etc.," 454), whose theological program drives him to deny that we can speak of Jesus as the head of a school. To the extent that Rengstorf is thinking of the structures and methods of learning reflected in later rabbinic literature, he is correct; but more is at stake in his denial when he affirms flatly: ". . . Jesus is nowhere the head of a school; He is the living Lord of His people." This is not just historical description and comparison; it is theological confession and apologetics.

[21] Culpepper (*The Johannine School,* 258–59) tries to isolate nine characteristics of the various schools he surveys: (1) emphasis on friendship or fellowship among disciples; (2) origins in a founder revered as an exemplary wise man; (3) teachings and traditions of the founder that are valued by disciples; (4) membership in the school, which membership is based on being a disciple of the founder; (5) common activities such as teaching, learning, studying, and writing; (6) communal meals; (7) rules and practices regarding admission, retention, and advancement within the school; (8) some degree of distance from society; (9) organizational means of ensuring the school's continued existence. Needless to say, not all these characteristics are found with equal strength or clarity in all the schools. The case for Philo's "school" is especially questionable. But, even if we do not insist on a precise list of characteristics, the "school" phenomenon in the Greco-Roman world is clear enough, and Jesus' disciples belong to this phenomenon, broadly understood. As "school" must be understood to have an elastic and variable sense, so too must "disciple." Wilkins (*The Concept of Disciple,* 11–32) holds that in classical Greek one can distinguish the following meanings of *mathētēs:* (1) early general use: "learner," "a diligent student of the matter under consideration"; (2) technical use, with a sense of direct dependence on a superior authority: (a) non-specific technical use: "adherent," someone who adopts the way of life of a cultural milieu; (b) specialized-technical sense: "institutional pupil." While these meanings persisted in the Hellenistic world, there was a tendency to use *mathētēs* especially in the sense of an adherent of a philosopher, a

great thinker of the past, or a religious figure (ibid., 32–42). One can see how, for the earliest Greek-speaking Christians, *mathētēs* would naturally fit the devoted adherents of the great master, Jesus.

[22] Among the works that have fostered the comparison between Jesus and Cynic philosophers are F. Gerald Downing, *Jesus and the Threat of Freedom* (London: SCM, 1987); idem, *Christ and the Cynics: Jesus and Other Radical Preachers in First Century Tradition* (Sheffield: JSOT, 1988); idem, *Cynics and Christian Origins* (Edinburgh: Clark, 1992); see also Ronald F. Hock, "Cynics," *Anchor Bible Dictionary*, 1. 1221–26. Various biblical scholars have used Cynic traditions to interpret the historical Jesus, with varying results; see, e.g., Burton Mack, *A Myth of Innocence. Mark and Christian Origins* (Philadelphia: Fortress, 1988) 67–69, 73–74; John Dominic Crossan, *The Historical Jesus. The Life of a Mediterranean Jewish Peasant* (San Francisco: Harper, 1991) 72–88, 295, 304, 338. For a critique of the whole approach, see Richard A. Horsley, *Jesus and the Spiral of Violence* (San Francisco: Harper & Row, 1987) 230–31; Hans Dieter Betz, "Jesus and the Cynics: Survey and Analysis of a Hypothesis," *JR* 74 (1994) 453–75, esp. 470–75; Witherington, *Jesus the Sage*, 117–45; idem, *The Jesus Quest. The Third Search for the Jew of Nazareth* (Downers Grove, IL: InterVarsity, 1995) 58–92 (disputing in particular the claims of Crossan); Paul Rhodes Eddy, "Jesus as Diogenes? Reflections on the Cynic Jesus Thesis," *JBL* 115 (1996) 449–69. In my opinion, the attempt to draw Jesus as a Cynic is an example of a common phenomenon in Jesus research: making much out of little. As Volumes One and Two of *A Marginal Jew* have shown at length, Jesus was above all a Jewish eschatological prophet in the guise of a miracle-working Elijah. There is little if anything in such a description that would tie him to the Cynic philosophical tradition. To be sure, as Witherington and Eddy stress in *Jesus the Sage* and "Jesus as Diogenes?" respectively, Jesus also represented the wisdom tradition of Israel, but it is *that* wisdom tradition, not the philosophical movement known as Cynicism, that is the primary context for interpreting Jesus' sapiential teaching. This is not to deny that various individual parallels can be drawn between Jesus and the Cynics, as Downing, Crossan, and others rightly point out: e.g., the deliberate flouting of certain social conventions, an itinerant life style, a call to detach oneself from the luxuries of life. However, the whole context and motivating force of Jesus' teachings and actions are different: the imminent coming of the kingdom of God to his people Israel, a kingdom already present through Jesus' miracles and teaching. Unlike the disciples of Jesus sent out on mission to the Jewish towns and villages of Galilee, the Cynics formed no social group, had no community base, and appeared primarily in the cities of the Greco-Roman world. Moreover, it is unclear whether one may even speak of the existence of Cynicism in and around Palestine in the early 1st century A.D. Cynicism seems to have suffered an eclipse if not a sort of death in the 2d and 1st centuries B.C., and a Cynic revival seems to begin only in the middle of the 1st century A.D., after Jesus' death. It is therefore highly questionable whether Cynics operated in the 1st-century peasant society of Galilee in which Jesus lived. Then, too, while the great cities of Palestine, along with their ruling elites and supporters, were Hellenized to varying degrees, scholars still debate how much of this Hellenization "trickled

down" to peasants in the countryside, especially in the case of Jewish peasants loyal to their religious traditions. In the end, the Cynic portrait of Jesus, especially as sketched by Crossan and Mack, fails to take seriously his Jewishness, his prophetic eschatology, and the specific socio-religious situation in the towns and villages of rural Galilee in the early 1st century A.D.

[23] Cohen, *From the Maccabees to the Mishnah*, 122.

[24] Ibid. This balanced view is preferable to the apologetic claim of Rengstorf (*"manthanō*, etc.," 455) that, despite "formal kinship . . . , there is . . . no inner relation" between the *talmîd* of later Rabbinic Judaism and the *mathētēs* of Jesus.

[25] While Elijah's call of Elisha is the clearest harbinger of the "prophet-disciple" relationship found in the Jesus movement, the OT provides much more of a background to the phenomenon of discipleship than Rengstorf allows in his *TDNT* article on *manthanō* and *mathētēs*, where he speaks of "the absence . . . of the master-disciple relation from the OT" (p. 427). As Wilkins points out (*The Concept of Disciple*, 43–91), the social reality of a master-disciple relationship extends far beyond the limited vocabulary of discipleship in the OT. (1) As for explicit terms, *talmîd* occurs only in 1 Chron 25:8, of an apprentice musician learning his trade. The verbal adjective and substantive *limmûd* ("taught," "accustomed," and, as a noun, "disciple") occur six times in the OT, always in the prophetic literature. While "my disciples" in Isa 8:16 might refer to God's disciples, more likely it refers to the disciples gathered around the prophet Isaiah, disciples who hear and bear witness to his prophecy (so Otto Kaiser, *Isaiah 1–12* [OTL; Philadelphia: Westminster, 1972] 120). When Deutero-Isaiah applies the *limmûd* terminology to the servant's (or Israel's) relation to Yahweh (Isa 50:4 *[bis]*; 54:13), the metaphor of Yahweh teaching someone who is like a disciple presupposes a recognizable group of people in Israel referred to as "taught ones" or "disciples"; see Claus Westermann, *Isaiah 40–66* (OTL; Philadelphia: Westminster, 1969) 225–29. (2) Beyond mere terminology, the social reality of the master-disciple relationship in Israel existed in various ways in circles of prophets (bands of prophets connected with Samuel, "sons of prophets" connected with Elijah and Elisha), scribes (active in families, temple administration, royal administration, and postexilic bureaucracy), and wise men (active in the clan, the city gate, the royal court, and schools). Whether there were formal scribal schools or wisdom schools in the OT period is debated—though Ben Sira seems to function within the context of some sort of school or academy—but at the very least ancient Israel was no stranger to various sorts of master-disciple relationships. The diverse expressions of discipleship found in the Israelite streams of prophecy, wisdom, and apocalyptic crystallize in a particular way in the relationship of Jesus and his disciples. Still, the Elijah-Elisha relationship probably provides the single clearest model. While some of this model may have been communicated to Jesus by the Baptist and his circle of disciples, the Baptist, on the whole, does not fit the pattern of an itinerant *miracle-working* prophet, especially *active in northern Israel*, who *issues a peremptory call to another individual to leave work and family to follow him* (we have no

proof that the Baptist acquired disciples in this manner). Consequently, trying to create an Elijah-Elisha relationship between the Baptist and Jesus may look attractive at first glance, but it breaks down under detailed analysis.

[26] In the development of stories about Elijah and Elisha around the time of Jesus, the idea of a master-disciple relationship is strengthened. In his *Jewish Antiquities,* Josephus retells a story from 2 Kings that mentioned elders sitting in front of Elisha (2 Kgs 6:32), but Josephus refers to them instead as "disciples" (*mathētai* in *Ant.* 9.3.4 §68). When 2 Kgs 9:1 says that Elisha sent one of the sons of the prophets on a mission, Josephus speaks of Elisha sending "one of his disciples" (*hena tōn autou mathētōn* in *Ant.* 9.6.1 §106). This development continues in rabbinic literature in the centuries after Jesus. Rengstorf (*"manthanō,* etc.," 437) observes that in *t. Soṭa* 4:7, "Elisha is called a *talmîd* of Elijah, who for his part is *talmîd* of Moses." Wilkins (*The Concept of Disciple,* 59) notes that a targum on 2 Kgs 2:12 (recounting Elisha's reaction to Elijah's being taken up into heaven in a fiery chariot) changes Elisha's cry to Elijah from "my father" to "my rabbi." Rengstorf (*"manthanō,* etc.," 434) also notes that the Aramaic of the targum renders the Hebrew *bĕnê-hannĕbîʾîm* ("the sons of the prophets") in 2 Kgs 2:15 (and elsewhere) as *talmîdê nĕbiyyāʾ* ("the disciples of the prophet").

[27] Throughout the argument about various sayings that follows, one point should be stressed: I am not concerned here in establishing, e.g., whether Mark, Q, or John represents the earliest form of a saying or what the exact wording of the earliest form of a saying is. At this point I seek only to establish by the various criteria (especially multiple attestation) that a particular trait, idea, or aspect of being a disciple of Jesus is not a mere invention of the early church but actually goes back to the ministry of the historical Jesus.

[28] It should be noted that the overenthusiastic rich man in Mark 10:17–22 does not ask to follow Jesus as a disciple; he rather asks the question: "What must I do to inherit eternal life?" As the tragic end of the story reveals, the rich man obviously did not suspect that, in his concrete case, inheriting eternal life would mean giving all his money to the poor and literally following Jesus (v 21). When Jesus calls him to make this sacrifice in order to be a disciple, the rich man goes away sad. To these three examples some might add the "implicit call" that Jesus issues to the blind Bartimaeus by the very fact that he cures him on his journey up to Jerusalem for Passover (Mark 10:46–52). As many critics have noted, the way Mark shapes the narrative mixes the form of miracle story with the form of call story; see *A Marginal Jew,* 2. 733–34. In a sense, the climax of the story is reached not when Bartimaeus gains his sight but rather when the final words of the narrative are spoken: "And he [Bartimaeus] *followed* [*ēkolouthei*] him [Jesus] on the way [i.e., the way up to Jerusalem and to the cross]." Nevertheless, one must distinguish the Bartimaeus story from the stories of Jesus calling the four disciples, Levi, and the rich man. These three stories are "call stories" in their very essence; they simply could not be told without the central element of Jesus calling people to follow him. In contrast, the element of "call story" in

the healing of Bartimaeus is intimated rather than stated and may belong more to Mark's redactional shaping than to the traditional miracle story.

[29] As noted above, the story in Matt 8:21–22 par. echoes but heightens the demand that Elijah makes on Elisha in 1 Kgs 19:19–21. There Elisha is allowed to go back to bid farewell to his parents (though Elijah's statement at the end of 19:20—often translated as indirect permission—is obscure in the Hebrew); Jesus brooks no such delay for the sake of filial piety. There is no proof that "Let the dead bury their dead" was ever a general proverb in the ancient Mediterranean world; it is much more likely a subversive aphorism of Jesus. On the history-of-religion background of Matt 8:21–22 par., see Hengel, *The Charismatic Leader*, 3–15; also Sanders, *Jesus and Judaism*, 252–55. Hengel (p. 7) rightly rejects various attempts to take the sting and shock out of Jesus' order by those who propose either a mistranslation from the Aramaic or a contorted interpretation of the blunt Greek command. Both Hengel and Sanders argue from the criterion of discontinuity to the authenticity of the logion. The proper burial of the deceased by close relatives or associates (especially the son of the deceased) was one of the most sacred obligations recognized throughout the ancient Mediterranean world; see, e.g., the examples from Corinth in Richard E. De-Maris, "Corinthian Religion and Baptism for the Dead (1 Corinthians 15:29): Insights from Archaeology and Anthropology," *JBL* 114 (1995) 661–82. Extolled by Jewish piety, it was one of the most important practical expressions of obedience to the fourth commandment of the Decalogue ("Honor thy father and thy mother"). There seems to have been no rejection of this obligation to give decent burial in early Christian practice—even when the deceased was not a relative (see, e.g., Acts 5:6, 9–10; 8:2).

[30] Various exegetes suggest that this Lucan logion may have stood in Q together with the other two sayings present in Matt 8:19–20 + 21–22 par.; so, e.g., Hengel, *The Charismatic Leader*, 4. However, Fitzmyer (*The Gospel According to Luke*, 1. 833) represents those commentators who think that Luke 9:61–62 comes from L or possibly even from Lucan redaction. For a list of authors pro and con, see Kloppenborg, *Q Parallels*, 604.

[31] For arguments in favor of this view, see *A Marginal Jew*, 2. 194 n. 68.

[32] Commentators continue to debate which group is referred to in the two clauses "for they were many and they followed him" at the end of Mark 2:15. There are three possibilities: (1) The reference is to the toll collectors and sinners mentioned earlier in 2:15; so Gundry, *Mark*, 125, 128. But (a) the disputed clauses have to jump over the closer noun "disciples" to refer back to two nouns at a fair distance; and (b) the statement "for they were many" would be hopelessly redundant after the phrase "many toll collectors and sinners." (2) The clause "for they were many" refers back to the disciples, but *kai ēkolouthoun autō* ("and they followed him") actually goes with the beginning of v 16 and has as its subject "the scribes of the Pharisees"; so Robert A. Guelich, *Mark 1–8:26* (Word Biblical Commentary 34A; Dallas: Word, 1989) 97–98,

102. While it is true that Mark can use *akoloutheō* in a neutral rather than a positive sense, nowhere in his Gospel does he depict the religious enemies of Jesus as "following" him. To refer *akoloutheō* to the enemies of Jesus in v 15 when it is used twice in the strong religious sense of heeding a call to discipleship in v 14 is especially harsh. (3) Hence the simplest explanation is that both clauses refer back to the immediately preceding phrase, "his disciples" *(tois mathētais autou)*. On this see Bruce Metzger, *A Textual Commentary on the Greek New Testament* (2d ed.; Stuttgart: German Bible Society, 1994) 67.

[33] *A Marginal Jew,* 1. 271–78.

[34] Reading with Hebrew manuscript B, "in the house of my instruction," *(bĕbêt midrāšî),* which (granted the constraints of a Hebrew construct form) actually means "my house of instruction." However, neither the Greek nor the Syriac translation has the possessive pronoun. Hence Patrick W. Skehan and Alexander A. Di Lella (*The Wisdom of Ben Sira* [AB 39; New York: Doubleday, 1987] 573, 575, 578) prefer the translation "in the house of instruction"; they may well be right.

[35] One may wonder whether Josephus' claim that he adhered to the Pharisaic movement at such an early age is not colored by hindsight.

[36] It is intriguing that Josephus includes the Essenes in this scenario. There is no sense that *they* sought out Josephus to make peremptory demands on him to follow them. One imagines that this would be even truer of the Qumran community, isolated as it was at the northwestern corner of the Dead Sea. As far as we know, the Qumranites did not send out envoys around Palestine to recruit new members. Like many a "monastic" community, they probably expected interested persons—the truly repentant—to seek them out. Perhaps the larger Essene movement, spread throughout Israel, was the prime source of new members at Qumran. No doubt, granted the fiercely sectarian nature of Qumran, with its dualistic worldview and apocalyptic scenario, once a person entered the community, there was a grave obligation to remain. In all this, I retain my view that Qumran was connected in one way or another with the Essene movement (see, e.g., *A Marginal Jew,* 1. 93–94, 336–39; 2. 25–27); the identification of Qumran as Sadducean suffers from many difficulties, as Fitzmyer (see article cited below) demonstrates. Admittedly, though, the debate on the identity of the Qumranites still rages; for a sampling of views, see Philip R. Davies, *Behind the Essenes. History and Ideology in the Dead Sea Scrolls* (Brown Judaic Studies 94; Atlanta: Scholars, 1987); Geza Vermes and Martin D. Goodman, *The Essenes According to the Classical Sources* (Oxford Centre Textbooks 1; Sheffield: JSOT, 1989) 12–13; Lawrence H. Schiffman, "The Sadducean Origins of the Dead Sea Scroll Sect," *Understanding the Dead Sea Scrolls* (ed. Hershel Shanks; New York: Random House, 1992) 35–49; James C. VanderKam, "The People of the Dead Sea Scrolls: Essenes or Sadducees?" ibid., 50–62; Shemaryahu Talmon, "The Community of the Renewed Covenant: Between Judaism and Christianity," *The Community of the Renewed Covenant* (Christianity and Judaism in Antiquity 10; ed. Eugene Ulrich and

James VanderKam; Notre Dame, IN: University of Notre Dame, 1994) 3–24; Joseph M. Baumgarten, "Sadducean Elements in Qumran Law," ibid., 27–36; Lawrence H. Schiffman, "The *Temple Scroll* and the Nature of Its Law: The Status of the Question," ibid., 37–55; Joseph A. Fitzmyer, "The Qumran Community: Essene or Sadducean?" *HeyJ* 36 (1995) 467–76.

[37] See, e.g., Jacob Neusner's treatment (*Introduction to Rabbinic Literature* [Anchor Bible Reference Library; New York: Doubleday, 1994] 600–608) of the stories in *The Fathers According to Rabbi Nathan* (*ʾAbot R. Nat.* 6:4–6) of how Rabbi Aqiba and Rabbi Eliezer decided to begin the study of Torah under famous teachers. Neusner (p. 591) tentatively dates *The Fathers According to Rabbi Nathan* to ca. A.D. 500. The complicated redaction history of this "extracanonical" tractate may stretch from the 3d to the 7th or 8th century; see H. L. Strack and G. Stemberger, *Introduction to the Talmud and Midrash* (Edinburgh: Clark, 1991) 246–47. For translations and commentaries, see Anthony J. Saldarini, *The Fathers According to Rabbi Nathan* (SJLA 11; Leiden: Brill, 1975); Jacob Neusner, *The Fathers According to Rabbi Nathan* (Brown Judaic Studies 114; Atlanta: Scholars, 1986).

[38] Needless to say, rabbis, like most teachers, were interested in having a large group of zealous students around them; see, e.g., the command in *m. ʾAbot* 1:1: ". . . raise up many disciples" *(haʿămîdû talmîdîm harbēh).* But this still left the inception of study largely to the initiative of the individual interested in studying. According to *m. ʾAbot* 1:4, Jose ben Joezer exhorted others: "Let your house be a reglar place of meeting [*bētĕkā bêt waʿad*] for the wise, and sit in the dust of their feet, and drink with thirst their words." According to *m. ʾAbot* 1:6, Joshua ben Perachiah advised: "Make [*ʾăśēh*, i.e., get] for yourself a teacher [*rab*], and acquire for yourself a companion [*ḥābēr*, i.e., a fellow student]. . . ." On the use of *rab* for a religious teacher without necessarily implying a fixed system of qualifications such as we find in the later rabbis, see Benedict T. Viviano, *Study as Worship. Aboth and the New Testament* (SJLA 26; Leiden: Brill, 1978) 12–13. No doubt the situation was still more fluid at the time of Jesus. The Gospels depict both Jesus (e.g., Mark 9:5; Matt 26:49; John 1:38,49; 3:2) and John the Baptist (John 3:26) being addressed with the title "Rabbi," although there is no positive evidence that either undertook "higher-level" study of Torah under some well-known teacher. Since we cannot find a clear parallel in the rabbinic tradition to the initiative practiced by Jesus, some scholars point to the motif of philosophical or religious leaders calling followers in the Greco-Roman tradition. While the parallels are not perfect, there is no need to ward them off in a polemical fashion, as does Rengstorf (*"manthanō,"* etc., 445).

[39] See, e.g., *Sipre* 305 on Deut 31:14: "Rabban Johanan ben Zakkai was riding on an ass, *and his disciples were walking behind him* [or: following after him]." The same statement is found in *b. Ketub.* 66b, with the same wording in the Hebrew for the key phrase I have italicized: *whyw tlmydyn mhlkyn ʾhrw.* An equivalent phrase is found in the Aramaic of *b. Ketub.* 72b, where Rabbah bar Bar Ḥana relates: "Once we were *walking behind* [or: going after] Rab ʿUqbaʿ. . . ." The Aramaic of the key

phrase is *q'zylnn* [or, corrected: *'zlynn*] *btryh*. Bar Ḥana also appears in *b. 'Abod. Zar.* 43a, where he says in the name of Rabbi Jehoshua ben Levi: "Once I *was walking after* [or: behind] the eminent Rabbi Eleazar Haqqapar on the road. . . ." The key phrase in Hebrew is *mhlk 'ḥr*. From these and other examples one may observe: (1) In these contexts, the phrase "go after" has the literal sense of "walk behind" someone who is walking or riding. It connotes the respectful position of a rabbinic disciple walking behind his master, while at times a servant will walk before. The phrase "walk behind" or "go after" does not serve as a dense, pregnant code-phrase that sums up the whole commitment to life as a disciple. It serves rather as a colorful detail introducing an anecdote. (2) The phrase "go after" or "walk behind" occurs in this usage in both Hebrew and Aramaic. (3) All the examples usually cited in the scholarly literature come from rabbinic collections later than the Mishna.

[40] Needless to say, in the ancient as well as the modern world, it was often necessary for the student to leave home for a period of time to receive instruction. This would certainly have been true of some rabbinic students. But this well-known necessity of student life is quite different from Jesus' peremptory call, which made leaving home, family, and property a necessary condition for anyone who would "follow" him in his itinerant ministry for an indefinite future. The difference between the obligations of following Jesus and the need to leave home temporarily to study under an eminent rabbi can be illustrated in a backhanded fashion in a legend about the great 2d-century rabbi Aqiba ben Joseph. The Babylonian Talmud preserves various forms (*b. Ned.* 50a; *b. Ketub.* 62b–63a) of the story that Aqiba left his wife and home for twelve years of study. When he was returning home, he overheard an unfriendly neighbor mock his wife about her being abandoned for so long. Aqiba's wife replied that she would consent to another twelve years if Aqiba desired it. Without making his presence known, Aqiba departed and studied for twelve more years. In the end, though, he did return to his wife and subsequently became both rich and famous. While the story in its present form is rightly considered a legend, in an indirect way it indicates that, however long the rabbinic student stayed away from home to study, the natural presumption was that he would return home when his studies were completed. (For the largely unreliable nature of talmudic narratives about the rabbis and for the minimum of historical information we have about Aqiba, see Strack and Stemberger, *Introduction to the Talmud and Midrash,* 66–68 and 79–80.) Alongside Aqiba, another unusual scholar of the tannaitic period was Simeon ben Azzai, who remained celibate; on him, see *A Marginal Jew,* 1. 341. As all admit, ben Azzai was a rare exception. As with Aqiba, so with ben Azzai: their special sacrifices were part of their particular stories, not part of the essence of rabbinic discipleship.

[41] See Rengstorf, "*manthanō,* etc.," 445. In due time, a distinction developed in rabbinic literature between a mere disciple *(talmîd),* who was still studying and was not allowed to make decisions in religious law as applied to concrete cases, and a "disciple of a sage" *(talmîd ḥākām),* who was so advanced in his studies and admired for his learning that he was allowed to make such decisions even though he had not yet been formally ordained a rabbi. On this, see Rengstorf, ibid., 432; Wilkens, *The*

Concept of Disciple, 93–94. The phrase "disciples of sages" is found as early as the Mishna, e.g., in *m. Mak.* 2:5; but not all agree that it bears here the later technical sense. In favor of the more general sense of "scholars" in this text is Samuel Krauss, *Die Mischna. IV. Seder. Nĕziqin. 4. u. 5. Traktat: Sanhedrin—Makkōt* (Giessen: Töpelmann, 1933) 344. The phrase can be found later on in many rabbinic texts, e.g., *b. Soṭa* 22a (but the reading of *ḥākām* after *talmîd* is disputed); *b. Sabb.* 114a.

[42] Strack and Stemberger, *Introduction to the Talmud and Midrash,* 15.

[43] On the shift in ordination practices (e.g., from the laying on of hands to simply a spoken formula, and from ordination by any rabbi to ordination by the patriarch), see ibid. See also Eduard Lohse, *Die Ordination im Spätjudentum und Urchristentum* (Göttingen: Vandenhoeck & Ruprecht, 1951) 28–66; David Daube, "The Laying on of Hands," *The New Testament and Rabbinic Judaism* (Peabody, MA: Hendrickson, 1956) 224–46; Hugo Mantel, *Studies in the History of the Sanhedrin* (Cambridge, MA: Harvard University, 1961) 206–21. A formal ordination ceremony for students does not seem to have existed before A.D. 70. In the view of some scholars, the use of the verb *sāmak* (literally, "to lean on," "to press") and the equivalent noun *sĕmîkâ* for rabbinic ordination may be witnessed as early as the Mishna; see, e.g., *m. Sanh.* 3:1; 4:4. However, other scholars think that at this early stage the verb is better translated as "appoint," with the sense of filling a vacancy in membership; see Mantel, *Studies,* 206 n. 225 (continuing on p. 207). Accordingly, some translators (e.g., Herbert Danby, *The Mishnah* [Oxford: Oxford University, 1933] 387; Philip Blackman, *Mishnayoth* [7 vols.; 2d ed.; New York: Judaica, 1963–64] 4. 253) prefer the weaker translation "appoint" at *m. Sanh.* 4:4, while others (e.g., Krauss, *Die Mischna. Sanhedrin—Makkōt,* 157–58; Jacob Neusner, *The Mishnah* [New Haven: Yale, 1988] 590) prefer the stronger translation "ordain." In the present context, the text in *Ḥag.* 2:2 clearly refers to laying hands on an offering; attempts to claim that originally the text referred to ordination must remain highly speculative (see Lohse, *Die Ordination,* 30–32, for the debate). Even Lohse, who claims (I think wrongly) that a set ordination rite existed among Jewish scholars by the time of the NT apostles, admits that for unambiguous information we must go to the two Talmuds (ibid., 32); he is perhaps too trusting of the talmudic data for his reconstruction of the situation in the latter half of the 1st century A.D.

[44] On this, see Gerhard Dautzenberg, *Sein Leben Bewahren. Psychē in den Herrenworten der Evangelien* (SANT 14; Munich: Kösel, 1966) 59–60. As Augustin George ("Qui veut sauver sa vie la perdra. Qui perd sa vie la sauvera," *Bible et vie chrétienne* 83 [1968] 11–24, esp. 22–23) points out, the precise contexts in which a saying like Mark 8:35 parr. is found in the four Gospels are most likely due to the evangelists or to earlier bearers of the Christian tradition who collected sayings of Jesus according to common themes or key words; similarly, Dautzenberg, ibid., 61. Hence it would be a methodological mistake to try to interpret the meaning of, e.g., Mark 8:35 in the mouth of the historical Jesus by using a Gospel's redactional context as a guide.

[45] Vincent Taylor, *The Gospel According to St. Mark* (2d ed.; London: Macmillan, 1966) 382; Dautzenberg (*Sein Leben Bewahren,* 51–53) discusses the basic similarities of grammatical structure, vocabulary, and thought as well as the differences found in the various forms of the logion. A useful chart illustrating the different forms can be found on p. 206 of Walter Rebell's article, " 'Sein Leben verlieren' (Mark 8.35 parr.) als Strukturmoment vor- und nachösterlichen Glaubens," *NTS* 35 (1989) 202–18. There is a vague echo of Mark 8:35 parr. in Coptic *Gos. Thom.* saying 67, but the thought is thoroughly transformed by the gnostic worldview: to know the All (i.e, the world of the divine, of light), one must know one's true inner self, which is consubstantial to the light. On the gnostic theology of this saying, see Michael Fieger, *Das Thomasevangelium. Einleitung, Kommentar und Systematik* (NTAbh 22; Münster: Aschendorff, 1991) 196–97.

[46] Hence I would not be as sure as George ("Qui veut sauver sa vie," 11) that all the forms of the aphorism found in the four Gospels "without doubt" go back to a single saying of Jesus.

[47] Gospel critics often distinguish between (1) a proverb, which speaks general truths in a collective voice and supports the traditional wisdom of the community, and (2) an aphorism, which speaks of concrete situations in an individual voice, inverting received views and so subverting traditional wisdom. While this may be a valid distinction from our point of view, we should remember that, for ancient Jews, both proverb and aphorism would fit under the very elastic term *māšāl.* On the distinctions, their validity, and their limitations, see Witherington, *Jesus the Sage,* 3–19, 147–65. On Mark 8:35 as a paradoxical, two-part *māšāl,* see Pesch, *Das Markusevangelium,* 2. 61.

[48] The manuscripts that omit "myself and" in Mark 8:35 include the early papyrus 45 (first half of the 3d century) and the important, if idiosyncratic, Codex Bezae (5th century).

[49] The classic text on this point is Frans Neirynck, *Duality in Mark. Contributions to the Study of the Markan Redaction* (BETL 31; Leuven: Leuven University, 1972).

[50] So Dautzenberg, *Sein Leben Bewahren,* 60–61. Although Mark is the shortest of the Gospels, it has the largest number of occurrences of the word "gospel" *(euaggelion).* While Matthew has four, Mark (excluding an occurrence in the canonical ending, 16:15) has seven. More striking still is the total absence of the noun "gospel" in the Gospels of Luke and John; it occurs only twice in Acts. On "gospel" in the theology of Mark, see Willi Marxsen, *Der Evangelist Markus* (FRLANT 67; 2d ed.; Göttingen: Vandenhoeck & Ruprecht, 1959) 77–101; Leander E. Keck, "The Introduction to Mark's Gospel," *NTS* 12 (1965–66) 352–70; Gerhard Dautzenberg, "Die Zeit des Evangeliums. Mk 1,1–15 und die Konzeption des Markusevangeliums," *BZ* 21 (1977) 219–34 and 22 (1978) 76–91; Detlev Dormeyer, "Die Kompositionsmetapher 'Evangelium Jesu Christi, des Sohnes Gottes' Mk 1.1. Ihre theologische und liter-

arische Aufgabe in der Jesus-Biographie des Markus," *NTS* 33 (1987) 452–68; M. Eugene Boring, "Mark 1:1–15 and the Beginning of the Gospel," *How Gospels Begin* (Semeia 52; ed. Dennis E. Smith; Atlanta: Scholars, 1991) 43–81. For possible reasons why both Matthew and Luke—independently of each other—dropped "for the sake of the gospel," see Rebell, " 'Sein Leben verlieren,' " 209 along with n. 1.

[51] On this, see Akira Satake, "Das Leiden der Jünger 'um meinetwillen,' " *ZNW* 67 (1976) 4–19; also Rudolf Bultmann, *Die Geschichte der synoptischen Tradition* (FRLANT 29; 8th ed.; Göttingen: Vandenhoeck & Ruprecht, 1970, originally 1921) 97. While Satake is correct in seeing the general context of the saying to be Jewish apocalyptic thought concerning the suffering of the just in this life and their corresponding reward in the next, he goes astray in denying that Mark 8:35 comes from the historical Jesus. His reasoning is odd: because the saying does not speak of the suffering of Jesus *and* the disciples, but only of the suffering of the disciples, it cannot come from the historical Jesus, who—according to Satake—certainly did speak of the possibility of his own future suffering. While I agree with the last part of Satake's reasoning, it hardly follows that every single saying that Jesus ever spoke about suffering would have to mention both his suffering and that of his disciples. This is all the more the case, if, as seems likely in Mark 8:35, Jesus is adapting a general proverb that is accordingly formulated in the third person singular *(hos gar ean . . .)*. Even Bultmann (ibid., 110) is less skeptical than Satake; the former accepts Mark 8:35 as authentic because it is filled with the power of Jesus' call to repentance and because it expresses a characteristic newness that goes beyond popular wisdom and piety and yet is not tied to apocalyptic or rabbinic Judaism.

[52] So George, "Qui veut sauver sa vie," 20. Rudolf Laufen (*Die Doppelüberlieferungen der Logienquelle und des Markusevangeliums* [BBB 54; Bonn: Hanstein, 1980] 321–22), along with a number of other critics, argues that "for the sake of myself" belongs even to the earliest Q form of the logion; however, he does not pay sufficient attention to the absence of the phrase in John 12:25. I find the agreement of two independent forms, one Lucan (Luke 17:33) and one Johannine, telling, especially when the phrase missing in both of their versions spoils the parallelism of the aphorism.

[53] Dautzenberg, *Sein Leben Bewahren,* 13–60; he is followed by many others, e.g., George, "Qui veut sauver sa vie," 11–13; Josef Sudbrack, " 'Wer sein Leben um meinetwillen verliert . . . ' (Mk 8,35)," *Geist und Leben* 40 (1967) 161–70. While the point is well taken, at times these interpreters seem engaged in a hermeneutical exercise that makes Jesus sound like Martin Heidegger (e.g., "existential anguish in the face of death"). One must remember that Hellenistic influence and apocalyptic dualism (entailing at times a dualism of body and soul) had an impact on 1st-century Judaism, including its anthropology (a factor recognized by Dautzenberg); such an influence seems clear in Matt 10:28 (contrast Luke 12:4–5). An ambiguity can also be noted in the use of the verb *apollymi* (*apolesei* in Mark 8:35), which can mean either "destroy" or "lose"; on this see Albrecht Oepke, "*apollymi,* etc.," *TDNT* 1 (1964)

394–97, esp. 394–95. It might be argued that the stronger sense of destroying (with the connotation of some personal act of will or fault) supplies the better antithesis to "saving" (*sōsai,* as in Mark 8:35), while the weaker sense of "losing" may supply the better antithesis to "finding" (*heurōn,* in the Matt 10:39 version of the aphorism). For the sake of inculcating the fact that the same verb is used in these sayings, I retain the translation "lose" throughout.

[54] For verbal parallels found in exhortations by military commanders to their troops to be brave in battle, see Johannes B. Bauer, " 'Wer sein Leben retten will . . . ' Mk 8,35 Parr.," *Neutestamentliche Aufsätze* (Josef Schmid Festschrift; ed. J. Blinzler, O. Kuss, and F. Mussner; Regensburg: Pustet, 1963) 7–10. Parallels in rabbinic literature are often cited by commentators; however, one should note that most of them (1) are later than the Mishna (but see the Aramaic saying of Hillel in *m. 'Abot* 1:13 concerning the ambitious quest for fame that ruins one's reputation) and (2) keep the traditional wisdom perspective of saving or losing one's physical life in this world. In this respect, the parallels are quite different in their thrust from the eschatological vindication Jesus promises.

[55] Parallels to the basic pattern of thought can be found in Jewish apocalyptic literature in the centuries before and after Jesus. For example, *1 Enoch* 108:10 reads: "He [i.e., the Lord] has assigned them [i.e., those who love God and suffer accordingly] their reward, for they were found to be such as loved heaven more than their life in the world, and even though they were trampled underfoot by evil men . . . , yet they blessed me." (The translation is by Michael A. Knibb, *The Ethiopic Book of Enoch* [2 vols.; Oxford: Clarendon, 1978] 2. 251; a slightly different translation is given by E. Isaac in James H. Charlesworth [ed.], *The Old Testament Pseudepigrapha* [2 vols.; Garden City, NY: Doubleday, 1983, 1985] 1. 88–89.) Fourth Ezra 7:88–91 speaks of the reward given to "those who have kept the ways of the Most High, when they shall be separated from their mortal vessel": "During the time that they lived in it, they laboriously served the Most High. . . . Therefore . . . , they shall see with great joy the glory of him who receives them. . . ." (The translation is by Michael Edward Stone, *Fourth Ezra* [Hermeneia; Minneapolis: Fortress, 1990] 236.)

[56] For the position that Luke 17:33 is simply Luke's rewriting of Mark 8:35, see, e.g., Josef Schmid, *Das Evangelium nach Lukas* (RNT 3; 4th ed.; Regensburg: Pustet, 1960) 277; with detailed argumentation, Josef Zmijewski, *Die Eschatologiereden des Lukas-Evangeliums. Eine traditions- und redaktionsgeschichtliche Untersuchung zu Lk 21,5–36 und Lk 17,20–37* (BBB 40; Bonn: Hanstein, 1972) 479–82.

[57] Striking examples of Luke's tendency to avoid doublets include the following: (1) Luke, contrary to Mark and Matthew, has only one account of the feeding of the multitude (Luke 9:10–17). (2) Contrary to Matthew, Luke takes over only the Q version of the prohibition of divorce (Luke 16:18), while omitting the Marcan version (Mark 10:1–12), which Matthew keeps (Matt 19:1–12) alongside the Q version (Matt 5:31–32). (3) The omission of the anointing at Bethany (Mark 14:3–9) may be

another example of such a tendency, since Luke has the story of the sinful woman anointing Jesus in the house of a Galilean Pharisee earlier in his Gospel (Luke 7:36–50). However, one should speak only of a "tendency" in Luke to avoid doublets; in some cases he lets them stand. For Luke's general tendency to avoid doublets and the reasons why he retains some, see Heinz Schürmann, "Die Dubletten im Lukasevangelium. Ein Beitrag zur Verdeutlichung des lukanischen Redaktionsverfahrens," *Traditionsgeschichtliche Untersuchungen zu den synoptischen Evangelien* (Kommentare und Beiträge zum Alten und Neuen Testament; Düsseldorf: Patmos, 1968) 272–78; idem, "Die Dublettenvermeidungen im Lukasevangelium. Ein Beitrag zur Verdeutlichung des lukanischen Redaktionsverfahrens," ibid., 279–89. See also Fitzmyer, *The Gospel According to Luke,* 1. 81–82; Kloppenborg, *Q Parallels,* 170.

[58] One of the most forceful proponents of this view is Laufen, *Die Doppelüberlieferungen,* 315–18. Laufen affirms that there is "no doubt" about the matter. Some other critics are more reserved in their judgments; e.g., Migaku Sato (*Q und Prophetie* [WUNT 2/29; Tübingen: Mohr (Siebeck), 1988] 21–22) counts Luke 17:33 par. among the sayings whose presence in Q is "quite possible, but uncertain." In reaching his judgment, Sato may rely too heavily on the mere counting of common words. In general, scholars who have investigated the Q material in great detail count Luke 17:33 par. among the Q sayings; so, e.g., Dieter Lührmann, *Die Redaktion der Logienquelle* (WMANT 33; Neukirchen-Vluyn: Neukirchener Verlag, 1969) 72; Paul Hoffmann, *Studien zur Theologie der Logienquelle* (NTAbh 8; Münster: Aschendorff, 1972) 42; Siegfried Schulz, *Q. Die Spruchquelle der Evangelisten* (Zurich: Theologischer Verlag, 1972) 444–46; Athanasius Polag, *Die Christologie der Logienquelle* (WMANT 45; Neukirchen-Vluyn: Neukirchener Verlag, 1977) 6; John S. Kloppenborg, *The Formation of Q* (Studies in Antiquity and Christianity; Philadelphia: Fortress, 1987) 230–32; David R. Catchpole, *The Quest For Q* (Edinburgh: Clark, 1993) 182 n. 84. I consider the presence of Luke 17:33 par. in Q to be much more probable than the theory of a mere rewriting of Mark 8:35 parr. However, the disagreement among scholars serves to remind us that, whenever we discuss Q, we are dealing with a hypothetical entity.

[59] For this suggestion see Alan Hugh McNeile, *The Gospel According to St. Matthew* (Grand Rapids: Baker, 1980, originally 1915) 148–49. He notes that *peripoieomai* and *zōogoneō* are used 10 and 11 times respectively in the LXX for the Hebrew *ḥāyâ,* "to live" (usually in pi'el or hip'îl with causative sense: "preserve alive" or "bring to life"). However, in an oral communication, Prof. Joseph A. Fitzmyer has indicated to me that he considers the Aramaic verb *šēzib* ("save," "rescue") the most likely candidate for the background of *sōzō.*

[60] In Luke 17:33, the most likely sense of *peripoieō* in the middle voice is "save or rescue (for oneself)," "preserve (for oneself)"; this is the sense favored by Walter Bauer for Luke 17:33 in his *Griechisch-deutsches Wörterbuch zu den Schriften des Neuen Testaments und der frühchristlichen Literatur* (ed. Kurt and Barbara Aland; 6th ed.; Berlin/New York: de Gruyter, 1988). Also possible is the sense "to gain," "to

acquire," "to win (for oneself)," though this seems less likely when the antithetical concept is "to lose" or "to destroy" *one's own life.* Similarly, the most likely sense of *zōogoneō* here is "to keep or preserve alive" (again, the choice of Bauer for Luke 17:33), though "to give life to," "to make alive" are also possible meanings of the verb.

[61] By a curious coincidence, both verbs occur only three times in the NT, and in the exact same three books: once in Luke, once in Acts, and once in 1 Timothy. Since *peripoieō* and *zōogoneō* occur only rarely in the NT and only in late NT works, at the very least one may conjecture that these two verbs probably do not represent the earliest Greek form(s) of the basic aphorism. Beyond this, it is difficult to judge whether these two verbs are the products of Luke's redaction of the traditional aphorism or whether they were already present in his version of the Q tradition. The presence of each verb once in Acts might argue for Lucan redaction in Luke 17:33, but both occurrences in Acts may reflect pre-Lucan tradition (*zōogoneisthai* in Stephen's trial speech in 7:19; *periepoiēsato* in Paul's farewell speech to the elders of Ephesus in 20:28); see Ulrich Wilckens, *Die Missionsreden der Apostelgeschichte. Form- und traditionsgeschichtliche Untersuchungen* (WMANT 5; 3d ed.; Neukirchen-Vluyn: Neukirchener Verlag, 1974, originally 1961) 220–24, 185 n. 2, 197 n. 2. While I lean toward the view that the two Greek verbs were already in the Q tradition known to Luke (Q^{Lk}), our uncertainty in the matter reminds us how hypothetical and tenuous conclusions about Q must remain. One cannot exclude the possibility that the choice of the two verbs or at least the variation in the verbs comes from Luke, who is replacing some verb such as *sōzō* ("save"), which he found in his source. Hence, in my retroversion of the primitive Mark/Q saying into Aramaic, I choose *šēzib* to translate the idea of "save" (thus favoring Mark's *sōzō*).

[62] It is noteworthy that Laufen (*Die Doppelüberlieferungen,* 321), who otherwise favors the Matthean form of the saying as more original, allows that Luke's construction with conditional relative clauses is more original; similarly, W. D. Davies and Dale C. Allison, Jr., *The Gospel According to Saint Matthew* (ICC; 3 vols.; Edinburgh: Clark, 1988, 1991, 1997) 2. 224. Various commentators claim that Matthew has been influenced by the attributive participles used substantively in the surrounding verses (10:37,40,41). That is possible but not certain, since a number of surrounding verses contain relative clauses (10:32,33,38,42).

[63] Ulrich Luz, *Matthew 1–7* (Minneapolis: Augsburg, 1989) 59.

[64] Among those Matthean commentators who attribute the participial construction, the verb "find," and the phrase "for the sake of myself" all to Matthean redaction is Gundry, *Matthew,* 201. The exact opposite view is proposed by Schulz, *Q. Die Spruchquelle der Evangelisten,* 444–45: Matt 10:39 represents almost perfectly the original Q form of the logion, the only open question being the phrase "for the sake of myself." In propounding his position, Schulz relies more on apodictic statements than on detailed argumentation. Even more uncertain is the question of the original

location of this logion in Q. While various commentators champion Matthew's or Luke's order (see Kloppenborg, *Q Parallels*, 170; Rebell, " 'Sein Leben verlieren,' " 207), Hoffmann (*Studien*, 5, 42) is probably correct in affirming that the original context in Q cannot be known.

[65] One might well argue that a verb referring to "wishing" (Mark 8:35 par.) or "seeking" (Luke 17:33) is a secondary addition to the primitive saying because (1) it upsets the balance between the two halves of the aphorism and (2) it is lacking in the forms found in Matt 10:39 and John 12:25. That may be true, but I incline to the view that, while a separate verb of willing or seeking was absent from the beginning in the Johannine form of the saying, it was present in the primitive Marcan-Q form of the saying. (1) As the Marcan or Lucan saying is constructed, a volitional verb like "wishing" or "seeking" has an essential place in the first half of the aphorism, while it would be out of place in the second half. "Wishing" or "seeking" conjures up the selfish, cowardly, and ultimately futile grasping at one's life by a disciple who fears the loss of self and paradoxically effects what he fears. Hence the volitional verb plays an important part in the first half of the aphorism; its upsetting of a perfect balance in the two halves is rhetorically justified. By the same token, such a verb would be out of place in the second half. The saying does not aim at exhorting masochistic disciples to wish for or ferret out suffering and martyrdom in their lives; but those who accept such a fate when it comes as the price of discipleship will preserve or save their lives in the eschatological kingdom. (2) While there is no separate verb of wishing in John 12:25, a certain volitional element is already contained in the verbs "to love" and "to hate." On the whole, therefore, I prefer the hypothesis that two different primitive forms of the aphorism circulated in the Aramaic tradition, the Johannine form being more perfectly balanced in structure than the Marcan-Q form.

[66] As I indicated above, other Aramaic verbs might lie behind the Greek verbs in the saying: e.g., for "to want" or "to wish," *bʿh* (properly, "to seek," "to request") is a possibility (see Matthew Black, *An Aramaic Approach to the Gospels and Acts* [Oxford: Clarendon, 1946] 178); for "to save" or "to rescue," *ḥyh* (in hapʿel), *nṣl*, or just possibly *yšʿ*. Some might prefer the hapʿel of the Aramaic verb "to live" (*ḥyh*) because it might help to explain *sōzō* in Mark and *zōogoneō* in Luke; at times both verbs translate forms of the Hebrew verb *ḥyh* in the LXX. For example, in Ezek 13:18, where the Hebrew uses the piʿel of *ḥyh* with the plural of *nepeš* in the sense of "keep people alive" or "save lives," the LXX renders the clause *kai psychas periepoiounto*. Significant for John 12:25's use of *phylassō* instead of Mark's *sōzō* or Luke's *peripoieomai* is Ezek 18:27, where the piʿel of *ḥyh* is rendered in the LXX as *houtos tēn psychēn autou ephylaxen* ("he has saved [or: shall save] his life"); see also Exod 1:16–17, where *peripoieomai* and *zōogoneō* are used in successive verses to translate forms of *ḥyh*. The LXX uses the verb *sōzō* for *ḥyh* in LXX Ps 29:4; Prov 15:27. Interestingly, in the LXX, *zōogoneō*, which appears there eleven times, always renders some form of *ḥyh*. For similar phrases expressing the idea of saving one's life in the MT, LXX, rabbinic literature, and pagan Greek literature, see Dautzenberg, *Sein Leben Bewahren*, 53–56. One weakness of this whole approach, however, is the pos-

sibility that the verbs *peripoieomai* and *zōogoneō* are the products of Luke's redaction. For the conjunction joining the two parts of the aphorism, I have chosen *wĕ*, which reflects the *kai* ("and") found in Matt 10:39 and John 12:25; the *kai* would reflect Semitic style perfectly. (I choose *wĕ* even before the letter *mem* because the use of *û* instead of *wĕ* before the letter *mem* is probably an example of the influence of Masoretic Hebrew in Biblical Aramaic.) The postpositive *de* ("but") found in the other forms of the aphorism may reflect adaptation to a more Grecized style.

[67] For a detailed study of John 12:25 compared with the Synoptic forms of the logion, see C. H. Dodd, "Some Johannine 'Herrenworte' with Parallels in the Synoptic Gospels," *NTS* 2 (1955–56) 75–86, esp. 78–81; idem, *Historical Tradition*, 338–43; Brown, *The Gospel According to John*, 1. 473–74; Schnackenburg, *Das Johannesevangelium. II. Teil*, 481–82.

[68] In the textual tradition of John 12:25, the "*omega*-verb" form *apollyei* is witnessed by a large number of early and important manuscripts: e.g., papyrus 66, papyrus 75, Codices Sinaiticus, Vaticanus, and Washingtonianus. Correcting in favor of the future tense of the classical form of the "*mi*-verb" *apollymi* (i.e., *apolesei*, which is found in all the other forms of the saying) are, e.g., Codices Alexandrinus, Bezae, and Koridethi. On this see BDR, 67 §92. Significantly, while some form of the verb *apollymi* occurs ten times in the Fourth Gospel, almost always in the mouth of Jesus, this is the only time that the *omega*-form of the verb appears. (Indeed, the *omega*-form of this verb is rare in the NT; for another example, see Rom 14:15.) This might be another pointer to pre-Gospel tradition as opposed to the creative hand of the evangelist.

[69] While the vocabulary is different, John's idea of "keeping" *(phylaxei)* one's life is similar to Luke's idea of "preserving" *(peripoiēsasthai, zōogonēsei)* one's life.

[70] Not only the overloading of the second half of the aphorism but also the specifically Johannine nature of the words and concepts *(kosmos, zōē aiōnios)* argue that the phrases "in this world" and "unto life everlasting" are later additions to the primitive form of the logion; see Barnabas Lindars, *The Gospel of John* (NCB; Grand Rapids: Eerdmans, 1972) 429. As Dodd (*Historical Tradition*, 340) points out, "not only is the word *kosmos* about four times as common in the Fourth Gospel as in all the others together, but the phrase *ho kosmos houtos* is peculiar to the Fourth Gospel, in which it occurs eleven times, while *zōē aiōnios* is more than twice as common in this gospel as in the three Synoptics."

In the view of some commentators, by the addition of *eis zōēn aiōnion* ("unto life everlasting"), John introduces into the saying a distinction (typical of his theology) between the physical, human life *(psychē)* of this world *(en tō kosmō toutō)* and the unchanging, eternal, divine life *(zōē)* made accessible through faith in the Son of God. This characteristically Johannine dualism, it is claimed, is foreign to the Synoptic forms of the logion, where *psychē* is the only word used for "life" and signifies the concrete existence of a human individual that may be either lost or saved both now and in the eschatological future. While the saying does exhibit Johannine dualism, the distinction between *psychē* and *zōē* is not so simple in this saying: despising one's present life *(psychē)* in this world means that one *will* preserve (future tense: *phylaxei*) "it" (i.e., one's *psychē*) unto life everlasting (denoting both duration and goal). So John's dualism, unlike that of a thoroughgoing Gnostic, does not simply write off embodied human existence in the present; there is a continuum between the believer's human existence now and final salvation in the future. To be sure, for John the emphasis is on the decision of faith now, which inexorably determines the future. This point is supported by another typically Johannine touch: the present tense of the verb *apollyei* ("lose" or "destroy"). While all the Synoptic forms have this verb (at least at some point in the saying) in the future tense (reflecting the Synoptics' future eschatology), John's realized eschatology naturally shifts the tense to the present: if one clings in unbelief to this present life as the ultimate value, one is already damned. Yet, typical of John's dialectical thought and expression, the future is not simply forgotten.

[71] In Dodd's view (*Historical Tradition,* 341), "the Johannine version of the saying [when stripped of the qualifying phrases added by the evangelist] is closer in shape to Matthew, closer in sense to Mark and Luke, but superior to them all in the combination of elegance with clarity." In contrast, Dautzenberg (*Sein Leben Bewahren,* 65) considers John 12:25 to be the most developed form of the saying. That may be true of the saying as it now lies in the Fourth Gospel; the easily discernible pre-Gospel form, however, looks quite primitive. Working under the influence of Dautzenberg, Rebell (" 'Sein Leben verlieren,' " 210) misses this point and so dismisses the Johannine form too quickly as a means for reconstructing the primitive form of the saying.

[72] Since the future tense "shall lose" *(apolesei)* is witnessed in all the Synoptic forms of the saying (and in the variant reading of John 12:25), since the present tense "lose" *(apollyei)* is most likely an editorial change occasioned by John's realized eschatology, and since the balancing verb "will preserve" *(phylaxei)* is in the future, I think it probable that the pre-Gospel form of John 12:25 had the future tense in both main verbs.

[73] For the use of love-hate in Greco-Roman pagan religion, see, e.g., the *Hermetic Corpus* 4.6. The opposition of the verbs "love" and "hate" *(ʾāhab* and *śānēʾ)* is common in the MT of the OT; in the LXX, *agapaō* ("to love") is more often opposed to *miseō* ("to hate") than is *phileō.* For "love" and "hate" used to express preference rather than diametrically opposed emotions, see, e.g., Deut 21:15–17; Gen 29:30–33. On this, see Dodd, *Historical Tradition,* 342.

[74] On the beatitudes, see *A Marginal Jew,* 2. 317–36.

[75] A mixed text resulting from the conflation of Matt 10:37–38 and Luke 14:26–27 is found in the Coptic *Gos. Thom.* saying 55: "Whoever will not hate his father and

his mother cannot become a disciple to me; and whoever will not hate his brothers and his sisters and will not carry his cross as I have will not be worthy of me." Here we have a parade example of how the *Gospel of Thomas* melds various phrases from various Synoptic Gospels to create its own form of a Gospel saying. On the whole, the saying is closer to Luke than to Matthew. The phrases "will not hate [as opposed to Matthew's "love]," *"his* father and *his* mother [with possessive pronouns, reflecting Luke's *heautou,* which is not in Matthew]," "brothers and sisters [Matthew has "son or daughter"]," and "cannot become a disciple to me" come from Luke. Yet at the end of the saying we see a clear trace of the redactional tendency of Matthew or his M tradition: "will not be worthy of me." The key words *mathētēs* (disciple), *stauros* (cross), and *axios* (worthy) appear in Greek in the Coptic text. The theme of imitating Jesus carrying his cross, which is implicit in the passages of the Synoptic Gospels, is made explicit by the addition in the *Gospel of Thomas:* "... carry his cross *as I have."* On the whole saying, see Fieger, *Das Thomasevangelium,* 165–67. A similar saying, with a similar conflation of Matt 10:37 and Luke 14:26 and a similar addition of "as I," is found in Gos. Thom. saying 101. The text, however, is fragmentary, and there is no mention of carrying one's cross; see Fieger, ibid., 256–57. Fieger's analysis of the parallels in Gos. Thom. to Mark 8:34–35 parr. shows that it is highly unlikely that *Thomas'* versions of these sayings are independent of the Synoptics.

[76] As soon as one tries to interpret Mark 8:34, one is faced with a text-critical problem. In the opening conditional clause, the reading "If anyone wishes to *follow (akolouthein)* after me" is supported by papyrus 45 (early 3d century) and Codices Ephraemi Rescriptus (5th century), Bezae (5th century), Washingtonianus (5th century), and Koridethi (9th century), as well as the majority of later manuscripts; the reading is thus supported by a combination of Caesarean, so-called Western, and Byzantine text types. However, some excellent early codices (Sinaiticus, Vaticanus [both representing the Alexandrian text type of the 4th century], and Alexandrinus [representing the Byzantine tradition of the 5th century]) favor the reading "to *come (elthein)* after me" instead. Opinions are divided. Many commentators (e.g., Laufen, *Die Doppelüberlieferungen,* 547 n. 15; Gundry, *Mark,* 434–35, with hesitation) argue in favor of "come" (supported by the great Alexandrian codices); the use of "follow" in the initial clause of 8:34 could be seen as a result of assimilation to the last clause in the verse, "follow *(akoloutheitō)* me," as well as to the Q form in Matt 10:38, resulting in a redundant statement in Mark 8:34. On the other hand, "come" in Mark 8:34 could be seen as an assimilation to the Marcan parallels (Matt 16:24 ‖ Luke 9:23) as well as to the Q parallel in Luke 14:27, all of which read *"come* after me." The substitution of "come" for "follow" may have resulted from the desire of scribes to avoid what seemed like an infelicitous and even illogical redundancy ("if anyone wishes to follow after me ... he must follow me"). "Follow" is the text favored by both the 3d and 4th editions of the *UBSGNT.* On the whole, I incline to accepting "follow" in 8:34a, though I admit there are good arguments on both sides. I think the redundancy is more apparent than real, since the first mention is conditional (*"if* anyone *wishes* to follow after me") versus the climactic command ("[then] follow me!"). Moreover, the apparent redundancy has a rhetorical purpose (*inclusio*

and chiastic structure in the verse), hammering home both the goal (following Jesus) and the means of reaching it (denying oneself, taking up one's cross). For critics intent on the historical Jesus, the whole question may be moot, since both "follow after" and "come after" might go back to the same Semitic phrase; hence the redundancy might be original and intentional on the part of Jesus.

[77] The chiasm is stronger in the Greek than in most English translations since in the opening conditional clause (protasis) the phrase "after me" is placed before the verb "follow," while in the concluding clause of the sentence (apodosis), "me" occurs after "follow" *(opisō mou akolouthein . . . akoloutheitō moi)*. One remembers that Mark 8:35 parr. was also marked by chiasm, though the two-part antithetical structure seen there is not found in Mark 8:34 parr.

[78] On this, see Gundry, *Mark,* 435. The full force of the 3d person of the Greek imperative is somewhat softened by the traditional English rendering *"let* him follow me." A rendering such as "he must follow me!" conveys better the imperative mood.

[79] It is difficult to guess what Semitic phrase might lie behind *aparnēsasthō heauton.* On p. 64 of the *Ergänzungsheft* (4th ed.; Göttingen: Vandenhoeck & Ruprecht, 1971) to his *Geschichte,* Bultmann, borrowing a suggestion from A. Fridrichsen, opines that "deny oneself" is a substitute for a more original "hate one's life [or: one's self]." The reflexive pronoun would represent *napšeh,* which may be reflected in the more literal *psychēn autou* of Mark 8:35 parr.; as we have seen, the Johannine parallel to Mark 8:35 has *ho misōn tēn psychēn autou; misei . . . tēn psychēn heautou* also occurs in Luke 14:26, but the presence of *psychē* in the list of things that must be hated may be due to Lucan redaction. Other suggestions for the Aramaic substratum include the verb *kěpar* ("deny," "renounce") in pe'al + *bě* + *napšeh* as object; for a slightly different form of this suggestion, see Gustaf Dalman, *Jesus—Jeshua. Studies in the Gospels* (New York: Ktav, 1971, originally 1929) 191.

[80] I shall deal with crucifixion in detail in a later chapter. For now, see Martin Hengel, *Crucifixion* (Philadelphia: Fortress, 1977); Joseph A. Fitzmyer, "Crucifixion in Ancient Palestine, Qumran Literature, and the New Testament," *To Advance the Gospel* (New York: Crossroad, 1981) 125–46; Gerald G. O'Collins, "Crucifixion," *Anchor Bible Dictionary,* 1. 1207–10.

[81] For the authenticity of Matt 19:12, see *A Marginal Jew,* 1. 342–45. For the authenticity of the eucharistic words of Jesus, see John P. Meier, "The Eucharist at the Last Supper: Did It Happen?" *TD* (Winter, 1995–96) 1–17.

[82] This is the message of the twin parables found in the special Lucan tradition: the parable of a man building a tower (Luke 14:28–30) and the parable of a king planning a military campaign (14:31–32): realize the tremendous cost before you throw yourself into the enterprise. It is not by accident that, in Luke's composition, these two parables follow upon the two Q logia on discipleship in 14:26 + 27: the obliga-

tion to hate father and mother and the obligation to carry one's cross. On all this, see Fitzmyer, *The Gospel According to Luke,* 2. 1060–63.

[83] Some commentators see the concluding imperative "follow me" as the summation of the first two imperatives, while others see it as the goal achieved by performing the actions described in the first two imperatives. Granted the brutal imagery and purposefully shocking rhetoric, this is a fine distinction that probably did not concern either Jesus or his audience.

[84] Hence, I do not see the force of the objection of Fitzmyer (*The Gospel According to Luke,* 1. 785–86), who prefers a suggestion stemming from D. F. Strauss that the original form of the saying may have referred to bearing Jesus' yoke (cf. Matt 11:29). When dealing with the Q form of this logion, Schulz (*Q. Die Spruchquelle der Evangelisten,* 431–33) draws too many far-reaching conclusions about the absence of the (saving) cross of Jesus from this saying. Not every saying can say everything, nor are we to suppose that the Q document as a whole said everything that could be said about the Christian faith of the people who used it.

[85] The attempts of various commentators to see the cross in this saying as a popular image used by Zealots, as a reformulation of the image of carrying a yoke (cf. Matt 11:29), as a wooden palisade carried by the followers of a military commander, as a cultic sign with which a follower was sealed, or as a demand that each and every disciple undergo literal martyrdom all miss the point of the forceful, even brutal rhetoric. On these various interpretations and the reasons for rejecting them, see Laufen, *Die Doppelüberlieferungen,* 309–13.

[86] See the text in W. A. Oldfather (ed.), *Epictetus* (LCL; 2 vols.; Cambridge, MA: Harvard University; London: Heinemann, 1925, 1928) 1. 229–30. Epictetus is hardly the first or only philosopher of the Greek or Roman world to use the cross in a philosophical or rhetorical context for purposes of teaching. Perhaps the most famous example comes from Plato's *Republic* 2.5.361e–362a, where it is argued that the completely just or innocent man will be scourged, tortured in all sorts of ways, and finally impaled on a stake (or crucified, the rare verb *anaschindyleuō* being used); for Greek text and translation, see Paul Shorey (ed.), *Plato. The Republic* (LCL; 2 vols.; London: Heinemann; New York: Putnam's Sons, 1930, 1935) 1. 124–25. Quotations from pagan Latin authors who use the cross symbolically and rhetorically are collected by Hengel, *Crucifixion,* 64–68. For the history of the cross mark, accompanied by abundant photographs, see Jack Finegan, *The Archeology of the New Testament* (rev. ed.; Princeton: Princeton University, 1992) 339–89.

[87] For a different argument in favor of the historicity of this logion, see Erich Dinkler, "Jesu Wort vom Kreuztragen," *Neutestamentliche Studien für Rudolf Bultmann* (BZNW 21; ed. W. Eltester; Berlin: Töpelmann, 1954) 110–29. Dinkler suggests a rather contorted tradition history that mixes together material from before and after the time of Jesus. Dinkler thinks that the historical Jesus was referring to the mark or

seal of the "tau" prophesied in Ezek 9:4. Although I think that this explanation is highly unlikely, it is favored by Pesch, *Das Markusevangelium,* 2. 60.

[88] As Kloppenborg (*Q Parallels,* 170) notes, most commentators accept this logion as a Q saying. Laufen (*Die Doppelüberlieferungen,* 546 n. 2) states that, as far as he knows, its presence in Q is not denied by any critic who holds the two-source theory of Synoptic origins.

[89] This is similar to the reconstruction of Laufen, *Die Doppelüberlieferungen* (see his arguments in favor of this wording on pp. 303–4), and of Schulz, *Q. Die Spruchquelle der Evangelisten,* 430–31. One must always remain hesitant about such reconstructions, all the more so in this case because "disciple" is a relatively rare word in Q.

[90] Pesch (*Das Markusevangelium,* 2. 61) favors Mark's form as more original, while Schürmann (*Das Lukasevangelium,* 1. 542) favors the Q form. Laufen (*Die Doppelüberlieferungen,* 305–8) suggests a primitive form that is basically Mark 8:34 minus the clause "let him deny himself and. . . ."

[91] On "dyadic personality," see Bruce J. Malina, *The New Testament World. Insights from Cultural Anthropology* (Atlanta: John Knox, 1981) 51–70. Needless to say, all sociological generalizations have to be tested against the details of the specific time and place with which one is dealing. For example, it may be that, because of socioeconomic pressures, the large, extended patriarchal family was breaking down in the Judea of the 1st century A.D. and that even a father of a nuclear family would have had difficulty making his will prevail in such a situation. For this hypothesis see Martin Goodman, *The Ruling Class of Judaea. The Origins of the Jewish Revolt against Rome A.D. 66–70* (Cambridge: Cambridge University, 1987) 68–75. At the same time, different conditions may have prevailed in Galilee, where Herod Antipas created a comparatively stable, if oppressive, situation during his reign (4 B.C.–A.D. 39); see *A Marginal Jew,* 1. 282–83.

[92] Once again, the brackets indicate possible additions by the Christian oral tradition or by the evangelists. I indicated the reasons for omitting the bracketed words above, when I treated Mark 8:35 parr. I emphasize again that what I am interested in at this point is the basic thrust of what the historical Jesus said, not the exact wording of the most primitive form of a particular logion. Hence I do not discuss here in detail which form of the promised reward is most original (cf. Mark 10:30 ‖ Matt 19:29 ‖ Luke 18:29–30); my focus is rather on the sacrifice Jesus demands. Many commentators suggest that the detailed list of rewards, the mention of persecutions, and the distinction between "in this present time" and "in the age to come" reflect the later experience and thought of Christian missionaries; see, e.g., Nikolaus Walter, "Zur Analyse von Mc 10:17–31," *ZNW* 53 (1962) 206–18, esp. 216–17, appealing to Bultmann, *Geschichte,* 115. Opposed to this is Gundry, *Mark,* 566–69. On itinerant Christian missionaries, see the famous essay of Gerd Theissen, "Legitimation and

Subsistence: An Essay on the Sociology of Early Christian Missionaries," *The Social Setting of Pauline Christianity. Essays on Corinth* (Philadelphia: Fortress, 1982) 27–67. From the start, we should be clear about what Mark 10:28–30 parr. and similar sayings do *not* tell us. We are not told about the practical arrangements that various individual disciples may have made concerning their homes and families. Was the break with home and family always as radical and permanent as the words of Jesus seem to demand? Caution is suggested by the one case we know of, namely, Simon Peter's (on this see Taylor, *Mark*, 433). Soon after Mark presents Peter and Andrew leaving their nets to follow Jesus (Mark 1:16–18), Mark depicts Jesus being hosted for a Sabbath-day meal in the house of Peter and Andrew in Capernaum and being served by Peter's mother-in-law (1:29–31). (Luke may be reordering things for logical and moral consistency when he places the story mentioning Simon Peter's house and mother-in-law [Luke 4:38–39] before the story of the call of Peter, with its concluding claim that Peter and his associates "left all things" to follow Jesus [Luke 5:1–11].) Later on in the public ministry, Jesus never seems to want for a boat, which at times is said to be supplied by his disciples (see, e.g., Mark 3:9; 4:1,35–36; John 6:16–17). Still later on, in the first Christian generation, we learn that Cephas (i.e., Simon Peter), the apostles, and the brothers of Jesus all go on missionary journeys *along with their wives* at the expense of the churches (1 Cor 9:4–7; see Gordon D. Fee, *The First Epistle to the Corinthians* [NICNT; Grand Rapids: Eerdmans, 1987] 403–4). We are left asking: To what extent and for how long did Simon Peter really leave his family and home during the ministry of Jesus—a ministry whose Galilean segment seems to have used Capernaum as a home base? (Gundry [*Mark*, 558] makes the intriguing suggestion that, in Mark's version of the logion, the omission of "wife" among those people the disciple leaves behind may be connected in some way with Peter's taking his wife on his missionary journeys. Yet most of the people mentioned in Mark 10:29 are in balanced pairs—"brothers or sisters or mother or father"—and hence the absence of "wife" may be explained rhetorically by the absence of "husband," the logion being addressed primarily to Peter and the Twelve.) In any event, we are reminded by all this that it is dangerous to use the sparse data we have in the NT to spin out sweeping sociological assertions about the Jesus movement and early Christianity. We must allow for the possibility of some discrepancy—even apart from Judas Iscariot—between what Jesus demanded of his disciples and what individual disciples may have actually done. To take an analogous example: for many centuries, Roman Catholic priests and religious have sincerely proclaimed, affirmed, and claimed to have followed the radical call of Jesus that we examine in these texts. It would be perilous to draw wide-ranging sociological conclusions about the actual lifestyles of these priests and religious from the religious rhetoric they sincerely embraced and thought they reflected. Similarly, one must exercise care in using the radical religious rhetoric of Jesus to draw sociological conclusions about how his individual disciples lived out his radical call in their concrete daily lives. Religious rhetoric and human reality do not always coincide.

[93] See, e.g., Friedrich Gustav Lang, "*Sola gratia* in Markusevangelium," *Rechtfertigung* (Ernst Käsemann Festschrift; ed. J. Friedrich, W. Pöhlmann, and P. Stuhl-

macher; Tübingen: Mohr [Siebeck]; Göttingen: Vandenhoeck & Ruprecht, 1976) 321–37. Lang's focus is the redactional theology of Mark, but even on this level he evinces a tendency to read Paul's theology into the evangelists.

[94] So Bultmann, *Geschichte*, 172–73; Fitzmyer, *The Gospel According to Luke*, 2. 1060–61 (who, however, points out Lucan redactional touches as well); Davies and Allison, *Matthew*, 2. 221.

[95] Despite some dissimilarity of wording in Matt 10:34–36 ‖ Luke 12:51–53, most commentators consider the logion Q material; see Kloppenborg, *Q Parallels*, 142. For a sorting out of what may be redactional in the Matthean and Lucan versions, see Schulz, *Q. Die Spruchquelle*, 258–59; most likely, Luke 12:52, which lacks a parallel in Matthew, is an addition. Davies and Allison (*Matthew*, 2. 218) argue that Matt 10:34 may more faithfully reflect a Semitic substratum with its wording: "to cast not peace into the earth but the sword." Matt 10:35 par. echoes Mic 7:6, a fact which might make some critics suspicious of a Christian creation. However, (1) the Synoptic texts do not reproduce exactly either the MT or the LXX. (2) More importantly, the idea that any citation or echo of the Jewish Scriptures must mean derivation from the church rather than from Jesus presupposes a rather strange picture of Jesus the Jewish prophet and teacher: someone who propounded his teaching about the fulfillment of Israel's prophecies and the proper way to do God's will in the last days without ever citing or alluding to the prophets or the Torah. This alienation of the historical Jesus from his own Jewish heritage is an unhappy aspect of traditional quests that must be overcome. Matt 10:36 ("and the enemies of a man [will be] the members of his own household") is probably a Matthean addition to the traditional Q logion because (1) it has no parallel in Luke; and (2) instead of being an allusion to the MT of Mic 7:6, as is v 35, it (unlike the LXX) represents an exact translation of the MT.

[96] See, e.g., Zech 13:3; *1 Enoch* 99:5; 100:1–2; *Jub.* 23:16; *2 Apoc. Bar.* 70:6. For "sword" as an image of divine judgment or punishment in the last days, see, e.g., Isa 66:16; Wis 5:20; *Jub.* 9:15; *1 Enoch* 62:12; 63:11; 90:19; 91:11–12; *2 Apoc. Bar.* 27:5; 40:1. It is with these prophetic and apocalyptic strains of thought that Jesus' teaching about breaking family bonds out of loyalty to him cohere rather than with traditional Israelite wisdom. Granted these prophetic and apocalyptic traditions at home in 1st-century Jewish Palestine, it is unnecessary to search abroad for influence from Greco-Roman Cynicism.

[97] Even the more skeptical form critics see some historical tradition behind Mark 3:21,31–35, although the judgment as to which verses are secondary varies from critic to critic. Bultmann (*Geschichte*, 28–29) thinks that vv 31–34 are a secondary anecdote created to fit with the original saying in v 35. Dibelius held the opposite view in the first edition of his *Formgeschichte*, although he modified his view later on; see the sixth edition of his *Formgeschichte*, 43–44. Whoever may be correct about which part of the story is original, both sides in the debate agree in general that this

disedifying tradition about the mother and brothers of Jesus probably goes back in some form to the public ministry; the criterion of embarrassment is applicable here. Bultmann even opines that Mark 3:21 was not simply spun out of 3:35, but rests on "good, ancient tradition."

[98] On *hoi par' autou* see Taylor, *Mark*, 236. In classical Greek, *hoi para tinos* referred to a person's envoys or ambassadors. In Koine Greek, the phrase broadened its meaning to refer to various sorts of people who are intimately connected with a person; possible translations include "agents," "adherents," "friends," "family," "relatives," or "parents." For "household" or "family," see LXX Prov 31:21; Sus 33 (both LXX and Theodotion); Josephus, *Ant.* 1.10.5 §193. The meaning "family" or "relatives" is shown to be the correct one for Mark 3:21 not by considering the phrase in the abstract but rather by interpreting it within the whole intercalated composition of 3:20–35: hostile family (3:21)—hostile scribes (3:22–30)—hostile family (3:31–35). As Gundry (*Mark*, 171) points out, another argument for the meaning "family" is based on Mark's "duality," his typical use of two more or less synonymous expressions, the second of which makes the first more specific; here *hoi par' autou* in v 21 is made more specific by *hē mētēr autou kai hoi adelphoi autou* in v 31. The extent to which Mark 3:20–21 is traditional or redactional is debated among commentators; see the views and authors listed in Guelich, *Mark 1—8:26*, 169–70. Guelich thinks that, while content and style argue that 3:20 (Jesus' return, the large crowds, the inability of the disciples to eat) comes from Marcan redaction, untypical Marcan usage suggests that 3:21 (his family goes out to seize him) may well come from pre-Marcan tradition—a view even Bultmann shares. Mark's redactional hand would then be seen primarily in the placement of the verse to create his typical "sandwiched" or "intercalated" order.

[99] For an exhaustive treatment of the parenthetical remarks in the Fourth Gospel, see Gilbert van Belle, *Les parenthèses dans l'évangile de Jean* (Studiorum Novi Testamenti Auxilia 11; Leuven: Leuven University/Peeters, 1985); for John 7:5, see p. 78. A less thorough treatment can be found in Tom Thatcher, "A New Look at Asides in the Fourth Gospel," *BSac* 151 (1994) 428–39. Van Belle shows that such parenthetical remarks are characteristic of the evangelist's style throughout the Gospel; hence a parenthetical remark should not be attributed automatically to the final redactor. John 7:5 in particular should not be attributed to the final redactor, since it ties in theologically and structurally with the theme of Jesus' mother and brothers in John 2:1–12 and 19:26–27.

[100] On this point, see *A Marginal Jew*, 2. 938–39. As most commentators agree, the reference to "my brothers" in the mouth of the risen Jesus in John 20:17 refers and points ahead to his disciples in 20:19. This makes plainer the message intimated at the cross (19:26–27): the believing disciples, not the unbelieving siblings, are the true brothers of Jesus.

[101] On the different ways in which the Synoptics treat the mother of Jesus, see Raymond E. Brown et al., *Mary in the New Testament* (Philadelphia: Fortress; New York: Paulist, 1978) 51–177.

[102] On Luke 11:27–28, see Bultmann, *Geschichte,* 29–30 (the pericope is classified as a biographical apophthegm); Dibelius, *Formgeschichte,* 162 (the pericope is classified as a chreia). Bultmann notes the similarity of motif between Luke 11:27–28 and Mark 3:31–35—though he denies any literary dependence of one text on the other. For Bultmann, Luke 11:27–28, which was a unity from the beginning, represents an "ideal scene," i.e., not a historical event in the life of Jesus. Fitzmyer (*The Gospel According to Luke,* 2. 926–29) shows how the pericope is to be interpreted positively in its Lucan context; similarly, Brown et al., *Mary in the New Testament,* 170–72. A more negative interpretation is given by I. Howard Marshall, *The Gospel of Luke* (Grand Rapids: Eerdmans, 1978) 480–82. T. W. Manson (*The Sayings of Jesus* [London: SCM, 1949, originally 1937] 88) likewise reads a negative tone into Jesus' response in 11:28, but he seems to be thinking of the hypothetical original situation in the life of Jesus rather than the redactional setting in Luke.

[103] See Meier (*A Marginal Jew,* 1. 57–58) for a comparison of the reliable tradition about James' martyrdom in Josephus with the more legendary treatment in Hegesippus, as recorded by Eusebius. For an overview of the NT data on James, see Florence Morgan Gillman, "James, Brother of Jesus," *Anchor Bible Dictionary,* 3. 620–21.

[104] This seems to me a much more probable interpretation than the idea that Mark and John were engaging in a fierce polemic against James, the family of Jesus, or the Jerusalem church in general. From the first generation of Christianity, the one person we know of who was engaged in prolonged controversy with James or those around him was Paul. Yet, for all his polemical outbursts, Paul never directly attacks James as someone lacking in faith. Still less does he engage in a direct polemic against the Jerusalem church, with which he wished to retain a relationship, however uneasy. By the time we come to the third Christian generation and the final composition of the Fourth Gospel, one wonders what possible purpose could be served by a polemic against the martyred James or against the Jerusalem church, which had long since passed from the scene. Not unlike some Hollywood cinema, certain types of NT criticism suffer from an excess of conspiracy theories.

[105] On this, see Rengstorf, "*manthanō,* etc.," 406–7.

[106] Hengel (*The Charismatic Leader,* 14) notes a few rabbinic anecdotes that, similar to call-stories in the Greek philosophical tradition, report some protest on the part of a family against the entrance of one of its members into a rabbinic school. The anecdote regularly ends with a reconciliation based on the honor that the student will later attain.

[107] I choose the phrase "historical disciple of the historical Jesus" with care. I do not deny that, on a few rare occasions, the evangelists may create a disciple "redactionally." In other words, for theological purposes, the evangelists may apply the title of disciple to someone who historically was not a disciple during Jesus' earthly ministry. One clear example is that of Joseph of Arimathea. In Mark 15:43, he is simply a "prominent councillor, who was himself eagerly awaiting the kingdom of God." More or less equivalently, Luke calls him in 23:50 "a councillor and a good and just man"; to make sure that there is no mistake, Luke adds in v 51 that "he had not agreed with their plan and actions [i.e., the actions of those who had asked for Jesus' death]"; Luke then continues with Mark: "who was eagerly awaiting the kingdom of God." Having experienced the break between his church and the synagogue, Matthew is uncomfortable with this ambiguous, in-between status of Joseph; hence in 27:57, Matthew makes Joseph "a rich man . . . who himself had become a disciple of Jesus [emathēteuthē tō Iēsou]." Having likewise experienced a traumatic break with the synagogue and espousing a dualistic theology that allows for no middle position, John remakes Joseph in the same way as Matthew: in John 19:38, Joseph is "a disciple of Jesus [mathētēs tou Iēsou], but a hidden one for fear of the Jews." Clearly, we are not dealing in Matthew or John with "a historical disciple of the historical Jesus," but rather the redactionally created status of a person who, in the earliest Gospel tradition, was not designated a disciple. Such a "redactional disciple" is of no interest to our historical project. A similar observation could be made about those Johannine comments in which Jesus is really the mouthpiece of the Johannine community rebuking Jewish Christians of low christology who apparently have remained in the synagogue. For example, supposedly speaking to "the Jews who had come to believe in him," the Johannine Jesus says (8:31–32): "If you abide in my word, truly you will be my disciples, and you will know the truth, and the truth will set you free." This echo of Johannine polemic toward the end of the 1st century A.D. tells us nothing about the historical disciples of the historical Jesus.

[108] Culpepper, *The Johannine School*, 225.

[109] Ibid.

[110] Disciples like Peter, Andrew, James, and John, who belonged to the inner circle of the Twelve, must receive separate treatment when we examine that group. For now, we are interested in them only insofar as they belong to and exemplify the traits of the larger group known as disciples. In John's Gospel, the anonymous "disciple whom Jesus loved" poses a special problem. On the one hand, the evangelist clearly labels him a disciple, indeed, *the* disciple par excellence (that is the sense of the polemical claim, "*the* disciple whom Jesus loved [more than all others]"). On the other hand, this disciple never appears in the Fourth Gospel before the Last Supper, hence, before the public ministry has reached its conclusion. He then appears—if we restrict ourselves to the passages where his identification is clear—only fleetingly at the Last Supper (John 13:23–25), the cross (19:26–27), and the empty tomb (20:2–10). He

may also appear simply as "another disciple" who is known to the high priest (18:15–16); he is probably not to be identified with the companion of Andrew in 1:35–39 (most likely Philip). With no information about the beloved disciple prior to the end of the public ministry, we lack the data necessary to decide whether he fits the three requirements we have abstracted from the Gospels. Needless to say, for those who think that the beloved disciple is only an ideal figure created by the evangelist and does not reflect some actual historical figure at the time of Jesus, there is no great problem: the beloved disciple is a redactional invention, pure and simple. Likewise, those conservative exegetes who still hold to the identification of the beloved disciple with John the son of Zebedee have no problem: as one of the Twelve, he obviously counts as a disciple. But what of those exegetes (including myself) who do not accept this identification but who hold that the figure of the beloved disciple, however legendary his Gospel portrait may be, is grounded in some historical figure? In my view, a tenable position is that the status of this historical person as a "disciple" in the strict sense is due to the veneration of this person by John's community or to the theological creativity of the evangelist. The very wording of the title, "the disciple whom Jesus *loved (ēgapa,* imperfect tense)," gives the impression of a group looking back to the sacred past when Jesus, during his earthly life, loved this follower; the wording would not make sense if the phrase were actually used during Jesus' ministry. The beloved disciple's status as a disciple may thus be redactional in the same sense as that of Joseph of Arimathea: the person really existed, but his status as a disciple in the strict sense is a post-factum honor.

[111] Robert P. Meye (*Jesus and the Twelve. Discipleship and Revelation in Mark's Gospel* [Grand Rapids: Eerdmans, 1968] 170–71) emphatically defends his opinion that the Gospel tradition nowhere identifies the women followers of Jesus, specifically the women named at the cross, as disciples. He points to the disjunction implied in Mark 16:7, when the young man at the empty tomb says to the two *women* who had been at the cross: "Go tell *his disciples. . . .*"

[112] See Quentin Quesnell, "The Women at Luke's Supper," *Political Issues in Luke-Acts* (ed. Richard J. Cassidy and Philip J. Scharper; Maryknoll, NY: Orbis, 1983) 59–79. Quesnell argues that Luke considers the women disciples from the following data: (1) Luke clearly uses "disciples" in Acts of both men and women (e.g., in Acts 9:1–2) and there is no reason to think his usage differs in the Gospel. (Actually, there is.) (2) The angel's address to the women at the tomb in Luke 24:6–7 reminds them of how Jesus in Galilee prophesied to them his death and resurrection; yet the Lucan passion predictions in Galilee (Luke 9:22,44) are directed to the disciples. (3) "The great throng of disciples" in Luke 19:37 would certainly include the women who had come up with him from Galilee (23:49,55). Quesnell stresses that he is investigating only the redactional view of Luke, not the actual situation of the historical Jesus. For a full discussion of the role of women in Luke, see Barbara E. Reid, *Choosing the Better Part? Women in the Gospel of Luke* (Collegeville, MN: Liturgical Press [Glazier], 1996).

[113] It cannot be stressed enough that here we are focused on a narrow question of historical reconstruction: were the female followers of Jesus thought of or called disciples during the ministry of the historical Jesus? Granted the very limited sources, a great deal of what follows must remain hypothetical. No attempt is made here to address the larger questions of the historical reality or the theological picture of women in the Gospels or in the NT in general—to say nothing of the still larger project of a feminist hermeneutic of the NT data. On these larger questions and projects, see Elizabeth M. Tetlow, *Women and Ministry in the New Testament* (New York/ Ramsey, NJ: Paulist, 1980); Elisabeth Moltmann-Wendel, *The Women Around Jesus* (New York: Crossroad, 1982, German original 1980); Elisabeth Schüssler Fiorenza, *In Memory of Her. A Feminist Theological Reconstruction of Christian Origins* (New York: Crossroad, 1983); idem, *Jesus. Miriam's Child, Sophia's Prophet* (New York: Continuum, 1994); Carla Ricci, *Mary Magdalene and Many Others. Women Who Followed Jesus* (Minneapolis: Fortress, 1994); Ingrid Rosa Kitzberger, "Mary of Bethany and Mary of Magdala—Two Female Characters in the Johannine Passion Narrative: A Feminist, Narrative-Critical Reader-Response," *NTS* 41 (1995) 564–86; Warren Carter, "Getting Martha out of the Kitchen: Luke 10:38–42 Again," *CBQ* 58 (1996) 264–80. Ricci struggles with the question of whether the women followers of Jesus should be regarded as disciples on pp. 179–92. Tetlow (*Women and Ministry*, 93–94) represents a common tendency in the literature to move almost immediately from the fact that certain women "followed" Jesus to the conclusion that these women were "disciples" of Jesus. It is this logical move from "followed" to "disciples" that must be examined more carefully.

[114] On the many exegetical problems connected with this list, see Brown, *The Death of the Messiah*, 2. 1152–60, 1169–71; Ben Witherington III, *Women in the Ministry of Jesus* (SNTSMS 51; Cambridge: Cambridge University, 1984) 118–23. I understand the Marcan list to contain three women who are expressly named. My treatment at this point concerns only the presence of devoted female adherents at the cross; I pass over for now other problems in the text. For the scholars who hold that Mark 15:40 was part of a pre-Marcan Passion Narrative, see the table of authors drawn up by Marion L. Soards, *The Death of the Messiah*, 2. 1516–17; to it may be added Martin Hengel, "Maria Magdalena und die Frauen als Zeugen," *Abraham unser Vater* (Otto Michel Festschrift; Arbeiten zur Geschichte des Spätjudentums und Urchristentums 5; ed. Otto Betz, Martin Hengel, Peter Schmidt; Leiden/Cologne: Brill, 1963) 243–56. Brown points out that Mark's awkward construction in 15:40–41 could create the impression of two groups of women: those named, who are specifically said to have followed and served Jesus in Galilee, and a larger unnamed group who are simply said to have come up with him to Jerusalem. Whether Mark really intends to differentiate the two types of women so sharply is unclear and, in my view, unlikely since, in a kind of *inclusio*, Mark mentions the larger group of women both at the beginning of v 40 and toward the end of v 41. In different ways, both Matt 27:55–56 and Luke 23:49 do away with the possible distinction. As for the problematic verb "serve" *(diakoneō)*, Brown (ibid., n. 29) thinks that Marcan usage (e.g., Mark 1:13,31) favors the meaning "to take care of material needs, particularly

food and drink." On p. 1170, he distinguishes this simpler meaning from the meaning of the verb in Luke 8:3, where, since the women are "serving" Jesus and the Twelve "out of their own means," the verb means "provide"; cf. Hengel, "Maria Magdalena," 247–48. On the problem of *diakoneō*, see my treatment of the Lucan texts below; cf. Hermann W. Beyer, "*diakoneō,* etc.," *TDNT* 2 (1964) 81–93 (with the questionable theologizing on the data typical of *TDNT*); John N. Collins, *Diakonia. Re-interpreting the Ancient Sources* (New York/Oxford: Oxford University, 1990) esp. 245–52 (with a theological agenda of his own).

[115] Winsome Munro ("Women Disciples in Mark?" *CBQ* 44 [1982] 225–41) thinks that Mark has purposefully suppressed the tradition of the women active in the Galilean ministry; unfortunately, her position on this point, like many of her positions throughout the article, rests on very fanciful hypotheses.

[116] On John's presentation of the women at the cross, see Brown, *The Death of the Messiah,* 2. 1013–26. John 19:25 does not mention that the women had followed Jesus in or from Galilee, but this is not surprising since Jesus' itinerant ministry in Galilee plays a remarkably small role in John's Gospel as compared with the Synoptics. Hence, the absence of any mention of women followers of Jesus in or from Galilee should not be taken to mean that women are unimportant in John's Gospel; see Raymond E. Brown, "Roles of Women in the Fourth Gospel," printed as Appendix II in *The Community of the Beloved Disciple* (New York/Ramsey, NJ/Toronto: Paulist, 1979) 183–98.

[117] Strictly speaking, John's Gospel, unlike the Synoptics, does not state that any of the women witnessed the burial, but the story of Mary Magdalene coming to the empty tomb early on Sunday morning (John 20:1–2) presumes that she had seen where Jesus was buried.

[118] Although, for clarity's sake, many translators create a second sentence starting with "and the Twelve" in v 1 (e.g., "and the Twelve were with him"), this distorts the overall unity of 8:1–3, which is one long, sprawling sentence. The pronouns/nouns *autos* (Jesus), *hoi dōdeka, gynaikes tines,* and *heterai pollai* are the subjects of the same verb, *diōdeuen* ("was traveling") in v 1; note the concatenation of *autos* . . . KAI *hoi dōdeka* . . . KAI *gynaikes tines* . . . KAI *heterai pollai.* Luke is putting Jesus, the Twelve, and certain women together, and the translator should not put them asunder. Some manuscripts read "served *him* [i.e., Jesus alone]" rather than "served *them* [i.e., Jesus and the Twelve]." For the arguments in favor of reading "him," see Robert J. Karris, "Women and Discipleship in Luke," *CBQ* 56 (1994) 1–20, esp. 5–10; abundant bibliography on women in Luke-Acts is also provided. While there are good manuscripts on both sides of the argument over 8:3, the plural reading is supported by a wide range of text types: e.g., Alexandrian (Codex Vaticanus, Washingtonianus), "Western" (Codex Bezae), Caesarean (family 13 [Ferrar group]), and the later Byzantine tradition (Codex Koridethi). The change to the singular reading may be explained by (1) the common tendency of Christian scribes to create a christocentric

reading and (2) the influence of the key Marcan text mentioning the women, Mark 15:41, which emphasizes that the women had followed *him* and served *him;* the parallel in Luke 23:49 takes over the pronoun in the singular. Hence I agree with Metzger (*Textual Commentary,* 120–21), Fitzmyer (*The Gospel According to Luke,* 1. 698), Collins (*Diakonia,* 245), and the 3d and 4th editions of the *UBSGNT* in reading the plural *autois* in Luke 8:3.

For discussions of the historical value and meaning of Luke 8:1–3, see Ben Witherington III, "On the Road with Mary Magdalene, Joanna, Susanna, and Other Disciples—Luke 8:1–3," *ZNW* 70 (1979) 243–48; idem, *Women,* 116–18; opposed to Witherington's views is David C. Sim, "The Women Followers of Jesus: The Implications of Luke 8:1–3," *HeyJ* 30 (1989) 51–62. One of the few full-scale treatments of the pericope can be found in Ricci, *Mary Magdalene.* On p. 127, Ricci notes that the "many other" women mentioned in 8:3 could be included among those whom Jesus had healed. However, in view of the text's distinction between "some" *(tines)* women in v 2 and "many other" *(heterai pollai)* women in v 3, Ricci thinks it more likely that the "many other" women are not included among those healed. On p. 54, Ricci sees Luke 8:1–3 as placing the group of women in the same close relation to Jesus that the Twelve enjoy, with the group called disciples standing farther off. Indeed, she even ventures the hypothesis (p. 129) that Luke intends to draw a parallel between the three women named in 8:2–3 and the inner circle of three men (Peter, James, and John) within the twelve apostles; here she echoes Hengel, "Maria Magdalena," 248.

[119] See *A Marginal Jew,* 2. 657–59.

[120] On the impossibility of deriving Luke 8:2–3 simply from Mark 15:40–41, see Ricci, *Mary Magdalene,* 27.

[121] One may therefore question Hans Conzelmann's claim (*The Theology of St Luke* [New York: Harper & Row, 1960] 47 n. 1) that "just as the male followers are turned into apostles, so the female followers are turned into deaconesses (v. 3)." Luke frequently uses the term "apostle" of the Twelve in both the Gospel and Acts; he never uses "deaconess" or any similar noun of the women named in Luke 8:2–3, who are never named after Luke 24:10 and who for all practical purposes disappear from his story after a passing reference in Acts 1:14. For the program Luke lays out in the Gospel Prologue, see Richard J. Dillon, "Previewing Luke's Project from His Prologue (Luke 1:1–4)," *CBQ* 43 (1981) 205–27, esp. 214–17.

[122] So Hengel, "Maria Magdalena," 243. This is not to engage in the caricatures sometimes propagated about the status of Jewish women around the time of Jesus. Conditions varied according to socioeconomic class, marital status, and legal context (public or private sphere). It is not true that a woman was simply and always equated with chattel. For the thesis that the Mishna oscillates between treating a Jewish woman as a person and treating her as chattel depending on whether control of her biological functions by a relevant male is at stake, see Judith Romney Wegner, *Chat-*

tel or Person? The Status of Women in the Mishnah (New York/Oxford: Oxford University, 1988) 3–19; for a brief statement of the situation, see Sims, "The Women Followers of Jesus," 54–55. Needless to say, the application of the mishnaic material to the time of Jesus calls for great caution. However, it is safe to say that, as a rule, Jewish religious teachers in the Palestine of the 1st century A.D. did not admit women to the circle of their male disciples undergoing instruction, to say nothing of having married women travel in the company of such teachers without the women's husbands being present. One should remember, though, that in the ancient Mediterranean world, women could and did provide monetary and material support to both rabbis and synagogues; see Witherington, "On the Road," 244.

Naturally, women would be taught their domestic religious obligations at home; in rare cases, a husband who was a rabbi might give more detailed instruction in private. But, as Wegner (*Chattel or Person?*, 161) observes: "The sages never envisaged the possibility of men and women studying [Torah] *together.*" On contact between Jewish teachers (or their students) and women, see (from a Christian source) John 4:27; and (from rabbinic sources) *m. 'Abot* 1:5; 2:7; *m. Soṭa* 3:4; cf. Viviano, *Study as Worship*, 11, 46. On the lack of formal instruction of women in Torah by rabbis, see Léonie J. Archer, *Her Price Is beyond Rubies. The Jewish Woman in Graeco-Roman Palestine* (JSOTSup 60; Sheffield: JSOT, 1990) 69–101; an attempt to deal with this tradition in a modern context can be found in Moshe Meiselman, *Jewish Woman in Jewish Law* (The Library of Jewish Law and Ethics 6; New York: Ktav/Yeshiva University, 1978) 34–42. On the question of scattered references to women trained in formal rabbinic learning, David Goodblatt ("The Beruriah Traditions," *Persons and Institutions in Early Rabbinic Judaism* [Brown Judaic Studies 3; ed. William Scott Green; Missoula, MT: Scholars, 1977] 207–29) argues that anecdotes mentioning the advanced rabbinic learning of Beruriah, the wife of Rabbi Meir, appear only in the Babylonian Amoraic stratum of talmudic literature and probably reflect a special situation in Babylonia ca. the 5th century A.D. While Archer is careful on this question of Beruriah, her book is sometimes marred by an uncritical use of material from the Talmuds for the conditions in Palestine around the turn of the era. The same can be said of Joachim Jeremias' appendix, "The Social Position of Women," in his *Jerusalem in the Time of Jesus* (London: SCM, 1969) 359–76, esp. 373.

As for Christian literature, we do not find clear reference to a devoted female disciple following a celibate male teacher in the Christian mission until we get to the highly imaginative (not to say romantic) *Acts of Paul (and Thecla),* composed around the end of the 2d century A.D.; see Wilhelm Schneemelcher, "Taten des Paulus und der Thekla," Edgar Hennecke and Wilhelm Schneemelcher (eds.), *Neutestamentliche Apokryphen* (2 vols.; 4th ed.; Tübingen: Mohr [Siebeck], 1968, 1971) 243–51. Needless to say, this dearth of data has not stopped some from offering fanciful hypotheses about the precise way in which women participated in the first-generation Christian mission; here we have a primary example of "historical imagination" that is almost all imagination and no history.

[123] For the possible redactional purposes that this tradition serves in Luke's overall theological program, see Witherington, "On the Road," 243–48.

[124] Sim ("The Women Followers of Jesus," 51–62) maintains that the well-to-do Joanna was not representative of Jesus' female followers. According to Sim, most of the women followers were poor, and so they pooled what little money they had in a common fund to support Jesus. While that is possible, Sim's conjectures about the socioeconomic and marital status of the women followers (e.g., most of the women followers were single) go far beyond the meager data we have.

[125] Hence it may go beyond what the text actually says to claim, as Ricci does (*Mary Magdalene,* 159), that the women in Luke 8:1–3 "have placed their patrimony at the disposal of the group [of Jesus and the Twelve]."

[126] Witherington (*Women,* 122) suggests, in reference to the women at the cross in Mark 15:40, that Mark does not use *hoi mathētai* of these women "because usually he reserves this word for the official witnesses or inner circle of Jesus, i.e., the Twelve." The weakness of this approach is intimated by the proviso "usually." In fact, Mark, who does not narrate Jesus' choice of twelve men to constitute the inner group until 3:13–19, uses "disciples" of Jesus' followers in 2:15–16,18,23; 3:7,9. Unless we reject everything that narrative criticism has taught us about Mark as story, the references to "disciples" in these verses cannot refer to a group that does not yet exist in the story. Moreover, coming right after the call of Levi (who is not one of the Twelve) to follow Jesus in 2:13–14, the references to "disciples" in 2:15–16 hardly argue for a restriction of the word to the Twelve, all the more so because these disciples are described as "many" (2:15), although only four of the Twelve (Peter, Andrew, James, and John) have been mentioned up until this point. The same basic point holds true of Luke's narrative as well. Matthew, rather than Mark, has a noted tendency to equate the disciples with the Twelve (Levi is turned into Matthew so that he will appear in the list of the Twelve). However, since Matthew never narrates the story of the choice of the Twelve, the exact extent of the group called "disciples" remains especially vague before the listing of the Twelve in Matt 10:2–4. John, who hardly ever mentions the Twelve during the public ministry (only at 6:67,70–71, where only Peter and Judas are clearly members of the group), gives no indication of a tendency to equate "the disciples" with "the Twelve," especially since John's ideal disciple, "the disciple whom Jesus loved," does not seem to be a member of the Twelve. In sum, one cannot explain the absence of references to women followers as "disciples" on the basis of a supposed but highly dubious equation of "the disciples" with "the Twelve" by the evangelists.

[127] On the historicity of the Bartimaeus story, see *A Marginal Jew,* 2. 686–90. One must be wary of making too strong a claim here, since the concluding statement in Mark 10:52 ("and he followed him on the road [or: way]") may well be an interpretive comment of Mark.

[128] On this, see A. E. Harvey, *Jesus and the Constraints of History* (Philadelphia: Westminster, 1982), esp. 1–10.

[129] As noted above, the Gospels supply multiple attestation of the use of the word "disciples" for the followers of the Baptist. However, one must be wary of possible anachronisms in the Christian presentation of the Baptist; at times, terms used by Jesus or the early Christians may have been retrojected onto the Baptist and his adherents. Still, given the references to "disciples" of the Baptist in Mark, Q, L, and John, I think it likely that the Baptist used *talmîdayyāʾ* of his intimate followers.

[130] On Luke's interest in women, an interest that can be verified simply on statistical grounds, see Ricci, *Mary Magdalene,* 63–64. By almost any measurement, he outstrips each of the other canonical Gospels. Ricci suggests (pp. 68–71) that this interest is to be explained not so much by Luke's temperament and social culture as by a special source or tradition at his disposal, a tradition handed on by women. As elsewhere in her book, here Ricci indulges in highly imaginative speculation.

[131] Apocryphal and gnostic works from the patristic period that contain references to Mary Magdalene, often presented as a favored follower of Jesus, include the Coptic *Gospel of Thomas,* the *Secret Gospel of Mark,* the *Gospel of Mary, Pistis Sophia,* the *Sophia of Jesus Christ,* the *Dialogue of the Savior,* the *Gospel of Philip,* and the *Acts of Philip;* on all this, see Raymond F. Collins, "Mary (Magdalene)," *Anchor Bible Dictionary,* 4. 579–81.

[132] The Greek text of the *Gospel of Peter* 12:50–51 reads in part: *orthrou de tēs kyriakēs Mariam hē Magdalēnē mathētria tou kyriou . . . ēlthen epi to mnēmeion* ("early in the morning on the Lord's Day [!], Mary Magdalene, a [female] disciple of the Lord . . . came to the tomb"). For a critical Greek text and commentary, see M. G. Mara (ed.), *Evangile de Pierre* (SC 201; Paris: Cerf, 1973) 62. Needless to say, one can speak only of the fragments of the *Gospel of Peter* we possess. Whether the work used *mathētria* in its narrative of the public ministry—indeed, whether there was a narrative of the public ministry in the *Gospel of Peter*—cannot be known at this stage of scholarship. Interestingly, even John Dominic Crossan (*The Cross That Spoke* [San Francisco: Harper & Row, 1988] 412), who thinks that the primitive core of the *Gospel of Peter* (a hypothetical "Cross Gospel") goes back to the early days of the church, does not include the reference to Mary Magdalene as a female disciple in his hypothetical "Cross Gospel." For my view that the *Gospel of Peter* comes entirely from the 2d century and evinces knowledge of some of the canonical Gospels (notably Matthew), see *A Marginal Jew,* 1. 116–18; cf. Mara, *Evangile de Pierre,* 213–15; Frans Neirynck, "The Apocryphal Gospels and the Gospel of Mark," *Evangelica* (BETL 60 and 99; 2 vols.; ed. F. van Segbroeck; Leuven: Leuven University/ Peeters, 1982, 1991) 2. 715–72, esp. 732–49; Brown, *The Death of the Messiah,* 2. 1317–49. Not surprisingly, the relatively sparse occurrences of *mathētria* in Koine Greek are found mostly in philosophical texts. In his *Historical Library* 2.52.7, Diodorus of Sicily (1st century B.C.) uses the word once in a metaphorical sense when he says that human arts become "disciples" [*mathētrias*] of nature in imparting various colors to objects; for the Greek text, see C. H. Oldfather et al. (eds.), *Diodorus*

of Sicily (LCL; 12 vols.; Cambridge: Harvard University; London: Heinemann, 1933–1967) 2. 56. In his *Lives of Eminent Philosophers* 4.2 and 8.42, Diogenes Laertius (3d century A.D.) refers to female students of Plato and Pythagoras; for the Greek text, see R. D. Hicks (ed.), *Diogenes Laertius. Lives of Eminent Philosophers* (LCL; 2 vols.; Cambridge, MA: Harvard University; London: Heinemann, 1925) 1. 374; 2. 358. The alternate form of the feminine noun, *mathētris,* is also rare and does not occur at all in the NT or early Christian literature. However, in his *On the Unchangeableness of God,* 2 [5]), Philo writes of Hannah, the mother of Samuel: *toutou ginetai mathētris kai diadochos Anna* ("of him [i.e., Abraham] Hannah becomes the disciple and successor"). In this context, Philo interprets Hannah allegorically as the gift of God's wisdom.

---

[133] Bultmann (*Geschichte,* 33, 58–59) considers the story a biographical apophthegm and an "ideal scene" (hence, not historical). In contrast, Dibelius (*Formgeschichte,* 293), while labeling it a legend, allows for some basis in historical reality, as does Marshall (*The Gospel of Luke,* 451). On the presentation of women in Luke-Acts in general and in Luke 10:38–42 in particular, see Mary Rose D'Angelo, "Women in Luke-Acts: A Redactional View," *JBL* 109 (1990) 441–61, esp. 454–55. I am not convinced by D'Angelo's argument that the redactional intent of Luke in the story of Martha and Mary is to discourage or restrict women's ministry in the church, a ministry represented by Martha's serving. (1) The thrust of Jesus' positive affirmation is that listening attentively to his word is the one necessary thing for any and every would-be disciple. That holds true for men as well as women, and in itself it restricts female ministry no more than male ministry. (2) In Luke's Gospel (as opposed to the two uses in Acts), the verb *diakoneō* ("serve" or "minister," the action of Martha in 10:40) is never used directly and unambiguously of "ministerial" activity such as preaching the word, performing liturgical actions, or acting as a leader of a faith-community. In contrast, it is used clearly to signify waiting on tables or playing the role of host(ess): so, e.g., 4:39; 12:37; 17:8. This is also the meaning of the word in the metaphorical speech of Jesus at the Last Supper in 22:26–27: faced with the self-centered disciples fighting over who among them is the greatest, Jesus compares his humble attitude and behavior toward his disciples with that of a person who waits at table. The verb *diakoneō* is used here to describe his humble demeanor, not to define any ministerial action he performs; note the *"like* one who serves" *(hōs ho diakonōn)* in 22:26–27. The image of waiting at table is reinforced by the overarching context of the Last Supper and by Jesus' vocabulary (*ho anakeimenos* ["the one reclining at table"] and *hina esthēte kai pinēte epi tēs trapezēs mou* ["that you may eat and drink at my table"]); cf. Collins, *Diakonia,* 246–47. The noun *diakonia* (service) occurs only at 10:40 ("Martha was busy with much service") in Luke's Gospel; it is in Acts, not in the Gospel, that it clearly carries the sense of various types of ministerial service in the church. (3) We have here a prime example of a basic rule of exegesis: the immediate context, not the remote context, is the primary guide to the interpretation of a unit. Given that the scene set by Luke in 10:38–42 is that of an itinerant dignitary being received by Martha into her home (v 38: *hypedexato:* "welcomed," "entertained as a guest"), the idea of hospitality and service at table is the natural meaning;

seeing references to leadership in the Christian church in 10:38–41 verges on patristic allegory.

The meaning of *diakoneō* in Luke 8:3 is less clear; the beneficence of the women toward Jesus and the Twelve while journeying through Galilee could refer to many kinds of support and service, not just serving at table, though that is not necessarily excluded. By the same token, male disciples are depicted as storing and distributing food in Mark 6:38,41. In John 6:12, it is explicitly said that it is the disciples' duty to gather up the leftovers. In John 4:8,31, the male disciples (cf. v 27) both buy food (cf. Mark 6:37) and then try to serve it to Jesus. Given all these passages, it is odd that some commentators insist on speaking of the "menial" task of procuring, preparing, or serving food to Jesus and his disciples; see, e.g., Collins, *Diakonia*, 245. The Gospels do not seem to view such activity as menial. In fact, "food service" within the circle of Jesus and his disciples is much more explicitly attributed to male than to female adherents.

[134] See Luke's description of Saul/Paul being educated in Torah at the feet of Gamaliel (Acts 22:3; is there an echo of this idea in Luke 8:35 + 38–39?); also in the later rabbinic literature, e.g., *m. 'Abot* 1:4.

[135] We should probably see a pun in the use of *merida* in Luke 10:42: (1) a "portion" of the food Martha is so concerned about preparing with great hustle and bustle: yet one dish will do; and (2) a "part," "lot," or "sharing" in the salvation Jesus brings through his word: this is what Mary has chosen by listening to Jesus. A literalistic limiting of *merida* to "a portion of food" may have contributed to the desire of scribes to "improve" the text. Despite the confused textual situation, "only one thing is necessary" is most likely the original reading; see Aelred Baker, "One Thing Necessary," *CBQ* 27 (1965) 127–37; Morley Stevenson, "Martha and Mary," *ExpTim* 28 (1916–17) 478; Metzger, *Textual Commentary*, 129; Witherington, *Women*, 102–3. In this I differ from Gordon D. Fee (" 'One Thing Needful'? Luke 10:42," *New Testament Textual Criticism* [Bruce M. Metzger Festschrift; Oxford: Clarendon, 1981] 61–75), who provides an excellent survey of the data, opinions, and arguments; on the question, see also Erling Laland, "Die Martha-Maria Perikope Lukas 10,38–42," *ST* 13 (1959) 70–85; Monika Augsten, "Lukanische Miszelle," *NTS* 14 (1967–68) 581–83.

[136] Richard A. Horsley (*Jesus and the Spiral of Violence. Popular Jewish Resistance in Roman Palestine* [San Francisco: Harper & Row, 1987] 209–84) appreciates the important question of the practical interaction of Jesus with local communities, but out of this valid insight he weaves highly imaginative scenarios.

[137] *A Marginal Jew*, 2. 617–1038.

[138] One wishes that one could be more specific about these "support groups," but the data do not support further speculation; for an attempt at such speculation, see Richard A. Horsley, *Sociology and the Jesus Movement* (New York: Crossroad,

1989) 105–29. Horsley suggests that the "Jesus movement" sought to revitalize local life in village communities in Jewish Palestine "in terms of egalitarian nonpatriarchal familial communities" (p. 128).

[139] Some might prefer to count these sedentary supporters as a separate circle among our concentric circles. However, since one of their major functions (and one of the major reasons we know about them) was the task of extending support to the itinerant Jesus with his entourage of itinerant disciples, I think it better to consider them as auxiliaries attached to the second circle.

CHAPTER 26

JESUS IN RELATION TO HIS FOLLOWERS

The Existence and Nature of the Twelve

I. DISCIPLES, APOSTLES, AND THE TWELVE: THE PROBLEM OF TERMINOLOGY

Having examined the outer circle of the crowds and the middle circle of the disciples, we move now to the inner circle of the Twelve.[1] Right away, some basic distinctions in terminology are in order. I use the phrase "the Twelve" to indicate a special group of twelve men who were not only disciples of Jesus but also formed an inner circle around him. In this I imitate the usage of Mark and John, who always speak of "the Twelve" absolutely (e.g., Mark 6:7; John 6:67). They never use phrases like "the twelve disciples" or "the twelve apostles."[2]

It is in Matthew that we come across the phrase "the twelve disciples" (Matt 10:1; 11:1; possibly 20:17). The problem with "the twelve disciples" is that it might be interpreted to mean that the group called the Twelve was coterminous with the group called disciples. In fact, Matthew, unlike Mark, may intend such an identification when he speaks of "the twelve disciples."[3] As we have already seen in our study of Jesus' disciples, the use of "the Twelve" as completely equivalent to "the disciples" does not reflect the historical situation of Jesus' ministry. For example, the toll collector Levi is called to be a disciple (Mark 2:13–15), but never appears in the list of the Twelve (Mark 3:16–19). Likewise, John's model "disciple whom Jesus loved"—who most probably is an idealized presentation of some historical follower of Jesus in or around Jerusalem[4]—does not seem to have belonged to the Twelve. Hence, in this initial survey of the data, I regularly avoid Matthew's "the twelve disciples" as open to misunderstanding.

Even more do I avoid the traditional Christian phrase "the twelve apostles," which is open to both conceptual and historical confusion.[5] During Jesus' public ministry, "apostle" (Aramaic šĕlîăḥ, Greek apostolos) was probably not used by him or his disciples as a fixed term for a particular group of his followers. At most, an Aramaic word like šĕlîḥîn ("messengers," "envoys") may have been used in an ad hoc sense when Jesus sent the Twelve out on a temporary mission. This is probably the sense of the word in its rare occurrences in Mark and Matthew (Mark 6:30; Matt 10:2). It is only when the Twelve return from the temporary mission on which Jesus has sent them that, for the one time in his Gospel, Mark uses the word: "And the apostles rejoined Jesus" (6:30).[6] The sense of "apostles" here is simply "those sent out on mission and now returning from that mission." Once the mission is over, the term disappears from Mark. Similarly, the only time Matthew uses the term in his Gospel is at the beginning of the missionary discourse, as Jesus prepares to send the Twelve out on their limited mission to Israel (10:2).[7] Thus, in both Gospels, "apostle" is purely an ad hoc term indicating a temporary function that the Twelve discharge; they are apostles only when actually out on mission.

It was in the early church that "apostle" (apostolos, "ambassador," "messenger") was first used as a set designation for a specific group—though different authors used the designation in different ways.[8] What is beyond doubt is that in the first Christian decades, "apostle" had a range of meanings that extended far beyond the Twelve. The pre-Pauline creed that Paul quotes in 1 Cor 15:3–7 creates a list of various persons who experienced appearances of the risen Jesus: "Cephas, then the Twelve, then . . . more than five hundred brothers . . . then James, then all the apostles"—all the apostles being obviously a wider category than the Twelve.

This was the mode of speaking of the primitive pre-Pauline church, and basically Paul adopted it as his own.[9] Though clearly not one of the Twelve, Paul fiercely vindicated his right to the title apostle (e.g., Gal 1:1,17; 2:8; 1 Cor 9:1–2; 15:9; 2 Cor 1:1; 11:5; 12:11–12; Rom 1:1,5). Ironically, it is uncertain whether Paul considered all the Twelve to be apostles.[10] He explicitly attributes apostleship to only one member of the Twelve, Peter (Gal 1:17–19; 2:8), though, in the context of Gal 2:1–10, John (the son of Zebedee) may also be understood to be an apostle. Two people who are not members of the Twelve are mentioned by Paul as being eminent apostles and Christians before Paul became one: a man named Andronicus and a woman named Junia

(Rom 16:7).[11] Paul also knows of "apostles of the churches," possibly envoys or missionaries sent out by local churches for particular tasks (2 Cor 8:23; Phil 2:25).[12]

The close connection, if not total identification, between the Twelve and the apostles in later Christian thought is due mainly to the theology of Luke. In Luke's version of Jesus' selection of the Twelve (Luke 6:13), Jesus "summoned his *disciples* [the larger group], and *from them* he chose *twelve, whom he also named apostles.*" While this text does not prove that Luke thought that only the Twelve were apostles, the title "apostle" obviously does not extend indiscriminately to all of Jesus' disciples and is attached in a special way to the Twelve.[13] In the story of the mission of the Twelve, Luke introduces the missionary discourse by stating that Jesus called together the Twelve (9:1); when these same people come back to Jesus to report on their mission, Luke says that "the apostles" returned (9:10).[14] At the beginning of Acts, Luke stresses the need to fill the position in the Twelve vacated by the apostate Judas (Acts 1:12–26). Matthias is then chosen by lot to take up the apostolate *(apostolē)* abandoned by Judas, and so he is numbered "with the *eleven apostles.*" That Matthias was already a witness of both the public ministry of Jesus and of Jesus' resurrection (Acts 1:21–22) and yet did not possess "apostleship" *(apostolē,* v 25) until he was chosen to be numbered with the "eleven apostles" (v 26) argues for the view that Luke makes the group called the Twelve and the group called the apostles coterminous.[15]

Yet the matter is not absolutely clear. Contrary to the striking but exceptional usage in Matt 10:2 ("the twelve apostles") and Rev 21:14 ("the twelve apostles of the Lamb"), Luke-Acts never employs the set phrase "the twelve apostles," which was to become a fixed formula in the later church. Moreover, while Luke's Gospel never clearly identifies anyone outside the Twelve as an apostle, Acts does depart from the customary Lucan way of speaking in Acts 14:4 + 14, where Barnabas and Paul are called "the apostles." It is unclear whether this divergence from ordinary Lucan usage is due to a source that Luke is using, whether "apostles" carries here the special sense of Christian missionaries sent out on a temporary mission by the local church of Antioch, or whether Luke's concept of apostle is not so completely identified with the Twelve as many critics claim.[16] Suffice it to say that Luke is the NT author who most consistently uses the labels "the Twelve" (or "the Eleven") and "the apostles" interchangeably or in close association. He is thus the main NT catalyst for the later Christian custom of speaking of "the twelve apostles."

From this quick survey, one can appreciate the varied and sometimes confusing uses of "Twelve," "disciples," and "apostles" in the NT. To avoid this terminological confusion, in what follows I will imitate Mark and John in speaking simply of the Twelve.[17] Naturally, the first question we must pose is whether the group called the Twelve existed during the ministry of the historical Jesus. Once the existence of the group is established, we can proceed to inquire about its characteristics and functions.

II. THE EXISTENCE OF THE TWELVE DURING JESUS' MINISTRY

That I should have to argue that there was a special group of twelve followers around Jesus during his public ministry may strike some readers as strange. Yet a number of distinguished critics throughout the 20th century have considered it probable or certain that the group called the Twelve actually arose in the early church and was later retrojected into the ministry of Jesus.[18] Hence there is a need to apply the criteria of historicity to the NT data to ascertain whether the Twelve existed as a group during Jesus' lifetime.

A. FIRST CRITERION: MULTIPLE ATTESTATION

In the first place, the existence of the Twelve during Jesus' ministry is supported by the criterion of *multiple attestation of sources and forms*.

(1) Mark mentions the Twelve 10 or 11 times in his Gospel: 3:14 (and possibly v 16); 4:10; 6:7; 9:35; 10:32; 11:11; 14:10,17,20,43. In recent decades, NT exegetes have paid a great deal of attention to Mark's redactional portrait of the Twelve—a portrait that some critics judge to be unrelievedly negative.[19] Granted Mark's theological focus on the Twelve, it is sometimes supposed that most, if not all, of his references to the Twelve come from his own redactional activity.[20] This conclusion, however, does not necessarily follow. For one thing, as Ernest Best points out, "disciples," not "the Twelve," is by far Mark's favorite designation for committed followers of Jesus.[21] Most critics would not want to draw from this the conclusion that the disciples are purely a redactional creation of Mark.

Moreover, there are positive reasons for thinking that at least some of Mark's references to the Twelve come to him from his tradition. Basing his view on the detailed analyses of Karl Kertelge and Günther Schmahl, Wolfgang Trilling argues that, while many of the Marcan references to the Twelve may well be redactional, at least two references seem firmly embedded in the pre-Marcan tradition.[22]

(a) The first reference comes in the introduction to the list of the twelve names in Mark 3:16–19, material that most critics recognize as pre-Marcan tradition.[23] To be sure, Mark 3:13–19 (the choice of the Twelve and the listing of their names) is, as it now stands, a product of Marcan composition. Nevertheless, the various repetitions, parenthetical explanations, and disruptions of syntax in Mark 3:13–19 create the overall impression that Mark is reworking and explaining an earlier tradition—a position that most commentators accept. In addition, as we shall see below, Luke has an independent tradition of the twelve names; therefore the list of the twelve names is not a Marcan creation out of thin air. Hence the introductory clause in Mark 3:14 ("and he made [= created, appointed] twelve")—or something similar to it—would have stood in the tradition as the title or introduction of the list.[24] Mark 3:16a ("and he made the Twelve") might represent a possible alternate form of the traditional introduction to the list, but unfortunately whether v 16a is part of the original Marcan text or a later gloss is uncertain.[25]

(b) The designation "the Twelve" was also embedded in the pre-Marcan passion tradition, specifically in reference to Judas as "one of the Twelve" *(heis tōn dōdeka)*—notably in 14:43, when Judas "hands over" Jesus at the arrest in Gethsemane.[26] This set phrase, "one of the Twelve" is also used of Judas in 14:10,20, though some would see these cases as Marcan redaction. In any event, the designation of Judas as "one of the Twelve" precisely when reference is made to his act of betrayal is clearly not a Marcan invention; for, as we shall see below, the independent tradition of John uses the same designation when speaking of Judas' act of betrayal ("Judas . . . was going to hand him over, [though Judas was] one of the Twelve," 6:71). In sum, the group called the Twelve is not a purely Marcan creation, but already existed in the tradition(s) he inherited, notably in the list of the Twelve and the tradition about Judas.

(2) The lists of the Twelve can shed further light on the question. While Matthew and Luke are almost entirely dependent on Mark for their references to the Twelve,[27] the slightly different lists of the names of the Twelve that they record (Mark 3:16–19 ‖ Matt 10:2–4 ‖ Luke 6:14–16 ‖ Acts 1:13) may indicate that in this material Matthew and/or Luke represents an independent tradition about the Twelve. If this be the case, then the commonly held view that the list of the Twelve in Mark 3:13–19 comes from pre-Marcan tradition would be confirmed by the independent parallels in M and/or L. The following table gives a quick overview of the four different lists of the Twelve and seems to argue for more than one form of the early Christian tradition that passed down the names of the Twelve.[28]

LISTS OF TWELVE

MARK 3:16–19	MATTHEW 10:2–4	LUKE 6:14–16	ACTS 1:13
First Group of Four			
Simon Peter	Simon Peter	Simon Peter	Peter
James [son of] Zebedee	Andrew his brother	Andrew his brother	John
John brother of James	James [son of] Zebedee	James	James
Andrew	John his brother	John	Andrew
Second Group of Four			
Philip	Philip	Philip	Philip
Bartholomew	Bartholomew	Bartholomew	Thomas
Matthew	Thomas	Matthew	Bartholomew
Thomas	Matthew the toll collector	Thomas	Matthew
Third Group of Four			
James [son of] Alphaeus	James [son of] Alphaeus	James [of] Alphaeus	James [of] Alphaeus
Thaddeus[29]	Thaddeus	Simon the Zealot[30]	Simon the Zealot
Simon the Cananean	Simon the Cananean	Jude [of] James	Jude [of] James
Judas Iscariot	Judas Iscariot	Judas Iscariot	———

Far from the variations in the lists of the Twelve disproving the group's existence during Jesus' lifetime, the Synoptists' disagreements within the basic agreement of their lists argue for a primitive oral tradition that underwent some changes before the Gospels were written.[31] Actually, the variations are hardly massive. Despite some commentators' sweeping statements about discrepancies in the lists, there is only one basic difference in the names: for the "Thaddeus" mentioned in tenth place in Mark and Matthew, Luke (in both Luke 6:16 and Acts 1:13) has "Jude [or Judas] of James" in eleventh place. Otherwise, not only are the other eleven names the same, but even the basic order of the names (three major blocks of four names each) is the same.

The first block of four names always begins with Peter and always continues (in varying order) with James and John (the sons of Zebedee), plus Andrew, the brother of Peter. The second block of four names always begins with Philip and always continues (in varying order) with Bartholomew, Matthew, and Thomas. The third block of four names always begins with James [the son] of Alphaeus and always continues with Simon the Cananean

[= the Zealot] and Judas Iscariot (always at the end of the list). The one variation in names, Thaddeus or Jude of James, is found, not surprisingly, in the third block of names. Understandably, the least known and most easily forgotten individuals were relegated to the third block—the one glaring exception being the notorious Judas, who is put at the end of the entire list for obvious reasons. If one considers that this list of twelve men (many of whom were otherwise unknown individuals) was handed down orally during the first and possibly second Christian generations, the surprising fact is that only one name varies in all four lists: Thaddeus versus Jude of James.

This one variation has been explained by some commentators in terms of alternate names for the same person, but this solution smacks of harmonization.[32] The variation may simply reflect the fact that the Twelve as a group quickly lost importance in the early church, and so the church's collective memory of them was not perfectly preserved. Another possible reason for the variation may lie in the fact that Jesus' ministry lasted for two years and some months. Considering Jesus' stringent demands on the Twelve to leave family, home, and possessions to be his permanent entourage on his preaching tours through Galilee and Judea, we should not be astonished that, sometime during the two years of the ministry, at least one member left the group. Any number of reasons might be suggested for the departure: voluntary leave-taking, dismissal by Jesus, illness, or even death. Whatever the cause, it may well be that one member of the Twelve departed and was replaced by another disciple. That Jesus would provide a replacement is itself significant. The Twelve were important precisely because their number symbolized and embodied the eschatological hopes of Israel and the eschatological message of Jesus: the restoration and salvation of all Israel, of all twelve tribes, in the last days.[33]

Granted the relatively minor variations in the twelve names within a context of overall agreement, is there sufficient reason to think that Matthew and/or Luke knew a list other than the one they received from Mark's Gospel? Or can the variations in Matthew and Luke/Acts be best explained simply by Matthew's and Luke's redactional changes in Mark's list? The answer may differ depending on whether we look at Matthew or Luke.

(a) Matthew's two notable divergences from Mark may be explainable simply from Matthew's editorial activity and theological viewpoint:

(i) As his whole Gospel shows, Matthew loves neat patterns; he will often reorder Mark and Q to create numerically arranged blocks of material. Hence it is hardly surprising that he reorders Mark's first block of four names; he elevates Andrew from fourth to second place to create two pairs of two brothers.[34] Having created pairs in the first block, Matthew continues the pattern throughout the list of the Twelve: e.g., "Philip *and* Bartholomew, Thomas *and* Matthew." Perhaps in this way he compensates for not taking over Mark's statement that Jesus sent out the Twelve "two by two" (Mark 6:7).

(ii) The variations in the second block of four names are likewise due to the First Evangelist's redactional activity: he changes the name of Levi the toll collector in Mark 2:14 to that of Matthew the toll collector in Matt 9:9. He thus assures that every named individual who is directly called to discipleship by Jesus winds up in the list of the Twelve.[35] The First Evangelist hammers home the identification by appending the designation "the toll collector" *(ho telōnēs)* to the name of Matthew in the list of the Twelve. But why is the name of Matthew placed last in the second block? Since no one else in the second block of names has a description attached to his name, the evangelist may have felt that the list would flow more smoothly if the lengthier phrase "Matthew the toll collector" was placed at the end of the second block.

In sum, it seems likely that the First Evangelist's list of the Twelve can be explained simply as his redactional reworking of Mark's list. Yet one cannot be absolutely sure of this. The list of the Twelve in Acts also puts Matthew at the end of the second block of names; only these two lists agree on this point. I tend to think that this correspondence is pure coincidence, but it warns us not to be too certain in our judgments.[36]

(b) The case of Luke-Acts is different and more complicated. To take Luke's Gospel first: some of the divergences from Mark can be explained, as in Matthew's list, by stylistic improvements. For instance, Luke as well as Matthew probably thought that putting Andrew right after Peter to create two pairs of two brothers produced a neater pattern.[37] Luke tends to avoid Hebrew and Aramaic words in his Gospel, so it is not surprising that he gives a translation of Simon the Cananean: Simon the Zealot.

However, there is a puzzling variation in Luke that is not paralleled in Matthew. Instead of Thaddeus, mentioned by Mark and Matthew in the second place of the third block of names, Luke has "Jude [i.e., Judas] of James" in the third place, Simon having been moved up to second place. This same "Jude of James" is found in the same place in the list of Acts. Stylistic reasons do not explain the change, nor apparently do theological agendas. Luke never mentions Jude of James outside his two lists; Jude of James is neither better known nor more theologically significant than Thaddeus, whom he replaces. That another Jude/Judas (in addition to Judas Iscariot) existed among Jesus' most intimate disciples is independently supported by a stray tradition in the Fourth Gospel's account of the Last Supper: "Jude [Judas], not the Iscariot," who is never mentioned elsewhere in the Fourth Gospel, suddenly appears to ask Jesus a question (John 14:22).[38] Thus, since the replacement of Thaddeus by Jude of James cannot be attributed to Luke's redactional activity, and since the existence of another Jude is independently witnessed by the Fourth Gospel, the most natural explanation is that Luke found this name in a list he inherited from his L tradition. In short, Luke rather than Matthew gives us solid evidence for a list of the Twelve independent of Mark's list.[39]

(c) Whether the Acts of the Apostles supplies us with still another independent tradition is doubtful. As was the case with Matthew, I think that the notable differences from Mark can be explained on redactional grounds.[40] In Acts 1:13, Luke seems to be meshing his Marcan tradition with his own special tradition (L); the conflated list seems further modified by Luke's redactional concerns in Acts. However, as we shall see, one divergence is difficult to explain on any grounds and leaves us unsure.

The most significant differences in the list of Acts 1:13 as compared with Luke 6:14–16 are as follows:

(i) In the first block of names, Luke follows Mark in keeping Andrew fourth.

(ii) With an eye to what will happen in Acts, Luke, for the only time in any of the lists, reorders the two sons of Zebedee by putting John before James in Acts 1:13. This change probably reflects two aspects of the story of the Twelve in the early chapters of Acts: John is the regular "sidekick" of Peter, and James is the first of the Twelve to die and so to drop out of the story of Acts.

(iii) The second block of names is somewhat puzzling in that the order is unique among the four lists: Philip, Thomas, Bartholomew, and Matthew. There is no discernible reason for this change, since both the list in Mark 3:18 and the list in Luke 6:14–15 read Philip, Bartholomew, Matthew, and Thomas. This divergence in order is the only serious argument in favor of seeing an independent tradition in Acts 1:13.[41]

(iv) The final difference is in the third block of names: the omission of Judas Iscariot. This is readily explained both by Judas' betrayal of Jesus, which has already been recounted in the Gospel (Luke 22:3–5,22–23,47–48), and by Judas' untimely death, which is about to be narrated in Acts (1:16–26).

In sum, the results of our survey are mixed. In my opinion, Matthew's list is purely a product of his redaction of Mark's list; no independent tradition is visible. The case of the list in Acts is more difficult, though I tend to think that it can be explained simply as a conflation of the lists found in Mark's and

Luke's Gospels, with further modifications due to Luke's program in Acts. Admittedly, the change of order in the second block of names is difficult to explain; one might perhaps appeal to a desire for variety on purely stylistic grounds. In contrast to Matthew's Gospel, though, the list that Luke presents in his Gospel (6:14–16) does not seem explicable simply as a redaction of Mark for stylistic or theological reasons. The replacement of Thaddeus by Jude of James finds no explanation in the theological program or stylistic preferences of Luke. Hence I think it most likely that Luke 6:14–16 represents a tradition of the names of the Twelve that is independent of the list in Mark 3:16–19. Therefore, the L tradition as well as the Marcan tradition witnesses both to the existence of the Twelve during the life of Jesus and to the names of the individuals who made up the Twelve.

(3) Besides tradition in Mark, and probably in L, the Johannine tradition gives independent attestation of the Twelve during Jesus' ministry. The fact that the Twelve are mentioned in John is all the more weighty because John has no special interest in the group called the Twelve. The Johannine tradition names important disciples or supporters of Jesus (e.g., Nathanael and Lazarus) who are not listed in the Synoptic catalogues of the Twelve; and the anonymous "disciple whom Jesus loved," the model of all discipleship, does not apparently belong to the Twelve. The few references to the Twelve that occur in John thus have the air of being relics or fossils embedded in primitive Johannine tradition.

In John's account of the public ministry, references to the Twelve are clustered—and, indeed, isolated—at the end of the Bread of Life discourse in John 6. Faced with desertion by many of his disciples, Jesus asks the Twelve whether they will leave him as well (6:67). Peter, acting as spokesman, proclaims his faith in Jesus as the Holy One of God (vv 68–69). Almost in a tone of sad musing, Jesus replies with a rhetorical question (v 70): "Have I not chosen you, the Twelve, and [yet] one of you is a devil?" In a characteristic aside, the evangelist explains Jesus' terse prophecy to the reader (v 71): "He spoke of Judas, [the son] of Simon Iscariot; for he was going to hand him over, [although] he was one of the Twelve."[42] Remarkably, this exhausts the direct references to the Twelve in John's account of the public ministry. Perhaps it is not accidental that these references are clustered at the end of John 6, the only chapter of John's Gospel that parallels the account of the Galilean ministry in the Synoptics, especially the "bread cycle" in Mark 6–8, which culminates in Peter's confession of faith at Caesarea Philippi.

There is one other reference to the Twelve, but it is only indirectly connected with the public ministry. In John 11:16, as Jesus prepares to go to Bethany to raise Lazarus from the dead, Thomas, "who is called Didymus [the Twin]," glumly remarks "to his fellow disciples": "Let us also go that we may die with him." In 14:5, Thomas reappears briefly at the Last Supper, asking querulously: "Lord, we do not know where you are going. How can we know the way?" It is, however, only in one of the resurrection appearances that Thomas is introduced with the specific identification, "Thomas, one of the Twelve, called Didymus . . ." (20:24).

Thus, directly or indirectly, the Fourth Gospel, which has no formal list of the Twelve, identifies Peter, Thomas, and Judas as members of the group. Though Andrew and Philip are never so identified, their prominence throughout the public ministry as a *pair* of disciples close to Jesus (1:35–46; 6:5–8; 12:21–22; cf. 14:8–9) may perhaps be taken as a hint that they were also known in the Johannine tradition as members of the Twelve. What is telling, though, is that we must piece this information together from fragments of a tradition about the Twelve that may have had some importance in the early Johannine community but apparently holds no great interest for the Fourth Evangelist. We are dealing with a tradition very different from the one we find in the Synoptics, with its precise enumeration of the names of the Twelve and its emphasis on the Twelve in the early part of the passion tradition.

(4) Besides Mark, John, and probably L, there may be an indirect reference to the Twelve[43] in the Q tradition, though this judgment depends on how we reconstruct the tradition underlying Matt 19:28 ‖ Luke 22:30. This Q logion has been placed by the two evangelists in strikingly different contexts; neither context can claim to be the original setting of the saying.[44] Matthew inserts the logion into Jesus' teaching on the dangers of wealth and on the reward awaiting disciples who leave family and home for his sake (Matt 19:23–30; cf. Mark 10:23–31); the larger context is Jesus' journey up to Jerusalem for the Passover and his passion. Luke instead places the Q logion in the mini-discourse that Jesus delivers at the Last Supper. The need to adapt the saying to each context may help explain why the first part of the saying is so different in Matthew and Luke and reflects the redactional concerns of the respective evangelists.[45] However, the final words of the saying are basically the same in both Gospels, as Jesus makes an eschatological promise to certain disciples:[46]

MATT 19:28	LUKE 22:30
you[47] shall sit	you shall sit
on *twelve* thrones	on thrones
judging the twelve tribes	judging the twelve tribes
of Israel	of Israel

Even if we had only the Lucan form of the saying, Luke's context of Jesus addressing his closest disciples at the Last Supper with the promise that they would "judge" (= rule? obtain justice for? pass judicial sentence on?)[48]

the *twelve* tribes of Israel might imply that the addressees are the Twelve. However, only the Matthean form of the saying makes this explicit. We must therefore face the problem of whether Luke has dropped the adjective "twelve" before "thrones" or whether Matthew has added it. Arguments can be mounted for either position, but I think it more likely that Luke has dropped the adjective "twelve" before "thrones."

First, Luke has made it clear from the larger context that he is thinking of the Twelve, "whom Jesus named apostles" (Luke 6:13). Luke alone states at the beginning of the Last Supper that "Jesus reclined at table and the *apostles* [reclined] with him" (22:14; Luke's source, Mark 14:17, speaks of "the Twelve"). The addressees of the Q logion in v 30 are described by Jesus in v 28 as "you . . . who have remained with me in my trials," a good description, in Luke's mind, of those who belonged to the Twelve (cf. Acts 1:21–22). Thus, unlike Matthew's context in Matthew 19, which speaks only of "disciples," Luke's context already makes it fairly clear that the audience addressed is the Twelve—an inference that then receives reinforcement from the mention of the *twelve* tribes in the saying. Indeed, granted Luke's characteristic care for style and his desire to avoid needless repetition, it is quite understandable why he would want to avoid the repetition of the word "twelve" within the space of three words.[49]

Second, Luke's chosen context—namely, the Last Supper—may have prompted him to drop the explicit reference to the *twelve* thrones at the final judgment. In Luke's ordering of the Last Supper material, Jesus has just predicted his betrayal by Judas, "one of the Twelve" (cf. Luke 22:3,47). Obviously, then, Judas, though one of the Twelve at the time of the Last Supper, will not persevere to be one of those seated on the thrones on judgment day; Matthias will take his place (Acts 1:15–26). Understandably, Luke wishes to soften an apparent clash between a prophecy of doom and a prophecy of reward for the same person (Judas). Or, to put the point more bluntly, he wishes to circumvent the embarrassment of having Jesus issue a prophecy about the Twelve that is not verified of one of their number. Accordingly, he drops the reference to the *twelve* thrones.[50]

In contrast, since Matthew inserts the Q saying into an instruction on discipleship during the journey to Jerusalem, and since Judas is not mentioned or even thought of in the larger Matthean context, Matthew naturally does not feel Luke's problem of clash or embarrassment. Indeed, since the preceding context in Matthew speaks only of "disciples" following Jesus (e.g., 19:10,13,23,25), *not* "the Twelve" or "the twelve disciples," the retention of "twelve" before "thrones" in the saying is necessary if the persons to whom the promise refers are to be made absolutely clear. On the whole, therefore, it seems more likely that the reference to *"twelve* thrones" and therefore to the circle of the Twelve is original in the Q saying.[51]

This promise to the Twelve makes perfect sense within the larger context of Jewish eschatological hopes in general and Jesus' eschatological proclamation in particular, as summarized in Volume Two of *A Marginal Jew*.[52] In other words, the core promise in Matt 19:28 par. meets the criterion of coherence. Even in OT and pseudepigraphic literature that is not itself apocalyptic (e.g., Tobit 13; Sir 36:1–17), the hope for the regathering or reconstituting of the tribes of Israel in the end time is expressed.[53] Such a hope fit perfectly into Jesus' proclamation of the coming of God's kingly rule, for Jesus addressed his proclamation not to the world indiscriminately but to Israel in its promised land. Reflecting his mission to all Israel in the end time, Jesus created the group called the Twelve, whose very number symbolized, promised, and (granted the dynamic power thought to be present in the symbolic actions of prophets) began the regathering of the twelve tribes. Accordingly, within his larger prophetic vision of God coming to rule Israel as king in the end time, Jesus promised in Matt 19:28 par. that his inner circle of the Twelve, the prophetic sign and beginning of the regathering of the twelve tribes, would share in the governance (or judgment?) of the reconstituted Israel. Matthew 19:28 par. thus gives us much more than a bare indication of the historical existence of the Twelve. It gives us an important statement of Jesus' eschatological vision and his intention in creating the Twelve as part of that vision.

Indeed, it is a vision that makes much more sense in the context of Jesus' ministry than in the context of the first generation of the early church, where the Twelve as an eschatological group (especially in relation to the idea of reconstituting the twelve tribes of Israel) disappear with surprising rapidity. In light of the quick demise of the Twelve as a visible and influential group in the early church (as distinct from some prominent individual members, such as Peter), one might mount a type of argument from dissimilarity or discontinuity. In the OT, intertestamental literature, and the NT, there is much talk about and many verbal pictures of the judgment of Israel, including scenes of courts and thrones, with various individuals on the thrones. Yet nowhere else in Jewish literature before or during the time of Jesus do we find the picture of twelve men sitting on twelve thrones sharing in God's prerogative of passing judgment on (or ruling?) eschatological Israel. In the NT, the Twelve are assigned various roles and are portrayed in various ways, both positive and negative; but the function assigned to the Twelve in Matt 19:28 par. remains unparalleled.

Thus, compared with pre-Christian Judaism and with the rest of the NT, the picture Jesus paints and the function he ascribes to the Twelve in Matt 19:28 par. are unique to this logion.[54] Being discontinuous on this point with both Judaism and early Christianity, the saying is best ascribed to the historical Jesus. Indeed, if one wants to claim that the saying was instead created by the early church, one must face a difficult question: Why would the early church have created a saying (attributed to the earthly Jesus during his public ministry) that in effect promised a heavenly throne and power at the last judgment to the traitor Judas Iscariot?[55] In the end, the criteria of coherence, discontinuity, and embarrassment all argue for the saying's origin in the public ministry.[56]

One minor objection to my whole argument, however, needs to be addressed. Even if we grant a reference to the Twelve in Matt 19:28 par., the Twelve appear only this one time in Q. Some critics, such as Philipp Vielhauer, use this as an argument against the existence of the Twelve during the life of Jesus.[57] Yet this is a very curious argument, since the word "disciple" (*mathētēs*) is almost as rare in Q as is the reference to the Twelve. There are only two absolutely clear cases of "disciple" in Q (Matt 10:24 ‖ Luke 6:40; Matt 11:2 ‖ Luke 7:18); all other suggested cases occur in either Matthew or Luke but not in both Gospels.[58]

Even more surprising is the fact that neither Q passage speaks directly of *Jesus'* disciples. In Matt 10:24 par., Jesus utters what seems to have been a general truth or proverb: "No disciple is above [his] teacher." The present contexts created by Matthew and Luke make clear that the reference is to the disciples of Jesus (see, e.g., Matt 10:25), but such an explicit reference does not exist in the saying taken by itself. In Matt 11:2 par., the word "disciples" is used of the disciples of John the Baptist, not those of Jesus.

Hence, strictly speaking, *no* Q text, taken by itself, speaks directly and unequivocally of the disciples of Jesus. Yet this does not cause NT critics to deny the existence of the historical disciples of the historical Jesus. The situation with the Twelve is somewhat similar. There is only one reference in Q; and, as is the case with "disciples," the reference to the Twelve is indirect rather than direct. Certain followers addressed by Jesus in Matt 19:28 will sit on twelve thrones judging the twelve tribes of Israel—a promise that makes no sense unless it is addressed to the Twelve.

In short, since the scarcity—or even absence!—of references to the disciples of Jesus in Q leads no one to deny the existence of such a group, the same should hold true of the one reference to the Twelve. All this simply reminds us of the fragmentary and random nature of the material preserved in Q. More particularly, it reminds us that Q is made up mostly of sayings, many of which would have been directed to Jesus' disciples or more specifically to the Twelve. There was no reason for Jesus to be constantly mentioning the identity of his audience in the sayings he was patently addressing to them.

(5) The final independent source to be investigated is, from the viewpoint of both literary composition and tradition history, the earliest: Paul's passing mention of the Twelve in 1 Cor 15:5. However, the special problems that this text involves lead me to consider it last.

What is especially noteworthy in 1 Cor 15:5 is that the mention of the Twelve comes, in a sense, not from Paul's own mouth or mind. The reference to the Twelve is rather embedded in an early pre-Pauline formula of faith (1 Cor 15:3–5), of which Paul is now reminding the Corinthians.[59] He says that it is a formula that he taught them when he converted them to Christianity; in fact, it is a formula that he himself learned when he became a Christian. This is the point of his somewhat convoluted introduction to the creedal formula: "I make known to you [i.e., I remind you], brothers, of the gospel that I announced to you, the gospel that you received [*parelabete*]. . . . For I handed on [*paredōka*] to you, first of all, what I myself received [*parelabon*] . . ." (vv 1 + 3). The vocabulary of handing on and receiving was used in the ancient world by philosophical schools, gnostic literature, and rabbinic circles (e.g., *m. ʾAbot* 1:1) to designate important traditions that were carefully passed down from teacher to student.[60] Paul uses the same terminology to introduce his narrative of the institution of the eucharist at the Last Supper (1 Cor 11:23–25).

Since Paul is writing to the Corinthians ca. A.D. 55–56, since he converted them ca. 50–51, and since he himself became a Christian and learned this primitive creed from other believers in Jesus somewhere around 31–34, we have here one of the earliest creedal statements of the church, a creed that was formulated only a few years after the events narrated (ca. 30).[61] The creedal formula probably underwent expansion over the years, with further recipients of resurrection appearances being added. But an early, if not the earliest, version had a basic four-part structure (1 Cor 15:3–5):

> Christ died for our sins according to the Scriptures,
>   and was buried,
> and was raised on the third day according to the Scriptures,
>   and appeared to Cephas [i.e., Peter] and then to the Twelve.

Now, practically no one has ever denied that Cephas (i.e., Peter) was a disciple of Jesus during the public ministry, and most critics would admit that he already had the name Cephas/Peter ("Rock") during that time.[62] Accordingly, I think that it goes against the natural thrust of the text to argue, as Vielhauer does, that the Twelve did not exist as such during the public ministry, but were rather called into existence in the postresurrection period, indeed precisely by a resurrection appearance. To support this view, Vielhauer lays great stress on the contradiction he sees between (1) the mention of the "Twelve" (not "Eleven") who are said to receive a resurrection appearance in 1 Cor 15:5 and (2) the tradition in all four Gospels that Judas betrayed Jesus—thus leaving only a circle of eleven men to receive a resurrection appearance.[63]

I think that Vielhauer sets up a false dichotomy between two different literary forms (creedal formula and Gospel narrative), which come from different "settings in life" *(Sitze im Leben)* in the early church, and which moreover function differently in their respective contexts.[64] The presence of "the Twelve" in the early and terse creedal formula of 1 Cor 15:5 simply underlines the essential symbolic significance of the Twelve, which would have been especially important to the earliest Christian Jews of Palestine: the Twelve represented the twelve tribes of Israel, which many Jews expected to be restored in the last days. This interpretation of the Twelve is supported by the Q logion (Matt 19:28 par.) that we have already examined. The symbolism of the number twelve was thus all important. Not surprisingly, the number quickly became the very name of the group, a set designation or stereotyped formula that could be used of this eschatological group even when membership changed or when—for a relatively brief time after Judas' defection—it lacked one member.[65] In a way, this fixed usage of "the Twelve" is intimated by the very wording of 1 Cor 15:5: first Cephas is mentioned alone, and then we hear of the Twelve, with no attempt to adjust or clarify the wording to indicate that, in the initial resurrection appearances, Cephas both stood apart from and yet was a member of the Twelve.

One might add here an observation about the way in which the nomenclature of the Twelve developed in the early church. As we can see from the independent witness of Paul, Mark, and John, "the Twelve," used absolutely as a substantive and not as an adjective modifying "disciples" or "apostles," was the earliest designation of this inner circle. Far from "the Eleven" being the early and natural way of referring to the circle when one member was missing, the phrase "the Eleven" occurs only in the second-generation stage of the Gospel tradition. Fittingly, it is Matthew and Luke, the two evangelists who supply detailed stories of Judas' death, who, out of their historicizing impulse for numerical exactitude, use the phrases "the eleven disciples" (Matt 28:16), "the eleven apostles" (Acts 1:26), or simply "the Eleven" (Luke 24:9,33).[66] This accountant-like precision is the sign of a late, not an early, stratum of the tradition. Not surprisingly, such precision is found in secondary, expansive narratives, not in an early, terse creedal formula that says only the essential. In brief, when one attends to the different literary forms of 1 Cor 15:3–5 and the Gospel narratives, coming as they do from different *Sitze im Leben* and having different functions, I think Vielhauer's supposed contradiction, on which he bases his denial of the Twelve's existence during Jesus' lifetime, evaporates.

Then, too, simply on a commonsense level, if one were to read a sentence like "President Smith appeared before Chairman Jones and the board of directors," one would not naturally think that President Smith appointed the board of directors (or Jones as chairman) in the moment when (or even after) he appeared before them. The natural sense of "Christ . . . appeared to Cephas and then to the Twelve" is that both Cephas and the Twelve existed as such before Christ appeared to them. This natural reading of 1 Cor 15:5 is supported by what we have already seen in our survey: namely, that the independent sources of Mark, John, L, and Q all think of the Twelve as a group around Jesus during his public ministry. Granted this widespread understanding of the Twelve in various streams of NT tradition, one would have to put forward weighty evidence to counter the plain and unaffected sense of 1 Cor 15:5, and Vielhauer produces no such evidence. Hence, the pre-Pauline formula in 1 Cor 15:3–5 is rightly placed alongside the Gospel traditions already examined as an independent witness to the existence of the Twelve during Jesus' ministry.

In sum, Mark, John, Paul, probably L, and probably Q give multiple attestation from independent sources that the Twelve existed as an identifiable group during the public ministry. A further point should now be noted. In addition to multiple attestation of *sources,* these texts also give us multiple attestation of *forms:* the Twelve are mentioned in narrative (Mark, John), sayings (Q, John), a catalogue-like list (Mark, probably L), and a creedal formula (1 Cor 15:3–5). In light of this broad spread of both sources and forms, suggestions that the Twelve arose only in the early days of the church must be judged pure conjecture with no real support in the NT texts.

B. Second Criterion: Embarrassment

Alongside the criterion of multiple attestation of sources and forms stands the criterion of *embarrassment,* a criterion already alluded to when we discussed Luke's redaction of the Q saying in Luke 22:30. Next to the bare fact of Jesus' death by crucifixion—one of the most horrific forms of execution in the ancient world—perhaps the most shocking event at the end of Jesus' career was his being "handed over" or "betrayed"[67] by his intimate disciple Judas, who in all four Gospels bears the mournful tag "one of the Twelve."[68]

Indeed, the parallel between the scandal of Jesus' cross and the scandal of Jesus' being handed over to the authorities by Judas—and the parallel ways in which these events were handled or explained by the church—is instructive. As for the cross, practically no one would deny the fact that Jesus was executed by crucifixion, for two obvious reasons: (1) This central event is reported or alluded to not only by the vast majority of NT authors but also by Josephus and Tacitus (criterion of multiple attestation of sources and forms). (2) Such an embarrassing event created a major obstacle to converting Jews and Gentiles alike (see, e.g., 1 Cor 1:23), an obstacle that the church struggled to overcome with various theological arguments. The last thing the church would have done would have been to create a monumental scandal for which it then had to invent a whole apologetic. Precisely because the undeniable fact of Jesus' execution was so shocking, precisely because it seemed to make faith in this type of Messiah preposterous, the early church felt a need from the beginning to insist that Jesus' scandalous death was "according to the Scriptures," that it had been proclaimed beforehand by the OT prophets, and that individual OT texts even spelled out details of Jesus' passion. That Jesus' death became increasingly surrounded by OT texts used apologetically has caused almost no one to deny the brute and brutal fact of Jesus' execution. Rather, it was precisely the disturbing fact of his crucifixion that called for an explanation and so called forth a flood of OT quotations and allusions.

My point is that, in this whole process, Jesus' crucifixion stands in clear parallel to Jesus' being handed over by Judas. The same two criteria, multiple attestation and embarrassment, may be invoked to establish the historicity of both events. That Judas handed Jesus over to the authorities is attested independently by Mark, by John, and by the stray tradition lying behind the very different accounts of Judas' death presented by Matthew and Luke (M in Matt 27:3–10 and L in Acts 1:16–20).[69] The criterion of embarrassment clearly comes into play as well, for there is no cogent reason why the early church should have gone out of its way to invent such a troubling tradition as Jesus' betrayal by Judas, one of his chosen Twelve. Why the church should have expended so much effort to create a story that it immediately had to struggle to explain away defies all logic. Rather, just like Jesus' death, Jesus' betrayal by Judas, a member of the intimate circle of the Twelve, called for an explanation and so called forth OT texts to soften the shock.

Not unlike the interpretation of Jesus' death, the earliest explanation of the betrayal may well have been the generic one: this has been prophesied, this has been written, this is according to the Scriptures. Just as the creedal formula in 1 Cor 15:3–5 contents itself with a generic "according to the Scriptures," so Mark 14:21 parr. explains in vague fashion: "The Son of

Man goes his way as it is written concerning him; but woe to that man through whom the Son of Man is handed over." A similar vague reference to the fulfillment of Scripture is found in John 17:12: "And not one of them [i.e., Jesus' disciples] was lost except the son of perdition [Judas], in order that the Scripture might be fulfilled."

A second, more developed stage of explanation can also be discerned. Just as in the Passion Narratives (e.g., the dividing of Jesus' clothing in Mark 15:24; cf. LXX Ps 21:19), references to Scripture passages are woven into the story of the betrayal without being explicitly cited. For example, indicating that one of the Twelve at the Last Supper will betray him, Jesus prophesies that "one of you will hand me over, the one who eats with me" (Mark 14:18, with a possible allusion to, but not a direct citation of, LXX Ps 40:10).

In a still further stage of theological explanation, John's Gospel (13:18) has Jesus cite LXX Ps 40:10 explicitly to show that the betrayal by Judas was prophesied: ". . . but in order that the Scripture be fulfilled, 'He who ate my bread lifted up his heel against me.' " Similarly, in the stories of Judas' death, explicit citations of Scripture are used to demonstrate that the tragedy had been prophesied (Matt 27:9–10; Acts 1:16,20). Jesus' being handed over by Judas thus parallels Jesus' death in a basic way: the shocking fact calls forth the Scripture texts—not vice versa. The betrayal by Judas is no more a creation of OT prophecy used apologetically than is Jesus' death. Indeed, in the case of Judas, one must admit that most of the Scripture texts cited apply to Judas only by a broad stretch of the imagination. We have here a prime example of the application of the criterion of embarrassment. An embarrassed church was evidently struggling with the scandalous fact of the betrayal—a fact that was too well known to deny—and did the best it could to find some OT texts that could qualify as prophecies of the tragedy. None of the texts cited, taken by itself, could have given rise to the idea of the betrayal of Jesus by one of the Twelve.[70]

We can therefore put together the following three points: (1) Judas was a member of the Twelve; this historical fact is supported by multiple attestation of sources (the Marcan and L lists of the Twelve; the pre-Marcan Passion Narrative lying behind Mark 14:10,20,43; John 6:71; and the special L tradition lying behind Acts 1:15–26). (2) Jesus was handed over to the authorities by Judas; this historical fact is supported by multiple attestation, as we have just seen. (3) Finally, as we have also just seen, that Jesus was handed over by Judas is also supported by the criterion of embarrassment. Hence, the fact that Judas, one of the Twelve, handed Jesus over to the authorities is firmly rooted in the historical tradition and so too, by logical consequence, is the existence of the group called the Twelve, to which Judas belonged.[71]

One regrets the need to plod through such detailed reasoning to prove what should be evident to anyone. But, by their strange denials of the obvious, critics like Vielhauer, Klein, Schmithals, and Crossan make it necessary to argue at length to demonstrate what most people have never doubted. The arguments these critics use to deny the betrayal by Judas vary, but they are all equally convoluted. To take the grand example: Vielhauer holds that Jesus was indeed handed over by one of his disciples. But, according to Vielhauer, it was the early church that used OT prophecies to create Judas, one of the Twelve, and to make him the one who handed Jesus over. Judas, like the Twelve, was retrojected by the church into the story of Jesus' passion and death.

Now, all this demands a very odd tradition history. On the one hand, the attempt of the early church to insert the Twelve (a group that supposedly arose only after Easter) back into the ministry of Jesus presupposes a desire to exalt the Twelve and magnify their status in the church. On the other hand, we are to suppose that, roughly around the same time, the church created the story that one of the Twelve was Jesus' betrayer. The two actions cancel each other out. Moreover, for the theory to work, one must suppose that, within a few years, the early church had totally forgotten the name of the disciple marked by the dubious distinction of having handed Jesus over to the authorities—not a likely lapse of memory for a religious movement that preserved lists of the names of the Twelve (Mark 3:16–19 parr.), of the four brothers of Jesus (Mark 6:3 par.), of the Seven Hellenists (Acts 6:5), of the earliest prophets and teachers at Antioch (Acts 13:1), and of various female followers of Jesus (Mark 15:40 parr.; Luke 8:2–3).[72]

Taking a somewhat different tack from Vielhauer, Günter Klein and Walter Schmithals hold that the story of Judas reflects some notorious case of apostasy in the early church. Schmithals, for instance, claims that Judas, one of the Twelve who experienced a resurrection appearance (as stated in 1 Cor 15:5), later committed apostasy, denounced the Christian community to the authorities, and so in that sense "handed Jesus over."[73] When the Twelve were retrojected into the life of Jesus, Judas the betrayer was likewise retrojected into the Passion Narrative.

Actually, an intriguing phenomenon can be detected as we watch Klein, Schmithals, Crossan, and other critics develop Vielhauer's basic approach or provide variations thereof: the more one tries to explain away the NT testimony about Judas, the member of the Twelve who handed Jesus over, the more one begins to write a novel whose plot has no empirical basis in the data of the NT documents. Even more intriguingly, when we look at the various reconstructions of Vielhauer, Klein, Schmithals, and Crossan, we notice one key agreement amid all their disagreements. Scan, if you will, the varied theories of these critics and observe the one point on which they all agree:

1. According to Klein and Schmithals, Judas, a member of the post-Easter group called the Twelve, betrayed the early church; he, his betrayal, and the whole group of the Twelve were subsequently retrojected into the life of Jesus.
2. According to Vielhauer, some disciple of Jesus did actually hand him over; it is the idea that the betrayer was one of the Twelve, along, of course, with the group called the Twelve, that was later retrojected into the life of Jesus.[74]
3. Crossan goes the German skeptics one better by streamlining the whole approach. He maintains both that Judas was a historical follower of Jesus and that he did actually hand Jesus over. According to Crossan, it was simply the post-Easter group called the Twelve (and consequently Judas' membership in the Twelve) that was retrojected into the life of Jesus.

Amid all these disagreements among the critics, one espies the all-determining point of agreement: come what may, the Twelve *must* not exist during the life of Jesus, for this would contradict all the portraits these critics paint of Jesus—especially the popular American one of Jesus the egalitarian Cynic with no concern for the future eschatology of the people Israel. Since the betrayer Judas, as one of the Twelve, is a chief obstacle to the critics' denial of the Twelve's existence during Jesus' ministry[75]—and of all that the Twelve imply for Jesus' mission and message—Judas must somehow be explained away. How exactly he is explained away is not all that important—witness the divergent theories of these critics.[76] What is determinative here is not historical data but the *a priori* decision that the Twelve did not—*must* not—exist during Jesus' ministry. From this one decision flow all the critics' convoluted and improbable tradition histories, created simply to avoid accepting a NT tradition that is supported by various criteria of historicity.[77]

Going through these strange theories is tiresome, to be sure. But at the very least, such an exercise makes us reflectively aware of why we affirm the historicity of certain significant aspects of Jesus' life, including the key data that he created a circle called the Twelve, one of whom handed him over to the authorities. As an extra dividend, our brief study of the Judas tradition serves another purpose: it refutes any wholesale rejection of the historicity of the Passion Narratives. Our examination of the betrayal by Judas has demonstrated that a relatively minor event in the Passion Narratives is nevertheless factual. We are not left with massive agnosticism beyond the mere fact that Jesus was crucified under Pontius Pilate. Therefore, if a specific incident in the Passion Narratives is to be judged a creation of the early church—which is certainly the case at times—the specific arguments for that position must be spelled out. A sweeping, global argument about OT prophecies creating the whole Passion Narrative will not do.

C. GENERAL FLOW OF THE TRADITION

In addition to the specific criteria of multiple attestation and embarrassment, we should ponder a final, more general consideration: the whole way in which the tradition about the Twelve crests and ebbs in the NT period argues in favor of the Twelve's origin in the life of the historical Jesus rather than in the first Christian generation.[78] If the group of the Twelve had arisen in the early days of the church and, for whatever reason, reached such prominence that its presence, unlike that of other church leaders (e.g., the Seven Hellenists, Barnabas, the prophets and teachers at Antioch), was massively retrojected into the Gospel traditions, one would have expected that the history of the first Christian generation would be replete with examples of the Twelve's powerful presence and activity in the church.

The exact opposite is the case. As we have seen, the Twelve are mentioned in the four Gospels, in the pre-Pauline formula in 1 Cor 15:5, and in the early chapters of the Acts of the Apostles (the group called the Twelve is never mentioned after Acts 6:2, while even references to "the apostles" diminish notably after chap. 8, disappearing entirely after 16:4). This exhausts all purportedly historical reports of the Twelve in the NT. They are mentioned again only fleetingly in Rev 21:14, an apocalyptic vision of the heavenly Jerusalem at the end of time ("the twelve apostles of the Lamb").

What should strike us immediately in this list are the gaping holes. The only writer from the first Christian generation whom we know by name and of whom we know any detailed facts is Paul. In his epistles, Paul alludes to his interaction with or compares himself to other church leaders—notably James, Peter, and John, but also Barnabas, Apollos, the apostles, and the brothers of Jesus. In stark contrast, what is glaringly absent in Paul's letters is any mention of the Twelve, the fossil of a reference preserved in the primitive creed of 1 Cor 15:5 being the sole exception that proves the rule. When we stop to consider how Paul goes on at length about his relations or struggles with Peter, James, John, Barnabas, Apollos, and various apostles or "pseudo-apostles" in the churches of Jerusalem, Antioch, Galatia, and Corinth during the 30s, 40s, and 50s of the 1st century, it is astounding that Paul never mentions his relations or interaction with the Twelve as a group. Likewise surprising is that Luke, for all the emphasis he puts on the Twelve as a living link between the time of Jesus and the time of the church, has increasingly little to say about the Twelve as the chapters of Acts pass on. The total silence from the rest of the epistolary literature of the NT—deutero-Paul, James, Peter, John, Jude, and Hebrews—is equally deafening.[79]

The only reasonable conclusion one can draw to explain the cresting and ebbing of references to the Twelve in the NT is the commonsense one: the Twelve are prominent in the story of Jesus because that is where they actually played a significant role. On the basis of their close relationship with Jesus, which they claimed had been restored and confirmed by a resurrection appearance, the role of the Twelve continued into the earliest days of the church; but it declined and disappeared with surprising rapidity.

The reasons for the swift disappearance or total absence of the Twelve from most of the NT are unclear. Perhaps some members of the Twelve, like the martyred James, the son of Zebedee, died in the first decade after the crucifixion; and no attempt was made to replenish a foundational group that was not viewed as ongoing in the church. Once this happened, it would make sense to speak of influential individuals like Peter, but it made little sense to continue to speak of the Twelve in regard to the present situation of the church, as opposed to remembering the Twelve's activity in the life of Jesus or in the earliest days of the church. Other explanations for the early disappearance of the Twelve are also possible: e.g., the power of the Twelve as a group was eclipsed by the ascendancy of individual leaders like Peter or James, or some other members of the Twelve imitated Peter in undertaking a mission to Diaspora Jews in the East or the West—thus leaving no visible group of twelve leaders "on the scene" in Palestine.

Whatever the reason or reasons for their disappearance, clearly the Twelve were present and active during the life of Jesus and the earliest days of the church; and, just as clearly, their presence and activity soon waned. So quickly did they fade from the scene that the majority of the names in the lists of the Twelve are just that—names and little more. This hardly coheres with a revisionist theory that would want to deny the Twelve's existence as a group during the ministry of Jesus and to postulate a sudden, meteoric rise of influence in the early church.[80] This is a prime example of ignoring the simple and obvious explanation that arises naturally from the NT data in favor of a convoluted theory that is based on next to no evidence.

As I laid out the proof for the existence of the Twelve during the public ministry, I necessarily alluded to the nature or function of this group. It is now time to go back and focus more directly on the question of why Jesus formed the Twelve. What did he expect them to be or do?

III. THE NATURE AND FUNCTION OF THE TWELVE

Inevitably, in the very act of arguing for the existence of the Twelve, we have already touched upon the nature and function of this group. What we need to do now is to collect, summarize, and develop the various insights we have already gained.

A. THE TWELVE AS EXEMPLARS OF DISCIPLESHIP

By binding the Twelve so closely to his person and mission, Jesus effectively made this group the standing exemplar of what being a disciple meant (as this has been spelled out in Chapter 25). The three conditions for discipleship (receiving a peremptory call from Jesus, following Jesus physically and thereby surrendering normal ties with one's family, and exposure to suffering) were especially exemplified by this inner circle of disciples whom Jesus chose to be "with him" (to use Mark's summary of their function) as he undertook his various preaching tours around Palestine. Other disciples may have come and gone. But, with the exception of the problematic Thaddeus/ Jude of James, the original disciples whom Jesus chose for the circle of the Twelve persevered in that group of high-profile followers throughout the successes and failures of the ministry. With the exception of Judas, they moved beyond the disaster of Calvary into the early days of the church. This stable, long-term association with Jesus would naturally mean that the Twelve, more than most followers, would have been the regular audience for Jesus' ministry of teaching and healing. Simply because of their stability and perseverance, and despite all their failings, the Twelve embodied in a public way and as a permanent lesson what Jesus meant by discipleship. Whether or not Jesus explicitly assigned them this function, de facto they fulfilled it, and this probably contributed in no small way to their influence in the earliest days of the church.

B. THE TWELVE AS PROPHETIC SYMBOLS OF THE REGATHERING OF THE TWELVE TRIBES OF ISRAEL

The basic intention of Jesus in creating the Twelve seems to have been more wide-ranging than simply providing a permanent example of discipleship. His intention apparently corresponded to the core of his proclamation to Israel: the coming of the kingdom of God, who would establish his rule definitively over a restored Israel.

As we saw in Volume Two of *A Marginal Jew,* in his proclamation of the kingdom Jesus was drawing upon the great story of Israel's election, apostasy, and restoration, as told in Israel's sacred writings.[81] As the Book of Genesis inculcates, the beginning of Israel's history lay in the choice Yahweh made among all the peoples of the earth, when he selected Abraham, Isaac, and Jacob as the forebears of a special nation. Through Jacob in particular, Yahweh formed for himself a people made up of twelve tribes, sprung from twelve patriarchs (Genesis 29–49), the sons of Jacob-renamed-Israel (hence, "the sons of Israel"). In his own person, King David welded the twelve tribes into a united kingdom (ca. 1000 B.C.), but rebellion soon tore that unity apart. Under David's grandson Rehoboam, the kingdom split into the northern kingdom of Israel and the southern kingdom of Judah (922 B.C.). In the 8th century, the Assyrians invaded and destroyed the northern kingdom (721 B.C.). In the biblical version of this history, the ten northern tribes were exiled and never returned to their land.[82] In the sixth century, Babylon invaded and overthrew the southern kingdom of Judah (587 B.C.), and so for a while the nation of Israel seemed extinguished. Within half a century, though, some of the exiles from the tribes of Judah, Benjamin, and Levi began returning to the former southern kingdom to start the rebuilding of Jerusalem (538 B.C.).

Despite the great hopes of prophets like Second and Third Isaiah, the restoration of Jerusalem and its temple was paltry and disappointing. Not surprisingly, Jews began to look forward in faith to a future in which God would gather all twelve tribes back to a restored promised land. According to many prophecies, "at the end of the days" Yahweh would recreate his people Israel as a whole. We hear this theme of the restoration of all Israel sounded in the prophet Micah (2:12; cf. 2:13; 4:9): "I will completely gather you, Jacob, [yes,] all of you; I will assemble the totality of the remnant of Israel. . . . and their king shall pass before them, and Yahweh at their head." After the prophecy about the birth of a scion of David in Isa 11:1–9, Isa 11:10–16 goes on to promise the regathering of Israel and Judah: "He [Yahweh] shall raise a signal-banner to the nations, and he shall gather the scattered people of Israel; and the dispersed people of Judah he shall assemble from the four corners of the earth" (11:12). The later Isaiah tradition continues this promise (e.g., Isa 59:15–21; 60).

Similar hopes are found in Jeremiah and Ezekiel. Speaking of the restoration after the exile, Jer 31:1 has God promise: "I shall be the God of *all* the tribes [or: clans] of Israel." At times, the Book of Jeremiah connects this hope with prophecies about a new King David who will rule over a restored kingdom made up of Israel and Judah (e.g., 30:3–9; cf. 33:14–26; 31:31–34). Similarly, the Book of Ezekiel (20:27–44) promises that God will gather Israel "from the lands in which you have been scattered. . . . on the holy mountain [of Zion] . . . the whole house of Israel—[yes,] the whole of it!—shall worship me. . . ." God the Good Shepherd will gather the scattered sheep of Israel (Ezekiel 34), and the kingdoms of Israel and Judah will be reunited, with "David" the prince reigning over them (37:15–28).

What is more striking is that certain postexilic books that are not essentially apocalyptic, such as Tobit, Baruch, and Ben Sira, continue and develop this hope for the restoration of the twelve tribes by God in the end time. The great hymn of praise in Tobit 13 exalts "our Lord, God, and Father," who will gather Israel "from all the nations among whom you [Israelites] have been scattered" (vv 4–5). The Lord, the great King, will bring them back to a rebuilt Jerusalem (v 16). In Baruch, likewise, a once mournful Jerusalem rejoices to see her exiled children brought back to her by God "from east and west" (Bar 4:21–5:9).

Despite the fact that he represents to a great degree the traditional wisdom of Israel, Ben Sira (writing ca. 180 B.C.) shares the eschatological hope that God will regather Israel in the end time (chap. 36). Praying that the "God of the universe" will renew the signs and wonders he worked through Moses at the exodus (36:6; in some enumeration systems, 33:6), Ben Sira begs God to hasten the end time (36:8 [33:10]) and gather *all* the tribes of Jacob, that they may inherit [the promised land] as in olden days" (36:11 [33:13]). Thus will "all the ends of the earth" come to know the eternal God (36:22 [36:19]). Especially significant for our picture of Jesus as the eschatological prophet in the guise of Elijah is the assertion by Ben Sira that, according to Scripture, the prophet Elijah is appointed by God to "establish the tribes of Israel [or: Jacob]" in the end time (48:10).

In spite of the great difference in literary genre, the theme of the regathering of Israel is likewise expressed in a very different book from the late 2d century B.C., 2 Maccabees. In 2 Macc 1:24–29, the priest Jonathan prays that God the Creator, King, and Savior, will gather the scattered people of Israel back to their homeland. A festal letter, urging the celebration of Hanukkah—connected as it is with Israel's experience of partial restoration—claims that certain objects from the temple, which Jeremiah hid at the time of the exile, will remain concealed "until God gathers together the assembly of [his] people and is merciful [to them]" (2:7). The letter then flows into a prayer that God, who has saved all his people, will "quickly . . . gather us together from every [country] under heaven to the Holy Place" (2:18).

The Jewish pseudepigrapha around the turn of the era also foster this "eschatology of regathering." Such disparate works as the *Psalms of Solomon* (1st century B.C.), the *Testament of Moses* (1st century A.D.), and the Qumran documents known as the *Temple Scroll* (2d century B.C.) and the *War*

Scroll (end of 1st century B.C.) all pray or prophesy that Israel as a whole, specifically all twelve tribes, will be reconstituted in the last days. *Ps. Sol.* 11:2–7 echoes phrases from Isaiah and Baruch in prophesying that God will gather the children of Israel from east and west. Resuming themes from Jeremiah and Ezekiel, *Ps. Sol.* 17:26–32 asserts that it will be the promised Davidic Messiah who "will gather a holy people . . . and will judge tribes of a people sanctified by the Lord their God. . . . he [i.e., the Lord Messiah] will assign them their divisions in the land according to their tribes. . . ." The end time is defined in capsule form as "those days" when God will bring about the gathering of the tribes of Israel (v 44). The *Testament of Moses,* which regularly thinks of Israel in terms of the twelve tribes (specifically, in terms of the two groups of two and ten tribes in 3:3–4; 4:8–9), prophesies in lyric form that "Israel" (presumably, all twelve tribes) will be exalted to the heights of heaven in the end time (10:8–9).

Even the fiercely sectarian community at Qumran, which views Israelite outsiders as subject to the same judgment as the Gentiles, nevertheless nourishes a hope for a reconstitution of the twelve tribes in the last days. According to the *War Scroll,* in the end time, twelve leaders (literally, "heads") of the priests are to serve continually before God; and "behind them, leaders of the Levites are to serve continually, twelve [in number], one for [each] tribe" (1QM 2:1–3). In the eschatological battle, the great military banner of the whole assembly will have written on it "people of God, the name of Israel and Aaron, and the names of the twelve tribes of Israel" (1QM 3:13–14). Similarly, the shield of the prince of the whole congregation will have written on it "his name, the name of Israel and Levi and Aaron, and the names of the twelve tribes of Israel . . . and the names of the twelve commanders of their tribes" (1QM 5:1–2). This constellation of the name of the eschatological prince of Israel, the names of the twelve tribes, and the names of the twelve commanders of the twelve tribes is especially relevant to Jesus' naming of an inner circle of twelve followers. Mention of the twelve tribes also surfaces in the *Temple Scroll.* In 11QTemple 18:14–16, the offering of first-fruits in the eschatological temple is apparently connected with the twelve tribes of Israel (though the text is fragmentary here). The significance of twelve leaders for the eschatological community of Israel may have been reflected in the makeup of Qumran's own community, if the *Rule of the Community* (or *Manual of Discipline*) is a safe guide to the community's governance around the turn of the era. We read in 1QS 8:1 that "in the council of the community [*ba'ăṣat hayyaḥad*] [there shall be] twelve men ['*îš*, taken by some to mean in this context laymen] and three priests, perfect in all that has been revealed from all the Torah. . . . " [83] Beyond the documents specific to Qumran, the perduring symbolic significance of the twelve patriarchs as the embodiment of the twelve tribes can be seen as well in the *Testaments of the Twelve Patriarchs*. Though the form of the *Testaments* that has come down to us shows clear Christian redaction, the collection has its roots in the pre-Christian period of Palestinian Judaism, as fragments of Qumran texts about the patriarchs Levi and Naphtali show.

The point of this quick survey is that the theme of the eschatological reconstitution of a fragmented Israel, the regathering of the twelve tribes of Israel, sometimes directly by God, sometimes by a human Davidic King or an Elijah, is not restricted to one current or one century of postexilic Israelite thought. From the major and minor prophets to the late narrative and wisdom literature, from what became the canonical OT to pseudepigraphic and Qumranite literature close to the time of Jesus, all sorts of literary forms representing various streams of postexilic Judaism testify to the lively and ongoing hope of the regathering of God's scattered people, the reassembling of the twelve tribes in the promised land. For all their many differences on matters eschatological, this "eschatology of restoration" [84] is the one point agreed on by such diverse writings of the second and first centuries B.C. as Ben Sira (with strong traditional sapiential—and some would say proto-Sadducean—tendencies), the *Psalms of Solomon* (to which some critics would attribute Pharisaic tendencies), and the *War Scroll* of Qumran (representing Essenes of a stringently sectarian and separatist stripe). Thus, for many Jews at the turn of the era, to hope for any sort of eschatological salvation from God meant necessarily to hope for the restoration of the whole people of Israel.

It is within this context of restoration eschatology that Jesus' prophetic proclamation and his institution of the Twelve must be understood. The coming of the kingdom of God, the object of Jesus' eschatological proclamation and hope, is inextricably bound up with the regathering of all Israel. Contrary to the popular presentations of liberal theology in the late 19th century, Jesus' proclamation of the kingdom of God is not primarily concerned with the inner peace of the individual soul; "kingdom of God" is a people-centered, Israel-centered symbol. Accordingly, Jesus does not address himself on equal terms to both Jew and Gentile—unlike the later Pauline mission. As the eschatological prophet wearing the mantle of Elijah, he addresses himself squarely to the people of Israel; personal encounters with Gentiles are ad hoc and rare events.

More importantly, Jesus addresses himself to the *whole* people of Israel. Far from restricting his mission exclusively to either the rich or the poor, to either the stringent Pharisees or the ordinary observant Jews (or even toll collectors and sinners), he embraces them all in his work—to the point of calling both Levi the toll collector and Simon the Zealot to discipleship. *All* Israel is the focus of this mission of the Elijah-like prophet of the end time. In this concern for the final fate of the whole restored people of Israel, Jesus stands in continuity with the mainstream Israelite tradition stretching from Isaiah and Jeremiah to Ben Sira and Qumran. There is no complete kingdom of God without a complete Israel.

It is within this overarching hope for the regathering in the end time of *all* Israel, all twelve tribes, that Jesus' choice of an inner circle of twelve disciples must be understood. As a Jewish prophet in the line of Isaiah, Jeremiah, and Ezekiel, Jesus well understood and often engaged in prophetic-symbolic gestures that proclaimed, and to some degree actualized, the kingdom: e.g., his prohibition of fasting coupled with his festive meals with toll collectors and sinners, his exorcisms, his "triumphal" entry into Jerusalem, his "cleansing" of the Jerusalem temple, and the symbolic gestures over bread and wine at the Last Supper.[85] Jesus was consciously performing such a power-laden, prophetic act when he constituted the Twelve.

As with most prophetic actions, the institution of the Twelve was not *merely* a "symbolic" gesture in the weak, modern sense of "symbolic," a gesture powerless in itself but pointing forward to something important that is about to happen. The symbolic actions of the OT prophets were understood by religious Israelites to be suffused with the reality they pointed to; they were charged with the power they unleashed. The various prophetic gestures of Isaiah (Isa 20:1–6: going naked in public), Jeremiah (Jer 13:12–14: smashing a wineflask), and Ezekiel (Ezek 4:1–8: lying on his side while gazing on a clay tablet with a picture of Jerusalem) dramatically prophesied destruction and exile. But, in the minds of the prophets and their followers, these symbolic gestures did not simply point forward to the future events they prophesied; the symbolic gestures unleashed the future events, setting them inexorably in motion.[86]

So too with Jesus' creation of the Twelve. (1) Granted the "eschatology of regathering the tribes" that was well known in Israel, (2) granted Jesus' claim to be the end-time prophet in the guise of Elijah (who was to regather the tribes),[87] and (3) granted the highly realistic sense of a prophet's symbolic actions—a sense Jesus repeatedly displays—the mere fact that Jesus the eschatological prophet chose to select twelve Israelite men from among his disciples to form a special group would, in the eyes of his adherents, set in motion the regathering of the twelve tribes, even before these twelve men actually did anything. It is within this overarching framework that the key promise made by Jesus to the Twelve, examined in our previous section, makes perfect sense: "You [that is, you Twelve who symbolize and embody the eschatological Israel right now] will sit on twelve thrones judging the twelve tribes of Israel [when the kingdom fully comes and the twelve tribes are restored]" (Matt 19:28 ‖ Luke 22:30). The creation of the Twelve thus coheres perfectly with Jesus' eschatological, people-centered message and mission: God is coming in power to gather and rule over all Israel in the end time.

C. THE TWELVE AS PROPHETIC MISSIONARIES TO ISRAEL

Once the Twelve were chosen by Jesus to symbolize the regathering of the twelve tribes, did these twelve Israelite men proceed to do anything in particular during the public ministry? While the matter is still hotly disputed among exegetes, I think it more likely than not that Jesus did send the Twelve out on a brief, urgent mission to various towns and villages of Israel.[88] In this way, the future ingathering of the twelve tribes, already realized in symbol by Jesus' gathering of twelve Israelite men around him, found further realization in another prophetic-symbolic action: the sending of the Twelve on mission to Israel, thus anticipating the great regathering of God's people on the last day.

The primary argument that the historical Jesus sent some of his disciples (be they the twelve disciples or other followers) on mission during his lifetime rests upon the multiple attestation of sources: Mark and Q have two different forms of a missionary discourse.[89] The two forms are found in various combinations in the three Synoptic Gospels:

1. Mark's terse version of a missionary charge to the Twelve is found in Mark 6:6–13. Even apart from comparisons with Q, it strikes one as an abridgement of or excerpt from some larger body of material in the pre-Marcan tradition.[90]
2. Faced with both a shorter Marcan and a longer Q form of the discourse, Luke shows his typical aversion to mixing Mark and Q by presenting two missionary discourses, one to the Twelve in Luke 9:1–6 (basically the Marcan form, with some touches from Q), and the other to the "seventy [or: seventy-two] disciples"[91] in Luke 10:1–12 (the Q form, with a few touches from Mark).[92] The seventy(-two) disciples seem to be an invention of Luke to facilitate keeping both forms of the discourse.[93] No trace of any such group of seventy(-two), active before or after Easter, is found elsewhere in the Gospels or the rest of the NT.
3. Displaying his tendency to mesh rather than separate sources, Matthew combines in one lengthy sermon addressed to the Twelve (Matt

10:1–42) both the Marcan and the Q forms of the missionary discourse, with further material supplied from the M tradition or from Matthew's own creative mind. Most commentators hold that Luke rather than Matthew is closer to the order—and often the wording—of Q.[94]

When analyzed, both the Marcan and Q forms of the discourse show signs of earlier traditions that have been edited.[95] Hence, there was a pre-Marcan and a pre-Q form of a missionary discourse circulating quite early in the first Christian generation. Comparing these two primitive forms, we can recover not the exact wording of an earlier form of the discourse but at least the main components of the tradition that existed prior to Mark or Q:[96]

1. The discourse began with some indication, either in an introductory narrative or in an initial saying, that Jesus was sending out his disciples on mission. As David Catchpole points out, the nucleus of sayings that most critics identify as the original core of the missionary charge would not have made sense in the oral or written tradition without some initial narrative or saying that indicated the purpose of the sayings.[97]

2. Jesus then gave instructions about conduct on the road. These included radical prohibitions against taking along money or provisions (e.g., silver coins, a knapsack, sandals, a staff, or two tunics)—or even stopping to greet people on the way (cf. 2 Kgs 4:29).[98] Such renunciation of the ordinary equipment for a journey was meant as a prophetic symbol of the urgent, eschatological, life-or-death nature of this brief mission, as well as a symbol of the disciples' total dependence on the God who was beginning to regather Israel through them.[99] In practical terms, this translated into an expectation of and dependence on the hospitality of a well-disposed householder.

3. Jesus proceeded to give instructions about how the disciples were to enter a house (a prospective base of operations) and greet the householder. Here the emphasis is more on the possibility of a positive reception and the eschatological peace such a reception would bring, though the possibility of rejecting this peace—the peace being conceived realistically as an entity in itself—is briefly mentioned.[100] From a practical point of view, the householder's positive reception would guarantee hospitality and support for the disciples, in particular food and drink, to which these messengers of the kingdom have a right.

4. Jesus complemented his instructions about an individual house with instructions about reception by a city as a whole. A positive reception by

a city would provide a wider arena in which the disciples could perform their basic tasks of proclaiming the kingdom and healing the sick. But the possibility of rejection looms larger here. If a city rejects their message, the disciples are to shake off the dust from their feet as a further prophetic symbol, this time of disassociation from those who willfully expose themselves to judgment when the kingdom comes.[101]

5. The ultimate basis of the all-determining seriousness of the mission, which will lead the recipients to either eschatological peace or eschatological judgment, rests upon a paradox: the powerful position of the seemingly impoverished missionaries. "He who accepts you accepts me, and he who accepts me accepts the One who sent me." To accept these messengers is to accept the one who authorizes their mission to Israel, namely, the eschatological prophet Jesus—just as to accept Jesus is to accept the one who authorizes his mission to Israel, namely, God. By the same token, spurning the messenger means spurning the sender. The two different forms of this saying (Matt 10:40 and Luke 10:16, each placed at the end of its respective discourse) are paralleled by alternate forms of the saying outside the missionary discourse, in Mark 9:37 and in John 13:20 (at the Last Supper; cf. John 12:44–45; 5:23). These, in turn, are echoed in the early patristic literature (Ignatius, *Eph.* 6:1; *Did.* 11:4).[102]

One might debate forever the exact wording and order of these components of the missionary discourse, as well as which components might be the most primitive.[103] Given the complicated question of the sources, certainty is not to be had. One might further question whether, even in the core of the discourse I have isolated, the various sayings were all spoken by Jesus on the same occasion. For instance, the fifth component is found in Mark and John outside any missionary discourse; hence various critics consider it a secondary addition to the basic pattern. Other scholars suggest the same for the first or the fourth component. In my view, at the very least, the second and third components (the prohibition of ordinary equipment for the journey and the instructions on conducting oneself in a house) lie at the heart of the mission tradition. Still, other scholars prefer to speak of various missionary sayings of Jesus instead of a single mission discourse. Granted the great diversity of opinion on the subject, I do not try to give any word-for-word reconstruction of *the* missionary discourse.

Nevertheless, the basic substance of a missionary charge by Jesus (whether or not all the sayings were spoken at one time and place) is fairly clear from the agreement-amid-differences between the pre-Marcan and Q forms of the discourse. Some of the sayings, whenever they were spoken, are "mission-specific," that is, they make sense only as part of a missionary charge or an instruction about a mission. Moreover, as Heinrich Kasting reminds us, these individual sayings need to be put into a larger context, that of Jesus' own mission to Israel.[104] As we saw in Volume Two, Jesus presented himself as the eschatological prophet *sent* by God to Israel—an Israelite prophet being by definition a person sent by God to speak God's word to God's people. Prior to any question of a mission of disciples sent by Jesus to Israel, there is the fundamental datum of Jesus' sense of mission, of his being sent by God to Israel.[105] As part of his own mission, Jesus undertook an itinerant ministry, reaching out to all types of Israelites, from the rich toll collector and the learned scribe to the poor beggar and the outcast "sinner." It was a mission filled with controversy and conflict—what else could an Israelite prophet expect?—a mission that culminated in his execution. For mission, of its nature, means that one is trying to win over people who do not, at least in the beginning, share one's views.

Granted this basic mission of Jesus to Israel, what sense would it make to speak of his disciples sharing his ministry if they did not in some sense share his mission? That Jesus should have sent his disciples out on a mission to Israel coheres perfectly with his own sense of identity (the eschatological prophet) and purpose (to summon, challenge, gather all Israel in view of God's coming kingdom). Hence, the argument from multiple sources receives support from the argument that highlights the basic coherence between what Jesus was claiming to do and what he asked his disciples to do if they agreed to follow him. The physical, literal following of this itinerant prophet-preacher-teacher flowed naturally into sharing his itinerant mission to Israel. Thus, in my view, it is quite probable from both the criterion of multiple attestation of sources and the criterion of coherence that, sometime during his ministry (perhaps more than once?), Jesus sent out disciples on a brief and urgent mission to Israel, after having given them instructions similar to those we find in the Gospels' missionary discourses.[106]

What is more questionable and harder to establish is the claim that Jesus sent out on this mission not just this or that group of disciples but specifically the Twelve. In other words, it is more difficult to establish the historicity of the mission *of the Twelve* in particular than of a mission of *some unspecified disciples*. A major reason for this difficulty is that the introductory narrative or original opening of the Q sermon is lost to us,[107] and many exegetes would assign the references to the Twelve at the beginning and end of Mark's version of the discourse to Mark himself.[108] In this view of things, the earliest version of the discourse did not name a specific audience—or, if it did, the audience's identity is now lost to us because of the rewriting of the evangelists.

I think, however, that, despite the methodological difficulties, we can still legitimately raise the question of the original addressees of Jesus' missionary instructions. While there can be no hard and fast proof in the matter, I incline to the view that Mark is correct in designating the Twelve as the audience,[109] though I admit that any argument in favor of this position must be indirect and complex.

(1) To begin with, one can construct a general argument on the basis of coherence with all that we have seen so far in this chapter. A good number of scholars reject the historicity of the mission of the Twelve during Jesus' ministry simply because they have already rejected the very existence of the Twelve during Jesus' ministry.[110] Once we have established the historicity of the Twelve during Jesus' lifetime—as I believe this chapter has done—the single greatest objection to the historicity of the mission of the Twelve disappears.

More positively, all that we have seen about the Twelve in this chapter—their being brought into existence by Jesus' conscious selection of specific individuals from among his disciples, their status as an inner circle of disciples who provided a stable example of what discipleship meant, the prophetic symbolism attached to their existence as twelve Israelite men representing the twelve tribes—all this makes them the most likely candidates for the persons Jesus would send on a brief, urgent mission to Israel. If the very existence of the Twelve was meant to symbolize the beginning of the eschatological regathering of Israel, who else would be better suited for a mission to Israel that would initiate, however symbolically, such a regathering?[111]

(2) If the mission of the Twelve is judged instead to be a retrojection from the time of the early church, the proponents of such a theory must face a serious objection. How can one claim that the mission of the Twelve is retrojected from the post-Easter period when there is absolutely no hard evidence that the Twelve ever undertook such a mission in the early church?[112] In fact, one reason for thinking that Jesus did send the Twelve on a mission during his lifetime is that the activity of the Twelve after Easter—as far as we can reconstruct it—does not jibe with such a mission.

As I have already noted, the Twelve as a group faded quickly from the scene after Easter. But what we can discern of their activity—basically from the Acts of the Apostles—argues for their more or less permanent residence and activity in the holy city of Jerusalem, the spiritual capital of Israel and the locus of Jesus' crucifixion and claimed resurrection. It is in Jerusalem that the Twelve apparently gave corporate witness to Jesus before the temple authorities, the citizens of Jerusalem, and the throngs of Jews from all over the world who crowded into Jerusalem during the great pilgrim feasts. Neither Acts nor any other NT source gives the slightest indication that, during the early days of the church, the Twelve as a group were active in Galilee or traveled around Israel on any sort of corporate, organized mission.

Instead, of all the members of the Twelve, only Peter stands out as often engaged in missionary journeys. Even in Acts, though, explicit statements about the travels of Peter bring us only as far as Samaria (Acts 8:14–25, in this case with John), not Galilee.[113] Interestingly, when we factor in knowledge obtained from Paul (Gal 2:11–14; 1 Cor 1:12; 3:22), we learn that Peter traveled to Syrian Antioch and possibly to Corinth—but again, we hear nothing of Galilee. More importantly, we hear nothing whatever in the NT about missionary journeys by the other members of the Twelve after Easter,[114] and certainly nothing about a coordinated mission undertaken by the Twelve as a group. Hence the problem of the "retrojection" theory: such a theory deletes a missionary journey of the Twelve present in all three Synoptic Gospels in favor of a missionary journey of the Twelve during the early days of the church for which there is not a shred of evidence. The simplest and easiest explanation of the account of the mission of the Twelve during the public ministry is that its origins do in fact lie back in the lifetime of Jesus. An explanation by way of retrojection from the early days of the church creates more problems than it solves.[115]

(3) A final consideration is likewise indirect and only suggestive, and perhaps it would not carry much weight with some critics. Yet I think it raises a point worth pondering. In the first Marcan narrative immediately after Jesus' initial proclamation of the kingdom (Mark 1:14–15), Jesus calls to discipleship two pairs of brothers, first Peter and Andrew and then James and John (Mark 1:16–20 ‖ Matt 4:18–22). To a large degree, the two calls are narrated in parallel fashion, but there is one conspicuous difference.[116] The first pair of brothers, Peter and Andrew, are summoned with a command-plus-promise that is unique in the Jesus tradition and, indeed, in the entire NT (Mark 1:17): "Come after me [= follow me], and I will make you become fishers of men [*halieis anthrōpōn*, i.e., fishers of human beings as opposed to fish]."[117]

In one sense, Jesus' use of a metaphor taken from fishing is hardly remarkable. In light of the importance of fishing throughout the ancient Mediterranean world, it is not surprising that metaphors connected with fishing are frequently found in religious and philosophical texts both in Greece and the Ancient Near East. The symbolic use of fishing was quite traditional: for example, Sumerian and Akkadian gods are depicted handling nets that catch men.[118] Wilhelm H. Wuellner has surveyed this "fishing" tradition at great length and argues that Jesus' usage must be seen within the larger context of Hellenistic culture, which had long since penetrated Palestine.[119] It is telling, though, that Wuellner cannot produce an exact parallel to the Marcan scene in which one historical human being promises to make others "fishers of men," with the metaphor carrying an obviously positive sense. The metaphor is especially intriguing in that the person speaking it is not himself a fisherman and does not apply the metaphor to himself.

The distinctiveness of the metaphor "fishers of men" in Mark 1:17 is all the more striking when we place Jesus in his own spiritual heritage, that of the Hebrew Scriptures and Palestinian Judaism.[120] Indeed, precisely within this heritage, I would argue on the basis of the criterion of discontinuity (as well as coherence) that the promise to make others "fishers of men" stems from the historical Jesus.[121] The exact phrase "fishers of men" never occurs in the OT, and the metaphor of fishing for human beings (or using a hook to catch them) is relatively rare. When it occurs, it always has a hostile sense of capturing or killing human beings.[122] The metaphor occurs at times in the Qumran literature, likewise in a negative context of destruction or judgment.[123] The metaphor of "catching men" is also found with a negative sense in later rabbinic literature. Thus, there is no real parallel to Jesus' positive, salvific use of the metaphor in the Jewish tradition before or after him.

Similarly, for all the various images used for mission and conversion in the Gospels and the rest of the NT, nowhere in this literature do we find the metaphor "fishers of men" used again.[124] This silence in Christian literature continues until the end of the 2d century A.D. Even when the metaphor begins to appear, it does so at first only in commentaries on NT books.[125] Clearly, then, "fishers of men" was not put on the lips of Jesus in Mark 1 because it was a favorite or common phrase in early Christianity. At the same time, this strange, different use of a negative metaphor in a positive, salvific sense—a striking image with a twist—coheres perfectly with the surprising, creative, and sometimes shocking parabolic speech of the historical Jesus.[126] It is not without significance that the "fishers of men" saying is that component of the call of Peter and Andrew that departs most notably from the OT story of the call of Elisha by Elijah (1 Kgs 19:19–21), the story on which Mark 1:16–20 may at least partially be modeled.

That the image "fishers of men" never occurs again even in the mouth of Jesus, indeed, even when he is calling other disciples, points up the fact that from the start it was tied to specific persons in a specific situation. Far from being a generic image applicable to many people in varied circumstances, "fishers of men" makes sense only at the moment when Jesus encounters some fishermen at their ordinary task, calls them away from their old task, and promises them a new but corresponding task. In other words, Jesus promises Peter and Andrew: "If you leave your ordinary work of fishing to follow me, I will in exchange have you fish for human beings, not fish." Jesus thus issues to these fishermen not only a call to discipleship ("follow me") but also a promise of corresponding future activity ("fishers of men") that he does not give, for example, to Levi the toll collector.

To sum up so far: from the beginning, the metaphor "fishers of men" was tied to a particular call issued to particular individuals. In no other case in the whole of the NT is this image applied to an individual follower of Jesus. More surprisingly, unlike later sermonizing, neither the Gospels nor the rest of the NT ever tries to turn the "fishers of men" metaphor into a general image applicable to all followers or all missionaries. Thus, the criteria of discontinuity and coherence argue that the "fishers of men" saying is a specific command-plus-promise that the historical Jesus spoke to specific disciples.

In addition, the very nature and function of the saying would have demanded that, from the start, it be passed down in the oral tradition in some sort of narrative framework. The saying would have made little if any sense in total isolation. As a matter of fact, the saying occurs only in the framework of the call of the fishermen Peter and Andrew. There is no rival tradition associating the saying with anyone else—not even with James and John, who, according to Mark, are soon called in a manner quite similar to that of Peter and Andrew (Mark 1:19–20 ‖ Matt 4:21–22).[127] Hence there is no solid reason to doubt that this strikingly different, not to say shocking, use of the metaphor of fishing for men was connected with the call of Peter and Andrew from the beginning.[128]

Once we have decided that this saying comes from the historical Jesus and was connected from the start with his call of Peter and Andrew, we need to attend more carefully to what precisely this saying about becoming "fishers of men" indicates. The logion of Mark 1:17, a command-plus-promise, implies that, after Peter and Andrew become disciples of Jesus (i.e., after they *follow* him), they will do something further: these two men, who once caught fish before Jesus called them to be disciples, will in the future fish for and catch human beings. Clearly, in the context of Jesus' proclamation of the coming kingdom and his attempt to gather all Israel in light of that coming, the image of fishing for human beings does not carry the negative, destructive sense found in the OT. Rather, it intimates the saving work these former fishermen will do in the future: they will assist Jesus ("I will make you") in winning adherents to his cause (i.e., fishing for human beings)—specifically, they will assist in gathering Israel in preparation for the kingdom's arrival.[129] The call of Peter and Andrew, therefore, is more than a call to discipleship; it is also a call to share in Jesus' mission to gather eschatological Israel.[130]

But where, we may ask, does Jesus fulfill this promise ("I will make you") to have Peter and Andrew share in his gathering of Israel ("fishers of human beings"), if not when he sends some of his disciples out on mission to Israel? This is the only opportunity that Jesus has during the public ministry to fulfill his promise to Peter and Andrew. Hence it stands to reason that, if Jesus did send some of his disciples out on mission—and I have shown that it is likely that he did so—Peter and Andrew, at the very least, were among those sent. Now, by the common witness of all four Gospels and Acts, Peter was the leader and spokesman not just of disciples in general but of the Twelve in particular. Moreover, in all four lists of the Twelve, both Peter and Andrew always stand in the first group of four; they were among the group's most prominent members. Are we to think that only Peter and Andrew, and not the rest of the Twelve, were sent out on mission by Jesus?

In my opinion, all these various considerations point, however indirectly, in the same direction: (1) Granted that the historical Jesus probably did send some disciples out on mission to Israel, (2) granted that Peter and Andrew, among all Jesus' disciples, are the most obvious candidates for a mission (having been promised by Jesus that he would make them fishers of men), and (3) granted that Peter was the leader and Andrew a prominent member of the Twelve, I think it likely—though not strictly provable—that the addressees of Jesus' missionary instructions as preserved in Mark and Q were the Twelve. In fact, granted the prophetic symbolism adhering to the Twelve, what other group would be more suited to joining Jesus in his appeal to all Israel in the end time?

Indeed, it is precisely in the light of the Twelve's symbolic significance that one can make the best sense of the brief mission of certain disciples to Israel during Jesus' public ministry. If one were to think only in terms of reasonable, pragmatic results from a carefully planned propaganda campaign, one might wonder what exactly Jesus hoped to accomplish by an apparently brief mission undertaken with such radical restrictions: no money for support, no shoes or change of garments for a long-term journey, and no traveling stick for defense or easy walking. No doubt, the mission of the Twelve did serve the purpose of spreading Jesus' message to a wider audience of Israelites. But it would be a mistake to think of the goal of the mission of the Twelve purely in such practical terms.

The mission of the Twelve, no less than the institution of the Twelve, was a symbolic, prophetic act. Carrying forward the eschatological thrust inherent in the creation of the Twelve, Jesus sent the group out on mission to Israel and thereby performed a further prophetic-symbolic gesture that embodied the events of the end time. By sending the Twelve to Israel, he pushed forward the process of regathering the scattered people of God, a process that God alone would complete when he came in full power (i.e., in his kingdom) and restored the twelve tribes.[131] The mission of the Twelve was thus something more than a piece of missionary strategy; it was one more prophetic-symbolic step toward the reconstitution of eschatological Israel.

Hence, I think the very significance of the Twelve as a special group chosen by Jesus coheres well with their being the audience to whom he directed his missionary instructions. Admittedly, since it is well nigh impossible to prove a negative in ancient history, I cannot prove that Jesus did not also send out other disciples on mission. Luke, after all, was willing to create the seventy-two as a second wave. In light of all we have seen, though, I think it more probable than not that *at least* the Twelve were sent out on mission, whether or not other disciples were dispatched as well.[132]

In brief, I readily admit that the mission of the Twelve does not enjoy the same high degree of probability that I would assign to the existence of the Twelve during Jesus' ministry and to their symbolic connection with the eschatological ingathering of all Israel. Nevertheless, in my opinion, that Jesus sent the Twelve out on a limited mission during his ministry is more probable than the hypothesis that some unattested mission of the Twelve during the early days of the church was retrojected into Jesus' lifetime—or that the mission of the Twelve was simply invented out of thin air.

Having established the existence of the Twelve during Jesus' ministry and having explored the nature and function of the group, we now turn our attention to what, if anything, can be said about the individual members of the Twelve, some of whom proved to be important leaders in the early church. Can anything be known about Jesus' relationship to at least some of these individuals?

NOTES TO CHAPTER 26

[1] For basic orientation and further bibliography, see J. B. Lightfoot, "The Name and Office of an Apostle," *Epistle of St. Paul to the Galatians* (Grand Rapids: Zondervan, 1957, originally 1865) 92–101; Julius Wellhausen, *Einleitung in den drei ersten Evangelien* (Berlin: Reimer, 1905) 112; Julius Wagenmann, *Die Stellung des Apostels Paulus neben den Zwölf in den ersten zwei Jahrhunderten* (BZNW 3; Giessen: Töpelmann, 1926); Kirsopp Lake, "The Twelve and the Apostles," *The Beginnings of Christianity. Part I. The Acts of the Apostles. Volume V* (Grand Rapids: Baker, 1979, originally 1933) 37–59; Nils Alstrup Dahl, *Das Volk Gottes* (Darmstadt: Wissenschaftliche Buchgesellschaft, 1963, originally 1941) 158–59; Werner Georg Kümmel, *Kirchenbegriff und Geschichtsbewusstsein in der Urgemeinde und bei Jesus* (SymBU 1; Zurich: Niehans, 1943) 3–7, 30–32; Hans von Campenhausen, "Der urchristliche Apostelbegriff," *ST* 1 (1947) 96–130; Rudolf Bultmann, *Theology of the New Testament* (2 vols.; London: SCM, 1952) 1. 37; Innozenz Daumoser,

Berufung und Erwählung bei den Synoptikern (Meisenheim am Glan: Hain, 1954) 74–82; Philipp Vielhauer, "Gottesreich und Menschensohn in der Verkündigung Jesu," *Aufsätze zum Neuen Testament* (TBü 31; Munich: Kaiser, 1965) 55–91; Günther Bornkamm, *Jesus of Nazareth* (New York: Harper & Row, 1960) 150; Günter Klein, *Die zwölf Apostel. Ursprung und Gehalt einer Idee* (FRLANT 77; Göttingen: Vandenhoeck & Ruprecht, 1961); Béda Rigaux, "Die 'Zwölf' in Geschichte und Kerygma," *Der historische Jesus und der kerygmatische Christus* (ed. Helmut Ristow and Karl Matthiae; Berlin: Evangelische Verlagsanstalt, 1962) 468–86; idem, "The Twelve Apostles," *Concilium* 34 (1968) 5–15; M. H. Shepherd, Jr., "Twelve, The," *IDB*, 4. 719; Karl Heinrich Rengstorf, *"dōdeka,* etc." *TDNT* 2 (1964) 321–28; Jürgen Roloff, *Apostolat—Verkündigung—Kirche* (Gütersloh: Mohn, 1965); Jean Giblet, "Les Douze. Histoire et théologie," *Aux origines de l'église* (RechBib 7; Bruges: Desclée, 1965) 51–64; Gottfried Schille, *Die urchristliche Kollegialmission* (ATANT 48; Zurich/Stuttgart: Zwingli, 1967); Meye, *Jesus and the Twelve;* Sean Freyne, *The Twelve: Disciples and Apostles* (London/Sydney: Sheed and Ward, 1968); Walter Schmithals, *The Office of Apostle in the Early Church* (Nashville/New York: Abingdon, 1969) 67–95, 231–88; Karl Kertelge, "Die Funktion der 'Zwölf' im Markusevangelium," *TTZ* 78 (1969) 193–206; Rudolf Schnackenburg, "Apostel vor und neben Paulus," *Schriften zum Neuen Testament* (Munich: Kösel, 1971) 338–58; Günther Schmahl, "Die Berufung der Zwölf im Markusevangelium," *TTZ* 81 (1972) 203–13; idem, *Die Zwölf im Markusevangelium. Eine redaktionsgeschichtliche Untersuchung* (Trierer Theologische Studien 30; Trier: Paulinus, 1974); Klemens Stock, *Boten aus dem Mit-Ihm-Sein. Das Verhältnis zwischen Jesus und den Zwölf nach Markus* (AnBib 70; Rome: Biblical Institute, 1975); Wolfgang Trilling, "Zur Entstehung des Zwölferkreises. Eine geschichtskritische Überlegung," *Die Kirche des Anfangs* (Heinz Schürmann Festschrift; ed. Rudolf Schnackenburg, Josef Ernst, and Joachim Wanke; Leipzig: St. Benno, 1977) 201–22; Ernest Best, "Mark's Use of the Twelve," *ZNW* 69 (1978) 11–35; Sanders, *Jesus and Judaism,* 98–106; Jacques Dupont, "Le nom d'Apôtres: a-t-il été donné aux Douze par Jésus?" *Etudes sur les évangiles synoptiques* (BETL 70; 2 vols.; ed. Frans Neirynck; Leuven: Leuven University/Peeters, 1985 2. 976–1018; Francis H. Agnew, "The Origin of the NT Apostle-Concept: A Review of Research," *JBL* 105 (1986) 75–96; W. Horbury, "The Twelve and the Phylarchs," *NTS* 32 (1986) 503–27; Raymond E. Brown, "The Twelve and the Apostolate," *NJBC,* 1377–81 (§ 135–57); Raymond F. Collins, "Twelve, The," *Anchor Bible Dictionary,* 6. 670–71.

[2] Strictly speaking, this is also true of Luke, who follows Mark in speaking of "the Twelve." However, as we shall see below, Luke seems to identify "the Twelve" with "the apostles," though he does not use "the twelve apostles" as a fixed formula.

[3] Meye (*Jesus and the Twelve,* 110–15) claims that, in Mark's redactional view, the Twelve and the disciples are coterminous groups. However, his thesis fails because (1) Levi the toll collector is explicitly called by Jesus to discipleship (Mark 2:13–15), but is not numbered among the Twelve, and (2) we are told as early as 2:15 (in the most probable interpretation of the Greek) that the disciples were many—at a time when, of the Twelve, only Peter, Andrew, James, and John have been mentioned; the Twelve

are not selected and named until 3:13–19. Given this larger context, when Mark says in 3:13 that Jesus "himself summoned whom he wished, and they went to him," the natural sense (especially after the sharp distinction between Jesus' disciples and the large crowd in 3:7) is that Jesus chose the Twelve out of a larger group of disciples. Luke thus interprets Mark correctly when he rewrites Mark 3:13 in Luke 6:13: "And he [Jesus] called his disciples, and chose from them twelve. . . ." (3) One might also note that, while the rich man in Mark 10:17–22 refuses Jesus' call to discipleship, Mark has no problem presenting Jesus as earnestly calling someone outside the Twelve to discipleship. Meye's contorted attempts (pp. 140–45, 157–59) to explain away the Levi incident, the many disciples in Mark 2:15, and the call of the rich man fail to convince.

In contrast to Mark, a number of Matthean redactional traits suggest that Matthew does equate the Twelve with the whole group of disciples. (1) This is probably why Matthew the Evangelist changes Levi's name to Matthew (Matt 9:9; contrast Mark 2:14), i.e., so that everyone who is called by Jesus to discipleship winds up in the list of the Twelve ("Matthew *the toll collector*" in Matt 10:3). (2) Thus, with no Levi as in Mark and no "disciple whom Jesus loved" as in John, no individual disciple is named or highlighted in Matthew who does not appear in his list of the Twelve. (3) By omitting any separate story of the selection of the Twelve (as found in Mark 3:13–19 ‖ Luke 6:12–16), Matthew avoids having to present Jesus calling the Twelve out of a larger group, presumably of disciples. Still, Matthew does retain Mark's story of the aborted call of the rich man; hence, the picture in Matthew is not absolutely clear. Perhaps one can say that Matthew presents the circle of the Twelve as *de facto* coterminous with the circle of disciples. On the whole question, see Stock, *Boten aus dem Mit-Ihm-Sein,* 199–203.

[4] For a defense of the position that some historical figure stands behind John's "disciple whom Jesus loved," see Oscar Cullmann, *Der johanneische Kreis* (Tübingen: Mohr [Siebeck], 1975) 67–88; Raymond E. Brown, *The Community of the Beloved Disciple* (New York/Ramsey, NJ/Toronto: Paulist, 1979) 31–34.

[5] What follows is not intended to be a complete survey of the use of "apostle" in the NT; it merely serves to explain why I choose to speak of "the Twelve" and not of "the twelve apostles." Defenders of the position that, during his earthly ministry, Jesus did not give the Twelve the title "apostles," understood as a fixed designation proper to them, include Dupont, "Le nom," 1017–18; Roloff, *Apostolat,* 144–45; Rigaux, "The Twelve Apostles," 8. For the somewhat ambiguous position of Karl Heinrich Rengstorf, see his article *"apostolos,"* TDNT 1 (1964) 429.

[6] In my view, the phrase "whom he also named apostles," which some important manuscripts (Sinaiticus, Vaticanus, Koridethi) read in Mark 3:14 after "and he appointed twelve," is not original; rather, it represents a harmonization with Luke 6:13, where the disputed phrase is found word for word (apart from 3:14, the verb for "named" [*onomazō*] never occurs in Mark, while Luke uses it three times in his two volumes). This harmonization, highlighted by the awkward position of the phrase in Mark 3:14, is hardly surprising since the Greek manuscript tradition evinces various

attempts to harmonize Mark's story of the selection of the Twelve with Matt 10:1–4 and Luke 6:12–16. Here I agree with Taylor (*The Gospel according to St. Mark*, 230), Meye (*Jesus and the Twelve*, 190), Pesch (*Das Markusevangelium*, 1. 203), and Hooker (*The Gospel According to Saint Mark*, 110–11) and disagree with Metzger (*TCGNT* [2d ed.], 69), who thinks that the external evidence is too strong to warrant the disputed phrase's omission. However, even he and his committee admit the shaky status of the phrase by putting it in brackets and assigning it a "C" rating, which indicates that the committee composing the text of the *UBSGNT* had difficulty deciding which variant to place in the text. The position of Guelich (*Mark 1—8:26*, 154) is similar to that of Metzger; definitely in favor of reading the disputed phrase is Gundry, *Mark*, 164.

[7] Curiously, it is in Matt 10:2, and not in Luke's Gospel, that we find the extremely rare NT locution, "the twelve apostles." The viewpoint of the late 1st-century church may be reflected ever so fleetingly here.

[8] In classical Greek, *apostolos* carries such meanings as a "naval expedition" and probably also the "commander" of such an expedition. In Josephus (in one or possibly two passages), it probably means "sending out"; in the papyri it signifies mostly a "bill of lading," less often a "passport" and also a "letter." In a few isolated cases, notably in the LXX (3 Kgdms 14:6 in Codex Alexandrinus [missing in Vaticanus]; Isa 18:2 in Symmachus), it means "ambassador, "delegate," "messenger." See Bauer, *Wörterbuch* (6th ed.), col. 200; Karl Heinrich Rengstorf, "*apostellō*, etc.," *TDNT* 1 (1964) 407–14.

[9] There is no need to engage in highly speculative theories about the Christian term "apostle" arising either from the rabbinic institution of the *šālîaḥ* (a legal agent sent out on a mission with the full authority of the sender)—an institution not documented before the time of Jesus—or from supposed gnostic apostles in Syria (a scholarly construct of Schmithals that is not witnessed in the early 1st century A.D.). The general OT concept of God sending certain messengers (especially the prophets) to Israel with authority, Jesus' sending of his disciples (especially the Twelve) on a limited mission to Israel during his public ministry, and the experience of appearances of the risen Jesus by the disciples (however one evaluates such claims) form a much more intelligible background and catalyst for the apostolate in the first days of the early church. Contrary to the theory of Klein, Paul the Apostle did not invent the concept or institution of the apostolate; he found the apostolate present in the early church and sought to claim the same status for himself (see, e.g., Gal 1:17–19; 2:8; 1 Cor 9:1–6; 15:7–9). On all this, see Brown, "The Twelve and the Apostolate," 1380–81.

[10] For the opinion (contrary to that of Klein or Schmithals) that the Twelve did count as apostles in the earliest days of the church, see Roloff, *Apostolat*, 57–60; Brown, "The Twelve and the Apostolate," 1381. An initial methodological problem is hidden in the word "count"—in whose eyes? Another problem, more properly exegetical, is that the key text in 1 Cor 15:3–8 is open to more than one interpretation:

(1) On the one hand, "all the apostles" in v 7, Paul's self-designation as "the least of the apostles" in v 9, and his claim that he has labored more than "all of them" in v 10 are taken by some to mean that Paul understands the Twelve in v 5 to be apostles. (2) On the other hand, since the "five hundred brethren" in v 6 probably did not all count in Paul's eyes as apostles, at least some persons or groups in the list were not automatically regarded as apostles simply because they witnessed a resurrection appearance. How, then, can we be sure that the Twelve counted as apostles simply because they are in the list as witnesses of the resurrection?

[11] See the philological discussion by Joseph A. Fitzmyer, *Romans* (AB 33; New York: Doubleday, 1992) 737–38. As James D. G. Dunn (*Romans* [Word Biblical Commentary 38 and 38A; 2 vols.; Dallas: Word, 1988] 2. 894–95) and many other recent commentators point out, (1) the Greek *Iounian* in Rom 16:7 is to be taken as a woman's name and (2) the clause *hoitines eisin episēmoi en tois apostolois* almost certainly means in this context "who are outstanding among the apostles," not "outstanding in the eyes of the apostles." Others mentioned by Paul who may rank in his mind as apostles include James "the brother of the Lord" (Gal 1:19—but the Greek is ambiguous) and Barnabas (if we may read together passages like 1 Cor 4:9; 9:6; Gal 2:9 and understand Paul's "we" to include Barnabas in the apostolate). The apostolic "we" may include Sylvanus and Timothy in 1 Thess 2:6–7 and Apollos in 1 Cor 4:6 (+ 9), but this is less likely.

[12] On 2 Cor 8:23, see Victor Paul Furnish (*II Corinthians* [AB 32A; Garden City, NY: Doubleday, 1984] 425), who prefers to translate the phrase as "representatives of the churches" to avoid the impression that these people are apostles in the same sense that Paul is. On Phil 2:25, see J. L. Houlden (*Paul's Letters from Prison* [Westminster Pelican Commentaries; Philadelphia: Westminster, 1970] 93), who holds that here Epaphroditus is called an "apostle" in the sense of a messenger of the Philippian church sent on Christian business.

[13] For a careful exegesis of Luke 6:12–16, see Fitzmyer, *The Gospel According to Luke*, 1. 613–20. Fitzmyer's judgment is that "this episode in the Lucan Gospel . . . equates with them [the Twelve] the apostles, ascribing even this title to Jesus himself . . ." (p. 616). On p. 618, Fitzmyer states that Luke restricts the title "apostle" to the Twelve. For the same opinion, see Conzelmann, *The Theology of St Luke,* 216 n. 1; Schürmann, *Das Lukasevangelium,* 1. 314–15; Josef Ernst, *Das Evangelium nach Lukas* (RNT; Regensburg: Pustet, 1977) 207–8; Eduard Schweizer, *The Good News According to Luke* (Atlanta: John Knox, 1984) 115; Peter K. Nelson, *Leadership and Discipleship. A Study of Luke 22:24–30* (SBLDS 138; Atlanta: Scholars, 1994) 44–45.

[14] To be sure, this equation between the Twelve and the apostles likewise occurs in Luke's source, Mark 6:7 + 30, but Mark does not proceed to develop this equation throughout his Gospel.

[15] On the passage, see Schneider, *Die Apostelgeschichte,* 1. 212–32; on p. 222, Schneider asserts that, in Luke-Acts, the Twelve and the apostles coincide; similarly, von Campenhausen, "Der urchristliche Apostelbegriff," 104, 115. This, in fact, is the major thesis of Klein in his *Die zwölf Apostel,* 202–16.

[16] Schneider (*Die Apostelgeschichte,* 2. 152, 159) thinks that "the apostles" in 14:14 stood in Luke's source and that Luke himself has introduced it in 14:4; so also Haenchen, *Die Apostelgeschichte,* 362 n. 5; Conzelmann, *Acts,* 108, 111; cf. Klein, *Die zwölf Apostel,* 211–13. Possibly the source used the term in the sense of the authorized messengers of the church at Antioch. Schneider speculates that Luke was willing to use the title in Acts 14 in order to create a parallel (in preaching the faith and working miracles) between Paul and Barnabas on the one hand and the twelve apostles on the other. The attempt to claim that "the apostles" in 14:4,14 is not the original reading in the Greek text of Acts is a solution born of desperation (*contra* Klein, pp. 212–13); Codex Bezae is the only significant witness to omit "the apostles" in v 14. In "The Apostles According to Luke," chap. 8 of her *Human Agents of Cosmic Power in Hellenistic Judaism and the Synoptic Tradition* (JSNTSup 41; Sheffield: JSOT, 1990) 109–23, Mary E. Mills apparently thinks that, in Acts, Luke presents Paul as an apostle parallel to the apostle Peter. This identification seems to stem from her emphasis on Luke's view of the apostles as disciples who, in Acts, perform wonders in the name of Jesus and by the power of that name. Her treatment does not distinguish carefully enough among various terms like "disciples," "apostles," and "the Twelve."

[17] The independent agreement of Mark and John in speaking simply of "the Twelve" indicates, in my view, that this was the earliest form of expression, going back to Jesus; see Rigaux, " 'Die Zwölf,' " 472. That Matthew at times (26:14,20,47) and Luke always speak simply of "the Twelve"—Luke never uses the fixed designations "the twelve disciples" or "the twelve apostles"—supports this view. Matthew's "twelve disciples" and Luke's identification (or at the very least close association) of "the Twelve" with "the apostles" both betray signs of secondary developments that culminate, as far as Christian tradition history is concerned, in Revelation's "the twelve apostles of the Lamb" and in the title of the *Didache,* "The Lord's Teaching through the Twelve Apostles to the Nations" (cf. *Epistle of Barnabas* 8:3).

[18] Adelbert Denaux ("Did Jesus Found the Church?" *LS* 21 [1996] 25–45) gives a convenient list of major critics (predominantly German) on both sides of the question. (In what follows, I add a few more scholars to his list.) Those who affirm the existence of the Twelve during Jesus' ministry include Julius Wagenmann, Werner Georg Kümmel, Lucien Cerfaux, Hans von Campenhausen, Jacques Dupont, Birger Gerhardsson, Béda Rigaux, Günther Bornkamm, Ulrich Wilckens, Jürgen Roloff, Anton Vögtle, Heinz Schürmann, Rudolf Schnackenburg, Martin Hengel, Helmut Merklein, E. P. Sanders, Joachim Gnilka, Raymond E. Brown, and Joseph A. Fitzmyer. Those who (with varying degrees of probability) deny it include Julius Well-

hausen (taking up a suggestion from Friedrich Schleiermacher), Johannes Weiss, Emmanuel Hirsch, Philipp Vielhauer, Günter Klein, Walter Schmithals, Herbert Braun, Gottfried Schille, Siegfried Schulz, Hans Conzelmann, and John Dominic Crossan. Extensive bibliography, mostly on German authors on both sides of the issue, can be found in the notes of Klein's *Die zwölf Apostel,* 34–37. For a brief summary of the arguments that many critics use to support the existence of the Twelve during Jesus' ministry, see Kümmel, *Kirchenbegriff,* 30–32; the summary is echoed by Klein in his rebuttal in *Die zwölf Apostel,* 35. It is astonishing that, although Klein's denial of the origin of the Twelve in Jesus' ministry is basic to his larger thesis about "the twelve apostles," he almost disdains to argue the point, giving only a cursory summary of the arguments of Vielhauer and like-minded scholars (pp. 35–37).

[19] Examples of studies on the Twelve (some of which do not always distinguish carefully between "disciples" and "the Twelve") include Theodore J. Weeden, Sr., *Mark—Traditions in Conflict* (Philadelphia: Fortress, 1971); Rigaux, "Die 'Zwölf' "; Meye, *Jesus and the Twelve;* Kertelge, "Die Funktion"; Schmahl, *Die Zwölf;* Klemens Stock, *Boten aus dem Mit-Ihm-Sein;* Augustine Stock, *Call to Discipleship* (Good News Studies 1; Wilmington, DE: Glazier, 1982); Ernest Best, *Mark. The Gospel as Story* (Edinburgh: Clark, 1983); idem, "Mark's Use of the Twelve"; Vernon K. Robbins, *Jesus the Teacher* (Philadelphia: Fortress, 1984); Shiner, *Follow Me!.*

[20] So Schulz, *Q. Die Spruchquelle der Evangelisten,* 335 n. 92.

[21] Best, "Mark's Use of the Twelve," 11–35. Vielhauer ("Gottesreich," 69) uses Mark's redaction in a different way to argue against the existence of the Twelve during Jesus' ministry: the historical existence of the Twelve is dubious because, from a literary point of view, the Twelve are only loosely connected with the narrative of Mark's Gospel. I find this a strange argument; the strict logical nexus between the historical existence of the Twelve and the way Mark works references to them into the redactional structure of his Gospel is difficult to grasp. Mark's literary structure is often loose and episodic. In fact, the same point could be made in regard to "the disciples" in Mark; yet hardly anyone would want to use this point to argue against the historical existence of Jesus' disciples.

[22] Trilling, "Zur Entstehung," 204–6; cf. Kertelge, "Die Funktion," 196–97. For a similar judgment, see Rigaux, "Die 'Zwölf,' " 470–82. One might ask whether even these authors too quickly assign most of the references to the Twelve to Mark's redaction. For one thing, the mere presence of the phrase "the Twelve" in sentences that introduce sayings of Jesus does not automatically prove that, in such instances, "the Twelve" has been introduced redactionally by Mark. If one should take, e.g., Pesch's view of Mark as a conservative redactor of large blocks of traditional material (especially in the Passion Narrative broadly understood), then, even in verses introducing sayings of Jesus, various references to the Twelve might belong to pre-Marcan tradition.

[23] Guelich (*Mark 1—8:26*, 155) sums up the matter well: "With few exceptions (e.g., Klein . . . and Schmithals . . .), the common consensus accepts the appointment of the Twelve (3:16–19) as a pre-Markan tradition. The Semitism behind 'to appoint' *(epoiēsen)*, the names of many who never appear again in Mark, the use of patronyms and surnames like Peter, Boanerges and Iscariot, and the presence of similar lists in Matt 10:2–4; Luke 6:14–16; Acts 1:13 support this consensus. The extent of Mark's redaction in 3:13–15, however, is more debatable." Guelich goes on to argue that even 3:13–15 evidences an underlying tradition. See also Karl-Georg Reploh, *Markus–Lehrer der Gemeinde*, (SBM 9; Stuttgart: Katholisches Bibelwerk, 1969) 43–50; Pesch, *Das Markusevangelium*, 1. 202–3.

[24] On this, see Schmahl, *Die Zwölf*, 64–65. The absence of the definite article before "twelve" in Mark 3:14 ("and he made [i.e., appointed] twelve") does not militate against the basic point that the pre-Marcan tradition knows of a special group of twelve disciples.

[25] For the arguments pro and con, see Metzger, *A Textual Commentary* (2d ed.), 69; he and his colleagues express their uncertainty by retaining the words in the text but within brackets. Guelich (*Mark 1—8:26*, 154) argues in favor of 3:16a being original in Mark's text: its function is to resume the thought "after the parenthesis of 3:14b–15."

[26] That Trilling reflects the consensus of Marcan redaction critics on this point can be seen from the chart (drawn up by Marion L. Soards) in Brown, *The Death of the Messiah*, 2. 1504–5. The vast majority of redaction critics listed in this chart who have examined Mark 14:43 consider it a part of the pre-Marcan Passion Narrative. The relation of the Judas tradition to the criterion of embarrassment will be treated below.

[27] As Kertelge ("Die Funktion," 196) notes, the one great exception is the indirect reference to the Twelve in Matt 19:28 par. (from Q).

[28] For basic exegesis and further bibliography, see the standard commentaries, including Pesch, *Das Markusevangelium*, 1. 202–9; Guelich, *Mark 1—8:26*, 153–66; Gundry, *Mark*, 163–70; Fitzmyer, *The Gospel According to Luke*, 1. 613–21; also Stock, *Boten aus dem Mit-Ihm-Sein*, 7–53.

[29] On the variant reading "Lebbaeus" instead of "Thaddeus" in some ancient texts, see the treatment of Thaddeus in the following chapter, under Section II, number 2.

[30] For "Simon the Zealot" as simply an alternate form of "Simon the Cananean," see the treatment of the individual members of the Twelve in the following chapter, under Section II, number 8.

[31] On this point, see Meye, *Jesus and the Twelve*, 200–201.

[32] So, rightly, Fitzmyer, *The Gospel According to Luke,* 1. 619–20. On p. 614, he points to the variations in the lists of the names of the twelve tribes (or twelve patriarchs) in the OT as a similar phenomenon. For a full study of these variations, see Phillip J. Rask, "The Lists of the Twelve Tribes of Israel" (Ph.D. dissertation; Washington, DC: The Catholic University of America, 1990). Actually, compared with the many variations in the names of the twelve tribes found in the OT, the pseudepigrapha, Qumran, Philo, Josephus, and the Book of Revelation, the variations in the four lists of the Twelve in the NT are relatively minor.

[33] Here I disagree with Sanders (*Jesus and Judaism,* 102), who thinks that Jesus was interested in the symbolism of the number twelve, but not especially in always having exactly twelve men in the group designated as "the Twelve": ". . . Jesus used the number 'twelve' symbolically, without anyone then, any more than later, being able to count precisely twelve [individual men in the group]." As a matter of fact, Mark, Matthew, and Luke do count precisely twelve men in the group, though Luke differs from the other two Synoptists with respect to one person's name. I do not understand how this particular group of men could symbolize the eschatological hopes connected with the number twelve and even be called by the set term "the Twelve" unless in fact during Jesus' ministry the members of the group were—at least most of the time—twelve in number. How the numerical symbolism of this group during the public ministry could be detached for any great length of time from the actual number of individuals in the group escapes me. To be sure, one must allow for the possibility of a short hiatus, when one member left the Twelve and was replaced by someone else. This may have happened during Jesus' ministry in the case of Thaddeus and Jude of James and after Jesus' ministry with Judas Iscariot and Matthias. But brief gaps do not amount to the conclusion that the number of disciples in the Twelve did not matter; the apparently historical phenomenon of replacement argues in the opposite direction.

[34] Like Luke-Acts, Matthew drops the Marcan parenthetical reference to the nickname that Jesus gave the sons of Zebedee ("Boanerges," which, Mark 3:17 claims, means "sons of thunder"). Matthew and Luke probably dropped the reference because (1) it disturbs the flow of the list, and/or (2) it may have been as puzzling to the later evangelists as it is to modern exegetes. For all we know, Matthew and Luke may have questioned Mark's interpretation of the nickname, but they had no alternative to offer. For a discussion of "Boanerges," see the treatment of John the son of Zebedee in the next chapter, under Section II, number 11. The grouping in pairs may allude to the lists of Jacob's sons/tribes in relation to their mothers. All the mothers delivered sons in pairs or multiples of two (see Gen 29:31–35:19).

[35] One problem remains: Why did the First Evangelist choose Matthew in the list of the Twelve to be the person who is identified with Levi? Various suggestions can be found in Rudolf Pesch, "Levi—Matthäus (Mc 2.14/Mt 9.9; 10.3): Ein Beitrag zur Lösung eines alten Problems," *ZNW* 59 (1968) 40–56; Mark Kiley, "Why 'Matthew' in Matt 9,9–13?" *Bib* 65 (1984) 347–51.

[36] Davies and Allison (*Matthew*, 2. 144–45) point out further minor agreements between the Matthean and Lucan lists vis-à-vis Mark. They leave open the possibility that Matthew and Luke reflect here a Q tradition, though for the most part they explain Matthew's list as his redaction of Mark; cf. Gundry, *Matthew*, 182–83 (who takes the unusual view that Luke used Matthew).

[37] Here is a prime example of a "minor agreement" of Matthew and Luke against Mark arising out of the coincidental desire of both writers to improve Mark's text. Similarly, that Luke, like Matthew, adds "his brother" after Andrew's name may be an accidental agreement and probably should not be used to argue for a Q list of the twelve names. Matthew may add "his brother" after Andrew's name to balance the same phrase used after the name of John, the brother of James. Perhaps Luke does not fully employ this balancing procedure (i.e., he does not append "his brother" after John's name) because James and John are treated differently than Andrew in Luke's Gospel. James and John have already been introduced as the sons of Zebedee (and hence brothers) back in Luke 5:10. But Andrew is absent from this Lucan version of the initial call of Peter, James, and John after the miraculous catch of fish (Luke 5:1–11). Therefore, as Luke mentions Andrew for the first and only time in his Gospel in the list of the Twelve (6:14), he supplies the explanation that he necessarily omitted when he dropped the Marcan version of the call of the first *four* disciples (Mark 1:16–20): Andrew was Peter's brother.

[38] On this text and the various changes made in the ancient versions to clarify the identity of this person, see Brown, *The Gospel According to John*, 2. 641. Schnackenburg (*Das Johannesevangelium. III. Teil*, 92) thinks that the Jude mentioned in John 14:22 surely belongs, in the mind of the evangelist, to the Twelve. While I do not think that this can be established with certainty, it is noteworthy that all the other *named* disciples who interact with Jesus during the Johannine Last Supper (Peter, Judas Iscariot, Thomas, and Philip) appear in the Synoptic lists of the Twelve. Hence I consider it possible, though not provable, that the Jude in John 14:22 is the Jude of James mentioned in Luke 6:16 ‖ Acts 1:13.

[39] Schürmann (*Das Lukasevangelium*, 1. 318–19) argues strongly for a non-Marcan source at Luke's disposal; he suggests, however, that this list of names had already been joined to the material behind Luke 6:12–13a in Q. Also in favor of Q is Schneider, *Die Apostelgeschichte*, 1. 206.

[40] Schneider (*Die Apostelgeschichte*, 1. 199) rightly claims that Luke reaches back to the material in his Gospel; see also Haenchen, *Die Apostelgeschichte*, 120; Conzelmann, *Acts of the Apostles*, 9.

[41] Admittedly, it is possible that the list in the Gospel of Luke has been partially assimilated to Mark and that Acts represents the more original form of the L tradition's list. This alternate explanation would not change the overall thrust of my argu-

ment, namely, that the list of the Twelve enjoys multiple attestation of sources (Mark and L).

[42] On the exegetical problems involved here, see Brown, *The Gospel According to John*, 1. 298; on pp. 301–2 he lists the parallels between John 6:67–71 and the various versions of the Synoptic scene of Peter's confession at Caesarea Philippi. The mention of Judas' father, Simon, and the attribution of "Iscariot" to Simon rather than to Judas (this is the reading of the best manuscripts in John 6:71) are unparalleled anywhere in the Synoptic tradition—another sign that John represents an independent tradition here.

[43] I purposely use the phrase "an indirect reference to the Twelve in the Q tradition" because Matt 19:28 par. does not directly name "the Twelve" with the fixed formula *(hoi dōdeka)* found elsewhere in the Gospels; we have here instead a reference to the Twelve by way of the image of "twelve thrones" (presuming for the moment the Matthean wording to be original). Nevertheless, Jesus speaks to certain close followers and promises them that at the last judgment they shall sit on *twelve* thrones judging (or ruling) the *twelve* tribes of Israel. Granted the knowledge of a leadership group called the Twelve in the early church, not only the Matthean and Lucan texts in their redactional contexts but also the traditional logion circulating in the early church could hardly refer to any group of persons except the Twelve.

[44] On this point, and on the logion in general, see Jacques Dupont, "Le logion des douze trônes (Mt 19,28; Lc 22,28–30)," *Etudes sur les évangiles synoptiques* (BETL 70; 2 vols.; ed. Frans Neirynck; Leuven: Leuven University/Peeters, 1985 706–43; Ingo Broer, "Das Ringen der Gemeinde um Israel. Exegetischer Versuch über Mt 19,28," *Jesus und der Menschensohn* (Anton Vögtle Festschrift; ed. Rudolf Pesch, Rudolf Schnackenburg, and Odilo Kaiser; Freiburg/Basel/Vienna: Herder, 1975) 148–65; Grundmann, *Das Evangelium nach Matthäus*, 435; Fitzmyer, *The Gospel According to Luke*, 2. 1411–19. That the final part of the saying, which is under discussion here, comes from Q is admitted by most scholars (e.g., Schulz, Hoffmann, Lührmann, Polag, Havener, Kloppenborg, Boring, and Catchpole). Some critics, however, prefer to see two independent traditions that have been preserved in M and L; so T. W. Manson, *The Sayings of Jesus* (London: SCM, 1949, originally 1937) 216–17. Sato (*Q und Prophetie*, 2, 23) remains dubious about the existence of the saying in Q. For a survey of views, see Kloppenborg, *Q Parallels*, 202. For a somewhat different approach, maintaining that Luke 22:30 is part of a pre-Lucan (and non-Marcan) tradition of the Last Supper, possibly even part of a special Lucan Passion Narrative, see Heinz Schürmann, *Jesu Abschiedsrede Lk 22,21–38. III. Teil einer quellenkritischen Untersuchung des lukanischen Abendmahlsberichtes Lk 22,7–38* (NTAbh 20/5; 2d ed.; Münster: Aschendorff, 1977, originally 1957) 36–63, 139–42; Schürmann feels less certain about some of his views in his "Afterword" to the 2d edition, pp. 168–70. Daniel Marguerat (*Le jugement dans l'évangile de Matthieu* [Le Monde de la Bible 6; 2d ed.; Geneva: Labor et Fides, 1995] 462) goes

too far when he claims that Rev 3:20–21 is another version of this logion. Rather, it displays some of the same apocalyptic motifs, but it does not use them in the same way or say the same thing.

[45] On the one hand, Matthew must try to insert the material into his larger teaching on the demands and rewards of discipleship in Matthew 19; the introduction of the theme of the Son of Man at the final judgment, a favorite theme of Matthew's, may be redactional in 19:28. On the other hand, Luke is obviously stitching together various disparate logia. Indeed, Luke 22:29–30a, with the themes of kingdom, covenant, and eating and drinking at Jesus' table fits awkwardly (with respect to both content and syntax) with v 30b (sitting on thrones and judging the twelve tribes of Israel). The composite nature of Luke 22:28–30 is examined by Broer, "Das Ringen," 149–50. Along with a number of other critics, Schulz (*Q. Die Spruchquelle der Evangelisten,* 332) thinks that Luke 22:30a is probably redactional. For the larger theological context of the Lucan form of the saying within Luke-Acts, see Jacob Jervell, "The Twelve on Israel's Thrones," *Luke and the People of God* (Minneapolis: Augsburg, 1972) 75–112. For various critics who champion Matthew's or Luke's form of the saying as more original, see Broer, "Das Ringen," 148 n. 2 (continued on p. 149).

[46] It is surprising that Klein (*Die zwölf Apostel,* 36) thinks that he can dismiss the question of the Q logion simply by noting that the word "regeneration" *(paliggenesia)* in Matt 19:28 makes the saying "suspect." This ignores the key point that likely Q material can be found only in the final words of Matt 19:28 ‖ Luke 22:30: ". . . you shall sit on (twelve) thrones, judging the twelve tribes of Israel." Quite properly, this is the part of the text that is put in bold print and underlined by Kloppenborg, *Q Parallels,* 202; cf. Rigaux, " 'Die Zwölf,' " 476. Q research, by definition, focuses on the material Matthew and Luke have in common, while omitting the material that is likely to come from Matthean or Lucan redaction—which is probably the case with Matthew's *paliggenesia.*

[47] For all the differences in the introductions to this logion in Matthew ("you who have followed me") and Luke ("you are the ones who have persevered with me in my trials"), there is an underlying similarity: Jesus is speaking not to the crowds in general but to followers who are especially close to him. *Contra* Broer ("Das Ringen," 163), there is no reason to doubt that the 2d person plural ("you shall sit") is original in the saying.

[48] For the different meanings of *krinō* that are possible here, see Dupont, "Le logion," 721–32. The two basic possibilities are (1) "to judge," namely, at the last judgment, with either (a) the positive nuance of "obtain justice for," "see justice done for," or (b) the negative nuance of "condemn" (a likely sense in Matthew's redactional theology); or (2) "govern," "rule," "exercise sovereignty over" (not the usual sense in the NT, but a sense witnessed in the OT and pseudepigrapha, and a possible sense in Luke's redactional context and theology). Needless to say, one meaning does not necessarily exclude the other; moreover, in light of the saying's strong OT and

Jewish eschatological flavor, one must allow for a Semitism in the use of the verb. (Broer's strange interpretation of *krinō* ["Das Ringen," 162–63] in terms of the followers of Jesus engaging in a judgment that annihilates Israel on the last day finds no basis in the Q saying taken by itself, apart from its redactional context in Matthew.) In any event, the reference to the twelve tribes of Israel, which did not exist as an empirical reality in Jesus' day but which were expected by at least some Jews to be regathered or reconstituted in the end time (see *A Marginal Jew,* 2. 237–88), points forward to some eschatological event (the final judgment) or situation (the kingdom of God fully come). Dupont (pp. 732–37) suggests that the curious mention of "thrones" in the plural in the scene of judgment in Dan 7:9 (while the Ancient of Days has a "throne" in the singular) may lie behind Jesus' promise to the Twelve. While the plural did provoke later rabbinic speculation and thoughts about the great ones or princes of Israel sharing in God's judgment, we cannot be sure that such speculation circulated in Jesus' day.

[49] Dupont ("Le logion," 721) notes that in this same verse Luke apparently makes another change for the sake of style: Matthew's more natural *krinontes tas dōdeka phylas tou Israēl* (probably reflecting Q) receives an unusual inversion (seen elsewhere in Luke's Greek style) in Luke's *tas dōdeka phylas krinontes tou Israēl*. Working with his theory of a pre-Lucan Last Supper tradition, Schürmann (*Jesu Abschiedsrede Lk 22,21–38. III. Teil,* 52) suggests that "twelve" before "thrones" was dropped in the pre-Lucan tradition to make possible a more general application of a saying that originally referred only to the Twelve.

[50] So Dupont, "Le logion," 720; Witherington, *The Christology of Jesus,* 141.

[51] So, among others, Roloff, *Apostolat,* 148–49; Trilling, "Zur Entstehung," 215; Fitzmyer, *The Gospel According to Luke,* 2. 1419; Witherington, *The Christology of Jesus,* 141; Schulz, *Q. Die Spruchquelle der Evangelisten,* 332; Marguerat, *Le jugement,* 462 n. 45 (though Schulz and Marguerat do not think that the saying goes back to the historical Jesus; so also Bultmann, *Geschichte,* 170–71). It is interesting to note that Vielhauer ("Gottesreich," 67), who rejects both the authenticity of Matt 19:28 par. and the existence of the Twelve during the ministry of Jesus, nevertheless states that, although the original form of the logion cannot be determined, the saying does refer to a promise that Jesus makes to the Twelve about ruling the twelve tribes of Israel. It might also be noted that, if one were to suppose that the original Q saying did not refer to the Twelve, the mere presence of the "twelve tribes" in the logion would not have given rise automatically or naturally to the numeral "twelve" before "thrones" in a secondary stage of the tradition. In the OT, the intertestamental literature, and the NT, we find many passages that speak of or depict the regathering or the judging of *all* Israel (sometimes the point of *all* the tribes is stressed), yet none of these depictions generates the idea of twelve thrones corresponding to the twelve tribes being judged or ruled. The twelve thrones in Matt 19:28 is most naturally explained as a correlative of the Twelve who are addressed.

[52] *A Marginal Jew,* 2. 237–506.

[53] That the idea of the regathering of the twelve tribes of Israel in the end time (or in the days of the Messiah) was a living hope in the time of Jesus is shown by many Jewish works, both OT and pseudepigrapha, which either were composed or continued to be read around the time of Jesus: e.g., Tobit (fragments of which have been found at Qumran; see Joseph A. Fitzmyer, "The Aramaic and Hebrew Fragments of Tobit from Qumran Cave 4," *CBQ* 57 [1995] 655–75); Baruch 4–5; Sir 36:10–13; 48:10; 2 Macc 1:27–29; 2:17–18; *Pss. Sol.* 11; 17:26–32,40–46; 1QM 2:1–3,7–8; 3:13–14; 5:1–2; 11QTemple 18:14–16. On these texts and their relation to the eschatological hopes connected with the idea of the Twelve, see Sanders, *Jesus and Judaism,* 95–106. More specifically, that the symbolism of the twelve patriarchs of Israel, instructing the twelve tribes and foreshadowing their history, was alive at the time of Jesus is shown by the basic form of the *Testaments of the Twelve Patriarchs.* While the *Testaments* in their present state display Christian redaction (the precise extent of which is still debated among critics), their roots reach back to the pre-Christian period in Palestine—witness the fragments of *Testaments* of some of the patriarchs at Qumran. On this point, see Howard Clark Kee, "Testaments of the Twelve Patriarchs," *The Old Testament Pseudepigrapha* (2 vols.; ed. James H. Charlesworth; Garden City, NY: Doubleday, 1983, 1985) 1. 775–80—though Kee minimizes Christian influence and pushes the date of the *Testaments* back farther (2d century B.C.) than I would.

[54] So Trilling, "Zur Entstehung," 216. The partial parallels brought forward by Dupont and others come from the later rabbinic literature.

[55] This point is made by Manson, *The Sayings of Jesus,* 217; similarly, Witherington, *The Christology of Jesus,* 141.

[56] For a list of critics maintaining or denying the saying's authenticity, see Schulz, *Q. Die Spruchquelle der Evangelisten,* 333 n. 80.

[57] Vielhauer, "Gottesreich," 69. In a curious variation on this argument, Sato (*Q und Prophetie,* 23) uses the absence of the concept of the Twelve elsewhere in Q to deny that Matt 19:28 par. is a Q saying. As I point out in the main text, the almost complete absence of *mathētēs* (referring to a disciple of Jesus) in Q shows, by way of analogy, how fragile such an argument is.

[58] For a list of all the passages, see Kloppenborg, *Q Parallels,* 224.

[59] A précis of the various reasons that lead to this judgment—a commonplace among NT exegetes—is given by Rigaux, "Die 'Zwölf,' " 469. Gordon D. Fee (*The First Epistle to the Corinthians* [NICNT; Grand Rapids: Eerdmans, 1987] 718) sums up the reasons quite well: (1) the fact that Paul says that this summary of "the gospel" is something he both "received" and "passed along" to the Corinthians; (2) the stylized form of the four statements in 1 Cor 15:3–5 in two balanced sets; (3) the repeated

hoti ("that") before each clause, which implies a kind of quotation, and (4) the appearance of several non-Pauline words in such a short compass. On this, see Joachim Jeremias, *The Eucharistic Words of Jesus* (London: SCM, 1966) 101–3. On specific questions concerning 1 Cor 15:3–5, see John Kloppenborg, "An Analysis of the Pre-Pauline Formula in 1 Cor 15:3b–5 in Light of Some Recent Literature," *CBQ* 40 (1978) 351–67; Jerome Murphy-O'Connor, "Tradition and Redaction in 1 Cor 15:3–7," *CBQ* 43 (1981) 582–89.

[60] For relevant texts, see Hans Conzelmann, *Der erste Brief an die Korinther* (MeyerK 5; Göttingen: Vandenhoeck & Ruprecht, 1969) 230.

[61] For these and other questions of Pauline chronology, see Robert Jewett, *A Chronology of Paul's Life* (Philadelphia: Fortress, 1979) 29–38; Jerome Murphy-O'Connor, *St. Paul's Corinth* (Wilmington, DE: Glazier, 1983) 129–52; Gerd Luedemann, *Paul Apostle to the Gentiles. Studies in Chronology* (Philadelphia: Fortress, 1984) 262–63; Joseph A. Fitzmyer, "Paul," *NJBC*, 1330–32 (§ 9).

[62] We have multiple attestation of sources for the claim that Jesus himself gave Simon the name Cephas (= Peter) during the public ministry: Mark 3:16; John 1:42; and probably the L list of the Twelve in Luke 6:12–16 (v 14). (Some might want to add the special M tradition in Matt 16:18.) There is no rival NT tradition that asserts that Simon's second name was conferred after Easter. Moreover, if one wanted to argue that Simon received the name Cephas/Peter only in the early days of the church, one would have to explain why and how a name given Simon (by whom?) so relatively late became the standard way of referring to him in so many different streams of NT tradition in the first, second, and third Christian generations (Paul, Mark, M, L, John, and the Petrine epistles). For a full treatment of the names Cephas and Peter, see the following chapter, under Section II, number 12.

[63] Vielhauer, "Gottesreich," 69–71.

[64] In addition, Vielhauer ("Gottesreich," 69) employs a facile distinction between a fixed group of twelve men who constituted a perduring institution and a group of twelve men who simply existed as a circle of persons at a particular point of time in the past. This is to set up a questionable dichotomy, especially for the fluid situation during the ministry of Jesus and the earliest days of the church. One may note in general that the language of "institution" and "office" *(Amt)* is used too quickly and loosely in German discussions of the Twelve.

[65] On this, see Joachim Jeremias, *New Testament Theology. Part One. The Proclamation of Jesus* (New Testament Library; London: SCM, 1971) 233–34. While I would readily admit that the present form of the story of the choice of Matthias in Acts 1:15–26 displays both legendary traits and Lucan redaction, I would not so quickly dismiss the underlying idea that, amid the eschatological fervor of the disciples' initial proclamation of Jesus' resurrection to their fellow Israelites, they selected

(by whatever means) a disciple to replace Judas—the restored circle of the Twelve thus perfectly mirroring the eschatological promise of a restored twelve tribes of Israel. To dismiss the entire tradition of the choice of Matthias as legendary or "secondary" with an apodictic statement (so Klein, *Die zwölf Apostel,* 36) instead of a detailed argument will not do. It is interesting to note that Schmithals (*The Office of Apostle,* 70) dismisses the selection of Matthias as legend in his main text, but then he apparently hesitates in n. 58: "The account of the later choice of Matthias, may, of course, go back to early traditions which told of a filling out of the circle of the twelve after Judas' apostasy." Haenchen (*Die Apostelgeschichte,* 128) allows that the assertion that Matthias and not Barsabbas became an Apostle by casting lots goes back to tradition and is not a Lucan invention. In favor of a historical core to the Matthias tradition is Rigaux, "Die 'Zwölf,' " 479.

[66] On this, see Rigaux, "Die 'Zwölf,' " 480; Trilling, "Zur Entstehung," 211. The 2d-century canonical ending of Mark's Gospel, probably a pastiche of resurrection-appearance stories from Matthew and Luke, also uses the late designation "the Eleven" (Mark 16:14). "The Eleven" also appears in Acts 2:14, but only because Peter is distinguished as leader and spokesman from the other eleven members of the recently reconstituted Twelve. Intriguingly, with that we exhaust all the occurrences of the word "eleven" *(hendeka)* in the NT. The word thus occurs only in stories contained in late NT writings, stories set in a postresurrection context. As we find in some other instances, the Fourth Evangelist retains the more primitive way of speaking. Although he knows that the Twelve existed during Jesus' public ministry, that Thomas and Judas were both members of the Twelve, and that Judas apostatized by betraying Jesus, John nevertheless refers to Thomas after the resurrection as "one of the Twelve" (John 20:24). In this matter, instead of sharing the historicizing tendencies of Matthew and Luke, John retains the primitive way of speaking found in the confessional formula of 1 Cor 15:3–5.

[67] Treatments of Judas commonly speak of his "betraying" Jesus and of the "betrayal." While I use this terminology at times for the sake of convenience and convention, "to betray" is not the most accurate translation for the NT verb *paradidōmi,* which is routinely connected with Judas' name in the Four Gospels. Strictly speaking, the verb means to "hand over" or "give over"; the verb is used in the NT narratives to affirm that Judas "handed over," "gave over," or "delivered" Jesus to the hostile authorities. To be sure, in the specific context of an intimate, trusted disciple handing over his supposedly revered teacher to authorities who may have him executed, the act of handing over may indeed constitute an act of betrayal, but that further meaning comes from the larger framework of the story, not from the particular verb employed. And what is the larger context in the various Gospels? Simply as a matter of fact, Luke explicitly names Judas the "betrayer" *(prodotēs,* 6:16), thus making clear how at least one NT author understood the terminology of "handing over." The woe that Jesus speaks at the Last Supper (Mark 14:21 parr.) over the one who hands him over indicates that Mark—along with Matthew and Luke—and probably the pre-Marcan tradition (so Pesch, *Das Markusevangelium,* 2. 346–53) likewise saw the

handing over in a negative light. Of Matthew's and John's evaluations of Judas' action we are hardly in doubt. But why, then, do the evangelists, including Luke, as well as the tradition before them, favor the verb *paradidōmi* ("hand over")? One possible answer is that the use of the verb *paradidōmi* allows the NT authors to interweave Judas' action with those of other persons, human and divine, who are said in one sense or another to hand Jesus over—notably God the Father, who, in a soteriological sense, hands Jesus over to his death (though here the verb is regularly put into the passive voice and the agent is left unexpressed); on all this, see Brown, *The Death of the Messiah*, 1. 211–13. What exactly constituted Judas' act of "handing over" is hotly debated among scholars; probably it was his cooperation in telling the authorities when and where they could most easily arrest Jesus without public notice or uproar (so Brown, "Overall View of Judas Iscariot," *The Death of the Messiah*, 2. 1401). Debates over Judas' motives, intentions, and moral culpability, while of theological interest, are insoluble from a purely historical point of view since we lack any firm data on these matters; the relevant statements in the Gospels and Acts represent early Christian theology. For a fanciful reconstruction, see William Klassen, *Judas. Betrayer or Friend of Jesus?* (Minneapolis: Fortress, 1996) 73–74. One is not surprised to see that Klassen's book ends on pp. 205–7 with "A Suicide Note from Judas Iscariot, ca. 30 C.E." The quest for the historical Judas, like the quest for the historical Jesus, often ends up giving us a novel.

[68] Trilling ("Zur Entstehung," 208) considers the tradition of the betrayal of Jesus by Judas, "one of the Twelve," the strongest argument in favor of the pre-Easter existence of the Twelve; see also Wagenmann, *Die Stellung*, 5. Quite rightly, Trilling thinks that the various attempts of critics to explain how Judas became a member of a post-Easter group of disciples called the Twelve (or was retrojected into a mythical pre-Easter group called the Twelve) fail to convince. In what follows in the main text, the sole focus is on Judas as an argument for the existence of the Twelve during the public ministry; no attempt is made to cover all the material or questions about Judas. For various approaches to Judas (sometimes with a great deal of novelistic and psychologizing tendencies), see Donatus Haugg, *Judas Iskarioth in den neutestamentlichen Berichten* (Freiburg: Herder, 1930); Roman B. Halas, *Judas Iscariot* (Studies in Sacred Theology 96; Washington, DC: Catholic University of America, 1946); K. Lüthi, *Judas Iskarioth in der Geschichte der Auslegung von der Reformation bis zur Gegenwart* (Zurich: Zwingli, 1955); Oscar Cullmann, "Der zwölfte Apostel," *Vorträge und Aufsätze 1925–1962* (ed. Karlfried Fröhlich; Tübingen: Mohr [Siebeck]; Zurich: Zwingli, 1966) 214–22; Wiard Popkes, *Christus Traditus. Eine Untersuchung zum Begriff der Dahingabe im Neuen Testament* (Stuttgart/Zurich: Zwingli, 1967) 174–81, 217–18; Bertil Gärtner, *Iscariot* (FBBS 29; Philadelphia: Fortress, 1971); J.-Alfred Morin, "Les deux derniers des Douze: Simon le Zélote et Judas Iskariôth," *RB* 80 (1973) 332–58, esp. 349–58; H. L. Goldschmidt and M. Limbeck, *Heilvoller Verrat? Judas im Neuen Testament* (Stuttgart: KBW, 1976); W. Vogler, *Judas Iskarioth* (Theologische Arbeiten 42; 2d ed.; Berlin: Evangelische Verlagsanstalt, 1985); H. Wagner (ed.), *Judas Iskariot* (Frankfurt: Knecht, 1985); Hans-Josef Klauck, *Judas—Ein Jünger des Herrn* (QD 111; Freiburg/Basel/Vienna:

Herder, 1987); Günther Schwarz, *Jesus und Judas* (BWANT 123; Stuttgart: Kohlhammer, 1988); Paul McGlasson, *Jesus and Judas. Biblical Exegesis in Barth* (American Academy of Religion, Academy Series 72; Atlanta: Scholars, 1991) 135–47; William Klassen, "Judas Iscariot," *Anchor Bible Dictionary,* 3. 1091–96; idem, *Judas;* Brown, "Overall View of Judas Iscariot," *The Death of the Messiah,* 2. 1394–1418.

[69] On this, see Rigaux, "Die 'Zwölf,' " 479.

[70] The betrayal of Jesus by Judas, "one of the Twelve," is a major stumbling block for the position of Vielhauer; ironically, in this dilemma, he mirrors the early church. The contorted reasoning by which he tries to show how the church derived from OT texts the idea that one of the Twelve betrayed Jesus fails to convince ("Gottesreich," 70). He is willing to allow as historical fact that one of Jesus' disciples betrayed him (why this much of the Judas tradition is accepted but not the rest is never made clear). The early church then sought Scripture texts (understood as prophecies) to explain this scandalous fact. The church invented the scene of Jesus' designation of the be-trayer at the Last Supper, creating the allusion to MT Ps 41:10 or LXX Ps 40:10 (a trusted friend who shared meals with the psalmist then attacks him)—an allusion that was later made explicit in John 13:18. The idea of betrayal by a table companion who had been a long-term follower of Jesus gave rise in turn to the idea of betrayal by one of the Twelve, once the group of the Twelve had arisen in the early church and then been retrojected into the life of Jesus. Not only is this theory in general convoluted and gratuitous, it also fails specifically because (1) the supposedly pivotal Psalm verse is never explicitly cited prior to John's Gospel; (2) in any event, the Psalm verse says nothing about *handing over* one's table companion *to his enemies,* a key element of the Judas tradition; (3) the complicated, multistage tradition history Vielhauer postu-lates demands a fair amount of time for the idea of betrayal by one of the Twelve to develop in the church, yet the tradition of the betrayal by Judas is already embedded in both the pre-Marcan and the pre-Johannine passion traditions; (4) finally, Viel-hauer's theory never explains adequately why or how the same name (Judas Iscariot [or Judas son of Simon Iscariot]) arose independently in both the pre-Marcan and pre-Johannine passion traditions as the name of the member of the Twelve who turned traitor. For a critique of Vielhauer's theory from a slightly different angle, see Sanders, *Jesus and Judaism,* 99–101.

[71] In his book *Who Killed Jesus?* (San Francisco: Harper, 1995) 75, John Dominic Crossan avoids the improbable hypotheses of Vielhauer and Klein by admitting that a disciple named Judas did actually betray the historical Jesus. But then Crossan pro-ceeds to deny the natural inference that the circle of the Twelve, to whom Judas be-longed, existed during Jesus' ministry. He does this by denying that Judas was a member of the Twelve. Judas could not have been a member of the Twelve since, claims Crossan, the Twelve as a fixed group did not exist during the ministry of Jesus. Instead of arguing this pivotal point at length, Crossan simply declares apodictically (ibid.): "I do not think he [Judas] was a member of the Twelve, because that symbolic

grouping of Twelve new Christian patriarchs to replace the Twelve ancient Jewish patriarchs did not take place until after Jesus' death. There are, for example, whole sections of early Christianity that never heard of that institution. But different and independent early Christian traditions knew about him [Judas]. . . ." This is a strange type of reasoning; these same arguments, used in the same sweeping manner, could just as easily prove the opposite since (1) different and independent early Christian traditions knew about the Twelve and (2) whole sections of early Christianity never heard about Judas or at least never mention him in the NT. Much more careful application of the criteria of historicity to the data is required.

[72] On this point, see Rigaux, " 'Die Zwölf,' " 478.

[73] Schmithals, *The Office of Apostle,* 69.

[74] Meye (*Jesus and the Twelve,* 208) rightly observes of Vielhauer's approach: "Judas is first stolen away from Jesus' company along with the whole pre-Easter circle of the Twelve . . . and then by a most intricate process returned to Jesus' company, with the Twelve, as a theological postulate." See also Eduard Schweizer, *Das Evangelium nach Markus* (NTD 1; 2d ed.; Göttingen: Vandenhoeck & Ruprecht, 1968) 71–72. Schille (*Die urchristliche Kollegialmission,* 148) thinks that the difficulty of explaining Judas' position in the later tradition of the Twelve is eased if we suppose that Judas belonged to the group of Galilean pilgrims around Jesus who went up with him to Jerusalem for the final Passover. How this explains the inexplicable escapes me.

[75] This point is stressed by Trilling, "Zur Entstehung," 208.

[76] Witness, indeed, the twists and turns of a single critic's position. In his article "Der Markusschluss, die Verklärungsgeschichte und die Aussendung der Zwölf," *ZTK* 69 (1972) 379–411, written after *The Office of Apostle,* Schmithals waffles on the question of whence and how Judas and the tradition about him arose. A number of suggestions are offered; my favorite is the following: "It is also possible that Mark wished to discredit as the 'betrayer of Jesus' a former disciple of Jesus who was named Judas Iscariot and who was appealed to as a bearer of tradition by Christian circles whom Mark is attacking in his Gospel." To make room for Judas in the list of the Twelve, Mark may have replaced Judas of James with Judas Iscariot. Oh, what a tangled web we weave. . . .

[77] Perhaps the basic lack of cogency in the various attempts to deny the existence of the Twelve during Jesus' ministry is reflected in the hesitation of Wellhausen (*Einleitung,* 112), one of the earliest proponents of the theory. He thinks it probable that the Twelve did not belong to the life of Jesus, but first appeared at the beginning of the apostolic period. Yet he adds that it is possible that they were Jesus' companions at the Last Supper and thus in a certain way were the "testamentary heirs of the Master."

[78] For this type of argument, see A. M. Farrer, "The Ministry in the New Testament," *The Apostolic Ministry* (ed. Kenneth E. Kirk; London: Hodder & Stoughton, 1946) 113–82, esp. 119–20.

[79] The same could be said for almost the entire corpus of the Apostolic Fathers. The use of "twelve" to mean the twelve apostles or disciples is limited to the title of the *Didache* (which is probably a secondary accretion to the body of the work) and to an indirect reference within an allegory of *Herm. Sim.* 9.17.1 (the twelve mountains represent the twelve tribes to whom the apostles preached the Son of God).

[80] Schmithals mentions yet completely misunderstands this point in *The Office of Apostle*, 69–70. He constructs the highly unlikely scenario of (1) a life of Jesus without the Twelve, (2) the sudden creation of the Twelve after Easter as a result of a resurrection appearance, (3) the conferral of such an important and lofty status on the Twelve in the early church that the group was retrojected into various streams of NT tradition (Mark, Q, L, and John), (4) the disintegration of the Twelve quite early on, as early as the apostasy of Judas and not later than the martyrdom of James the son of Zebedee, and consequently (5) the almost total absence of the Twelve from the rest of the traditions and writings of the 1st-century church. (6) Things become more complicated if one adds refinements from his later article, "Der Markusschluss," 398–401 (e.g., Mark was the first to retroject the Twelve into the public ministry). Such a convoluted hypothesis, with a meteoric rise followed by a meteoric fall, strains credulity and in the end is totally unnecessary.

[81] Here I resume briefly what was spelled out at length in *A Marginal Jew*, 2. 237–88. While the treatment in Volume Two focused upon the tensive symbol "the kingdom of God," here the focus is rather on the prophetic hope that the twelve tribes of Israel would be restored in the end time.

[82] Historical reality was probably not so simple, but we are concerned here with the biblical story as known and believed by Jews of Jesus' time.

[83] On this text, see Sherman E. Johnson, "The Dead Sea Manual of Discipline and the Jerusalem Church of Acts," *The Scrolls and the New Testament* (ed. Krister Stendahl with James H. Charlesworth; New York: Crossroad, 1992, originally 1957) 129–42, esp. 133–34; Bo Reicke, "The Constitution of the Primitive Church in the Light of Jewish Documents," ibid., 143–56, esp. 151–52; Joseph A. Fitzmyer, "The Qumran Scrolls, the Ebionites, and Their Literature," ibid., 208–31, esp. 223. While the Qumran text is useful for confirming the importance of the symbol of twelve men as leaders of eschatological Israel, any direct dependence of either Jesus or the Jerusalem church on the structures at Qumran is highly questionable (cf. Reicke, "The Constitution," 152). Johnson ("The Dead Sea Manual," 134) thinks that the group of twelve ruled over a community of apocalyptic expectation at Qumran, just as the Twelve in the early church were the Jerusalem community's council for the coming Messianic Age (appealing to the Q saying in Matt 19:28 par.). It should be noted that

1QS 8:1 itself is in part ambiguous, since it is not entirely clear whether the three priests belonged to the group of twelve men or were distinct from them (which is indicated when 'îš is translated as "laymen"). For example, Reicke ("The Constitution," 151), thinks that the twelve men were not laymen. A. Dupont-Sommer (*The Essene Writings from Qumran* [Gloucester, MA: Peter Smith, 1973] 90 n. 4) thinks of a council of 15 members, 12 laymen and 3 priests; this view is also held by Geza Vermes, *The Dead Sea Scrolls in English* (3d ed.; London: Penguin, 1987) 4. The translation supplied by *The Dead Sea Scrolls. Volume 1. Rule of the Community and Related Documents* (Princeton Theological Seminary Dead Sea Scrolls Project; ed. James H. Charlesworth; Tübingen: Mohr [Siebeck]; Louisville: Westminster/John Knox, 1994) leaves the matter ambiguous on p. 35 by writing "(lay)men." Scholars also differ as to which NT group the three priests should be compared, since no special Christian group bore the label "priests" (as distinct from "presbyters") in the 1st century. Some think of Peter and the two sons of Zebedee in the Synoptic Gospels, while others think of the three pillars (James, Cephas, and John) in Gal 2:9.

[84] A major proponent of "restoration eschatology" as an important background for understanding the historical Jesus is E. P. Sanders; see his *Jesus and Judaism*, 77–119.

[85] For a full study of these and other symbolic actions of Jesus, see Maria Trautmann, *Zeichenhafte Handlungen Jesu. Ein Beitrag zur Frage nach dem geschichtlichen Jesus* (FB 37; Würzburg: Echter, 1980). Trautmann's treatment of the constituting of the circle of the Twelve is found on pp. 168–233. Trautmann's argument is different from mine in that she does not think that the Q logion in Matt 19:28 par. (which, in her view, contained the reference to the "twelve thrones") goes back to the historical Jesus. She instead argues that Q contained a list of the names of the Twelve, that the Q missionary discourse contained Matt 10:5b–6, which in its earliest form was a saying of the historical Jesus addressed to the Twelve, and that therefore the Q missionary discourse was addressed to the Twelve. While I do not agree with what I consider a tenuous line of reasoning, I do concur in her conclusions: namely, that the historical Jesus did create and send out the Twelve as an extension of his own call to all Israel in the end time. In Trautmann's opinion, Jesus' intention to regather the lost sheep of the house of Israel fulfilled in particular the hopes of the Book of Ezekiel. See also Morna D. Hooker, *The Signs of a Prophet. The Prophetic Actions of Jesus* (Harrisburg, PA: Trinity, 1997).

[86] For the dynamic power of the prophets' symbolic actions, see Gerhard von Rad, *Old Testament Theology* (2 vols.; Edinburgh/London: Oliver and Boyd, 1962, 1965) 2. 95–98: "For antiquity, the sign, like the solemn word . . . , could not only signify a datum but actually embody it as well; this means that it could act creatively, and in early cultures it probably had an even greater power to do so than the word. . . . Jahweh himself acts in the symbol, through the instrument of his prophet. The symbol was a creative prefiguration of the future which would be speedily and inevitably realised. When the prophet, by means of a symbolic act, projects a detail of the future

into the present, this begins the process of realisation. . . . This way of regarding symbolic actions, which was only opened up by the study of comparative religion, is therefore basic for exegesis." See also J. Lindblom, *Prophecy in Ancient Israel* (Philadelphia: Fortress, 1962) 165–73; Georg Fohrer, *Die symbolischen Handlungen der Propheten* (ATANT 54; 2d ed.; Zurich/Stuttgart: Zwingli, 1968); Trautmann, *Zeichenhafte Handlungen;* David Stacey, *Prophetic Drama in the Old Testament* (London: Epworth, 1990).

[87] On this, see the Conclusion to Volume Two of *A Marginal Jew.*

[88] As I indicate below, this formulation is not meant to exclude the possibility that Jesus also sent out other disciples on mission or that he sent out disciples more than once. On the question of the missionary discourse of Jesus and the mission of the Twelve (or of disciples in general), see, besides the standard commentaries, E. Schott, "Die Aussendungsrede Mt 10. Mc 6. Lc 9. 10," *ZNW* 7 (1906) 140–50; Ferdinand Hahn, *Mission in the New Testament* (SBT 47; Naperville, IL: Allenson, 1965) esp. 41–46; Joachim Jeremias, "Paarweise Sendung im Neuen Testament," *Abba. Studien zur neutestamentlichen Theologie und Zeitgeschichte* (Göttingen: Vandenhoeck & Ruprecht, 1966) 132–39; Heinz Schürmann, "Mt 10,5b–6 und die Vorgeschichte des synoptischen Aussendungsberichtes," *Traditionsgeschichtliche Untersuchungen zu den synoptischen Evangelien* (Kommentare und Beiträge zum Alten und Neuen Testament; Düsseldorf: Patmos, 1968) 137–49; Heinrich Kasting, *Die Anfänge der urchristlichen Mission* (BEvT 55; Munich: Kaiser, 1969) esp. 124–26; F. W. Beare, "The Mission of the Disciples and the Mission Charge: Matthew 10 and Parallels," *JBL* 89 (1970) 1–13; G. Testa, "Studio di Mc 6, 6b–13 secondo il metodo della storia della tradizione," *Divus Thomas* 75 (1972) 177–91; Schmithals, "Der Markusschluss," 379–411; Gerd Theissen, "Wanderradikalismus. Literatursoziologische Aspekte der Überlieferung von Worten Jesu im Urchristentum," *ZTK* 70 (1973) 245–71; Siegfried Schulz, " 'Die Gottesherrschaft ist nahe herbeigekommen' (Mt 10,7/Lk 10,9). Der kerygmatische Entwurf der Q-Gemeinde Syriens," *Das Wort und die Wörter* (Gerhard Friedrich Festschrift; ed. Horst Balz and Siegfried Schulz; Stuttgart: Kohlhammer, 1973) 57–67; Michi Miyoshi, *Der Anfang des Reiseberichts. Lk 9,51—10,24* (AnBib 60; Rome: Biblical Institute, 1974) 59–94; Arland D. Jacobson, "The Literary Unity of Q. Lc 10,2–16 and Parallels as a Test Case," *Logia. Les paroles de Jésus—The Sayings of Jesus* (BETL 59; Joseph Coppens Memorial; ed. Joël Delobel; Leuven: Peeters/Leuven University, 1982) 419–23; Rudolf Pesch, "Voraussetzungen und Anfänge der urchristlichen Mission," *Mission im Neuen Testament* (QD 93; ed. Karl Kertelge; Freiburg/Basel/Vienna: Herder, 1982) 11–70; Gerhard Schneider, "Der Missionsauftrag Jesu in der Darstellung der Evangelien," ibid., 71–92; Hubert Frankemölle, "Zur Theologie der Mission im Matthäusevangelium," ibid., 93–129; Klemens Stock, "Theologie der Mission bei Markus," ibid., 130–44; Donald Senior and Carroll Stuhlmueller, *The Biblical Foundations for Mission* (Maryknoll, NY: Orbis, 1983) 141–60, 250–51, 266; Christopher M. Tuckett, "Paul and the Synoptic Discourse," *ETL* 60 (1984) 376–81; Risto Uro, *Sheep among the Wolves. A Study on the Mission Instructions of Q* (Annales Academiae Scientiarum Fennicae, Dissertationes Humanarum Litterarum 47; Helsinki: Suomalainen Tiede-

akatemia, 1987); Gnilka, *Jesus von Nazaret,* 166–93. For a list of scholars for and against the historicity of the mission, see Laufen, *Die Doppelüberlieferungen,* 525–26 nn. 387, 388, 389, 391, and 393. The two extremes among various positions can be seen on the one hand in Bultmann's *Geschichte* (155–56: originally the Risen One spoke in this discourse, that is to say, we have here a community-formation; other, less skeptical, views are noted in the 4th ed. of the *Ergänzungsheft* [1971], 59) and on the other hand in Manson's *The Sayings of Jesus* (73: "The mission of the disciples is one of the best-attested facts in the life of Jesus"). While some critics like Beare ("The Mission," 13) wholeheartedly adopt Bultmann's view, many are less skeptical than Bultmann but less confident than Manson.

[89] Manson (*The Sayings of Jesus,* 73–74) claims that there were also mission charges in the special M and L material, but this view is highly questionable. At the other extreme, David Catchpole (*The Quest for Q* [Edinburgh: Clark, 1993] 152–58) espouses the unlikely minority view that, in the missionary discourse, Mark is dependent on Q; against this view is Uro, *Sheep among the Wolves,* 101 n. 17. The majority opinion (missionary discourses in both the Marcan and the Q traditions) is presented and defended at length by Laufen, *Die Doppelüberlieferungen,* 201–301; see also Hahn, *Mission,* 41–42; Fitzmyer, *The Gospel According to Luke,* 1. 751. Some commentators treat two parallels from the Coptic *Gospel of Thomas* (saying 73 = Luke 10:2 par.; saying 14b = Luke 10:8–9 par.) as independent sources, but most likely the two parallels are dependent on the Synoptic Gospels. On this question, see Fitzmyer, ibid., 2. 842–43; Michael Fieger, *Das Thomasevangelium. Einleitung, Kommentar und Systematik* (NTAbh 22; Münster: Aschendorff, 1991) 71–76 (for saying 14), 205–6 (for saying 73); and my observations on saying 14 as a typical theological collage in *A Marginal Jew,* 1. 137–38, 165 n. 142. Sometimes an argument against the historicity of the mission during Jesus' ministry is constructed from the total silence of John's Gospel. This is a prime example of the danger of an argument from silence. The christological concentration of the Fourth Gospel focuses an intense spotlight on the person of Jesus, to such an extent that many themes present in the Synoptics virtually disappear in John. Accordingly, in John there is no call of the Twelve, no mission of the Twelve (Jesus is the one *sent,* period), no miracles performed by the Twelve, and in general no great development of what we would call "ecclesiological" motifs. Yet, just as there are a few "fossil" references to the Twelve (6:67,70–71; 20:24), showing that the group was known in the Johannine tradition, so there may be traces of a memory that Jesus sent his disciples out on mission during his lifetime. This is one possible explanation of the puzzling statement of Jesus to his disciples during the story of the Samaritan woman at the well, early in the public ministry (4:38; cf. 17:18): "I sent [*apesteila,* aorist tense] you to reap what you had not labored over." While allowing for a proleptic reference to the postresurrection mission, Brown (*The Gospel According to John,* 1. 183) also accepts the possibility of a reference to a mission during the ministry of Jesus. He rightly notes echoes of Luke 10:1–2 in John 4:35–38.

[90] So Bultmann, *Geschichte,* 155–56; Reploh, *Markus—Lehrer der Gemeinde,* 53. This should not be taken to mean, however, that Mark knew or used Q. For reserva-

tions about seeing Mark's mission discourse as an excerpt or abridgement (especially of Q), see Uro, *Sheep among the Wolves,* 36–39, 98–99.

[91] For the arguments for and against reading "seventy" or "seventy-two" in Luke 10:1, see Bruce M. Metzger, "Seventy or Seventy-Two Disciples?" *NTS* 5 (1958–59) 299–306; Sidney Jellicoe, "St Luke and the 'Seventy(-Two),' " *NTS* 6 (1959–60) 319–21; also Metzger, *Textual Commentary* (2d ed.), 126–27; Fitzmyer, *The Gospel According to Luke,* 2. 845–46. At present, there seems to be no clear solution to the problem.

[92] For the complicated mutual influences, see Miyoshi, *Der Anfang,* 74–75.

[93] Laufen (*Die Doppelüberlieferungen,* 202–3) is too diffident about the possibility of Luke's creativity here. Fitzmyer (*The Gospel According to Luke,* 2. 845) comments on the seventy(-two): "It is impossible to think that the number was part of 'Q,' since this verse [Luke 10:1] is from Luke's own pen"; see also Miyoshi, *Der Anfang,* 76–80. Even stronger in favor of a Lucan creation is Uro (*Sheep among the Wolves,* 62–66), who points out the clash between the Q logion lamenting the small number of laborers (Luke 10:2 par.) and Luke's immediately prior statement (10:1) that Jesus was sending out "seventy(-two) others." In any case, Luke is not overly concerned about two historically distinct missions. In his mini-discourse at the Last Supper (Luke 22:35), he has Jesus refer back to his instructions in the missionary discourse: "When I sent you without wallet, bag, or sandals. . . ." Yet, while the Lucan setting at the Last Supper demands that Jesus be speaking to his twelve apostles (sent out in chap. 9), the exact succession of nouns ("wallet, bag, sandals") with the same Greek words is found instead in Jesus' instructions to the seventy(-two) in Luke 10:4: *ballantion . . . pēran . . . hypodēmata.* Of these, only *pēran* appears in the instructions to the Twelve in 9:3.

[94] Schulz (*Q. Die Spruchquelle der Evangelisten,* 404, 408) spells out the reasons for this view. See Kloppenborg (*Q Parallels,* 72) for a long list of critics who hold that Luke's order is closer to Q; only Beare and Harnack are listed as favoring the Matthean order.

[95] For detailed attempts to discern the earlier material lying behind the Marcan and/or Q forms of the discourse, see Hoffmann, *Studien,* 236–311; Laufen, *Die Doppelüberlieferungen,* 246–60; Uro, *Sheep among the Wolves,* 73–96. The similarities yet differences among these reconstructions of the Q material should remind us how fragile any hypothetical reconstruction of the exact extent and wording of Q is. But the analyses undertaken by the above-named critics make clear enough the basic phenomenon of older tradition being reworked by Q. Likewise, the reworking of older tradition is discernible in the Marcan form both (1) in the transition from indirect discourse with *hina* clause (Mark 6:8) by way of an accusative participle (v 9a, apparently as the subject of an understood infinitive) to direct discourse (v 9b) and (2) in the softening (vv 8–9) of some, but not all, of the radical prohibitions preserved in Q

(cf. Luke 10:4); on this, see Pesch, *Das Markusevangelium,* 1. 326. As Uro points out (ibid., 103), it would never have crossed Mark's mind—especially in such a terse set of instructions—to state explicitly that Jesus permitted a staff, a piece of equipment taken for granted by any ancient traveler, unless the tradition he was editing had prohibited it.

[96] Like most critics, I do not include in this outline elements from the present forms of the discourse in which influences from the later Christian mission can be detected: e.g., the insistence on staying in the same house (Luke 10:7) seems to presuppose a fairly lengthy sojourn in a given town while the (Christian) missionaries set up a stable (Christian) community. In my outline, my intention is to highlight the five basic elements, not all the further explanatory details, which are taken mostly from Q.

[97] Catchpole, *The Quest for Q,* 180. Catchpole thinks in particular that Luke 10:3 par. was the beginning of the mission charge in Q and that the text probably ran: "Go. Behold, I am sending you as sheep in the midst of wolves." Uro (*Sheep among the Wolves,* 75–76) likewise retains this verse for the beginning of the Q discourse.

[98] For a list of the various interpretations of the prohibition of greeting anyone on the road, see Fitzmyer, *The Gospel According to Luke,* 2. 847. While it occurs only in Luke 10:4, Uro (*Sheep among the Wolves,* 77–78) argues for its inclusion in Q.

[99] Sato (*Q und Prophetie,* 311–12) stresses that this forgoing of all the usual supplies for traveling is an example of a prophetic-symbolic action, this time on the part of the disciples sent by Jesus. Sato makes the intriguing suggestion that the poor, defenseless disciples were thus acting out in their own lives the eschatological beatitudes and ethic inculcated by Jesus in the Sermon on the Mount/Sermon on the Plain (Lk 6:20–21,27–36 par.). It is generally accepted by exegetes that the permission in Mark 6:8–9 to carry a staff and to wear sandals is a secondary softening of the radical demands reflected in the Q form of the discourse (so Taylor, *The Gospel According to St. Mark,* 304); an unconvincing minority view on this subject is espoused by Gundry, *Mark,* 308. However, I see no reason to hold, as Laufen does (*Die Doppelüberlieferungen,* 252–53), that the radical prohibitions of Q were originally mere hyperbole; Sato (*Q und Prophetie,* 311) rightly rejects this view. The original situation of a brief, urgent mission to nearby Jewish towns in Palestine did not make the radical demands impossible to fulfill. The situation was quite different once lengthy, and sometimes overseas, missions came into view; hence, perhaps, the Marcan modifications. Hoffmann (*Studien,* 241) takes the prohibitions quite literally, suggesting that the radical prohibition of bread and a traveler's (or beggar's) bag—supplies that even the wandering Cynic philosophers took with them—was meant to show that Jesus' disciples surpassed even the Cynics in their severe abstention from ordinary possessions. On the larger Cynic-Christian question, see F. Gerald Downing, "Cynics and Christians," *NTS* 30 (1984) 584–93; cf. Theissen, "Wanderradikalismus," 255–56. Pesch (*Das Markusevangelium,* 1. 328) sees a similar surpassing of the Essenes, who were allowed to have weapons and sandals when on journeys; on this, see Josephus, *J. W.*

2.8.4 §124–127. As Catchpole points out (*The Quest for Q*, 182), Q's radical prohibition of any and every means of support while traveling runs contrary to human instinct, Cynic practice, Jewish assumptions as seen in the rabbinic literature, the rules of the Essenes, and the practice of certain Christian missionaries known to us (e.g., Mark 6:8–9; Paul's usual practice). Thus, one might argue from the criterion of discontinuity that these radical prohibitions come from Jesus (cf. p. 188). At times critics bring forth as a parallel to these prohibitions a rabbinic prohibition against bringing certain things into the temple precincts (*m. Ber.* 9:5): "One must not enter upon the Hill of the House [i.e., the holy mount of the temple] with one's staff and with one's shoes and with one's money belt and with the dust that is on one's feet. . . ." This is a good example of how not to use rabbinic texts. At first glance, the verbal parallel is dazzling, but closer inspection shows that the agreement is purely verbal; the context and thrust of the two sayings are quite different. The mishnaic passage is intent on the proper reverential attitude and behavior of Jerusalem pilgrims toward the temple mount, with a special concern for not profaning the sacred with the elements of ordinary daily life. The context of the mission discourse is one of eschatological urgency in a crisis situation and of a total dependence on God that makes the disciples dispense with all the usual equipment for a journey. On this point, see Laufen, ibid., 254. Thus, the attempt of some commentators (e.g., Walter Grundmann, *Das Evangelium nach Markus* [THKNT 2; 6th ed.; Berlin: Evangelische Verlagsanstalt, 1973] 124) to use this mishnaic passage to interpret the disciples as pilgrims verges on patristic allegory.

[100] Catchpole (*The Quest for Q*, 184–85) sees in this weighty eschatological peace that the disciples are charged to bring to the welcoming host the real reason why they are not to engage in a casual, superficial exchange of "peace" *(šālôm)* on the road. While this is possible, Catchpole's position is not entirely firm, since the prohibition of giving a greeting on the road in Luke 10:4 *(kai mēdena kata tēn hodon aspasēsthe)* does not use the key word "peace" *(eirēnē)* that is the greeting to the host in Luke 10:5. See, however, the equating of the verb "greet" and the noun "peace" in Matt 10:12–13 (in the context of entering a house).

[101] Guelich (*Mark 1—8:26*, 322–23) mentions three possible meanings of the symbolic gesture: (1) Since Jews customarily shook dust from their feet when returning from Gentile territory, the city that rejects the message of the regathering of Israel is considered no longer Israelite but pagan. A problem with this approach is that firm proof of such an attitude and/or practice comes only from later rabbinic literature; cf. *m. Tohar.* 4:5; *m. Ohol.* 2:3 (but it should be noted that neither of these two passages speaks explicitly of Jews returning from pagan lands and shaking off the dust from their feet). (2) The gesture symbolizes the termination of any further contact and communication between the disciples and the unbelieving city, thus denying it any further opportunity to hear their message of the kingdom or benefit from their ministry of healing. (3) The gesture shows that the messengers have conscientiously completed their task and are now "washing their hands" of any further responsibility for the unbelieving city. Clearly, one interpretation need not exclude the other; such sym-

bols are of their nature multivalent. Jeremias (*Theology of the New Testament,* 238) interprets the gesture slightly differently: ". . . they [the Twelve] are to shake the dust which their feet have stirred up from their cloaks"; cf. Neh 5:13; Acts 18:6. Sato (*Q und Prophetie,* 313 n. 610) strongly rejects this interpretation. In any event, the significance of the act remains basically the same. For other possible interpretations (especially in reference to passages in Acts), see Henry J. Cadbury, "Dust and Garments," *The Beginnings of Christianity. Part I. The Acts of the Apostles* (5 vols.; ed. F. J. Foakes Jackson and Kirsopp Lake; Grand Rapids: Baker, 1979, originally 1933) 5. 269–77.

[102] Commentaries usually point to the well-known rabbinic institution of the *šālîaḥ* (a fully authorized legal agent) and to the famous dictum repeated frequently in rabbinic writings (e.g., *m. Ber.* 5:5): "The *šālîaḥ* of the man is as the man himself" (*šĕlûḥô šel ʾādām kĕmôtô*). The problem, though, is that neither the legal institution of the *šālîaḥ* nor the relevant saying has been proven to exist in the early 1st century A.D. A more likely background to Jesus' saying is the OT tradition of Yahweh sending his prophet with authority to speak to Israel his powerful word of salvation and/or judgment—especially the deuteronomistic idea of the rejected prophets sent to call a recalcitrant Israel to repentance in the last hour before disaster strikes. The OT background coheres well with the way that Jesus presents himself to Israel as the eschatological prophet. A modification, however, must be noted in that Jesus the eschatological prophet now sends his disciples with his authority just as God has sent Jesus with his authority. On this last point, see Schulz, *Q. Die Spruchquelle der Evangelisten,* 412–13.

[103] Amid all the disagreements among scholars, certain tendencies dominate. For instance, Kloppenborg (*The Formation of Q,* 192–93) suggests for "the core of the tradition" about mission a shorter list of components: at least the "equipment instruction" (Luke 10:4 ‖ Mark 6:8–9) and the instructions concerning acceptance (Luke 10:5–7 ‖ Mark 6:10) and rejection (Luke 10:10–11 ‖ Mark 6:11). Hahn (*Mission,* 43–44) thinks that the common basic pattern, already enlarged in Q, consisted of what I count as the first four components, though he admits that there are problems about the first one. In the end, Hahn judges that, although certain core elements go back to the historical Jesus (e.g., Luke 10:8–11), the larger pattern of the discourse must be ascribed to the early church (p. 46). Similar to Hahn's reconstruction is that of Uro, *Sheep among the Wolves,* 101–2. Uro (p. 106) suggests that the common antecedent of the Marcan and Q forms of the discourse comprised something like Luke 10:4–11, minus Luke 10:7c ("not from house to house") and 10:8b ("eat what is set before you"). Pushing still further back, Uro postulates an earlier form of the tradition, made up of the prohibitions of equipment for travel and the instructions about houses (pp. 106–8). Quite different from these approaches is the hypothesis of Schürmann ("Mt 10,5b–6," 148–49): the original kernel and main part of the whole mission pericope was Luke 10:1 + Matt 10:5b–6 + Luke 10:8–11; for a critique of this position, which has not found much acceptance in subsequent studies, see Uro, *Sheep among the Wolves,* 108–9.

[104] Kasting, *Die Anfänge,* 125–26.

[105] It is hardly by accident that we have wide multiple attestation for a saying of Jesus in which he correlates (in one way or another) the act of accepting one of his disciples, the act of accepting himself, and the act of accepting God: so, e.g., Matt 10:40: "He who receives you [plural: in context, the twelve disciples sent on mission], receives me, and he who receives me receives the One who sent me." For the various forms of this saying, see Luke 10:16 (with the verbs "hear" and "reject," *akouō* and *atheteō*); Matt 10:40 (with the verb "receive," *dechomai*); John 13:20 (with the verb "receive," *lambanō;* cf. John 12:44–45; 5:23); and more distantly Mark 9:37 (with the verb "receive," *dechomai*). In all these sayings, Jesus refers in reverential periphrasis to God as "the One who *sent* me" (*apostellō* in the Synoptic tradition, *pempō* in John). These sayings, in turn, form just one piece of the evidence for Jesus' sense of *being sent,* which, in various sayings and under various images, is witnessed in all the major streams of the Gospel tradition. It is not without reason that Martin Hengel ("The Origins of the Christian Mission," *Between Jesus and Paul* [London: SCM, 1983] 48–64) remarks (p. 62): "If anyone is to be called 'the primal missionary,' he [Jesus] must be."

[106] On this, see Hengel, *The Charismatic Leader,* 74. In contrast, Hoffmann (*Studien,* 262–63) is willing to speak only of Jesus' disciples "sharing in" his work or ministry. What this "sharing in" exactly involved, why it demanded that a group of people leave family, home, and employment for a long stretch of time to follow Jesus around Palestine, and how in particular the Twelve "shared in" Jesus' ministry is never made clear. In contrast, Catchpole (*The Quest for Q,* 188) strongly affirms that the original mission charge, which he isolates in Luke 10:3,4,5–7,9,10a,11a,12, stems from the historical Jesus. Fitzmyer (*The Gospel According to Luke,* 1. 753) remains reserved on the question: "There is no reason to question it [the mission of the disciples during Jesus' ministry] in the long run, even though the evidence from the Synoptics amounts at most to a plausibility." I would upgrade "plausibility" to "probability."

[107] A number of exegetes think that Matthew's introduction (Matt 10:1,5a) is dependent on Mark 6:7 and that Luke 10:1 is probably due mostly to Lucan redaction (so Schulz, *Q. Die Spruchquelle der Evangelisten,* 404; Miyoshi [*Der Anfang,* 73] thinks that Luke 10:1–2a is redactional); in any case, it would not represent Q. On all this, see Laufen, *Die Doppelüberlieferungen,* 201–5; M. Eugene Boring, *The Continuing Voice of Jesus* (Louisville: Westminster/John Knox, 1991) 206. Slightly more confident is Uro (*Sheep among the Wolves,* 74–75), who, with great hesitation, relies upon minor agreements between Matt 10:1 and Luke 9:1 to suggest that the Q discourse was introduced by wording such as: "And summoning his disciples, he gave them authority to heal illnesses. And he said to them. . . ."

[108] For example, Guelich (*Mark 1—8:26,* 319) thinks that Mark's hand is most evident in the framework (6:7,12–13): "Vocabulary, style and content point to Mark's

own redaction based to a large extent on the calling of the Twelve in 3:13–19"; see also p. 321. The view that Mark is largely responsible for the framework of the mission discourse is shared by Hoffmann (*Studien*, 238) and Uro (*Sheep among the Wolves*, 26–39) and is argued in detail by Reploh, *Markus–Lehrer der Gemeinde*, 50–58; and Stock, *Boten aus dem Mit-Ihm-Sein*, 82–97. Dissenting from this view are Ernst Lohmeyer, *Das Evangelium des Markus* (MeyerK 1/2; Göttingen: Vandenhoeck & Ruprecht, 1967, originally 1937) 113; Pesch (*Das Markusevangelium*, 1. 326–27); and Gundry (*Mark*, 307), who think it likely that the tradition had a narrative framework (or at least an introduction) prior to Mark.

[109] Those in favor of a mission of the Twelve during Jesus' ministry include Schneider ("Der Missionsauftrag," 83–84), who in turn cites Pesch, *Das Markusevangelium*, 1. 331.

[110] For example, Kasting (*Die Anfänge*, 124–25), who is open to the possibility of the mission of the disciples in general, is negative on the question of the mission of the Twelve because he first of all doubts that the Twelve existed during Jesus' ministry.

[111] On this point, see Pesch, *Das Markusevangelium*, 1. 331.

[112] On this, see C. K. Barrett, *The Signs of an Apostle* (Philadelphia: Fortress, 1972) 31–32 (but note his qualifications); Gundry, *Mark*, 307.

[113] The only possible exception—and one that needs a little reading between the lines for support—is found in Acts 9:31–32. In v 31, Luke gives one of his summaries of the life of the early Palestinian church. It begins: "Now the church throughout the whole of Judea and Galilee and Samaria was enjoying peace. . . ." Then, after the summary is completed, Luke introduces two miracle stories involving Peter (9:32–43: the healing of Aeneas and the raising of Dorcas, both situated in Judea) with the words "And Peter, passing through every region [*dia pantōn*], came down to the saints who lived in Lydda." (Since Christians are already present in the towns Peter visits, his visit is as much a "pastoral" as a "missionary" one; Conzelmann calls it "an inspection tour.") Whether the vague *dia pantōn* of v 32 is meant to reach back and include Galilee from v 31 is questionable, especially since there is no direct linkage between the two miracle stories in Judea and the preceding summary. In his division of the pericopes, for instance, Haenchen (*Die Apostelgeschichte*, 280) connects v 31 with the story of Paul in chap. 9 (after persecution comes peace), while with v 32 he begins a new section. Schneider (*Die Apostelgeschichte*, 2. 50) leaves open whether *dia pantōn* refers to the regions mentioned in v 31 or to all the Christian communities that Peter as the "Jerusalem inspector" is calling upon. In addition, Conzelmann (*Acts of the Apostles*, 76) notes that *pantōn* could refer either to people or to places.

[114] Many exegetes interpret 1 Cor 9:5 to mean that Paul is mentioning the travels (apparently at church expense) of "the rest of the apostles and the brothers of the Lord and Cephas [= Peter]." (Other exegetes, however, interpret the verse in reference

to the married state of other missionaries as compared to Paul's celibacy.) In any case, as we have already seen, Paul never gives any explicit indication that he considers all of the Twelve to be "apostles." Hence it would be questionable to see the Twelve included here in the group called "the rest of the apostles" and then to draw conclusions about the journeys of the Twelve. (Indeed, "apostles" in 9:5 may refer not to apostles in the full, "plenipotentiary" sense that Paul claims for himself but in the looser sense of missionaries or delegates sent out by individual churches.) For the various problems involved in this verse, see Conzelmann, *Der erste Brief an die Korinther,* 181; Fee, *The First Epistle to the Corinthians,* 402–4.

[115] A prime example of the convoluted theories in which critics become entangled once they adopt the retrojection theory can be found in Schmithals, "Der Markusschluss," 398–409. The document Mark supposedly redacted to create his Gospel is said to have contained a story of the risen Jesus appearing to the Twelve and sending them out on mission. Mark deleted this material from his resurrection story for the sake of his "messianic secret" theory. He then retrojected the resurrection appearance to the Twelve (which, according to the Vielhauer-Klein-Schmithals school of thought, created the Twelve as a fixed group) back into Mark 3:13–19 (the call of the Twelve), while the mission charge was retrojected into Mark 6:7–13 (the mission discourse).

[116] There are other, minor differences as well: the call of James and John is shorter in that Jesus' words are not quoted, yet it is more detailed in that the father of James and John (Zebedee), the hired men, the work of mending (or folding) the nets, and a boat are all mentioned. These differences make me wary of the theory that the story of the call of James and John is simply a secondary creation, manufactured on the model of the call of Peter and Andrew. This is not to deny that a literary parallel has been created between the two calls and that, in the present state of the story, the second call makes complete sense only in connection with the first call. On all this see Rudolf Pesch, "Berufung und Sendung, Nachfolge und Mission. Eine Studie zu Mk 1,16–20," *ZKT* 91 (1969) 1–31, esp. 8–18; Reploh, *Markus—Lehrer der Gemeinde,* 27–29; Guelich, *Mark 1—8:26,* 49–52; Gundry, *Mark,* 72.

[117] For basic exegesis and further bibliography, see Jindřich Mánek, "Fishers of Men," *NovT* 2 (1958) 138–41; Charles W. F. Smith, "Fishers of Men. Footnotes on a Gospel Figure," *HTR* 52 (1959) 187–203; Otto Betz, "Donnersöhne, Menschenfischer und der davidische Messias," *RevQ* 3 (1961) 41–70, esp. 53–61; Werner Bieder, *Die Berufung im Neuen Testament* (ATANT 38; Zurich: Zwingli, 1961) 7–15; Schulz, *Nachfolgen und Nachahmen,* 97–116; Anton Vögtle, "Exegetische Erwägungen über das Wissen und Selbstbewusstsein Jesu," *Gott in Welt* (Karl Rahner Festschrift; 2 vols.; Freiburg/Basel/Vienna: Herder, 1964) 1. 608–67, esp. 616–18; Wilhelm H. Wuellner, *The Meaning of "Fishers of Men"* (New Testament Library; Philadelphia: Westminster, 1967); Hans Dieter Betz, *Nachfolge und Nachahmung;* Francis Agnew, "Vocatio primorum discipulorum in traditione synoptica," *VD* 46 (1968) 129–47; Günter Klein, "Die Berufung des Petrus," *Rekonstruktion und Inter-*

pretation. Gesammelte Aufsätze zum Neuen Testament (BEvT 50; Munich: Kaiser, 1969) 1–48 (with *Nachtrag;* originally *ZNW* 58 [1967] 1–44); Reploh, *Markus— Lehrer der Gemeinde,* 27–35; Ernest Best, *Following Jesus. Discipleship in the Gospel of Mark* (JSNTSup 4; Sheffield: JSOT, 1981) 166–74.

[118] Otto Betz, "Donnersöhne," 53. Betz's article represents a highly imaginative weaving together of many different texts from the OT, Qumran, the NT, and the *Testaments of the Twelve Patriarchs.*

[119] In his *The Meaning of "Fishers of Men,"* Wuellner presents a wide-ranging survey of literary and iconographic uses of fish/fisherman imagery in the ancient world. The book, however, suffers from many problems. There is a basic lack of methodological rigor: various terms like "fish," "fishing," "fisher," "hunter," "fowler," "nets," "catch," "snare," and even "shepherd" are readily associated and even declared interchangeable. In the words of Howard Clark Kee in his review of Wuellner's book (*JBL* 87 [1968] 220–21), "the inevitable consequence . . . is methodological chaos." Wuellner casts his own net far and wide in the manner of Carl Jung and Joseph Campbell, with a resulting lack of historical and textual precision. As Klein ("Die Berufung des Petrus," 48 [in the *Nachtrag* to the original article]) rightly points out, the metaphor "fishers of men" is read arbitrarily into all sorts of texts where it does not appear; for, in Wuellner's archetypal mind, everything is connected with everything else. Thus, the tradition of "men-fishing" is seen in "Jewish legendary tradition about angels . . . chasing the daughters of men in Gen., ch. 6 . . ." (p. 69). "Inspired by the classical Greek *paideia* ideal, 'man-fishing' and 'disciple-making' *(mathēteuein)* become interchangeable" (p. 71). "In the appointment of the shepherd boy David to the royal authority of shepherding Israel we have the closest analogy to the New Testament account of Galilean fishermen being called to be fishers of men" (p. 100). That Wuellner's overarching hermeneutical and theological project, rather than the sober exegesis of individual texts, is at the heart of his work is clear when, within the compass of two sentences, he contrasts John the Baptist and Qumran on the one hand and "the Pharisaic and Sadducean 'center' " (equated with "the rabbis") on the other by showing how they disagreed on what Paul Tillich calls the New Being (pp. 121–22).

[120] In so situating Jesus, I by no means deny the Hellenistic influence in Palestine at the turn of the era, though this point has at times been overemphasized in some recent works on the historical Jesus. For all the Hellenistic influences abroad in Palestine, the primary context to be investigated when one is inquiring after the meaning of a metaphor used by a 1st-century Palestinian Jew (from rural Galilee) as he addresses other Jews in a religious situation must be that Jew's own spiritual heritage, witnessed by the flow of Jewish-Palestinian traditions from the OT through the "intertestamental" period (e.g., Qumran) down to the later rabbinic literature (the last being used with care to avoid anachronisms). To prefer to these sources Lucian of Samosata (2d century A.D.) or Diogenes Laertius (3d century A.D.) is questionable methodology.

[121] All too often, in the study of this pericope, a judgment against historicity is allowed to flow directly from a judgment about the form-critical category of the pericope: e.g., an apophthegm that is an ideal scene (Bultmann), a paradigm (Dibelius),
an etiological disciple-legend, an etiological missionary-legend, or a call story. Actually, there is some truth in each of these labels, yet none of them nor all of them together can decide automatically the question of whether some historical event lies at
the origin of Mark 1:16–20. I readily grant that the call of Elisha by Elijah (1 Kgs
19:19–21), the desire to exalt certain leaders in the early church (e.g., Peter, James,
and John), the desire to see every Christian vocation as grounded in the primordial
call of the disciples by Jesus, and the desire to ground the ongoing missionary activity
of the church in the command of Jesus have all had their influence on the narrative.
This is simply to reiterate the basic form-critical insight about the *Sitz im Leben* of the
church molding and carrying the Jesus tradition. Similar claims could be made about
the Gospel narratives of Jesus' crucifixion. Yet hardly anyone draws from the legendary, etiological, midrashic, or parenetic nature of these narratives the conclusion
that Jesus was not crucified. Pesch ("Berufung und Sendung," 1–3) rightly protests
against form-critical judgments being allowed to determine a priori judgments about
historicity. Having made this vital distinction, Pesch (p. 25) has no logical problem
defending the basic historicity of Mark 1:16–18 while at the same time deciding that
the pericope's form-critical category is that of a "missionary etiology."

[122] See Jer 16:16 for the metaphors of fishers and hunters: "Behold, I [am] sending
for many fishers [= the enemies of Israel, e.g., the Babylonians]—oracle of Yahweh—
and they shall catch them [i.e., the Israelites, like fish]. And after that I shall send for
many hunters, and they shall hunt them down from upon every mountain and from
upon every hill and from the clefts of the crags." In the LXX, the word for "fishers"
is the same as in Mark 1:17: *haleeis* (also spelled *halieis*). The oracle of doom in Jer
16:16 is immediately preceded by an oracle prophesying Israel's return from exile to
the promised land (16:14–15). While this latter oracle is out of place in the overall
context of doom in Jeremiah 16 (cf. Jer 23:7–8; see John Bright, *Jeremiah* [AB 21; 2d
ed.; Garden City, NY: Doubleday, 1965] 112–13), its position in the final form of the
book could possibly—this can be nothing more than a surmise—have suggested to
Jesus the novel, salvific twist that he gave to the originally negative image of fishing
for men. At the very least, Jer 16:14–15 fits in with the idea of the regathering of all
Israel, the mission of Jesus that he shared with the Twelve. While Mánek ("Fishers of
Men," 138–41) rightly sees a possible connection between "fishers of men" and Jer
16:15–16, he engages in unsubstantiated speculation when he reads into the simple
metaphor of Mark 1:17 the whole Ancient Near Eastern cosmological myth of the
struggle between God and the forces of chaos, death, and the underworld, symbolized by water. Mánek leaps too quickly from the homely metaphor of fishing to the
cosmic myth of God's triumph over the water-monster of chaos; cf. Gundry, *Mark*,
72. For the metaphor of hooks used to catch fish, see Ezek 29:4–5, where Yahweh
puts hooks into the jaws of the crocodile Egypt to draw Egypt up from the Nile with
all the fish of the Nile sticking to Egypt's scales; Yahweh then casts the crocodile into
the desert to perish. Amos 4:2 predicts that, on the day of judgment, the affluent

women of Samaria will be dragged away with fishhooks. Habakkuk 1:14–17 states
that Yahweh has made human beings like the fish of the sea; the wicked person pulls
them up with his hook to devour them. Thus, in the OT, the images of fishing for
human beings or hauling them up with hooks regularly refer to judgment and destruction. For the image of "catching" men (with the root *ṣwd*) in later rabbinic literature, see Str-B, 1. 188; see also Hengel (*The Charismatic Leader*, 76–78) on the lack
of direct parallels to Mark 1:17 in the OT, Qumran, the rabbinic literature, and the
Greek diatribe.

[123] Images of nets, fishing, and fishers in a context of judgment and destruction
occur in 1QH 3:26 (the nets of the wicked were spread out over the face of the waters); and 5:7–8 (using the same words for "fishers" and "hunters" that are found in
Jer 16:16). Otto Betz ("Donnersöhne," 53) thinks that the fishers in the latter text are
the angels executing punishment at the last judgment, but the text is not entirely clear.

[124] As Smith ("Fishers of Men," 187) points out, Mark 1:17 is not a case of an
image that was first applied to Christ and then was transferred secondarily to his followers, since nowhere in the NT is Christ described as a fisherman. This is significant
when one considers how some other descriptions or metaphors applied to Christ
(e.g., shepherd [pastor], teacher, overseer, servant, the one sent [apostle]) are also applied to church leaders. A clear reason for this difference appears when, for example,
one contrasts the images of shepherd and fisherman. As Best points out (*Following
Jesus*, 171–72), at least a shepherd cares for his sheep for some time before using
them for food. In contrast, the first encounter between fish and fisherman is fatal and
final. The only point of fishing (unlike shepherding) is killing and eating the fish—
hence the strangeness of the metaphor Jesus chooses.

[125] Wuellner, *The Meaning of "Fishers of Men,"* 134.

[126] Hengel (*The Charismatic Leader*, 78) suggests that the "fishers of men" logion
might be compared to other paradoxical and provocative sayings of Jesus, such as
"Let the dead bury their dead" (Matt 8:22 par.). This view is much more likely than
Smith's strange assertion ("Fishers of Men," 188) that "the possibility that Jesus . . .
used well-known figures in an entirely new sense seems remote." As Wuellner recognizes (*The Meaning of "Fishers of Men,"* 138–39), such a claim totally misses the
striking and at times shocking originality and creativity of Jesus in his sayings and especially his parables. Likewise questionable is Smith's idea that Jesus used the
metaphor "fishers of men" in basically the same negative or menacing sense as did the
OT and Qumran. In other words, Jesus was commissioning Peter and Andrew to
gather the people for judgment, which Smith seems to understand largely in terms of
condemnation and punishment. This hardly jibes with the overall thrust of Jesus' mission; in view of the coming kingdom of God, he sought to gather and restore Israel
precisely to save it from final condemnation (so rightly Gundry, *Mark*, 72). It is in this
sense that "he who does not gather with me scatters" (Matt 12:30 par.). Those who
refused to be "caught" or gathered into the restored Israel would be subject to judg-

ment in the sense of condemnation. In arguing for the authenticity of Mark 1:17, some might want to invoke as well the criterion of multiple attestation of sources, since Luke 5:10 presents Jesus speaking a variant form of the saying to Simon (= Peter): "Fear not; from now on you [in the singular, addressed only to Peter] will be catching [zōgrōn] men [anthrōpous, i.e., human beings as opposed to fish]." Whether one sees Luke 5:10 as an independent version or as a redactional rewriting of Mark 1:17 depends on one's overall view of the sources and tradition history of the story of the miraculous catch of fish in Luke 5:1–11. Since I think (1) that behind Luke 5:1–11 lies a story of a postresurrection appearance of Jesus (a point seen clearly in the parallel in John 21:1–11) and (2) that the present form of Luke 5:1–11 arises from a retrojection of this story into the public ministry as well as from a rewriting of the story in the light of the call story in Mark 1:16–20, I incline to the view that Luke 5:10 represents a redactional adaptation of Mark 1:17. On this, see A Marginal Jew, 2. 896–904; cf. Fitzmyer, The Gospel According to Luke, 1. 559–64; Agnew, "Vocatio," 137–38. Consequently, I do not appeal to the criterion of multiple attestation in my argument in favor of the authenticity of Mark 1:17. In favor of seeing Luke 5:10 as Lucan redaction of Mark 1:17 is Pesch ("Berufung und Sendung," 5–7), who notes various Lucan stylistic traits; Fitzmyer (ibid., 563), who suggests that Luke's reformulation of the metaphor sought to avoid the disturbing image of fishing for men (with the concomitant idea of killing and eating them) by substituting the verb zōgreō, which means "to capture [someone] alive." Marshall (The Gospel of Luke, 205) points out that zōgreō is used in the LXX in the sense of sparing persons or saving them from death; see, e.g., Num 31:15,18; Deut 20:16. There is no need, therefore, to appeal, as does Hengel (ibid., 76), to a translation variant of the Aramaic word ṣayyād ("hunter" or "fisher") to explain the genesthai halieis of Mark 1:17 and the zōgrōn of Luke 5:10. Even less is there a need to see the summons to Peter in Luke 5:10 as more primitive in the history of the tradition than Mark 1:17, as does Klein, "Die Berufung des Petrus," 11–48. Despite his defense of his approach (pp. 32–35), Klein's analysis is marred by his failure to undertake a detailed analysis of John 21:1–14 in tandem with his initial analysis of Luke 5:1–11. Instead, John 21:1–14 is treated only toward the end of the article, with a resulting failure on Klein's part to understand correctly the interplay between the resurrection-appearance tradition (standing behind John 21:1–14) and the call story of Mark 1:16–20 as Luke (or his special tradition?) creatively meshes them in Luke 5:1–11. Klein also fails to appreciate Luke's redactional hand not only in Luke 5:1–11 but also in his treatment of Peter elsewhere in the Third Gospel.

[127] It may be, however, that in Mark's redactional understanding, the same promise is understood to apply to James and John as well, since they too are fishermen.

[128] This is not to decide the redactional question of how far Mark has rewritten the tradition behind Mark 1:16–20. As usual, Pesch ("Die Berufung und Sendung," 7–8) sees Mark as a conservative redactor who has made only a few additions; Reploh (Markus—Lehrer der Gemeinde, 29–30) allows for a somewhat larger amount of Marcan redaction; see also Best, Following Jesus, 166–68. In my view, no matter

which of these two approaches is taken, the core of the saying in Mark 1:17 and its connection with a tradition about the call of Peter (and Andrew) are prior to Mark's redaction. The details of that call and even its chronological position in Jesus' public ministry (its being placed near the beginning could be due to Marcan redaction) do not affect my basic argument.

[129] On this, see Pesch, "Berufung und Sendung," 21–22.

[130] A similar interpretation is presented by Wuellner, *The Meaning of "Fishers of Men,"* 152.

[131] Needless to say, I am not advocating here Albert Schweitzer's dubious hypothesis (*Geschichte der Leben-Jesu-Forschung* [Siebenstern-Taschenbuch 79/80; 2 vols.; Munich/Hamburg: Siebenstern Taschenbuch, 1966, originally 1906] 2. 402–50) that Jesus expected the kingdom of God to come fully before his disciples finished their mission and that therefore he would not see them again in this present age. Curiously, Schweitzer rested a good part of his theory on the shaky basis of Matt 10:23 ("When they persecute you in one city, flee to the next. For amen I say to you, you shall not have finished [going through] the cities of Israel until [or: before] the Son of Man comes")—a verse whose origin, tradition history, and meaning are among the most difficult to determine in the whole Gospel tradition. In my opinion, Matt 10:23 is a saying not of the historical Jesus but of a Christian prophet; see *A Marginal Jew,* 2. 339–41.

[132] This comes close to the carefully enunciated position of Vögtle, "Exegetische Erwägungen," 617: "Thus, up to the present moment it is not possible to decide whether Jesus sent out specifically the Twelve and only the Twelve or instead a larger circle of disciples. . . ." Similarly, Hahn, "Die Nachfolge Jesu," 29–30.

CHAPTER 27

JESUS IN RELATION TO
HIS FOLLOWERS

The Individual Members of the Twelve

I. THE SEVERE LIMITS OF THIS QUEST

Having said as much as we can about the Twelve as a group in the previous chapter, we are naturally led by our historical curiosity to ask what we can know about various individual members of the group. With the exception of a few persons, the sobering answer is: next to nothing.

Here is a classic lesson in the distinction between ontology and epistemology, between what did exist in the 1st century A.D. and what we can know of it today. That each member of the Twelve lived in the 1st century, that each went through the usual stages of childhood and adulthood, that each had a life-changing encounter with Jesus that resulted in his becoming first a disciple and then one of the Twelve, that each experienced the effects of Jesus' crucifixion and then belief in his resurrection,[1] that each was a significant figure in the Jerusalem church in the early 30s, that, in short, each had an eventful life that would be fascinating to know today—all these assertions are either certain or at least quite probable (with the obvious exception of Judas Iscariot in regard to the time after Jesus' death). But none of these assertions nor all of them together tell us anything specific about the individual members of the Twelve. With the exception of very few of them, the lives of the Twelve, however full and exciting they may have been in the 1st century, have been lost to our ken forever.

However obvious this truth may seem, it must be hammered home because all of our academic desires war against it. In the ancient world, it was the apocryphal Gospels and Acts—imitating and building on the canonical Gospels and Acts of the Apostles—that tried to fill in the gaping holes in our knowledge with popular piety and bizarre imagination (the two sources often overlapping). Today, it is the pressure in academia to discover something new and so make the morning headlines that pushes professors and doctoral students to rummage through the apocryphal literature—Nag Hammadi being a perennial favorite—to come up with the latest find about the Apostle Thomas alias Didymus alias Jude alias Thaddeus, the twin brother of Jesus.

All in vain. If the Coptic *Gospel of Thomas* and the rest of the Nag Hammadi material contain no new reliable information about the historical Jesus—and, in my opinion, they do not[2]—they certainly hold no new revelations about the historical Bartholomew or the historical Jude of James. If we restrict our question to what we can know about the individual members of the Twelve during the public ministry of Jesus, then the answer, apart from a few special cases, must be almost entirely negative. In fact, even if we extend our glance into the early church, the result is still zero, with a few precious exceptions.

To document this inverse insight (i.e., one comes to know that there is nothing further to know), I will examine in turn each member of the Twelve, touching only in passing on the endless pious legends or gnostic fantasies of a later period. Most of the space given to each individual will be taken up with pointing out that later legends yield no historical data for our quest. The little that can be affirmed with some probability usually derives from hypotheses about the meaning of obscure nicknames, patronymics, or places of origin (e.g., Simon the Zealot, Judas Iscariot). In the end, of all the members of the Twelve, only Peter and, to a lesser degree, the sons of Zebedee emerge from the shadow of the group to stand on their own as knowable individuals.

II. SURVEYING THE INDIVIDUAL MEMBERS OF THE TWELVE

1. Bartholomew

To start with the absolute dead ends: Bartholomew is mentioned in all four lists of the Twelve, and nowhere else in the NT. His name is possibly a patronymic, i.e., his name in Aramaic was perhaps *Bar Talmai,* meaning "Son of Tolmi" (cf. LXX Josh 15:14) or "Son of Tholomaeus" (cf. Josephus,

Ant. 20.1.1 §5).[3] Obviously, that tells us nothing. From about the 9th century onwards—notice how relatively late is the tradition—Bartholomew was often identified in Christian thought with Nathanael, who is mentioned only in John's Gospel (1:45–51; 21:2). Unless one adopts the erroneous notion that John's Gospel thought of most disciples as members of the Twelve (hardly a central group for the Fourth Gospel!), there is no basis for such an identification.[4]

2. Jude of James (and Thaddeus)

Jude (or Judas or Judah) of James is even more of an unknown, occurring only in the Lucan lists of the Twelve (Luke 6:16; Acts 1:13). Mostly likely "of James" means "son of James," though "brother" has at times been supplied instead. Of the James (= Jacob) who is Jude's father we know absolutely nothing, except that there is no reason to identify him with any other James in the NT. It is possible, but by no means certain, that Jude of James is to be identified with the "Judas, not the Iscariot" who asks Jesus a question at the Last Supper in John 14:22.[5] Since, in Luke and Acts, Jude of James occupies the slot filled by Thaddeus in the Marcan and Matthean lists, Christian imagination was quick to harmonize and produce a Jude Thaddeus, a conflation that has no basis in reality.

Nor is there any reason to identify Jude of James with Jude the brother of Jesus. John 7:5 notes bitterly that the brothers of Jesus did not believe in him during the public ministry, an impression reinforced independently by the negative picture of Jesus' brothers in Mark 3:21–35. Hence Jude the brother of Jesus was hardly a member of the Twelve. However, it is probably Jude the brother of Jesus, and not Jude of James, who is designated as the author in the opening verse of the Epistle of Jude.[6] In any case, the dividing line between the two Judes became blurred at times in later Christian tradition. Moreover, not unlike Bartholomew, Jude (whichever of the two) sometimes became conflated with other NT notables, including Thomas (e.g., in the opening of the Coptic *Gospel of Thomas*) and Simon the Cananean.[7] On Thomas and Simon, see below.

Once one rejects the identification of Jude of James with Thaddeus, there is nothing to be known or said about the latter—except that, by way of Jude, he too became identified with the ever-popular Thomas.[8] In later piety, "Jude Thaddeus" was hailed as the saint of the impossible, and he continues to fulfill that role by doing the impossible. He forces NT critics to admit: "We do not know."

3. James of Alphaeus

James "of Alphaeus" (probably in the sense of James the son of Alphaeus) always begins the third group of four names in the lists of the Twelve. That is all we know about him. This nescience has not stopped but rather encouraged critics to identify him with all sorts of other NT worthies named James. (When we remember that the English name "James" actually translates "Jacob" in the Greek text, we need not be surprised that there are so many persons called James in the NT.) There are no grounds for identifying James of Alphaeus—as church tradition has done—with James "the Less" (or "the Younger" or "the Small," whatever *tou mikrou* means in Mark 15:40).[9] A more tantalizing suggestion points out that Levi the tax collector is likewise called "the (son) of Alphaeus" in Mark 2:14. It is thus possible, though not provable, that Levi (called to be a disciple) and James (called to be not only a disciple but also one of the Twelve) were brothers. Even if that is so, it tells us nothing further unless we indulge in the uncritical identification of Levi the toll collector with Matthew.

4. Matthew

As I have pointed out a number of times, both the Marcan and the Lucan Gospels distinguish between Levi, a toll collector whom Jesus calls to be a disciple (Mark 2:14 ‖ Luke 5:27), and Matthew, who appears in the lists of the Twelve, who has no description after his name, and about whom nothing else is known (Mark 3:18 ‖ Luke 6:15). It is the Matthean Gospel that creates a cross-reference and identification, first by changing Levi's name to Matthew in the story of Jesus' call of a toll collector (Matt 9:9) and then by adding to Matthew's name in the list of the Twelve the description "the toll collector" (Matt 10:3). Whatever reasons the First Evangelist may have had for his editorial alterations, the change of names is a redactional intervention of a Christian evangelist toward the end of the 1st century and tells us nothing about an original member of the Twelve named Matthew.[10]

5. Philip

Philip presents us with an interesting pattern. In the Synoptics and Acts, he exists as an individual nowhere outside the lists of the Twelve. In contrast, he is one of the more prominent disciples in John's Gospel, usually appearing in the company of Andrew. Philip is probably the unnamed companion of Andrew in the incident in which John the Baptist points out Jesus to two of the Baptist's disciples (John 1:35–40,43–44).[11] If so, Philip along with Andrew is presented as a former disciple of the Baptist who transfers his allegiance to

Jesus. Philip is said to be from Bethsaida, "the city of Andrew and Peter" (1:44)—thus explaining why Philip should be a regular companion of Andrew.[12] Philip and Andrew both play a role in John's version—and only in John's version—of the feeding of the five thousand (6:6–9). Because they both bear Greek rather than Hebrew or Aramaic names, Philip and Andrew stand out in the group of the Twelve. This may explain why some Greek (i.e., non-Jewish) pilgrims, coming to Jerusalem for Passover, approach Philip to ask for an interview with Jesus and why Philip takes along Andrew when he presents the request to Jesus (12:20–22). At the Last Supper, Philip briefly appears as an interlocutor when he says to Jesus (14:8): "Lord, show us the Father, and it is enough for us."

This last passage should warn us that Philip, like everyone else in John's Gospel, can serve as a mouthpiece or symbol of Johannine theology. Philip seems conveniently and strategically placed at key points in the public ministry, appearing with Andrew at its beginning (chap. 1), middle (chap. 6), and end (chap. 12). One cannot help but detect here the deft theological hand of the evangelist. Hence it is difficult to know how much of the special Johannine material about Philip may reach back to reliable information about him circulating in the early church. Since no particular theological points seem to be scored by the assertions that Philip was from Bethsaida and that he was a companion of Andrew, these may be nuggets of historical tradition. Critics have likewise been willing to grant that Philip, along with Andrew and Peter, may well have met Jesus for the first time in the circle of the Baptist's disciples. Given the rivalry between the Johannine Christians and the followers of the Baptist that existed toward the end of the 1st century, the idea that some of Jesus' closest disciples (and by implication Jesus himself) were formerly disciples of the Baptist would be a strange tradition for the Fourth Evangelist to have invented out of thin air.[13]

Even if we accept these points as historical, they tell us very little about Philip as an individual. We know nothing about his activity in the early church. He is not to be identified with the Philip who is one of the seven leaders of the Hellenists (Acts 6:5; 8:4–13,26–40; 21:8–9). Confusion between the two Philips may have begun as early as the Church Father Papias in the 2d century.

6. Andrew

Our treatment of Philip in John's Gospel included the three times he appears with Andrew; hence it is convenient to discuss Andrew here. This may surprise the reader who might have expected Andrew to be treated later on alongside his brother Peter. Strange to say, though, the NT does not place

Andrew in Peter's company on a regular basis.[14] It is Mark who most frequently joins Andrew to Peter, but even in Mark the cases are relatively few. Jesus calls Peter and Andrew together to become "fishers of men" in Mark 1:16–18 ‖ Matt 4:18–20. However, there is no such pairing in Luke's equivalent story of the miraculous catch of fish (5:1–11), where Andrew is notably absent when James and John are designated the partners of Simon (Peter) in Luke 5:10. Mark—and only Mark—also mentions Andrew in the company of Peter, James, and John at the beginning of the healing of Peter's mother-in-law (1:29). With the exception of the list of the names of the Twelve (Mark 3:18), Andrew disappears from the rest of the public ministry in Mark. At the end of the public ministry, Mark brings Andrew back (13:3) in the company of Peter, James, and John at the beginning of Jesus' eschatological discourse in chap. 13, thus creating an *inclusio* with the initial call story.

Apart from a few parallels to Marcan pericopes in Matthew and Luke and the four lists of the Twelve, Andrew figures nowhere else in the Synoptics and Acts. Given the prominence of Peter and John in the early chapters of Acts (cf. Gal 2:9), as well as the account of the martyrdom of James the brother of John in Acts 12:2, it is remarkable that Andrew completely disappears from Acts and hence the history of the early church after his name is listed among the Eleven in Acts 1:13. Thus, unlike the two sons of Zebedee, who are regularly mentioned together, Peter usually appears in the NT without any mention of Andrew. Indeed, except in John's Gospel, Andrew remains practically a cipher.

7. Thomas

Thomas reflects the same curious pattern we observed with Philip (and, to a lesser degree, with Andrew): in the Synoptics, he appears nowhere outside the lists of the Twelve, while he receives some prominence in John's Gospel. Unlike Philip, though, he surfaces relatively late in the Fourth Gospel, almost at the end of the public ministry. He is never mentioned prior to the narrative of the raising of Lazarus in chap. 11. Even then, he appears only in a single verse. In response to Jesus' announcement that, in spite of danger, both master and disciples will return to Judea, Thomas makes the glum and unintentionally ironic remark (11:16): "Let us also go that we may die with him." Thomas then disappears from the narrative, only to resurface at the Last Supper as one of Jesus' interlocutors. In the querulous style that seems proper to Thomas in John's Gospel, Thomas objects to Jesus' puzzling affirmation that the disciples know the way Jesus is going. Thomas protests (14:5): "Lord, we do not know where you are going. How can we know the way?" This provides the perfect "setup" for one of Jesus' great "I am" declarations (14:6): "I am the way and the truth and the life." Thomas disappears again until the narratives of the resurrection appearances. There we meet the famous story of the doubting Thomas, who, having missed the first appearance of the risen Jesus to his disciples, stubbornly demands tactile proof of the resurrection. When the risen Jesus offers him just that, Thomas responds with the climactic christological confession in the Gospel narrative (20:28): "My Lord and my God!" After this theological coup, the passing mention of Thomas in 21:2 is anticlimactic—as is, indeed, a good part of the epilogue in chap. 21.

Even more than is the case with Philip, all the passages in the Fourth Gospel involving Thomas look suspiciously like theological vehicles of the evangelist. Such is the case with 11:16, which literary analysis has shown to be a redactional addition to a primitive story of the raising of Lazarus.[15] That Thomas' interventions act as ironic foils or introductions to Jesus' revelatory statements is especially clear in 14:5. As for the great christological declaration in 20:28, it serves as the capstone of the high christology of preexistence and incarnation characteristic of the Fourth Gospel. By way of *inclusio*, 20:28 soars back to the Prologue of the Gospel, which twice calls the Word "God" (1:1,18). Thus, all of Thomas' appearances in John's Gospel are largely molded if not totally created by the evangelist.

The one intriguing detail that might contain a nugget of historical information about Thomas is embedded in Thomas' name. Three times (11:16; 20:24; 21:2 [final redactor]), the Fourth Gospel translates the Hebrew *(tĕʾôm)* or Aramaic *(tĕʾômāʾ)* word for "Thomas" into its Greek equivalent, *didymos,* which means "twin." In the 1st century A.D., these Hebrew and Aramaic words were common nouns that were not regularly used as personal names; the Greek *didymos,* however, was employed as a proper name.[16] (This helps explain the redundant-sounding references in Christian writings to "Didymus Thomas.") It may be, then, that the Hebrew or Aramaic designation "Thomas" was actually the second name or nickname of a person whose real name we do not know.

Strange to say, despite John's insistence on translating the name three times, we are never told who was Thomas' twin. Christian imagination, stimulated by the triple translation and the puzzling silence, soon remedied the oversight. Becoming a favorite of gnosticizing groups, the enigmatic Thomas, identified with Jude (Judas), was declared to be the twin brother of Jesus himself—a simple enough identification for a religious movement that prized mystical or even pantheistic identification of the saved with the savior. A veritable "school" of Thomas arose in gnosticizing circles, generating a number of books that are highly entertaining but totally devoid of historical data about the member of the Twelve called Thomas.[17] In the end, if we discount Johannine theology and later gnosticizing legends, we know next to nothing about the historical Thomas, to say nothing of his historical twin.

8. Simon

Simon the Cananean (or the Zealot) bears one similarity to Thomas: all that we might know about him is hidden in an enigmatic second name or designation.[18] For Simon the Cananean appears nowhere outside the lists of the Twelve, thus replicating the scarcity of Thomas in the Synoptic Gospels and Acts. Our only hope for learning something about Simon comes from the description of him as *ho Kananaios* (usually translated as "the Cananean") in Mark 3:18 ‖ Matt 10:4 and as *ho zēlōtēs* (usually translated as "the Zealot") in Luke 6:15 ‖ Acts 1:13. Practically all critics agree that Simon "the Cananean" and Simon "the Zealot" are the same person, "Zealot" being a translation into Greek *(zēlōtēs)* of the Aramaic word for "zealous" or "jealous" *(qan'ānā'),* represented by the transliteration "Cananean." This difference in presenting the designation in Greek mirrors quite well the evangelists' usual practice when it comes to Semitic words. Here as elsewhere, Mark and Matthew are not adverse to transliterating an Aramaic word into Greek. As is his wont, Luke avoids the Semitic word attached to Simon's name and supplies instead a translation in Greek, a translation that perhaps already existed in the L tradition of the list of the Twelve.

Doubtless, within the circle of the Twelve, the designation *qan'ānā'* served the practical purpose of distinguishing this Simon from the leader of the group, the other Simon, who also bore a second Aramaic name, *kēpā'* (= Cephas, Peter). But what more precisely did the *qan'ānā'* attached to the name of Simon "the Cananean" originally signify? At times one comes across the affirmation, more often made than argued, that Simon was or had been a member of the Zealots, an organized group of ultranationalist freedom-fighters who took up arms against the occupying forces of Rome. Sometimes this dubious interpretation is then parlayed into the suggestion that Jesus was a Zealot or at least was sympathetic to the Zealot cause, though perhaps without taking up arms himself.[19] Although popular for its "relevance," this position is highly questionable. As scholars like Morton Smith and Shaye Cohen have correctly argued, the organized revolutionary faction that Josephus calls "the Zealots" came into existence only during the First Jewish War, specifically during the winter of A.D. 67–68 in Jerusalem.[20] To make Simon the Cananean a "Zealot" in the narrow sense of a member of this organized group of armed rebels is hopelessly anachronistic.

The evangelists' attribution of the name "Zealot" or "Cananean" to

Simon reflects instead an older and broader use of the term *qanʾānāʾ*: a Jew who was intensely zealous for the practice of the Mosaic Law and insistent that his fellow Jews strictly observe the Law as a means of distinguishing and separating Israel, God's holy people, from the idolatry and immorality practiced by neighboring Gentiles. In the view of such scholars as J.-Alfred Morin, "zealots" in the early 1st century A.D. were Jewish rigorists, prepared to use violence to enforce Israel's separation from the Gentiles. In imitation of Israelite heroes like Phinehas the priest, Elijah the prophet, Jehu the king, and Mattathias the priest, these rigorists punished or even executed Jews who, in their eyes, were unfaithful to the Mosaic Law.[21] Phinehas was perhaps the greatest model for this "zealot" tradition; apart from Simon the Cananean, the only instance in prerabbinic Judaism of an individual Israelite bearing the additional name of "the Zealot" is found in 4 Macc 18:12, where Phinehas is called "the Zealot Phinehas" *(ton zēlōtēn Phinees)*.

While individual zealous defenders of the Law might at times vent their anger at the Gentiles, especially the hated Roman rulers, their "street justice" was aimed primarily against "apostate" Jews. Philo of Alexandria speaks of myriads of Jews who are watchful "zealots of the laws [*zēlōtai nomōn*], pitiless toward those who do anything to annul them" *(De Specialibus Legibus* 2.46 §253). This inward thrust toward other Jews rather than an outward thrust toward Rome would have been especially true in Galilee during the ministry of Jesus, for Galilee was directly ruled not by a Roman governor but by a Jewish prince, the tetrarch Herod Antipas, who was usually clever enough not to offend the religious sensibilities of his Jewish subjects. Moreover, Herod Antipas maintained his own army and imposed his own taxes. Hence, it makes no sense to talk about Galilean zealots at the time of Jesus' ministry taking up arms against the Roman legions occupying their country. Except in times of military crisis, there were no Roman legions in Herod's Galilee for Simon or other supposed "zealots" to oppose.[22]

Actually, one need not suppose that all Jewish "zealots" were self-appointed judges who took the law into their own hands in order to punish "fallen-away" Jews. This idea of vigilante justice is certainly not the only sense of "zeal" or "zealot" found in various NT passages. For example, the high priests and other officials in Jerusalem are said to be "filled with *zēlos*" (here in the sense of "jealousy") when they arrest the apostles (Acts 5:17). Or to take an autobiographical account: twice in his letters (Gal 1:13–14; Phil 3:6), Paul designates himself as "zealous" or as a "zealot" *(zēlōtēs)* in his observance of ancestral Jewish tradition. In each case, the context mentions his persecution of the early church.[23] Luke echoes this theme in his presentation of Paul as well, for the Lucan Paul calls himself "a zealot of God" (Acts 22:3) who persecuted the church (22:19). If Luke's account of Paul's pre-Christian days bears any resemblance to historical reality, Paul's persecution of Christian Jews was in keeping with a legal mandate he had received and was not the vigilante justice of a self-appointed judge (Acts 9:1–2). In any case, it is clear that zealotry in the NT did not always mean armed rebellion against Rome or extralegal street justice. Indeed, it did not always connote violence of any sort. For example, in Acts 21:20, James and the Jerusalem elders inform Paul that many Christian Jews in the Holy City are "zealots of the Law" *(zēlōtai tou nomou)*. In still more general terms, Paul can assert that Jews as a whole have zeal *(zēlon)* for God (Rom 10:2), which hardly means that Jews as a whole are willing to take up arms against fellow Jews or Rome.

But to return to the particular case of Simon the Zealot: in the early 1st century A.D., any pious Jew who was zealous for the strict observance of the Mosaic Law, who publicly harassed nonobservant Jews and tried to coax or bully them back into observance, and who was fiercely opposed to the incursion of pagan-Gentile influence into the life of Palestinian Jews might well merit the accolade of "the Zealot" from his admiring coreligionists. Faced with the various senses of "zeal" and "zealot" in the NT, we cannot be sure precisely how Simon may have manifested his zeal and to what extent his zeal may have involved violence, though we can safely rule out the anachronistic idea that he belonged to the organized group of Zealots described by Josephus.

In a sense, the precise nature of Simon's zealotry is beside the point. What is important for our understanding of the groups around Jesus is that Simon's call to discipleship and then to membership in the Twelve demanded a basic change in his outlook and actions. No doubt this held true, in one way or another, of the rest of the Twelve as well. Still, the change in Simon's case must have been especially jarring. After all, Jesus insisted on hobnobbing with the religious "lowlife" of Palestinian Judaism, "the toll collectors and sinners" (Mark 2:15–17). So regularly and openly did Jesus share table fellowship with them that he was mocked by some stringently observant Jews as "an eater and a drinker, a friend of toll collectors and sinners" (Matt 11:19 par.). Going beyond table fellowship, Jesus called at least one toll collector, Levi, to discipleship (Mark 2:14; cf. Luke 19:1–10), just as he called Simon the Zealot to discipleship.[24]

For toll collectors, sinners, and Simon the Zealot all to be rubbing elbows in Jesus' company tells us something about Jesus and something about his followers. The decidedly "mixed bag" of Jesus' followers mirrors perfectly the Nazarene's outreach and call to *all* Israel, the people of God that was about to be regathered and reconstituted as the twelve tribes of the end time.

There was no room for narrow sectarianism or puritanical exclusivity in this eschatological outreach. Jesus' inclusive call to community correspondingly demanded a new attitude on the part of those who accepted his call: Simon would have to accept the former toll collector Levi as a fellow disciple just as much as Levi and company would have to learn to live with Simon. The kingdom-proclamation of Jesus, which sought to embrace all of Israel, had no room for the separatism of 1st-century Qumran—or, for that matter, for the divisiveness of some forms of 20th-century liberation theology. In the end, Simon's designation as "the Zealot" and Simon's presence in the Twelve indicate just the opposite of what the purveyors of Jesus the violent revolutionary or freedom-fighter would have us think. Jesus sought not a sectarian war that would pit Jew against Jew or against anyone else. He sought to bring all Israel together in preparation for the final coming of God as king. It was for this eschatological cause that Simon the Zealot, like the rest of the Twelve, had to learn to be zealous.

9. Judas Iscariot

Judas Iscariot has already been treated in the previous chapter, since his tragic fate serves the positive function of helping to establish the existence of the Twelve before Easter. Down through the ages, Judas has been a magnet for the artistic imagination of Christians. Literature and the pictorial arts have expanded his story and personality to such huge proportions that it is difficult to remind even critical readers that we know only two basic facts about him: (1) Jesus chose him as one of the Twelve, and (2) he handed over Jesus to the Jerusalem authorities, thus precipitating Jesus' execution. These two starkly contrasting facts are the colliding flints that have set ablaze Christian fantasy ever since.[25]

Actually, we can see the midrashic expansion of the basic facts already beginning in the Gospel treatments of Judas. To take but one example: stark, dark, laconic Mark gives us no motive for Judas' act of betrayal. Money is mentioned and given to Judas only after he spontaneously makes the offer to hand over Jesus to the high priests (Mark 14:10–11). As usual, Matthew is not satisfied with Mark's enigmatic narrative that leaves so many questions unanswered. Here as elsewhere in his redaction of Mark, Matthew clarifies by introducing motive (26:15): Judas initiates his offer to betray Jesus with the question, "What are you willing to give me?" Matthew thus makes everything clear: Judas was avaricious; he betrayed Jesus for money.

The motive of greed is developed in a somewhat different way in the Johannine tradition. Only in John's Gospel is Judas identified as the person who objects to the anointing of Jesus with costly myrrh at Bethany (John

12:1–8 parr.; see vv 4–5): "Judas Iscariot, one of his disciples, the one who was about to hand him over, said: 'Why was this myrrh not sold for 300 denarii, and [the money] given to the poor?' " With a typical Johannine aside, the author turns to his audience to explain in v 6: "Now he [Judas] said this not because he was concerned about the poor, but because he was a thief. Being in charge of the [common] money box, he used to filch what was put into it." For John, Judas wasn't simply a greedy traitor; he was first a greedy thief. To hammer the point home, the Fourth Evangelist repeats the detail of Judas being the disciples' "treasurer" at the moment when Judas leaves the Last Supper to betray Jesus (13:28–30).

On the question of motivation, Luke takes a different tack, one also found in the Johannine tradition. In the story of Judas' going to the high priests to plan the betrayal, Luke, unlike Matthew, keeps the mention of money where Mark put it, after Judas' offer to betray Jesus (Luke 22:4–5 ‖ Mark 14:10–11). For Luke, Judas' motivation is demonic rather than human; it stems from Satanic influence rather than from base greed. Accordingly, the Lucan pericope begins (22:3): "Satan had entered into Judas. . . . And going away, he [Judas] conferred with the high priests. . . . "[26] In supplying this motivation, Luke may be drawing upon some special tradition, for the same motivation appears independently in John's Gospel alongside the more mundane explanation that Judas was a thief (John 13:2,27 [almost the exact words of Luke 22:3]; cf. 6:70–71). The Matthean motive of greed and the Lucan motive of demonic possession thus become intertwined in John.

In recent decades, modern writers imbued with a sense of civil rights and social justice have protested against this demonizing of Judas. Not content with this exegetical exorcism, some have even sought to rehabilitate him as a poor, misunderstood disciple. While one must applaud the authors' Christian charity, one must remain critically aware of the fact that painting Judas in glowing colors is just as much an exercise of artistic imagination as painting him in sinister ones.[27] The two bare facts enunciated above are almost all that we know about the historical Judas. Beyond them lies theological speculation or novel writing, with the dividing line between the two activities not always clear-cut.

As with a number of other members of the Twelve (Didymus Thomas, Simon the Cananean, Simon Peter), one of the few clues we have for Judas' background or personal history is his second name or nickname: Iscariot(h). As with Simon the Cananean, the second name Iscariot probably served the practical function of distinguishing Judas from other well-known persons called Judas or Jude (e.g., Jude of James and Jude the brother of Jesus). The exact meaning or etymology of Iscariot is lost to us now; perhaps it was already lost to the evangelists.[28] There is no greater proof of our ignorance than the seemingly endless string of interpretations offered. While a discussion of all the interpretations ever given "Iscariot" would fill a book, the following are among the ones most frequently cited:[29]

(a) Judas was a member of the *sicarii*, i.e., Jewish terrorists who used daggers to assassinate political enemies. Sometimes this dubious identification is further extended to make Judas a Zealot, though identifying Zealots and *sicarii* is a historical blunder that should have long since been laid to rest. Not only is the derivation of Iscariot from the Latin word *sicarius* dubious on philological grounds; more to the point, many historians claim that the *sicarii* arose as an identifiable group only in the 40s or 50s of the 1st century A.D., too late for Judas' betrayal of Jesus (ca. A.D. 30). Moreover, if Judas had been a *sicarius*, one would have expected him to assassinate Jesus by stabbing him while the latter was in a crowd—the approved method among *sicarii*–and not to have handed him over to the supposedly hated authorities.

(b) Iscariot has been derived from the Semitic root *šqr* ("to lie," "to be false") and indicates that Judas is "the man of lies" or "the liar" par excellence. One problem here is that Judas is not presented in the NT as someone who is habitually lying; to hand a person over to his enemies does not necessarily involve lying to him.

(c) Judas is regularly referred to in the NT as the one who "handed over" Jesus to the authorities; hence Iscariot may be derived from the Semitic root *skr* (or *sgr*), which in the pi'el or hip'îl forms of the verb can mean "hand over." Once again, it is questionable whether one can get from this Semitic verb to the name "Iscariot." One would also have to explain the strange redundancy of passages like Mark 3:19: "Judas Iscariot, the very one who [*hos kai*] handed him over." Mark, after all, seems to know how to translate Hebrew and Aramaic words into Greek; and he uses a different set of words to indicate such translations (e.g., *ho estin* in 3:17).

(d) Others connect Iscariot with a Semitic word describing Judas' former work: he was a red dyer according to some, a fruit grower according to others. Some have even suggested that the word means that Judas had red hair or a ruddy complexion. Even if any of these etymologies were correct—a highly questionable point—it would be of no help to the historian seeking to probe the life or motivation of Judas.

(e) Perhaps the most popular view is that "Iscariot" refers to Judas' place of origin. If Judas was from the town of Kerioth in Judea (see Josh 15:25), he would be in Hebrew "a man from Kerioth," *'îš qĕriyyôt*, whence "Iscariot." Some critics who support this solution draw a further intriguing implication from the location of the town. If Kerioth was in fact a town in Judea, the designation "Iscariot" would make Judas the only member of the Twelve who clearly came from Judea rather than Galilee—an outsider in the circle of the Twelve. Some scholars press the point still further by emphasizing that Judas' name in Hebrew *(Yĕhûdâ)* fits in perfectly with his supposed place of origin (Judea, i.e., OT Judah [*Yĕhûdâ*]). This last argument is weak, since we are hardly to suppose that every Jew named Judas came from Judea. To take but one example: Jude (= Judas), the brother of Jesus, was presumably born in Nazareth of Galilee. All these suggestions may be beside the point, though, since it is by no means certain a town called Kerioth ever existed in Judea.[30]

Accordingly, other scholars put forward the names of towns that certainly did exist, e.g., Askar near Shechem, Jericho, or Kartah in Zebulun. Still others, relying upon the usage of later targums, take Iscariot to mean "the man from the city," i.e., Jerusalem. Thus, while deriving Iscariot from a place-name is a common solution, the designated place is as disputed as the name Iscariot. In addition, all of these suggestions suffer from philological objections.

One minor point, however, favors the theory that "Iscariot" does refer to some place-name. Three times in John's Gospel (6:71; 13:2,26), Judas is apparently called not "Judas Iscariot" but rather "Judas [son] of Simon Iscariot."[31] John is presenting here a tradition independent of the Synoptics, who never identify Judas' father. If Judas' father likewise bore the name Iscariot, many interpretations (e.g., "man of lies," "the one who handed [Jesus] over") fall by the wayside, since they refer only to Judas' actions. While a reference to a trade would still be a possibility, since Judas might have taken up the trade of his father, the most likely explanation why both father and son should bear the same name Iscariot would be that it designated the town from which both came. That does not get us very far since, as we have seen, a number of towns vie for the dubious honor, with no clear winner.

In the end, all these subtle theories of etymology lack solid proof, and so "Iscariot" tells us even less than "Didymus" or "Cananean." The nickname, like the person, remains an enigma.

We are now left with the three members of the Twelve who are presented in the Synoptics as the innermost circle around Jesus: Peter, James, and John. Whether this circle of three reflects historical reality or Mark's theology of the "messianic secret," which envelops various events during Jesus' ministry in an aura of mystery, is difficult to say. According to Mark, the innermost three were privileged to witness Jesus' raising of the daughter of Jairus (Mark 5:37) and his transfiguration (Mark 9:2). They were also chosen by Jesus to be with him during his prayer in Gethsemane (Mark 14:33), but failed to do so, falling asleep instead.

The problem is that, apart from Mark, we have no independent attestation in the NT of this special, separate group of three disciples within the circle of the Twelve. The group of three appears nowhere in John's Gospel nor, for that matter, anywhere else in the NT outside of the Synoptics. In my opinion, Matthew and Luke do not present the threesome in any scenes that are independent of Mark. In fact, Matthew drops the three in his retelling of the raising of the daughter of Jairus (Matt 9:23–26), and Luke does not single them out in his version of the prayer in Gethsemane (Luke 22:39–46). Luke does present Peter as a partner with James and John in the story of the miraculous catch of fish (Luke 5:10), but this configuration may arise from Luke's meshing of the Marcan story of the call of the first disciples (Mark 1:16–20) with a story that originally referred to a resurrection appearance (cf. John 21:1–14).[32] If this is the case, Luke 5:10 does not represent independent attestation of the group of three. In any event, the Lucan passage refers to the relationship of the three before their call to follow Jesus, not to their special place within the Twelve.

Moreover, the group of three is not Mark's only subgroup within the Twelve. As we have already seen, Mark deftly frames the public ministry with stories about the first four disciples: Peter, Andrew, James, and John. Their presence in 1:16–20 (their call) and 1:29 (the healing of Peter's mother-in-law) is neatly balanced by their presence in 13:2, where they serve as the esoteric audience of Jesus' eschatological discourse in chap. 13. In light of all these convenient configurations in Mark's Gospel, one must be wary of treating a special group of three—or four—as a historical phenomenon. While there is no way of proving the point, the group of three may be a creation of Mark's redactional activity.[33] In any case, not much hangs on its existence. Let us move on to the individual members of the group.

10. James

James and John are said by Mark to be the sons of Zebedee, and there is no particular reason to doubt the designation. Granted, the various Matthean and Lucan passages that speak of the "sons of Zebedee" are probably all derived directly or indirectly from Mark. We do, however, have multiple attestation for "the [sons] of Zebedee," since they are mentioned—but neither numbered nor named—by the final redactor of the Fourth Gospel in John 21:2. More to the point, the fact that James and John are the sons of Zebedee is neither exploited for some theological purpose nor expanded by legendary accretions within the NT. Hence, merely from a commonsense point of view, there is no reason to question the historicity of the relationship.

It is easier to treat James first, for a simple reason: if we leave the material that touches both brothers to our treatment of John, there is next to nothing to say about James, since he is never mentioned in the NT without a reference to his brother. This holds true even of the one passage in the NT where James, alone among the Twelve, receives a dubious distinction: he is martyred by Herod Agrippa I ca. A.D. 44 (Acts 12:1–2), thus apparently fulfilling a prophecy attributed to Jesus in Mark 10:39. As far as we know, James was the first of the Twelve to be killed for his faith.[34] In fact, he is the only member of the Twelve whose martyrdom is explicitly recounted in the NT, though John 21:18–19 probably refers indirectly to the martyrdom of Peter. Indeed, apart from James and Peter, there is no solid proof that any members of the Twelve were martyred. Later Christian tradition, but not the NT, dubbed this James "the Great(er)" to distinguish him from the other persons named James in the NT, especially the "James the Less" (literally, "James the Small") mentioned in Mark 15:40.[35] Not until the 6th or 7th century did legend connect James the Greater (= Santiago) with mission work in Spain.

11. John

While there has been confusion in Christian tradition and even in scholarship over the various persons called James in the NT, the conflation of and confusion among various historical figures reach a high point when we come to John the son of Zebedee. Many NT scholars today would distinguish five different persons, most, if not all, of whom were collapsed into John the son of Zebedee by Christian tradition. The five distinct figures—whom the NT never conflates—are (1) John the son of Zebedee, (2) the anonymous "disciple whom Jesus loved" in the Fourth Gospel (identified by modern critics with everyone from Lazarus to Matthias), (3) the anonymous author of the Fourth Gospel, (4) the anonymous author of the three Epistles that bear the name of John, and (5) the apocalyptic seer who wrote the Book of Revelation and who does call himself John.[36] In what follows, I restrict myself to what can be stated with fair probability about John the son of Zebedee during the public ministry, with a quick glance at the early days of the church. I will pass over briefly what has already been noted in reference to the special group of four or three within the Twelve.

Mark presents James and John being called by Jesus while they are mending or arranging the nets in the boat of their father Zebedee (1:18–20). Since hired workers are also mentioned, Mark's picture is one of a relatively prosperous family fishing business on the Sea of Galilee. Luke instead presents James and John not as workers for their father but rather as business partners with Simon Peter (their fishing activities are not connected in this way in Mark 1:16–20). Luke's picture may result from a redactional meshing of

Mark 1:16–20 with a traditional resurrection story about a miraculous catch of fish (cf. John 21:1–14). In any event, neither the Marcan nor the Lucan tradition presents the sons of Zebedee as desperately poor. It is well to remember that the fishing business on the Sea of Galilee was a lively and prosperous one, at least for those who owned or oversaw the operations.[37] The romantic idea of Jesus calling only the impoverished to discipleship finds no confirmation in the sons of Zebedee—nor, for that matter, in Peter with his house and family in Capernaum, nor in Levi the toll collector at Capernaum.

In the Synoptics (as opposed to Acts), the lists of the Twelve always put James before his brother John. Some sort of priority is also implied by the way in which James at times is first identified as "the son of Zebedee" and then John is identified as the brother of James (Mark 1:19 ‖ Matt 4:21; Mark 3:17 ‖ Matt 10:2; cf. Matt 17:1). Many critics draw the conclusion that James was the elder brother. While this may well be true, other explanations are possible: e.g., special reverence among early Christians for James, the first of the Twelve to be martyred.[38] In any case, all four lists of the Twelve place James and John in the first group of four names, a testimony to their importance to the early church that is confirmed in Acts and (in the case of John) Galatians.

The important status—or perhaps some character trait—of James and John is also indicated, according to Mark 3:17, by the peculiar name Jesus gives them: *Boanērges,* which Mark translates as "sons of thunder." In this, the two brothers parallel Simon, who likewise receives a name from Jesus (*Petros,* Peter = "stone" or "rock"); in neither case does Mark explain what prompted Jesus to confer the name, title, or description. In fact, Mark never indicates—unlike the Gospels of Matthew and John in dealing with "Peter"—when these names were conferred. That the name *Boanērges* did actually come from Jesus, and was not an invention of the early church, may be indicated by the fact that Matthew and Luke do not take over the name and that the rest of the NT shows no interest in or even knowledge of such a designation for the sons of Zebedee.

As R. Alan Culpepper points out, one must distinguish two questions here:[39] (1) What is the etymology and meaning (scientific or popular) of *Boanērges?* (2) What is meant by the translation Mark gives the name, i.e., "sons of thunder" (whether or not that is the etymologically correct meaning)? The first question has produced a lengthy list of learned hypotheses. If Mark is at all correct in his translation, the first part of the word, *boanē-* must represent the Hebrew or Aramaic *bĕnê,* "sons of." All sorts of explanations have been offered as to why the straightforward *bĕnê* has been rendered in Greek by the awkward *boanē,* but no theory is totally satisfactory.[40]

As for the second half of the word, *-rges,* a number of Semitic roots have been suggested: *rgš* ("commotion," "tumult"), *rgz* ("anger," "hot temper," "agitation," "excitement"), *rʿš* ("to quake," "to shake"), *rʿm* ("thunder"). Some critics, however, throw up their hands in despair, asserting that Mark's transliteration is hopelessly corrupt and his interpretation hopelessly wrong, and so the original meaning has been lost.[41]

If we do not give in to despair but instead put the components of the first and second halves of *Boanērges* together, a number of possible interpretations arise, e.g., "sons of the quaking (heavens)" or "those with a loud voice." Most popular, however, remains the view that Mark is basically correct in his interpretation—however garbled his transliteration may be—and that the true meaning is "sons of thunder."

All this, however, only shifts the problem to our second question, namely, what did Mark (or originally Jesus) mean by the name, "sons of thunder"? Again, suggestions are legion: the brothers spoke with a loud voice; or, being disciples of the Baptist, they witnessed the voice from heaven, spoken in thunder, at Jesus' baptism. More common is a psychological interpretation: James and John were impetuous, hot-tempered, or even (in the broad sense of the word) Zealots. This last named opinion has been championed by noted scholars like Otto Betz,[42] but the obvious question remains: if James and John were Zealots, why was the clear label *Kananaios* or *Zēlōtēs* not applied to them in Mark 3:17 parr. as it was applied to Simon the Cananean (or Zealot) in 3:18 parr.?

Zealots aside, there seems to be some basis in three Synoptic stories (Mark 9:38–39 par.; Luke 9:52–56; Mark 10:35–40 par.) for the claim that James and/or John was impetuous and hot-tempered.

In Mark 9:38, John reports to Jesus that someone who "does not follow us" is performing exorcisms in Jesus' name and hence "we forbade him" to do so. Jesus responds with openhearted liberality (v 39): "Stop forbidding him; for there is no one who can perform a miracle in my name and be able immediately to speak evil against me." A number of exegetes find either the strikingly unique role of John as a spokesman for the Twelve or the inclusive approach of Jesus a good argument for the basic historicity of this apophthegm. However, (1) the description of this independent exorcist as someone "who does not follow *us*" (rather than "you," i.e., Jesus); (2) the idea of competing persons or groups performing religious actions "in the name" of Jesus (cf. Acts 2:38; 3:6,16; 4:10,18,30; 5:28,40–41; cf. 1 Cor 1:13,15; 5:4); (3) the allied story of the sons of Sceva in Acts 19:11–17, which revolves around the question of who has the right to perform exorcisms in the name of Jesus; and (4) the scriptural echoes from Num 11:24–29 all make this story sound suspiciously like a creation of the early church.[43]

Another story, found only in Luke (9:52–56), recounts how a particular

Samaritan village refused to receive Jesus hospitably as he journeyed up to Jerusalem for his final Passover. James and John officiously ask Jesus: "Lord, do you want us to command fire to come down from heaven and destroy them?" Jesus, however, rebukes their Elijah-like zeal and goes off to another town. One cannot dismiss this story out of hand, since it fits in well with what we have seen in Volume Two of *A Marginal Jew*. Jesus consciously presented himself to his disciples as the miracle-working, Elijah-like prophet of the end time. In keeping with this conception, two of Jesus' disciples naturally, if somewhat impetuously and self-importantly, ask whether they should act in the manner of Elijah, who twice commanded fire to come down from heaven to consume soldiers who had been sent by the king to arrest him (2 Kgs 1:9–12). Jesus' rebuke would be aimed at both the disciples' presumption and their misunderstanding of the saving thrust of his mission to Israel.

However, while historically possible, the story in Luke 9:52–56 bears many traits of Lucan redactional theology: the great journey of Jesus to Jerusalem for the final Passover, the Lucan interest in the Samaritans, a christology that portrays Jesus as the prophet who performs the works of Elijah but who is greater than Elijah, Jesus' teaching on non-retaliation, his readiness to forgive enemies "who know not what they do," the proper understanding of discipleship, and the universality of salvation.[44] Moreover, the precise clause that mentions James and John as the speakers is somewhat awkward in the Greek (v 54a). Literally, it reads: "But seeing, the disciples James and John said. . . ." Nowhere else in the Gospels or Acts are James and John introduced in a pericope with the bare title "the disciples." This awkwardness leads Culpepper, along with many other scholars, to suggest that the proper names "James and John" were added secondarily to a story that originally spoke of "the disciples" in general.[45] For all these reasons, I am leery of using this story to establish particular character traits of the historical James and John.

A final story that is often cited to explain the name "sons of thunder" is the request of James and John that Jesus give them the coveted seats at his right and left when he begins his reign (Mark 10:35–40 par.). Bultmann inclines to the view that the whole story comes, in various stages, from the early church; but I think that there are reasons for holding that the core of the narrative stems from an encounter between the historical Jesus and the sons of Zebedee.[46]

(a) While it is true that Mark seems to go out of his way to present the disciples in a bad light, James the son of Zebedee poses a special case. James was the first of the Twelve—as far as we know—to suffer martyrdom (at the hands of Herod Agrippa I ca. A.D. 44; cf. Acts 12:2). Are we to suppose that the early church—and even Bultmann views the core of the tradition as pre-Marcan—went out of its way to invent a negative picture of the protomartyr of the Twelve? Did early church tradition even before Mark revel in presenting notable disciples in a bad light?

(b) Then, too, the picture of Jesus in this story is a strange one if it is simply the product of a church that is trying to proclaim and win converts for Jesus the Messiah and risen Lord. In the larger context of Mark 10, Jesus has just displayed for the third time his foreknowledge by prophesying in amazing detail the events of his passion, death, and resurrection (Mark 10:32–34). With his love of stark contrasts, Mark immediately introduces the two uncomprehending brothers, who plan to ask for privileged places at Jesus' right and left when his rule over Israel begins.[47] At first, the ambitious brothers cagily hide their precise intention and try to have Jesus grant them a spiritual blank check: "Teacher, we want you to do for us whatever we ask you to do" (10:35). Jesus refuses to give the blank check; instead he must ask: "What do you want me to do for you?" The all-knowing prophet does not know what these two members of his own inner group are up to and must ask them to explain.

The power and status of Jesus become even more problematic at the end of the exchange, when Jesus explains why he cannot guarantee what they request: "As for sitting on my right or left, that is not mine to give; but [it is to be given] to those for whom it has been prepared [namely, by God]."[48] The emphasis on Jesus' lack of knowledge and power in this pericope is striking.

(c) Equally striking for a church facing persecution and possible martyrdom is Jesus' refusal to promise any reward to those who suffer for him. On the one hand, this runs remarkably contrary to promises of reward supposedly made by Jesus elsewhere in the Gospels, including just a few verses previous in Mark 10:29–30. On the other hand, it is hard to imagine that the early church thought that Jesus' refusal to promise a reward in 10:39–40 was an effective exhortation to suffering. Did the church actually think that inventing a story in which Jesus refuses to promise prominent disciples a reward for their sufferings would encourage latter-day followers to suffer for Christ? This is strange religious propaganda on the part of a church seeking converts and struggling to stiffen the resolve of its beleaguered members.

(d) Nothing in the theological atmosphere of this pericope is specifically Christian. While elsewhere in his Gospel Mark presents Jesus predicting in detail his death, resurrection, and coming on the clouds of heaven at the end of the present age as the Son of Man, the request of James and John in regard to the future is expressed with surprising vagueness. They wish to sit at Jesus' right and left "in your glory." What this sitting refers to is unclear. Some critics think in terms of the messianic banquet; but the usual terminolcgy of the Gospels for banquets is reclining at table *(anakeimai, anaklinomai, katakeimai, kataklinomai, anapiptō)*, not sitting *(kathizō, kathēmai)*.[49] The imagery may instead suggest sitting on thrones, sharing in Jesus' function of ruling or judging Israel. If, as I have argued above, Jesus did promise the Twelve that they would sit on twelve thrones, judging the twelve tribes of Israel (Matt 19:28 par.), the request of James and John for the thrones closest to Jesus would cohere perfectly with his promise. Their petition touches not on some future reward open to all believers but on the privilege proper to the Twelve.

In true rabbinic fashion, Jesus parries their request with a question (10:38): "Are you able to drink the cup of which I am drinking, or be baptized with the baptism with which I am being baptized?" This puzzling imagery is a far cry from the detailed, point-by-point summary of the passion in 10:33–34; rather, it coheres perfectly with the enigmatic, parabolic speech of Jesus. In the OT and intertestamental Judaism, the cup is an ambiguous image. It symbolizes the destiny one is to undergo, the cup that God gives the individual or the nation to drink.[50] But whether that destiny is one of joy or sorrow or even death has to be determined from the context.

The second image, the surprising symbol of "baptism," helps specify the nature of the cup. "Baptism" in this saying hardly points to Christian influence. To begin with, both John the Baptist and Jesus practiced baptism as a Jewish rite before Christians came on the scene and appropriated the ritual. More to the point, we must remember that the Hebrew, Aramaic, and Greek verbs for "to baptize" (Hebrew *ṭābal*, Aramaic *ṭĕbal*, Greek *baptizō*) originally meant simply "to dip or immerse in water." Throughout the OT, the imagery of being engulfed by flood waters or of being immersed in water conjures up the idea of dire perils, fierce suffering, or imminent danger of death.[51]

The cup of Mark 10:38 thus receives a more precise and negative connotation by being joined to the image of baptism. It is a cup full of suffering. Jesus is asking James and John, who are so eager to share his power, whether they have the strength to share the fierce sufferings that may engulf Jesus like a flood. It is, however, only in the larger context of Mark 10 and later Christian history that these nebulous images can be referred specifically to Jesus' cross and to the disciples' martyrdom. Taken in isolation, the symbols in Jesus' question in 10:38 remain indeterminate. Jesus asks the brothers whether they are ready to share whatever suffering Jesus may have to undergo to fulfill his mission. What that suffering may be and whether it will involve a violent death at the hands of his enemies is never stated. Indeed, coming right after the third and most detailed passion prediction (10:33–34), v 38 is surprising in its vagueness.

(e) In this pericope (10:35–40), Jesus' lack of knowledge and power is paralleled by the absence of any christological designation or title. This absence is glaring because the pericope is surrounded by two weighty Son of Man sayings: the third prediction of the Son of Man's passion (10:33–34) and the assertion that the Son of Man will give his life as a ransom for many (10:45). All in all, then, the exchange between the sons of Zebedee and Jesus in 10:35–40 is remarkably lacking in Christian traits and coheres quite well with what we know of the historical Jesus and of his relationship with the Twelve. In particular, it coheres with the sayings of Jesus examined in chap. 25, in which he made exposure to danger and suffering an essential part of being one of his disciples.

(f) Finally, the criterion of embarrassment may also come into play insofar as Jesus' prophecy that James and John would both drink of Jesus' cup and be baptized with Jesus' baptism may not have been completely fulfilled. The natural sense of the passage is that Jesus is speaking to both brothers of a fate that awaits the two of them equally, a fate that will mirror his own. However, while James was soon martyred for his faith (ca. A.D. 44; cf. Acts 12:2), to that extent sharing the fate of Jesus, we have no firm proof that John ever suffered martyrdom or even some persecution aimed specifically and solely at him. This must be stressed in the face of later patristic legends—legends perhaps arising out of a desire to see Mark 10:35–40 completely fulfilled—that invented a martyrdom for John as well.[52] Apart from the suffering John endured with other members of the Twelve (Acts 4:1–31; 5:17–42), nothing is recorded by any 1st-century or early 2d-century writer about a specific persecution that John alone underwent, to say nothing of a martyr's death.

In this, John differs notably not only from his brother James but also from Stephen, Peter, Paul, and James the brother of Jesus.[53] If John had been martyred, the silence about his fate compared to that of the other great leaders of the 1st-century church is difficult to explain, as is the rise of the later patristic legend about John's dying a natural death in his old age. In my opinion, the silence about John is best explained by the supposition that he did not suffer martyrdom or any special persecution. In fact, all we can say of John the son of Zebedee after Easter is that he remained in Jerusalem in the company of the Twelve in the early days of the church (Acts 1:13), was active with Peter in Jerusalem as well as in Samaria (Acts 3:1,3–4,11; 4:13,19; 8:14,17) and that, along with James (the brother of Jesus) and Peter he was considered a leader ("pillar") of the Jerusalem community as late as the "Jerusalem Council" held ca. A.D. 49 (Gal 2:9).[54] After that, we must admit total ignorance of John's life and fate.

However, we may accept as historical the bare fact of John's activity in the Jerusalem church after Easter and his association in particular with Peter. This much is supported by the multiple attestation of the stories in Acts plus Paul's rather different narrative of his dealings with the Jerusalem church in Gal 2:9. If John was reputed to be one of the "pillars" of the Jerusalem church along with James and Cephas (= Peter), then he must have been a significant leader in the life of the Jerusalem church, alongside James and Peter, in the years prior to the Jerusalem council of which Paul speaks in Galatians 2. This is precisely what the early chapters of Acts indicate. Moreover, in Acts, John is simply the "sidekick" of Peter, having no voice or function of his own. Why Luke or his tradition would have bothered to invent the role of John (instead of, say, Peter's brother Andrew) as Peter's silent and otiose partner if there had been no basis for this in historical reality is hard to say.

As best we can tell, then, Jesus' prophecy was not fulfilled with respect to John as it was to James; and so the criterion of embarrassment may be invoked in support of the basic historicity of the exchange in Mark 10:35–40.[55] If one grants the historicity of this pericope, it is significant not only for our knowledge of individual members of the Twelve and their relation to Jesus but also for Jesus' view of the possibility of persecution and violence against himself, a topic we must address in a later chapter.

To return to our consideration of *Boanērges:* our study of the three passages that are often cited to explain the term has had a largely negative result. Contrary to claims commonly made, it is doubtful that the name is best explained psychologically as referring to the impetuous religious zeal of the sons of Zebedee. The best supports for such a view of the two brothers, Mark 9:38–39 and Luke 9:52–56, are of doubtful historicity. The one passage with a good claim to historicity, Mark 10:35–40, witnesses not to the brothers' fiery religious zeal but to their blind ambition. In the end, one must wonder whether Mark or the early church knew the original reason why Jesus conferred the name *Boanērges* on the brothers. After all, Mark, while translating the term, makes no attempt to explain it, and Matthew and Luke both drop it.

Faced with this exegetical dead end, one may wish to consider the intriguing alternative that Culpepper offers.[56] He thinks that, instead of interpreting the name in a negative, psychological sense referring to the character or temperament of the brothers, we should remember the OT tradition of name-giving as a way of uttering a promise or conferring a task. Possibly Jesus called the brothers "sons of thunder" because he realized or wished to foster their potential as thundering witnesses for his proclamation of the kingdom. This would fit in neatly with my opinion that Jesus did in fact send the Twelve out on mission to proclaim the kingdom. But are we to suppose that James and John were so superior to the rest of the Twelve in their powerful proclamation that Jesus singled them out with this name? In the last analysis, we must admit that we are left with mere conjecture.

12. Peter

On the evangelical principle that the first shall be last, Peter, who is always mentioned first in the four lists of the Twelve, comes last in our survey. A more secular reason for keeping him to the end is the large number and difficult nature of the NT passages in which he appears. He is the most frequently mentioned, the most actively engaged, and hence the most prominent of the Twelve.[57]

Countless monographs and articles have been written on Peter in the NT, and so our first problem is how to limit our thumbnail sketch of Peter to the essentials. Since our study is focused on the relation of the historical Jesus to the historical Peter, the following restrictions apply:

(a) We are concerned with Peter only during the public ministry of Jesus. His later career in the early church will be mentioned only briefly, lest subsequent events be read back into Jesus' ministry.

(b) Within the time frame of the public ministry, we are concerned with Peter as a historical figure. The evangelists' use of him as a theological symbol, positive or negative, is not our concern.[58]

(c) Alone among the Twelve, Peter remains a source of fierce theological conflict down to our own day because of debates about the papacy that have arisen between Roman Catholics on the one side and Eastern Orthodox and Protestant Christians on the other. These conflicts are the proper domain of church history and Christian theology. They have no place in a historical investigation of how one 1st-century Palestinian Jew named Jesus related to another 1st-century Palestinian Jew named Simon, alias Peter.

(d) Gospel narratives that I have already studied and judged to be creations of the early church will not be examined here again. For example, in Volume Two of A Marginal Jew, a lengthy treatment of the story of Jesus' walking on the water concluded that neither the Marcan nor the Johannine version of Jesus' walking on the water goes back to an event in the life of the historical Jesus. A fortiori, the story of Peter walking on the water (Matt 14:28–32), which Matthew adds to the Marcan narrative, does not belong in a sketch of the historical Peter. For similar reasons, stories such as the miraculous catch of fish, the cursing of the barren fig tree, the paying of the temple tax, and the healing of Simon's mother-in-law will not be mentioned.[59] By the same token, I will not repeat here my arguments in favor of material already judged to be historical.

A brief sketch of the historical Peter would include the following items:[60] A Palestinian Jew known to us by the Greek name Simon (the equivalent Hebrew name being *Šimʿôn,* Symeon in Greek transliteration)[61] was a fisherman with a wife, family, and home in Capernaum, a Jewish town on the northwest coast of the Sea of Galilee.[62] Somewhere around the year A.D. 28 or 29 he was called by Jesus to become one of his disciples. This call is portrayed in three different ways:[63] (a) In Mark 1:16–20, Simon, engaged in his ordinary work on the Sea of Galilee, is called along with his brother Andrew and just before James and John. (b) In Luke 5:1–11, after a miraculous catch of fish on the Sea of Galilee, Simon is called in his boat along with his fishing partners James and John. (c) In John 1:35–42, Andrew and Philip, disciples of the Baptist, are directed to Jesus by the Baptist, apparently near the Jordan River; Andrew then brings Simon to meet Jesus.[64]

Significantly, in all these versions, Simon (soon to be named Peter) is never the first to be called to discipleship, absolutely speaking. His call takes place along with other disciples and, in John's Gospel, after two other disciples have met Jesus. (Hence Peter's first place in all four lists of the Twelve cannot be explained, as some scholars try to do, by the supposed fact that he was the first disciple to be called.) The Fourth Gospel's indication that Peter and other disciples first met Jesus in the circle of the Baptist's disciples may well be true,[65] even though a permanent relationship between Peter and Jesus may have been established only after Jesus began his independent ministry in Galilee. It was perhaps in this latter context, while Peter and Andrew were engaged in fishing, that Jesus called them to follow him with the promise that they would become "fishers of men [*anthrōpōn,* human beings]" (Mark 1:17).

All four Gospels (plus Acts) present Peter as the spokesman and/or leader of the disciples in general or the Twelve in particular (see, e.g., Mark 1:36; 8:29; 9:5; 10:28; 14:29,37; Matt 15:15; 16:18; 17:24; 18:21; Luke 12:41; John 6:68). This, rather than the dubious claim that he was the first to be called by Jesus, explains at least in part why Peter is always named first in the four lists of the Twelve (representing Marcan and L traditions).[66] The Synoptics also present him as the first-named in a special inner group of three or four disciples, though, as we have seen, the historicity of such a group during the ministry of Jesus is problematic.[67]

All four Gospels also testify in various ways to the fact that this leader of the Twelve, whose original name was Simon, received a second name or nickname, *Kēpā*ˀ in Aramaic (transliterated as *Kēphas* in Greek), which was then translated as *Petros* in Greek. The Aramaic masculine noun *kēpā*ˀ has a range of meanings including "rock," "rocky crag," or "stone," while the Greek masculine noun *petros* means specifically "an isolated rock" or "a small stone," but at times "rock" or "stone" in general.[68] From Mark (3:16), John (1:42), and possibly Matthew (16:18) we have multiple attestation that Jesus was the one who gave Simon this second name—or (according to Matthew) its special interpretation.[69]

The nickname *Kēpā*ˀ turned out to have a fate quite different from that of *Boanērges* (Mark 3:16), the nickname that Jesus gave the sons of Zebedee. Despite the fact that Mark supplied a translation for it, *Boanērges* disappeared along with its translation in any and all NT traditions after Mark. In contrast, the Aramaic *Kēpā*ˀ (Grecized as *Kēphas,* "Cephas") and the Greek *Petros* ("Peter") had such staying power that, in most NT traditions about Peter outside the four Gospels, they practically obliterated the original name Simon. From a designation, nickname, or second name, *Kēphas* and then *Petros* ultimately became the bearer's proper name. There is an intriguing, though only partial, parallel here to "Jesus" and "Christ."

The transition from designation or nickname to proper name must have occurred quickly. Already in the first Christian generation, Paul (writing to mostly Gentile converts in Greece and Asia Minor) refers to Peter regularly with the Aramaic "Cephas" (1 Cor 1:12; 3:22; 9:5; 15:5; Gal 1:18; 2:9,11,14), rarely with the Greek "Peter" (only in Gal 2:7–8), and never with "Simon." In Acts, Luke uses the Hebrew form "Symeon" of Peter only in the mouth of James the brother of Jesus, apparently to create an archaizing, Semitic feel, as James delivers his speech at the Council of Jerusalem (Acts 15:14). Otherwise, Acts always speaks of "Peter." Perhaps sharing Luke's archaizing intention, the pseudonymous Second Epistle of Peter uses the form "Symeon Peter" in its introduction (2 Pet 1:1); otherwise both 1 and 2 Peter use only "Peter" (though only in 1 Pet 1:1 and 2 Pet 1:1), never "Simon."[70]

Reflecting both its roots in early Aramaic tradition and the whole history of Peter's name in a nutshell, the Gospel of John has Jesus prophesy as soon as he meets Peter: "You are *Simon,* son of John; you shall be called *Cephas* (which is translated as *Peter*)" (1:41–42). John is the only evangelist to use "Cephas," which otherwise appears only in Paul. In addition, John is the only NT writer who regularly uses the compound name "Simon Peter," though he also uses "Peter" alone. Looking at these various NT patterns, we can see that Jesus' choice of a new name for Simon, whatever the reason for or meaning of this name, "took," even to the point of eclipsing Peter's original name, Simon.

What else can be said about the historical Peter? Peter's role in the chain of events surrounding Jesus' arrest and crucifixion is supported by multiple attestation in the Marcan and Johannine passion traditions.[71] Peter was present at the Last Supper and at the arrest of Jesus in Gethsemane. He followed Jesus to the place where a hearing was held by the high priest and his councillors before Jesus was handed over to Pilate. However, under questioning by bystanders, Peter lost his nerve, denied that he was a follower of Jesus, and fled.

That is the last we know of Peter during the public ministry. Since Peter's subsequent career is not the concern of this study, I need only note that, shortly after Jesus' crucifixion, Peter claimed that the risen Jesus had appeared to him (1 Cor 15:5; Luke 24:34; cf. John 21:1–14). Peter apparently became a rallying point for other disciples and a leader of the Jerusalem church in its early days (Gal 1:18; 2:7–9; Acts 1–12). After suffering imprisonment a number of times, he left Jerusalem and engaged in missionary work outside Palestine, certainly at Antioch (Gal 2:11–14) and possibly at Corinth (1 Cor 1:12; 3:22). The NT hints at a martyr's death (John 21:18–19), and 1 Pet 5:13 (cf. 2 Pet 1:13–15; 3:1), along with early patristic witnesses such as 1 Clement (5:4) and Ignatius in his letter to the Romans (4:3), may point to Rome as the place of execution. Later church tradition placed Peter's martyrdom on the Vatican hill. Archaeological excavations under St. Peter's Basilica in Rome, carried out in the 1940s and 50s, are consistent with this location, though not all scholars accept them as proof that Peter was buried in the Vatican necropolis found under the Basilica.[72]

With this, I exhaust what most NT scholars would agree upon if they had to write a sketch of the historical Peter. Once we descend to specific sayings and actions connected with Peter, both the interpretation of individual passages and the judgment about their historicity become more difficult. Major points of debate include the following:

(a) It is not clear when precisely in the public ministry Jesus gave Simon his new name "Cephas" (= "Peter"). In John 1:42, as soon as Jesus meets Simon for the first time—before the public ministry has actually begun—Jesus utters the new name "Cephas" along with its translation "Peter." It is unclear whether this is meant to indicate that Simon would begin to be called Peter forthwith or whether it merely prophesies that Simon would be called Peter at some future date. The evangelist, however, regularly calls this figure Peter or Simon Peter from the beginning to the end of his Gospel—indeed, even before Jesus formally announces the new name (cf. John 1:40,42,44).[73]

Mark (and Luke following him) observes the time line or story line more carefully. Mark always uses "Simon" until Jesus constitutes the Twelve in

3:13–19. It is at that point that Jesus' bestowal of the new name is mentioned (3:16). Ever after, with the one exception of Jesus' rebuke to the sleeping "Simon" in Gethsemane (14:37), Mark always uses "Peter." Luke imitates this pattern: after the appointment of the Twelve (6:12–16), Luke never uses "Simon" for Peter during the public ministry. Only at the Last Supper, when Jesus promises to pray for Peter during the crisis of the passion (22:31), does the name "Simon" reappear. As in Mark 14:37, it is on the lips of Jesus in direct address.[74]

Matthew is not unlike John in insisting on the name Peter from the beginning, although he places the formal bestowal (or interpretation?) of the name more than halfway through the ministry. While Mark speaks only of "Simon" in the call of the first four disciples (1:16), Matthew (4:18) pointedly substitutes "Simon who is called Peter." Matthew proceeds to speak regularly of "Peter" throughout the public ministry and the Passion Narrative. At times, however, "Simon" is used—usually in connection with "Peter" (10:2; 16:16–17), though once alone (17:25).

All the more curious, then, is the relatively late location (16:13–20) of Jesus' pronouncement of a formal beatitude on Simon and the apparent conferral on him of the name "Peter." Matthew is more interested in ordering large blocks of thematic material (chaps. 14–18 focus on ecclesiological concerns) than in presenting a logical plot or time line. Actually, since Matthew speaks of "Simon Peter" making his profession of faith in 16:16, before Jesus tells "Simon Bar-Jonah" (v 17) that "you are Peter" (v 18), one wonders whether Matthew understands Jesus' pronouncement to be the conferral of a new name or simply the authoritative, theological interpretation of a second name Simon already bore.

This suggestion may sound strange to most Christian readers of the famous passage Matt 16:13–20. Technically, however, Matthew never says explicitly that, near Caesarea Philippi, Jesus confers on Simon a new name that Simon did not previously bear. Both Matt 4:18 and 10:2 speak simply of "Simon who is called Peter," without Mark's explanation that Jesus "conferred the name Peter on Simon" (Mark 3:16). Indeed, if one were reading Matthew in isolation, one might get the impression that, in 16:18, the Matthean Jesus is simply giving a theological interpretation to a name that Simon bore even before he met Jesus. However, when one reads Matthew in the light of redaction criticism, it seems fairly clear that Matthew understands his statements in 4:18 and 10:2, expressed with the passive participle *legomenos* ("called"), in the sense of Mark 3:16: Simon was called Peter because Jesus had conferred (as early as the event alluded to in Matt 10:2) or would confer (at Matt 16:18) that name upon him.

In sum, on the one hand, it is highly probable that Simon was called Peter during the public ministry and that this name was given him by Jesus. On the other hand, the exact time or occasion of the conferral of the name cannot be known. Moreover—however paradoxical this may seem—Jesus may have intended that the name *Kēpāʾ* be used of Simon only by other people, not by Jesus himself. Admittedly, this suggestion sounds quite strange, but it is supported by a curious detail that enjoys wide multiple attestation. In varied scenes in all four Gospels, when Jesus directly addresses Peter, he regularly uses, in the vocative, the name "Simon," not "Peter" or "Cephas." [75] This usage, which sits awkwardly with Jesus' conferral of the name "Peter," is witnessed by the special traditions of all four Gospels: the rebuke in Gethsemane (Mark 14:37); the beatitude Jesus addresses to Peter (Matt 16:17); the question about the payment of the temple tax (Matt 17:25); Jesus' promise to pray for Simon (Luke 22:31); and the triple question about Peter's love for Jesus (John 21:15–17). The name Jesus confers is not the name Jesus uses: what one makes of this paradox is hard to say. One possibility is that Jesus intended the new name *Kēpāʾ* to indicate Simon's relationship to the other disciples, not to Jesus. Once again, though, we must admit that we are left guessing.

(b) The question of the conferral of the name "Cephas" ("Peter") on Simon has already brought into play the famous and much debated scene near Caesarea Philippi in Matt 16:13–20. In this passage, a centuries-old battleground between Catholics and Protestants, Peter proclaims Jesus to be the Messiah and the Son of God (v 16). Jesus in turn proclaims that Simon bears (or will bear) the name Peter and that upon this rock Jesus will build his church (v 18); moreover, Jesus will give Peter the keys of the kingdom of heaven, i.e., the power to bind and loose (v 19). Granted the limits of our quest, we cannot delve into the history of the use of this text in the Christian church down through the centuries. [76] Our probe has to be restricted to two key questions:

(i) At some point in the public ministry, did Peter, as a spokesman for the other disciples, make a striking profession of faith in Jesus? [77] If we put the question in such general terms, I think that the answer is yes. In very different contexts and with very different words, both Mark (8:27–29) and John (6:67–69) depict Peter declaring his faith when Jesus asks the disciples about their faith in him or their commitment to him. [78] Matthew and Luke basically follow Mark, but each evangelist's report of Peter's confession differs in its wording as well as in its context.

In Mark 8:27–29, Jesus had led his disciples outside of Galilee into the area around Caesarea Philippi (modern Banias), northeast of the Sea of

Galilee. Unlike John's setting (John 6:66–67), there is no sense of immediate crisis as many disciples turn their backs on Jesus. Instead, Jesus presses the question of his mysterious identity—the *basso continuo* of Mark's Gospel. In response to Jesus' question about what people in general say of him (Mark 8:27), the disciples respond with various labels: John the Baptist, Elijah, or one of the prophets (v 28). Jesus then insists on the disciples voicing their own opinion (v 29): "But you—who do you say that I am?" Peter responds with true Marcan terseness: "You are the Messiah."

In 9:18–20, Luke presents the basic Marcan scene with a number of changes. The reference to the region around Caesarea Philippi is dropped; the last time Luke mentioned a location, it was Bethsaida (9:10), on the northeast corner of the Sea of Galilee. Placed in a typically Lucan context of prayer, the Marcan scene unfolds with only small redactional changes, the most striking being that Peter's response is made more laconic even as the title he chooses is lengthened (9:20): "Peter answered: 'The Messiah of God.' "

It is in Matthew, though, that not only the christological title but also the whole scene is expanded (16:13–20). The locale near Caesarea Philippi is kept, but Matthew raises the christological ante from the start by having Jesus ask (v 13): "Who do people [*anthrōpoi*] say that the Son of Man [*ton huion tou anthrōpou*] is?" In the disciples' reply (v 14), Matthew adds the suffering prophet Jeremiah to the names taken over from Mark. When Jesus in v 15 presses for the disciples' own opinion, "Simon Peter" (a rare combination in Matthew, but common in John) responds with a solemn double title (v 16): "You are the Messiah, the Son of the living God." Matthew has thus created a christological synthesis by drawing together in one pericope the three key titles Messiah, Son of God, and Son of Man. To this high christology Matthew typically adds a high ecclesiology in vv 17–19, with the beatitude addressed to Simon, who is called Peter, who will be the rock on which the church will be built, and who will receive the keys of the kingdom to bind and loose.

The scene of Peter's confession in John's Gospel (6:67–69) is almost completely different. It comes at the end of Jesus' Bread of Life discourse, which culminates in the shocking references to eating Jesus' flesh and drinking his blood (6:35–58). We then learn that Jesus is speaking in the synagogue at Capernaum (v 59), therefore within Galilee proper rather than far to the northeast near Caesarea Philippi. Unlike the Synoptic scenes, the Johannine narrative culminates in a crisis when many former disciples refuse to follow Jesus anymore because of his disturbing claim that he himself is the bread of life that they must eat (6:66). In all this, we are probably overhearing a late

1st-century debate among Christian Jews over the high christology and eucharistic theology championed by some Johannine Christians but rejected by others. In the midst of this crisis, the Johannine Jesus turns to the Twelve, who have never been mentioned previously in John's Gospel and who now appear out of nowhere. To them Jesus addresses a question (v 67): "You do not want to go away as well, do you?" "Simon Peter" answers for the group in typically Johannine terms (vv 68–69): "Lord, to whom shall we go? You have the words of eternal life, and we have come to believe and know that you are the Holy One of God." While "Simon Peter" corresponds to Matthew's usage in Matt 16:16, and while "Holy One of God" is somewhat similar in form to Luke's "Messiah of God," one can see how vastly different from the Synoptics' scene John's presentation is.

Clearly, each evangelist has molded the scene of Peter's confession according to his own theological concerns. Amid all the differences, especially the huge differences between the Synoptics and John, the basic agreement on one point is all the more striking: at a pivotal point in his ministry, Jesus asked the disciples a probing question about their faith or commitment. Peter, replying for the group, proclaimed his faith in Jesus by using some hallowed title or designation taken from the OT or Jewish tradition.

In light of this fundamental accord amid all the differences in the narratives of Mark and John, I think it probable that Peter did make such a profession of faith in Jesus some time during the public ministry. Beyond this bare affirmation, though, we cannot go. Almost all the other details of the narratives either contradict each other (e.g., Caesarea Philippi or Capernaum? Messiah or Holy One?) or clearly reflect the theological concerns of the individual evangelists (e.g., Luke's emphasis on prayer, Matthew's synthesis of christology and ecclesiology, John's christology of preexistence and incarnation).

(ii) Methodologically, when one is trying to answer historical questions, one must distinguish carefully between Peter's profession of faith in Jesus, which occurs in some form in all four Gospels, and Jesus' lengthy reply praising Peter, which appears only in Matt 16:17–19. It is the latter saying that is a storm center of exegetical and theological controversy, the very first step in the debate being whether it is a saying of the historical Jesus or a product of the early church.

One must admit that, at first glance, Matt 16:17–19 seems to reflect a Christian ecclesiology penned by an evangelist rather than a prophecy spoken by a Jew named Jesus ca. A.D. 28–30: "Happy [*makarios*] are you, Simon Bar-Jonah, for flesh and blood has not revealed this to you but my Father in heaven. And I say to you that you are Peter [*Petros*], and upon this rock [*epi tautē tē petrạ*] I shall build my church [*ekklēsian mou*], and the gates of the underworld [*hạdou,* Hades] shall not prevail against it. I shall give you the keys of the kingdom of heaven; and whatever you bind on earth shall be bound in heaven, and whatever you loose on earth shall be loosed in heaven."

To be sure, when Matt 16:17–19 is read as an integral part of the Gospel of Matthew, it is clearly a statement of Christian theology and polity. Nevertheless, conservative exegetes argue that, if Matt 16:17–19 (or some reconstructed Aramaic tradition standing behind it) were taken by itself, it would be intelligible in the mouth of the historical Jesus.[79] A conservative brief in favor of historicity might be argued as follows:

The historical Jesus was intent not on "saving souls" in an individualistic sense but on regathering the whole of Israel in preparation for the final coming of God's kingdom. His was a prophetic mission that focused on the entire people of God, not on individuals and not, à la Qumran, on a faithful remnant separated from the sinful mass of Israelites. The corporate nature of his mission would necessarily raise the question of how the people of Israel— most of whose history had been shaped by kings, native or foreign—was to be ordered or governed in "the last days."

We have already seen expressions of Jesus' sense of his corporate mission to Israel, a mission into which he co-opted his disciples. The historical Jesus sent his disciples, including most probably the Twelve, out on mission to begin the gathering of God's people, a gathering that God would bring to completion on the last day. Moreover, Jesus had promised the Twelve, who were to "sit on twelve thrones" (Matt 19:28 par.), a share in the rule of this Israel of the end time. In this context of a people-centered mission of the eschatological prophet, it was quite natural for Jesus to speak more specifically of his plans for the ordering and governing of this Israel that God was calling into being.

Focusing on the leader and spokesman of the Twelve, who had just proclaimed his faith, Jesus, who so often played with words and images, played with Simon's nickname. Simon was indeed *kēpāʾ*, "rock," for on this rock, this foundation within the foundational group of the Twelve, Jesus would build his eschatological assembly or congregation (Matt 16:18ab: *ekklēsia* in the Greek, perhaps *qahălāʾ* or *kĕnîštāʾ* in the Aramaic).[80] One should not read Christian ecclesiology into the original sense of *ekklēsia* here. In the mouth of Jesus, the word signifies not the later Christian church, local or universal, but rather the people of Israel gathered together to hear and worship God, as it did in the desert after the exodus (e.g., LXX Deut 4:10; 9:10; 18:16; 23:2–3; 31:30). In the 1st century A.D., Christians hardly had a monopoly on the Greek word *ekklēsia*—or the Hebrew and Aramaic words that might lie behind it. The word *ekklēsia* occurs some 96 times in the Septuagint.[81] In the passages that translate a Hebrew text we possess (including the fragments of Ben Sira), the Septuagint's *ekklēsia* represents some form of the root *qhl*, most often the noun *qāhāl* ("gathering," "meeting," "convocation," "assembly," "congregation"). It is in this sense that Peter was to be the rock for the eschatological congregation of Israel. There may also have been an allusion in the imagery to the patriarch Abraham, who was the rock from which Israel was first hewn (Isa 51:1–2).

The further metaphor of building a community need hardly reflect a specifically Christian concern for organization. Building the congregation of the end time was a metaphor used at Qumran as well as in the early church. For example, in 4QpPs37 3:16, Qumran interpreted Ps 37:23–24 to mean that God "has established him [the Teacher of Righteousness] to build for himself [God] a congregation . . ." [*libnôt lô ʿădat*]."[82] This Hebrew text could easily be translated into Greek as *oikodomein heautō ekklēsian,* basically the same words that we find in Matt 16:18. The sectarian scrolls of Qumran remind us that, around the turn of the era, a fiercely apocalyptic Jewish community could also be intensely interested in the organization of God's people both before and after the final victory over evil.

By his leadership, Peter the Rock was to be a firm defense against all the destructive powers of sin and death (the Greek *hadēs,* the Hebrew *šĕʾôl*) that would assault the assembly of God's people in the final battle between good and evil (Matt 16:18c).[83] There may be an echo here of Jewish lore that spoke of the cosmic rock on which the Jerusalem temple was supposedly built; this temple rock was the entrance way to both heaven and the underworld.[84] In any case, as the leader appointed by Jesus and sharing Jesus' authority, Peter was to be like Eliakim, the majordomo of the royal palace of King Hezekiah of Judah (Isa 22:20–25). The prophet Isaiah promised Eliakim that Yahweh would place on Eliakim's shoulder "the key of David" (administrative power over the palace): "He shall open and no one shall shut, and he shall shut and no one shall open" (v 22) . . . and he shall be a glorious throne for the house of his father" (v 23).

The key-like authority of Peter was to be exercised especially in teaching the Israel of the end time the true will of God, i.e., what was permissible or impermissible to do according to God's Law. This power is summed up in the allied metaphors of binding (declaring an action illicit or invalid) and loosing (declaring it licit or valid). Peter's authoritative teaching, addressed to Israel here on earth, would be ratified by God in heaven and so would be a sure defense against the hostile powers of sin and death seeking to destroy the eschatological assembly.

Thus, a plausible case can be made that Matt 16:17–19 is a charge that the historical Jesus gave to the leader of the Twelve during the public ministry. To be sure, Matt 16:17–19 lacks multiple attestation of sources, but critics sometimes accept other sayings of Jesus that lack multiple attestation when the sayings cohere perfectly with Jesus' core message and mission (e.g., the Lord's Prayer or Jesus' saying on "the finger of God" in Luke 11:20 par.). In the opinion of various conservative exegetes, Matt 16:17–19 should be accepted on such grounds. At the very least, such arguments show that the passage cannot be simply dismissed with a wave of the hand.

Nevertheless, serious arguments weigh heavily in favor of the passage coming from a post-Easter situation in the church. I agree that Matt 16:17–19 cannot be rejected simply because it lacks multiple attestation. But one must face honestly the specific history of tradition and redaction in which Matt 16:17–19 is embedded. It does not appear in Matthew's Gospel as a completely isolated unit. It is part of Matthew's overall redaction and expansion of Mark's version of Peter's confession at Caesarea Philippi. Most critics, for example, would admit that "Son of the living God" in 16:16 was Matthew's own addition to Mark's more restricted confession of "the Messiah" in Mark 8:29. We must therefore take seriously the clear signs of Matthew's heavy redaction of this pericope, which may include even the whole of v 17.

Furthermore, the claim that 16:18 goes back to the historical Jesus is especially difficult to defend because of the special status of the word *ekklēsia* ("church," "assembly") in the Gospels in particular and in the NT in general. The word *ekklēsia* occurs 114 times in the NT. With the exception of three occurrences in Matthew (16:18; 18:17 *bis*), the word never appears in the Gospels. It rather occurs throughout Acts, almost all of the Pauline Epistles, Hebrews, James, 3 John, and the Book of Revelation. With very few exceptions,[85] *ekklēsia* always refers to the Christian church, either local or universal. Throughout the NT, there seems to be a tacit rule that "church" language belongs after Easter, not before.

Luke, sometimes considered the first church historian, is a striking case in point. He is admirably careful in the sober distinction he makes in his use of *ekklēsia*. Despite the fact that he is so concerned about the history of the early church that he writes a companion volume to his Gospel (the Acts of the Apostles), and despite the fact that he is intent on highlighting points of continuity between the time of Jesus and the time of the church, Luke is nevertheless punctilious in not retrojecting the vocabulary of *ekklēsia* into his Gospel. Various words for "people" (including the people of God), "company," or "crowds" are used in his Gospel, but *ekklēsia* is not employed until Luke begins in Acts to depict a clearly organized group of believers in Jerusalem, held together by the leadership of Peter and the other apostles (see 5:11, the first occurrence).

It is against the backdrop of this strong post-Easter usage of the rest of the NT that one must judge the three occurrences of *ekklēsia* in Matthew. The position that *ekklēsia* in Matt 16:18 comes from the usage of the early church, and not from the historical Jesus, is strengthened by the fact that most exegetes would readily grant that the two other occurrences, in Matt 18:17, reflect early church discipline.[86] In fact, the whole pericope of Matt 18:15–20 seems to be an instruction on how to administer discipline in the local church when a sinful church member proves recalcitrant. If private fraternal correction and even the urging of two or three comrades prove futile (18:15–16), the person bringing the charge is to appeal to the church (*tē ekklēsia*, 18:17). If the sinful member refuses to listen even to the church, he is to suffer ostracism or shunning from the community ("let him be to you like a pagan or a toll collector"). The authority of the local church—for this is what *ekklēsia* clearly means here—is then asserted by a double formula that repeats Matt 16:19, only now in the plural (18:18): "Amen I say to you, whatever you bind on earth shall be bound in heaven, and whatever you loose on earth shall be loosed in heaven." In the end, this authority is guaranteed by the presence of Jesus, even in the smallest of local communities (18:20): "For where two or three are gathered together in my name [*eis to emon onoma,* echoing phrases in the early church that speak of doing something in the name of Jesus], there am I in their midst."

One need not belabor the point. The whole of Matt 18:15–20 reflects a way of handling disciplinary problems in a local Christian church with a Jewish-Christian background. This church treats the problem of recalcitrant sinful members with a system of excommunication and readmission, all the while appealing to the presence of the risen Jesus in its midst, conferring upon it the power to "bind" (excommunicate) and "loose" (readmit to the community). One must therefore face the critical question: if Matt 18:15–20, which contains the only other Gospel references to *ekklēsia* as well as the power to bind and loose, is judged to be an articulation of the theology and polity of the early church, is there much hope of salvaging Matt 16:18–19 as the lone case in the NT where a Gospel passage containing *ekklēsia* comes from the historical Jesus? To be sure, a position upholding the authenticity of Matt 16:18–19 might be thought possible when the unit is considered in the abstract. However, when one reads Matt 16:18–19 in light of all the other *ekklēsia* passages in the NT, especially Matt 18:15–20, is such a position really the most probable solution? I think not. Moreover, we have in 16:18 not a reference to "the church" or "a church" but to "*my* church"—the church of Jesus, who has just been declared by Peter to be the Messiah, the Son of the living God. It is difficult to imagine such a usage in the mouth of the historical Jesus.

Besides the context of all the *ekklēsia* passages in the NT, there is another context in which Matt 16:17–19 may be read, and this too argues for a post-Easter origin of our much disputed text. This other context is Johannine, specifically John 20:23 and 21:15–17, both of which relate appearances of the risen Jesus.[87] Although neither passage uses the word *ekklēsia*—the word never appears in the Fourth Gospel or the First Epistle of John—both supply verbal and/or substantive parallels to Matt 16:17–19.

John 20:23 belongs to the first appearance of the risen Jesus to the assembled disciples on Easter Sunday evening.[88] In v 23, Jesus conveys authority to his disciples in a charge similar in style and thrust to the charge he gives to Peter in Matt 16:19. Both John 20:23 and Matt 16:19 have the same structure of a two-part statement, one part referring to a positive action of the church (loosing, forgiving), the other to a negative action (binding, holding fast), each part in turn having two corresponding halves, the first in the active voice, the second in the passive voice. In Matthew, the negative action comes first; in John, the positive. In each statement, Jesus confers on the chief disciple (in Matthew) or on the whole group of disciples (in John) some sort of authority over the church:

MATT 16:19	JOHN 20:23
What you bind on earth	Whose sins you shall forgive,
shall be bound in heaven.	they are forgiven them.
And what you loose on earth	Whose [sins] you shall hold fast,
shall be loosed in heaven.	they are held fast.

To be sure, the communal audience and the concern about sin in the community also create a strong parallel between John 20:23 and Matt 18:18. However, as with Matt 16:18–19, the context in John 20:23 is one of universal scope, the audience being the whole company of disciples assembled on Easter Sunday. It is from this company of disciples that the whole future church—and not just some local community—will spring. The solemn, programmatic, and universal nature of the scene thus suggests a parallel to Matt 16:18–19 as well as to 18:18.

More specifically focused on Peter is the charge of the risen Jesus in John 21:15–17. The basic theme of Jesus investing Peter with authority over the whole church is the main link with Matt 16:18–19, but even in some minor details there are intriguing points of contact between the two texts. With a locution unusual for Matthew, the chief disciple is referred to in Matt 16:16

as "Simon Peter"; that is the typically Johannine form of his name, which, in fact, introduces Jesus' dialogue with Peter in John 21:15. In both texts, Jesus addresses Peter with a patronymic. In fact, Peter's patronymic is found only in these two NT texts—though the patronymic varies in the two traditions. In Matt 16:17, Jesus exclaims: "Happy are you, Simon Bar-Jonah [i.e, son of Jonah]." In John 21:15,16,17, Jesus thrice asks: "Simon, son of John, do you love me?" [89]

The basic connection between these two texts, however, is one of substance rather than form. In both Matt 16:18–19 and John 21:15–17, Jesus singles out Peter from among the other disciples mentioned in the context, conferring on Peter alone a special function in and authority over Jesus' church or flock. In each passage, the metaphors are sweeping: (1) In Matthew 16, Peter is the rock of Jesus' church and the majordomo in the Messiah's palace. He has the keys of the kingdom; therefore, his authoritative decisions here on earth are ratified by God in heaven. (2) In John 21:15–19, Peter stands in the place of Jesus, who, in the body of John's Gospel, had sole claim on being the good shepherd (John 10:1–18), a claim he proved by laying down his life for his sheep. Now, after the resurrection, Peter alone is commissioned by the risen Jesus to shepherd, feed, and tend the lambs and sheep of the flock, proving his role as shepherd by laying down his life as a martyr in imitation of Jesus. The authority Peter receives directly from Jesus apparently extends to the whole church without restriction: upon Peter the Matthean Jesus builds *"my* church," and Peter is commissioned by the Johannine Jesus to feed *"my* lambs, *my* sheep"—hardly one particular local community.

Beyond all these individual points of comparison, there is one overriding parallel to ponder. We have already seen that the immediate parallel to Matt 16:18–19, namely, Matt 18:15–20, reflects the situation of the church after Easter; the one conferring authority upon and present in the local church is the risen Jesus. Likewise, the two other major parallels to Matt 16:18–19 outside of Matthew's Gospel, namely, John 20:23 and John 21:15–17, are both situated within post-Easter appearances of the risen Jesus either to all the disciples or to Peter in particular. Indeed, some exegetes suggest that behind John 21:1–19 we may discern the faint outlines of the narrative of the primordial appearance of the risen Jesus to Peter, the appearance mentioned in passing in 1 Cor 15:5 and Luke 24:34, but never narrated in full—except perhaps in John 21.

Thus, the post-Easter context, implicit or explicit, of all the major parallels to Matt 16:18–19 argues persuasively that the Matthean Jesus' charge to Peter originally had the same context. As we saw in Volume Two of *A Mar-*

ginal Jew, when treating the Lucan and Johannine traditions of the miraculous catch of fish, the general flow of the Gospel tradition is from a post-resurrection setting to a preresurrection setting, not vice versa.[90] One can easily see, for instance, why the story of the miraculous catch of fish might be retrojected from a post-Easter setting into the public ministry. It is difficult to see why the church would go out of its way to project into post-Easter settings events that actually took place during the public ministry. In my opinion, John 20:23 and 21:15–17 argue forcefully that Matt 16:18–19 is another example of the same dynamic of retrojection.

This judgment receives some confirmation when we broaden our search for parallels beyond Gospel traditions. In Gal 1:15–17, Paul gives us a first-hand account of the experience of a first-generation Christian who claimed to have received an appearance from the risen Jesus and to have been commissioned by him to be an apostle.[91] The vocabulary Paul uses to describe the appearance and its effects has some striking similarities to Matt 16:16–17. In Galatians 1, Paul is at pains to insist that he has not received his gospel message from human beings but from a revelation given by God the Father and Jesus Christ (Gal 1:1,11–12). Describing this revelation, Paul says (1:15–17): "But when it pleased him [i.e., God the Father] who set me apart from my mother's womb and called me by his grace *to reveal [apokalypsai] his son [ton huion autou]* to me . . . I did not confer with *flesh and blood [sarki kai haimati,* i.e., weak human beings]." Paul emphasizes that he did not at that time go up to Jerusalem to confer with the other apostles, although he concedes in v 18 that three years later he did visit Cephas (i.e., Peter).

In Matt 16:16–17, we have a similar concatenation of key words and ideas. In v 16, Peter declares Jesus to be *the Son of God (ho huios tou theou).* Jesus replies with a beatitude felicitating Peter because *flesh and blood (sarx kai haima)* has not *revealed (apekalypsen)* this to Peter, but rather God the Father. The vocabulary of Matt 16:16–17 thus echoes the very early Christian idea that an appearance of the risen Jesus was a kind of apocalyptic revelation, disclosing to the recipient that Jesus was the risen Son of God (cf. Rom 1:4; Acts 10:40–41; 13:33).[92] These Pauline parallels in vocabulary and thought thus support what we have already seen from the Gospels: Matt 16:16–19 is best understood as a scene originally laid in a post-Easter setting, a scene that Matthew or his tradition has retrojected into the public ministry. In short, while Matt 16:16–19 is of great importance for the history of the early church in general and of Peter in particular, it falls out of consideration when we restrict our study to the historical Peter during the public ministry.[93]

(c) Treating Mark's presentation of Peter's confession near Caesarea Philippi necessarily entails treating as well the aftermath of that confession in

Mark 8:30–33. In rapid-fire succession, Jesus first responds to Peter's assertion that Jesus is the Messiah by strictly charging *(epetimēsen)* them (the disciples in general, for whom Peter was the spokesman) to speak to no one
about him (i.e., about him as Messiah, v 30). In v 31, Jesus proceeds to utter
the first of the three great predictions of his passion, death, and resurrection;
these predictions are the structural pillars of Mark 8:31–10:52. In v 32, Peter
responds to Jesus' prediction of his passion by remonstrating *(epitiman)* with
him. In v 33, Jesus, seeing this revolt against the prophecy of his passion as
something that endangers all his disciples, firmly rebukes *(epetimēsen)* Peter
in the sight of the other disciples with the shocking words: "Get behind me,
Satan, for you think not the thoughts of God but the thoughts of men [*anthrōpōn*, human beings]." In the aftermath (vv 34–38) of this sharp exchange, Jesus impresses upon the crowd as well as his disciples the message
of the cross: those who would follow Jesus must take up their own crosses if
they would share in his victory.

As almost all exegetes would admit, what we have in 8:30–33 is a Marcan
composition, clearly tied together by such stylistic traits as the repetition of
the key word *epitimaō* (carrying the various nuances of "sternly enjoin,"
"sternly remonstrate with," "sternly rebuke").[94] At least some of the verses
are probably creations of Mark or the Christian tradition he inherits. For example, Jesus' surprising injunction to the disciples in 8:30 to say nothing to
anyone about the messiahship Peter has just acknowledged is most likely a
creation of Mark himself, a prime example of the Marcan "messianic secret"
(cf. 9:9). While Mark may not have created the three predictions of Jesus'
passion, death, and resurrection out of whole cloth, in their present form
they are most likely the product of early Christian preaching and catechesis.[95] In any event, their careful placement at Mark 8:31; 9:31; and
10:33–34 are clearly the result of Mark's editorial activity as he structures a
major part of his Gospel.[96]

Whatever one thinks of 8:32–33 as a whole, one naturally tends to be less
skeptical about the historicity of Jesus' rebuke to Peter: "Get behind me,
Satan." Although the saying lacks multiple attestation, the criterion of embarrassment certainly comes into play.[97] In the larger context of Mark's
Gospel, one could take the Greek of Jesus' rebuke *(hypage opisō mou)* to
mean "return to your place as a true disciple, following after me." However,
the sense of the rebuke taken by itself, especially with the vocative "Satan,"
might well be "out of my sight, you Satan!"[98] Some would prefer to see this
rebuke as a creation of an anti-Peter faction in the early church rather than
an outburst from an exasperated Jesus, but I do not find this approach persuasive. Admittedly, Peter was involved in various disputes in the first-

generation church, notably with Paul and James (Gal 2:11–14). Yet even Paul's polemical remarks in Galatians—which must be balanced against his implicit recognition of Peter's importance—do not descend to the depths of calling Peter satanic.[99] The truly unbridled polemics against Peter must await the later gnostic literature. Hence I think it probable that Jesus' fiery rebuke to Peter as Satan is historical.

The trouble is that, granted the thoroughgoing Marcan composition of Mark 8:30–33, we cannot be sure of the historical context of Jesus' rebuke. If we assign Jesus' command to silence to Marcan redaction, the first prediction of the passion to Christian catechesis, and its placement in this passage to Mark, Peter's presumptuous remonstrance with Jesus and Jesus' fiery retort float in a vacuum. If Jesus' rebuke to Peter is historical, what occasioned it? Once we use form and redaction criticism to dissolve the unity of 8:30–33, there is no interpretive framework for the rebuke. We are free to imagine and supply any substitute we like, but the substitute is the product of our imagination just as Mark's framework was the product of his.

Perhaps the most imaginative framework created by modern critics is the one that draws together the two key sayings in Mark 8:29–33: Peter's confession that Jesus is the Messiah (v 29) and Jesus' rebuke branding Peter as Satan (v 33). According to this reconstruction, the original response of the historical Jesus to Peter's proclamation that Jesus was the Messiah was the rejection of Peter's confession and the branding of Peter as Satan, perhaps because Peter's idea of messiahship was infected with a national-political zealotry. This, some would claim, is the original historical event that Mark's redaction has obscured. While such a juxtaposition of opposites is intriguing, it labors under many difficulties.

First of all, as we have seen above, multiple attestation of sources does make it likely that, at some pivotal moment in the public ministry, Peter made a profession of faith in Jesus. However, the wording of that profession differs in our Gospel sources, and we cannot reconstruct it with certainty. Second, even apart from our uncertainty about the wording of Peter's confession, there is a telling objection to the idea that Mark 8:29–33 contains a tradition recalling that the historical Jesus rebuked Peter for calling him the Messiah. Such a hypothesis has to presuppose that, in the early days of the oral tradition prior to Mark, Christian catechesis passed down a story about Jesus rejecting a confession of his messiahship as something satanic. The problem here is that the earliest Christians, basically "Jews for Jesus," were intent on nothing so much as persuading their fellow Jews that, despite the scandal of the cross, Jesus was the Messiah. It is extremely difficult to imagine that the very Christians who were giving themselves totally to spreading

their faith in Jesus as the Messiah, the very Christians who made this affirmation the central tenet of their religion, were at the same time preserving
and spreading a story in which Jesus branded as satanic a confession of his
messiahship by his chief disciple, who was a prominent leader of the early
church. In my view, the conjecture that unites Mark 8:29 directly with 8:33
and sees in this creation a historical event cannot construct a plausible tradition-history for such a pericope in the early church.

We are left, then, with a fascinating but exasperating historical nugget for
which we have no larger context. What moved Jesus to rebuke Peter with the
sharp epithet of "Satan"? Did Peter reject some statement Jesus made about
his expectation of or readiness for suffering and death as part of his role as
the eschatological prophet? Or was Peter revolting against Jesus' more general teaching that all the disciples must be ready to undergo suffering and
persecution? Given the fact that the historical Jesus spoke Aramaic, is it possible that, in his mouth, as opposed to the setting in Mark's Gospel, the Aramaic word śāṭānāʾ was used to mean not the proper name of the devil but
simply "adversary," a common meaning of śāṭānāʾ?[100] In other words, might
Jesus have been saying that Peter had become his adversary instead of his disciple because he opposed the unwelcome message of the necessity of suffering either for Jesus or for all disciples?

One quickly sees our problem: the criterion of embarrassment suggests
that Jesus' "Satan saying" is authentic, but the criterion cannot supply a historical context to help us choose among various possible settings. The
"Satan saying" certainly confirms that Peter's relationship with Jesus was
tension-filled, as was his relationship with Paul, James, the Jewish high
priest, Herod Agrippa I, and no doubt the Roman authorities who executed
him at a later date. Hence the "Satan saying" also fits the criterion of coherence, for it jibes with the picture we get of Peter from many sources. But,
in the end, all this gives us is an aspect of Peter's personal profile, and nothing more.[101] Constructing grand hypotheses from this shred of evidence is ill
advised.

(d) Up until now, the traditions dealing with Peter have been Marcan,
Matthean, and Johannine. There is one saying of Jesus referring to Peter that
is found only in the special Lucan (L) tradition; but it is, if anything, more
difficult to evaluate than the logia we have just examined.

In the expanded Lucan form of the Last Supper, just after Jesus' institution
of the eucharist (Luke 22:15–20) and his prediction of his betrayal
(22:21–23), Jesus delivers a mini-discourse to the twelve apostles on the subject of true leadership: being a leader means being the servant of everyone
else (22:24–30, a mixture of Marcan, L, and Q traditions).[102] At this point,

immediately before he reworks the Marcan tradition of Jesus' prediction of Peter's betrayal (22:33–34), Luke abruptly inserts a saying of Jesus, addressed to Peter, that has no parallel in any other Gospel tradition (22:31–32):

> 31 "Simon, Simon, behold, Satan has sought you [plural, *hymas*, i.e., all the apostles] to sift [you, plural] like wheat.

> 32 But I have prayed for you [singular, i.e., for Simon alone] that your [singular] faith may not fail completely [*eklipē*, i.e., come to an end, give out, die].

> And you [singular], once you have turned back [i.e., once you have repented or been converted], strengthen your brothers."

Faced with these puzzling two verses, the origin of which is hotly disputed among exegetes, we should begin by interpreting the vv 31–32 within the immediate Lucan context. Structurally, these two verses act as a bridge between the mini-discourse on true leadership, which consists in serving all (vv 24–30), and Jesus' prediction that Peter would deny him three times before daybreak (vv 33–34). The mini-discourse has stressed that the one who is "the greatest *(ho meizōn)* among you" (i.e., among the Twelve), the one who is the leader *(ho hēgoumenos),* must be like the servant who waits at table *(ho diakonōn,* vv 26–27). In Luke's redaction, the use of "the leader" in the singular (v 26) might just carry a veiled reference to Peter in particular.[103] If so, the focus then shifts from Peter to the whole circle of the Twelve, who have remained faithful to Jesus during his various trials. They are promised that, in the kingdom, they will sit on thrones judging the twelve tribes of Israel (vv 28–30).

In a sense, vv 31–32 continue the theme of the Twelve, but now with a focus on the relationship of Peter the leader ("Simon, Simon") to the circle of the Twelve (the "you" whom Satan has sought to sift). Peter must be the servant of the rest in their time of greatest trial and temptation, which is about to break upon them in Jesus' passion. Jesus' intercessory prayer will guarantee that Peter's faith (i.e., his fidelity or loyalty to Jesus), on which the others depend, will not fail completely. Yet, the reference to Peter having to "turn back," i.e., undergo repentance or conversion, hints at some failure on his part, which, however, will not prove fatal. Recovering from this fall or failure, Peter will exercise his servant-leadership by strengthening his brothers. The change from the plural "you" (i.e., the Twelve at table with Jesus) to the plural "your brothers" may indicate that Peter is commanded to strengthen *(stērison,* an imperative) a wider circle than just the Twelve.

Jesus' hint that Peter will in some sense suffer a fall sparks Peter's protestation of total loyalty, even if it entails imprisonment and death (v 33). This, in turn, calls forth Jesus' prediction of Peter's triple denial (v 34). One sees, therefore, how vv 31–32 both prepare for and at the same time soften the blow of Jesus' prediction of Peter's denial.[104] As elsewhere, Luke, if he cannot delete, at least reduces the negative tone of Gospel traditions dealing with Peter. In the present case, Peter's triple denial—present in both the pre-Marcan and pre-Johannine Passion Narratives—was too deeply rooted in the primitive Gospel tradition to be blithely deleted by Luke. The best Luke can do is to cushion the shock both before and after the scandalous event.

Now that we have seen the connections that vv 31–32 have with the immediate context, we can examine the style and substance of this puzzling prediction about Satan sifting the apostles. With a double address indicating emphasis and perhaps passionate concern (cf. "Martha, Martha" in Luke 10:41), the Lucan Jesus reveals (idou, behold) that the events about to unfold in his passion are not a series of chance happenings of minor importance. Peter and the Twelve are caught up in a cosmic, dualistic struggle between Satan and Jesus. Since the temptation narrative, Satan has abstained from direct and open attacks on Jesus (or the Twelve). Now, as the crisis of the passion breaks in on the scene, Satan seeks to bring about not only the death of Jesus but also, through it, the apostasy of the twelve apostles, the official eyewitnesses of the public ministry, the living link to any possible future for believers.[105] In a way reminiscent of the opening scenes in the Book of Job, Satan asks permission from God to sift the Twelve like so much wheat, that is, to throw them into such confusion and distress that their faith will completely fail when confronted with the fierce trials of the passion.[106]

In this time of peril, Jesus judges it sufficient to pray for Peter alone in order to counter Satan's petition. Luke thus creates a stark juxtaposition of Satan's petition for the Twelve and Jesus' petition for Peter before the throne of God as the passion begins. Jesus asks that, for the sake of the perseverance of the Twelve, Peter's faith not give out, fail completely, come to an end (the sense of the verb eklipē in v 32). Needless to say, in Luke's theology, Jesus' prayer is effective. The petition of the advocate of Peter is stronger than the petition of the adversary or accuser (= śāṭān) of the Twelve.[107] But, while Peter's loyalty does not fail totally, v 32 intimates that he does suffer a partial fall, namely, in his triple denial, a fall of which he needs to repent ("and you, once you have turned back [epistrepsas] . . .").

Not satisfied with this preemptive softening of the story of Peter's denial, Luke softens the denial narrative itself. By this, I do not mean that Luke fails to take Peter's denial of Jesus seriously. He certainly does take it seriously, presenting Peter in his first denial as immediately claiming no knowledge of Jesus: "I do not know him" (Luke 22:57). However, in Luke, unlike Mark and Matthew, Peter's denials do not increase in intensity and climax with Peter cursing and swearing—perhaps with Jesus as the implied object of the curse.[108] Moreover, no sooner does Peter utter his third denial than Jesus, the efficacious intercessor, brings about the fulfillment of his own petition by turning (*strapheis,* 22:61) and looking at Peter.[109] This immediately causes Peter first to remember Jesus' prediction and then to rush out of the courtyard, weeping bitter tears of repentance. Thus, even by the end of the scene of the triple denial, the power of Jesus' prayer and the sincerity of Peter's repentance are displayed. One wonders whether Luke intends to imply deftly that Jesus' *turning* to look at Peter, causing Peter to remember Jesus' prediction (22:31–34), causes Peter likewise to *turn* back in repentance.

Be that as it may, we need not be surprised when, at the death of Jesus, we are told that at a distance from the cross there stood not only the women followers (as in the other three Gospels) but also *all* of Jesus' male acquaintances (22:49: *pantes hoi gnōstoi autō),* a phrase probably meant to include Peter and the rest of the Eleven as eyewitnesses of the passion.[110] Thus, according to Luke, Peter's failure was only momentary. He has already "turned back" to the point of coming to Calvary with the rest of the Eleven to witness Jesus' death—as is to be expected of the official eyewitnesses deputed to give testimony in the Acts of the Apostles.

Given this Lucan program of almost instantaneous rehabilitation, one is not surprised to learn that it is Peter (alone, according to Luke, cf. John 20:3) who runs to the empty tomb on Easter Sunday morning (Luke 24:12) and leaves amazed at what has happened. By Easter Sunday evening, Peter is gathered with the rest of the Eleven and the other disciples (24:33). This whole group steals the thunder of the returning Emmaus disciples by announcing to them that "the Lord truly has been raised and has appeared to Simon" (v 34). Thus, even before the risen Jesus appears to the assembled disciples, Peter has fulfilled the rest of Jesus' petition: turning back from his failure at the triple denial, he has strengthened his "brothers" ("the Eleven and those with them") by telling them of Jesus' resurrection appearance to him—again, him alone.

This strengthening of Peter's "brothers" will continue throughout the early chapters of Acts. Jesus had pointedly said that Peter would strengthen his "brothers," which for Luke indicates more than just the twelve apostles, since the usage of "brothers" in Acts refers to disciples in general, not to the apostles in particular.[111] Peter will strengthen the brothers—the whole growing church in Acts—by guiding the election of Matthias, preaching the first post-Easter sermon to the Jews gathered in Jerusalem on Pentecost, leading the Jerusalem church in its first days, inflicting disciplinary punishment when necessary, paying pastoral visits to other churches around Palestine, and baptizing Cornelius, the first clearly Gentile convert. Thus, the deceptively simple prophecy in Luke 22:31–32 sketches in a nutshell the entire career of Peter through the rest of the Gospel and into Acts.

Considering how perfectly 22:31–32 fits into the immediate context of the Last Supper, how exactly it prophesies the cushioned fall and speedy rehabilitation of Peter during his triple denial and the rest of the passion, and how presciently it looks forward to his postresurrection ministry in the Gospel and Acts, I am tempted to think that this small unit is a creation of Luke himself. It fits the larger literary and theological framework of Luke too snugly to be a stray L tradition inserted secondarily at a convenient spot in the Last Supper narrative. The view that 22:31–32 is a Lucan creation can be supported to some degree by traits of vocabulary and style that reflect his redactional hand.[112]

Nevertheless, in fairness I must admit that many Lucan experts see here instead Luke's reworking of an earlier saying (or sayings) that circulated in the L tradition, perhaps without any connection to the Last Supper.[113] Possible original settings and meanings of the earlier form of the L saying are suggested, but naturally any such suggestion must remain highly speculative. While I think the claim of a traditional saying reworked by Luke less likely, I am sufficiently impressed by the weight of Lucan scholarship favoring this view to render a final judgment of *non liquet* ("not clear") on Luke 22:31–32. In other words, I judge it unclear whether the verses are Luke's own creation or his creative adaptation of an L tradition. Granted this uncertainty, I am leery of using 22:31–32 (in what earlier form or setting?) to reconstruct some hypothetical episode in the life of the historical Jesus and the historical Peter.[114]

(e) Our consideration of Luke 22:31–32 has already touched upon the story of Peter's denial of Jesus after the latter's arrest. We will have to return to these events when we treat the Passion Narratives; here the sole interest is verifiable incidents in Peter's life. Despite the complexities of the four variant narratives of Peter's denial in the four Gospels, a judgment about the historicity of the denial tradition is easier than a judgment on Luke 22:31–32.[115] Two criteria seem satisfied by the denial tradition: embarrassment and multiple attestation.

First, in all four Gospels, Peter's denial of Jesus is, after the betrayal by Judas, the single most embarrassing incident involving a disciple. That such a story should have been invented out of whole cloth after Easter, when Peter was a significant leader of the early church, is difficult to believe. As noted above, Peter's relationship with Paul and James was at times filled with tension and disagreement over the handling of the Gentile mission (Gal 2:11–14). But there is no indication from first-generation Christianity of a wholesale campaign to defame or discredit Peter in such a thoroughgoing manner.[116] Such campaigns belong to certain branches of 2d-century Gnosticism.

One should remember a practical point here. For all their differences, Peter, James, Paul, and other first-generation Christian Jews were all engaged in a single, extremely difficult task: to convince their fellow Jews (as well as skeptical Gentiles, once the mission was broadened) that a condemned and crucified Jew named Jesus had been raised from the dead as Messiah and Lord. After naming the various witnesses of the resurrection, including both Peter and James, Paul remarks to the Corinthians in 1 Cor 15:11: "Therefore, whether I or they [proclaimed this creed to you and to others], so we proclaimed and so you believed."

Indeed, in the primitive creedal formula that Paul himself taught the Corinthians ca. A.D. 50 and recalled to them some five years later in 1 Corinthians 15, Peter was proclaimed by the early church to have been the first to receive an appearance of the risen Christ (1 Cor 15:5; cf. Luke 24:34). For Christian missionaries to have engaged in a fierce campaign to discredit Peter's basic credentials as a trustworthy disciple would have been to cut the ground out from under their own feet. The primordial witness to the resurrection would have been disallowed by the very missionaries trying to convince others of the resurrection and of the truth of the creed that extolled Peter as witness to the resurrection. One is reminded of a picture of a snake biting its own tail. Such a convoluted tradition-history smacks of 20th-century professors spinning out theories in their studies rather than 1st-century Christian-Jewish missionaries struggling to gain converts to their new faith. In this case, the criterion of embarrassment is also the criterion of missionary pragmatism.

The second criterion supporting the story of Peter's denial is multiple attestation of sources. The argument here is not that all four Gospels narrate the denial in narratives that show a basic core of agreement amid differences in detail. That global argument is not valid, for the versions in Matt 26:69–75 and Luke 22:56–62 depend solely on Mark 14:66–72 and so supply no multiple attestation of independent sources.[117] John 18:15–18,25–27, however, does seem to represent an independent version of the incident, as the detailed studies of scholars like C. H. Dodd, Raymond E. Brown, Rudolf Schnackenburg, and Robert T. Fortna have demonstrated.[118] In a crazy-quilt pattern that is not explainable simply by his redactional tendencies, John is at times closer to Mark and Matthew, more often closer to Luke; but frequently he goes his own way with some curious details.[119] Hence we have two independent sources, one from the pre-Marcan passion tradition and one from the pre-Johannine.

I should emphasize that all I am interested in establishing here is the basic historicity of Peter's denial of Jesus. Whether there were actually three denials or whether the threefold denial is a typical example of the "law of threes" in storytelling (the same action or statement being repeated three times for emphasis or heightened suspense moving toward a climax) is unclear and, in the end, not important for our quest.[120] The differences we find in the designation of the individual interrogators of Peter, the precise time and placement of the denials, the number of cockcrows, and the manner in which suspense is created and then resolved may all be due to the narrative skill of oral storytellers and the evangelists.

As for the further question of Jesus' prediction of Peter's denial during or after the Last Supper, agnostics and believers on my mythical committee of scholars locked up in the Harvard Divinity School library would no doubt have different views on the question—a question that is not of paramount importance. One should note, though, that the prediction of Peter's denial is witnessed in both the Marcan and Johannine traditions (Mark 14:29–31 ‖ John 13:37–38). Therefore, at the very least, it is not a late addition to the passion tradition. Then, too, history is full of cases in which leaders like Abraham Lincoln, Martin Luther King, Jr., or Oscar Romero have sensed beforehand the possibility of imminent violent death or betrayal. Faced with the possibility of legal arrest or illegal "street justice" in Jerusalem, Jesus knew all too well the weaknesses of his close followers, especially Peter. It would not have taken a great amount of imagination to have foreseen how the shaky disciples might react when faced with a crisis. In the end, though, whether the prophecy of Peter's denial was actually spoken by Jesus or was created secondarily out of the story of the denial is a question that may be insoluble and one that I am willing to waive.

Nevertheless, from the two criteria of embarrassment and multiple attestation, I conclude that the basic event of Peter's denial of Jesus after the latter's arrest sometime around Passover ca. A.D. 30 is factual, supplying a shattering conclusion to Peter's following of the historical Jesus. Humanly speaking, the public ministry ended in disaster for the disciple as well as for the prophet he followed. Indeed, looking back on all that we have seen of Peter, we can observe an interesting pattern. Even allowing for later legendary expansions, we are probably justified in detecting in Peter a tendency to blow hot and cold, to act with impetuous boldness only to retreat when trouble arises. Standing up and caving in weave a double strand that runs through Peter's career, extending from his role as follower in the public ministry to his role as leader in the early church. For all the pulpit rhetoric about sin and repentance, change and transformation, what is remarkable is how much Peter remains the same in various NT sources, both before and after Easter. Some may find this consoling, others depressing.

Yet, for all his weaknesses, Peter remains, after Jesus, the most fascinating figure in the Gospel tradition; for he bridges in a singular way the ministry of the historical Jesus and the mission of the early church. In the end, neither his prominent role among the disciples during the public ministry nor the belief that he was the first to see the risen Jesus can explain fully his special place in early church history. It is precisely the combination of the two vastly-different-yet-surprisingly-similar stages of his life that created his unique impact on Christian history and his enduring hold on Christian imagination.

III. CONCLUSION:
JESUS IN RELATION TO HIS FOLLOWERS

For the last four chapters, we have been tracing the contours of the various kinds of people who could be said, in one way or another, to have followed Jesus. Using "followers" as an umbrella term, we have found the rough outlines of three concentric circles of followers around Jesus: the crowds, the disciples, and the Twelve. One must stress the qualifier "rough" in our sketch, since, especially in the outer circle of the crowds and even in the middle circle of the disciples, an individual's relation to Jesus over the two or more years of his public ministry could have been quite fluid. People may have dropped in or out of a given circle or passed from one to another. Practical considerations as well as degrees of commitment would have dictated shifts.

For instance, while Jesus and the Twelve apparently kept a common purse, supplied with donations from sympathizers, and while they counted on hospitality from sedentary supporters during preaching tours, this support system could not have sustained the crowds. After a period of enthusiastic following, many would have had to return to their usual work to sustain themselves and their families. Even the Gospels do not depict Jesus feeding the multitudes every day.

It was perhaps this very fluidity of relationships that led Jesus, on the practical as distinct from the theological level of his mission, to establish the inner circle of the Twelve. Over a two-year period, the prophet and teacher would have wanted some stable inner circle to act as the regular audience for his preaching and teaching and the regular source of assistance in his mission. In sum, we must think of our sketch of the three circles as a heuristic model in motion, not as a still photograph. To review each circle briefly:

(1) The criteria of the multiple attestation of sources and of the final fate of Jesus argue that Jesus did in fact attract large crowds. The crowds were large enough and followed Jesus long enough to persuade those politically successful partners, Caiaphas and Pilate, that a preemptive strike against a possible disturber of the peace would be wise. Their decision, after some two years of activity on Jesus' part, suggests that there had been no massive falling away of followers at some point during the ministry. At the same time, we must admit that we can only speak vaguely of "large" crowds, without being able to specify what numbers or types of people made up the crowds. No doubt the vast majority qualified as "poor" in one sense or another, since the vast majority of the population of Palestine would have so qualified. Yet stories that are more specific about the individuals who interact with Jesus indicate that some of his supporters were or had been people of means. As the eschatological Elijah sent to begin the ingathering of all Israel, Jesus, unlike the Qumranites, did not restrict his attention to one particular stripe of Israelites.

While we may make some generalizations about the crowds, there are other generalizations that should be avoided. The Gospels do not equate the crowds with "sinners," those Jews who had in practice rejected God's commandments and adopted Gentile ways. Nor do the Gospels equate the crowds with "the people of the land," a label applied in later rabbinic literature to ordinary Jews who were not punctilious in observing the purity laws and tithing. As a matter of fact, unlike the label "sinners," the Gospels never use the phrase "people of the land" of any group. We would be wise to follow their lead.

(2) More can be said about the middle circle of disciples, for which there is abundant multiple attestation. Disciples of Jesus must be carefully distinguished from other adherents, such as sedentary supporters, who do not technically qualify as disciples. This reminds us that we should not take the label "disciple" for granted or use it loosely. With few exceptions, the word "disciple" is lacking in the proto- and deutero-canonical books of the OT, the OT pseudepigrapha, and the nonbiblical books at Qumran. The word occurs in Philo and Josephus, but relatively rarely. Josephus is the first major Jewish author to use "disciple" language to describe master-disciple relationships in the OT, including those of the followers of the prophets Elijah and Elisha.

It may be that the terminology of discipleship reflects the influence of Greco-Roman culture and was relatively new within Palestinian Judaism when Jesus—perhaps in imitation of the Pharisees or the Baptist—picked it up and used it to describe a special type of follower. Indeed, so special was the meaning Jesus gave "disciple" that, with the exception of Luke writing his Acts of the Apostles, it was not adopted by 1st-century Christians as their usual self-designation.

Reflecting the biblical tradition of Elijah calling Elisha to follow him, Jesus called certain adherents to follow him in a very specific sense as disciples. Three factors went into being a genuine disciple of Jesus: (a) Jesus took the initiative in issuing a peremptory command to follow him, a command that brooked no opposition or delay. (b) By the word "follow" Jesus meant literally, physically accompanying him on his preaching tours and therefore leaving behind one's home, parents, and livelihood—with no indication of a geographical or temporal limit on the commitment. (c) Such an open-ended commitment that demanded abandonment of home and livelihood could entail not just risk but also hostility and suffering, even at the hands of one's own family, as Jesus knew from his own experience. Thus, Jesus' demands on his disciples were radical and absolute; following him as a disciple was something far different from following him as part of the crowd. Yet for all these radical demands that created a sharp identity with sharp borders, Jesus and his disciples regularly crossed spiritual borders by associating and eating with such social and religious lowlifes as "toll collectors and sinners."

If Jesus' hobnobbing with toll collectors and sinners upset the stringently pious, Jesus' traveling entourage of women followers, notably Mary Magdalene, probably disturbed them even more—especially since some, if not all, of the women apparently followed Jesus without benefit of husbands as chaperons. Strangely, these women who followed Jesus in a literal, physical sense are never explicitly called "disciples" by the evangelists. Some critics might attribute this to the evangelists' androcentric point of view. Other explanations are also possible: (a) The evangelists may have lacked any narratives of specific women being called by Jesus to follow him. Or (b) the evangelists may simply be echoing in wooden fashion their Aramaic sources, which had no feminine form of the word "disciple" (talmîdā'). Whatever the linguistic situation, the women proved themselves disciples in deed if not in word not only by the economic support they gave Jesus during his journeys but also by their following him even to the cross, after the male disciples had betrayed, denied, or abandoned him.

Besides the disciples, Jesus enjoyed support from other adherents, men and women who accepted his message but did not leave their homes and families to follow him. When possible, they expressed their support by offering him hospitality during his journey—and perhaps by economic contributions as well. No doubt, some of the people healed by Jesus would have figured among these sedentary supporters, though some, like Mary Magdalene, responded to their cures by following Jesus literally. Perhaps we might think of the sedentary supporters as the "auxiliaries" or "support groups" of the disciples who made up the middle circle.

(3) Jesus' relations with the crowds and with his disciples flowed from and reflected his basic proclamation of the coming of God's kingdom and of the gathering of eschatological Israel in light of that coming. As with his miracles, so with his relations with the crowds and disciples, Jesus' message about the imminent future (kingdom of God and gathering of Israel) was also the program he began to realize in the present. In other words, as with his proclamation of the kingdom of God and his miracles, so with his formation of groups of followers, future eschatology and realized eschatology were inextricably intertwined. Nowhere is this more so, and nowhere does his eschatological vision appear more clearly, than in his formation of the inner circle of the Twelve.

It is by his choice of the Twelve that Jesus states most emphatically that God's definitive rule over the world is unthinkable without the fulfillment of the prophetic hopes uttered so often during and after the Babylonian exile: all Israel, all twelve tribes, will be regathered in the end time. Jesus' message of the kingdom of God is not some vague statement about eternal life. It is a prophet's proclamation that God is about to fulfill his promises to Israel by recreating his chosen people as they were meant to be. The kingdom of God is from start to finish a people-centered, Israel-centered message addressed to Jesus' fellow Jews. As with his healings and exorcisms, so with his formation of the Twelve, Jesus embodies this message in the present moment in a dramatic action that not only portends but also begins to realize the future promise. The twelve Israelite men chosen by Jesus evoke the twelve patriarchs (the sons of Jacob/Israel) and the twelve tribes—Israel as it was in the beginning and shall be at the end, only better (a typical apocalyptic hope).

Despite doubts from some critics, the multiple attestation of sources and forms argues convincingly that the Twelve were indeed a creation of Jesus during his ministry and not a retrojection of the early church into the Gospel story. Mark, John, and the special tradition of Luke all speak of the Twelve. In addition, a Q saying of Jesus (Matt 19:28 par.) confirms that Jesus connected the Twelve with the fate of eschatological Israel. In the end time, the Twelve would sit on twelve thrones, ruling or judging the restored twelve tribes of Israel.

So fixed was the name and function of the Twelve that, even when Judas

Iscariot betrayed Jesus and thus fell away from the group, the early church still spoke of the risen Jesus' appearance to the Twelve (1 Cor 15:5). As a matter of fact, Jesus' betrayal by Judas, one of the Twelve, adds the criterion of embarrassment to the criterion of multiple attestation as a strong argument for the Twelve's existence during Jesus' ministry. Moreover, while a few members of the Twelve, notably Peter and the sons of Zebedee, were prominent leaders of the early church in Jerusalem, most of the Twelve and the Twelve as a group disappear very quickly after Easter. The idea that they were such a significant and dominant group in the early church that they were massively retrojected into the Marcan, Q, L, and Johannine traditions is contradicted by the actual flow and ebb of their career.

The Twelve functioned in a number of ways during the public ministry. They embodied in a fairly permanent fashion what it meant to be a disciple of Jesus. More importantly, they formed a corporate, prophetic symbol that both prophesied and began to realize the regathering of the twelve tribes in the end time. In my opinion, the realization of this future regathering of the tribes was further symbolized and initiated by a brief mission to Israel with which Jesus entrusted the Twelve (and perhaps other disciples as well).

That the Twelve were important primarily as a group symbolizing the restored Israel and not as individuals is reflected in the fact that most of the Twelve are little more than names to us. We are left trying to guess a few details from their nicknames, patronymics, or places of origin. Even Judas Iscariot becomes an individual only at the end of the story, when he stands out in the Twelve by standing apart from the Twelve in his betrayal. Whether Peter, James, and John actually formed a special group of three within the Twelve during the public ministry is difficult to say. In any case, they stand out as the three members of whom a little more can be known. Only Peter, however, emerges as what literary critics would call a "round" as opposed to a "flat" character. This may be due in part to the fact that the Gospels preserve more of his history—and perhaps even of his character—than that of any other member of the Twelve. The Gospels' special interest in Peter is due in turn to the leadership role he exercised both during the ministry and in the early days of the church.

With this we exhaust what can be said of the various followers of Jesus. While the three concentric circles must remain sketchy, at least our quest for the historical followers of the historical Jesus has yielded some insights. Contrary to some present-day presentations of Jesus, we have come to see that the followers were not some amorphous blob around him. He himself chose to distinguish from those who followed him merely physically (the crowds) a special group of people (the disciples) who were willing to follow him with a costly commitment that bespoke deep personal adherence to his message and his person. From this circle in turn he took the initiative in singling out the Twelve as a prophetic symbol of end-time Israel.

By these very choices, Jesus, for all the "charismatic" elements of his conduct, in effect gave a specific shape to his ministry by supplying it with certain structures, however vague and fluid they may have been. Such structures, while by no means as complex as those described at Qumran, flowed from the same basic concern as Qumran's: eschatological Israel. Both the Essenes at Qumran and the disciples of Jesus formed religious movements of eschatologically oriented Palestinian Jews. As such, both were focused on the people of Israel, which had never been experienced historically and would never be imagined eschatologically as an amorphous blob.

This should be kept in mind when some present-day questers apply the adjective "egalitarian" to Jesus, though precise definitions of the term are often not supplied.[121] If one thinks of Jesus' open-ended address to all Israelites, including toll collectors and sinners, of his free-wheeling table fellowship with these social or religious pariahs, of his message of good news to the poor in particular (while not excluding the affluent who were well disposed toward him), of his acceptance of women followers, of his lack of concern for what the powerful or influential might think of himself or his disciples, and of his insistence that his disciples must show love, compassion, and forgiveness toward all, "egalitarian" expresses well the leveling influence his message would have had on Israelite society of the time. But what a present-day historian must not do is retroject modern thought about social classes, revolution, utopian egalitarianism, and theoretical anarchy into the mind of a 1st-century Palestinian Jew for whom Israel always had been and always would be, in one way or another, an ordered society.

The eschatological prophet bearing the mantle of Elijah apparently thought he had something to do with ordering end-time Israel. Significantly, when Jesus instituted the particular structure of the Twelve for the Israel of the end time, he chose to stand over against the circle of the Twelve as its founder instead of making himself one of its members, even possibly its leader and spokesman à la Peter. As the prophets Jeremiah and Ezekiel stood over against the Israel they addressed, even though they themselves were Israelites passionately committed to the future of their people, so too Jesus stood over against the circle of twelve men he had formed, the twelve men who embodied the Israel he had been sent to gather. He gave them a structure to which he himself did not belong.

As a matter of fact, the circle of the Twelve was not the only incipient structural element Jesus provided for those who followed him on the path of discipleship. As I have argued in Volume Two, without creating a separatist sect, Jesus used certain distinguishing practices to form and give identity to the disciples who followed him.[122] The practice of baptism, the rejection of voluntary fasting yoked with festive meals celebrated with the outcasts of Israel, the rejection of divorce (and perhaps the use of oaths and vows), the special prayer we call the Lord's Prayer, the fierce demands made on those who followed him literally on his itinerant ministry, the inner circle of the Twelve symbolizing eschatological Israel, the mission of the Twelve and perhaps other disciples to Israel—all these incipient structural elements shaped the contours of a clearly distinguished group of disciples, even as Jesus sought with them and through them to reach out to all Israel.[123] This outreach to *all* Israel did indeed have a certain egalitarian thrust to it. But as the inner circle of the Twelve as well as George Orwell reminds us, in an egalitarian society all are equal, but some are more equal than others. The eschatological program of Jesus did not envision the Israel of the future, any more than the Israel of the past, as totally devoid of structure and order.

One must carefully distinguish these considerations on incipient structural elements in the ministry of the historical Jesus from a much more complicated question that mixes historical and theological perspectives: Did Jesus found or intend to found a (or: the) church? Any attempt to answer such a question must of necessity deal with the historical elements from Jesus' public ministry that I have listed above. It is a historical fact that certain personages and practices from the ministry of the historical Jesus continued as or became key personages and practices in the early church. From the teaching on divorce to the leadership of Peter within the circle of the Twelve, too many links exist to deny any connection whatever between Jesus' ministry and the rise of the early church.

At the same time, one must honestly face the massive elements of discontinuity. Jesus the Jew addressed his fellow Israelites and sought to gather all Israel into the community of the end time. It was apparently only at the consummation of Israel's history that he thought Gentiles would be brought into the kingdom (see, e.g., Matt 8:11–12 par.).[124] He was not interested in creating a separatist sect or a holy remnant à la Qumran, and he never sent his disciples on a formal mission to the Gentiles.[125] The idea that his special religious community within Israel would slowly undergo a process of separation from Israel as it pursued a mission to the Gentiles in this present world—the long-term result being that his community would become predominantly Gentile itself—finds no place in Jesus' message or practice.

While the early church as we know it would not have arisen without the ministry of the historical Jesus as a necessary precondition, the ministry of

Jesus, taken by itself, did not create the early church. The immediate matrix of the church is the crucifixion of Jesus, the claim by some of his disciples that he had risen from the dead and appeared to them, and their experience of an outpouring of the Holy Spirit, unleashing a vigorous mission first to Israel and then increasingly to the Gentiles. One can see immediately from this statement that faith claims as well as empirically verifiable historical claims play a great role in a description of the origins of the church. Of necessity, therefore, the question of the rise of the church and of its continuity with yet discontinuity from the ministry of the historical Jesus lies beyond the limits of our quest. We are concerned with the various religious groups with which the historical Jesus interacted during his ministry. The new religious group that arose as a consequence of his death and belief in his resurrection lies beyond the narrow horizons of this present work.[126]

Having surveyed the various groups of people attracted to Jesus and to his vision of what the people of Israel were called to be, we must now turn our gaze to other groups and movements in Israel which fostered alternate visions of the people's present and future. Jesus must be understood in relation to those Israelites who did not follow him as well as to those who did.

NOTES TO CHAPTER 27

[1] Here we must allow an exception for the only case of a change of names in the lists of the Twelve: Thaddeus in the lists of Mark and Matthew versus Jude of James in the Lucan lists. If this change means that some original member of the Twelve dropped out of the group during the public ministry, the latter assertions made above in the main text would not hold for that individual. Likewise, as is noted in the main text, they did not hold for Judas Iscariot.

[2] On the negative results of sifting the Nag Hammadi material for information about the historical Jesus, see *A Marginal Jew,* 1. 123–39. For a review of the debate that is more favorable to the "autonomy" if not the "independence" of the sayings tradition in the *Gospel of Thomas,* see Robert McL. Wilson, "The Gospel of Thomas Reconsidered," *Divitiae Aegypti* (Martin Krause Festschrift; ed. Cäcilia Fluck et al.; Wiesbaden: Reichert, 1995) 331–36. See also James M. Robinson and Christoph Heil, "The Lilies of the Field: Saying 36 of the *Gospel of Thomas* and Secondary Accretions in Q 12.22b–31," *NTS* 47 (2000) 1–25.

[3] For a useful summary of traditions about Bartholomew in both the NT and later literature, see Michael J. Wilkins, "Bartholomew," *Anchor Bible Dictionary,* 1. 615. The only questionable judgment in the article is: ". . . to reject categorically the identification [between Bartholomew and Nathanael] is . . . unwarranted." It *is* warranted by the basic philosophical principle that what is gratuitously asserted may be gratuitously denied. Even the status of Bartholomew's name as a patronymic is un-

clear, since, as E. P. Blair points out ("Bartholomew," *IDB*, 1. 359), in NT times certain names that may technically have been patronymics seem to have been used as independent proper names. Moreover, other patronymics in the lists of the Twelve are not expressed with the use of *bar* (Aramaic for "son") but rather with the Greek genitive case, the Greek noun *huios* ("son") being understood: e.g., "James the [son] of Zebedee."

[4] Sometimes it is argued that (1) since, in John 1:45–46, Philip introduces Nathanael to Jesus, and (2) since, in the three Synoptic lists of the Twelve, Bartholomew's name follows Philip, Bartholomew was the patronymic of Nathanael. But (1) in John's Gospel, it is Andrew, not Nathanael, with whom Philip is regularly associated (1:35–44; 6:5–9; 12:21–22), and (2) the connection between Philip and Bartholomew is not kept in the list of Acts 1:13.

[5] For the various people named Jude (= Judas) in the NT and for the attempts by scribes to rewrite the name in John 14:22 as "Judas the Cananean" or as "(Judas) Thomas," see Brown, *The Gospel According to John*, 2. 641. Brown concludes: "In the face of such confused evidence, no decision [on the identity of the Judas in 14:22] is possible."

[6] For the problem of who is intended by the real author of the Epistle of Jude when he uses the designation "Jude, servant of Jesus Christ and brother of James," see Jerome H. Neyrey, *2 Peter, Jude* (AB 37C; New York: Doubleday, 1993) 44–45.

[7] More material may be found in Robert D. Miller II, "Judas" (entry number 7), *Anchor Bible Dictionary*, 3. 1090. Identification of Jude with "the Cananean" or "the Zealot" is seen in some Coptic and Old Latin versions of John 14:22, while identification with Thomas is seen in some versions of the Syriac.

[8] Much is made by some critics of the name "Lebbaeus," which is found in some manuscripts of Mark and Matthew in place of or along with "Thaddeus." All sorts of theories of equivalencies or substitutions (either merely of the names or of actual historical persons) are suggested; see, e.g., Taylor, *The Gospel According to St. Mark*, 233–34; Davies and Allison, *The Gospel According to Saint Matthew*, 2. 156; JoAnn Ford Watson, "Thaddeus (Person)," *Anchor Bible Dictionary*, 6. 435. In my view, "Thaddeus" (by itself) is the original reading in both Mark and Matthew. (1) In Mark 3:18, "Lebbaeus" is found only in Codex Bezae and a number of the Old Latin manuscripts; it is therefore restricted to only a part of the so-called Western textual tradition. Quite rightly, the *UBSGNT* (4th ed.) assigns the reading "Thaddeus" an "A" (certain) status. (2) In Matt 10:3, the readings are more varied: "Thaddeus," "Thaddeus who is called Lebbaeus," "Lebbaeus who is called Thaddeus," etc. While the testimony of the textual witnesses is more confused, the *UBSGNT* (4th ed.) rightly prefers "Thaddeus" and assigns it a "B" (almost certain) rating. In favor of the unadorned "Thaddeus" in Matt 10:3, I think an argument can be mounted from the conclusions we reached about the sources of the lists of the Twelve: apart from the present case, there is no reason to suppose that the Matthean list of the Twelve is de-

rived from any source beyond the Marcan list. Consequently, once one decides in favor of the simple "Thaddeus" in Mark, it is difficult to see what redactional reason would have led Matthew, with no other source in front of him, to change "Thaddeus" to "Lebbaeus." Whether "Lebbaeus" arises merely out of scribal confusion in the copying of certain manuscripts or whether exegetical difficulties in reconciling the various NT lists of the Twelve led some Christian scribes to change the name on purpose is hard to say. For the theory that "Lebbaeus" arose from an effort to introduce Levi into the list of the Twelve ("Lebbaeus" being a Latinism for "Levi"), see Barnabas Lindars, "Matthew, Levi, Lebbaeus and the Value of the Western Text," *NTS* 4 (1957–58) 220–22. In any event, "Lebbaeus" is not original in the text of either Mark or Matthew; hence it has no relevance to our treatment of the historical existence of the Twelve during the ministry of Jesus. The confusion over Lebbaeus arose among Christian scribes, not among Jews following Jesus or even among the earliest Palestinian Jewish Christians.

[9] All we know about "James the Less" is summed up in one NT verse, namely Mark 15:40: one of the women standing at a distance from the cross of Jesus was "Mary the mother of James the Less and Joses [= Joseph]." "James the Less and Joses" should not be identified with the James and Joses mentioned as brothers of Jesus in Mark 6:3. Granted the insights of redaction and narrative criticism, one must ask why Mark confers the distinguishing designation "the Less" on the James of 15:40. The only reasonable answer is: to distinguish him from the other persons named James already mentioned in the narrative, namely, James the son of Zebedee and James the brother of Jesus. Granted that Mark has already assigned the latter James a very clear and impressive identity (the brother of Jesus), how is the reader of Mark's Gospel supposed to know that the James of 6:3 is to be identified with a James who, in 15:40, is designated by a completely different label? And what would be Mark's purpose in introducing a new and confusing label for the same person? Rather, to make clear to the reader that the same James was meant in 15:40 as in 6:3, Mark would either have to use the phrase "the brother of Jesus" in 15:40 or have to repeat the names of all four brothers as listed in 6:3. On this whole question, see *A Marginal Jew*, 1. 355 n. 21.

[10] On this, see John P. Meier, *The Vision of Matthew* (Theological Inquiries; New York/Ramsey, NJ/Toronto: Paulist, 1979) 23–25.

[11] On this possibility, see *A Marginal Jew*, 2. 194 n. 68; also Rudolf Schnackenburg, *The Gospel According to St John. Volume One* (London: Burns & Oates; New York: Herder and Herder, 1968) 310–11.

[12] On the geographical and political problems involved in pinpointing NT Bethsaida, see *A Marginal Jew*, 2. 690–92, 738–39; on the excavations at Bethsaida, see Heinz-Wolfgang Kuhn and Rami Arav, "The Bethsaida Excavations: Historical and Archaeological Approaches," *The Future of Early Christianity* (Helmut Koester Festschrift; Minneapolis: Fortress, 1991) 77–106. Since Pliny in his *Natural History,*

Eusebius, and Jerome all refer to Bethsaida as being in Galilee, when strictly speaking it was just outside Galilee on the northeast shore of the Sea of Galilee, slightly east of the Jordan River, John cannot be taxed too severely for using a loose, popular way of referring to the town. On the problem of the Johannine tradition of Bethsaida as the city of Peter vis-à-vis the Marcan tradition of Capernaum, see the treatment of Peter below.

[13] On this whole question, see *A Marginal Jew*, 2. 116–30.

[14] When one considers that Peter is rarely associated with Andrew in the Synoptic tradition after their initial call and is never yoked with him in any information we have from the early church, this very silence may be the best argument for the historicity of the claim that Andrew was connected with Peter in their initial call by Jesus—be that understood in terms of Mark 1 or John 1. For Andrew, see Dennis R. MacDonald, "Andrew (Person)," *Anchor Bible Dictionary*, 1. 242–44. As Peter M. Peterson (*Andrew, Brother of Simon Peter. His History and Legends* [NovTSup 1; Leiden: Brill, 1958] 17–23) points out, the Eastern Christian tradition that connects Andrew with Byzantium (later Constantinople) is not earlier than the 8th or 9th century. Peterson also thinks that the references to Andrew in John's Gospel are legendary (p. 47).

[15] See the analysis of the Lazarus story in *A Marginal Jew*, 2. 800–822; for v 16, see p. 807.

[16] The matter is further complicated by the fact that while "Thomas" was not regularly used as a proper name in Hebrew or Aramaic, the Greek *Thōmas* was used as a proper name in Greek-speaking regions. It may be, as Brown suggests (*The Gospel According to John*, 1. 424), that the Greek name *Thōmas*, because it resembled the Semitic noun, was adopted by Jews in areas where they spoke Greek.

[17] The Nag Hammadi material on Thomas comprises the 2d-century Coptic *Gospel of Thomas* and the 3d-century *Book of Thomas the Contender*, both of which reflect a negative view of matter and sexuality and so favor a radical asceticism. The same traits are found in the 3d-century *Acts of Thomas*, originally composed in Syriac. On "the school of St. Thomas," see Bentley Layton, *The Gnostic Scriptures* (Garden City, NY: Doubleday, 1987) 359–65. That "Jude Thomas (also called Didymus)" is Jesus' twin brother is clearly asserted in *Thom. Cont.* 138:7–19; *Acts of Thomas*, chaps. 11; 31; 39. In contrast, the idea is at best only intimated in the Coptic *Gospel of Thomas*, which rather presupposes the "consubstantial" identity of every saved person (to be sure, including Thomas) with the savior, since the inner being of every saved person is divine. An intriguing point here is that in the one work of "the school of St. Thomas" that clearly dates from the 2d century, namely, the Coptic *Gospel of Thomas*, Thomas is actually a peripheral figure who hardly belongs to the traditional material in the book. He is introduced as the author of the work in the clearly redactional opening sentence, but figures prominently in only one other logion, the lengthy

saying 13, where Simon Peter and Matthew are also mentioned but Thomas is exalted as the possessor of the secret knowledge of Jesus' nature. This logion stands in tension with the rival logion just before it, saying 12, where James the Just (the brother of Jesus) is exalted as the leader of the disciples after Jesus departs. On this tension, see Gilles Quispel, " 'The Gospel of Thomas' and the 'Gospel of the Hebrews,' " *NTS* 12 (1965–66) 371–82, esp. 380. Hence the *Gospel of Thomas,* the earliest apocryphal and gnosticizing work that was put under the name of Thomas, does not present a tradition really rooted in that person and does not clearly inculcate the idea that Thomas is Jesus' twin brother. As already noted, the reading "Judas Thomas" in some Syriac texts of John 14:25 may also reflect the developing legend of Thomas as the twin brother of Jesus if the "Judas" mentioned in the texts is understood as Jude the brother of Jesus. As Quispel points out (ibid., p. 380), it is surprising to see such a critical scholar as Helmut Koester ("*Gnōmai diaphoroi.* The Origin and Nature of Diversification in the History of Early Christianity," *HTR* 58 [1965] 279–318, esp. 296–97) favoring the idea that Christianity came to Edessa through the work of Thomas, who was in fact Jude, the twin brother of Jesus. How one can be so skeptical about the historical Jesus and yet so credulous about the twin brother of Jesus, Jude Thomas, boggles the mind.

[18] As for the first name, "Simon [Greek *Simōn*]" was an ordinary Greek name that was used by Greek-speaking Jews around the turn of the era to represent the similar-sounding Semitic name *Šimʿôn.* The LXX usually renders the Semitic name with the Greek form *Symeōn,* although some late deuterocanonical books (Ben Sira, 1 and 2 Maccabees) use the native Greek form *Simōn.* The tendency is just the opposite in the NT. The form that regularly occurs in the NT is the native Greek *Simōn,* while the use of *Symeōn* is relatively rare, occurring only in late NT books and only in references to the OT or in passages that intend to convey a venerable or Semitic tone: Luke 2:25,34; 3:30; Acts 13:1; 15:14; 2 Pet 1:1; Rev 7:7. The Hebrew *Šimʿôn* and its Greek transliteration *Symeōn* are rendered as "Simeon" or "Symeon" in most English translations, while the Greek *Simōn* is represented by "Simon." This convention is followed in my references to Simon the Zealot and Simon Peter. See Joseph A. Fitzmyer, "Aramaic *Kephaʾ* and Peter's Name in the New Testament," *Text and Interpretation* (Matthew Black Festschrift; ed. Ernest Best and R. McL. Wilson; Cambridge: Cambridge University, 1979) 121–32 (= *To Advance the Gospel* [New York: Crossroad, 1981] 112–24).

[19] One of the most famous proponents of this view was S. G. F. Brandon, *Jesus and the Zealots. A Study of the Political Factor in Primitive Christianity* (Manchester: Manchester University, 1967). On the whole question of Jesus' relation to the political situation in Jewish Palestine, see the essays collected in *Jesus and the Politics of His Day* (ed. Ernst Bammel and C. F. D. Moule; Cambridge: Cambridge University, 1984). Of special interest are J. P. M. Sweet, "The Zealots and Jesus," pp. 1–9; E. Bammel, "The Revolution Theory from Reimarus to Brandon," pp. 11–68; G. M. Styler, "Argumentum e silentio," pp. 101–7; E. Bammel, "The Poor and the Zealots,"

pp. 109–28. One notes in some of these essays a lack of a critical definition of who precisely the Zealots were.

[20] On this point, see Morton Smith, "Zealots and Sicarii. Their Origins and Relation," *HTR* 64 (1971) 1–19; Shaye J. D. Cohen, *Josephus in Galilee and Rome* (Columbia Studies in the Classical Tradition 8; Leiden: Brill, 1979); idem, *From the Maccabees to the Mishnah* (Library of Early Christianity 7; Philadelphia: Westminster, 1987) 164–66; see also Fitzmyer, *The Gospel According to Luke*, 1. 619. For a good overview of the whole question of Zealots, other factions involved in the First Jewish War (the provisional government under the priestly and lay aristocrats, the sicarii, the group led by John of Gischala, the group led by Simon bar Giora), and the larger problem of Jewish revolutionary movements in Palestine, see David Rhoads, "Zealots," *The Anchor Bible Dictionary*, 6. 1043–54, with a helpful bibliography appended. Standard works on the question that represent a wide variety of views include F. J. Foakes Jackson and Kirsopp Lake, "The Zealots," *The Beginnings of Christianity. Part I. The Acts of the Apostles. Vol. I* (ed. F. J. Foakes Jackson and Kirsopp Lake; Grand Rapids: Baker, 1979, originally 1920) 421–25; William R. Farmer, *Maccabees, Zealots, and Josephus. An Inquiry into Jewish Nationalism in the Greco-Roman Period* (Westport, CT: Greenwood, 1973, originally 1956); Brandon, *Jesus and the Zealots*; Oscar Cullmann, *Jesus and the Revolutionaries* (New York: Harper & Row, 1970); Martin Hengel, *Was Jesus a Revolutionist?* (Philadelphia: Fortress, 1971); idem, *Victory over Violence* (Philadelphia: Fortress, 1973); idem, *The Zealots* (Edinburgh: Clark, 1989); David Rhoads, *Israel in Revolution: 6–74 C.E.* (Philadelphia: Fortress, 1976); J.-Alfred Morin, "Les deux derniers des Douze: Simon le Zélote et Judas Iskariôth," *RB* 80 (1973) 332–58; D. Hill, "Jesus and Josephus' 'Messianic Prophets,' " *Text and Interpretation* (Matthew Black Festschrift; ed. E. Best and R. McL. Wilson; Cambridge: Cambridge University, 1979) 143–54; Emil Schürer, *The History of the Jewish People in the Age of Jesus Christ* (4 vols.; revised and edited by Geza Vermes, Fergus Millar, and Matthew Black; Edinburgh: Clark, 1973–87) 2. 598–606; Seán Freyne, *Galilee from Alexander the Great to Hadrian: 323 B.C.E. to 135 C.E.* (Center for the Study of Judaism and Christianity in Antiquity 5; Notre Dame, IN: University of Notre Dame; Wilmington, DE: Glazier, 1980); Tessa Rajak, *Josephus. The Historian and His Society* (Philadelphia: Fortress, 1983); Richard A. Horsley and John S. Hanson, *Bandits, Prophets, and Messiahs* (Minneapolis: Seabury, 1985); Richard A. Horsley, *Jesus and the Spiral of Violence* (San Francisco: Harper & Row, 1987); Martin Goodman, *The Ruling Class of Judaea* (Cambridge: Cambridge University, 1987); Lester L. Grabbe, *Judaism from Cyrus to Hadrian. Volume Two: The Roman Period* (Minneapolis: Fortress, 1992) 457–59; Monette Bohrmann, *Flavius Josephus, the Zealots and Yavne* (Bern: Lang, 1994).

[21] Simeon and Levi, the sons of Jacob, are also mentioned in this tradition (cf. Gen 34:25–31 and the negative evaluation in Gen 49:5–7); on this see William R. Farmer, "Zealot," *IDB*, 4. 936–39. Important texts that make explicit the reference to "zeal" in the violent acts of these heroes include Num 25:10–13 (Phinehas); Sir 45:23–24

(Phinehas); 1 Macc 2:54 (Phinehas); 1 Macc 2:15–28 (Mattathias); Sir 48:2 (Elijah); *Jub.* 30:5–20 (Levi); Jdt 9:2–4 (Simeon).

[22] Often connected with an erroneous idea of "Zealots" is the highly questionable picture of the Galilee of Jesus' time as a cauldron constantly boiling over with revolutionary fervor. Against such a view is Freyne, *Galilee from Alexander the Great to Hadrian,* 208–55; cf. *A Marginal Jew,* 1. 282–83.

[23] On Phinehas-like "zeal" and the pre-Christian Paul, see Martin Hengel, *Acts and the History of Earliest Christianity* (Philadelphia: Fortress, 1979) 83–84; Terence L. Donaldson, "Zealot and Convert: The Origin of Paul's Christ-Torah Antithesis," *CBQ* 51 (1989) 655–82; Jürgen Becker, *Paul Apostle to the Gentiles* (Louisville: Westminster/John Knox, 1993, German original 1989) 66–69. A study that suffers from too quick a leap from zealot traditions in the broad sense to *the* Zealot movement is Mark R. Fairchild, "Paul's Pre-Christian Zealot Associations: A Re-examination of Gal 1.14 and Acts 22.3," *NTS* 45 (1999) 514–32.

[24] On the evidence for Jesus' table fellowship with toll collectors and sinners, see *A Marginal Jew,* 2. 1035 n. 317 (continued on pp. 1036–37).

[25] For an overview of the problems connected with Judas Iscariot, see Brown, *The Death of the Messiah,* 2. 1394–1418.

[26] One is reminded of how Boïto and Verdi were unsatisfied with Shakespeare's skimpy motivation for Iago's "betrayal" of Othello. To fill in the lacuna, they wrote for Iago the famous aria "Credo in un Dio crudel" ("I believe in a cruel God") to provide a deeper, theological motive for Iago's otherwise unfathomable villainy.

[27] One is at a loss to know what to make, e.g., of Klassen's summation of "Judas in Recent Discussion" in his article on "Judas" in *Anchor Bible Dictionary,* 3. 1096: "The numerous novels about Judas in the 20th century and their revisions of the traditional point of view (not to mention contemporary movies or musicals in which he figures) *signals the continuing search for the Judas of history*" (italics mine). Here everything that is wrongheaded about the modern quest for the historical Jesus is raised to the *n*th power. Stranger still is the approach of Günther Schwarz (*Jesus und Judas,* 237), who mixes hypothetical Aramaic reconstructions with theological speculation to arrive at a supposedly historical conclusion: Jesus wished to die, he controlled his death to the point of fixing the time, and he gave Judas a specific role to play in arranging the death, a role that Judas obediently played. A good antidote to all this unbridled imagination is the sane and modest approach of Klauck, *Judas,* 137–46.

[28] So Gustav Dalman, *Die Worte Jesu* (Leipzig: Hinrichs, 1898) 42.

[29] For reviews and evaluations of theories, see Morin, "Les deux derniers des Douze," 349–58; Albert Ehrman, "Judas Iscariot and Abba Saqqara," *JBL* 97 (1978)

572–73; Yoël Arbeitman, "The Suffix of Iscariot," *JBL* 99 (1980) 122–24; Klauck, *Judas*, 40–44; Schwarz, *Jesus und Judas*, 6–12; Klassen, "Judas Iscariot," 1091–92; idem, *Judas*, 32–34; Brown, *The Death of the Messiah*, 2. 1410–16. For the two different spellings of Iscariot, *Iskariōth* and *Iskariōtēs*, and for text-critical variations, see Klauck, ibid., 40–41; Brown, ibid., 1411–13.

[30] See Brown, *The Death of the Messiah*, 2. 1414.

[31] The textual tradition is, however, quite divided. Not surprisingly, the *UBSGNT* (3d ed.) gives the reading a "C" rating in each passage, indicating that, because of a considerable degree of doubt, the committee had difficulty in deciding which variant to place in the text. For the arguments in favor of *Iskariōtou* (modifying *Simōnos*, Judas' father), see Metzger, *Textual Commentary* (2d ed.), 184, 204–5. Perhaps the best argument in favor of "Iscariot" belonging with "Simon" rather than with "Judas" is that it is the more difficult reading, one that would quickly invite correction from Christian scribes who knew the usage of the Synoptic Gospels. Why they would thrice change a reading in John's Gospel that agreed with the Synoptics (i.e., "Judas Iscariot") to create an otherwise unheard-of reading is difficult to explain.

[32] See *A Marginal Jew*, 2. 896–904; similarly, Rudolf Pesch, *Simon-Petrus. Geschichte und geschichtliche Bedeutung der ersten Jüngers Jesu Christ* (Päpste und Papsttum 15; Stuttgart: Hiersemann, 1980) 36.

[33] Another possibility is that the idea of an inner group of three is a garbled retrojection of the situation in the Jerusalem church of the first Christian generation, when, for a time, James *the brother of Jesus*, Cephas (= Peter) and John (the son of Zebedee) were the "pillars" of the Jerusalem community (see Gal 2:9)—James the son of Zebedee and brother of John having already been martyred by Herod Agrippa I (Acts 12:2). In this case, not only was an early Christian leadership group of three read back into Jesus' public ministry, but in the process James the son of Zebedee was substituted for James the brother of Jesus—necessarily so, since it was well known that the brothers of Jesus did not believe in him during his public ministry. If this (admittedly, highly speculative) hypothesis were true, it would mean that the idea of the innermost group of three was not invented by Mark but already existed in some of the traditions he inherited. Such a hypothesis would also weaken the argument of Pesch (*Simon-Petrus*, 23) for the historical existence of the group of three during the public ministry; Pesch points out that Peter, James (the son of Zebedee), and John did not function as a leadership group in the early church.

[34] Admittedly, we have no 1st-century attestation for the martyrdom of James the son of Zebedee apart from Acts 12:2. As a matter of fact, though, almost all recent commentators on Acts seem to accept the basic historicity of the bare fact of James' martyrdom by Agrippa I without further ado. This acceptance is reasonable. The whole of Acts 12:1–23, "not distinctively Lucan in style," is almost an isolated block within the flow of the larger narrative of Acts; it "is more easily detachable from the

main thread of narrative in Acts than any other [paragraph]" (Barrett, *Acts,* 1. 568). This is even more true of the fleeting reference to the killing of James in v 2. As Barrett goes on to say (p. 569), "it is hard to see how the progress of Luke's story is affected" by the brief notice about James' martyrdom. Hence many would agree that Luke has not invented the passing reference to James' death but rather has inherited it from a Jewish-Christian Palestinian source (see Fitzmyer, *Acts,* 486). One notices that neither in the bare fact of James' martyrdom nor in its position in the Lucan narrative does any great theological agenda seem to be served. The one-sentence statement in v 2 cries out for some further elaboration, which it duly received in ancient legends and in modern scholarly speculation; see, e.g., Josef Blinzler's—in my view, unlikely—hypothetical reconstruction of the juridical context of James' execution in "Rechtsgeschichtliches zur Hinrichtung des Zebedäiden Jakobus (Apg xii,2)," *NovT* 5 (1962) 191–206; also highly speculative is Oscar Cullmann's "Courants multiples dans la communauté primitive. A propos du martyre de Jacques fils de Zébédée," *RSR* 60 (1972) 55–68. The very fact that the sober notice in Acts 12:2 has not received such elaboration by the time it reaches Luke speaks in favor of its reliability.

[35] On the various persons called James in the NT and the problem of distinguishing among them, see Donald A. Hagner, "James (Person)," *Anchor Bible Dictionary,* 3. 616–18. Hagner (p. 617) considers it probable that Matthew identifies the Salome mentioned by Mark (15:40) at the cross of Jesus with the mother of the sons of Zebedee (Matt 27:56). I instead see here a conscious redactional change on Matthew's part. To soften the negative picture of James and John in Mark 10:35–45, Matthew, in his parallel story, had their mother make the initial request that James and John be seated at Jesus' right and left in his kingdom (Matt 20:20). Once Matthew had introduced this specific woman among the followers of Jesus going up with him to Jerusalem (and hence to the cross), the evangelist's accountant-like mind did not want to waste her; she therefore appears among the women at the foot of the cross in the place of Salome, who is not mentioned in Mark (or, for that matter, Matthew) prior to the scene at the foot of the cross. Any further speculation about Salome in relation to James and John is without foundation.

[36] Perhaps some scholars would like to add the final redactor of the Fourth Gospel—if, as I think likely, he is not identical with the author of the Johannine Epistles. For the reasons why one should not identify John the son of Zebedee, the author of the Fourth Gospel, the final redactor of the Gospel, and the anonymous "disciple whom Jesus loved," see B. W. Bacon, "John and the Pseudo-Johns," *ZNW* 31 (1932) 132–50; Pierson Parker, "John the Son of Zebedee and the Fourth Gospel," *JBL* 81 (1962) 35–43; Brown, *The Community of the Beloved Disciple;* Rudolf Schnackenburg's excursus, "Der Jünger, den Jesus liebte," *Das Johannesevangelium. III. Teil* (HTKNT 4/3; Freiburg/Basel/Vienna: Herder, 1975) 449–64; Joachim Kügler, *Der Jünger, den Jesus liebte* (SBB 16; Stuttgart: KBW, 1988) 439–48; Brendan Byrne, "Beloved Disciple," *Anchor Bible Dictionary,* 1. 658–61. On the more debated question of the separate identity of the author of the Johannine Epistles vis-à-vis the author of the Fourth Gospel, see Raymond E. Brown, *The Epistles of John* (AB 30;

Garden City, NY: Doubleday, 1982) 14–30, 69–115. The separate identity of the John who wrote the Book of Revelation was maintained by some even in the patristic period; no serious scholar today would identify him with the authors of the Fourth Gospel or the Johannine Epistles. Raymond Collins ("John [Disciple]," *Anchor Bible Dictionary*, 3. 883–86) sums up the present critical consensus well (p. 885): "Historical criticism has . . . shown that all five works [John, 1–2–3 John, Revelation] could not have been written by the same author, and that it is highly unlikely that John, the son of Zebedee, was the author of any one of them." For a rear-guard conservative attempt to maintain the link between John the son of Zebedee and the Fourth Gospel, see John A. T. Robinson, *The Priority of John* (Oak Park, IL: Meyer-Stone, 1985). For a conservative approach to the Gospel that remains critical and intellectually respectable, see Martin Hengel, *The Johannine Question* (London: SCM; Philadelphia: Trinity, 1989). For a survey of critical thought and legendary musings on John the son of Zebedee down through the ages, see the fine overview of R. Alan Culpepper, *John, the Son of Zebedee. The Life of a Legend* (Studies on Personalities of the NT; Columbia, SC: University of South Carolina, 1994).

[37] This is a major point made throughout Wuellner's *The Meaning of "Fishers of Men"*; see also Culpepper, *John, the Son of Zebedee*, 9–15.

[38] The weakness of this explanation is that Acts, the very book that recounts the martyrdom of James (12:2), is also the sole NT book that lists John before James (1:13).

[39] In what follows, I am dependent on the summary of opinions given by Culpepper, *John, the Son of Zebedee*, 38–40.

[40] For a consideration of the problem and a speculative solution by way of a Greek copyist's play on words, see Randall Buth, "Mark 3:17 *Boneregem* and Popular Etymology," *JSNT* 10 (1981) 29–33. Of such speculative solutions there is no end. D. R. G. Beattie, for example, suggests that an original *r'm* ("thunder") was misread as *r's* by a scribe who thought that the final *mem* was a *samek* instead, thus producing the strange *-rges* ending of the Greek noun. See his "Boanerges: A Semiticist's Solution," *Irish Biblical Studies* 5 (1983) 11–13.

[41] See Gustaf Dalman, *Grammatik des jüdisch-palästinischen Aramäisch* (Darmstadt: Wissenschaftliche Buchgesellschaft, 1960, originally 1905) 144 n. 2; idem, *Die Worte Jesu*, 33, 39–40; Bauer, *Wörterbuch* (6th ed.), col. 287.

[42] Betz, "Donnersöhne," 41–51.

[43] For arguments for and against historicity, see Eino Wilhelms, "Der fremde Exorzist," *ST* 3 (1949) 162–71; Jacques Schlosser, "L'exorciste étranger (*Mc* 9,38–39)," *RevScRel* 56 (1982) 229–39; E. A. Russell, "A Plea for Tolerance (Mk 9.38–40)," *Irish Biblical Studies* 8 (1986) 154–60; Culpepper, *John, the Son of Zebedee*, 41–43.

I do not find the arguments for historicity proposed by critics like Russell convincing. (1) Some argue for historicity on the grounds that the early church would not have created a story with such a "liberal" perspective advocating tolerance. This supposes a strange monolithic view of the first-generation church, one hardly in keeping with the debates we overhear in the Pauline epistles. If there is any truth to the idea that some of the sayings of Jesus come from Christian prophets, one could well imagine some of them espousing a "liberal" position on the exercise of charismatic authority in Jesus' name. (2) The idea that a noted disciple would represent a view that Jesus would then reject is hardly an argument for historicity when one is dealing with the Gospel of Mark, where Jesus regularly rebukes his disciples for their lack of understanding. (3) To be sure, this pericope is unique; it is the only Gospel story where John the son of Zebedee acts as the lone spokesman for the disciples in an exchange with Jesus. Perhaps this is the sole—though tenuous—argument for historicity that gives one pause. However, as Culpepper suggests (p. 43), it is possible that the nickname "sons of thunder," given by Jesus in the positive sense of powerful witnesses to his message, was later (mis-)interpreted by the church in a negative, psychological sense to refer to John's impetuous zeal. As one can see from the apocryphal Gospels and Acts, not all the legends that sprang up about early disciples and church leaders were laudatory or edifying. Thus, while I admit certitude is not to be had, I incline to the view that the anecdote about the independent exorcist does not go back to the ministry of the historical Jesus. Many critics, however, argue for the story's historicity; see Karl Ludwig Schmidt, *Der Rahmen der Geschichte Jesu* (Darmstadt: Wissenschaftliche Buchgesellschaft, 1969, originally 1919) 236; Taylor, *The Gospel According to St. Mark*, 406; Pesch, *Das Markusevangelium*, 2. 109; Gundry, *Mark*, 520–21. For arguments against historicity, see Bultmann, *Geschichte*, 23–24; Ernst Lohmeyer, *Das Evangelium des Markus* (MeyerK 1/2; Göttingen: Vandenhoeck & Ruprecht, 1967, originally 1937) 195; Ernst Haenchen, *Der Weg Jesu* (2d ed.; Berlin: de Gruyter, 1968) 327; Hooker, *Mark*, 229. Dibelius (*Formgeschichte*, 159 n. 2) seems uncertain. In favor of the view that in vv 38–39 Mark composed new material for his discipleship discourse is Harry Fleddermann, "The Discipleship Discourse (Mark 9:33–50)," *CBQ* 43 (1981) 57–75.

[44] For Lucan composition and theological themes, see Fitzmyer, *The Gospel According to Luke*, 1. 826–27.

[45] Culpepper (*John, the Son of Zebedee*, 44) thinks that a misunderstanding of the nickname "sons of thunder" by the early church (or possibly by Luke) in terms of impetuous zeal led to the introduction of James and John into this story. Likewise in favor of the possibility that "James and John" is a secondary addition to the story is Marshall, *Luke*, 406. Bultmann (*Geschichte*, 24) sees the whole story as arising from the missionary experience of the early church; Grundmann (*Das Evangelium nach Lukas*, 201) remains uncertain. Josef Ernst (*Das Evangelium nach Lukas* [RNT; Regensburg: Pustet, 1977] 317) takes something of a mediating position: the story goes back to an experience that Jesus had during his public ministry and that the disciples had before and after Easter, but Luke has inserted the story into the "fictive journey

through Samaria." Ernst (p. 318) hesitates over the historicity of the role of James and John in the story.

[46] See Bultmann, *Geschichte*, 23; for arguments in favor of the basic authenticity of Mark 10:38–39, see Sanders, *Jesus and Judaism*, 147. On the problems of interpreting the pericope, see Georg Braumann, "Leidenkelch und Todestaufe (Mk 10:38f.)," *ZNW* 56 (1965) 178–83; André Feuillet, "La coupe et le baptême de la passion," *RB* 74 (1967) 356–91; S. Légasse, "Approche de l'épisode préévangélique des fils de Zébédée (Marc x. 35–40 par.)," *NTS* 20 (1974) 161–77. Against the view that Mark 10:35–40 grew by various stages in the oral tradition, Légasse points to the chiastic structure at the heart of the whole story: sit at right and left hand (v 37)—drink of cup, be baptized with baptism (v 38)—drink of cup, be baptized with baptism (v 39)—sit at right and left hand (v 40). Hence Légasse thinks that the oral form of the story behind Mark 10:35–40 was a unit from the beginning.

[47] Mark may intend the reference to places on Jesus' right and left as ironic, since, as it turns out, those are the places reserved for the two brigands crucified with Jesus (15:27).

[48] For an alternate interpretation of the elliptical Greek—one that takes the Greek *all'* to mean "except," not "but"—see Gundry, *Mark*, 578. I find Gundry's interpretation less likely in the overall context. In any case, as Gundry points out, even his interpretation has Jesus disclaiming ultimate authority in preparing and assigning the seats of highest honor; the passive verb ("has been prepared") is a divine passive, indicating that God is the one who has prepared and apportioned various eschatological rewards.

[49] On this, see Légasse, "Approche," 170–74; Légasse, however, rejects the connection with Matt 19:28 par. In my view, he restricts unduly the imagery of Matt 19:28.

[50] God presents his holy ones, i.e., faithful Israelites, with a cup filled with blessing or salvation (e.g., Pss 23:5; 116:13). The wicked must drink to the dregs the cup of wine that is the wrath of God (e.g., Pss 11:6; 75:8 [MT 75:9]; Isa 51:17,22; Jer 25:15; 49:12; Hab 2:15–16). The symbol of the cup of judgment is widespread in the intertestamental literature: 1QpHab 11:14–15; 4QpNah 4:6 (fragmentary, but the sense is clear from the larger context); *Pss. Sol.* 8:14; *2 Apoc. Bar.* 13:8; *Bib. Ant.* 50:6. Even the good must taste the cup of death; see *T. Abraham* 1:3 in Recension A: "But even to him [the righteous Abraham] came the common and inexorable bitter cup of death and the unforeseen end of life." In the *Martyrdom and Ascension of Isaiah* 5:13, we find "the cup" used absolutely of the martyrdom of the prophet by the wicked ruler; but Christian influence may be at work here. On the symbolism of the cup in OT and NT, see J. L. Kelso, "Cup," *IDB*, 1. 748–49.

[51] For the imagery of being overwhelmed by water or of sinking into the deep, see, e.g., 2 Sam 22:5 (cf. Ps 18:4); Ps 69:2–3; Ps 42:7 (MT 42:8). (In Symmachus' transla-

tion of Ps 69:3, *baptizō* is used for the verb *ṭāba*ʿ, "to sink.") The Greek *baptizō* translates the Hebrew *ṭābal* in LXX 4 Kgdms 5:14 (= MT 2 Kgs 5:14) in the literal sense of immersing oneself in water. We find *baptizō* used metaphorically of extreme distress or ruin engulfing a person or a group in LXX Isa 21:4 and in Josephus, *J. W.* 4.3.3 §137. In all, *baptizō* occurs four times in the LXX, in both the literal and the metaphorical senses of the verb. The metaphorical use of *baptizō* for being over-whelmed as by a flood is also known in pagan Greek literature; see, e.g., Diodorus of Sicily, 1.73 §6; Plutarch, *Galba,* 21 §2. However, more important for Jesus' metaphorical use of the term may have been the baptism practiced by John the Bap-tist and himself, along with John's special title *ho baptistēs* or *ho baptizōn,* which probably represents a participial form of the Aramaic *ṭĕbal.* That the historical Jesus did speak of the sufferings that might await him under the imagery of baptism is sup-ported by multiple attestation of sources, namely, Mark 10:38–39 and the special L tradition in Luke 12:50 (which, admittedly, shows signs of Luke's redactional hand): "I have to be baptized with a baptism, and how distressed I feel [or: how governed I am by this thought] until it be accomplished!" In favor of the authenticity of Luke 12:50 is Grundmann, *Das Evangelium nach Lukas,* 271. In favor of a Lucan creation on the basis of Mark 10:38 is Helmut Koester, *"synechō," TDNT* 7 (1971) 885 n. 77; against this theory is Marshall, *The Gospel of Luke,* 547–48; also Légasse, "Ap-proche," 165–70. To take "cup" and "baptism" in Mark 10:38 to refer to the Chris-tian sacraments, as does Braumann ("Leidenkelch," 178–83), does violence to the text even on the level of Mark's Gospel because (1) the order of the symbols is wrong (baptism should come first, then the cup of the eucharist); (2) it makes no sense to ask disciples whether they *are able to (dynasthe)* drink the cup and be baptized; if inter-preted in reference to Christian rites, these are essential acts for all believers, not some special feat that a few chosen followers may be able to endure; (3) one is reading into the use of "baptism" in Mark 10:38 Paul's idea of being united to Christ's death through Christian baptism (e.g., Rom 6:3–5), an idea not expressed in Mark's Gospel. A more nuanced approach to the possibility of a sacramental reference is of-fered by Feuillet, "La coupe," 383–91.

[52] Besides the influence of Mark 10:35–40, the legends may also have been affected by the identification made at times between John the son of Zebedee and John the au-thor of the Book of Revelation, who was exiled to the island of Patmos because of his Christian witness (Rev 1:9). So confused and garbled do later patristic and liturgical references to "John" become that at times John the son of Zebedee seems to be con-fused with the martyred John the Baptist. Here one sees the danger of invoking pa-tristic witnesses from later centuries to determine the historical fate of John the son of Zebedee. For detailed treatment of John the son of Zebedee in patristic literature, see Culpepper, *John, the Son of Zebedee,* 107–250; a brief refutation of the patristic tradition about John's supposed martyrdom is found in Taylor, *The Gospel Accord-ing to St. Mark,* 442; cf. Feuillet, "La coupe," 360–62. For earlier debate on the ques-tion, see Eduard Schwartz, "Über den Tod der Söhne Zebedäi," *Johannes und sein Evangelium* (Wege der Forschung 82; ed. Karl H. Rengstorf; Darmstadt: Wis-

senschaftliche Buchgesellschaft, 1973) 202–72; J. H. Bernard, "Die Traditionen über den Tod des Zebedäussohnes Johannes," ibid., 273–90; Friedrich Spitta, "Die neutestamentliche Grundlage der Ansicht von E. Schwartz über den Tod der Söhne Zebedäi," ibid., 291–313. Schwartz replied to Spitta in "Noch einmal der Tod der Söhne Zebedaei," *ZNW* 11 (1910) 89–104; Schwartz was supported in his view by Johannes Weiss, "Zum Märtyrertod der Zebedäiden," ibid., 167. A more recent attempt to uphold the historicity of the martyrdom of John as well as James, based on a highly questionable appeal to the two witnesses in Rev 11:3–13, can be found in Michael Oberweis, "Das Martyrium der Zebedäiden in Mk 10.35–40 (Mt 20.20–3) und Offb 11.3–13," *NTS* 44 (1998) 74–92.

[53] Stephen's martyrdom is narrated in Acts 7:54–60. Paul's martyrdom is intimated in Acts 20:25–38; 21:11 and in 2 Tim 4:6–18; it is affirmed in *1 Clem.* 5:1–7 and intimated by Ignatius of Antioch, *Rom.* 4:1–3. Peter's martyrdom is "prophesied" in John 21:18–19 and is likewise affirmed or alluded to in the same passages of *1 Clement* and Ignatius. On Ignatius, see the comment by William R. Schoedel, *Ignatius of Antioch* (Hermeneia; Philadelphia: Fortress, 1985) 176: "Thus the selection here [in *Rom.* 4:3] of Peter and Paul no doubt reflects Ignatius' awareness of a tradition about their [Peter and Paul's] joint presence and their martyrdom in Rome which significantly bolstered the prestige of that city's Christian community." For a more reserved opinion on this Ignatian passage, see Pheme Perkins, *Peter. Apostle for the Whole Church* (Studies on Personalities of the NT; Columbia, SC: University of South Carolina, 1994) 138–39. The martyrdom of James the brother of Jesus is recounted in Josephus, *Ant.* 20.9.1 §200 (see *A Marginal Jew,* 1. 57–59).

[54] For the possible meaning of the metaphor of "pillars," see C. K. Barrett, "Paul and the 'Pillar' Apostles," *Studia Paulina in Honorem Johannis de Zwaan Septuagenarii* (ed. J. N. Sevenster and W. C. van Unnik; Haarlem: Bohn, 1953) 1–19; Günter Klein, "Galater 2,6–9 und die Geschichte der Jerusalemer Urgemeinde," *Rekonstruktion und Interpretation* (BEvT 50; Munich: Kaiser, 1969) 99–128; Ulrich Wilckens, *"stylos,"* TDNT 7 (1971) 732–36; Roger D. Aus, "Three Pillars and Three Patriarchs: A Proposal Concerning Gal 2:9," *ZNW* 70 (1979) 252–61. One sees in the theory of Schwartz ("Über den Tod," 202–6) the danger of jumping to the conclusion that Mark 10:35–40 must refer to martyrdom and must be a *vaticinium ex eventu:* Schwartz reasons that, since Mark 10:35–40 must be a prediction after the fact, and since John as well as his brother James must therefore have been martyred by Herod Agrippa I ca. A.D. 43 or 44, the John mentioned as one of the three pillars in Gal 2:9 must be some other John! Schwartz's reasoning is challenged by Bernard, "Die Traditionen," 273–90; and Spitta, "Die neutestamentliche Grundlage," 291–313.

[55] If we accept the basic insight that Jesus presented himself as a prophet sent by God to Israel, then we need not be at all surprised that he would utter prophecies about individuals as well as the whole nation. Prophets like Amos, Isaiah, and Jere-

miah utter a good number of prophecies concerning individuals (e.g., Jeroboam II, Amaziah, Hezekiah, Shebna, Eliakim, Pashhur, Hananiah, and Zedekiah). The OT is also acquainted both with prophecies that were not fulfilled (e.g., the prophecy that Jeroboam II would die by the sword in Amos 7:11), at least fully or literally, and with later attempts to reinterpret apparently failed prophecies in order to make them coincide with subsequent history (e.g., Dan 9:2,24).

[56] Culpepper, *John, the Son of Zebedee,* 40.

[57] The bibliography on Peter, both the historical person and the theological symbol, is vast. A few works that can supply the reader with an overview of the problems and further bibliography are Oscar Cullmann, *Peter. Disciple—Apostle—Martyr* (2d ed.; London: SCM, 1962); Raymond E. Brown, Karl P. Donfried, and John Reumann (eds.), *Peter in the New Testament* (Minneapolis: Augsburg; New York/Paramus/ Toronto: Paulist, 1973); Wolfgang Dietrich, *Das Petrusbild der lukanischen Schriften* (BWANT 5/14; Stuttgart: Kohlhammer, 1972); Jack Dean Kingsbury, "The Figure of Peter in Matthew's Gospel as a Theological Problem," *JBL* 98 (1979) 67–83; Pesch, *Simon-Petrus;* Arthur H. Maynard, "The Role of Peter in the Fourth Gospel," *NTS* 30 (1984) 531–48; Rudolf Schnackenburg, "Petrus im Matthäusevangelium," *A cause de l'évangile* (Jacques Dupont Festschrift; LD 123; Paris: Cerf, 1985) 107–25; Carsten Peter Thiede, *Simon Peter. From Galilee to Rome* (Grand Rapids: Academie/Zondervan, 1986); Kevin Quast, *Peter and the Beloved Disciple. Figures for a Community in Crisis* (JSNTSup 32; Sheffield: JSOT, 1989); Arthur J. Droge, "The Status of Peter in the Fourth Gospel: John 18:10–11," *JBL* 109 (1990) 307–11; Arlo J. Nau, *Peter in Matthew* (Collegeville, MN: Liturgical Press, 1992); Perkins, *Peter;* João Tavares de Lima, *"Tu serás chamado Kēphas." Estudo exegético sobre Pedro no quarto evangelho* (Analecta Gregoriana 265, Series Facultatis Theologiae: sectio B, 89; Rome: Gregorian University, 1994). (A separate bibliography on Matt 16:17–19 will be given below.)

[58] On the distinction between "the historical Simon" and "the Peter of faith," see Pesch, *Simon-Petrus,* 1–8.

[59] For Jesus' walking on the water, see *A Marginal Jew,* 2. 905–24; for the miraculous catch of fish, see 2. 896–904; for the cursing of the barren fig tree, see 2. 884–96; for the paying of the temple tax, see 2. 880–84; and for the healing of Simon's mother-in-law, see 2. 707–8. The last-named story received the judgment of *non liquet* ("not clear" either way); the rest were judged to be creations of the early church.

[60] What follows is meant to be a consensus statement, a summary of what most scholars would accept as historical. I realize that various items have been disputed by individual scholars; for example, Günter Klein has rejected the historicity of Peter's denial of Jesus after the latter's arrest. I will examine some of these disputed items in greater detail after presenting the summary.

[61] Fitzmyer ("Aramaic *Kepha'*," 122) supports the commonly held view that "the use of both Symeon and Simon [of Peter in the NT] reflects the well-known custom among Jews of that time of giving the name of a famous patriarch or personage of the Old Testament to a male child along with a similar-sounding Greek/Roman name." Theoretically possible, though less likely, is the view that, during his fishing days in Galilee in the 20s and 30s of the 1st century, Peter simply bore the Semitic name of Symeon *(Šim'ôn)*, while the Greek Simon was introduced to designate him when the Gospel story was first told in Greek. On Simon as a common name for Jews around the turn of the era, see Joseph A. Fitzmyer, "The Name Simon," *Essays on the Semitic Background of the New Testament* (SBLSBS 5; Missoula, MT: Scholars, 1974) 105–12. For a full listing of the occurrences of "Simon," "Symeon," "Peter," and "Simon Peter" in the Gospels, see Pesch, *Simon-Petrus*, 25–27.

[62] That the historical Peter was a fisherman is supported directly only by the Marcan tradition (Mark 1:16–18; I consider Matt 17:24–27 to be a Christian creation), but the picture of Peter as a fisherman receives indirect support from the picture of Peter leading a fishing expedition in John 21:1–14 (admittedly, however, in a postresurrection context). Likewise supported only by the Marcan tradition is the placing of Peter's home in Capernaum (1:29–31), though some would now seek to support this location of his house with present-day archaeological discoveries. An emphatic claim that Peter's house at Capernaum has been discovered is made by Virgilio C. Corbo, "Capernaum (Place)," *Anchor Bible Dictionary*, 1. 866–69; more cautious in their approach are Jerome Murphy-O'Connor, *The Holy Land* (2d ed.; Oxford: Oxford University, 1986) 188–91; Jack Finegan, *The Archeology of the New Testament. The Life of Jesus and the Beginning of the Early Church* (rev. ed.; Princeton: Princeton University, 1992) 107–11; and Leslie J. Hoppe, *The Synagogues and Churches of Ancient Palestine* (Collegeville, MN: Glazier/Liturgical Press, 1994) 81–89. The difficulty that the Marcan picture of Peter living in Capernaum stands in conflict with the passing remark of John 1:44 that Bethsaida was the city of Peter and Andrew is solved in different ways by different commentators; see, e.g., Brown, *The Gospel According to John*, 1. 82. Some harmonize by suggesting that Peter and Andrew were originally from Bethsaida but moved to Capernaum when Peter married (so Pesch, *Simon-Petrus*, 10–12); others point out that, while Peter may have lived in Capernaum, his fishing activity along the northern shore of the Sea of Galilee may have caused him to keep a small house in Bethsaida (on the northeast shore) as well as a larger family house in Capernaum (on the northwest shore). Such a minor point is of no concern to our quest. As with the datum that Jesus was a woodworker (Mark 6:3; see *A Marginal Jew*, 1. 280), most critics seem willing to accept the idea that Peter was a fisherman and was connected with Capernaum in one way or another on the commonsense grounds that there is no particular reason why these details would have been invented. It may be noted that, in Mark, Q, and John (Mark 1:21; 2:1; 9:33; Matt 8:5 ‖ Luke 7:1; Matt 11:23 ‖ Luke 10:15; John 2:12; 4:46; 6:17,24,59), we have multiple attestation for Capernaum being an important focus of Jesus' Galilean ministry; moreover, there is no doubt that fishing was a major business in Capernaum.

That Peter was married—and remained so during his Christian missionary activities—is supported by a curious multiple attestation of sources: Mark 1:29–31 and 1 Cor 9:5. His connections with both Bethsaida and Capernaum as well as the exigencies of his trade may point to his being able to speak both Aramaic and Greek; if that be true, his knowledge of Greek would certainly have helped him later on in his journeys to Antioch, Corinth (?), and Rome.

[63] For a survey of the different traditions of the call of Peter, see S. O. Abogunrin, "The Three Variant Accounts of Peter's Call: A Critical and Theological Examination of the Texts," *NTS* 31 (1985) 587–602.

[64] In reference to John 1:35–42, I use the word "call" to discipleship only analogously. For the most part, John 1 does not depict the peremptory command to follow Jesus that we find in the Synoptics. The one exception is Jesus' command to Philip, "Follow me" (John 1:43).

[65] See *A Marginal Jew*, 2. 116–30. Pesch (*Simon-Petrus*, 15, 19–20) suggests that it was Andrew who, after he was baptized by the Baptist, stayed in the circle of his disciples and so became acquainted with Jesus. Perhaps the Fourth Gospel is correct in claiming that Andrew brought Peter to Jesus, though this encounter might have taken place back in Galilee instead of by the Jordan.

[66] I say "at least in part" because one must also allow for the influence (1) of the early Christian belief that the risen Christ appeared first to Cephas (= Peter; 1 Cor 15:5; cf. Luke 24:34) and (2) of Peter's leadership and missionary activity in the first Christian generation. Christian belief and the evangelists' redactional activity no doubt account for some of the Gospel references to Peter's role as leader or spokesman, but there is enough multiple attestation of sources to point to a leadership role played by the historical Peter during the ministry of Jesus. However, this still leaves us asking the question why Peter was a leader and/or spokesman during the public ministry. One is left theorizing about natural character (in Peter's case, with many weak as well as strong points) or some appointment or designation by Jesus (favored by such texts as Matt 16:18–19; Luke 22:31–32; and John 1:42, which will be considered below).

[67] As I have noted, a major problem with the inner group of three (Peter, James, and John) is that it is attested only by the Marcan tradition (including parallel passages dependent on Mark) and fits in nicely with Mark's "messianic secret." Taken individually, the Synoptic stories that mention the inner group of three differ in their historical verifiability. I think that the raising of the daughter of Jairus (Mark 5:21–43 parr.) reflects an event in the life of Jesus; see *A Marginal Jew*, 2. 777–88. In contrast, the transfiguration of Jesus (Mark 9:2–8 parr.) is, of its nature, a type of esoteric religious experience that does not allow of historical verification such as we seek in this quest; see my remarks in *A Marginal Jew*, 2. 972. The special role of the three disciples during Jesus' agonized prayer in Gethsemane (Mark 14:32–42 parr.) is difficult to sustain

on historical grounds when Mark himself stresses that the threesome were asleep during the whole episode. As for an inner group of four (Peter, James, John, and Andrew) receiving special teaching from Jesus, the only relevant passage is Mark 13:3, which designates the audience for the eschatological discourse. Many critics consider 13:3 to belong to Mark's redactional introduction to the discourse, harking back by way of *inclusio* to the call of the original four disciples in chap. 1, but placing Andrew last in view of the inner group of three that has been mentioned during the public ministry. It is telling, for instance, that Rudolf Pesch, despite the many changes of opinion between his first and second major study of Mark's eschatological discourse, still inclines to the view that the foursome mentioned in 13:3 are probably Mark's contribution; compare his *Naherwartungen. Tradition und Redaktion in Mk 13* (Kommentare und Beiträge zum Alten und Neuen Testament; Düsseldorf: Patmos, 1968) with his *Markusevangelium*, 2. 264–318, especially 273–75.

[68] Pre-Christian documentation of the meaning of Aramaic *kēpāʾ* can be found in various Qumran fragments: 11QtgJob 32:1 (translating Hebrew Job 39:1); 11Qtg-Job 33:9 (translating Hebrew Job 39:28); 4QEn[c] 4 iii 19; 4QEn[c] 4:3; 4QEn[a] 1 ii 8. The Greek feminine noun *petra* means "a large and solid rock." Strictly speaking, therefore, *petros* and *petra* should be distinguished in meaning; however, some scholars claim that they were often used interchangeably. Sustaining this position is Oscar Cullmann, *"petra," TDNT* 6 (1968) 95–99; cf. Fitzmyer, "Aramaic *Kephaʾ*," 121–32, esp. 131; and emphatically Crys C. Caragounis, *Peter and the Rock* (BZNW 58; Berlin/New York: de Gruyter, 1989) 9–16. However, Peter Lampe argues by way of a corrective that the use of *petros* in the sense of "rock" was not all that common in ancient Greek; see his "Das Spiel mit dem Petrusnamen—Matt. xvi. 18," *NTS* 25 (1978–79) 227–45, esp. 240–41; see also Pesch, *Simon-Petrus*, 27–34 (notably under the influence of Lampe). As for the use of these words as proper names, Fitzmyer ("Aramaic *Kephaʾ*," 127–30) points to an occurrence of *kpʾ* in an Aramaic papyrus from Elephantine in Egypt that dates from the late 5th century B.C. He argues forcefully that the word is used in this text as an Aramaic proper name; but, as he notes, not all scholars are convinced of this position. More to the point, no occurrence of *kēpāʾ* as an Aramaic proper name for a man has been so far documented in Palestine around the turn of the era. As for *Petros*, despite the claims of Caragounis (*Peter and the Rock*, 17–25), no firm and unambiguous evidence for its use as the proper name of a man can be dated to the first half of the 1st century A.D. For critiques of Caragounis' positions, see the reviews of his book by Gérard Claudel, *Bib* 71 (1990) 570–76; John P. Meier, *CBQ* 53 (1991) 492–93.

[69] As we shall see, the precise sense of "you are Peter" in Matt 16:18 (conferral of new name or interpretation of an already used name?) is disputed. Luke 6:14 also states that Jesus gave the name Peter to Simon, but here Luke is dependent on Mark 3:16, while Matt 16:18 and John 1:42 are independent traditions. On Peter's name in its various forms, see Cullmann, *"petra,"* 95–99; *"Petros, Kēphas,"* ibid., 100–112; J. K. Elliott, *"Kēphas: Simōn Petros: ho Petros.* An Examination of New Testament Usage," *NovT* 14 (1972) 241–56; Fitzmyer, "Aramaic *Kephaʾ*," 121–32; Caragou-

nis, *Peter and the Rock;* Timothy Wiarda, "Simon, Jesus of Nazareth, Son of Jonah, Son of John: Realistic Detail in the Gospels and Acts," *NTS* 40 (1994) 196–209.

[70] For the text-critical problem connected with Symeon (alternate reading: Simon) in 2 Pet 1:1, see Metzger, *Textual Commentary* (2d ed.), 629. Along with Fitzmyer ("Aramaic *Kepha'*," 122 n. 4), I do not think that Luke in Acts 15:14 intends to refer to someone else named Symeon (e.g., the Symeon Niger of Acts 13:1). That some other Symeon, possibly Symeon Niger, was meant in a source but that Luke thought the source referred to Simon Peter is suggested by Fitzmyer in his "Acts of the Apostles," *JBC*, 2. 195 §75; cf. Paul J. Achtemeier, "An Elusive Unity: Paul, Acts, and the Early Church," *CBQ* 48 (1986) 1–26. While this is possible, I think it more likely that the occurrence of the Semitic name precisely in the mouth of James is probably a conscious stylistic choice on the part of Luke, who wishes to give a Semitic or even "Holy-Bible" flavor to James' speech; cf. Richard J. Dillon, "Acts of the Apostles," *NJBC*, 752 §83.

[71] Some critics would include in the multiple attestation what they consider to be an independent Lucan Passion Narrative. Critical disputes over Luke 22:31–32 and the tradition of Peter's denial of Jesus will be handled in detail below.

[72] On the martyrdom tradition, see Perkins, *Peter,* 138–39, 38. On the whole question of Peter's connection with Rome and the excavations under St. Peter's Basilica, see Jocelyn Toynbee and John Ward Perkins, *The Shrine of St. Peter and the Vatican Excavations* (New York: Pantheon, 1957); Erich Dinkler, "Die Petrus-Rom-Frage. Ein Forschungsbericht," *TRu* 25 (1959) 189–230, 289–335; 27 (1961) 33–64; Margherita Guarducci, *The Tradition of Peter in the Vatican in the Light of History and Archaeology* (Vatican City: Vatican Polyglot Press, 1963); Daniel W. O'Connor, *Peter in Rome* (New York: Columbia University, 1969); Engelbert Kirschbaum, *Die Gräber der Apostelfürsten. St. Peter und St. Paul in Rom* (3d ed.; Frankfurt: Societäts-Verlag, 1974); Pesch, *Simon-Petrus,* 113–34; John E. Walsh, *The Bones of St. Peter* (Garden City, NY: Doubleday, 1982).

[73] On parallels with OT and Jewish narratives in which a change of name signifies a call to a new role in salvation history (e.g., Abram and Abraham, Jacob and Israel, Sarai and Sarah), see Pesch, *Simon-Petrus,* 28; cf. Tavares de Lima, *"Tu serás chamado Kēphas,"* 67–72. The parallels with Abram, Sarai, and other change-of-name stories in Genesis suggest that the narrator understands the change of Simon's name to Cephas/Peter to become operative as soon as Jesus announces the new name.

[74] Cf. Luke 24:34, where "Simon" is used by the disciples after Easter in what appears to be an early kerygmatic formula. On the redactional tendencies of each evangelist in his use of "Simon," "Peter," and "Cephas," see Elliott, *"Kēphas,"* 241–56—though Elliott's views on Synoptic relationships and his text-critical judgments would not meet with universal acceptance.

[75] I say "regularly" because the rule is not ironclad. At the Lucan Last Supper, after Jesus prefaces his warning about an imminent crisis and his promise of prayer with an initial "Simon, Simon" (Luke 22:31), he proceeds to predict Peter's denial with the vocative "Peter" (22:34). Many critics see here a clue that points to distinct sources; whether the change of names really signifies this is debatable. Luke 22:31–34 does serve, however, as an objection against the claim that the use of "Simon" for Peter in the later chapters of the Gospels necessarily carries with it a connotation of Peter's failure to be a true disciple.

[76] For a survey of opinions in the various periods of interpretation, see Joseph Ludwig, *Die Primatworte Mt 16,18.19 in der altkirchlichen Exegese* (NTAbh Band 19, Heft 4; Münster: Aschendorff, 1952); Franz Obrist, *Echtheitsfragen und Deutung der Primatsstelle Mt 16,18f. in der deutschen protestantischen Theologie der letzten dreissig Jahre* (NTAbh Band 21, Heft 3/4; Münster: Aschendorff, 1961); Joseph A. Burgess, *A History of the Exegesis of Matthew 16:17–19 from 1781 to 1965* (Ann Arbor, MI: Edwards Brothers, 1976). For a sampling of present-day approaches, see Anton Vögtle, "Messiasbekenntnis und Petrusverheissung. Zur Komposition Mt 16,13–23 par.," *BZ* 1 (1957) 252–72; idem, "Zum Problem der Herkunft von 'Mt 16,17–19,' " *Orientierung an Jesus* (Josef Schmid Festschrift; ed. Paul Hoffmann et al.; Freiburg/Basel/Vienna: Herder, 1973) 372–93; Oscar Cullmann, "L'apôtre Pierre instrument du diable et instrument de Dieu," *New Testament Essays* (T. W. Manson Memorial; ed. A. J. B. Higgins; Manchester: Manchester University, 1959) 94–105; Johannes Ringger, "Das Felsenwort," *Begegnung der Christen* (Otto Karrer Festschrift; ed. Maximilian Roesle and Oscar Cullmann; Stuttgart: Evangelisches Verlagswerk; Frankfurt: Knecht, 1959) 271–347; Josef Schmid, "Petrus 'der Fels' und die Petrusgestalt der Urgemeinde," ibid., 347–59; André Legault, "L'authenticité de Mt 16:17–19 et le silence de Marc et de Luc," *L'église dans la bible* (Studia 13; Bruges: Desclée de Brouwer, 1962) 35–52; Ernst Haenchen, "Die Komposition von Mk vii 27-ix 1 und par.," *NovT* 6 (1963) 81–109; Kenneth L. Carroll, " 'Thou Art Peter,' " *NovT* 6 (1963) 268–76; Robert H. Gundry, "The Narrative Framework of Matthew xvi 17–19," *NovT* 7 (1964) 1–9; Jacques Dupont, "La révélation du Fils de Dieu en faveur de Pierre (Mt 16,17) et de Paul (Ga 1,16)," *RSR* 52 (1964) 411–20; François Refoulé, "Primauté de Pierre dans les évangiles," *RevScRel* 38 (1964) 1–41; Erich Dinkler, "Petrusbekenntnis und Satanswort. Das Problem der Messianität Jesu," *Zeit und Geschichte* (Rudolf Bultmann Festschrift; Tübingen: Mohr [Siebeck] 1964) 127–53; Reinhart Hummel, *Die Auseinandersetzung zwischen Kirche und Judentum im Matthäusevangelium* (BEvT 33; 2d ed.; Munich: Kaiser, 1966) 59–64; Brown et al., *Peter in the New Testament,* 83–101; André Feuillet, " 'Chercher à persuader Dieu' (Ga 1:10a). Le début de l'Epître aux Galates et la scène matthéenne de Césarée de Philippe," *NovT* 12 (1970) 350–60; Günther Bornkamm, "The Authority to 'Bind' and 'Loose' in the Church in Matthew's Gospel," *Jesus and Man's Hope* (2 vols.; ed. Dikran Hadidian et al.; Pittsburgh: Pittsburgh Theological Seminary, 1970, 1971) 1. 37–50; Georg Strecker, *Der Weg der Gerechtigkeit* (FRLANT 82; 3d ed.; Göttingen: Vandenhoeck & Ruprecht, 1971) 201–6; Paul Hoffmann, "Der Petrus-

Primat im Matthäusevangelium," *Neues Testament und Kirche* (Rudolf Schnacken-burg Festschrift; ed. Joachim Gnilka; Freiburg/Basel/Vienna: Herder, 1974) 94–114; Max Wilcox, "Peter and the Rock: A Fresh Look at Matthew xvi. 17–19," *NTS* 22 (1975–76) 73–88; Christoph Kähler, "Zur Form- und Traditionsgeschichte von Matth. xvi. 17–19," *NTS* 23 (1976–77) 36–58; Franz Mussner, *Petrus und Paulus—Pole der Einheit* (QD 76; Freiburg/Basel/Vienna: Herder, 1976) 11–22; Ferdinand Hahn, "Die Petrusverheissung Mt 16,18f.," *Das kirchliche Amt im Neuen Testament* (Wege der Forschung 189; ed. Karl Kertelge; Darmstadt: Wissenschaftliche Buchge-sellschaft, 1977) 543–61; John P. Meier, *The Vision of Matthew* (Theological In-quiries; New York/Ramsey/Toronto: Paulist, 1979) 106–21; Lampe, "Das Spiel"; J.-M. van Cangh and M. van Esbroeck, "La primauté de Pierre (Mt 16,16–19) et son contexte judaïque," *RTL* 11 (1980) 310–24; Stephen Gero, "The Gates or the Bars of Hades? A Note on Matthew 16.18," *NTS* 27 (1981) 411–14; M.-A. Chevallier, " 'Tu es Pierre, tu es le nouvel Abraham' (Mt 16/18)," *ETR* 57 (1982) 375–87; J. Duncan M. Derrett, "Binding and Loosing (Matt 16:19; 18:18; John 29[*sic*]:23)," *JBL* 102 (1983) 112–17; Bernard P. Robinson, "Peter and His Successors: Tradition and Redaction in Matthew 16.17–19," *JSNT* 21 (1984) 85–104; Pierre Grelot, "L'origine de Matthieu 16,16–19," *A cause de l'évangile* (Jacques Dupont Festschrift; LD 123; Paris: Cerf, 1985) 91–105; Richard H. Hiers, " 'Binding' and 'Loosing': The Matthean Authorizations," *JBL* 104 (1985) 233–50; Herbert W. Basser, "Derrett's 'Binding' Reopened," *JBL* 104 (1985) 297–300; Augustine Stock, "Is Matthew's Pre-sentation of Peter Ironic?" *BTB* 17 (1987) 64–69; Joachim Gnilka, " 'Tu es, Petrus.' Die Petrus-Verheissung in Mt 16,17–19," *MTZ* 38 (1987) 3–17; P. Grelot, " 'Sur cette pierre je bâtirai mon Eglise' (Mt 16,18b)," *NRT* 109 (1987) 641–59; Gérard Claudel, *La confession de Pierre* (EBib n.s. 10; Paris: Gabalda, 1988); Joel Marcus, "The Gates of Hades and the Keys of the Kingdom (Matt 16:18–19)," *CBQ* 50 (1988) 443–55; Hildebrecht Hommel, "Die Tore des Hades," *ZNW* 80 (1989) 124–25; Caragounis, *Peter and the Rock,* 61–119; Davies and Allison, *The Gospel According to Saint Matthew,* 2. 602–52; Ulrich Luz, "Das Primatwort Matthäus 16.17–19 aus wirkungsgeschichtlicher Sicht," *NTS* 37 (1991) 415–33; A. del Agua, "Derás narrativo del sobrenombre de 'Pedro' en el conjunto de Mt 16,17–19," *Salmanticensis* 39 (1992) 11–33; François Refoulé, "La Parallèle Matthieu 16/16–17—Galates 1/15–16 réexaminé," *ETR* 67 (1992) 161–75; Christian Grappe, "Mt 16,17–19 et le récit de la Passion," *RHPR* 72 (1992) 33–40.

In this initial probe, I treat Matt 16:17–19 as a unit, as it now lies in Matthew's Gospel. This is not meant to prejudge the further question of whether the various phrases in the unit come from the same stratum or from different strata of the tradi-tion. It may be, for instance, that the end of v 16, the whole of v 17, and the begin-ning of v 18 are Matthew's redactional additions, creating a bridge between the Marcan story of Peter's confession and the special promise to Peter, which comes from a tradition of a resurrection appearance; on this, see Vögtle, "Zum Problem," 372–91.

[77] When, with reference to Peter's declaration in Mark 8:29, we use phrases like "profession" or "confession" of faith in Jesus, we must be careful not to import into

the words the later sense of Christian creedal formulas. Within the context of a quest for the historical Jesus, a phrase like "faith in Jesus" must be understood analogously to the statement in 1QpHab 8:1–3 that the Qumranites put their faith or trust in the Teacher of Righteousness: ". . . the doers of the Law in the house of Judah, whom God will rescue from the house of judgment because of their toil and their faith in [or: trust in; or: fidelity to] the Teacher of Righteousness." In other words, the Qumranites accepted the Teacher of Righteousness as the legitimate teacher, approved by God, who taught the true, eschatological interpretation of the Torah and the prophets. In this sense, they displayed "their faith in the Teacher of Righteousness" (ĕmūnātām bĕmôrēh haṣṣedeq). Similarly, the disciples could be said to "believe in Jesus" in the sense that they accepted his proclamation of the kingdom of God, present yet soon to come, and therefore accepted him as the Elijah-like prophet of the end time, the one appointed to gather together and restore Israel.

[78] As elsewhere, I consider John to represent a source independent of the Synoptics. For the view that John is dependent here on the Lucan redaction of the story of Peter's confession, see Pesch, Simon-Petrus, 37. Pesch (ibid., 37–40) holds to the historicity of Peter's confession of Jesus as Messiah in the region of Caesarea Philippi as presented in Mark 8:27–30; in my opinion, he never offers sufficient reasons for holding so strictly to the historicity of Mark's account. See also Tavares de Lima, "Tu serás chamado Kēphas," 128–33.

[79] In favor of authenticity (though in diverse settings in Jesus' life) are, e.g., Cullmann, Peter, 165–217 (at the Last Supper); Gundry, "The Narrative Framework," 1–9 (against Cullmann's theory of the Last Supper). For a hypothetical Aramaic retroversion of Matt 16:16–19, see Grelot, "L'origine," 98. Grelot, however, thinks that the full form of this traditional unit belongs in the framework of an appearance of the risen Jesus to Peter. Not all agree with the view that a large number of Aramaisms are found in Matt 16:17–19 and that behind the present Greek text lay a Semitic original. On this, see Kähler, "Zur Form- und Traditionsgeschichte," 38–43; he, too, suggests a resurrection appearance as the original narrative framework.

[80] Pesch (Simon-Petrus, 29–32), who prefers "stone" as the original meaning of the name Petros, suggests that Jesus saw Peter as the precious stone, be that in the sense of a foundation stone, a cornerstone, or a decorative stone, within the structure he was creating, namely, the circle of the Twelve, who in turn symbolized the restored twelve tribes of Israel.

[81] One must qualify this number with "some" because of variant readings. One must also remember that, for certain books in the LXX (e.g., Judith, 1 Maccabees), we lack a Hebrew original.

[82] On this, see Jeremias, New Testament Theology, 168. Other relevant Qumran passages that use similar metaphors include 4QFlor 1:6; 1QH 6:24–26; see Gnilka, " 'Tu es, Petrus,' " 12–13.

[83] Probably the reference to Hades is first of all to the power of death; but, around the turn of the era, the realm of death and the realm of sin or evil were sometimes intertwined in Jewish and Christian eschatology. See, e.g., Luke 10:15; 16:23; Rev 20:13–15; cf. Josephus, *Ant.* 18.1.3 §14. For all the fine distinctions we may make between sin and death, Paul in particular (e.g., Romans 5–8) and early Christians in general saw both sin and death as destructive powers that God would defeat in the end time.

[84] See Gnilka, " 'Tu es, Petrus,' " 12.

[85] In the few places in the NT where the word carries another sense, the relevant text is often quoting or alluding to an OT passage (e.g., Acts 7:38; Heb 2:12) and points typologically to the Christian church. The sense of a purely secular or political assembly is very rare (see the special case of Acts 19:32,39,40).

[86] This holds true despite the famous parallels in the disciplinary rules of Qumran (1QS 5:24–6:1; CD [MS A] 9:2–8; cf. 5Q12). Matt 18:15–17, like the Qumran passages, presumes a local, organized community with clear procedures for disciplining recalcitrant members. This reflects the situation of local communities in the early Christian church, not a group of itinerant disciples interacting directly with an itinerant Jesus. On the Qumran parallels to this Matthean text, see Joachim Gnilka, "Die Kirche des Matthäus und die Gemeinde von Qumran," *BZ* 7 (1963) 43–63; W. D. Davies, *The Setting of the Sermon on the Mount* (Cambridge: Cambridge University, 1966) 221–24.

[87] Although both John 20:23 and 21:15–17 obviously come from the Johannine tradition, there is an attenuated type of multiple attestation at work here insofar as John 20:23 represents the hand and mind of the evangelist (no special role for Peter in the resurrection appearances), while John 21:15–17 comes from the hand and mind of the final redactor, who seems to be more amenable to a pastoral role for Peter after Easter.

[88] Though Peter is not explicitly mentioned as being present at this resurrection appearance, the statement in the next verse (20:24) emphasizes that "Thomas, *one of the Twelve,* was not *with them* when Jesus came." The natural inference is that, with Thomas singled out as the member of the Twelve who was not present in the group of disciples to whom Jesus appeared, Peter is presumed to be present in the group.

[89] For various explanations of the difference in the patronymics in Matt 16:17 and John 21:15–17, see Davies and Allison, *The Gospel According to Saint Matthew,* 2. 622; Elliott, *"Kēphas,"* 244 (who argues that Jonah is original); Claudel, *La confession,* 327–30 (who argues that John is original). In my view, the most likely explanation of the difference is that the original name of Peter's father, whether it was Jonah *(yônâ)* or John *(yôḥānān),* was inadvertently garbled in the decades-long oral tradition of either the Matthean or the Johannine community. Such garbling is not a

merely theoretical possibility: LXX manuscripts at times interchange the two names (see, e.g., LXX 1 Chr 26:3). There is no way of knowing which form of the name is historically correct, although the rarity of Jonah as a proper name around the turn of the era might argue that the original name was John and that it was changed by Matthew (or his special tradition) to Jonah for theological purposes (e.g., the sign of Jonah in Matt 12:39 and 16:4; Peter's role as a true prophet; or the initial unwillingness of both Jonah and Peter to go to the Gentiles [Jonah 1:1–3; Acts 10]); see Joachim Jeremias, "*Iōnas*," *TDNT* 3 (1965) 406–10. Other—and in my opinion, less likely—theories include the following: (1) Peter had been a Zealot; bar-Jonah derives from an Akkadian word for "terrorist." (2) The tradition of the Johannine community changed the original name Jonah (not commonly used at the time) to the more common and popular John. (3) The change was inadvertent and was caused by the common occurrence of the name John at the time.

[90] See *A Marginal Jew*, 2. 899–901. That Matt 16:17–19 is a post-Easter saying is one of the basic points that make up what Luz ("Das Primatwort," 415) considers the present-day critical consensus among Protestant and Catholic exegetes.

[91] On the question of possible contacts between Gal 1:15–16 and Matt 16:17–19, see Dupont, "La révélation," 411–20; Refoulé, "Primauté," 1–41; Feuillet, " 'Chercher,' " 350–60. I do not think it likely that either passage is directly dependent on the other; rather, a similar experience in first-generation Christianity has called forth similar concepts and language. One must not, however, overlook the differences as well as the similarities: e.g., "flesh and blood" function in a somewhat different way in Gal 1:16 than in Matt 16:17.

[92] In both form and substance, Matt 16:17–19 bears resemblances to various Jewish traditions dealing with a revelation given to an apocalyptic seer—which is certainly one way in which a 1st-century Palestinian Jew might have interpreted the tradition of an appearance by the risen Jesus. On this, see Kähler, "Zur Form- und Traditionsgeschichte," 46–55; he lists as examples of beatitudes spoken to recipients of revelation 4 Ezra 10:57; *Joseph and Aseneth* 16:14; *3 Enoch* 4:9; *Memar Marqah* 2 §9; the *Gospel of Bartholomew* 1 §8; the *Apocalypse of Paul;* the *Pistis Sophia;* and the Ethiopic *Apocalypse of Mary*. See also George W. E. Nickelsburg, "Enoch, Levi, and Peter: Recipients of Revelation in Upper Galilee," *JBL* 100 (1981) 575–600.

[93] It is because of this exegetical decision that I do not include here a detailed treatment of the many disputed questions about individual elements in Matt 16:17–19: e.g., whether Peter himself (as distinct from his confession, his faith, or perhaps Jesus himself) is identified as the rock on which Jesus will build his church, whether the "it" that the gates of Hades will not overcome is the rock or the church, and whether the power to bind and loose refers primarily to authoritative teaching, or to the power to excommunicate from and admit to the community, or to some other function (e.g., exorcism). These and many other questions, while important to a thorough exegesis

of the passage, cease to be of importance to our investigation once we decide that the sayings do not come from the public ministry.

If pressed to summarize my own views on the Simon-Cephas-Peter controversies, I would favor the following theses:

1. During the public ministry, Simon already bore the second Aramaic name or nickname *kēpāʾ* ("rock"), a name probably given him by Jesus. As far as we know, *kēpāʾ* was not ordinarily used as a proper name for a Jewish male in Palestine at the time of Jesus.

2. In the early days of the church, the Aramaic *kēpāʾ* was quickly given a corresponding Greek form by adding an "s," thus creating *Kēphas*, a Greek noun of the first declension.

3. Likewise early on (if we may judge by the multiple attestation of Paul, the pre-Marcan, and the pre-Johannine tradition), the transliterated form *Kēphas* was translated into Greek by using the noun *Petros*. While *kēpāʾ* would have been more naturally rendered by the feminine noun *petra* ("rock"), the masculine form *petros* (which could at times mean "rock," though its more ordinary meaning was "stone") was more suited for the name of a man. Again, as far as we know, *petros* was not ordinarily used as a Greek proper name in the first half of the 1st century A.D.

4. Unlike *Boanērges,* the Aramaic nickname for the sons of Zebedee, Peter's nickname was apparently considered to be of great significance. Unlike *Boanērges,* *kēpāʾ* was remembered and used early and late in the 1st century (from Paul to John), and its meaning was considered so important that it was not only transliterated but also translated into Greek with *Petros,* which in due time became the standard usage among Greek-speaking Christians.

5. That at least some Christians saw theological meaning in Peter's name is shown by Matt 16:18.

6. Although the number of Semitisms in Matt 16:17–19 has been overrated, at least a portion of these verses probably goes back to an Aramaic tradition. One possible retroversion of the key Petrine statement in 16:18 would be *ʾantāh hûʾ kēpāʾ wěʿal kēpāʾ dēn ʾebnêh qěhālî.* According to this retroversion, there was in the original Aramaic a double use of *kēpāʾ* to refer both to the person named "Rock" (i.e., Simon) and to the rock on which Jesus would build his assembly. Thus, the second occurrence of *kēpāʾ* would most naturally refer back to the first.

7. This is probably how the Greek translator(s) of the Aramaic tradition understood the statement. However, because of the difficulty of the different genders of *petros* and *petra* noted above in point (3)—and perhaps because *Petros* as Simon's Greek name was already a given in the early church—the Greek version of Matt 16:18 kept the substance of the wordplay in a slightly attenuated form by playing on *Petros* (new name of Simon)/*petra* (common noun).

---

[94] Here I agree with Gundry (*Mark,* 450–51) in stressing the common point in all the occurrences of *epitimaō,* viz., severity of tone; cf. Carl Kazmierski, "Mk 8,33—

Eine Ermahnung an die Kirche?" *Biblische Randbemerkungen* (Rudolf Schnacken-burg Festschrift; 2d ed.; Würzburg: Echter, 1974) 103–12, esp. 106–7. This tells against Pesch's attempt (*Das Markusevangelium*, 2. 47) to distinguish sources by dis-tinguishing the different nuances of *epitimaō* in v 30 and vv 32–33.

[95] On this, see Hooker, *The Gospel According to Saint Mark*, 204–5.

[96] See Grundmann, *Das Evangelium nach Markus*, 166.

[97] It is not simply Christians of later centuries who have felt the embarrassment: Luke, who often seeks to spare Peter, drops the whole incident of Peter's rebuke to Jesus and Jesus' rebuke to Peter. In Luke 9:20–21, Luke moves swiftly from Peter's confession of faith through Jesus' command to be silent to the first passion predic-tion. Despite the criterion of embarrassment, Pesch (*Simon-Petrus*, 41–42) thinks that nothing in Mark 8:31–33, including the "Satan word," goes back to an event in the life of Jesus. While the criterion of embarrassment is, in my view, a weighty con-sideration, Taylor's attempt (*The Gospel According to St. Mark*, 379) to add to it a criterion of lifelike narrative (as seen in Mark 8:32–33), a narrative that supposedly comes from original (i.e., Peter's) testimony, is not convincing. Lifelike narrative can be found in any good novel; see *A Marginal Jew*, 1. 180–82.

[98] See Grundmann, *Das Evangelium nach Markus*, 171; Hooker, *The Gospel Ac-cording to Saint Mark*, 206–7. Gundry (*Mark*, 432–33) stresses the series of move-ments in the story to support his view that Jesus' command means that Peter is ordered "to go back to his position among the disciples, where he belongs, following after Jesus . . . , not taking him [i.e., Jesus] aside by walking ahead of him or at least beside him." In favor of this view is the ordinary sense of *opisō mou* (as opposed to *eis ta opis*, as seen in John 6:66, with the sense of leaving Jesus entirely), which occurs in Mark 1:17,20; and notably here in 8:34 in the sense of following Jesus as a disci-ple. The problem with this view is that (1) the other Marcan examples of *opisō mou* are attached to *deute, aperchomai,* and *erchomai,* not with *hypagō,* as in 8:33; and (2) the direct address of "Satan" makes a call to discipleship aimed at a person so named difficult to understand.

[99] So, rightly, Lohmeyer (*Das Evangelium des Markus*, 170 n. 1) against Bultmann (*Geschichte*, 276–77), who judges the whole exchange between Peter and Jesus in Mark 8:31–33 to be actually a polemic that the Pauline form of Hellenistic Chris-tianity aimed at the Jewish Christian position represented by Peter. Thus, for Bult-mann, none of this material, including the "Satan word," goes back to Jesus. Bultmann, in turn, connects this view with the highly questionable position that Matt 16:17–19 was the original ending of the story of Peter's confession, an ending that Mark deleted and replaced with the Pauline polemic against Peter. One may note in passing that Bultmann's model of a lapidary Pauline-Hellenistic Christianity fiercely attacking a Petrine Jewish Christianity is hopelessly simplistic and outmoded; see

Raymond E. Brown, "Not Jewish Christianity and Gentile Christianity, but Types of Jewish/Gentile Christianity," *CBQ* 45 (1983) 74–79.

[100] For the Aramaic *śāṭān* as a common noun in the sense of "adversary," see, e.g., 4QTLev ar[a] 1:17. On this interpretation, see Meinrad Limbeck, "Satan und das Böse im Neuen Testament," in Herbert Haag (ed.), *Teufelsglaube* (Tübingen: Katzmann, 1974) 273–388, esp. 292–93; Pesch, *Das Markusevangelium*, 2. 54. Pesch points out that (1) Jewish writings around the time of Jesus did not identify Satan with any historical human being and that (2) Satan would be expected to think "the thoughts of the devil," not "the thoughts of men." (Gundry [*Mark*, 451]) tries to answer this second point, but not very effectively.) There may be a weak echo here of 2 Sam 19:23, where David calls Abishai, one of his overzealous followers, a *śāṭān* because he urges the king to execute his former enemy, Shimei. On this text, see Peggy L. Day, "Abishai the *śāṭān* in 2 Samuel 19:17–24," *CBQ* 49 (1987) 543–47.

[101] See Pesch, *Das Markusevangelium*, 2. 55; he denies the historicity of the scene in Mark 8:31–33, while admitting that the idea of Jesus calling Peter *śāṭān* may go back to some memory of how Peter resisted Jesus' message of the necessity of suffering.

[102] On the clearly composite nature of the material in Luke 22:24–30, see Fitzmyer, *The Gospel According to Luke*, 2. 1411–19. We probably have in this pericope a mixture of sayings of the historical Jesus, creations of the early church, and Lucan redaction (especially the use of the Last Supper as the overarching context). Nevertheless, there is an underlying unity of theme; on this, see Peter K. Nelson, *Leadership and Discipleship. A Study of Luke 22:24–30.*

[103] The plural form of the participle *(hēgoumenoi)* is used to refer to the leaders of the local church community in Heb 13:7,17,24; a somewhat vaguer usage occurs in Acts 15:22.

[104] See Fitzmyer, *The Gospel According to Luke*, 2. 1422.

[105] On the theme of apostasy in Luke, see Schuyler Brown, *Apostasy and Perseverance in the Theology of Luke* (AnBib 36; Rome: Biblical Institute, 1969).

[106] Gustav Stählin (*"exaiteō,"* *TDNT* 1 [1964] 195) thinks that the verb "to seek" or "to ask" means that the devil is demanding the surrender of the Twelve in the sense that he is asking God to hand them over to be tested, just as Satan asks God to hand over Job in Job 1–2. But Stählin may be pressing a point too far when he claims that in Luke 22:31 the devil "is the anti-Messiah who winnows (cf. Mt. 3:12) or sifts the wheat." The precise imagery involved in the "sifting" *(siniasai)* is unclear. Most likely it is an allusion to Amos 9:9: "I shall shake the house of Israel among all the nations as one shakes with a sieve." Still, there is no real parallel in the wording between the LXX form of this passage and Luke 22:31; the contact, if there be one, is on the level of thought, not words. Commentators debate the exact application of the imagery to

the Twelve; on the various theories, see Marshall, *The Gospel of Luke*, 820–21. Whatever the precise picture one conjures up, the general sense is one of tribulation and upset caused by fierce temptation and trials. Some commentators also see in the reference to "turning back" and "strengthening" the brothers an allusion to 2 Sam 15:20, in which King David, fleeing from his rebellious son Absalom, tells the foreigner Ittai the Gittite that he should not follow him into exile: "Return and take your brothers with you; [may the Lord show you] mercy and faithfulness." This is at best a weak echo, since David is urging a foreigner who has come into his service only recently to abandon him, while the foreigner insists on staying with him.

[107] See Dietrich, *Das Petrusbild*, 123–24. One wonders whether there might be an allusion here to the scene in Zech 3:1–10, where Joshua the high priest (= Peter?) is accused by Satan but defended by Yahweh through his angel (= Jesus?). While barely possible, such an echo smacks more of patristic allegory.

[108] See Fitzmyer, *The Gospel According to Luke*, 2. 1459, 1465; Brown, *The Death of the Messiah*, 1. 604–5. Dietrich (*Das Petrusbild*, 149), however, rejects the idea that Luke tends to spare Peter in the denial narrative. While there is no climax in Peter's three denials, Dietrich traces a climax in the three accusers and their accusations (ibid., 155). On the opposite side, Schuyler Brown (*Apostasy and Perseverance*, 70) sees a Lucan softening of Peter's denial in the fact that Luke has Peter simply deny his personal acquaintance with Jesus in 22:57 ("I do not know him"), not his profession of faith in Jesus as Messiah. For Brown, Peter's sin is one of cowardice, not loss of faith.

[109] See Fitzmyer, *The Gospel According to Luke*, 2. 1425, 1460–61; Frank J. Matera, *Passion Narratives and Gospel Theologies* (Theological Inquiries; New York/ Mahwah, NJ: Paulist, 1986) 171. Brown (*The Death of the Messiah*, 1. 608) points out that it is Jesus' looking upon Peter rather than the cockcrow that is "the primary impetus for Peter to remember" Jesus' prediction of Peter's denial—and perhaps as well Jesus' promise that Peter would "turn back" and strengthen his brothers. Brown also notes (p. 608 n. 37) that the verb "to turn" *(strephō)* often has "theological import" in Luke-Acts.

[110] For various interpretations of "all his acquaintances," see Raymond Brown, *The Death of the Messiah*, 2. 1171–73. See also Grundmann, *Das Evangelium nach Lukas;* Ernst, *Das Evangelium nach Lukas*, 640; Charles H. Talbert, *Literary Patterns, Theological Themes, and the Genre of Luke-Acts* (SBLMS 20; Missoula, MT: Scholars, 1974) 113–14. Dietrich (*Das Petrusbild*, 125) rejects a reference to Peter and the rest of the Eleven; in favor of such a reference is Jack Finegan, *Die Überlieferung der Leidens- und Auferstehungsgeschichte Jesu* (BZNW 15; Giessen: Töpelmann, 1934) 33 n. 2 (continued on p. 34); Schuyler Brown, *Apostasy*, 70. In my view, it is difficult to take the phrase *"all* his acquaintances" seriously (even if it is hyperbolic) and at the same time exclude Peter and the rest of the Eleven. To be sure, the phrase may include other Galilean men who followed Jesus, but it is hard to cham-

pion this inclusive reference while at the same time excluding Peter and the rest of the Eleven. Faced with the firmly rooted tradition that the disciples had fled after Jesus' arrest (an idea present in both the pre-Marcan and the pre-Johannine passion traditions), Luke may have felt that his rewriting of the story to include Peter and the rest of the Eleven at the cross demanded a certain diplomatic vagueness of expression; see Finegan, ibid., agreeing with Maurice Goguel.

[111] See Fitzmyer, *The Gospel According to Luke*, 2. 1423.

[112] That Luke 22:31–34 is essentially a Lucan reformulation of Mark 14:27–31, coupled with some of Luke's creative writing, is sustained by Finegan, *Die Überlieferung*, 14–15. Among possible traces of Luke's redactional hand in vv 31–32 may be listed *idou* ("behold"), the name and role of "Satan," the infinitive introduced by the genitive article *tou* (*tou siniasai*, "to sift"), the verb *deomai* ("to pray"), the verb *ekleipō*, interest in Jesus' prayer, and some typically Lucan words at the end of v 32 (*epistrephō, stērizō,* and the plural *adelphoi* used of the Christian faithful).

[113] Fitzmyer (*The Gospel According to Luke*, 2. 1421), who shares this view, lists various proponents of the idea that 22:31–32 is an L tradition that Luke inherited; they range all the way from the skeptical Rudolf Bultmann (*Geschichte*, 287–88) to the conservative Vincent Taylor, *The Passion Narrative of St Luke* (SNTSMS 19; Cambridge: Cambridge University, 1972) 65. See also Dibelius (*Formgeschichte*, 201), who mentions the possibility that the reference to Peter's leadership among the disciples after the passion is a prophecy after the fact.

[114] If, as I think is the case (see Brown, *The Death of the Messiah*, 1. 64–75), Mark is Luke's only continuous source for his Passion Narrative, any special L tradition behind Luke 22:31–32 would have been inserted only secondarily by Luke into the Marcan framework of the Last Supper. Strange to say, Günter Klein ("Die Verleugnung des Petrus," *Rekonstruktion und Interpretation* [BEvT 50; Munich: Kaiser, 1969] 49–98) tries to use Luke 22:31–32 to disqualify as unhistorical the tradition of Peter's denial of Jesus, which is firmly rooted in the pre-Marcan and pre-Johannine passion traditions. Since the placement of 22:31–32 at the Last Supper—and probably in the whole Passion Narrative—is not original, indeed, since the original narrative setting of 22:31–32 (if it is not simply a Lucan creation) is unknown, the floating and historically suspect tradition of Luke 22:31–32 can hardly be used to cast doubt on the denial tradition, which is on much firmer historical ground. On the denial by Peter and Klein's denial of the denial, see below.

[115] While the majority of scholars favor the historicity of the core event behind the denial stories in the Gospels, some noted scholars, including Maurice Goguel, Rudolf Bultmann, and Alfred Loisy in his later career denied the historicity of Peter's denial. Perhaps the most famous proponent of a judgment against historicity is Günter Klein ("Die Verleugnung des Petrus," 49–98). Against Klein's rejection of historicity, the following observations may be made:

1. Peter's denial is, as Klein claims, a unit that can be isolated within the Passion Narrative, a discrete unit that is easily removed without disturbing the larger story. That fact, however, simply flows from the special subject matter: it is the one large unit in the pre-Marcan and pre-Johannine Passion Narratives that focuses upon someone other than Jesus while Jesus is absent entirely from the stage. The short pericope dealing with the female witnesses at the cross can also be isolated and easily omitted, but that hardly proves that the presence of women witnesses at the cross is unhistorical. On the question of the denial narrative as a discrete unit, see Dodd, *Historical Tradition,* 84 n. 1.

2. Klein quickly dismisses the version of the story in John without giving sufficient consideration to the question of John representing an independent source. As throughout the three volumes of *A Marginal Jew,* I hold that John represents an independent tradition, a position that has been validated again and again. The detailed studies of scholars like Dodd, Brown, Schnackenburg, and Fortna have confirmed this point with respect to the denial narrative; for their work, see the treatment of the criterion of multiple attestation below. In brief, the multiple attestation of Mark and John makes Klein's rejection of historicity highly questionable.

3. As I have already indicated above, Klein's attempt to play off Luke 22:31–32 against the denial tradition is curious. (a) The multiple attestation of Mark and John shows that Peter's denial is deeply rooted in the passion tradition, while we are uncertain about the original narrative setting of Luke 22:31–32 (if, indeed, it is not a Lucan creation). At the very least, the present form and setting of the saying is due to Luke—and likewise, therefore, whatever tension exists between it and the denial tradition. Yet Luke is willing to have the two types of sayings stand side by side, a fact that leads to my next point. (b) Contrary to Klein, I think that the *mē eklipē hē pistis sou* ("that your faith may not fail") need not be taken as hopelessly opposed to the tradition of Peter's denial. Certainly, Luke did not take it that way. The verb *ekleipō* can contain within itself the idea of "totally," as when it is used to say that one's years "come to an end" (Heb 1:12, citing LXX Ps 101:28), one's money "gives out" or "runs out" (1 Macc 3:29; Luke 16:9), or one "dies" or "is destroyed" (Gen 49:33; Tob 14:11; LXX Ps 17:38; Wis 5:13; *J.W.* 4.1.9 §68; *Ant.* 2.7.5 §184). Thus, it is not eisegesis to take Luke 22:32 to mean that Jesus prayed that Peter's faith not fail completely or be destroyed. Clearly, Luke does not think that Peter's faith simply came to an end, died, or in that sense failed totally. Hence, in Luke's mind, Jesus' prayer is effective, Peter's denial notwithstanding. In my opinion, the strict antithesis between Luke 22:31–32 and the denial tradition is in Klein's head, not in Luke's text; Klein should have attended more closely to the meaning and implication of the verb *ekleipō.* (c) Klein, like Bultmann before him, must claim that the participle *epistrepsas* ("having turned back") in Luke 22:32 is an addition by Luke to an earlier tradition that knew nothing of Peter's denial of Jesus; neither Klein nor Bultmann produces solid evidence for such a thesis. On all this, see Marshall, *The Gospel of Luke,* 821–22; Dietrich, *Das Petrusbild,* 121–36.

4. Klein's own explanation of the origin of the story of Peter's denial is nothing

short of "historical imagination"—not historical reconstruction—at its worst. Klein posits, without any real proof, that, in the early church, Peter was *successively* the head of the Twelve, then the leader of the apostles, and after that a member of the three Jerusalem pillars. Having left each group to join the next—hence, the triple denial!—Peter finally struck out on his own as a missionary, coming in this capacity to Rome. Needless to say, there is no proof that Peter's role in any one of the three groups mentioned necessitated his leaving his leadership or membership in the other groups. Galatians 2:7–9 indicates just the opposite: Peter was both an apostle and one of the three pillars; nowhere in or outside of the NT is it ever said that Peter ceased to be one of the Twelve. Klein's whole theory must stand as one of the most contorted and convoluted pieces of interpretation in the history of 20th-century exegesis. Since even Klein finds the highly speculative theory of Eta Linnemann ("Die Verleugnung des Petrus," *ZTK* 63 [1966] 1–32) unlikely because it lacks any basis in verifiable events in the early church, the reader will excuse me for not examining it in detail.

More open to some historical event involving Peter's denial of Jesus during the passion, an event that lies behind literary texts that are clearly artificial in their present formulation, is (besides Dodd and Brown) Max Wilcox, "The Denial Sequence in Mark xiv. 26–31, 66–72," *NTS* 17 (1970–71) 426–36. For the history of the interpretation of the Marcan version of the story (in a monograph that admittedly pursues a conservative theological hermeneutic), see Robert W. Herron, Jr., *Mark's Account of Peter's Denial of Jesus. A History of Its Interpretation* (Lanham, MD/New York/London: University Press of America, 1991).

[116] On the argument from embarrassment, see Brown, *The Death of the Messiah*, 1. 615. On Paul's view of Peter, see Eduard Lohse, "St. Peter's Apostleship in the Judgment of St. Paul, the Apostle to the Gentiles," *Greg* 72 (1991) 419–35; cf. Martin Karrer, "Petrus im paulinischen Gemeindekreis," *ZNW* 80 (1989) 210–31. On the question of polemics against Peter, see Terence V. Smith, *Petrine Controversies in Early Christianity* (WUNT 2/15; Tübingen: Mohr [Siebeck], 1985). While one may readily admit that Mark and John, for instance, have a more reserved, and at times negative, view of Peter than do Matthew and Luke-Acts, one does not find in any of the canonical Gospels the wholesale rejection of Peter witnessed in some writings of the 2d and 3d centuries.

[117] For a study establishing this position on the denial story, see Neil J. McEleney, "Peter's Denials—How Many? To Whom?" *CBQ* 52 (1990) 467–72. He shows that Matthew's and Luke's variations in the story are to be explained by their editorial tendencies (e.g., Matthew's penchant for pluralizing and Luke's staging technique) and do not require an appeal to a special source beyond Mark. In favor of Luke representing at least in part another tradition of the denial, indeed, one earlier than Mark's, see Bultmann, *Geschichte*, 290.

[118] For a defense of John's independence in the denial tradition, see Dodd, *Historical Tradition*, 83–88; Brown, *The Gospel According to John*, 2. 836–42; idem, *The Death of the Messiah*, 1. 610–14; Schnackenburg, *Das Johannesevangelium. III. Teil*, 258–73; Robert T. Fortna, "Jesus and Peter at the High Priest's House: A Test Case for the Question of the Relation between Mark's and John's Gospels," *NTS* 24 (1978) 371–83. On John's presentation of the triple denial and its divergences from the Synoptics, see also Quast, *Peter and the Beloved Disciple*, 71–89. A convenient table of the similarities and differences among the four evangelists in their denial narratives is found in Brown, *The Death of the Messiah*, 1. 590–91.

[119] One particularly puzzling detail is the reference to "another disciple . . . known to the high priest," who asks the female gatekeeper to let Peter into the courtyard of the high priest (John 18:15–16). Bultmann (*Das Evangelium des Johannes*, 499 n. 6) suggests with hesitation that the Fourth Evangelist invented this disciple to explain how Peter obtained entrance into the high priest's palace. The natural objection to this line of reasoning is that none of the three Synoptists felt any such need to explain Peter's access. In fact, one could easily join part of v 15 ("Now Simon Peter was following Jesus . . . and he entered with Jesus into the high priest's palace") to v 17 ("Then the girl who was the doorkeeper said to Peter . . .") and no one would notice the absence of v 16 and the "other disciple," so superfluous are they to the whole narrative. Moreover, this "other disciple" (who may or may not be intended to be identified with "the disciple whom Jesus loved") plays no further role—theological or purely narrative—in the story of Peter's denial. As Brown (*The Gospel According to John*, 2. 841) rightly observes, "to invent a disciple of Jesus who inexplicably was acceptable at the palace of the high priest is to create a difficulty where there was none." Hence Schnackenburg (*Das Johannesevangelium. III. Teil*, 266–67) concludes that the other disciple was already present in the Fourth Evangelist's (non-Synoptic) source; the same is probably true of the curious detail (v 18) of the fire being a "coal fire" *(anthrakian)*. Such considerations even lead Dibelius (*Formgeschichte*, 217) to conclude that this other disciple was a historical figure. In any event, in light of all these considerations, it is very difficult to see the other disciple simply as a redactional addition made by the Fourth Evangelist to Mark's version of the story.

[120] Fortna ("Jesus and Peter," 378–79), e.g., holds that Mark's version hints at an originally single denial that has been expanded into three; but Fortna also holds—rightly, I think, against Kim Dewey ("Peter's Curse and Cursed Peter," *The Passion in Mark* [ed. Werner H. Kelber; Philadelphia: Fortress, 1976] 96–114)—that, if such an expansion took place, it was already present in the pre-Marcan and pre-Johannine stages of the Passion Narrative.

[121] See, e.g., John Dominic Crossan, *The Historical Jesus* (San Francisco: Harper, 1991) 261–64, 341. Unlike some other authors, Crossan does supply a definition; see his *Jesus. A Revolutionary Biography* (San Francisco: Harper, 1994) 71: ". . . radical egalitarianism . . . [means] an absolute equality of people that denies the validity of

any discrimination between them and negates the necessity of any hierarchy among them." That, in turn, would demand a careful definition of what qualifies as "radical" and "absolute"—to say nothing of "discrimination" and "hierarchy," terms that are often used in present-day America for whatever aspects of society one does not like. More to the point, Crossan himself (ibid.) senses the immediate objection that a great deal of this involves "anachronistically retrojecting" modern ideology back into 1st-century Jewish Palestine. For all his attempts at a reply, I think that the objection stands. One would do well to attend to the methodological cautions voiced by Goodman's *The Ruling Class of Judaea.*

[122] *A Marginal Jew,* 2. 449–50.

[123] On this point, see John P. Meier, "Dividing Lines in Jesus Research Today," *Int* 50 (1996) 355–72, esp. 366–67. I do not mention here Jesus' words and actions over bread and wine at the Last Supper, since this particular symbolic practice, while it was carried over by and became very important to the early church, did not shape the disciples' lives during the public ministry. For the historicity of Jesus' words and actions over bread and wine at the Last Supper, see my article, "The Eucharist at the Last Supper: Did It Happen?" *TD* 42 (1995) 335–51.

[124] See *A Marginal Jew,* 2. 309–17.

[125] Even if statements like Matt 10:5–6 ("Do not go to Gentiles and do not enter a Samaritan city; rather, go only to the lost sheep of the house of Israel") and 15:24 ("I was sent only to the lost sheep of the house of Israel") are judged to be creations of the early church, they reflect what seems to have been the actual practice of Jesus and his disciples during the public ministry.

[126] The way theologians today pose the question of whether Jesus founded the church is more methodologically sophisticated than was often the case in the past. For a full treatment of this key theological question, which can only be touched upon here, see Gerhard Lohfink, *Jesus and Community* (Philadelphia: Fortress; New York/Ramsey, NY: Paulist, 1984). Lohfink encapsulates his whole approach in the opening of his Preface (p. xi): "Critical theology has long asked emphatically if the historical Jesus really founded a church. Yet it has become increasingly clear that this question is posed in the wrong way. It is not much of an exaggeration to say that Jesus could not have founded a church since there had long been one—God's people, Israel." See also Denaux, "Did Jesus Found the Church?" 25–45, esp. p. 38: "We are now sufficiently equipped to formulate our own answer to the question of whether Jesus founded a Church. When it is a question of the possibility whether there is one well-determined act of founding in Jesus' life by which he formally established his Church, then our answer is negative. When we think, however, of the coming into existence of the Church in terms of a process in several phases which go back to the whole Christ event, to which also the church-founding moments in the earthly life of Jesus obviously belong, then our answer is expressly positive." Michael A. Fahey

("Church," *Systematic Theology. Roman Catholic Perspectives* [2 vols.; ed. Francis Schüssler Fiorenza and John P. Galvin; Minneapolis: Fortress, 1991] 3–74) speaks on p. 19 of the church as "the community that emerged from Jesus' preaching, life, death, and resurrection. . . ." Joseph Ratzinger ("Ein Versuch zur Frage des Traditionsbegriffs," in Karl Rahner and Joseph Ratzinger, *Offenbarung und Überlieferung* [Freiburg/Basel/Vienna: Herder, 1965] 41) thinks that "only a series of historical shocks [e.g., the execution of Stephen and later of James, the flight of Peter from Jerusalem] . . . brought the primitive community to the point . . . of creating the church instead of the kingdom." See further Francis Schüssler Fiorenza, *Foundational Theology. Jesus and the Church* (New York: Crossroad, 1984).

PART TWO

JESUS THE JEW AND HIS JEWISH COMPETITORS

CHAPTER 28

JESUS IN RELATION TO COMPETING JEWISH GROUPS

The Pharisees

I. INTRODUCTION

Jesus' wide-ranging itinerant ministry throughout Israel, his summoning of many disparate types of Israelites to follow him, his creation of the Twelve, symbolizing the reconstituted twelve tribes of Israel, and his journeys to Jerusalem during the pilgrim feasts, where great crowds would be gathered—all these activities make clear that Jesus the eschatological prophet did not intend to form an elite group or esoteric sect within or apart from Israel. He intended instead to address, challenge, and regather the whole of God's people, the whole of Israel, in expectation of the coming kingdom of God.

If, from the viewpoint of empirical Jewish history, Jesus was a failure—and he was—his failure was due at least in part to the fact that other individuals and groups were competing alongside him and his disciples for influence and leadership in Israel at a critical stage of its history. For example, behind the Christian theology in John 3:22–30 is the somewhat embarrassing memory that, for a while after Jesus emerged from the Baptist's circle to begin his own ministry, John the Baptist and Jesus were competing for disciples with similar methods, including baptism.

Jesus and the Baptist were hardly the only 1st-century Jewish gurus attracting individual Jews in search of a higher or stricter way of living their Judaism. In his autobiography (*Life* 2 §11), Josephus (ca. 37– ca. 100) mentions a certain Bannus, a desert ascetic with whom he claims to have spent three years of his life, from age 16 to 19, after having tried out the other main Jewish groups (Pharisees, Sadducees, and Essenes). John the Baptist, Bannus, and the Qumranites were probably only a few manifestations of the larger phenomenon of Jewish individuals preaching repentance and practicing ritual lustrations in the Jordan valley around the turn of the era.[1] We can only wonder how many other holy men, ascetics, prophets, apocalyptic seers, or zealous religious nationalists in the isolated nooks and crannies of Palestine attracted young Jews on a spiritual quest. The huge library that we awkwardly dub "the intertestamental writings" or "the OT pseudepigrapha" reminds us that there were probably many religious leaders in Palestine of whom we are largely ignorant.

But individual holy men who were contemporaries of Jesus would not have been the greatest source of competition for the Nazarene and his recently formed movement. Especially in matters religious, the ancient Mediterranean world, unlike our own, respected tradition over innovation, ancient and venerable institutions over a cult or "superstition" that was automatically suspect because it was new. Jesus, "the new kid" on the religious block of Palestinian Judaism, had to compete against a number of religious and political movements that had become fixtures on the wall of Israel's history for almost two centuries prior to his appearance. The most famous of such movements—thanks to Josephus' essays on them—though hardly the only ones, are the Pharisees, the Sadducees, and the Essenes.[2]

Hence, to understand Jesus "in relation to . . . ," as we are attempting to do in Volume Three, we must understand not only his positive relation to his followers but also his negative relation to his competitors or opponents in the public arena of Jewish religion and politics in the early 1st century A.D. An initial caution: one must not confuse the limited task of this chapter (on the Pharisees) and the following ones (on the Sadducees, the Essenes, and other groups) with an attempt to write a history of Judaism at the turn of the era in the manner of Emil Schürer or to survey the state of Jewish institutions, parties, practices, and beliefs in the manner of E. P. Sanders.[3] The focus of these chapters remains "*Jesus* in relation to his competitors," and just enough will be said about his major competitors to illuminate his interaction with them—if, indeed, such interaction occurred. As we shall see, the net effect of this narrow focus is to restrict our concern mainly to the Pharisees, the chief topic of this chapter.[4] However, before we attempt to draw a thumbnail sketch of the Pharisees and later on of the Sadducees—the only two religious-political Jewish groups with whom Jesus did clearly interact—it might be helpful to step back for a moment and review briefly the origins of these major competitors of Jesus' movement.

II. BY WAY OF BACKGROUND:
A BRIEF HISTORY OF ORIGINS[5]

A. Tensions within Israel from the Beginning

That there should have been competing parties within Israel at the turn of the era is hardly a surprise to those who know the history of Israel as reflected in the OT. As early as the Book of Genesis, the internecine strife among the twelve sons of the patriarch Jacob serves as a perfect symbol of the tensions and at times open warfare that regularly threatened to rip the people of Israel apart.[6] Civil strife and even civil war occurred from the time of the formation of a monarchy (or monarchies) in Israel in the 11th and 10th centuries B.C. The national unity that was achieved at such a high price under King David (reigned 1000–962) and King Solomon (reigned 961–922) was short-lived. The nation was split into two rival kingdoms, Israel (in the north) and Judah (in the south) in 922. Ongoing dynastic warfare, internal court intrigues, debates among competing parties as to which international suzerain should be embraced as an ally, the erosion of morale by prophets foretelling doom, and blind arrogance in the face of overwhelming foreign forces led to the destruction of the northern kingdom by Assyria in 721 and of the southern kingdom by Babylon in 587.

When in 539 the Persian King Cyrus allowed Jewish exiles from the southern kingdom to begin rebuilding the temple in Jerusalem, party strife was not long in reigniting over control of the temple and its high priesthood.[7] This internal strife became aggravated in the 3d and 2d centuries by increasing tensions over encroaching Hellenistic culture, which some Jews embraced and others resisted.[8] Resistance came to a head when some Jerusalem priests collaborated with the Syrian monarch Antiochus IV Epiphanes to push through a thorough Hellenization of Jerusalem. When Antiochus desecrated the temple and sought to suppress basic Jewish practices like circumcision in 167, the priest Mattathias, his son Judas Maccabeus, and their whole Hasmonean family sparked a revolt.[9]

B. The Hasmoneans as a Source of Tension

After Judas' death in battle in 160, his brothers (notably Jonathan and Simon) continued the struggle. They succeeded in throwing off the yoke of Syrian oppression only to end up establishing their own form of monarchy. By gradual steps, Jonathan (ruled 160–143), Simon (143–134), and Simon's son John Hyrcanus I (134–104) established the Hasmonean dynasty in Israel.

Paradoxically, the Hasmonean rulers became the new occasion for civil strife. They became increasingly Hellenistic in their style of ruling and living.[10] They also insisted on holding the high priesthood despite their doubtful claim to be legitimate high priests, and they united the offices of high priest and king in one ruler (at least by the time of Aristobulus I in 104–103). Worse still, they oscillated between various warring parties and proved quite ruthless in suppressing any party out of favor. Thus did these successors of Judas the freedom fighter become a cause of dissension rather than unity for their compatriots. As time passed, some deeply religious Jews may have considered the Hasmonean monarchs the worst of both worlds: tyrannical kings who were not of the legitimate line of David and worldly high priests who were not of the legitimate line of Zadok, the priest who served David and Solomon.[11]

It was out of these turbulent times of the early Hasmonean rulers that the major Jewish groups known to us from Josephus and the NT were born. While some scholars trace either the Pharisees or the Essenes back to the Babylonian exile or the restoration of Jerusalem in the 6th century B.C.,[12] our first sure glimpses of them and their labels reach back—by way of Josephus—only to the period after the Maccabean revolt in the 2d century B.C., when the Hasmoneans Jonathan, Simon, and John Hyrcanus were consolidating their power.[13]

C. THE ESSENES AND THE QUMRANITES

By the middle of the 2d century, the Essenes, especially the subgroup that fled to Qumran, seem to have coalesced into a separatist sect in the strict sense of the word.[14] The precise origins of the Essenes are hotly debated among scholars. Some historians suggest that both the Essenes and the Pharisees stemmed from a group of "faithful" or "loyal" people ("Hasideans," *Ḥăsîdîm* in Hebrew, *Asidaioi* in Greek), who at first supported the Maccabean revolt.[15] According to this view, some Hasideans, interested only in the strict observance of the Law and not political machinations, became increasingly alienated from the Hasmoneans because of their royal and high-priestly ambitions. These dissenters withdrew into sectarian conventicles and became the Essenes. In due time, the more radical wing of the Essenes, under the leadership of a priest known as the Teacher of Righteousness, finally broke away entirely from the temple community in Jerusalem and created an isolated settlement of the pure in the Judean desert at Qumran, on the northwest corner of the Dead Sea. Some historians trace this break to ca. 152 B.C., when the Hasmonean ruler Jonathan accepted appointment as Jewish high priest from the pagan Syrian king Alexander Balas.[16] Other Hasideans, however, continued to try to work with the Hasmoneans, provided they could get their own religious-political program enacted into law. These politically active Hasideans supposedly became the Pharisees.[17]

Some scholars, however, doubt the origin of either the Essenes or the Pharisees from the shadowy "Hasideans," who quickly disappear from view.[18] Others suggest that only the Pharisees, but not the Essenes, emerged from the Hasideans.[19] Still other critics theorize that the Essenes were ultra-conservative Jews who had returned to Palestine from Babylon upon hearing of the success of Judas Maccabeus, only to be alienated by the assimilation of many Palestinian Jews to Hellenistic culture.[20] In my opinion, given the present state of scholarship with its welter of conflicting theories, it is better to admit that the precise origins and precursors of both the Essenes and the Pharisees remain a mystery. A major reason for our ignorance is that Josephus (*Ant.* 13.5.9 §171–72) simply presents both of them, without further ado, as already existing during the reign of the Hasmonean Jonathan (160–143 B.C.). He never tells us when or how they arose.[21]

In any event, the Essenes saw themselves as the true, faithful Israel that alone knew and observed God's will as Israel entered the great final struggle of its history "at the end of the days."[22] All other Jews were polluted by an illegitimate priesthood offering unclean sacrifices according to an erroneous calendar in a defiled temple. The Essenes themselves formed the true spiritual temple; their rigorous study and practice of the Law substituted for cultic sacrifices until such time as they could regain and purify the temple.[23] Because of their separatist views and lifestyle, they did not compete actively in the public arena of religion and politics in Jerusalem in the same way the Pharisees and Sadducees did. This held true, a fortiori, of the separatists at Qumran.

D. The Pharisees and the Sadducees under the Hasmoneans

The disappearance of the "Hasideans" and the withdrawal of the Essenes left the Pharisees and the Sadducees as the major opponents in the struggle for power in Jerusalem under the Hasmoneans, who were not above switching sides. John Hyrcanus I apparently began his reign with the support of the Pharisees; but, after falling out with them, he favored the Sadducees (*Ant.* 13.10.5 §288–96).[24] The Pharisees continued in opposition during the reigns of Aristobulus I and Alexander Jannaeus (103–76), which were marked by severe civil strife.[25] However, the pious Queen Salome Alexandra (76–69, usually thought to be the widow of Jannaeus) sought to resolve the internal turmoil plaguing her kingdom by handing over effective power in domestic affairs to the Pharisees (*J. W.* 1.5.1–3 §107–114; *Ant.* 13.15.5–13.16.6 §401–432). Back in the saddle, the Pharisees took such violent revenge on their political adversaries that the queen had to provide safe havens for the erstwhile supporters of Aristobulus I and Jannaeus.

Still, relative peace reigned until Salome Alexandra's death, when the struggle between her two sons, Aristobulus II (ruled 69–63) and Hyrcanus II (high priest 76–69 and 63–41; ruled 47–41) plunged Israel into a new period of civil disturbance. The picture presented by Josephus is murky. Many scholars think that the Sadducees favored Aristobulus, the de facto ruler and high priest, while the Pharisees supported Hyrcanus. The reality may have been more complicated, with both people and aristocrats divided and switching sides more than once.[26] The Roman general Pompey finally decided matters in 63 by imprisoning Aristobulus, accepting Hyrcanus as high priest, and making Palestine a part of the Roman province of Syria.

E. Herod the Great

Amid the chaos caused in Palestine by the shifting sands of Roman politics, a wily politician from Idumea named Antipater and his son Herod (the future King Herod the Great) used Hyrcanus II as a tool for gaining political power. Once Herod assumed the throne as King of Judea (officially in 40 B.C., in reality in 37), he ruthlessly destroyed or marginalized all political opponents, though some Pharisees sought influence indirectly through palace intrigues.

If anything, the Sadducees probably suffered more than the Pharisees during Herod's reign, since the king took brutal measures to cow the aristocracy, which was mostly Sadducean. Josephus tells us that after Herod took Jerusalem in 37, he put to death Hyrcanus II and all the members of the Sanhedrin, with the exception of a favored Pharisee, Samaias. (An alternate version of the slaughter, perhaps more believable for its more modest claim, states that Herod killed 45 of the most prominent supporters of Antigonus, the son of Aristobulus II.)[27]

Throughout his reign, Herod almost always chose high priests from among priestly families other than the Hasmoneans. It was hardly by accident that some of these families hailed from Babylon or Egypt; this made them still more dependent on Herod's support. The king became all the more convinced of the wisdom of this policy after making the tactical error of appointing the 17-year-old Hasmonean Aristobulus III, the grandson of Hyrcanus II, as high priest in 36/35 B.C. When Herod saw how fervently the Jewish people in the temple acclaimed Aristobulus during the feast of

Sukkot, the king quickly arranged for the teenage high priest to meet with an unfortunate accident in a swimming pool.[28]

Thus, with the Jerusalem aristocracy diminished and afraid, with the Hasmoneans killed, marginalized, co-opted, or married (Herod first married the Hasmonean Mariamme I and then killed her), and with the reigning high priest almost totally under Herod's thumb, no organized political opposition was possible. For all practical purposes, during Herod's autocracy the Pharisees and Sadducees could exist openly only as what modern scholars would label "voluntary associations."[29] Granted their small numbers and lack of popular support, the Sadducees probably saw their influence reduced during this period even more than that of the Pharisees.[30]

F. The Roman Prefects and Procurators

After Herod the Great died (4 B.C.) and his incompetent son Archelaus was replaced in A.D. 6 by a new system of Roman prefects ruling Judea as a Roman province, a different type of political constellation arose. On the one hand, Rome preferred to govern "barbarian" populations at the borders of its empire through local monarchs (hence Herod the Great) or local aristocracies. On the other hand, from the time of the Persian Empire onwards, *the* local aristocrat who had represented the Jews of Judea to the suzerain and vice versa was the high priest in Jerusalem.[31] This had been the general modus vivendi for about half a millennium; Herod's autocratic rule, which eclipsed the high priest's power, was, in comparison, a short interlude. After the failure of Archelaus, the Romans solved the problem in Judea—or thought they did—by resuming the traditional approach that had worked fairly well in the past.

Meanwhile, in Galilee and Perea, another son of Herod the Great, Herod Antipas (reigned 4 B.C.–A.D. 39), proved to be a much abler ruler (technically, "tetrarch") than Archelaus had in Judea. Accordingly, Rome kept Antipas in place until much later. (He was finally deposed in A.D. 39 for the politically indiscreet move of asking the emperor Caligula to make him a king.) On the whole, Antipas was careful not to offend Jewish sensibilities in public. Hence we hear of no great unrest or uprising by the populace during his reign. Needless to say, this peaceful situation was due, at least in part, to Antipas' ever-watchful eye that nipped the slightest danger to public order in the bud. It was this policy that led to the execution of John the Baptist.[32] As far as the Pharisees in Galilee are concerned, little can be said. Indeed, some recent scholars have even suggested that the presence of the Pharisees in Galilee during the reign of Antipas (and hence during the public ministry of

Jesus) was minimal or nonexistent.[33] Be that as it may, there is no reason to think that the Pharisees controlled either the political or the religious scene in Galilee during the time of Jesus.[34]

The political and religious situation in the new Roman province of Judea had a quite different configuration. The Roman prefect, domiciled at Caesarea Maritima with his auxiliary troops, acted as the local military commander, administered the financial affairs of Judea for Rome, maintained a garrison of troops in Jerusalem for security, and had ultimate life-and-death power over everyone in the province who was not a Roman citizen.[35] In practice, though, he let the high priest in Jerusalem, along with the priestly and lay aristocrats around him, run most aspects of internal Jewish life—*provided* the native aristocracy maintained good order among the Jews and saw to the collection of taxes and customs.[36]

This forced the high priest to engage in a delicate balancing act. He had to serve as the chief buffer and mediator between the often overbearing Roman prefect and Jewish sensitivities—especially when the prefect came up to Jerusalem with his troops to enforce order during the great feasts—while at the same time trying to persuade his fellow Jews to comply with Roman demands for order and taxes. In negotiating this balancing act, his immediate mainstay and support were the wealthy and influential priestly and lay aristocrats in Jerusalem. Since many—though not all—of these wealthy aristocrats inclined to the Sadducean position, the Sadducean party probably came out of the political wilderness and regained the upper hand during the years of the Roman prefects and procurators.[37]

This political arrangement was a fragile one, as can be seen by the very short tenure of most high priests and, indeed, most prefects and procurators from A.D. 6 to 66. The two great exceptions among the prefects were Valerius Gratus (ruled A.D. 15–26) and his successor Pontius Pilate (26–36).[38] Intriguingly, the one great exception among the high priests was Joseph Caiaphas, who managed to stay in office from 18 to 36. Apparently he mastered the balancing act and learned to work hand in glove with Valerius Gratus and Pontius Pilate. It may be no accident that Caiaphas was deposed from the high priesthood as soon as Pilate was removed from his prefecture.

Whatever later Jews and Christians may have thought of Caiaphas and Pilate, they were in their own day skillful masters of pragmatic politics, which at least minimized major disturbances and bloodshed. As a result, from the viewpoint of high-level Jewish and Roman politics in Judea, the time of Jesus' adulthood and ministry was the most stable (though not entirely peaceful) period in the 1st century A.D. To be sure, the high-handed and insensitive Pilate ignited a number of dangerous political-religious conflicts: e.g., introducing military standards with the emperor's medallions into Jerusalem and using money from the temple treasury to build an aqueduct.[39] In general, however, both prefect and high priest apparently worked effectively to prevent conflicts from exploding into a full-scale uprisings. In the end, it was a conflict of Pilate with the Samaritans, not the Jews of Judea, that caused his recall to Rome (*Ant.* 18.4.1–2 §85–89). If Caiaphas and Pilate worked well as a team at the time of Jesus' trial and execution, it was because they were well practiced in the game.

This tacit arrangement may have suited the high priests and the Jerusalem aristocracy—and hence the Sadducean party that was well represented among them. But it tended to leave the Pharisees out in the cold. It is not surprising that Josephus has practically nothing to narrate about them during the rule of the Roman prefects and procurators. With no direct political power, the Pharisees had to seek levers of power by indirect means. They probably redoubled their efforts during this period to spread their influence among the common people, most of whom never became Pharisees themselves. Still, according to Josephus, ordinary Jews were much impressed by the widespread reputation that the Pharisees enjoyed for their exact knowledge of the Mosaic Law.[40] Thus, that the Pharisees would be the major religious group questioning and debating Jesus, who was also active among the common people, should come as no surprise.

In addition, if Anthony J. Saldarini is correct in suggesting that the Pharisees were strongly represented in the "retainer class" of Judean society—that is, the class of low-level bureaucrats, functionaries, and educators on whom the aristocrats depended to keep everyday government operating—then the Pharisees would have had a kind of "backstairs" access to power.[41] Thus, both through their influence on the mass of Jews who belonged to no party and through their influence as servants of the people in power, they may at times have been able to persuade or pressure the high priests and the aristocrats to adopt their views and practices. This would have been made easier by the fact that, as Josephus indicates, at least some priests were Pharisees (see *Life* 39 §197).

Nevertheless, one must be careful not to overstate this very limited political influence, which in fact is exaggerated by Josephus to the point of claiming that Sadducees assuming public office had to obey the regulations of the Pharisees. It is noteworthy that this claim is never made in his earlier *Jewish War* but only in his later *Antiquities* (written ca. A.D. 94), and then only in one passage (*Ant.* 18.1.4. §17). His presentation in *Antiquities* is perhaps colored by the subsequent influence of the Pharisaic party on emerging rabbinic Judaism and possibly also by the competition among Jewish groups for Roman favor at the end of the 1st century.

While the Pharisees as a group apparently lacked direct political power during direct Roman rule in the period before A.D. 70, at least a few individual Pharisees seem to have risen high in the Jerusalem power structure. For example, in Acts 5:34, Luke mentions Gamaliel, "a Pharisee," as a respected lawyer and an influential member of the counselors around the high priest. One must be cautious here: we have no other attestation of this Gamaliel (known by scholars as Gamaliel I) as a Pharisee, and Luke makes a glaring historical error about 1st-century Jewish-Palestinian history right at the beginning of Gamaliel's speech (5:36–37).[42] Hence some scholars have wondered whether Luke is any better informed when he claims that Gamaliel was a Pharisee. Yet there is one reason for thinking that Luke is right: Gamaliel's son, Simeon (or Simon) I.[43]

Josephus tells us that Simeon I was a Pharisee, the offspring of a prominent Jerusalem family, and a key member of the moderate coalition government in the early days of the First Jewish War (*Life* 38 §190–96), a coalition that sought unsuccessfully to counter the more extreme rebels.[44] We also hear of a Pharisaic *priest* who was a member of the delegation sent by the revolutionary government to relieve Josephus of his military command in Galilee in the early days of the revolt (*Life* 39 §197). In short, while the Pharisees as a group were kept largely on the sidelines of political power during the rule of the Roman prefects and procurators,[45] their reputation and influence with the common people, perhaps their indirect influence as the retainer class in government (if one accepts Saldarini's opinion), and at times their direct influence through prominent individuals like Gamaliel I and Simeon I allowed them to have some leverage on Judean society.

G. The New Situation after A.D. 70

By the end of the First Jewish War, the capture of Jerusalem, the destruction of the temple, the defeat of the rebels, and the extinction of any sort of independent temple-state in Judea brought about a sea change in the Jewish power structure of Judea. The burning of the temple in A.D. 70 meant the demolition of the power base of the priestly aristocracy. The capture of Jerusalem likewise entailed the slaughter or imprisonment of large numbers of priestly and lay aristocrats, many of whom were probably Sadducees; we know, however, of priests (including Josephus) who survived the disaster.[46] Qumran was also destroyed by the Romans in 68, and the Essenes as a distinct group disappeared from Judean society. The extremists among the rebels, such as the Zealots and the Sicarii, also perished, either in Jerusalem or later on in the last Jewish-held fortresses of Judea, notably Masada in 73/74. Apocalyptic groups that might have welcomed the war would either have perished or have been discredited. In short, the only Jewish group to survive intact with significant numbers and the respect of the common people was the Pharisees.[47] They did not so much conquer their Jewish rivals as outlive them.

Various Pharisees, along with other Jews willing to resettle under Roman auspices—probably including both priests and scribes—gathered in the Judean town of Yavneh (Jamnia) by the Mediterranean coast.[48] There they founded a type of academy *(yĕšîbâ)* dedicated to preserving pre-70 legal traditions and developing them so as to adapt Jewish practice to a very different post-70 era. Under these emergency conditions, the Pharisees coalesced with other pious and learned Jews who had survived the war; thus did they mutate into the early rabbinic movement.[49] The first significant leader at Yavneh was Johanan ben Zakkai; whether he was a Pharisee or not is unclear, though many scholars have so identified him.[50] In any event, some early rabbinic teachers (e.g., the conservative Eliezer ben Hyrcanus) most likely did stand in the Pharisaic tradition.[51] In particular, Gamaliel II, the son of Simeon I and a Pharisee, became a prominent leader at Yavneh in the 90s. He may have received some sort of official recognition from the Roman government, perhaps becoming the first of those Jewish officials who would eventually come to bear the title of *nāśî* ("patriarch") by the time of Judah the Patriarch, the compiler of the Mishna, around A.D. 200–220.[52] Hence, while it would be hopelessly simplistic to equate the pre-70 Pharisees with the post-70 rabbinic movement, the Pharisees were no doubt a major influence on and contributor to the new form of Judaism emerging at Yavneh. The rabbis were their spiritual heirs and successors.

III. THE PROBLEM OF SOURCES AND METHOD

The brief historical outline I have just sketched as a kind of chronological grid for the reader has been kept skeletal on purpose. In particular, the outline has been restricted as much as possible to verifiable external events. Next to nothing has been said about the beliefs of the Pharisees and Sadducees, and purposely so, since so much of what was once traditionally affirmed about them in histories of the NT period is questioned by critics today. The sole primary sources for our knowledge of these groups, sources that were once cited with naive faith in their total reliability and with remarkable blindness to their mutual (or even self-) contradictions, are now viewed with a much more skeptical eye by many scholars. The three sources for our knowledge of the Pharisees and Sadducees are (in chronological order) the

NT (Paul, the four Gospels, and Acts, ranging from the 50s to ca. 100), Josephus (whose works range from the 70s to ca. 100), and the rabbinic literature (the first work of which is the Mishna, ca. 200–220).[53] Each of these sources labors under serious problems.

A. The New Testament as a Source[54]

One way of appreciating the difficulty of obtaining "objective" historical knowledge about the Pharisees or Sadducees is to realize that the first document in the whole of world literature to use the word "Pharisee" is the Epistle to the Philippians, penned by Paul of Tarsus ca. A.D. 56–58. In Phil 3:5—a highly polemical passage—Paul boasts against his Jewish or Jewish-Christian opponents that he was "according to the Law a Pharisee."[55] After Philippians, the next document to use the word is the Gospel of Mark (ca. A.D. 70), where the "Pharisee(s)" occurs in narratives and sayings twelve times: ten times in Mark's narrative voice, once in the question of an anonymous speaker, and once in a saying of Jesus. In addition, Mark's Gospel is the first document in world literature to use the word "Sadducee."[56] Given the struggle over identity in which early Judaism and Christianity were locked in the 1st century, neither Paul nor Mark can be expected to be a neutral or "objective" historical source when it comes to describing the Pharisees or Sadducees. In addition, one must remember that both authors were writing to communities outside Palestine that were predominately Gentile.

Still, approached critically, Paul could be a valuable witness, especially since, alone among all our sources, he himself was certainly—at least for a while—a Pharisee in the pre-70 period. (Josephus' claim to have been a follower of the Pharisees' school of thought from his youth is enunciated only in his late work *The Life* and, as we shall see below, is open to serious doubt.)[57] Unfortunately, Paul mentions having been a Pharisee only once in all his epistles (Phil 3:5), and then only in passing in the midst of a scathing attack on his Jewish or Jewish-Christian opponents. If Paul is to be used at all, it must be as an indirect witness. This is a delicate business at best, but better than nothing. By reading between the lines in Paul's epistles, one can try to intuit the *sort of* Pharisaism—and Pharisaism was no monolith in the 1st century A.D.—that Paul had known and embraced.

Once one comes to the Gospels, one has much more material, but the material is highly problematic. Even in the earliest Gospel, Mark, the picture of Jesus clashing with the Pharisees may reflect to a great degree the struggle between the early church and the Pharisees during the first Christian generation.[58] The polemic already heard in Mark becomes increasingly vitriolic in the later Gospels of Matthew and John.[59] While Luke may at times sound more irenic in his Gospel and Acts, it is Luke's theological program (e.g., continuity in salvation history) rather than reliable history from the pre-70 period that we are probably hearing.[60] In the end, it is salutary to remember that with Phil 3:5, the four Gospels, and Acts, our NT sources for the Pharisees are exhausted. The Sadducees get even shorter shrift. Neither Paul nor John mentions them, and so we are reduced to the Synoptics and Acts.[61] Thus, a significant portion of the NT never mentions either group.

B. JOSEPHUS AS A SOURCE

One might expect more from the Jewish historian Josephus. Indeed, a number of scholars consider him our main, if not only, reliable source for the main Jewish "schools of thought" (or "philosophical schools," two attempts to translate into English Josephus' description of these Jewish groups as *haireseis*).[62] Yet his systematic treatments of the Pharisees, Sadducees, and Essenes are limited to three blocks of material isolated within the vast expanse of his writings. Even in the case of the Pharisees, the group that was destined to have the greatest impact on subsequent Jewish history, Josephus restricts mention of them to fourteen different passages, of which only nine provide some deliberate, reflective discussion of their beliefs or activities.[63] More to the point, what the cagey Josephus does say is not free of ambiguity. While his depiction of the Essenes is unfailingly laudatory, and his view of the Sadducees almost always negative, his treatment of the Pharisees has created a lively debate among 20th-century Josephan scholars. The range of modern interpretations of Josephus' stance vis-à-vis the Pharisees includes the following options (not all of which are mutually exclusive):[64]

1. Josephus consistently portrays the Pharisees as students of the Law or as a scholar-class who championed the twofold Law, written and unwritten. They enjoyed great power over the common people and so over all Jewish life in Palestine.[65]

2. Josephus is at times inconsistent in his portrayal of the Pharisees. The reason for this is that Josephus uses sources (e.g., Nicholaus of Damascus, the court historian of Herod the Great), especially for the Pharisees in the Hasmonean and Herodian periods. The mingling of various sources with his own views explains the inconsistency of his evaluations of the Pharisees.[66]

3. Josephus' presentation is thoroughly anti-Pharisaic in all his works.[67]

4. Josephus shifts from a more anti-Pharisaic view in the *War* to a more pro-Pharisaic view in the *Antiquities* because of changes in his own life and

beliefs and/or because of political changes in post-war Palestine as various Jewish groups compete for Roman favor and Rome searches for a group that could represent Roman interests to ordinary Palestinian Jews.[68]

5. Josephus is neither pro- nor anti-Pharisaic; he is against anyone who disturbs the Roman order and peace in society. Hence the Pharisees are negatively portrayed when they disturb social peace and are positively portrayed when they foster it.[69]

6. Josephus the Hasmonean aristocrat and priest always disliked the Pharisees, from the beginning to the end of his political and literary career. He displays his dislike clearly in the *War*, written in the decade after the First Jewish War (fought A.D. 66–70). The opposition Josephus had experienced during the war from a delegation sent to Galilee from Jerusalem to relieve him of command—three out of the four members had been Pharisees—and the bribery Simeon I (a Pharisee) had used to undermine Josephus' political support in Jerusalem still rankled as he wrote the *War* in the 70s. Accordingly, in the narrative sections of the *War*, he portrays the Pharisees in an almost unrelievedly negative light.

But in the *Antiquities*, written in the 90s, Josephus modifies his anti-Pharisaic presentation in the direction of a somewhat more favorable (and therefore mixed) picture.[70] This might have something to do with the healing of wounds with the passing of time. More likely, it has something to do with Josephus' survival instinct. Josephus, the Talleyrand of 1st-century Judaism, was nothing if not a survivor who knew how to wind up on the winning side. His shift toward a mixed portrait of the Pharisees may reflect the Pharisees/rabbis' increasing influence by the 90s. Gamaliel II, the son of Simeon I and therefore a Jewish leader in the Pharisaic tradition, probably received some sort of official recognition from the Roman government in the 90s. Hence Josephus may feel a need to modify his completely negative picture of the Pharisees in the direction of a more nuanced presentation, with a juxtaposition of light and dark elements. Such a mixed picture is not incongruous in the *Antiquities*, since Josephus shifts his presentations of a number of Jewish notables (e.g., Aristobulus I, Alexander Jannaeus, and Herod the Great) to create portraits more complicated than those found in the *War*.

Finally, by the late 90s, Josephus feels so sure that the Pharisees and their spiritual heirs, the rabbis, are the wave of the future that he claims mendaciously that he had been a follower of the Pharisaic school of thought since he was 19 (*Life* 2 §12). One surmises, though, that he utters these words through clenched teeth, for even in the *Life* he cannot refrain from some unflattering statements about individual Pharisees (i.e., the bribery used by

Simeon I to get a delegation sent to Galilee to remove Josephus from command and the underhanded behavior of the largely Pharisaic delegation).[71] One notes in particular the curious praise given Simeon I (*Life* 38 §191–92) right in the midst of the story of how he tried to use bribery to undermine Josephus' command in Galilee (*Life* 38–39 §189–203). The awkward juxtaposition shows two things. The betrayal still smarts; but, if Simeon's son, Gamaliel II, is now a rising star in Jewish politics in Palestine, Simeon must be duly praised.[72] Josephus is reconciling himself to living with the winners, but he does not like it.

This sixth view is my own. I realize that my accusation that Josephus is simply lying in *Life* 2 §12 when he claims to have been a Pharisee from his youth may sound harsh and extreme. Yet Josephus' portrait of himself as a sincere young man carefully testing all the religious options available before he makes a final commitment (*Life* 2 §9–12) is self-contradictory. He claims that, about the age of 16, he began testing successively the three main philosophical schools of the Pharisees, the Sadducees, and the Essenes. He stresses that he acquired knowledge of each school in great detail not by mere theoretical study but by the hard training and great exertion demanded of one who "passed through" *(diēlthon)* all three schools.[73] Not satisfied even with this exhaustive trial, he became for three years the zealous disciple of a desert ascetic named Bannus. After achieving this experience of all the desirable options, at the end of three years he returned to Jerusalem. At the age of 19 he began his public career,[74] becoming a follower of the Pharisaic school of thought.

Now this narrative of the sincere young searcher after philosophical truth, however appealing to a Greco-Roman audience (one is reminded of the similar stories of Galen, Justin Martyr, and Apollonius of Tyana),[75] cannot possibly be true as told. The numbers simply do not add up. Josephus himself tells us elsewhere that entrance into the Essenes demanded at least a *three*-year period of trial (an initial year of probation followed by a two-year period of initiation), and the Qumran scrolls more or less confirm this picture.[76] Since Josephus' own story in *Life* 2 §10–11 presupposes that the Pharisees and Sadducees also demanded an arduous "novitiate" through which one had to pass, one is left wondering how all three groups could have been experienced in such detail and rigor all within three years, when a thorough novitiate in the Essenes alone took three years. But then Josephus goes on to claim that, after passing through the preparatory stages of all three groups, he also spent *three* years with Bannus. To make things worse, he also claims that this entire period of testing began when he was around 16 and that, after he had finished the entire period, including the three years with Bannus, and returned to Jerusalem to enter public life, he was *then* 19 (*Life* 2 §12).

Unless Josephus is practicing a new type of new math, something is very wrong with his story.[77] In my opinion, what is wrong is that, in old age, he is clumsily manufacturing a lengthy period during which he supposedly tested the major Jewish religious options of the time, all to stress that in the end his loyalty throughout his adult life was to the Pharisees alone. Even apart from the impossible arithmetic of this apologetic in old age, a reader thoroughly versed in the *War* and the *Antiquities* would be quite amazed by this sudden jack-in-the-box claim in *Life* 2 §12. No one reading through the two great historical works of Josephus would ever guess that the author was himself a Pharisee for the whole of his adult life.[78] Nowhere in the *War* or the *Antiquities* does he clearly associate himself with the Pharisees. Indeed, especially in the *War,* where his picture of the Pharisees is quite negative in the narrative sections, his ideal group seems to be the Essenes, to whom he devotes the most space and the highest praise when he describes the four major "schools of thought" (*War* 2.8.1–14 §118–66).

Indeed, even in the *Life,* one searches in vain for some discernible impact of Josephus' Pharisaic allegiance on the rest of the narrative. One might have expected, for example, that the matter of Josephus' allegiance to the Pharisees would have come up in his dealings with the delegation sent to Galilee by the provisional revolutionary government in Jerusalem to relieve him of command. Three of the four officials are Pharisees; and yet in all the negotiations, this common bond with Josephus is never mentioned. In fact, in order to counter the Galileans' "love" of Josephus because of his natural gifts and achieved status, the delegates are instructed to stress that they too, like Josephus, are natives of Jerusalem, knowledgeable of the customs of their fathers, and, in the case of two of them, priests (*Life* 39 §198). One would have thought that an obvious further point of comparison would have been that three out of the four delegates are Pharisees, just like Josephus. Yet that point is never raised.[79] Likewise, Simeon I's use of bribery to undermine Josephus would be all the more reprehensible if this were a case of one Pharisee-in-revolt stabbing another Pharisee-in-revolt in the back. Yet this point likewise is never brought up.[80]

In the end, Josephus' claim to have been a life-long Pharisees floats in the isolated vacuum of *Life* 2 §12. It makes no sense in its own context, has no precedent in Josephus' previous works, and has no impact on what Josephus writes subsequently. A true literary Melchizedek (cf. Heb 7:3), it has neither father nor mother in Josephus' past volumes nor any progeny in the rest of his *Life* or *Against Apion*. One wonders whether it is not the awkwardness of Josephus' lie (plus perhaps his continued dislike of the Pharisees) that prevents him from saying simply "and so I became a Pharisee" or "and so I am now a Pharisee" at the end of *Life* 2 §12. The slightly ambiguous Greek (*tē Pharisaiōn hairesei katakolouthōn*, which probably means "becoming a follower of the Pharisaic school of thought") may be the closest he can bring himself to making a claim which he does not want to make but which he thinks he had better make in order once again to wind up on the winning side.[81]

The upshot of all this is clear. We may not naively approach Josephus as the one totally reliable source about the Pharisees on the grounds that he was himself a Pharisee for the whole of his adult life. What we are dealing with is a Jerusalem aristocrat and anti-Pharisaic Hasmonean priest who found it convenient toward the end of his life to declare that he had been a Pharisee for all of his public career when in fact he had not. To be sure, this does not negate the fact that Josephus' narratives and summaries about the Pharisees are important sources both because he draws from still earlier sources and because he was an eyewitness to some important events. But his statements about the Pharisees must be approached with caution, just like the NT and the rabbinic literature.

C. THE RABBINIC LITERATURE AS A SOURCE

It was common among older Jewish scholars to rely heavily on the Mishna (ca. A.D. 200–220), the Tosepta (3d century), the Palestinian (or Jerusalem) Talmud (5th century), and the Babylonian Talmud (6th century)[82] as well as the rabbinic midrashim from various centuries to reconstruct the historical Pharisees and Sadducees. More recently, Jewish scholars like Jacob Neusner and Shaye Cohen, as well as Christian scholars like E. P. Sanders and Anthony Saldarini, have urged greater caution in the use of rabbinic literature to delineate the very different conditions of Judaism in pre-70 Palestine.

The most obvious reason for caution is the problem of dating and attribution. Even the earliest rabbinic collection, the Mishna, was compiled almost 200 years after the time of Jesus. To be sure, various legal decisions and sayings in the Mishna are attributed to sages who lived before or roughly around the time of Jesus (e.g., Hillel and Shammai). But if we must be extremely cautious in accepting sayings attributed to Jesus in Mark or Q as actually coming from the historical Jesus—even though Mark and Q were written down only a generation after Jesus's death, when possibly some people who had known Jesus were still living—we must a fortiori be cautious about presuming that sayings attributed to Hillel and Shammai actually come from them or their time period.

Then, too, there is the problem of knowing when the rabbinic documents are talking about the group that the NT and Josephus call "Pharisees" (*Pharisaioi* in Greek). The rabbinic writings speak at times of *pĕrûšîm* or *pĕrûšîn* in Hebrew (the corresponding Aramaic form is *pĕrîšayyāʾ*), but it is by no means always clear when or if *pĕrûšîn* should be translated as "Pharisees." In itself, the word *pĕrûšîn* could mean simply "separated ones" or "separatists." [83] In various rabbinic contexts, the word seems to refer to excessively pious people, extreme ascetics, sectarians who have separated themselves from the mainstream of Judaism, or even "heretics." [84]

In a few contexts, though, *pĕrûšîn* seems to mean "Pharisees." This is especially true when *pĕrûšîn* is contrasted in a legal debate with an antithetical group called *ṣaddûqîm* or *ṣaddûqîn,* most likely the "Sadducees" mentioned by the NT and Josephus.[85] Since both the NT and Josephus present the Pharisees and Sadducees as antithetical groups, and since the Sadducees as a clearly defined group seem to have disappeared after A.D. 70, the rabbinic passages that present *pĕrûšîn* and *ṣaddûqîn* locked in debate most probably preserve traditions that reach back to pre-70 Palestinian Judaism.[86]

Even such a cautious approach has its problems, including problems of text criticism. Some later manuscripts of rabbinic works seem at times to have substituted references to *ṣaddûqîn* for the original word *mînîm,* "heretics," out of fear that Christian censors might take *mînîm* to refer to Jewish Christians. Hence one cannot always be sure that the opposition between *pĕrûšîn* and *ṣaddûqîn* is original in the passage; without that opposition, *pĕrûšîn* might simply mean "religious deviant."

An additional problem is that the Mishna, the earliest of the rabbinic collections, contains only one extended passage where the two groups are opposed to each other, thus making the meaning of "Pharisees" and "Sadducees" fairly certain. The key passage is *m. Yad.* 4:6–8.[87]

In 4:6, the Sadducees reject the Pharisees' view that the Scriptures render one's hands unclean, while other works, like those of Homer, do not. The Pharisees are defended by Joḥanan ben Zakkai, who compares the Pharisees' view on Scripture to their view on bones: the bones of an ass do not defile, while those of a high priest do. As the Sadducees accept the latter view, so they should accept the former since the principle is the same: the higher our esteem for some object, the greater its power to transmit uncleanness. In this passage, then, the Pharisees are singled out as being concerned with questions of purity and as holding views on contracting impurity by touch that another Jewish group considered too stringent. Especially striking in this passage is that, while Joḥanan ben Zakkai is presented as defending the Pharisees' position, he seems to do so as an outsider, speaking of the Pharisees in the third person.[88]

In *m. Yad.* 4:7, the Sadducees protest against two further positions of the Pharisees. The Pharisees hold that the unbroken stream of a liquid flowing from a clean vessel to an unclean vessel does not render the first vessel and its contents unclean; it does not act as a connective transmitting uncleanness.[89] The Pharisees retort that the Sadducees declare clean a stream of water that flows from a cemetery; if *that* cannot convey uncleanness, a fortiori neither can the stream of a liquid from one vessel to another. Here the Pharisees are again presented as holding a detailed position about a minor matter of purity, this time in reference to containers of liquids. Also implied is their sensitivity about uncleanness coming from corpses.

Also in *m. Yad.* 4:7, the Sadducees protest against the Pharisaic view that a person is legally reponsible for the injury caused by his ox or ass, but not for injury caused by his male or female slave. The Sadducees argue that, if a person can be liable because of the actions of his animals, concerning which the Law imposes no obligations, certainly he is liable because of the actions of his slaves, concerning whom the Law imposes obligations on their owners. The Pharisees deny the Sadducees' reasoning, pointing instead to the fact that one's slaves, but not one's animals, have intelligence and therefore personal responsibility. Here the Pharisees are shown to be concerned with questions of civil law, legal responsibility for damages, and the principle that legal responsibility arises from the perpetrator's knowledge and intention.

The text in *m. Yad.* 4:8 is still more problematic, since manuscripts of the Mishna speak of an argument between a Galilean heretic *(mîn)* and the Pharisees. However, Stemberger argues that the original opponent of the Pharisees may have been a Sadducee, not a heretic.[90] The Sadducee objects to the way in which the Pharisees draw up the document granting a divorce (a *gēṭ*). The Pharisees write down in the document the name of the ruler (as a way of dating the document) as well as the name of Moses, which appears in the concluding formula. The Pharisees reply that the Sadducees likewise write the name of the ruler and the name of God on the same page of documents they draw up; indeed, they put the name of the ruler at the top of the page and the name of God at the bottom. Here the Pharisees are presented as concerned not only with the question of divorce but more precisely with the details of how a bill of divorce should be properly composed.

To be noticed in all these disputes is that the Mishna apparently sides in each case with the Pharisees. This does not prove that mishnaic material is automatically Pharisaic material; but it does show that in some cases the Mishna clearly transmits the positions of the Pharisees, and does so approvingly. Surprisingly, though, the Mishna hands down more legal traditions about the Sadducees (nine) than about the Pharisees. As we have seen, the Mishna transmits only five legal views of the Pharisees that are specifically contrasted with those of the Sadducees: three concerning issues of purity (Scripture, an unbroken stream of a liquid, and water flowing from a cemetery),[91] one concerning civil law on legal responsibility in cases of injury, and one concerning the proper writing of a bill of divorce. The small number of legal rulings attributed to the Pharisees in the Mishna is remarkable if one holds, as do most scholars, that the rabbis were the inheritors and successors of the Pharisees.

When we turn to the Tosepta, we find only one passage where the Pharisees and Sadducees appear in a dispute. In *t. Ḥag.* 3:35, the Sadducees hold that the menorah, the golden lampstand in the temple, cannot be rendered unclean, while the Pharisees hold that it can. Once again, the two groups are divided on a question of purity, in this case regarding part of the cult apparatus in the temple.

If we may suppose that the obscure group called the Boethusians are understood by the Tosepta to be the Sadducees or a subgroup of them, we may add another text.[92] In *t. Yad.* 2:19–20, the Boethusians hold that a daughter may receive an inheritance from her father, while the Pharisees reject the idea. Here we have another dispute over civil law.[93]

In the end, one must admit that the yield from these rabbinic passages about the Pharisees in debate with the Sadducees is meager. Scholars naturally seek to find some other way to mine the rabbinic corpus, especially the Mishna, for further material that can be attributed with fair probability to the Pharisees. In the past, a common but uncritical route was to declare that "the sages" and/or "the scribes" mentioned in the rabbinic literature were identical with the Pharisees. The identification was sometimes not even argued; it was simply presupposed. Such an approach is rejected by many scholars today as begging the question or arguing in a circle.[94]

Perhaps the most famous attempt to find a more critical way of sifting the rabbinic material for information about the Pharisees is that of Jacob Neusner. To provide a wider data base on the Pharisees, Neusner engaged in a massive three-volume project, *The Rabbinic Traditions about the Pharisees before 70.* This trilogy sought to excavate the earliest stratum of the Mishna (along with scattered traditions from the later rabbinic corpus), a stratum that would have a good claim to go back to the pre-70 period. While his scholarship is admirable and his criteria exacting, critics have pointed out that one cannot presume that the pre-70 legal traditions preserved in the Mishna and other rabbinic writings are necessarily Pharisaic.[95]

After all, the Pharisees were not the only Palestinian Jews before 70 who studied the Law and formulated individual rules for concrete behavior (*hǎlākâ* in the singular, *hǎlākôt* in the plural), as the Dead Sea scrolls and various OT pseudepigrapha show. In other words, not all pre-70 *hǎlākâ* abstracted from the rabbinic corpus by modern scholars has to be *hǎlākâ* unique to or especially characteristic of the Pharisees. Pharisaism was not, in the strict sense of the word, a sect that cordoned itself off from a supposedly apostate Israel, as Qumran did.[96] Living among and necessarily interacting with other Palestinian Jews, especially when large crowds went up to the temple for the great feasts, Pharisees no doubt followed practices that were not unique to them but rather shared by mainstream Judaism—a mainstream that also included the high priestly families, priests of no particular party, Sadducees, various Jews with apocalyptic leanings, and the mass of ordinary Jews who belonged to no special group.[97]

In addition, it is more often presupposed than proved that great pre-70 sages like Hillel and Shammai were in historical fact Pharisees.[98] They may well have been, and many modern scholars have declared them so. But the historical arguments in favor of identifying them as Pharisees are tenuous. The best that can be said is that one may probably identify Gamaliel I and Simeon I as pre-70 Pharisees. In itself, the mere fact that *m. ʾAbot* 1 puts these two at the end of a line of teachers who include the great pre-70 sages like Hillel and Shammai provides a thin basis for declaring the latter pair Pharisees. In general, the tannaitic rabbis (up to the compilation of the Mishna ca. 200–220) were not terribly interested in maintaining that their predecessors were Pharisees. That claim becomes somewhat more prominent in the teaching of the amoraic rabbis (from the compilation of the Mishna down to the compilation of the Babylonian Talmud).[99] Were the early rabbis simply uninterested in post-biblical history? Or did they want to deny their origins in just one group among the many competing movements in the pre-70 period? Or were they playing down their Pharisaic connections for the sake of defusing party strife and creating a grand coalition of diverse views? Or did the later rabbis emphasize connections with the Pharisees because they were intent on creating a "myth of origins" and continuity to bolster their authority? There may be some truth in all of these explanations.

In brief, then: one should be cautious about appealing to the earliest stratum of the Mishna and other rabbinic works as evidence for Pharisaic positions.[100] This does not mean that rabbinic writings should be excluded as evidence for the pre-70 period. Rather, each claim must be tested on its own merits. If some legal opinion or practice found in rabbinic literature is said to be Pharisaic or, more generally, to go back to the pre-70 period, arguments in favor of that judgment should be given.

D. THE METHOD TO BE ADOPTED

By now we can appreciate the difficulties of using the three major sources for knowledge of the Pharisees and Sadducees, especially in relation to the historical Jesus. How, then, should we proceed, granted the problems of dating and the bias evinced by all the sources? In a sense, our problem is not all that much different from the problem of using the various NT sources to reconstruct the historical Jesus. As in any historical endeavor, particularly involving ancient history, the same basic criteria of historicity apply.

Take, for example, the Pharisees: probably the most important criterion for reconstructing the historical Pharisees is the criterion of multiple attestation of sources and forms. The Pauline epistles, the Gospels, Acts, Josephus' *Jewish War, Antiquities,* and *Life,* and the rabbinic literature (primarily the Mishna) represent very different types of literature: letters, kerygmatic stories of Jesus' life, death, and resurrection, histories and (auto)biographies written in the Greco-Roman mode, and collections of legal opinions and wisdom sayings. These works were written by very different types of individuals: some Jews, some Jewish Christians, some Gentile Christians, with different levels of education and socioeconomic status, and most certainly with different beliefs. They were written or compiled at different periods of time: Paul in the 50s of the 1st century A.D., Mark and Q around A.D. 70, Josephus from the 70s through the late 90s of the 1st century, and the Mishna at the beginning of the 3d century. The location of composition also differed: all but the Mishna and other early rabbinic writings were most likely written outside Palestine.[101]

As far as we know, there is no literary dependence connecting Paul, Q, Mark, John, the special sources of Matthew and Luke, Josephus, and the Mishna. Therefore, agreement on specific points about the Pharisees on the part of such different authors with such different biases, living and writing in so many different times and places, argues well for historicity. Granted the varied extent and intent of our three major sources, one cannot hope that all three (or even two) of them will always speak about the same belief, legal ruling, or practice and specifically attribute it to the Pharisees. But at least when two out of three do so, we have good reason to suppose a historical basis for the attribution. In addition, a statement about the Pharisees that runs counter to the usual biases of a given author deserves consideration on grounds of the criterion of embarrassment.

IV. THE PHARISEES

A. A Few 20th-Century Portraits of the Pharisees[102]

The dirty little secret of NT studies is that no one really knows who the Pharisees were—though many thought they did before a wave of more critical studies hit the academic beach in the 1970s. As Joseph Sievers bluntly remarks, "we know considerably less about the Pharisees than an earlier generation 'knew.' "[103] The history of 20th-century research is strewn with many portraits of the Pharisees, most of which are discarded today.

Some scholars, attempting a sociological approach, depicted the Pharisees as "plebeian" urbanite Jews, drawing support from the city proletariat as they struggled against the boorish landed aristocracy, the Sadducees, whose uncouth ways reflected their rural background. The leaders of the Pharisees were the scribes, and the Pharisees in general dedicated themselves to the study of the Law. They extolled learning, while the Sadducees held scholarship in contempt.[104]

In a similar vein, other scholars emphasized that the Pharisees were enlightened liberals, consciously fighting against the hidebound conservative Sadducees. What triggered the revolution of the Pharisees was the transformation of an old agrarian society to an increasingly urbanized one, a society where the Pentateuchal laws were often not applicable. The unwritten laws introduced by the Pharisees were adapted to the new urban society; hence the Pharisees came to dominate all areas of Jewish life in Palestine, including the cult. In such a scenario, the Pharisees are usually portrayed as a class of lay scholars, opposed to an antiquated religious system tied to animal sacrifices and a single temple, where alone the fullness of Jewish worship could be offered. Seeking to reject or at least reform this obsolete priestly system, the Pharisees championed a progressive, populist religion centered on the study of the written and oral Law and spread through the democratic, lay institution of the synagogue. In effect, the Roman legions simply helped the Pharisees' program achieve complete success by destroying Jerusalem, its temple, and its Sadducean priesthood, which was tied to a literalistic understanding of Scripture. Unwittingly, the Roman army opened up the future to the purified, pacifist religion of the Pharisees, which, without further ado, is more or less equated with rabbinic Judaism.[105]

A more recent, and much more scholarly grounded, reconstruction has been offered by Jacob Neusner.[106] He has argued that the Pharisees were driven by an ideal of priestly holiness. They sought to eat their daily food in a state of ritual purity proper to priests in the Jerusalem temple. Far from withdrawing into an esoteric sect à la Qumran, the Pharisees sought by strict observance of purity rules to extend the holiness of the temple into the sphere of everyday Jewish living and eating. Neusner's suggestion builds on the view of earlier scholars that the Pharisees strove to have the whole Jewish people fulfill the command in Lev 19:2 that summed up the Holiness Code of Leviticus: "You shall be holy, for I, the Lord your God, am holy."

Neusner has made this approach more specific by emphasizing that the ideal of holiness pursued by the Pharisees was the priestly holiness proper to the temple and that the Pharisees achieved their program by the careful handling of food in all its aspects: proper harvesting and paying of tithes on the harvest, proper purity of vessels used for food, proper purity of those taking part in ordinary daily meals. Once the Pharisees gave up aggressive political activity after the end of the Hasmonean dynasty, they became, as it were, a holy dining club.[107] Neusner's reconstruction has been criticized by various scholars, notably E. P. Sanders, who sees no indication in the earliest rabbinic material of the ideal of pursuing priestly purity in everyday Jewish eating.[108]

Problematic also is the claim that the Pharisees chose to withdraw from public life and political activity once Herod the Great consolidated control of his kingdom. A more likely explanation is that they were forced to the sidelines by Herod's autocratic rule and ruthless elimination of opponents. Nevertheless, some Pharisees did participate at times in the political life of Herod's court. At the beginning of Herod's reign, when he killed many of his political opponents, he spared the Pharisee Pollion and his disciple Samaias out of gratitude. Some years prior, when Herod had been put on trial before the Sanhedrin as a commoner, either Pollion or Samaias (Josephus is confused and confusing on this point) had predicted that Herod would one day kill both Hyrcanus II and the judges trying Herod—a prophecy that turned out to be all too true. In addition, when Herod was later besieging Jerusalem at the beginning of his reign, Samaias urged the Jerusalemites to admit the new king (Ant. 14.9.4 §172–76; cf. 15.1.1 §3). Herod's respect for Pollion and Samaias proved lasting. Even when Herod forced all the people to take an oath of loyalty to him, he exempted Pollion, Samaias, and most of their disciples, who refused to take the oath (Ant. 15.10.4 §370).[109] Apparently at least a few Pharisees retained influence at Herod's court.

Relations, though, were not alway so friendly, especially when some Pharisees tried to use indirect, not to say underhanded, means to exercise political influence (e.g., cabals with some of the highly placed women in Herod's court).[110] In one extreme case, Pharisaic political action became overt: in the uprising against the Roman census under Quirinius in A.D. 6, a Pharisee named Saddok joined Judas the Galilean in leading the revolt.[111]

The failure of Judas' uprising perhaps persuaded other Pharisees of the wisdom of keeping a low political profile. Indeed, to a large degree, the Pharisees continued to be kept on the sidelines by the policy of the Roman prefects and procurators, who dealt primarily with the high priest and the Jerusalem aristocrats. This de facto political marginalization of the Pharisees hardly proves that they were not eager to exercise indirect political influence in the corridors of power or even to regain direct political control. If Acts may be believed, at least some individual Pharisees (e.g., Gamaliel I in Acts 5:34) were influential in the councils of the high priest during direct Roman rule.

Moreover, it is difficult to explain how, given this supposedly withdrawn, apolitical, or even quietist and pacifist group, some noted Pharisaic leaders played an important political role in Jerusalem in the events leading up to the revolt against Rome in A.D. 66. When the young priest Eleazar stopped the twice-daily sacrifice for Rome and the emperor, thus inviting war, leading citizens met in council with the chief priests and the most esteemed of the Pharisees to try to head off disaster (*J. W.* 2.17.3 §411; cf. *Life* 5 §21). After the revolt began, some Pharisees were involved in its early stages (e.g., Simeon I, a Pharisaic member of the provisional government, and the three Pharisees in the delegation sent to relieve Josephus of his command in Galilee).[112] Even more, it is difficult to understand why the victorious Romans, those quintessential political animals, should ferret out as their possible collaborators in post-70 Judea a quietist dining club that supposedly had had no political experience or interest since about 37 B.C. Some 20 years or so after A.D. 70, the Romans moved to recognize Gamaliel II, the scion of a distinguished Pharisaic family, as a representative of and to Judean Jews. This does not argue well for the Pharisees being totally removed from political life in Judea during the previous century.

B. A MINIMALIST SKETCH BY WAY OF SIX POINTS

Perhaps part of the problem with these sociological and political approaches to the Pharisees is that the scholars who employ them try to know more about the pre-70 Pharisees than the sources now available allow. In what follows, I will use the sources and method described above not to flesh out a full-drawn portrait of the Pharisees, which may not be possible in any case, but rather to sketch a basic outline, a bare minimum that is supported by more than one source.

(1) To begin with, let us assert the obvious: the Pharisees (as well as the Sadducees) were a Jewish group with both political and religious interests,

active in Palestine prior to the First Jewish War. This most basic of all points, which fortunately is not in dispute and therefore need not be argued at length, is abundantly supported by all three sources.

(a) Indeed, in the 50s of the 1st century, Paul of Tarsus, a former Pharisee, gives autobiographical witness to the existence of the Pharisees in Phil 3:5. Since Paul became a Christian sometime in the early or mid–30s, and since he apparently presumes that the Pharisees continue to exist as a well-known group at the time he is writing to the Philippians,[113] he supplies firsthand evidence for the existence of the Pharisees in the first half of the 1st century A.D.

(b) In complementary fashion, Josephus claims to have been a follower of the Pharisaic movement from the time he was 19 (*Life* 2 §12), that is, around A.D. 56 (just around the time Paul is writing Philippians!). While I have argued above that Josephus is lying about having become a Pharisee at 19, his claim, however untrue, would be sheer nonsense and would not help him at all unless it was generally known that a "school of thought" *(hairesis)* called the Pharisees did in fact exist in Palestine in the 50s and continued to do so up to and during the First Jewish War (as is clear from Simeon I and the three Pharisees in the delegation sent to relieve Josephus of his command in Galilee).

(c) Finally, when the later rabbinic sources refer to legal arguments between two groups called *pĕrûšîn* and *ṣaddûqîn*—and some of these arguments refer to conditions that perdured only as long as the Jerusalem temple still stood—the only antithetical groups that could be reasonably identified with the disputants in these texts are the Pharisees and the Sadducees. Thus, at least on the fundamental truth of the existence of the Pharisees in the pre-70 period, all three sources agree.

(2) The Pharisees enjoyed a reputation for their exact or precise *(akribēs)* interpretation of the Mosaic Law. The vocabulary of "exactness" or "precision" is a point on which Luke and Josephus conspicuously agree.[114] The precise opinions about relatively minor points of legal observance found in the Pharisees-Sadducees disputes in rabbinic literature support this picture.

Josephus, perhaps as part of his negative portrait of the Pharisees, stresses that they enjoyed a *reputation* (expressed by the verb *dokeō*) for exact *knowledge* of the Mosaic Law and ancestral customs. It may have been intentional on Josephus' part that his narratives about the Pharisees leave the impression that the group was not always so punctilious and exacting when it came to *acting* legally or morally.[115] Still, Paul's portrait of himself as a "zealot" when it came to keeping the "traditions of my forefathers" (Gal 1:14), even to the point of persecuting the nascent church, as well as his insistence that he was "blameless according to the justice in the Law" (Phil 3:6, which makes sense only if he is referring to his conduct),[116] shows that the Pharisees were interested in correct behavior as well as correct interpretation. The fierce polemic of the Gospels against the Pharisees, however exaggerated and one-sided, presumes a group that expressed itself both in the precise enunciation of rules and in the punctilious observance of them. At the same time, this precision must not be taken to betoken harshness in judgment. Rather, both the NT (Gamaliel's advice in Acts 5:33–40) and Josephus (*Ant.* 13.10.6 §294; cf. 20.9.1 §199, §201) show—and the Mishna tractate *Sanhedrin* suggests—that the Pharisees tended toward leniency when passing judgment.[117]

(3) The struggle between Jesus (or early Christians) and the Pharisees over questions of law reflects a wider struggle raging in Israel around the turn of the era over the proper interpretation of the Mosaic Law. The Jerusalem temple and the Mosaic Law were the two great unifying and yet paradoxically divisive symbols of the Jewish religion. For the Qumranites, the differences over the right use of the temple and the right interpretation of the Law were so great that they felt constrained to cut themselves off from all other Jews, who, in the eyes of Qumran, had gone astray. While divisions did not run quite so deep among Pharisees, Sadducees, and other Jews, differences over the interpretation of the Mosaic Law and the practical consequences thereof (including temple worship) helped give each Jewish group its distinctive form.[118]

Needless to say, each group wanted to think that many of its teachings were found in the Mosaic Law or were at least deducible from it. In reality, when examined with a cold, critical eye, the legal positions of Pharisees, Sadducees, and Qumranites all show historical developments far beyond the letter of the Mosaic Law. The key question is how each group explained such developments. The Qumranites appealed to ongoing revelation and prophetic inspiration.[119] The Sadducees apparently observed various traditional practices distinctive of their group. While it is very difficult to say how they saw these distinctive traditions vis-à-vis the Mosaic Law, my guess is that, unlike the Pharisees, they were not engaged in an active campaign among the common people to convince all Jews that they should observe specifically Sadducean traditions in daily living.[120]

In my view, what made the Pharisees distinctive was that they openly admitted that some of their legal views and practices were not to be found as such in the written Mosaic Law, that such practices were instead venerable "traditions" that had been handed down by the "fathers" or the "elders," and that such practices nevertheless were God's will for all Israel. Unlike the Sadducees, they were actively engaged in trying to convince ordinary Jews to observe Pharisaic traditions in their daily lives. However, while the Pharisees struggled to have their views accepted by the common people, they did not consider the common people or other Jews heinous sinners or beyond the pale simply for not agreeing to follow Pharisaic practice.

As with the language of "accuracy" in legal interpretation, so with the language of "traditions of the fathers [or: elders]," the NT and Josephus basically agree in their descriptions of the Pharisees. Speaking in Gal 1:13–14 of how he outstripped many Jews of his own age group in his observance of "Judaism," Paul the former Pharisee stresses that he was "extremely zealous for my ancestral traditions [or: the traditions that stem from my forefathers, *tōn patrikōn mou paradoseōn*]." [121]

Similar language can be found in Josephus when he distinguishes the Pharisees from the Sadducees on the question of law (*Ant.* 13.10.6 §297) during the reign of John Hyrcanus: "The Pharisees have handed down [*paredosan*] to the common people [*tǭ dēmǭ*] certain laws [*nomima*] that come from the tradition [literally: "the succession," *diadochēs*] of the fathers [*paterōn*], laws that have not been written down in the laws [*nomois*] of Moses." [122] Josephus seems to be saying that, because these special Pharisaic laws are not found in the written Law of Moses, the Sadducees reject them. In other words, the Sadducees hold that only the laws written down (apparently, in the Law of Moses) should be considered normative for all Israelites. Therefore, one is not obliged to observe the (Pharisaic) laws that stem "from the tradition of the fathers [*ek paradoseōs tōn paterōn*]." [123]

During the early part of Hyrcanus' reign, when the Pharisees enjoyed his favor, they apparently were able to impose their special laws on the people. Once they lost Hyrcanus' favor, and during the subsequent reigns of Aristobulus I and Alexander Jannaeus, such Pharisaic laws seem to have been rescinded. When, however, Salome Alexandra assumed the throne and restored the Pharisees to favor, they once again imposed on the people their special laws, which had been abrogated by Hyrcanus. Josephus (*Ant.* 13.16.2 §408) pointedly describes these laws *(nomima)* as those "the Pharisees had introduced in accordance with the tradition of the fathers [*kata tēn patrǭan paradosin*]." Luke (Acts 22:3) echoes the ancestors/fathers theme found in both Paul and Josephus when he has Paul describe his Pharisaic instruction at the feet of the Pharisee Gamaliel as being "according to the accuracy [*akribeian*] of the ancestral law [*patrǭou nomou*]." [124]

Mark speaks of "the elders" rather than "the fathers," but his basic depiction of the Pharisees' special tradition is the same. While Mark's statement is somewhat garbled, perhaps because he is a Gentile with less than perfect knowledge of Judaism, or perhaps because the dispute is refracted through the lens of Diaspora Judaism and its debate with Christianity, he stands in basic agreement with Paul, Luke, and Josephus. In 7:1, Mark depicts "the Pharisees and some of the scribes coming from Jerusalem" to Jesus. (This statement that the Pharisees come from Jerusalem may, like John's Gospel, preserve the memory that the pre-70 Pharisees were centered in Jerusalem and did not enjoy a notable presence in Galilee.) In v 3, Mark notes in an all-too-generalizing aside that "the Pharisees and all the Jews do not eat without . . . washing their hands, since they hold to the tradition of the elders [tēn paradosin tōn presbyterōn]." Mark's sweeping claim about hand-washing appears to be erroneous, but the important point that links Mark with Paul, Luke, and Josephus is the sense (however confused) that the Pharisees are champions of ancestral traditions that are not found in—and that the Marcan Jesus (7:6–13) declares contrary to—the written Mosaic Law.[125]

We have, therefore, the multiple attestation of Paul (speaking as an ex-Pharisee in the 50s), Mark (writing around 70), Luke (writing ca. 80–90), and Josephus (writing ca. 75–100) that the Pharisees were especially characterized by their fierce devotion to the traditions of the fathers or elders. These traditions comprised various laws and practices that were not found in the written Law of Moses but that the Pharisees themselves taught, observed, and tried—when they had political power under the Hasmoneans (i.e., early in the reign of John Hyrcanus I and during the reign of Queen Salome Alexandra)—to impose on the Jewish people in general. The Sadducees, in particular, rejected these traditions, claiming that they were not normative precisely because they were not found in the Mosaic Law.

In a certain indirect and attenuated sense, we also have support for this characteristic of the Pharisees from the Mishna. However, one must carefully distinguish what the Mishna (and, even more, later rabbinic sources) says from the statements of our 1st-century authors. The rabbinic sources, especially the later ones, present a doctrine about "the dual Torah" not found in the portrait of the Pharisees painted by Paul, Mark, Luke, and Josephus. The rabbinic corpus—in particular, the two Talmuds—holds that the Law that God gave to Moses on Sinai was handed down in two forms: the written Torah known to us as the Pentateuch, "the five books of Moses," and the oral Torah passed down by a chain of oral tradition from Moses to the rabbinic sages.[126]

Some scholars think that a primitive or embryonic expression of the idea of the dual Torah is found at the beginning of the mishnaic tractate Pirqê 'ābôt (The Sayings [or: The Chapters] of the Fathers). In m. 'Abot 1:1 we are told: "Moses received [qibbēl] the Torah from Sinai and passed [mĕsarah] it on to Joshua, and Joshua [passed it on] to the elders [cf. Mark's use of "tradition of the elders"], and the elders [passed it on] to the prophets, and the prophets [passed it on] to the men of the Great Assembly." No critical scholar today would accept this claim of unbroken tradition as serious history. But the significant point here is that, perhaps for the first time, the Mishna is enunciating this theory of unbroken oral tradition (designated as "Torah"),[127] reaching from Moses to the vague period after the return from the Babylonian exile (represented by the mythic entity, "the Great Assembly").[128] Notice, however, that the passage does not use phrases like "the two Torahs" or "the oral Torah" and "the written Torah." Such phraseology, along with the detailed theory attached to it, appears only in later rabbinic literature. Rather, the key passage in *m. ʾAbot* 1 is formulating a theory of text and tradition that will ultimately blossom as the doctrine of the dual Torah, but the full doctrine is a later rabbinic development.

The rest of chap. 1 of *m. ʾAbot* continues the chain from the ahistorical "Great Assembly" of the postexilic period down to the First Jewish War (A.D. 66–70): Simeon the Just and Antigonus of Socho (ca. 200 B.C.) are first and second in the chain.[129] They are followed by the famous five "pairs" *(zûgôt)* of teachers: Josi ben Joezer and Josi ben Joḥanan (early 2d cent. B.C.), Joshua ben Peraḥiah and Mattai (or Nittai) the Arbelite (late 2d cent. to early 1st cent. B.C.), Judah ben Ṭabbai and Simeon ben Sheṭaḥ (early 1st cent. B.C.), Shemaiah and Abṭalion (mid-1st cent. B.C.), and finally the celebrated duo, Hillel and Shammai (late 1st cent. B.C. to early 1st cent. A.D.), who bring us down to the period of Herod the Great and the turn of the era.[130]

While we cannot be absolutely sure that any of these teachers (some of whom are little more than names to us)[131] were actually Pharisees, it is important to examine closely the two persons who come second-to-last and last in the list in chap. 1. Following Hillel and Shammai is Gamaliel I.[132] Two things should be noted about Gamaliel I. On the one hand, it is at least probable from the fact that Acts 5:34 calls him a Pharisee and that his son Simeon I is designated a Pharisee by Josephus (*Life* 38 §191) that Gamaliel I was indeed a Pharisee. On the other hand, surprisingly, the chain of tradition carefully constructed in *m. ʾAbot* 1 seems, in a sense, to be broken when we come to Gamaliel I.[133] From Moses on down, *m. ʾAbot* 1 scrupulously traces the teachers who "hand on" (*māsar, m. ʾAbot* 1:1) and "receive" (*qibbēl, m. ʾAbot* 1:2–12) the oral Torah. In particular, all the pairs down to Hillel and Shammai are said to receive the tradition from their predecessors. Yet, as we move from Hillel and Shammai to Gamaliel I ("Rabban Gamaliel") in *m. ʾAbot* 1:16, the vocabulary of "receiving" disappears.

Consequently, it is not explicitly claimed in *m. ʾAbot* 1 that Gamaliel stands in the direct line of tradition traced from Moses through the great pairs. Looking at the process the other way round, we must admit that

Gamaliel's possible status as a Pharisee cannot automatically be read back-wards into the chain of famous pairs that includes Hillel and Shammai. Simeon I, the son of Gamaliel I and (according to Josephus) a Pharisee, is placed right after Gamaliel I, but once again the language of receiving tradition is not used.[134]

In fact, it is only by reasoning back from the apparent connections of Gamaliel and Simeon with the House of Shammai (e.g., *m. ʿOr.* 2:12; *m. Beṣa* 2:6)[135] that we find in the tannaitic traditions that we can conclude with some probability that the Houses (or Schools) of Hillel and Shammai were Pharisaic. The route of this reasoning is admittedly indirect and circuitous: from Simeon the Pharisee (so Josephus) back to his father Gamaliel the Pharisee (so Acts), then back to the (Pharisaic) House of Shammai with which these two Pharisees are sometimes associated in rabbinic literature, and then back to the (Pharisaic) House of Hillel that is the counterpart of the (Pharisaic) House of Shammai. A circuitous route, to be sure, but perhaps the best route we have for arguing that historically the two Houses in the pre-70 period were Pharisaic. Gamaliel I and Simeon I are also among our best routes for demonstrating the Pharisaic connection with the nascent rabbinic movement, since Simeon's son and grandson, Gamaliel II and Simeon II, were prominent leaders in the rabbinic academies at Javneh and Usha.

But to return to my main point, the doctrine of the dual Torah: taking stock of the NT, Josephus, and the Mishna, I would suggest that chap. 1 of *m. ʾAbot* may represent something of a watershed. Earlier than the Mishna, we have in the NT and Josephus the idea that the Pharisees strove mightily to convince all Jews to observe not only the Mosaic Law but also certain "traditions of the fathers [or: elders]" not found in the Mosaic Law. Significantly, no claim is made by the sources written in the 1st century A.D. that these ancestral traditions were given by God to Moses on Sinai and were then passed down solely by word of mouth—without any of them ever being written down—to the 1st-century sages.[136] Nor is the claim made that these traditions not only are to be observed but also constitute an oral Torah enjoying the same status and weight as the written Torah of Moses.

These two points (unbroken oral chain from Sinai and equal status with the written Torah) do not appear until the Mishna and the later rabbinic writings. Even in the Mishna, the theory remains embryonic; the full-blown doctrine of the oral Torah *(tôrâ šebĕal peh)* standing alongside the written Torah *(tôrâ šebiktab)* and handed down by memory through constantly repeated recitation develops throughout the rabbinic period. Hence, in my view, it would be anachronistic to retroject the full doctrine of the dual Torah into the Pharisees' much simpler claims about their ancestral traditions.

Nevertheless, (1) the fact that *m. ʾAbot* 1 is speaking, one way or another, of traditions that come down by succession from "the elders" and (2) the fact that *m. ᵓAbot* 1 ends this line of tradition with two notable figures of the 1st century A.D. who are called Pharisees in other sources (Gamaliel I and his son Simeon I) point to a likely tradition history. The relatively simple idea of the Pharisees that, alongside the written Mosaic Torah, they possessed normative traditions not present in the Mosaic Torah, traditions that had been handed down by their forefathers, was developed in the second and subsequent centuries A.D. into the rabbinic doctrine of the dual Torah.

The important point for us is that the Mishna and other rabbinic writings thus witness indirectly (by a sort of argument from hindsight) to the earlier stage of Pharisaic thought reported by Paul, Mark, Luke, and Josephus. Be it ever so obliquely, the Mishna supports the multiple attestation of our 1st-century authors in regard to the Pharisees' zeal for the traditions of the fathers, to which they attribute normative status for all Israel. Another valuable point that results from this probing of the tradition history of the dual Torah is that we have a parade example of how Pharisaic tradition both precedes and then flows into the Mishna, but also how the Mishna and subsequent rabbinic works substantially transform the Pharisaic tradition that they received.

(4) Granted the importance of these traditions of the fathers, it would help greatly in our attempt to sketch the Pharisees if we could know what the subject matter or at least the general focus of these traditions was. One way of trying to identify the nature of these traditions is to apply the criterion of multiple attestation of sources. On the one hand, various Gospel traditions, often from different Gospel sources, attest to certain concerns of the Pharisees. On the other hand, the early stratum of the Mishna (or, in a few cases, the Tosepta) that transmits traditions about Pharisees in general or about Gamaliel I and Simeon I in particular (identified as Pharisees by Luke and Josephus, respectively) reflects a similar cluster of concerns. This cluster of concerns, attested both by early Gospel traditions and early mishnaic traditions, includes the following:[137]

   a. *purity rules concerning food and vessels containing food and liquids:* Mark 7:1–23; Matt 23:25–26; cf. Gamaliel I, *m. ᶜOr.* 2:12; Gamaliel I, *t. ᶜAbod. Zar.* 4:9. Connected with this is the allied concern about clean and unclean hands: Mark 7:1–5; cf. the Pharisees in *m. Yad.* 4:6.
   b. *purity rules concerning corpses and tombs:* Matt 23:27–28; cf. the Pharisees in *m. Yad.* 4:7.
   c. *purity or sanctity of the cult apparatus* in the Jerusalem temple, and proper way of worshiping and offering sacrifice in the temple: Matt

23:16–22; cf. the Pharisees in *t. Ḥag.* 3:35; Gamaliel I, *m. Šeqal.* 6:1; Simeon I, *m. Ker.* 1:7; also (indirectly) Josephus in *Ant.* 18.1.3 §15 and 18.1.4 §17.

d. *tithing, priests' shares and dues:* Matt 23:23; cf. Gamaliel I (indirectly), *m. Peʾa* 2:5–6; Gamaliel I, *t. Sanh.* 2:6; also Hillel and Shammai, *m. ʿEd.* 1:2.

e. *proper observance of the sabbath and holy days,* especially in regard to work and travel: Mark 2:23–28; 3:1–6; Luke 13:10–17; 14:1–6; John 5:1–18; 9:1–34; cf. Gamaliel I, *m. Roš. Haš.* 2:5; Simeon I, *m. ʿErub.* 6:2; *m. Beṣa* 2:6 (indirectly).

f. *marriage and divorce,* including writing the bill of divorce and the grounds for divorce: Mark 10:1–12 par. (cf. Luke 16:18 par.); cf. the Pharisees in *m. Yad.* 4:8; Gamaliel I, *m. Yebam.* 16:7; Gamaliel I, *m. Giṭ.* 4:2–3; also, the Houses of Hillel and Shammai, *m. Giṭ.* 9:10.

From attestations of the stories and sayings of Gamaliel I and Simeon I, one can extend the data base to include many attestations of these concerns in the teachings of the House (= School) of Hillel and the House of Shammai, the two leading "schools" in Palestinian Judaism of the 1st and 2d centuries A.D. As Neusner points out, there are reasons for thinking that both Gamaliel I and Simeon I not only were Pharisees but also stood in the tradition of the Shammaites. By association, then, the House of Shammai would qualify as part of the Pharisaic tradition; and so, again by association, would the correlative House of Hillel. As the lengthy chart drawn up by Neusner at the end of his second volume of *The Rabbinic Traditions* plainly shows, both Houses attest to the legal concerns listed above.[138] Admittedly, all this reasoning is somewhat convoluted and indirect. Nevertheless, the correlation between these tannaitic traditions about Gamaliel I and Simeon I—broadened out secondarily to include the Houses of Hillel and Shammai—and similar concerns attributed to the Pharisees in the Gospels makes it likely that we have here a constellation of legal emphases typical of—though not necessarily unique to—the Pharisees.

At this point in the argument, I should underscore how I am using the criterion of multiple attestation. I am speaking in general terms of major emphases and concerns of the Pharisees as witnessed by two or three different bodies of religious and/or historical literature that ultimately stem from 1st-century Palestine. In particular, it must be stressed that I am not claiming at this point in the argument that the historical Jesus actually spoke any of the sayings in the list above.

Fortunately, that claim is not necessary for the present line of reasoning.

All that is needed for this delineation of Pharisaic concerns through multiple attestation of sources is that various Christian works, most reflecting traditions from the pre-70 period (certainly at least Mark and Q), attest to certain Pharisaic concerns that are also attested in Josephus or a very early stratum of rabbinic literature. Right now I am merely trying to establish the fact that certain practices and beliefs were characteristic of the pre-70 Pharisees—and not necessarily the fact that the historical Jesus actually debated with the Pharisees about these practices or beliefs.

(5) Not surprisingly, most of what is attributed to Pharisaic teaching in the NT and the Mishna refers to legal rulings or opinions regarding concrete behavior *(hălākôt)*. Such legal opinions are almost always the type of material that provides a basis for a clash between Jesus and the Pharisees as reported in the Gospels. This is hardly surprising, and indeed enjoys a certain degree of verisimilitude, since ancient Judaism, like later Judaism, stressed ortho*praxis* more than ortho*doxy*.

Nevertheless, Judaism was not devoid of all doctrinal beliefs. Monotheism and the special chosen status of Israel are two examples of beliefs held by most if not all Palestinian Jews around the turn of the era. Hence it is not startling that, within Palestinian Judaism, Pharisees should hold particular doctrines. Here it is Josephus, rather than the Mishna, who directly supports the statements of the NT.[139]

(a) All three Synoptic Gospels as well as Acts single out the Sadducees as in some way special because they deny the resurrection of the dead. When Mark introduces the Sadducees—they appear only once in his Gospel, in the dispute over the resurrection of the dead (12:18–27) toward the end of Jesus' ministry—Mark does something that he does nowhere else when presenting a particular group of Jesus' opponents for the first time. He adds a relative clause that pinpoints the distinguishing characteristic of the Sadducees (12:18): "And there come to him [Jesus] the Sadducees, who say that there is no resurrection." The natural implication is that this doctrinal stance differentiates the Sadducees from most, if not all, other Jews or Jewish groups. Indeed, this implication may be given a more precise focus by the way Mark positions the dispute over the resurrection within his collection of Jerusalem dispute stories (Mark 11:20–12:37). Mark places Jesus' dispute with the Sadducees over the resurrection right after a dispute story involving the Pharisees (along with the Herodians), who ask about the coin of tribute. This positioning may at least *imply*—though it does not explicitly state—that the distinguishing trait of the Sadducees, their denial of the resurrection, distinguishes them in particular from the Pharisees.[140] Luke goes on to affirm this difference between Sadducees and Pharisees clearly in Acts 23:6–9 (cf. Acts 4:1–2; 5:17).[141]

Josephus likewise asserts that the Pharisees differ from the Sadducees on this point. These assertions occur in two of the passages where he presents Pharisaism as a kind of Greek philosophical school familiar to his Greco-Roman audience (*J. W.* 2.8.14 §163; *Ant.* 18.1.3 §14). Specifically, the Pharisees take on the coloration of the Stoics (cf. *Life* 2 §12). In these two passages, Josephus affirms clearly that the Pharisees, unlike the Sadducees, believe in the immortality of the soul, a place of reward and punishment after death, and—in at least one passage—the resurrection of the body (*J. W.* 2.8.14 §163; though his Gentile audience may have understood Josephus' ambiguous language to refer to reincarnation instead).[142]

The Mishna does not line up Pharisees and Sadducees in opposition to each other precisely on this point. Yet it may contain a faint reverberation of the controversy. In *m. Sanh.* 10:1, the Mishna excludes from a share in the world to come anyone who says that there is no resurrection of the dead—or, in a variant (and probably later) version of the text, anyone who says that the resurrection of the dead is not taught in (or deducible from) the Mosaic Torah.[143] If this latter form of the text is original, it could well refer to the Sadducees, who may have denied the normative status of belief in the resurrection specifically on the grounds that it was not taught in the Torah (perhaps the reason for the strange type of argument used against them in Mark 12:18–27).[144] If, however, the shorter form of *m. Sanh.* 10:1 is original, a reference to the Sadducees in particular becomes less clear; nevertheless, they could be one of the groups included in the general condemnation. In brief, it may be—though it cannot be proved from the Mishna taken by itself—that *m. Sanh.* 10:1 preserves an echo of the pre-70 argument between the Pharisees and the Sadducees on the resurrection and so provides indirect confirmation of what we know from Josephus and the NT.

(b) This single item of doctrine concerning immortality and/or resurrection is a meager fragment that seems to hang almost alone in midair. At first glance, it does not seem connected with much else that is reported about the Pharisees. Yet this belief in immortality and/or resurrection would seem to argue that the Pharisees had some characteristic beliefs about eschatological and/or apocalyptic events. The sources, though, are all but silent about them. If one could accept the formerly common view that certain works classified among the OT pseudepigrapha (e.g., the *Psalms of Solomon* and the *Book of Jubilees*) were Pharisaic in authorship, we would be able to sketch a Pharisaic doctrine about salvation history, the Messiah, and a restored Jerusalem and temple in the end time. Unfortunately, ascription of these works to the Pharisees is considered dubious or impossible by many critics today.[145]

One other, admittedly indirect and speculative, way of discerning Pharisaic views of messianism and eschatology is to look at the one known Pharisee who speaks to us in his own voice from the pre-70 period, namely, Saul/Paul of Tarsus. I readily grant that this approach is fraught with difficulty. The Paul who speaks to us in his epistles is a formerly zealous Pharisaic Jew who became a zealous Christian Jew some 15 years or more before he penned the first epistle (1 Thessalonians) that has come down to us.

Yet much of the personal as well as the theological bedrock of the old Saul is visible beneath all the Christian superstructure. At times, the reappearance of the personal bedrock is almost comical. For all Paul's theology of justification by faith apart from the works of the Law, for all his insistence on the bankruptcy of human religious achievements exalting themselves in the eyes of God, Saul the super-achiever is quite proud of his missionary success, quite demanding when it comes to the moral behavior of his Gentile converts, and quite ready to lay down precise rules of conduct (from grounds for marital separation in mixed marriages to the proper head-covering of women during public worship).

Similarly, there is a certain Jewish—and I would suggest Pharisaic—theological substratum both supporting and presupposed by Paul's specifically Christian beliefs.[146]

(i) No doubt the Christian claim that the crucified Jesus of Nazareth was the promised Jewish Messiah had seemed shocking to Saul the Jew. Becoming a Christian meant for him overcoming and accepting the scandal of the cross. This whole struggle intimates, however, that, for Paul, becoming a Christian did not entail accepting for the first time the idea that there was to be a promised Messiah. Paul's struggle was over what the precise nature of this Messiah was to be, not whether there would be a Messiah. But as scholars have often noted in recent years, belief in a coming Messiah was by no means universal in Judaism around the turn of the era; it was a specific belief proper to specific groups.[147] Hence it is reasonable to infer that the messianic hope that was part of Paul's belief-system before he became a Christian stemmed from his specifically Pharisaic beliefs. These beliefs naturally underwent massive realignment when Paul accepted the crucified Jesus as Messiah.[148]

(ii) Likewise, as a Pharisee, Paul would have believed in a resurrection of the dead "in the last days." (While belief in the resurrection was not unique to the Pharisees, it was a distinguishing characteristic of their movement, and the acceptance of this belief by Paul the Jew is most naturally explained by his adherence to Pharisaism.) For Paul, the great turnabout of Christian faith involved coming to believe that one specific individual, the crucified Messiah Jesus, had already been raised to eternal life—and so, in a sense, the last days had already begun.

(iii) In most of his epistles, Paul thinks it natural to support his views about Christ, the flow of salvation history, the place of Israel and the church, and the end of time by interpreting various OT texts in a creative fashion—specifically, in an eschatological, messianic light. Since we find such creative reinterpretation of OT texts for the sake of contemporary eschatological and messianic agendas both at Qumran and in various OT pseudepigrapha, it is likely that Paul's way of reading the Jewish Scriptures from an eschatological and messianic perspective did not begin simply after he became a Christian. If the Pharisees engaged in the exact, precise interpretation of *all* the Scriptures, and not just some legal texts, it is hardly surprising that their exegesis should have had an eschatological and messianic as well as a legal (halakic) dimension.

(iv) It goes without saying that the Mosaic Law looms large in Paul's thought. He presupposes that it plays an important role within the flow of Israel's history as God guides that history towards its consummation (e.g., Rom 3:27–8:4; 9:30–10:4). Indeed, the life of Paul the Jew was so wrapped up in the Mosaic Law that he can sum up his traumatic break with his Pharisaic past (Gal 1:13: "my former way of life in Judaism") and the place the Law had in that past with a laconic paradox (Gal 2:19): "Through the Law I died to the Law that I might live to God." The precise meaning of this paradox is much debated among exegetes; but, whatever its sense in its immediate context, it points to the centrality of the Law in Paul's life as a Pharisee and the rupture that leaving that life meant for him.[149]

Now, we must not leap to the conclusion that the eschatological and/or messianic substratum that we may find at the basis of Paul's Christian theology can be attributed to all Pharisees at the time of Paul, to say nothing of all Pharisees from about 150 B.C. to A.D. 70. But Paul may well reflect one type of 1st-century Pharisee whose legal study and practice were part of a larger theological vision. This vision would have encompassed the sweep of salvation history from Israel's election and reception of the Law through Israel's ongoing sanctification by careful study and observance of the Law down to the fulfillment of the promises contained in the Law and the prophets: the coming of the Messiah, the resurrection of the dead, the final judgment, and the blessings of the last days.

While this reconstruction of one type of Pharisaism from Paul's presuppositions is admittedly hypothetical, it does serve to remind us that the religious life of the Pharisees was no doubt much fuller and richer than a dry list of legal observances would imply. In addition, it is likely that the Pharisees, over more than two centuries of existence before the destruction of Jerusalem, developed characteristic forms of prayer and communal life. What they were is now lost to us, though some elements may have flowed into and been preserved by the synagogue liturgies of the rabbinic period.

(6) One final element of Pharisaic doctrine, highlighted only by Josephus, must remain rather vague because of the way Josephus presents it: the interaction between divine providence ("fate" in Josephus' terminology) and human effort (put philosophically, "free will"). In his three static descriptions of the major Jewish movements, Josephus attempts to present the Essenes, Pharisees, and Sadducees as equivalents of the great and venerable philosophical schools of Greco-Roman culture; hence they struggle with the same weighty questions. (This may be one reason why Josephus speaks of "fate" [*heimarmenē*] when one might have expected "divine providence.")[150] The apologetic aim and the attempt at cross-cultural comparisons should make us wary from the start. The approach that Josephus uses to draw the comparison and at the same time to differentiate the main Jewish groups among themselves involves the application of the two categories of immortality/resurrection and fate/human effort.

We have already examined Pharisees' beliefs about immortality/resurrection under point 5. In applying the grid of fate/human effort to the Jewish groups, Josephus, at least in *Antiquities* 13, places the Essenes and the Sadducees at the two ends of the spectrum.[151] The Essenes, says Josephus, hold that fate is the mistress of human lives and decrees all events; hence the Essenes leave everything to God (*Ant.* 13.5.9 §172; 18.1.5 §18). In contrast, the Sadducees "entirely do away with fate," affirm that *all things* lie in the power of human beings, and exalt every human's ability to choose good or evil (*J. W.* 2.8.14 §164–165; *Ant.* 13.5.9 §173).

Immediately, what we know from Qumran should make us leery of this simple and perhaps simplistic pattern.[152] To be sure, the documents that reflect the theology of the Qumran community or of the wider body of Essenes (e.g., *The Rule of the Community*, the *Hodayot Psalms*, the *Damascus Document*) put great emphasis on God foreordaining all things and humanity being unable to extricate itself from sin by its own puny efforts. There is a strong tone of predestination and a clear accent on the hopeless corruption of all "flesh." Nevertheless, these same documents extol repentance, conversion, a decision to enter the purified community of Qumran, and a demanding and detailed observance of the Law, which every member is expected to keep. As with a good deal of both the OT and the NT, and in keeping with the unmediated juxtapositions of opposites typical of the Semitic mind, affirmations of divine omnipotence, human impotence, and predestination lie side by side with urgent calls to conversion and fierce moral endeavor. While Josephus, for the sake of his neat classification, chooses to emphasize the first half of the Essene paradox, one may ask whether he does full justice to the second.

As we shall see in the next chapter, it is much more difficult to speak of the Sadducees and their beliefs, since we have no statements on these matters from the Sadducees themselves and have to rely largely on the claims of their various enemies. Still, it is difficult to believe that a group of Jerusalemite Jews (including priests) who revered the Pentateuch as sacred text and who engaged in regular prayer and sacrifice celebrated in the Jerusalem temple (as at least the priests did) had no room in their belief-system for faith in God's guidance of Israel through its history and of individual believers through their lives. As with the Essenes, so with the Sadducees, Josephus may be emphasizing those aspects of their religious lives which were most obvious and striking to the outsider. As wealthy lay and priestly aristocrats engaged in conducting public affairs and/or public liturgy, the Sadducees would naturally be concerned with the importance of human effort and decision in the arena of political, economic, and religious policy. Simply as a matter of survival amid the chaotic events of the ancient Near East, the aristocratic leaders of the nation would instinctively tend toward a pragmatic, *realpolitik* approach to life, including religious life.

All this leads us to approach Josephus' statements on Pharisaic beliefs concerning fate and human choice with due caution. Indeed, when we look at Josephus' three expositions of the subject, in his three great descriptions of the Jewish schools, we notice that his presentations are not entirely consistent.[153]

In the first passage (*J.W.* 2.8.14 §162–63), Josephus begins with the blanket statement that the Pharisees "attribute *all things* to fate and to God." He immediately proceeds to modify this absolute claim with a two-part thesis: on the one hand *(men)*, moral activity, be it good or evil, lies "for the most part" *(kata to pleiston)* in the power of human beings; on the other hand *(de)*, fate "comes to the assistance of [or: cooperates with] each person." While both fate and free will are therefore affirmed and held in tension, the rhetorical structure of the whole does not give them equal weight. (1) Josephus' initial absolute statement attributing all things to fate, (2) the restriction of human freedom to the individual's moral activity—and that only "for the most part"—and (3) the structure of the whole presentation, with the theme of fate forming an *inclusio* in an A-B-A' pattern, clearly put the emphasis on the power of fate.[154] Since the Essenes' exaltation of fate alone is not treated in this first exposition of the schools, the Pharisees have to play the role of the stark opposite of the Sadducees, who reject fate. This may help explain why the passage tilts the Pharisees' position in the direction of the almighty grip of fate.

In contrast, in his second description of the schools and of the Pharisaic position (*Ant.* 13.5.9 §172), Josephus seems to divide up the spheres of fate and human action almost on a half-and-half basis. "On the one hand *(men)*, some things [*tina*], *but not all things* [contrast the absolute claim in the first description!] are the work of fate.[155] On the other hand *(de)*, some things [*tina*] happen or do not happen, depending upon what we do [literally: depending on ourselves]." Here events are divided up fairly equally. There is no sense of an all-encompassing and all-controlling fate in the Pharisees' belief-system, since this second exposition makes clear that such an extreme position is held instead by the Essenes. The Pharisees thus move to the middle position.

Josephus' third exposition of the schools (*Ant.* 18.1.3 §13), which uses the vocabulary of mixing, blending, or fusion *(krasis),* is itself something of a blending of the two other statements.[156] We are told that the Pharisees think that *all things* are accomplished by fate; yet the Pharisees do not deprive the human will of the initiative and choice that lie within its power. These two truths can stand side by side because it has pleased God that there be a certain mixture or fusion. Josephus tries to explain this unclear metaphor of fusion with another metaphor that is still less clear: by God's decree, the human will, with its power to choose good or evil, is allowed to join the deliberative meetings that fate holds in its council chamber.

In a way, this balanced statement is reminiscent of the second description; indeed, Josephus insists that this balance or blending is the result of God's gracious will to arrange matters so. Nevertheless, as in the first description, (1) *all things* are said to be determined by fate—a point that is reinforced by the affirmation that the very balance between fate and free will is the result of God's decision—and (2) human freedom is not extended to all events, but only to one's moral choice between good and evil. Thus, Josephus' two former expositions undergo a certain "fusion" in this third exposition.

Clearly, Josephus is not interested in a detailed and systematic account of Pharisaic belief on this subject. His descriptions, when taken all together, seem driven more by his desire (1) to position the Pharisees between the Essenes and the Sadducees and (2) to compare the Pharisees to the Stoics, who, at least in some of their philosophical writings (e.g., those of Chrysippus), acknowledged the important role of the human will in moral actions and yet attributed every action to fate.

Nevertheless, there may be a certain truth to Josephus' description of the Pharisees' position. The emphasis on fate (predominant in the first description) correlates well with the Pharisees' vision of Israel's history being inexorably directed by God toward a cosmic consummation, at which he will raise and judge the dead. The emphasis on free choice in the arena of good and evil correlates well with the Pharisees' inculcation of Israel's responsibility to obey the holy will of the holy God as revealed in the Law and explicated in the traditions of the fathers, a responsibility that is expressed in accurate and detailed observance of all commandments. In the end, though, one wonders whether the juxtaposition of an affirmation of God's total control and an emphasis on human responsibility really differentiated the Pharisees all that much from most other Jews.[157]

Our listing of all six basic points about the Pharisees and, in particular, the problematic nature of the sixth point, should warn us not to imagine that one or another of these points made a Pharisee a Pharisee. What characterized the Pharisees as Pharisees was no one belief or practice. One can describe the Pharisees only by creating a *Gestalt*, a configuration of beliefs and practices that converge to form an organic whole that we call Pharisaism. It was this organic whole that made Pharisees distinctive *within*—but *not* shut off *from*—pre-70 Judaism. This is what all six points, taken together, are intended to signify.

Yet even such a configuration does not capture the full reality of the Pharisees, who did not constitute a separatist conventicle like Qumran. With almost all other Palestinian Jews the Pharisees shared in what we might call "mainstream" or "common" Judaism:[158] the belief that Israel was God's chosen people, that God had given Israel the gift of the Mosaic Law, that he had imposed on Israel the boundary-marking obligations of circumcision, sabbath observance, rules of purity (e.g., with respect to food, sexual activity, and treatment of the dead), and the cycle of feasts and sacrifices in the Jerusalem temple, to be observed according to the (solar-)lunar calendar generally accepted by 1st-century Jews apart from the Essenes. With their special *hălākâ*, the Pharisees might develop and mold these basic elements of the Law to fit their own views, but the basic elements were something they held in common with almost all Jews.

Even beyond these "common components" of Judaism, the Pharisees were hardly unique among their coreligionists in stressing zealous study and practice of the Law. The Essenes, particularly the Qumranites, probably outstripped them in this regard. Thus, it is only when we put all the components together, those characteristic of the Pharisees and those shared with other Jews, that the full flesh-and-blood reality of the Pharisees, as opposed to a cardboard caricature, begins to emerge.

C. Summary: A Minimalist Sketch of the Pharisees

Keeping in mind this wider Jewish context in which the Pharisees were embedded, we are now in a position to draw up a brief sketch of the Pharisees' history and specific beliefs. If we were to delineate a thumbnail portrait of the Pharisees, it might look like this: The Pharisees were a particular religious and political group of devout Jews that arose at the beginning of the Hasmonean period, somewhere around 150 B.C. They represented one specific religious and political response to the crisis of Hellenization unleashed by Antiochus IV and his Jewish supporters, a crisis that continued into the reign of the Hasmonean princes and kings.

In the face of a perceived threat to the continued existence of Jews as a distinct ethnic, cultural, and religious entity in the ancient Near East, the Pharisees emphasized the zealous and detailed study and practice of the Mosaic Law, the careful observance of legal obligations in concrete areas of life such as tithing, purity laws (especially concerning food, sexual activity, and the proper treatment of the dead), the keeping of the sabbath, marriage and divorce, and temple ritual. As they developed their characteristic legal observances, they correspondingly developed a theory that justified these observances: they possessed a normative body of traditions—the traditions of the fathers (or the elders)—which went beyond the written Mosaic Law but which was (or at least should be) incumbent on the whole people of Israel.

These legal obligations did not float in a vacuum as a desiccated list. They expressed concretely the response of Israel, God's holy people, to the holy God who had given Israel the Law to mark it out from all the peoples of the earth. Fidelity to God and his Law carried a sure reward. Those Israelites who proved faithful to the Law would be raised from the dead on the last day, acquitted at the final judgment, and given a share, along with all the just, in the world to come. The wicked and the apostates who had forsaken the Law or even persecuted its faithful adherents would be punished forever and would have no share in the world to come.

At least some Pharisees, like Saul/Paul, understood Pharisaic practice and belief within an overarching (perhaps apocalyptic) view of salvation history, where the Law had a salvific role leading up to the coming of the Messiah. One characteristic element of Pharisaic Judaism was its zeal in spreading its own view of Judaism among the people at large. Hence it is not surprising that, while neither the Gospels nor Josephus presents the mass of Palestinian Jews as Pharisees, they present the Pharisees as active and influential among the common people. The Sadducees, restricted largely to the priestly and lay aristocracy in Jerusalem, seem to have shown no such zeal in propagating their views beyond their elite group.

Amid all these theological descriptions, we must not forget that the Pharisees were not only a religious movement but at the same time a political party or "political interest group." [159] Here we must remember that our idea of separation of church and state was quite foreign to the ancient Mediterranean world. Throughout OT history, the political life of the Israelite or Jewish state was inextricably intertwined with the struggle for what various groups saw as proper Israelite belief and practice. That struggle continued during Hasmonean rule. During that period, the Pharisees, when they were in a position to do so, were quite willing to use the power of the state to impose their legal practices on the general population. Such seems to have been the case during the early part of the reign of John Hyrcanus, and it was certainly true throughout the reign of Salome Alexandra. During the latter reign, they used their power in domestic affairs to wreak bloody vengeance on their foes. Despite the frequency with which scholars have applied "pacifist" to the Pharisees, the label does not square with the historical record.

Both Herod's despotic rule and the Roman prefects' use of the high priests as their go-betweens with the Jewish people of Judea pushed the political activity of the Pharisees to the sidelines. But there is no solid proof that, during the 1st century A.D., the Pharisees ever gave up their aspirations to political power. They never withdrew completely from the political arena to become merely a pious group of laymen pursuing holiness through meals celebrated in ritual purity with fellow Pharisees. In other words, Pharisaism never became a quietist sect. Be it through intrigues in Herod's palace, agitation among the common people, or Pharisaic retainers serving the ruling class (if one accepts that interpretation of the Pharisees' socioeconomic status), the Pharisees continued to seek political power, by indirect if not direct means. [160]

At least some of them regained political power during the coalition government that the more moderate factions set up in Jerusalem at the beginning of the revolt (A.D. 66–67). After the war, the Pharisees coalesced with other devout and studious Jews at Yavneh to form the beginnings of the rabbinic movement. In due course, the leader of this movement (the *nāśî* or "patriarch") gained a certain amount of recognition from the Roman government. By that time, however, the Pharisees as a distinct group had receded into past history even as their spiritual heirs and continuators, the rabbis, began to gain control of Palestinian Judaism.

We have, then, a bare minimum, a brief sketch of what can be said about the pre-70 Pharisees.[161] Let us turn now to the Gospels to see what can be said about the historical Jesus' relation to or interaction with the Pharisees.

D. JESUS' RELATION TO THE PHARISEES

If our question were one of redaction criticism, namely, how Jesus relates to the Pharisees in a given Gospel and how this relationship reflects the theology of the Gospel's author, our task would be fairly simple. In a given Gospel, we would treat each of the pericopes and sayings where the Pharisees appear, note any changes the evangelist makes vis-à-vis his sources, and correlate the results with the overall theology of the evangelist. A good deal of the material in the Synoptics would comprise (1) the various dispute stories *(Streitgespräche)* in Mark (as well as their reworked forms in Matthew and Luke) and (2) the woes against the Pharisees and the lawyers/scribes in Luke and Matthew (largely Q material).[162] However, as soon as we engage in such redaction-critical studies of each of the Gospels, these studies show how problematic is any attempt to reconstruct the relation of the *historical* Jesus to the *historical* Pharisees.

For example, compared to Mark, both Matthew and Luke tend to introduce references—especially negative references—to the Pharisees in passages where the Pharisees do not appear in Mark. For instance, in the story of the healing of the paralytic in Mark 2:1–12,[163] the adversaries who think Jesus is speaking blasphemy when he declares the paralytic's sins forgiven are designated by the vague phrase "some of the scribes" (Mark 2:6 ‖ Matt 9:3). In contrast, Luke, both at the beginning of the story (Luke 5:17) and at the moment of criticism (5:21), introduces "Pharisees" alongside "teachers of the law" or "scribes" as Jesus' adversaries. If, then, Luke can introduce Pharisees into this story as he creatively rewrites Mark, how can we be sure that Mark or Mark's source has not introduced Pharisees into dispute stories where the original adversaries either were vague "scribes" or had no label whatever?

To take another example, this time from Mark's redactional hand: as Joanna Dewey has shown,[164] the cycle of Galilean dispute stories in Mark 2:1–3:6 is carefully composed to create an artistic and theological pattern:

1. "Some scribes" think but do not openly say that Jesus is blaspheming in the story of the healing of the paralytic (Mark 2:1–12). The story con-

tains an obvious cross-reference to the accusation of blasphemy at Jesus' trial before the Sanhedrin (Mark 14:53–65, esp. v 64). Quite fittingly for the Marcan cross-reference, the Sanhedrin scene, just like the healing of the paralytic, has scribes but lacks Pharisees.

2. "The scribes of the Pharisees"—probably scribal leaders of the Pharisaic party—complain not to Jesus but to his disciples about Jesus' eating with sinners and toll collectors (2:13–17). The theme of "Pharisees" is thus introduced indirectly.

3. Some unnamed people[165] ask Jesus why the disciples of John and the disciples of the Pharisees practice voluntary fasting while Jesus' disciples do not (2:18–22). Again, the Pharisees appear indirectly, in this case offstage.

4. At last, the Pharisees appear on stage in person and interact with Jesus. They directly challenge him—not about his own actions, but about those of his disciples, who are plucking grain *on the sabbath* (2:23–28).

5. In 3:1–6, the healing of the man with the withered hand *on the sabbath* in the synagogue, the adversaries are unnamed at the beginning of the story (3:1).[166] However, since this narrative follows immediately upon the story of the Pharisees objecting to Jesus about his disciples plucking grain *on the sabbath,* the adversaries are probably intended by Mark to be understood as Pharisees. The adversaries watch Jesus to see whether his healing activity on the sabbath will give them a pretext to accuse him. When he both heals the man with the withered hand and defends his action theologically, Mark tells us that "the Pharisees, going out [so they are thought to have been present in the synagogue, most probably as the adversaries], took counsel with the Herodians on how they might destroy him [Jesus]" (3:6).

The artistic and theological hand of Mark is clear. The cycle of five stories is arranged in a concentric pattern around key themes: (1) healing—(2) eating—(3) fasting—(4) eating—(5) healing. At the same time, though, the stories are driven by an ever increasing tone of antagonism and an ever more direct attack on Jesus himself. In keeping with this increasing antagonism, the Pharisees gradually appear on stage, become the only named group to confront Jesus directly with a hostile interrogation (in the fourth pericope), and in the climax to the whole cycle emerge as the lead agents in the plot to kill him.

Granted this artistic and artificial pattern created by Mark's theological program, and granted that this idea of the Pharisees as the lead agents in bringing about Jesus' death finds no echo even in the Marcan Passion Narrative, the use of this cycle of dispute stories to determine exactly when, in what circumstances, and on what issues the historical Jesus clashed with the historical Pharisees is a dubious procedure. This is especially true of the climactic fifth pericope. As we have seen, the Pharisees are not named in the body of the fifth pericope, but are rather inferred from the larger Marcan structure. Moreover, if one holds, as many critics do,[167] that the conclusion in 3:6 (or at least the mention of the Pharisees there) is Mark's redactional addition to the whole cycle of dispute stories, then the Pharisees' presence in the most hostile and deadly confrontation of the cycle evaporates as soon as historical as opposed to literary questions are asked.

In the corresponding cycle of Jerusalem dispute stories at the end of the public ministry (Mark 11:27–12:37), the yield is even more meager. The major partners in dispute or dialogue are "the high priests, scribes, and elders" (11:27, symbolizing the Sanhedrin, which in Mark will condemn Jesus to death in 14:53–65), the Sadducees (12:18), a lone sympathetic scribe (12:28), and the scribes in general (12:35–38). The Pharisees appear—again, in the company of the Herodians—only in the question about the coin of tribute (12:13–17); this is the only time they come on stage in Jerusalem. One wonders whether the curious combination of "Pharisees and Herodians" in 12:13 is a cross-reference created by Mark to "Pharisees with Herodians" in 3:6. With this *inclusio*, he may intend to tie together the Galilean dispute stories (2:1–3:6) with the Jerusalem dispute stories (11:27–12:37).[168] In sum, Mark's artistic and theological compositions must make us wary of presuming that every reference to the Pharisees goes back to an actual incident in the life of the historical Jesus.

As we have seen already, this holds true a fortiori of Matthew and Luke, where Pharisees—especially in Matthew's favorite tag, "scribes and Pharisees"—multiply as stage props. It is telling that, in the collection of woes spoken by Jesus against his adversaries, Luke 11:39–52 still preserves a distinction between woes spoken against the Pharisees (11:39–44) and woes spoken against the lawyers (11:45–52), a distinction that most likely stood in Q.[169] In contrast, Matthew conflates these woes into one long tirade against the monolithic "scribes and Pharisees" (Matt 23:2–36). In a number of passages, Matthew replaces Mark's hostile "scribes" with "Pharisees" (e.g., Mark 3:22 ‖ Matt 9:34 and 12:24; Mark 12:12, where the understood subject is "the high priests and the scribes and the elders" from 11:27, as compared with Matt 21:45, where the expressed subject is "the high priests and the Pharisees"). While the borders between the various opponents of Jesus in Matthew's Gospel tend to be blurred, the Pharisees stand out as the opponents par excellence. Though the Pharisees multiply also in Luke's narrative as compared with Mark's, the Lucan portrait is less monochromatic and un-relievedly hostile than the Matthean one.

Although the absence of large blocks of legal and moral material tends to create a different configuration of adversaries in John, the Fourth Gospel does not lack for references to the Pharisees, references that clearly reflect the evangelist's situation in late 1st-century Christianity. Instead of being one of several Jewish parties or groups, the Pharisees are *the* controlling group in Judaism, period.[170] They, and they alone among the traditional Jewish movements, are blithely equated with the set Johannine phrase "the Jews" *(hoi Ioudaioi)* when it is used in the special Johannine sense of "the authorities hostile to Jesus." This equation is especially striking in the story of the healing of the man born blind (chap. 9). Here the "Pharisees," alias the "Jews" (9:13 + 18), are said to have the power to expel fellow Jews from the synagogue if they profess faith in Jesus as the Messiah (9:22). Indeed, the Pharisees are said to hold such power of expulsion even over the "rulers" *(archontōn)* of the Jewish people (12:42). Such a situation is simply inconceivable in the political and religious conditions of Palestinian Judaism around A.D. 28–30.

In short, as in Matthew, so in John, the post-70 situation of Judaism vis-à-vis Christianity strongly colors the presentation of the Pharisees. The Pharisees of Matthew and John are largely the post-70 Pharisees and their allies who are swiftly on their way to becoming the early rabbis of tannaitic Judaism. Hence one must take great care in using either Matthew's or John's Pharisees to reconstruct the historical Pharisees who interacted with Jesus ca. A.D. 28–30.[171]

Still, one should not dismiss any and every aspect of the Matthean or Johannine picture out of hand without at least examining it for possible archaic traits. For example, John's Gospel places Pharisees only in and around Jerusalem, as does in general Luke's Acts of the Apostles (cf. Mark 7:1). This coheres with the views of those scholars who find little or no proof of widespread and successful Pharisaic activity in Galilee during the early 1st century A.D. Here as elsewhere in his Gospel, for all his theological development, John sometimes preserves startling bits of historical data, especially in regard to Jerusalem and its environs. It may well be that, in the early 1st century A.D., Pharisaism as a group phenomenon was largely restricted to Jerusalem and the larger towns of Judea. In general, it seems to have been an urban rather than a rural movement, demanding as it did a certain level of learning and a certain modicum of leisure (and material resources?) to engage in regular study and punctilious practice of the Law.

Thus, it is perhaps Mark's artificial theological schema, keeping Jesus in

Galilee and away from Jerusalem until the final fatal week of his life, that necessitates putting most interaction with the Pharisees in Galilee. Historically,
it may well be that interaction with the Pharisees, for the most part, took
place in and around Jerusalem, when Jesus came on pilgrimage to the great
feasts—just as John's Gospel intimates.

Reviewing all these data about the Pharisees in the Gospels, we find ourselves faced with a problem not unlike the one faced by those examining
Jesus' miracles. The basic fact that the historical Jesus claimed to work miracles and that certain actions performed by him were hailed by his followers
as miracles during his lifetime is easily established by the criteria of historicity. But to move beyond that global affirmation to discern which individual
miracle stories may actually go back to startling actions performed by Jesus
is extremely difficult. The sweeping generalization is easy to make; the precise judgment about the individual cases took up a good part of Volume Two
of *A Marginal Jew,* with a certain number of miracle stories falling into the
limbo of *non liquet* (not clear).[172]

In a way, the situation is even more difficult with the problem of Jesus and
the Pharisees. A dispute story that does in fact go back to the historical Jesus
could easily have suffered the secondary insertion of the word "Pharisees" at
a later date, when a Christian editor wanted to specify who the originally unnamed opponents were. Still, the fundamental similarity to miracle stories
remains: the global affirmation that Jesus did interact with Pharisees is much
easier to establish than the historicity of individual incidents involving them.

The basic fact that Jesus at times addressed, debated with, talked about, or
in general interacted with Pharisees enjoys multiple attestation of sources
and forms. Indeed, every single Gospel source contains such material: e.g.,
Mark (especially in dispute stories: 2:16,18,24; 3:6; 7:1–5; 8:11; 10:2;
12:13); Q (woes in Luke 11:39–44 par.); M (Matt 5:20; 21:45; 23:2);
L (7:36–50; 11:37–38; 13:31; 15:2; 17:20; 18:10–14); and John (3:1; 7:32,
45, 47–48; [8:13;] 9:13,15–16,40; 11:46–47,57; 12:19,42).

Needless to say, my argument is not that every passage I have just listed by
way of example goes back to the historical Jesus. Some of Mark's theological
patterns (Mark 3:6 + 12:13), some of Luke's narrative introductions to Jesus'
sayings (e.g., Luke 15:2; 17:20), some of the Matthean statements about the
Law and morality (e.g., Matt 5:20), and John's general picture of the Pharisees as having ultimate control over Palestinian Judaism (e.g., John 12:42)
are either suspect or patently redactional. Clearly, the struggle between
Christian Jews and Pharisaic Jews in the period of A.D. 30–100 has left a
strong imprint on the four Gospels.

Nevertheless, the broad sweep of attestation, with Pharisees represented in every source and in many different literary forms (general narratives, dispute stories, woes, sayings about entrance into the kingdom of heaven, parables) does suggest some historical basis in the career of the historical Jesus. At the very least, a number of the Gospel scenarios involving the Pharisees enjoy a certain probability:[173]

1. Jesus the eschatological seer clashes with Pharisees over his radical view on marriage and divorce. This scenario enjoys a fair amount of verisimilitude because (a) the House of Hillel and the House of Shammai were divided precisely on the grounds for divorce, and (b) Jesus' stance is based on the eschatological hope that the end time would restore the Creator's intention for what he had created in the beginning (i.e., the permanent union of one man and one woman in marriage, Mark 10:1–12).

2. Jesus the prophet pronounces woes à la Amos or Isaiah on Pharisees and others who reject his message (Q material in Luke 11:39–44).

3. Jesus the spinner of parables includes the antithetical figures of a Pharisee and a toll collector, familiar actors on the Palestinian stage, in a parable (L material in Luke 18:10–14).

4. Jesus the teacher finds a sympathetic ear among individual Pharisees, despite the general coolness, if not antipathy, of the group toward him (Nicodemus in John 3:1,10; 7:47–52; to a lesser degree, Simon in Luke 7:36–50).

Indeed, granted that Jesus sought to address the whole of his people in order to confront them with his vision of the consummation of Israel's history and the proper way Israel was to prepare for it, and granted that he was especially active among the common people and at times drew large crowds—granted all this, which Jewish group would he most likely collide and debate with if not the Pharisees? After all, according to Josephus, the Pharisees were the Jewish party most active and influential among the common people.

In contrast, the Qumranites had withdrawn to the desert. The Essenes in general lived their sectarian program in their own conventicles. The Sadducees were apparently a relatively small group of priestly and lay aristocrats, who did not campaign vigorously to win over the common people to their beliefs. Moreover, contrary to some popular presentations, there was no organized revolutionary group such as the Fourth Philosophy or the

Zealots active in Palestine ca. A.D. 28–30. The only significant Jewish group seeking to influence the religious views and practical behavior of ordinary Palestinian Jews "at ground level" ca. A.D. 28–30 was the Pharisees.

It is hardly a wonder, then, that Jesus would have interacted more with them than with any other Jewish movement or party. Both Jesus and the Pharisees shared a consuming desire to bring all Israel, not just an esoteric sect or a privileged elite, to the complete doing of God's will as laid out in the Law and the prophets. No doubt Jesus and the Pharisees would have agreed on many basic points: God's free election of Israel, his gift of the Law, the need to respond wholeheartedly to the Law's demands in one's everyday life, God's faithful guidance of Israel through history to a future consummation involving the restoration of Israel, a final judgment, the resurrection of the dead, and perhaps some sort of eschatological or messianic figure as God's agent in the end time.

At the same time, disagreements were inevitable, (1) granted the peculiar mix of present-yet-future eschatology that implicitly put Jesus himself at the center of the eschatological drama that he proclaimed, (2) granted the eschatological significance he attributed to some of his "miracles," (3) granted some of his unusual teaching on *hălākâ* that flowed from his eschatological message: e.g., (a) the total prohibition of divorce; (b) celibacy as one possible way of serving the kingdom; (c) the rejection of voluntary fasting; and (d) the neglect or rejection of various familial obligations and purity rules (e.g., refusing to grant a follower time to bury his dead father; possibly a lack of concern about food laws).[174]

If some of the woes against the Pharisees go back to the historical Jesus, then the debate between the Pharisees and himself became at times fierce and vituperative—which is quite typical of the defaming of adversaries practiced in the ancient Mediterranean world. It is especially typical of the ways various Jewish groups attacked one another around the turn of the era. One hears similar accusations in Qumran literature (perhaps at times directed against the Pharisees!)[175] and in various OT pseudepigrapha such as *1 Enoch* and the *Psalms of Solomon*. Polite ecumenical dialogue among different religious groups is a happy modern invention. Even the House of Hillel and the House of Shammai, according to rabbinic literature, engaged in some nasty clashes.[176]

However, especially in view of the tragic history of later Christian polemics against Judaism, it must be stressed that the biting rhetoric used by Jews, including Jesus, in religious debates with their coreligionists should not be translated by Gentile audiences into a rejection of Judaism in general or of the Jewishness of one's adversaries in particular (the fiercely sectarian group at Qumran is the exception that proves the rule). Fiery denunciation was a revered rhetorical tradition from the prophets Amos and Hosea onwards, and Jesus the prophet saw himself as standing in their line. Moreover, one must remember that a particular verbal attack that Jesus may have uttered against individual Pharisees with whom he happened to be debating would take on a much more sweeping meaning when it was stitched together with other polemical statements and turned into a programmatic denunciation of "scribes and Pharisees" in general (e.g., in Matt 23:1–36).

In particular, when treating Jesus' relationship to the Pharisees, one should bear in mind that the earliest strata of the Gospel traditions supply no basis for thinking that Jesus' clashes with the Pharisees were the major reason why he was put to death. Indeed, as to both issues and actors, there is a remarkable "disconnect" in the Gospels between Jesus' disputes with the Pharisees during the public ministry and his arrest and execution at the end of his life. The whole Marcan Passion Narrative, as well as the primitive form of the Johannine Passion Narrative, never presents the Pharisees as a group taking part in the trial, condemnation, or execution of Jesus.[177] The united witness of the passion traditions points to the interaction of the disciple Judas, the high priest Caiaphas, various priestly, scribal, and aristocratic officials around Caiaphas, and the Roman prefect Pontius Pilate, who had the last word. Especially in contrast to their abundant presence in the stories of the public ministry, the Pharisees as a group are notable by their absence in the Passion Narrative.[178]

Therefore, a summary of what we can say with fair probability about Jesus' relation to the Pharisees might run like this: All Gospel sources testify to Jesus' interaction with Pharisees during the public ministry. The tone of the interaction is often adversarial. This is not surprising, since both Jesus and the Pharisees were competing to influence the main body of Palestinian Jews and win them over to their respective visions of what God was calling Israel to be and do at a critical juncture in its history.

Debate between Jesus and the Pharisees tended to be of a halakic (legal, behavioral) rather than of a doctrinal nature. Such debate probably involved questions like divorce, fasting, tithing, purity rules, observance of the sabbath, and in general the relative importance of various external observances. As part of the prophet-like polemic of Jesus against his debating partners, he may at times have proclaimed woes against Pharisees and attacked them in open or veiled ways in some of his parables. Nevertheless, the counter-indications in the Gospels that some Pharisees were willing to give Jesus a serious hearing (e.g., Luke 7:36–50; John 3:1–2) may serve as a reminder that the interaction need not always have been as negative as later Christians portrayed it.

It is difficult to be more specific than this. Clearly, to take every Gospel story involving the Pharisees as a video-taped replay of historical events from ca. A.D. 30 or to ignore the massive expansion of the Pharisees' role in the Gospels of Matthew and John as part of their polemical agendas is to abandon the quest for the historical Jesus in favor of Christian theology. Indeed, the difficulty of knowing when a reference to the Pharisees goes back to an original historical incident and when it may be a secondary insertion makes imperative an important distinction in method. One must not simply identify the question of the historical Jesus' relation to the Pharisees and the much larger question of the historical Jesus' relation to the Mosaic Law. Gospel traditions about Jesus' relation to the Mosaic Law could be quite historical even though the insertion of the Pharisees into the debates as the specific partners might be secondary.

Hence, while touching briefly on various legal questions in this section on the Pharisees, I purposely reserve a treatment of Jesus' teaching on the Law to a later chapter in Volume Four. The Pharisees were not the only 1st-century Palestinian Jews concerned with the Mosaic Law, nor were they probably the only Jews concerned with Jesus' teaching about the Law. While the Pharisees had their own views and practices regarding matters like divorce and purity rules, these basic topics belonged to the common concerns of "mainstream" Judaism. When Jesus addressed such topics and especially when he proclaimed new, startling, and disturbing rules governing such topics, he was addressing and potentially upsetting the lives of all pious Jews, not just Pharisees. Accordingly, these topics are more properly treated under the question of Jesus' relation to the Mosaic Law, the common treasure of all Jews, as opposed to the more narrow question of Jesus' relation to the Pharisees.

While the Pharisees loom large in the Gospels' depiction of Jesus' relation to Jewish groups, they were not the only group with whom Jesus interacted. In chapter 29, we will seek to broaden our focus by surveying the main opponents of the Pharisees, the Sadducees. Then, in chapter 30, we shall complete our survey by looking at other Jewish groups, including the Essenes and the Samaritans, who may at times have had contact with Jesus. Obviously, though, from all that we have seen in this chapter on the Pharisees, the next group to be examined is naturally the Sadducees.

NOTES TO CHAPTER 28

[1] On the whole question of the Baptist and baptizing movements, see *A Marginal Jew*, 2. 19–233; also Joseph Thomas, *Le mouvement baptiste en Palestine et Syrie (150 av. J.-C.—300 ap. J.-C.* (Universitas Catholica Lovaniensis 2/28; Gembloux: Duculot, 1935); Knut Backhaus, *Die "Jüngerkreise" des Täufers Johannes. Eine Studie zu den religionsgeschichtlichen Ursprüngen des Christentums* (Paderborner Theologische Studien 19; Paderborn: Schöningh, 1991); Robert L. Webb, *John the Baptizer and Prophet. A Socio-Historical Study* (JSNTSup 62; Sheffield: JSOT, 1991) 95–216.

[2] There is no lengthy, formal treatment of the Jewish "schools of thought" in Josephus' *Life* or *Against Apion*. There is one systematic presentation in the *Jewish War* (2.8.1–14 §118–66, with a fairly lengthy and laudatory treatment of the Essenes), two in the *Antiquities* (13.5.9 §171–73; 18.1.2–6 §11–25). The first and third treatments include the "Fourth Philosophy" of Judas the Galilean (and Saddok the Pharisee); the second treatment, which omits the "Fourth Philosophy," is relatively brief. Josephus uses the label "the Fourth Philosophy" to designate a group of religious radicals (under the leadership of Judas the Galilean and Saddok the Pharisee) who fomented resistance against the Roman census imposed by Quirinius for purposes of taxation after Archelaus, the son of Herod the Great, was deposed by the Romans in A.D. 6 (*J.W.* 2.8.1 §118; *Ant.* 18.1.1 §3–9). It should be noted that Josephus does not identify this Fourth Philosophy, which was crushed by the Romans, with the Zealots, who were one of the revolutionary groups fighting for control of Jerusalem during the First Jewish War. While Josephus probably wishes his readers to see a certain "unholy succession" stretching from the Fourth Philosophy through the many social disturbances caused by "brigands" or "bandits" under Roman rule down to the Zealots and other radical revolutionaries during the First Jewish War, there was in reality no single long-term, organized, armed resistance movement against Roman rule between the time of Judas the Galilean (if, indeed, arms were involved in his resistance) and the outbreak of the First Jewish War. For the view (contrary to the one often found in historical surveys of the period) that Judas' Fourth Philosophy did not engage in violent rebellion and did not lead an armed revolt against Rome, see Richard A. Horsley and John S. Hanson, *Bandits, Prophets, and Messiahs. Popular Movements in the Time of Jesus* (Minneapolis: Seabury/Winston, 1985) 190–99. Horsley and Hanson see Judas and Saddok as standing in the tradition of scholarly martyrs practicing nonviolent resistance rather than armed revolt against Rome. Whether this can be squared with Josephus' statements that Judas "incited his countrymen to revolt" *(eis apostasin enēge tous epichōrious)* and that his followers were told not to shrink from the killing that might be incumbent on them *(mē exaphiōntai phonou tou ep' autois)* is at least debatable. Horsley and Hanson support their position by translating *apostasin* by the mild "resistance" instead of "revolt" and by interpreting the ambiguous *phonou tou ep' autois* ("murder," "killing" that somehow is "upon them") as something that might befall the resisting Jews, not something they might have to engage in. But how Judas and Saddok could seriously hope that the Jewish

nation could "make a bid for independence" (*Ant.* 18.1.1 §4) solely on the basis of nonviolent resistance against Rome is unclear. In any event, the point that is important for us is that the Fourth Philosophy did not share the lengthy historical continuity of the Pharisees, Sadducees, and Essenes, stretching back to the middle of the 2d century B.C. (even granting the fact that the Qumran community apparently suffered a hiatus in its settlement near the Dead Sea in the latter part of the 1st century B.C.). Nor did the Fourth Philosophy provide an ongoing organization between A.D. 6 and 70 that a zealous Jew could join and to which Jesus might relate positively or negatively. Neither the Fourth Philosophy nor the Zealots existed as an organized political or military group at the time of Jesus, and hence they are not treated in this chapter. For more on "zealots" and "zealotry," see the treatment of Simon the Cananean (Zealot) in section II, number 8, in chapter 27 of this volume, and in section V in chapter 30. For Horsley and Hanson's presentation of the Zealots, see *Bandits*, 216–41.

³ The old classic is Emil Schürer's *The History of the Jewish People in the Age of Jesus Christ* (rev. and ed. Geza Vermes, Fergus Millar, Matthew Black, and Martin Goodman; 3 vols. [vol. 3 having two parts]; Edinburgh: Clark, 1973–1987). While containing valuable information, the volumes display an obvious tension between older views on Jewish parties and institutions and newer insights. See the outmoded presentation of the Pharisees in 2. 388–90 and the near-contradiction to this presentation in n. 20 on p. 389, which takes into consideration the work of scholars like Jacob Neusner. Much more up-to-date, if controversial, is E. P. Sanders's *Judaism. Practice and Belief. 63 BCE–66 CE* (London: SCM; Philadelphia: Trinity, 1992); see also Jacob Neusner, *First Century Judaism in Crisis* (augmented ed.; New York: Ktav, 1982, originally 1975); idem, *Judaism in the Beginning of Christianity* (Philadelphia: Fortress, 1984); Martin Goodman, *The Ruling Class of Judaea. The Origins of the Jewish Revolt against Rome A.D. 66–70* (Cambridge: Cambridge University, 1987). For the larger historical context, see Lester L. Grabbe, *Judaism from Cyrus to Hadrian. Volume Two: The Roman Period* (Minneapolis: Fortress, 1992); Peter Schäfer, *The History of the Jews in Antiquity* (Luxembourg: Harwood, 1995, German original 1983).

⁴ A comprehensive bibliography on the Pharisees would fill a whole volume. A useful overview with a short bibliography can be found in Anthony J. Saldarini, "Pharisees," *Anchor Bible Dictionary*, 5. 289–303; his fuller, sociologically oriented treatment, is contained within his *Pharisees, Scribes and Sadducees in Palestinian Society* (Wilmington, DE: Glazier, 1988). Another good, brief introduction is Günter Stemberger, *Pharisäer, Sadduzäer, Essener* (SBS 144; Stuttgart: KBW, 1991); the English translation, *Jewish Contemporaries of Jesus* (Minneapolis: Fortress, 1995), is not always reliable. The huge work that championed a new, more critical sifting of the rabbinic material on the Pharisees is Jacob Neusner, *The Rabbinic Traditions about the Pharisees before 70* (3 vols.; Leiden: Brill, 1971); a long bibliographical essay can be found in 3. 320–68. Neusner has summarized his findings in a number of subsequent works; a convenient digest of his three volumes can be found in Jacob

Neusner, *The Pharisees. Rabbinic Perspectives* (Hoboken, NJ: Ktav, 1973); see also his more popular presentation, *From Politics to Piety. The Emergence of Pharisaic Judaism* (Englewood Cliffs, NJ: Prentice-Hall, 1973). In his *Judaism: The Evidence of the Mishnah* (Chicago/London: University of Chicago, 1981), he seems to modify his position about being able to extract knowledge concerning the pre-70 Pharisees from the Mishna. For his debate with E. P. Sanders on the precise nature of the Pharisees, see Jacob Neusner, *Judaic Law from Jesus to the Mishnah. A Systematic Reply to Professor E. P. Sanders* (South Florida Studies in the History of Judaism 84; Atlanta: Scholars, 1993); see also his *The Mishnah before 70* (Brown Judaic Studies 51; Atlanta: Scholars, 1987). For the views of Sanders, see his *Jesus and Judaism*, 49–50, 174–211, 275–93; *Jewish Law from Jesus to the Mishnah* (London: SCM; Philadelphia: Trinity, 1990), esp. 97–254; idem, *Judaism. Practice & Belief*, 380–451. A lengthy review of Sanders' views on the Pharisees can be found in Martin Hengel and Roland Deines, "E. P. Sanders' 'Common Judaism,' Jesus and the Pharisees," *JTS* 46 (1995) 1–70. For a survey of scholarship on the Pharisees during the 19th and 20th centuries, see Roland Deines, *Die Pharisäer* (WUNT 101; Tübingen: Mohr [Siebeck], 1997). A do-it-yourself survey of scholarly articles on the Pharisees during the 20th century (mostly by Jewish authors) is made available by a two-volume work edited and introduced by Jacob Neusner, *Origins of Judaism. Volume II. The Pharisees and Other Sects* (2 parts; New York/London: Garland, 1990), with each part a separate volume. The articles that are relevant to scholarship on the Pharisees include: Albert I. Baumgarten, "Josephus and Hippolytus on the Pharisees," 1. 31–55; Roger T. Beckwith, "The Pre-History and Relationships of the Pharisees, Sadducees and Essenes: A Tentative Reconstruction," 1. 57–100; Shaye J. D. Cohen, "The Significance of Yavneh: Pharisees, Rabbis, and the End of Jewish Sectarianism," 1. 101–27; Samuel S. Cohon, "Pharisaism: A Definition," 1. 135–44; Louis Finkelstein, "The Pharisees: Their Origin and Their Philosophy," 1. 167–243; Henry A. Fischel, "Story and History: Observations on Greco-Roman Rhetoric and Pharisaism," 1. 245–74; Ralph Marcus, "Pharisees, Essenes, and Gnostics," 1. 379–83; idem, "The Pharisees in the Light of Modern Scholarship," 1. 385–96; Jacob Neusner, "From Exegesis to Fable in Rabbinic Traditions about the Pharisees," 1. 401–7; idem, "History and Purity in First-Century Judaism," 1. 409–25; idem, " 'Pharisaic-Rabbinic' Judaism: A Clarification," 1. 426–46; idem, "The Rabbinic Traditions about the Pharisees in Modern Historiography," 1. 448–78; idem, "The Use of the Later Rabbinic Evidence for the Study of First-Century Pharisaism," 1. 479–92; Jacob Z. Lauterbach, "A Significant Controversy between the Sadducees and the Pharisees," 2. 1–33; idem, "Sadducees and Pharisees. A Study of Their Respective Attitudes towards the Law," 2. 34–56; idem, "The Pharisees and Their Teachings, Part I, The Pharisees," 2. 57–79; idem, "The Pharisees and Their Teachings, Part II, The Pharisees' Attitude toward Law and Tradition," 2. 81–102; idem, "The Pharisees and Their Teachings, Part III, The Pharisaic Ideas of God and Israel," 2. 103–29; Jacob Neusner, "The Rabbinic Traditions about the Pharisees before A.D. 70: The Problem of Oral Transmission," 2. 155–72; Ellis Rivkin, "Defining the Pharisees: The Tannaitic Sources," 2. 173–217; idem, "Pharisaism and the Crisis of the Individual in the Greco-Roman World," 2. 219–45; Cecil Roth, "The Pharisees in the Jewish Revolution of 66–73," 2. 255–72;

Daniel R. Schwartz, "Josephus and Nicolaus on the Pharisees," 2. 327–41; Morton Smith, "The Description of the Essenes in Josephus and the Philosophumena," 2. 343–83; Solomon Zeitlin, "The Origin of the Pharisees Reaffirmed," 2. 471–83; idem, "The Pharisees and the Gospels," 2. 485–536. Other works include I. Abrahams, *Studies in Pharisaism and the Gospels* (New York: Ktav, 1967, originally 1917, 1924); Richard Laqueur, *Der jüdische Historiker Flavius Josephus* (Darmstadt: Wissenschaftliche Buchgesellschaft, 1970, originally 1920); Robert Travers Herford, *The Pharisees* (Boston: Beacon, 1924, 1952); George Foot Moore, *Judaism in the First Centuries of the Christian Era. The Age of the Tannaim* (2 vols.; New York: Schocken, 1971; originally 1927, 1930); Ben Zion Bokser, *Pharisaic Judaism in Transition* (New York: Arno, 1973, originally 1935); Louis Finkelstein, *The Pharisees. The Sociological Background of Their Faith* (2 vols.; 2d rev. ed.; Philadelphia: Jewish Publication Society of America, 1940); Hugo Odeberg, *Pharisaism and Christianity* (St. Louis: Concordia, 1964; Swedish original, 1943); Leo Baeck, "The Pharisees," *The Pharisees and Other Essays* (New York: Schocken, 1947) 3–50; W. D. Davies, *Introduction to Pharisaism* (FBBS 16; Philadelphia: Fortress, 1967, originally 1954); idem, *The Setting of the Sermon on the Mount* (Cambridge: Cambridge University, 1963); Morton Smith, "Palestinian Judaism in the First Century," *Essays in Greco-Roman and Related Talmudic Literature* (ed. Henry A. Fischel; New York: Ktav, 1977, essay originally 1956); A. F. J. Klijn, "Scribes, Pharisees, Highpriests and Elders in the New Testament," *NovT* 3 (1959) 259–67; Claude Gruber-Magitot, *Jésus et les pharisiens* (Paris: Robert Laffont, 1964); Asher Finkel, *The Pharisees and the Teacher of Nazareth* (Arbeiten zur Geschichte des Spätjudentums und Urchristentums 4; Leiden/Cologne: Brill, 1964); A. Michel and J. Le Moyne, "Pharisiens," *DBSup*, 7 (1966) 1022–1115; John Bowker, *Jesus and the Pharisees* (Cambridge: Cambridge University, 1973); Clemens Thoma, "Der Pharisäismus," *Literatur und Religion des Frühjudentums* (ed. Johann Maier and Josef Schreiner; Würzburg: Echter/Mohn, 1973) 254–72; Rudolf Meyer and H. F. Weiss, *"Pharisaios," TDNT* 9 (1974) 11–48; Solomon Zeitlin, "Jesus and the Pharisees," *Jewish Expressions on Jesus. An Anthology* (ed. Trude Weiss-Rosmarin; New York: Ktav, 1977) 148–56; Ellis Rivkin, *A Hidden Revolution* (Nashville: Abingdon, 1978); Peter Schäfer, "Einleitung," *Studien zur Geschichte und Theologie des rabbinischen Judentums* (AGJU 15; Leiden: Brill, 1978) 1–22; idem, "Zur Geschichtsauffassung des rabbinischen Judentums," ibid., 23–44; idem, "Die sogenannte Synode von Jabne," ibid., 45–65; idem, "Das 'Dogma' von der mündlichen Torah im rabbinischen Judentum," ibid., 153–97; idem, "Die Torah der messianischen Zeit," ibid., 198–213; Shaye J. D. Cohen, *Josephus in Galilee and Rome. His Vita and Development as a Historian* (Columbia Studies in the Classical Tradition 8; Leiden: Brill, 1979); idem, *From the Maccabees to the Mishnah* (Library of Early Christianity 7; Philadelphia: Westminster, 1987) 143–64; Jacob Neusner (with Alan J. Avery-Peck), "The Quest for the Historical Hillel: Theory and Practice," *Formative Judaism. Religious, Historical, and Literary Studies* (Brown Judaic Studies 37; Chico, CA: Scholars, 1982) 45–63; idem, "Literature and Society: The Unfolding Literary Conventions of Hillel," ibid., 87–97; Jacob Neusner, "The Pharisees in the Light of the Historical Sources of Judaism," ibid., 71–83; idem, "The Myth of the Two Torahs: A Prolegomenon," *Formative*

Judaism: Religious, Historical and Literary Studies. Third Series: Torah, Pharisees, and Rabbis (Brown Judaic Studies 46; Chico, CA: Scholars, 1983) 7–11; idem, "The Meaning of *Torah shebeʿal Peh,* with Special Reference to Mishnah Tractates Kelim and Ohalot," ibid., 13–33; idem, "Josephus's Pharisees: A Complete Repertoire," ibid., 61–82; idem, "Judaism after the Destruction of the Temple," ibid., 83–98; idem, "The Formation of Rabbinic Judaism: Methodological Issues and Substantive Theses," ibid., 99–144; Gary G. Porton, "Diversity in Postbiblical Judaism," *Early Judaism and Its Modern Interpreters* (ed. Robert A. Kraft and George W. E. Nickelsburg; Atlanta: Scholars, 1986) 57–80; Irving M. Zeitlin, *Jesus and the Judaism of His Time* (Cambridge/New York: Polity/Blackwell, 1988); John Kampen, *The Hasideans and the Origin of Pharisaism. A Study in 1 and 2 Maccabees* (SBLSCS 24; Atlanta: Scholars, 1988); Seth Schwartz, *Josephus and Judaean Politics* (Columbia Studies in the Classical Tradition 18; Leiden: Brill, 1990); Alan F. Segal, *Paul the Convert. The Apostolate and Apostasy of Saul the Pharisee* (New Haven/London: Yale University, 1990); Lawrence H. Schiffman, *From Text to Tradition. A History of Second Temple and Rabbinic Judaism* (Hoboken, NJ: Ktav, 1991) 103–12; Ruqaiyyah Waris Maqsood, *The Separated Ones. Jesus, the Pharisees and Islam* (London: SCM, 1991); Steve Mason, *Flavius Josephus on the Pharisees. A Composition-Critical Study* (SPB 39; Leiden: Brill, 1991); Peter Schäfer, "Der vorrabbinische Pharisäismus," *Paulus und das antike Judentum* (ed. Martin Hengel and Ulrich Heckel; WUNT 58; Tübingen: Mohr [Siebeck], 1991) 125–75; Martin Hengel, "Der vorchristliche Paulus," ibid., 177–293; Roland Deines, *Jüdische Steingefässe und pharisäische Frömmigkeit* (WUNT 2/52; Tübingen: Mohr [Siebeck], 1993); Hannah Safrai, "Jesus und die Pharisäer," *Lernen in Jerusalem—Lernen mit Israel* (Veröffentlichungen aus dem Institut Kirche und Judentum 20; ed. Martin Stöhr; Berlin: Institut Kirche und Judentum, 1993) 50–58; David Goodblatt, *The Monarchic Principle. Studies in Jewish Self-Government in Antiquity* (Texte und Studien zum antiken Judentum 38; Tübingen: Mohr [Siebeck], 1994); Klaus-Stefan Krieger, *Geschichtsschreibung als Apologetik* (Texte und Arbeiten zum neutestamentlichen Zeitalter 9; Tübingen/Basel: Francke, 1994); Alan Watson, *Jesus and the Jews. The Pharisaic Tradition in John* (Athens, GA/London: University of Georgia, 1995); idem, *Jesus and the Law* (Athens, GA/London: University of Georgia, 1996); John C. Poirier, "Why Did the Pharisees Wash Their Hands?" *JSJ* 47 (1996) 217–33; Joseph Sievers, "Who Were the Pharisees?" *Hillel and Jesus* (ed. James H. Charlesworth and Loren L. Johns; Minneapolis: Fortress, 1997) 137–55; Joel Marcus, "Scripture and Tradition in Mark 7," *The Scriptures in the Gospels* (BETL 81; ed. C. M. Tuckett; Leuven: Leuven University/Peeters, 1997) 177–95; Lester L. Grabbe, "Sadducees and Pharisees," *Judaism in Late Antiquity. Part Three. Where We Stand: Issues and Debates in Ancient Judaism. Volume One* (Handbook of Oriental Studies, Part One, The Near and Middle East 40; ed. Jacob Neusner and Alan J. Avery-Peck; Leiden: Brill, 1999) 35–62. For bibliography on Josephus and the Pharisees, see Louis H. Feldman, *Josephus and Modern Scholarship* (New York/Berlin: de Gruyter, 1984) 551–75; idem, *Josephus. A Supplementary Bibliography* (New York/London: Garland, 1986).

In general, one may observe that most of the Christian presentations of the Pharisees earlier in this century were uncritical in that they took at face value the presentations of the Gospels and then tried to harmonize them as best they could with the works of Josephus and the rabbinic literature (if, indeed, the latter two corpora were even used). The result was more often Christian theology than historical description: the unique goodness of Jesus' gospel of grace had to be highlighted by being set over against the legalistic, "works-righteousness" religion of the Pharisees. Worse still, uncritical acceptance of ancient anti-Jewish polemic was sometimes mixed with modern anti-Semitism. While certainly not anti-Semitic, Christian scholars as different as Rudolf Bultmann and Joachim Jeremias fell prey in various ways to a certain apologetic tendency. Christian scholars who reacted against these negative caricatures of Pharisees (e.g., Robert Travers Herford, George Foot Moore, John Bowker) fell ironically into the opposite problem of uncritically adopting the approach of older Jewish scholars. On the Jewish side, there was naturally much better use of the rabbinic literature and, to a certain degree, Josephus; but various sources were often synthesized and harmonized without critical concern for the dating of the sources, the literary forms employed, the problem of authorial bias, and the ultimate question of historical usefulness in describing the pre-70 period. All too often, the Pharisees would be swiftly equated with the "sages" and the "scribes," so that most of the tannaitic material wound up being treated as Pharisaic. Attributions to particular teachers would be accepted without questioning, and the teacher would be declared (or assumed) to be a Pharisee on the basis of generally accepted tradition. Similarly, traditions about the pre-70 sages or the tannaitic rabbis that were attested only in the Talmuds were taken as historically reliable. Even the Gospels, while purged of their anti-Jewish polemic, were cited uncritically for the positions of the historical Jesus. At times, the 19th- and 20th-century struggles among Orthodox, Conservative, and Reform Jews would shine through what was supposed to be a description of the struggles between the Pharisees and the Sadducees at the turn of the era. Happily, the work of scholars like Neusner, Cohen, Goodblatt, and Goodman on the Jewish side and of scholars like Smith, Sanders, and Saldarini on the Christian side—for all the many differences among them—has marked a much more historically critical period in research on the Pharisees in particular and on ancient Judaism in general. On all this, see the brief review of scholarship by Saldarini in "Pharisees," 289–91; also the older review by Marcus in "The Pharisees," 390–95.

[5] The reader may remember that, in Volume One of *A Marginal Jew,* I mentioned that, instead of having one chapter on the history of Jewish Palestine around the turn of the era at the beginning of the entire work, I decided that it would be more useful to intersperse reviews of historical background throughout the work as they proved relevant to particular topics. Hence, in this section, I offer a historical review from the perspective of the major Jewish groups or parties.

[6] One possible interpretation of the history of strife within Israel from the time of the Judges down to Antiochus Epiphanes can be found in Morton Smith, *Palestinian Parties and Politics that Shaped the Old Testament* (2d ed.; London: SCM, 1987).

[7] See, e.g., the speculative reconstruction of Paul D. Hanson, *The Dawn of Apocalyptic* (rev. ed.; Philadelphia: Fortress, 1979); cf. Joseph Blenkinsopp, "Interpretation

and the Tendency to Sectarianism: An Aspect of Second Temple History," *Jewish and Christian Self-Definition. Volume Two. Aspects of Judaism in the Graeco-Roman Period* (ed. E. P. Sanders, A. I. Baumgarten, and Alan Mendelson; Philadelphia: Fortress, 1981) 1–26, esp. 13; idem, "A Jewish Sect of the Persian Period," *CBQ* 52 (1990) 5–20.

[8] See in particular Martin Hengel, *Judaism and Hellenism* (2 vols.; Minneapolis: Fortress, 1974); Blenkinsopp, "Interpretation and the Tendency to Sectarianism," 1–26. As Porton observes ("Diversity," 58), "the issue . . . was not Hellenism per se; rather, the issue must have been to determine exactly when one had become *too* Hellenized."

[9] The first members of the Hasmonean dynasty are often referred to as the Maccabean rulers, though the adjective is not accurate. As far as we know, only Judas bore the title "Maccabeus" (see *Ant.* 12.6.1 §266). The original meaning of this title or nickname is disputed; "hammer" is a popular explanation. Contrary to a number of assertions by Josephus (*Ant.* 12.10.6 §414, 419; 12.11.2 §434), but in accordance with his more reliable statement in *Ant.* 20.10.3 §237, Judas never ruled formally as high priest (let alone king). The rulers of the dynasty that was gradually set up after him are more properly called "Hasmonean," after the supposed name of the great-grandfather of Mattathias, the father of Judas (at least this is what Josephus tells us in *Ant.* 12.6.1 §265). Whether that is the true origin of the name is disputed; "Hasmonean" may have originally derived from a place name such as Heshmon or Hashmonah. Interestingly, the books of the Maccabees know only the word "Maccabeus," not "Hasmonean"; Josephus knows both words; and the rabbinic literature uses only "Hasmonean," in the form of *běnê ḥašmônā'î* ("the sons of Ḥashmonai"; see, e.g., *m. Mid.* 1:6). Needless to say, Josephus' account of the Hasmonean dynasty must be used with due attention to his redactional tendencies and the resulting adaptation of his sources; see Louis H. Feldman, "Josephus' Portrayal of the Hasmoneans Compared with 1 Maccabees," *Josephus and the History of the Greco-Roman Period* (Morton Smith Memorial; SPB 41; ed. Fausto Parente and Joseph Sievers; Leiden: Brill, 1994) 41–68.

[10] The precise extent of the Hellenization of Hasmonean rule and its deeper meaning for the Hasmoneans' commitment to Judaism remain a subject of scholarly debate. One must allow that real history is a messy matter and that it is quite possible that the Hasmonean rulers combined a Hellenizing policy in some areas with great fidelity to Judaism—as they interpreted it—in other areas. On this, see Albert I. Baumgarten, "Invented Traditions of the Maccabean Era," *Geschichte—Tradition—Reflexion. Band I. Judentum* (Martin Hengel Festschrift; ed. Hubert Cancik, Hermann Lichtenberger, and Peter Schäfer; Tübingen: Mohr [Siebeck], 1996) 197–210.

[11] On this, see Jean Le Moyne, *Les Sadducéens* (EBib; Paris: Gabalda, 1972) 384–85; Le Moyne thinks that this was one of the major reasons for Pharisaic opposition to the Hasmoneans.

[12] Solomon Zeitlin ("The Origin of the Pharisees," 471–83) holds that the Pharisees arose shortly after the restoration, "i.e., during the latter part of the fifth century BCE." This is echoed by Irving M. Zeitlin, *Jesus and the Judaism of His Time,* 16. This approach continues the uncritical tendencies of ancient authors who sought to make certain religious movements respectable by making them ancient, whatever the facts of the case. A prime example is Josephus' claim (*Ant.* 18.1.2 §11) that the Jews "from the most ancient times" had three philosophies: Pharisees, Sadducees, and Essenes. In a similar vein, Pliny the Elder (*Natural History* 5.15 §73) states that the Essenes have existed "through thousands of ages"—a claim not too many historians would care to support today.

[13] Josephus never gives a precise date for the rise of the various Jewish movements or "schools of thought," perhaps because he did not know or perhaps because the rise of the schools involved a gradual process that defies exact dating. On the whole question, see Albert I. Baumgarten, *The Flourishing of Jewish Sects in the Maccabean Era: An Interpretation* (Supplements to *JSJ* 55; Leiden: Brill, 1997) 15–33. In the *War,* the Pharisees first appear, without much of an introduction, at the time of Salome Alexandra (ruled 76–69; see *J. W.* 1.5.2 §110). The great essay on the four Jewish "schools" (the Fourth Philosophy, Essenes, Pharisees, and Sadducees) does not appear in the *War* until the end of the reign of the ethnarch Archelaus and the setting up of a Roman province in Judea in A.D. 6 (*J. W.* 2.8.1 §117). In *Ant.* 13.5.9 §171, a very short essay on the Pharisees, the Sadducees, and the Essenes appears parenthetically during the reign of the Hasmonean Jonathan (ruled 160–143). That the Pharisees and the Sadducees were already active as powerful political parties is seen from the story of why John Hyrcanus (ruled 134–104) switched allegiance from the Pharisees to the Sadducees (*Ant.* 13.10.5 §288–98). The third essay on the "schools" occurs in the *Antiquities,* as in the *War,* after the deposition of Archelaus (*Ant.* 13.1.1 §4); as in the *War,* the Fourth Philosophy is included, only to be distinguished from the three ancient and respectable schools.

[14] The *Book of Jubilees* may be read as a last-gasp attempt by a priest of Essene tendencies to vindicate the old solar calendar for the Jerusalem temple and so to avoid the kind of schism we see at Qumran. Such a schism, in fact, occurred soon afterwards, perhaps because the Hasmoneans made clear that they were holding on to both the high priesthood and the (solar-)lunar calendar, recently introduced into the temple liturgy. (One must allow, however, for a previous, less structured schism involving at least some Essenes who distanced themselves from the Jerusalem establishment.) If, with James C. VanderKam, one favors a dating of *Jubilees* between 161–152 B.C., the Qumran schism may be placed somewhere around 150. On this, see James C. VanderKam, *Textual and Historical Studies in the Book of Jubilees* (HSM 14; Missoula, MT: Scholars, 1977) 287–88; idem, "The Origin, Character, and Early History of the 364-Day Calendar: A Reassessment of Jaubert's Hypothesis," *CBQ* 41 (1979) 390–411; idem, "The Putative Author of the Book of Jubilees," *JSS* 26 (1981) 209–17; idem, "2 Maccabees 6,7A and Calendrical Change in Jerusalem," *JSJ* 12 (1981) 52–74; idem, "Jubilees, Book of," *Anchor Bible Dictionary,* 3.

1030–32; cf. John J. Collins, *The Apocalyptic Imagination* (New York: Crossroad, 1987) 63–67. For a slightly different view, see George W. E. Nickelsburg, *Jewish Literature between the Bible and the Mishnah* (Philadelphia: Fortress, 1981) 73–80; Nickelsburg, however, still places *Jubilees* before the founding of Qumran. Recent research on calendars at Qumran makes it clear that, while *Jubilees* rejects a solar calendar, both solar and lunar factors figured into calendrical considerations at Qumran, thus reflecting what is found in *1 Enoch;* on this, see James C. VanderKam, *Calendars in the Dead Sea Scrolls: Measuring Time* (The Literature of the Dead Sea Scrolls: London/New York: Routledge, 1998). In my remarks on the Essenes and Qumran, I am well aware that the precise relationship between the Essenes as a whole and the special group of Essenes at Qumran is still very much debated. (Indeed, some still question whether the Qumranites were Essenes.) Hence I keep my observations as brief and general as possible, especially since, as I shall indicate below (chapter 30, section I), there is no proof that Jesus ever interacted with the Essenes or Qumran—thus obviating a detailed treatment in *A Marginal Jew.*

[15] See, e.g., Finkelstein, *The Pharisees*, 2. 573; Marcus, "The Pharisees in the Light of Modern Scholarship," 388; cf. the revised Schürer, *The History of the Jewish People,* 2. 401.

[16] A number of scholars suggest that Jonathan is the "Wicked Priest" mentioned in the Qumran documents (see 1QpHab 8:8; 9:9; 11:4; 4QpPs[a] [= 4QpPs 37] 4:8); the many candidates are listed by Murphy-O'Connor ("The Judean Desert," 139–40), who considers Jonathan to be "the current favorite"; cf. Joseph A. Fitzmyer, *Responses to 101 Questions on the Dead Sea Scrolls* (New York/Mahwah, NJ: Paulist, 1992) 91. A different point of view is offered by Florentino García Martínez (*The Dead Sea Scrolls Translated* [2d ed.; Leiden: Brill; Grand Rapids, Eerdmans, 1996] lv), who holds that the "Wicked Priest" was a title "applied to the various Hasmonean High Priests, from Judas Maccabaeus [?] to Alexander Jannaeus. . . ."

[17] In favor of tracing the Pharisees back to the Hasideans is Hengel, "Der vorchristliche Paulus," 226.

[18] See Cohen, *From the Maccabees to the Mishnah,* 161. Schiffman (*From Text to Tradition,* 104) discounts the origin of the Pharisees from the Hasideans, who were probably not a party or a sect, but simply a loose association of pious Jews; cf. Porton, "Diversity," 61.

[19] For a review of the literature and a discussion of the whole question, see Kampen, *The Hasideans.* Kampen points out how little we know of the group called the Hasideans, apparently a scribal leadership group in Jerusalem who were galvanized into revolt not by a general "crisis of Hellenization" but by the specific steps taken by Antiochus IV against circumcision, sabbath, and the temple cult. Kampen rejects any connection of the Hasideans with the Essenes, but thinks it probable that in the scribal circles of the Hasideans lie the origins of the later movement known as Phari-

saism. That may well be; but, when one remembers that the only testimony we have about *hoi Asidaioi* ("the Hasideans") is the scant information found in 1 Macc 2:42; 7:12–17; and 2 Macc 14:6, one must remain cautious about creating connections between a group that is glimpsed for a fleeting moment during the revolt of Judas Maccabeus and a political-religious party that emerges sometime later on during the reign of the early Hasmonean rulers. Kampen appeals to the "early Hasidim" *(ḥăsîdîm hāri'šōnîm)* mentioned in the rabbinic literature (e.g., *m. Ber.* 5:1) to fill out the picture of the Hasideans and to build an argument in favor of connecting the Maccabean Hasideans with the later Pharisees; not everyone will find this approach convincing.

[20] As Jerome Murphy-O'Connor notes, William Foxwell Albright suggested a Babylonian origin for the Essenes in *From Stone Age to Christianity* (2d ed.; Garden City, NY: Doubleday, 1957) 376. Murphy-O'Connor himself is one of the most prominent proponents of such a view in recent years. See his magisterial essay on reconstructing the history of the Essenes, "The Essenes and Their History," *RB* 81 (1974) 215–44; idem, "The Judean Desert," *Early Judaism and Its Modern Interpreters* (ed. Robert A. Kraft and George W. E. Nickelsburg; Atlanta: Scholars, 1986) 119–56, esp. 139–43. In critical dialogue with Murphy-O'Connor is Philip R. Davies, *Behind the Essenes. History and Ideology in the Dead Sea Scrolls* (Brown Judaic Studies 94; Atlanta: Scholars, 1987). In my opinion, attempts to reconstruct the history of the Essenes—and of Judaism in general just before the turn of the era—from the Dead Sea Scrolls labor under two difficulties: (1) decoding the many cryptic or symbolic references in the Qumran documents, which are open to various interpretations; and (2) producing a theory of the relative chronology of the documents and of the various sources within the documents that can command general agreement among scholars. As far as dating is concerned, I think that these difficulties have not been overcome and perhaps cannot be overcome without new archaeological and literary discoveries that could act as external controls on hypotheses. Hence I do not make a great deal of use of the Dead Sea Scrolls in my attempt to sketch the history of the period that produced the Pharisees and the Sadducees.

[21] See Rivkin, "Pharisaism and the Crisis of the Individual," 223–26.

[22] This paragraph must be understood as a generalizing statement about basic outlook and tendencies. Existing as they did for over 200 years, the Essenes no doubt developed and subdivided into various groups (apparently including both celibate and married Essenes), the prime example of division being the Qumranites.

[23] The exact nature of the Essenes' participation in or exclusion from the sacrificial cult of the Jerusalem temple is debated among contemporary scholars because of the paucity and contradictory nature of the evidence. It may well be that Essene practice varied depending upon the prevailing religious and political circumstances during the roughly 200-year period we are reviewing.

[24] I consider the account of this event (involving Yannai, i.e., Alexander Jannaeus, not John Hyrcanus) in *b. Qidd.* 66a to be a secondary, garbled version of the story found in Josephus. According to Josephus, Hyrcanus, a disciple of the Pharisees, holds a banquet for the Pharisees at which he asks them to offer any criticism they may have of his way of life. The Pharisees instead praise him, while a certain Eleazar (*not* called a Pharisee by Josephus) purposely sows dissension by suggesting that Hyrcanus give up the high priesthood because of rumors that he was born illegitimate. Since the rumors are false, Hyrcanus becomes furious; and *all* the Pharisees become indignant (hence we may conclude that Eleazar is not one of them). Then Jonathan, a Sadducee, falsely tells Hyrcanus that Eleazar uttered his slander with the approval of the Pharisees. Jonathan spurs Hyrcanus on to test the Pharisees by asking them what punishment Eleazar deserves. The Pharisees, being lenient on the subject of punishment, suggest scourging and chains. Hyrcanus, thinking that the offense deserves the death penalty, concludes angrily from the leniency of the Pharisees that they had approved of Eleazar's slander. Jonathan fans Hyrcanus' anger and so induces him to join the party of the Sadducees.

When this coherent story is compared to the version found in the Talmud, one notices three reasons for considering the talmudic version secondary: (1) The talmudic version of the story does not make sense as it stands; there is a lacuna in the flow of the narrative. To make sense of the narrative, one must supply the element of the Pharisees suggesting only scourging, not execution, as the penalty for the man who insulted the king; this element is found only in Josephus' version of the story. (2) The end of the talmudic story reflects the rabbinic doctrine of the dual Torah, oral as well as written, a doctrine that, as far as we can tell, was not enunciated in the pre-70 period; indeed, it was not fully developed before the two Talmuds. (3) Elsewhere in the Talmud, Abaye, the rabbinic sage (ca. A.D. 280–339) who tells this story about "Yannai," is said to have claimed that John Hyrcanus and Alexander Jannaeus were the same person (*b. Ber.* 29a). Taken together, these three points offer strong evidence that the talmudic version of the story is a late, secondary, and confused reworking of the story in Josephus, be the dependence direct or indirect. It is also possible, though not likely, that both Josephus and the talmudic story are dependent on some (now lost) common source; see Neusner, "Josephus's Pharisees," 61–82, esp. 71–75. Le Moyne (*Les Sadducéens,* 51–59) favors the idea of a common source; much less likely is his opinion (put forth with hesitation) that the Talmud is correct in assigning the rupture with the Pharisees to the reign of Jannaeus. On the whole question, see Albert I. Baumgarten, "Rabbinic Literature as a Source for the History of Jewish Sectarianism in the Second Temple Period," *Dead Sea Discoveries* 2 (1995) 16–57.

In any event, the details of the anecdote in Josephus may to a certain extent be legendary and are best not pressed. It should be emphasized, though, that the story as presented by Josephus does not put the blame for the break with Hyrcanus on the Pharisees, who are singled out as being by nature lenient on the subject of punishment (§294). Moreover, Eleazar, the troublemaker in the story, is *not* identified as a Pharisee (contrary to the summaries given by some authors); indeed, *all* the Pharisees (§292) are indignant with him. This is perhaps one example of the mixed picture of the Pharisees in the *Antiquities* (note the negative statement about them at the beginning of the anecdote in §288). It does not support Mason's thesis *(Flavius Josephus on the Pharisees)* that Josephus' picture of the Pharisees is negative throughout his works.

²⁵ That the Pharisees actually unleashed a bloody civil war against Alexander Jannaeus is asserted sometimes by modern historians writing on the period; so Hengel, "Der vorchristliche Paulus," 177–293, esp. 246. Actually, to arrive at this position, one must read between the lines of Josephus; see Moore, *Judaism,* 1. 63–65; Sanders, *Judaism. Practice & Belief,* 380–81 (who gives here a good summary of the reasons for thinking that the Pharisees were involved in leading the opposition to Jannaeus); see also his *Jewish Law from Jesus to the Mishnah,* 86. In any case, it seems probable that the Pharisees acted as an opposition party all the way from the last days of Hyrcanus through the reigns of Aristobulus I and Jannaeus down to the beginning of Salome Alexandra's reign.

²⁶ This is the opinion of Le Moyne, *Les Sadducéens,* 46–48. He admits, though, that his view is contrary to the majority opinion. Part of the problem in this dispute is that Josephus' narrative of this period is less than crystal clear. For instance, it is unclear from *Ant.* 14.1.2 §4–7 and *War* 1.6.1 §120–122 whether Aristobulus forced Hyrcanus to give up the high priesthood as well as the kingship. However, *Ant.* 14.6.1 §97 and 20.10.4 §243–244 indicate that Aristobulus did become high priest in the place of Hyrcanus. The latter passage also tells us that, after Pompey arrested Aristobulus and sent him to Rome, he restored Hyrcanus to the high priesthood. See Schäfer, *The History of the Jews in Antiquity,* 76–78. A complete reconstruction of the course of events depends, admittedly, on reading between the lines in Josephus. It remains possible that, in this very fluid and unstable period, some Jews refused to recognize Aristobulus as the legitimate high priest. See also Sanders, *Judaism. Practice & Belief,* 383; but compare the doubts of Moore, *Judaism,* 1. 72. For the view that "the Sadducean hierarchy" fought on the side of Aristobulus to the bitter end, see Günther Baumbach, "Der sadduzäische Konservativismus," *Literatur und Religion des Frühjudentums* (ed. Johann Maier and Josef Schreiner; Würzburg: Echter/Mohn, 1973) 201–13, esp. 206.

²⁷ For the killing of "all those in the Sanhedrin and Hyrcanus himself, except for Samaias," see *Ant.* 14.9.4 §175; for the slaughter of the 45 leading members of Antigonus' party *(hairesis),* see *Ant.* 15.1.2 §6. On this problem, see Baumbach, "Der sadduzäische Konservativismus," 206.

²⁸ The story is told briefly in *J.W.* 1.22.2 §437 and more fully in *Ant.* 15.3.3 §50–56.

²⁹ On various types of associations in the Greco-Roman world, see Frederick W. Danker, "Associations, Clubs, Thiasoi," *Anchor Bible Dictionary,* 1. 501–3; also the

various essays in John S. Kloppenborg and Stephen G. Wilson (eds.), *Voluntary Associations in the Graeco-Roman World* (London/ New York: Routledge, 1996).

[30] On this, see E. P. Sanders, *The Historical Figure of Jesus* (London: Penguin, 1993); idem, *Judaism. Practice & Belief*, 387.

[31] For the defense of this view, see Goodblatt, *The Monarchic Principle*, 6–29. See also Sanders, *Judaism. Practice & Belief*, 388.

[32] On this, see *A Marginal Jew*, 2. 171–76.

[33] The extent of Pharisaic presence in Galilee (if any existed) is still debated among scholars. Sean Freyne (*Galilee from Alexander the Great to Hadrian 323 B.C.E. to 135 C.E.* [University of Notre Dame Center for the Study of Judaism and Christianity in Antiquity 5; Wilmington, DE: Glazier; Notre Dame, IN: University of Notre Dame, 1980] 305–34) is willing to accept at least part of the Gospel picture of some Pharisees (of a non-rigid type) present and active in Galilee, while Richard A. Horsley (*Archaeology, History, and Society in Galilee* [Valley Forge, PA: Trinity, 1996] 151–53) for the most part rejects the idea of Pharisees active in the synagogues of Galilee in the pre-70 period as a Christian construct. For the view that Pharisees were not active to any great degree in Galilee in the pre-70 period, see Morton Smith, *Jesus the Magician* (San Francisco: Harper & Row, 1978) 157; Cohen, *Josephus in Galilee and Rome*, 226; Neusner, "Preface," *Origins of Judaism*, 1. x; the revised Schürer (*The History of the Jewish People*, 2. 329–31) takes a similar view of the "Torah scholars" or scribes. Saldarini (*Pharisees, Scribes and Sadducees*, 291–97) surveys the various views and arguments and concludes that the evidence "is too ambiguous to permit a certain conclusion concerning the Pharisees' presence in Galilee" in the pre-70 period. He suggests that, "if they were there, they were a minor and probably relatively new social force. . . ." (Yet he seems a little more confident about the Pharisees' presence in pre-70 Galilee in his article "Pharisees," 295). For the view that literate residents of cities in the Hellenistic age were the pool from which members of ancient Jewish sects were drawn, see A. I. Baumgarten, "He Knew that He Knew that He Knew that He Was an Essene," *JJS* 48 (1997) 53–61, esp. 59. This coheres with Josephus' remark that *the cities* bear witness to the virtue of the Pharisees (*Ant.* 18.1.3. §15).

[34] It is for this reason that I do not dwell on the situation in Galilee in this subsection but rather focus on Judea, where Pharisees certainly did exist. On the question of the political and religious situation in Galilee during the reign of Herod Antipas, see the convenient summary in E. P. Sanders, "Jesus in Historical Context," *TToday* 50 (1993) 429–48, esp. 438–41.

[35] On the problem of the exact extent of the prefect/procurator's authority in capital cases, see the revised Schürer, *The History of the Jewish People*, 1. 367–72.

[36] See *Ant.* 20.10.5 §251: After the death of Herod and the removal of Archelaus, "the form of government [in Judea] was an aristocracy, and the high priests were entrusted with the leadership of the people." On this, see the revised Schürer, *The History of the Jewish People,* 1. 376–77; Sanders, *Judaism. Practice & Belief,* 485–90. In the period from A.D. 6 to 41, the high priest was appointed by the competent Roman governor, either the legate of Syria or the prefect of Judea.

[37] See Baumbach, "Der sadduzäische Konservativismus," 208. Even Le Moyne, who usually accepts at face value the claim of Josephus and the rabbinic literature that the Sadducees had to submit to the regulations of the Pharisees in matters of temple and worship, allows that the Sadducees regained some power under direct Roman rule and that the Pharisees did not have control of Jewish life in Jerusalem during this period; see *Les Sadducéens,* 393–98. How this squares with Le Moyne's picture of the Sadducees and the Pharisees elsewhere in his book is not clear.

[38] The difference here may be due, at least in part, to Tiberius' preference for keeping provincial governors in office for long periods of time. Various reasons are given for this preference by Tacitus (*Annals* 1.80; cf. 3.69; 6.39) and Josephus (*Ant.* 18.6.5 §172–176): e.g., a preference for making a single long-term decision instead of facing recurring problems, a mean-spirited desire not to have too many people enjoy high positions, his desire to send potential rivals away from Rome for lengthy periods of time, a fatalism about humanity's proneness to corruption and extortion, and a belief that, by leaving a single man in office for many years, extortion would be moderated because the perpetrator would become sated. The most likely reason, according to Robin Seager (*Tiberius* [Berkeley/Los Angeles: University of California, 1972] 173–74), is that Tiberius disliked decision-making and change for the sake of change. Hence Seager thinks that Tiberius preferred to leave "competent and unambitious men," once they had been found, in office as long as possible. This policy would argue in favor of Pilate's basic competence. One must admit, though, that Tiberius may simply have been less interested in the provinces than was Augustus. On the increasing "frozen sluggishness" of Tiberius' governance of the provinces, see Michael Grant, *The Roman Emperors* (New York: Scribner's Sons, 1985) 24. Still, whatever Tiberius' reasons, Valerius Gratus and Pontius Pilate would not have been kept in office for so long if they had been bungling incompetents who constantly created problems for Rome.

[39] On the military standards, see *J. W.* 2.9.2–3 §169–74; *Ant.* 18.3.1 §55–59; Philo in his *Embassy* 38 §299–305 probably refers to the same incident, though the matter is not entirely clear. On the aqueduct, see *J. W.* 2.9.4 §175–77; *Ant.* 18.3.2 §60–62. The classic study on Pilate is by Jean-Pierre Lémonon, *Pilate et le gouvernement de la Judée. Textes et monuments* (EBib; Paris: Gabalda, 1981). Actually, the number of major clashes between Pilate and the Jews of Judea is relatively small, granted his ten-year rule in a very difficult border province. A milder, revisionist view of Pilate is espoused by Brian C. McGing, "Pontius Pilate and the Sources," *CBQ* 53 (1991) 416–38. For a balanced assessment of the position of the high priest, see Sanders,

Judaism. Practice & Belief, 458–94; see also Baumbach, "Der sadduzäische Konservativismus," 208–9.

[40] See, e.g., *J.W.* 2.8.14 §162; *Ant.* 13.10.5 §288; 13.15.5–13.16.1 §401–406; 18.1.3 §15; 18.1.4 §17. Three points should be noted about these passages: (1) The context often suggests that Josephus is lamenting rather than celebrating the Pharisees' influence over the common people. (2) Josephus may at times exaggerate the influence of the pre-70 Pharisees in view of their ascendancy in the post-70 period. (3) The one passage (*Ant.* 18.1.4 §17) in which Josephus claims that Sadducees entering public office must obey the regulations of the Pharisees because of the latter's influence on the common people is most likely an exaggeration since (a) it is not made in any of the other passages describing the Pharisees' influence and (b) it does not jibe with many of Josephus' own narratives. Nevertheless, as Cohen points out (*From the Maccabees to the Mishnah,* 163), although the post-70 NT writings, Josephus, and the rabbinic corpus all tend to exaggerate the power of the Pharisees (e.g., they sit in the chair of Moses, even the Sadducees must follow their rules, they control the Sanhedrin), even these exaggerations tell us something: (1) That all three bodies of literature, for all their exaggerations, would agree on choosing the Pharisees as the powerful group indicates the Pharisees must have enjoyed some sort of authority or influence among the Jewish people even before 70. (2) The agreement of all three *post-70* bodies of literature in focusing on the Pharisees (e.g., the agreement of Matthew and John in portraying the Pharisees as the great adversaries of Jesus and therefore of the churches of their own day) points to an organic connection between the pre-70 Pharisees and the proto-rabbinic movement after 70.

[41] See Saldarini, *Pharisees, Scribes and Sadducees,* 4–5, 35–49, 87–88, 99–106. On p. 313, Saldarini defines "retainer class" as "those who served the needs of the ruler and governing class, including soldiers, bureaucratic government officials, educators, religious leaders. They shared the life of the governing class to some extent, but had no independent base of power or wealth (in contrast to the modern middle class)." In all fairness, it should be noted that not all students of the period accept this description of the Pharisees as belonging to the retainer class. If—as I shall argue in the next chapter—a large part of the priestly and lay aristocracy in Jerusalem belonged to or at least favored the Saducean party, it would have been natural, not to say expedient, for many of the bureaucrats and other officials who directly served them to have leaned in that direction as well.

[42] Luke has Gamaliel, speaking sometime in the mid–30s, "remember" the past event of the popular movement led by Theudas, when in fact Theudas formed his following ca. A.D. 44–46, when Cuspius Fadus was procurator of Judea (*Ant.* 20.5.1. §97–99). The Lucan Gamaliel then claims that "after" Theudas there arose Judas the Galilean, who is correctly said to have been active "in the days of the census" (taken by Quirinius), hence in A.D. 6 (*Ant.* 18.1.1 §1–4). To try to harmonize Luke and Josephus (e.g., by claiming that there was an earlier Theudas) or to try to claim that Luke is right and Josephus is wrong is pure apologetics. On the historical problem of

Luke's presentation of Gamaliel, see Bruce Chilton, "Gamaliel," item 2, *Anchor Bible Dictionary*, 2. 904–6; on various solutions, see Barrett, *Acts,* 1. 292–96. Barrett (p. 292) states that it is unclear why Haenchen (*Apostelgeschichte,* 207 n. 2) should doubt that Gamaliel was a Pharisee.

[43] Strictly speaking, there is no absolute proof that the Gamaliel said to be the father of Simeon I in *Life* 38 §190 is the Gamaliel said to be a Pharisee in Acts 5:34. But since the father of the Pharisee Simeon may be presupposed to be a Pharisee as well, since Simeon's father would presumably have been alive and active in Jerusalem around the time of the incident recounted in Acts 5:34, and since a number of passages in the Mishna speak of a famous and respected sage called Rabban Gamaliel the Elder (e.g., *m. Roš. Haš.* 2:5; *m. Giṭ* 4:2; *m. Soṭa* 9:15), apparently active in Jerusalem in the pre-70 period, the deduction seems a reasonable one. The search for the pre-70 Pharisees would be helped if one could be sure that Luke's claim—witnessed nowhere else, including Paul's epistles—that the Pharisee Paul had studied in Jerusalem under the Pharisee Gamaliel I (Acts 22:3) is historically true. Some scholars are willing to accept the claim: e.g., W. C. van Unnik, *Tarsus or Jerusalem* (London: Epworth, 1962); Hengel, "Der vorchristliche Paulus," 177–293, esp. 223. Others (e.g., Schneider, *Die Apostelgeschichte*, 2. 42–43), however, are wary of this claim, found only in a speech obviously constructed by Luke as part of his portrait of Paul. The claim fits perfectly into Luke's apologetic picture of Paul as the true and faithful Jew (see Günther Bornkamm, *Paulus* [Stuttgart: Kohlhammer, 1969] 27). One has to wonder why being a student of Gamaliel—a striking proof of his authentic Jewish credentials—would be omitted by the historical Paul from all the lists of his Jewish traits that he draws up when arguing with his real or hypothetical opponents in Phil 3:5; 2 Cor 11:22; and Rom 11:1. That Paul did receive formal instruction in Jewish Scriptures and Pharisaic tradition while residing in Jerusalem is more than probable from the use of the OT (reflecting various text types) and the mode of theological argumentation found in his epistles. But the connection with Gamaliel must remain a question mark and therefore will not be appealed to in my arguments. I do think, however, that it is more likely than not that Gamaliel I was a Pharisee, as was his son Simeon I. They provide an important linchpin for constructing a connection between the pre-70 Pharisees (including the Houses of Hillel and Shammai) and the post-70 rabbis.

[44] See Goodman, *The Ruling Class,* 164, 183–87, 209, and in general 152–97.

[45] On the difference between Roman prefects and procurators (both usually referred to by the umbrella term "governor"), see *A Marginal Jew,* 1. 100–101 n. 8.

[46] Schwartz (*Josephus and Judaean Politics,* 72–78) thinks that a fair number of priests, including priests from the upper echelons who lived in Galilee, escaped the war unharmed and continued to operate in post-70 Palestine. He goes on to suggest (pp. 87–95) that, while in the *War* Josephus champions the high priests as leaders in a post-70 Palestine, in the *Antiquities* he denigrates the memory of the high priests and favors priests of his own class ("well-to-do lower priests") as candidates for govern-

ing Judaea. This last point is highly speculative. Le Moyne (*Les Sadducéens,* 399) suggests that we have some indications that the Sadducees continued to exist during the century following the destruction of Jerusalem. Unfortunately, as often happens in Le Moyne's book, he argues uncritically from many different strata of rabbinic material, early and late. It may well be that individual Sadducees survived the disaster of 70; the religious-political party of the Sadducees, however, seems to disappear as an influential group after 70.

[47] This is not to claim that all other Jewish groups in Palestine disappeared overnight. It is quite plausible that various remnants of the Sadducees or the Qumranites (even more so, the scattered communities of Essenes) survived the war and continued to live in Palestine. Some of them may have even joined forces with or been assimilated to the Pharisees/proto-rabbis at Yavneh. But of no other group besides the Pharisees can it be said that they survived the war "intact with significant numbers and with the respect of the common people." Bokser (*Pharisaic Judaism in Transition,* 1–3) makes the philosophical/theological argument that, after the disaster of 70, Pharisaism alone, among all the competing Jewish groups, had "survival value amid the new conditions which that disaster had called into being."

[48] Schwartz (*Josephus and Judaean Politics,* 99–109) suggests that some groups of priests may have held themselves aloof from Johanan ben Zakkai at the beginning of the academy of Yavneh after 70 and entered the early rabbinic movement only when Gamaliel II came to power (ca. 85–90). Still other groups of priests may have kept their distance from the Yavnean academy and established their own corporate existence. When one remembers that surviving members of the Herodian family (notably, Agrippa II) were still on the scene and were probably vying for influence with Rome, one realizes how fluid the situation in Palestine immediately after 70 must have been.

[49] The problem of the exact relationship between the pre-70 Pharisees and the post-70 rabbis at Yavneh and how the first may have mutated into the second is hotly debated among scholars today. For a sampling of major approaches and opinions, see the monumental work of Neusner, *The Rabbinic Traditions;* idem, "Mr. Sanders' Pharisees and Mine," *SJT* 44 (1991) 73–95; idem, " 'Pharisaic-Rabbinic' Judaism: A Clarification," 426–46; Cohen, "The Significance of Yavneh," 101–27; idem, *From the Maccabees to the Mishnah,* 154; Stemberger, *Pharisäer, Sadduzäer, Essener;* Schäfer, "Der vorrabbinische Pharisäismus," 125–75; Sanders, *Jewish Law from Jesus to the Mishnah;* idem, *Judaism. Practice & Belief,* 380–451. Cohen (p. 103) warns that scholars often presume "that we know a good deal more about Yavneh than we really do"; similarly, Neusner, " 'Pharisaic-Rabbinic' Judaism: A Clarification," 445. Schäfer ("Die sogenannte Synode," 45–64) seems somewhat more trusting of the reports about what Johanan ben Zakkai did at Yavneh; but he also acknowledges ("Der vorrabinische Pharisäismus," 170) the difficulty of reconstructing the process by which the pre-70 Pharisees mutated into the post-70 rabbis. Cohen suggests that the great contribution of Yavneh was the creation of a society that tolerated disputes without producing sects. Still, Neusner sees signs of a fierce struggle

between the Hillelites and the Shammaites during the Yavnean period. Likewise, one thinks of the conflicts that rabbinic tradition connects with the names of Gamaliel II and Eliezer ben Hyrcanus.

⁵⁰ Cohen, "The Significance of Yavneh," 106, 111. Schwartz (*Josephus and Judaean Politics,* 201–5) thinks that Johanan ben Zakkai's control in Yavneh may have been relatively brief and unsuccessful in rallying other Jewish groups (priests, Pharisees, Herodians) around him. Schwartz suggests that it was the rise of Gamaliel II that was "the most important event in the formation of Rabbinic Judaism," since Gamaliel succeeded in uniting various competing Jewish groups (e.g., Pharisees, priests) at Yavneh.

⁵¹ See Neusner, " 'Pharisaic-Rabbinic' Judaism: A Clarification," 427–38; idem, "The Formation of Rabbinic Judaism: Methodological Issues and Substantive Theses," 99–144. Neusner sees Eliezer ben Hyrcanus as a continuator of pre-70 Pharisaism in the post-70 period ("The Formation," 130), while Johanan ben Zakkai was more of an innovator, addressing the new period created by the destruction of the temple. Neusner thinks that, on the basis of the extant laws culled from the earliest stratum of the rabbinic material, we lack irrefutable proof that Johanan was a Pharisee before 70 (pp. 131–32). For a full study of Eliezer, see Bokser (*Pharisaic Judaism),* who sees in Eliezer affinities to the *hălākâ* of the Sadducees and the *hălākâ* of the Shammaites.

⁵² See Goodblatt, *The Monarchic Principle,* 130–231. Goodblatt holds that it was Roman intervention from without rather than merely the evolution of a Jewish institution from within that brought about the revolutionary change after A.D. 70 from priestly to lay "monarchy"—i.e., from the rule of a high priest in Jerusalem to that of a lay leader (later called "patriarch") in Yavneh in Judea and later in Usha, Beth Shearim, Sepphoris, and Tiberias in Galilee. Against Goodblatt's theory, Schwartz (*Josephus and Judaean Politics,* 206–8) suggests that it was Agrippa II who chose and promoted Gamaliel II. For the contrarian view that the Jewish patriarch was never a civil ruler but only a religious leader recognized by Rome, see Martin Goodman, "The Roman State and the Jewish Patriarch in the Third Century," *The Galilee in Late Antiquity* (ed. Lee I. Levine; New York/Jerusalem: The Jewish Theological Seminary of America, 1992) 127–39.

⁵³ Other possible sources all seem to be secondary in one or another sense; so, e.g., the statements of Hippolytus (ca. A.D. 170–ca. 236) about the Pharisees in his *Refutation of All Heresies* (also called the *Philosophumena*) 9.18 §2—9.29 §4; for the Greek text, see Paul Wendland (ed.) *Hippolytus Werke. Dritter Band. Refutatio Omnium Haeresium* (GCS 26; Leipzig: Hinrichs, 1916) 256–63. Whether one thinks that Hippolytus depends directly on Josephus or on a pro-Pharisaic revision of Josephus by a later Jewish author (so Baumgarten, "Josephus and Hippolytus on the Pharisees," 31–55), no new reliable information is attainable from Hippolytus. Even if one holds with Smith ("The Description of the Essenes in Josephus and the Philoso-

phumena," 343–83, esp. 381–83) that Josephus and Hippolytus used a common source for their descriptions of Jewish groups, in the end the hypothetical source would provide us with no new reliable information about the Pharisees that could not be obtained from sifting critically our three major sources. Smith's approach to Hippolytus is made questionable not only by Baumgarten's arguments but also by the study of Josephus' use of his sources by Cohen; see his *Josephus in Galilee and Rome*, 24–66, esp. p. 49 n. 88. While certain passages from the Dead Sea scrolls are identified by some scholars as containing veiled references to the Pharisees (e.g., the "seekers after smooth things"), the very nature of Qumran's esoteric code makes the use of these texts problematic.

[54] For brief overviews of the NT books that mention the Pharisees, see Stemberger, *Pharisäer, Sadduzäer, Essener*, 24–39; Saldarini, "Pharisees," 294–98.

[55] The meaning of Paul's claim to have been a Pharisee is clear whether or not we think that our text of Philippians consists of one or more than one original letter and whether or not we see Paul's opponents as Jews or Jewish Christians.

[56] This point about the priority of Paul and Mark in usage is stressed at the very beginning of his work by Stemberger, *Pharisäer, Sadduzäer, Essener*, 7.

[57] On Paul and Josephus as sources for Pharisaism, see Segal, *Paul the Convert*, xi.

[58] See, e.g., Michael J. Cook, *Mark's Treatment of the Jewish Leaders* (NovTSup 51; Leiden: Brill, 1978) (Cook's theory of sources has been called into question by a number of critics); Joanna Dewey, *Markan Public Debate* (SBLDS 48; Chico, CA: Scholars, 1980); Elizabeth Struthers Malbon, "The Jewish Leaders in the Gospel of Mark: A Literary Study of Marcan Characterization," *JBL* 108 (1989) 259–81; Jack Dean Kingsbury, *Conflict in Mark. Jesus, Authorities, Disciples* (Minneapolis: Fortress, 1989). Saldarini *(Pharisees, Scribes and Sadducees)* gives detailed treatments of Pharisees, scribes, and Sadducees in Mark and Matthew (pp. 144–73) and in Luke-Acts and John (pp. 174–98).

[59] For various views of the apologetic and polemical situation in Matthew, see Davies, *The Setting;* Gerhard Barth, "Das Gesetzesverständnis des Evangelisten Matthäus," Günther Bornkamm, Gerhard Barth, and Heinz Joachim Held, *Überlieferung und Auslegung im Matthäusevangelium* (WMANT 1; 5th ed.; Neukirchen-Vluyn: Neukirchener Verlag, 1968) 54–154; Wolfgang Trilling, *Das wahre Israel* (SANT 10; 3d ed.; Munich: Kösel, 1964); Reinhart Hummel, *Die Auseinandersetzung zwischen Kirche und Judentum im Matthäusevangelium* (BEvT 33; Munich: Kaiser, 1966); Sjef van Tilborg, *The Jewish Leaders in Matthew* (Leiden: Brill, 1972); Hubert Frankemölle, *Jahwebund und Kirche Christi* (NTAbh 10; Münster: Aschendorff, 1974); Alexander Sand, *Das Gesetz und die Propheten* (Biblische Untersuchungen 11; Regensburg: Pustet, 1974); David E. Garland, *The Intention of Matthew 23* (NovTSup 52; Leiden: Brill, 1979); Jack Dean Kingsbury, "The Devel-

oping Conflict between Jesus and the Jewish Leaders in Matthew's Gospel: A Literary-Critical Study," *CBQ* 49 (1987) 57–73; idem, *Matthew As Story* (2d ed.; Philadelphia: Fortress, 1988); Amy-Jill Levine, *The Social and Ethnic Dimensions of Matthean Salvation History* (Studies in the Bible and Early Christianity 14; Lewiston, NY/Queenston, Ontario: Mellen, 1988); J. Andrew Overman, *Matthew's Gospel and Formative Judaism* (Minneapolis: Fortress, 1990); Anthony J. Saldarini, *Matthew's Christian-Jewish Community* (Chicago/London: University of Chicago, 1994); Celia M. Deutsch, *Lady Wisdom, Jesus and the Sages* (Valley Forge, PA: Trinity, 1996). For the overall question of conflict and polemic in Fourth Gospel, see J. Louis Martyn, *History & Theology in the Fourth Gospel* (rev. ed.; Nashville: Abingdon, 1979); Raymond E. Brown, *The Community of the Beloved Disciple* (New York/Ramsey, NJ/Toronto: Paulist, 1979); Urban C. von Wahlde, "The Terms for Religious Authorities in the Fourth Gospel: A Key to Literary Strata?" *JBL* 98 (1979) 231–53; idem, "The Johannine 'Jews': A Critical Survey," *NTS* 28 (1982) 33–60; idem, "The Relationships between Pharisees and Chief Priests: Some Observations on the Texts in Matthew, John and Josephus," *NTS* 42 (1996) 506–22.

[60] See J. A. Ziesler, "Luke and the Pharisees," *NTS* 25 (1978–79) 146–57; S. G. Wilson, *Luke and the Law* (SNTSMS 50; Cambridge: Cambridge University, 1983); Joseph B. Tyson, *The Death of Jesus in Luke-Acts* (Columbia, SC: University of South Carolina, 1986); Jack T. Sanders, *The Jews in Luke-Acts* (Philadelphia: Fortress, 1987); John T. Carroll, "Luke's Portrayal of the Pharisees," *CBQ* 50 (1988) 604–21 (with abundant bibliography); Joseph A. Fitzmyer, "The Jewish People and the Mosaic Law in Luke-Acts," *Luke the Theologian. Aspects of His Teaching* (New York/Mahwah, NJ: Paulist, 1989) 175–202; Mark Allan Powell, "The Religious Leaders in Luke: A Literary-Critical Study," *JBL* 109 (1990) 93–110; Jack Dean Kingsbury, *Conflict in Luke. Jesus, Authorities, Disciples* (Minneapolis: Fortress, 1991); David B. Gowler, *Host, Guest, Enemy and Friend: Portraits of the Pharisees in Luke and Acts* (Emory Studies in Early Christianity 2; New York: Lang, 1991); Frank J. Matera, "Jesus' Journey to Jerusalem (Luke 9.51–19.46): A Conflict with Israel," *JSNT* 51 (1993) 57–77.

[61] The exact number of occurrences of *Pharisaios* in the NT is uncertain because of alternate readings in some texts; one count lists 97 occurrences in all: 29 in Matthew, 12 in Mark, 27 in Luke, 19 in John, 9 in Acts, and 1 in Philippians. Alternate readings could bring the total count up to 99. By contrast, there are only 14 occurrences of *Saddoukaios* in the NT: 7 in Matthew, 1 in Mark, 1 in Luke, and 5 in Acts. At least on the redactional level of the Gospels, the Pharisees are much more important to the story of Jesus than the Sadducees.

[62] See Stemberger, *Pharisäer, Sadduzäer, Essener,* 10; Mason, *Flavius Josephus on the Pharisees,* 375. On the problem of translating *hairesis,* see Saldarini, *Pharisees, Scribes and Sadducees,* 123–27; Mason, *Flavius Josephus on the Pharisees,* 125–28.

[63] The count is that of Mason, *Flavius Josephus on the Pharisees,* 43 with n. 8. All in all, Josephus uses the word "Pharisee(s)" 44 times: 7 times in the *War,* 31 times in the *Antiquities,* and 6 times in his *Life.*

[64] For a survey of the range of opinions among modern scholars, see Mason, *Flavius Josephus on the Pharisees,* 18–39. For an example of a combination of explanations, see Sanders, *Judaism. Practice & Belief,* 410.

[65] This position is often based on an uncritical meshing of Josephus' statements with those of the later rabbinic literature. See, e.g., Finkelstein, *The Pharisees,* 1. 82–100, 2. 570–625; Rivkin, *A Hidden Revolution,* 179; cf. Schiffman, *From Text to Tradition,* 107.

[66] So, e.g., Schwartz, "Josephus and Nicolaus," 327–41; cf. Moore, *Judaism,* 1. 62 n. 4. Schwartz combines the source-theory with the suggestion that in the *War,* Josephus tried to portray the Pharisees as a largely apolitical religious group not involved in the revolt against Rome; hence very little of Nicholaus' damaging portrait of a troublesome political party is allowed to come to the surface. In the *Antiquities,* however, more of the source material from Nicholaus is allowed to speak—probably because of Josephus' carelessness—and so the Pharisees appear as more involved in politics and even in the revolt. While practically all scholars admit that Josephus used sources in writing about the Pharisees, not all of Schwartz's arguments in favor of a source theory are valid: e.g., (1) the presumption that hostile statements about the Pharisees must come from a source because they could not come from Josephus the (supposed) Pharisee; (2) the claim that the *War* reflects Josephus' attempt to portray the Pharisees as uninvolved in politics. Josephus is certainly responsible for choosing *where* in the *War* he will introduce the Pharisees to his readers. That he selects the reign of Salome Alexandra (*J. W.* 1.5.1 §107–12) and proceeds to depict the Pharisees during her reign as all-powerful, ruthless, and vengeful politicians does not support Schwartz's position.

[67] This is the view defended at length and with great care by Mason in his *Flavius Josephus on the Pharisees;* see his concluding statement on p. 373. For a critique of some of Mason's views, see Sanders, *Judaism. Practice & Belief,* 533–34 n. 22; 532 n. 9.

[68] With various differences in emphases and perspectives, this view is propounded by Laqueur *(Der jüdische Historiker),* Smith ("Palestinian Judaism"), Neusner ("Josephus's Pharisees"), and Cohen *(Josephus in Galilee and Rome).* The differences among the various authors must be respected. For instance, the detailed thesis of Cohen in a full-length book allows for more nuances than the programmatic essay of Smith. On p. 151 n.171, Cohen notes some inconsistencies in the *Antiquities'* supposedly pro-Pharisaic presentation: "It [the *Antiquities*] has several passages which are quite nasty to the Pharisees. . . ." Schäfer ("Der vorrabbinische Pharisäismus,"

168–70) agrees in general with the Smith-Neusner reading of how the Pharisees are presented in Josephus' works, but warns against hasty conclusions about the historical Pharisees on the basis of Josephus' tendentious presentation. Schäfer also notes correctly that (1) the picture of the Pharisees in the *Antiquities* is not completely positive, and (2) it is erroneous to claim that, under Herod, the Pharisees simply disappeared as a political party.

[69] Saldarini, *Pharisees, Scribes and Sadducees,* 131.

[70] Schwartz (*Josephus and Judaean Politics,* 200) recognizes the mixed picture of the Pharisees in the *Antiquities.* He concludes that Josephus is moving "close to Pharisaism without actually adhering to it." He goes on to suggest that this ambiguous relationship to Pharisaism was the chief characteristic of the early rabbinic movement. Therefore, reasons Schwartz, Josephus in the *Antiquities* is moving toward rabbinic Judaism.

[71] *Life* 38–64 §189–335. Those who advocate nuanced interpretations of Josephus' view of the Pharisees often point out that the three static, synthetic treatments of the philosophical schools in the *War* and the *Antiquities* serve an apologetic purpose (presenting the Jewish groups as honorable schools of thought comparable to the great Greek philosophical schools) that sets these passages apart from other statements about Jewish groups in Josephus' works. Hence the noble tone of the systematic presentations does not always jibe with what is said of the Pharisees in the narratives.

[72] Josephus struggles to put the best face on a story that cannot help but present him at odds with a leading Pharisee in the provisional Jerusalem government and with a largely Pharisaic delegation sent to Galilee. Notice how Josephus (*Life* 38 §192) claims that the highly intelligent and politically skillful Simeon was at odds "with me then [*tote,* at that time]." How long a space of time *tote* encompasses is not made clear; we never hear of a friendly relationship between Simeon and Josephus before or after this particular story. Is enduring enmity being reinterpreted as a temporary tiff? Cf. Cohen, *Josephus in Galilee and Rome,* 145, 238.

[73] While the verb *dierchomai* can mean simply "go through," "pass through," the prefix *dia-* can have an intensive force giving the verb the sense of "complete," "reach, arrive at (the end of something)," or "go through in detail."

[74] I follow Mason (*Flavius Josephus on the Pharisees,* 347–51) in taking *ērxamēn politeuesthai* in the strong sense of "I entered public life," "I began to engage in public affairs," "I began my career in government." (Notice the proximity of the phrase to "I returned to the city [*polin,* i.e., Jerusalem]" and the immediately following narrative, Josephus' embassy to Rome.) This strong, political sense is the more common usage in Josephus. Also witnessed in Josephus, however, is the weaker sense ("live,"

"conduct oneself," "lead one's life"), which ties this phrase closer to the participle *katakolouthōn*: "I began to conduct my life by following the Pharisaic school of thought" or "I began to govern my life by the rules of the Pharisees" (so H. St. J. Thackeray in the LCL translation of the *Life*). Both senses are witnessed in Jewish and Christian literature around the turn of the era, and either sense is compatible with the basic point I am making.

[75] On this, see Cohen, *Josephus in Galilee and Rome,* 106.

[76] Actually, one could read *War* 8.1.7 §137–38 to mean that more than three years is required before one fully enters the community; but a total of three years is also a possible interpretation. The Qumran scrolls are not as clear about the total time of probation and initiation. Possibly the *Rule of the Community* (alias the *Manual of Discipline,* 1QS) treats the case of an outsider entering the settlement at Qumran while the *Damascus Document* (CD) and the *Rule of the Congregation* (1QSa) may be dealing with children born within Essene communities scattered throughout Palestine. Likewise possible is a reflection of different disciplines at different time periods during the sect's existence. In any event, according to the *Rule of the Community,* instruction is given for an indeterminate amount of time, after which the candidate undergoes an examination (1QS 6:15–16). If the candidate passes the examination, he then undergoes one year of training (6:16–17). If he passes the test at the end of that year, he is permitted to touch "the purity" (pure solid food and the vessels that contain them?), but his property, while transferred to the community's custody, is not yet merged with that of the community (6:18–21). At the end of the second year, if the candidate passes another examination, he becomes a full member of the community and his property is merged with that of the community (6:21–22). Hence, while 1QS does not add up the total time of probation and initiation, it is certainly more than two years and so agrees roughly with Josephus' report of three years. The rules of admission are vaguer in the *Damascus Document* (CD 13:11–12), but some period of examination and then approval by the *měbaqqēr* ("examiner," "overseer") is prescribed. *The Rule of the Congregation* seems to deal with the special case of a child born to members of an Essene community; he is instructed for ten years and then becomes a full member of the community at age 20. This is intriguing in light of Josephus' claim that he thoroughly passed through the arduous initiation processes of all three major groups (plus three years with Bannus!) from age 16 to age 19. On the question of initiation into Qumran or the Essenes, see the various views in Edmund F. Sutcliffe, *The Monks of Qumran* (London: Burns & Oates, 1960) 104–6; Suitbert H. Siedl, *Qumran. Eine Mönchsgemeinde im Alten Bund* (Bibliotheca Carmelitica II/2; Rome: Desclée, 1963) 286–91; Mathias Delcor, "Le vocabulaire juridique, cultuel et mystique de l' 'initiation' dans la secte de Qumran," *Religion d'Israel et Proche Orient Ancien* (Leiden: Brill, 1976) 363–88; Jean Giblet, "L'initiation dans les communautés esséniennes," *Les rites d'initiation. Colloque Liège/Louvain 1984* (ed. Julien Ries; Louvain: Centre d'histoire des religions, 1986) 397–412; Geza Vermes, *The Complete Dead Sea Scrolls in English* (New York: Penguin, 1997) 32–34.

[77] The difficulty of accepting Josephus' account at face value is noted by Harold W. Attridge, "Josephus and His Works," *Jewish Writings of the Second Temple Period* (CRINT 2/2; ed. Michael E. Stone; Assen: Van Gorcum; Philadelphia: Fortress, 1984) 185–232, esp. 186; cf. Le Moyne, *Les Sadducéens*, 28–29. Different authors try to come to terms with the difficulty in different ways. Geza Vermes and Martin D. Goodman (*The Essenes According to the Classical Sources* [Oxford Centre Textbooks 1; Sheffield: JSOT, 1989] 57) offer this gentle judgment: "It is hard to see how so long a period [of probation and initiation] can be fitted into the chronology of Josephus' life, and it may be suspected that his description of his education has been idealised." Tessa Rajak (*Josephus. The Historian and His Society* [Philadelphia: Fortress, 1983] 30–38) tries to save the reliability of Josephus' account by allowing for "some rhetorical exaggeration." Her case is not helped by her questionable assumptions that Josephus had had a Pharisaic education before he began his experiments with the various schools and that Bannus may have been involved in political activism. A scholar seeking a more convincing way out of Josephus' obvious self-contradiction might try to find refuge in alternate readings of the Greek text. Unfortunately for such a scholar, the number *hekkaideka* ("sixteen") in *Life* 2 §10 and the numbers *treis* ("three") and *enneakaidekaton* ("nineteen") in §12 do not have any alternate readings in the critical apparatus of Benedikt Niese's critical edition, *Flavii Josephi Opera* (2d ed.; 6 vols.; Berlin: Weidmann, 1955) 4. 322–23. To attempt hypothetical emendations when the text is quite clear in what it says would be a solution of desperation. See Cohen, *Josephus in Galilee and Rome*, 107. Quite emphatic in denying the truthfulness of the entire account of *Life* §10–12 is Gohei Hata, "Imagining Some Dark Periods in Josephus' Life," *Josephus and the History of the Greco-Roman Period* (Morton Smith Memorial; SPB 41; ed. Fausto Parente and Joseph Sievers; Leiden: Brill, 1994) 309–28, esp. 310–12, 327–28. However, Gohei Hata's argument is hurt by a lively use of imagination (freely admitted by the author) to fill in the blank spots in our knowledge of Josephus' life.

[78] See Mason (*Flavius Josephus on the Pharisees*, 324–41), where he rightly refutes attempts by some critics to detect hints of Josephus' supposed Pharisaism scattered throughout his works.

[79] On this, see Mason, *Flavius Josephus on the Pharisees*, 336–38, 368–69.

[80] Notice, in this regard, how Josephus describes his emergence from his place of refuge in the temple to rejoin the Jerusalem leaders after the radical Menahem had been put to death (*Life* 5 §21): "I once again associated with the high priests and the leading men of the Pharisees." Just as one would not get the impression from this sentence that Josephus was a high priest, so no reader would get the impression that he was a Pharisee.

[81] Mason (*Flavius Josephus on the Pharisees*, 342–56) offers a valiant and ingenious attempt to make sense of the passage by taking it to mean that, when Josephus decided to enter public life, he had to conform externally to the observances of the Pharisees,

since the Sadducees and everyone else entering public life had to make this concession to be accepted by the people (for a similar view, see Stemberger, *Pharisäer, Sadduzäer, Essener*, 10–11 with n. 2 on p. 11). The problems with this interpretation are numerous: (1) It is useless to argue about what the logical flow of thought in *Life* 2 §10–12 demands; the story makes no sense either in itself or in the wider context of Josephus' writings. Josephus is simply lying. That is why his becoming a Pharisee after his initial experience of the Pharisees apparently proved unsatisfactory (hence his turning from the three "schools" to the unscholastic Bannus) is so difficult to understand. (2) Mason presumes that Josephus' claim in *Ant*. 18.1.4 §17 that the Sadducees (and presumably others) who wished to assume public office had to conform to the rules of the Pharisees is historically true. But as Neusner, Cohen, Sanders, and many other recent scholars of Judaism have pointed out, such a description does not square with the realities of Judean politics during the period of direct Roman rule. The very narratives of Josephus, as distinct from his idealized systematic summaries of the three schools, point to what other ancient sources confirm: during direct Roman rule, the Jewish official in Judea with real power under the prefect/procurator was the high priest, supported by the priestly and lay aristocrats. The bulk of Josephus' *narratives* does not support the idea that the high priest, the priests as a group, or the aristocrats as a group had to bow as a general rule to the wishes of the Pharisees in order to operate in public—a claim made nowhere in Josephus' works outside of *Ant*. 18.1.4 §17. (This unique claim cannot be simply equated with Josephus' statements elsewhere that the Pharisees enjoyed great influence among the people.) It may well be, as I have suggested above, that in certain cases the high priest and the aristocrats around him yielded diplomatically on individual points for the sake of public harmony and peace. But there is no basis for the claim that, as a rule, a priestly aristocrat entering public life would have had to conform his external life wholesale to the observances of the Pharisees. Here one sees a weakness in Mason's otherwise fine study: a lack of a critical correlation of the idealized systematic portraits of the Jewish groups (a) with what de facto happens in Josephus' own narratives and (b) with what most critical historians today hold to have been the actual political situation in Judea during direct Roman rule. (3) In the end, Mason's interpretation of *Life* 2 §12, while theoretically possible, demands reading a great deal into a few words. While not as clear as one might wish (perhaps because Josephus wishes it to be unclear), *tē Pharisaiōn hairesei katakolouthōn* most naturally means "becoming a follower of the Pharisees' school of thought." Since we are never told that Josephus was previously a Sadducee or anything else (the whole story in *Life* 2 militates against such an idea), we do not have the option of supposing that, as in *Ant*. 18.1.4 §17, a particular Sadducee remained a Sadducee while externally conforming to Pharisaic rules. If Josephus conformed totally to the Pharisaic way of life, what was he if not a Pharisee, since he had never been anything else? The meaning of Josephus' statement is clear; it just happens to be a lie. Perhaps the only weighty objection to my theory that Josephus is lying is the one proposed to me in a private communication by the great Josephus scholar Louis H. Feldman. As Feldman observes, the *Life* is a controversial and apologetic work in which Josephus is defending himself against adversaries (notably, Justus of Tiberias) who had made charges against Josephus' public conduct. In such circumstances, could

Josephus have afforded to face his critics with such a blatant lie? Would he not be weakening his own defense and opening himself up to further attack from his foes? Such an objection does give one pause. Yet one must attend to the precise nature of Josephus' claim and where he makes it in his narrative. It may not be purely by accident that the claim that he became a follower of the Pharisaic school of thought occurs in a dependent circumstantial clause, modifying the main statement that, at the age of 19, he began his public career. One may wonder how many people in the late 90s of the 1st century A.D. could claim to know what religious choice Josephus had made at the age of 19—to say nothing of proving what they knew (cf. Josephus' gibe at Justus of Tiberias in *Life* 65 §359–360). As for Josephus' conduct later on, nowhere does Josephus claim that his whole adult life displayed unbroken loyalty to Pharisaism. In other words, who in the late 90s would be in a position to dispute the very narrow claim that Josephus makes about his religious commitment at the age of 19?

[82] These dates are purposely left vague, since especially the Babylonian Talmud went through many stages of redaction. Its main form and content seem to have been set by the sixth century, but Stemberger holds that the Babylonian Talmud "attained its (almost) final shape in the eighth century. . . . Even later explanations . . . have made it into the text via marginal glosses" (Strack and Stemberger, *Introduction to the Talmud and Midrash*, 233, 225). In light of still later insertions of conjectures into the text, Stemberger (p. 225) cites David Goodblatt's observation that, in a certain sense, the Babylonian Talmud "reached its present state only in the last century [i.e., the 19th century]."

[83] The Greek form *Pharisaios* comes from the Aramaic rather than the Hebrew form of the word; the Hebrew form, however, is the form used in rabbinic literature when "Pharisee" is meant. See Meyer-Weiss, *"Pharisaios,"* 12. The reader will notice that I do not attempt any deduction about the origin or nature of the Pharisees from the supposed etymology of their name, since the original meaning of the Hebrew or Aramaic word is still disputed among scholars. While many take *pĕrûšîn* to mean "separated ones," from the verb *prš* ("to separate"), other scholars prefer another meaning of *prš*, "to explain," "to interpret" (i.e., the Scriptures); for an intriguing interpretation of the name "Pharisees" as coming from *pārôšîm* (= "specifiers," reflecting their vaunted *akribeia*), see A. I. Baumgarten, "The Name of the Pharisees," *JBL* 102 (1983) 411–28. Still other scholars prefer a double entendre. Even if one accepts the often-championed meaning "separated" as original, the question remains: from whom or what? (On this, see Baeck, "The Pharisees," 3–4; Moore, *Judaism*, 1. 60–62; Marcus, "The Pharisees," 385–86; Cohon, "Pharisaism: A Definition," 137–39.) Does the name refer to separation from the Hasmoneans (e.g., John Hyrcanus and his court), from cooperation with the Sadducees, from the political arena in general, from the mass of ordinary Jews who were not sufficiently observant for the Pharisees, from things that were legally unclean, or from the unclean Gentiles (thus, with the sense of being God's "separated," i.e., "holy" people)? An additional problem is that, while it is often held that the name "Pharisee" was first coined as an insulting label by the Sadducees or other opponents (so, among many others, Zeitlin,

"The Pharisees and the Gospels," 487), this too is hypothesis rather than historical fact. Sievers ("Who Were the Pharisees?") points out that the theory of an insulting label labors under some difficulties. For example, Paul and Josephus—the only two 1st-century authors who claim to be or have been Pharisees—use the designation *Pharisaios* without any sense that it conveys insult or opprobrium. Indeed, in the context of Phil 3:5, Paul uses "Pharisee" alongside of a number of other designations to indicate his honorable and upright status as a Jew: "circumcised . . . of the people of Israel, of the tribe of Benjamin, a Hebrew of Hebrews, according to the law a Pharisee. . . ." Moreover, the use of the verb *pāraš* in 4QMMT (see Elisha Qimron and John Strugnell [eds.], *Qumran Cave 4. V. Miqṣat Ma'aśe Ha-Torah* [DJD 10; Oxford: Clarendon, 1994] 58–59) to describe the proud, righteous stance of the separatist community (presumably Qumran) vis-à-vis mainstream Judaism (". . . and you know that we have separated [presumably the qal form *pārašnû*] ourselves from the multitude of the people") shows that such an expression of holy separation was, at least in one case around the turn of the era, not the mocking designation of opponents but the freely chosen self-description of a sectarian group. Once the theory of "origin in insult" becomes suspect, likewise suspect is the explanation that "Pharisee" was usually avoided in the tannaitic literature because of its origin as an insult and that the rabbis therefore preferred to use terms like "sages," "scribes," and "associates" for the Pharisees (cf. Stemberger, *Pharisäer, Sadduzäer, Essener,* 50). Granted all this uncertainty, I think it unwise to base a historical understanding of the Pharisees on dubious etymological explanations.

[84] For a consideration of these types of texts, see Stemberger, *Pharisäer, Sadduzäer, Essener,* 41–46. Stemberger includes in his list of "unusable or questionable texts" *m. Ḥag.* 2:7 (*pĕrûšîn* mentioned in an ascending scale of sensitivity to impure garments); *m. Soṭa* 3:4 (a puzzling reference to a *pĕrûšâ* woman and to the wounds [or: blows] of the *pĕrûšîn*); *t. Šabb.* 1:15 (a *pārûš* who suffers from a genital discharge); various midrashic references to the obligation of the people of Israel to be *pĕrûšîn* because God is *pĕrûš*, "holy" (*Sipra Shemini* 12:3–4 on Lev 11:44; *Sipra Qedoshim* 1 on Lev 19:2; *Mek. Baḥodesh* 2 on Exod 19:6); *t. Soṭa* 15:11–12 (*pĕrûšîn* who abstain from meat and wine because of the destruction of the temple); *t. Ber.* 3:25 (*pĕrûšîn* equated with *mînîm* in the sense of "deviant" or "heretic"); and the famous list of seven types of *pĕrûšîn*, attested in various passages (e.g., *'Abot R. Nat.* B 45 and A 37; *y. Ber.* 9.7.14b; *y. Soṭa* 5.7.20a; a commentary on the list, found in *b. Soṭa* 22b, may indicate that an editor interpreted the list in terms of the Pharisees). While one might argue that one or another of these texts contains a reference to Pharisees, the critical consensus today assigns to most, if not all, of these texts meanings such as "extremely pious persons," "ascetics," "holy people," or "religious deviants." See also Rivkin, "Defining the Pharisees," 173–217; Bowker, *Jesus and the Pharisees,* 1–38.

[85] This cautious approach is urged by Rivkin and is supported by Stemberger (*Pharisäer, Sadduzäer, Essener,* 40–41), who finds Neusner's method in his *The Rabbinic Traditions* too ready to accept an unbroken continuity between the pre-70 Pharisees and the rabbis.

[86] This is the correct starting point taken by Rivkin, "Defining the Pharisees," 173–217. The problem arises when he proceeds to declare that the Pharisees are synonymous with the *ḥăkāmîm* ("sages") and *sōpĕrîm* ("scribes") of rabbinic literature. Such a blanket identification is highly questionable in a quest for the historical Pharisees of the pre-70 period.

[87] I realize that later rabbinic material also contains cases of the opposition between *pĕrûšîn* and *ṣaddûqîn*. For instance, Lauterbach ("A Significant Controversy," 1–33) chooses the dispute between the two groups over when and where the high priest should place incense in the censer on Yom Kippur (outside or inside the veil that separated the Holy of Holies from the rest of the temple?) as a starting point for discussing the differences between the two parties. The earliest account of the controversy is in a *baraita* in the halakic midrash *Sipra* on Leviticus, a tradition that is then recycled in the tractate *Yoma* in both the Palestinian and Babylonian Talmuds (with some significant changes in the latter). It may well be that the dispute goes back to the pre-70 period; it certainly coheres with the Pharisees' concern about the proper performance of the temple cult (Lauterbach's [pp. 22–23] insistence that the Pharisees were a progressive, liberal group that had less regard for the sacrificial cult than the Sadducees betrays modern concerns [cf. p. 33]). Nevertheless, as always, there is the problem of dating the tradition; Strack and Stemberger (*Introduction to the Talmud and Midrash*, 287) judge that, while the basic core of *Sipra* goes back to the second half of the 3d century A.D., "this text [i.e., the basic core] in particular certainly underwent an extensive subsequent development which has yet to be adequately clarified." Hence I prefer to err on the side of caution by restricting myself to the Mishna and Tosepta.

[88] See Cohen, "The Significance," 113.

[89] This is only one possible interpretation of this obscure passage about *niṣṣôq*. The meaning of the word and therefore of the dispute has been interpreted in various ways by experts in rabbinics; for different opinions (e.g., "aqueduct," "honey"), see Le Moyne, *Les Sadducéens*, 212. The most likely meaning, though, is an unbroken or uninterrupted stream of liquid. On this as well as on the question of water from the cemetery, see Stemberger, *Pharisäer, Sadduzäer, Essener*, 47. A similar tradition about a stream of liquid, expressed in somewhat different language (*hmwṣqwt*, in MMT as opposed in *nṣwq* in Mishnaic Hebrew) but apparently agreeing with the Saducean position, is found in the so-called Halakic Letter from Qumran (4QMMT). A convenient translation for the general reader can be found in lines 58–61 (of the composite text of Elisha Qimron and John Strugnell) as printed in García Martínez's *The Dead Sea Scrolls Translated*, 78 (cf. the fragmentary texts on pp. 81–83). Scholars will want to consult the original Hebrew text along with transcriptions, translation, commentary, and photographs in *DJD*; see Elisha Qimron and John Strugnell (eds.), *Qumran Cave 4. V. Miqṣat Maʿaśe Ha-Torah* (DJD 10; Oxford: Clarendon, 1994); the text in question can be found on p. 53, lines 55–58, commentary on p. 161–62. Since the Qumranites were founded by a Jerusalem priest (the Teacher of Righteous-

ness) and continued to be led by dissident priests originating from Jerusalem, it is hardly surprising that some of their halakic views should coincide with those of the Sadducees, who were well represented among (though not totally identical with) the Jerusalem priests who remained loyal to the temple and its rulers. This agreement on some halakic points is hardly sufficient to identify the Qumranites as Sadducean. Rather, it points to a common background in the Jerusalem priesthood and the temple establishment. In this, I agree with James C. VanderKam, "The People of the Dead Sea Scrolls: Essenes or Sadducees?" *Understanding the Dead Sea Scrolls* (ed. Hershel Shanks; New York: Random House, 1992) 51–62, esp. 58–62; the opposite view is taken by Lawrence H. Schiffman, "The Sadducean Origins of the Dead Sea Scroll Sect," ibid., 36–49. Cohen (*From the Maccabees to the Mishnah,* 159) takes a different tack: in the rabbinic literature, while *ṣaddûqîn* may usually mean what the NT and Josephus mean by the "Sadducees," at times it may refer to the "Zadokites" at Qumran; he thinks that this is the case in *m. Yad.* 4:7. For a salutary caution about deducing too much too quickly from the fragmentary 4QMMT, see John Strugnell, "MMT: Second Thoughts on a Forthcoming Edition," *The Community of the Renewed Covenant* (Christianity and Judaism in Antiquity Series 10; Notre Dame, IN: University of Notre Dame, 1994) 57–73.

[90] Stemberger, *Pharisäer, Sadduzäer, Essener,* 48; he points to the concluding statement in 4:8 that the Lord is (truly) "the Just One" *(haṣṣaddîq),* possibly a final gibe at the "Sadducees," whose name could be taken to mean (in a popular rather than a scientific etymology) "the just ones." On the origin of the name "Sadducees," see the next chapter.

[91] I include in my count the Pharisees' retort to the Sadducees in 4:7: the Sadducees hold that a channel of water flowing from a cemetery is clean. Presumably, the Pharisees hold the opposite. One might count a fourth Pharisaic position on purity, since 4:6 states as part of the argument that, according to the Pharisees, the bones of a dead ass do not transmit uncleanness, but the bones of the high priest do. In this case, though, the Sadducees share the Pharisees' view.

[92] Some scholars consider "Boethusians" synonymous with "Sadducees"; others suggest that the Boethusians were a subgroup of the Sadducees or that we are dealing with two groups with certain affinities. It may be that two similar groups that were originally distinct came to be equated by the compilers of the Mishna and Tosepta. On this, see Porton, "Diversity," 68.

[93] I do not examine cases where the opposition of Pharisees to Sadducees is clearly introduced secondarily into a tradition where the Pharisees were originally lacking; so, e.g., *b. Yoma* 19b when compared with the earlier version of the legendary narrative in *t. Yoma* 1:8; similarly, *'Abot R. Nat.* A 5 as compared to B 10. For a review of later texts that give us no new historical information about the Pharisees, see Stemberger, *Pharisäer, Sadduzäer, Essener,* 52–64. In particular, Stemberger (p. 61) is quite skeptical about the historical worth of the narrative *baraitot* (i.e., teachings and say-

ings in the Talmuds supposedly coming from the tannaitic period) that mention the Pharisees and the Sadducees in the Babylonian Talmud.

[94] So Stemberger, *Pharisäer, Sadduzäer, Essener*, 50.

[95] See, e.g., Cohen, "The Significance," 111 n. 21; also 110 n. 18; Schäfer, "Der vorrabinische Pharisäismus," 130–32. Neusner seems to concede this point in some of his later writings; see, e.g., Neusner, *Judaism. The Evidence of the Mishnah*, 70. Other problems are pointed out by Schäfer, "Einleitung," 1–22, esp. 1–3.

[96] The debate over whether Pharisaism was a sect is bedeviled by the fact that different authors use different definitions of "sect," and even the same author may alter his position from one work to another. So, e.g., Cohen inclines to the position that the Pharisees were a sect in his "The Significance," but thinks in his *From the Maccabees to the Mishnah* (p. 172) that the Pharisees, "at least in the first century, seem not to have been a sect but a more amorphous group. . . ." By a sect I understand a group within a larger religious community that separates itself in some visible way from the larger community because the sect claims exclusive possession of the truth, a truth that it asserts the larger community has lost, abandoned, or perverted; the sect is thus the only true, authentic, and legitimate expression of the community's religious tradition. This self-understanding seems true of the Qumranites, but not of the Pharisees. If, however, one omits the idea that the larger community has completely perverted the truth and allows for a less rigid understanding of exclusivity, "sect" can be understood in a broader sense so as to include the Pharisees. This seems to be the approach of Saldarini, "Pharisees," 294; cf. Baumgarten (*The Flourishing of Jewish Sects*, 1–41), who opts for a broad definition of sects that allows him to apply the label to Sadducees, Pharisees, Essenes, Qumran, the Fourth Philosophy, and the followers of John the Baptist and of Bannus. The problem of defining "sect" is also broached in Stephen G. Wilson, "Voluntary Associations: An Overview," *Voluntary Associations in the Graeco-Roman World* (ed. John S. Kloppenborg and Stephen G. Wilson; London/New York: Routledge, 1996) 1–15.

[97] See Mason (*Flavius Josephus on the Pharisees*, 174–75), where Mason makes the point that, while the Pharisees stand closer to Josephus' own thought than do the Sadducees, the agreement is due not to the fact that Josephus is a Pharisee but to the fact that the Pharisees espouse certain positions of mainstream Judaism that are shared by Josephus and by the Jewish people in general.

[98] Sievers ("Who Were the Pharisees?" 139) points out that the first written testimony we have that explicitly connects Hillel and Shammai with the Pharisees is Jerome's commentary on Isaiah, written in the first decade of the 5th century A.D. Commenting on Isa 8:14, Jerome states that the Nazareans, a Jewish-Christian sect, hold that the scribes and the Pharisees originated from Shammai and Hillel.

[99] See Cohen, "The Significance of Yavneh," 112–14. Cohen states that the identification of the rabbis with the Pharisees becomes secure and central for the first time only in the early medieval Scholia to the Scroll of Fasting.

[100] At the same time, I wish to make clear that my extreme caution is for the sake of my method and goal. I do not mean to discourage others from trying to widen the data base of our knowledge of Pharisaic traditions by various lines of reasoning. Indeed, scholars like Sanders have done notable work in this area. However, for the sake of my limited goal here in Volume Three, I prefer to restrict myself to an assured minimum.

[101] I realize that certain scholars think that some NT documents may have been written in Palestine: e.g., Mark (in Galilee around the time that the First Jewish War was erupting), Matthew (placed vaguely somewhere around the Galilean-Syrian border in the post-war period), and at least some of Paul's captivity epistles (Philippians at Caesarea Maritima). Along with many other critics, I find none of these suggestions likely.

[102] For a brief summary of the many different portraits of the Pharisees in 19th- and 20th-century scholarship, see Saldarini, "Pharisees," 289–91; an older review of scholarship can be found in Marcus, "The Pharisees in the Light of Modern Scholarship," 385–96. Here I simply summarize a few representative stances.

[103] Sievers, "Who Were the Pharisees?" 138. Sievers proceeds to list and describe twelve individuals who are the only persons from the pre-70 period whom we can name and identify as Pharisees. Yet, at the end of his descriptive catalogue, he admits (p. 153) that the Pharisaic identity or even the historicity of several individuals on the list of the twelve is doubtful.

[104] So Finkelstein, *The Pharisees,* 1. 73–100, 2. 570–625.

[105] This is a composite sketch that, in different ways, reflects the approaches of Lauterbach, "A Significant Controversy," 1–33; idem, "The Sadducees and Pharisees," 34–56; idem, "The Pharisees and Their Teachings," 57–129; Baeck, "The Pharisees," 3–50; Cohon, "Pharisaism: A Definition," 135–44; Finkel, *The Pharisees;* Rivkin, *A Hidden Revolution;* idem, "Defining the Pharisees," 173–217; idem, "Pharisaism and the Crisis of the Individual," 219–45. The claim that the entire theory and background of the Pharisees was nonpolitical and quietist runs counter to a good deal of what Josephus tells us; yet the claim is made by Roth, "The Pharisees in the Jewish Revolution," 255–72. Likewise unfounded is the claim that the pre-70 Pharisees were anti-temple, anti-sacrifice, and anti-priesthood. This type of claim is found not only among the older Jewish scholars but also among Christian scholars who find such tendencies theologically satisfying; see, e.g., W. D. Davies, *Introduction to Pharisaism,* 13–14.

[106] Neusner has presented his position in a voluminous number of writings; a short summary of his view can be found in his "Preface," *Origins of Judaism. Volume II* (2 parts; ed. Jacob Neusner; New York/London: Garland, 1990) 1. v–xii, esp. ix.

[107] See, e.g., his book-length presentation of the theory of the Pharisees' withdrawal from politics in his *From Politics to Piety*. On p. 14, Neusner states: "Hillel evidently transformed the Pharisees from a political party to a table-fellowship sect."

[108] See, e.g., his essay "Did the Pharisees Eat Ordinary Food in Purity?" in *Jewish Law from Jesus to the Mishnah*, 131–254. Sanders holds (1) that it was impossible for lay people to eat ordinary food in full purity and (2) that there is no indication at all that the Pharisees wished to do this, though they did make a few minor gestures toward attaining a higher degree of purity than most people.

[109] On Josephus' muddled presentation of the incidents involving Pollion and Samaias, see Mason, *Flavius Josephus on the Pharisees*, 261–63. Note that only Pollion is explicitly said to be a Pharisee; Samaias is only his "disciple." On this, see Sievers, "Who Were the Pharisees?" 141.

[110] See *J.W.* 1.29.1–2 §568–71; *Ant.* 17.2.4 §41–45; cf. Mason, *Flavius Josephus on the Pharisees*, 116–19.

[111] While Josephus includes Saddok the Pharisee as a companion of Judas the Galilean in his (later) account of the revolt in *Ant.* 18.1.1 §4, he is silent about the Pharisee's involvement in the revolt in his (earlier) parallel account in *J.W.* 2.8.1 §118 (likewise, when he resumes his narrative about Judas in *Ant.* 18.1.6 §23). The omission of Saddok in the account in the *War* could be explained simply by the shorter treatment of Judas' revolt in the *War,* itself notably shorter than the *Antiquities*. However, in the account of Judas' revolt in the *War,* Josephus may be pursuing the apologetic aim that pervades that work: the revolt was the work of brigands, hotheads, and irresponsible, marginal groups; none of the major Jewish groups was responsible for it. In the *Antiquities,* a much longer work written about two decades later, when the crisis has receded, Josephus is more open about the involvement of various groups, including the Pharisees, in the revolt. (At any event, portraits of notables in the *Antiquities* tend to produce more of a mixed picture.) This may explain why, in *J.W.* 2.8.1 §118, Josephus insists that Judas had a school of thought *of his own (idias haireseōs),* being in no way similar to the other schools, while in *Ant.* 18.1.6 §23, he says just the opposite: in its doctrine, Judas' Fourth Philosophy agrees entirely with the view of the Pharisees, except for the former's almost unconquerable passion for national liberty.

[112] Hengel ("Der vorchristliche Paulus," 247) interprets these various indications of political involvement by Pharisees to mean that, from A.D. 6 to 66, the Pharisees were politically split into pro-revolt and anti-revolt camps. While that does not necessarily follow from the data, it is quite likely that, in political as well as in religious

matters, the Pharisees were not a monolithic block. For example, the fiery eschatological and messianic beliefs apparently espoused by the Pharisee Saul of Tarsus were not necessarily held by all Pharisees of the time.

[113] Notice how all the other elements of self-description listed by Paul in v 5, while rooted in his past, would refer to religious and social realities that would hold true for all or at least some Jewish men at the time Paul was writing Philippians: circumcised on the eighth day, born of the stock of Israel and of the tribe of Benjamin, and "a Hebrew of Hebrews" (probably referring to his knowledge of Hebrew and/or Aramaic, despite being from a Greek-speaking, Diaspora Jewish family). There is no reason to think that the phrase "according to the Law a Pharisee" does not likewise refer to a present as well as a past religious-social reality in Judaism.

[114] For Luke, see *akribeia* in Acts 22:3; *akribēs* in Acts 26:5 (where the Lucan Paul calls Pharisaism "the most exact school of thought of our religion," *tēn akribestatēn hairesin tēs hēmeteras thrēskeias*); for Josephus, see, e.g., *J. W.* 1.5.2 §110 (the Pharisees form the group that has the reputation [*dokoun*] of expounding the laws very precisely [*akribesteron*]; similarly, *J. W.* 2.8.14 §162 *(met' akribeias)*; *Ant.* 17.2.4 §41 *(ep' exakribōsei)*; *Life* 38 §191 *(dokousin . . . akribeiō)*. While Paul does not use this vocabulary, his insistence on his zeal and blamelessness as a Pharisee certainly coheres with it.

[115] See Mason, *Flavius Josephus on the Pharisees,* 106–13; 373. This point is missed by the revised Schürer, *The History of the Jewish People,* 2. 388.

[116] So, e.g., J. B. Lightfoot, *St. Paul's Epistle to the Philippians* (Grand Rapids: Zondervan, 1953, reprint of 1913 ed.) 147: ". . . he [Paul] had left nothing undone which the law required." See also Ernst Lohmeyer, *Die Briefe an die Philipper, an die Kolosser und an Philemon* (MeyerK 9; 13th ed.; Göttingen: Vandenhoeck & Ruprecht, 1964) 130. Hengel ("Der vorchristliche Paulus," 240) thinks that Paul's reference to himself as a "zealot" points to his education as a Pharisee in Jewish Palestine, more precisely in Jerusalem.

[117] See Sanders, *Judaism. Practice & Belief,* 419–20. Despite his attempt at damage control, Mason (*Flavius Josephus on the Pharisees,* 228 n. 77) cannot explain away Josephus' positive evaluation of the Pharisees in *Ant.* 13.10.6 §294. There Josephus says absolutely that "the Pharisees are *by nature* lenient in matters of punishment." Josephus could have said that the Pharisees are *more* lenient than the Sadducees (the escape hatch Mason proposes); Josephus chooses instead a blanket, unqualified assertion about the Pharisees' very nature. That this assertion is to be understood positively seems likely from the larger context of §293–296: the Pharisees refuse to support the death penalty for someone who has spoken insultingly of doubts about John Hyrcanus' legitimacy; they hold that being scourged and bound by chains would be sufficient punishment.

[118] Cohen ("The Significance," 105) thinks that Josephus, by his emphasis on the philosophical and theological differences among the three Jewish *haireseis,* obscures the point that the Pharisees were distinguished from their opponents by their peculiar exegetical principles and legal rulings.

[119] A prime example is the pesher on Habakkuk. The basis of this commentary's authority is that, while God told Habakkuk to write about what would happen in the final generation, God did not reveal to him the "consummation of the end." This mystery, namely, the true and full meaning of all that the prophets wrote, has now been revealed to the Teacher of Righteousness. This involves some new form of revelation, for the time of the last days has been extended and goes far beyond what the prophets said (1QpHab 7:1–8). Hence the sin of the traitorous apostates boils down to this: they did not hearken to the words of the Teacher of Righteousness coming from the mouth of God, which amounts to not believing in the new covenant that God has made (1QpHab 2:1–4). Here we come very close to some Christian claims: God has acted anew in the end time, establishing a new covenant and revealing the fulfillment of his promises, which was not revealed even to his prophets. In this whole approach, the Qumranites are worlds away from the Pharisees, not to mention the Sadducees. For the probable ways in which the various groups justified their special practices and beliefs, see Sanders, "Did the Pharisees Have Oral Law?" *Jewish Law from Jesus to the Mishnah,* 126–27; Lawrence H. Schiffman, "The Qumran Scrolls and Rabbinic Judaism," *The Dead Sea Scrolls after Fifty Years. A Comprehensive Assessment* (2 vols.; ed. Peter W. Flint and James C. VanderKam; Leiden: Brill, 1999) 2. 552–71, esp. 558–59. Sanders thinks that the Sadducees, "like all good fundamentalists," either found biblical support for the traditions they championed or at least claimed that they could find such support. (Sanders, though, cautions that they probably could have defended almost anything by exegesis.) Hence, for them, there was no normative tradition outside of the written Torah because, they claimed, everything they believed and did was contained in the written Torah. In any case, it would appear that the Sadducees rejected not oral traditions per se but rather the particular traditions of the Pharisees. But here we run into the basic problem of trying to reconstruct the detailed theology of the Sadducees when so little is said about them in the ancient sources, and that almost entirely by their enemies.

[120] The reader is asked to excuse me for not providing detailed proof of these statements about the Sadducees here; they will be treated at length in the next chapter.

[121] Strictly speaking, the possessive pronoun *mou* ("my") in Gal 1:14 depends upon the noun *paradoseōn* ("traditions"). But, as many translations intimate, the sense of *mou* seems connected rather with the adjective *patrikōn* ("pertaining to" or "stemming from the fathers"). On the meaning of the phrase and for various Jewish parallels, see Franz Mussner, *Der Galaterbrief* (HTKNT 9; Freiburg/Basel/Vienna: Herder, 1974) 80.

[122] As Mason notes (*Flavius Josephus on the Pharisees*, 100, 105, 231), Josephus usually employs *nomoi* and *nomima* interchangeably for "laws." The need to explain the special Pharisaic position on ancestral traditions not written in the Law of Moses leads him, by way of exception, to make a distinction in this passage between the written laws *(nomoi)* of Moses and the laws *(nomima)*, i.e., the traditions of the fathers, not written in the Law of Moses.

[123] The precise meaning of this passage in *Antiquities* is disputed. I have adopted the interpretation of Sanders ("Did the Pharisees Have Oral Law?" 99–100; see also Mason, *Flavius Josephus on the Pharisees*, 240–43): when Josephus says that the Sadducees accept only the laws *(nomima)* that are written, he means "written down in the laws of Moses." As Sanders argues, this meaning is made likely by the antithetical parallel Josephus creates between the Sadducees' position and that of the Pharisees, who hand down laws from the fathers that are not written in the laws of Moses. Sanders observes (p. 100), "Josephus states—whether correctly or not—that the Sadducees rejected pharisaic traditions because they were not in the Bible" (cf. *Ant.* 18.1.4 §16). The opposition is thus between laws written down in the Law of Moses and laws not written down in the Law of Moses. In this, Sanders disagrees with the view of Schäfer ("Das 'Dogma' von der mündlichen Torah," 153–97, esp. 189–91), who sees Josephus' antithesis as referring primarily to "written" versus "not written"; Josephus would not necessarily be stating that the Sadducees reject the derivation of the "traditions of the fathers" from Moses. One should note that Sanders goes on to say (p. 108) that his own explanation of the difference between Sadducee and Pharisee on tradition "does not explain *why* various views were or were not accepted. The Sadducees . . . rejected the idea of an afterlife. Had they wished to accept it, they could have found biblical texts which support the view. . . . We do not explain the inner workings of Sadduceeism when we say that they rejected what is not biblical, since it lay with them to decide what was biblical and what not." It should be noted that neither Josephus nor the NT ever explicitly claims that the Sadducees acknowledged only the five books of Moses as Sacred Scripture, rejecting the Prophets and the Writings from this category. (1) To begin with, such a notion presupposes a closed canon of Scripture, a complete "Bible"; the Jewish canon was still in flux in the early 1st century A.D.; see Eugene Ulrich, *The Dead Sea Scrolls and the Origins of the Bible* (Grand Rapids/Cambridge, UK: Eerdmans; Leiden: Brill, 1999). (2) The idea that the Sadducees rejected the Prophets and Writings as Sacred Scripture seems to come from some Fathers of the Church, who misunderstood Josephus' distinction between the Pharisees and Sadducees on the basis of laws written or not written in the books of Moses; see Moore, *Judaism*, 1. 68.

[124] There may be another echo of this theme in the Lucan Paul's speech of defense before the Jews in Rome, when he protests (Acts 28:17) that he has done nothing against the people of Israel or against "the ancestral customs [*tois ethesi tois patrōois*]." Here, though, as Paul speaks before Diaspora Jews in Rome, the reference may be to Israelite laws and customs in general. That the Torah in general is meant in

v 17 is the opinion of Schneider, *Die Apostelgeschichte*, 2. 414 n. 27. In my opinion, the situation is different in Acts 22:3, where the Lucan Paul specifically mentions Gamaliel (identified as a Pharisee in 5:34) and connects his name with the key theme of *akribeia* ("accuracy," "precision"), the hallmark of the Pharisees in Josephus.

[125] That the sweeping claim in Mark 7:3 makes not just the Pharisees but also "all Jews" the champions of "the traditions of the elders" may reflect the polemical stance of early Christianity vis-à-vis Judaism ca. A.D. 70. All Jews, seen as the adversaries of the nascent Christian movement, are now lumped together by Mark with the Pharisees, the particular debating partners of Jesus during the public ministry. The later, Diaspora situation may also be reflected in the focus on the washing of hands. In Sanders' view (*Jewish Law from Jesus to the Mishnah*, 39–40, 90–91, 163–64, 260–63), the early rabbinic evidence shows that Pharisees washed their hands for purity reasons before handling the priests' food or before eating their own holy meals— but not on all the occasions mentioned in Mark's sweeping statement. Mark's incorrect assertion may be influenced by the practice of Diaspora Jews washing their hands or engaging in other lustrations in connection with prayers or the synagogue service.

[126] See Neusner, "The Myth of the Two Torahs," 7–11. In Neusner's view, the "myth of the two Torahs" appears only rarely until we reach the two Talmuds; the myth came to full expression by ca. A.D. 400. See also Cohen, "The Significance," 111; Sanders, "Did the Pharisees Have Oral Law?" *Jewish Law from Jesus to the Mishnah*, 97–130; Sanders differentiates the various terms found in early rabbinic literature (basically the Mishna and the Tosepta) and concludes that neither the phrase "the words of the scribes" nor the term *hălākâ* is equated with the Torah. The approach of Schäfer ("Das 'Dogma' von der mündlichen Torah," 153–97) is somewhat different, but he agrees that only in amoraic times was the "dogma" that the whole oral Torah went back to Moses fully and firmly established. One is astonished to see Rivkin ("Defining the Pharisees," 217) claiming that Josephus, Paul, the Gospels, and the tannaitic literature agree that the Pharisees were the scholar class of the twofold Law. He mixes together not only different strata of rabbinic material from various periods but also the notably different statements of Josephus and NT authors. Also claiming that Josephus and the NT speak of the oral Law is Irving M. Zeitlin, *Jesus and the Judaism of His Time*, 11–12.

[127] In his notes on *m. 'Abot* 1:1, Philip Blackman takes *tôrâ* to mean "the Oral Tradition or Oral Torah"; see his *Mishnayoth* (7 vols; 2d ed.; Gateshead [England]: Judaica Press, 1990) 4. 489. Actually, "Torah" in *m. 'Abot* 1:1 could refer both to the written Torah and to the oral interpretive traditions surrounding it. In any case, Torah is being used here in a sense wider than just the written document we call the Pentateuch. On the whole question, see Anthony J. Saldarini, *Scholastic Rabbinism. A Literary Study of the Fathers According to Rabbi Nathan* (Brown Judaic Studies 14; Chico, CA: Scholars, 1982) 6–7.

[128] Benedict Viviano (*Study as Worship. Aboth and the New Testament,* 6), a scholar who is fairly trusting of the reliability of the traditions in *m. ʾAbot* (see p. 2), comments: "Whether such a body [as the Great Synagogue] actually existed is uncertain." More emphatic is Goodblatt in *The Monarchic Principle* (pp. 80–82): The idea of "the Great Council" or "the Great Synagogue" or "the Great Assembly" (*kĕneset haggĕdôlâ,* cf. *m. ʾAbot* 1:1), in the sense of a "regularly meeting national council" during the Persian or Seleucid period, is "an ahistorical concept," "an imaginary institution conjured up by the rabbis of Roman Palestine." It is found for the first time in the Mishna. In my opinion, the arguments Goodblatt puts forth to sustain his position are convincing.

[129] It is extremely difficult to date most of these shadowy figures. For example, the Simeon the Just mentioned in rabbinic material has been identified by various scholars as either Simeon I (310–291 or 300–270 B.C.), the son of Onias I, or Simeon II (219–199 B.C.), son of Onias II. Indeed, other scholars have identified some of the Simeon traditions with Simon Maccabee and Simeon, the son of Gamaliel I. On the confusion, see Neusner, *The Rabbinic Traditions,* 1. 58. Hence the dates given for the pairs in the main text must remain rough approximations.

[130] For a detailed study of traditions about these and other pre-70 sages, see volume one on "The Masters" in Neusner's trilogy, *The Rabbinic Traditions.*

[131] See, e.g., the attempt to describe the person and teachings of Hillel in the various essays in James H. Charlesworth and Loren L. Johns (eds.), *Hillel and Jesus* (Minneapolis: Fortress, 1997). Personally, I remain skeptical about knowing much about the historical individual called Hillel beyond the bare fact that he was a distinguished Jewish teacher, active in Jerusalem around the time of Herod the Great, and that, more likely than not, he was a Pharisee. See the sober estimation of Robert Goldenberg, "Hillel the Elder," *Anchor Bible Dictionary,* 3. 201–2: "Precisely on account of the importance that came to be attached to Hillel's name, the task of extracting biographical information from the legends that surround him is extremely difficult." In a similar vein, Neusner, *From Politics to Piety,* 42–43; Neusner (with Avery-Peck), "The Quest for the Historical Hillel," 45–63; Cohen, *From the Maccabees to the Mishnah,* 156–57.

[132] It is possible that the reference is to Gamaliel II, but Viviano (*Study,* 28) defends the attribution to Gamaliel I. Viviano notes that the break in the chain of tradition is explained by some scholars either as "a digression on the descendants of Hillel" or as "a later insertion made for tendentious reasons. . . ."

[133] On this, see Neusner, *The Rabbinic Traditions,* 18.

[134] On this, see Sievers, "Who Were the Pharisees?" 143. The vocabulary of receiving *(qibbēl)* is resumed briefly in *m. ʾAbot* 2:8, where Joḥanan ben Zakkai is said to

have received a tradition from Hillel and Shammai. But *qibbēl* does not provide a leit-motiv in chap. 2 as it did in chap. 1. Did 2:8 once follow immediately upon 1:12–15? That is suggested by the fact that the *'Abot de Rabbi Nathan* moves immediately from the traditions about Hillel and Shammai to Joḥanan ben Zakkai (*'Abot R. Nat.* A 14). For a translation of version A of the *'Abot de Rabbi Nathan,* see Jacob Neusner, *The Fathers According to Rabbi Nathan* (Brown Judaic Studies 114; Atlanta: Scholars, 1986) 103–7. The transition between Hillel and Joḥanan is different in version B of the text, but the same basic phenomenon of moving from Hillel to Joḥanan without mentioning Gamaliel or Simeon occurs. For a translation of version B, see Anthony J. Saldarini, *The Fathers According to Rabbi Nathan* (SJLA 11; Leiden: Brill, 1975) 144–67. Saldarini discusses the complexities of the versions of the chain of tradition in the mishnaic *'Abot* and in the two versions of the *'Abot de Rabbi Nathan* in his *Scholastic Rabbinism.* Another possible theory is that the order of the Mishna is original and that the absence of the *qibbēl* formula in the case of Gamaliel and Simeon is due to the fact that the sages compiling the Mishna wished to suppress the fact that Gamaliel and Simeon received their tradition from the House of Shammai rather than from the House of Hillel.

[135] On the connection of Gamaliel I and Simeon I with the House of Shammai, see Neusner, *The Rabbinic Traditions,* 1. 344–45, 375–76, 380, 387. On the importance of Gamaliel I and Simeon I as the only two pre-70 sages named in the Mishna whom extra-mishnaic literature identifies as Pharisees, see Neusner, "The Use of Later Rabbinic Evidence," 486. The number of named Pharisees could be extended slightly if we could identify the Pollio(n) mentioned by Josephus with the Abṭalion who appears in rabbinic literature as one member of the "pair" Shemaʿiah and Abṭalion. (The relevant passages in Josephus that mention Pollio and/or his disciple Samaias are *Ant.* 14.9.4 §175; 15.1.1 §3; and 15.10.4 §370.) In favor of the identification of Pollio with Abṭalion (and against scholars who reject it, e.g., Solomon Zeitlin), see Louis H. Feldman, "The Identity of Pollio, the Pharisee, in Josephus," *JQR* 49 (1958–59) 53–62; Viviano, *Study as Worship,* 18. On various opinions concerning this identification, see Strack and Stemberger, *Introduction to the Talmud and Midrash,* 71. Against the identification of Pollio with Abṭalion is Neusner, *The Rabbinic Traditions,* 1. 159. Neusner points out some of the questionable historical reasoning involved in making the identification. Moreover, nothing in the rabbinic traditions about Shemaʿiah and Abṭalion hints at involvement with Herod; such involvement is at the heart of the stories about Pollio and/or Samaias in Josephus. A further difficulty is that, in Josephus, Samaias is the disciple of Pollio, while, in rabbinic literature, Shemaʿiah is never represented as Abṭalion's disciple, but rather his colleague.

[136] On this point, see Neusner, "The Rabbinic Traditions about the Pharisees before A.D. 70," 155–72. Neusner rejects as anachronistic the theory of Birger Gerhardsson in his *Memory and Manuscript* (ASNU 22; Lund: Gleerup; Copenhagen: Munksgaard, 1961) that the pre-70 Pharisees used the system of strictly oral formulation and transmission of tradition that we find later on in the rabbis. The NT, Josephus, and the rabbinic literature all testify to the fact that the Pharisees had extra-biblical

traditions; but we have no reliable information on how exactly the Pharisees preserved and transmitted them. The Pharisees may have used both oral and written means.

[137] The list of citations is meant to be illustrative, not exhaustive. The list does not mean to claim that the Gospel texts and the passages from the Mishna or Tosepta are discussing exactly the same point or taking the same approach to the subject matter; it simply highlights similar legal concerns or materials, attributed independently in both corpora to the Pharisees. Similarly, I am not claiming that we can know with certainty that, on some specific occasion, Gamaliel I or Simeon I spoke the very words or performed the precise deeds attributed to them in the Mishna or the Tosepta. It suffices that certain halakic concerns were connected by the earliest rabbis with the two great figures whom we know with good probability to have been Pharisees in the pre-70 period. (1) The fact that the number of sayings or stories attributed to Gamaliel I and Simeon I is surprisingly small despite their being the forebears of the rabbinic leaders Gamaliel II and Simeon II and (2) the probability that some of their teachings may have been suppressed because Gamaliel I and Simeon I inclined to the views of the Shammaites suggest that those teachings that have survived, despite the ultimate triumph of the Hillelites, may well reflect the views of these two pre-70 Pharisees.

[138] On Gamaliel I and Simeon I as connected with the tradition of the House of Shammai, see Neusner, *The Rabbinic Traditions,* 344–45, 386–87. The full list of the topics discussed by the two Houses is given by Neusner, ibid., 2. 345–53. While this list contains many other topics as well, it attests abundantly to all the legal concerns I have extracted from the traditions about Gamaliel I and Simeon.

[139] Neusner often emphasizes the great difference between the picture of the Pharisees in the rabbinic material, where they are associated with particular legal rulings and opinions *(hălākôt)* and the picture of the Pharisees in Josephus, where they are an influential philosophical school (as well as a political party) teaching specific doctrines like the immortality of the soul, the resurrection of the body, and the Providence of God (expressed by the Greek philosophical term "fate") that nevertheless leaves space for human decision and cooperation; see, e.g., *From Politics to Piety,* 66, 80; idem, "The Use of Later Rabbinic Evidence," 486–87 (where the Gospels are also set over against the rabbinic portrait). In my opinion, the differences between Josephus and the rabbinic material may be explained at least in part by the great differences in the literary genre, intent, and audience of each set of works; the differences do not necessitate the theory that, in the beginning, the Pharisees were a political party but ceased to be so after Herod the Great came to power. To a certain degree, the NT provides a middle term between Josephus and the Mishna insofar as the NT presents the Pharisees both as holding certain doctrines (e.g., resurrection of the dead) and observing certain special rules (e.g., concerning eating food and tithing).

[140] This view runs counter to the position of Jack Dean Kingsbury ("The Religious Authorities in the Gospel of Mark," *NTS* 36 [1990] 42–65), who holds that Mark

presents the various groups of Jewish authorities as forming a united front against Jesus; Mark does not stress the distinctiveness of the various groups. It seems to me, however, that the distinctiveness of the Sadducees vis-à-vis the Pharisees is at least implied by Mark in the way he introduces the Sadducees in 12:18, after having related the dispute story involving "some of the Pharisees and the Herodians" in 12:13–17. By starting the next dispute with the statement "and there come to him [Jesus] Sadducees, who [*hoitines*, precisely because they are Sadducees] say there is no resurrection" (12:18), Mark implies that this is the distinguishing characteristic of the Sadducees, which differentiates them from the aforementioned Pharisees (and presumably the Herodians). Unlike Luke, who usually neglects the distinction between the simple relative pronoun *hos* and the compound relative *hostis,* Mark may be using *hoitines* in 12:18 with its qualitative or even causative connotation; see Max Zerwick, *Graecitas Biblica* (5th ed.; Rome: Biblical Institute, 1966) 70–72 (#215–20). One should also note that, right after the dispute over the resurrection, Mark tells us that "one of the scribes" recognizes approvingly that Jesus has delivered a good refutation of the Sadducean position (12:28). This scribe (who might be understood to be a Pharisaic scribe, though that is not said) is clearly distinguished from the defeated Sadducees. The most likely implication is that he, like Jesus, accepts the doctrine of the resurrection of the dead.

[141] In Acts 23:8, Luke claims that the Sadducees reject not only the resurrection but also the existence of any angel or spirit, while the Pharisees affirm all these realities. We have no other witness in the NT, Josephus, or the early rabbinic literature to the Sadducees' denial of angels or spirits; and it is difficult to see how the Sadducees could have denied absolutely the existence of angels, since "the angel of the Lord" plays a significant role in certain parts of the Pentateuch. On this, see Haenchen, *Die Apostelgeschichte,* 567 n. 1. Perhaps Luke is reflecting in a garbled way the idea that the Sadducees rejected the explosion of speculation about angels and demons that was current in Jewish apocalyptic, mystical, and magical circles around the turn of the era, while at least some Pharisees were open to such developments. On the whole question, see the treatment of the Sadducees in the next chapter.

[142] See Mason, *Flavius Josephus on the Pharisees,* 156–69. Actually, there is only a thin line between certain conceptions of resurrection of the body and certain conceptions of reincarnation. However, the train of thought in *J. W.* 2.8.25 §163 suggests a definitive, once-and-for-all passing of the soul of the good person into a new body as a form of eternal reward (as opposed to the "eternal punishment" that "the wicked suffer"). This is strikingly different from at least some ideas about reincarnation, which often involve the possibility of passing through a lengthy succession of many bodies as part of a process of purification or punishment as one moves toward the desired goal of existence without a body or even the total extinction of the human person with his or her individual consciousness.

[143] The Hebrew of the longer form of the text of *m. Sanh.* 10:1 reads at this point: *hāʾômēr ʾên tĕḥiyyat hammētîm min-hattôrā* ("he who says that the making-alive

[i.e., the resurrection] of the dead is not [derivable or demonstrated] from the Torah"). But both the preponderance of textual witnesses of the Mishna and the likelihood of the shorter reading generating the longer one (rather than vice versa) argue for the originality of the shorter reading, without the final two words *min-hattôrâ;* the resulting sense is: "he who says that there is no resurrection of the dead." For arguments in favor of the shorter reading being original, see Le Moyne, *Les Sadducéens,* 169–70; in a private communication to me, Prof. Anthony J. Saldarini also argues in favor of the originality of the shorter reading. Scholars, however, remain divided on the question; both Danby and Neusner print the longer text in their translations, though Danby gives the shorter text in a footnote. In sum, complete certainty is not to be had. When one reads of the resurrection of the dead in this text, one must remember that, at this period, the idea of resurrection was a fluid one and need not entail one fixed conception of what the resurrection would be like or what sort of body it would involve. For the variety of conceptions of immortality and resurrection in Judaism at the turn of the era, especially in the Qumran material, see John J. Collins, *Apocalypticism in the Dead Sea Scrolls* (New York/London: Routledge, 1997) 110–29. For a brief general survey of the various approaches to death found in the OT and early Judaism, see Günter Fischer's excursus, "Versuche des AT zur Lösung des Todesproblems," in his monograph *Die himmlischen Wohnungen. Untersuchungen zu Joh 14,2f* (Europäische Hochschulschriften series 23, vol. 38; Bern: Herbert Lang; Frankfurt: Peter Lang, 1975) 128–37.

[144] Notice how (1) the Sadducees present a hypothetical case that is based on what *Moses wrote* in the Pentateuch (Deut 25:5), the Scriptures they apparently held to be normative above all others; and how (2) Jesus' scriptural argument does not appeal, e.g., to Dan 12:1–3,13, which clearly mentions resurrection, or even to ambiguous texts like Ezek 37:1–14, Isa 25:6–9, or Ps 22:27–29, which could conceivably be interpreted of the resurrection, but rather to the great epiphany of Yahweh in Exod 3:6, even though this demands a contorted argument to arrive at the implied truth of resurrection. For the sake of argument, Jesus accepts the ground rules of the debate as laid out by the Sadducees. On Mark 12:18–27, see chapter 29, Section II.

[145] See Mason, *Flavius Josephus on the Pharisees,* 7–9.

[146] As James D. G. Dunn (*The Theology of Paul the Apostle* [Grand Rapids/Cambridge, UK: Eerdmans, 1998] 716) remarks, "Paul's faith remained in large measure the faith and religion of his fathers—more so than many commentators on Paul have realized." See Dunn's treatment of "the stable foundation of Paul's theology" on pp. 716–22. For various attempts—some more critical than others—to trace the Jewish or specifically Pharisaic background/substratum of Paul's thought, see H. J. Schoeps, *Paul. The Theology of the Apostle in the Light of Jewish Religious History* (Philadelphia: Westminster, 1961, German original 1959); W. D. Davies, *Paul and Rabbinic Judaism* (rev. ed.; New York/Evanston, IL: Harper & Row, 1967); Ulrich Wilckens, "Die Bekehrung des Paulus als religionsgeschichtliches Problem," *Rechtfertigung als*

Freiheit. Paulusstudien (Neukirchen-Vluyn: Neukirchener Verlag, 1974) 11–32; E. P. Sanders, *Paul and Palestinian Judaism* (Philadelphia: Fortress, 1977); Segal, *Paul the Convert;* Hengel, "Der vorchristliche Paulus," 177–293; Jürgen Becker, *Paul Apostle to the Gentiles* (Louisville: Westminster/John Knox, 1993, German original 1989) 40–51; Karl-Wilhelm Niebuhr, *Heidenapostel aus Israel. Die jüdische Identität des Paulus nach ihrer Darstellung in seinen Briefen* (WUNT 62; Tübingen: Mohr [Siebeck], 1992) 48–57, 108–9; Jerome Murphy-O'Connor, *Paul. A Critical Life* (Oxford: Clarendon, 1996) 52–70. Hengel ("Der vorchristliche Paulus," 254) argues that pre-70 Pharisaism was much more strongly eschatological, theocratic-political, dualistic, prophetic-apocalyptic, and mystical than the rabbinic texts would lead one to suppose.

[147] See, e.g., the various essays in *Judaisms and Their Messiahs at the Turn of the Christian Era* (ed. Jacob Neusner, William S. Green, and Ernest Frerichs; Cambridge: Cambridge University, 1987); also the programmatic essay of James H. Charlesworth, "From Messianology to Christology: Problems and Prospects," *The Messiah. Developments in Earliest Judaism and Christianity* (ed. James H. Charlesworth; Minneapolis: Fortress, 1992) 3–35, along with the other detailed essays in the volume.

[148] Without much support in the relevant data, some earlier scholars uncritically considered "eschatological messianism" as "a specific feature of Pharisaism" (so, e.g., Baeck, "The Pharisees," 27). Today scholars speak much more guardedly about messianic beliefs among the Pharisees and, indeed, in pre-70 Palestinian Judaism in general; see the essays in James H. Charlesworth (ed.), *The Messiah* (Minneapolis: Fortress, 1992); cf. John J. Collins, *The Scepter and the Star* (New York: Doubleday, 1995). Since many critics (though not all) now doubt the Pharisaic provenance of the *Psalms of Solomon,* we lack firsthand evidence of messianic belief among the pre-70 Pharisees. Nevertheless, although Josephus regularly plays down or suppresses references to messianism and national future eschatology when recounting Jewish beliefs (notice the absence of such themes in his account of the Essenes, as compared with what we now know from the Dead Sea Scrolls), there may be a hint of messianic belief among at least some Pharisees in Josephus' account of the intrigues in Herod's palace (*Ant.* 17.2.4 §41–45). Not only are the Pharisees at court presented as claiming to have prophetic powers that they exercise in favor of their patrons (some critics see here confusion with the Essenes), they even promise a eunuch named Bagoas that, in the future, when Herod and his descendants are removed from the throne, he will receive power to marry and beget children, one of whom will rule the people as king. With all sorts of echoes from OT texts possibly standing behind this strange prophecy (see, e.g., Isa 56:1–5), we may have a garbled echo of one kind of Pharisaic messianism from the pre-70 period. On the whole question of the Pharisees and eschatology, especially in comparison and contrast with other Jewish groups, see Albert I. Baumgarten, *The Flourishing of Jewish Sects in the Maccabean Era: An Interpretation* (Supplements to *JSJ* 55; Leiden: Brill, 1997), esp. chap. 5.

[149] For various interpretations of Gal 2:19, see Ernest De Witt Burton, *The Epistle to the Galatians* (ICC; Edinburgh: Clark, 1921) 132–35; Mussner, *Der Galaterbrief,* 179–82; Hans Dieter Betz, *Galatians* (Hermeneia; Philadelphia: Fortress, 1979) 121–23; Frank J. Matera, *Galatians* (Sacra Pagina 9; Collegeville, MN: Liturgical Press, 1992) 95–104; James D. G. Dunn, *The Epistle to the Galatians* (Black's NT Commentary; Peabody, MA: Hendrickson, 1993) 143–45.

[150] Mason (*Flavius Josephus on the Pharisees,* 136) points out that "fate" is "never a supreme or even autonomous entity" in Josephus. Josephus often uses it interchangeably with "God," for "it is simply the executive aspect of the divine will." Elsewhere Josephus calls the same reality "providence" *(pronoia);* see, e.g., *J.W.* 1.30.5 §593; 2.18.1 §457; 3.8.7 §391; 7.11.4 §453; *Ant.* 2.5.1 §60; 2.16.6 §349. On *pronoia* in Josephus' *Antiquities,* see Harold Attridge, *The Interpretation of Biblical History in the Antiquitates Judaicae of Flavius Josephus* (HDR 7; Missoula, MT: Scholars, 1976) 71–107, 154–165; Attridge detects in Josephus' use of *pronoia* in the *Antiquities* a certain shift away from the more "fatalistic" language of the *War.* As Smith ("Palestinian Judaism in the First Century," 79–80) points out, Josephus is not so far off the mark as we might think in describing different forms of Judaism as different philosophical schools. To a Hellenized Gentile steeped in the syncretistic Greco-Roman culture of the 1st century A.D., Judaism would have looked very much like a philosophy, with venerable teachings passed down in schools with a chain of succession (at least among the Pharisees). By the 1st century, *philosophia* connoted to many a Hellenized person not so much abstract metaphysical speculation about being and becoming as a combination of beliefs, rites, and rules of behavior that we might well call a religion.

[151] Despite the lengthy treatment of the Essenes in *War* 2, Josephus does not discuss there their view of fate and free will. In the rhetorical context of *War* 2, this tends to make the Pharisees, set in bipolar opposition to the Sadducees, the proponents of the absolute power of fate—a position that Josephus, however, tempers with the statement that the Pharisees allow that humans "for the most part" have free will in moral choices. On this, see Mason, *Flavius Josephus on the Pharisees,* 203–4.

[152] See the revised Schürer, *The History of the Jewish People,* 2. 394.

[153] Note that only in the case of the Pharisees do all three of Josephus' static expositions of the Jewish schools take up the question of fate and free will.

[154] So, rightly, Mason, *Flavius Josephus on the Pharisees,* 152.

[155] Mason (*Flavius Josephus on the Pharisees,* 204) remarks that the phrase "not all things" almost sounds like a pointed correction of the presentation in *War* 2. Mason goes on to insist that the differences between *War* 2 and *Antiquities* 13 on this point are not major. I am not so sure. True, Josephus refers the reader of *Antiquities* 13

back to the *War* for a more precise or detailed account of the schools. Mason reasons (p. 205): "Evidently, then, Josephus does not think that his self-contradiction is significant." One is reminded of many a prolific exegete who claims that what he said in a later work does not contradict—at least in a "significant" way—what he said in an earlier work. What the author (ancient or modern) claims and what is the case may be two different things.

[156] I think this is a more exact description of what Josephus says than the claim of Mason (*Flavius Josephus on the Pharisees,* 293) that, in his third exposition, Josephus abandons the model of balancing *(tina . . . tina)* that he used in *Antiquities* 13 and returns to the "cooperation" model of *War* 2. Rather, he seems to be consciously attempting a "fusion" of the two former expositions.

[157] It may well be that, in both *War* 2 and *Antiquities* 13, Josephus makes fate and free will the central issue distinguishing Pharisees from Sadducees; on this, see Mason, *Flavius Josephus on the Pharisees,* 132. This simply reminds us that we must not move too quickly and naively from Josephus' portrait of the Pharisees to the historical reality of the Pharisees. See also Sanders, *Judaism. Practice & Belief,* 418–19. As an instance of the Pharisees' belief on fate and free will, the famous saying in *m.* ʾ*Abot* 3:15 is often cited: *hakkol ṣāpûy wĕhārĕšût nĕtûnâ* ("all [is fore]seen [by God], but freedom is given [to man]"). One must note, however that (1) the parallel is created only when one supplies a number of understood words to the laconic aphorism, (2) nothing in the saying identifies it as specifically Pharisaic, and (3) the attribution of the saying to Aqiba comes from the larger redactional context (3:13) and does not introduce 3:15 itself.

[158] In his earlier work, *Paul and Palestinian Judaism* (1977), Sanders spoke especially in terms of a holistic "pattern" or "structure" or "type" of the Jewish religion. By this he meant a largely presupposed pattern, seldom discussed explicitly, that had to do with how one "got into" or "stayed in" the covenant community of Israel. In his more recent *Judaism. Practice & Belief* (1992), Sanders tends to speak in terms of "Common Judaism" (see pp. 47–76). Here he is thinking more in terms of a list of various practices and beliefs, explicitly discussed in the sources, that show similarity in behavior and belief as one "stays in" the covenant community. This is not intended to reintroduce the erroneous notion of a monolithic "orthodox" Judaism in the pre-70 period or to deny the reality of competing groups with different practices, beliefs, and agendas. It simply acknowledges that, for all their differences, the vast majority of 1st-century Palestinian Jews shared certain basic religious practices and beliefs. If one can speak of Judaism in the 20th century, despite all the differences among Orthodox, Conservative, Reform, and Reconstructionist Jews, one can speak in global terms of Palestinian Judaism in the 1st century. Analogously, if one can speak of Christianity today, in the face of incredible differences and disagreements in belief and practice, one can speak of Christianity in the 1st century. Acknowledging real differences within a given religious movement does not mean denying that the given religious movement exists as a discrete and discernible entity.

[159] This is the phrase used by Saldarini, "Pharisees," 293. It is in keeping with this role that they come to the fore in Josephus' narrative in times of change, crisis, or transition in government.

[160] Curiously, Irving M. Zeitlin (*Jesus and the Judaism of His Time*, 14) first claims, against the evidence, that the Pharisees were not a political party at all and yet later on refers to them as a party. He also makes the strange assertion that, during the reign of Salome Alexandra, the Pharisees wielded only religious, not political authority (contrast *J. W.* 1.5.1 §107–14).

[161] Some readers may notice that I have not raised the vexed problem of the *ḥăbērîm* ("fellows," "associates"), pious Jews who banded together to observe strict purity, taking upon themselves some of the special priestly laws of purity, observing the laws of tithing meticulously, and sharing communal meals in an "association" or "fellowship" *(ḥăbûrâ)*. Various opinions exist among scholars as to their identity: the *ḥăbērîm* were the same as the Pharisees, a subgroup of the Pharisees, a group that partially overlapped the Pharisees, or another pious Jewish group that was not Pharisaic. Different views can be found in Beckwith, "The Pre-History," 79; Neusner, "Preface," *Origins of Judaism*, 1. viii; Sanders, *Jesus and Judaism*, 180–88; idem, *Jewish Law from Jesus to the Mishnah*, 152–55; idem, *Judaism. Practice & Belief*, 440–443; the revised Schürer, *The History of the Jewish People*, 2. 398–99. Saldarini ("Pharisees," 300) cautions that *ḥăbērîm* in itself simply means "ones' fellows" (e.g., one's townsfolk or social familiars); it does not necessarily imply any technical meaning or special organization. (One should also note that most of the *ḥăbērîm* passages that are cited in this discussion seem to belong to the 2d century A.D.) At the very least, then, I think it probable that one cannot simply identify Pharisees and *ḥăbērîm* as the same body of people. In general, the equation sometimes found in older literature, according to which the Pharisees equaled the rabbis who equaled the *ḥăbērîm*, is now questioned by many scholars, and rightly so. I do not spend time trying to identify the *ḥăbērîm* because, in any case, the *ḥăbērîm* make no appearance in the NT material under any equivalent Greek term; they are known only from the rabbinic sources. Hence the question of the relation of the historical Jesus to the *ḥăbērîm* does not arise. If, de facto, he related to some of them, it was because they happened to be Pharisees as well.

[162] For a pericope-by-pericope study of Jesus and the Pharisees in all four Gospels, see Wolfgang Beilner, *Christus und die Pharisäer* (Vienna: Herder, 1959). The Pharisees have been studied by experts in each of the Gospels; for Matthew, see the works of Strecker, Hummel, and Kingsbury; for Mark, see Dewey and Kingsbury; for Luke, see Carroll; for John, see von Wahlde.

[163] On this story, see *A Marginal Jew*, 2. 679–80.

[164] Dewey, *Markan Public Debate*.

[165] See *A Marginal Jew,* 2. 498 n. 195. For the pericope in its redactional and original forms, see pp. 439–50.

[166] On the story as a whole, as well as the identification of the adversaries, see *A Marginal Jew,* 2. 681–84.

[167] The classification of either the whole of Mark 3:6 or at least the mention of the Pharisees as redactional spans the exegetical spectrum from skeptical (Bultmann, *Geschichte,* 54) through moderate (Schweizer, *Das Evangelium nach Markus* [NTD 1; 12th ed.; Göttingen: Vandenhoeck & Ruprecht, 1968] 40) to conservative (Guelich, *Mark 1—8:26,* 139). In keeping with his thesis of Mark as a conservative redactor, Pesch (*Das Markusevangelium,* 1. 188) attributes 3:6 and the Pharisees to a pre-Marcan collection of dispute stories that extended from 2:1 to 3:6. That simply moves the question back one step. Were the Pharisees an original part of the separate unit 3:1–6 or were they added by the pre-Marcan collector of traditions?

[168] In the NT, the constellation of "the Pharisees and the Herodians" or "the Pharisees . . . with the Herodians" occurs only in these two Marcan verses. Matt 22:16, which is a rewriting of Mark 12:13, says more diffusely: "They [the Pharisees] send to him [Jesus] their disciples with the Herodians." This exhausts the occurrences of the much-disputed "Herodians" in the NT. See chapter 30, section IV.

[169] For the complicated relationship between Matthew 23 and Luke 11 and for different opinions on what part of the material originally stood in Q, see Kloppenborg, *Q Parallels,* 106–15. On the complex tradition history of the woes, see Kloppenborg, *The Formation of Q,* 139–48; Catchpole, *The Quest for Q,* 256–62. For Matthean redaction of the material, see Donald A. Hagner, *Matthew* (Word Biblical Commentary 33A and 33B; Dallas: Word, 1993, 1995) 2. 653–73; for Luke's redaction, see Fitzmyer, *The Gospel According to Luke,* 2. 941–53. In Luke's mind, the "lawyers" *(nomikoi)* and the "teachers of the Law" *(nomodidaskaloi)* are probably equivalent to "scribes" *(grammateis);* cf. Luke 11:53 ("the scribes and the Pharisees") at the end of the woes addressed to the Pharisees and the lawyers; 5:17 ("Pharisees and teachers of the Law") + 5:21 ("the scribes and the Pharisees"); 20:46–47 (referring to "the scribes," but reminiscent of the woes against the lawyers in chap. 11). The word *nomikos* is practically unique to Luke among the evangelists; the only other occurrence in the Gospels may be in Matt 22:35, but its attestation there is uncertain because of variant readings in the manuscripts. The compound noun *nomodidaskalos* is unique to Luke among the Gospels.

[170] Correspondingly, John's Gospel never mentions the Sadducees nor, for that matter, scribes *(grammateis),* lawyers *(nomikoi),* or teachers of the Law *(nomodidaskaloi).*

[171] That both Matthew and John, independently of each other, should choose the Pharisees as the symbol and surrogate for the early rabbinic movement against which

they are struggling is in itself a good argument for heavy Pharisaic presence in and influence on nascent rabbinism at the end of the 1st century.

[172] For the global affirmation of the reputation of the historical Jesus as a miracle worker, see *A Marginal Jew,* 2. 617–645. For the treatment of individual miracles stories, see ibid., 646–1038.

[173] The argument here is one from converging indicators: (1) certain topics that we have already identified as characteristic concerns of the Pharisees (2) also occur in pericopes in which Jesus interacts with the Pharisees, (3) and these topics at times enjoy multiple attestation of sources and/or forms (e.g., Jesus' teaching on divorce).

[174] For Jesus' present-yet-future eschatology, see *A Marginal Jew,* 2. 237–506; for the eschatological significance of his miracles, ibid., 2. 399–404, 404–23; for Jesus' celibacy, ibid., 1. 332–45; for the rejection of voluntary fasting, ibid. 2. 439–50.

[175] A phrase occurring a number of times in the Dead Sea scrolls that is often interpreted as referring to the Pharisees is "the seekers after smooth things" (*dôrĕšê (ha)ḥălāqôt;* see 1QH 2:15,32; 4QpNah 1:2,7; 2:2,4; 3:3,6–7; cf. CD 1:18). Saldarini ("Pharisees," 301) thinks instead that the phrase refers to a broad coalition opposing Alexander Jannaeus; it would have included, but not been identical with, the Pharisees. Some authors see even more extensive references to the Pharisees at Qumran: e.g., "Ephraim" used as a code word for the Pharisees, "the builders of the wall [or: the barrier]" (*bônê haḥayiṣ;* see CD 4:19; 8:12,18), or the unnamed opponents referred to in the so-called Halakic Letter (4QMMT). This view was proposed by Schiffman in his "The Sadducean Origins of the Dead Sea Scroll Sect," 35–49, esp. 41–42. His view that the Qumranites were not Essene but Sadducean has been opposed, rightly in my view, by VanderKam, "The People of the Dead Sea Scrolls: Essenes or Sadducees?" 50–62. For a more recent formulation of Schiffman's view, see his "The Qumran Scrolls and Rabbinic Judaism," *The Dead Sea Scrolls after Fifty Years. A Comprehensive Assessment* (2 vols.; ed. Peter W. Flint and James C. VanderKam; Leiden: Brill, 1999) 2. 552–71, esp. 559 n. 24: ". . . Qumran origins are to be located in a group of Sadducees." In any event, I am more hesitant than many others to identify various code words in the Dead Sea scrolls as referring specifically to the Pharisees; in this, I agree with Cohen, who suggests that deciphering the symbolic labels of Qumran "is best left to the cryptanalysts of the CIA" (*From the Maccabees to the Mishnah,* 153). Hence I have not included the Dead Sea scrolls among the major sources of our knowledge about the Pharisees alongside the NT, Josephus, and the early rabbinic literature.

[176] See Neusner, "Sanders's Pharisees and Mine," 247–73, esp. 258. Neusner notes the disagreement between the rabbinic reports of rough confrontations between the Houses and Josephus' claim that the Pharisees stood out vis-à-vis the Sadducees because the Pharisees were affectionate toward one another. On this, see Sanders, *Jewish Law from Jesus to the Mishnah,* 87–89. In dealing with later rabbinic traditions,

one must allow for rhetorical exaggeration and legend-building. I very much doubt that the pre-70 followers of Hillel and Shammai actually killed one another or caused one another grave physical injury because of scholastic disputes on the fine points of the Torah.

[177] Even when the Gospels of Matthew and John do connect the Pharisees with the Passion Narrative, they are placed at the very beginning or end of the story: see John 18:3; Matt 27:62. Even these secondary traditions, which can hardly claim to represent the original historical events, never place the Pharisees at the heart of the action, Jesus' trial and execution.

[178] I stress the Pharisees *as a group*. It is possible that some scribes or officials and even some priests advising the high priest may have been Pharisees—though this is never said—but there is no indication of the Pharisees acting as a group in the Passion Narrative proper.

CHAPTER 29

JESUS IN RELATION TO COMPETING JEWISH GROUPS

The Sadducees

I. THE PROBLEM OF IDENTIFYING THE SADDUCEES

A. INTRODUCTION TO THE PROBLEM

For a number of reasons, our attempt to identify the Sadducees will be less complicated and circuitous than our treatment of the Pharisees.[1] First of all, much of the initial spade work, such as the sketching of a historical grid, the evaluation of primary sources, and the interpretation of key texts has already been done in chapter 28. More specifically, examining key passages on the Pharisees in the NT, Josephus, and the rabbinic literature has entailed looking at what those passages say about the Sadducees as well. While the results of that examination will be recalled here, there is no need to repeat the detailed exegesis of all the texts cited and probed in the previous chapter.[2]

A second reason for our less circuitous treatment is that the fund of information on the Sadducees is even more meager—and even more biased—than that on the Pharisees.[3] Bias in texts mentioning the Sadducees is an especially severe problem because, unlike the case of the Pharisees, we lack material emanating from either a contemporary or a sympathetic spokesperson.

As we have seen, this is not true of the Pharisees. In Paul—and some would add Josephus—we have a 1st-century writer who was himself a Pharisee. In any case, Josephus claimed to be a Pharisee, and he certainly knew some prominent Pharisees firsthand. Granted, his presentation of the Pharisees in the narratives of his *Jewish War* is almost entirely negative. But at least in the *Antiquities,* Josephus makes some positive statements in the narratives that mention the Pharisees. Moreover, in his three static descriptions of the Pharisees as one of the Jewish "schools of thought" *(haireseis),* Josephus is intent on presenting Pharisaism as a venerable and respectable philosophical school within Judaism. Accordingly, his static descriptions of the Pharisees are mostly positive, though not necessarily always accurate.

The various works of rabbinic literature, centuries later in their final forms, display—as one would expect—a basically positive stance toward the Pharisees. It is telling that in the mishnaic disputes between the Pharisees and the Sadducees that we studied in chapter 28, the Mishna always favors the Pharisees. As we move to the later rabbinic literature, we notice an increased desire to create a line of continuity between the Pharisees and the rabbis.

Even the NT, despite its polemics against the Pharisees, does not lack a few favorable comments. For all its ambiguity, John's Gospel seems ultimately favorable toward the Pharisee Nicodemus (John 3:1–15; 7:50–52; 19:38–42). In Acts, Luke makes the high priests and the Sadducees the unrelenting enemies of the Christians in Jerusalem, while the Pharisee Gamaliel urges tolerance (5:34–39) and some Pharisees in the Sanhedrin want at least to consider Paul's claims (23:6–10).[4]

In contrast, from the whole of ancient literature, no individual Sadducee speaks to us in his own voice, and no 1st-century author presents a positive portrait of the group.[5] If the Sadducees as a group produced writings reflecting their point of view, they have not survived.[6] Consequently, for a portrait of the Sadducees, we must rely upon our three major sources (the NT, Josephus, and the rabbinic literature), all of which are hostile to the Sadducees in varying degrees.

Any attempt to arrive at a reliable historical portrait of the Sadducees runs into special difficulties in sifting the rabbinic literature. As Anthony Saldarini points out, while the "Sadducees are mentioned a moderate number of times in rabbinic literature, the references are scattered over various types of literature from different periods."[7] Increasingly, in later rabbinic literature, the Sadducees become stereotypical opponents of rabbinic Judaism; the texts show no great concern for or knowledge of the Sadducees' historical identity in the 1st century A.D. The polemic at times becomes so fierce in the Babylonian Talmud that the Sadducees are no longer seen as really Jews but rather as heretics.[8] Compounding the problem, variant forms of the same story about the Sadducees will use different designations for their opponents (e.g., the Pharisees, the sages, or a vague "they").

These basic problems are aggravated further by problems of text criticism in the rabbinic manuscripts. As we saw in chapter 28, rabbinic references to the Pharisees proved problematic at times because we could not always be sure when the Hebrew word *pĕrûšîn* meant "Pharisees" and when it meant something like "ascetics," "separatists" or "religious deviants." The problem was one of proper translation. In the case of the Sadducees, the problem is still more fundamental: we cannot always be sure that the word *ṣaddûqîn* that we now find in our printed texts of rabbinic works actually stood there in the original manuscripts. Later Christian censorship, or Jewish fear of it, seems to have led Jewish scribes at times to substitute *ṣaddûqîn* for an original *mînîm* ("heretic" or "deviant") or *gôyîm* ("Gentiles"), words that could be taken to refer to Jewish Christians or Christians in general.[9] There also seems to have been occasional confusion in the manuscripts between Sadducees and Samaritans. Hence we cannot always be certain that a given text originally referred to the Sadducees.[10]

In addition, there is the problem of the unclear relationship between the Sadducees and a priestly group in Jerusalem known as the Boethusians.[11] The Boethusians never appear in the NT or Josephus; they are unique to rabbinic literature, appearing in some parts of it (e.g., the Tosepta) much more often than in other parts (e.g., the Mishna). The absence of written attestation of such a group prior to the 3d century must make one wary. Moreover, within the rabbinic literature, one version of a tradition will feature Boethusians while another version of the same tradition will have Sadducees instead. Sometimes the two groups seem identical, sometimes not. When we combine all these special problems with the usual one of weighing the date and the attribution of traditions in the rabbinic literature, we can appreciate the great caution that must be observed in using the rabbinic sources for historical knowledge of the Sadducees in the pre-70 period. In my opinion—and in keeping with the procedure observed in chapter 28—it is best to restrict ourselves, for the most part, to the relatively few cases where *ṣaddûqîn* is clearly opposed to *pĕrûšîn* in the Mishna.[12]

B. A Few Clear Lines in a Fuzzy Portrait

Gathering up what we have already seen here and there throughout the previous chapter, we can make the following certain or probable statements about the pre-70 Sadducees. In this summary, the assertions that most scholars would consider certain or highly probable are presented first. As we move further along through the summary, the claims gradually become more hypothetical.

1. Existence

The existence of the Sadducees as a religious-political group active in Judea around the turn of the era is supported by the multiple attestation of the NT, Josephus, and the rabbinic literature. Since the fact of their existence is not seriously questioned, and since we have already seen the key texts on the Sadducees in chapter 28, the point need not be argued at length here. Still, we should notice as a warning sign that the multiple attestation we have for the Sadducees is not as strong as that for the Pharisees. For example, in the NT, the Sadducees are mentioned only in the Synoptics and Acts, and even there relatively rarely. Indeed, in the Synoptics, only one pericope, Jesus' dispute with the Sadducees over the resurrection of the dead (Mark 12:18–27 parr.), focuses directly on the Sadducees and their teaching.[13] They are slightly more prominent in Acts, though they are mentioned only in passing and always in a negative light (4:1; 5:17; 23:6–8).

2. A Brief History[14]

Despite the paucity of references, it is possible to sketch the bare outlines of a history of the Sadducees. Josephus first mentions them, in one of his static descriptions of the three schools of thought (*Ant.* 13.5.9 §171–72), during the reign of the Hasmonean Jonathan (160–143 B.C.). We hear nothing about them during the subsequent reign of his brother Simon (143–134). Although John Hyrcanus I (134–104), the son of Simon, originally favored the Pharisees, the Sadducees succeeded in luring him away to their own party (*Ant.* 13.10.5 §288–96). Presumably—though this is not explicitly stated by Josephus—the Sadducees continued to support and be supported by Aristobulus I (104–103) and Alexander Jannaeus (103–76).[15] In this very limited sense, one might speak of these three Hasmonean rulers as Saducean high priests. Thus, the Sadducees conceivably could have enjoyed uninterrupted power under the Hasmonean rulers for roughly half a century.

The accession of Queen Salome Alexandra (76–69) and her support of the Pharisees spelled the eclipse and even the endangerment of the Sadducees by their vengeful rivals, the Pharisees (*J. W.* 1.5.1–3 §107–14; *Ant.* 13.15.5–13.16.6 §410–32). After Salome Alexandra's death, it is not clear whom exactly the Sadducees supported and how they fared during the chaotic period marked by the struggle between her two sons, Hyrcanus II and Aristobulus II (along with the latter's son, Antigonus). This troubled interval came to an end when, with Rome's support, Herod the Great ascended the throne in 37 B.C. During his reign, Herod installed a number of high priests whose families came from Babylon and Egypt, a policy that probably aimed at marginalizing the royal-and-priestly Hasmoneans and perhaps the aristocratic Sadducees as well. Herod thus created a new elite of high priestly families, unrelated to the Hasmoneans and dependent solely on his favor.[16] Certainly, under Herod's autocracy, the Sadducees could not hope to recoup the power they had once enjoyed under Hyrcanus I and had lost under Salome Alexandra. While there is some indication of the Pharisees' backstairs influence in Herod's court, we hear nothing similar of the Sadducees.

The Sadducees' fortunes apparently changed for the better with the institution of direct Roman rule in Judea.[17] Under the Roman prefect (later, procurator), the high priest was allowed, to a great degree, to manage the day-to-day affairs of his fellow Jews in Jerusalem and Judea, provided he maintained public order and the regular flow of tax revenues to Rome. To help him accomplish his tasks, the high priest relied primarily on the priestly and lay aristocracy around him in Jerusalem—in other words, on an elite group that was (as we shall see below) largely, though not entirely, Sadducean.[18]

Direct Roman rule thus spelled for the Sadducees a return to at least some of the power they had wielded under Hyrcanus I. One high priest during this period (Ananus the Younger, who held office in A.D. 62) is specifically identified as a Sadducee by Josephus. As I shall argue below, a number of other high priests during this time were probably Sadducees as well. Significantly, no high priest during direct Roman rule is ever said to have been a Pharisee, though some Jerusalem priests were Pharisees.[19] That the Sadducees as an organized group did not survive the destruction of Jerusalem in A.D. 70 suggests that most of them remained in the city, struggling with other Jewish factions while fighting the Romans till the bitter end. The internecine warfare within Jerusalem, as well as the Roman assault upon it, ended up killing a good number of the Sadducean aristocracy, both priest and lay, thus destroying the group as an effective political force.[20]

3. Socioeconomic and Political Status

From the direct testimony of Josephus, indirectly supported by the NT and rabbinic literature, we can say a few things about the socioeconomic and political status of the Sadducees—which, in turn, helps us fill in more of their history. According to Josephus *(Ant.* 13.10.6 §298; 18.1.4 §16), the Sadducees, on the one hand, were few in number and lacked a following among the common people; on the other hand, they enjoyed "the confidence of the wealthy alone" and were "the most prominent" or "leading" men *(tous . . . prōtous)* among the Jews. This combination of wealth, prominence, and leadership is hardly surprising. In Judean society of the time, social promi-

nence was largely based on wealth (especially the ownership of land) and political power or influence, often accompanied by a distinguished genealogy.
These were the usual attributes of the aristocracy.

For the period of direct Roman rule, the most prominent Jews in Judea
would naturally have included the present and former high priests, as well as
their high priestly families.[21] Under the Roman governor, the high priest,
supported by his family and associates, managed the ordinary affairs of his
fellow Jews. He enjoyed not only religious power over the temple and political power over the Jews of Judea but also great wealth from large landhold-
ings and the special dignity that in ancient societies derived from a carefully
guarded genealogy reaching back to ancient times—an important condition
for being high priest. As we shall see, our sources do, in fact, connect the Sadducees, at various points in their history, with the high priest and his entourage. As the Sadducees supported him, so they gained support from him.

The list of prominent and wealthy Jews in Judea would have included lay
aristocrats as well as priestly ones.[22] They, too, would have numbered among
the few and wealthy prominent citizens who belonged to the Sadducees.
Given this concentration of aristocrats in the Saducean party, and given the
party's connections to at least some high priests, we need not be surprised
that historically reliable reports from our three main sources usually place
the Sadducees in and around Jerusalem.

That the party of the Sadducees, while including aristocratic laymen, was
rooted first of all in the old-time high priestly families and their supporters is
suggested by the most probable etymology of the name Sadducee. The Hebrew ṣaddûqîn most likely comes from the name Zadok (in Hebrew ṣādôq),
the priest of Jerusalem who served both King David and King Solomon.[23]
The Jerusalem priests who traced their ancestry from Zadok and thus based
their claims to legitimacy and authority on him are called "sons of Zadok"
(benê ṣādôq) in various passages of the OT and intertestamental literature.[24]

These sons of Zadok seem to have controlled the Jerusalem temple and the
high priesthood from the time of the rebuilding of the Jerusalem temple (ca.
520–515 B.C.) after the Babylonian exile down to the disruption and revolt
caused by the Hellenizing policies of Antiochus IV (reigned 175–164 B.C.).
The victory of the Hasmonean family and their assumption in due time of the
high priesthood meant that a priestly family that did not claim to stem from
Zadok now occupied the supreme priestly office. While some of the sons of
Zadok had been discredited by their association with the Hellenizing policy
of Antiochus IV, and while others had been killed in the war unleashed by the
Hellenization crisis, some faithful sons of Zadok survived the war with their
honor intact. But they now found themselves displaced from the pinnacle of

religious (and political) power—the high priesthood—by the interloping Hasmoneans.

This may explain why, at this juncture, the sons of Zadok, along with their priestly and lay supporters, mutated into a party called the Sadducees. The Sadducees saw themselves as representing or supporting the Zadokites, the legitimate high priestly family, against the Hasmonean intruders.[25] Perhaps this also explains why, when we first meet the Pharisees and Sadducees contending with each other for power under John Hyrcanus I, the Hasmonean monarch starts out with the support of the Pharisees. The Sadducees—the old-line aristocratic priests who counted themselves sons of Zadok, along with the old-line lay aristocracy that supported them—apparently formed the opposition.

In due time, though, the Sadducees seem to have decided that limited power under a non-Zadokite high priest was better than no power at all.[26] As we have seen, the Sadducees succeeded in drawing Hyrcanus away from the Pharisees and to their own party, a party centered on the traditional Zadokite priests but including lay aristocrats as well. They were the "old-boy network" in Jerusalem as distinct from the *arrivistes* Hasmoneans. That may explain in part why some of the Hasmoneans were willing to join forces with the Sadducees: the support of the Zadokite priests and their followers could enhance the Hasmonean high priest's patina of legitimacy, while the Sadducees could regain some power. It was a holy horse trade.

In short, then, we should conceive of the Sadducees as a religious movement and a political party, made up mostly of old-time aristocratic priests and laymen, focused on Jerusalem, its temple, and its high priesthood.[27] Thus, Josephus' assertion that the Sadducees were not large in number only stands to reason. In the ancient Mediterranean world, the traditional aristocracy of a given country was always composed of a relatively small number of people situated on or near the top of the political, economic, and social pyramid.

Unlike the Pharisees, the Sadducees did not have a great amount of influence with the common people. Perhaps this might be explained in part by the fact that, at least during direct Roman rule, the Sadducees were accustomed to issuing orders backed up by police power, and so felt little need to rely heavily on moral suasion, exemplary living, and exact knowledge of the Scriptures, as did the Pharisees. Needless to say, the usual tension in ancient Mediterranean society between the poor common people and the rich and powerful elite played its part as well.

In describing the Sadducees, however, we should avoid simplistic identifications. As we have seen, not all Sadducees were priests, and not all priests were Sadducees. Likewise, not all aristocrats were Sadducees. Just as Josephus mentions a Pharisee who was a priest (Jozar, a member of the delegation sent to relieve Josephus of his command in Galilee), so he also mentions a Pharisee who was a prominent citizen of Jerusalem, though not a priest (e.g., Simon I, son of Gamaliel I).[28] Moreover, since in ancient Mediterranean society aristocrats had various retainers and clients, some "hangers on" among the Jewish laity in Jerusalem may have been Sadducees even though they were not rich noblemen.[29] Similarly, some members of the "lower" priesthood, who did not enjoy great wealth or political power, may have taken their cue from the priestly aristocrats among the Sadducees.

In brief, while we should think of the Sadducees as composed mainly of the priestly and lay nobility, we should remember that the religious and political reality in 1st-century Palestine may have been more complicated than we can detect today. Perhaps a small number of the common people, especially some residents of Jerusalem who were fiercely dedicated to temple piety and the exaltation of the temple state, may have been counted among the Sadducees too. But they would have been the exception, not the rule.

4. The Sadducees and the High Priesthood

When we come to the question of whether the high priest himself was always, regularly, or just occasionally a Sadducee during the period of direct Roman rule, matters become more speculative because the sources are largely silent on this question. In fact, the party affiliation of only a few high priests under Hasmonean, Herodian, and Roman rule is expressly stated by our sources. In addition, few individual Sadducees can be identified by name—a problem that, as we have seen, holds true for the Pharisees as well.

Still, a few things are fairly certain. As we have already seen, in the late 2d century and early 1st century B.C., John Hyrcanus I switched allegiance from the Pharisees to the Sadducees, and his successors Aristobulus I and Alexander Jannaeus probably continued to support the Sadducees. Whether we should speak of these three high priests (and monarchs) as Sadducean high priests or high priests who supported and were supported by the Sadducees is hard to decide. In the struggle between Hyrcanus II and Aristobulus II, some critics claim that the two rulers were supported by Pharisees and Sadducees respectively, but the historical record is so murky during this period of civil strife that it is difficult to reach a firm conclusion.

Not trusting Hasmoneans, Sadducees, or Pharisees—indeed, not trusting any of the Jewish groups previously in power—Herod the Great appointed some high priests whose families hailed from Babylon and Egypt. This policy was meant to guarantee the high priests' dependence on himself alone. During direct Roman rule, the only high priest whose party affiliation is specified is Ananus II (alias Ananus the son of Ananus or Ananus the Younger). Josephus clearly labels this Ananus II a Sadducee *(Ant.* 20.9.1 §197–203). Although Ananus II held the office of high priest for only three months in A.D. 62, he is a pivotal figure for our knowledge of the Sadducees, for Ananus II was the son of Ananus I (alias Ananus the Elder), who is known to Christians as Annas from his cameo appearances in Luke 3:2; John 18:13,24; and Acts 4:6. To Christians he is famous not because he was the father of a number of high priests, but because he was the father-in-law of Joseph Caiaphas, the high priest at the time of Jesus' arrest and crucifixion.

The picture of Annas that we get from the Gospels, Acts, and Josephus *(Ant.* 20.9.1 §198) is of a powerful manipulator of the political scene even after he was dismissed from office in A.D. 15.[30] He was probably responsible at least in part for the selection of Ananus II (as well as other members of his family) as high priest. If, then, his son, Ananus II, was a Sadducee, it is highly likely that Annas, who was to some extent "calling the shots" behind the scenes, was a Sadducee as well. It is hard to imagine that this *doyen* of a powerful and well-represented high priestly family did not set the political tone for his sons, who needed his help to succeed him.

This conclusion, in turn, has significant consequences. For Josephus *(Ant.* 18.2.1–2 §26–34; 20.9.1 §197–98) tells us that, although Annas was dismissed from office by the Roman prefect Valerius Gratus in A.D. 15, he enjoyed the unique good luck of seeing five of his sons and one son-in-law become high priests. According to Josephus, the five sons of Ananus who became high priests were Eleazar (A.D. 16–17), Jonathan (A.D. 37), Theophilus (A.D. 37–41), Matthias (A.D. 43?), and Ananus II (A.D. 62).[31] The one son-in-law, Joseph Caiaphas, is mentioned by Josephus in *Ant.* 18.2.2 §35 and 18.4.3 §95 as well as in Matt 26:3,57; Luke 3:2; John 11:49; 18:13–14, 24,28; and Acts 4:6—though only John 18:13 states that Annas was his father-in-law.[32] Granted, we are involved here in a lengthy chain of reasoning. But if we conclude that Ananus I was both a Sadducee and a major reason why his sons (one a known Sadducee) and son-in-law became high priests, then it is fairly probable that, from Ananus I to Ananus II, seven high priests under direct Roman rule were Sadducean.

Now, direct Roman rule down to the beginning of the First Revolt lasted some 60 years (A.D. 6–66). If we add up the years that these seven Sadducean high priests held office, the sum amounts to roughly 34 years. This would mean that during more than half of the period of direct Roman rule, a Sadducee certainly or probably occupied the office of high priest.[33]

If we may trust certain statements of Luke in Acts, the case for the Sadducean orientation of the house of Annas receives further support,[34] for in the first clash between the apostles and the high priests narrated in Acts, Annas and Caiaphas are both presented as operating within the circle of the Sadducees. In Acts 4:1–2, "the priests and the captain of the temple and the Sadducees" are annoyed by Peter and John proclaiming, in the specific case of Jesus, the resurrection from the dead.[35] They arrest the apostles and hold them for trial.

The next day, various officials gather for the trial; according to 4:6, they include "Annas the high priest and Caiaphas and John and Alexander, and all who were of high-priestly lineage." As so often is the case, Luke is confused about the details, but probably right about the big picture. Notice, for instance, how Annas, not Caiaphas, receives the title "high priest"—perhaps a muddled recollection that Annas was the true leader of the clan and holder of power, no matter who in the family occupied the office of high priest at a given moment (cf. Luke 3:2).

Despite his confusion over this item, Luke's overall picture, though, may well be accurate: the Jerusalem priests who are high temple officials with the power to arrest their fellow Jews are placed in the company of the Sadducees (v 1). All the members of the official group of v 1 are said to be annoyed at Peter's proclamation of resurrection from the dead (v 2)—as we would expect of temple authorities with a Sadducean bent. Then, in v 6, at least some of the priestly temple authorities referred to globally in v 1 are specified: not surprisingly, they include Annas, Caiaphas, and John (an alternate form of Jonathan, one of Annas' sons?).[36] While these priests are not explicitly called Sadducees in this verse, the general flow of the narrative in 4:1–6 intimates at least some connection. Still, Luke is not as clear as he might be. The wording of 4:1 is open to the interpretation that the priests and the Sadducees were simply two different groups that happened to be working together against the apostles.

Luke is clearer in Acts 5:17, which begins the second trial narrative, this time involving all the apostles. In 5:17, we are told: "Rising up, the high priest and all those with him, the party of the Sadducees, were filled with jealousy. . . ." At first sight, this verse seems straightforward enough, though it is encumbered with a grammatical problem. The high priest quite naturally takes the lead, though we should remember that, in the light of 4:6, Luke may be thinking of Annas rather than Caiaphas.[37] "All those with him" is a general way of referring to all his supporters. The grammatical problem comes with the phrase that immediately follows, which literally reads: "the being party of the Sadducees [hē ousa hairesis tōn Saddoukaiōn]."[38] Perhaps the best way of understanding the phrase is to take it as standing in apposition to the previous phrase: "the high priest and all his supporters, *namely,* the party of the Sadducees." This gives even greater precision to the statements in Acts 4:1–6: the group of supporters around the high priest is identified with the party of the Sadducees. In context, this statement implies that Annas (or, less likely, Caiaphas) is a Sadducee.[39] Thus, while Acts 4:1–6 and 5:17 do not give us any new information about Annas and his household, they do confirm the Sadducean slant of his family, a point that we have already deduced by other means.[40]

While this overview of high priests who were certainly, probably, or possibly Sadducean during direct Roman rule is fairly convincing, we should note a further significant point. In contrast to these high priests under direct Roman rule who were or may have been Sadducees, there is no high priest during this period who is known to have been a Pharisee. Indeed, it is telling how Josephus describes the four members of the delegation sent by the Jerusalem authorities to relieve him of his command in Galilee *(Life* 39 §197): "On the one hand, two of them were members of the common people and of the Pharisaic school, Jonathan and Ananias; on the other hand, the third, Jozar, was of priestly stock, and he too [was] a Pharisee; but Simon, the youngest of the group, was of a high priestly family." Notice that, after mentioning the party affiliation of the other three members of the delegation, Josephus feels no need to state explicitly whether Simon was or was not a Pharisee. It may be that Josephus takes for granted that mentioning Simon's high priestly origin excludes the possibility of his being a Pharisee.

In any case, granted that the high priest under the Roman prefect or procurator had to exercise his rule through or in cooperation with his fellow priestly and lay aristocrats based in Jerusalem, his personal beliefs or tendencies were perhaps not the single most important factor when it came to policy decisions. From the practical point of view, he had to work with the largely— though not entirely—Sadducean nobility if he was to govern effectively.

5. *Hălākâ*

As for Sadducean beliefs and practices, we are poorly informed. It is well to remember that, as with the Pharisees so with the Sadducees, we are dealing with a group that existed for over 200 years in a Palestinian society that was undergoing massive changes around the turn of the era. No doubt both the Pharisees and the Sadducees developed and mutated along with the society in which they were embedded. Yet all we have are "flat," static descriptions of their beliefs and practices, with no historical sense of their developments and mutations. With that caveat in mind, let us recapitulate what we learned about the legal rules and practices of the Sadducees in chapter 28:

(a) The Sadducees rejected the claims of the Pharisees that the latter possessed "traditions of the fathers [or: elders]" that were not contained in the written Law of Moses but that were nevertheless incumbent on all Israelites. This basic affirmation has often been broadened by later interpreters to mean that the Sadducees were wooden conservatives who accepted only the literal meaning of Scripture and rejected all legal traditions, opinions, and rulings *(hălākôt)* not found as such in Scripture. Some authors, from Church Fathers like Origen and Jerome onward, even stretched this position to mean that the Sadducees accepted as canonical Scripture only the Pentateuch, rejecting the other two parts of the canon, the Prophets and the Writings, accepted by the Pharisees.[41] This latter claim is simply anachronistic, since we cannot speak of a clearly defined and definitively closed canon of Jewish Scriptures in the pre-70 period. Nor is there any indication that the Sadducees in principle rejected most of the books that eventually entered the Jewish canon as the Prophets and the Writings.

It may well be that the Sadducees exalted the five books of Moses to a unique status that was so lofty that no other books, however sacred and revered, were thought to occupy the same level of authority. Yet this position would not have distinguished the Sadducees from later classical rabbinism. From the Mishna to the Babylonian Talmud, later rabbinic literature, written at a time when the three-part canon of Torah-Prophets-Writings was firmly established, sometimes gives indications of distinctions made within the canon, distinctions that exalt the primacy of the Pentateuch.[42]

As for the Sadducees being wooden literalists who rejected any tradition not clearly found in the Pentateuch, both common sense and the Mishna argue against such an idea.[43] Simply from a practical point of view, the Pentateuch gives only the broadest kind of directions for the performance of the liturgy by the high priest and other priests—and the Pentateuch speaks of the Tabernacle (or Tent of Meeting) in the wilderness, not the ornate temple (re)built by Herod the Great in Jerusalem. Hence, to carry out the daily liturgy in the Jerusalem temple, to say nothing of the complicated rituals of the great feasts, the priests would have had to develop, pass down, and rely upon all sorts of traditional rubrics not written in the Torah. As with any trade in the ancient Near East, the sons of officiating priests no doubt learned their sacred trade largely by observing and imitating what their fathers did. Thus, at least those Sadducees who were officiating priests (a fortiori, the high priest) had in effect their own "traditions of the fathers," guiding their conduct of the temple liturgy.

The same would hold true of the liturgical calendar governing the temple. The Pentateuch does not dictate the details of a whole yearly calendar for the temple liturgy. It seems likely that, during the early Second Temple period, the Jerusalem priests used a 364-day solar calendar, traces of which are preserved in *1 Enoch, Jubilees,* and Qumran literature.[44] Indeed, various sectarian groups, especially the Essenes, held tenaciously to the solar calendar even after the Jerusalem priests switched to a (solar-)lunar calendar sometime in the first half of the 2d century B.C. Surely the early Sadducees were aware of the change, a change that was not clearly founded in the Pentateuch and that probably helped to provoke the schism of the Qumranites, who continued to protest against the switch. Yet the Sadducees held firmly to the relatively new temple calendar—a prime example of their vindicating the special traditions of the Jerusalem temple, even when such traditions were relatively new and not contained in the written Torah. In fact, in a backhanded way, Josephus also testifies to special Sadducean traditions. Even in his exaggerated claim that the Sadducees, willingly or not, had to observe Pharisaic rules when assuming any office *(Ant.* 18.1.4 §17), Josephus indirectly testifies to the existence of Sadducean rules, which the Sadducees in office supposedly had to ignore in favor of the Pharisees' directives.

The later rabbinic literature likewise supplies us with stories—some, at least, obviously legendary—about Sadducean high priests either giving way to Pharisaic liturgical usage or insisting on observing their own ways. The most famous and well-attested story concerns a dispute about when and where the high priest should begin to burn incense as he enters the holy of holies on Yom Kippur.[45] While the particular anecdotes related by the rabbis may not be historical, the rabbinic literature, like Josephus, apparently preserves the memory that the Sadducees had their own liturgical traditions, which were at variance with the Pharisees'. Interestingly, the dispute over burning incense on Yom Kippur (likewise the dispute over the burning of the red heifer) seems to take for granted that high priests are Sadducees (or Boethusians).

(b) Even apart from the rubrics for temple liturgies, where we might expect the Sadducean priests to have evolved their own special practices, the Mishna indicates that the Sadducees, priestly or otherwise, championed particular legal rulings and opinions concerning human conduct *(hălākôt)* that are not contained as such in the written Mosaic Law. As we saw when treating the Pharisees in chapter 28, the most reliable example of such Sadducean *hălākôt* is found in the disputes between the Pharisees and the Sadducees laid out in *m. Yad.* 4:6–8. From these disputes we can gather the following:

(i) In *m. Yad.* 4:6, the Sadducees reject the (relatively new?) view of the Pharisees that the scrolls of Scripture render the hands that touch them unclean. The Sadducees do, however, accept the commonly held view that the bones of human beings render a person unclean, while the bones of animals do not. Thus, the dispute is over a *hălākâ* on purity, and one in which the Sadducees show themselves less rigorous and demanding than the Pharisees—and perhaps less amenable to recent innovations.

(ii) In *m. Yad.* 4:7, the Sadducees hold that an unbroken stream of liquid flowing from a clean vessel to an unclean vessel renders the first vessel and its contents unclean as well. Again, we have a Sadducean *hălākâ* on purity, and this time the Sadducees seem more rigorous than the Pharisees, who do not think that the second vessel renders the first unclean.

(iii) In the argument of *m. Yad.* 4:7, it is also stated by the Pharisees that the Sadducees hold that a stream of water flowing from a cemetery is clean. The position of the Pharisees is not explicitly stated here, but the view of the Sadducees on this subject of purity seems lenient rather than rigorous. In any case, these three examples show that the Sadducees had *hălākôt* on detailed points of purity.[46]

(iv) In *m. Yad.* 4:7, contrary to the Pharisees, the Sadducees hold that, just as an owner is liable for harm done by his ox or his ass, so is he liable for the harm done by his slave. The Pharisees, arguing on the grounds of individual human responsibility, maintain instead that the owner is responsible for harm done by his animals but not by his slave.

Three important points should be noted about the Sadducees' view in this argument over liability. First, their *hălākâ* extends in this case outside laws of purity to civil law, specifically to what we would call torts.[47] Second, the Sadducees take the more rigorous view of the owner's legal responsibility in tort law. This coheres with Josephus' claim that, in judicial matters, the Sadducees tended toward rigor but the Pharisees toward leniency.[48] Third, one may nevertheless wonder whether this example coheres entirely with Josephus' neat distinction between the Sadducees, who rejected the power of fate in human lives and stressed the responsibility of human beings for their own actions, and the Pharisees, who tried to maintain both the overriding power of fate and some limited human freedom. In this mishnaic example of liability for damage, the Pharisees are the ones who base their position simply on the principle of the freedom and responsibility of each human individual, even a slave, while the Sadducees make no allowance for this factor in their legal position.

(v) As we have seen, there is a problem of textual criticism in *m. Yad.* 4:8, where the Pharisees are arguing with either a Sadducee or a *mîn* (some sort of deviant Jew). If we think that the original form of this mishna referred to a Sadducee, then the passage shows that the Sadducees had their own way of drawing up a document granting a divorce (i.e., a *gēṭ*). This form differed from that of the Pharisees. Here the Sadducees' hălākâ concerns the laws governing marriage and divorce.

(c) Beyond these key passages in the mishnaic tractate Yadayim, other scattered traditions may preserve authentic Saducean hălākâ prior to A.D. 70. For example, it may be that Sadducees objected in principle to the ʿerûb, a legal fiction created by the Pharisees to mitigate the restrictions on local movement imposed by the sabbath. The ʿerûb was a legal means of "fusing" or joining adjacent houses. In effect, it extended the limits of one's house and so permitted freer movement and also the carrying of certain objects into streets or alleys on the sabbath. In m. ʿErub 6:1, we find a vague reference to "a Gentile or someone who does not recognize the ʿerûb." Some see here a veiled reference to a Sadducee.[49] More pertinent is m. ʿErub 6:2: Gamaliel II recalls how his father, Simeon I (a pre-70 Pharisee), ordered Gamaliel to hurry to place utensils in an alley way shared with a Sadducee. This would allow Simeon to set up an ʿerûb. But if the Sadducee, who did not recognize the institution of the ʿerûb, put his vessels in the alley first, he effectively impeded the setting up of the Pharisaic ʿerûb. In this mishna, then, the Pharisees are involved in mitigating the rigor of the sabbath observance by the ʿerûb, while the Sadducees remain the rigorists.[50]

(d) However, the stereotype of the Sadducees as rigorists, at least in matters of criminal justice, is rendered questionable by a tradition in m. Mak. 1:6.[51] The problem treated in this mishna is the proper punishment of false witnesses in a case involving the death penalty. Under what circumstances should the false witnesses themselves be put to death if their lie is discovered? The Sadducees hold that the false witnesses should themselves be executed only if the falsely accused person has already been executed. The Sadducees invoke the principle of the Torah found in Deut 19:21: "A life for a life."[52] If the accused's life has not yet been taken, then the false witnesses' lives should not be taken.

On the other side of the debate stand "the sages" (ḥăkāmîm)—who should not automatically be equated with the Pharisees.[53] The sages counter the Sadducees' citation of Deut 19:21 with Deut 19:19: "Then shall you do unto him [i.e., the false witness] as he intended to do unto his brother [i.e., the accused]." The sages stress that the false witness is still liable to the death penalty even if he only intended to have his "brother" executed, without being able to see the intention realized because his false testimony is discovered after his "brother" has been sentenced to death but before his "brother" has been executed. In other words, since Deut 19:19 states that the evil the false witness intended against another is to be inflicted on the false witness himself, the sages argue that the false witness is to be put to death even if his false testimony has been discovered before the execution of the accused. At the same time, the sages claim to uphold the principle of "a life for a life" by holding that the false witness is to be executed only if the death sentence has already been passed on the accused, making the latter, as it were, already a dead man.

In this whole question, then, the sages, like the Sadducees, could be said to adhere to the letter of the law. They simply emphasize a different "letter," that is to say, a different verse of the same passage from Deuteronomy. The sages latch onto the verse (Deut 19:19) that justifies the more rigorous answer to the question of how a false witness is to be punished, while the Sadducees seize upon the verse (Deut 19:21) that allows a milder answer.

Further examples of disputes over *hălākâ* between Sadducees and Pharisees—or Sadducees and sages—could be given, but the main point is clear. The Sadducees had *hălākôt* of their own, but the various legal rulings and opinions they followed do not seem to have formed a neat, seamless whole, governed by one set principle.

On the one hand, some of these Sadducean *hălākôt* simply rejected the innovations and additions to the Mosaic Law created by the Pharisaic traditions: e.g., the claim that the scrolls of Scripture rendered hands unclean or the Pharisaic invention of the ʿerûb, which clearly has no basis in the written Torah. In the first case, the Pharisees are imposing a burden not contained in the Law, a burden that the Sadducees reject. In this case, then, the Sadducees are the more lenient party. In contrast, in the case of the ʿerûb, the Sadducees prove to be the rigorists. According to certain modern scholars, some of these Sadducean *hălākôt* might be explained by a firm Sadducean principle: the adherence to the letter of the Mosaic Law. However, in the question of the death penalty for false witnesses, both Sadducees and sages adhere to the letter of the Law while appealing to different verses of the Law—and this time, the Sadducees emerge as the lenient party. Thus, adherence to the letter of the Law does not explain in every case what is distinctive about Sadducean *hălākôt*, just as it does not always make the Sadducees the rigorists in a dispute.

On the other hand, not all of the Sadducean *hălākôt* can be explained by this principle of adherence solely to the written Torah, i.e., the principle that rejects all innovations or additions to the written Torah. In the cases of the unbroken stream of liquid, the stream of water flowing from a cemetery, the liability of the owner for the harm done by his slave, and the proper form of a document of divorce, the written Mosaic Law gives no prescriptions covering the details over which the Sadducees and the Pharisees argue. Whatever the reasoning process or scriptural citations that might have been adduced to support these Sadducean traditions (and such supports, when present, are often secondary elements in the rabbinic tradition), the Sadducees in fact observed certain legal rules that cannot be found in the Pentateuch. Therefore, the mere fact of having such traditions did not, in itself, essentially distinguish the Sadducees from the Pharisees.[54]

What, then, *was* the essential difference between the Sadducees and Pharisees in matters of *hălākâ?* The meager historical record leaves us unsure, but perhaps the real difference lay in the way that the two groups understood their respective *hălākôt.* The Pharisees apparently considered that their venerable "traditions of the fathers," which they freely admitted were not present as such in the written Torah, were nevertheless normative for all Israel. This explains why, when they were in power under Hyrcanus I and later under Salome Alexandra, they enshrined their traditions in the laws governing the whole nation *(Ant.* 13.10.6 §296; 13.16.2 §408). This also explains why they took pains to be active and influential among the common people; when out of power, they sought to persuade the people to follow their traditions voluntarily.

How the Sadducees, in contrast, understood their special traditions is not clear. One possible explanation is that the Sadducees were like some Christian fundamentalists who champion what they call the "literal" interpretation of Scripture as the sole rule of faith and yet hold to various dogmas of Christian orthodoxy that in fact are not contained as such in Scripture—though the fundamentalists manage to find them in the Bible by highly creative and imaginative exegesis. Similarly, the Sadducees may have claimed that all their additional traditions were actually present in the written Torah or at least clearly derived from it. After all, creative exegesis can find in Scripture whatever creative exegetes want to find.[55] In brief, then: both the Pharisees and the Sadducees had legal traditions not found in the Torah. The difference, say some scholars, was that the Pharisees readily admitted this and yet maintained that their venerable and ancient "traditions of the fathers" were obligatory for all Israelites, while the Sadducees claimed that their special traditions were found in or were directly derived from the Torah.[56]

Another possible explanation, though, is that the Sadducees were content to defend and observe their special traditions both in their private lives and when they were exercising some public office—but without claiming that their special traditions were obligatory for all Jews and therefore should be imposed on all Jews in their daily lives.[57] The Sadducees were quite willing to argue in learned debate with the Pharisees and, indeed, even with their own teachers about which traditions were the right ones. But they had no zealous desire to force their particular traditions upon the whole nation as something normative for all Israelites.[58] They objected to the Pharisaic "traditions of the fathers" not simply because they thought that such traditions were wrong but also and perhaps primarily because they objected to any one party's traditions being imposed on the whole nation as mandatory for all.[59] It was perhaps in this limited sense that they held to "Scripture alone." But this hardly makes the Sadducees wooden literalists or fundamentalists.[60]

In the end, though, we must admit that we are only guessing when we try to discern the inner rationale behind the positions of the Pharisees and the Sadducees on their respective hălākôt. The sources do not give us sufficient information to form a sure conclusion.

6. Doctrine

It was perhaps in the area of what we would call doctrine, as distinct from hălākôt, that the Sadducees resisted most strongly any innovation that went beyond the clear teaching of the Pentateuch.[61] This may explain their rejection of some beliefs favored by the Pharisees:

(a) The most obvious example is the Sadducees' rejection of belief in the resurrection of the dead (J.W. 2.8.14 §165; Ant. 18.1.4 §16; Mark 12:18–27 parr.; Acts 23:8).[62] In this, the Sadducees' sober estimation of what the Pentateuch—and indeed, almost all of the books later taken into the Jewish canon—presupposes and teaches coincides perfectly with modern scientific exegesis. (One might ask as an aside whether this makes modern scientific exegesis "literalistic" like the Sadducees.) The Pentateuch in particular and, with few exceptions, the Jewish canon in general contain no affirmation of the resurrection of the body, a blessed eternal life, or any set of rewards and punishments meted out to the good and the bad beyond the grave. Only a highly ingenious argument (either by Jesus or by the Pharisees) could find such doctrines in the five books of the Torah.

Hence, instead of the pejorative label "literalistic," it might be fairer to say that here the Sadducees were sober exponents of the plain meaning of the text, a meaning upheld by modern critics as the original sense intended by the author(s)—though the Sadducees, needless to say, did not think in such terms. Once again, the Pharisees prove to be the innovators, for their doctrine of the resurrection of individual deceased Israelites is not taught explicitly in any sacred book later taken into the Jewish canon of Scripture, save for the Book of Daniel. And let us remember that Daniel was written only a decade or two before the Sadducees and Pharisees began to crystallize as parties. Thus, at least within mainstream Judaism, the Pharisees were championing a fairly new doctrine.[63] In contrast, the conservative Sadducees, while rejecting belief in bodily resurrection and eternal life, probably held to the common opinion contained in the Pentateuch and elsewhere in the sacred literature of Israel: namely, that the dead descended to a tenuous, shadowy existence in the underworld (Sheol), where there were no separate rewards or punishments for the good and the evil.

(b) Belief in the resurrection of the dead, reward and punishment after death, and a happy eternal life for the virtuous are all various expressions of what lies at the heart of Jewish apocalyptic eschatology: the transcendence of death for the individual believer and for the faithful of Israel as a whole.[64] If the Sadducees rejected the entire idea of postmortem reward and/or resurrection, and therefore the individual's transcendence of death, we may safely assume that they likewise rejected in general the whole apocalyptic movement that flourished in Judaism from the 3d century B.C. to the 1st and 2d centuries A.D.—a movement that was much broader than Pharisaism. As with the Pharisees' traditions of the fathers, so with the apocalyptic writers' visions of resurrection and eternal life: the Sadducees remained, in their own eyes, the solid rock of sober conservatism, holding fast to the normative revelation of Judaism's central document, the Torah, in the face of a flood of new and suspect ideas.

Does this mean that the Sadducees must have had no eschatological hopes at all? Not necessarily.[65] Already in the Torah and more explicitly in the pre-exilic prophets, there are intimations of a this-worldly eschatology centered on the Davidic king and/or the Jerusalem temple on Mt. Zion. Both politically and religiously, the Sadducees were focused on the temple-state of Judea, with its center in Jerusalem. Certain of the sacred writings of Israel (e.g., Isaiah) inculcated the belief that God had given this temple-state to his chosen people. He continued to sustain it amid all adversities, and at some future date he would reveal his full glory dwelling within it.

It is therefore at least conceivable that some, if not all, Sadducees cultivated an eschatological hope for the exaltation of Mt. Zion in the last days à la Isa 2:1–5 or Isa 60:1–22: all the Gentiles would come bearing gifts to the temple, as indeed some Gentiles already did in the 1st century A.D. A Davidic or Hasmonean king could have been included in this scenario, but the priestly and lay aristocracy may have preferred to dispense with that particular hope. All this, I admit, is speculation on my part. I simply wish to emphasize that the Sadducees' rejection of more recent apocalyptic eschatology need not have entailed the wholesale rejection of more traditional eschatological hopes for an ideal future in this world, centered upon Jerusalem and the temple they controlled.

(c) The Sadducees' rejection of apocalyptic theology no doubt involved the rejection of the luxuriant angelology and demonology that supplied the drama of the end time with a huge cast of characters, often with distinct names and functions. This rejection offers us one possible way of understanding a puzzling statement made by Luke in Acts 23:8: "The Sadducees say that there exists neither resurrection nor angel nor spirit, while the Pharisees affirm all of these." [66] This supposed denial of angels and spirits by the Sadducees is problematic, since it is attested nowhere else.[67] Some scholars resolve the difficulty by having it refer to the highly developed angelology of apocalyptic, not to angels in general.[68]

But restricting Luke's statement to apocalyptic angels does not satisfy many critics. It does not really explain the puzzle that, while the Sadducees' denial of the resurrection is attested in both Josephus and the Synoptics—and echoed later on in rabbinic literature—neither Josephus nor the rabbis nor the NT, apart from Acts 23:8, says anything about the Sadducees' denial of angels or spirits. More to the point, to restrict Luke's sweeping, unqualified statement ("nor angel nor spirit") to the special case of the highly evolved angelology and demonology of apocalyptic is arbitrary. The natural sense of the statement is the denial of any angel or spirit whatsoever.

Yet there is a grave difficulty with understanding Luke's assertion in this natural sense: the Sadducees certainly revered the Torah as normative. And the Torah speaks in various passages either of "the angel of the Lord" (a sort of visible representation or spokesman of Yahweh) or of a group of angels obviously subservient to Yahweh (e.g., Jacob's dream of the angels of God ascending and descending on a ladder reaching up to heaven in Gen 28:12) or of individual kinds of angels with individual tasks (e.g., the cherubim who guard the way to the tree of life in the Garden of Eden in Gen 3:24). One possible solution would be to refer Acts 23:8 to angels who intervene now, in present history as opposed to the sacred past, to convey a new revelation or to work a miracle. But this approach likewise suffers from a gratuitous restriction of a sweeping statement to a specific case.

David Daube takes a different tack by suggesting that "angel" or "spirit" refers here not to preternatural beings from heaven but rather to the human soul or spirit that survives death and exists in an interim state prior to the resurrection.[69] However, while "angel" and "spirit" are at times interchangeable when an author speaks of heavenly beings (see, e.g., Heb 1:13–14), the use of "angel" and "spirit" in the same breath (so in Acts 23:8) for the immortal soul of a deceased human prior to the resurrection is unusual and harsh. In fact, there is no Jewish or Christian text from the 1st century A.D. that clearly equates "spirit" and "angel" in the sense of a human being's postmortem, interim mode of existence before the resurrection. Moreover, both the phrasing of Acts 23:8 (*mēte aggelon mēte pneuma*, "neither angel nor spirit") and even more the word order of v 9 (*ei de pneuma elalēsen autō ē aggelos,* "What if a spirit has spoken to him, or an angel?") seem to make a clear distinction between spirit and angel as two different kinds of beings.[70]

Acts 23:8 therefore remains a puzzle. One must leave open the possibility that on this point Luke is simply mistaken,[71] either because he has taken over erroneous information about the Sadducees from some source (there would be more of the same in the patristic church) or because he has made an erroneous deduction from the Sadducees' denial of the resurrection. Luke certainly knows about this denial from the story of Jesus' dispute with the Sadducees over the resurrection in Mark 12:18–27. Luke reproduces this dispute story in Luke 20:27–40, where, in v 36, Jesus affirms that humans who attain to the resurrection of the dead are *isaggeloi* (a rare adjective meaning "like the angels"). Moreover, Luke strengthens this point by adding a statement to the Marcan story: risen human beings are "sons of God," a phrase that occurs at times in the OT and intertestamental literature to describe angels.[72] Thus, the close connection between risen human beings and angels in the dispute story on the resurrection may have led Luke to draw the erroneous conclusion that Sadducees denied the existence of angels as well as the resurrection of humans. Still, this is only one explanation among many; the puzzle of Acts 23:8 remains.

(d) Just as Luke alone tells us that the Sadducees denied angels or spirits, Josephus alone tells us that the Sadducees totally rejected ("did away with") fate (= divine providence). According to Josephus, the Sadducees claimed that all things lie in the power of human beings; every human has the ability to choose between good and evil. As we saw in our treatment of the Pharisees, this broad generalization about the Sadducees deserves to be read with a critical eye.

For apologetic reasons, Josephus is intent on presenting the Essenes, the Pharisees, and the Sadducees to his cultured Greco-Roman audience as three venerable schools of thought (or philosophical schools, *haireseis*) within Judaism. Pressing his typology, Josephus describes the three schools by imposing on them the template of the fate/free will debate that was a major issue in the main Greek philosophical schools. In *Ant.* 13.5.9 §171–73 (cf. *J.W.* 2.8.14 §162–65; *Ant.* 18.1.2–5 §11–22), Josephus neatly distributes the three main positions among the three Jewish schools: the Essenes attribute everything to fate; the Pharisees, in one way or another, combine fate and human freedom; and the Sadducees simply deny fate. As we saw, this monochromatic picture of the Essenes as fatalists situated on one end of the philosophical spectrum hardly does justice to the complicated picture we find in the sectarian documents of Qumran: a juxtaposition of God's control of all things and of humans' responsibility to choose and act rightly.

Extrapolating from this comparison between Josephus' neat model and the complex reality of Qumran, we may at least wonder whether the sleek and simple portrait of the Sadducees, situated symmetrically by Josephus at the other end of the spectrum, does full justice to their position. After all, the Sadducees revered the Pentateuch, with its dominant themes of God's choice of Israel as his special people, his guidance of Israel's history and of the lives of individual patriarchs, his miracles performed to deliver Israel from Egypt and conduct it safely through the desert to the promised land, and his revelation to Israel of particular laws and ceremonies that were not made known to the pagan nations.

Nor was it simply the great figures of Israel's history, such as Abraham and Moses, to whom God showed his special care and interest. The very laws of the Pentateuch claim that God cares for and vindicates the widow, the orphan, and the poor day laborer. The reward-and-punishment theology behind the laws in the Torah presume, especially in Deuteronomy, that God will reward those who keep his laws and will punish those who do not. If we doubt Luke's assertion in Acts 23:8 that the Sadducees deny the existence of angels and spirits because it is contradicted by their presence in the Pentateuch, should we not also doubt Josephus' claim that the Sadducees deny divine providence when that assertion is abundantly contradicted by the presence of divine providence throughout the Pentateuch?

Moreover, it is hard to comprehend how those Sadducees who were officiating priests could regularly offer prayers and sacrifices in the Jerusalem temple, thanking God for past benefactions, begging him to forgive sins (especially on Yom Kippur!), and petitioning him for his blessing on Israel (notably the blessings of rain and an abundant harvest) when their complete denial of God's providential concern for and involvement in this world would render all such prayers meaningless, even laughable. The same would hold true of the Sadducean laity who regularly attended the ceremonies of the great feasts in the temple. Are we to imagine that for some 200 years, the Sadducees as a group engaged in mass hypocrisy, focusing their religious concern on a temple whose prayers and sacrifices, conducted often by Sadducean priests, contradicted what the Sadducees really believed and openly professed as their teaching?

While such a damning portrait of the Sadducees is not unheard of in modern scholarship (they are often made the convenient "bad guys" or "heavies" of ancient Jewish history), it hardly seems supported by the evidence.[73] I think it more reasonable to suppose that, just as Josephus exaggerated a major tendency of Essene theology, turning the Essenes into fatalists for the sake of his neat pattern of Jewish philosophical schools, so too he exaggerated a major tendency of the pragmatic Sadducees, whose obligation to run the temple and govern Judean Jews during direct Roman rule naturally made them concentrate on human initiative, actions, and obligations. This is an almost universal trait in effective politicians and rulers, whether or not they make room for divine providence in their religious thought.[74] Moreover, from a theological point of view, the Sadducees may have been influenced by that stream of postexilic Jewish thought which tended to stress the transcendence of God, thus downplaying—though not explicitly denying—his guidance of human history. One should also remember the theologically valid and perfectly reasonable concern that, according to Josephus, moved the Sadducees in this direction: the desire to remove God from any involvement in evil.[75]

This, I think, is all we can say about the Sadducees. Even more than in the case of the Pharisees, our discussion of the Sadducees has had to rely on indirect arguments, reading between the lines, and hypotheses—only to produce a very fragmentary picture. We must resign ourselves to the fact that, short of the discovery of new documents from the ancient Mediterranean world, the Sadducees will remain for us very shadowy figures.

II. JESUS' DISPUTE WITH THE SADDUCEES OVER THE RESURRECTION OF THE DEAD (MARK 12:18–27 PARR.)[76]

A. Introduction to the Sadducees in the Gospels

As soon as we turn to the presentation of the Sadducees in the Gospels, we are struck by how different it is from the Gospels' depiction of the other opponents of Jesus. In contrast to multiple appearances by stock adversaries like the Pharisees, the scribes, the chief priests, and the elders, the Sadducees appear only once in Mark's Gospel. The occasion is their debate with Jesus over the question of the resurrection of the dead (Mark 12:18–27 parr.).[77] Apart from this lone Marcan story and its Synoptic parallels (Matt 22:23–33; Luke 20:27–38), the Sadducees are virtually absent from the Gospels as well as from the rest of the NT. The only exceptions are two pericopes into which Matthew inserts the Sadducees secondarily as stage props alongside the Pharisees (Matt 3:7; 16:1,6,11–12).

Accordingly, the Sadducees are completely absent from the letters of Paul. This is at first glance surprising, since Paul is writing during the 50s of the 1st century, when the Sadducees were ascendant in the Jerusalem power structure. The Sadducees are likewise absent from the Gospel of John, who is otherwise well informed about matters Jewish in pre-70 Jerusalem. Actually, the silence of Paul, John, and other NT authors supports the picture of the Sadducees we get from Josephus: the Sadducees were a small, inbred group of priestly and lay aristocrats centered in Jerusalem.

Understandably, then, Paul had no occasion to mention them when writing to largely Gentile churches outside Palestine. A fortiori, the other NT authors, composing their works probably after A.D. 70 and outside Palestine, would find no reason to play up a tiny aristocratic Jewish party that had since disappeared as an organized group from the Palestinian landscape. In contrast, the Pharisees, already present in some Gospel traditions before 70, supplied the evangelists with a convenient, if tendentious, symbol for the nascent rabbinic movement that emerged out of the fiery crucible of 70.

Hence one sign that Mark's Gospel lies somewhere near the bloody borderline of 70—give or take a few years—is that, among all the 1st-century Christian writings later taken into the NT, it alone preserves from some pre-Gospel source an account of one particular clash between Jesus and the Sadducees. All Matthew and Luke can do is take over Mark's story into their Gospels; they have nothing substantive to add on Jesus' relations with the Sadducees.[78] If, then, the dispute over the resurrection in Mark 12:18–27 does contain some historical recollection from Jesus' ministry, it is a unique NT relic that deserves to be enshrined alongside the few stories about the Sadducees in Josephus.

B. THE FORM-CRITICAL CATEGORY OF THE PERICOPE

Mark 12:18–27 fits into Bultmann's category of a *Streitgespräch* (a "dispute story," "conflict story," or "controversy dialogue"), which consists of a hostile exchange between Jesus and some opponent(s).[79] Characteristically, the opponents pose a question about or a challenge to the teaching or practice of Jesus and/or his disciples. Jesus replies with a short, incisive, and sometimes witty argument, including at times a counterquestion, a metaphor or axiom, or a citation of Scripture. His argument defeats the opponents, at least in the opinion of the Christians composing and listening to the dispute story.

Mark 12:18–27 exhibits most of these traits. The Sadducees, whose basic stance as deniers of the resurrection mark them as opponents of Jesus from the start, approach him with an objection to belief in the resurrection of the dead (v 18). The objection is based on the levirate law governing the marriage of a widow to her brother-in-law in Deut 25:5 (v 19). The Sadducees implicitly argue that resurrection of the dead would lead to bizarre consequences in the case of a widow who had been married in serial fashion to six men who were all brothers of her deceased husband (vv 20–23). The hostility of the Sadducees is clear from their mocking example of one woman married to seven men; the whole point of their question and of the large number of husbands is to expose belief in the resurrection to ridicule.

After an initial rebuke to the Sadducees for their ignorance of both the Scriptures and the power of God (v 24), Jesus replies first by rejecting the Sadducees' underlying assumption about the *manner* of the resurrection, i.e., that the condition of people raised from the dead will be basically a continuation of their former earthly condition, marriage and sexual activity included (v 25). In the risen state, says Jesus, there will be no more marriage; to that extent, those who rise from the dead will be similar to the angels. Then he cites Exod 3:6, God's revelation of himself to Moses in the burning bush, as a proof of the *fact* of the resurrection (v 26).[80]

While the pericope ends without an explicit statement of the reaction of the opponents (amazement, anger, plans to kill Jesus), Jesus' emphatic concluding words in v 27 ("you are very much in error") plus the reaction of the scribe who asks the next question of Jesus in v 28 because he sees that Jesus had "answered them well" serve as a sufficient indication to the Marcan audience that Jesus has defeated his opponents.[81] Thus, Mark 12:18–27 is a good example of the form of a dispute story.

C. The Placement of the Dispute within Mark's Gospel

Mark has carefully arranged two sets or cycles of dispute stories *(Streitgespräche):* one in Galilee near the beginning of the public ministry, the other in Jerusalem toward the end of the ministry. The Galilean cycle occurs at 2:1–3:6, after Jesus has begun his ministry in Galilee but before his Galilean ministry reaches its climax in chaps. 6–9. Similarly, Mark places the Jerusalem dispute stories (11:27–12:37) after the initial events of Jesus' ministry in Jerusalem (triumphal entry, cursing of the fig tree, and "cleansing" of the temple in 11:1–25), but before the climactic events of Jesus' death and resurrection (14:1–16:8).

A basic function of the Jerusalem dispute stories is to depict the increasing hostility between Jesus and the various Jewish groups in Jerusalem, a hostility that will lead to Jesus' death a few days later. In each encounter, Jesus is presented, at least implicitly, as the authoritative teacher victorious over his enemies in every dispute. The cumulative effect of Jesus' triumphs is that a well-disposed scribe finds himself agreeing with Jesus (12:28), that no one else dares challenge Jesus any further (12:34), and that Jesus can in turn pose a question about the scribes' teaching on the Messiah, a question that receives approbation from the crowd but no answer from the scribes (12:37). Jesus concludes his treatment of the scribes, who have been present from the beginning of the first dispute in 11:27, by roundly denouncing them for their religious ostentation, oppression of the poor, and hypocrisy (12:38–40).

The Christian audience of Mark's Gospel could no doubt surmise what this series of clashes would lead to, but Mark leaves nothing to surmise. At the end of Jesus' parable of the evil tenants of the vineyard (12:1–12), Mark states that Jesus' opponents wished to arrest him, since they realized that this parable, which branded them as the murderers of the son of the owner of the vineyard, was aimed squarely at them. Yet they dared not arrest Jesus in public, since they feared the crowd, which listened gladly to him (12:12; cf. 12:37).

This predicament of the authorities links up neatly with the opening of the Passion Narrative, where the chief priests and the scribes plan to arrest Jesus stealthily, to avoid any riot among the people who are in Jerusalem for the feast of Passover (14:2). Hence it is important that Judas Iscariot seek the right time (14:11: *eukairōs*) to hand Jesus over to the authorities. Not surprisingly, the time chosen is at night, when Jesus is away from the crowd and outside the city at Gethsemane (14:32–50). Mark thus clearly, if artificially, binds the final disputes in Jerusalem to the story of Jesus' arrest and death.

Still, for all Mark's artifice and linkage, the cycle of Jerusalem dispute stories, examined one by one, turns out to be a mixed bag of goods, much more so than the Galilean cycle. The first dispute (11:27–33), on the authority of Jesus, acts as something of a rubric over the whole cycle, since it issues a general challenge to Jesus' authority. What has unleashed this challenge is not clear in the story itself, though Mark's ordering of the material makes the triumphal entry and the cleansing of the temple the most likely provocations.[82] The next pericope, the parable of the evil tenants of the vineyard (12:1–12), does not technically fall under the category of a dispute story. However, in Mark's overarching composition, it may well serve as a further polemical reply of Jesus to the initial challenge of "the high priests, the scribes, and the elders" in 11:27. There is no change of time, place, or audience at 12:1; and so the opponents who do not react to Jesus at the end of the first dispute story (11:33) are the same people who do react at the end of the parable: they seek to arrest him (12:12).

The third pericope in the cycle (12:13–17) is the query about paying the coin of tribute to Caesar. The question is posed by the curious combination of "some of the Pharisees and the Herodians" (v 13). The only other time in the whole of the NT that this strange alliance of adversaries surfaces is at the end of the Galilean cycle of dispute stories (3:6), where the Pharisees take counsel with the Herodians on how to destroy Jesus. The alliance's reappearance at 12:13 is Mark's way both of binding the two cycles together and of indicating by way of cross-reference the deadly intent of these questioners. Thus, the Jerusalem cycle points forward once again to the imminent passion.

The next dispute story (12:18–27) is our major concern, the debate over the resurrection. As we have seen, it brings another group of opponents, the Sadducees, on the scene. It is followed by what is usually called a "scholastic dialogue" *(Schulgespräch)* rather than a dispute story, since—at least in Mark's version—the scribe who questions Jesus about the greatest commandment (12:28–34) is well disposed toward him and is praised by Jesus at the end of the exchange. It is then that Jesus turns the tables by asking the crowd about the muddled teaching of the scribes on the Messiah (12:35–37); this is followed by Jesus' denunciation of the scribes (12:38–40). The story of the widow's mite (12:41–44) may serve as something of a coda to the whole cycle insofar as one can read it not so much as a praise of the self-sacrificing generosity of the widow as rather Jesus' excoriation of the temple authorities for their exploitation of the poor.[83]

This rapid survey of the Jerusalem dispute cycle reveals how heterogeneous the material is, both in form and in substance.[84] While there are verbal and thematic links among the pericopes, we do not have the same tight, concentric structure and interweaving of themes that we find in the Galilean cycle of dispute stories. Indeed, some of the pericopes making up the Jerusalem cycle are not, strictly speaking, dispute stories at all. It may be that Mark's primary intent in welding together this Jerusalem cycle is not so much a full treatment of each question that is raised as rather the moving forward of the plot by creating the sense of a gathering storm: various Jewish groups—chief priests, scribes, elders, Pharisees, Herodians, and Sadducees—line up against Jesus, only to be defeated by him. All this, implies Mark, only enrages them the more and drives them to carry out the plan that the Pharisees and Herodians broached back in 3:6: they must destroy Jesus. The Jerusalem dispute stories are thus, in Mark's composition, the immediate spark that starts the conflagration of the Passion Narrative.[85]

Thus, we can see how the focus of our concern, the Sadducees' dispute over the resurrection, fits into this overall purpose of Mark. One reason that Mark, who otherwise shows no knowledge of or interest in the Sadducees, places the Sadducees' debate with Jesus over the resurrection at this point in his Gospel may be that it helps swell the chorus of diverse opponents as the passion approaches.

In addition, there may be a thematic reason for Mark's positioning of this debate within the cycle of disputes just before Jesus' passion and death. It is fitting that the one dispute story in the whole Gospel that focuses directly on the theme of death and resurrection should be followed so closely by the story of Jesus' own death and resurrection. That Jesus should prove the doctrine of the resurrection from the dead to a group of his adversaries just before he is put to death by his adversaries, only to rise from the dead on the third day, is an irony worthy of John's Gospel. In fact, if we define "dispute story" in a precise and restricted fashion—so that neither the scholastic conversation with the well-disposed scribe nor Jesus' question about the scribes' teaching on the Messiah qualifies—the debate with the Sadducees about death and resurrection is the last dispute story in Mark's narrative before Jesus' death and resurrection.[86]

Mark thus shows himself a true literary artist in being able to take a number of heterogeneous pericopes and forge them into the Jerusalem cycle of dispute stories by imposing on them an overriding theme and purpose. At the same time, though, we must remember not to read into the different dispute stories, when analyzed as isolated units, the overarching themes that Mark has secondarily imposed on them. In particular, we should notice that the theme of Jesus' own death and resurrection and, indeed, the whole Christian approach to the problem of death and resurrection, are absent from the Sadducees' dispute when 12:18–27 is removed from Mark's artificial framework and examined as a discrete unit of tradition. Taken by itself, the Sadducees' debate moves within the thought-world of 1st-century Judaism, not 1st-century Christianity. With this in mind, let us now turn to this isolated unit and examine its structure in detail.

D. The Structure of Mark 12:18–27

Some 20th-century exegetes have dissected Mark 12:18–27 into a number of different pieces of tradition, which are then assigned to different chronological stages in the story's development.[87] However, the methodological starting-point for any analysis of a pericope must be the inspection and delineation of the pericope's structure as it now stands in the text. Any theories about some verses being secondary additions must come later.

That this ten-verse pericope is held together from start to finish by the themes of death and resurrection, a basic belief in God's normative revelation in the Torah, references to Moses, citations of Scripture, and discussions about marriage and the cessation of marriage is clear from even a cursory inspection of the text. What is more striking, on closer examination, is how carefully structured and balanced this compact pericope is. The pericope as a whole is divided into two major parts, each part having in turn two subsections:

(1) In Part One (vv 18–23), the Sadducees are the grammatical subject of v 18; seizing the initiative, they become the speakers throughout Part One. (a) In the first subsection (v 19), the Sadducees cite Deut 25:5 (conflated with Gen 38:8) on levirate marriage. They thus highlight the normative will of God, revealed in Scripture, which governs the precise case they are about to present in the second subsection. (b) In the second subsection (vv 20–23), they pose the fictitious (and mocking) case of seven brothers, each of whom in turn marries the same woman. These successive marriages are undertaken in keeping with the law of levirate in Deut 25:5, in a vain attempt to provide legal offspring to the deceased husband of the first marriage. After vv 21–22 carefully describe the case in detail, with each husband dying without producing a child, v 23 springs the mocking trap-question: When these persons rise from the dead—really, in the mind of the Sadducees, *if* they should ever rise—which of the seven brothers, all of whom lawfully had this woman as their wife during their earthly existence, will have her as his wife in his risen existence? This second subsection then ends with an *inclusio:* the final clause in v 23 ("for the seven had her as wife") harks back to the opening clause of v 20, at the beginning of the exposition of the fictitious case ("there were seven brothers").

(2) In Part Two (vv 24–27), Jesus becomes the grammatical subject (v 24) and the speaker throughout Part Two, replying to the question of the Sadducees in two subsections (v 25 and vv 26–27). His two-part answer corresponds (a) to the Sadducees' basic denial of the *fact* of the resurrection (stated in v 18) and (b) to the underlying reason for their denial: their (erroneous) way of conceiving of the *manner* or mode of the resurrection (expressed in their bizarre example in vv 20–23). Jesus announces the two parts of his answer in v 24 when he asks in a mocking rhetorical question (corresponding neatly to the Sadducees' mocking question in v 23): Are not you Sadducees in error about the resurrection because you are ignorant of (a) the Scriptures, which testify to the *fact* of the resurrection, and (b) the power of God, which causes people who rise from the dead to possess a very different *manner* or mode of life from their earthly existence? Jesus then takes up these two points in chiastic (i.e., inverted) order: first (b), then (a). In other words, Jesus first deals with the more superficial or "presenting" problem; he corrects the Sadducees' misconception about the *manner* of the resurrection. Then he moves on to the more fundamental point of the *fact* of the resurrection. Both point (b) and point (a) are introduced by rebuking rhetorical questions: "Is it not for this reason . . . ? " (v 24) and "Have you not read . . . ? " (v 26).

In v 25 (point [b]), Jesus explains how God's power, raising the dead to life, brings them into a thoroughly different type or *manner* of existence: *like* (*hōs* [manner!]) the angels in heaven, they do not engage in marriage or sexual activity. Hence the whole problem the Sadducees have posed about levirate marriage (vv 20–23) does not apply to the radically altered existence of those who have risen from the dead.

Verses 26–27 (point [a]) begin with "but concerning" *(peri de),* marking a clear break in the text to indicate that Jesus is moving from point (b) to point (a).[88] Jesus now proves the *fact* of the resurrection (v 26: *hoti* [fact!] *egeirontai*), the denial of which defines the Sadducees as a group (v 18). As the Sadducees based their argument against the resurrection on the revelation of God's will in the Mosaic Torah (Deut 25:5, cited in v 19), so Jesus bases his argument for the resurrection on God's revelation of his very self in the Mosaic Torah, specifically in his revelation of his identity to Moses in the burning bush (Exod 3:6, cited in v 26). In v 27a, Jesus takes this self-revelation of God, who chooses to manifest himself precisely as the God who protects and saves the lives of his chosen people (i.e., the God of Abraham in v 26), and then builds on it. Jesus adds as a second premise the observation—obvious to ancient Jews—that the savior God who defines himself by his relation to Abraham, Isaac, and Jacob is the God not of dead, moldering corpses but of living persons. Hence the unspoken conclusion: God the protector and savior of the patriarchs and of his chosen people will raise Abraham and all faithful Israelites to life. The conclusion, however, that Jesus puts into words is rather his initial point in v 24, now strengthened in v 27b: the Sadducees are *very much* in error because their denial of the resurrection is tantamount to a denial of the God of Abraham, Isaac, and Jacob.

In brief, this pericope is a marvelously compact structure composed of balanced parts and subsections and sustained by straightforward and inverted (chiastic) parallelism. One could run through a list of all the individual words, phrases, and themes that cooperate in assembling this carefully contoured whole: e.g., the Sadducees' statement "Moses wrote" *(Mōysēs egrapsen)* in v 19, corresponding to Jesus' claim about "the book of Moses" *(tē biblǭ Mōyseōs)* in v 26; "for the seven had her as wife" at the end of v 23, harking back to "there were seven brothers" at the beginning of v 20—thus creating an *inclusio* for the second subsection of Part One; "you are in error" *(planasthe)* in v 24, corresponding to "you are very much in error" *(poly planasthe)* in v 27—thus creating an *inclusio* between the beginning and the end of Jesus' reply in vv 24–27, the whole of Part Two. More important, both halves of the pericope, the Sadducees' question and Jesus' answer, turn on the two problems of the manner and the fact of the resurrection, i.e., the "how" (*hōs* in v 25) and the "that" (*hoti* in v 26) of the resurrection. Both parts of Jesus' answer are introduced by rebuking rhetorical questions (v 24 + v 26). Faced with such an intricately articulated unit of tradition with common words, phrases, and themes forming a complex network of references back and forth across the whole pericope, I find it a priori difficult to accept the theory that this pericope grew haphazardly in stages, with various verses being added by various hands at various times.

Nevertheless, such observations do not solve the issue definitively. We must now turn to a more thorough, verse-by-verse exegesis of the pericope to see whether its flow of thought confirms our initial impression of unity or instead makes the theory of multiple stages of redaction more likely. A greater appreciation of the details and subtleties of the text will also aid us in our subsequent discussion of whether this tradition ultimately goes back to an incident in the ministry of Jesus or is simply a creation of the early church.

E. EXEGESIS OF MARK 12:18–27[89]

(1) Part One (vv 18–23) begins in v 18 with the Sadducees taking the initiative in coming to Jesus with their trick question that aims at making belief in the resurrection of the dead—and anyone like Jesus who holds it—look ridiculous.[90] For a Christian audience, the identification of the Sadducees as the group that, by definition *(hoitines),* holds that there is no resurrection of the dead immediately brands them as a circle of people who stand in theological opposition to Jesus.[91] No doubt the story presumes that this identification of Sadducees as deniers of the resurrection is known to Jesus. Hence, while the question they pose ostensibly deals with the effects of the law of levirate when the resurrection finally takes place, it is obvious to both sides from the very beginning of the debate that the Sadducees intend by their question to attack belief in the resurrection and so Jesus' credibility as a reliable teacher.

The need to define the Sadducees as deniers of the resurrection when they first appear in this story seems to indicate that, unlike the Pharisees, scribes, chief priests, or elders, the name "Sadducee" could not be presumed to be immediately intelligible to a Christian audience. Indeed, as we have seen, this pericope is the only Gospel tradition circulating in the early church (as opposed to a few redactional insertions by Matthew) that spoke of the Sadducees. Small wonder they had to be identified.[92]

(a) In v 19 (the first subsection of Part One), the Sadducees address Jesus politely as "teacher" (with *rabbi* probably standing behind this word in any hypothetical Aramaic or Hebrew source). In the early 1st century A.D., the title *rabbi* was not yet tied to an elite circle of learned Jews who had engaged in lengthy formal study under famous masters and who were then ordained to the rabbinate.[93] Instead, the address on the lips of the Sadducees simply recognizes Jesus as a Jew who has a de facto reputation for effective teaching among the people and who has therefore attracted a following. The address does not necessarily indicate that the Sadducees really accept his authority.

The Sadducees lay the groundwork for their question by appealing to the authority of Moses in the Pentateuch, that part of the Jewish Scriptures that all Jews, whatever their theoretical positions about other sacred books, accepted as the holy and normative revelation of God's will for his chosen people ("Moses wrote *us*"). It is surprising to see how many 20th-century commentators explain the choice of the Pentateuch by the Sadducees—and by Jesus in his reply—on the grounds that the Sadducees rejected all other works of Scripture.[94] As we have seen, there is no basis for this claim when the ancient sources are read critically. It may well be that for Sadducees, as for many other Jews, the Pentateuch enjoyed a unique preeminence among sacred works. But that hardly translates into outright rejection of all the other works that later entered the Jewish canon of Scripture. A better explanation might be that, at a time when the Jewish canon was still in flux, the best "ground rules" for a dispute among Jews who differed in their theological outlook were for both sides to draw their Scriptural citations and their arguments from the universally revered written Torah of Moses.[95]

The Sadducees cite a paraphrastic version of Deut 25:5, the law of levirate ("brother-in-law").[96] The law provided that if a man died before his wife had a child, the dead man's brother (i.e., the widow's brother-in-law) should take the widow as his wife. The first child of that second union would count legally as the child of the dead man, continuing his name and lineage and preserving his ancestral property within his family.[97] The text the Sadducees cite is actually a conflation of an abbreviated form of Deut 25:5 with Gen 38:8. In the latter text, the patriarch Judah orders his son Onan to perform the levirate duty for Tamar, the widow of Onan's deceased brother Er. Onan is told to "raise up seed for your brother," a phrase not found in Deut 25:5 but present in the Sadducees' citation in Mark 12:19. The insertion of Gen 38:8 thus conveniently introduces the terminology of "raising up" into this dispute on the resurrection.[98] Interestingly, the form of Deut 25:5 found in Mark 12:19 does not correspond exactly to the Septuagint or to any other ancient Greek translation. At one point it is closer to the Hebrew text than is the Septuagint, while at another point it renders the Hebrew text loosely, while the Septuagint is more precise.[99] The overall impression, then, is that

Mark 12:19 does not come from the Septuagint but rather represents an independent and sometimes loose translation of the Hebrew text (possibly an Aramaic targum?).[100]

The Sadducees' purpose in citing the levirate law precisely as Mosaic may be to underscore their view that, if Moses had foreseen or known about the resurrection of the dead, he would not have sanctioned an institution like levirate marriage, which creates a hopeless legal imbroglio at the resurrection—as the following case is meant to make clear. Perhaps the text from Gen 38:8 is woven into Deut 25:5 to make a further subtle point amid all the talk about "resurrection" *(anastasis)* and "rising (from the dead)" *(anistamai)*. If the whole thrust of the law of levirate is to "raise up seed" for the deceased brother (as the interpolated text from Gen 38:8 says), the implication is that such extreme action is necessary in this life because this is the only life there is, and any "raising up" must be done here. The fierce, desperate drive to create offspring, even by the legal fiction of considering the first child of the second marriage the child of the dead husband, implies that having physical descendants to carry on one's name is the only kind of immortality that the dead brother will ever have, and so his surviving brother must make sure that he has it.

(b) The second subsection (vv 20–23) of Part One proposes a fictitious and purposely bizarre case that falls under the levirate law and that is meant to highlight what an absurd result and hopeless quandary any resurrection of the dead would produce in the case of levirate marriage. The point could have been made with a simple example involving two brothers, one of whom dies childless. But in typical folkloric as well as biblical style, the number of brothers is expanded to seven, the number of fullness and completeness,[101] to underline the utter idiocy of the risen state in such a situation. It is an old theological gambit: win the theoretical debate by making a laughingstock of your opponent.

The point is drawn out in vv 20–21 by mentioning the first three brothers individually (three being, along with seven, a favorite number in oral stories, including jokes). Then, after the first three have been listed, the end-result of the whole process is summarized, since the issue has been made abundantly clear: "And the seven [brothers] did not leave seed [v 22a], and last of all, the woman died [v 22b]."

The main point is also drawn out and emphasized by repetition at both the beginning and the end of the trap-question in v 23: "At the resurrection, when they rise, of which of them shall she be the wife?" To drum home the inexorable absurdity of the situation, created precisely by punctilious observance of the Mosaic Law, the Sadducees add as their parting shot: "For the seven [brothers all] had her as wife [during their earthly lives]." Hence all seven have a right to her and her sexual activity in their risen state.[102]

Now, to appreciate the full force of the ridiculous situation painted by the Sadducees, one must understand an important distinction in Jewish society between polygyny and polyandry. On the one hand, polygyny (one husband with multiple wives at the same time) was known and accepted among Israelites in early biblical times, was still found among political leaders during the monarchical period, and survived in scattered instances through the time of Jesus into the rabbinic period.[103] On the other hand, the idea of polyandry (one wife with multiple husbands at the same time) would have seemed both highly offensive and supremely silly to 1st-century Jews embedded in a patriarchal society—a fortiori if they were contemplating the final state of human salvation beyond this present world.

Thus, it is probably not by accident that the Sadducees seek to discredit the idea of resurrection not by posing the problem of a husband with multiple wives—some ancient Jews might have seen the reconstitution of a polygynous marriage as part of the joys of the risen state—but rather by conjuring up the culturally repulsive prospect of a polyandrous marriage. Since resurrection of the dead would potentially involve polyandry for all those Jewish women involved in levirate marriages, the only logical alternative, in the view of the Sadducees, is to deny the whole idea of resurrection as implicitly excluded by the Mosaic Law, specifically the law of levirate. Because polyandry is impossible, the resurrection is impossible.[104] It is a clever, if convoluted and grotesque, argument. No doubt, in the world of the story, we may presume that the Sadducees are congratulating themselves on their cleverness. They think they have won by wit.

(2) However, as Part Two (vv 24–27) begins, Jesus immediately responds with the cannon blast of his own mocking, rhetorical question. In true rabbinic fashion, Jesus counterattacks by parrying the Sadducees' question with another question. What is absurd, says Jesus, is not the idea of resurrection but the ignorance of you Sadducees, who pride yourselves on your clever but erroneous arguments drawn from Scripture: "Is it not because of this that you are in error, namely, because you are ignorant of both the Scriptures and the power of God?"[105] By mentioning the double object of their ignorance, the Scriptures and God's power, Jesus' question introduces the two subsections of Part Two (v 25 and vv 26–27). On the one hand, by not understanding the Scriptures correctly, the Sadducees have failed to grasp that these Scriptures—indeed, the very Mosaic Torah they so highly revere—do teach the *fact* of the resurrection. On the other hand, by not understanding how

God's power on the last day will radically transform human existence, they have failed to grasp the *manner* or mode of the new and different life God will create for his people.

Jesus then proceeds, in the two subsections, to treat these two errors in reverse (chiastic) order: first, manner of resurrection, then, fact of resurrection. This reverse order makes sense, since Jesus must first dispel the erroneous idea about the nature or *manner* of the resurrection, which to the Sadducees excludes a priori any serious consideration of the subject. Only then can Jesus go on to offer a positive scriptural proof of the *fact* of resurrection.

(a) Accordingly, the first subsection (v 25) takes up the *manner* of the resurrection—or, more specifically, God's transformative power, which is manifested in the new and very different conditions of life that the resurrection creates.[106] Jesus begins by taking up the Sadducees' phrase from v 23, "when they rise." He not only affirms but also strengthens the phrase: "when they rise *from the dead.*" Coming at the beginning of Jesus' reply, the phrase emphasizes that he is speaking of a real resurrection of formerly dead people; the personal identity of those who once died with those who now rise is implicitly asserted.

And yet personal identity does not mean identity or complete continuity between one's former mode of earthly existence and the way one will exist after being raised from the dead. Along with the continuity of the person comes a massive discontinuity in the manner of one's life. The basic relationship between male and female, molded as it is in this world by marriage, sexual activity, and procreation, is utterly and definitively altered and transcended in the risen state. Men will not marry and women will not be given in marriage. Rather, says Jesus, using a simile to suggest the basic change in the manner of human existence, both men and women will be *"like* [*hōs*] the angels in heaven."

Now, one must understand this statement from the perspective of 1st-century Judaism, not of later Christianity. The idea that angels are "pure spirits," lacking any material component, body, or sexuality, became common in Christian theology only toward the end of the patristic period.[107] As is clear from the story of the "sons of God" (i.e., angelic beings) having sex with and procreating by means of the "daughters of men" (i.e., human women) in Gen 6:1–6, angels in the OT and early Judaism were thought to have highly rarefied or refined bodies (made, e.g., of fire), including sex organs. Hence the seraphim in the vision of Isaiah in Isa 6:1–3 cover their "feet" (a euphemism for genital organs) with two of their six wings out of reverence for the thrice-holy God they proclaim.

The story in Gen 6:1–6 of some angels ("the sons of God") having sex with human women became an object of great speculation around the turn of the era, as *1 Enoch* 6–11 clearly shows.[108] Such sexual activity is totally unacceptable because, as God explains in *1 Enoch* 15:6–7, he has created the angels to be immortal. Since they dwell in heaven and possess eternal life, God does not create wives for them, though they are sexual beings.[109] They are to remain celibate, since there is no need for them to reproduce their own kind. Ideas of cultic purity may also have played a role in the depiction of angels as celibate, since they were believed to perform priestly functions in the heavenly sanctuary. Such conceptions are especially strong at Qumran and may partly explain why at least some Essenes at some period in the sect's history practiced celibacy. They believed that their worship in the sectarian community shared in the heavenly worship of the angels; thus, they, like the angels, needed to be celibate. Such celibacy, practiced on earth, may also have been seen as a preparation for their joining the company of the angels after death.[110]

It is within this theological milieu that we must understand Jesus' statement that human beings at the resurrection will be "like the angels in heaven." Jesus is not saying that humans will be transformed into angels, will become immaterial, or will cease to be sexual beings. Rather, at the resurrection, God's power will cause humans to undergo a radical transformation of their existence; they will receive refined bodies like the angels. *Like* the angels, these risen humans will be made immortal by God's power. Though sexual beings, they will not engage in sexual activity or marriage, since, like the angels, they will have no need to reproduce themselves in view of death.

Jesus' point is clear: once one understands the manner of human existence after the resurrection, created solely by God's power, which transcends all puny human conceptions, the whole objection of the Sadducees collapses. Instead of being the mockers, the Sadducees become the mocked, since their gross ignorance of what the manner of risen life will be reveals a much more serious ignorance: that of the limitless power of God. Belief in the resurrection is based not on anthropology, that is, on a particular conception of what humans are made of (e.g., a mortal body and an immortal soul), but on theology, who God is and what he can do.[111] It is here that the Sadducees are most gravely in error. One begins to see the seriousness of Jesus' accusation.

(b) Having removed the obstacle of an erroneous conception of what the *manner* or mode of resurrection will involve for human existence, Jesus moves on to prove the basic point at issue: the *fact* of the resurrection. Needless to say, the proof comes not from philosophical speculation about human nature but from the only authority that could prove such a fact for most 1st-century Palestinian Jews, namely, the revelation of God in Scripture. Just as

the Sadducees appealed to the core of God's revelation to Israel, the Pentateuch, so does Jesus. But, while the Sadducees invoked an obscure piece of
hălākâ (law governing specific human conduct) from Deut 25:5 to rule the
resurrection of the dead out of court, Jesus homes in instead on the central
revelation of God to Israel, the theophany to Moses in the burning bush
(Exod 3:6): "I [am] the God of Abraham, the God of Isaac, and the God of
Jacob."[112] As in the first subsection, so in the second, for Jesus the fundamental issue is the nature and power of God, not the nature and potential of
humanity. It is *theo*-logy in its root sense that binds the two halves of Jesus'
response together.[113]

To us moderns, Jesus' scriptural text seems, at first sight, to have as little to
do with the resurrection as did the Sadducees' text. To understand how Jesus'
argument from Scripture functions in Mark 12:18–27, we must bear in a
mind a number of related points:

(i) First of all, any attempt to evaluate Jesus' argument from Exod 3:6
brings us face-to-face with a basic hermeneutical problem: the cultural
chasm that separates us moderns from this 1st-century Palestinian Jew. Actually, this is a problem that extends far beyond the quest for the historical
Jesus. What is cogent proof to one group of people conditioned by a particular culture at a particular time in history will not necessarily be cogent or
even intelligible to another group of people conditioned by another culture
in a different period of history.

For example, Jesus' scriptural argument about the resurrection may not
seem cogent to a modern Western theologian, just as some of the modern
Western theologian's arguments for the existence of God might not have
seemed cogent or even intelligible to Abraham, Isaac, and Jacob, or perhaps
to a 20th-century peasant in Southeastern Asia. Like many other realities
conditioned by culture, the cogency of an argument may not be easily trans-
latable from one culture into another. It is with this sense of the cultural rela-
tivity of cogency that we must grapple with Jesus' argument, just as we
grappled with the Sadducees' argument.

(ii) To appreciate the cultural presuppositions of Jesus' argument, many
commentators point to the arguments for the resurrection used by later rabbis, especially in the Babylonian Talmud. In a lengthy passage in the tractate
Sanhedrin 90b–91a, a number of rabbis are presented giving various arguments from Scripture in favor of the resurrection. What immediately strikes
us moderns as we read these arguments is that the rabbis' texts seem to have
as little to do with the resurrection as does the text Jesus chooses. The rabbis
use their texts in contorted and tendentious ways, seizing upon the future
tense of a verb or a reference to a long-dead person in order to argue that the
text can have its full meaning only if there is a resurrection. Obviously, such

an approach, which ignores the immediate context and the plain sense of the text when read in context could not be taken seriously by modern exegetes or theologians trained in historical-critical thinking.

Needless to say, the rabbis from the 1st to the 5th centuries A.D. were not operating according to such modern criteria. Their starting point was their community of faith that already held to belief in the resurrection. Already confident that God does in fact raise the dead and that he had revealed this truth to Israel in the Scriptures, the rabbis readily found clues and intimations of resurrection in texts whose literal sense has nothing to do with the subject. Almost reveling in their own intellectual dexterity, they mostly ignored the few truly probative texts, such as Daniel 12, in favor of passages that, to us moderns, are bereft of even a hint of resurrection.

(iii) Perhaps we should not be so surprised at this kind of argument, for it corresponds to the psychological mechanism usually at work in apologetics. Down through history, theological arguments may ostensibly be aimed outward to confute nonbelievers and to bring them to acknowledge the truth defended by the apologist. In reality, such arguments are often aimed inward instead and function as confirmation and reassurance to those in the community who already hold the faith that is being attacked by outsiders. So it is with the scriptural arguments for resurrection offered by both the rabbis and Jesus. In addition, since both Jesus and the rabbis are speaking to particular faith communities that share common cultural presuppositions, they also display a tendency to construct arguments from Scripture in which certain steps or rules of logic are taken for granted and not explicated.

(iv) Still, one must be careful about blithely declaring Jesus' mode of argumentation in Mark 12:26–27 to be "rabbinic."[114] While, as we have seen, there are similarities, there are also differences. The rabbis' arguments, being constructed by trained scholars at a later date, follow certain hermeneutical rules developed by the rabbis, including the so-called seven *middôt* (exegetical rules) of Hillel. Not surprisingly, the type of argument employed in the early 1st century A.D. by a Galilean Jew from Nazareth, a person who had never received any advanced training in interpreting Scripture, does not operate in strict accordance with these rules and so might be found wanting by the later rabbis.[115]

Thus, it may not be purely accidental that none of the rabbis in *b. Sanhedrin* use Exod 3:6, the passage chosen by Jesus, to prove the resurrection. Indeed, the precise way Jesus uses Exod 3:6 to prove the resurrection finds no exact parallel in the OT, intertestamental Judaism, the NT, and rabbinic literature.[116] As a matter of fact, the full formula (with "I [am] the God of Abraham . . ." etc.), quoted by Jesus in Mark 12:26, never occurs again in the OT.[117] Nor is it commonly cited in full in the various retellings of the burning bush story in major Jewish authors around the turn of the era. In the NT, the full formula occurs only in Stephen's speech in Acts 7:32, within a sweeping précis of Israelite history. A briefer form occurs in Peter's kerygmatic speech in Acts 3:13, as Peter begins to proclaim Jesus' death and resurrection. But, as in the OT so in the NT, nowhere outside of Mark 12:26 is the text used to prove the general resurrection of the dead.

(v) If Jesus' argument from Exod 3:6 is unique within the OT, ancient Judaism, and NT Christianity, is it also uniquely arbitrary, even by the standards of ancient hermeneutics? I think not. While Jesus' use of Exod 3:6 obviously goes beyond the literal sense of the text as determined by modern historical-critical exegesis, it is in touch with and develops the meaning that the text had taken on in the larger context of the OT and ancient Judaism.[118]

Taken at face value, "I [am] the God of Abraham, the God of Isaac, and the God of Jacob" might be understood simply to mean that a particular God, whose identity is otherwise unknown, identifies himself by listing some of his most famous worshipers. In this understanding, "the God of X" means nothing more than the God whom a famous ancestor named X, once alive but now dead, worshiped at some time in the past. While one can find some passages where the formula "the God of X" does mean this, this is not the usual sense of formulas referring to "the God of the fathers" in the OT and early Judaism. In context, these formulas are meant to conjure up the idea of how God freely chose these individuals and their descendants to be his own people and how he acted as their shield, protector, and savior when they were endangered by life-threatening perils.[119]

This is clearly the sense in which the formula is used in the grand theophany of Exodus 3, as Yahweh reveals himself for the first time to Moses and commissions him to free his people Israel from the slavery of Egypt through the foundational event of the exodus. Right after proclaiming in 3:6 that "I [am] . . . the God of Abraham, the God of Isaac, and the God of Jacob," Yahweh proceeds in vv 7–8 to say that he has seen the affliction of "*my* people" (not *Moses'* people) and has heard their cry for liberation from their oppressors. Yahweh himself, the God of their fathers, will "come down" to deliver the descendants of Abraham, Isaac, and Jacob from Egypt and lead them up from that prison house of slavery into the promised land. Frequently throughout the rest of the OT, the evocation of "the God of the fathers" intimates a renewal of this basic promise of God to his people to continue the protecting, saving, liberating activity that he showed of old to the patriarchs and to the exodus generation.

One can begin to see, then, how Jesus extends this weighty sense of the formula "the God of Abraham, the God of Isaac, and the God of Jacob" to the ultimate liberation of God's people from the eschatological oppressor, the enslaving power of death. By a final, definitive exodus up from the prison house of the grave, the God who was, is, and always will be the protector and savior of Israel will lead his faithful people into the promised land of the risen life.

(vi) Interestingly, this use of the three great patriarchal figures as pledges or symbols of sharing in the final salvation that will transcend this present world coheres with another saying of Jesus, which we verified as authentic in Volume Two.[120] In a Q saying (Matt 8:11–12 ‖ Luke 13:28–29), Jesus speaks prophetically of the eschatological pilgrimage of the Gentiles into the kingdom of God, where they will share with the three patriarchs of Israel in the heavenly banquet: "Many from east and west shall come and shall recline [at table] *with Abraham and Isaac and Jacob* in the kingdom of God." This union of Gentiles with the (formerly) dead patriarchs at the eschatological feast certainly intimates the trio's resurrection. The coherence of Mark 12:26 with this Q saying reminds us that Jesus' argument from Exod 3:6 is both intelligible and cogent only *within* the context of Jesus' eschatological proclamation and only *to* the people who have already accepted his proclamation.

(vii) Perhaps Jesus' "proof" from Exod 3:6 involves a further line of argument as well. When God wills to manifest himself to Moses in Exodus 3, he first identifies himself by way of the three patriarchs in v 6. Even when he reveals "Yahweh" as his "personal" name, he insistently binds this special name to the title with which he began the theophany (Exod 3:15). Moses is ordered to tell the Israelites: "Yahweh, the God of your fathers, the God of Abraham, the God of Isaac, and the God of Jacob, has sent me [Moses] to you [Israel]. This is my name forever."

Now, in the OT, especially when used of a deity, a name is not simply an arbitrary label slapped on something, a superficial tag that could just as well be interchanged with any other tag. The OT does not flippantly ask, "What's in a name?" For the OT, there is a great deal in a name. Especially in the case of a deity, the name expresses or reveals the inner being, nature, and power of the deity. It allows the worshiper to invoke the deity properly and to call on his saving power effectively. If, then, God chooses to identify himself, to name himself, to define himself, by identifying his being with his relationship with Abraham, Isaac, and Jacob, one may ask: How is it that the eternal, all-powerful God can identify and define himself by his relationship to some moldering corpses of long-dead men? How can that be the self-chosen, self-defining name of the one true God? For OT faith, the answer is, it cannot. The God of all life and all the living cannot be named, defined, and understood by his relationship with the dead.

(viii) In a sense, Jesus both sharpens and develops this line of thought in v 27a. Not unlike some of the rabbis arguing for the resurrection, Jesus appears, consciously or unconsciously, to be constructing an implicit syllogism—or so, at least, it seems to our Western eyes. Indeed, it might help our hermeneutical grappling with Jesus' argument if we tried to make his implicit syllogism explicit.

We have already seen that, by using Exod 3:6 as his starting point and scriptural proof-text, Jesus has highlighted the fact that God defines himself in terms of the three patriarchs. No believing Jews would deny that point, enshrined as it is in the foundational revelation of God to Moses. Universally accepted, it may serve as the major premise of Jesus' argument. Jesus then moves to his minor premise in v 27a: "He [the God who defines himself as the God of Abraham, Isaac, and Jacob] is not the God of the dead but of the living." [121] In effect, Jesus is again appealing to the Jewish Scriptures, but now not to a single text but to their common witness. Apart from a few late apocalyptic passages, the Jewish Scriptures regularly assert that the one true God has no relationship with the dead, who are, by definition, unclean and defiling. It is a source of lament in the OT that death means the end of one's relationship with God (see, e.g., Isa 38:18–19; Pss 6:6; 30:8–10; 88:4–12). God has nothing further to do with persons once they die. The Psalmist can imagine no more negative metaphor of his dire straits than to compare himself with those who are already dead, "like those whom you [O God] remember no more because they are cut off from your hand" (Ps 88:5). As the Psalmist says in Ps 6:6: "In death there is no remembrance of you [O God]. In the realm of the dead who shall praise you?" Death cuts off even the most devout Israelite from the worship of God, because the one true God, the living God, is the God of the living and only of the living. He has and can have nothing to do with the dead; that is the job description of the false, dead, pagan gods. For the OT, God and the dead are matter and antimatter. The real God has a real relationship only with the really living. This is an axiomatic truth for believing Israelites, and so Jesus can use it as his minor premise without needing to argue the point.

One sees, then, where Jesus' argument is headed. If we tried to tease out the thrust of his argument in the form of a syllogism, it would run something like this:

1. *Major Premise:* According to God's self-chosen definition, the very being of God involves being the God of Abraham, Isaac, and Jacob. This is his permanent self-definition.
2. *Minor Premise:* But, as the whole of the OT proclaims, God is God only of the living, not of the defiling, unclean dead, with whom he has no relation.

3. *Unspoken Conclusion:* Therefore, if God's being is truly defined by his permanent relationship to the three patriarchs, the three patriarchs must be (now or in the future) living and in living relationship to God.[122]

In the concrete arena of debate set up by the Sadducees and accepted by Jesus, this life beyond death in God's presence is understood in terms of resurrection. Moreover, since the formula "I am the God of Abraham, the God of Isaac, and the God of Jacob" has as its precise purpose in Exodus 3 the proclamation of the continuation of God's saving action to the patriarchs' descendants, this hope of resurrection is held out to all their faithful offspring. Jesus thus grounds the hope of resurrection firmly in the primordial revelation of God to Moses and the chosen people—and ultimately in the very being of the God who, by definition, is related to the people he saves. To understand the God of Israel correctly is to accept the resurrection. To reject resurrection is to misunderstand God's primordial revelation to Israel and ultimately God himself. Hence the bite of Jesus' final, reinforced rebuke to the would-be teachers and leaders of Israel in v 27b: "You are *very much* in error." This *inclusio* with Jesus' opening question in v 24 ("Is this not the reason why you are in error?") clinches his argument rhetorically as well as theologically.

Having worked through the exegesis of Mark 12:18–27, we can appreciate the harmonious convergence of what we saw in the analysis of the literary structure of the pericope with what we have just seen in a thorough exegesis of the unit. The analysis of the structure revealed a svelte, compact composition, carefully constructed out of two major parts, each with two subdivisions. The whole was held together by a unity of subject matter and debating partners, by key words and themes, and by literary techniques like parallelism and *inclusio*. The exegesis of the pericope now shows a corresponding unity in the flow of the argument back and forth: the Sadducees, who deny the resurrection, cite the Pentateuch and develop a theological argument from it to object to the resurrection, while Jesus, in chiastic order, replies with a theological argument to parry the objection and then cites the Pentateuch to prove the resurrection.

This correspondence between a finely articulated literary structure on the one hand and coherent theological content on the other argues well for the original unity of the pericope, as opposed to the view that the present form of the debate grew in a number of stages by various additions. In my opinion, it is unlikely that this unit, a perfect fusion of well-crafted literary design and carefully developed theological argumentation, is the accidental product of different authors composing at different times. Rather, at some set time, one Christian author from the first generation of the church composed this story of the Sadducees' dispute with Jesus, be it in oral or written form. The logical corollary of this insight is that the pericope as it now stands is a Christian product. After all, during his ministry, the historical Jesus was a participant in disputes; he did not compose dispute stories. The question we must now ask is whether the historical Jesus actually engaged in a dispute with the Sadducees on the resurrection, a dispute that became the origin and matrix of the Christian composition in Mark 12:18–27.

F. The Debate on the Resurrection of the Dead: An Incident from the Ministry of the Historical Jesus?

Two final questions remain in our investigation of Mark 12:18–27: (1) Was this dispute story on the resurrection first composed by Mark himself or by an earlier teacher in the first Christian generation? (2) Does the story preserve some incident from the ministry of the historical Jesus, or is its content from start to finish a creation of the early church?

(1) Interestingly, few commentators hold that Mark created the dispute story on the resurrection out of whole cloth. Even skeptical exegetes like Bultmann and Hultgren discern behind the present pericope a pre-Marcan unit that underwent subsequent redaction.[123] The reasons for not assigning the entire unit to Mark's creative talent are clear.

On the macro-level: the string of Jerusalem dispute stories lacks the neat concentric structure and thematic links that the Galilean cycle of dispute stories evinces in Mark 2:1–3:6.[124] Yet, even in the Galilean cycle, on which Mark has imposed a fair amount of unity, most exegetes discern earlier pre-Marcan material. Indeed, as we saw in Volume Two, the problem of why the disciples of Jesus do not fast probably goes back to the actual teaching of the historical Jesus.[125] If, then, even the fairly well-ordered and unified Galilean cycle of dispute stories reflects Marcan reworking of older material, a fortiori it would seem that the more disjointed Jerusalem cycle is not the creation of Mark from start to finish. One gets the impression instead of various individual dispute stories—probably not even a cycle or collection[126]—that Mark has brought together as best he could to dramatize the heightening tensions between Jesus and his opponents just before the passion.

On the level of the individual dispute in Mark 12:18–27: Mark shows no interest in the Sadducees beyond this one story. He does not even attempt to link the incident in some concrete way with the Passion Narrative that is about to follow. This is all the more striking when one remembers that, to a

great extent, the Sadducees arguing with Jesus about the resurrection represent the party whose leaders were probably the main Jerusalem authorities
involved in Jesus' arrest and trial. Yet Mark makes no connection whatever
between the Sadducees in the dispute story of Mark 12 and the high priest,
the chief priests, and elders who plan and carry out Jesus' arrest and trial in
Mark 14. In fact, if we knew nothing except Mark's Gospel, we would never
think—indeed, does Mark?—that there is some connection between the Sadducees on the one hand and the high priest, the chief priests, and the elders
on the other. One gets the impression that Mark is taking over and using for
his own purposes a story involving a group about which he otherwise evinces
neither knowledge nor concern.

The focus of Mark 12:18–27 is likewise atypical of Mark's theological
concerns. While Mark is naturally intent on proclaiming the death and resurrection of Jesus—chaps. 14–16 are obviously dedicated to that task—
Mark shows no interest outside of 12:18–27 in the question of the precise
nature of the risen state of believers and the proper way that the general resurrection might be proven from Scripture. For Mark as for the rest of the NT,
eternal life and/or the resurrection of believers flows from and is grounded in
the work, death, and resurrection of Jesus, not the revelation of God to
Moses in the burning bush.

A small telltale sign that Mark 12:18–27 does not represent a free creation
of the evangelist is that only here in the whole of Mark's Gospel is the resurrection designated by the use of the noun *anastasis* ("resurrection" in vv
18,23). In speaking of the resurrection elsewhere, Mark uses the verbs
anistēmi and *egeirō,* but never the noun *anastasis.* This is true not only when
the resurrection of Jesus is directly the topic (e.g., *anistēmi* in 8:31; 9:31;
10:34; *egeirō* in 14:28; 16:6), but even when the bewildered disciples discuss
among themselves "what rising from the dead means" *(ti estin to ek nekrōn
anastēnai)* or when Herod Antipas imagines that John the Baptist has risen
(egēgertai) from the dead (6:14,16). Hence the double occurrence of *anastasis* in 12:18,23 may be a fingerprint of the pre-Marcan author left on the dispute story.

While Mark did not create the narrative in 12:18–27, it is possible that the
present form of the pericope contains some phrases added by the evangelist.
Two in particular are often singled out by commentators.[127] Both candidates
occur in the last verse (v 23) of Part One (vv 18–23) of the pericope.

Verse 23 begins: "At the resurrection, when they rise [*en tē anastasei,
hotan anastōsin*]. . . ." The redundancy is striking.[128] Since Mark's literary
style is noted for its "duality" (Mark's tendency to say the same thing twice),

it could be that the second phrase, "when they rise," is his addition.[129] Yet the whole of v 23, as it poses the trap-question to Jesus, reflects one overriding rhetorical intention: to highlight the dilemma faced by anyone who wishes both to maintain belief in the resurrection and, at the same time, to offer a satisfactory answer to the Sadducees' riddle. Hence the repetitive "when they rise" may intend both to emphasize the difficulty that the woman's complicated marital situation poses to belief in the resurrection and to intimate the mocking skepticism of the Sadducees. The surface meaning of "when they rise" may include the sotto voce meaning of "if, indeed, they rise."

The second possible addition by Mark comes at the end of v 23. Right after the trap-question is posed ("Of which of them shall she be the wife?"), the text adds the apparently unnecessary and anticlimactic clause, "for the seven had her as wife." Possibly, in a moment of pedantry, Mark added this clause; yet other explanations for the clause's presence can be offered. This seemingly unnecessary clause, like the unnecessary "when they rise," may purposely overload the verse with repetitions in order to underline the difficulty, if not the impossibility, of solving the dilemma the Sadducees pose. The reminder of the *seven* brothers also reinforces the mocking tone of skepticism. Moreover, we have seen how this well-structured pericope uses *inclusio* to bind the various parts of the story together. We may have here another example. The clause "for the seven had her as wife," which stands at the end of the fictitious case the Sadducees have proposed, harks back to the opening words of the case in v 20 ("there were seven brothers"), thus forming an *inclusio*. At the same time, the clause sums up the whole case, explained at length in vv 20–22. In brief, in my opinion, both of the two supposed Marcan insertions in v 23 could well have stood in the pre-Marcan text. Pesch may thus be correct in maintaining that Mark took over this pericope unchanged.[130] Still, one must admit that the suggestion that Mark added the two disputed clauses in v 23 cannot be completely excluded.

(2) In any case, it is most likely that the dispute story in Mark 12:18–27, minus perhaps a few short phrases, circulated in the pre-Marcan tradition of the first Christian generation. To be sure, as a full narrative *about* Jesus, as distinct from sayings *of* Jesus, the text of the story as we have it is a Christian composition. But does this story preserve the recollection of some actual incident in the ministry of Jesus? While various critics have suggested that not only the present text of the narrative but also the incident narrated is purely a Christian creation, other scholars have argued that behind Mark 12:18–27 lies an actual debate between Jesus and the Sadducees over the question of

the general resurrection.[131] In my opinion, two criteria of historicity argue for the authenticity of the basic story, though not the exact wording of the pericope.

(a) *Discontinuity.* The criterion of discontinuity applies in a number of different ways.[132]

(i) First, there is discontinuity with respect to the whole tendency of the Synoptic tradition to create dispute stories. Most critics admit that the early church composed at least some of the Synoptic dispute stories, at times building them around authentic sayings of Jesus, at times creating them out of whole cloth. The lengthy dispute over hand washing, korban, and purity rules (Mark 7:1–23 par.) and the dispute over the plucking of grain on the sabbath (Mark 2:23–28) may be examples of this tendency. What is to be noted about these possible creations of the early church is that the stock adversaries appearing in these and other disputes with Jesus—as well as in the denunciations of his opponents by Jesus—are almost invariably the scribes (alternately lawyers) and/or the Pharisees (see, e.g., Mark 2:6,16,18,24; 3:6,22; 7:1; 8:11; 10:2; 11:27; 12:13,35,38; Matt 22:34; 23:2–36; Luke 11:37–53). In the Jerusalem disputes, high priests and elders appear at times as well (e.g., Mark 11:27).

As we look through the growth of the dispute-story tradition in the Synoptics, what is striking is the total lack of any tendency to create or multiply stories involving the Sadducees. Mark 12:18–27 parrs. stands alone in the NT as the only dispute story in which Jesus directly debates with the Sadducees.[133] Apart from Matt 16:1–12 (cf. Matt 3:7), in which Matthew adds Sadducees to the Pharisees in order to create a symbol of the united front of Judaism, the Gospel tradition shows no interest in increasing references to Sadducees, even as supporting characters, in stories about Jesus.

(ii) Likewise discontinuous with other Gospel dispute stories are the obscure topics of the law of levirate and sexual activity after the general resurrection. When Christian Jews in Palestine created dispute stories in the pre-70 period, they dwelt on topics that reflected their actual debates with their fellow Jews. Here we touch on the basic point of *Sitz im Leben:* the early church tended to preserve or create traditions that served a particular purpose or met a practical need in its internal life or external struggles. Not surprisingly, the Christian Jews of pre-70 Palestine, like Jesus before them, clashed with their fellow Jews on practical questions like observance of sabbath and purity. Such debates naturally tended to create dispute stories on these and similar topics. These dispute stories helped crystallize the positions and guide the practices of Christian Jews in everyday life. Such stories are thus expressions of Christian-Jewish *hălākâ.*

The atypical dispute with the Sadducees over the general resurrection does not fit this pattern of Christian Jews debating other Jews over proper halakic observance. Simply because of their socioeconomic standing, most Christian Jews had no occasion to engage in debate with priestly or lay aristocrats of the Sadducean party resident in Jerusalem. As we can see in Acts, when such clashes did occur, they quite naturally took place between the Sadducees and the leaders of the Christian-Jewish community in Jerusalem. Their conflict focused on the question of Jesus' death and resurrection, not on the general resurrection of the dead and certainly not on the law of levirate.[134] There is no indication that Christian Jews of Palestine—or any other first-generation Christians, for that matter—were exercised over the problem of whether or with whom a wife involved in a levirate marriage would have sex after the general resurrection. In brief, the dispute makes sense as a historical clash between the Sadducees and Jesus during the latter's Jerusalem ministry. The dispute hardly makes any sense as a creation of the early church. Not surprisingly, those critics who claim that the dispute was created by the church must be highly creative themselves in imagining what *Sitz im Leben* called it forth.[135]

(iii) This point brings us to a much more important discontinuity between Mark 12:18–27 and the early church: the way in which the question of the general resurrection is treated and grounded. As we can see in the parade example of Paul's debate with those Corinthian converts who questioned the idea of the resurrection of the dead on the last day (1 Corinthians 15), first-generation Christians based their hope of a general resurrection on the resurrection of Christ (see, e.g., 1 Cor 15:12–13). To put the matter in philosophical terms, Jesus' own resurrection, already accomplished, was seen as the efficient and/or exemplary cause—the energizing archetype—of the resurrection of believers, still to come. This nexus between the resurrection of Christ and the resurrection of believers is hardly unique to 1 Corinthians 15. It can be found in both the authentic and pseudonymous letters of Paul, the four Gospels, Acts, 1 Peter, and the Revelation of John.[136] In contrast, it never occurs to any Christian author in the NT to base the Christian hope of resurrection on a single verse from the Jewish Scriptures—especially not Exod 3:6. The whole approach to speaking about and arguing for the general resurrection of the dead in Mark 12:18–27 is remarkably lacking in a specifically Christian viewpoint.[137]

(iv) This point brings us in turn to a further discontinuity that separates Jesus' argument for the general resurrection not only from Christians after him but also from Jews before and after him in the Greco-Roman period. If Jesus' use of Exod 3:6 as *the* scriptural proof for the general resurrection strikes us as strange, it apparently struck his Jewish contemporaries as well as later Christians in the same way. As far as we can tell from the sources available to us, there was no Jewish exegetical tradition before or after Jesus in ancient times that used Exod 3:6 to argue for the general resurrection. When belief in the resurrection of the dead—or alternately, belief in immortality—appeared late in the OT period (e.g., Daniel 12; 2 Macc 7:10–11; Wis 2:21–5:23), no appeal was made to Exod 3:6. The exegetical treatment of Exod 3:6 in the writings of intertestamental Judaism likewise shows no parallel to Jesus' use of it to ground belief in the general resurrection. Most striking of all is that later rabbinic arguments for the resurrection, notably in *b. Sanh.* 90b–92a, use all sorts of OT texts, many of which bear as little ostensible relationship to the resurrection as does Exod 3:6.[138] Yet none of these talmudic arguments employs Exod 3:6.[139] Here, strange to say, the authors of the NT are at one with the later rabbis of the Babylonian Talmud. Jesus' appeal to Exod 3:6 was apparently so idiosyncratic that it found no resonance in either Jewish or Christian arguments for the resurrection in the ancient period—apart from Christian authors of later centuries who cited or borrowed from Mark 12:18–27.[140]

Even the formula Jesus uses from Exod 3:6 ("I [am] the God of Abraham, the God of Isaac, and the God of Jacob") occurs only once again in the NT, in a slightly different form, in Acts 7:32 ("I [am] the God of your fathers, the God of Abraham and Isaac and Jacob"), within Stephen's speech before his martyrdom. In this "speech for the defense," Stephen constructs an overview of salvation history stretching from the call of Abraham to Solomon's construction of the Jerusalem temple. A large part of the speech's narrative is given over to the story of Moses, who is seen as a type of Christ (cf. 7:35). The citation of Exod 3:6 in Acts 7:32 occurs, quite properly, during the narration of the call of Moses by God speaking from the burning bush. Indeed, Acts 7:30–34 is a digest of Exod 3:1–10. The important point for us is that Acts 7:32, the only example in the NT of a citation of the full formula of Exod 3:6 apart from Mark 12:26, simply reproduces the natural sense of the Exodus text. No reference to or proof of the general resurrection is read into the text by Stephen the orator or Luke the writer.

The only other NT passage where Exod 3:6 is cited (or better, alluded to) is Acts 3:13, though here the citation is not as full as in Acts 7:32. Acts 3:13 stands at the beginning of Peter's kerygmatic speech in Solomon's Portico after the healing of the lame man at the Beautiful Gate of the temple. Peter solemnly announces the resurrection of Jesus with a tissue of OT allusions: "The God of Abraham and the God of Isaac and the God of Jacob, the God of our fathers, glorified his servant Jesus, whom you handed over and denied in the presence of Pilate, although he had determined to release him. . . . " [141] The opening string of titles could be from Exod 3:6, though Exod 3:15 or 3:16 could equally be the source, since the formula of self-revelation from 3:6 ("I [am] . . .") is missing in Acts 3:13. The assertion that God "glorified his servant" probably echoes the reference to the suffering servant in Isa 52:13. For Luke, this glorification is made up of Christ's resurrection, ascension, and being seated at the right hand of God. The designation "God of Abraham . . ." has special value for Luke in this kerygmatic sermon because it stresses that the one God has been planning and directing the whole course of salvation history from beginning to end, from Abraham's call to Christ's glorification. [142]

Thus, while the titles of God from Exod 3:6 are brought into relation with (though not made a proof of) Jesus' resurrection, no link is forged in Acts 3:13 between Exod 3:6 and the general resurrection of the dead. In other words, while Luke uses Exod 3:6 twice in Acts—indeed, he is the only NT author to use the text outside of Mark 12:26 parr.—it never enters his mind to connect it with the general resurrection. This is all the more remarkable when one remembers that Luke knows this application of the text because he takes over the dispute story of Mark 12:18–27 in Luke 20:27–38. Hence, although he knows the tradition that Jesus interpreted Exod 3:6 as a proof-text of the general resurrection, Luke, no more than any other NT author, has the slightest inclination to imitate his Master's unique hermeneutic. Jesus' use of Exod 3:6 to prove the fact of the general resurrection finds no precise parallel either in early Judaism before or after him or in the 1st-century Christian movement that flowed from his own teaching.

To sum up, then: In the debate in Mark 12:18–27, Jesus handles both the *how* (manner) and the *that* (fact) of the resurrection quite differently from the early Christians. Jesus answers the *how* by a comparison to the angels and the *that* by an appeal to Exod 3:6. The early Christians, instead, handle both the *how* (see Phil 3:21) and the *that* (see 1 Cor 15:12–20) simply by pointing to the risen Jesus. At the same time, Jesus' arguments, especially his grounding of the resurrection in Exod 3:6, are not those of Judaism before or after him. The various concepts and motifs that flow into Jesus' double answer are indeed drawn from the OT and early Judaism, but Jesus forges them into a new, creative whole. The criterion of discontinuity fits Mark 12:18–27 to a remarkable degree.

(b) *Coherence*. [143] Some critics have doubted the historicity of the dispute with the Sadducees over the resurrection because they maintain that the historical Jesus never spoke about a general resurrection of the dead. Such scholars reason that Jesus expected the imminent coming of the kingdom, and so his gaze was resolutely fixed on the empirical Israel in front of him. He was totally taken up with his contemporaries, who were the object of his passionate call to repentance and renewal in view of the kingdom's coming. He had no time for or interest in speculation about a general resurrection of the dead. That a Palestinian Jew could be intensely interested in future eschatology and/or apocalyptic expectations and yet not be concerned about the resurrection of the dead seems verified by the documents authored by the Qumran community. There we find eschatological and/or apocalyptic expectations, but little if anything about a general resurrection of the dead.[144]

Nevertheless, to claim that Jesus never spoke of the general resurrection is to go too far and at the same time to miss a subtle but important point. To be sure, at the heart of Jesus' proclamation was the kingdom of God, soon to come yet somehow already present in his ministry. With the sense of urgency that such a belief engendered, Jesus' thought and action aimed squarely at convincing and converting those who were, in his eyes, at risk of final condemnation: his contemporaries—or, as the gentle and nonjudgmental Jesus preferred to call them, "this evil generation."[145] This main goal of his mission, and not speculation about the fate of the long-since departed, naturally occupied most of his attention and preaching. He was interested above all in making sure that the living, standing on the threshold of the final kingdom, would "enter into the kingdom" or "enter into life."[146]

In contrast, the idea of a general resurrection, by definition, involved the dead, not the living. Such a resurrection beyond this world of time and space would be the final step into the kingdom for those who had already died, not for those still living when the kingdom of God came in full reality. Accordingly, the resurrection would be a matter for God, not Jesus, to take care of. Jesus had his hands full with "this generation." We need not be surprised, then, that the general resurrection either was mentioned only in passing by Jesus or remained implicit within his proclamation of the kingdom. But mentioned or alluded to it was.

(i) As we have already seen in the exegesis of Mark 12:26, an important Q saying of Jesus implies the general resurrection.[147] Speaking of the eschatological pilgrimage of the Gentiles into the kingdom of God, Jesus prophesies (Matt 8:11 par.): "Many from east and west shall come and shall recline [at table] with Abraham and Isaac and Jacob in the kingdom of God." Thus, in his role as the eschatological prophet, Jesus foretells that, on the last day, the Gentiles will recline with the long-dead patriarchs (notice: the same three as in Mark 12:26) at the heavenly banquet, the metaphor for final salvation. Thus, the final stage of the kingdom is not just a continuation of this present world in some improved or even miraculous form. The presence of Abraham, Isaac, and Jacob, feasting together with the Gentiles in the kingdom, indicates that, in some sense, the final kingdom is discontinuous with and transcends this present world.

More to the point, the very picture of the long-dead patriarchs now joining Gentiles (including, presumably, those still living when the end time comes) at a banquet intimates some sort of resurrection. It is typical of Jesus, however, that we never get beyond symbols, metaphors, and intimations. Jesus is not interested in giving detailed scenarios of the last day. He is a prophet and a poet, not a systematic theologian. Still, if Jesus is at all serious about this prophecy, the last day seems to involve some kind of resurrection. But it lies on the periphery, not at the center, of his vision.

(ii) In a few cases, though, it does seem that Jesus spoke in passing—and yet directly—of the resurrection. Within a "Lucan symposium," made up of various sayings collected by Luke around the theme of a banquet, we find an L saying in which Jesus urges his host to be generous in extending hospitality to those who cannot pay him back in this life. Using a form of beatitude similar to the pattern found at the beginning of the Sermon on the Mount/Plain, Jesus provides motivation for his exhortation by promising a future reward beyond this present world (Luke 14:14): "And you will be happy, for . . . you will be rewarded at the resurrection of the just." As in the beatitudes of the Sermon, Jesus proclaims the reversal of all values and the radical demand of gratuitous love in the light of the last day, understood in 14:14 in terms of the resurrection.[148]

(iii) We have already looked briefly at the woes that Jesus the eschatological prophet spoke against the cities of Galilee that rejected him (a Q saying).[149] As we saw, the mention of Chorazin alongside Bethsaida and Capernaum as cities where Jesus worked argues for historicity. This saying is not something spun out of other Gospel material—in fact, Chorazin is never mentioned elsewhere in the NT—and there is no evidence of any early Christian missionary activity at Chorazin. Similarly, despite the fact that Matt 11:21 par. presupposes a large number of miracles worked in Bethsaida, we have only a single narrative recounting a lone miracle worked by Jesus in Bethsaida (Mark 8:22–26). Hence this Q saying is probably a fossil reflecting activities of Jesus that were otherwise lost to the Gospel tradition. The saying also coheres with the picture of Jesus as the eschatological prophet calling Israel to repentance in view of the imminent judgment. We hear echoes of the fiery mentor, John the Baptist, continuing to speak through his former disciple.

In this Q saying (Matt 11:21–24 ‖ Luke 10:13–15), Jesus proclaims: "Woe to you, Chorazin! Woe to you, Bethsaida! For if in Tyre and Sidon [OT archetypes of evil Gentile cities opposed to God and his people Israel] had been worked the miracles that have been worked in you, long ago they would have repented in sackcloth and ashes. But it will go easier with Tyre and Sidon on the day of judgment than with you." Then Capernaum, the city specially favored by Jesus' extended ministry, is threatened even more graphically: "You will descend to Hades [the abode of the dead or hell]." That the Gentile citizens of Tyre and Sidon will be arraigned alongside the Jewish citizens of Chorazin, Bethsaida, and Capernaum "on the day of judgment" and will suffer a less grievous fate presupposes some sort of afterlife or coming to life. Granted the stock apocalyptic scenario of the gathering together of scattered groups, including the dead, to a final judgment, the most likely implication is that "the day of judgment" will involve some sort of resurrection of the dead.

(iv) A similar prophecy of Jesus about the final judgment can be found in the Q tradition about "the sign of Jonah." In Matt 12:41–42 ‖ Luke 11:31–32, Jesus excoriates his unresponsive contemporaries by comparing them once again with more responsive Gentiles. In a two-part saying, with each part perfectly parallel to the other, Jesus foretells: "The queen of the south [i.e., the queen of Sheba] shall rise up at the judgment with the men of this generation and shall condemn them. For she came from the ends of the earth to hear the wisdom of Solomon. And behold, something greater than Solomon is here. The men of Nineveh will rise up at the judgment with this generation and shall condemn it. For they repented at the preaching of Jonah. And behold, something greater than Jonah is here." Typical of the indirect, enigmatic style of Jesus is his reference to "something" (*not* "someone") greater being present before his audience's eyes. As is his custom, he points directly not to himself but to the kingdom of God, already present in his words and works ("here"). This is not the way the post-Easter church proclaimed its christology in its various forms.

As with the previous saying, we are presented with a scenario of judgment day, with Gentiles from the past faring better than Jesus' Jewish contemporaries. Here, unlike the examples of Tyre and Sidon, the Gentiles have in fact been responsive to Israel's great wisdom teacher (Solomon) and to one of its great prophets of repentance (Jonah). One might discern here a self-portrait of the historical Jesus (wisdom teacher and eschatological prophet of repentance); but, as usual, it is at best an indirect, allusive reference. The main point of the saying is that the queen of Sheba and the Ninevites, all Gentiles, shall not simply fare better at the final judgment than Jesus' Jewish contemporaries but will even take an active part in witnessing against and condemning them. The scene is clearly that of the general judgment. Since both the queen of Sheba and the Ninevites died many centuries ago and yet will appear alongside Jesus' contemporaries (some of whom are probably presumed to be still living when the final judgment arrives), the natural inference is that this final judgment involves some sort of resurrection.[150]

(v) In Mark 9:43–47 ‖ Matt 18:8–9 ‖ Matt 5:29–30, we find various forms of a string of sayings concerning the seriousness of "scandal" (in the weighty theological sense of something that will lead one into serious sin or apostasy). In Mark 9:43–47, Jesus warns his disciples: "If your hand scandalizes you, cut it off. It is better for you to enter into life maimed than with two hands to depart into Gehenna, into the inextinguishable fire. And if your foot scandalize you, cut it off. It is better for you to enter into life lame than with two feet to be cast into Gehenna. And if your eye scandalize you, pluck it out. It is better for you to enter into the kingdom of God with one eye than with two eyes to be cast into Gehenna."[151]

In Matt 5:29–30, within the Sermon on the Mount, only two of these sayings, on the eye and the hand, are reproduced, probably with a specific application to impure glances and touches, since the larger context is the second antithesis (on adultery). A compressed form of Mark's three sayings is found in Matt 18:8–9. Verse 8 combines the sayings about hand and foot (the first two sayings of Mark) into one saying: "If your hand or foot scandalize you. . . ." Verse 9 continues with the separate Marcan saying on the eye. Whether or not some of the Matthean forms of the saying represent Q or M tradition as opposed to a mere reworking of the Marcan sources is debated among scholars.[152] In any event, we have in Mark's source (Mark 9:42–50 is clearly a hodgepodge collection of stray sayings) and possibly in the Q document a few sayings of Jesus that speak in most graphic and concrete terms about the entrance of a person with his or her bodily limbs into the kingdom or into eternal punishment. A resurrection of the body is presupposed.

The shocking imagery used in these sayings plus the uncompromising demand for a radical decision in view of imminent judgment cohere well with the style and content of the authentic message of the historical Jesus. Interestingly, while one can find some parallels to these arresting images in later rabbinic literature, the rest of the NT and the Apostolic Fathers offer no exact parallels.

(vi) In Volume Two, I argued at length for the authenticity of Jesus' prophecy at the Last Supper about his own final fate (Mark 14:25): "Amen I say to you that I shall no longer drink of the fruit of the vine until that day when I drink it new in the kingdom of God."[153] In the face of approaching death and the seeming failure of his mission to all Israel, Jesus consoles himself (much more than his disciples) with the hope that God will vindicate him beyond death and will bring him to participate in the final banquet in the kingdom. The picture painted by this logion remains remarkably indistinct: there are no christological titles, no references to Jesus' death as sacrificial or saving, no references to resurrection or parousia, no indication that Jesus will be the host at the banquet or that he will be rejoined there by his disciples. Specifically Christian ideas about the consummation are simply lacking. Rather, in this saying, the historical Jesus expresses his hope that God will bring him out of death when the kingdom fully comes and will seat him at the final banquet, presumably alongside the great patriarchs and even the Gentiles (cf. Matt 8:11–12 par.). Once again, the imagery of sharing in the heavenly banquet beyond death intimates but does not openly proclaim the idea of a general resurrection on the last day—but *not* a unique resurrection of Jesus within ongoing human history.

As the reader will have noticed, I have not spent a great deal of time arguing about the wording of the six texts I have just reviewed. I have not even considered at length the question of whether these sayings go back to the historical Jesus. In some cases, I have done that already; in other cases, I think the brief indications of why the sayings might be considered authentic will suffice for the moment. My major point in treating these six sayings is not so much the details of each logion but rather their cumulative effect. They provide us with an argument from multiple attestation of sources and forms for the basic assertion that Jesus spoke at various times, in various ways, and under various images, of a final judgment on the last day and that, sometimes overtly but more commonly indirectly, he referred to the general resurrection of the dead as part of this eschatological event. In one way or another, this idea is expressed or implied in sayings found in Mark, Q, L, and possibly M.

While the tradition that stands behind the Gospel of John also contains the idea of a general resurrection (e.g., John 5:28–29), the complicated nature of Johannine eschatology and the various stages of tradition and redaction in the Fourth Gospel make it extremely difficult to trace an individual saying on future eschatology back to the historical Jesus. Suffice it to say that the pre-Johannine tradition, for all its differences from the Synoptics, agrees with the other Gospel sources in attributing references to the general resurrection to Jesus.[154] In any event, the multiple attestation of sources and forms makes it highly probable that the historical Jesus did at times speak in passing or allude to the general resurrection of the dead on the last day, though it was not usual for him to make this subject the direct object of his preaching.

This last point might, at first glance, create an objection to seeing a historical incident behind the debate with the Sadducees in Mark 12:18–27. Actually, the exact opposite is true. If Jesus generally spoke only in passing or allusively of a general resurrection, what would be the one kind of event that would cause him to address the question directly? Precisely the type of event that Mark 12:18–27 depicts: the only Jewish movement that explicitly denied any future resurrection or final judgment beyond this present world was moved by Jesus' passing references to confront him on the subject, forcing him to spell out and defend his implied position. It is therefore not by accident but rather in keeping with everything we have seen that the only time Jesus focuses the theological spotlight directly on the subject of the general resurrection is when he is directly challenged on the matter by the only Jewish group that would be likely to dispute his position, namely, the Sadducees.

In short, while the argument from coherence has to be built up gradually, saying by saying, its cumulative impact in the case of the debate with the Sadducees is fairly impressive. Hence I maintain that, when the arguments from discontinuity are joined to the arguments from coherence, the most probable conclusion is that the debate with the Sadducees over the resurrection in Mark 12:18–27 does reflect an actual incident in the ministry of the historical Jesus that took place, naturally enough, in Jerusalem.[155] Whether Jesus engaged in any other debates with the Sadducees we cannot say.[156] Such clashes, perhaps spread out over a number of visits to Jerusalem (as the Fourth Gospel indicates), might help explain the growing opposition of "the chief priests and elders," which ultimately led to Jesus' arrest. But we must admit that we lack the hard evidence to make these suggestions anything more than speculation.

In any event, Mark 12:18–27 is a unique and precious relic that allows us to appreciate more fully Jesus' own views on what the future coming of the kingdom would mean. The historical Jesus believed that, at some point in the eschatological drama, past generations would rise from the dead and that faithful Israelites would share in a new type of life similar to that of the angels, one that left behind old relationships established by marriage and sexual activity. The final state of the kingdom would thus entail a transcendence of this present world, not simply an improvement of it. In bringing about this new world, the God of creation and covenant, the God of Abraham, Isaac, and Jacob, would fulfill his deepest commitment to the people of Israel to be their savior and protector, even beyond death. In the end, Jesus proclaims this particular view both of the manner of the resurrection and of the scriptural proof of the resurrection not on the basis of some hallowed tradition but simply on the basis of his own authority.[157] He knows that this is so, he teaches it is so, and that is the end of the matter. We have here the peremptory, authoritative, it-is-so-because-I-say-it-is-so style that is typical of the charismatic leader. There is no "Amen I say to you" in Jesus' pronouncement on the resurrection; but that introductory phrase, so characteristic of Jesus' teaching style, sums up well the air of direct, authoritative, intuitive knowledge that marks this eschatological prophet from Nazareth. One can understand why the Sadducees in particular and the Jerusalem establishment in general would find this Galilean upstart difficult to take or tolerate.

NOTES TO CHAPTER 29

[1] Detailed discussion of the sources, texts, and bibliographical material concerning the Sadducees can be found in Le Moyne, *Les Sadducéens*. Other books and articles that deal with or touch on the Sadducees include: Lauterbach, "A Significant Controversy," 1–33; S. W. Baron, *A Social and Religious History of the Jews* (2 vols. 2d ed., New York: Columbia University, 1952) 2. 36–44; Robert North, "The Qumrân 'Sadducees,'" *CBQ* 17 (1955) 164–88; A. C. Sundberg, "Sadducees," *IDB*, 4. 160–63; Victor Eppstein, "When and How the Sadducees Were Excommunicated," *JBL* 85 (1966) 213–24; Davies, *Introduction to Pharisaism*, 12–13, 24; Clemens Thoma, "Auswirkungen des jüdischen Krieges gegen Rom (66–70/73 n. Chr.) auf das rabbinische Judentum," *BZ* 12 (1968) 30–54; Joachim Jeremias, *Jerusalem in the Time of Jesus* (London: SCM, 1969) 222–32; Samuel Sandmel, *The First Christian Century in Judaism and Christianity: Certainties and Uncertainties* (New York: Oxford University, 1969); Alexander Guttmann, *Rabbinic Judaism in the Making* (Detroit: Wayne State University, 1970) 127–32; Rudolf Meyer, *"Saddoukaios,"* *TDNT* 7 (1971) 35–54; Bowker, *Jesus and the Pharisees*, 8–12; Günther Baumbach, "Der sadduzäische Konservativismus," *Literatur und Religion des Frühjudentums* (Würzburg: Echter/Mohn, 1973) 201–13; idem, "Das Sadduzäerverständnis bei Josephus Flavius und im Neuen Testament," *Kairos* 13 (1971) 17–37; M. Stern, "Aspects of Jewish Society: The Priesthood and Other Classes," *The Jewish People in the First Century. Volume Two*, 561–630; Karlheinz Müller, "Jesus und die Sadduzäer," *Biblische Randbemerkungen* (Rudolf Schnackenburg Festschrift; 2d ed.; ed. Helmut Merklein and Joachim Lange; Würzburg: Echter, 1974) 3–24; Gillis Gerleman, "Das übervolle Mass. Ein Versuch mit *haesaed,"* *VT* 28 (1978) 151–64; the revised Schürer, *History of the Jewish People*, 2. 404–14; Ernst Bammel, "Sadduzäer und Sadokiden," *ETL* 55 (1979) 107–15; Beckwith, "The Pre-History," 57–100; Cohen, *From the Maccabees to the Mishnah*, 143–64; Otto Schwankl, *Die Sadduzäerfrage (Mk 12, 18–27 parr)* (BBB 66; Frankfurt: Athenäum, 1987) 14–62; Saldarini, *Pharisees, Scribes and Sadducees*, 79–237, 298–308; idem, "Sadducees," *The HarperCollins Bible Dictionary* (ed. Paul J. Achtemeier; San Francisco: HarperSanFrancisco, 1996) 957–58; David Daube, "On Acts 23: Sadducees and Angels," *JBL* 109 (1990) 493–97; Schwartz, *Josephus and Judaean Politics*, 58–109; Gary G. Porton, "Sadducees," *Anchor Bible Dictionary*, 5. 892–95; Sanders, *Judaism. Practice & Belief*, 317–40; Grabbe, *Judaism from Cyrus to Hadrian. Volume Two*, 484–87; Feldman, "Josephus' Portrayal of the Hasmoneans," 41–68.

[2] Hence this treatment of the Sadducees will not repeat the entire collection of references to texts in the NT, Josephus, and the rabbinic literature that was given in chapter 28; only key references will be supplied here.

[3] On the difficulty of investigating the Sadducees, see Müller, "Jesus und die Sadduzäer," 3–6. A prime example of the meager nature of our knowledge is our uncertainty about the original pronunciation of the name Sadducee in Hebrew; for basic philological information, see North, "The Qumrân 'Sadducees,' " 164–88; Meyer, "Saddoukaios," 35–36; Le Moyne, Les Sadducéens, 155–57. The earliest Hebrew text to mention the Sadducees is the Mishna (ca. A.D. 200). There, in the originally unvocalized text, we have the spelling ṣdwqyn (or ṣdwqym) in the masculine plural; the rare masculine singular is ṣdwqy; the corresponding feminine singular and plural are ṣdwqyt (or ṣdwqh) and ṣdwqywt respectively. There is some dispute about the original vocalization and hence the proper pronunciation of these forms. Some scholars suggest that the primitive form of the masculine singular (an adjective expressing origin or relation) was ṣĕdûqî; secondarily, the letter daleth (d) was doubled ("secondary gemination") to produce the later commonly used form, ṣaddûqî. While this is a theoretical possibility, there is no extant attestation of such a primitive form from the ancient period; at times, though, various modern authors use this vocalization. The three Gospels, Acts, and Josephus—no example of the noun is found in the OT Pseudepigrapha written in Greek—all attest to the Greek noun Saddoukaioi (they all use the noun only in the plural). The Greek noun is probably derived from the hypothetical Aramaic form ṣaddûqay (masculine singular absolute state; no example of the word in Jewish Aramaic from around the turn of the era has yet been found). Hence the Greek Saddoukaioi gives us indirect attestation of the pronunciation of the Hebrew form as ṣaddûqîn. This is of some importance when it comes to the question of the etymology and original meaning of the term; on this, see below.

[4] Other Lucan passages are more ambiguous. For example, a Pharisee invites Jesus to dine with him (Luke 7:36–50), but the former's attitude toward the sinful woman and Jesus' reception of her casts him in an unfavorable light. The intention of the Pharisees who urge Jesus to flee Galilee because Herod Antipas seeks his life (Luke 13:31) has been interpreted both positively and negatively by exegetes. In Acts 15:5, we hear of Pharisees who have become Christians, but they prove to be troublemakers. In all such reports, one must naturally make allowances for Luke's redactional theology.

[5] See Jacob Neusner, The Idea of Purity in Ancient Judaism (SJLA 1; Leiden: Brill, 1973) 112. Le Moyne (Les Sadducéens, 46, 59) thinks that Josephus' dislike of the Sadducees may explain why, as a group, they are almost invisible in his narrative apart from the three static descriptions of the Jewish schools. For a survey of the treatment of the Sadducees in the Gospels and Acts, see Le Moyne, Les Sadducéens, 121–35; Saldarini, Pharisees, Scribes and Sadducees, 144–98.

[6] Curiously, Le Moyne (*Les Sadducéens*, 321) insists that there must have been a Sadducean literature, which totally disappeared after A.D. 70. But how do we know that?

[7] Saldarini, *Pharisees, Scribes and Sadducees*, 226.

[8] Meyer (*"Saddoukaios,"* 46) uncritically attributes this relatively late view of the Sadducees to the rabbinic tradition in general. It does not hold for the Mishna.

[9] On the whole problem of the censorship of the rabbinic texts mentioning Sadducees, see Le Moyne, *Les Sadducéens*, 95–102; Saldarini, *Pharisees, Scribes and Sadducees*, 226.

[10] The problem is compounded for those who think that, at times in the rabbinic literature, *ṣaddûqîn* refers not to the Sadducees, the priestly and lay aristocracy in Jerusalem, but rather to those "sons of Zadok" who are the Essenes or Qumranites mentioned in the Dead Sea Scrolls. Personally, I remain skeptical of this suggestion, though the possibility cannot be entirely ruled out.

[11] On the Boethusians, see Le Moyne, *Les Sadducéens*, 332–40 (on their history and identity), 177–98 (on their legal opinions); Saldarini, *Pharisees, Scribes and Sadducees*, 226–28; Grabbe, *Judaism from Cyrus to Hadrian. Volume Two*, 486. In Saldarini's view (p. 227), the conflation and confusion of the Sadducees and Boethusians suggest that the authors of the rabbinic literature "did not understand the first century realities and thus throw doubt on the reliability of all the texts about the Sadducees and Boethusians." I do not give much consideration to the Boethusians for two reasons: (1) Since they are not mentioned by any 1st-century author, any attempt to identify them must remain highly speculative. (2) Since our concern is "Jesus in relation to" various Jewish groups, the fact that Jesus is never presented as coming into contact with the Boethusians makes a detailed treatment of them irrelevant to our goal. A hypothesis about the relation of the Boethusians to the Sadducees will be sketched below.

[12] Here I differ noticeably from the approach taken by Le Moyne in his detailed study of the Sadducees, *Les Sadducéens*. While his volume is a treasure trove of texts and information, and while Le Moyne does reject obviously late legends, a thoroughgoing critical stance is lacking. Le Moyne jumps too quickly back and forth from the Mishna and the Tosepta to the two Talmuds, mixing in other rabbinic works along the way.

[13] The appearance of the Sadducees yoked with the Pharisees in Matt 3:7 and 16:1,6,11–12 is almost certainly a redactional creation of Matthew since (1) the phrase "Pharisees and Sadducees" is unique to Matthew in the NT and (2) the presence of the Sadducees in chaps. 3 and 16 is clearly due to Matthew's reworking of Q and Marcan traditions that lacked them (cf. Luke 3:7–9 [the audience is simply "the

crowds who came to be baptized" by John] and Mark 8:11–21 [the adversaries are the Pharisees and Herod]). On this, see Müller, "Jesus und die Sadduzäer," 6 n. 6; also Meyer ("*Saddoukaios*," 52), who remarks that, although Matthew uses the term *Saddoukaioi* more than Mark, he seems "even further from the historical reality [than Mark]." To be sure, as Saldarini (*Pharisees, Scribes and Sadducees,* 157–73) points out, an alliance or coalition of Pharisees and Sadducees against a new faction centered around Jesus would not be unthinkable. But Saldarini never addresses in detail the inter-Synoptic relationships that indicate that what we have in these Matthean texts is simply Matthew's redaction of Mark for his own theological purposes. In my opinion, the unlikely pairing of Pharisees and Sadducees under the rubric of their common teaching (Matt 16:12) reflects Matthew's theological presentation of the various Jewish groups as a united front against the Baptist and Jesus. Once these redactional additions of Matthew are omitted, the presence of the Sadducees in the Gospels is reduced to the Marcan dispute story on the resurrection of the dead.

[14] This brief sketch presumes the broader historical grid presented in chapter 28.

[15] See the revised Schürer, *The History of the Jewish People,* 2. 413.

[16] See Stern, "Aspects of Jewish Society," 570, 604–5; Bowker, *Jesus and the Pharisees,* 10–11; Sanders, *Judaism. Practice & Belief,* 319. It is significant that, for his first appointment to the high priesthood, Herod the Great broke with (more recent) tradition by reaching outside the Hasmonean family to choose Hananel, a Babylonian (so *Ant.* 15.3.1 §40, though *m. Para* 3:5 says he was from Egypt; see Le Moyne, *Les Sadducéens,* 391 n. 4; Meyer, "*Saddoukaios,*" 45), who presided in 37 and 35 B.C. (Aristobulus III, Herod's sole experiment in choosing a Hasmonean high priest, was allowed to preside only for one year, in 36 B.C., before this fatally popular teenager met a highly untimely though carefully arranged death. After the crowds in the temple during the feast of Tabernacles had shown great enthusiasm for Aristobulus, Herod had this newly installed high priest drowned in a pool at Herod's palace in Jericho, though Herod made it appear that Aristobulus' death was a tragic accident that occurred while he was playing with friends in the pool; see *Ant.* 15.2.5. §23— 15.3.3 §56.) A much more lengthy term of office was enjoyed by a Herodian high priest, Simon, son of Boethus, whose family hailed from Alexandria in Egypt. Herod had wished to marry Simon's daughter, Mariamme II; appointing her father high priest gave instant status to the family. (It is probable that Simon was Mariamme's father and the high priest appointed by Herod [so *Ant.* 15.9.3 §320–22; 17.4.2 §78; 18.5.1 §109; but see the confusing statement in 19.6.2 §297]; however, some critics think that Boethus himself was the father of Mariamme and the high priest whom Herod appointed, Simon being instead her brother.) Some scholars (e.g., Le Moyne, Meyer) suggest that both Hananel and Boethus belonged to the old Zadokite line: Hananel stemming from those Zadokite priests who had not returned to Palestine after the Babylonian exile, and Boethus being related to Onias IV (or Onias III, see Le Moyne, p. 66), a legitimate Zadokite priest who had fled to Egypt during the Hellenizing reforms of Antiochus IV and founded a temple at Leontopolis. This sugges-

tion, while speculative, would help clarify the flow of events: (1) Herod's appointment of Hananel and Simon not only reached outside the Hasmonean family but also sought to marginalize—even delegitimize—the Hasmonean priests by installing old-line Zadokite priests, with the not-so-subtle propaganda message that Herod, the rebuilder of the Jerusalem temple and the true King of the Jews, was replacing the usurpers with legitimate high priests who did not claim the kingship. He may also have intended to provide a counterbalance to the Sadducees in Jerusalem by bringing in families of the Zadokite line who could claim that they had not been compromised first by the Hellenizers and then by the Hasmoneans. (2) If the family of Boethus was Zadokite, one can understand why, by the time of direct Roman rule, priests from this family (the Boethusians of rabbinic literature) might have begun to associate with the Sadducees: both saw themselves as the descendants or supporters of "the sons of Zadok," the old-line legitimate high priests. They had good reason to form a common front against both the remnants of the Hasmonean family and the Pharisees. Over time an alliance may have formed between the two groups. This might explain why the rabbinic literature easily interchanges and tends to equate the Boethusians and the Sadducees: both claimed descent from Zadok and hence were willing to form alliances with each other (including by marriage), thus leaving the Hasmonean priests out in the cold. While details are hard to come by, it may well be that, between them, the Boethusian and the Sadducean groups supplied most of the high priests under direct Roman rule. It must be stressed repeatedly, though, that this does not mean that the Sadducees and their allies were simply and solely priests. The old-line aristocratic lay families, who considered both the Hasmoneans and the Herodians upstarts, would have naturally gravitated toward the old-line aristocratic families of priests. On the whole question of the relationship between aristocrats and the Sadducees, see Sanders, *Judaism. Practice & Belief,* 317–40. On theories about the relation of the Boethusians to the Sadducees, see Le Moyne, pp. 337–39; Saldarini (*Pharisees, Scribes and Sadducees,* 228) considers Le Moyne's theory that the Boethusians were a subgroup of the Sadducees and may have been identical with the Herodians "very doubtful." In any event, there would be no reason why pious Jews would in principle or a priori reject a given high priest simply because he had been appointed by Herod. The Jewish Scriptures do not indicate that one particular official alone has power to appoint a high priest. At various times in Israel's history, various monarchs and officials, both Jewish and Gentile, did in fact appoint the high priest. While the new policy of Herod the Great and the Roman governors, which favored frequent changes of high priests, may have weakened respect for the office, there is no evidence that most Palestinian Jews refused to recognize the legitimacy of a given high priest solely on the grounds that Herod the Great or a Roman governor had appointed him. Legitimate descent would have been the key factor.

[17] Jeremias (*Jerusalem in the Time of Jesus,* 232) seriously misreads the sources when he claims that the Sadducees declined in political importance during the first half of the 1st century A.D. See, on the contrary, *Ant.* 20.10.5 §251; cf. Schwartz, *Josephus and Judaean Politics,* 61.

[18] Le Moyne (*Les Sadducéens*, 393–94) thinks that there are three events that may suggest that, during direct Roman rule and the rule of Agrippa I (A.D. 41–44), the criminal justice system administered in Jerusalem followed the Sadducean *hălākâ*: (1) the incident of the woman caught in adultery (John 7:53–8:11); (2) the stoning of Stephen, one of the seven Hellenist leaders in the Jerusalem church (Acts 7:54–60); and (3) the case of the daughter of a priest who, when found guilty of unchastity, was burned alive (see *m. Sanh.* 7:2; *t. Sanh.* 9:11; cf. Lev 21:9). While this may be true, we must admit a number of problems: (1) Not all scholars would admit that all three cases reflect historical incidents. (2) The first two incidents could have been cases of "street justice" inflicted on individuals by a lynch mob—all the more so if, as seems likely, Jewish courts in Jerusalem lacked the power during this period to inflict the death penalty.

[19] As we saw in chapter 28, the delegation sent to Josephus in Galilee to relieve him of his command included a Pharisaic priest named Jozar as well as two Pharisaic laymen from the common people, Jonathan and Ananias (*Life*, 39 §197). From the rise of the Hasmoneans down to the destruction of Jerusalem, the only high priest we might designate as a Pharisee would be John Hyrcanus in the early years of his reign, when he favored the Pharisees. What "being a Pharisee" would have meant in the early days of the Pharisaic movement, especially for a monarch often engaged in leading Gentile mercenaries into war against other Gentiles, is hard to say. As for Hyrcanus II, he was apparently (if we may trust Josephus) such a weak and easily manipulated person that it is difficult to think of him as firmly situated in any camp by his own choice.

[20] Goodman (*The Ruling Class*, 83) says that the destruction of the temple "saw the end of the Sadducees." At the same time, it must be emphasized that individual priests—and so perhaps individual Sadducees—did survive the disaster of A.D. 70 and figured in the nascent rabbinic movement in Palestine. Some scholars suggest that there was a direct underground connection between the Sadducees and the medieval Jewish group know as the Karaites, who opposed rabbinic Judaism and rejected the Talmud. While it is theoretically possible that some Jews after A.D. 70 continued to read the works of the Sadducees in private and that such a practice ultimately led to the rise of Karaitism in the 8th–9th centuries A.D., there is no firm evidence for such a connection or, indeed, even for written works of the Sadducees. See Sandmel, *The First Christian Century*, 95 n. 1; Le Moyne, *Les Sadducéens*, 137–41.

[21] So Stern, "Aspects of Jewish Society," 610. As Le Moyne observes (*Les Sadducéens*, 44), it is somewhat astonishing that Josephus, in his three static descriptions of the Jewish schools, never mentions priests or high priests as important members of the Sadducean group; moreover, Josephus explicitly calls only one high priest (Ananus ben Ananus) a Sadducee when describing the period of direct Roman rule. But Le Moyne wisely cautions against an argument from silence. In his depiction of the three schools in the *Jewish War*, Josephus' longest and most laudatory description

is reserved for the Essenes; yet he never mentions priests as an important element in their movement. We know otherwise from the Qumran literature. Could Josephus' silence in these instances have something to do with his being a priest of Hasmonean descent instead of being either a Sadducean or an Essene priest of Zadokite descent?

[22] Sanders (*Judaism. Practice & Belief,* 329) thinks that the lay aristocrats are given the designation "the powerful" *(dynatoi)* or "the best known" *(gnōrimoi)* in Josephus and "the elders" *(presbyteroi)* in the NT. In Sanders' opinion, both priestly and lay leaders are covered by terms like "the first [or: leading] people" *(prōtoi),* "the rulers" or "the magistrates" *(archontes),* and "the leaders" or "the eminent" *(hoi en telei).*

[23] Both Zadok and Abiathar served David as priests (2 Sam 20:25) in the 10th century B.C. Abiathar made the tactical error of supporting David's son Adonijah in the struggle over the succession to the throne, while Zadok supported Solomon (1 Kings 1). When Solomon succeeded in becoming the new king, Abiathar was banished (1 Kgs 2:27) and Zadok became, without a rival, the leading priest serving Solomon in Jerusalem (2:35).

Even those scholars who reject the derivation of the name Sadducees *(ṣaddûqîn)* from the priest Zadok *(ṣādôq)* admit that it is the common opinion—and, in my view, the right one; in favor of a derivation from Zadok see, e.g., the revised Schürer, *The History of the Jewish People,* 2. 413; Cohen, *From the Maccabees to the Mishnah,* 159; Sanders, *Judaism. Practice & Belief,* 25. If we put aside unlikely or fantastic theories (on which see Le Moyne, *Les Sadducéens,* 159), the chief rival theory is the derivation of the name from the Hebrew adjective ṣaddîq ("just," "righteous"). It was espoused by a number of the Church Fathers, including Epiphanius and Jerome. This theory has in its favor the double daleth *(d)* as its central consonant. But almost all critics (e.g., Sundberg, "Sadducees," 160; Saldarini, *Pharisees, Scribes and Sadducees,* 226 n. 60) admit that the passage of the long î sound in the second syllable to a long û sound is difficult if not impossible to explain (so even Le Moyne, who seems nevertheless to be partial to ṣaddîq as an explanation, although he professes agnosticism at the end of his treatment). North's attempt ("The Qumrân 'Sadducees,' " 165–66) to explain the passage from long î to long û by appealing to the Akkadian form ṣaduq ("innocent") is forced, since we are speaking about a name *(ṣaddûqîn)* that was formulated in Palestinian Hebrew and/or Aramaic in the 2d century B.C. The appeal to an Akkadian form might be justified if there were absolutely no other viable explanation; as it is, the priest Zadok provides us with not only a viable but also a more probable alternative. Moreover, if we accepted ṣaddîq as the source of the name Sadducees, we would have to ask why the Sadducees, at the very beginning of their existence as a distinct party, would have been singled out as "just" or "righteous"— either as a proud self-designation or as a mocking sobriquet bestowed by their opponents. One might have expected instead that the designation "the righteous" would have been conferred on the Pharisees. The Sadducees may have proven themselves over time to have been exacting, rigorous, or even severe in their judgments, as Josephus claims. But since we first hear of their political activities in the narrative sections of Josephus when they are out of power (i.e., when Hyrcanus I is allied with the Pharisees), they seem to have received their name before they had much of a chance to compile a record of judicial decisions or a reputation for stringency in judgment. (As a variation of the hypothesis of a derivation of the name Sadducee from ṣaddîq, I should mention as a curiosity Gerleman's article, "Das übervolle Mass," 151–64. From a study of ṣaddîq in the OT, Gerleman concludes that a special sense of the adjective is "fair, temperate, moderate, modest." Without any investigation of the name Sadducee, he immediately declares that this name is derived from ṣaddîq and means "the moderate" or "the modest" men, as opposed to the excessive Pharisees.)

Since the derivation from ṣaddîq labors under so many difficulties, the name Zadok *(ṣdwq)* seems the better explanation. One might object that, in this alternate explanation, there is likewise a philological problem in the passage from ṣādôq to ṣaddûqîn. But such a passage is readily intelligible once we notice that the Hebrew proper name ṣdwq (ṣdq only in 1 Kgs 1:26) seems to have received various vocalizations when it was transliterated into Greek. Some of the Greek renderings of the name doubled the *d* and vocalized the Hebrew *w* as *ou;* on this, see the revised Schürer, 2. 405–6. For example, there are ten passages in Ezekiel, Ezra, and Nehemiah where the LXX text (in some, and sometimes all, of the major codices) reads *Saddouk* or *Saddouch* as the transliteration of the Hebrew ṣdq; see Ezek 40:46; 43:19; 44:15; 48:11; Ezra 7:2 (= LXX 2 Esdras 7:2); Neh 2:4,29 (= 2 Esdras 13:4,29); 10:21 (= 2 Esdras 20:22); 11:11 (= 2 Esdras 21:11); 13:13 (= 2 Esdras 23:13). The Lucianic recension (a later recension of the Greek OT) almost always reads *Saddouk.* A manuscript of the Greek text of the *Ascension of Isaiah* reads *Saddouk* in 2:5. Josephus *(J.W.* 2.17.10 §451; 2.21.7 §628; cf. *Life* 39 §197) mentions a person named *Ananias Saddouki.* Since this Ananias is a Pharisee, *Saddouki* cannot mean Sadducee; its most likely meaning is "son of Zadok," which gives us another example of the vocalization of the Hebrew ṣdq with a double *d* and the vocalization *ou.* A medieval manuscript of the Mishna, the Codex de Rossi 138, at times vocalizes the name of a Rabbi Zadok; the vocalized form is sometimes ṣaddûq. Thus, we have the attestation of the LXX, the Lucianic recension, Josephus, and the Codex de Rossi 138 for one way of pronouncing the proper Hebrew name ṣdwq in ancient times: ṣaddûq. Le Moyne objects that most of these witnesses were copied by Christian scribes, who may have been influenced by the form *Saddoukaioi* in the NT. While that is a possibility, the broad range of attestation of the Greek *Saddouk(i)* (or the Hebrew ṣaddûq) in ancient and medieval documents makes it difficult to attribute this intriguing orthographic phenomenon entirely to Christian scribes.

If, then, we derive the name Sadducees from the proper name Zadok, is it clear that the Zadok referred to is Zadok the priest who functioned in Jerusalem under David and Solomon? Two other suggestions have been made: (1) The rabbinic commentary on the *Pirqê ʾAbôt,* the *ʾAbot de Rabbi Nathan* in versions A and B, contains two forms of a story that derives the name Sadducees from a disciple of Antigonos of Sokho named Zadok (*ʾAbot R. Nat.* A5 and B10). While Le Moyne gives some credence to the tradition, most critical scholars deny any historical value to this story for a number of reasons: (a) The date of composition of *ʾAbot de Rabbi Nathan* should make one wary of using it for reconstructing Jewish history for the 2d century B.C.; its primitive core dates from the third century A.D., but it continued to receive additions over the next few centuries. (b) The story in 'Abot de Rabbi Nathan also explains the origin of the Boethusians through a disciple of Antiochus named Boethus. Since almost no one would accept this explanation of the origin of the Boethusians (in reality, the group most probably took its name from Boethus, the father of Simeon, a Herodian high priest), it is difficult to see why the explanation of the origin of the Sadducees should be accepted. In the end, most scholars consider the story in 'Abot de Rabbi Nathan to be a legend based on a scholarly deduction; see the revised Schürer, 2. 406-7. Strack-Stemberger (Talmud and Midrash, 70) call the story a "historically worthless anecdote"; similarly, Sundberg, "Sadducees," 160; Stern, "Aspects of Jewish Society," 609; Saldarini, Pharisees, Scribes and Sadducees, 227 ("historicity . . . doubtful." Even Le Moyne (p. 116), after arguing for a kernel of historicity, salvages very little from the story, indeed, only the fact that, toward the end of the 2d century B.C., a split took place between the Pharisees and Sadducees over the subject of the resurrection of the dead and retribution after death—a point that most scholars draw anyway from Josephus' presentations. (For a curious attempt to date the origin of the Sadducees during Herod the Great's reign, see Bammel, "Sadduzäer," 107–15.) Guttmann (Rabbinic Judaism, 127–32) also argues for the basic historicity of the story in 'Abot de Rabbi Nathan, but his approach to the sources and the historical period is uncritical. (2) Some scholars simply play the agnostic and suggest that the Zadok who was the source of the name Sadducee is otherwise unknown to us. While that is a theoretical possibility, it is strange that a person who had such a great impact on Jewish history that he gave his name to a major Jewish party at the turn of the era should at the same time have totally disappeared from the pages of that history without leaving a trace. Especially since Josephus and Luke give us reason to see some connection between the Sadducees and the high priests of Jerusalem, the most natural supposition is to connect the Zadok who is the source of the name Sadducee with Zadok, the famous priest of Jerusalem.

[24] While scholars sometimes claim that the descendants of Zadok monopolized the Jerusalem priesthood or at least the high priesthood in the preexilic period, this cannot be proven; see George W. Ramsey, "Zadok (Person)," Anchor Bible Dictionary, 6. 1034–36, esp. 1035–36; cf. the hypothetical reconstruction of the history of the priesthood during and after the Babylonian exile by Joseph Blenkinsopp, "The Judaean Priesthood during the Neo-Babylonian and Achaemenid Periods: A Hypothetical Reconstruction," CBQ 60 (1998) 25–43. To be sure, parts of the postexilic Book of Ezekiel attempt to assign non-Zadokite levitical priests (or "Levites") to lesser duties in the temple, while restricting service at the altar to the priests who are "the sons of Zadok (běnê ṣādôq)," a special group within "the sons of Levi" (Ezek 40:45–46; 43:19; 44:9–31; 48:11). In reality, though, a broader group, "the sons of Aaron," seems to have served at the altar along with "the sons of Zadok." It is probable, however, that the sons of Zadok filled the office of high priest through the Second Temple period until the disruption caused by the Hellenization policy of Antiochus IV in the first part of the 2d century B.C. In the Hebrew text of Sir 51:12 (ix), which is probably an independent hymn from the time of Ben Sira but not by him, the audience is

urged to give thanks to the God who chose "the sons of Zadok as [his] priests." Skehan and Di Lella (*The Wisdom of Ben Sira, 659*) take this verse to refer in particular
to the Zadokites who were still the high priests in Jerusalem. Indeed, this mention of
the sons of Zadok follows after the lengthy praise of the Zadokite high priest Simeon
in Sir 50:1–24; in 50:24, Ben Sira prays that God will not abrogate his covenant with
Simeon's descendants, the Zadokite priests. Thus, the phrase "sons of Zadok" in the
Second Temple period would point in the direction not just of the priesthood in general but of the high priesthood and the high priestly families in particular. If, then—as
seems to be the case—the name Sadducees *(saddûqîn)* is derived from Zadok *(sādôq),*
this is an important indicator of the roots of the Sadducees in the old-line high priestly
families of Jerusalem.

This state of affairs would also explain the importance of "the sons of Zadok" in
some of the main Qumran documents: 1QS 5:2,9 (but probably not 9:14); 1QSa
1:2,24; 2:3; 1QSb 3:22; CD 3:21–4:1; 4:3 (cf. 5:5); 4QFlor 1:17 (but the meaning
here is unclear). The community of Qumran seems to have been founded by a group
that rejected the Hasmonean high priests because they were not of the sons of Zadok
and therefore (in the eyes of the Qumranites) were illegitimate high priests. The leaders (including the Teacher of Righteousness) and some of the members of the original
Qumran community probably belonged to the old-line high priestly families of Jerusalem who based their control of the office on Zadok and his descendants and who
therefore fiercely resented the Hasmonean interlopers. For different readings of the
evidence relating to the sons of Zadok at Qumran, see Geza Vermes, *The Dead Sea
Scrolls in English* (4th ed.; London: Penguin, 1995) 1–40; Murphy-O'Connor, "The
Essenes and Their History," 215–44; Philip R. Davies, *Behind the Essenes. History
and Ideology in the Dead Sea Scrolls* (Brown Judaic Studies 94; Atlanta: Scholars,
1987) 51–72. The presence of the phrase "sons of Zadok" at Qumran is all the more
striking in that the phrase is absent from all other intertestamental Jewish writings;
see Le Moyne, *Les Sadducéens,* 86, and in general 85–93. Le Moyne (pp. 92–93)
thinks that, at Qumran, only a part of the priests counted as "sons of Zadok," who
constituted the leadership group.

[25] Just as, from one point of view, the Qumranites might be considered extreme
Pharisees, insofar as they exalted purity rules and observed them even more stringently than the Pharisees, so, from another point of view, the Qumranites might be
considered extreme Sadducees, insofar as some of the founding members of Qumran
were apparently Jerusalem Zadokite priests who refused, unlike the Sadducees who
remained in Jerusalem, to accept the ministrations of the Hasmonean high priest in
the Jerusalem temple. For somewhat similar observations, see the revised Schürer,
The History of the Jewish People, 2. 413. In reality, while sharing various similarities
with both main parties, the Qumranites were neither Pharisees nor Sadducees; rather,
they established a unique identity for themselves. Josephus rightly distinguishes the
Essenes as a third school of thought.

[26] The pro-Hasmonean First Book of Maccabees has the dying Mattathias (the father of Judas Maccabeus) reminding his sons that "Phinehas, our father, because of

his fierce zeal, received a covenant of an eternal priesthood" (1 Macc 2:54). Since Phinehas was thought to have been an ancestor of Zadok (1 Chr 6:3–8,49–53; Ezra 7:1–5), Mattathias' assertion may reflect a Hasmonean bid for legitimacy in the eyes of the Sadducees. A supposed "Phinehas-connection" might have made collaboration with the upstart Hasmoneans somewhat more palatable to the Sadducees, who cherished the Zadokite line of priests. Technically, the Sadducees did not have to reject a non-Zadokite high priest in principle, since the Pentateuch, the normative core of Sadducean belief, simply demanded that the high priest be a descendant of Aaron— as, no doubt, the Hasmonean priests were (or were thought to be). On this, see Le Moyne, *Les Sadducéens,* 387–89; cf. Jonathan A. Goldstein, *I Maccabees* (AB 41; New York: Doubleday, 1976) 8; Meyer, *"Saddoukaios,"* 43–44.

[27] For all his questionable and tendentious assertions, Lauterbach ("The Sadducees and Pharisees," 35) is right on this point. A similar position is held by Stern, "Aspects of Jewish Society," 609; Jeremias, *Jerusalem in the Time of Jesus,* 228–30 (though his reasoning is somewhat curious). Eppstein's article ("When and How the Sadducees Were Excommunicated," 145–56) is an example of fantasy wedded to uncritical use of the sources: his conclusion is that ca. A.D. 60–61, the sages made it "impossible for any Jew believing in Sadducean halakhah to enter the temple. . . ."

[28] For Jozar, see *Life* 39 §197; for Simon, son of Gamaliel, see *Life* 38–39 §189–96.

[29] See Le Moyne, *Les Sadducéens,* 350. On p. 353, Le Moyne notes that we have some indirect evidence for Sadducean scribes insofar as the NT speaks of "the scribes of the Pharisees" (Mark 2:16; "the Pharisees and their scribes" in the Lucan redaction of Mark [Luke 5:30]) and "some scribes of the party of the Pharisees" (Acts 23:9). One may reasonably infer that if one of the two major religious-political parties had scribes, the other did as well. It is difficult to imagine what else Mark's "the scribes of the Pharisees" might indicate. In a somewhat similar vein, Josephus says that the Sadducees "consider it a virtue to dispute with the teachers *(didaskalous)* of the wisdom that they follow." The Sadducees, therefore, cultivated some kind of educational and scribal activity proper to their own party. All this warns us against accepting the all-too-common view of the Sadducees (as well as the Jerusalem priests in general) as ignoramuses with respect to Jewish Scripture and tradition, the Pharisees alone being the wise and educated group. That is a caricature of the rabbinic literature, not a sober historical portrait. See also Jeremias, *Jerusalem in the Time of Jesus,* 231. Commenting on John Hyrcanus' switch from the Pharisees to the Sadducees, Saldarini (*Pharisees, Scribes and Sadducees,* 88) suggests that the Sadducees were a rival group of retainers competing with the Pharisees. Whether or not that was true at the time of John Hyrcanus, I doubt that we can call the Sadducees a group of retainers during direct Roman rule. The high priest with the priestly and lay aristocracy around him effectively governed a great deal of day-to-day Jewish life in Judea—subject to the Roman governor.

[30] See Bruce Chilton, "Annas (Person)," *Anchor Bible Dictionary,* 1. 257–58. The confusion in Luke 3:2; Acts 4:6; and John 18:13,24 over whether Annas (reigned A.D. 6–15) or Caiaphas (A.D. 18–36) is the high priest in office at the time of Jesus' death (ca. A.D. 30) may be explained at least partially by Annas' continued influence after he was deposed from office. In fact, references to Annas as high priest (*archiereus,* traditionally translated in the singular as "high priest"), while technically incorrect, are understandable on two grounds: (1) He remained the true power behind the throne of his sons and son-in-law. (2) Since the NT and Josephus use the plural form *archiereis* (traditionally translated as "chief priests") to designate members of the high priestly families (including former high priests and future candidates), it was but a small step to use *archiereus* in the singular of a former high priest. Present-day reporters do something similar when they address a former president of the United States with the title "President." On the question of the meaning of the plural *archiereis,* I am following the opinion of Sanders, *Judaism. Practice & Belief,* 327–28; cf. the revised Schürer, *The History of the Jewish People,* 2. 232–36; similarly, Stern, "Aspects of Jewish Society," 602–3; Goodman, *The Ruling Class,* 120 n. 13. The major competing theory is that of Jeremias, *Jerusalem in the Time of Jesus,* 175–81: the chief priests were the independent body of priests who permanently governed the affairs of the Jerusalem temple and priesthood. They included such officials as the captain of the temple guard and the temple treasurer. Actually, the difference between these two theories would not amount to much in practice. No doubt, most of the chief temple authorities were chosen from relatives of former high priests or the presently reigning high priest. Other theories about the meaning of *archiereis* (e.g., the heads of the 24 priestly divisions; the priestly members of the Sanhedrin mentioned in the NT) are highly unlikely, since they cannot explain all the occurrences of the term in the NT and Josephus. The occurrence of the plural *archiereis* in the NT and Josephus for a whole group of Jewish priests living at the same time is striking; perhaps it has something to do with the rapid turnover of high priests during direct Roman rule.

[31] For Eleazar, see *Ant.* 18.2.2 §34; for Jonathan, see 18.5.3 §123; for Theophilus, see ibid.; for Matthias, see 19.6.4. §316; for Ananus II, see 20.9.1 §197. Although Josephus underlines in *Ant.* 20.9.1 §198 the fact that Ananus I (i.e., the NT Annas) had five sons who became high priests, there is some confusion in his two accounts in *Ant.* 18 and 19 (§123 and §313–16) over who succeeded Jonathan in the priesthood, Theophilus or Matthias. Some scholars suggest that Jonathan and Theophilus may have been alternate names for the same son of Annas. However, Louis H. Feldman, in the LCL edition of Josephus (*Josephus,* 9. 362–63 n. a), rejects this suggestion because (1) the names Jonathan and Theophilus are similar but not the same in meaning and (2) it is improbable that Josephus, himself a priest, would make a mistake about such an important matter as the succession of high priests.

[32] Only Josephus tells us that Caiaphas' proper name was Joseph; on the other hand, Josephus does not say that Annas was the father-in-law of Caiaphas. Only John

18:13 vouches for that. But since no theological or polemical point seems to be scored by this marital connection, many exegetes and historians are willing to accept the claim. Caiaphas' connection through marriage with Annas, reflecting the latter's continued political influence, would certainly jibe with the amazing picture of four or five sons of Annas filling the office of high priest at various times from A.D. 16 to 62.

[33] Thoma ("Auswirkungen," 34) goes so far as to claim that all or almost all of the high priests from A.D. 6 to 70 were Sadducees. But such a claim goes beyond what one can establish with the present supply of data.

[34] The testimony of Acts is used with confidence by Stern, "Aspects of Jewish Society," 610. Le Moyne (Les Sadducéens, 135) distinguishes: he is mistrustful of the information on the Sadducees in Acts 4 and 5, but accepting of the data in Acts 23:8.

[35] Barrett (Acts, 1. 219) thinks that "we must suppose" that the priests just mentioned prior to the Sadducees in 4:1 shared the viewpoint of the Sadducees. Meyer ("Saddoukaios," 53) thinks that the statement about the Sadducees in Acts 4:1–2 "implies that temple politics and theology were controlled by the Sadducees, which is in accordance with the historical facts."

[36] The Codex Bezae actually changes "John" to "Jonathan." While a few scholars maintain that this is the original reading, it is almost certainly a correction by a Christian scribe who knew—perhaps from Josephus' Antiquities—that Annas had a son named Jonathan. In any event, the final person named, Alexander, is unknown.

[37] So Stern, "Aspects of Jewish Society," 611 n. 2; Barrett (Acts, 1. 282) feels certain that Annas is meant.

[38] The participle ousa is difficult to explain. Two possibilities are mentioned by Barrett (Acts, 1. 282–83, though the two options are sometimes conflated into one position): (1) The use of the redundant participle ōn is typical of both Acts and Egyptian papyri; hence, it need not be translated. (2) At times, ōn can carry the sense of "current," "existent," or "local"; this is the translation chosen by Kirsopp Lake and Henry J. Cadbury in The Beginnings of Christianity. Part I. The Acts of the Apostles, 4. 56–57. Perhaps the sense is that, unlike the Pharisees and the Christians, who still exist in Luke's day, the Sadducees existed at the time of the events narrated, but have disappeared as an organized group after A.D. 70.

[39] Meyer ("Saddoukaios," 53) perhaps exaggerates a little when he says flatly of the narrative in Acts 5:17–42: "The high priest is a Sadducee. . . ." Luke never makes so explicit a statement, but Meyer's assertion is a valid inference from the text in its larger context.

[40] There are other possible candidates for the label of Sadducean high priest. (1) One is the high priest who presided over Paul's trial after he was arrested in Jerusalem

(Acts 23). Luke tells us that the high priest's name was Ananias (23:2), and here Luke is sustained by Josephus. Since Paul's Jerusalem trial would have taken place ca. A.D. 57, and since the high priest for the whole period from 47 to 59 was Ananias, son of Nedebaeus, Luke is correct this time in his use of both name and title (as we see from Josephus' reports about Ananias in *Ant.* 20.5.2 §103; 20.6.2 §131; and 20.9.2–4 §205–14). While Luke does not call Ananias a Sadducee, the flow of the narrative intimates a connection. The trial starts with a hostile Ananias having Paul struck (23:1–2). The wily Paul then divides his potential opposition by proclaiming his belief in the resurrection of the dead (v 6). Predictably, this doctrine divides the Pharisees and the Sadducees, rendering at least some of the former sympathetic, while presumably (from Luke's emphasis on division, shouting, and disorder) the Sadducees become quite hostile. The Roman tribune has to rescue Paul and bring him to the army barracks (v 10). The next day, about forty conspirators hatch a plot to assassinate Paul; they even bind themselves by an oath not to eat or drink until they have succeeded (vv 12–13). The conspirators ask "the chief priests and elders" to aid the plot by requesting that Paul be brought back for further inquiry (vv 14–15), and the authorities comply with the plotters' request.

Now, if one looks at the flow of the narrative from 23:1 to 23:15, one notices that (a) from the beginning Ananias is shown to be fiercely hostile to Paul; (b) the same fierce hostility is shown during the trial by the Sadducees, but not the Pharisees; and (c) this fierce hostility is continued by the assassins, in whose plotting Ananias, along with his priestly and lay associates, concur. In 24:1, Ananias and the elders pursue the matter before the governor Felix at Caesarea Maritima. When they fail to make progress, they plan another assassination attempt in 25:1–3. No one statement in this narrative but rather the overall context suggests that Ananias' persistent and even deadly hatred of Paul is a quality that associates him not with the Pharisees but with the Sadducees, who probably are understood as sponsors, if not members, of the conspiracy. At the very least, Ananias stands on the Sadducees' side of the divide and connives to accomplish what they and the plotters desire. If we add Ananias to our list of Sadducean high priests, the Sadducees' hold on the office from A.D. 6–66 rises to roughly 46 out of 60 years. Nevertheless, one must admit that, in this case, our argument is quite indirect. Moreover, one must make allowances for part of Luke's theological program in Acts: namely, the high priests and the Sadducees are the implacable enemies of the early Christians, while the Pharisees are at least potential sympathizers. (2) Stern ("Aspects of Jewish Society," 611) argues from rabbinic literature that the high priestly house of Phiabi was affiliated with the Sadducees. If this be true, then we could also rank Jesus son of Phiabi (appointed by Herod the Great), Ishmael son of Phiabi (A.D. 15), and Ishmael son of Phiabi (A.D. 59–61) as Sadducean high priests (the two Ishmaels are probably different persons). Once again, though, the argument is tenuous and indirect. (3) Le Moyne (*Les Sadducéens*, 337–39, 347) thinks that the Boethusians constituted a priestly group within the larger group of Sadducees. If one accepts Le Moyne's view, then it follows that the high priests whom Le Moyne assigns to the Boethusian family also count as Sadducees: Simon, son of Boethus (23–6 B.C.); Joazar, son of Boethus (5–4 B.C., 3 B.C.–A.D. 6); Eleazar, brother of Joazar (4 B.C.), Simon Cantheras, son of Boethus (A.D. 41), Elioneus, son of Cantheras (A.D. 44). If this line of reasoning is adopted, then the Sadducees emerge as dominating the high priesthood for a good part of the Herodian/Roman period. However, the identification of the Boethusians as a group within the Sadducees is far from certain. In sum, one can see from all these complicated arguments that it goes beyond the available evidence to claim, as Müller ("Jesus und die Sadduzäer," 6) does, that from A.D. 6 to 70, the Sadducees supplied all or almost all of the high priests.

[41] On this, see Grabbe, *Judaism from Cyrus to Hadrian. Volume Two*, 486; Le Moyne, *Les Sadducéens*, 358.

[42] On this, see Moore, *Judaism*, 1. 239–40; the revised Schürer, *The History of the Jewish People*, 2. 319–20; Le Moyne, *Les Sadducéens*, 359 n. 6. According to the revised Schürer, while rabbinic Judaism placed the Prophets and the Writings alongside the Pentateuch as the canon of Holy Scripture, "at no time were they [the Prophets and the Writings] placed on the same footing; the Torah has always occupied the higher place." At times the rabbis distinguish between the *tôrâ* (the five books of Moses, the original and full revelation of God to Israel) and the *qabbālâ* ("tradition," i.e., the Prophets and the Writings, which are seen as collections of traditions, handing down the original revelation to subsequent generations with reinforcement and explanation). An early example of this can be found in *m. Ta'an.* 2:1, where Joel 2:13 is cited as *qabbālâ* in the sense of post-Pentateuchal Scriptures—in this case, the Prophets. (Danby's translation of *qabbālâ* in this text as "protest" is questionable.) Other examples of *qabbālâ* in this sense can be found in both Talmuds; this distinction intimates a certain preeminence of the five books of Moses within the Jewish canon. A similar distinction is made in *m. Meg.* 3:1 between *tôrâ* ("Law," i.e., the Pentateuch) and *sĕpārîm* ("Books," i.e., the Prophets and the Writings). The mishna states that the *tôrâ* may be purchased with the proceeds from the sale of *sĕpārîm*, but not vice versa—thus indicating the superior value of the Pentateuch over the other parts of the Jewish canon of Scripture.

[43] See Sanders, *Judaism. Practice & Belief*, 333–34. Sanders points out that Hyrcanus I would have had to exercise judgment in serious criminal cases, including capital cases; yet the Pentateuch gives only the broadest indications about the correlation between crime and punishment in such cases. In setting penalties, Hyrcanus would have had to follow some traditional rules that supplemented the written Torah; and these, presumably, would have been Sadducean after he switched to their party. The practical problem of Sadducees without any traditions outside of the written Torah is felt by Goodman (*The Ruling Class*, 74), who nevertheless fails to draw the logical conclusion. He opines instead that the traditionless Sadducees must have been left "at rather a loss when cases came before them that had not been explicitly dealt with in the written sources." The celebrations of intricate temple liturgies under Sadducean high priests around the turn of the era and the examples of Sadducean *hălākôt* in the Mishna argue otherwise.

[44] See James C. VanderKam, "The Origin, Character, and Early History of the 364-Day Calendar: A Reassessment of Jaubert's Hypotheses," *CBQ* 41 (1979) 390–411. At the same time, VanderKam (*Calendars in the Dead Sea Scrolls,* 110–16) points out the differences between *Jubilees,* which simply rejects a lunar calendar, and *1 Enoch* and Qumran fragments, which allow for lunar elements in their calendrical computations. Making matters more complicated, the indications of the calendrical fragments from Qumran suggest that the Qumranites in turn did not agree entirely with the views seen in *1 Enoch.* Moreover, one must remember that multiple copies of *Jubilees* have been found at Qumran, where it was apparently a revered work. It may well be, then, that views on calendrical questions at Qumran were complex and went through various phases during the roughly 200 years of the community's history.

[45] Contrast *m. Yoma* 5:1 with *t. Yoma* 1:8 (Boethusian high priest); *y. Yoma* 1, 5, (Boethusian high priest); *y. Yoma* 1, 5, (Sadducean high priest; identical with the *Sipra* on Lev 16:13); *b. Yoma* 53a; and *b. Yoma* 19b (both texts in the Babylonian Talmud speak of a Sadducean high priest). Many critics seem willing to accept this dispute between Pharisees and Sadducees on when the high priest should begin to burn the incense on Yom Kippur (before or after entering the holy of holies?) as a historical, pre-70 dispute between the two parties (but for doubts about the historicity of any material about the Sadducees that comes from the amoraic period, see Sundberg, "Sadducees," 162–63). Supposedly, the Sadducees maintained that the high priest should place the incense on the burning coals before he entered the holy of holies (the *dĕbîr*), while the Pharisees claimed that he should do so after entering. For a detailed study of the various forms of the tradition, see Le Moyne, *Les Sadducéens,* 249–60; Le Moyne is dependent on Lauterbach's essay ("A Significant Controversy," 1–33) for his interpretation. According to the tendentious interpretation of Lauterbach, the Sadducees held "superstitious," "primitive" notions of God and cult, while the "enlightened" Pharisees were the "progressive liberal group," which supported a "purer" conception of God with "less regard for the sacrificial cult," which the Pharisees sought to "democratize and spiritualize." Modern controversies among the various wings of Judaism peep through here. Nevertheless, Le Moyne accepts this explanation except for the qualification "superstitious." In favor of the historicity of the dispute is the wide attestation of the core tradition (stripped of various legendary accretions), which deals with a minor detail of ritual that would have had no relevance after the destruction of the Jerusalem temple. Caution, though, seems advisable: (1) One has to consider that when the description of the burning of the incense on Yom Kippur first appears in rabbinic literature, namely, in *m. Yoma* 5:1, there is no indication of any dispute between two parties. Sadducees and Pharisees do not appear in the text, and it is simply said—without any sense that the point is controversial—that the high priest begins to burn the incense after he enters the holy of holies (thus the Mishna's description coincides with the Pharisaic position). The idea of a controversy (involving a Boethusian—not a Sadducean—high priest) first appears in the Tosepta. Moreover, the whole legal world of *m. Yoma* 1:3–7 is "charming and fanciful" (so Sanders, *Judaism. Practice & Belief,* 396). (2) In practice, how would

the high priest, while manipulating various objects, manage to put the incense on the burning coals once he was in the closed, unlit holy of holies? It would be easy enough to start burning the incense when he was still in the holy place (the *hêkāl,* the sanctuary), where the candelabra *(měnôrôt)* would shed light. (3) Again, in practice, how would anyone besides the high priest know exactly when he began to burn the incense (see Lev 16:17: no one is to be in the Tent of Meeting from the time the high priest enters until the time he exits)? (4) There are many cases in rabbinic literature of disputes arising among rabbis about rituals that had ceased with the destruction of the temple. Few critical historians would claim that all these disputes go back in fact to the pre-70 period. Actually, acceptance of this dispute about incense as historical would only strengthen the basic point I am making in the main text, namely, that the Sadducees had their own liturgical traditions. Whether this dispute over when to begin burning the incense on Yom Kippur shows that the Sadducees always represented the literal and more traditional sense of the text is debatable. Interestingly, scholars disagree on whether the literal sense of the text of Lev 16:12–13 favors the Sadducean or the Pharisaic point of view. My own opinion is that the natural sense of Lev 16:12–13 favors the Pharisaic interpretation (so also Sanders, p. 335); hence, in this case, the Sadducees are not the ones championing the literal sense of the text.

[46] If one is willing to include the testimony of the Tosepta, we may add the dispute in *t. Ḥag.* 3:35 (cf. *y. Ḥag.* 3, 8, 79d): the Sadducees hold that the menorah cannot be rendered unclean, while the Pharisees hold that it can. Here again, the Pharisees seem the more rigorous in a matter of purity. Le Moyne (*Les Sadducéens,* 103, 292–93, 323–24) tends to accept this as a genuine, pre-70 tradition on the grounds that the rabbis would not have invented a tradition in which the Sadducees mock the Pharisees.

[47] If we may include the testimony of *t. Yad.* 2:20 (cf. *y. B. Bat.* 8, 1, 16a; *b. B. Bat.* 115b–116a), the *hălākâ* of the Sadducees (in the Tosepta, the Boethusians) in the area of civil law also included matters of inheritance. Once again, though, we must notice that the Mishna (*m. B. Bat.* 8:2) does not present the tradition as a dispute between the Sadducees and the Pharisees; nevertheless, Le Moyne (*Les Sadducéens,* 299–306) considers the tradition historical.

[48] However, the relevant examples in Josephus deal with criminal, not civil, law; see *Ant.* 13.10.5 §288–96 (which displays the leniency of the Pharisees on the question of the punishment of Eleazar, who insulted John Hyrcanus); 20.9.1 §200 (which displays the severity [or savagery] of the Sadducean high priest Ananus ben Ananus in the execution of James, the brother of Jesus, and certain other Jews). Another possible example of the severity of Sadducees in criminal law is the strange question of executing a person by burning him or her alive "externally," i.e., burning the whole exterior part of his or her body, as opposed to the supposedly Pharisaic method of introducing a wick or thread into the person's mouth, extending it to the stomach, and then igniting it so that the person is burned "internally," with the physical integrity of

the body being preserved (cf. *m. Sanh.* 7:2). In this mishna, Rabbi Eliezer ben Zadok recounts an incident in which a priest's daughter who committed adultery was burned alive "externally." However, there are problems with seeing in this mishna evidence of a Sadducean-Pharisaic dispute over *hălākâ*. The text in *m. Sanh.* 7:2 mentions neither Pharisees nor Sadducees; one can arrive at the position that "external" burning was the Sadducean as opposed to the Pharisaic position only by combining rabbinic texts from various periods and arguing from inference. Moreover, whether the Sadducean form of executing a person by fire "externally" can be considered all that much more severe or cruel than the "internal" Pharisaic form is debatable. On the whole question, see Le Moyne, *Les Sadducéens*, 236–38. In any case, as we shall see below, the Sadducees took the less severe side of the argument on when and under what conditions false witnesses could be put to death in a case involving the death penalty (*m. Mak.* 1:6). It is therefore at least questionable whether the Sadducees were always the more severe party when it came to punishing criminals.

[49] So the revised Schürer, *The History of the Jewish People*, 2. 411 n. 36 (connecting 6:2 with 6:1).

[50] Le Moyne (*Les Sadducéens*, 201–4) remains unsure whether *m. 'Erub.* 6:2 proves that the Sadducees were opposed in principle to the practice of the *'erûb*. He thinks that the Sadducees' opposition is a likely inference, but that the text does not offer firm proof. I must admit that I do not understand his difficulty.

[51] On this passage, see Le Moyne, *Les Sadducéens*, 227–33

[52] Strictly speaking, in *m. Mak.* 1:6, the Hebrew wording of the law of talion is that found in Exod 21:23–24. However, the second citation is clearly from Deut 19:19, and the deviation from the wording of the law of talion in Deut 19:21 is very slight (*tahat* instead of *bĕ*).

[53] Le Moyne (*Les Sadducéens*, 227) shows his usual tendency of conflating Jewish groups when he translates the words introducing the opponents of the Sadducees in *m. Mak.* 1:6 as "[But] the teachers [Pharisees] said to them. . . ." He then proceeds to adduce a number of later rabbinic texts as partial parallels, once again not noticing that the neat opposition of "Pharisees" and "Sadducees" is lacking.

[54] On false ways of distinguishing Sadducees from Pharisees, see Saldarini, *Pharisees, Scribes and Sadducees*, 303. In particular, one should avoid the simplistic formula that the Sadducees were Sadducees because they rejected oral traditions and held only to the written Torah; see, e.g., the muddled presentation in the revised Schürer, *The History of the Jewish People*, 2. 407–8. As we have seen, the Sadducees as well as the Pharisees had traditions not found in the written Torah. Moreover—and this point is often overlooked—we have no way of knowing whether the non-Scriptural traditions of the Pharisees and Sadducees from the pre-70 period were oral,

written, or both. As we saw in chapter 28, one must not explain the Sadducees' position in terms of the rabbinic doctrine of the dual Torah (oral and written), a doctrine that probably was not developed in explicit fashion before the 3d century A.D.

[55] See Sanders, *Judaism. Practice & Belief,* 335–36.

[56] Sanders (*Jewish Law,* 107) puts it this way: "The distinction, then, would be that the Pharisees were *conscious* of having *non-interpretative traditions,* while the Sadducees claimed that their traditions were based on interpretation [of Scripture]."

[57] For a similar view, see Lauterbach, "The Sadducees and the Pharisees," 37; also Le Moyne, *Les Sadducéens,* 375. Lauterbach thinks (p. 46) that "the Sadducees distinguished strictly between the absolutely binding written laws and their own additional laws and decisions. The latter they considered merely as temporary decrees and ordinances, . . . issued for the time being by the ruling authorities as necessary for the welfare of the community. . . ." The Sadducees, says Lauterbach, admitted the right of previous generations of priests and teachers to create such laws, but these laws could not stand on the same level as the written laws in the Pentateuch. The priestly leaders of any given time had the authority to decide whether traditional laws from a previous period should be maintained or abolished. Lauterbach mars this scholarly technical analysis by proceeding to engage in polemic (pp. 47–48): the Sadducees became "blind slaves to the letter of the Law without regard for its spirit. . . ." The religious law was allowed to degenerate into "mere formalism and ritualism. . . ."

[58] One might object that the (solar-)lunar calendar observed in the temple became obligatory for all Israelites, not just the Sadducees. But since the Hasmoneans and Pharisees likewise accepted the (solar-)lunar calendar, it cannot be considered a specifically Sadducean tradition as opposed to Pharisaic traditions. The acceptance of the (solar-)lunar calendar by the Sadducees does show, however, that the Sadducees were not opposed in principle to change and to the adoption of new regulations that could not be found in the Pentateuch.

[59] One might speculate on whether the Sadducees opposed the Pharisees' "traditions of the fathers" because they instinctively intuited in the Pharisees' position the implicit danger that traditions that were normative for all Israelites would become in effect a second Torah, on equal footing with the written Torah. If this was the Sadducees' rationale, they prophesied unawares. In fact, the Pharisees' position on the traditions of the fathers did finally blossom—much later on in the rabbinic literature—into the explicit doctrine of the dual Torah.

[60] Part of the problem in modern discussions is the presumption that everyone agrees on what the "literal" meaning of Scripture is. Sandmel (*The First Christian Century,* 70), for instance, connects the supposed biblical literalism of the Sadducees with the Protestant principle of *sola Scriptura* ("the Bible alone"); in a somewhat similar vein, Baron, *A Social and Religious History,* 2. 36–38. More frequently, though,

scholars tend to associate biblical literalism not with Protestantism in general but with Protestant fundamentalists (see Davies, *Introduction to Pharisaism*, 12–13, 24). Whether the label "literal" should be so easily given over to fundamentalists is questionable. All too often, fundamentalists are allowed to proclaim that they are defending the "literal" meaning of Scripture, when what is being defended is a naive (mis)reading of an ancient text by a modern person ignorant or dismissive of the ancient languages, cultures, laws, and religious ideas that are the proper context for understanding the sacred text. For the fundamentalist, the "literal" meaning of Scripture is what pops into the head of a modern person as he or she reads the sacred text not within the original ancient context but rather within a modern one, without any critical sense of the hermeneutical distance between the two contexts. One must ask why this curious approach should be called "literal" interpretation. Is it not rather the historical-critical exegete, reading the ancient text in the ancient context that gives some direction to understanding the mind of the original authors of the literature, who should be seen as seeking the "literal" meaning of the text? Given this conceptual and terminological confusion, perhaps it would be better to call a moratorium on the debate over whether the Sadducees were "literalists." A similar problem arises even with the designation "conservative," which is often laden with unspoken value judgments. It is perhaps sobering for any over-confident scholar to notice that, while Lauterbach ("The Sadducees and the Pharisees," 34–56) declares the Sadducees to have been extreme conservatives and the Pharisees progressive liberals, Beckwith ("The Pre-History," 57–100) asserts that the Pharisees were the conservative traditionalists, while the Sadducees were a reform movement.

[61] One wonders whether, in the area we call "doctrine," the Sadducees did not so much develop a doctrine of their own as resist the innovations and developments seen in Pharisaic doctrine. Porton ("Sadducees," 892) makes the intriguing observation that, when Josephus lists the various doctrinal positions of the Sadducees in his static descriptions of the Jewish schools of thought, no single doctrine occurs in all of the lists. Apparently, reasons Porton, no one element in their collection of beliefs stood out so prominently that it automatically came to mind whenever Josephus wrote about the Sadducees. However, we should remember that the Synoptics, Acts, and the *'Abot de Rabbi Nathan* all make denial of the resurrection and/or reward and punishment beyond this life *the* defining aspect of Sadducean belief, an aspect also mentioned by Josephus in two of his three descriptions of the Jewish schools of thought. This aspect, at least, seems to have struck a number of different observers as salient. Hence I put denial of resurrection first in my list of Sadducean doctrines.

[62] While Josephus and Acts indicate that denial of the resurrection is a major point dividing Sadducees from Pharisees, the Synoptics never mention that the Sadducees and the Pharisees are at odds precisely on this point. However, since Luke obviously knows that this is a point of division (Acts 23:8) and yet does not introduce that information into his redacted form of Mark 12:18–27 (cf. Luke 20:27–40), one must be cautious about creating an argument from silence. It could be that, in placing the dispute story about the resurrection right after the story of the Pharisees and Herodians

questioning Jesus about the coin of tribute (Mark 12:13–17), Mark presupposes but does not mention that the resurrection of the dead is a point of division between the Pharisees and the Sadducees. It should be noted that the Mishna never explicitly states that the Sadducees deny the resurrection. Rather, as we saw in chapter 28, *m. Sanh.* 10:1 simply asserts that no one who says that there is no resurrection will have a share in the age to come; the Sadducees are never mentioned in this text. Even when, much later in *b. Sanh.* 90b, we have an anecdote about the Sadducees debating Gamaliel II on the resurrection, the precise point at issue is whether there is adequate scriptural proof of the resurrection, not whether the resurrection will happen; see Le Moyne, *Les Sadducéens,* 171. There may be an indirect reference to the Sadducees' denial of the resurrection in *m. Ber.* 9:5, where some manuscripts read that the Sadducees perverted the truth by saying that there is only one "age" or "world" ('ôlām)—namely, this one, and no age to come. But some manuscripts read "heretics" (mînîm) instead of "Sadducees."

[63] Postmortem existence and/or some form of resurrection seems to be envisioned for the righteous in *1 Enoch* 22–27 (part of the Book of the Watchers, late 3d to early 2d century B.C.) and the *Epistle of Enoch* 91–105 (late 2d to early 1st century B.C.). One should remember, though, that (1) *1 Enoch* probably represents a particular type of apocalyptic Judaism that later found welcome at Qumran rather than among Jews in general, and (2) the concept of "resurrection" is still vague and embryonic in these passages. In the opinion of Collins (*Apocalypticism in the Dead Sea Scrolls,* 112–13), the Book of the Watchers in *1 Enoch* contains that oldest Jewish reference to "a differentiated life after death" (*1 Enoch* 22:9), i.e., reward for the good and punishment for the evil. In the *Epistle of Enoch,* we are told that "the righteous shall rise from sleep" (*1 Enoch* 91:10). Collins notes, though, that these passages do not speak of a resurrection *of the body* as such, nor of a return of the persons who are raised from the dead to life on earth. Collins thinks that the reference is to the resurrection of the human spirit and its transformation into an angel-like existence.

[64] On this, see John J. Collins, "Apocalyptic Eschatology as the Transcendence of Death," *CBQ* 36 (1974) 21–43.

[65] Meyer (*"Saddoukaios,"* 46) thinks that the "Sadducean outlook . . . rested ultimately on a particularist eschatology."

[66] A minor exegetical puzzle in Acts 23:8 is why Luke lists three items denied by the Sadducees ("neither resurrection nor angel nor spirit") and then says that the Pharisees affirm "both" (amphotera). There are two common ways of explaining the apparent inconsistency: (1) "Neither angel nor spirit" is understood as one item ("angel" and "spirit" are coordinated by mēte . . . mēte, as opposed to the simple mē negating "resurrection"); this verbal distinction corresponds to a conceptual distinction: aggelon and pneuma refer to the heavenly world of spirits, while anastasin refers to the resurrection of the human body. (2) The word amphotera is being used here loosely to mean "all," not "both"; such usage is possible in Hellenistic Greek; see

Bauer, *Wörterbuch* (6th ed.), col. 93. As a matter of fact, Luke uses *amphoterōn* in the sense of "all" in Acts 19:16, where the pronoun refers to the *seven* sons of Sceva.

[67] See Sandmel, *The First Christian Century,* 56 n. 71; Meyer, *"Saddoukaios,"* 53–54. Saldarini (*Pharisees, Scribes and Sadducees,* 185) is mistaken in claiming that the denial of angels is common to Luke and Josephus. Strange to say, Goodman (*The Ruling Class,* 78–79) accepts the Sadducees' denial of "the mediating authority of angels and spirits" without hesitation and with no sense of the difficulties involved in his position.

[68] See, e.g., Moore, *Judaism,* 1. 68; the revised Schürer, *The History of the Jewish People,* 2. 411; Meyer, *"Saddoukaios,"* 53–54.

[69] Daube, "On Acts 23," 493–97; a similar view is found in Le Moyne, *Les Sadducéens,* 133. In favor of this view, Daube adduces the fact that, when Josephus discusses the Pharisees and Sadducees in *J. W.* 2.8.14 §165, he links together the ideas of (a) the continued existence of the soul after death, (b) the resurrection of the body, and (c) the idea of postmortem punishment of the wicked. While this is true, one should note two points: (1) This configuration of ideas is true of the treatment of the Pharisees. But, when Josephus speaks of the Sadducees, he simply says that they do away with (a) the immortality of the soul and (b) punishments and rewards "in the underworld [literally: down in Hades]." Josephus does not explicitly speak of "resurrection" in this passage about the Sadducees (§165), even by way of circumlocution, as he does in the preceding passage about the Pharisees (§163). (2) We do not find an explicit link between denial of resurrection and denial of an interim state of the soul coupled with rewards or punishments in any of Josephus' other treatments of the Sadducees.

[70] Daube appeals to *ho aggelos . . . autou* in Acts 12:15 as a case where *aggelos* may mean the immortal soul of the departed (in this case, says Daube, the soul of Peter, who has in fact been liberated from prison by an angel but who is thought by some of the Christians in the house to have been executed). However, the meaning of this text is anything but clear; many critics (e.g., Haenchen, *Die Apostelgeschichte,* 328; Conzelmann, *Acts,* 95; Schneider, *Die Apostelgeschichte,* 2. 106 n. 59) see here a reference to some sort of guardian angel who resembles the person he protects.

[71] So Sandmel, *The First Christian Century,* 56 n. 71.

[72] On this, see Fitzmyer, *The Gospel According to Luke,* 2. 1306. Examples include Gen 6:2; Pss 29:1; 89:7; Job 1:6; 2:1; 38:7. Significantly, in Gen 6:2, the LXX translates the Hebrew *běnê hā'ĕlōhîm* ("the sons of God") literally as *hoi huioi tou theou* ("the sons of God," though a later hand in the Codex Alexandrinus substitutes "angels" for "sons"), while, in Job 1:6, the LXX gives the interpretive translation, *hoi aggeloi tou theou* ("the angels of God"). The use of "sons of God" or "sons of heaven [= God]" for what we would call angels continues in the intertestamental and Qum-

ran literature; see, e.g., *1 Enoch* 6:2 ("the angels, the sons of heaven"); 11QMelch 2:5 ("the sons of heaven"); 2:14 ("sons of God"); 1QapGen 2:5 ("the sons of heaven"). For the idea that the Qumranites thought not so much in terms of resurrection of the dead as in terms of fellowship with the angels even now, a fellowship that would be consummated after death when the members of the Qumran community made the transition to an angelic existence in heaven, see Collins, *Apocalypticism at Qumran*, 110–29.

[73] Grabbe (*Judaism from Cyrus to Hadrian. Volume Two*, 484) observes that the Sadducees have tended to be "the whipping boys of most writers, whether Jewish or Christian." Contrast the caricatures in the revised Schürer (*The History of the Jewish People*, 2. 412); Meyer, "*Saddoukaios,*" 46 (where Josephus' description of the Sadducees is said to amount to atheism in practice); Müller, "Jesus und die Sadduzäer," 3–24; and Goodman (*The Ruling Class*, 79) with Sanders' rejection of polemical generalizations about the Sadducees and the Jerusalem aristocracy (*Judaism. Practice & Belief*, 336–39). Josephus' general hostility toward the Sadducees is reflected in his comment in *J.W.* 2.8.14 §166 that the Sadducees' behavior is rather boorish (*agriōteron*, possibly "savage") even toward one another and that the Sadducees are as rude (*apēneis*, possibly "rough" or even "cruel") in their dealings with those like themselves (*homoious*) as they are toward others (*allotrious*). Two things should be noted about Josephus' comment: (1) The exact meaning of some of the Greek terms is not clear. Who are "those like themselves" (members of other Jewish groups, parties, and sects? all their fellow Jews?), and who are "the others" (those outside the groups? enemies? foreigners?)? One can also adjust the gravity of his accusation depending on whether one translates some of the adjectives as "boorish" and "rude" or as "savage" and "cruel." (2) This polemical statement, coming in the decade after the end of the First Jewish War, may reflect Josephus' deep anger toward the ruling group in Jerusalem (largely Sadducean) that agreed to relieve him of his command in Galilee. However, time does not seem to have softened Josephus' viewpoint. In *Ant.* 20.9.1 §199, Josephus calls the Sadducees *ōmoi* ("severe," "savage," "fierce," "heartless," or "cruel") in their judicial decisions. On all this, see Le Moyne, *Les Sadducéens*, 43, 352. As for the common portrait of the Sadducees as worldly skeptics imbued with (or corrupted by) Hellenistic culture, there is no reason to think that, by the period of direct Roman rule, the Sadducees were any more or less Hellenized than the Pharisees; see Sundberg, "Sadducees," *IDB*, 4. 162; cf. Saldarini, *Pharisees, Scribes and Sadducees*, 302–3; Smith, "Palestinian Judaism," 81. As Saldarini observes, trying to offer the Romans the basic cooperation necessary to protect the temple-state of Judea from destruction while at the same time preserving the religious and national identity of Jews proved to be a very difficult balancing act for the Sadducees. One can surmise that there were divisions within the ranks of the chief priests on the subject. On the one hand, Caiaphas stayed in power for the record time of A.D. 18 to 36, presumably because he maintained a good working relationship with Pontius Pilate. On the other hand, some of the high-placed temple priests were involved in the initial stages of the revolt against Rome in A.D. 66. It is no doubt a mistake to try to depict all Sadducees during the period of direct Roman rule as being of one mind on politi-

cal and cultural questions. Not all of them were quislings, and not all of them were revolutionaries.

[74] On the problem of Josephus' claim that the Sadducees rejected divine providence, see Le Moyne, *Les Sadducéens,* 37–40; Saldarini, *Pharisees, Scribes and Sadducees,* 304. As Le Moyne points out, if one were to take Josephus literally (as, e.g., Goodman [*The Ruling Class,* 79] does), the Sadducees would be practical atheists, the equivalent of the "fool" in Pss 14:1 and 53:2. Despite Meyer's assertion (*"Saddoukaios,"* 46) that Josephus apparently refers to the Sadducees as though they were Epicureans, Josephus himself never assimilates the Sadducees to Epicureans or atheists. In his three static descriptions, he presents the Sadducees as one of the three venerable philosophical schools of Judaism. Hence scholars have suggested various ways of softening or restricting Josephus' claim about the Sadducees' denial of providence: (1) The Sadducees denied providence in relation to the individual, but not in relation to the governance of the world and Israel. (2) The Sadducees simply denied the possibility of prophesying future events, as practiced by the Essenes and the Pharisees. (3) The Sadducees simply desired to avoid attributing to God responsibility for the evil in the world. (4) The Sadducees did not believe in God's apocalyptic intervention in world history; they denied a divine providence that was guiding the world inexorably to an apocalyptic consummation. While there may be some truth in these interpretations, especially the third and the fourth, I think that the best solution is to maintain that Josephus has exaggerated one aspect of the Sadducees' position in order to provide a neat pattern of three philosophical stances for his presentation of the three Jewish schools. With respect to the Sadducees' position on providence, it may be helpful to note that some scholars see Ben Sira as a sort of "proto-Sadducee," and not without reason; cf. Meyer, *"Saddoukaios,"* 49. Ben Sira was a cosmopolitan man of affairs, a statesman and scribe (Sir 39:1–11), devoted to the Jerusalem temple and its priesthood (50:1–21), a teacher of aristocratic youth in Jerusalem (7:1–17; 9:17–10:3; 14:3–19; 31:1–31; 33:19–33), an exponent of human freedom and responsibility (15:11–20), and a conservative theologian who had no place in his thought for immortality, reward and punishment after death, or resurrection of the body (38:20–23; 41:1–13). Yet, despite his great insistence on humanity's power to choose between good and evil and its responsibility for doing so, Ben Sira strongly affirmed God's control of his good creation, his guidance of Israel throughout its history (36:1–17; 42:15–43:35; 44:1–49:16), and the efficacy of sincere prayer (22:27–23:6; 34:18–35:24; 38:9). Could not the later "full-blown Sadducees" have done the same?

[75] On the possible influence of postexilic Jewish theology on the Sadducees, see Saldarini, *Pharisees, Scribes and Sadducees,* 122. In *J.W.* 2.8.14 §164, Josephus associates the Sadducees' denial of fate with their desire to "place God outside of doing or overseeing [*ephoran*] anything evil." When used of the gods in pagan Greek discourse, the verb *ephoraō* often means more than simply "look" or "observe"; it can carry the sense of "oversee," "watch over," or "visit." Hence Josephus seems to be referring not simply to God's foreknowledge of but also his involvement in evil.

[76] Besides the standard commentaries on Mark, see David Daube, "Four Types of Question," *The New Testament and Rabbinic Judaism* (Peabody, MA: Hendrickson, 1956) 158–69; F. Dreyfus, "L'argument scripturaire de Jésus en faveur de la résurrection des morts (*Marc*, XII, 26–27)," *RB* 66 (1959) 213–24; Gilles Carton, "Comme des anges dans le ciel," *BVC* 28 (1959) 46–52; Sebastián Bartina, "Jesús y los saduceos. 'El Dios de Abraham, de Isaac y de Jacob es "El que hace existir",' " *EstBib* 21 (1962) 151–60; E. Earle Ellis, "Jesus, the Sadducees and Qumran," *NTS* 10 (1963–64) 274–79; Alfred Suhl, *Die Funktion der alttestamentlichen Zitate und Anspielungen im Markusevangelium* (Gütersloh: Gerd Mohn, 1965) 67–72; D. H. van Daalen, "Some Observations on Mark 12,24–27," *Studia Evangelica. Vol. IV* (TU 102; ed. F. L. Cross; Berlin: Akademie, 1968) 241–45; William Strawson, *Jesus and the Future Life* (rev. ed.; London: Epworth, 1970) 201–10; Baumbach, "Das Sadduzäerverständnis," 31–35; Antonio Ammassari, "Gesù ha veramente insegnato la risurrezione!" *BibOr* 15 (1973) 65–73; Karlheinz Müller, "Jesus und die Sadduzäer," *Biblische Randbemerkungen* (Rudolf Schnackenburg Festschrift; 2d ed.; ed. Helmut Merklein and Joachim Lange; Würzburg: Echter, 1974) 3–24; Robert H. Gundry, *The Use of the Old Testament in St. Matthew's Gospel* (NovTSup 18; Leiden: Brill, 1975) 20–21; Arland J. Hultgren, *Jesus and His Adversaries. The Form and Function of the Conflict Stories in the Synoptic Tradition* (Augsburg: Minneapolis, 1979) 123–31; D. M. Cohn-Sherbok, "Jesus' Defense of the Resurrection of the Dead," *JSNT* 11 (1981) 64–73; F. Gerald Downing, "The Resurrection of the Dead: Jesus and Philo," *JSNT* 15 (1982) 42–50; Elizabeth Schüssler Fiorenza, *In Memory of Her* (New York: Crossroad, 1983) 143–45; Jean-Gaspard Mudiso Mbâ Mundla, *Jesus und die Führer Israels. Studien zu den sog. Jerusalemer Streitgesprächen* (NTAbh n.s. 17; Münster: Aschendorff, 1984) 71–109; J. Gerald Janzen, "Resurrection and Hermeneutics: On Exodus 3.6 in Mark 12.26," *JSNT* 23 (1985) 43–58; François Vouga, "Controverse sur la résurrection des morts (Marc 12,18–27)," *LumVie* 35/no. 179 (1986) 49–61; Otto Schwankl, *Die Sadduzäerfrage (Mk 12,18–27 parr)* (BBB 66; Frankfurt: Athenäum, 1987); idem, "Die Sadduzäerfrage (Mk 12,18–27) und die Auferstehungserwartung Jesu," *Wissenschaft und Weisheit* 50 (1987) 81–92; Jack Dean Kingsbury, "The Religious Authorities in the Gospel of Mark," *NTS* 36 (1990) 42–65; M. Reiser, "Das Leben nach dem Tod in der Verkündigung Jesu," *Erbe und Auftrag* 66 (1990) 381–90; Frédéric Manns, "La technique *al tiqra* dans les évangiles," *RevScRel* 64 (1990) 1–7; P. G. Bolt, "What Were the Sadducees Reading?" *TynBul* 45 (1994) 369–94. A much fuller bibliography can be found in Schwankl's monograph, pp. 641–78.

[77] Throughout this treatment of Mark 12:18–27, the word "resurrection"—unless the context clearly indicates otherwise—refers to the general resurrection of the dead on the last day, not to the unique resurrection of Jesus at Easter. Given the precise question debated in Mark 12:18–27, this comes down in practice to the resurrection of faithful Israelites, who will be "like angels in heaven"; in other words, we are dealing with the resurrection of the just.

[78] As we have seen, Luke says more about the Sadducees in Acts, but this material involves the interaction of the Sadducees with the early Jerusalemite Christian Jews

and (later on) with Paul. Luke has nothing further to say about the focus of our inquiry, Jesus' relations with the Sadducees. The vast majority of critics accept the view that Matthew and Luke are dependent on Mark for their versions of Jesus' debate with the Sadducees, though some allow for Luke's use of a variant tradition in the first part of Jesus' reply to the Sadducees' question (Luke 20:34b–36); on this, see Hultgren, *Jesus and His Adversaries,* 123–26; Mudiso Mbâ Mundla, *Jesus und die Führer,* 71. Since, along with scholars like Fitzmyer (*The Gospel According to Luke,* 2. 1299), I doubt that Luke is using any special tradition here, my focus will be almost entirely on the Marcan form of the story. On the possibility of independent forms of the tradition preserved in the patristic literature—one of Hultgren's main arguments for non-Marcan tradition in Luke's form of the dispute—see below.

[79] For Mark 12:18–27 as a *Streitgespräch,* see Bultmann, *Geschichte,* 24. Dibelius (*Formgeschichte,* 40) classifies it as a paradigm "of the less pure type"; Taylor (*The Gospel according to St. Mark,* 480) calls it a "pronouncement-story." It is unclear why Pesch (*Markusevangelium,* 2. 230) instead calls it a *Schulgespräch* ("scholastic dialogue").

[80] The complicated nature of the debate, with two distinct foci that demand two distinct answers from Jesus, helps explain why this dispute story does not end with a single pithy aphorism, as do some others. The matter being debated is simply too complex for such a neat solution.

[81] Sometimes there is no indication whatever of the opponents' reaction; see, e.g., the Marcan version of the question about divorce in 10:1–12. After Jesus speaks in v 9 a concluding axiom to the Pharisees (if, indeed, we include them in the story, which has a notable text-critical problem in v 2), he enters a house to explain his teaching privately to his disciples (a typical Marcan device). Neither the Pharisees' nor the disciples' reaction to Jesus' startling revocation of divorce is mentioned. See also Mark 2:17 (on eating with tax collectors and sinners) and 2:28 (on plucking grain on the sabbath); in both cases, the *Streitgespräch* ends with a saying of Jesus without any reaction being noted.

[82] For the possibility that Jesus' practice of baptizing, continuing that of the Baptist, may have been the nub of the historical debate that lies behind the present form of the dispute story, see *A Marginal Jew,* 2. 163–67.

[83] For this interpretation, see Addison G. Wright, "The Widow's Mites: Praise or Lament?—A Matter of Context," *CBQ* 44 (1982) 256–65; against this interpretation is Gundry, *Mark,* 730–31.

[84] While it is common and convenient to speak in general terms of a Jerusalem cycle of dispute stories, in reality not all the pericopes in this cycle are, in the strictest sense of the form-critical category, "dispute stories" or *Streitgespräche;* for more carefully differentiated categories, see Mudiso Mbâ Mundla, *Jesus und die Führer Israels,* 299–302. Seeking to find some underlying theme to the heterogeneous Jerusalem dis-

pute stories, John R. Donahue makes the intriguing suggestion that the three exchanges about the coin of tribute, the resurrection, and the first commandment all
have a unified *theo*-logical scope; they focus on God, not on Christ. See his "A Neglected Factor in the Theology of Mark," *JBL* 101 (1982) 563–94, esp. 570–81.

[85] At the same time, one should remember that, in Mark's plot, the dispute stories
have in turn been unleashed on the empirical level by the triumphal entry and the
"cleansing" of the temple and on the supernatural level by Jesus' prophetic-symbolic
act of the cursing of the fig tree.

[86] On Mark's interpretation of 12:18–27 within his larger composition, see Mudiso
Mbâ Mundla, *Jesus und die Führer*, 108–9; Schwankl, *Die Sadduzäerfrage*, 421–34.

[87] Many exegetes rely on Bultmann's analysis (*Geschichte*, 25), according to which
the pericope was created in two stages by the early church: (1) 12:18–25, in which we
see the early church debating with the scribes of the Sadducees' party; and (2)
12:26–27, which never existed separately; it was created as an addition to 12:18–25
and may reflect theological discussions within the church. This position is developed
in a bizarre way by Suhl, *Die Funktion*, 67–72. Hultgren (*Jesus and His Adversaries*,
123–31) pushes Bultmann's approach even further by suggesting that the two pre-
Marcan units of tradition were 12:19–23,25 (addressing the problem of marriage in
the Christian community for those whose spouses have died) and 12:26–27a (presenting an apologia for the resurrection), which were then linked by the addition of
12:18,24,27b. As we shall see below, such tradition-histories are open to serious objections on literary, theological, and historical grounds. In favor of the unity of the
pericope, see van Daalen, "Some Observations," 242; Ammassari, "Gesù ha veramente insegnato," 66; Mudiso Mbâ Mundla, *Jesus und die Führer*, 72–74; Schwankl,
Die Sadduzäerfrage, 304–9. Vouga ("Controverse," 57) favors the unity of the pericope, but sees it entirely as the product of one group of Hellenistic-Jewish Christians
in debate with other Jewish Christians; his reconstruction of the groups and their
controversies is highly speculative.

[88] A prime example of how *peri de* ("but concerning") can be used as a marker in
the text to indicate that the speaker or writer is moving from one topic or question to
another is found in 1 Corinthians. There Paul uses *peri de* a number of times (e.g.,
1 Cor 7:1,25; 8:1; 12:1; 16:1,12) to move from one question to another and, indeed,
even to move from one aspect of a question to another (see 1 Cor 7:1,25). Strange to
say, some commentators use the presence of *peri de* in Mark 12:26 to argue that vv
26–27 were added to the unit at a later date. Yet few, if any, exegetes would claim that
every time in 1 Corinthians we find *peri de* indicating a move to a new topic, *peri de*
is a sign of a later addition by another author. More to the point, vv 26–27 are essential to the completeness of Jesus' argument. The Sadducees' basic problem is their denial of the fact of the resurrection (v 18); their fictitious case (vv 20–23) is simply a
way of validating their denial. Hence, after Jesus deals with the erroneous conception

of the manner of resurrection presupposed by their case (v 25), he must still address the basic problem of their denial (vv 26–27). As Schwankl (*Die Sadduzäerfrage,* 382) puts it, "Without the *hoti* ['that'] (v 26a), the *hotan* ['when'] (v 25a) would remain hypothetical."

[89] This verse-by-verse exegesis focuses on Mark 12:18–27 as an isolated unit of early Christian tradition, circulating in oral or written form prior to its reception into Mark's Gospel. Therefore, with a few exceptions, the exegesis prescinds from the overarching theology of Mark's Gospel and the further meaning such a theology gives this pericope once it is embedded in Mark's larger story.

[90] While it is true that belief in the resurrection put Jesus on the same side of the theological debate as the Pharisees, belief in the resurrection (or at least in some form of afterlife) was hardly limited at the turn of the era to Pharisees, as various apocalyptic works that are not specifically Pharisaic indicate. The Qumranites apparently held to some sort of individual survival beyond death, though very few passages in the Dead Sea Scrolls speak of resurrection. The Qumranite belief in an angel-like existence after death is not all that different from the belief in the immortality of the soul that we find in various Jewish authors in the Diaspora, notably Philo and the author of the Wisdom of Solomon.

[91] This seems to be a case where the classical distinction between the simple relative *hos* and the compound relative *hostis,* which can convey the sense of the specific nature or quality of the antecedent, may hold true even in NT Koine Greek; see Zerwick, *Graecitas Biblica,* 70–72 (§215–20).

[92] One might speculate that when the narrative was first formed by some Christian Jew in Palestine during the first Christian generation, the identification of the Sadducees in v 18b was not necessary and that it was added when the tradition was handed on outside Palestine. While this is possible, even the original version of the story might have wanted to underline from the start the point at issue in the story. After all, denial of the resurrection is not the only defining characteristic of the Sadducees; it is simply the one debated here.

[93] Notice how John the Baptist is addressed as *rabbi* in John 3:26.

[94] So, e.g., Gundry, *Mark,* 701.

[95] In a written communication, David Noel Freedman suggested to me a simple, commonsense explanation: in a dispute like this, if the first party quotes from Moses, it makes sense for the second party to quote from the same source.

[96] The word "levirate" comes from the Latin *levir,* "the brother of one's husband," i.e., a wife's brother-in-law.

[97] The abbreviated form of Deut 25:5 in Mark 12:19 drops out the detail that the brothers are living together and so the idea of the preservation of the ancestral property within the family as a motivation for the law of levirate. The focus thus shifts to the childless wife and her destiny.

[98] See Pesch, *Das Markusevangelium*, 2. 231.

[99] For a comparison of text forms, see Gundry, *The Use of the Old Testament*, 45. In Deut 25:5, the Hebrew text's "and if he has no child" (literally, "and there is no child to him," *ûbēn ʾēn-lô*) is translated loosely in Mark 12:19 as "and he leave no child" *(kai mē aphē teknon);* the LXX renders the Hebrew construction more exactly with *sperma de mē ē autō* ("and there is no seed to him"). However, Mark 12:19 is closer to the Hebrew in the use of *teknon* ("child") for *bēn* ("son" or generically "child") than is the LXX's use of *sperma* ("seed"). Mark 12:19 differs from LXX Deut 25:5 in other details as well and cannot be considered simply a taking over of the LXX form of the text. As for Gen 38:8, Mark 12:19 uses the compound verb *exanastēsē* ("raise up") instead of the LXX's simple *anastēson*. Mark's choice is curious, since the simple verb would fit more exactly with the noun *anastasis* ("resurrection") and the verb *anistamai* ("rise") in vv 18,23,25. This may be a sign that Mark is simply taking over a text citation that was already fixed in the tradition instead of either taking over the LXX or creating his own translation.

[100] One might argue that all this corresponds perfectly with the findings of Gundry (*The Use of the Old Testament*, 1, 28, 147–50), who notes that Mark's citations of the OT that are introduced by a formula (i.e., "formal quotations") are almost entirely Septuagintal, while all sorts of patterns of agreement and disagreement with the LXX and the MT are found in Mark's allusive quotations (i.e., those that lack a formal introduction and that flow from and into the context). Actually, while Gundry counts Mark 12:19 among the allusive quotations, the introduction "Moses wrote us that . . . ," together with the clear indication that the reference is to the law of levirate in Deuteronomy, might be taken to make Mark 12:19 a formal quotation of Deut 25:5. After all, (1) the Sadducees clearly intend to cite normative Mosaic Scripture, (2) the *hoti* in v 19 is considered by some exegetes the equivalent of quotation marks (see, e.g., Gundry, *Mark,* 701; Mudiso Mbâ Mundla, *Jesus und die Führer,* 75), and (3) v 20 clearly ends the quotation and begins afresh by proposing to Jesus a hypothetical case that exemplifies the law of levirate. (By the way, conflation with another OT text does not prevent a text from being a formal quotation; see Mark 1:2.) If we count Mark 12:19 as a formal quotation—which I am inclined to do—then it diverges notably from the purely LXX form almost always found in such quotations in Mark. This may be one indication among many that Mark himself has not created this story out of whole cloth.

[101] It is possible that there is a vague allusion here to the seven successive husbands of Sarah in Tob 3:8,15; 6:13; 7:11. Less likely is an allusion to the seven brothers mar-

tyred by Antiochus IV in 2 Macc 7:1–41; the theme of resurrection is present in the passage, but not the theme of marriage. On this, see Gundry, *Mark*, 705.

[102] The whole thrust of the Sadducees' fictitious case presupposes that those Jews who maintain a resurrection of the dead think that sexual relations will be restored at that time. Commentators (e.g., Mudiso Mbâ Mundla, *Jesus und die Führer*, 87) proceed to call upon later rabbinic literature both to illustrate and to question this view, but the whole approach is problematic: (1) We are faced with the usual problem of using texts composed centuries later in a different cultural situation to explain a 1st-century text. (2) Even if rabbinic texts are employed, it is not always clear whether the texts are referring to the intermediate reign of the Messiah, the final resurrection of the dead, or the existence of the souls of the righteous in heaven. The continuation of physical activities like eating and procreation are understandably denied for the last named of these three states, while at least some texts seem to allow for such physical activities in the other two states of existence. But in the very fluid situation of early 1st-century Palestinian Judaism, it is a mistake to look for some normative view on the precise conditions of human existence after the resurrection. The Sadducees' line of attack apparently presupposes that at least one popular view of the matter was that sexual activity—and probably many other bodily activities proper to this present world—resumed after the resurrection.

[103] See Victor P. Hamilton, "Marriage (Old Testament and Ancient Near East)," *Anchor Bible Dictionary*, 4. 559–69, esp. 565. On polygamy (always polygyny) among Palestinian Jews around the time of Jesus, see Jeremias, *Jerusalem in the Time of Jesus*, 90, 93, 369. In his article "Polygamy," *The Oxford Dictionary of the Jewish Religion* (ed. R. J. Zwi Werblowsky and Geoffrey Wigoder; New York/Oxford: Oxford University, 1997) 540, Daniel Sinclair states that the rabbis accepted polygamy as legally valid, although very few rabbis had more than one wife.

[104] One might understand the dilemma posed by the Sadducees in a somewhat different way: namely, since polyandry is impossible, the wife can be the wife of only one of her seven husbands. But on earth she had been equally and legally the wife of all seven brothers, with no offspring giving one marriage a privileged status over the others. Thus, there is no criterion for assigning her to one rather than another brother. (Some commentators cite the mystical medieval Jewish work called the Zohar for the view that a twice-married wife would be restored to her first husband; but such a late work can hardly be employed to illumine a 1st-century debate.) In the end, this line of argument seems to come down to the same problem I am emphasizing: the polyandrous situation remains, with no way of resolving it. Hence I would take the question of the Sadducees in v 23 not as a serious request for a criterion for choosing among the seven brothers but rather as a way of pointing out the lack of any criterion and therefore the perduring polyandrous union—something that is understood to be ridiculous and unacceptable to all sides, not only on earth now but all the more so in heaven at the resurrection.

[105] In this translation of v 24, I take the initial *dia touto* ("because of this") to point forward to the participle (*mē eidotes,* "not knowing," i.e., "because you do not know"). Exegetes like Suhl (*Die Funktion,* 69) and Gundry (*Mark,* 705–6) argue that *dia touto* must instead point backward to what the Sadducees have said in the previous verses. This is not necessarily so. (1) In itself, the demonstrative *touto* may point either backward or forward. (2) Suhl and Gundry object that the phrase *dia touto* points forward only when it is followed by a *hoti* clause, a *hina* clause, an infinitive phrase, or a noun. (Clear examples of *dia touto* pointing forward with a *hoti* causal clause are found in John 5:16 + 18.) But the participial phrase *mē eidotes* in Mark 12:24 has, by the common consent of exegetes, a causal sense ("because you do not know") and therefore is the functional equivalent of a *hoti* causal clause. That Mark does not supply another example of this construction elsewhere in his Gospel is hardly surprising; Mark's Gospel is full of unusual locutions and grammatical structures that occur only once in his work. In any event, the dispute over the precise reference of *dia touto* does not invalidate the observations that Jesus mentions two realities that the Sadducees do not know (the Scriptures and the power of God) and that Jesus proceeds to treat these two realities in chiastic order. As Mudiso Mbâ Mundla (*Jesus und die Führer,* 90) points out, the LXX background of the verb *planaō* favors the negative religious idea of culpable transgression of the revealed will of God, and not just purely intellectual error.

[106] C. K. Barrett is probably right that *dynamin* ("power") in v 24 means in particular the eschatological power of God. More dubious is his appeal to the famous synagogue prayer the *Eighteen Benedictions* (the *Amidah* or *Shemoneh Esreh*). In the traditional order of that prayer, the first benediction *(Aboth)* praises the God of Abraham, the God of Isaac, the God of Jacob, who is the "shield [i.e., protector] of Abraham" (thus, says Barrett, paralleling Jesus' proof from Exod 3:6 in v 26). The second benediction *(Geburoth)* praises God as the "powerful" and "strong" one, who displays his eschatological power by "making the dead to live" (thus paralleling Jesus' theological argument in v 25). While the parallel is intriguing, it runs into a major problem: the date of a fixed order and text of the *Eighteen Benedictions.* In the *EncJud,* 2. 839–40, the article "Amidah" states that the exact order and wording of the *Eighteen Benedictions* probably varied in the pre-70 period. "Attempts to reconstruct the 'original' text of the *Amidah* or to ascertain the date when each section was 'composed' are pointless. . . . It was probably in the early geonic [i.e., post-talmudic] period only that definite versions of the *Amidah* were established and committed to writing. . . ."

[107] In the article "Angels," *The Oxford Dictionary of the Christian Church* (3d ed.; ed. F. L. Cross and E. A. Livingstone; Oxford: Oxford University, 1997) 61–63, it is noted that the immaterial and spiritual nature of angels was not fully recognized until Dionysius the Pseudo-Areopagite (ca. A.D. 500) and Gregory the Great (A.D. 540–604). Origen had held that angels had ethereal bodies, a position apparently shared by Augustine of Hippo. On the sense of "like the angels" in Mark 12:25, see van Daalen, "Some Observations," 241.

[108] See also *Jubilees* 5:1–2 (cf. 10:1–14); CD 2:16–21; 4Q 180.

[109] In the context of *1 Enoch* 15:1–7, this is said by way of contrast to the Watchers (the rebellious angels), who gave way to their sexual desires and had intercourse with human women. Responding to this perversion of the original divine plan for them, God, who formerly did not create wives for them in their immortal state, now provides them with wives and children, apparently as part of his intention to allow their sinful actions to have their full natural—or rather, unnatural—results. This, in turn, will redound to the final punishment of the Watchers and their offspring.

[110] Similar ideas are also found in *1 Enoch* 104:1–6: the righteous will rejoice "like the angels"; *2 Apoc. Bar.* 51:10: the righteous "will be like the angels. . . ." Some commentators (e.g., Mudiso Mbâ Mundla, *Jesus und die Führer*, 92; Schwankl, *Die Sadduzäerfrage*, 378) see a further point in Jesus' comparison of risen persons with the angels: the Sadducees are in error as well because they deny the existence of angels. This denial, in turn, contributes to their erroneous denial of the resurrection. However, as we have seen, that the Sadducees denied the existence of angels is by no means certain, since the reliability of Luke's assertion in Acts 23:8 is disputed.

[111] See Schwankl, *Die Sadduzäerfrage*, 574–77.

[112] A modern scholar would probably begin his exegesis of this verse by noting that it occurs in a passage made up of Yahwist and Elohist (some would add: Priestly) traditions, with 3:6 usually being assigned to the Elohist. Needless to say, Jesus and his contemporaries did not think in such terms; they read the whole Pentateuch as the work of Moses.

[113] So van Daalen, "Some Observations," 244; Strawson, *Jesus and the Future Life*, 204; Schwankl, *Die Sadduzäerfrage*, 378–79. The idea that all this takes place by God's power alone (cf. *tēn dynamin tou theou* in v 24) may explain the switch from the vocabulary of *anastasis* and *anistēmi* (12:18–19,23,25) to the passive voice of *egeiro* in v 26: "But concerning the dead, that they are raised up [divine passive: namely, by the power of God]. . . ."

[114] Lohmeyer's judgment (*Markus*, 257) is often quoted: Mark 12:18–27 is "an excellent example of the rabbinism of Jesus."

[115] On this, see D. M. Cohn-Sherbok, "Jesus' Defense of the Resurrection of the Dead," *JSNT* 11 (1981) 64–73. A parallel to Jesus' mode of argumentation is sought in Philo by F. Gerald Downing, "The Resurrection of the Dead: Jesus and Philo," *JSNT* 15 (1982) 42–50. In my view, Downing's attempt at finding a parallel is strained and verges at times on circular reasoning. To achieve the parallel, Downing must declare Mark 12:25–26a to be a later addition. The literary structure and the flow of theological thought in 12:18–27 make this highly unlikely. As a matter of fact,

almost all of the critics who detect a later addition in the pericope identify it as
vv 26–27.

[116] On the surprising absence of the full formula in the rest of the OT and in intertestamental texts, see Schwankl, *Die Sadduzäerfrage,* 396–403. It is instructive to
see how Exod 3:6 is treated in major Jewish authors around the turn of era, as they
retell (or fail to retell) the story of the theophany in the burning bush: (1) in *Jubilees*
48:1–4, the author surprisingly skips over the theophany of Sinai, alluding to it only
cryptically in v 1 with the words "And you know what was related to you on Mount
Sinai." The author seems to be rushing on to the parts of the Moses story that interest him more. (2) As the exception that proves the rule, the Jewish poet Ezekiel the
Tragedian (2d cent. B.C.), writing in Greek, cites the full formula, though the wording
is somewhat changed and expanded because of the demands of the Greek iambic
trimeter in which he writes. In his *Exagōgē* ("Leading Out"), 104–7, Ezekiel has God
tell Moses from the burning bush: "God am I of those your fathers three, / of Abram,
Isaac, Jacob, I am He. / Mindful of my promises to them, / to save my Hebrew people
I am come. . . ." The text in Greek reads (as preserved in Eusebius' *Praeparatio Evangelica,* 9.29.8; see Karl Mras [ed.], *Eusebius Werke. Achter Band. Die Praeparatio
Evangelica* [GCS 43/1; Berlin: Akademie, 1954] 530, lines 23–26): *egō theos sōn,
hōn legeis, gennētorōn /Abraam te kai Isaak kai Iakōbou tritou /mnēstheis d'ekeinōn
kai et' emōn dōrēmatōn /pareimi sōsai laon Hebraiōn emon.* Ezekiel faithfully reproduces the sense of the original; no further theological deduction is drawn from this
self-revelation, certainly not the resurrection of the dead. This example from Ezekiel
does require a modification in Schwankl's sweeping statement (p. 397) that the full
formula of Exod 3:6 is found "nowhere else in the OT and in [early] Judaism." (3) In
the fragments of summaries of the work of Artapanus (3d to 2d cent. B.C.), the theophany in the bush is summarized in a few brief sentences, with God's words reduced
to one sentence: ". . . a divine voice bade him campaign against Egypt, rescue the
Jews, and lead them to their ancient homeland." This brevity is all the more remarkable in light of the extensive legends Artapanus tells about Moses' career in Egypt. (4)
In his *De Vita Mosis (On the Life of Moses),* 1.12–14 §65–84, Philo skips over the introductory v 6 when retelling the story of Exodus 3 and proceeds to give a homiletic
paraphrase of the rest of Exodus 3–4 that is, in his typical fashion, highly allegorical
and moralizing. Given his middle-Platonic philosophy, Philo naturally focuses not on
"the God of Abraham, Isaac, and Jacob" but rather on the mysterious "I am who
am" *(egō eimi ho ōn),* which receives a metaphysical interpretation as "the Existent
One"; to him alone existence belongs. Only then do we get a reference to "the God of
Abraham, Isaac, and Jacob." But this "name" of God is almost denigrated by Philo.
He claims that God allows the use of such an improper title—for God stands in relationship to nothing—out of indulgence for human weakness. The name is somewhat
excused by making the three patriarchs symbols of three virtues. Similar approaches
can be found in *De Mutatione Nominum (On the Change of Names)* 2–4 §11–29 and
De Abrahamo (On Abraham), 10–11 §50–55. (5) In Pseudo-Philo's *Biblical Antiquities* (1st cent. A.D.), there is no retelling of the theophany in the burning bush. Rather,
after chap. 9 recounts the legend of Moses' birth, chap. 10 jumps to a very brief nar-

rative of the oppression of Israel, the bare statement that God sent Moses to the Israelites and so freed them from the Egyptians. After a quick mention of the plagues, Israel is depicted moving to the Red Sea, pursued by the Egyptians. Then, in 10:4, we are told: "And Moses cried out to the Lord and said: Lord God of our fathers, did you not say to me, 'Go and tell the sons of Israel, "God has sent me to you" '?" The crossing of the Red Sea follows. Even in this ever-so-brief reference to the theophany in the bush, the reader is not told when "the Lord God of our fathers" delivered his command to Moses. (6) Josephus presents a free rendering of the theophany of Exodus 3 in *Ant.* 2.12.1–4 §264–76. Most of the words of God, spoken directly by the Deity in Exodus 3, are narrated instead in the third person. Exodus 3:6 does not appear at all. In sum, then, in major Jewish authors retelling the Exodus story around the turn of the era, the self-revelation of God in Exod 3:6 is either ignored, briefly repeated or paraphrased, or even denigrated. It is never the object of positive theological reflection (Philo's reflection is quite negative), and it enters the mind of no one to connect the verse with the doctrine of the resurrection. As we shall see below, all this contrasts sharply with the use of the verse by Jesus to prove the resurrection; the discontinuity argues well for the historicity of the dispute reflected in Mark 12:18–27. Indeed, even if we look forward into the later rabbinic commentaries on the Book of Exodus, we still do not find Jesus' interpretation of Exod 3:6. Since the *Mekilta* (2d to 3d century A.D.) begins only with Exodus 12, it lacks a detailed commentary on our text. When we come to *Exodus Rabbah* (ca. 10th century A.D.), the comment on Exod 3:6,15 has nothing in common with Jesus' interpretation. Commenting on Exod 3:6, the midrash tells us that God revealed himself in the voice of Moses' father. Moses, thinking that it was his father, answered: "Here am I. What does my father desire?" God replies: "I am not your father, but the God of your father. I have come to you gently so that you might not be afraid. [I am] the God of Abraham, the God of Isaac, and the God of Jacob." Moses rejoiced and said: "Behold, my father is included among the patriarchs. Moreover, he must be great, for he is even mentioned first." Later, commenting on Exod 3:15, the midrash states that now Moses notices that the name of his father is no longer mentioned with the patriarchs. God explains: "At first, I used every kind of persuasion, but from now on I will speak only words of truth with you." Obviously, this concern about Moses' father has nothing to do with Jesus' appropriation of Exod 3:6. In fact, the mention of Moses' father is precisely the phrase that Jesus omits from his citation.

[117] I use the phrase "full formula" to refer to those citations of Exod 3:6 that include the initial "I [am]" (the verb "am" is understood in the Hebrew text; in Greek translations it is sometimes expressed, sometimes not). Actually, the citation in Mark 12:26 is not the fullest form possible, since it omits "the God of your father" before "the God of Abraham" etc. The omission may be purposeful on Jesus' or Mark's part, since it does not fit Jesus' argument. His argument rests on the link the text affirms between the God of the living and people who have died. But the text of Exodus does not say that Moses' father is dead at the time of the theophany in the burning bush. If he were thought to be still alive, his presence in the formula alongside dead persons would muddle the thrust of the argument. (Interestingly, the original reading

of Exod 3:6 at this point is not absolutely certain; the Samaritan Pentateuch, some LXX manuscripts, Acts 7:32, and Justin Martyr in his *First Apology* 63:7 [but in paraphrased form] read the plural "your fathers.") Not only does the full formula of Exod 3:6 never occur elsewhere in the OT, but even the title "the God of Abraham, Isaac, and Jacob" is rare in the OT. Outside of the context of the theophany in the bush (therefore, including Exod 3:15,16; 4:5), it occurs in the variant form "God of Abraham, Isaac, and Israel" only three times: 1 Kgs 18:36; 1 Chr 29:18; 2 Chr 30:6.

[118] On Jesus' development of the implicit thrust of the text's meaning, when read in a new situation, and on the larger question of the open-ended meaning of texts as they move through history, see Schwankl, *Die Sadduzäerfrage,* 394–95.

[119] On this, see Dreyfus, "L'argument scripturaire," 216–20; Schwankl, *Die Sadduzäerfrage,* 388–92; on a different tack, Janzen, "Resurrection and Hermeneutics," 43–58. On "the God of the fathers," see the famous essay by Albrecht Alt, "Der Gott der Väter," *Kleine Schriften zur Geschichte des Volkes Israel* (3 vols.; 4th ed.; Munich: Beck, 1968) 1. 1–78. Examples of the use of some form of the God-of-the-fathers formula with the sense of "the savior and protector of the patriarchs and their children" include *Jubilees* 45:3; Wis 9:1; 1QM 13:7–9; 3 Macc 7:16; the Prayer of Manasseh 1; the *Testament* [or: *Assumption*] *of Moses* 3:9; and the first benediction in the *Eighteen Benedictions.* From the *Testaments of the Twelve Patriarchs,* one might add *T. Reuben* 4:10; *T. Simeon* 2:8; *T. Joseph* 2:2; 6:7; and *T. Gad* 2:5. See also the Hebrew text of Sir 51:12. Dreyfus hammers home the point that in these passages, the mention of the God of the fathers emphasizes not the fidelity of the patriarchs toward God but rather the mercy and protection that God bestowed on the patriarchs.

[120] *A Marginal Jew,* 2. 309–17.

[121] Taking Mark 12:27 as the minor premise in Jesus' implicit syllogism seems better than taking it as the conclusion of his argument. The assertion that "God is not the God of the dead but of the living" was not, among 1st-century Palestinian Jews, a highly disputed point for which Jesus would have had to argue at length. Rather, it was an axiomatic truth that almost all Jews of that time and place would have readily accepted. As Strawson (*Jesus and the Future Life,* 208) puts it, "Jesus could not think of God and of dead people at the same time." Hence the assertion's natural function is as the minor premise of the implicit syllogism. As a readily accepted, even self-evident truth, it is a useful stepping stone from the universally revered text of Exod 3:6 to the disputed conclusion (left unspoken but obviously understood in Mark 12:27 as the whole point of the *Streitgespräch*) that there is a resurrection of the dead. On all this, see Schwankl, *Die Sadduzäerfrage,* 403–6. Schwankl points out the similarities of Jesus' syllogistic reasoning to that of the rabbinic arguments for the resurrection in *b. Sanh.* 90b–92a. At the same time, there are notable differences: (1) What functions as the minor premise in the rabbinic arguments is usually a sentence that relates directly to the Scripture citation, emphasizing or exploiting some detail of the text (a future verb form, a particular pronoun or noun). (2) The conclusion is usu-

ally stated explicitly. In contrast, (1) Jesus' minor premise introduces a new thought by way of an axiomatic truth (and not some reasoning about the wording of Exod 3:6, such as "It says not 'I was,' but rather 'I am' "). (2) The conclusion is left unspoken, but it is obviously implied in Jesus' final condemnation of the Sadducees' view (i.e., denial of the resurrection) as a great error.

[122] Exegetes argue over whether the implication of Jesus' argument is that the patriarchs are already raised from the dead or at least are already living in God's presence (so Pesch, *Markusevangelium*, 2. 234) or simply that even now the souls of the dead in Sheol are enjoying a foretaste of the definitive blessedness (cf. Luke 16:22–31) that they will receive in full when they are raised from the dead on the last day (so Mudiso Mbâ Mundla, *Jesus und die Führer*, 101). Like many theological distinctions that arise from a close reading of a biblical text, this question may go beyond the immediate horizon of either the historical Jesus or the Christian author of the pericope. In a similar vein, it is sometimes observed that Jesus' argument, if valid, has as its logical conclusion not the resurrection of the dead but the immortality of the soul; on this, see Ellis, "Jesus, the Sadducees and Qumran," 274–79. While the firm distinction made between the concept of immortality and the concept of resurrection represented a valid reaction by biblical theology against an older systematic theology, the very fluid ideas and images of postmortem existence among Jews at the turn of the era should warn us against imposing our sharply differentiated theological concepts of various eschatological states on this pericope. Once one accepts Jesus' idea of human life after the resurrection being akin to that of the angels with their rarefied, heavenly bodies, the distinction between resurrection of the body and immortality of the soul, while real, is not as vast as is sometimes supposed. More to the point, one must attend to the concrete rhetorical situation depicted in the debate of Mark 12:18–27. The either-or alternative defined by the Sadducees in the first half of the debate is resurrection or no resurrection. No third option is allowed by the Sadducees or suggested by Jesus, who accepts the arena of combat as set up by the Sadducees. Thus, any afterlife affirmed during the debate is presupposed by both sides to refer to the resurrection.

[123] Bultmann, *Geschichte*, 25; Hultgren, *Jesus and His Adversaries*, 123–31. Bultmann seems to hold that the entire pericope is pre-Marcan; while his position on the tradition-process is more complicated than Bultmann's, Hultgren apparently thinks that most, if not all, of the pericope is pre-Marcan.

[124] Compare the evaluation of the Galilean cycle of dispute stories in Joanna Dewey (*Markan Public Debate* [SBLDS 48; Chico, CA: Scholars, 1980] 131–97) with the evaluation of the Jerusalem cycle in Mudiso Mbâ Mundla, *Jesus und die Führer Israels*, 299–302; Schwankl, *Die Sadduzäerfrage*, 434–38.

[125] See *A Marginal Jew*, 2. 439–50.

[126] See Mudiso Mbâ Mundla, *Jesus und die Führer*, 299–302.

[127] On these two candidates, see Mudiso Mbâ Mundla, *Jesus und die Führer,* 72; Schwankl, *Die Sadduzäerfrage,* 420–21.

[128] Some critics advocate the view that "when they rise" is a Marcan addition by pointing out that the phrase is missing in some important Greek manuscripts, including Sinaiticus, Vaticanus, Ephraemi Rescriptus, Bezae, and Washingtonensis. But this is to confuse two questions: whether the phrase belongs to the original text of Mark and whether it existed in the pre-Marcan tradition that the evangelist edited. The first question can be answered, at least in part, by an inspection of the Greek mansucripts and versions; the second cannot. The textual confusion at the beginning of v 23 is so great that it is difficult to be confident about the original Marcan wording. However, it is probable that the phrase "when they rise" belongs to the original Marcan text. There is no reason why later Christian scribes would have gone out of their way to insert it, while it is perfectly understandable that some of them felt the redundancy to be stylistically jarring. Removing "when they rise" rather than "at the resurrection" would strike such scribes as the preferred solution because both Matthew and Luke omit "when they rise" while retaining "at the resurrection" (see Matt 22:28 ‖ Luke 20:33). That Matthew and Luke agree in the omission—one of the "minor agreements" of Matthew and Luke against Mark—is readily explainable. Both often correct Mark for better style, and the redundancy here is glaring. On all this, see Metzger, *Textual Commentary* (2d ed.), 93. Another possibility is that the close proximity of two words beginning with *anast-* may have occasioned the accidental omission of one of them.

[129] See Frans Neirynck, *Duality in Mark. Contributions to the Study of the Markan Redaction* (BETL 31; Leuven: Leuven University, 1972).

[130] Pesch, *Das Markusevangelium,* 2. 229; also Mudiso Mbâ Mundla, *Jesus und die Führer,* 72, 108; more hesitant is Schwankl, *Die Sadduzäerfrage,* 420–42—though he finally dismisses the question of the few possible additions by Mark as "irrelevant."

[131] Against an origin in the ministry of the historical Jesus are Bultmann and Hultgren; in favor, Pesch and Schwankl.

[132] Schwankl (*Die Sadduzäerfrage,* 466–587) argues for historicity by using the criteria of both discontinuity and coherence, as I do here. However, he places relatively little emphasis on discontinuity, while basing most of his argument on coherence. I would reverse the emphasis, not only because coherence, left to itself, is not the strongest of criteria but also because I consider the argument from discontinuity to be impressive.

[133] Not even the redactional creations of Matthew are exceptions to this sweeping statement. In 3:7, Matthew simply creates a group of "many of the Pharisees and Sadducees" to supply an audience for John the Baptist's denunciation of trust in the ex-

ternal guarantees of religion. The Pharisees and Sadducees do not engage in a dispute with John, let alone with Jesus (who has not yet appeared on the scene as an adult). In 16:1, Matthew substitutes his theological odd couple, "the Pharisees and Sadducees," for "the Pharisees" of Mark 8:11 as the persons who ask Jesus for a sign from heaven. Yet Matt 16:1–4 is not properly a dispute story in which Jesus debates some legal or doctrinal question with the Pharisees and Sadducees; still less is Jesus' warning to his disciples to beware of the leaven of the Pharisees and Sadducees (Matt 16:5–12) a dispute story narrating a debate between Jesus and his opponents. These Matthean texts are the only examples of a later redactor introducing—ever so marginally—the Sadducees into the text. Notice that, in all the examples of Matthean redaction, the Sadducees never stand alone. They are put alongside the stock Pharisees as symbols of the united front of Judaism against Jesus (and the church).

[134] The one exception is Acts 23:6–10, but here we have the singular case of a wily Paul speaking not specifically of Jesus' resurrection but in general terms of the resurrection of the dead as a political ploy. He casts the question of resurrection in global terms in order to identify himself as a Pharisee and so to set the Pharisees against the Sadducees (v 6): "Brothers, I am a Pharisee, a son of Pharisees; I am on trial because of [Israel's] hope, [namely,] the resurrection of the dead." On this, see Schneider, *Die Apostelgeschichte,* 2. 332.

[135] This is especially apparent in the reconstruction of Hultgren, *Jesus and His Adversaries,* 123–31.

[136] See, e.g., the argument from the risen Christ as the "firstfruits" of the resurrection in 1 Cor 15:20–22; see also 1 Thess 4:13–18; 5:9–10; 1 Cor 6:13–14; 15:44–49; 2 Cor 3:18; 4:10–15; Rom 8:17,29; 14:7–10; Phil 3:20–21; Col 1:13–20; 2:9–15; 2 Tim 2:8–13. The same basic affirmation is found in the Epistle to the Hebrews, but it is made with different categories: the exaltation or perfection (rather than the resurrection) of Christ and the salvation or perfection of believers (rather than the general resurrection); see, e.g., Heb 2:8–10; 5:7–10. See also Acts 4:2; 26:23; 1 Pet 1:3–5,18–21; 3:18–4:7; Rev 1:5. The whole structure of the four Gospels aims at making the death and resurrection of Jesus, the climax of the story, paradigmatic for the believer. On all this, see David Michael Stanley, *Christ's Resurrection in Pauline Soteriology* (AnBib 13; Rome: Biblical Institute, 1961); Scott Brodeur, *The Holy Spirit's Agency in the Resurrection of the Dead: An Exegetico-Theological Study of 1 Corinthians 15, 44b–49 and Romans 8, 9–13* (Tesi Gregoriana, Serie Teologia 14; Rome: Gregorian University, 1996).

[137] This is denied by Suhl (*Die Funktion,* 68), who attempts to understand Mark 12:18–25 in terms of a Christian defense of the resurrection of Jesus against the Law, which presupposes that there is no resurrection. Verses 26–27, declared a later Christian addition, supposedly address the problem of the first cases of death in the Christian community. Suhl's arbitrary exegesis reflects the larger theological concerns of Bultmann and Marxsen, lacks an adequate treatment of the Jewish background of the

material (especially the Sadducees), never adverts to the unique and isolated situation of Exod 3:6 within Jewish and Christian exegetical traditions, and overlooks the many elements in the text that bind it together as a literary whole. On the lack of Christian traits in this pericope, see van Daalen, "Some Observations," 243; Jeremias, *New Testament Theology,* 184 n. 3.

[138] Some critics (e.g., D. E. Nineham, *The Gospel of St Mark* [Pelican NT Commentaries; Harmondsworth: Penguin, 1963] 321) have pointed to a supposed similarity between Jesus' argument in Mark 12:26–27 and statements in 4 Macc 7:19 and 16:25 that Abraham, Isaac, and Jacob did not die, "but live unto God [*alla zōsin tō theō*]." Such critics suggest that this similarity shows that Jesus' argument was actually a stock argument of the Pharisees. This suggestion suffers from a number of difficulties: (1) The exegetical basis of Jesus' argument, Exod 3:6, is totally absent from these supposed parallels. (2) The phrase stating that the patriarchs "live unto God" finds its proper parallel not in Mark 12:18–27 but rather in Luke's redactional addition to the Marcan pericope in Luke 20:38b: "For all [humans] live unto him [i.e., God]" *(pantes gar autō zōsin)*. (3) There is nothing to indicate that 4 Maccabees, written in Greek in the Diaspora by a Jew well acquainted with middle Platonic, neo-Pythagorean, Stoic, and Philonic philosophical ideas, is a product of Pharisaic theology in particular. Apart from the problematic cases of the writings of Paul and Josephus, we cannot identify a single document from the 1st century A.D. that was certainly written by a Pharisee. Ammassari ("Gesù ha veramente insegnato," 70–71) points out that in the much later Midrash Ha-Gadol, we find in a variant reading on Exod 3:6 a hint of the idea of immortality. However, (1) this midrashic collection belongs to the medieval period, and (2) the idea of immortality is connected with Moses' father via the phrase "the God of your father" in Exod 3:6—the very phrase that Jesus omits from his citation of Exod 3:6 in Mark 12:26.

[139] See the chart drawn up by Schwankl, *Die Sadduzäerfrage,* 278. Schwankl counts 17 discussions on proving the resurrection in *b. Sanh.* 90b–92a, with 22 OT passages cited. (One could extend this list with other discussions in *b. Sanh.* 90b–92a that touch tangentially on the topic of resurrection, but which do not provide a new scriptural argument as *proof* of the resurrection. The results would not be altered by such an extension.) The texts examined by Schwankl include citations from the Torah (Exodus, Numbers, and Deuteronomy), the Prophets (Joshua, Isaiah, Jeremiah), and the Writings (the Song of Songs, the Psalms, Proverbs, and Daniel). Of these 22 passages, only Dan 12:2 and Dan 12:13 (each cited once) would qualify as resurrection texts by modern historical-critical standards. Isaiah 25:8 and 26:19 (each cited once) might also qualify, though it is unclear whether the original reference of these two texts was to the resurrection of the individual on the last day or to the restoration of the people Israel after some historical disaster such as exile. But at least both of them are open to being interpreted of the resurrection without resorting to contorted exegesis. Contorted exegesis (from a modern viewpoint) is what is needed to extort a reference to the resurrection from the other 18 texts employed. For example, in *b. Sanh.* 90b, an illustration of how the doctrine of the resurrection can be derived from the

Torah is offered by citing Num 18:28: "And you [the Levites] *shall* give from it [the tithes collected from the Israelites] the 'heave offering' [i.e., the *těrûmâ*, the priestly dues] of Yahweh to Aaron the priest." The rabbinic argument then points out the obvious: Aaron did not live forever; in fact, he did not even enter Palestine, whose harvest was to supply the priestly dues (which were to be rendered only in Palestine). Hence, if this command of Num 18:28, expressed with a verb with a *future* sense, is to be fullfilled, Aaron must be raised from the dead so that Israel may fulfill this injunction by giving him the priestly dues prescribed in Num 18:28.

Among the proof texts taken from the Book of Exodus, 6:4 and 15:1 are cited, but not 3:6. Schwankl (p. 406 n. 232) conjectures that perhaps the lack of any verb in the key statement "I [am] the God of Abraham . . ." discouraged the rabbis from using Exod 3:6, since they could not play off the reading "I *am* the God of Abraham" (in the present, suggesting Abraham's continued existence) against a hypothetical reading "I *was*. . . ."

[140] Hultgren (*Jesus and His Adversaries,* 124–25) claims that the fragments of the dispute story on the resurrection that we find in Justin's *Dialogue with Trypho* 81.4, *On the Resurrection* 3 (attributed to Justin), and the pseudonymous *Epistle of Titus* are independent of the three Synoptics; to the contrary, Mudiso Mbâ Mundla, *Jesus und die Führer,* 71. I think that a careful inspection of the texts shows that we have in these passages typical examples of the meshing and/or paraphrasing of Gospel texts by patristic authors. (1) The text in the *Dialogue with Trypho* is a case in point: (a) To begin with, one should attend to the larger context. Justin is defending the idea of a thousand-year reign of Christ on earth by quoting or alluding to various Scripture texts. He first cites Isa 65:17–25, then alludes to Rev 20:4–6, and finally appeals to Jesus' saying about risen persons being like angels (a form of Luke 20:36). As he then moves on to another point, he cites a form of Ezek 3:17–19 and 33:7–9. What is to be noted here is that all the other citations or allusions in the larger context come from the written books of Scripture. The most natural supposition is that the same is true of Jesus' saying about the risen state. (b) When we examine the OT citations in this context, we see that, while Justin is citing the LXX, there are various divergences from the LXX scattered throughout his quotations. This is especially true of the quotation from Ezekiel in *Dialogue* 82.3, where Justin abbreviates and paraphrases with abandon. If Justin treats the hallowed and centuries-old LXX in this way, need we be surprised that he cites a Gospel text in the same manner? (c) When we look at Jesus' saying in the Greek of the *Dialogue* 81.4, we notice that it follows the basic order of thought in Luke 20:36: after the resurrection, believers will neither marry nor be given in marriage, but will be like angels, being children of the God of the resurrection. But, just as with the OT texts, what Justin offers the reader is an intriguing paraphrase, conflation, and abbreviation of the Lucan text. Since Justin is arguing about a future event and is speaking in his own voice in the future tense, the verbs about marrying are likewise thrown into the future. (One should also note that the Greek verb used for "to marry" varies in some of the manuscripts of all three Synoptic Gospels, and so it is not surprising that variant forms occur here.) While Mark and Matthew state that risen persons will be "like angels" with the simple Greek phrase

hōs aggeloi, Luke uses instead the rare compound adjective "angel-like" *(isaggeloi),* which Justin reproduces. Luke's clarifying phrase ("for neither can they die any more") is dropped, thus assimilating Justin's text at this point to the simpler text of Mark and Matthew. Most interesting of all is the way Justin collapses the final bit of reasoning that Luke had added to Mark's text. Luke writes: ". . . and they are sons of God, being sons of the resurrection." Justin folds this into the dense and somewhat ungainly "being children of the God of the resurrection" (Justin is not noted for his polished Greek style). What we have, in effect, is a reworking of Luke in view of the surrounding context of Justin's argument and of the alternate Marcan text. One wonders whether Justin at this point is citing from memory or possibly is influenced by the homiletic traditions of his church. After all, one must remember: the canonical Gospels not only drew upon and fixed oral tradition; since the Gospels were regularly heard in Christian assemblies, they also created oral tradition. (2) A similar homiletic reworking is found in the tract *On the Resurrection* 3. The citation begins with the expansion of the Marcan tradition that we find in Luke 20:34–35, which contrasts the earthly state with the risen one: "The sons of this age marry and are given in marriage; but the sons of the age to come neither marry nor are given in marriage" (here the phrase "sons of the age to come" reflects Luke 20:35 ["but those counted worthy to attain to that age"], but is recast so as to provide a perfect parallel to "the sons of this age"; hence also the point of marrying and being given in marriage is repeated in the negative). The comparison with the angels *(hōs aggeloi en tō ouranō)* follows exactly the wording unique to Matthew. Once again, we are in the presence of a text produced by both homiletic adaptation and conflation of text forms, perhaps cited from memory. (3) As for the *Epistle of Titus,* it was probably written "in connection with the Priscillianist movement in the ascetic circles of the Spanish church in the course of the 5th century" (A. de Santos Otero, "The Pseudo-Titus Epistle," *New Testament Apocrypha* [2 vols.; ed. Edgar Hennecke and Wilhelm Schneemelcher; Philadelphia: Westminster, 1965] 2. 143). That a version of Jesus' saying that was independent of the Synoptic Gospels would have survived into the 5th century (and in Spain) strains credulity. Moreover, the *Epistle of Titus* is composed in barbarous Latin, apparently by someone who knew neither Latin nor Greek very well. To use such a text to reconstruct a supposedly independent version of a Greek logion is a highly dubious procedure. In addition, the author of the *Epistle of Titus* shows knowledge of Matthew, Luke, John, 1 Corinthians, 2 Corinthians, Galatians, and Revelation. With such a broad knowledge of books of the NT, sometimes quoted quite freely in a paraphrastic form, there is no need to appeal to a special independent form of the logion in Mark 12:25 parr., especially when the author ignores the original sense of Mark 12:25 parr. by applying his statement "such are to be called angels" not to risen believers in general but to celibates in particular, and apparently while they are still living on earth.

[141] While Wilckens (*Missionsreden,* 38) sees a reference here to Exod 3:6,15, he cautions that we cannot be certain that Luke intended such a reference, since "the God of Abraham, Isaac, and Jacob" had become a well-known designation of God in early Judaism. Luke expresses the thought of Acts 3:13 more tersely in the apostles'

speech in 5:30: "The God of our fathers raised Jesus, whom you killed, hanging [him] on a tree."

[142] So Wilckens, *Missionsreden,* 160, 164.

[143] For a detailed consideration of the argument from coherence, see Schwankl, *Die Sadduzäerfrage,* 511–78.

[144] See Collins, *Apocalypticism in the Dead Sea Scrolls,* 110–29. Needless to say, those scholars who deny that Jesus' proclamation involved future eschatology would a fortiori deny that he would have engaged in a debate about the general resurrection. For a discussion and refutation of the claim that the general resurrection of the dead was not a part of Jesus' message, see Schwankl, *Die Sadduzäerfrage,* 512–15.

[145] That the historical Jesus did use the word "generation" (*dôr* in Hebrew, *dār* in Aramaic, *genea* in Greek) in a pejorative sense to refer to his sinful and unrepentant contemporaries seems likely in view of the distribution of the term *genea* in the NT. The pejorative sense employed by Jesus is scattered throughout every Gospel source except John (multiple attestation in Mark, Q, M, and L), and yet it is almost entirely lacking in the sparse use of *genea* elsewhere in the NT. The only two NT occurrences outside the Gospels that are similar to Jesus' pejorative usage are both citations of LXX Deut 32:5 (and possibly LXX Ps 77:8). They are found (1) at the conclusion of Peter's Pentecost sermon in Acts 2:40 ("save yourselves from this crooked generation"), where Luke may purposely make Peter echo the exhortations of Jesus to Israel to create one of his parallels between the time of Jesus and the time of the church (though Luke is also probably intending to allude to LXX Deut 32:5 or LXX Ps 77:8); and (2) in the moral exhortation of Phil 2:15, where Paul urges his Christian converts to remain spotless and innocent "in the midst of a crooked and perverted generation," where the pejorative label is now applied not to Israel but to the Gentile world; here the citation of LXX Deut 32:5 is word for word. Otherwise, the occurrences of *genea* outside the Gospels are restricted to general references to one's contemporaries or to long periods of time (usages also found in the Gospels, but rarely on the lips of Jesus). Interestingly, the Gospels never attribute to Jesus the precise phraseology of LXX Deut 32:5: "a crooked and perverted generation"; the closest parallel is found in Matt 17:17 ‖ Luke 9:41: "a faithless and perverted generation."

[146] While various "entrance into the kingdom" sayings may be the product of the early Christian tradition or the evangelists, multiple attestation of sources (Mark, Q, M, and John) argues that this was one of Jesus' regular ways of speaking of salvation. See, e.g., Mark 9:43,45,47; 10:15,23–25; Matt 5:20; 7:13,21; 19:17; John 3:5.

[147] See *A Marginal Jew,* 2. 317.

[148] In favor of the beatitude of 14:14 coming from the historical Jesus are Marshall, *Luke,* 583; Ernst, *Lukas,* 440. Indeed, one must wonder whether the haste with

which some exegetes deny that this saying is authentic is prompted in part by dismay at seeing Jesus urge generosity on the basis of a sure reward on the last day. Bultmann (*Geschichte,* 108) denies the authenticity of 14:14 because it does not fit Jesus' "new and individual piety, which outgrew Judaism." The material in Luke 14:12–14 is "specifically Jewish" (p. 220), including, no doubt, the idea of reward. Such an idea may bother some Christians, but the promise of an eschatological reward as the motive for action is firmly ensconced in the teaching of the Jew named Jesus.

[149] *A Marginal Jew,* 2. 620, 692.

[150] Nevertheless, the phrase "shall rise up with" (*egerthēsetai/ anastēsontai meta,* with an Aramaic phrase like *qûm ʿim* in the background) should not be pressed as though it primarily referred to the general resurrection. The primary meaning of this Semitic phrase is "to appear in court with someone." However, granted the context, one cannot exclude a secondary allusion to the final resurrection; on this, see Schwankl, *Die Sadduzäerfrage,* 543–44.

[151] For Gehenna used as a metaphor of eschatological punishment of the wicked by fire, see Duane F. Watson, "Gehenna," *Anchor Bible Dictionary,* 2. 926–28. Of the 12 occurrences of the word in the NT, all but one (Jas 3:6) are found in the mouth of Jesus in the Synoptic Gospels. Moreover, it occurs in Mark, Q, and M, thus supplying an argument from multiple attestation of sources for the use of the word by the historical Jesus.

[152] Davies and Allison (*Matthew,* 1. 523 and 2. 765) favor the view that Matthew is reworking his Marcan source in two different ways; so also Gundry, *Matthew,* 88–89, 363. Yet doublets in Matthew sometimes signal a Mark-Q overlap; Pesch (*Markusevangelium,* 2. 116) prefers the view that Matt 5:29–30 comes from Q. Ulrich Luz (*Matthew 1–7* [Minneapolis: Augsburg, 1989] 291–92) also thinks that Matthew may be drawing on a Q version of the sayings.

[153] *A Marginal Jew,* 2. 302–9.

[154] For instance, I think that John 5:28–29 ("Do not marvel at this, for an hour is coming in which all those in the tombs shall hear his voice and shall come forth, those who have done good to a resurrection of life, those who have done evil to a resurrection of judgment") is not an invention of the final redactor of the Fourth Gospel, correcting the realized eschatology of the evangelist. Rather, it represents an earlier stage of eschatological teaching in the Johannine tradition. In my view, the Fourth Evangelist reinterpreted this traditional future eschatology in terms of his own realized eschatology. Hence 5:25 ("An hour is coming *and is now here* when the dead shall hear the voice of the Son of God, and those who hear shall live") should be seen as the evangelist's reworking of the older tradition found in 5:28–29 (see Brown, *The Gospel According to John,* 1. 218–21). But to argue this point at length would take us too far afield.

¹⁵⁵ Those who hold that Luke's version of the story, esp. Luke 20:34–36, represents an alternate form of the primitive tradition might argue for authenticity from the criterion of multiple attestation of sources (Mark + L). However, along with many Lucan commentators, I think that 20:34–36 is best explained as Luke's creative redaction of his Marcan tradition, perhaps with a glance at the LXX Maccabean literature; on this, see Schwankl, *Die Sadduzäerfrage,* 442–61; for the opposite view, Mudiso Mbâ Mundla, *Jesus und die Führer,* 79; and, more extensively, David E. Aune, "Luke 20:34–36: A "Gnosticized" Logion of Jesus?" *Geschichte—Tradition—Reflexion. Band III. Frühes Christentum* (Martin Hengel Festschrift; ed. Hermann Lichtenberger; Tübingen: Mohr [Siebeck], 1996) 187–202. Arguments for historicity from philological considerations (at best, confirmatory in nature) can be found in *Die Sadduzäerfrage,* 579. Perhaps the most curious objection to the historicity of Mark 12:18–27 is that of Haenchen (*Der Weg Jesu,* 411): If he had known Jesus' saying in Mark 12:25, Paul would have cited it when writing his defense of the resurrection in 1 Corinthians 15. Since he does not, the saying and therefore the whole pericope are a product of the early church. The answer to Haenchen's objection is obvious: Paul's knowledge of the sayings of Jesus was, as far as we can tell, fairly limited. Hence I think the burden of proof must lie on the side of anyone who maintains that, in spite of his limited knowledge, Paul would nevertheless have known this idiosyncratic Marcan pericope that stands isolated within the Synoptic tradition.

¹⁵⁶ In favor of such a view is Baumbach, "Das Sadduzäerverständnis," 31–35; Müller, "Jesus und die Sadduzäer," 8–11. Their attempts to assign certain Gospel sayings and dispute stories to Jesus' clashes with the Sadducees are quite speculative.

¹⁵⁷ See Dibelius, *Formgeschichte,* 141–42; Schwankl, *Die Sadduzäerfrage,* 508–9, 563–66.

CHAPTER 30

JESUS IN RELATION TO COMPETING JEWISH GROUPS

The Essenes and Other Groups

In this chapter, we shall deal with other Jewish groups that existed—or are thought to have existed—alongside Jesus and his followers in 1st-century Palestine. The extent to which Jesus interacted with these various groups is debatable, and each case must be judged on its own merits. We shall consider in turn the Essenes/Qumranites, the Samaritans, the scribes, the Herodians, and the Zealots—a very mixed bag, as we shall see. Among these groups, certainly the most fascinating and widely discussed candidate in our own day is the group called the Essenes, along with its famous subgroup, the inhabitants of Qumran.[1]

I. THE ESSENES AND QUMRAN

A. INTRODUCTION: THE NARROW FOCUS OF THIS SECTION

While the Essenes have been treated in passing in our survey of the Pharisees and of the Sadducees, the reader might well expect at this juncture a large, detailed treatment of the Essenes and Qumran. Both the initial fervor with which the first Qumran scrolls (discovered in 1947) were studied in the 1950s and the renewed interest in Qumran literature today, now that all the Qumran fragments are finally available to scholars, naturally foster such expectations.

Regrettably, I must disappoint these expectations. The theme running through Volume Three of *A Marginal Jew* is the *relation* of the historical Jesus to various Jewish groups, be they followers or competitors. The goal of Volume Three, therefore, is not a complete study of various Jewish groups considered in themselves, but rather a description of Jesus' interaction with these groups in order to understand Jesus better. Now, while the Gospels do present Jesus associating with or reacting to Pharisees, Sadducees, and Samaritans, neither the Gospels nor the rest of the NT says a word about Jesus interacting with the Essenes or the Qumranites. In fact, the words "Essene" and "Qumran" occur nowhere in the NT.[2] The compliment is returned by the Essenes: despite sensationalistic claims to the contrary, the Qumran documents never mention or allude to Jesus of Nazareth. Hence, if the question to be answered in this section is simply "What does the NT directly say about Jesus' relation to or interaction with the Essenes and/or Qumran?" the answer must be brutally brief: nothing.[3]

While this answer is perfectly correct, one can sympathize with the reader who desires some enlightenment as to the conflicting claims made about Qumran's relation or similarity to Jesus and/or early Christianity. After all, beyond the question of Jesus' direct relation to or interaction with Qumran, there lies the legitimate question of similarities in religious views and practices, even if Jesus never met a single Qumranite in his life. Then, too, there is always the possibility that, in his journeys around Palestine, Jesus was influenced indirectly by Essene tendencies, even if he never interacted directly with the Essenes. Hence I offer in this section a brief consideration of the similarities and dissimilarities that various scholars have seen between Jesus and the Qumran (as well as the wider Essene) movement. Actually, it is to the early church rather than to the historical Jesus that the Qumran material supplies a large number of intriguing parallels.[4] However, a study of parallels between Qumran and the church belongs to a history of early Christianity, not to a quest for the historical Jesus.

Before we engage in some sober comparisons between Jesus and Qumran (or the Essenes in general), I should mention in passing some not-so-sober attempts to see references to Jesus in the Qumran scrolls. Barbara Thiering, an Australian scholar, has tried to show that John the Baptist was the Teacher of Righteousness who founded the Qumran community and that Jesus was the Wicked Priest who opposed him.[5] Going Thiering one better, Robert H. Eisenman, a professor at the State University of California, Long Beach, has claimed that the Teacher of Righteousness was none other than James, the brother of Jesus, and that Saul/Paul of Tarsus was "the Man of Lies" denounced in the *Pesher on Habakkuk* (1QpHab 2:2).[6] As a matter of fact, fanciful ideas about Jesus and Qumran have a venerable pedigree, reaching back to the early days of research on the Dead Sea scrolls. While some scholars, like André Dupont-Sommer, simply suggested that the Teacher of Righteousness foreshadowed Jesus in the pattern of their two careers,[7] others, like Jacob L. Teicher, could not resist the temptation of declaring that Jesus *was* the Teacher of Righteousness.[8] Going in the opposite direction, John Mark Allegro, whose technical work on Qumran texts left something to be desired, expressed at first great skepticism about how much we could know about the historical Jesus. Later on, Allegro cut the Gordian knot by declaring that Jesus had never existed; he was created out of hallucinatory fantasies arising from eating sacred mushrooms.[9] The reader can evaluate the weightiness of these suggestions without much prompting from me.[10] Suffice it to say that the tabloid-damaged minds that find all these theories fascinating never seem to notice that, if any one of these theories were true, it would necessarily invalidate all the other theories they find attractive. For some, playing endlessly with bizarre hypotheses is a satisfying end in itself.

While wildly popular in the media, these sensationalistic approaches are generally dismissed today by serious scholars for two reasons:

(1) These hypotheses rest for the most part on the academic equivalent of reading tea leaves or interpreting Rorschach inkblots. Certain Qumran documents use code words or symbolic names to refer to key figures in the history of the Qumran community. Short of finding the Qumran equivalent of the Rosetta stone, we have no sure way of identifying the persons to whom the code words allude. One is reminded of the eternal hunt for the identity of the beloved disciple in John's Gospel.

(2) More to the point, Jesus' public ministry lasted roughly from A.D. 28 to 30. Thus, for the theories of Thiering or Eisenman to be correct—and each one's theory excludes the other—a number of significant documents discovered at Qumran (supposedly referring to Jesus) would all have to have been written in the last few decades of the community's existence, i.e., from A.D. 30 to 68. Yet both paleographic evidence and radiocarbon dating suggest that most of these documents go back to the 2d or 1st centuries B.C.—though some manuscripts might possibly be assigned to the early decades of the 1st century A.D. Moreover, unless we imagine that we hold in our hands the autographs of these works, the writing of the originals must be dated earlier than the dates assigned to the texts in our possession. In short, the dates of composition of the key Qumran documents are prior to the dates of Jesus' public ministry.[11] Hence these documents could not possibly refer to him or to the people around him. The theories of academics like Thiering and Eisenman are the stuff of pulp fiction and late-night talk shows. Instead of wasting

time on them, let us move on to those points of comparison between Jesus and the Essenes on which many scholars agree.

B. Jesus and Qumran/the Essenes: Caveats on Comparisons

Before we begin listing similarities and dissimilarities between the *historical* Jesus and Qumran in particular or the Essenes in general, five preliminary observations on method are in order:

(1) All too often in the past, comparisons were carried out in a manner that ignored everything scholars had learned about source, form, and redaction criticism of the Gospels. For instance, when the subject of the Mosaic Law was raised, the Jesus compared with the Qumran material was not the *historical* Jesus but rather the *Matthean* Jesus as presented in the Sermon on the Mount.[12] The idea that the Sermon on the Mount was a composition created by the Christian evangelist Matthew somewhere around A.D. 80–90 and that the Jesus portrayed in Matthew's Gospel reflected, at least in part, the Christian theology of Matthew did not seem to impinge on the consciousness of the enthusiastic compilers of parallels. Our inquiry in this section is strictly limited to comparisons between Qumran and the historical Jesus.

(2) Some of the parallels we will consider involve larger questions about Jesus' teaching on the Mosaic Law or his stance vis-à-vis various Jewish hopes for a Messiah. These topics will be treated at length in subsequent chapters in Volume Four. For now, we must content ourselves with brief summary statements about Jesus' positions on these topics. The justification of these statements will be presented in the later treatments.

(3) We are comparing the views of Qumran, a highly structured community that existed in one place for roughly two hundred years and left behind extensive firsthand documentation, with the views of an itinerant prophet whose ministry lasted probably less than three years (toward the end of Qumran's existence) and who did not leave behind anything written by himself. Therefore, we should not be surprised at the difficulty inherent in making such comparisons and at the relatively meager results from them.

(4) Certainly in the case of Qumran and the Essenes and probably in the case of Jesus, we must allow that views developed or changed. However, since we know next to nothing about the chronological order of events in Jesus' ministry between his being baptized by John and his final days in Jerusalem, almost nothing can be said about the development of his views. In the case of Qumran, a number of theories concerning the stages of development of Qumran's main documents and the theological views contained therein have been put forward, but none has gained general assent.[13] Therefore,

since we lack a firm sense of "before" and "after," our comparisons must remain synchronic. In other words, in the absence of a reliable chronological grid for tracing the development of the theological ideas we will survey, the following comparisons will be limited to describing similarities and differences in thought, language, and social structures. No claims will be made as to whether these similarities between Jesus and Qumran existed at the same precise moment in history or whether Qumran influenced Jesus—or vice versa.

(5) Not all scholars agree on whether certain documents that were found at Qumran and that are often used to compare Qumran and Jesus were actually composed at Qumran and are representative of Qumran's views. Examples of disputed cases included the *Temple Scroll* and the *Damascus Document*, both written in Hebrew, as well as the *New Jerusalem* text, written in Aramaic. Nevertheless, I think that these documents can be used judiciously when making comparisons. For example, the multiple manuscripts of the *New Jerusalem* text (at least six copies were found at Qumran) and the *Damascus Document* (eight manuscripts were found in Cave 4) argue well for their being accepted by and popular with the Qumran community, whatever their ultimate origin. Whether the *Temple Scroll* was composed in or outside of Qumran is likewise debated. In any case, it certainly shows affinities with documents that are clearly of Qumranite origin (e.g., the *Rule of the Community*, the *Commentary on Nahum*, the *Pesher on Habakkuk*, and the *Hodayot Psalms*).

In short, then, faced with these methodological difficulties, we can offer only a generalizing, impressionistic study that is synchronic rather than diachronic. Nothing more is attempted or claimed. At times, when it is impossible to be more precise, I will speak in undifferentiated fashion of comparisons between Jesus on the one hand and Qumran/the Essenes on the other. Such an approach should not be taken as indicating that the terms "Essene" and "Qumranite" are coterminous or interchangeable categories in historiography. Rather, such an approach simply indicates the poverty of our sources and the limits of our knowledge. Still, since, in my view, Qumran was a subgroup and prime expression of the larger Essene movement, some generalizations encompassing both Qumran and the Essenes are not totally out of order. At other times, when our sources do draw distinct pictures of the Essenes in general and the Qumranites in particular—for instance, in matters concerning money and possessions—I will be more precise and specify the group with whom Jesus is being compared.

C. Jesus and Qumran/the Essenes:
Points of Comparison and Contrast

With these caveats in mind, we turn now to the question of similarities and dissimilarities between Jesus and Qumran/the Essenes. As often happens in comparative religion, the similarities have tended to attract more attention than the dissimilarities. Long lists of similarities or points of contact began to be compiled soon after the major documents from Cave 1 at Qumran were published. Some of the items on these lists are little more than verbal similarities that lose their importance as soon as one examines the different contexts in which they appear. Other items are without significance because they simply reflect the common soil of the Jewish Scriptures from which both the Essene and Jesus movements sprang.[14] Still other items are more substantive, but may simply reflect common religious ideas circulating in Palestinian Judaism around the turn of the era, especially among eschatologically minded Jews. Not being specific to Jesus and Qumran, they are parallels only in a broad sense.

Even when we narrow down the similarities to those more specific to Jesus and Qumran/the Essenes, they still range over a wide spectrum of topics. For convenience' sake, I will gather these similarities and dissimilarities—somewhat artificially—under three major categories: (1) eschatology, (2) attitude toward the temple, and (3) rules governing behavior. As we shall see, as soon as we start investigating the similarities, we will inevitably stumble across dissimilarities that are inextricably intertwined with them. Hence the major similarities and corresponding dissimilarities will be treated together in this section. In the next section, I will give special attention to some notable dissimilarities that emerge from the overview in this section and that I think deserve further consideration.

1. Eschatology

(a) Early on in the research into Qumran's theology, less than accurate attempts were made to distinguish Qumran's eschatology from that of Jesus. Jesus' view of the kingdom of God supposedly differed from Jewish eschatological views of the day in that it involved a tension between the "already" of Jesus' ministry and the "not yet" of the full, final coming of the kingdom. In contrast, Qumran supposedly evinced only a fervent expectation of an imminent end of the present order.[15]

Such claims can hardly be sustained today. While documents like the *War Scroll* show that Qumran eagerly awaited a final battle waged by the sons of light (the Qumranites) against the sons of darkness (everyone else), with victory for the Qumranites ushering in a new state of affairs,[16] Qumran's eschatology also had a "realized" or "present" dimension. In Qumran, though, this present dimension was experienced especially in the liturgy of the community, supposedly celebrated in the company of the angels. In view of Jesus' emphasis on "the kingdom of God," it is striking to see how much the theme of God's kingship pervades these angelic liturgies.[17] In communal worship, the Qumranites believed that they were already joined with the angels in heaven as they worshiped the divine king. Accordingly, death for the individual seems to have been viewed as a final union with the heavenly hosts. How exactly this realized element relates—if it does—to the victory of the community living at the time of the final battle and to the rare references at Qumran to resurrection is not clear.[18]

Qumran's eschatological view of the present also had a more negative element: the present time is a time of testing and suffering for the community, a time in which all Israelites are called to decide for or against the renewed covenant and the true interpretation of the Law as found at Qumran. It is in this sense that the so-called *Halakic Letter* (4QMMT, 95–108) can speak of the "end of days" already beginning.[19] In Qumranite theology, this time of conflict seems to culminate in the coming of the two Messiahs and the great final war, led by the royal Messiah. This whole period of struggle, included within "the end of days," still belonged to the present world of time and space. Final salvation (involving perhaps the resurrection of the dead?) was to lie beyond this period.[20]

Jesus' eschatology likewise held together the paradox of present and future elements. As we have seen, in Jesus' view, the kingdom of God (i.e., God exercising his power in the end time to liberate and gather Israel) was already present in Jesus' ministry, a ministry that nevertheless proclaimed and pointed forward to a definitive future coming of the kingdom in full power. As we saw in our treatment of the Sadducees (Mark 12:18–27), Jesus also believed in a general resurrection of the dead at the end of time. In a way similar to Qumran, Jesus leaves unclear how this resurrection fits into the rest of his eschatological scenario. Yet, unlike Qumran, Jesus is notably unapocalyptic in that he does not supply a timetable for the eschatological events. An even more striking difference from Qumran lies in Jesus' inclusion of some Gentiles in the eschatological banquet with the (apparently risen) patriarchs, while some of Jesus' fellow Israelites are to be excluded (Matt 8:11–12). In Qumran's view, all Gentiles and all Israelites outside the Essene community would ultimately perish.

As for the realized element in the eschatological paradox of already/not yet, one may conjecture that there was a difference in emphasis. The religious commitment of Jesus' disciples was intensely focused on the person of Jesus himself, who made the kingdom palpable for them by his healings and exorcisms, his table fellowship with religious outcasts, and his parables, which aimed at drawing the listener into an experience of the kingdom. All this, crammed into a two-and-a-half-year ministry, would have tended to heighten the disciples' experience of the kingdom as already present. In contrast, by the time of Jesus, the Qumran community had been in existence, with some interruptions, for roughly a century and a half. Its realized eschatology found expression especially in the routinized liturgy of the group. I think it therefore a reasonable surmise—though nothing more than a surmise—that Jesus' eschatology was more highly realized than that of Qumran at the same period. In any case, though, both of these Jewish eschatological movements held in tension realized and future elements. This paradoxical tension cannot be claimed as a unique factor in Jesus' eschatological stance.

(b) Some of the Qumran documents speak directly of the community's messianic expectations.[21] While there is fleeting reference to some sort of eschatological prophet (Elijah?), the key figures are two Messiahs: a priestly Messiah of the house of Aaron (no doubt thought of as the legitimate high priest of the end time), and a lay royal Messiah, who would lead Israel in its final battle and govern it after the victory (1QS 9:11).[22] Granted the whole history of the Davidic monarchy in preexilic Judah, granted the dual leadership of the high priest Joshua and the Davidic prince Zerubbabel after the exile (Zech 3:1–4:14; 5:9–15), and granted references to a Davidic figure in other Qumran documents, this royal Messiah is probably thought of as a son of David, though he is never directly called such in the *Rule of the Community*. In 1QSa 2:12–21, the priestly Messiah clearly takes precedence over the royal Messiah, although both have honored places at the eschatological banquet of the community.[23]

The figure of an eschatological prophet like Elijah, which is at best dim at Qumran, seems to be the eschatological role that Jesus chose for himself.[24] In addition, some of Jesus' disciples, perhaps aware of a family tradition that Joseph, Jesus' putative father, was descended from David, may have combined the idea of physical descent from David with the implications of Jesus' exorcising activity. As we have seen, King Solomon, the literal son of David, was considered in some Jewish traditions to be the exorcist par excellence.[25] Consequently, some of Jesus' disciples, having witnessed Jesus' exorcising activity over an extended period and having heard of Jesus' supposed Davidic lineage, may have reached the conclusion that Jesus was the messianic Son of David, an exorcist in the tradition of Solomon.

During most of his ministry, however, Jesus apparently gave no great encouragement to the idea that he was the Davidic Messiah. Yet the two symbolic actions he performed as he came to Jerusalem for his last Passover—the "triumphal entry" and the "cleansing" of the temple—may have been intended as an expression of a royal messianic claim over David's ancient capital and the temple first built by Solomon, the Son of David.[26] That would help to explain why he was arrested and tried at this particular visit to Jerusalem and why Pilate condemned him to death on the charge of claiming to be King of the Jews.

One further parallel between Jesus and Qumran with respect to the eschatological Messiah may be found in Jesus' answer to the messengers sent by John the Baptist (Matt 11:2–6 par.).[27] In response to the vague and open-ended question, "Are you the one who is to come?"—i.e., are you the final protagonist in the eschatological drama—Jesus replies indirectly. Rather than focus directly on himself by using some title, he focuses instead on the miracles he has been performing, miracles that echo OT prophecies, especially those of Isaiah (29:18–19; 35:5–6; 26:19; 25:8; 61:1–2; cf. 11:1–9): the blind see, the lame walk, lepers are cleansed, the deaf hear, the dead are raised. Then, pointedly, he crowns all these miraculous acts with the greatest eschatological act of all, prophesied by Isaiah: "And the poor have good news proclaimed to them." All these activities sharply distinguish his ministry of healing and consolation from the Baptist's fiery threat of judgment.

A remarkable parallel in thought—and, in a few instances, language—is found in a fragment from Cave 4 at Qumran, 4Q521.[28] Emile Puech has labeled it a "Messianic Apocalypse," though Florentino García Martínez categorizes it as a wisdom text that exhibits belief in the resurrection (hence the label "Resurrection Fragment").[29] The second column of the second fragment of this text begins with a prophecy that the heavens and the earth will hear (or obey) his (i.e., God's) Messiah (apparently in the singular).[30] In order to offer hope to those who seek the Lord, the text prophesies the marvelous deeds that the Lord (i.e., God) will work for the faithful members of Israel (the pious, the just, and the poor), apparently in the days of the Messiah, which is also called "the eternal kingdom." With allusions to Ps 146:7–8 and passages in Isaiah, the text promises that the Lord will set captives free, give sight to the blind, straighten those who are bent, heal the wounded, revive the dead, "and bring good news to the poor" (Isa 61:1).[31]

While the direct parallels between this text and Matt 11:5 par. lie in the four saving acts of healing the wounded, giving sight to the blind, raising the dead, and proclaiming good news to the poor,[32] the overall context and "feel" of the two passages are surprisingly similar. These acts that heal and comfort are the fulfillment of prophecy, especially as found in the Book of

Isaiah; they occur in the eschatological and/or messianic period of salvation for Israel. In each text, there is an astonishing order of climax. The various miraculous acts rise in a crescendo to the announcement of the resurrection of the dead. Yet trumping even that spectacular end-time feat is the still greater act of salvation: proclaiming good news to the poor (or meek).

To be sure, there are differences in the two texts. Typically, the fulfillment of prophecy that the Qumran text promises for the future is declared by Jesus to be already present in the miracles he works and the message he proclaims. This in turn involves another difference. While the Messiah is mentioned at the beginning of the Qumran text, the "Lord" (Hebrew: ʾădōnai) who performs the saving deeds is clearly the Lord God, not the Messiah. In Matt 11:2–6 par., it is Jesus who is performing all the saving acts listed. Still, there may not be a strict opposition here. On the one hand, the Qumran text may presuppose that the Lord performs his saving deeds through his Messiah, though this is never said in the fragment preserved for us.[33] On the other hand, Jesus undoubtedly understands all he does to be the vehicle of the coming of God in power. Hence the passive voice Jesus uses ("lepers are cleansed ... the dead are raised") may be employed to point away from himself to God as the one who ultimately accomplishes these eschatological deeds.

It is striking that both lists of eschatological wonders reach a climax in an allusion to Isa 61:1, in which the prophet speaks of his end-time mission to Israel: "The spirit of the Lord Yahweh [is] upon me because Yahweh has anointed me; to proclaim good news to the poor he has sent me." This allusion at the culmination of each list naturally conjures up the image of the eschatological prophet in both texts. The Qumran text might thus be read as meshing the images of Messiah (explicitly mentioned at the beginning of the fragment) and eschatological prophet (who may be alluded to near the end of the fragment, insofar as the Lord's "proclaiming good news to the poor" presumably involves some human spokesman). Calling on later rabbinic texts, John J. Collins even suggests that the text may be intimating that God will raise the dead through the eschatological prophet like Elijah.[34]

This idea of the eschatological prophet like Elijah (if it is present in 4Q521) would cohere perfectly with all that we have seen about the self-image intentionally projected by the historical Jesus. In the case of Matt 11:2–6, the overall context of the ministry of the historical Jesus naturally leads us to read this text as referring to the eschatological prophet wearing the mantle of the miracle-working Elijah. To be sure, the title Messiah is nowhere mentioned in Matt 11:5 par., though that does not mean that the concept is absent from the text. Indeed, since the prophetic figure in Isa 61:1 affirms that he owes his prophetic mission to the fact that "Yahweh has *anointed* [*māšaḥ*] me," he may also be considered a messianic figure in some sense, though not a royal Davidic sense.

All in all, the parallels are remarkable. Since 4Q521 was possibly not a composition of Qumran itself but rather an outside document preserved in Qumran's library,[35] we may venture a further conjecture. It may be that Jesus chose to answer the Baptist's question with the theme of the fulfillment of Isaiah's prophecies of healing and comfort because this theme was cherished among various groups of pious Jews around the turn of the era. This end-time hope may even have included the figure of an eschatological, miracle-working prophet (in the guise of Elijah?). At the very least, 4Q521 shows that the reply of Matt 11:5 is completely intelligible in the mouth of Jesus the Jew in 1st-century Palestine and need not be assigned to the creativity of the early church.

2. Attitude toward the Temple

Around the turn of the era, the Jerusalem temple and the Mosaic Law were the two central religious symbols of Palestinian Judaism. Being so pivotal to Jewish life, they were also the two great battlefields for power and control. Intended to be unifying symbols, they became major sources of division. Perhaps even more than the Mosaic Law, the Jerusalem temple, along with its governing priesthood, liturgical rituals, and liturgical calendar, became the focal point of Qumran's dispute with and separation from the rest of Palestinian Judaism.[36] Yet one must be careful when speaking of Qumran's rejection of or opposition to the Jerusalem temple that stood in its day. Qumran's ultimate objection to the temple was that Qumranites did not control it and run it according to their rules.

This dispute over the temple probably reaches back to the days when the Hasmoneans acquired possession of the high priesthood in the middle of the 2d century B.C.[37] Not being Zadokites, the Hasmoneans had, in the eyes of the Qumranites, no legitimate claim on the high priesthood. Indeed, some scholars have suggested that the Teacher of Righteousness was a Zadokite priest who thought that he, instead of a Hasmonean, should be high priest— or even that he had in fact functioned as high priest during the chaotic period stretching from the death of the high priest Alcimus (159 B.C.) during the Maccabean revolt down to the assumption of the high priesthood by Judas Maccabeus' brother Jonathan (ca. 150 B.C.). Not only were the Hasmonean high priests illegitimate in the eyes of Qumran, the ritual they used was likewise incorrect. Worst of all, the (solar-)lunar calendar introduced into the temple sometime in the first half of the 2d century B.C. was deemed to be a false calendar by the Qumranites, who held to the older solar calendar (though perhaps with some correlations with a lunar calendar). Hence all the festivals in the temple were being celebrated on the wrong days.

The entire temple liturgy was therefore invalid, and only a restoration of the Qumran priesthood with its proper liturgy and calendar could rectify the present unclean situation of the temple. Such a restoration was eagerly awaited by the Qumranites. In fact, it may be that Qumran expected two stages of eschatological restoration. First, the Qumranites would control a huge temple in a purified Jerusalem. However fanciful its description, this temple was apparently thought to belong to the present era of history. Scholars sometimes refer to it as a "utopian" or "idealized" temple. It would be administered by the legitimate priesthood according to the laws and calendar of Qumran. The function of the *Temple Scroll* at Qumran may have been to supply the legal directions to run this renewed temple.[38] Later on, in the new creation, an eschatological temple would be built.

In any event, the temple, be it in its present, interim, or eschatological state, was central to Qumran's theology. Naturally, in the unclean present period of Hasmonean or Roman control, Qumranites avoided the defiled temple in Jerusalem. The Qumran community itself, by its worship in the company of angels, careful study of the Mosaic Law, and stringent observance thereof, served as a spiritual temple until the Jerusalem temple could be properly restored (see 1QS 8:5–15). Thus did they "prepare the way of the Lord in the desert" (1QS 8:13–14, citing Isa 40:3).

Jesus' attitude toward the temple was also a complicated one, though in a different way. We have from the historical Jesus no lengthy, programmatic statement about the temple such as we find in the *Temple Scroll*. We have to piece together his view as best we can from various sayings and actions.

We have multiple attestation for the fact that Jesus himself frequented the temple. The Synoptics depict him doing so during the single visit to Jerusalem that they mention from his public ministry, namely, at the end of his life.[39] In contrast, John's Gospel narrates five visits to Jerusalem over a number of years. In all the Gospels, the fact that Jesus goes up to the temple, teaches in the temple, and—in the Synoptics—celebrates the Passover with a lamb slain in the temple according to the temple's ritual is taken for granted as an obvious datum that needs no explanation and generates no dispute. In this, Jesus stood with "mainstream" Palestinian Jews, who, no matter what they thought of the particular reigning high priest, revered the temple as the one sacred place chosen by God for lawful sacrifice.

This attitude of Jesus, which was basically accepting of the temple *in the present order of things,* is also borne out by various sayings of Jesus that take the temple and its ritual for granted as obligatory. We find attestation of such an attitude in sayings from every Gospel source: (1) Jesus commands those he heals of leprosy to go to an officiating priest and offer—obviously in the Jerusalem temple—the sacrifice prescribed by the Mosaic Law (Mark 1:44; cf. the L tradition in Luke 17:14). (2) While Jesus stresses that justice, mercy, and fidelity are more weighty obligations than the paying of tithes, he nevertheless affirms the obligation of tithing to the temple priesthood (a Q tradition in Matt 23:23 ‖ Luke 11:42). (3) Jesus demands reconciliation with one's brother before one offers a sacrifice at the altar in the temple. But, after reconciliation, one is to return to offer one's gift (an M tradition in Matt 5:23–24). (4) In a saying of the M tradition, Jesus affirms the sanctity of the temple and its altar, for the temple is the dwelling place of God (Matt 23:16–21). (5) In a parable of the L tradition, Jesus takes for granted the temple as the supreme locus of prayer for all Jews, Pharisees and toll collectors alike (Luke 18:9–14). (6) Whether or not Jesus' statement to the chief priest Annas in John 18:20 actually comes from the historical Jesus, this saying sums up very well Jesus' activity in the temple as it is presented in all four Gospels: "I always taught in a synagogue and in the temple." Significantly, in this saying the temple is nonchalantly put alongside the synagogue as a basic institution of Jewish prayer and teaching. Indeed, even in the very act of declaring that neither Jerusalem nor Mount Gerizim nor any sacred place is of determinative significance in the eschatological hour that has arrived with him, the Johannine Jesus still intimates the superiority of the Jerusalem temple over the Samaritans' (John 4:22): "You [Samaritans] worship what you do not know; we [Jews] worship what we do know, for salvation is from the Jews."

Even if we do not think that all of these narratives and sayings are authentic—the sayings in John are especially problematic—we still have widespread multiple attestation of both sources and forms for Jesus' acceptance of the Jerusalem temple in his own day. This unperturbed acceptance of the temple in every Gospel source (Mark, Q, M, L, and John) and in both narratives and sayings is all the more impressive because there is no countervailing tradition in the Gospels that Jesus throughout his public ministry shunned the temple and refused to take part in its festivals. Unlike the Qumranites (and most likely the Baptist), the historical Jesus—and here the Fourth Gospel probably gives the more accurate picture—regularly went up to the temple, joined in the temple feasts, and used the temple as a solemn auditorium for addressing large numbers of his fellow Jews. Simply from a practical point of view, if Jesus the preacher, teacher, and prophet wanted to address the whole of Israel, where else could he hope to find a large part of this audience during the great feasts? In sum, then, Jesus clearly accepted the Jerusalem temple *as part of the present order of things.*

The rub, of course, is in that final proviso. During the course of his ministry, Jesus takes for granted the temple as the proper place for Jews to offer sacrifice, to pray, and to be instructed. Yet, as his ministry comes to a close, Jesus indicates that this present order of things, ordained by God in the Torah, will soon come to an end. Both the Marcan and the Johannine traditions (Mark 11:15–17; John 2:13–17) *narrate* versions of the so-called cleansing of the temple, which most likely is a symbolic, prophetic action by which Jesus foretells and, in a sense, unleashes the imminent end of the present temple. Likewise, Mark, Q, L, and John contain *sayings* attributed to Jesus that prophesy the destruction of the present temple (Mark 14:58 [cf. Mark 13:2]; Matt 23:37–38 ‖ Luke 13:34–35; Luke 19:41–44; John 2:19). Thus, in addition to an argument from multiple attestation of sources and forms, we have here as well an argument from coherence: the sayings about the temple explain the otherwise puzzling prophetic action of Jesus in the temple.[40]

Hence, from one vantage point, Jesus' attitude toward the temple does parallel that of Qumran: a distinction is made between the present order and the last days. Yet, for Qumran's present practice, the distinction means the exact opposite of what it means for Jesus. For Qumran, the present temple is not to be entered or used because it is defiled; only after a future purification and renewal will a utopian or an eschatological temple be used by the Qumranites to offer fitting worship. For Jesus, the present temple, whatever its failings, is the temple willed by God for the supreme acts of worship by all Jews.[41] It is, however, an institution that belongs to and is doomed to disappear with this present age. Apparently the full coming of the kingdom of God in power would do away with the temple Jesus and his contemporaries used. Whether Jesus expected some new or better temple to be built after the present one disappeared is unclear.[42] Different versions of a saying witnessed in both Mark and John (Mark 14:58; John 2:19) indicate that some sort of a new temple would be built after the present one was destroyed. It is difficult to say, though, whether we should interpret this prophecy symbolically— e.g., of the restored Israel of the end time or of Jesus' disciples—or literally of some future temple building.[43]

In the end, we begin to see an intriguing pattern arising in the comparison between Jesus and the Qumranites. In both cases, we find major concerns of Palestinian Judaism—e.g., messianic figures and the temple—interpreted within an eschatological context that draws a distinction between the present time-period and a new age of salvation that will be brought into being by God working through human agents. Within this overarching context, though, the detailed scenario of how these two periods interrelate differs notably. Turning from the future to the present, we must now see whether Jesus and Qumran differed notably in another major area of Jewish concern, namely, rules governing human behavior.

3. Rules Governing Behavior

I use this vague category rather than "interpretation of the Mosaic Law" or "morality" because our comparisons cover such a wide range of legal, ethical, and ritual material. At times, the question at hand is related to the Mosaic Law, at times not. At times, the question is ethical, at times ritual. Needless to say, our neat distinctions among legal, ethical, and ritual matters would seem strange to Palestinian Jews around the turn of the era. The later rabbis would label the matters treated here as *hălākâ:* rules, decisions, or opinions regarding individual human actions insofar as such actions are in keeping with or contrary to God's will for his people Israel.[44] Some of the questions listed below will be discussed at greater length in the treatment of the Mosaic Law in Volume Four. Hence all that is presented here is a brief catalogue for the sake of a comparison between Jesus and Qumran.

It is often said that Jesus and Qumran share an ethical radicalism arising from their intense eschatological expectations.[45] To an extent this is true, but this eschatological radicalism can work itself out in different ways and with very different results. Sometimes, Jesus and Qumran both appear extremely stringent and demanding on the same issue—for instance, divorce. At other times, eschatological radicalism leads to opposite outcomes: for example, Qumran's extreme rigor in matters of ritual purity and observance of the sabbath is glaringly different from Jesus' relative laxity on the same issues. One sees, then, the need for briefly listing some individual items of behavior.

(a) On *sexual* matters, Jesus and the Essenes tend in the same direction: stringent standards and prohibitions. (Modern presentations of a "relevant" Jesus usually ignore this dimension of his teaching and practice.) Both Jesus and the Essenes demand strict restraints on thoughts and actions that could lead to improper sexual activity. In a sense, one could call both Jesus and the Essenes extreme conservatives. Jesus and at least some Essenes practiced celibacy, while affirming monogamous marriage for most people as part of the present order of creation. However, while these general statements are true, they need further clarification and nuance.

(i) Josephus (*J.W.* 2.8.2 §120) tells us that the Essenes avoid (sensual) pleasures as evil and consider self-control and refusal to submit to the passions as virtue. While they reject marriage for themselves, they accept it for the human race in general as necessary for procreation. Josephus bases the Essenes' avoidance of marriage on women's inability to control their sexual impulses and so to be faithful to one man (!). While we may see in Josephus' portrait a mixing of Stoic teaching on the control of one's passions with traditional Near Eastern misogyny, his emphasis on the Essenes' restraint and control in sexual matters is confirmed by the Dead Sea Scrolls.

At Qumran, we meet with various rules that take a strongly puritanical stance toward sexual activity. At the very beginning of the *Rule of the Community,* one of the basic obligations of Qumranites is declared to be "no longer to walk [i.e., to conduct oneself morally] in the stubbornness of a guilty heart and lustful eyes [literally: eyes of fornication] to do every kind of evil" (1QS 1:6–7). Actions with one's hands and exposure of one's genitals are strictly regulated. A Qumranite who walks naked in the sight of one of his confreres without a constraining reason is to be punished for six months (1QS 7:12).[46] Likewise, a Qumranite who pulls his penis out from under his garment or has holes in his garment so that his nakedness is exposed is to be punished for 30 days (1QS 7:13).[47]

We do not hear the same detailed regulations coming from Jesus. As a matter of fact, detailed regulations on moral and legal matters do not loom large in the sayings of the historical Jesus. Even more remarkably, apart from the two special cases of divorce and celibacy (see below), relatively little of the Gospel material that can claim to come from the historical Jesus deals with sexual matters.[48] Mark 9:42–47 contains general warnings about actions that "scandalize," i.e., actions that can lead oneself or others into sin. While sexual sins would no doubt be included here, they are not singled out for particular treatment. For that, we must go to Matthew's M tradition (Matt 5:27–28), which brands looking at a woman with lustful intention as an act of adultery in one's mind and will ("heart").[49] The additional statements about scandal by eye or hand that follow in Matt 5:29–30 may be Matthew's way of applying to the area of sexuality the general exhortation against scandal by hand, foot, or eye in Mark 9:43–47.

Perhaps one reason that we have so little from the historical Jesus on sexual topics is that, apart from the two special cases of divorce and celibacy, where he diverged from mainstream Judaism, his views *were* those of mainstream Judaism. Hence there was no pressing need for him to issue or for the earliest Christian Jews to enshrine moral pronouncements about matters on which all Law-abiding Jews agreed. If almost all Jews agreed that acts of fornication and adultery were wrong, there was no reason for Jesus, who shared these views (see, e.g., Mark 7:21–22; Luke 16:18), to exegete the obvious. Beyond these basic moral strictures, Jesus apparently had no interest in the details of sexual behavior that loom large, for instance, in the Mishna (e.g., the various problems connected with a menstruating woman, the type of woman a priest could marry, uncleanness resulting from a sexual discharge).

These were not the areas in which Jesus' stringency in sexual matters manifested itself. Rather, for clear examples of his rigor in matters related to sex—examples that may parallel the views of Qumran—we must focus on the two questions of divorce and celibacy.

(ii) The historical Jesus held that marriage was to be monogamous and indissoluble and that any divorce (with remarriage understood as the natural consequence) was equivalent to adultery (Mark 10:2–12; Matt 5:32 ‖ Luke 16:18; cf. 1 Cor 7:10–11). The Q saying as preserved in Luke 16:18, with its striking male-centered perspective, may represent the earliest attainable form of Jesus' teaching: "Every man who divorces his wife and marries another woman commits adultery, and the man who marries a woman divorced from her husband commits adultery."

The teaching of the Qumranites on divorce is not so easily summarized, since it is found in different forms in different documents (11QTemple 57:17–19; CD 4:20–5:2) and is open to various interpretations.[50] Does the prohibition in the documents focus on polygamy, divorce, or remarriage after the death of a spouse? Does the prohibition concern the present era or only the eschatological future? Does the prohibition hold for all Israelites or just specific persons, in particular the king? We shall treat these problems in Volume Four. Suffice it to say for now that Qumran had a very negative attitude toward divorce. In fact, many scholars think that Qumran, like Jesus, prohibited divorce entirely. My personal opinion, however, is that Qumran's prohibition of divorce, while stringent, was less than total. Indeed, some statements in the *Damascus Document* and the *Temple Scroll* may indicate that the Qumranites (or the Essenes) allowed divorce in at least some circumstances.[51]

(iii) Religious celibacy is a complicated problem in the case of both Jesus and the Qumranites (and the Essenes in general). As we saw in Volume One, the NT says nothing directly about Jesus' marital status.[52] Some scholars read the silence as meaning that Jesus, like almost any other Jew of his day, would have been married. His marriage was so taken for granted that none of his contemporaries and no NT book commented on it. However, the silence, though ambiguous, more likely should be read the other way. The NT does inform us about Jesus' mother Mary, his putative father Joseph, his four brothers James (= Jacob), Joses (= Joseph), Simon (= Simeon), and Jude (= Judah), his unnamed and uncounted sisters, and the various named women who followed and ministered to him (notably Mary Magdalene). Other women who did not literally follow him around Galilee (e.g., Martha and Mary) are also named. The Gospels even tell us forthrightly of unseemly tensions between Jesus on the one hand and his mother and brothers on the other. Granted this surprising amount of information, total silence about Jesus' wife and children and his relations with them would be exceedingly strange.

Hence the silence more likely points in the opposite direction: Jesus, like Jeremiah the prophet before him, desert-ascetics such as the Baptist and Bannus alongside him, and a few figures in rabbinic literature after him, lived a celibate life. Having seen what a strong and perduring influence the Baptist had on Jesus,[53] we may conjecture that the Baptist influenced Jesus in this area as well. Jesus' celibacy and the jibes it may have occasioned from his opponents may be the context for his shocking statement that some men make themselves eunuchs for the sake of the kingdom of heaven (Matt 19:12).[54] However, unlike the picture we are about to trace of the Essenes, there is no indication that Jesus ever made celibacy a requirement for those who wished to join his movement.

When we turn to the Essenes and Qumran, we again encounter problems about the practice of celibacy. Here, though, the problems do not come from total silence in the sources, but rather from mixed signals. Philo, Pliny the Elder, and Josephus all testify to the celibacy of the Essenes. In addition, Pliny locates the celibate Essene community in the area near the western shore of the Dead Sea, close to where the ruins of Qumran were found. Thus, the Greek and Latin sources from the 1st century A.D. agree that the Essenes practiced celibacy.

A serious problem arises, however, when we compare these sources with those Dead Sea Scrolls that most likely mirror the life and beliefs of the Essenes in general or the Qumran community in particular. In the Dead Sea Scrolls, we find no explicit statement that the Qumranites were celibate. Indeed, the *Damascus Document* presumes the existence of wives and children (CD 7:6–9; 19:2–5) and forbids polygamy (4:20–5:2). The *Rule of the Congregation* (1QSa) specifically includes "children along with women" in "the congregation of Israel in the last days" (1QSa 1:1,4). In fact, 1QSa 1:9–10 dictates that a young man who belongs to the congregation may not have sexual relations with a woman until he is a full 20 years old.

At the same time, the *Rule of the Community* (1QS), perhaps the most basic and normative document for life at Qumran itself, lacks such passages. There is no specific provision made in the community for wives and children, and consequently there is no prohibition of polygamy or divorce. This rule seems to envision a community made up only of males. How all this is to be sorted out remains the focus of lively debate among scholars. A likely solution is that one must distinguish various groups among the Essenes and perhaps even at Qumran—as well as allowing for possible variations in practice in different stages of the movement's history, which encompasses roughly 200 years.[55]

Such a distinction is not a modern invention concocted to rescue scholars from an academic dilemma. It is firmly grounded in Josephus' *Jewish War.* Right at the beginning of his most extensive—and highly laudatory—presentation of the Essenes, Josephus emphasizes and explains their practice of celibacy (*J. W.* 2.8.2 §120–121). Thus, the reader naturally goes through the rest of Josephus' essay on the Essenes with the impression that all of them were celibate. Suddenly, at the end of his presentation, almost as an afterthought, Josephus notes that there is another order or class *(tagma)* of Essenes who marry (*J. W.* 2.8.13 §160–161). This other order considers the continued procreation of the human race so important that they feel obliged to do their duty in this regard. As though to make up for this concession on the part of the married Essenes, Josephus hastens to add information about their stringent testing of their wives-to-be and their great restraint in having no intercourse with their wives during pregnancy. That this married group is the exception rather than the rule is made likely not only by Josephus' placement of it in a sort of appendix to his treatment of the Essenes in the *Jewish War* but also by his shorter essay on the Essenes in *Ant.* 18.1.5 §18–22, where he speaks only of celibate Essenes (§21).

This distinction attested by Josephus may help explain the apparently conflicting evidence. Philo and Pliny probably knew of the Palestinian Essenes more by reputation than by firsthand contact. In addition, they may have used reports that emphasized the most unusual aspects of Essene life, such as celibacy. Indeed, especially in the case of Philo, philosophical or rhetorical purposes may have favored mention of the exotic celibate Essenes and silence about the more pedestrian married Essenes. On such matters, we may rightly suppose that Josephus was better informed, since he had lived his early life in Palestine and was, in addition, of priestly lineage. Even if we harbor doubts about his touching account of the spiritual odyssey of his teenage years (*Life* 2 §7–12), he may well have had personal contact with Essenes before the disaster of A.D. 70. His superior knowledge may be reflected in the fact that he knows how to distinguish the married from the celibate Essenes.

This diversity of observance among the Essenes may help to explain the different pictures we receive from the Qumran material. The *Damascus Document* may be addressed, in at least some of its ordinances, to the wider community of Essenes living throughout Palestine, some of whom were married. This is suggested by the curious way in which the topic of wives and children is introduced in 7:6–7 of Manuscript A (and similarly in 19:2–3 of Manuscript B): "And [or: but] if they reside in camps according to the rule of the land and take wives and beget children. . . ." The "and if" may imply that an exception to the usual situation is being made. This in turn might explain the phrase "according to the rule of the land": if these members live in communities scattered throughout the land of Israel, then they may have family lives like the ordinary Jews living around them.

This might also explain why the author feels a need to provide a supporting text from the Torah (Num 30:17), which seems aimed at demonstrating that marriage and childbearing are in keeping with the Law. Thus, even the *Damascus Document,* precisely in the way it broaches the question of married Essenes, may intimate that the regular, normative, or ideal condition of Essenes, the condition that is taken for granted and therefore not explained, is the celibate state. In my opinion, the celibate state is likewise taken for granted in the *Rule of the Community.* That is why the *Rule of the Community,* which was written specifically for life at Qumran, makes no exceptions regarding married Essenes. I think it likely, therefore, that the Qumranites, at least for part of their history, practiced the celibacy that was the Essene ideal, though marriage was allowed for some groups living outside Qumran. Alternately, one might conjecture that a certain group within the Qumran community (perhaps the priestly leaders?) observed celibacy, while others did not—though I think this solution less likely.[56]

In any case, the reasons for celibacy were probably quite different for Jesus and for the Qumranites. Jesus' shocking statement about those who make themselves eunuchs *for the sake of the kingdom of heaven* suggests that somehow he saw his celibacy as part of his total, radical dedication to the proclamation of the coming kingdom and the task of regathering all Israel as this present age drew to a close. As Jeremiah, the tragic prophet, had seen himself called to celibacy as a sign "embodying" the crisis and judgment looming over Israel (Jer 16:1–4), so Jesus, the eschatological prophet, may have seen his celibacy as a sign that the present order of things was soon to cease. For those totally dedicated to the kingdom, there could be no "business as usual." Proclaiming the kingdom and calling Israel to repentance and renewal were to be his all-consuming mission. There was no time for an ordinary life, no space for a private existence.

One might even venture a further conjecture. The dispute with the Sadducees on the resurrection (Mark 12:18–27) showed us that Jesus held a particular view about the new and different life of those raised from the dead on the last day. Those raised to eternal life would be "like the angels." That is to say, while they would have human bodies, those bodies would be endowed with a new and different type of existence. With no danger of death, there would be no need to beget offspring. Hence there would be no marriage or sexual activity. In this, the bodies of the risen would be like the rarefied bodies—sexual but celibate—of the angels. Thus, it is possible that the eschatological prophet, proclaiming and realizing to some degree the coming kingdom in his own life, took upon himself as a prophetic sign the celibate state that he thought all the risen members of Israel would share on the last day. Admittedly, this last point is sheer conjecture. More solid is the supposition that Jesus, like Jeremiah, saw celibacy as part of his all-consuming service to the God who was coming to Israel in judgment and mercy.

While the Qumranites or the Essenes in general may have seen celibacy from an eschatological perspective as well, the precise reasons for celibacy probably differed from those of Jesus.[57] In view of the great concern that Qumran displays about purity rules in general and sexual activity in particular, celibacy may have simply been the extreme but logical extension of this focus on purity of the body. This becomes all the more likely when we consider the purity rules for priests engaged in the temple liturgy in Jerusalem. While actually engaged in ministering at the altar in the temple, the priests were obliged to abstain from sexual activity. This abstinence was, of course, temporary.

Qumran, however, saw itself, in its daily study of the Law, stringent observance thereof, and regular worship in the company of the angels, as the present substitute for the defiled temple in Jerusalem. If, then, the Qumranites were perpetually involved in temple service, one could easily see how the idea of perpetual celibacy might arise, especially since the community was led and spiritually molded by priests. This idea would be all the stronger because of the presence of the perpetually celibate angels at Qumran's liturgies. Thus, a stringent priestly concern for ritual purity in the temple might have led the community to share in the angels' celibacy as well as in their worship.[58]

An alternate version of this theory of purity harks back to what scholars call the OT theology of the Holy War.[59] While Israel was engaged in "the battles of the Lord," waging war against the pagan enemies of God and his people, the soldiers in the field were obliged to abstain from sexual activity. God and/or his angels were thought to be in their camp.[60] Their war, after all, was simply an extension of their service and worship of God. Since, as the *War Scroll* shows, the Qumranites looked forward to an eschatological battle in which they would fight and definitively conquer all of God's enemies, they may have seen themselves in the present as the army preparing spiritually for that battle. In constant readiness for the Holy War, they may have observed the ritual purity demanded of warriors so engaged.

To sum up, then: the celibacy of Jesus on the one hand and of the Essenes or Qumranites on the other may well have shared an eschatological basis.

Beyond that common basis, though, the precise nature of the eschatological mind-set favoring celibacy probably differed widely. For Jesus, celibacy was a prophetic sign of the coming and yet already present kingdom of God. For Qumran, it was a priestly expression of the stringent ritual purity demanded of those who were the living temple of God and who therefore enjoyed the company of the angels as they worshiped God and prepared for the final Holy War.

(b) On the question of taking *oaths,* both Jesus and the Essenes show disapproval of the multiplication and the frivolous use of oaths.[61] For both, major factors in this negative attitude are the obligation always to speak the truth and the obligation to avoid irreverence for God and God's name. In *J.W.* 2.8.6 §135, Josephus states that anything the Essenes say has more weight than an oath, so great is their reputation for truthfulness. In fact, they avoid an oath as something worse than perjury. In their view, if a person cannot be believed unless he invokes God, he is already branded a liar. The Essenes' rejection of oaths on principle may explain in part why Herod the Great dispensed them from an oath of loyalty to himself (*Ant.* 15.10.4 §371).[62]

Yet Josephus modifies these absolute statements by noting that candidates for membership in the Essenes must take frightening oaths before they are admitted to full membership (*J.W.* 2.8.7 §139). Such oath-taking is confirmed by 1QS 5:8, where the novice entering the community at Qumran binds himself by oath "to return to the Law of Moses." The rite of entrance into the community probably took place at the community's annual feast of the renewal of the covenant, when the blessings and curses of the covenant were recited and all the members replied "Amen, Amen"—thus, in effect, renewing the oath they had all taken at their entrance (1QS 1:18–2:19).

Similarly, the *Damascus Document,* addressing the wider community of Essenes throughout Palestine, speaks of the "oath of the covenant" taken when the children of members who were already enrolled in the community reach the age for their own enrollment (CD 15:5–13). The *Damascus Document* also provides us with a possible explanation of the tension already noted in Josephus' statement about Essene oaths. Although the text of CD 15:1–4 is not perfectly preserved, it seems to prohibit all oaths using divine names like "God" and "Lord" and also all oaths that invoke the Mosaic Torah. Significantly, an exemption is made for the oaths taken by those entering the community "with the curses of the covenant" (15:1–2).[63] Apparently these curses of the covenant could be used as a way of swearing when one is under judicial examination (15:3). This interpretation coheres well with the section of the *Damascus Document* explicitly titled in the text "concerning the oath" (CD 9:8–12). One member of the community is not to make another member swear in private. One is to swear only before judges and at their bidding. In addition, when an object is stolen and the thief cannot be identified, the owner may utter "the oath of the curse" against the thief who has not confessed.[64]

A certain tension in the treatment of oaths can also be found in the NT. In the Sermon on the Mount, Jesus forbids all oaths (Matt 5:33–37; cf. Jas 5:12). Yet this isolated M tradition must be balanced against another M tradition: Jesus' polemic against the (supposed) teaching of the Pharisees concerning which oaths are binding and which not (Matt 23:16–22). On the level of Matthew's Gospel, though, there may not be a strict contradiction, since the vitriolic polemic of Matthew 23 has a mocking, *ad hominem* tone to it. The thrust of the passage is to criticize and reject casuistic teaching on oaths rather than to propose an alternate teaching on the topic.[65] For Matthew, part of the horror of Peter's denial of Jesus during the passion may be that Peter seals his denial with an oath (Matt 26:72,74).

Curiously, apart from the variant form of Matt 5:33–37 in Jas 5:12, the rest of the NT seems to be ignorant of a total prohibition of oaths. Early and late, Paul uses oaths in his epistles (1 Thess 2:5; 2 Cor 1:23; Gal 1:20; Phil 1:8; Rom 1:9). John, the seer of the Book of Revelation, sees nothing wrong with an angel swearing an oath in the name "of the One who lives forever and ever" (Rev 10:5, citing Dan 12:7). In a way, even Mark presents Jesus as uttering a type of oath when the Pharisees ask for a sign from heaven (Mark 8:11–13). Jesus' brief reply in v 12—usually translated as "No sign shall be given to this generation"—is actually the abbreviated form of an OT oath formula that includes a conditional curse: "If a sign is given to this generation [by me, may God do so-and-so to me in punishment]." [66] But if, as is usually the case, an oath is understood to be the invocation of God (either by naming him or by using a surrogate noun like "heaven") to bear witness to the truth of what the oath-taker says, Mark 8:13 as it stands hardly qualifies as an oath.

In any event, the total prohibition of oaths in Matt 5:34 may indeed come from the historical Jesus. It is discontinuous with the practice of both Judaism before him and most of Christianity (notably Paul) after him—James 5:12 being the sole exception.[67] Thus, in comparison to Essene discipline, Jesus' *total* prohibition of oaths parallels his *total* prohibition of divorce. While, on both questions, stringent Essene practice tended in the same direction of prohibition, the Essenes did not adopt a total ban on either oaths or (perhaps) divorce.

(c) Moving from oaths in general to a particular type of oath or vow, we can find a slight parallel between Jesus' objection to the devious use of a vow and a similar prohibition in the *Damascus Document.*

In Mark 7:1–23, we have a large composite passage that polemicizes against the Pharisees' use of the "tradition of the elders." [68] Jesus claims that, at times, keeping this tradition in effect annuls the basic commandments of God in Scripture (vv 7–8). In a subunit, 7:9–13, Jesus contrasts God's commandment in the Decalogue to honor (and therefore support economically) one's father and mother with the pious subterfuge of dedicating part of one's goods to God and therefore removing it from the fund of support on which one's parents might rely. In v 11, Jesus refers to this kind of vow, which dedicates some possession or property to a sacred purpose, with the Aramaic (and Hebrew) word *qorbān* (which Mark aptly translates as *dōron,* "gift"). [69] Jesus does not object to vowed gifts as such, but rather to the devious use of them to avoid one's prior and overriding obligation to one's parents.

The question of whether the substance of Mark 7:9–13 (not the exact wording) goes back to the historical Jesus is difficult to answer, since the unit has no parallel elsewhere in the Gospels. Hence multiple attestation is lacking. At the very least, we can assign the unit to pre-70 Palestine, Mark's Gospel having been written somewhere around A.D. 70. The Aramaic *qorbān,* which was later translated as "gift" when this pre-Marcan tradition was put into Greek, offers sufficient indication of a Palestinian provenance.

In theory, the tradition could have been invented by first-generation Christian Jews in Palestine. However, we have no evidence from any source that such an abstruse question about *qorbān* occupied Christian Jews in Palestine in the decades after Jesus death and constituted a dividing line between themselves and other Jewish groups. As both the letters of Paul and the Acts of the Apostles indicate, major questions like circumcision, food laws, struggles over leadership within the church, and relations with Gentile Christians made up the agenda of the increasingly beleaguered Christian Jews in Palestine between A.D. 40 to 66.

By default, therefore, I think it more likely that the *qorbān* dispute originated in a debate between Jesus and certain other Palestinian Jews (possibly of the Pharisaic persuasion) who differed with him on the validity or revocable nature of a vow that deprived one's parents of support. [70] The objection from early form critics like Bultmann that the unit has Jesus citing Scripture and arguing about a particular question of *hălākâ* carries weight only for those who maintain the strange image of a 1st-century Jewish teacher in Palestine who never quoted Jewish Scriptures in arguments and never discussed concrete moral and ritual behavior with his fellow Jews. [71] The various and at times conflicting views on oaths and vows found in the *Damascus*

Document, Philo, Josephus, and the later rabbinic literature suggest that the subject was a lively topic of debate in Judaism at the turn of the era.[72] That a popular teacher like Jesus would have expressed his views on the subject, especially if it helped score a point against a debating partner, coheres perfectly with what we know of both Jesus and Palestinian Judaism at the time.

As a matter of fact, the problem of annulling an oath or a vow arises in the *Damascus Document* as well. To be sure, the word *qorbān* does not appear as such in CD 16:1–20, a fragmentary text that continues the treatment of oaths and vows begun in column 15. Yet, within the larger context of various questions about when one should annul an oath or a vow, a case similar to Jesus' pronouncement about *qorbān* is mentioned.[73] Two fragmentary lines (CD 16:14–15) read: "[Let no] man sanctify [i.e., dedicate to God and so set apart from another's use] the food of [his mouth], for this is what he [i.e., God through the prophet Micah in Mic 7:2] said: 'Each man entraps his neighbor with a ban [*ḥērem,* the dedication of something to the exclusive use of God].' "[74]

While the situation is not the same as that denounced by Jesus in Mark 7, there is an underlying similarity. In each case, a basic obligation of an Israelite toward his fellow Israelites (supporting one's parents or sharing food with a needy neighbor) is subverted by vowing part of one's possessions (money or food) to God. In each case, such devious use of a pious practice to avoid a primary religious duty is rejected. In their common stance, both Jesus and the Essenes, rather than displaying direct dependence of one on the other, stand together in the age-old prophetic tradition of Israel, which regularly censured external displays of piety that subverted the deeper religious intent of the Torah.

In sum, then, both the Essenes and Jesus expressed a disdain for oaths, especially when needlessly multiplied or sworn in a frivolous manner. However, it appears that Jesus, when addressing his own followers, forbade any swearing at all. When addressing his debating partners, probably the Pharisees, Jesus pointed out the inconsistencies or difficulties that their limited acceptance of oaths involved. In contrast, while they were in principle opposed to oaths, both the Essenes in general and the Qumranites in particular used solemn oaths to celebrate and renew the members' entrance into their community. It may be that, beyond that, some stringent groups like the Qumranites forbade all oaths. As the *Damascus Document* indicates, though, at least some Essenes allowed a limited use of oaths and vows.

(d) As to their views on *wealth and property,* the positions of Jesus and the Essenes once again register both similarities and differences.[75] As for Qumran, the *Rule of the Community* orders that after an indeterminate period of instruction and an initial examination (1QS 6:15–16), the candidate for entrance into the community undergo one further year of training (6:16–17). If he passes the examination at the end of that year, the candidate is allowed to touch "the purity" (perhaps ritually pure solid food and its vessels). His property, however, while given over to the custody of the "overseer" or "examiner" *(hammĕbaqqēr)* of the community's possessions, is not yet merged with that of the community (6:18–21).

After a second year and another examination, the candidate becomes a full member of the community. He is allowed to share the pure drink of the community; in other words, he can now participate fully in the community's meals. Moreover, his property is completely merged with the community's (6:21–22). Apparently, then, full members of the Qumran community practiced a complete community of goods or—from the viewpoint of the individual's ownership of personal property—poverty.[76] This boundary-marker that separated the Qumranites from the outside world was taken most seriously. If it was discovered that a member had lied about his property or money, he was to be punished by being excluded from sharing the pure food of the community for one year and was to be fined one-fourth of the food allotted him (6:24–25). Sharing all goods with other members without any charge was a distinguishing sign of belonging to the community. Hence no Qumranite was to accept food, drink, or goods from outsiders without paying for them—no doubt from the common treasury (5:16–17).

This Qumranite life of shared goods and individual poverty largely coincides with the composite picture of Essene life that results from putting together various statements of Philo and Josephus.[77] (At times, though, traits specific to the Essene communities scattered around Palestine surface in their accounts.) According to Philo and Josephus, groups of Essenes lived together and shared common meals under their leaders (*Apol.* 11.5; *Prob.* 12 §85–86; *J.W.* 2 §129–133). Having only contempt for wealth, the Essenes practiced a total community of goods. Hence all new members had to hand over their possessions to the group, thus obliterating economic differences within the brotherhood (*J.W.* 2.8.3 §122–123).

In return for the surrender of all their property, the new members received a small pickax, a loin cloth, and a white robe (§137).[78] A particular officer of the community saw to the members' needs, including food, clothing, and care of the sick and aged (*Apol.* 11.13; *Prob.* 12 §87). Individual members were allowed without special permission from their leaders *(epimelētai)* to help others in need, but any assistance given to the members' relatives required the permission of the financial administrator *(epitropos)* (*J.W.* 2.8.6 §134). The members earned their livelihood mainly, though not entirely, through farming, raising livestock, and various crafts. The money earned by these activities was given to the person appointed treasurer. Commerce and the making of weapons were absolutely prohibited (*Apol.* 11.8–10; *Prob.* 12 §78). In sum, while there are some differences, on the whole the descriptions of Josephus and Philo point to the community life of Qumran described in the *Rule of the Community.*

The *Damascus Document,* while not as detailed on questions of the disposal of members' property, clearly differs in some ways from the picture presented both in the *Rule of the Community* and in Philo and Josephus. This difference no doubt derives from the fact that the *Damascus Document* addresses not a quasi-monastic community such as Qumran but rather the various Essene settlements dispersed throughout the towns of Israel. These Essenes are probably the "other order" of Essenes described briefly by Josephus (*J. W.* 2.8.13 §160–161). In these settlements or "camps," at least some Essenes married and had children. Hence the disposition of property would naturally differ from that of a more monastic group, since the strict observance of poverty (in conjunction with the community of goods) practiced at Qumran was not feasible. No matter how much the inner life of the scattered Essene communities might be cordoned off from the towns in which the sectarians lived, economic reality exerted its influence and required some interchange with ordinary Jews living around them.

Accordingly, the Essenes in the *Damascus Document* were allowed to trade with non-Essenes, provided they informed the "overseer" or "examiner" *(mĕbaqqēr)* in their settlement. Commerce, however, could have no place in the relations among community members. Fellow Essenes were to be given what they needed out of charity (CD 13:14–16).[79] Thus, in place of a strict regimen of holding all goods in common stood a strict regimen of charitable giving. The Essenes living in towns were obliged to contribute at least two days' wages per month to a common fund, which was administered by the overseer and the judges of the community to relieve the needs of the sick and the poor (CD 14:12–16).

For all the differences between the quasi-monastic Qumranites and the Essenes living in towns, both groups clearly shared one goal: to avoid the accumulation of vast amounts of private property in the hands of relatively few individuals. In other words, they sought to avoid the wide economic and social gaps between haves and have-nots that plagued most of ancient Mediterranean society. The spirit of community and brotherhood was to be fostered by seeing to it that everyone lived on the same socioeconomic level and shared his goods with those in need. No doubt, this was easier to achieve with the Qumran discipline of total surrender of a member's property to the community. Only a certain approximation of the ideal was possible in Essene communities where married men possessing some property had to support their wives and children as well as contribute to a common fund.

Once again, Jesus' teaching on wealth and poverty shows both similarities with and differences from the Essenes'. That Jesus saw wealth as a danger to total commitment to God and acceptance of his proclamation of the kingdom is supported in varying degrees by the criteria of multiple attestation of sources and forms, embarrassment, discontinuity, and coherence.

(i) In the *Marcan* tradition, Jesus proclaims, to the astonishment of his disciples, that it is extremely difficult for a rich man to be saved. To impress the idea firmly on the resistant minds of his disciples, Jesus employs one of his most arresting metaphors: "It is easier for a camel to pass through the eye of a needle than for a rich man to enter the kingdom of God." [80] Then he adds a comforting afterthought to cushion the shock of his sweeping pronouncement: "It [i.e., the salvation of a rich man] is impossible for humans, but not for God; for all things are possible for God" (Mark 10:23–27). As we shall see, the substance of this teaching is supported by other Gospel stories and forms. Emphasis on the dangers of wealth coheres with Jewish apocalyptic thought in general, which took a dim view of the wealthy. It also coheres with Jesus' own radical lifestyle and that of his immediate disciples insofar as his ministry meant leaving one's work and home. Jesus and his disciples had to depend on a precarious support system of voluntary donations of money and goods and on the hospitality offered by those well-disposed sedentary adherents who were (paradoxically) relatively well-off. [81]

In Mark's redaction, [82] what occasions this teaching by Jesus is his encounter with a rich man who asks him in the most fawning fashion what he must do to *"inherit* eternal life" (Mark 10:17–22). [83] (One wonders whether inheriting was the way he came to his earthly wealth as well.) Jesus replies coolly with a summary reference to some of the Ten Commandments. The rich man insists that he has kept all these commandments from his youth. Jesus then raises the stakes to test the man's sincerity and commitment. One thing still is lacking, says Jesus—perhaps not without some irony, since the "one thing" involves everything the man has. Jesus orders the rich man to sell whatever he possesses, to give it to the poor, and then to follow him in the literal, physical sense demanded of disciples. The rich man's initial enthusiasm collapses in the face of Jesus' radical demand. The story, which is a mixture of a scholarly dialogue and a call story, ends on a tragic note. The man's face fell on hearing Jesus' demand. "He went away sad, for he had many possessions" (Mark 10:22).

Does this story go back to some incident in the life of Jesus? To be sure, the story serves a theological and literary purpose in this section of Mark's Gospel (8:27–10:52), dominated as it is by the three predictions of Jesus' passion, death, and resurrection. Having twice foretold his passion (8:31; 9:31), Jesus begins his fateful journey to Jerusalem (10:1). On his way, he issues various teachings on diverse states of life as well as on the challenges those states will pose for his followers (and in Mark's eyes, for future Christians if they wish to follow Jesus, metaphorically speaking, on the way of the cross). Jesus first addresses the question of marriage and divorce (10:2–12), then the place of children in the kingdom (10:13–16), then the dangers the rich face on the way to salvation (10:17–27), and, finally, the great rewards promised to and fierce demands made upon his immediate disciples, especially the Twelve (10:28–31,35–45). Significantly, embedded in this treatment of rewards and demands is the third and fullest prediction of the passion (10:32–34).

Still, despite the fact that the story of the rich man conveniently fits Mark's theological agenda in chap. 10, some of the criteria of historicity argue for its origin in Jesus' ministry. First, there is the criterion of embarrassment. The rich man greets Jesus in a highly unusual and fawning manner. Kneeling before Jesus, he asks, "Good teacher, what must I do to inherit eternal life?" (10:17).[84] Jesus brusquely rejects the adulation—which will prove to be superficial—with the (to Christians) shocking reply, "Why do you call me good? No one is good except God alone" (10:18).[85] It is difficult to imagine that the post-Easter church, as it sought to win converts to its faith that the risen Jesus was Lord, Messiah, and Son of God, went out of its way to create this particular answer. Indeed, so troubled is Matthew by Jesus' reply that he changes Mark's text to the innocuous "Why do you ask me *about* what is good?"—which leads neatly into the reference to the Ten Commandments (Matt 19:17–18).

Likewise embarrassing—and discontinuous within the bounds of the Marcan tradition—is the unique failure of Jesus' peremptory call to have its desired effect. Elsewhere in Mark, Jesus' explicit or implicit call to discipleship, to the circle of the Twelve, or to mission is always effective (Mark 1:16–20; 2:13–14; 3:13–19; 6:7–13,30; 10:46–52). The failure of Jesus to win over the rich man stands out like a sore thumb. The magnetic appeal of the charismatic Jesus is seen to have its limits.

Also dissimilar to the other Marcan stories of Jesus calling individuals to discipleship is the demand that the rich man sell everything he has, give it all to the poor, and then follow Jesus as a (totally impoverished) disciple. Interestingly, Jesus does not make such a precise and detailed economic demand on the other individuals he calls to discipleship, e.g., Peter, Andrew, James,

John, or Levi. Admittedly, they must leave their present occupations and homes for the indefinite future to follow Jesus. But nothing is said about their being obliged to sell all their possessions and give them to the poor. The very fact that, after Peter's call to discipleship, he can still host Jesus in his home at Capernaum, where his mother-in-law serves the whole group a meal, indicates that at least Mark did not think that every call to discipleship involved a call to total self-impoverishment (Mark 1:29–31).[86] Nor was such a sweeping obligation imposed later on upon people entering the Christian church of the first generation.[87]

Thus, Jesus' demand of complete self-impoverishment as a condition for discipleship seems unique to—and tailored to—the special case of this rich individual. It is situation-specific: the unheard-of rigor of Jesus' condition is meant to unmask the insincerity and lack of commitment of this affluent flatterer, who knows how to kneel but not how to give. In brief, then, the criteria of embarrassment and dissimilarity argue well for the basic historicity of the incident and of Jesus' warning about the dangers of wealth, occasioned by the rich man's refusal to accept Jesus' call.

(ii) In the *Q tradition*, we hear the positive reason why Jesus and his followers can waive any interest in wealth. In Matt 6:25–33 ‖ Luke 12:22–31, Jesus exhorts his followers not to be anxious about food, clothing, and the other goods that this world considers the necessities of life.[88] They should instead trust the providential care of the Creator who is also their Father. Provided that they keep their minds and lives fixed solely on the center of Jesus' preaching, the kingdom of God, the Father will take care of the rest. Here is a prime example of how Jesus weaves together OT wisdom themes concerning the uselessness of anxiety in the face of God's governance of creation with his major eschatological theme of the kingdom. The traditional exhortations of wisdom receive a new motivation and direction as they are set within the overarching framework of the coming yet present kingdom of God.[89]

In effect, Jesus sets before his followers a clear either/or choice. In typical apocalyptic style, Jesus stresses that two competing forces, the divine and the demonic, are struggling to control human hearts. Caught between the two opponents, humans have no hope of being completely autonomous individuals, free of both contending powers. Their only chance to choose lies in selecting which of the two forces will dominate their lives, which of the two masters they will serve. Human nature being what it is, humans try to have it both ways and avoid a final choice. But that is already to have made the wrong choice.

Another Q saying (Matt 6:24 ‖ Luke 16:13) sharpens this message to a fine point.[90] Jesus sternly rebukes humanity's universal penchant for straddling the fence by insisting, "No one can serve [or: be a slave of] two lords. For either he will hate the one and love the other, or he will cling to the one and despise the other." Most striking in this logion is how Jesus then concludes the brief contrast by making the general choice between the two masters more specific: "You cannot serve God and Mammon."

The word "Mammon" (in Greek: *mamōnas*) represents the Aramaic word *māmōnāʾ* (Hebrew: *māmôn*). The Hebrew form of the word occurs in some of the Qumran documents as well as in the Mishna.[91] In both of these collections of Jewish literature, it has the general sense of "wealth," "riches," "money," "property," or "value," with none of the demonic overtones of idolatry that Jesus gives it in Matt 6:24 par.[92] Indeed, in the Mishna, it is the normal word for "money" or "wealth." So far is *māmôn* from being the quintessence of evil that, in exegeting the *Šĕmaʿ* ("Hear, O Israel . . ."), the Mishna explains the command to love God "with all your strength" to mean "with all your wealth" (*māmônekā* in *m. Ber.* 9:5).[93]

Quite different, then, is the imaginative use Jesus makes of the word. By creating a stark opposition between serving Mammon and "serving" (i.e., worshiping and obeying) God, Jesus personifies Mammon as a false god. He thus confronts every hearer with the primordial choice with which the prophets confronted Israel: the true God or the false idols—which will you worship and obey? Money and property can become so all-absorbing an interest that possessions begin to possess the possessor rather than vice versa. It is precisely Jesus' call to total dedication to the kingdom of God that exposes money as the great alternate object of total dedication, an object that brooks no rivalry. Both the Father of Jesus and Mammon are jealous gods. Jesus therefore presses the point that there can be no compromise; one must choose. In brief, the presence of this Aramaic word *māmônāʾ* (transliterated as *mamōnas*) in a Greek saying, the appearance of *mamōnas* only in the sayings of Jesus within the NT, the unusual and imaginative use of this common Aramaic word to depict a demonic force or false god pitted against the true God in an eschatological struggle, and the coherence of this radical eschatological morality with the demands of Jesus seen elsewhere in the Gospels all argue for the authenticity of this saying.[94]

Jesus' criticism of wealth in the Q tradition is balanced by his concern for the poor. A prime example is Luke's stark version of the first beatitude, "Happy are [you] poor" (Luke 6:20), generally held by scholars to be more original than Matthew's "Happy are the poor in spirit" (Matt 5:3).[95] Similarly, many think that Luke's version of the Parable of the Great Supper (14:16–24), with its concern for the poor and the sick, represents the original form of the parable more closely than does Matthew's version (22:2–10), which transforms a simple supper into a royal wedding feast that serves as an allegory of salvation history.[96]

(iii) The special *Lucan* tradition (L) contains a great amount of material dealing with wealth and poverty.[97] However, since such themes are a major theological concern of Luke and apparently of his church, the origin of these L traditions in the ministry of the historical Jesus is, in some cases, open to serious question. For example, we have already seen that the present form of the parable of Lazarus and the rich man (Luke 16:19–31), made up of a number of different traditions, is probably a composition of Luke.[98] Nevertheless, the sheer amount of L material dealing with the topic of wealth is impressive, and most scholars would be willing to admit that some of the sayings go back to Jesus. But which ones?

The difficulty of deciding that question can be seen, for example, in the Parable of the Rich Fool (Luke 12:16–21). The parable takes up a common theme in the OT prophetic and wisdom literature: the folly of heaping up wealth and luxury in the illusory hope that one can control one's future. What the fool fails to understand is that death can, at any moment, put a sudden end to all one's grandiose plans, and then the piled-up wealth passes to someone else. To be sure, this parable could go back to Jesus. He was both a prophet and a wisdom teacher. But is there anything in this parable that could not just as easily have come from any imaginative Jewish prophet or wisdom teacher of the time or from some disciple of Jesus who had picked up the master's way of spinning out a parable? While I tend to think that the parable does come from Jesus, I readily admit that one cannot be sure.[99]

Perhaps a better candidate is the curious incident with which Luke prefaces this parable. A man from the crowd listening to Jesus asks him to insert himself into a family quarrel about dividing an inheritance (12:13–14). Jesus brusquely dismisses the petition with a rhetorical question that was probably as shocking to Christian ears as was "Why do you call me good?" in Mark 10:18. For in Luke 12:14, Jesus responds to the petitioner with the dismissive remark, "Man, who appointed me judge or arbitrator over [the two of] you?" This from the evangelist who insists in Acts that God has appointed Jesus Lord and Messiah, the judge of the living and the dead (Acts 2:36; 10:42; 17:31)! Hence the criterion of embarrassment suggests that this incident does go back to the historical Jesus.[100] The blunt statement that no one had appointed Jesus the judge of humans and their affairs does not sound like an invention of a church that was struggling to promote faith in Jesus as Lord and eschatological judge.

But what did the historical Jesus mean by his brusque rhetorical question?

Unlike revered teachers of the Law who were asked at times to decide questions of inheritance and who were honored to play such an influential role in society, Jesus the eschatological prophet is expressing here his disdain (not to say contempt) for minor matters of property when he has a pressing mission to proclaim the kingdom of God to all Israel. The implied rebuke to the speaker is that he should be asking Jesus for something much more vital than an earthly inheritance. One is tempted to say that he should be repeating—but with sincerity—the question of Mark's shallow rich man: "What must I do to *inherit* eternal life?"

To sum up: not all the examples cited in this brief survey of sayings about wealth need go back to the historical Jesus, though I think that many of them probably do. My main point, however, is that, whether we agree on this or that saying, the overall argument from multiple attestation of sources and forms indicates that the historical Jesus did take a strong stance against excessive concern about or trust in money and property. He himself had left behind his occupation as a woodworker and apparently lived off voluntary donations and offers of hospitality. His peremptory call to his disciples to follow him physically on his itinerant ministry naturally tended to detach them from their work, homes, and property for an indefinite future. In at least one case, Jesus even demanded that a rich man sell all his goods, give them to the poor, and follow him literally. The failure of the rich man to rise to the challenge was a perfect example of the fact that, at the most basic level of their existence, humans are the total slaves of either God or money. One or the other dominates and shapes their lives and choices, however much they try to straddle the fence. Rich people are thus in grave spiritual danger; their salvation is nothing short of a miracle possible to God alone.

And yet, for all this criticism of wealth as a potential false god seducing people from loyalty to the one true God, Jesus did not demand that all those who adhered to him in a spiritual sense, all those who in some way believed in him or accepted his message, had to forsake their livelihoods and homes or had to sell all they had and give it to the poor. If that had been the case, there would have been no Marthas and Marys providing a support system of hospitality as Jesus and his entourage traveled the roads of Palestine. There would have been no female companions who were affluent enough to help support him and his disciples "out of their means"—means that apparently they had not simply given up. There would have been no rich and repentant Zacchaeus, supplying Jesus with hospitality while promising to give *half* of his goods to the poor and to make up for any fraud he had perpetrated with fourfold restitution.

To be sure, Jesus always remained critical of wealth as a dangerous temptation. He directed a major part of his ministry to the poor of Palestine and felicitated them rather than the rich as the ones for whom the kingdom was meant. But this did not translate into a one-size-fits-all policy on wealth and poverty when it came to dealing with his adherents. From some he demanded that all their goods be given to the poor. From others he demanded an open-ended commitment as disciples, which involved leaving behind their homes, work, and property—but with nothing being said about selling off every-thing and giving the proceeds to the poor.[101] From still others he demanded support and hospitality, given from the supply of goods these adherents had and presumably would continue to have.

Here in particular Jesus differed from the Qumranites. To become a mem-ber of Qumran one *had* to surrender all of one's goods—not to the poor in general but to the community one joined. The community considered itself the community of "the poor"—with good reason, since the economic poverty of the individual was real and stark. At the same time, we should re-member that we are dealing here with the vocabulary of poverty, which is suffused with a long theological tradition stemming from the OT, especially the Psalms and the prophetic literature. The mere presence of this theological vocabulary of poverty in various OT, Jewish, and Christian texts should not automatically be taken as a complete and sober description of economic des-titution. The specific theological context must always be taken into account. At Qumran, the surrender of personal goods, while certainly a rejection of money as the center of one's life, also guaranteed that the novice would be supplied with basic necessities from the community that now assumed re-sponsibility for the new member's welfare. The Essenes who lived in towns scattered throughout Israel represented a different situation from that of ei-ther Jesus or the Qumranites. In the regimen of such Essenes, jobs were held in Jewish towns, money was made, and one's wife and children were thus supported. But, within the sectarian Essene group one belonged to, one was obliged to make regular fixed contributions to the common fund that aided the sick and the destitute. The yawning chasms between rich and poor that marred ordinary society were thus carefully avoided, though the abstemious life of the Essenes in towns was hardly as stark as that of the inhabitants of Qumran.

Intriguingly, then, while Jesus, the Essenes living in towns, and the Qum-ranites all expressed and lived out a sharp critique of a society that made money its secret god, all three structured this critique in markedly different ways as they lived and moved in or apart from regular Jewish society. It may not be purely accidental that the self-designation of Jesus and the Qumran-ites differs on this point. The Qumranites proudly called themselves "the poor," echoing the spirituality of many OT psalms and prophets. The label accurately described the economic poverty of every individual who was a full member of Qumran, proclaimed Qumran's spiritual stance of being totally dependent on God while renouncing the false supports of this world, and perhaps also intimated an underlying political message overheard likewise in the psalms, prophets, and intertestamental literature: we are the party of God that is temporarily and unjustly out of power.

Jesus' use of the word "poor" in relation to himself is strikingly different. As the eschatological prophet, he singles out the poor in his audience and felicitates them (Luke 6:20 par.); he proclaims good news to the poor (Luke 7:22 par.; cf. 4:18); he demands that a rich man sell all his goods and give the profits to the poor before he can follow Jesus (Mark 10:21 parr.); he reminds his disciples that they always have the poor with them, while they will not always have him (Mark 14:7 par. ‖ John 12:8).[102] What is remarkable in all these statements is that Jesus implicitly sets himself over against and distinguishes himself from the poor, about whom he is so concerned. In Mark 14:7 par., as in a number of other Gospel texts, someone speaks of giving money to the poor, *not* to Jesus. Zacchaeus promises to give half of his possessions to the poor, not to the Jesus who has invited himself to Zacchaeus' house (Luke 19:8). At the Johannine Last Supper, the disciples think that the departing Judas may be leaving to give some money to the poor from the common purse he held for Jesus' group (John 13:29). Most pointedly, Jesus—unlike some later Christians—never directly calls himself "poor," and he does not make that word the defining title of his entire movement. I do not intend by these observations to deny that, from an economic viewpoint, Jesus was poor (Matt 8:20 par.: "the Son of Man has nowhere to lay his head"), or that his lifestyle may be appealed to by Christians as a basis for a spirituality of poverty. But one must notice that, unlike the Qumranites, Jesus does not define himself or his whole group with the word "poor." Jesus says that he wishes to help the poor, not that he is one of the poor. His historical self-understanding and self-designation should not be distorted by later theological views or a desire to assimilate him to Qumran.

D. Jesus and Qumran/the Essenes: Notable Points of Contrast

Having run through this list of similarities and dissimilarities, I think it important—even at the risk of some repetition—to focus on certain notable points of contrast between Jesus and Qumran. I do so in part for pedagogical reasons, since often these points of contrast are not given due consideration, especially in the popular literature on the subject that tends to exalt the similarities between Jesus and Qumran, if not their supposed identity.

However, before we examine individual points of contrast, the great overarching difference between the two historical phenomena we are studying should be underscored. The Essenes were a Jewish sectarian movement in Palestine that spanned some two hundred years of what is vaguely called the intertestamental period. They arose as a distinct sect in Palestine in the early-to-middle period of the second century B.C. and perdured as an organized group in Palestine until the First Jewish War (A.D. 66–70). The subgroup of Qumranites settled at Qumran in the wilderness of Judea between the middle and end of the second century B.C. and lasted until A.D. 68. The Qumran community was founded by the Teacher of Righteousness, an anonymous figure who no doubt belonged to the priestly aristocracy in Jerusalem and who may even have functioned for a while as high priest. After their founding, the Qumranites constructed a series of buildings, developed a highly complex internal organization with detailed rules for daily life, and supported an industrious scribal group that both copied manuscripts brought in from outside the community and produced a whole new corpus of religious literature proper to Qumran.

A thumbnail description of Jesus of Nazareth could hardly be more different. A Jewish layman from Nazareth in Galilee, a woodworker with no professional education as a scribe or a student of the Law, Jesus spent two years and some months (A.D. 28–30) traveling around Palestine, mostly in Galilee and on pilgrimages to the Jerusalem temple. In his itinerant ministry, he harked back to the ancient tradition of the oral prophets of Israel rather than to the more recent tradition of learned scribes composing apocalypses and other esoteric literature. We cannot even be sure that Jesus could read, though it seems more probable that he could.[103] Neither he nor his immediate disciples produced any written work during his public ministry. His group of disciples, including the inner circle of the Twelve, did not break with mainstream Judaism during Jesus' ministry. They continued to frequent the temple and take part in the festivals presided over by the reigning high priest Caiaphas. Therefore, strictly speaking, they did not qualify as a sect in the sense that the Qumranites did.[104]

More specifically, Jesus seems to have combined in his ministry a number of different religious roles: an eschatological, miracle-working prophet in the guise of Elijah, an exorcist, a prophet who felt commissioned to gather the scattered tribes of Israel together in the end time and who created a nucleus of twelve followers to begin the process, a religious guru who gathered male and female disciples around him and had them follow him on his itinerant ministry, a teacher of *hǎlākâ* (specific rules of concrete behavior in keeping with the Jewish Law), a wisdom teacher and spinner of parables who taught the common people, and—possibly toward the end of his ministry—a prophet who made at least implicit claims about being the Messiah. Such claims may have led to his execution by the Roman prefect Pontius Pilate under the accusation of trying to make himself "the King of the Jews." In the case of the Teacher of Righteousness, some Qumran texts have been interpreted as indicating that he was put to death by his enemies. While this interpretation is not impossible, in my opinion there is no clear and convincing evidence that the Teacher of Righteousness met a violent end at the hands of the ruling authorities in Jerusalem.[105] Likewise, we have no indication that the Teacher of Righteousness, during his lifetime, ever claimed to be the Messiah. Any parallel between the Teacher of Righteousness and Jesus on these points would have to be restricted to persecution by the reigning high priest—though, obviously, the persecution would be for very different reasons: a rival high priest championing rival ritual rules in the temple as opposed to a disruptive lay prophet and possible messianic claimant.

It is under this vast overarching canopy of basic differences between the centuries-old institution of Qumran and the two-year itinerant ministry of an eschatological prophet, healer, and lay teacher from Galilee that any individual dissimilarities must be viewed. As with the list above, it is convenient, though somewhat arbitrary, to gather prime examples of contrast under major headings.

1. Approach to detailed hǎlākâ

Qumran in particular and the Essenes in general display a fierce, stringent and—no doubt in the eyes of most Palestinian Jews—extreme observance of the Law, both in and beyond its letter. The documents of Qumran and the ancient descriptions of the Essenes evince an intense interest in interpreting, developing, and specifying the exact observance of *hǎlākâ*. One need only think of the prohibition of defecating on the sabbath or spitting in the assembly of the congregation, of the frequent lustrations that are required of the sectarians, or of the observance of ritual purity to the point of at least some members of the Qumran community remaining celibate. Strict punishment is meted out for offenses like guffawing foolishly or stretching out one's left hand to perform certain actions.[106] To take but one Essene document in particular: the *Damascus Document* ranges widely over rules dealing with the ordeal of a wife suspected of adultery, the diagnosis of skin diseases, the impurity that results from bodily fluids and childbirth, fraudulent arrangements of marriages, and the purity of the temple and of Jerusalem. It includes various dietary laws that go beyond the requirements of the written Torah as well as a penal code to deal with transgressions of the community's discipline. To take another example: the so-called *Halakic Letter* (4QMMT) concerns itself with the details of temple and purity rules, e.g., whether, when sacrificing pregnant animals, one may sacrifice the mother and her son on the same day, or whether a flowing liquid carries impurity from one container to another.

In contrast, Jesus, as presented in the Synoptic Gospels, explicitly rejects a fierce focus on purity rules and on what he considers in general to be minor points of the Law. More significant, though, in all four Gospels, is the glaring absence of the vast majority of the legal concerns treated in the Qumran documents. As we shall see in Volume Four, this absence is not to be interpreted as Jesus' rejection or abrogation of the written Mosaic Law. As a Palestinian Jew of the 1st century, Jesus takes the Mosaic Law for granted as the normative expression of God's will for Israelite conduct. The Law is certainly subject to interpretation; but, however it is interpreted, it is *the* revelation of God's will for his people Israel. Jesus, however, shows no interest in the details of *hălākâ* as developed by the Essenes, and at times he fulminates against excessive concern with the minutiae of the Law (Matt 23:23 ‖ Luke 11:42). So far is he from being obsessed with purity rules that he readily dines with public sinners and toll collectors (Mark 2:13–17; Luke 19:1–10; Matt 11:19 ‖ Luke 7:34), deals with and even touches lepers (Mark 1:40–45; Luke 17:11–19; Matt 11:5 par.), and is apparently not disturbed by the purity questions that would have to arise when unchaperoned women accompany and serve him during his itinerant ministry (Luke 8:1–3).

There is no evidence that for the historical Jesus—as opposed to later Christian systematic theologians—this freewheeling approach to the details of the Law and *hălākâ* was grounded in some grand overriding principle, such as the love commandment or an interim ethic, valid for the short time before the kingdom of God comes in all its fullness.[107] Rather, there seems to be a certain ad-hoc quality to Jesus' pronouncements on the Law and halakic observances. His attitudes and actions seem to be ultimately grounded in his prophetic-charismatic authority, so well summed up in his characteristic, peremptory introductory phrase: "Amen I say to you. . . ." The underlying assumption of so much of Jesus' actions and teachings is that he knows directly and without scribal study and deductions what God's will is in any given legal question. As with his position on the resurrection of the dead in his debate with the Sadducees, so with his treatment of the Mosaic Law and *hălākâ*, Jesus exudes the air of "it is so because I say it is so." Two notable examples of this approach are the question of observance of the sabbath and purity rules.

(a) Scholars continue to debate the historicity of individual stories of Jesus running afoul of certain observant Jews because of his "liberal" views on the sabbath rest.[108] Details of the individual stories and, in some cases, their connection with miracle-working, may be secondary. But, since we find such disputes multiply attested in Marcan (Mark 2:23–28; 3:1–6), L (Luke 13:10–17; 14:1–6), and Johannine (John 5:1–18; 9:1–17) traditions, it seems likely that Jesus was known to have held less-than-stringent views about the extent to which one was obliged to abstain from work on the sabbath.

Especially intriguing is one of Jesus' sayings on the sabbath rest embedded in a number of different stories of healing on the sabbath. In Mark 3:1–6, the healing of a man with a withered hand on the sabbath, Jesus simply asks his adversaries whether it is licit on the sabbath to do good or evil, to save a life or kill it (3:4). In the Matthean parallel to this story (Matt 12:9–14), however, Matthew substitutes a different rhetorical question that proposes a concrete case: "Which of you, if you have a sheep that falls into a pit on the sabbath, will not take hold of it and draw it out? Of how much greater value is a human being than a sheep?" (Matt 12:11–12). The Lucan parallel (Luke 6:6–11) basically follows Mark's form of the story. Yet, in the separate story of Jesus healing a man with dropsy (Luke 14:1–6), the rhetorical question found in Matt 12:11 resurfaces in a variant form: "Which of you, if you have a *son* or an *ox* that falls into a *well* will not immediately draw him [or it] out [even] on the sabbath?" (Luke 14:5).

The question of Synoptic relationships is difficult to decide here. It may be that a stray Q logion on sabbath observance was inserted by Matthew into a Marcan dispute about healing on the sabbath while Luke chose to insert it into a dispute story from his special L tradition. Alternately, the differences in the two rhetorical questions might well be explained not by different uses of the Q document by Matthew and Luke but simply by variant oral traditions that came to Matthew and Luke in different forms: (1) Matt 12:11 speaks of a sheep in a pit, while Luke 14:5 speaks of a son or an ox in a well; (2) Matthew's argument is an a fortiori argument ("of how much greater value . . . ? ") while Luke's is more a pari (one would do the same thing in both cases).

This particular argument of Jesus becomes all the more fascinating when put into the context of Jewish disputes about the legality of particular acts on the sabbath. Jesus was hardly the only Jewish teacher around the turn of the era engaging in such debates. The Mishna (compiled ca. A.D. 200) records disagreements between the House of Hillel and the House of Shammai on the issue of sabbath observance, some of which may indeed reach back to the pre-70 period (see, e.g., *m. Šabb.* 1:4–8). Nor were disagreements on the sabbath confined to the Pharisees. The Sadducees would seem to have been stricter than the Pharisees on at least some aspects of sabbath observance since—as we saw in our treatment of the Sadducees—they did not allow the extension of the distance that one could walk on the sabbath by the legal fiction of the *ʿerûb* (the joining or "fusion" of houses). As already noted, the Essenes were extremely strict on sabbath observance. In fact, contrary to the agreement Jesus presumes in his argument, the Essenes prohibited the drawing of a newborn animal out of a cistern or pit into which it had fallen on the sabbath (CD 11:13–14). The corrupt state of the manuscript of the *Damascus Document* at this point leaves matters somewhat unclear, but apparently the Essenes did not permit a man who had similarly fallen into "a place of water" to be helped out with a ladder, rope, or utensil (although 4Q265 7 i 7–8 allows a garment to be thrown to him as a lifeline). Contrary to the strictness of the Essenes on this point, the Babylonian Talmud (whose compilation is usually dated to about the 5th century A.D.) specifically allows placing objects in a well to help an animal out on the sabbath (*b. Šabb.* 128b).[109]

The way various Jewish parties and sects debated sabbath observance thus clarifies the thrust of Jesus' argument. Jesus presumes both a knowledge of the strict *hălākâ* forbidding any help to the fallen animal and a general rejection—both by himself and by his audience—of this view as being too strict. He builds on this basic agreement to try to convince his audience that healing a sick person is a similar example of reasonable leniency and mercy exercised on the sabbath. If such reasonable leniency be acceptable for animals in distress, how much more for humans in distress! It would seem, then—if we accept this logion as coming from the historical Jesus—that Jesus is not directly arguing with the Essenes but is rather arguing with fellow Jews who, like himself, would consider Essene rules on sabbath observance as too strict. However, granted the fluid and pluralistic situation in pre-70 Judaism, it is also possible that the strict prohibition found in the CD 11:13–14 was held not only by the Essenes but by other Jewish rigorists as well. In that case, Jesus would not necessarily have been referring to Essenes in particular. In any event, the saying of Jesus in Matt 12:11 ‖ Luke 14:5 is a clear example of how the lenient view of Jesus regarding the sabbath rest, as represented in the Gospels, directly contradicts the stringent approach of the Essenes.

(b) The concern that any observant Jew had about the proper observance of the food laws in the Pentateuch was naturally intensified by the purity-minded Essenes. At Qumran, the stringent control of the basic act of eating assumed the form of taking meals in common according to a set ritual. Only those members of the community who had gone through the process of initiation and who had not incurred censure since then could partake of the pure meals of the community ("the purity of the many"), which were presided over and blessed by a priest (1QS 6:4–5,16–17).[110] The sacral nature of these meals was intensified by their implicitly eschatological character. The description of the regular communal meal in 1QS 6:4–5 is echoed in the prophetic portrait of the communal meal of the last days that will be celebrated when the two Messiahs have come (1QSa 2:17–21). If it be true that the Pharisees sought to turn every meal into a holy, priestly event, a fortiori this was true of the Qumranites.[111]

Hence nothing could be further from the spirit and practice of Qumran than Jesus' free-wheeling wining and dining with the social and religious "riffraff" of Israel, the toll collectors and sinners (Matt 11:18–19 par.; Mark 2:13–17; Luke 19:1–10; cf. Matt 8:11–12 par.; Mark 14:25). Jesus' meals were communal in a very different sense. As the eschatological prophet sent to gather all Israel in the end time, he purposely sought out the religiously and socially marginalized and dramatically celebrated their inclusion in the Israel of the end time by joining them in table fellowship. The type of purity demanded by Qumran would have been out of the question in such an open situation. If Jesus' undifferentiated approach to communal meals raised such hackles among the Pharisees and other pious Jews, one can only imagine what the reaction of any Qumranite would have been.[112]

But perhaps that is the point. While we hear in the Gospels of criticism from the Pharisees, there is telling silence about any reaction from the Essenes or Qumranites, rigorists who made the Pharisees look liberal by comparison. While the Pharisees and Jesus, for all their differences, inhabited the same public space and therefore would meet and debate and clash over meal practice, there is no mention of criticism from Qumran probably because Jesus and Qumran did not exist in the same spiritual universe. Jesus was so far beyond the Qumran pale, religiously if not geographically, that the Qumranites either knew nothing of him or immediately dismissed him from serious consideration if they did hear about him. Jesus and the Pharisees clashed at times because they took each other seriously. Qumran could not have taken Jesus seriously and would have had nothing to do with him. That, most likely, is what the Gospels' silence about Qumran betokens. This is one reason why any attempt to compare and contrast Jesus with Qumran is almost beside the point. In a real sense, whether the Qumranites knew about him or not, Jesus did not exist for Qumran. One is reminded of Otto von Bismarck's doubts about the likelihood of war between a land power like Germany and a naval power like Britain: a land rat and a water rat—where would they fight?[113]

2. Interest in Calendars

As we have seen, Qumran was deeply concerned about which calendar should regulate Jewish feasts.[114] Qumran apparently held to an older solar calendar (though perhaps with some correlations with a lunar calendar), while the priests in control of the Jerusalem temple employed a lunar calendar (though corrected by solar observations). The introduction of the lunar calendar into the liturgy of the Jerusalem temple in the 2d century B.C. may in fact have been one of the causes precipitating the withdrawal of the Teacher of Righteousness and his followers from the temple and their founding of the Qumran community. What is so striking in Jesus' teaching and practice, by comparison, is the total lack of concern with or pronouncements about which religious calendar one should observe. As far as we can tell from the four Gospels, Jesus, along with the vast majority of Jews, followed as a matter of course the festal calendar observed by the priests controlling the Jerusalem temple. What was a burning issue and a reason for schism for the Qumranites does not even appear on Jesus' mental horizon. In this, he was very much a part of "mainstream" Palestinian Judaism.[115]

3. Hatred or Love of Enemies

In a number of its writings, notably the *Rule of the Community* (1QS 1:9–11; 2:4–3:6) and the *War Scroll*, Qumran positively inculcates hatred for all those outside the community. Such outsiders were "the sons of darkness," comprising both Gentiles and all those Jews who did not accept the views and practices of the Qumranites ("the sons of light"). Such a sense of separation from and fierce opposition to the rest of the world is explainable in political and social terms by the Qumranites' past history of withdrawal from and persecution by the Jerusalem priesthood in control of the temple. This political and social experience resulted in a worldview that was starkly dualistic, seeing the whole cosmos, invisible as well as visible, in terms of two armed camps engaging in an eschatological struggle for the soul of the individual and the future of the world.[116]

While Jesus' own worldview was formed by Jewish eschatology tinged with apocalyptic, his sense of a final struggle between God and Satan did not translate into an extreme exclusionary view in which all Gentiles and all Jews outside his own group were automatically destined to eternal destruction. His outreach to all Israel, sinners and toll collectors included, his prophetic vision that many Gentiles would take part in the eschatological banquet, and his ministry of exorcising demoniacs (thus waging war on evil spirits rather than evil humans) modified the tendency inherent in Jewish apocalyptic to see everything in black and white, good and bad, "them and us." Correspondingly, instead of a positive command to hate those outside his own group of followers, Jesus stressed in his direct teaching, his parables, and his praxis the message of love, compassion, mercy, and forgiveness. This core message is richly and multiply attested in the traditions of Mark, Q, M, and L (e.g., Mark 2:1–12,13–17; 11:25; 12:28–34; Matt 5:21–26,38–48; 6:12, 14–15; 18:10–14,15,21–35; Luke 7:36–50; 9:51–55; 10:25–37; 15:1–32; 18:9–14; 19:1–10; cf. John 8:1–11). Perhaps most striking is his command to love even one's enemies and persecutors, together with his exhortations to show compassion and forgiveness to sinners. The direct command to love one's enemies in Q (Matt 5:44 par.) is reinforced both by other Q sayings (e.g., Matt 5:46–48 par.; 5:39–42 par.) as well as by similar ideas in L and M parables (the Good Samaritan, the Lost Coin, the Prodigal Son, and the Unforgiving Servant; see also Mark 11:25). This inclusive thrust of Jesus, reaching out to gather the scattered sheep of the house of Israel, stands in stark contrast to the exclusive sectarianism of Qumran, which saw itself alone as the true Israel. In short, at Qumran extreme sectarianism tended to express itself theologically in extreme dualism, while Jesus' all-embracing approach tended to mitigate—without abolishing entirely—the dualistic tendencies of apocalyptic.[117]

4. Hierarchical Leadership

Not surprisingly for a group whose leadership emerged from the temple hierarchy in Jerusalem, the Qumran community was a highly organized hierarchical society with precedence given to priests and Levites (see, e.g., 1QS 1:18–2:23; 6:3–5; 8:1–4; 1QM 2:1–3).[118] By comparison, Jesus' movement shows a very low level of organization during his public ministry.[119] In previous chapters, we were able to sketch in rough fashion three concentric circles around him: crowds following him, disciples called by him, and the circle of Twelve chosen by him and sent out on a short-term mission. But this incipient organization, if it may be called that, was fluid at best, and there is much we do not know about it. To what extent donations and the hospitality of sedentary supporters were organized into some sort of regular support system and to what extent they all remained ad hoc we cannot say. It stands to reason that the popular support for Jesus that was originally spontaneous may have begun to take on some regular contours and rhythm over the course of the two years Jesus traveled around Galilee and up to Jerusalem, but we can offer only educated guesses. We hear tantalizing references to a common purse in Jesus' group, disbursements to the poor from it, and ongoing support by the women of means who traveled with Jesus (John 12:4–8; 13:29; Luke 8:1–3), but no more substantive information is forthcoming. Capernaum in Galilee and Bethany/Jerusalem in Judea may have developed as "bases of operation," but again we lack the data to draw firm conclusions. It is a sociological commonplace that an enthusiastic charismatic movement formed around a gifted leader will, given enough time, tend toward institutionalization, routinization, and rationalization; such tendencies can be found in the early church.[120] But, apart perhaps from Jesus' creation of the Twelve, there seems to be very little of that in the public ministry. And needless to say, the emphasis on priestly control at Qumran finds no echo in the lay movement led by the Jewish layman called Jesus. Perhaps this contrast between Qumran's sectarian self-awareness as the highly organized community of the "new covenant" (CD 6:19; 19:33) versus Jesus' loose eschatological movement reaching out to all Israel may help to explain why the noun "covenant" is an important term for Qumran and why, with the exception of Jesus' words over the cup at the Last Supper (probably: "the covenant in my blood"), it is entirely absent from the sayings of Jesus as preserved for us in the Gospels.[121] Unlike Paul and the Epistle to the Hebrews, we hear nothing from the historical Jesus about a "new covenant." [122]

5. Miracle Working

As Volume Two of A Marginal Jew demonstrated at great length, Jesus' reputed ability to work miracles was a major part of his ministry and self-definition.[123] In contrast, in the Qumran scrolls neither the Teacher of Righteousness nor the awaited Messiahs (with the possible exception of 4Q521) are depicted as miracle workers. The types of healings and exorcisms that form a good part of the portrait of Jesus in the Gospels are largely lacking at Qumran. In the narrative material at Qumran, one can find partial parallels in (1) the Genesis Apocryphon, where Abraham prays and lays hands on a sick Pharaoh in order to rebuke an evil spirit causing a plague (1QapGen 20:28–29); and (2) the fragmentary Prayer of Nabonidus, where a Jewish exorcist (Daniel?) forgives King Nabonidus' sins in God's name and thus apparently frees the king from the "evil disease" plaguing him (4QPrNab 6).[124] In both cases, we are dealing with (a) stories of demonic obsession rather than possession, (b) stories in which a holy person prays to God for another's relief instead of directly commanding the evil spirit to leave,[125] and (c) stories that are midrashic reworkings of older texts about ancient heroes. In contrast, both Mark and Q, written a generation after the ministry of the historical Jesus, recount or refer to exorcisms in the strict sense, in which Jesus directly commands an evil spirit that has invaded and taken up the body and psyche of an individual to leave.

To cast our net a bit wider: the literature in the Qumran library clearly shows that the Qumranites knew about various practices of magic, incantations, and divination (including astrology and dream interpretation), but on the whole the legal texts found at Qumran are either silent on the subject or allow only the casting of lots to discern God's will.[126] In Qumran's dualistic and eschatological worldview, magic and divination were generally thought to belong to the evil sphere of present existence and were doomed to be destroyed at the final judgment. Knowledge of the future was to be gained by the inspired exegesis of Scripture, as found in Qumran's *pēšer* commentaries, and not by magic or divination. To be sure, Josephus recounts a few anecdotes—usually dismissed by scholars as legendary—about individual Essenes operating in Jerusalem (indeed, in the thick of royal politics), who were known for their prophetic ability.[127] Even Josephus, though, has no stories of an individual Essene noted for working a whole series of miracles. In all this, we are far from the role of the miracle-working eschatological prophet wearing the mantle of Elijah that Jesus consciously assumed.

In sum, the differences between Jesus and Qumran/the Essenes were many and profound. It is no wonder, then, that the two did not interact during the public ministry. Still, the foregoing exercise in comparison and contrast remains helpful insofar as it reminds us that Jesus and his movement were one expression of a larger phenomenon in Palestine at the turn of the era: Jewish eschatological groups with radical lifestyles, fervent hopes for Israel's future, and tense or hostile relations with the priestly establishment in Jerusalem. Unlike the Qumranites, though, the itinerant Jesus actively addressed, engaged, and wooed the whole of Israel. Not surprisingly, then, while both Jesus and the Qumranites met with personal disaster at the hands of the Roman authorities, his impact, unlike theirs, survived in an ongoing movement that transcended his own time and place.

II. THE SAMARITANS

A. INTRODUCTION: WHY HERE?

At this point, the reader may wonder at my ordering of the material. After all, the Samaritans are mentioned by name in the Gospels, while the Qumranites/Essenes are not. Yet I have placed the treatment of the Samaritans after that of the Qumranites. Why? Put simply, the Qumranites/Essenes were, for all their differences from mainstream Palestinian Judaism (in which I include the Pharisees, the Sadducees, the priests, and common people), clearly Jews. The status of the Samaritans vis-à-vis 1st-century Palestinian Jews was at best ambiguous. A number of Gospel passages apparently view them as neither fully Jewish nor fully Gentile. Some later rabbinic texts reflect a similar ambivalence. At least in the eyes of some, then, the Samaritans were marginal in the literal sense of straddling the margins or borders between the Jewish and Gentile worlds. Their proper classification, as well as a detailed description of their historical origins, remains as problematic for modern historians as it was for 1st-century writers.

B. PROBLEMS OF TERMINOLOGY AND DEFINITION

To repeat a basic theme of this volume: our concern is not a general and all-encompassing treatment of the Samaritans.[128] Our focus is instead a narrow one: Jesus *in relation to* the Samaritans. Granted this restriction, what do we mean when we talk about the *Samaritans* who might have interacted with Jesus? The label *Samaritan* is a slippery one. Different authors have defined Samaritans in terms of geography, physical descent, or religion—as well as by various combinations of all three perspectives.[129]

1. Geography

One might define Samaritans predominately in terms of geography: Samaritans were the inhabitants of the region called Samaria, located in 1st-century Palestine to the north of Judea and to the south of Galilee on the western side of the Jordan River. Its capital city was also originally called Samaria, though in the 1st century B.C. Herod the Great had rebuilt it and renamed it Sebaste in honor of Augustus Caesar (the Greek equivalent of *Augustus* being *Sebastos*).[130] As we shall see, the population group defined in these geographical terms might better be called "Samarians." [131]

2. Physical Descent or Ethnic Makeup

One might also define the Samaritans predominately in terms of physical descent or ethnic makeup: Samaritans were the presumed descendants of the Israelite tribes of Ephraim and Manasseh (main components of the northern kingdom of Israel), with some admixture over the centuries of non-Israelite groups from the Assyrian and Hellenistic empires. This ethnic approach, more than the geographic one, has the virtue of clarifying matters for the situation we find in the 1st century A.D. For, by the 1st century, the region of Samaria was inhabited by a number of different ethnic groups, the exact percentages of which are not known.[132] They probably included Samaritans (in the third sense defined below), Jews, other indigenous Semitic populations of the Syrian-Palestinian region that had been Hellenized, descendants of the Assyrian, Babylonian, and Persian ruling classes, and descendants of the Greek conquerors from the time of Alexander the Great. Hence, not everyone who was geographically a "Samarian" was ethnically or religiously a "Samaritan."

3. Religion

One might also define the Samaritans predominately in terms of their religion: Samaritans were those Semites (a) who worshiped the God Yahweh, (b) but who, in distinction from mainstream Jews, revered Mt. Gerizim (near ancient Shechem in Samaria) instead of Mt. Zion in Jerusalem as the one valid place to build an altar or temple for the public worship of Yahweh, (c) who maintained that their line of Levitical priests functioning on Mt. Gerizim were the legitimate priests of the Mosaic dispensation, as opposed to the priests functioning in the Jerusalem temple, and (d) who accepted only the five books of Moses (the Pentateuch) as authoritative Scripture, to the exclusion of the still fluid corpus of the Prophets and the Writings developing alongside the Pentateuch in mainstream Judaism. Part of the problem here is that the three ways of defining Samaritans partially overlap while not perfectly coinciding with one another.

Since the Gospels naturally tend to view the Samaritans from a religious point of view, and since some elements of the religious definition of Samaritans peek through the story of Jesus and the Samaritan woman at the well in John 4 (the longest single treatment of Samaritans in the Gospels), in what follows I will use the religious definition as best suited to the purposes of our quest. Another reason for using the religious definition is that it avoids the pitfall of imagining that everyone who lived in the region of Samaria was a Samaritan in the religious sense of the term. By the 1st century A.D., there were notable pockets of Hellenized pagans in Samaria, especially in its capital city of Sebaste (the OT city of Samaria). Such pagans were "Samarians" geographically but not "Samaritans" religiously.

Beyond the minimal definition of Samaritan religion sketched above, it is difficult to be precise about the details of Samaritan religion in the 1st century A.D. Religious writings by Samaritans themselves date from centuries later, the earliest compositions coming from the 3d or 4th century A.D. Our major sources from the 1st century A.D. are Josephus and (secondarily) Luke-Acts and the Gospel of John. None of these gives us a disinterested picture of the Samaritans. In particular, Josephus' account, in the estimation of most critics, is hostile to the Samaritans, though it is unclear whether we should place the hostility at the door of the author or of his sources.[133] Paradoxically, then, we might almost count it a blessing that so few passages in the NT mention the Samaritans in relation to Jesus, since our ignorance of 1st-century Samaritanism would leave us ill-equipped to exegete a large body of Gospel material on the subject.

C. The Problem of the Historical Origins of the Samaritans

If we define Samaritans in the religious terms sketched above, any attempt to determine when and how the Samaritans emerged as a distinct group is fraught with difficulty. In the ancient period, both Samaritans and Jews created narratives describing the Samaritans' origins, but neither narrative tradition is historically reliable. In a glorious anachronism, traditional Samaritan theology places the basic split between Samaritanism and Judaism as far back as the 11th century B.C., at the time of the priest Eli (active toward the end of the period of the Judges according to 1 Sam 1:9–4:18).[134] The wicked Eli is said to have moved the sanctuary from its true locus, Mt. Gerizim near Shechem, to Shiloh. Eli thus created both an illegitimate place of worship and an illegitimate priesthood. All future antagonism between Samaritans and Jews is traced to this primordial break with authentic Israelite religion, centered on Mt. Gerizim and preserved by the Samaritans, the direct descendants of the Israelite tribes of Ephraim and Manasseh.

The Jewish version of events is not so wildly anachronistic, but neither is it historically accurate. Strictly speaking, the OT never applies the term "Samaritans" to the special religious group centered around the cult place located on Mt. Gerizim. In the OT, the Hebrew term commonly translated by modern scholars as "Samaritans" *(haššōmĕrōnîm)* occurs only at 2 Kgs 17:29, within a highly polemical passage. In v 29, the noun *haššōmĕrōnîm* simply means "the inhabitants of Samaria," who are said to have created "high places" for false worship in the northern kingdom of Israel.[135] This text in turn is part of a larger tendentious narrative, 2 Kgs 17:2–41, which has gone through a number of stages of tradition and redaction.[136] In its present state, the text tells a clear though inaccurate story. According to this narrative, the northern kingdom of Israel, because of its terrible sin of idolatry, was destroyed by Yahweh. (Samaria [*šōmĕrôn*], the capital city, was in fact captured by the Assyrians in 722/721 B.C.) The Assyrians sent Israel (presumably most or all of the northern kingdom's population is meant) into exile, an exile apparently viewed as permanent. The Assyrians then brought into the former northern kingdom various foreign populations to settle "the cities of Samaria in place of the sons of Israel" (2 Kgs 17:24). When, out of ignorance, these new groups did not worship Yahweh, "the God of the land," Yahweh sent lions to kill some of them. The king of Assyria remedied the situation by sending back one of the deported Israelite priests to teach the new settlers "the proper way to worship the God of the land" (2 Kgs 17:27). In v 28, the priest is said to settle at Bethel (*not* Shechem or Mt. Gerizim), the cult site that the OT regularly regards as the center of the idolatrous worship of the northern kingdom (cf. 1 Kings 12–13; Amos 7:10–17; Jer 48:13). The result—at least according to the OT narrative—was that the new settlers adopted a syncretistic polytheism that offered sacrifice to Yahweh alongside the various national gods brought in by the mixed population. Perhaps with a side glance and swipe at the religious group we call the Samaritans, the final redactor of 2 Kings 17 concludes his narrative with the following summation: "And these nations worship [literally, 'fear'] Yahweh, but they [also] serve their idols—[as do] also their sons and the sons of their sons. As did their fathers, [so] do they until this very day" (2 Kgs 17:41).

Josephus backs ups and elaborates upon this polemical narrative in *Ant.* 9.14.1–3 §277–291. Indeed, his retelling of the story is the first unambiguous use of 2 Kings 17 as anti-Samaritan propaganda. Josephus makes a point of describing the newly installed immigrants in the northern kingdom as coming from Chouthos (= OT Kuthah), which Josephus claims is in Persia. Hence he refers to them as "Chutheans" or "Chuthites" (*chouthaioi* in §288), a name he then applies to the Samaritans (§290). Josephus makes this identification in a context in which he highlights the syncretistic rites that he claims have continued among the Chutheans-alias-Samaritans down to his own day. Thus does Josephus create a clear link between the Samaritans of his own day and the descendants of the pagans settled by the Assyrians in the former northern kingdom. Understandably, Josephus' statements in the *Antiquities,* traditionally understood as hostile references, had a great impact on all subsequent understanding of the Samaritans, since, taken as a whole, his narratives about the Samaritans constitute the largest single written source from around the turn of the era.[137]

While good propaganda, this version of events is bad history. Sifting through the literary sources and the archaeological remains, many present-day historians hold that only a small part of the population of the northern kingdom of Israel was actually exiled by the Assyrians.[138] Primary targets of the Assyrian policy would have been the upper classes, especially in the capital city of Samaria. Correspondingly, those foreigners who were then brought into the former northern kingdom were probably settled in a few urban areas, the most notable being the capital city, where a new ruling class was installed. In subsequent Palestinian history, it was often this ruling class in Samaria (best called "Samarians") that came into conflict with the Jewish leaders in Jerusalem. Most of the population in the rural areas and small towns of the former northern kingdom would probably have remained native Israelite. In sum, then, 2 Kings 17 gives us no direct information about the cultic community centered on Mt. Gerizim that the NT calls "Samaritans."

Consequently, how a historian is supposed to get from 2 Kings 17 and its tendentious description of Israelite history after the destruction of the northern kingdom to the emergence of the Samaritans as a distinct religious group a few centuries before Jesus is hard to say. Our sources give us little hard data about the state of things in the former northern kingdom during most of the Assyrian, Babylonian, and Persian rule of Palestine (i.e., from the 8th to the 4th century B.C.). What can be said is that there are no positive indications of a cultic group identifiable with the Samaritans or of any "schism" between such a group and Jerusalem. While the precise historical details of the religious reform of King Josiah of Judah (reigned 640–609 B.C.) are still debated among scholars, it seems clear that his attempts to win northern Israelites back to the Jerusalem temple did not collide with any rival cult at Shechem or with any cultic group we could equate with the Samaritans of the NT period. Indeed, the Book of Deuteronomy or some part thereof apparently played an important role in Josiah's reforms; that same book wound up as part of the Samaritan Pentateuch. Moreover, within Deuteronomy, Mt. Gerizim is mentioned (11:29; 27:12) without any censure or slur. In fact, in both passages, Mt. Gerizim is associated with the positive cultic ritual of pronouncing blessings, while Mt. Ebal opposite it is connected with the ritual of pronouncing curses. Clearly, the supposed "schism" between Samaritans and worshipers of Yahweh in the kingdom of Judah had not yet taken place (if it ever did). Likewise telling is the consistent attitude of the southern prophets before, during, and after the Babylonian exile (e.g., Isaiah, Jeremiah, Ezekiel, Haggai, and Zechariah). In the writings attributed to them, hope is expressed for the restoration and union of the two kingdoms of Israel and Judah. This hope contravenes any idea that the northern tribes had been permanently and irrevocably contaminated by some polytheistic or syncretistic pagan religion. Neither do we find in these prophetic writings any idea of the "ten lost tribes" of northern Israel, exiled from their land by the Assyrians (contrast the presence of this idea in 4 Ezra 13:40, written at the end of the 1st century A.D.).

After the destruction of Jerusalem and the exile of the leaders of the southern kingdom of Judah by the Babylonians (587/586 B.C.), and after some

Judeans (i.e., "Jews") were allowed to return to Jerusalem under subsequent Persian rule (Cyrus began his rule in Babylon in 539/538 B.C.), we hear of the efforts of Nehemiah and Ezra to rebuild the walls and temple of Jerusalem as well as to dissolve mixed marriages between Jews and non-Jews.[139] In this endeavor, they meet opposition from various adversaries, including the political officials ruling in Samaria. The narrative in the Books of Ezra and Nehemiah is muddled, and the chronological problems it raises are intractable. Suffice it to say that there is no clear evidence that the opposition Nehemiah and Ezra faced at various times in the 5th (or possibly also the 4th) centuries B.C. came mainly from a distinct religious group centered around Mt. Gerizim and known as the Samaritans.[140] To be sure, that Samaritans were the main source of opposition is how Jews and Christians of a later date came to read and tell the story (so, e.g., Josephus in *Ant.* 11.2.1–2 §19–30 and 11.4.3–9 §84–119). But from Third Isaiah, Haggai, Zechariah, Nehemiah, and Ezra, modern historians discern instead indications of internecine quarrels among various Jewish groups in the south, notably between those Jews who had returned from the Babylonian exile and those Jews who had been left behind in Judah. Mixed up with these quarrels was the friction between the Jewish leaders in Jerusalem and the local rulers in Samaria, acting as agents of their Persian overlords. What should be noted is that the group the NT calls Samaritans is totally absent from the OT narrative of these disputes.

Some scholars claim that a ray of light is shed on the Samaritans during the murky Persian period by 5th-century papyri emanating from the Jewish colony of Elephantine in Egypt. To request aid in the rebuilding of their own temple, which had been destroyed, these Egyptian Jews sent letters both to Bagoas, the governor—and hence imperial agent—of Judea and to Delaiah and Shelemiah, the sons of Sanballat, the governor of Samaria, likewise an agent of the Persian empire. Far from indicating that a "schism" had already taken place between Jews and Samaritans, this correspondence tells us nothing about Samaritans understood in a religious sense. As R. J. Coggins points out, the city of Samaria, to which the letter is sent (as well as to Jerusalem), was a center of local political power, but was never the center of the Samaritan religion or priesthood. Mt. Gerizim near Shechem was.[141]

Likewise less than enlightening are Josephus' accounts of the origin of the Samaritan temple at the end of the Persian period and the dealings of both Samaritan and Jewish priests with Alexander the Great.[142] These stories are so laced with legendary elements that historians are divided on what if anything can be salvaged as reliable historical data.[143] Some authors suggest that, when Alexander destroyed the city of Samaria because of a revolt against his rule, large numbers of its inhabitants fled to Shechem, which was in fact rebuilt ca. 331 B.C.[144] This in turn may have led to Shechem's becoming a religious center of the emerging Samaritan religion. But we must admit that at this point we are mostly in the realm of speculation. Perhaps the greatest lesson to be drawn from all these frustrating attempts to sketch the origins of Samaritanism is that one must carefully and consistently distinguish "Samarians," the inhabitants and rulers of the city and territory known as Samaria, from "Samaritans," the adherents of an Israelite religious group centered around Mt. Gerizim/Shechem. If this distinction is maintained, a review of the available evidence only underlines our ignorance of the origins of the Samaritan religion prior to the Hellenistic period.

With all this uncertainty, it is not surprising that scholars disagree on when or how the Samaritans came to build their temple on Mt. Gerizim. Some (e.g., Abram Spiro, Bo Reicke) place the event toward the end of the Persian period, ca. 388 B.C.[145] Others prefer a later date in the 4th century, soon after the beginning of the Hellenistic period inaugurated by Alexander the Great.[146] The exact site of the Samaritan temple on Mt. Gerizim has so far eluded archaeologists, and some scholars suggest that the cult site was much more modest in size than Josephus' remarks might lead us to expect. In this regard, it is well to remember that Samaritan traditions stress the holiness of Mt. Gerizim and the altar Moses supposedly commanded to be built there, and not a temple building as such. This stands in contrast to the OT and later Jewish traditions that focused on the temple built on Mt. Zion.[147]

Interestingly, in line with this point, no Samaritan temple is mentioned in the first Jewish (and deuterocanonical) text that clearly refers to the Samaritans (though not by that name). This highly polemical text, Sir 50:25–26, forms part of the end of the Book of Ben Sira (if we may put aside the text-critically problematic chap. 51). In Sir 50:25–26, we read, according to the Hebrew text preserved in manuscript B, a couplet in the form of a numerical proverb:[148] "My soul loathes two nations [gôyîm], and the third is not [even] a people ['am: those who dwell in Seir [= Edom] and Philistia, and the foolish nation [gôy nābāl] that lives in Shechem." [149]

The Hebrew text contains a number of philological problems. For instance, should one press nābāl ("foolish") to carry the weighty sense of one who rebels against God or denies the existence and power of the true God— thus implying that the Samaritans, by their use of a rival sanctuary, in effect reject the true God of Israel? And should one see here the distinction, common in later Jewish texts, between gôyîm understood as "Gentiles" and 'am understood as the chosen people Israel? In any event, by putting those who dwell at Shechem in the same basic category as the Edomites and the Philistines, traditional enemies of Israel, Sir 50:25–26 apparently intends to deny the Samaritans any claim to be part of Israel, the chosen people of God. Perhaps Ben Sira shares the view of the final redactor of 2 Kings 17, who, as we have seen, implies that the Samaritans are a mixed race practicing a polytheistic religion. As we have also seen, Josephus is completely in accord with this tendency, which he underscores by calling the Samaritans "Chutheans," i.e., people from the region of Kuthah, one of the pagan populations brought in by the king of Assyria after the fall of the northern kingdom of Israel (see 2 Kgs 17:24).[150]

Muddled accounts of the Samaritans and their religious stance continue down into Hasmonean times and beyond. We are told, for instance, in 2 Macc 6:2 (cf. 5:23) that, under pressure from the Hellenizing policies of the Seleucid monarch Antiochus IV (175–164 B.C.), the Samaritans accepted Hellenistic influence in their sanctuary by naming their temple *Zeus Xenios* (Zeus the Friend of Strangers).[151] The text does not say explicitly that the Samaritans took the initiative in requesting this name for their temple. Not surprisingly, in *Ant.* 12.5.5 §257–264, Josephus gives a more hostile version of events: the Samaritans disown all kinship with and similarity to the Jews and willingly petition Antiochus IV to have their unnamed temple named *Zeus Hellēnios* (the Greek Zeus). The historical fact may simply be that the Samaritans, feeling themselves in a perilous position, did not resist Antiochus' Hellenizing policies with the same zeal as that shown by Judas Maccabeus and his followers. In any event, after the triumph of the Hasmonean leaders over the Seleucids, relations between Samaritans and Jews went from bad to worse. The ambitious Hasmonean rulers extended their territory to include Samaria; but, unlike some of the native populations elsewhere (e.g., Idumea), the Samaritans refused to be co-opted by the Judaism of Jerusalem. A climax in the deterioration of relations was reached during the reign of the Hasmonean monarch and high priest John Hyrcanus, who destroyed the Samaritan sanctuary on Mt. Gerizim in 128 B.C. and the town of Shechem ca. 107 B.C.[152] From this time onward, relations between Samaritans and Jews were extremely strained, although the ups and downs of history brought them at times into more amicable dealings with each other.

Looking back on this obscure and tangled history, we should at least learn to avoid certain facile statements often found in both popular and scholarly presentations. For example, writers often argue over when the "schism" between Samaritans and Judaism took place. The more cautious commentators rightly reject the idea of a single break at one moment in time. They prefer to speak of a gradual drifting apart or a series of breaks interwoven with occasional and temporary rapprochements. But one must ask whether the very concept of "schism" is appropriate here. "Schism" presupposes some original unity or union. If we are speaking of Samaritans and *Jews,* we must ask in what sense these two groups were ever united. This question in turn brings us back to our initial problem of terminology and definitions. "Jews" (*Ioudaioi* in Greek, *yĕhûdîm* in Hebrew, *yĕhûdāʾîn* in Aramaic) take their name from the tribe of Judah and the territory referred to in Hellenistic and Roman times as Judea (*Ioudaia* in Greek, *yĕhûdâ* in Hebrew, *yĕhûd* in Aramaic).[153] After the Babylonian exile in the 6th century B.C., some of the "Jews" who had been exiled from Judah to Babylonia returned to their native land in Palestine, many with the specific intention of rebuilding the Jerusalem temple on Mt. Zion. There they interacted with various natives of Judea who had not been forced into exile; the interaction was not always a happy one.[154] If one understands the phrase "Palestinian Jews" to designate the ethnic-geographical-religious community that resulted from these events and interaction, and if one understands the distinctive religious practices and beliefs of this community to constitute "Palestinian Judaism," then Samaritans, descended in some sense from a number of the northern tribes of Israel (most likely Ephraim and Manasseh) and focused religiously on the sanctuary on Mt. Gerizim, never belonged to the group we label Palestinian Jews and never practiced the corresponding religion we call Judaism. In keeping with this historical situation as well as with their self-understanding, the Samaritans refer to themselves in their major religious works as "Israel" but not as "Jews."[155]

Perhaps, then, a better way of conceiving of the state of affairs around the turn of the era is that both Samaritanism and Judaism were latter-day forms of the ancient religion of Israel, a Palestinian religion that believed in and worshiped the God Yahweh as the unique God of Israel according to the prescriptions contained in the five books of Moses. Over the centuries, this religion had developed distinctive practices such as circumcision of infants, the prohibition of eating pork, the observance of every seventh day as a day of rest, an emphasis on the need to have one central sanctuary, and annual celebrations of special feasts of pilgrimage to this central sanctuary (e.g., Passover, Pentecost, Tabernacles). This core religion of Israel experienced various traumas, transformations, and developments under the assaults and influences of the Assyrian, Babylonian, Persian, and Hellenistic empires.

During the last centuries before the turn of the era—though at different times and in different ways—Samaritanism and Judaism emerged from the crucible of all this historical turmoil as two major expressions of the ancient religion of Israel, the ancient worship of Yahweh. Neither religion was immediately derived from the other and neither broke away from the other.[156] There was no one, definitive moment of schism.[157] Indeed, not only was there no one definitive moment of schism; in a real sense, there was no schism at all. This helps explain the strange symbiosis of these two latter-day forms of ancient Israelite religion, at times in fierce opposition to each other, at times in uneasy rapprochement.[158]

It is within this unclear and fluctuating situation in the 1st century A.D. that we must place the few Gospel texts that speak of Jesus' relation to the Samaritans. Before we begin, though, one point should be emphasized. From all we have seen, we can already exclude one popular presentation of the Samaritan religion in the 1st century A.D.: namely, that it was a type of syncretistic polytheism combined with Jewish elements. Far from being polytheists in practice or belief, the Samaritans tended to represent a rather conservative expression of Israelite religion, more rigorous than many Jews in their observance of the sabbath and more wary of religious innovations— a characteristic that may partly explain their restriction of the canon of sacred books to the Pentateuch. As for syncretism, to the cold eye of the historian of religions, the Samaritans would probably appear no more syncretistic than their Jewish or later Christian neighbors in the eastern Mediterranean world.

D. The Problems of the Gospel Texts

The canonical Gospels offer relatively little material on Jesus and the Samaritans. What they do offer stands in basic agreement with what we know from sources outside the NT. At the same time, though, the passages dealing with Samaritans in the Gospels add nothing essentially new to our knowledge of the Samaritans. Moreover, as many exegetical studies indicate, the Gospel references to Samaritans may tell us more about the situation of the early church as it pursued its mission in Palestine than they do about the historical Jesus.[159] The easiest way to gain an overview of what, if anything, these references may tell us about Jesus' relation to the Samaritans is to undertake a rapid survey of each Gospel or Gospel source in turn:[160]

1. "Samaria" and "Samaritans" do not occur at all in either Mark or Q, our two earliest written sources of Gospel material. This in itself may serve as an initial indicator that Jesus' interaction with Samaritans was probably not all that extensive. This point is confirmed indirectly by Matthew.

2. In Matthew, "Samaritans" occurs only in the negative command Jesus gives the Twelve at the beginning of the missionary discourse (Matt 10:5b–6): "Do not go to the Gentiles, and do not enter a city of Samaritans [*eis polin Samaritōn mē eiselthēte*]; go rather to the lost sheep of the house of Israel." While one cannot prove absolutely that this saying is a product of the early

church—possibly created by stringently conservative Christian Jews who opposed a wider mission to Samaritans and Gentiles—any claim that these words come from the historical Jesus faces a number of difficulties.

(a) As it stands, Matthew's missionary discourse (10:5–42) is a creation of Matthew himself, who has conflated the missionary discourses found in Mark and Q. (This a commonplace in NT exegesis that can be demonstrated easily enough by comparing the missionary discourses in Mark 6:7–11; Matt 10:5–42; Luke 9:3–5; and Luke 10:2–12.)[161] Yet the prohibition of a mission to Gentiles or Samaritans spoken in Matt 10:5b–6 is found in neither the Marcan nor the Q form of the discourse. Clearly, then, Matthew himself has chosen to insert this prohibition into the traditional missionary discourses that he has inherited and combined. Consequently, the key prohibition of entering a Samaritan town must come either from Matthew's redactional creativity or from his special M tradition.

(b) An argument in favor of the prohibition being a purely Matthean creation might be constructed on the basis of a parallel logion found later in the Gospel. At 15:24, Matthew inserts a similar negative statement into his reworked version of Mark's story of the Syrophoenician woman who begs Jesus to exorcise her daughter (Mark 7:24–30). (To be exact: the Syrophoenician woman of Mark's story becomes a Canaanite woman in Matthew's version, Matt 15:21–28.) Only in the Matthean form of the story (at Matt 15:24) does Jesus apply to himself a description that echoes his command to the Twelve in Matt 10:6: "I was sent only to the lost sheep of the house of Israel." Since Matt 15:24 is not only a Matthean insertion into the Marcan story but also clearly a product of Matthew's own creative activity as he redacts this Marcan pericope, the suspicion arises that the same is true of the insertion of Matt 10:5b–6 into the Marcan and Q traditions of the missionary discourse. However, the case is far from clear. The presence in 10:5b–6 of a number of rare words or phrases gives one pause. The phrase "to the Gentiles" (eis hodon ethnōn) occurs only here in the NT, and "a city of Samaritans" (polin Samaritōn) occurs only here in Matthew. Hence the presence of M tradition that Matthew has redacted for his own purposes is a possibility, some would say even a probability.[162]

(c) In any event, at least the saying in Matt 15:24 would have to be considered unhistorical in its present context, since we have already judged on other grounds that the underlying Marcan story about the Syrophoenician woman does not reach back to the historical Jesus. A fortiori, that must be true of Matthew's editorial addition to the story.[163]

While these considerations do not prove beyond a doubt that Matt 10:5b–6 is a creation of the early church, they do place the burden of proof on anyone who would claim that this missionary directive goes back to the historical Jesus. My own view is that this saying is more likely a product of some group within the first Christian generation that opposed widening the proclamation of the gospel to groups other than Jews. Still, one must note an important paradox here. The saying in Matt 10:5b–6 may not be "authentic" in the sense of having been said by the historical Jesus. Yet it may be "authentic" in a broader sense. Namely, if we may put aside the question of the intentions of its creator(s), the saying seems to reflect accurately what in fact happened during the public ministry: neither Jesus nor his immediate disciples pursued a formal, programmatic mission to the Samaritans *as a group* in the way that they pursued such a mission to their fellow Jews in Galilee and Judea. In addition, we should take note of the telling point of view presupposed in Matt 10:5b–6: Samaritans are not Gentiles, but neither do they belong to "the house of Israel"—even to those Israelites considered "lost." Thus, the saying in Matt 10:5b–6, coming probably from Christian Jews of the first generation of the church, captures well the ambiguous status and marginality of Samaritans in the eyes of both Christians and Jews in the 1st century A.D.

The fact that Jesus did not undertake a formal mission to the Samaritans as a group does not, however, exclude the possibility of occasional encounters with or references to Samaritans—which is precisely what we find in the Gospels of Luke and John. Nevertheless, while they supply more extensive references to Samaritans, Luke and John must be approached with suspicion as sources for the historical Jesus' interaction with Samaritans. Of all the NT authors, it is only Luke (explicitly) and John (implicitly) who refer to Christians preaching the gospel to Samaritans in the early days of the church (see Acts 1:8; 8:1,5–25; 15:3; cf. John 4:35–38). The possibility that Christian history is being read back into the public ministry of Jesus is thus quite real.

3. Luke mentions Samaritans both in narratives about Jesus and in the words of Jesus:[164]

(a) The narrative material includes the healing of the ten lepers, one of whom turns out to be a Samaritan (Luke 17:11–19). Actually, it is only in the second half of this story that the one grateful recipient of healing, who returns to thank Jesus, is said to be a Samaritan (v 16b). In Volume Two of *A Marginal Jew,* I noted how the opposition of the one grateful Samaritan and the blasé attitude of the other nine (presumably Jews) may foreshadow Luke's story of the spread of the Christian gospel as told in the Acts of the Apostles: the persecution of Christians in Jerusalem leads to a mission to Samaria (8:2–25).[165] Luke's schematic vision of many Jews rejecting the gospel while at least some inhabitants of Samaria accept it may be prefigured in his distinction in the story of the ten lepers: only the Samaritan has faith *(pistis)*, and so only the Samaritan is not only healed physically *(iathē,* as were the other nine) but also saved spiritually (with the full symbolic sense of *sesōken* in v 19). While I think that the story of the ten lepers represents L tradition rather than a pure Lucan creation and that the L tradition is not simply a reworking or a variant of the healing of the leper in Mark 1:40–45, I do not feel that, given the many Christian and specifically Lucan concerns in Luke 17:11–19, the details of the story can be confidently traced back to the historical Jesus. Hence I would not want to insist on the presence of a *Samaritan* leper in the story as historical. This is not a question of being sure that the detail comes from the early church; it is simply a question of reaching the frustrating but frequent judgment *non liquet* (not clear).

(b) The other Lucan narrative involves a brief reference to the beginning of Jesus' great journey up to Jerusalem, a journey that in Luke's story reaches all the way from chap. 9 to chap. 19 and so forms a major compositional element in the Gospel.[166] Almost as soon as Jesus begins this fateful journey, we are told (9:52–53) that he seeks to enter a village of Samaritans, but they refuse to receive him "because he was traveling to Jerusalem [for the feast of Passover]." At the very least, the competition between the rival sanctuaries of Mt. Gerizim and Mt. Zion, each one being the goal of pilgrims at Passover, is echoed in this verse. The disciples James and John react angrily to this rebuff, suggesting in a both officious and bloodthirsty manner (v 54), "Lord, do you wish that we call down fire from heaven and destroy them?" Jesus replies by rebuking his vengeful disciples rather than the inhospitable village. He then solves the problem pragmatically by going off to a different village (vv 55–56). (Whether this other village is inhabited by Samaritans in the religious sense is not said; Luke's grasp of Palestinian geography in this section of his Gospel is shaky at best.)

In itself, there is nothing improbable in this story: we see the temperamental "sons of thunder" (thus are James and John designated in Mark 3:17, though not in Luke) clashing with the merciful Jesus. At least, coherence favors the historicity of the incident, and various commentators detect a pre-Lucan substratum beneath all the Lucan redaction.[167] Yet the presence and function of this story at a pivotal redactional moment in Luke's overarching composition raise doubts. We stand at the solemn beginning of Luke's great journey narrative, with all sorts of OT allusions and key Lucan motifs ringing in vv 51–52: "Now it came to pass that when the days for his [i.e., Jesus'] being taken up were being fulfilled, he set his face firmly to go to Jerusalem; and he sent messengers before his face; and going, they entered a village of Samaritans. . . . "[168] One must also remember that Luke is building here on a

Marcan framework and that in Mark, as in Matthew, this final journey apparently goes through Perea across the Jordan and up to Jerusalem by way of Jericho—a common route for Jewish pilgrims wishing to avoid the hostility of Samaritans.[169] True, it remains possible that the incident recounted in Luke 9:52–56 actually took place on some other journey to or from Jerusalem (as, e.g., in John 4).[170] But once, again, serious doubts about redactional creativity leave us with a *non liquet* in regard to Luke 9:51–55.

(c) Luke's most famous reference to Samaritans comes in the Parable of the Good Samaritan (10:30–37). This involves us in the much larger problem of trying to judge whether an individual parable that lacks multiple attestation of sources goes back to the historical Jesus or is a product of the early church—a problem to which we must return in a later chapter. Some critics, such as Gerhard Sellin, have argued that Luke himself has created the parable of the Good Samaritan, along with the dialogue between Jesus and a lawyer that frames it.[171] If Sellin is correct, then any use of the parable to understand the views of the historical Jesus is illegitimate. Sellin's position, though, depends upon many individual judgments—from the structure and classification of different forms of parables to the theological views of Luke on the Mosaic law—that are, to say the least, debatable. Along with many critics, I consider it more likely that, while the Parable of the Good Samaritan shows the redactional style and theology of Luke in its final form and placement, it is not simply a creation of Luke but goes back to his special L tradition.[172] The introductory dialogue between a lawyer and Jesus on the two commandments of love (Luke 10:25–29) seems to be Luke's recycling of a tradition also found in Mark 12:28–34 ‖ Matt 22:34–40. The exact nature of the source Luke is using (Mark? Q? L?) is debated by scholars. In any case, Luke's need to refashion an older tradition to make it a suitable introduction to the Parable of the Good Samaritan and the fact that nevertheless the introduction does not perfectly fit what it is supposed to introduce probably indicate that the parable itself is an earlier tradition taken over by Luke and reworked for his larger theological and literary plan. Whether the parable goes back to the historical Jesus is more difficult to say, though Christian piety and sentiment, if not hard-nosed critical arguments, certainly favor the idea.[173]

Even if we should allow that the substance of the parable goes back to Jesus, what exactly would that tell us about the historical Jesus and the historical Samaritans? In this parable, Jesus uses a Samaritan as a tool in his usual rhetorical strategy of reversing the expectations of his complacent audience: a poor, wounded man (presumably a Jew coming down from Jerusalem, perhaps from worshiping at the Jerusalem temple) is helped not by a

Jewish priest or Levite (ministers of the Jerusalem temple) but rather by a despised Samaritan (who, by definition, rejects the Jerusalem temple). In the Lucan context, the parable helps to redefine (or better: it refuses to define) who one's neighbor is (10:29). Implicitly, the parable tells us that "one's fellow," whom the Book of Leviticus commands us to love (Lev 19:18), is not only the fellow member of our own religious or ethnic community but any and every human being in need.[174] Explicitly, though, the parable ends not with a definition of who one's neighbor is but rather with a command to act as a neighbor to anyone in need. In any event, the Parable of the Good Samaritan is a call to show mercy and compassion to all the suffering members of our human community, irrespective of religious or ethnic barriers. All this supposes that Jesus deplores the hostile relations between Samaritans and Jews of his day (an idea supported by the anecdote in Luke 9:52–56), although that is not the major thrust of the parable. Admittedly, even if all this is true, it does not get us very far. We are left with the meager datum that, while not undertaking a formal mission to Samaritans, Jesus took a benign view of them.[175]

4. In John as in Luke, we find both a narrative about Jesus' relation to the Samaritans and a saying mentioning the Samaritans.

(a) The narrative is the famous encounter of Jesus with the Samaritan woman at the well (John 4:4–42). Here we meet the problem of the relation of tradition, redaction, and possible historical core on a massive scale. No critical scholar would deny that the story as it stands in John 4 reflects John's own theology and his way of structuring a story to serve that theology. The narrative betrays typical theological concerns of John and typical Johannine vocabulary.[176] Especially prominent as a structuring device of the whole story is what we might call a "christology of encounter." As elsewhere in the Fourth Gospel (the gathering of the first disciples in John 1:35–51; the blind man who gradually comes to see who Jesus really is in 9:1–39), a person (or a group of persons) who has not previously met Jesus "bumps into him," struggles to understand and articulate who he is, and runs through a series of titles or descriptions, usually in a carefully arranged ascending order of prominence. This is certainly true of the Samaritan woman, who is guided by Jesus on a spiritual journey that leads her from an initial, slightly hostile reference to Jesus as "you, a Jew" (4:8) through descriptions of him as *kyrios* ("sir" or "lord" in 4:11,15), an ironic question about whether he is greater than the patriarch Jacob (4:12), and an affirmation that he is a prophet (4:19), to the climactic though hesitating suggestion to her fellow Samaritans that this Jew may be the awaited Messiah (4:25 + 29). After encountering Jesus themselves, the Samaritans conclude this narrative essay in christology with the choral acclamation: "This is truly the Savior of the world" (v 42). Fittingly, then, right in the midst of the story, during an interlude in the action, Jesus seems to refer prophetically to the future mission of the early Christian church to the Samaritans (vv 31–38; cf. Acts 8).[177]

All this makes one wary of claiming that behind this magnificent theological composition, foreshadowing as it does the Christian mission to the Samaritans, lies a particular event from the life of the historical Jesus. Yet, whether such an event lies there or not, what is striking about John 4 is that it is the most explicit and well-informed passage about Samaritans in the NT. For instance, there is indeed a well at the foot of Mt. Gerizim. The evangelist is probably quite correct in informing us that Samaritans and Jews do not use the same utensils (v 9, with an indirect reference to purity rules).[178] The narrative also correctly implies that it would be most unusual for a Jewish man to speak with a Samaritan woman (with a possible reference to suspicions about the ritually impure state of Samaritan women and their loose morals).[179] More significantly, for the only time in the NT, explicit mention is made of the competition between Samaritan worship on Mt. Gerizim (though the name itself is not spoken) and Jewish veneration of Jerusalem and its temple (v 20).[180] For all the supposed anti-Judaism of John's Gospel, it is in this story that Jesus is most directly identified as "a Jew"—as distinct from another monotheistic religious group of Semites in Palestine—and that he clearly vindicates the correct stance of the Jews vis-à-vis the Samaritans on the proper place for the public, communitarian worship of God ("we [Jews] worship what we know," v 22). Indeed, Jesus sums up his Jewish view of things vis-à-vis that of the Samaritans in the lapidary pronouncement: "Salvation is from the Jews." One suspects that this is not a pure redactional creation of the evangelist especially noted for his polemic against "the Jews." In addition, the Samaritan woman's expectation of a Messiah who is a prophet, teacher, or revealer figure (v 25) confirms for the 1st century what we learn from later Samaritan sources: the Samaritans awaited an eschatological figure called the Taheb. The Taheb was not a royal Davidic figure but more of a prophet-teacher-revealer like Moses (cf. Deut 18:15,18).[181] In sum, as in many other narratives in the Fourth Gospel, we seem to be hearing in John 4 early Christian-Jewish tradition that is well informed about the situation in 1st-century Palestine. Whether or not this material goes back in part to the historical Jesus, we find in John 4 an important contribution to or confirmation of our fragmentary knowledge of Samaritans in the 1st century A.D.[182]

(b) Finally, in John 8:48 we have a saying that uses the word "Samaritan." However, in this case, the saying is spoken not by Jesus but by his adversaries. In fact, it is a slur that they hurl against Jesus in the midst of a hot exchange of invectives: "Do we not say well that you are a Samaritan and are possessed by a demon?" This slur may refer either to the supposed illegitimate origins of the Samaritans (and thus indirectly to the supposedly illegitimate birth of Jesus) [183] or more likely to the supposed magical powers of the Samaritans (e.g., Simon Magus, Dositheus), attributed in this saying to their consorting with demonic agents. James D. Purvis ingeniously spells out this point by placing it within the larger context of the developing polemic of chap. 8.[184] He suggests that the double charge made by Jesus' adversaries refers back to (1) Jesus' accusation that the Jews are "not of God" (8:47) and not Abraham's children (8:39–40), an accusation that echoes the sort of charge that *Samaritans* would make against Jews, and (2) Jesus' claim to be of heavenly or divine origin ("from above") and therefore "not of this world" (8:23)—a claim that his adversaries twist into an accusation of being possessed by a *demon*. It is telling that in v 49 the Johannine Jesus thinks it sufficient to reply to the adversaries' double charge with a single denial: "I am not possessed by a demon." Clearly, then, in the mind of the evangelist, the charge of being a Samaritan and the charge of being possessed are two alternate ways of saying the same disparaging thing. Whatever the precise historicity of the debate in John 8—a great deal of which reflects the polemic between John's community and Jews or Jewish Christians at the end of the 1st century A.D.[185]—the saying in 8:48 voices the common disdain with which observant Jews viewed Samaritans.

In the end, we must admit we are not left with very much by way of hard data about the historical Jesus' interaction with or views about the Samaritans.[186] At best, there is a multiple attestation in Lucan and Johannine traditions that Jesus stood over against the typical Jewish views of the day in that he held a benign view of Samaritans, even when that attitude was not reciprocated. In addition, both Luke and John suggest that Jesus had positive, though passing, encounters with particular Samaritans. But, by either explicit statement or telling silence, all the Gospels agree that there was no programmatic mission to the Samaritans during Jesus' lifetime.

III. THE SCRIBES

In the interest of full disclosure, I begin this section with a simple admission. The only reason why Jewish scribes are treated in this chapter is the necessity to correct popular misconceptions about them.[187] Actually, scribes do not belong in a chapter or a book dealing with Jesus' relationship to different Jewish religious groups because the scribes *in their capacity as scribes* did not

form or belong to any one religious group in Palestinian Judaism at the time
of Jesus. Yet that is the popular misconception about them, one that stems
from their depiction in the Synoptic Gospels and to a lesser degree in later
rabbinic literature. From the Synoptics, many Christian readers garner the
impression that the scribes were by definition a unified group of people who
had formally studied the Mosaic Law in great detail,[188] who were therefore
acknowledged experts in religious, moral, and legal questions, and who accordingly wielded great social influence and political power, notably by having representatives sitting alongside the chief priests and the lay elders on the
Jerusalem Sanhedrin. In its most extreme form, this approach presupposes—
rather than argues—that all scribes were Torah scholars (alias wise men,
sages, rabbis, or sophists) and all Torah scholars were scribes. Curiously, the
basic scribal function of writing and copying documents is often underplayed or forgotten.

Such a portrait is hopelessly simplistic, not least of all because it forgets
that in the ancient Mediterranean world, the word "scribe" had a wide range
of meanings. It was a designation that applied to various figures up and
down the social, educational, and political ladder. It could mean different
things at different times and in different places. As Anthony Saldarini suggests, an equivalently ambiguous title in today's society would be "secretary."[189] The word can apply to a lowly drudge taking notes of meetings and
typing them into a computer in a corporate cubicle, or a trusted and well-
paid assistant to the CEO of the same corporation, or a major functionary on
the board of trustees running the corporation, or a minor bureaucrat in the
city, state, or federal government, or the Secretary of State of the United
States, fourth in the line of succession if the President should die in office.
One cannot write one sentence defining what "secretary" must mean always
and everywhere in the United States today. Likewise, one cannot write one
sentence that defines what a scribe was in the ancient Mediterranean world
in general or in 1st-century Palestine in particular.

The starting point for understanding the idea of scribe in the ancient world
is the idea of writing.[190] Just as relatively few people in the ancient Mediterranean world could read a lengthy, complicated document, so even fewer
people could write such a document. Writing lengthy documents—as opposed to scratching one's name on a document or writing a few lines of an
I.O.U. or quick note—was an acquired skill that demanded a good amount
of training. Hence it was a distinct profession, one that was little needed in a
primitive agrarian society, but one that was increasingly needed as cities,
large-scale commercial ventures, military organizations, religious and educational institutions, government bureaucracies and—needless to say—tax col-

lection developed. As such needs arose, scribes wrote, copied, and kept records for tax purposes and military musters, annals for government archives, sacred religious texts for temples, and, in due time, literary works for the educated elite.[191]

In various times and places, scribes could be found on most levels of the social ladder. They included poorly educated scribes in villages, writing marriage contracts, other legal records, and personal correspondence for the illiterate villagers. At times, their scribal activity may have supplied them with only part-time employment; hence, they would have had to have other means of support. Such scribes would also have been natural go-betweens when villagers had to deal with bureaucrats higher up in the government. In more developed societies, scribes could be found in middle-level bureaucratic positions in government and religious institutions. In large cities, there would have been sufficient demand to allow some scribes to set up private businesses of writing and copying documents. Royal courts and major temple establishments would have allowed some scribes to rise high in social standing and in at least indirect power as they advised rulers, executed government orders, undertook diplomatic missions, delivered messages from one official to another, and helped educate the children of the elite. Both priests and laity would have been represented in higher scribal circles.

In ancient Israel before the Babylonian exile, the major locus of scribes would naturally have been the royal court, the military, and the temple (or temples in the northern kingdom). There may have been schools in Jerusalem and elsewhere to train the scribes in their profession, but direct evidence is lacking. The most famous Jerusalem scribe from the preexilic period is Baruch, the friend and amanuensis of the prophet Jeremiah. Called a *sōfēr* ("scribe") in Jer 36:26,32, Baruch shows intriguing connections between prophetic and scribal activity within the larger context of the Jerusalem royal palace and temple. Indeed, a seal impression recovered from a royal archive suggests that Baruch may have been a royal scribe and perhaps a member of a prominent scribal family.[192]

During the Persian rule in Judea after the return from the Babylonian exile, scribal activity was probably limited in large part to the government and temple bureaucracies in Jerusalem, neither of which would have been all that extensive. The most famous Jewish scribe of the early postexilic period—at least in the view of the Books of Ezra and Nehemiah—was the priest and community leader Ezra. To what extent the title "scribe" as applied to Ezra signifies that he held a definite position in the Persian governmental structure (even governor?) is debated among scholars.[193] Certainly, the Book of Ezra pictures him as the chief local civic and religious official, though some critics see his exalted position combining the roles of scribe and priest as a retrojection of the prominent position of later priest-scribes of the Second Temple period. Be that as it may, at the very least Ezra was a scholar and teacher of the Mosaic Law who had great influence and impact on the postexilic Jewish community in Jerusalem as it struggled to rebuild the city and its temple. As the example of Ezra indicates, in postexilic Jerusalem the roles of priest/ Levite, community leader, and scribe at times overlapped, though no doubt laymen were scribes as well. More specifically, Ezra represents a striking case of a scribe who combined in one person the functions of a high civic official, a student and teacher of the Law, and a priestly leader (though not high priest!) of the worshiping community.

Needless to say, it would be a mistake to take the unusual case of Ezra as typical of postexilic Jewish-Palestinian scribes in general.[194] Yet the creation, transmission, and gradual canonization of the Mosaic Pentateuch would have given a special aura and cast to at least some Jewish scribes in Palestine that would have had no exact correlative in the Greco-Roman world. Further changes in the position of scribes apparently took place in Palestine during the Ptolemaic period, when the Hellenistic rulers of Egypt controlled Judea. Especially under the administrative reforms of Ptolemy II Philadelphus, the local bureaucracy grew significantly and the demand for scribes increased accordingly, not only in Jerusalem but also in towns and villages.[195] Not only Jerusalemites but also small-town and rural populations needed more documents, and the status and influence of scribes in Palestinian society naturally grew.

It is within this context of increased scribal activity and Hellenistic influence that we can best understand a figure like Jesus Ben Sira, the author of the deuterocanonical/apocryphal Book of Sirach (written sometime in the early 2d century B.C.). He is a well-educated and much-traveled ambassador, expert in the Law, exponent of Israel's wisdom tradition, and teacher of the youth drawn from the Jerusalem elite.[196] In his famous portrait of the scribe in Sir 38:24–39:11, he melds into one ideal type the scribe, the sage, the Law expert, the government official, the teacher, and most notably the pious, holy man, deeply attached to the temple and its priesthood—in short, the archetype of the learned Jew leading the devout life. Here we have an expansion and religious exaltation of the idea (and ideal) of a scribe that would be largely unintelligible to a pagan Greek or Roman audience, where a scribe was usually either a professional writer/copyist or a lower-to-middle-level bureaucrat.

To be sure, most Jewish-Palestinian scribes would not have been the authors of important religious works like Ben Sira and would not have fully embodied the ideal portrait Ben Sira paints, but many would have been involved in copying and transmitting sacred documents to subsequent generations of Jews. At least some of these scribes would have been in a position to become religious teachers and leaders in groups of pious Jews dedicated to careful study and practice of the Law. During the Maccabean revolt (167–164 B.C.), some deeply religious scribes were involved in the resistance to the Hellenizing policies of the Syrian king Antiochus IV Epiphanes. They may have been associated with the shadowy group known as Hasideans (1 Macc 4:24; 7:12–14), though the texts are not clear on this point.[197] In 2 Macc 6:18–31, we hear of the noble resistance of the elderly and highly influential scribe Eleazar, who chose torture and martyrdom rather than betray the Mosaic Law.[198]

The religious aura that was beginning to surround the figure of the Jewish scribe in Palestine was broadened still more in certain apocalyptic circles, as can be seen from the Book of Daniel, *1 Enoch,* the Qumran fragments of the *Book of the Giants,* 4 Ezra, and *2 Baruch.*[199] In *1 Enoch,* Enoch is twice called "the scribe of righteousness" (12:4; 15:1) and carries out the functions of both prophet and wisdom teacher. In this apocalyptic perspective, a scribe like Enoch, Ezra, or Baruch is not just a writer, and not just a religious or social leader, but more importantly a recipient, guardian, and teacher of apocalyptic revelation, an author of apocalyptic literature, a sage, and a preacher of repentance and doom to Israel, the whole world, and angelic powers. All this is a far cry from a copyist of marriage contracts in a village. The one underlying constant in this shifting and expanding understanding of a scribe is the rare, revered, and sometimes almost magical power to write lengthy documents, including those of religious or even esoteric import. While Jesus may have been a sage as well as a prophet, he was definitely not a scribe.[200]

Strikingly different from this Jewish-Palestinian vision of the ideal scribe (be it in Ben Sira or *1 Enoch*) is the regular meaning of scribe in Jewish-Hellenistic literature that was strongly oriented to the larger pagan Greco-Roman world. For instance, the author of the *Letter of Aristeas* (probably written in Alexandria in the 2d century B.C.) and Josephus both mention educated and wise Jews around their own time who were students and teachers of the Law. But, in keeping with Greco-Roman usage, they do not call such revered figures scribes. To their way of thinking, the title scribe, when used of persons around their own time, refers to copyists, secretaries, or government bureaucrats, not to learned and venerable sages.[201] To this extent, the usage of the Synoptic Gospels (the original text of John's Gospel never mentions scribes)[202] reflects more the milieu of Jewish Palestine than that of the larger Greco-Roman world, although it hardly gives us a completely accurate and differentiated picture of scribes at the time of Jesus. Because of their overriding theological agendas, the Synoptists tend to present the Jewish scribes as a homogenized group of teachers of the Law and community leaders who are united in their opposition to Jesus—though, as we shall see, there are a few exceptions to the rule and some stylistic variations among the evangelists. We turn now to the three Synoptic Gospels.

Mark lays out the basic picture of the scribes that Matthew and Luke follow with minor modifications. To Mark's mind, which seems to move between the poles of Galilee and Jerusalem, scribes are especially associated with Jerusalem and hence with opposition to Jesus. During the public ministry, Mark portrays hostile scribes as coming from or residing in Jerusalem (3:22; 7:1,5; the passion predictions in 8:31; 10:33). The references in 3:22 and 7:1,5 create the impression of some sort of investigatory commission sent from Jerusalem to question or attack Jesus' activity in Galilee. One is therefore not surprised that, when Jesus finally comes to Jerusalem at the end of the public ministry, his interaction with the scribes, presented alongside other Jewish leaders, is almost entirely negative. This interaction occurs in two contexts: the Jerusalem dispute stories (11:18,27; 12:28,32 [the only positive references to a scribe in the whole Gospel],35,38) and the Passion Narrative (14:1,43,53; 15:1,31). In contrast, throughout the whole Gospel, there are only a few instances where Mark mentions scribes who are clearly resident in Galilee (possibly 1:22; 2:6,16; the geographical setting in 9:11,14 is unclear).

In both venues, the scribes in Mark are presupposed to be teachers learned in the Mosaic Law and/or officials enjoying authority and prestige within Jewish society. Mark may take for granted that this learning and authority are connected with the scribes' professional ability to write texts, but curiously this point is never explicitly made by either Mark or any other evangelist.[203] That Mark does not simply equate scribes with Pharisees is indicated by what is the most likely reading of Mark 2:16, which speaks of "the scribes of the Pharisees," i.e., those professional scribes who belonged to and were teachers in the party of the Pharisees.[204] By implication, other Jewish parties would have had their scribes too, though Mark never says this outright. As noted above, the scribes are regularly depicted as hostile to Jesus, who in turn is said by Mark 1:22 to teach the people with authority "and not like the scribes"—which, on the face of it, suggests that the Jewish scribes have no real authority to teach.[205] It is remarkable that Mark felt it necessary to undertake such a preemptive strike (in the first chapter of the Gospel, before the scribes have actually appeared on the stage of the narrative!) to deny that Jewish scribes have any teaching authority. One may infer from this polemic that, among Jews whom Mark or his tradition knew, at least some scribes did enjoy such authority.[206] Ominously, early on in the public ministry, the scribes in 2:6–7 already judge that Jesus has committed blasphemy—the very charge on which he will finally be condemned by the Jerusalem Sanhedrin, of which the scribes form a part (14:64). The polemic against the scribes' teaching authority, which surfaces at various points in the public ministry, is matched at the very end of the public ministry by Jesus' biting critique of their ostentatious religious behavior, which he claims only masks their exploitive practices (Mark 12:38–39).

This tone of Christian polemic continues into the Marcan Passion Narrative, though in a different key. Scribes are mentioned alongside the chief priests and (at times) the elders as plotting the death of Jesus and as constituting one of the three parts of the (putative) Jerusalem Sanhedrin, before which Jesus is put on trial. These Jerusalem scribes are thus thought to exercise major political and religious power in Jerusalem, naturally under the supreme authority of the Roman governor. Granted this pervasively hostile depiction of the scribes, it is striking that Mark relates one story in which a sympathetic scribe in Jerusalem agrees with Jesus on the question of the two greatest commandments of the Law (Mark 12:28–34). This one pericope, which flows against the basic Marcan current in particular and the Synoptic tradition in general, most likely goes back to early tradition and perhaps even to an actual event in Jesus' life. Its presence in Mark's Gospel may also indicate that relations with Judaism are not so completely ruptured in Mark's community (at Rome?) that Mark cannot conceive of a Jewish scribe being in accord with Jesus' teaching on the proper place of love of God and love of neighbor within the Mosaic Law (contrast the Matthean parallel!).[207]

Matthew's picture of Jewish scribes agrees basically with Mark's, though the tone is, if possible, even darker.[208] In a foreshadowing of the Passion Narrative, scribes act as official interpreters of the Law along with the chief priests in Jerusalem as early as the Infancy Narrative (2:4–5). It is not lost on Matthew that the scribes' expertise in this story is put at the service of King Herod, who uses it to try to put the infant Jesus to death. The final involvement of the Jerusalem scribes in Jesus' death is thus prefigured at the beginning of the Gospel.

Still, for Matthew, it is the Pharisees, even more than the scribes, who are the adversaries par excellence of Jesus during the public ministry. In some passages, Matthew substitutes the Pharisees for the scribes mentioned in the Marcan tradition he inherited (see Matt 9:11 ‖ Mark 2:16; Matt 9:34 and 12:24 ‖ Mark 3:22; Matt 21:45 ‖ Mark 12:12; Matt 22:34 ‖ Mark 12:28). The scribes, however, still function as opponents during the public ministry, especially when they are in the company of the Pharisees. Hence, the Pharisees who ask for a sign in Mark 8:11 become in Matt 12:38 "some of the scribes and Pharisees." The fact that Matthew's alternate version of this incident in Matt 16:1 identifies the hostile petitioners as "the Pharisees and the Sadducees" reveals how much Matthew tends to blur distinctions among Jewish groups for the sake of constructing his "united front of Jewish leaders" against Jesus.[209]

This blurring of borders becomes all the clearer in Matthew's redaction of the great list of woes in chap. 23. Matthew's catalogue of woes is aimed in undifferentiated fashion at "the scribes and the Pharisees" (23:13,15,23,25, 27,29; cf. 23:2; also 5:20; 12:38; 15:1 [in reverse order]) while the equivalent catalogue in Luke 11:42–53 (probably reflecting the original Q tradition) distinguishes the Pharisees and the lawyers as separate groups.[210] Matthew's refrain-like repetition of this tag "scribes and Pharisees" at various points in the public ministry might conjure up the impression of a total identification of the two groups. Yet Matthew never explicitly makes such an identification,[211] perhaps because, as we shall see below, Matthew knows of the existence of Christian scribes while he knows of no Christian Pharisees. However, whenever the scribes are associated with the Pharisees during the public ministry, they are always seen in a negative light.

Likewise negative is the scribes' role in the Jerusalem dispute stories and the Passion Narrative, though the scribes do not appear as lead agents in these narratives as frequently in Matthew as they do in Mark. More often, Matthew speaks simply of the chief priests and the elders. At first glance, this might lead the modern reader to suppose that Matthew has a better sense than Mark of the political realities at the time of Jesus: in Jerusalem, the chief priests and the lay aristocrats (the elders) were the major political players under Pilate, with scribes in a merely supporting role. Alternately, one might interpret Matthew's usage as indicating that he seeks to spare the scribes full responsibility for the death of Jesus. Both of these approaches, however, seem unlikely. At times, Matthew does present the scribes alongside the chief priests (or Caiaphas) and the elders as one of the three constitutive elements of the Sanhedrin (26:57 + 59; 27:41; cf. the passion predictions in 16:21; 20:18). Hence his omission of the scribes from some of the passages he inherits from Mark may be purely a matter of stylistic variation, without much significance for theology or history.[212] After all, Matthew, contrary to Mark, pointedly places all three groups at the cross as they mock Jesus—thus reconstituting the hostile Sanhedrin on Golgotha. In addition, in 21:15 Matthew adds a scene in which the chief priests and the scribes object to Jesus' performing miracles in the temple and being acclaimed as Son of

David. Thus, scribes remain opponents of Jesus in Matthew's Gospel, though their prominence as a distinct group is somewhat diminished when compared to Mark's presentation. In all of these purposeful changes by Matthew, we have clear examples of his highly symbolic, theological, and polemical view of scribes. Accordingly, we are not surprised that the Marcan exchange between the sympathetic scribe and Jesus on the greatest commandment of the Law is changed by Matthew in 22:35 into a hostile question posed by a Pharisee (who, in many Greek manuscripts, is called a lawyer).[213] Apparently, Matthew has difficulty conceiving of a Jewish scribe during the final clash in Jerusalem expressing basic agreement with Jesus.

In striking contrast, Matthew twice hints at the existence of Christian scribes in his community or tradition (13:52; 23:34). In a more ambiguous passage (8:19), Matthew depicts a scribe offering to follow Jesus. Jesus' sharp response about the cost of discipleship ("foxes have holes and birds of the air have nests . . .") leaves one unsure as to whether the scribe is meant to be taken in a positive (sincere if naive) or negative (unsubstantial and rejected) light.[214] In any event, these two (or three) positive references to scribes indicate that, for Matthew, the problem with the Jewish scribes is not ultimately that they are scribes but that they are Jews who refuse to believe in Jesus. Scribe, in itself, refers to a profession, not a religious stance or a sectarian group.

Like Matthew, Luke basically follows Mark's leitmotiv in his presentation of Jewish scribes, though with his own variations on the theme. If anything, the portrait of the scribes becomes vaguer in Luke's Gospel compared to Mark's. During the public ministry, the scribes regularly appear in the company of the Pharisees and seem more or less assimilated to them. In a style similar to Matthew's, Luke repeatedly uses the tag "the scribes and the Pharisees" or "the Pharisees and the scribes."[215] Again like Matthew, and following Mark's basic approach, Luke associates the scribes with the chief priests and at times the elders in the context of the passion predictions and the Passion Narrative. Yet the picture is not quite the same as the one created by Matthew's redaction of Mark. Luke complicates matters by introducing into his Gospel the categories of "lawyer" (*nomikos,* in the sense of a person learned in the Mosaic Law) and "teacher of the Law" *(nomodidaskalos).*[216] Granted his vague and homogenizing usage, Luke probably understands these two categories as more or less equivalent to that of scribes.[217] For instance, Luke concludes the two catalogues of woes against Pharisees and *lawyers* with a general reference to *scribes* and Pharisees (11:53). In addition, Luke speaks of "the Pharisees and the lawyers" in 7:30 and 14:3 and of "Pharisees and teachers of the Law" in 5:17—apparently just as stylistic variations of his more usual "the scribes and the Pharisees" (which he uses when he picks up the phrase from 5:17 in 5:21).

Luke carries his general portrait of the scribes from the Gospel into Acts, though there he gives the portrait some new details. In particular, during Paul's trial before the Sanhedrin, Luke indicates that some scribes belong specifically to the party of the Pharisees (23:9; cf. Mark 2:16) and hence, by implication, that other scribes might belong to other parties (in the immediate context, the Sadducees). Thus, at least in Acts, scribes are not totally assimilated to the Pharisees. This is all the more true since, in Acts, we have the unique Lucan reference to a Gentile scribe. Displaying his wider Greco-Roman cultural background, Luke in Acts 19:35 speaks of a "scribe" at Ephesus, who is some sort of city clerk, secretary, or other kind of bureaucrat—a type of scribe quite different from the one we see in Luke's Gospel. To this extent, at least, Luke faithfully reflects the divergence of Jewish-Palestinian from pagan Greco-Roman usage.

The upshot of this brief survey is that one must beware of taking the presentation of the scribes in the Synoptics as sober history. The portrait and activities of the scribes are filtered through Christian theology and polemic—and perhaps at times ignorance of the pre-70 Palestinian situation.[218] What, then, can be said of the historical Jesus' relation to the historical scribes? One can speak in only general terms. Most likely, Jesus would have encountered various types of scribes as he traveled through Galilee and Judea and as he stayed in Jerusalem during the festivals. In Galilee, he may have met and at times debated with village scribes equipped with a very limited education. (One may wonder whether Jesus himself learned basic Hebrew and something of the Hebrew Scriptures from such a village scribe in Nazareth.) More educated scribes would have been employed both privately and by the government in larger towns like Capernaum, which was a border crossing important to Herod Antipas for tolls. Insofar as the skilled and learned among Galilean scribes would have been employed at least at times by pious Jews or Jewish groups in copying the Pentateuch and other religious scrolls, some of the scribes would probably have acquired a reputation for knowledge of the Law and skill in its interpretation. From a practical point of view, at Jewish religious meetings on the sabbath (*synagōgai* in this fluid sense), the scribes would have been the natural persons to read and explain the sacred scrolls to the public. Hence, while not all scribes would have enjoyed great religious learning or authority to teach, some among them, especially those belonging to or working for groups of pious, zealous Jews (be they Pharisees or not), would have possessed such a reputation. It may be this particular phenomenon that the Gospels later blow up into a broad and polemical generalization.

Jesus may have encountered still more educated, socially prominent, and affluent scribes in Jerusalem. Here scribes would have had a wide range of opportunities for employment, from the private business of copying both civil and sacred documents to jobs in the government bureaucracy (including law courts), controlled on the local level by the high priest along with the priestly and lay aristocracy around him—all under the watchful eye of the Roman prefect, who would have needed his own scribes when he visited Jerusalem during the festivals. Especially in the holy city, some learned scribes in the tradition of Ben Sira may have combined the vocations of writer-copyist, student-teacher-interpreter of the Mosaic Law, government bureaucrat, and member and perhaps leader of a pious group (including but not necessarily restricted to Pharisaism). If it be true that, during the time of Jesus, Pharisees were especially concentrated in Jerusalem, then it stands to reason that those scribes who belonged to and helped guide the Pharisaic movement would likewise have been more readily found in Jerusalem than in Galilee. If some of the dispute stories of the Gospels actually go back to events in the public ministry of Jesus, it is possible that, though the narrative framework of Mark later placed these clashes in Galilee, they may actually have taken place in Jerusalem.

It likewise stands to reason that, when the priestly and lay aristocracy, in concert no doubt with the Roman prefect, moved to have Jesus arrested, some scribes would have been involved, especially in the Jewish "hearing" (however informal that may have been). Contrary to the impression given by the Synoptics, the scribes as a group would not have sat alongside Caiaphas, the chief priests, and the lay aristocrats as a distinct power-group within a national Sanhedrin judging Jesus (a very questionable picture on many different historical grounds). High-level scribes may well have been among the trusted councillors meeting with and advising Caiaphas (hence, a *synedrion* in the general sense of a meeting or a session) as well as among the secretaries taking notes or writing up charges, but they hardly enjoyed political or religious authority distinct from or on a coequal level with his. In this sense, they were indeed "retainers," dependent for power and resources on their rich and aristocratic overlords.[219]

One can see, then, that to speak of Jesus in relation to the Jewish scribes in the same way that one speaks of Jesus in relation to the Pharisees or the Sadducees or the Samaritans (or hypothetically the Essenes) is an example of an ahistorical confusion of different categories. Basically, one is mixing up religious-political movements unique to Judaism and Palestine with a profession widespread throughout the ancient Mediterranean world, though one that had developed in special ways within Palestinian Judaism. That Jesus at times dealt, dialogued, or debated with various types of Jewish scribes is indeed likely. But that the Jewish scribes were a homogeneous religious group with a united theological agenda as well as with a distinct power base, a homogeneous group that formed part of the united front against Jesus, is hopelessly wrong. Hence, given the tendency of the Synoptics to supply scribes as stock characters in disputes with Jesus or in plots against him, one must be very wary of appealing to any particular Gospel pericope for information about specific historical incidents involving Jesus' interaction with Jewish scribes.[220]

IV. THE HERODIANS

When one comes to the Herodians, one gets the impression that rarely has so much been made of so little NT data.[221] The Greek word *Hērōdianoi* (= "Herodians") occurs nowhere prior to the 1st century A.D., and in the 1st century it occurs only in Mark 3:6 (at the end of the healing of the man with the withered hand); 12:13 (at the beginning of the question about the coin of tribute); and in the Matthean passage dependent on Mark 12:13, Matt 22:16.[222] Matthew does not take over "Herodians" from Mark 3:6 in the parallel verse (Matt 12:14). Surprisingly, Luke, for all his interest in the Herodian dynasty and its clients, never mentions a group called the Herodians. In spite of or perhaps because of this scarcity of data, theories about who the Herodians were have multiplied over the centuries, modern scholars vying with Church Fathers to see who can be more imaginative or bizarre.

If we pass over the silliest explanations (though it is hard to decide which theories deserve that accolade the most), we may list major options for defining the Herodians as follows:[223] (1) a religious sect that claimed Herod was the Messiah, though proponents of this theory disagree on whether the monarch so hailed was Herod the Great (reigned 37–4 B.C.), Herod Antipas (4 B.C.–A.D. 39), Herod Agrippa I (A.D. 41–44), or Herod Agrippa II (A.D. 48–ca. 93); (2) more vaguely, a religious sect founded or favored by Herod the Great; (3) the Essenes; (4) the Sadducees or the Boethusians, the latter understood as a group closely related to the Sadducees or as a subset thereof; (5) a political party that supported a particular Herodian monarch or the Herodian dynasty in general; (6) officials, courtiers, or household servants of Antipas; (7) soldiers of Antipas; (8) Jews who disliked direct Roman rule by the prefects and who therefore wanted the territory of Antipas (or possibly Agrippa I, prior to A.D. 41) to be extended to the limits of the former kingdom of Herod the Great; (9) followers of the Jewish revolutionary, Judas the Galilean (= Judah the Gaulonite, who led a revolt in A.D. 6), or, more generally, extreme opponents of Roman rule; (10) a Roman sodality or *collegium* founded in honor of Herod the Great, similar to the sodalities founded in Rome to honor various emperors after their deaths; (11) Jews who belonged to the northern tetrarchies of Palestine, which were governed at various times by various members of the Herodian dynasty; (12) publicans or tax collectors; (13) the scribes; (14) a group called *běnê bathyra* (= the sons of the city of Bathyra) in rabbinic sources. Some of these theories have been combined with each other in varying configurations and with different members of the Herodian dynasty being chosen as the referents. Complicating matters still further is that, while some authors think that Mark is historically accurate in placing the Herodians at the time of Jesus, other critics detect an anachronistic reference to supporters of either Agrippa I or Agrippa II.[224]

What can be said in favor of most of these theories? Not much. What we can say is that the NT form *Hērōdianoi* (with its *-ianoi* ending) is not the proper Greek form for "Herodians." The proper Greek form is rather *Hērōdeioi,* which we find once (but only once) in Josephus.[225] The NT form seems based on a presumed or theoretical Latin form *Herodiani* (*-iani* being a regular Latin ending). The other two famous cases of such Greek nouns with Latin endings are *Kaisarianoi* (= Latin *Caesariani,* meaning in various contexts Caesar's troops, his partisans, or his household servants)[226] and *Christianoi* ("Christians" in Acts 11:26; 26:28; 1 Pet 4:16, perhaps in imitation of *Hērōdianoi* or *Kaisarianoi,* and perhaps with the mocking sense of the household servants or slaves of their master, the crucified Christ). Another, though less well-known, example is *Pompēianoi,* the followers or supporters of Pompey the Great.[227] In light of these (admittedly few) parallels from the beginning of the Christian era, the most likely meanings of *Hērōdianoi* would include the household servants or slaves of Herod, his officials or courtiers (high officials sometimes being ex-slaves), and more generally all the supporters of Herod's regime, whether or not they belonged to an organized group or party.[228] Since "Herod," in imitation of "Caesar," had become the name of a dynasty, which Herod is meant cannot be determined from the word itself.

Can the two Marcan dispute stories (the first is also a miracle story) in which the Herodians appear shed any further light on this shadowy group and its possible interaction with the historical Jesus? The two incidents recounted by Mark ostensibly take place during Jesus' public ministry (A.D. 28–30): the healing of the man with the withered hand in 3:1–6 is situated in Galilee early on in the public ministry while the question about the coin of tribute in 12:13–17 is situated in Jerusalem during Jesus' final days. In both cases, the Herodians appear suddenly alongside the familiar Pharisees and just as suddenly disappear from the ongoing narrative. In both cases, the Pharisees are mentioned first: "the Pharisees took counsel with the Herodians" in 3:6; "and they [presumably the chief priests, scribes, and elders of 11:27] send to him [Jesus] some of the Pharisees and [some] of the Herodians" in 12:13. And in both cases, the two groups are presented as working together with deadly enmity toward Jesus.

Both stories likewise have a political dimension, covert or overt. (1) In 3:6, the political reference is implicit. Insofar as the Pharisees wished to "destroy" [apolesōsin] Jesus by capital punishment—let us remember that we are dealing here with Mark's story, not necessarily with historical events—they would have needed the cooperation of the tetrarch Herod Antipas, who held the power to inflict capital punishment in his tetrarchy, made up of Galilee and Perea.[229] Granted their deadly intent, their conspiring with "the Herodians" in particular makes perfect sense within the story world of Mark 3:6. (2) The political thrust of the question about the coin of tribute is obvious. Loyalty to Rome would naturally be a concern of supporters or servants of Antipas, who held his power by Rome's favor and who ultimately lost it by Rome's disfavor.

Granted the political tone of the two stories, if we were then to take these two stories along with their references to the Herodians as historical, the Herodians would be best understood as the servants, courtiers, or officials of Herod Antipas. That they should have fixed their attention on Jesus is hardly surprising. It was, after all, Herod Antipas who imprisoned and executed John the Baptist, the mentor of Jesus, merely on the suspicion that John might become the focus of some future revolt.[230] Antipas had eliminated the danger with a preemptive strike. Nothing would be more natural than for "that fox" (cf. Luke 13:32) to be on the lookout for other prophets who, like John, might pose a potential danger because of their ability to attract large and enthusiastic crowds. Jesus, an erstwhile disciple of John, would have been all the more worrisome in that, unlike the Baptist, he moved widely around Galilean towns and villages instead of restricting himself to the environs of the Jordan. That he spoke regularly about some sort of coming kingdom made things only more disturbing. If the belief that Jesus was a descendant of King David actually circulated among the common people during the public ministry, that belief would have made his activity positively alarming to supporters of Antipas, who himself harbored hopes of assuming the official title of king. Hence, while the Pharisees' interest in or opposition to Jesus would have been basically religious, the Herodians' concern would have been basically political—though in 1st-century Palestinian Judaism the two interests usually overlapped. Hence the presence of the Herodians in these two stories enjoys a certain coherence with the historical situation in Palestine.

By the same token, though, the neat combination of religious and political interests in these two stories should set off an alarm bell in the critic's mind. Mark is presenting us with a highly unusual yoking of Pharisees and Herodians as joint plotters against Jesus early on in Galilee (3:6) and then as joint questioners of him (12:13) not long before his execution in Jerusalem. Is this simply the evangelist's special way of dramatizing what he considers the united opposition of Jewish-Palestinian religious and political groups against this unconventional prophet and preacher? At the very least, the symmetrical positioning of these two dispute stories in Mark's Gospel must be judged more theological art than sober history. The combination of Pharisees and Herodians occurs first at the climax of the Galilean cycle of dispute stories, questions, and clashes (Mark 2:1–3:6) early on in the public ministry and then for a second time in the Jerusalem cycle of dispute stories, questions, and clashes (Mark 11:27–12:44) at the end of the public ministry. In a broad sense, then, the union of Pharisees and Herodians brackets the public ministry, foreshadowing early on in Galilee the deadly opposition of religious and political forces that would finally bear fruit in Jerusalem. (That this is Marcan theological polemic and not historical record is intimated even by Mark's own Passion Narrative; the primitive passion tradition, to which Mark is largely tied, knows nothing of Pharisees or Herodians being involved in Jesus' trial and death.)

The historical reliability of the first mention of the Pharisees conspiring with the Herodians to do away with Jesus (3:6) is weakened further by our uncertainty about whether the Pharisees enjoyed a significant presence in Galilee in the early 1st century A.D. A more fatal weakness, however, is that the dispute story in 3:1–6 is, in its present form (especially because of the presence of v 6!), hardly credible as a historical event. As we have seen, one of the remarkable aspects of the story of Jesus healing the man with the withered hand on the sabbath is that, quite literally, Jesus *does* nothing.[231] That is to say, he performs no action whatever. He does not touch the man, lay hands upon him, seize him by the hand, or raise him up, as is the case in some other Gospel accounts of Jesus' miracles. Jesus simply issues two verbal orders: the man is to stand up in the sight of the congregation and to stretch forth his hand (vv 3 + 5). On doing that, the man finds his hand healed. Since Jesus has engaged in no physical activity whatever, it is unbelievable that the Pharisees, who differed among themselves on precise points of sabbath observance, would think that they could have Jesus put to death merely for speaking healing words on a sabbath. And once one excludes the historicity of the supposed conspiracy mentioned in 3:6 (namely, to execute Jesus on grounds of breaking the sabbath by speaking words), the historical participation of the Herodians in such a conspiracy is concomitantly excluded. One of the two appearances of the Herodians in Mark thus disappears as a historical datum.

Other secondary considerations also make one suspicious about the historicity of these two events. For example, in both incidents, Mark's combination of the Pharisees and the Herodians occurs only in an introductory (12:13) or a concluding (3:6) verse; it plays no part in the body of either story. Indeed, within the larger compass of the two cycles of dispute stories, this combination comes out of nowhere and then immediately disappears. Whether we assign these framing verses to the hand of Mark or to the hand of some pre-Marcan collector of dispute stories (3:6 concludes the entire cycle of disputes in 2:1–3:6), they are usually considered editorial constructs.[232] It is thus difficult to argue that the combination of Pharisees and Herodians, present only in these two framing verses composed by a redactor, reaches back to the original forms of these stories circulating as isolated units in the oral tradition—to say nothing of possible historical events behind the oral tradition. As we have already seen, such is clearly not the case in 3:6. In my view, while certainty is impossible, 12:13 is more easily understood as a similar case of redactional creation by Mark for the sake of symmetry as he positions his two cycles of disputes stories in Galilee and Jerusalem.[233] As noted above, the combined forces of the Pharisees and Herodians, while not lacking historical verisimilitude in Jerusalem during the last days of Jesus' life, have no discernible impact or even echo in the Marcan account of the passion.

To be sure, I do not intend to deny the existence of a group of servants, officials, and other supporters around Herod Antipas, a group that both we and Mark can legitimately label "Herodians." The onetime use of the similar label *Hērōdeioi* by Josephus (though in *J.W.* 1.16.6 §319 he is speaking of Herod the Great) may supply an argument from analogy for the likelihood of such a group with such a designation at the time of Herod Antipas.[234] Moreover, as noted above, it is quite probable that Herod Antipas would have been concerned about Jesus and would have tried to learn more about him or even to take action against him. Despite their redactional tendencies, both Mark and Luke may well echo historical reality when they refer to Antipas' unhealthy interest in Jesus (Mark 6:14–16; Luke 9:7–9; 13:31–32; 23:6–12; cf. 8:3; Acts 13:1). Antipas might even have attempted to use his servants and allies to spy on, oppose, and discredit Jesus in public; spy systems were quite common in the 1st-century Roman empire. At the very least, verisimilitude favors the idea of Antipas' vigilance and interference; it may even be that such verisimilitude influenced Mark as he formulated his dramatic presentation. Thus, I see no need to deny in principle that, at times during the public ministry, "Herodians" in the sense of supporters, officials, or servants of Antipas may have argued with or set verbal traps for Jesus. The precise question before us, though, is whether Mark 3:6 and 12:13 supply any specific historical information about particular incidents involving Jesus and the Herodians. On balance, the presence of Herodians as sidekicks of the Pharisees precisely in the concluding verse of the healing on the sabbath (unhistorical on the face of it) and in the introductory verse of the coin of tribute—and nowhere else—arouses too much critical suspicion to serve as the firm basis of an argument in favor of historicity. In my view, the curious combination is best attributed to the redactional activity of either Mark or a pre-Marcan collector of dispute stories. Hence Mark 3:6 and 12:13, as they stand in Mark's text, tell us nothing reliable about particular incidents in the life of the historical Jesus. Once we have made this judgment, disputes about whether Mark is referring to Herod Antipas or anachronistically to Herod Agrippa I or Herod Agrippa II are irrelevant to the quest for the historical Jesus.

V. THE ZEALOTS

The question of the Zealots was treated when we considered Simon the Cananean (alias Simon the Zealot) in Chapter 27, which examined the individual members of the Twelve.[235] Here we need recall only a few key points that touch on the question of how Jesus related to the various Jewish groups or parties of his day. (1) If we take Zealot to mean what Josephus almost always takes it to mean, i.e., an organized and armed group of revolutionaries rebelling against Roman rule in Palestine, then it is beside the point to ask whether and how Jesus interacted with the Zealots. The Zealots in this sense of the word did not emerge as a distinct group until the First Jewish Revolt (A.D. 66–70), more specifically during the winter of A.D. 67–68 in Jerusalem, as various political groups jostled and maneuvered for control of the revolt. By definition, therefore, it is hopelessly anachronistic to talk about Jesus being a Zealot or even about his being sympathetic to the Zealots, understood in this narrow sense of the word. (2) Speaking of Jesus' relation to zealots makes sense only if we take zealot in an older and broader sense. In this sense, a zealot was any Jew (a) who was intensely zealous for the practice of the Mosaic Law, (b) who insisted that his fellow Jews strictly observe the Law as a means of separating Israel from the idolatrous and immoral Gentiles round about, and (c) who, in some cases, might use harassment, violence, or even murder to force his fellow Jews to practice strict separation from the Gentiles and their way of living. However, not every Jew zealous for the Law used violence as a means of expressing such zeal.

Simon the Zealot, one of Jesus' chosen Twelve, was apparently a zealot in this broader sense. To what extent he may have engaged in violent activity before being called by Jesus to discipleship and membership in the circle of the Twelve is not know to us and, in a sense, is beside the point. What is to the point is that Jesus called this Simon (1) to a communal life that involved associating (indeed, even eating and drinking at festive meals) with "toll collectors and sinners [i.e., Jews who did not observe the Law]" and (2) to a group of disciples that included Levi the toll collector. The company Simon had to keep as a disciple of Jesus clearly indicates that Simon had to say farewell to his former way of thinking about and acting toward his fellow Israelites. Jesus' inclusive outreach to all of Israel in the end time, his emphasis on mercy and forgiveness, his rejection of retaliation, and his exhortation to love even one's enemies lay at the opposite end of the Palestinian-Jewish spectrum from violence-prone zealotry.

To be sure, there will always be writers who claim that the evangelists have suppressed the true historical Jesus—i.e., Jesus the violent revolutionary who was executed for trying to launch a revolt against Rome—and have substituted for this embarrassing figure the meek and loving Jesus of the Gospels. In a sense, there is no point arguing with such convinced conspiracy-theorists. The massive amount of Gospel traditions brought forward by scholars to disprove the conspiracy theory only proves to the conspiracy-theorists the all-pervasive nature of the cover-up. There is something of a Catch–22 in this position. On the one hand, the conspiracy-theorists claim that the cover-up has been so massive and all-pervading that it deceives most scholars. Yet, on the other hand, we are asked to suppose that the evangelists were surprisingly inept in their cover-up. Inadvertently they left in the Gospels sufficient material to make clear to those with eyes to see—namely, the conspiracy-theorists—the suppressed truth of Jesus the armed revolutionary.

Apart from the difficulty of explaining how most Palestinians around the time of Jesus could so quickly and easily forget what Jesus was all about and why he was executed, the fatal flaw of this approach is its presupposition that there was one or more organized and armed groups of Jewish revolutionaries active in Palestine ca. A.D. 28–30. As far as we can tell, there was not. To be sure, Palestine at the time of Jesus saw more than enough of banditry, social unrest, and popular prophetic movements. But, as far as the historical record permits us to judge, there were no organized, armed groups of Jewish revolutionaries active during Jesus' public ministry. Needless to say, the facts notwithstanding, Jesus the Zealot will remain perennially popular in mass-media presentations, just as he will remain totally anachronistic. We are once again reminded that a sober and nuanced evaluation of the complicated political, social, and economic situation of Palestine in the early 1st century A.D. has never been a strong point of popular presentations of the historical Jesus.

With this, we come to the end of our consideration of the various Jewish groups with whom Jesus may have interacted during his public ministry. The results of our survey in this chapter are admittedly meager. (1) While one can draw up an intriguing list of similarities and differences between Jesus and the Essenes/Qumranites, there is no proof that Jesus ever interacted face to face with representatives of this movement. At best, there is a possibility that he may have alluded to some of their practices or beliefs, such as sabbath observance—though only to distinguish his own position from theirs. This lack of contact is not really surprising: Jesus and the Qumranites in particular existed in different worlds spiritually and even, to a certain extent, geographically. (2) Geographical separation also distinguished the Samaritans, who, in addition—at least in the judgment of some scholars—have the strange distinction of being labeled Israelites but not Jews. That Jesus held a benign view of the often-reviled Samaritans and on a few occasions had passing, positive encounters with some individual Samaritans is supported by multiple attestation of sources and forms. But, beyond that, not much can be said. (3) What can be said about the scribes is that they really do not belong in a list of Jewish parties or sects. They were a profession, not a religious sect or party united around one particular theological agenda. During his itinerant ministry, Jesus probably interacted with various types of scribes who enjoyed different levels of education and social status, but the polemical presentations of scribes as a unified religious group alongside the Pharisees or as a special part of the national Sanhedrin reflect later theological debates, not the historical record. (4) As for the Herodians, we are left with two dispute stories in Mark that mention them ever so briefly. Their presence in both passages may be due to Marcan or pre-Marcan Christian redaction of earlier traditions. This is not to deny that supporters, servants, or even officials of Herod Antipas had reason to be interested in Jesus. They may at times have engaged Jesus in debate or sought to discredit him in public. But the few Gospel passages that mention the Herodians (whoever exactly they may have been) are dubious sources for reliable historical information about specific historical events involving Jesus. (5) Finally, as for the Zealots, understood as an armed and organized group of Jewish revolutionaries fighting Rome, they simply did not exist at the time of Jesus.

While the results of our survey in this chapter are thus quite meager, they still make a positive contribution to our overall quest for the historical Jesus. First, like a great deal of research on the historical Jesus, they serve the purpose of clearing the field of oft-repeated but highly dubious claims about the groups with which Jesus interacted, about the main audience he addressed, and therefore about his basic aim in his ministry. Second, and more positively, what we have seen in this chapter confirms our basic contention that Jesus saw himself as the eschatological prophet sent to *all* Israel in the end time as he sought to prepare the chosen people for God's final act of regathering the twelve tribes. Jesus' message and ministry were addressed to the whole of the Jewish people, not to some sectarian or elite group. While especially aimed at the poor, marginalized, or lost sheep in Israel (which made up most of the population anyway), it excluded no Israelite a priori. Hence we need not be surprised that Jesus spent most of his time and energy speaking of the great questions that involved all Israel rather than of specific and detailed rules that might fascinate this or that Jewish sect or movement. To the extent that he would have engaged a particular group in discussion, it would most likely have been the Pharisees, the other religious movement of the time that was especially active among the common people. To a lesser extent, during his pilgrimages to Jerusalem, he would at times have addressed the representatives of the Jewish leaders who controlled the temple, including those who belonged to the Sadducean party. It was by clashing with this small but powerful Jerusalem elite who worked hand in glove with the Roman prefect that he finally sealed his fate.

We have now come to the end of our survey of Jesus' real or putative relationships to all the major Jewish groups, movements, or sects active in Palestine during his ministry. Still, there remains one very important relationship to be investigated—though it is a notably different sort of relationship: that of Jesus to the Mosaic Law. In a sense, it is the relationship that determined all his other relationships. Jesus' interactions with the Pharisees, the Sadducees, and the common people took place under the sacred canopy of the Mosaic Law, the reality that ultimately defined how one Palestinian Jew related to another. Since the Law was the all-pervading and defining factor of Jewish life in Palestine, it is not surprising that we have bumped into it at every turn in our quest, whether we were considering stories of Jesus healing on the sabbath, his teaching on practices like oaths or divorce, or his relationship to the Pharisees, the Sadducees, and the Essenes.

And yet Jesus' relationship to the Law is a different sort of a relationship from those studied in this volume. It is a relationship not to other persons or groups but to an abstract and all-pervasive principle of Jewish life. It is also a relationship that bundles together a whole series of enigmas. Hence the question of Jesus' relationship to the Mosaic Law is reserved to Volume Four, where other major enigmas and riddles of Jesus' public ministry (his parables, his self-designations, and finally his death) will be considered.

All that remains to be done now is to draw to a conclusion this survey of the relationship of Jesus the Jew to other Jewish groups and individuals.

NOTES TO CHAPTER 30

[1] The bibliography on Qumran and the Essenes is now all but uncontrollable and has spawned volume-length bibliographies of its own. See, e.g., Bastiaan Jongeling, *A Classified Bibliography of the Finds in the Desert of Judah 1958–1969* (STDJ 7; Leiden: Brill, 1971); F. García Martínez and D. W. Parry, *A Bibliography of the Finds in the Desert of Judah 1970–95: Arranged by Author with Citation and Subject Indexes* (STDJ 19; Leiden: Brill, 1996); references to works treating Qumran in relation to Jesus are given according to topics in the index of *A Bibliography of the Finds,* 541–42. For a brief selection of monographs and articles on varied topics connected with Qumran, see the works listed in *A Marginal Jew,* 1. 104–5 nn. 31–37; 2. 287–88 nn. 116–23. As indicated in previous chapters, I accept the majority view that the Qumranites were one particular expression of the larger Essene movement. This view is outlined and vindicated as the consensus position by James H. Charlesworth in his introductory overview, "Qumran Scrolls and a Critical Consensus," in the volume of collected essays, James H. Charlesworth (ed.), *Jesus and the Dead Sea Scrolls* (Anchor Bible Reference Library; New York: Doubleday, 1992) xxxi–xxxvii. This consensus is substantiated by the arguments of James C. VanderKam, "The People of the Dead Sea Scrolls: Essenes or Sadducees?" *Understanding the Dead Sea Scrolls* (ed. Hershel Shanks; New York: Random House, 1992) 50–62. I do not find alternative theories (e.g., that the Qumranites were Zealots or Sadducees, or that the Qumran library was really a library taken from Jerusalem and therefore simply reflects mainstream Judaism) convincing. For the intriguing but not entirely persuasive view that the Qumranites had gone into schism vis-à-vis other Essenes, see Gabriele Boccaccini, *Beyond the Essene Hypothesis* (Grand Rapids/Cambridge, UK: Eerdmans, 1998). Boccaccini is quite right to emphasize that the Essene movement was larger and more varied than its expression at Qumran, but the idea of a schism lacks evidence in the texts. A more radical approach, mixing certitude with agnosticism, is that of Lena Cansdale, *Qumran and the Essenes* (Texte und Studien zum Antiken Judentum 60; Tübingen: Mohr [Siebeck], 1997). According to Cansdale, the scrolls found at Qumran definitely do not come from or reflect the Essenes (pp. 58–66); they come from one or more unnamed and otherwise unknown sects that existed within the many strands of Second Temple Judaism (see p. 194). Likewise questioning an easy identification of the Qumran community with the Essenes, but not as certain about defini-

tively excluding the Essenes, is Phillip R. Callaway, *The History of the Qumran Community* (Journal for the Study of the Pseudepigrapha Supplement 3; Sheffield: JSOT, 1988). On this ongoing debate, see also Johann Maier, "Theories of Qumran," *Judaism in Late Antiquity. Part Three. Where We Stand: Issues and Debates in Ancient Judaism. Volume One* (Handbook of Oriental Studies, Part One, The Near and Middle East 40; Leiden: Brill, 1999) 81–98; Albert I. Baumgarten, "The Current State of Qumran Studies: Crisis in the Scrollery. A Dying Consensus," ibid., 99–119. On the complicated philosophical and methodological problems involved in arguing from and about the archaeological finds at Qumran and Ain Feshkha, see Ferdinand Rohrhirsch, *Wissenschaftstheorie und Qumran* (Novum Testamentum et Orbis Antiquus 32; Freiburg: Universitätsverlag Freiburg; Göttingen: Vandenhoeck & Ruprecht, 1996).

[2] To be accurate, one should make a distinction here. As we shall see, the name "Essenes" is used in various ancient sources (e.g., Josephus). The word "Qumran" does not occur in ancient sources as the designation of a sectarian Jewish community commonly associated with the Essenes. Indeed, this usage postdates and flows from the archaeological discoveries near a wadi that the Arabs called Qumran (hence the name of the ruins: Khirbet Qumran) in the 1940s and 1950s.

[3] Charlesworth ("Qumran Scrolls and a Critical Consensus," xxxv) considers it part of the scholarly consensus on Qumran that "none of the Dead Sea Scrolls refer to him [Jesus], and they do not mention any follower of Jesus described in the New Testament." One possible avenue of indirect contact between Qumran and Jesus might be John the Baptist, the mentor of Jesus. However, as I indicated in my treatment of the Baptist (*A Marginal Jew*, 2. 19–233), I tend to doubt the claim that the Baptist had been a member of the Qumran community (pp. 25–27). For other positions on the connection of the Baptist to Qumran, see James C. VanderKam, "The Dead Sea Scrolls and Christianity," *Understanding the Dead Sea Scrolls*, 188–90 (a possibility); Otto Betz, "Was John the Baptist an Essene?" ibid., 205–214 (probable that the Baptist had lived at Qumran); Joseph A. Fitzmyer, *Responses to 101 Questions on the Dead Sea Scrolls* (New York/Mahwah, NJ: Paulist, 1992) 106–8 (not unlikely that the Baptist was a member of the Qumran community).

[4] See, e.g., Jerome Murphy-O'Connor (ed.), *Paul and Qumran* (London: Chapman, 1968); James H. Charlesworth (ed.), *John and the Dead Sea Scrolls* (New York: Crossroad, 1972, 1990).

[5] Barbara E. Thiering, *Redating the Teacher of Righteousness* (Sydney: Theological Explorations, 1979); other works by her include *The Gospels and Qumran* (Sydney: Theological Explorations, 1981); *The Qumran Origins of the Christian Church* (Sydney: Theological Explorations, 1983); *Jesus and the Riddle of the Dead Sea Scrolls* (San Francisco: Harper, 1992); *Jesus of the Apocalypse. The Life of Jesus after the Crucifixion* (London/NY: Transworld, 1997).

[6] Robert H. Eisenman, *Maccabees, Zadokites, Christians, and Qumran* (SPB 34; Leiden: Brill, 1983); idem, *James the Just in the Habakkuk Pesher* (Leiden: Brill, 1986); idem, *James, the Brother of Jesus* (New York: Viking, 1996).

[7] André Dupont-Sommer notes the striking similarities between the Teacher of Righteousness and Jesus, but at the same time underlines the many differences in his *The Essene Writings from Qumran* (Gloucester, MA: Peter Smith, 1973) 371–73.

[8] Jacob L. Teicher, "The Dead Sea Scrolls: Documents of the Jewish Christian Sect of Ebionites," *JJS* 2 (1951) 67–99.

[9] His earlier skepticism can be found in John Mark Allegro, *The Dead Sea Scrolls. A Reappraisal* (2d ed.; London: Penguin, 1964); his later fantasies in his *The Sacred Mushroom and the Cross* (Garden City, NY: Doubleday, 1970). For a polemic against the early approaches of both Dupont-Sommer and Allegro, see Jean Carmignac, *Christ and the Teacher of Righteousness* (Baltimore/Dublin: Helicon, 1962).

[10] Brief but devastating critiques can be found in Fitzmyer, *Responses to 101 Questions on the Dead Sea Scrolls,* 109–110, 127, 161–66; Hartmut Stegemann, *The Library of Qumran* (Grand Rapids: Eerdmans; Leiden: Brill, 1998) 12–33. A longer refutation of some particularly bizarre claims can be found in Otto Betz and Rainer Riesner, *Jesus, Qumran and the Vatican: Clarifications* (New York: Crossroad, 1994). It needs to be stressed that not all popularization has been of the sensationalistic type; fortunately, responsible authors have also made the findings of scholarship accessible to the educated lay person. Examples include Joachim Gnilka, "Jesus—Ein Essener?" *BK* 26/1 (1971) 2–5; Hartmut Stegemann, "Die Bedeutung des Qumranfunde für das Verständnis Jesu und des frühen Christentums," *BK* 48/1 (1993) 10–19; idem, "Jesus and the Teacher of Righteousness," *Bible Review* 10/1 (1994) 42–47, 63; Wolfgang Stegemann, "Qumran, Jesus und das Urchristentum," *TLZ* 119 (1994) 388–408; Hans Maas, *Qumran. Texte contra Phantasien* (Stuttgart: Calwer, 1994); Klaus Berger, *The Truth under Lock and Key? Jesus and the Dead Sea Scrolls* (Louisville: Westminster/John Knox, 1995, German original 1993).

[11] On this, see Stegemann, *The Library of Qumran,* 9–11; a useful inventory of the contents of each of the Qumran caves can be found on pp. 67–79. See also Callaway, *The History,* 209.

[12] An example of this approach is Kurt Schubert, "The Sermon on the Mount and the Qumran Texts," *The Scrolls and the New Testament,* 118–28. To be sure, the core of the Sermon on the Mount goes back to a short, primitive sermon in the Q document. But even this Q sermon is composed of various units, some reaching back to the historical Jesus, some not. As can be seen from these remarks, I do not share the theory of Hans Dieter Betz on the growth of the Sermon on the Mount in early Christian

tradition. For his thesis, see his *The Sermon on the Mount* (Hermeneia; Minneapolis: Fortress, 1995).

[13] For example, Jerome Murphy-O'Connor, Hartmut Stegemann, and Gabriele Boccaccini are all first-rate Qumran scholars, and yet they disagree on the question of the relative order and dating of the documents found at Qumran, on the question of which documents were composed by the Qumranites themselves, by the Essene movement in general, or by other streams of Judaism, and on the question of the precise relationship of Qumran to the larger Essene movement and of the Essene movement to Judaism in general. Without consensus on these questions, no overall theory of the development of Qumran (or Essene) thought can hope to win general acceptance.

[14] So Jerome Murphy-O'Connor, "Qumran and the New Testament," *The New Testament and Its Modern Interpreters* (ed. Eldon Jay Epp and George W. MacRae; Atlanta: Scholars, 1989) 55–71, esp. 63. In his overview essay, James H. Charlesworth ("The Dead Sea Scrolls and the Historical Jesus," *Jesus and the Dead Sea Scrolls*, 1–74) purposely casts his net far and wide to gather in all possible parallels; he then, however, sorts out these parallels into various categories: traits that Jesus shared with most other Jews, traits that may show either Jesus' similarity or his reaction to the Essenes, and traits that may have made Jesus stand out as different from most other Jews.

[15] Though not put in such stark terms, there is something of this distinction in the presentation of W. D. Davies, *The Setting of the Sermon on the Mount* (Cambridge: Cambridge University, 1963) 219–21.

[16] In this connection, Collins (*Apocalypticism in the Dead Sea Scrolls*, 56–62) notes the complex meaning of the hallowed phrase "the end of days" (*'aḥărît hayyāmîm*) in the Qumran documents. This future period encompasses both a time of testing for the community and the dawning of the age of salvation, including the coming of the messiah(s) and, at least in some passages, the final war. However, "the end of days" does not include the final stage of salvation that will follow upon the eschatological battle. See also John T. Willis, "The Expression *be'acharith hayyamim* in the Old Testament," *ResQ* 22 (1979) 54–71; Annette Steudel, "*'hryt hymym* in the Texts from Qumran," *RevQ* 16 (1993–95) 225–46.

[17] The set phrase "kingdom of God," so central to Jesus' preaching, is not a fixed locution at Qumran. Similar phrases, though not the exact equivalent, can be found, e.g., in 1QM 6:6 (echoing Obad 21): *wĕhāyĕtâ lĕʾēl yisrāʾēl hammĕlûkâ* ("and to the God of Israel shall [belong] the kingly rule [or: kingdom]"). It is striking how it is precisely in the Qumran document that concentrates on the theme of sharing in the angelic liturgy, the *Songs of the Sabbath Sacrifice*, that we find an exceptionally strong emphasis on the images of the divine king and his kingdom. On this, see *A Marginal*

Jew, 2. 266–67. The presence of the angels in the council of the congregation of the last days is mentioned in passing in 1QSa 2:8–9.

[18] In the view of Torleif Elgvin ("Early Essene Eschatology: Judgment and Salvation According to *Sapiential Work A,*" *Current Research and Technological Developments on the Dead Sea Scrolls* [STDJ 20; ed. Donald W. Parry and Stephen D. Ricks; Leiden: Brill, 1996] 126–65), the combination of realized and future elements in Essene eschatology existed already at an early stage of the community's theological development; see also George W. E. Nickelsburg, "The Qumranic Transformation of a Cosmological and Eschatological Tradition (1QH 4:29–40)," *The Madrid Qumran Congress* (STDJ 11; 2 vols.; ed. Julio Trebolle Barrera and Luis Vegas Montaner; Leiden: Brill, 1992) 2. 649–59.

[19] This is the interpretation Collins (*Apocalypticism in the Dead Sea Scrolls,* 61–62) gives to an admittedly fragmentary passage. The numbering of lines is according to the composite text supplied by García Martínez, *The Dead Sea Scrolls Translated,* 79. For the relevant individual fragments of 4Q397 (Fragments 14–21 [= 4Q398 14–17 I; 4QMMT C 1–17]) in the original Hebrew with English translation, see Florentino García Martínez and Eibert J. C. Tigchelaar, *The Dead Sea Scrolls Study Edition* (2 vols.; Leiden: Brill; Grand Rapids: Eerdmans, 1997, 1998) 2. 800–801, line 13.

[20] One must readily admit that one arrives at this synthetic view only by combining various statements from various Qumran documents; this certainly is the case with Collins' fine work, *Apocalypticism in the Dead Sea Scrolls.* In addition, one must always remember that apocalyptic thought does not put a high premium on logical consistency. Hence any reconstruction of the end-time scenario as envisioned by Qumran must remain tentative.

[21] As shall become clear when we treat directly the question of a or the messiah(s) in a later chapter, scholars are divided on the proper use of the term "messiah." Suffice it to say that here I restrict the word to eschatological figures who are either called "The Anointed One" (Hebrew: *māšîaḥ,* Aramaic: *mĕšîḥāʾ*) or who, in the larger context of the text, are said directly or indirectly to be anointed (e.g., the prophetic figure in Isa 61:1). Other scholars prefer to extend the meaning of "messiah" to any figure who is to perform a saving function for Israel in the eschatological drama. For the range of messianic figures at Qumran—a royal Davidic Messiah, the Messiah of Aaron and the Messiah of Israel, a teacher/priest/prophet figure, some sort of heavenly or angelic figure, and a Son of God figure—see Collins, *The Scepter and the Star.* I do not treat here the remarkable parallel between 4Q246 (with the phrases "will be great," "he shall be called Son of God," "they shall call him Son of the Most High," and "his kingdom is an everlasting kingdom") and the Lucan annunciation to Mary (specifically Luke 1:32–35), since this does not concern the words or deeds of the historical Jesus. Moreover, it is not certain that the text refers to a Jewish messianic fig-

ure. On 4Q246, see ibid., 154–72. See also Frank Moore Cross, "Notes on the Doctrine of the Two Messiahs at Qumran and the Extracanonical *Daniel Apocalypse (4Q246)*," *Current Research and Technological Developments on the Dead Sea Scrolls* (STDJ 20; ed. Donald W. Parry and Stephen D. Ricks; Leiden: Brill, 1996) 1–13. For the debate on whether the "Son of God" mentioned in 4Q246 represents a negative figure (e.g., a false divine king like Antiochus IV Epiphanes) or a positive Jewish messianic figure, see Edward M. Cook, "4Q246," *Bulletin for Biblical Research* 5 (1995) 43–66 (in favor of the negative interpretation); and John J. Collins, "The Background of the 'Son of God' Text," *Bulletin for Biblical Research* 7 (1997) 51–62 (in favor of the positive interpretation). For a sampling of different views on the nature, origin, and development of messianic expectations in the Dead Sea scrolls, see, e.g., George J. Brooke, "The Messiah of Aaron in the *Damascus Document*," *RevQ* 15 (1991–92) 215–30; Michael A. Knibb, "The Interpretation of *Damascus Document* VII, 9*b*–VIII, 2*a* and XIX, 5*b*–14," ibid., 243–51; Emile Puech, "Préséance sacerdotale et Messie-Roi dans la Règle de la Congrégation (1QSa ii 11–22)," *RevQ* 16 (1993–95) 351–65; Johann Maier, "Messias oder Gesalbter? Zu einem Übersetzungs- und Bedeutungsproblem in den Qumrantexten," *RevQ* 17 (1996) 585–612; Hartmut Stegemann, "Some Remarks to *1QSa*, to *1QSb*, and to Qumran Messianism," ibid., 478–505; James H. Charlesworth, "Introduction: Messianic ideas in Early Judaism," *Qumran-Messianism* (ed. James H. Charlesworth, Hermann Lichtenberger, and Gerbern S. Oegema; Tübingen: Mohr [Siebeck], 1998) 1–8; idem, "Messianology in the Biblical Pseudepigrapha," ibid., 21–52; "Challenging the Consensus Communis Regarding Qumran Messianism (1QS, 4QS MSS)," ibid., 120–34; Hermann Lichtenberger, "Messianic Expectations and Messianic Figures During the Second Temple Period," ibid., 9–20; Gerbern S. Oegema, "Messianic Expectations in the Qumran Writings: Theses on their Development," ibid., 53–82; idem, "Tradition-Historical Studies on 4Q252," ibid., 154–174; Ferdinand Dexinger, "Reflections on the Relationship Between Qumran and Samaritan Messianology," ibid., 83–99; John J. Collins, "Jesus, Messianism and the Dead Sea Scrolls," ibid., 100–119; Craig A. Evans, "Are the 'Son' Texts at Qumran 'Messianic'? Reflections on 4Q369 and Related Scrolls," ibid., 135–53; Johannes Zimmermann, "Observations on 4Q246–The 'Son of God,' " ibid., 175–90; Martin G. Abegg and Craig A. Evans, "Messianic Passages in the Dead Sea Scrolls," ibid., 191–203; (the *Qumran-Messianism* volume concludes with a "Bibliography of Messianism and the Dead Sea Scrolls," 204–14, compiled by Martin G. Abegg, Craig A. Evans, and Gerbern S. Oegema); Craig A. Evans, "Jesus and the Dead Sea Scrolls," *The Dead Sea Scrolls after Fifty Years. A Comprehensive Assessment. Volume Two* (ed. Peter W. Flint and James C. VanderKam; Leiden: Brill, 1999) 573–98.

[22] The key text is 1QS 9:11 because it is the only passage where "the Messiahs of Aaron and Israel" are clearly and unambiguously mentioned together. Collins (*Apocalypticism in the Dead Sea Scrolls,* 77–80; *The Scepter and the Star,* 74–77) argues effectively that other passages in the Qumran literature reflect the idea of the dyarchy of a priestly Messiah and a royal Messiah, though the other documents do not use the precise phrase "the Messiahs of Aaron and Israel." The title in the singular, "the

Messiah of Aaron and Israel," occurs three times in the *Damascus Document* (CD 12:23–13:1; 14:19; 19:10–11), and "a Messiah from Aaron and from Israel" is found in CD 20:1. Though one could take these passages to refer to a single Messiah, Collins is probably correct in seeing even here a reference to dyarchy. This is also the opinion of James VanderKam, "Messianism in the Scrolls," *The Community of the Renewed Covenant*, 211–34, esp. 228–31. VanderKam holds that the occurrences of the singular form of *měšîaḥ* in the disputed CD passages are probably instances of "a singular construct noun which is to be understood with each of two (or more) absolutes" (p. 230). He lists various examples from both the OT (Gen 14:10; Judg 7:25) and Qumran (1QM 3:13–14; 5:1).

[23] Along with Collins (*The Scepter and the Star*, 75–76), I take "the priest" and "the Messiah of Israel" in the *Rule of the Congregation* (1QSa 2:12–21) to be the Messiahs of Aaron and Israel, though the fragmentary nature of the text makes a firm decision difficult.

[24] This view of Jesus is the upshot of Volume Two of *A Marginal Jew*; see, e.g., 1039–49. For the eschatological prophet at Qumran, see Collins, *The Scepter and the Star*, 116–23. Apart from the clear reference in 1QS 9:11, one must rely either on mere scraps that mention Elijah (or a prophet) or inferences from certain eschatological passages (notably 4Q521, on which see below).

[25] On this, see *A Marginal Jew*, 2. 688–90.

[26] These weighty and difficult topics will be discussed at length when we treat the last days of Jesus. Suffice it to say for now that both events enjoy multiple attestation in the Marcan and Johannine traditions, as well as support from the criteria of coherence and embarrassment.

[27] See *A Marginal Jew*, 2. 131–37, 400–401.

[28] On this passage, see Emile Puech, "Une apocalypse messianique (4Q521)," *RevQ* 15, no. 60 (1992) 475–522; James D. Tabor and Michael O. Wise, "4Q521 'On Resurrection' and the Synoptic Gospel Tradition. A Preliminary Study," *Journal for the Study of the Pseudepigrapha* 10 (1992) 149–62; Collins, *The Scepter and the Star*, 117–22; idem, *Apocalypticism in the Dead Sea Scrolls*, 87–89; Craig A. Evans, "Jesus and the Dead Sea Scrolls from Qumran Cave 4," *Eschatology, Messianism, and the Dead Sea Scrolls* (ed. Craig A. Evans and Peter W. Flint; Grand Rapids/Cambridge, UK: Eerdmans, 1997) 91–100, esp. 95–97.

[29] See Puech, "Une apocalypse messianique (4Q521)," 475–522; Geza Vermes, "Qumran Forum Miscellanea I," *JJS* 43 (1992) 299–305, esp. 303–4 for 4Q521; García Martínez, *The Dead Sea Scrolls Translated*, 394–95 and 510; cf. Vermes, *The Dead Sea Scrolls in English* (4th ed.), 244–45. Vermes (*The Dead Sea Scrolls*, 244)

notes that 4Q521 is made up of eleven fragments and possibly six further tiny pieces. Fragment 2, the largest fragment, contains parts of three columns; it is the second column that contains the material that interests us here. Puech dates the manuscript to somewhere around 100–80 B.C.

[30] Puech ("Une apocalypse messianique," 487) thinks that the text "very probably" speaks of "his Messiah" in the singular.

[31] Perhaps the most important line in this text is line 12, which reads in the unvocalized Hebrew: *ky yrp' ḥllym wmtym yḥyh 'nwym ybśr* ("for he shall heal the mortally wounded [or: the pierced], and shall make the dead to live; he shall announce good news to the poor").

[32] In addition, one might understand the reference to straightening those who are bent as roughly equivalent to "the lame walk."

[33] See Collins, *Apocalypticism in the Dead Sea Scrolls*, 88.

[34] Ibid., 89. The earliest of the texts that Collins cites is at the very end of *m. Soṭa* 9:15: *ûtĕḥiyyat hammētîm bā' 'al yĕdê 'ēliyyāhû zākûr lĕṭôb* ("The resurrection of the dead comes through Elijah of blessed memory").

[35] Granted, in light of the small amount of data we have to deal with, it is difficult to decide whether the thought is proper to Qumran. Vermes (*The Dead Sea Scrolls in English*, 244) argues that there is nothing clearly sectarian in the text. In particular, "the Messiah" is apparently referred to in the singular (without the additions "of Aaron" or "of Israel"), and the resurrection makes one of its rare appearances at Qumran. Yet Collins (*Apocalypticism in the Dead Sea Scrolls*, 89) points to some contacts with the Qumran sectarian literature and so leaves the question open.

[36] Needless to say, one cannot create a dichotomy between the Jerusalem temple and the Mosaic Law. However, one should remember that the Jerusalem temple as such, as opposed to its surrogate, the Tent of Meeting in the wilderness during the time of Moses, is not described or regulated in the Pentateuch. Even the liturgical regulations that are given in the Pentateuch and that are clearly intended to apply to the later temple are general and sketchy. The Pentateuch hardly supplies a full book of liturgical directions governing all the minutiae of daily liturgical life in the temple. It was up to the Jerusalem priesthood to develop their own *hălākâ* to cover such matters. In light of this, it is striking to note how much of, e.g., the *Halakic Letter* at Qumran concerns itself with details of the priesthood, the temple, the temple calendar, the temple liturgy (especially sacrifices), and purity questions affecting the temple, even in those areas where the Pentateuch gives no ruling—though, naturally, the Qumranites claim that their positions are the true interpretation of "the book of Moses and . . . the words of the prophets."

[37] The brief historical references here presume the historical overviews given in the previous chapters dealing with the Pharisees and the Sadducees.

[38] This is the view of Lawrence H. Schiffman, "Temple Scroll," *Anchor Bible Dictionary*, 6. 348–50, esp. 349. The fragmentary state of the Aramaic *New Jerusalem* text (of which at least six copies were found at Qumran) does not permit us to decide whether the apocalyptic vision in the text refers to the interim temple or the final eschatological temple, though Collins (*Apocalypticism in the Dead Sea Scrolls*, 59–60) inclines toward the former.

[39] Luke's Infancy Narrative also depicts Jesus in the temple in a quite positive context when he is brought to it as an infant and when, as a twelve-year-old, he accompanies his parents (Luke 2:22–52). Such scenes are, at least in their present state, the product of Christian theology. But we may note that here Luke is in agreement with the other Gospel traditions in seeing nothing problematic in Jesus' presence at and participation in temple activities. There is no known countervailing tradition that can be considered historical.

[40] On the question of Jesus and the temple, see Sanders, *Jesus and Judaism*, 61–90.

[41] Technically, the cultic legislation contained within the five books of Moses does not mention the Jerusalem temple as such, but rather the Tabernacle or Tent of Meeting in the wilderness. However, especially in Deuteronomy's stress on the single legitimate sanctuary for performing the ritual sacrifice of animals, the reality of the Jerusalem temple shines through the ostensible scenario.

[42] On the idea of a new temple in Jewish thought around the turn of the era, see Sanders, *Jesus and Judaism*, 77–90.

[43] With his typical high christology, the Fourth Evangelist reinterprets this saying by referring the building or raising up of the temple to Jesus' resurrection (John 2:21–22). The whole question of the "cleansing" of the temple and Jesus' prophecy will have to be revisited when we study the final days of Jesus in Jerusalem before his death. Here our only concern is to appreciate the similarities and differences in the eschatological outlook of Jesus and Qumran.

[44] A comprehensive study of *hălākâ* at Qumran within the larger history of Jewish *hălākâ* remains a *desideratum*. Earlier studies on the subject include the pioneering work of Lawrence H. Schiffman, who uses the category *hălākâ* (which actually is not attested at Qumran in its later technical rabbinic sense) in his *The Halakhah at Qumran* (SJLA 16; Leiden: Brill, 1975). He continued his work in *Sectarian Law in the Dead Sea Scrolls* (Brown Judaic Studies 33; Chico, CA: Scholars, 1983). There he argues that the Qumran sectarians did not have the later rabbinic concept of an oral Torah distinct from the written Torah; rather, they derived all their laws from what

they considered to be inspired biblical exegesis. See also his "The *Temple Scroll* and the Nature of Its Law: The Status of the Question," *The Community of the Renewed Covenant* (ed. Eugene Ulrich and James VanderKam; Notre Dame, IN: University of Notre Dame, 1994) 37–55; here he stresses the similarities of Qumran *hălākâ* to that of the Sadducees. On this, see also John Strugnell, "MMT: Second Thoughts on a Forthcoming Edition," ibid., 57–73. Other studies on aspects of Qumran *hălākâ* include Joseph M Baumgarten, *Studies in Qumran Law* (SJLA 24; Leiden: Brill, 1977); idem, "The Purification Rituals in *DJD* 7," *The Dead Sea Scrolls. Forty Years of Research* (STDJ 10; ed. Deborah Dimant and Uriel Rappaport; Leiden: Brill, 1992) 199–209; Lawrence H. Schiffman, "Laws Pertaining to Women in the *Temple Scroll*," ibid., 210–28; Daniel R. Schwartz, "Law and Truth: On Qumran-Sadducean and Rabbinic Views of Law," ibid., 229–40; Moshe Weinfeld, "Prayer and Liturgical Practice in the Qumran Sect," ibid., 241–58; Joseph Baumgarten, "The Disqualifications of Priests in 4Q Fragments of the 'Damascus Document,' a Specimen of the Recovery of pre-Rabbinic Halakha," *The Madrid Qumran Congress* (STDJ 11; 2 vols.; ed. Julio Trebolle Barrera and Luis Vegas Montaner; Leiden: Brill, 1992) 2. 503–13; Menahem Kister, "Some Aspects of Qumranic Halakhah," ibid., 2. 571–88; and the whole range of essays dedicated to the problem of legal issues in Qumran texts in *Legal Texts and Legal Issues* (STDJ 23; ed. Moshe Bernstein, Florentino García Martínez, and John Kampen; Leiden: Brill, 1997).

[45] On the question of radicalism at Qumran and in Jesus' teaching, see Herbert Braun, *Spätjüdisch-häretischer und frühchristlicher Radikalismus: Jesus von Nazareth und die essenische Qumransekte* (BHT 24; 2d ed.; 2 vols.; Tübingen: Mohr [Siebeck], 1969). The category of "late Judaism" has since been abandoned for "early Judaism" around the turn of the era.

[46] The phrase "without a constraining reason" is my attempt to render a difficult phrase in the text of 1QS. The main manuscript from Cave 1 reads literally "and he is not a man" *(wĕlôʾ hāyâ ʾĕnôš)*. This is probably a scribal error. The last word in the phrase should probably be read in accordance with manuscript G as *ʾānûs* ("forced," "constrained"). What the constraint might be (illness? weakness? incontinence?) is not clear.

[47] On the translation of *yād* ("hand") as a euphemism for "penis," see Charlesworth's note on his translation in *The Dead Sea Scrolls*, 1. 33 n. 185. The prohibition of self-exposure may be connected with the great care with which the Essenes were said to defecate and urinate; see *J. W.* 2.8.9 §147–149; cf. 1QM 7:6–7; 11QTemple 46:13 *(mĕqôm yād,* "place of the hand" = "latrine"). For the stringency of Essene rules regarding excrement, see Albert I. Baumgarten, "The Temple Scroll, Toilet Practices, and the Essenes," *Jewish History* 10 (1996) 9–20. It is typical of the general contrast between the Essenes and the historical Jesus that parallel material in the sayings of the latter are nonexistent.

[48] For example, the famous story of the adulteress brought before Jesus in John 7:53–8:11 is fraught with weighty textual as well as historical problems; see my observations in *A Marginal Jew,* 1. 268–69 and the relevant notes. Even if the basic event were historical, we would be left with the mind-numbing truism that Jesus considered adultery to be a sin but urged mercy and forgiveness toward the woman so involved (8:11).

[49] In this stricture against lustful intentions and glances, both Qumran and Jesus stand within a lengthy OT and Jewish tradition; see, e.g., Job 31:1; Sir 23:4–6; 26:9–11; cf. *Pss. Sol.* 4:4–6; and a good number of passages in the later rabbinic literature and the *Testaments of the Twelve Patriarchs.* Granted this coherence with the whole OT and Jewish tradition, it is difficult to judge how much of this saying or of the many other sapiential and ethical sayings attributed to Jesus in the Gospels actually comes from him. The difficulty is increased in the case of a saying like Matt 5:27–28 because it is found only in the M tradition. While the antithetical pattern ("you have heard that it was said . . . but I say") might easily be the work of Matthew or the cultivators of the M tradition before him, the basic content of the instruction in v 28 could go back to Jesus, though positive proof is lacking. At the very least, I doubt that many would want to argue that the instruction in v 28 is contrary to Jesus' own views.

[50] Whether 11QTemple was written by Qumranites or by some other eschatologically oriented Jewish-Palestinian group is disputed among scholars. But since this longest of all Qumran manuscripts existed at Qumran in multiple copies, we may suppose that at the very least it was highly esteemed by the Qumranites, whatever its ultimate origin. On the *Temple Scroll,* see Lawrence H. Schiffman, "Temple Scroll," *Anchor Bible Dictionary,* 6. 348–50.

[51] This is the position suggested by Tom Holmén, "Divorce in CD 4:20–5:2 and in *11QT* 57:17–18: Some Remarks on the Pertinence of the Question," *RevQ* no. 71, tome 18/3 (1998) 397–408. He points out that CD 13:14–18 and 11QTemple 54:4–5; 66:8–11 may be read as allowing divorce in certain circumstances. Hence he thinks that, read in their respective contexts, the texts in the title of his article do not refer to a prohibition of divorce.

[52] *A Marginal Jew,* 1. 332–45. The reader is referred to the notes on those pages for all relevant references, ancient and modern; they will not be repeated here.

[53] This is the burden of the whole of Part One of *A Marginal Jew,* 2. 19–233.

[54] See *A Marginal Jew,* 1. 342–45. It is sometimes suggested that Jesus was referring to and praising the Qumranites, who, like himself, practiced celibacy for eschatological reasons. Yet the shocking use of self-castration as a metaphor for religious celibacy would have seemed strange praise indeed to the ears of the Qumranites.

They specifically excluded castrated men from their holy assembly; see 4QMMT 42 in the reconstructed version of García Martínez, *The Dead Sea Scrolls Translated*, 78.

[55] An obvious example: it is highly unlikely that the Teacher of Righteousness and his priestly followers who left Jerusalem to found the community at Qumran were celibates. As functioning priests in the Jerusalem temple, they would have been expected to marry and procreate children to continue the priestly line. If celibacy began to be practiced at Qumran—and I think that this is likely—we must confess our ignorance of the precise time and occasion of the practice's inception.

[56] Part of the problem here is how one interprets the ambiguous archaeological testimony from the cemetery at Qumran. The main burial ground near the buildings contains only male skeletons, but the skeletons of some women and children were discovered in fringe or secondary cemeteries at a greater distance from the buildings. Various solutions are possible: e.g., Qumran was a focus of pilgrimage by the larger Essene sect (including married members) during the great pilgrimage festivals, when most "mainstream" Jews would go up to Jerusalem. If this were the case, it is reasonable to suppose that at times women and/or children might have died during their stay at Qumran. Other scholars claim that the remains of women and children date from a much more recent period.

[57] Various theories about the reasons for celibacy at Qumran are proposed by A. Marx, "Les racines du célibat essénien," *RevQ* 7 (1969–71) 323–42; Hans Hübner, "Zölibat in Qumran?" *NTS* 17 (1970–71) 153–67; and Anton Steiner, "Warum lebten die Essener asketisch?" *BZ* 15 (1971) 1–28.

[58] On this view, see Elisha Qimron, "Celibacy in the Dead Sea Scrolls and the Two Kinds of Sectarians," *The Madrid Qumran Congress* (STDJ 11; 2 vols.; ed. Julio Trebolle Barrera and Luis Vegas Montaner; Leiden: Brill, 1992) 1. 287–94.

[59] It should be noted that "Holy War" is our way of describing the belief expressed in the OT that the enemies of Israel were the enemies of God, that the wars Israel fought were therefore undertakings sanctioned by and dedicated to their God, and that God ("the divine warrior") fought with and for Israel in their battles. See, e.g., Exod 14:13–14; 15:3; Josh 8:1; Judg 5:31; 1 Sam 23:4. A careful observance of ritual purity was thus incumbent on the army in the field because God or his angels were in the camp.

[60] This is clearly the belief of the *War Scroll,* as it describes the Israelite soldiers who are to be "perfect in spirit and flesh" for the great eschatological battle (1QM 7:5–7): "And any man who is not clean from a [sexual] discharge on the day of battle shall not go down with them [i.e., with the rest of the holy army to the battle], for the angels of holiness [will be] together with their hosts . . . and no nakedness shall be seen in their surroundings [taking the shorter emended reading of 4QM1 fragments 1–3 line 8 against the longer reading in 1QM 7:7]."

⁶¹ Like a number of other topics listed here, this question will have to be revisited when Jesus' relation to the Mosaic Law is examined. Only the bare essentials are noted here. For basic information on Matt 5:33–37, see Meier, *Law and History,* 150–56. For the difference between the *Damascus Document* and the *Temple Scroll* on the regulation of oaths and vows, see Lawrence H. Schiffman, "The Law of Vows and Oaths (*Num* 30, 3–16) in the Zadokite Fragments and the Temple Scroll," *RevQ* 15 (1991–92) 199–214. Since the *Damascus Document* and the *Rule of the Community* seem to have been the two most basic rule books, I focus in what follows on these two documents.

⁶² This is the suggestion of Sanders, *Jewish Law,* 53. However, in the narrative that immediately follows, Josephus bases Herod's leniency toward the Essenes on the favorable prophecy of the Essene Manaemus, who told the boy Herod that he would become king of the Jews (*Ant.* 15.10.5 §373–379). It would seem that, in contrast, the Pharisees, who did not reject oaths in principle, were fined by Herod for refusing to take the oath of loyalty (*Ant.* 17.2.4 §42). Yet this passage stands in tension with Josephus' claim in *Ant.* 15.10.4 §370 that Herod also exempted the noted Pharisaic teacher Pollion along with Samaias and their disciples. Were these Pharisees alone exempted while other Pharisees were fined?

⁶³ On the close connection between covenant and curse, see Douglas Stuart, "Curse," *Anchor Bible Dictionary,* 1. 1218–19.

⁶⁴ Sanders (*Jewish Law,* 53) tries to solve the tension among the various sources by suggesting differences on the subject of oaths between the Essenes represented in the *Damascus Document* and those represented in the *Rule of the Community* at Qumran. While that may well be, both documents (as well as Josephus) speak of a solemn oath that is taken by one entering the community.

⁶⁵ For a somewhat different view, see Sanders, *Jewish Law,* 55–56. Sanders thinks that Jesus holds all the oaths listed in Matt 23:16–22 to be of equal seriousness; they are all oaths taken in the name of God himself. According to Sanders, Jesus teaches that it is better not to swear at all. But if a person does swear, he must realize that all oaths are sworn in the name of God and are therefore binding.

⁶⁶ On such oath formulas, see Marvin H. Pope, "Oaths," *IDB,* 3. 575–77. OT examples include Ruth 1:17; 1 Sam 3:17; 14:44; 2 Sam 3:35; 1 Kgs 2:23. For the grammatical forms in Hebrew, see Paul Joüon and T. Muraoka, *A Grammar of Biblical Hebrew* (2 vols.; Rome: Biblical Institute, 1991) 2. 618–21; the authors note the mutual contamination of oath and curse formulas. They also identify Mark 8:12 as an example of this Hebraic construction in the NT.

⁶⁷ On the question of the relation of Matt 5:34 and James 5:12 and their possible common source, see Ernst Kutsch, "Eure Rede aber sei ja ja, nein, nein," *EvT* 20 (1960) 206–18; Paul S. Minear, "Yes or No: The Demand for Honesty in the Early

Church," *NovT* 13 (1971) 1–13; Meier, *Law and History,* 150–56; Gerhard Dautzenberg, "Ist das Schwurverbot Mt 5,33–37; Jak 5,12 ein Beispiel für die Torakritik Jesu?" *BZ* 25 (1981) 47–66; Peter H. Davids, "James and Jesus," *Gospel Perspectives. The Jesus Tradition Outside the Gospels. Volume 5* (ed. David Wenham; Sheffield: JSOT, 1984) 63–84; Patrick J. Hartin, *James and the Q Sayings of Jesus* (JSNTSup 47; Sheffield: JSOT, 1991); William R. Baker, " 'Above All Else': Contexts of the Call for Verbal Integrity in James 5:12," *JSNT* 54 (1994) 57–71; Luke Timothy Johnson, *The Letter of James* (AB 37A; New York: Doubleday, 1995) 55–57, 327–28.

[68] On the development of the various units that make up Mark 7:1–23, see Jan Lambrecht, "Jesus and the Law: An Investigation of Mk 7, 1–23," *ETL* 53 (1977) 24–82; Robert P. Booth, *Jesus and the Laws of Purity. Tradition History and Legal History in Mark 7* (JSNTSup 13; Sheffield: JSOT, 1986); Guelich, *Mark 1—8:26,* 360–62, 372–74. It is safe to say that Mark 7:1–23 is not a historical report of a single incident that occurred at one time in the life of Jesus, but a composite of various sayings originating partly in the ministry of Jesus and partly in the life of the first-generation church. Our focus here is solely on Mark 7:9–13.

[69] See Joseph A. Fitzmyer, "The Aramaic *Qorbān* Inscription from Jebel Hallet eṭ-Ṭûri and Mk 7:11/Mt 15:5," *Essays on the Semitic Background of the New Testament* (SBLSBS 5; Missoula, MT: Scholars, 1974) 93–100; Karl H. Rengstorf, *"korban, korbanas,"* TDNT 3 (1965) 860–66; A. I. Baumgarten, *"Korban and the Pharisaic Paradosis,"* *Journal of the Ancient Near Eastern Society* 16–17 (1984–85) 5–17; Sanders, *Jewish Law,* 51–57; Max Wilcox, "Corban," *Anchor Bible Dictionary,* 1. 1134. In the OT, *qorbān* carries only the general idea of a gift, offering, or sacrifice. In the LXX, *qorbān* (as distinct from *qurbān,* "supply," "procurement") is always rendered by *dōron,* a rendering found also in Mark and Josephus. While the Greek transliterated form *korban* occurs nowhere else in the NT or the LXX, Josephus uses it in *Ant.* 4.4.4 §73, in a context in which he is explaining the tithes due to priests according to various laws in the Pentateuch. He then proceeds: "Those who designate themselves *korban* to God—a word that means 'gift' in Greek—if they wish to be relieved of this religious obligation, must pay the priests a sum of money. . . ." (Note that Josephus, like Mark, first uses *korban* [the Semitic word *qorbān* transliterated into Greek, as in Mark 7:11] and then translates it with the Greek word *dōron,* "gift.") While in the *Antiquities* text the word *korban* occurs in a discussion on how to be released from vows (note the similar context in CD 16), in *Ag. Ap.* 1.22 §167 Josephus uses *korban* of oaths *(horkoi),* but once again interprets the word to mean "God's gift" *(dōron theou).* In this shift in meaning from vow to oath there is a similarity in CD 16, where the vocabulary of oath *(šĕbûʿâ)* easily slides into the vocabulary of vow *(neder).* (The precise distinctions between oaths and vows created by later rabbis and Christian theologians may not have been all that clear to ordinary Jews at the turn of the era. Indeed, Baumgarten [*"Korban,"* 8 n. 21] notes that "Philo does not seem to have known the distinction between vows and oaths." But if Philo, the greatest Jewish genius produced by the ancient Jewish Diaspora, did not know this

distinction, how many ordinary Jews inside or outside Palestine knew it? Hence the later rabbinic material on this question must be used with caution for Jewish texts around the turn of the era.)

The use of *qorbān* with the meaning of a gift vowed to God is attested by an Aramaic ossuary inscription from Jebel Hallet eṭ-Ṭûri: "Everything that a man may find to his profit in this ossuary [is] an offering *(qrbn)* to God from the one within it." (For a different view on the ossuary inscription, see Baumgarten, *"Korban,"* 7; Sanders, *Jewish Law,* 55.) Even the phrasing (speaking of what may be to another person's profit—hence there was probably something of value in the ossuary besides the bones) is reminiscent of Mark 7:11: "Whatever [support] you might have gained from me is Corban, that is, a gift [to God]. . . ." Similar phrasing can be found in rabbinic literature (e.g., *m. Ned.* 6:7). In rabbinic literature, the words *qorbān* and *qônām* are found with the idea of an offering to God that therefore becomes forbidden to humans; see, e.g., *m. Ned.* 1:4, where it is used for food that is forbidden to a person (a case similar to CD 16:14–15). In some passages, the sense of dedication to God fades away, leaving simply the sense of something forbidden to another. In *m. Ned.* 4:6, we see the development of a further meaning of *qônām:* a protestation or even a curse called down upon a person. Such developments apparently lie beyond the time frame of Mark 7:9–13. The problem of people using casuistry and subterfuge to escape from vows they have made when using *qorbān* and similar words is discussed in *m. Ned.* 2:5.

One intriguing point about this material should be noted. The texts in Josephus and the ossuary inscription use *korban/qorbān* not absolutely but with a genitival or datival construction indicating that the gift is given or belongs to God. While he does not use the word *korban,* Philo makes the same point in *Hypothetica* 7:3: the vow dedicating an object gives that object irrevocably *to God* and therefore bars it from all ordinary use. Perhaps, therefore, one might distinguish between those gifts that were literally vowed to the temple (and so to God) and those gifts that were in some vaguer sense dedicated to God and thus withdrawn from ordinary use. The latter type—which would include the ossuary inscription—would involve a true religious dedication to God, but not to the temple. If this be the case, the typology of Baumgarten (*"Korban,"* 6–7) needs further refinement when applied to the pre-rabbinic period. Baumgarten jumps from the use of *qorbān* as a formula of actual dedication to the temple (here he places the text from Josephus' *Antiquities*) to the use of *qorbān* as a vow formula by which some object was forbidden to oneself or to another person in the same way in which a dedicated animal was forbidden (*kĕqorbān,* "as though it were *qorbān*"; here he places the ossuary inscription). It seems to me that the explicit statement on the ossuary (*qrbn ʾlh,* "an offering to God"), in the light of the statements of Josephus and Philo, demands a more explicitly *theo*-logical understanding of *qorbān* in this text.

---

[70] In favor of historicity are Pesch, *Markusevangelium,* 1. 376; (apparently) Baumgarten, *"Korban,"* 16–17; Booth, *Jesus and the Laws of Purity,* 94–96; Guelich, *Mark 1—8:26,* 362. It is sometimes objected that the Pharisees would not have allowed a subterfuge like *qorbān,* since the opposite opinion about *qorbān* is taught in

the Mishna. As usual, one must beware of automatically equating the teachings of pre-70 Pharisees with positions held in the Mishna. Moreover, the mishnaic material is complex, reflecting various stages and conflicting opinions in an ongoing debate in Judaism. For example, in *m. Ned.* 9:1, we hear of a variety of views about the grounds that would justify the annulling of a vow that a man had made to the detriment of his father and mother. The fact that assorted views on the question were allowed to stand side by side at the time of the composition of the Mishna suggests that earlier this matter was still unsettled. One might observe that, even in this mishnaic passage, it is a question of what grounds would allow a man to annul his vow; nothing is said about his having a strict obligation to annul it. More telling still is the anecdote related in *m. Ned.* 5:6. A man had made a vow that prevented his father from receiving any food from him. To provide the father with food, the man engaged in an elaborate subterfuge *via* a legal fiction. The story presupposes that (1) vows like this were in fact made and (2) no simple way of annulling them was available. On the story, see Baumgarten, *"Korban,"* 10–12. A similar situation is presupposed by Philo's treatment of oaths and vows in his *Hypothetica* 7:3–5. He takes a strict view of the irrevocability of a vow, even when it works to the detriment of members of one's family. In Philo's presentation, ways of annulling the vow are quite limited (refusal of the gift by the officiating priest or—expressed in vague terms by Philo—declaration by some ruler). The strictness of his view comes close to the position rejected by Jesus. It may therefore be, as Pesch suggests (*Markusevangelium,* 1. 375), that *m. Ned.* 5:6 represents the early state of casuistry around the time of Jesus, when the position that Jesus excoriates was a live option. At the very least, CD 16, Philo, Mark 7:11, and *m. Ned.* 5:6 suggest that there was a lively debate around the turn of the era about vows that could deprive one's parents or neighbor of vital support and about the possibility of annulling such vows. In brief, the mishnaic material does not rule out the possibility that the substance of Mark 7:9–13 goes back to Jesus.

[71] See, e.g., Bultmann, *Geschichte,* 51 (discussing texts like Mark 7:9–13). Even Bultmann, though, accepts the possibility that "here and there" the use of a Scripture text might go back to Jesus, although he claims that such a case cannot be verified by scholars today. I think that the wiser approach is to admit that, theoretically, the Scripture citation in a given pericope might come from either Jesus or the early church and that each case is to be decided on its own merits, not on an a priori judgment against the origin of Scripture citations in the mouth of the historical Jesus.

[72] This is a major point of Baumgarten's article, *"Korban,"*; see esp. pp. 8–10.

[73] So Rengstorf, *"korban, korbanas,"* 864.

[74] As often with the use of Scripture at Qumran (and in the NT), the original meaning of the text is "bent" to serve the purpose of the latter-day interpreter. The original meaning of Mic 7:2 is quite general. It is part of a lament over the apparently universal triumph of evil in society. Mic 7:2 as a whole reads in the MT: "The pious man has

perished from the land; and there is no one upright among men. All of them lie in ambush to shed blood; one man hunts his brother [i.e., his fellow Israelite] with a net [ḥērem]." The Essene interpreter "bends" and particularizes the meaning of the second half of v 2 by understanding the noun ḥērem ("net") in its other possible meaning: "something dedicated to God and so withdrawn from any profane use." The verb ṣûd ("hunt") then naturally takes on its other possible meaning: "catch," "capture," or "entrap." Thus, a very general condemnation of injustice in society is narrowed down to the very special case of using the dedication of one's goods to God to avoid sharing them with one's neighbor in need. Remarkably, the Essene interpreter achieves this practical application of the text not by changing the wording of the text (except for the substitution of "one's fellow" for "one's brother") but by choosing alternate meanings for two key words.

[75] This subject is quite complicated, but space allows only for a schematic overview here. For a detailed study of the Qumran/Essene texts, with special emphasis on the Qumran *Rules* tradition and the *Damascus Document,* see Catherine M. Murphy, *The Disposition of Wealth in the Literature and Practice of the Qumran Community and Its Relevance for the Study of the New Testament* (Ph.D. dissertation; Notre Dame, IN: University of Notre Dame, 1999). My brief summary of the views of the Essenes on money and property also depends on the presentation of Geza Vermes and Martin D. Goodman, *The Essenes According to the Classical Sources* (Sheffield: JSOT, 1989) 4, 8–9.

[76] One should therefore speak of "poverty" at Qumran in a qualified sense. To be sure, living conditions were quite stark, and the individual possessed nothing he could call his own apart from the community. On the other hand, as long as he remained a member in good standing, the Qumranite could be sure of basic shelter, food, and whatever else he needed to perform his work for the community (e.g., scribal materials). Hence the Qumranites, for all their individual poverty, enjoyed—precisely because of their voluntary poverty in a religious institution—a social safety net that the poor individual adrift in the outside world did not have. One often meets this paradox of surrender and safety in religious institutions of voluntarily poor people.

[77] The major sources for these statements are Book Two of Josephus' *Jewish War* (*J. W.*) and two works of Philo, *That Every Good Man Is Free* (*Quod omnis probus liber sit,* abbreviated *Prob.*) and his *Apology for the Jews* (*Apologia pro Judaeis,* abbreviated *Apol.*). The *Apology* is probably to be identified with Philo's *Hypothetica;* two extracts from this work are preserved in Eusebius' *Praeparatio Evangelica.* For the *Apology,* I use the reference system found in the LCL edition of F. H. Colson, vol. 9, pp. 437–43.

[78] In *Apol.* 11.12, Philo states that warmer clothing was supplied in winter time; however, he stresses that all clothing belonged to the common property of the group.

[79] The meaning of CD 13:14–15 is disputed. There the members are forbidden to buy from or sell to "the Sons of Dawn." If Joseph M. Baumgarten and Daniel R. Schwartz are correct in their commentary on the *Damascus Document* in Charlesworth (ed.), *The Dead Sea Scrolls,* 2. 55 n. 203, the phrase "the Sons of Dawn" refers to fellow members of the covenant community (cf. 4Q298). Obviously, this prohibition makes sense only if the Essenes were allowed to engage in commerce with non-Essenes, as is also implied by 13:15–16 (informing the overseer is required for trading). Geza Vermes (*The Complete Dead Sea Scrolls in English,* 142) notes the uncertain meaning of the Hebrew text of CD 13:14–15. He translates it thus: "No member of the Covenant of God shall give or receive anything from the sons of Dawn *(shahar)* [or: of the Pit *(shahat)*] except for payment." Interestingly, in his one-volume work, *The Dead Sea Scrolls Translated. The Qumran Texts in English* (p. 43), García Martínez corrects the text to read "the sons of the pit." However, in Florentino García Martínez and Eibert J. C. Tigchelaar, *The Dead Sea Scrolls. Study Edition* (2 vols.; Leiden: Brill; Grand Rapids: Eerdmans, 1997, 1998) 1. 573, the text reads "the Sons of Dawn."

[80] As Taylor (*The Gospel According to St. Mark,* 431) and Pesch (*Markusevangelium,* 2. 141) rightly observe, various attempts to soften or rationalize Jesus' intentionally absurd imagery (e.g., *kamēlos,* "camel," is a scribal mistake for *kamilos,* "a ship's cable"; "the eye of the needle" was the name of a low, narrow gate in Jerusalem's city walls) miss the whole point of the drastic word-picture: the impossible (*adynaton* in v 27). For ordinary Palestinian peasants, the camel was the largest animal and the eye of a needle was about the smallest opening they would ever see. Jesus' metaphorical mentality was given to bringing clashing, violent, disturbing images together to impress his message on his audience: e.g., castration for the sake of the kingdom of God, bread as his body and wine as his blood, wolves in sheep's clothing, mourning at a wedding feast. As history has shown, the forcefulness of his imagery helped ensure the longevity of his message.

[81] See, e.g., *1 Enoch* 94:8–9; 96:4–8; 100:6; 103:5–8.

[82] Some exegetes, such as Pesch (*Markusevangelium,* 2. 135–46), think that a primitive form of Mark 10:23–27 actually goes back to the historical incident recounted in 10:17–22. That may well be, but I prefer to leave open the possibility that the substance of vv 23–27 reflects a separate tradition conveying general comments of the historical Jesus on the dangers of wealth.

[83] The concepts of eternal life and of inheriting (eternal) life were at home in Jewish eschatological literature at the turn of the era; see, e.g., *Pss. Sol.* 3:12; 9:5; 13:11; 14:4,7–10; *1 Enoch* 37:4; 40:9; 58:3; cf. Dan 12:2; 2 Macc 7:9.

[84] "Good teacher" is a very unusual address to a Jewish teacher in a 1st-century Palestinian context; combined with the act of kneeling, it represents, for the time and

place, an unheard-of gesture of reverence. Part of the irony (or tragedy) of the story is that such unparalleled adulation proves hollow when tested.

[85] Jesus' rejection of the highly unusual adulation reflects perfectly a characteristic of his mission that is commonly agreed upon by scholars: the all-consuming center of his proclamation was the coming kingdom of God, not his own person and status. The emphasis on the truth that "God alone is holy" may be intended to echo the great prayer called the Šĕmaʿ (Deut 6:4): "Hear, O Israel, the Lord [is] our God, the Lord alone. . . ." (Gundry's attempt [Mark, 553] to interpret Mark 10:18 to mean that Jesus implies that his goodness derives from his divine sonship is contorted exegesis, even on the level of Mark's redaction.) The allusion to the Šĕmaʿ may in turn have a connection with what at first glance seems to be a fairly random citation of commandments by Jesus. If we may take Jesus' reference to "God alone" (v 18) to stand for the "first table" of the Decalogue, i.e., the commandments prescribing our obligations toward God, then Jesus' listing of certain specific commandments (v 19) may be intended to stand for the "second table" of the Decalogue, i.e., the commandments prescribing our duties toward our neighbor. This would be especially likely if, as Pesch (Markusevangelium, 2. 139) suggests, mē aposterēsēs ("do not defraud"), unusual in a listing of the Ten Commandments, is understood as a summary of the concluding commandment(s) prohibiting the coveting of one's neighbor's wife, house, or other possessions. One might further hypothesize that the fourth commandment, "honor your father and mother"—which referred especially to material and monetary support in one's parents' old age—is transferred to last place because (1) it allows the list of obligations toward one's fellow human beings to end with a positive rather than a negative commandment (what we are to do rather than what we are to avoid) and (2) the idea of positively doing good toward other human beings, notably through material and monetary support, leads neatly into Jesus' positive command to give all one's possession to the poor and then to follow him. While all of this may be true of the present structure of Mark's pericope, one would hesitate to suggest that all these closely woven literary and theological threads go back to the original incident.

[86] On this, see Gundry, Mark, 563. Typically, it is Luke, in his redactional reworking of the story of the call of the first disciples, who ends the narrative with the sweeping statement, ". . . they left all things and followed him" (Luke 5:11; cf. Mark 1:18,20). However, not even Luke claims in this pericope that Jesus made leaving all things an explicit condition for following him. On the story of the miraculous catch of fish, see A Marginal Jew, 2. 896–904. That the Lucan Jesus does not expect everyone who accepts or believes in him to surrender all his property is clear from the story of Zacchaeus in Luke 19:1–10. To be sure, Peter does assert in Mark 10:28 that he and his fellow disciples have left "all things" and followed Jesus. While Jesus reassures his disciples that anyone who has left family or possessions "for my sake" will receive abundant reward in this life and the next (10:29–31), neither he nor Peter says anything about selling all of one's possessions and giving them to the poor.

[87] With respect to the "communism" of the early Jerusalem church, one should remember that (1) Luke's idealistic portrayal of this total sharing, which is largely restricted to two summary statements (2:44–45; 4:32–37), must be read with a critical eye (see Schneider, *Die Apostelgeschichte,* 1. 290–95); and (2) the story of Ananias and Sapphira makes clear that such sharing was voluntary. Peter emphasizes (Acts 5:4) that the sinful couple were not obliged to sell their property and that, once it was sold, they were free to keep the money for themselves. Their sin lay in lying "not to men but to God."

[88] For an excellent detailed analysis of the structure and content of this passage, see Richard J. Dillon, "Ravens, Lilies, and the Kingdom of God (Matthew 6:25–33/Luke 12:22–31)," *CBQ* 53 (1991) 605–27. Dillon apparently attributes the substance of the passage to the historical Jesus.

[89] On this, see Hoffmann, *Studien,* 327; Polag, *Christologie,* 76–77; Schulz, *Q. Die Spruchquelle der Evangelisten,* 149–57. Hoffmann suggests that the exhortation to heap up one's treasure in heaven rather than on earth (Matt 6:19–21 ‖ Luke 12:33–34) originally belonged to this Q context and so was likewise grounded in the eschatology of the kingdom. Against some present-day tendencies to separate wisdom and apocalyptic in the Q tradition, Schulz (p. 156) observes that cosmology, ethics, and apocalyptic were already an inseparable unity in Jewish apocalyptic literature. See, e.g., *1 Enoch* 2:1–5:10.

[90] With the exception of Luke's addition of "household slave" *(oiketēs)* at the beginning of his form of the logion, the two versions of this Q saying are word-for-word the same in both Matthew and Luke—a relatively rare phenomenon in the Q tradition. That Luke has added *oiketēs* to the Q tradition is the opinion of most commentators; so Fitzmyer, *The Gospel According to Luke,* 2. 1106. Indeed, two out of the four occurrences of the word in the NT are Lucan, the other texts being Acts 10:7; Rom 14:4; and 1 Pet 2:18. That "household slave" is Luke's addition to the Q saying is a significant judgment, since it therefore suggests that the version of the saying we have in the Coptic *Gospel of Thomas* from Nag Hammadi is not an independent one but is rather (as so often) dependent on Luke. *Gospel of Thomas* 47 reads: ". . . it is impossible for a *servant* to serve two masters; otherwise [the Greek particle *ē* is taken over here in the Coptic text] he will honor the one and offend the other." As a matter of fact, the second part of the saying in the *Gospel of Thomas* does not make a great deal of sense, since the second half of the choice ("or he will cling to the one and despise the other" is dropped). The Greek *ē* ("or") in the Coptic text calls for the other, balancing *ē* of the Greek text ("either . . . or"). Moreover, the specification "servant" sticks out in saying 47 because the axioms just before and after it speak in general terms of "a man" or "no man."

[91] See, e.g., 1QS 6:2; 1Q27 (the *Book of the Mysteries*) fragment 1, column 2, line 5 (probably); CD 14:20; 11QtgJob 2:8 on Job 27:17 (though the more usual word for "wealth" in Qumran literature is *hôn*). For the Mishna, see, e.g., *m. Ber.* 9:5; *m.*

Sanh. 4:1; *m.* '*Abot* 2:12. On all this, see Max Wilcox, "Mammon," *Anchor Bible Dictionary,* 4. 490.

[92] One finds in Sir 31 (34):8 a saying that approaches the dichotomy Jesus sets up: "Happy the rich man who is found perfect, and [who] has not turned aside after mammon." If, along with the Greek, Syriac, and Latin texts, we prefer '*āšîr* ("rich man") to the simple '*îš* ("man") of MS B of the Cairo Geniza (so Skehan and Di Lella, *The Wisdom of Ben Sira,* 381), we immediately detect a notable difference between the views of Ben Sira and those of Jesus. Jesus felicitates the poor, not the rich (see Luke 6:20,24), while Ben Sira felicitates the rich man who does not let riches turn him aside from the right path. (If one counts Ben Sira as a deuterocanonical book of the OT, it is the only OT book in which the Hebrew word *māmôn* appears.)

[93] In the later targums, the noun *māmônā*' often has the sense of "dishonest gain" or "a bribe"; but, in such cases, *māmônā*' is regularly accompanied by some qualifying phrase indicating the idea of dishonesty; see F. Hauck, *"mamōnas," TDNT* 4 (1967) 388–90. Indeed, one of the other rare occurrences of the word "mammon" in the sayings of Jesus (Luke 16:9) has the Greek phrase *mamōnas tēs adikias,* "the mammon of iniquity," i.e., "dishonest gain," which corresponds literally to an Aramaic phrase found in the targums, *māmôn dišqar.* In slightly better Greek, this appears as *adikọ mamônạ* in Luke 16:11 (cf. 16:13).

[94] *Contra* Bultmann, *Geschichte,* 91 (who ignores the tightly woven chiastic and triadic structure of Matt 6:24 par.); and in agreement with Davies and Allison, *Matthew,* 1. 643.

[95] See *A Marginal Jew,* 2. 320–21. Intriguing similarities between Matthew's form of the beatitudes and groupings of beatitudes at Qumran have been studied by Emile Puech; see his "Un Hymne essénien en partie retrouvé et les Béatitudes," *RevQ* 13, nos. 49–52 (1988) 59–88; idem, "4Q525 et les péricopes des béatitudes en Ben Sira et Matthieu," *RB* 98 (1991) 80–106. The larger conclusions he draws concerning Matthew's sources and composition of the beatitudes remain questionable. The sapiential rather than eschatological thrust of the beatitudes in 4Q525 is underscored by Craig A. Evans, "Jesus and the Dead Sea Scrolls from Qumran Cave 4," *Eschatology, Messianism, and the Dead Sea Scrolls* (ed. Craig A. Evans and Peter W. Flint; Grand Rapids/Cambridge, UK: Eerdmans, 1997) 91–100, esp. 95.

[96] This is not to say that Luke's version lacks any allegory of salvation history; Fitzmyer (*The Gospel According to Luke,* 2. 1053) sees allegory in the two stages of the invitation, symbolizing the proclamation of the good news first to the Jews and then to the Gentiles. On the whole, though, Matthew has allegorized the parable much more thoroughly. (As an aside, I would note that I doubt that the version of the parable in the Coptic *Gospel of Thomas* [saying 64] represents a primitive stage of the tradition. Much more likely, it represents a later conflation of the Matthean and Lucan forms, with all traces of salvation history removed because of gnostic tendencies.)

[97] See Luke T. Johnson, *The Literary Function of Possessions in Luke-Acts* (SBLDS 39; Missoula, MT: Scholars, 1977).

[98] See *A Marginal Jew*, 2. 822–30.

[99] For arguments for and against the authenticity of the parable, see Marshall, *Luke*, 521–22.

[100] *Contra* Bultmann, *Geschichte*, 57.

[101] In John 12:6; 13:29, we hear only fleeting references to a common purse (more precisely, a "money box," *glōssokomon*) that was supposedly held, administered, and pilfered by Judas. The desire to portray Judas in as negative a light as possible is obvious in John's theology (he is a devil, 6:70–71); yet the idea of a common purse for Jesus' disciples is certainly plausible, given their itinerant lifestyle and their various affluent supporters. Unfortunately, we lack further data that would allow us to be more specific and to engage in comparisons with the common treasury at Qumran.

[102] The saying in Mark 14:7 par. ‖ John 12:8 is especially intriguing since it both enjoys multiple attestation and makes a sharp distinction between the poor and Jesus: "The poor you always have with you, but me you do not always have."

[103] On this question, see *A Marginal Jew*, 1. 268–78.

[104] On the problem of defining the category of "sect," see *A Marginal Jew*, 2. 449–50.

[105] On this disputed question, see the treatments by Geza Vermes in his *The Dead Sea Scrolls. Qumran in Perspective* (Philadelphia: Fortress, 1977) 142–56; Fitzmyer, *Responses to 101 Questions on the Dead Sea Scrolls*, 57–58. To be sure, passages in the *Pesher on Habakkuk* (1QpHab), the *Pesher on Nahum* (4Q169), and the *Thanksgiving Hymns* (1QH) speak clearly of the persecution that the Teacher of Righteousness and his followers suffered; see, e.g., 1QpHab 11:5–8. However, as Vermes notes (pp. 153–54), attempts to prove that the Wicked Priest put the Teacher to death rest on ambiguous texts. For example, 4QpPs[a] 3–10 iv 8–9 speaks of the Wicked Priest trying to kill the righteous man. While the reference could be to the Teacher of Righteousness, the singular "righteous man" could easily have a general sense as in the usage of the Psalms. One must also take into account similar passages that speak of attempts to slay the Teacher and/or members of the community but then speak of the deliverance God grants the righteous. Vermes sums up his treatment of the question as follows (p. 154): ". . . we neither know who the founder of the Essenes was, nor how, nor where, nor when he died." Hence my wording in the main text: "there is no clear and convincing evidence."

[106] The precise meaning of this last offense is obscure. Vermes (in the 4th edition of his *The Dead Sea Scrolls in English*, 80) translates 1QS 7:15 as "whoever has drawn out his left hand to gesticulate. . . ." Charlesworth (*The Dead Sea Scrolls*, 1. 33) translates instead: "whoever stretches out his left hand in order to recline on it. . . ."

[107] One must be careful here not to read into the various sayings and actions of the historical Jesus the overarching theological structures and implicit systems of, e.g., the Sermon on the Mount in Matthew's Gospel or Paul's statements on the Law and the love command. Still more must we be on guard against finding in the scattered statements of Jesus on morality/legal observances some outline of Christian ethics or moral theology.

[108] See the comments and notes on the pericopes treated in *A Marginal Jew*, 2. 681–85, 710–11. I do not repeat all the observations and bibliography here.

[109] On this point, see Schiffman, *The Halakah at Qumran*, 121–22. The Tosepta (*t. Šabb.* 14:3), perhaps reflecting an intermediate stage of the tradition, records the ruling that, if an animal falls into a cistern (or well) on the sabbath, it should be provided with food to keep it alive. Only after the sabbath was it to be removed from the pit. Schiffman observes that the Amoraim were apparently more lenient, permitting the placing of pillows or cushions to allow the animal to come up. Lutz Doering ("New Aspects of Qumran Sabbath Law from Cave 4 Fragments," *Legal Texts and Legal Issues* [STDJ 23; ed. Moshe Bernstein, Florentino García Martínez, and John Kampen; Leiden: Brill, 1997] 251–74) notes (p. 274) that, in reference to the observance of the sabbath, "the Qumran texts always seem to advocate the strictest approach when different views are recorded in the various ancient Jewish literatures."

[110] On this point, see both Josephus (*J. W.* 2.8.7 §138–139) and 1QS 6:16–17. Geza Vermes (*The Dead Sea Scrolls. Qumran in Perspective*, 94) suggests that the "new wine" *(tîrôš)* mentioned in 1QS 6:4–6 and 1QSa 2:17–20 actually refers to unfermented grape juice, as distinct from *yayin*, regular wine; but see also the remarks of W. Dommershausen, *"yayin,"* *TDOT* 6 (1990) 59–64, esp. 61, 64.

[111] See Vermes and Goodman, *The Essenes According to the Classical Sources*, 11.

[112] The reaction would have been even fiercer if, as Mark 7:14–23 claims, Jesus (at least in theory) rejected the binding nature of the Law's distinction between clean and unclean foods. Needless to say, such a radical challenge to a central element of the Mosaic Law would have called forth strong opposition not only from Qumranites but from pious Jews of almost any persuasion. As we shall see, however, the historicity of Jesus' rejection of the food laws is questioned by various scholars.

[113] See Louis L. Snyder, *The Blood and Iron Chancellor* (Princeton, NJ: Van Nostrand, 1967) 1.

[114] For a thorough survey of the problem, see VanderKam, *Calendars in the Dead Sea Scrolls;* see also Joseph M. Baumgarten, *Studies in Qumran Law* (SJLA 24; Leiden: Brill, 1977) 101–42; Shemaryahu Talmon, "The Calendar of the Covenanters of the Judean Desert," *The World of Qumran from Within* (Jerusalem: Magnes; Leiden: Brill, 1989) 147–85; Strugnell, "MMT: Second Thoughts," 61–62; Johann Maier, "Shîrê ʿOlat hash-Shabbat. Some Observations on Their Calendric Implications and on Their Style," *The Madrid Qumran Congress* (STDJ 11; 2 vols.; ed. Julio Trebolle Barrera and Luis Vegas Montaner; Leiden: Brill, 1992) 2. 543–60; Uwe Glessmer, "The Otot-Texts (4Q319) and the Problem of Intercalations in the Context of the 364-Day Calendar," *Qumranstudien* (Schriften des Institutum Judaicum Delitzschianum 4; ed. Heinz-Josef Fabry, Armin Lange, and Hermann Lichtenberger; Göttingen: Vandenhoeck & Ruprecht, 1996) 124–64.

[115] Even if Jesus purposely anticipated the official Passover meal a day early at the Last Supper or at least gave the Last Supper some overtones of a Passover meal, such action would have been occasioned by the special situation of Jesus' surmise that he might not be able (because of the imminent threat of arrest or death) to celebrate the regular Passover meal with his disciples the next night. It would have had nothing to do with Jesus' observance of a Qumran calendar or any other special calendrical views. On the chronology of Jesus' last days, see *A Marginal Jew,* 1. 386–401.

[116] For a discussion of the nature and origin of dualism at Qumran with extensive bibliography, see Bernt Besch, *Der Dualismus in den Kernschriften von Qumran* (Rome: St. Thomas Aquinas University, 1996); see also Jörg Frey, "Different Patterns of Dualistic Thought in the Qumran Library," *Legal Texts and Legal Issues* (STDJ 23; ed. Moshe Bernstein, Florentino García Martínez, and John Kampen; Leiden: Brill, 1997) 275–335.

[117] It should be remembered that anyone who believes in a personal transcendent Creator distinct from the world he creates necessarily holds to some form of dualism; the question in each case is the intensity and precise form of the dualism espoused.

[118] For a brief summary, see Vermes, *The Dead Sea Scrolls. Qumran in Perspective,* 86–115; see also Nathan Jastram, "Hierarchy at Qumran," *Legal Texts and Legal Issues* (STDJ 23; ed. Moshe Bernstein, Florentino García Martínez, and John Kampen; Leiden: Brill, 1997) 349–76.

[119] Perhaps we might take as a symbol of the difference the contrast between the insistence in the *Rule of the Congregation* that members of the community participating in the messianic banquet are to sit "each according to his glory" (1QSa 2:11–21) and Jesus' emphasis on voluntarily taking the lowest place and letting the host (God at the eschatological banquet?) tender the invitation to "go higher" (Luke 14:10). However, I offer this contrast only as a symbol of the difference in spirit between the two movements because, in its original historical context, the advice in Luke 14:10 was probably a piece of prudential, worldly wisdom meant to guide proper conduct

at an ordinary banquet. It is rather Luke's redaction (see 14:7,11) that gives it an eschatological thrust; see Fitzmyer, *The Gospel According to Luke,* 2.1043–48. This distinction between Jesus tradition and Lucan redaction is ignored by Marshall, *Luke,* 581–83.

[120] See, e.g., Bengt Holmberg, *Paul and Power* (Philadelphia: Fortress, 1978) 161–92; idem, *Sociology and the New Testament* (Minneapolis: Fortress, 1990); see also Abraham J. Malherbe, *Social Aspects of Early Christianity* (Baton Rouge/London: Louisiana State University, 1977); Gerd Theissen, *Sociology of Early Palestinian Christianity* (Philadelphia: Fortress, 1978); idem, *The Social Setting of Pauline Christianity;* Howard Clark Kee, *Christian Origins in Sociological Perspective* (Philadelphia: Westminster, 1980); Richard A. Horsley, *Sociology and the Jesus Movement* (New York: Crossroad, 1989).

[121] On the covenant at Qumran, see Vermes, *The Dead Sea Scrolls. Qumran in Perspective,* 163–69; Raymond F. Collins, "The Berith-Notion of the Cairo Damascus Covenant and Its Comparison with the New Testament," *ETL* 39 (1963) 555–94; Shemaryahu Talmon, "The Community of the Renewed Covenant: Between Judaism and Christianity," *The Community of the Renewed Covenant* (ed. Eugene Ulrich and James VanderKam; Christianity and Judaism in Antiquity 10; Notre Dame, IN: University of Notre Dame, 1994) 3–24.

[122] On "covenant" in the eucharistic words at the Last Supper, see John P. Meier, "The Eucharist at the Last Supper: Did It Happen?" *TD* 42 (1995) 335–51; I take the word "new" in the phrase "the new covenant in my blood" in Luke 22:20 (cf. 1 Cor 11:25) to be a Christian expansion and interpretation of the words of Jesus.

[123] *A Marginal Jew,* 2. 509–1049.

[124] On these two texts, see *A Marginal Jew,* 2. 588–90.

[125] Indeed, Armin Lange ("The Essene Position on Magic and Divination," *Legal Texts and Legal Issues* [STDJ 23; ed. Moshe Bernstein, Florentino García Martínez, and John Kampen; Leiden: Brill, 1997] 377–435) thinks that, in the *Genesis Apocryphon* story of Abraham curing Pharaoh, the prayer "is the true means of exorcism . . . the laying on of hands is only an accompanying ritual" (p. 383).

[126] In the following remarks, I am dependent on the overview of Qumran's attitude toward magic and divination presented by Lange, "The Essene Position," 377–435.

[127] See the tales about the Essene prophets Judas (*J. W.* 1.3.5 §78–80 ‖ *Ant.* 13.11.2 §311–313), Simon (*J. W.* 2.7.3 §111–113 ‖ *Ant.* 17.13.3 §345–348), and Manaemus (*Ant.* 15.10.5 §373–378). Interestingly, all three of these Essenes are portrayed as active in Jerusalem and in royal circles in particular. Whoever these Essenes may have been, they seem to have been quite different from the reclusive scribes at Qumran. We

are reminded once again that the Essene movement was broader than its manifestation at Qumran and may, in some cases, have differed from Qumran quite notably in both theory and practice.

[128] For general orientation and detailed bibliographies, see James Alan Montgomery, *The Samaritans. The Earliest Jewish Sect* (New York: Ktav, 1968, originally 1907); Moses Gaster, *The Samaritans. Their History, Doctrines, and Literature* (The Schweich Lectures; London: The British Academy, 1925; reprint: Munich: Kraus, 1980); David Daube, "Jesus and the Samaritan Woman: The Meaning of *sygchraomai*," *JBL* 69 (1950) 137–47; Abram Spiro, "Samaritans, Tobiads, and Judahites in Pseudo-Philo," *PAAJR* 20 (1951) 279–355; idem, "Steven's Samaritan Background," in Johannes Munck, *The Acts of the Apostles* (AB 31; Garden City, NY: Doubleday, 1967) 285–300; John Macdonald, *The Theology of the Samaritans* (NT Library; London: SCM, 1964); G. Ernest Wright, *Shechem. The Biography of a Biblical City* (New York/Toronto: McGraw-Hill, 1964); J. D. Purvis, *The Samaritan Pentateuch and the Origin of the Samaritan Sect* (HSM 2; Cambridge, MA: Harvard University, 1968); idem, "The Samaritans and Judaism," *Early Judaism and Its Modern Interpreters* (ed. Robert A. Kraft and George W. E. Nickelsburg; Atlanta: Scholars, 1986) 81–98; idem, "The Fourth Gospel and the Samaritans," *NovT* 17 (1975) 161–98; Hans G. Kippenberg, *Garizim und Synagoge* (Religionsgeschichtliche Versuche und Vorarbeiten 30; Berlin: de Gruyter, 1971); John Bowman, *The Samaritan Problem. Studies in the Relationships of Samaritanism, Judaism, and Early Christianity* (Pittsburgh Theological Monograph Series 4; Pittsburgh: Pickwick, 1975); R. J. Coggins, *Samaritans and Jews. The Origins of Samaritanism Reconsidered* (Growing Points in Theology; Atlanta: John Knox, 1975); idem, "The Samaritans and Acts," *NTS* 28 (1982) 423–34; idem, "The Samaritans in Josephus," *Josephus, Judaism, and Christianity* (ed. Louis H. Feldman and Gohei Hata; Detroit: Wayne State University, 1987) 257–73; idem, "Issues in Samaritanism," *Judaism in Late Antiquity. Part Three. Where We Stand: Issues and Debates in Ancient Judaism. Volume One* (Handbook of Oriental Studies, Part One: The Near and Middle East 40; ed. Jacob Neusner and Alan J. Avery-Peck; Leiden: Brill, 1999) 63–77; Mathias Delcor, "Vom Sichem der hellenistischen Epoche zum Sychar des Neuen Testamentes," *Religion d'Israel et Proche Orient Ancien* (Leiden: Brill, 1976) 389–403; Rita Egger, *Josephus Flavius und die Samaritaner* (Novum Testamentum et Orbis Antiquus 4; Freiburg: Universitätsverlag; Göttingen: Vandenhoeck & Ruprecht, 1986); Nathan Schur, *History of the Samaritans* (Beiträge zur Erforschung des Alten Testaments und des Antiken Judentums 18; Frankfurt: Peter Lang, 1989); Iain Ruairidh Mac Mhanainn Bóid, *Principles of Samaritan Halachah* (SJLA 38; Leiden: Brill, 1989); Menachem Mor, "I. Samaritan History. 1. The Persian, Hellenistic and Hasmonaean Period," *The Samaritans* (ed. Alan David Crown; Tübingen: Mohr [Siebeck], 1989) 1–18; Léon Poliakov, *Les Samaritains* (Paris: Editions du Seuil, 1991); Robert T. Anderson, "Samaritans," *Anchor Bible Dictionary*, 5. 940–47; Alan David Crown, *A Bibliography of the Samaritans* (ATLA Bibliography Series 32; 2d ed.; Metuchen, NJ/London: American Theological Library Association/Scarecrow, 1993); Alan David Crown, Reinhard Pummer, and Abraham Tal (eds.), *A Companion to Samaritan Studies* (Tübingen: Mohr [Siebeck], 1993); Jean-Daniel Macchi, *Les Samaritains: Histoire d'une légende*

(Le Monde de la Bible 30; Geneva: Labor et Fides, 1994); M. Böhm, *Samarien und die Samaritai bei Lukas* (WUNT 2/111; Tübingen: Mohr [Siebeck], 1999; Ingrid Hjelm, *The Samaritans and Early Judaism: A Literary Analysis* (JSOTSup 303; Sheffield: JSOT, 2000).

[129] Indeed, as can be seen from what follows, it is extremely difficult to keep the three perspectives entirely separate.

[130] See Peter Richardson, *Herod King of the Jews and Friend of the Romans* (Minneapolis: Fortress, 1996, 1999) 77–79. The terminology here is confusing, since originally, in the writings of the OT (with a few possible exceptions), it was the *city*, not the *region*, that was called Samaria. In the OT, the whole region is referred to by such names as Ephraim or Israel; scholars speak of the northern kingdom of Israel. After the destruction of the city by the Assyrians, the name Samaria came to be used of the whole Assyrian province. Then, after Herod rebuilt and renamed the capital city Sebaste, the name Samaria was used not of the city but only of the region; this is the regular NT usage (but see the text-critical problem in Acts 8:5). On all this, see James D. Purvis, "Samaria," *Anchor Bible Dictionary*, 5. 914–21.

[131] On this, see Coggins, *Samaritans and Jews,* 9; idem, "Issues in Samaritanism," 6–7. Differing from Coggins in emphasizing Samaritan nationhood and geography is Schur, *History of the Samaritans,* 14–19.

[132] Richardson, *Herod,* 139.

[133] The typical tendency of scholars to read Josephus as hostile to the Samaritans is seen, e.g., in Coggins, *Samaritans and Jews,* 10, 93–99; idem, "The Samaritans in Josephus," 260–71. Opposed to this idea of Josephus' hostility is Egger, *Josephus Flavius,* 310–14. She holds that, in general, Josephus shows true historical objectivity when dealing with the Samaritans, understood as the religious group centered on Mt. Gerizim. Egger does well to emphasize the importance of distinguishing between what I call "Samarians" in the geographical sense (all inhabitants of Samaria) and "Samaritans" in the religious sense. However, her suggestion that Josephus was clear and consistent in using terms like *Samareis, Samareitai, Chuthaioi* in the original draft of his work and that it was his Greek-speaking collaborators who confused his terminology is highly speculative.

[134] On this, see Macdonald (*The Theology of the Samaritans,* 17), relying on the account in the Samaritan writing known as *Chronicles II.*

[135] The Greek translates the Hebrew at this point in 2 Kings 17 as *Samaritai,* hence the common English translation "Samaritans." I. W. Slotki (*Kings* [Soncino Bible; London: Soncino, 1950] 268) sums up well the sense of the original Hebrew text when he states that *haššōmĕrōnîm* refers "to the Israelites who had formerly inhabited the district. The new settlers made use of the places of worship which the former inhabitants had erected." Interestingly, the Samaritans themselves derive their name

not from the geographical region of Samaria (taken from the name of the capital city, Samaria [šōmĕrôn]), but rather from the term šāmĕrîm [their form of the Biblical Hebrew šōmĕrîm], "keepers [of the Law]." This is a regular usage in *Chronicles II*. On this, see Coggins (*Samaritans and Jews*, 10–11), who also discusses there the alleged reference to Samaritans in 2 Chr 13:11.

[136] See the extended treatment of the passage in Macchi, *Les Samaritains*, 47–72; also Coggins, *Samaritans and Jews*, 13–19. Different commentators see different stages of tradition and redaction, but almost all agree on the complicated, multistage nature of the tradition history of the chapter. For example, John Gray (*I & II Kings* [OTL; Philadelphia: Westminster, 1963] 579–98) discerns a primitive report, perhaps from the Annals of Israel, redacted and added to by a number of later hands, including the Deuteronomic redactor and perhaps a priestly historian of the sanctuary at Bethel. For short and sane comments on the overall sense of the passage, see J. Robinson, *The Second Book of Kings* (Cambridge Bible Commentary; Cambridge, UK: Cambridge University, 1976) 160–63; Terence E. Fretheim, *First and Second Kings* (Westminster Bible Companion; Louisville: Westminster/John Knox, 1999) 193–94.

[137] As noted above, Egger (*Josephus Flavius*) is one of the few authors who dissent from this consensus on the hostile attitude of Josephus toward the Samaritans understood as a religious group.

[138] On the situation after the destruction of the capital of Samaria, see Macchi, *Les Samaritains*, 120–33, 173–74; Schur, *History of the Samaritans*, 26.

[139] Fortunately, our focus on Jesus' relationship to the Samaritans dispenses us from plunging into the complicated problem of the chronological order and the precise dating of the activity of Nehemiah and Ezra.

[140] On this, see Macchi, *Les Samaritains*, 34–35; also Bowman, *The Samaritan Problem*, 4. It cannot be emphasized enough that one must distinguish from (the later) Samaritans in the religious sense certain political figures, especially imperial officials, in the provinces of Samaria and Ammon such as Sanballat and Tobiah (see, e.g., Neh 2:10,19; 6:1–2; 13:4–9,28). Only when we get to Josephus is the political struggle over the rebuilding of Jerusalem reinterpreted in terms of conflict with Shechem and hence with the Samaritans. This point is not sufficiently appreciated by Macdonald, *Theology of the Samaritans*, 24; Schur, *History of the Samaritans*, 31–32.

[141] Coggins, "Issues in Samaritanism," 66.

[142] *Ant.* 11.7.1–7 §297–347. One also finds a garbled version of the story in the post-Talmudic scholion to the 1st-century A.D. Aramaic *Megillat Ta'anit* (see also the variant version in *b. Yoma* 69a). A translation of the scholion along with a discussion of the anachronisms contained in it can be found in Appendix C of vol. 6 of the LCL

edition of Josephus (ed. Ralph Marcus), pp. 517–19. The proliferation of legends about Alexander the Great in both pagan and Jewish literature makes one leery of accepting Josephus' account of the relations between Alexander, the Samaritans, and the Jews, including the story of the apostasy of the Jewish priest Manasses to the Samaritans and Alexander's permission to build a Samaritan temple.

[143] See Coggins, *Samaritans and Jews,* 95–97. The one shred of truth in the whole story may be that the origins of the Samaritan temple lie somewhere around the shift from the Persian to the Hellenistic era. Schur (*History of the Samaritans,* 35–36) is more ready to accept Josephus' account of events during the time of Alexander than I would be.

[144] See Wright, *Shechem,* 172–80; Coggins, *Samaritans and Jews,* 106–9. Coggins discusses the possible relevance of the discovery of skeletons, Samaria papyri, and Shechem-like pottery in a cave in the Wadi Daliyeh to Alexander's destruction of Samaria and the supposed flight to Shechem. Perhaps the most significant archaeological datum is the simple fact that Shechem was reoccupied late in the 4th century B.C. and continued to be occupied until the late 2d century B.C. These dates correlate neatly with the activity of Alexander the Great and that of the Hasmonean monarch John Hyrcanus, respectively.

[145] Spiro, "Samaritans," 312 (continuation of n. 67 from p. 311); Bo Reicke, *Neutestamentliche Zeitgeschichte* (3d ed.; Berlin/New York: de Gruyter, 1982) 24–29.

[146] So, e.g., Wright, *Shechem,* 178; similarly, Kippenberg, *Garizim und Synagoge,* 57.

[147] It is sometimes claimed that the very existence of a temple on Mt. Gerizim would indicate that a definitive, irrevocable break had already taken place between Samaritans and Jews. Yet a temple built by Jewish colonists in Egypt existed at Elephantine in the 6th to 5th centuries B.C., and another Jewish temple in Egypt existed from the middle of the 2d century B.C. until ca. A.D. 71 at Leontopolis. Neither of these temples seems to have created an irrevocable breach between the Egyptian Jews who worshiped there and the Jewish authorities in Jerusalem. While this is certainly true—and while one is therefore reminded that Deuteronomy's law of only one temple for the public cult of Yahweh may not always have been understood and enforced as stringently as scholars formerly imagined—one should also note two aggravating differences in the case of the sanctuary on Mt. Gerizim: (1) This temple existed within the traditional promised land of Israel and not in the Diaspora; hence, from a practical point of view, it could serve as a rival pilgrimage site for people living in Israel. (2) The Mt. Gerizim temple came to be understood by the Samaritans and the Jews alike as a *rival* to that of Jerusalem; such seems to have been the intent of the additions the Samaritans made to the Decalogue (after Exod 20:17 and Deut 5:18), ordering that an altar of sacrifice be constructed on Mt. Gerizim. The Samaritan version of the Pen-

tateuch also presents Moses ordering the construction of an altar on Mt. Gerizim in Deut 27:4 (a version of the text that some scholars hold to be earlier than that of the MT). Thus, Mt. Gerizim came to be claimed as the one legitimate sanctuary of Yahweh, with Mt. Zion's claim being rejected. As far as we know, no such claim was ever made for the sanctuaries in Elephantine or Leontopolis. In any event, the somewhat confusing stories about disputes between Jews and Samaritans in Egypt (*Ant.* 12.1.1 §10; 13.3.4 §74–79, possibly a doublet) may indicate that by the 2d century B.C. conflicts between Jews and Samaritans had spread into the Diaspora and were focused on the question of whether Jerusalem or Gerizim was the true sanctuary.

[148] On this text, see Skehan and Di Lella, *Ben Sira,* 558; perhaps, as Coggins claims ("Issues in Samaritanism," 68), too much of the standard OT story is taken as sober history in their comment.

[149] Instead of "those who dwell in Seir," the Greek translation has "those who dwell on the mount of Samaria." Almost all recent critics accept the Hebrew text as the original form; see Coggins, "Samaritanism," 73.

[150] At times, Josephus also calls the Samaritans "Shechemites" (see, e.g., *Ant.* 11.8.6–7 §340–347). Coggins (*Samaritans and Jews,* 10) suggests that Josephus purposely used *Samaritai* of the community at Shechem "to imply a contemptuous association with the by this time paganized city of Samaria. . . ." More frequent in both Josephus and the Mishna is the use of the designation "Chutheans," a usage that shows even more clearly than that of *Samaritai* that the account in 2 Kings 17 was now being associated in a polemical manner with the community at Shechem.

[151] The Greek of 2 Macc 6:2 is not entirely clear. The key phrase referring to the inhabitants of Mt. Gerizim is *kathōs etygchanon hoi ton topon oikountes.* The *NAB* takes this to mean "as the inhabitants requested," while the *NRSV* translates it as "as did the people who lived in that place" and the *NEB* "following the practice of the local inhabitants." The *New Jerusalem Bible* also uses "requested" in its translation, but indicates in a note on the verse that this translation is chosen in light of Josephus' narrative, while the Greek of 2 Macc 6:2 could simply mean that "being themselves hospitable, the Samaritans chose this epithet." I think it wise not to read Josephus' hostile interpretation of events into a translation of the admittedly obscure 2 Macc 6:2. Indeed, so difficult is an accurate interpretation that Goldstein (*II Maccabees,* 268, 273) purposely leaves a blank at this point in his translation ("in accordance with the . . . of the inhabitants of the place"). He suggests that one could complete the thought contained in the verb *etygchanon* with either "in accordance with the practice" or "in accordance with the name." In his opinion, taking the text to mean that the inhabitants "obtained" or "obtained by request" this name is possible but not likely because of the imperfect tense of the verb. In any case, in 2 Macc 6:2 the inhabitants of Mt. Gerizim do not take the initiative in the way portrayed in Josephus' account.

[152] Scholars still debate the exact dates of these events, with some suggesting that the destruction of both the Samaritan temple and Shechem took place ca. 107 B.C.; so D. S. Russell, *The Jews from Alexander to Herod* (The New Clarendon Bible, OT, vol. 5; London: Oxford University, 1967) 63. Wright (*Shechem,* 183–84) favors distinguishing the two events. In any case, the basic facts are not in dispute.

[153] On the whole vastly complicated question of defining who was a Jew in the ancient world, see the various essays of Shaye J. D. Cohen in his collection, *The Beginnings of Jewishness* (Berkeley, CA: University of California, 1999).

[154] Coggins (*Samaritans and Jews,* 5–6) rightly warns against taking the narrative of the Chronicler and Ezra-Nehemiah as sober, objective history. It is instead idealized, sacred history that seeks to legitimate those Judeans who went into exile and then returned to Jerusalem as the true Israel.

[155] On this whole question, see Purvis, "The Samaritans and Judaism," 90–95. While I agree with the substance of Purvis' remarks, I question his view that Samaritanism should be considered part of Judaism "broadly defined." At this point, though, the argument becomes semantic rather than substantive.

[156] Hence I think it inappropriate to speak of the Samaritans as the earliest or oldest Jewish sect in the manner of such scholars as Montgomery or Gaster. A better formulation is that of Macchi, *Les Samaritains,* 43: "Therefore, the Samaritans should not be considered as a Jewish sect but rather as another branch of the religion of Yahweh, centered around a holy place different from Jerusalem."

[157] On the inappropriateness of the term "schism," see Coggins, *Samaritans and Jews,* 162–65. Coggins does at times, though, refer to Samaritans as part of "that larger complex which constitutes the Judaism of the last pre-Christian centuries" (p. 163). For the reasons given above, I think "Israel" would be a better umbrella term than Judaism. Interestingly, elsewhere Coggins is more nuanced; see, e.g., "Issues in Samaritanism," 75–76: "Just as it is clearly wrong to regard the Samaritans as Gentiles *tout court,* so it [is] equally impossible to treat them as Jews *tout court.* . . . if pressed to describe themselves, they [the Samaritans] would have used the name 'Israelites' rather than 'Samaritans.' " Similarities between Samaritans and Qumranites (to a lesser extent, Sadducees) are often pointed out (see, e.g., Anderson, "Samaritans," 942; Bowman, *Samaritan Problem,* 91–118); but common traditions or tendencies rather than direct dependence of one group on another seem the best explanation.

[158] See Josephus' disparaging statement about the Samaritans' fluctuating attitude toward the Jews: sometimes they call themselves their kinsmen, sometimes they claim to be of another race (*Ant.* 9.14.3 §291). This oscillating attitude may have been shared by the Jews as well, even into the Christian era.

[159] Notice, e.g., the focus of Purvis, "The Fourth Gospel and the Samaritans," 162, 191.

[160] It should be noted that works that offer surveys of Samaritan history or theology often do not treat the NT texts in a critical manner; see, e.g., Schur, *History of the Samaritans,* 80–82.

[161] For bibliography on the missionary discourses and the question of their sources, see the treatment on the mission of the Twelve in chapter 26 of this volume; see in particular Laufen, *Die Doppelüberlieferungen,* 201–301; Hahn, *Mission,* 41–42; Fitzmyer, *The Gospel According to Luke,* 1. 751; Uro, *Sheep among the Wolves,* 101 n. 17.

[162] On this question, see Stephenson H. Brooks, *Matthew's Community. The Evidence of His Special Sayings Material* (JSNTSup 16; Sheffield: JSOT, 1987) 49–50.

[163] See my treatment in *A Marginal Jew,* 2. 659–61.

[164] The attempts of some critics (see, e.g., Bowman, *Samaritan Problem,* 74–89) to see many points of contact between Luke-Acts and the Samaritans is, in my opinion, strained.

[165] *A Marginal Jew,* 2. 701–5. However, whether Philip's mission to Samaria should be understood as involving Samaritans in the religious sense is not entirely clear. The judgment depends partially on whether we read in Acts 8:5 that Philip, one of the seven leaders of the Hellenists (see Acts 6:5), went down to *a* city of Samaria or to *the* city of Samaria. The Greek manuscripts differ on this point; some (e.g., papyrus 74, A, and B) include the definite article while others (e.g., C, D, and the Byzantine tradition) omit it. If we read "the city of Samaria," then Philip's mission would not involve Samaritans in particular, since the city of Samaria (rebuilt in the 1st century B.C. by Herod the Great as Sebaste) had become largely paganized. If instead we read "a city of Samaria," it is likely—especially in light of 8:25—that Samaritans are meant. The fourth edition (1993) of the *UBSGNT* reflects the uncertainty of the manuscript testimony by putting the definite article in brackets in the main text and giving the reading a "C" rating. This indicates that the editorial committee inclines to the position that the article "may be regarded as part of the text, but . . . in the present state of New Testament textual scholarship this cannot be taken as certain" (p. 2*). In the 2d edition of his *Textual Commentary,* Metzger states (p. 311) that the external evidence supports the inclusion of the article, while internal considerations favor its absence. Metzger suggests that the reading with the definite article be translated "the [main] city of Samaria," which could be interpreted as either Sebaste (the paganized capital) or Nablus/Shechem (the hub of the Samaritan religion). But by what right do we interpolate "main" into the text? In any event, Samaritans are certainly mentioned as the audience of missionary preaching in 8:25: As Peter and John return to Jerusalem after completing Philip's initial work, they proclaim the gospel in "many villages of

the Samaritans." Given all these textual and conceptual difficulties, it is not surprising that the major commentaries are divided in their treatment of Acts 8:5. Haenchen (*Apostelgeschichte*, 252) favors the article, but notes the opposite opinion. Conzelmann (*Acts of the Apostles*, 62) thinks that "Luke believes that the region of Samaria has only one city—the city of the same name." Schneider (*Apostelgeschichte*, 1. 487) holds that the reading with the article is to be preferred, but whether Luke thinks that the capital city of Samaria is Sebaste or Shechem is unclear. Fitzmyer (*Acts of the Apostles*, 402) is more willing to give serious consideration to the reading without the article, which is the definite choice of Lake and Cadbury (*The Beginnings of Christianity. Part I: The Acts of the Apostles*, 4. 89). Barrett (*Acts of the Apostles*, 1. 402–3) gives a thorough discussion of all the possibilities without indicating a firm choice. In all these arguments pro and con, there is an underlying problem that is not always discussed: Luke's hazy notions about Palestinian geography, especially when it comes to Samaria. Would he have been aware of the difference in religious makeup between *the (capital) city of Samaria* and *villages of Samaritans* in the region of Samaria? In other words, throughout this treatment we have been at pains to distinguish conceptually between Samarians and Samaritans. Did Luke instead, like some modern scholars, inadvertently identify the two groups?

[166] Besides the standard Lucan commentaries (e.g., Fitzmyer, *The Gospel According to Luke*, 1. 823–32; Marshall, *Luke*, 400–408), see Michi Miyoshi, *Der Anfang des Reiseberichts. Lk 9,51–10,24* (AnBib 60; Rome: Biblical Institute, 1974) esp. 6–32; Edgar Mayer, *Die Reiseerzählung des Lukas (Lk 9,51–19,10): Entscheidung in der Wüste* (Europäische Hochschulschriften, Reihe 23, vol. 554; Frankfurt: Peter Lang, 1996) esp. 203–6.

[167] See, e.g., Miyoshi, *Der Anfang*, 6–16. The difficulty of deciding what belonged to the pre-Lucan form of the story is clear from the oscillation in Dibelius' criticism. While in the 1st edition of his *Formgeschichte* he thought that the story behind Luke 9:52–56 was a "personal legend" about James and John, by the 3d edition (*Formgeschichte*, 44–45) he had reversed himself and decided that the primitive story originally spoke of anonymous disciples, who were later identified with James and John, perhaps to give an explanation of the name "sons of thunder." Helmut Flender (*St Luke Theologian of Redemptive History* [Philadelphia: Fortress, 1967] 33–34) sees Lucan tradition in vv 51b,52b, and 53ff. If truth be told, beyond saying that Luke is probably redacting an earlier story in these verses, we are largely in the dark.

[168] The Lucan motifs that dominate 9:51–56 include the theme of ascension as the goal of the Lord's way (which *must* pass through death and resurrection in the city of destiny, Jerusalem), the rejection of the Lord by some and yet his acceptance by others, the need for the disciples to follow the way of the Lord (including his experience of rejection), the commission they receive from the Lord to prepare his way, the mercy of the Lord toward ignorant sinners (whom he seeks to save rather than destroy), and echoes of an Elijah-christology. Both Miyoshi and Mayer place this pericope firmly within the larger theological and literary project of Luke, whose major

themes and structures it faithfully mirrors. OT allusions include the "taking up" of Enoch and Elijah, the theme of the rejected and martyred prophets of Israel, and possibly the prophecy about sending messengers before the face of the Lord in Mal 3:1.

[169] While the text of Mark 10:1 (cf. Matt 19:1) is probably inaccurate (". . . into the territory of Judea [and] across the Jordan"—but see the variant readings), the general intent seems to be to indicate the roundabout path to Jerusalem by way of Perea (cf. *peran tou Iordanou*) and the road through Jericho (cf. Mark 10:46). A direct north-south route from Galilee through Samaria to Jerusalem would not lead through Jericho near the Jordan; yet this is how Luke portrays the end of Jesus' journey to Jerusalem (see Luke 18:35; 19:1,28–29).

[170] See Marshall, *Luke*, 404.

[171] Gerhard Sellin, "Lukas als Gleichniserzähler: Die Erzählung vom barmherzigen Samariter (Lk 10:25–37)," *ZNW* 65 (1974) 166–89; 66 (1975) 19–60.

[172] In favor of Lucan redaction of an earlier tradition, see Marshall, *Luke*, 444–50; Fitzmyer, *The Gospel According to Luke*, 2. 882–90 (with further bibliography). For the history of interpretation, see Werner Monselewski, *Der barmherzige Samariter* (BGBE 5; Tübingen: Mohr [Siebeck], 1967); Hans Gunther Klemm, *Das Gleichnis vom barmherzigen Samariter. Grundzüge der Auslegung im 16./17. Jahrhundert* (BWANT 6/3; Stuttgart: Kohlhammer, 1973). For consideration of the parable from various historical, theological, and literary angles, see Joachim Jeremias, *The Parables of Jesus* (NT Library; London: SCM, 1963) 202–5; John Dominic Crossan, *In Parables* (San Francisco: Harper & Row, 1973) 57–66; John Drury, *The Parables in the Gospel* (New York: Crossroad, 1985) 132–35; John R. Donahue, *The Gospel in Parable* (Philadelphia: Fortress, 1988) 128–34; Bernard Brandon Scott, *Hear Then the Parable* (Minneapolis: Fortress, 1989) 189–202. For a series of essays applying a structuralist approach to this parable, see John Dominic Crossan (ed.), *The Good Samaritan* (Semeia 2; Missoula, MT: Scholars, 1974). For larger hermeneutical issues, see Sandra Wackman Perpich, *A Hermeneutic Critique of Structuralist Exegesis, with Specific Reference to Lk 10.29–37* (Lanham, MD: University Press of America, 1984); Llewellyn Welile Mazamisa, *Beatific Comradeship. An Exegetical-Hermeneutical Study on Lk 10:25–37* (Kampen: Kok, 1987); James I. H. McDonald, "The View from the Ditch—and Other Angles," *SJT* 49 (1996) 21–37. Many commentators agree with the general approach of Fitzmyer: the core of the parable comes from the L tradition; Luke has framed it with an introductory question (v 29b) and a concluding command (v 37b). I think it significant that the parable (or example story) depends for its full impact on all sorts of details of Jewish-Palestinian life that are presupposed rather than explained; this may argue for pre-Lucan tradition.

[173] The entire argument of the Jesus Seminar in favor of the parable's coming from Jesus is simply that this story "redraws the map of both the social and the sacred world" and is therefore a prime example of "the provocative public speech of Jesus";

see Robert W. Funk, Roy W. Hoover, et al., *The Five Gospels* (New York: Macmillan, 1993) 324. Apparently no early Christian, while engaged in tearing down the sacred walls separating Jews, Samaritans, and Gentiles, would have ever thought to use such provocative public speech to redraw social and sacred maps. Why this is so is not explained.

[174] It should be noted that the Hebrew word used in the love command of Lev 19:18 is *rēăkā* ("your fellow [man]," "companion," "friend"), not the adjective *qārôb* (used as a substantive: "the one near to you"—which can mean "relative"). The standard English translation "neighbor" reflects the LXX Lev 19:18 *(ton plēsion)*; while the adverb *plēsion* means "near," "close by," as a substantive it often signifies "neighbor," a regular meaning in the NT. Interestingly, the Vulgate reads "amicum tuum," a closer rendering of the Hebrew.

[175] This exhausts explicit references to Samaritans in Luke's Gospel. Some might see a garbled reference in Luke 13:1 ("the Galileans whose blood Pilate had mingled with the blood of their sacrifices") to Pilate's attack on and slaughtering of a gathering of Samaritans on Mt. Gerizim (*Ant.* 18.4.1 §86–87). But this remains highly speculative, and nothing can be concluded that aids our particular inquiry. On the question of the possible historical backgrounds for 13:1, see Fitzmyer, *The Gospel According to Luke,* 2. 1006–7.

[176] Note, e.g., the themes of water, Spirit, eating and drinking, Jesus as the supersession of traditional religious institutions, realized eschatology, the lack of understanding on the part of the disciples, and the ultimately cosmic dimensions of the work that Jesus is to bring to perfection. Barrett (*The Gospel According to St John,* 191) emphasizes that the evangelist has written the story as a whole and that therefore it is impossible "to isolate a pre-Johannine nucleus of the story." Even Brown (*The Gospel According to John,* 1. 175–76), while defending a substratum of traditional material, acknowledges the evangelist has formed it "into a superb theological scenario." For a semiotic analysis of the whole story, see Hendrikus Boers, *Neither on This Mountain Nor in Jerusalem. A Study of John 4* (SBLMS 35; Atlanta: Scholars, 1988); a bibliography on John 4 can be found on pp. 201–7. For general bibliography on the passage, see Haenchen, *John 1,* 213–16.

[177] See Oscar Cullmann, *Der johanneische Kreis* (Tübingen: Mohr [Siebeck], 1975) 49–52.

[178] John 4:9 is often translated in more general fashion as "Jews have no dealings with Samaritans" (so *RSV*) or something similar. The root sense of the verb in question, *sygchraomai,* is "use together." Hence scholars like Daube ("Jesus and the Samaritan Woman," 143) and Coggins (*Samaritans and Jews,* 139) suggest that, in the specific context of John 4, the idea is that Jews will not use utensils used by Samaritans because of considerations of purity. This contextual interpretation of the verb fits perfectly with the details of the dramatic scene in John 4: Jesus is thirsty and wants

a drink of water from "Jacob's well," but he has no utensil or vessel with which to draw the water (see v 11: Jesus has no *antlēma* with which to draw the water). Hence the translation of the *NAB* may reflect better John's intention: "Jews use nothing in common with Samaritans." Yet this interpretation, however attractive, is not without its philological difficulties, as is pointed out by D. R. Hall, "The meaning of *sygchraomai* in John 4:9," *ExpTim* 83 (1971–72) 56–57. However, Hall's own counterargument suffers from weaknesses as well. In light of both the immediate Johannine and larger Jewish-rabbinic context, I prefer Daube's approach ("use in common"), though I admit the alternate translation ("have dealings with") remains a possibility.

[179] The text often cited in this regard is *m. Nid.* 4:1: "Kuthean women [= Samaritan women; literally: "daughters of Kutheans"] are [considered unclean as] menstruants from their cradle." One must allow, however, for the activity of censors, who sometimes introduced *kûttîm* (Kutheans) into rabbinic texts as a substitute for other designations. One should also note that rabbinic views on Samaritans vary greatly from text to text.

[180] Interestingly, this is presupposed in the Lucan passages we have examined (especially 9:53), but it is never explicitly stated anywhere in Luke's Gospel.

[181] The etymology of the term "Taheb" is disputed, though it may well be the participial form of the verb *tûb*, "to return," hence "the returning one" (or possibly, with a transitive sense, "the one who restores"). The Taheb was a very malleable figure in Samaritan thought and, in various writings, is associated with different eschatological expectations; see Ferdinand Dexinger, "Taheb," *A Companion to Samaritan Studies*, 224–26. The origin of the figure no doubt lies in the eschatological hopes ignited by the promise that God would raise up a prophet like Moses (Deut 18:15,18); Jews, Samaritans, and Christians all developed these hopes in different ways. Interestingly, at times the Taheb is said to be a descendant of Jacob. Is there possibly a connection between this idea and the ironic question of the Samaritan woman to Jesus in John 4:12: "Surely you are not greater than our father Jacob, who gave us the well . . . ? "

[182] While many critics would admit some contact between a stage or stratum of Johannine tradition and the Samaritans (see Brown, *Community of the Beloved Disciple*, 22–23 n. 31, 35–40), few would be willing to accept the claim of Bowman (*Samaritan Problem*, 59) that the Gospel of John addressed itself to the "heretical" Dosithean wing of 1st-century Samaritan religion. In any event, there seems to be some narrative source that the Fourth Evangelist is using as he composes 4:4–42. Both Fortna and von Wahlde detect tradition behind the present story, though they differ on whether it belonged to the cohesive "Sign Source" or "Gospel of Signs" that the evangelist supposedly used; see Fortna, *The Fourth Gospel and Its Predecessor*, 108–9; von Wahlde, *The Earliest Version of John's Gospel*, 83–90.

[183] See my remarks in *A Marginal Jew*, 1. 227–29.

[184] Purvis, "The Fourth Gospel and the Samaritans," 195–96; see also Brown, *The Gospel According to John*, 1. 358.

[185] See, e.g., Brown, *Community of the Beloved Disciple*, 76–78.

[186] Since our focus is the relation of the historical Jesus to the Samaritans, I do not consider here the views of scholars who see Samaritan influence in the speech of Stephen in Acts 7 or in the theology of the Epistle to the Hebrews. In my opinion, though, such views lack solid proof.

[187] For basic orientation and bibliography, see Christine Schams, *Jewish Scribes in the Second-Temple Period* (JSOTSup 291; Sheffield: JSOT, 1998); see also Saldarini, *Pharisees, Scribes and Sadducees*, 144–98, 241–76; idem, "Scribes," *Anchor Bible Dictionary*, 5. 1012–16; David E. Orton, *The Understanding Scribe. Matthew and the Apocalyptic Ideal* (JSNTSup 25; Sheffield: JSOT, 1989) 39–133. I have also drawn upon a seminar paper on "Jesus and the Scribes" by Eric Stewart, a doctoral student at the University of Notre Dame. For older (and sometimes uncritical) literature, see the revised Schürer, *History of the Jewish People*, 2. 322–36; Joachim Jeremias, *Jerusalem in the Time of Jesus*, 232–45; idem, *"grammateus,"* TDNT 1 (1964) 740–42. On wider issues, see William V. Harris, *Ancient Literacy* (Cambridge, MA/London: Harvard University, 1989).

[188] Schams (*Jewish Scribes*, 15–35) points out how *Schriftgelehrte*, as an artificial category conflating scribes, sages, rabbis, wise men, and sophists, has had long life in German scholarship; a striking example of the conflation is seen in Schürer, *History of the Jewish People*, 2. 324: "In New Testament times, this process [by which the scribes replace the priests and Levites as the real teachers of the Law to the people] was already complete: the scribes are represented as the undisputed spiritual leaders of the people. Usually, they are alluded to as *grammateis*, 'Scripture experts,' 'the learned,' . . . to correspond with the Hebrew *swprym*." A similar conflation of evidence, titles, and roles can be seen in the works of Jeremias and Orton. It should also be noted that the depiction that we get at times in the Mishna of scribes as the authoritative teachers in postexilic Israel between the time of the writing of the Hebrew Scriptures and the rise of the rabbis is likewise of dubious historical value. Interestingly, when the Mishna and Tosepta speak of scribes around their own time, they usually mean professional writers and copyists, not learned teachers of Torah. On the various meanings of "scribe" in the Mishna and Tosepta, see Schams, *Jewish Scribes*, 218–34, 297–98.

[189] Saldarini, *Pharisees, Scribes and Sadducees*, 242.

[190] The Hebrew verb *sāpar* means "to count" in qal and "to recount," "to enumerate," "to make known," "to tell" in pi'el. The noun designating the permanent in-

strument and record by which these actions are done, especially in the context of court, army, government bureaucracy, or temple, is *sēfer,* the (written) document, scroll, or letter. Accordingly, the person who draws up or copies the *sēfer* is the *sōfēr* in Hebrew (qal active participle), the *safrā'* in Aramaic. The Greek word for scribe is *grammateus* (from *gramma,* "something drawn," "letter," which comes in turn from *graphō,* "to carve," "to engrave," "to paint," "to draw," and then generally "to write"). In the LXX, it is used to translate *sōfēr* and less often—but notably in the Pentateuch—*šōṭēr* (a type of scribe or officer in charge of organization). It is the regular NT Greek word for "scribe."

[191] One should remember that, especially in the case of texts of great religious or literary importance for the community, the manuscripts copied by scribes would be read not only in private or in small groups by the educated elite but also at times in public to assemblies of the illiterate masses.

[192] On this, see Jack R. Lundbom, "Baruch," *Anchor Bible Dictionary,* 1. 617.

[193] For different opinions on the position and functions of Ezra, see Schams, *Jewish Scribes,* 50–57.

[194] On the complicated question of scribes in the Chronicler's writings, see Joseph Blenkinsopp, "Sage, Scribe and Scribalism in the Chronicler's Work," *The Sage in Israel and the Ancient Near East* (ed. John G. Gammie and Leo G. Perdue; Winona Lake, IN: Eisenbrauns, 1990) 307–15.

[195] On this, see Schams, *Jewish Scribes,* 291–92.

[196] While this section clearly presents an idealized picture of the pious Jewish scribe, I take the basic elements of Ben Sira's portrait of the scribe to be largely auto-biographical; so Di Lella, "Sirach," *NJBC,* 507 (#64). For extensive commentary on Sir 38:24–39:11, see Skehan and Di Lella, *Ben Sira,* 445–53. Schams (*Jewish Scribes,* 98–106) acknowledges that Ben Sira witnesses to a partial overlap between the positions and functions of some scribes and those of wise men, but rightly warns against deducing from this a total identification of scribes and wise men.

[197] On the difficulties involved in interpreting the relevant texts in 1 and 2 Maccabees, see Saldarini, *Pharisees, Scribes and Sadducees,* 251–54; Schams, *Jewish Scribes,* 113–24.

[198] The ideal portrait of Eleazar should not be taken as typical of all Jewish scribes, even in the narrow compass of the Maccabean literature. Other scattered references in the Maccabean literature depict scribes in such varied roles as military officials, diplomats, or census-takers.

[199] For the relevant passages of *1 Enoch* and the *Book of the Giants* (4QEnGiants), see Schams, *Jewish Scribes,* 92–97.

[200] For the importance of writing and of divinely inspired scribes as a strategy for undergirding the authority of a religious tradition or document in various streams of intertestamental Judaism, notably the *Book of Jubilees*, see Hindy Najman, "Interpretation as Primordial Writing: *Jubilees* and Its Authority Conferring Strategies," *JSJ* 30 (1999) 379–410. Faced with the fierce insistence of *Jubilees* on sacred writing as a basis of religious authority in matters of divine revelation, one is struck by the stark contrast with the style of an oral, oracular, itinerant (illiterate?) popular prophet like Jesus of Nazareth, a prime example of the charismatic religious figure who dares to claim that something is so simply because he says it is so.

[201] See Saldarini, *Pharisees, Scribes and Sadducees,* 259–66. Saldarini observes (p. 265) that the grandson of Ben Sira faithfully renders his grandfather's use of the Hebrew word *sôfēr* ("scribe") as *grammateus* in his Greek translation when the word occurs in the body of the Hebrew text referring to one learned in the Law (see, e.g., Sir 38:24). Yet, when the grandson writes on his own in his preface to his translation, he refers to people learned in the Law without using the word "scribe" (see his *Prologue,* 1–14). Schams (*Jewish Scribes,* 125–27) notes that, in all of Philo's extensive writings, he refers to scribes *(grammateis)* only twice: in one case, they are Gentile scribes of the Roman prefect of Egypt; in the other case, Philo mentions the "scribes of the [Israelite] army" when commenting on Deut 20:5–8. On pp. 129–43, Schams deals with Josephus' use of *grammateus;* she carefully distinguishes between his usage in his retelling of the biblical history (where he basically follows the usage of the biblical books, with some additional emphasis on scribes at court and in the army) and his relatively few references to scribes in the Roman period (where he basically follows common Greco-Roman usage). See also her remarks on pp. 283–86. As Schams notes, part of the confusion we feel in dealing with our varied sources may result from the overlap and yet lack of complete identity between the meanings of the Hebrew *sōfēr* and the Greek *grammateus.*

[202] As almost all critics of John's Gospel agree, the story of the woman taken in adultery (John 7:53–8:11) and therefore the mention of "the scribes and the Pharisees" in 8:3 do not belong to the original text of the Gospel. Added to the text of John's Gospel at a later date (and therefore lacking in many early manuscripts), this stray pericope appears in some Greek manuscripts of Luke's Gospel; and, indeed, both the theology and the literary style have a Lucan air about them. On all this, see Brown, *The Gospel According to John,* 2. 332–38; Metzger, *Textual Commentary* (2d ed.), 187–89; and the text and notes of *A Marginal Jew,* 1. 268–69. There are no absolutely clear examples of *grammateus* in Q. The overall pattern is that Matthew seems to insert *grammateus* into Q material where it is lacking in the Lucan parallel. A few cases are debatable. For example, Matt 23:13 || Luke 11:52 and Matt 23:29 || Luke 11:47 might be passages where *grammateus* did occur in Q since the Lucan texts or contexts contain the roughly equivalent *nomikos.* Still, granted Matthew's general redactional tendency to add *grammateus* to Q material elsewhere, that seems to be the more likely explanation here as well. Hence we are reduced in what follows to examining in turn the occurrences of the word in Mark, Matthew, and Luke. Part of the methodological problem here is that there is no sure way at

times of distinguishing redactional creations of Matthew and Luke from occurrences of *grammateus* in special M or L traditions.

[203] On this, see Schams, *Jewish Scribes,* 162.

[204] For the reasons for taking "the scribes of the Pharisees" as the original reading, see Metzger, *Textual Commentary* (2d ed.), 67. While this exact locution is found nowhere else in the NT, the meaning of the phrase is reflected in the slightly longer and clearer phrase "some of the scribes of the party of the Pharisees" in Acts 23:9.

[205] On Mark 1:22 and the larger question of teaching authority in Mark, see Richard J. Dillon, " 'As One Having Authority' (Mark 1:22): The Controversial Distinction of Jesus' Teaching," *CBQ* 57 (1995) 92–113; Scaria Kuthirakkattel, *The Beginning of Jesus' Ministry According to Mark's Gospel (1,14–3,6)* (AnBib 123; Rome: Biblical Institute, 1990) 128–32. Dillon holds that the scribes in Mark are not authorities of a lesser degree but rather teachers without authority. He also points out that, while scribes appear in both the Galilean and Jerusalem sections of the Gospel, Pharisees, with the exception of 12:13, seem restricted to Galilee (and its environs). Mark, says Dillon, sees the scribes more in relation to questions of teaching and the Pharisees more in relation to questions of practice. One may observe, though, that (1) the fact that some Marcan texts mention the Pharisees and the scribes together and (2) the general truth that Jewish teaching is often teaching about practice make the distinction less than ironclad.

[206] On this, see Saldarini (*Pharisees, Scribes and Sadducees,* 152), who may not, however, give sufficient weight to the polemical negation of scribal authority in Mark 1:22; similarly, Schams, *Jewish Scribes,* 149. That Mark is reflecting the position of Jewish scribes in Roman synagogues is possible, but the Roman inscriptions sometimes invoked to support this view date from centuries later.

[207] At the same time, one must not press this single text beyond what it says. At the end of the exchange, Jesus affirms that the scribe is "not far from the kingdom of God," not that he is in it or is a disciple of Jesus. The following two pericopes (12:35–37,38–39) cast the scribes in a negative light, and so the brief positive note is immediately tempered.

[208] Much more space could be dedicated to the details of Matthew's presentation of scribes. But since our purpose here is to understand the situation of the historical Jesus, a study of the theological and literary reworking of Mark and Q by Matthew would not serve our goal, since it would not contribute to the quest for the historical Jesus.

[209] On Matthew's lack of interest in clearly differentiating various Jewish groups, see Schams, *Jewish Scribes,* 182–84.

²¹⁰ That Luke understands the "lawyers" *(nomikoi)* to be equivalent to the scribes is suggested by his redactional conclusion (11:53) to the woes against the Pharisees and the lawyers: "As he [Jesus] was going away from there, the *scribes* and the Pharisees began to be fiercely hostile. . . ."

²¹¹ The fact that, in the Matthean Passion Narrative, the scribes have a major role, while the Pharisees appear only in 27:62 (in the special Matthean story of the setting of the guard at Jesus' tomb), suggests that Matthew himself did not totally equate the two groups.

²¹² Schams *(Jewish Scribes,* 185) thinks that no pattern can be found in Matthew's omission or inclusion of various Jewish groups in his Passion Narrative; he simply evinces a general preference for pairs.

²¹³ For the text-critical problem, see Metzger, *Textual Commentary* (2d ed.), 48–49.

²¹⁴ One reason for thinking that the scribe is presented in a negative light in Matthew is that he addresses Jesus with the vocative *didaskale* ("teacher"), a form of address that is regularly used by nonbelievers. In Matthew, those who believe in Jesus regularly use the vocative *kyrie* ("lord"). As for the original text in Q, certainty is impossible. But it seems more likely that Matthew has made the petitioner a scribe, while Luke 9:57 represents the Q tradition more faithfully by speaking vaguely of "someone" *(tis).* Schams *(Jewish Scribes,* 181) seems to be in the minority in supposing that here as elsewhere in the Q material, Matthew rather than Luke preserves the original version of the material.

²¹⁵ Only twice in Luke's Gospel do the scribes appear alone: (1) in 20:39, when some of them approve Jesus' answer to the Sadducees (hence once again they are implicitly assimilated to the Pharisees, who believe in the resurrection of the dead, as Luke makes clear in Acts); (2) in 20:46, where Jesus warns his disciples of the scribes' ostentation, hypocrisy, and exploitation of widows.

²¹⁶ As noted above, some Greek manuscripts read *nomikos* in Matt 22:35, but the text is uncertain.

²¹⁷ Schams *(Jewish Scribes,* 165–72, 177) thinks that, in his Gospel, Luke intends to identify Jewish scribes as lawyers; she sees this as a narrowing of the category of scribe in Luke, who supposedly avoids presenting scribes as teachers of the people in general and authorities with some political power. In my view, the overall vagueness of Luke's portrait of the scribes makes this latter point difficult to prove.

²¹⁸ Herein lies a serious problem, for, apart from the Synoptics and Josephus, we have very little information from 1st-century A.D. sources concerning the nature and

functions of Jewish scribes in Palestine during the time of Jesus. See Schams, *Jewish Scribes,* 275, 280.

[219] So Saldarini, *Pharisees, Scribes and Sadducees,* 274.

[220] Caution is all the more advisable since, without attestation of *grammateus* in the most likely reconstruction of Q and the original text of John, we are left with Mark as our sole main source, with additional passages that are unique to Matthew or Luke. In the case of material unique to Matthew or Luke, it is usually very difficult to decide whether we are dealing with tradition or redactional creations. This, in effect, leaves us with a single source, Mark. Granted that at least some of the Marcan instances look very much like redactional stock characters introduced at the beginnings of pericopes or in generalizing summaries (e.g., the passion predictions), the amount of material that can be considered seriously as a source for knowledge of the historical Jesus is quite small. Perhaps the story of the scribe who basically agrees with Jesus on the greatest commandments is the best candidate for historicity simply because it goes so contrary to Mark's hostile portrait of the scribes—though, strictly speaking, this gets us only to pre-Marcan tradition in the first Christian generation. This is the reason why, in my conclusions in the main text, I restrict myself to general observations.

[221] For initial orientation and further bibliography, see B. W. Bacon, "Pharisees and Herodians in Mark," *JBL* 39 (1920) 102–12; Elias J. Bikerman [*sic*], "Les Hérodiens," *RB* 47 (1938) 184–97; H. H. Rowley, "The Herodians in the Gospels," *JTS* 41 (1940) 14–27; Constantin Daniel, "Les 'Hérodiens' du Nouveau Testament sont-ils des Esséniens?" *RevQ* 6 (1967) 31–53; idem, "Les Esséniens et 'Ceux qui sont dans les maisons des rois' (*Matthieu* 11, 7–8 et *Luc* 7, 24–25)," *RevQ* 6 (1967) 261–77; idem, "Nouveaux arguments en faveur de l'identification des Hérodiens et des Esséniens," *RevQ* 7 (1970) 397–402; Abraham Schalit, *König Herodes. Der Mann und Sein Werk* (SJ 4; Berlin: de Gruyter, 1969) 479–80; Harold W. Hoehner, *Herod Antipas* (SNTSMS 17; Cambridge: Cambridge University, 1972) 331–42; W. J. Bennett, Jr., "The Herodians of Mark's Gospel," *NovT* 17 (1975) 9–14; Bruce Chilton, "Jesus *ben David*: reflections on the *Davidssohnfrage*," *JSNT* 14 (1982) 88–112, esp. 104–5; Dieter Lührmann, "Die Pharisäer und die Schriftgelehrten im Markusevangelium," *ZNW* 78 (1987) 169–85, esp. 170–71; Klaus Wengst, *Pax Romana and the Peace of Jesus Christ* (Philadelphia: Fortress, 1987) 195–96 n. 14; Freyne, *Galilee, Jesus and the Gospels,* 37–38, 92, 126, 140–41, 248; idem, "Urban-Rural Relations in First-Century Galilee: Some Suggestions from the Literary Sources," *The Galilee in Late Antiquity* (ed. Lee I. Levine; New York/Jerusalem: Jewish Theological Seminary of America, 1992) 75–91; Willi Braun, "Were the New Testament Herodians Essenes? A Critique of an Hypothesis," *RevQ* 14 (1989) 75–88; Lester L. Grabbe, *Judaism from Cyrus to Hadrian. Volume Two: The Roman Period* (Minneapolis: Fortress, 1992) 501–2; Stegemann, *The Library of Qumran,* 267–68; Richardson, *Herod,* 259–60. See also the standard commentaries on Mark, e.g., Pesch, *Markusevangelium,* 1. 187–97; Guelich, *Mark 1–8:26,* 130–41; Gundry, *Mark,* 154–55.

[222] Despite its presence in papyrus 45 (3d century), the reading "of the Herodians" at Mark 8:15 in some Greek manuscripts is almost certainly secondary; the vast majority of manuscripts, early and late, favor "of Herod." Hence the *UBSGNT* (4th edition) rightly gives "of Herod" an "A" ("certain") rating in this verse. As Metzger observes (*Textual Commentary* [2d ed.], 83), "of the Herodians" is a scribal alteration influenced by Mark 3:6 and 12:13.

[223] A classic enumeration of possible theories was offered by Rowley, "The Herodians," 14–22. Daniel then added lengthy arguments in support of identifying the Herodians as Essenes, arguments largely refuted by Braun, "Were the New Testament Herodians Essenes?" 75–88. In Stegemann's view (*The Library of Qumran*, 267), the Essenes are not only "the center of Judaism in the time of Jesus" but also both "the scribes" and "the Herodians." Chilton ("Jesus *ben David*," 104–5) has put forth the unusual explanation based on the rabbinic phrase *běnê bathyra*.

[224] See, e.g., Bacon, "Pharisees," 109–12. For arguments against this view, see Richardson, *Herod*, 260.

[225] This word is found in *J. W.* 1.16.6 §319, but nowhere else in Josephus; see Abraham Schalit, *Namenwörterbuch zu Flavius Josephus* (Leiden: Brill, 1968) 51 (col. 3).

[226] The Greek form *Kaisarianoi* is found, e.g., in the 2d century A.D. in the philosopher Epictetus, *Discourses* 1.19.19; 3.24.117 (actually written by Arrian) and in the historian Appian, *Bellum civile* 3.91 (in reference to Octavian); the meaning is "domestic servants of Caesar" or "members of Caesar's household"—though it should be remembered that at times such people might hold important positions. The Latin adjective from which the Greek form is derived, *Caesarianus,* is found already in the 1st century B.C. and functions as the equivalent of the genitive *Caesaris;* see, e.g., the biographer Cornelius Nepos (1st century B.C.), *Atticus* 7.1. For *Caesariani* in the sense of Caesar's troops, see, e.g., *Bellum alexandrinum* 59.1; *Bellum africanum* 13.1 (both works have been attributed, not without contradiction, to Aulus Hirtius); Annaeus Florus, *Epitome* 2.13.66. *Caesarianus* has the meaning of a servant or member of Caesar's household in Martial, *Epigrams* 9.79. On the *-ianoi* Greek forms, see Bikerman "Les Hérodiens," 193–96; Rowley, "The Herodians," 24–26.

[227] Again, the Latin form is found already in the 1st century B.C.; see, e.g., Julius Caesar, *Bellum civile* 3.46, and the Greek formation on the basis of the Latin form is found in the 2d century A.D. in Appian, *Bellum civile* 3.82. This example is not discussed by Bikerman.

[228] Lührmann ("Die Pharisäer," 170) emphasizes that the comparable terms in Josephus seem to refer not to an organized Herodian party but more generally to those people who sided with Herod the Great. He thinks that the same general sense holds true for Mark's "Herodians" and that therefore an equation of them with fixed parties like the Pharisees or the Sadducees is a mistake. Schalit (*König Herodes,*

479–81) suggests more specifically that the Herodians were people from various strata of society who were drawn to support Herod (the Great) because of the financial advantage involved. Schalit goes on to conjecture that, as part of their propaganda among the common people who were not well-disposed toward Herod, the Herodians tried to spread the idea that Herod was the embodiment of the Messiah. This is highly speculative.

[229] The verb "destroy" *(apollymi)* in Mark 3:6 is usually interpreted by commentators as referring to putting Jesus to death. This is in line with Mark's later use of the verb in the context of the final clash in Jerusalem. In 11:18 the chief priests and scribes seek to "destroy" Jesus, which in turn becomes their plot to "kill" him in 14:1, which in turn involves their handing him over to the political authority of Pilate in 15:1. In reference to persons, Mark always uses *apollymi* in the strong sense of to kill or to destroy life.

[230] On this point, see my treatment in *A Marginal Jew,* 2. 56–62, 171–76; cf. Lührmann, "Die Pharisäer," 171. Bennett ("The Herodians," 13–14) goes so far as to suggest that Mark has created the *Hērōdianoi* as a literary and theological means of linking the enemies of John the Baptist with the enemies of Jesus.

[231] See the treatment in *A Marginal Jew,* 2. 681–84.

[232] For a list of scholars holding to redactional creation, see Guelich, *Mark 1–8:6,* 132–33 (though Guelich himself argues against this position); cf. *A Marginal Jew,* 2. 730 n. 15. The question of Marcan versus pre-Marcan activity in collecting and editing the dispute stories has been touched upon a number of times in *A Marginal Jew;* see, e.g., 2. 494 n. 183; 2. 728 n. 6.

[233] On the whole question of Mark's redaction, see Braun, "Were the New Testament Herodians Essenes?" 83–84.

[234] We should note, though, that Josephus also uses phrases like "some of Herod's picked men" *(tōn Hērōdou tines epilektōn)* in *J.W.* 1.18.2 §351 and "those who favored the side [or party] of Herod" *(tous ta Hērōdou phronountas)* in *Ant.* 14.15.10 §450. Hence whether *Hērōdeioi,* which occurs only once in Josephus, can be considered a fixed term for Herod's "party" is unclear. A fortiori, the striking absence of *Hērōdianoi* in 1st-century literature apart from the two passages in Mark and the single passage of Matthew dependent on Mark could argue for Mark's invention of this precise label—though not, I think, of the group of Herodian supporters or servants designated by the label. That Mark, with his penchant for Latinisms, may actually have invented the Greek term *Hērōdianoi* is not as strange a claim as may first appear. Greek proper nouns based on a person's name and ending in *-ianoi* are rare in the 1st century A.D.; indeed, *Hērōdianoi* may be among the very earliest literary examples of the form. The clearest parallel in 1st-century Greek literature is *Christianoi,* which, from the viewpoint of literary attestation (only Acts and 1 Peter), is later than Mark's

Hērōdianoi. The construction of similar nouns ending in *-ianoi* multiplies in later Greek.

[235] See Chapter 27, section II., "Surveying the Individual Members of the Twelve," under point 8, Simon the Cananean, along with the bibliographical references in the notes.

INTEGRATING JESUS' JEWISH RELATIONSHIPS INTO THE WIDER PICTURE

After all we have seen in Volume Three about Jesus the Jew and his relationships to other Jews in Palestine, we naturally ask the question: how does this fit—or does it fit—into what we learned about the historical Jesus in Volumes One and Two of *A Marginal Jew?* The problem with using a methodical, step-by-step process in our quest for Jesus is that we can lose a sense of the whole—if, indeed, there is a whole to sense. Hence, at the end of Volume Three, it is time to step back, take a deep breath, and try to understand how the insights gained in this volume cohere with those of the first two volumes.[1] Do all these varied conclusions converge to create an intelligible sketch of Jesus, stretching from his origins through the beginning of his ministry up to the full range of his interaction with his fellow Palestinian Jews during that ministry? Answering this question will in turn open the way to grappling with the remaining enigmas surrounding this enigmatic Jew, enigmas that will be the topic of our fourth and final volume.

I. THE ROOTS OF JESUS THE JEW IN THE JUDAISM AND THE GALILEE OF THE FIRST CENTURY

1. Birth and Family

Somewhere around 7–6 B.C., a Jew named *Yēshûaʿ*, a shortened form of the Hebrew *Yĕhôshûaʿ* (Joshua) was born in the hillside town of Nazareth in

lower Galilee. The Infancy Narrative traditions that locate his birth in Bethle-
hem of Judea (traditions isolated in chap. 2 of Matthew and Luke respec-
tively) are probably later Christian theological dramatizations of the belief
that Jesus was the royal Davidic Messiah. The name of Jesus' mother was
Miryam or Miriam (= Mary); his putative father's name was *Yôsēf* (= Joseph).
All four Gospels, the Acts of the Apostles, Paul, Josephus, and some early
Church Fathers speak of brothers. Mark, followed by Matthew, names four:
Jacob (= James, a leader later on in the Jerusalem church), Joseph, Judah
(= Jude or Judas), and Simon (= Simeon). Reflecting the patriarchal culture of
the day, Mark and Matthew mention sisters, but do not enumerate or name
them. At the very least, then, there were seven children in the family who survived to adulthood. Mary likewise survived to see the public ministry of her
son. In notable contrast to other family members, Joseph, the father of the
family, does not appear on the stage of the Gospel narratives during the public ministry. This is usually interpreted to mean that he had died before Jesus
emerged into public view.

While this information about Jesus' family is quite meager, it may have one
intriguing link with Jesus' public ministry. One cannot help but notice how
every name in Jesus' family harks back to the beginnings of Israel's history:
the patriarch Jacob (= James), who received the name Israel; the twelve sons
(and tribes) of Israel (including Judah, Joseph, and Simeon); Miriam, the sister of Moses; and finally Joshua/Jesus, the successor of Moses and leader of
Israel into the promised land. It may not be totally by accident that the adult
Jesus saw himself called, as the Elijah-like prophet, to begin the regathering
and renewal of the twelve tribes of Israel in the end time. As one of his symbolic-prophetic acts, he gathered around himself an inner circle of twelve
disciples, whom he in turn sent out on a limited, symbolic mission to Israel.

One is tempted to speculate—and it can be nothing more than speculation—that Jesus' intensely Jewish way of conceiving of his religious mission
may reflect his rearing in a pious northern-Israel family, a family that shared
the reawakening of Jewish national and religious identity in Galilee in the
wake of the Hasmonean conquest of the north in the late 2d and early 1st
centuries B.C. For the first time since the reign of King Solomon in the 10th
century B.C., the northern regions of Israel had been reintegrated with the
rump state in the south (Judea in the narrow sense) into one Israel, one kingdom of the Jews (Judea in the wider sense), with its capital in the temple-city
of Jerusalem. This almost mythical "return to the beginnings" in Israel's political and religious life may have had its impact on devout Jews of the
Galilean countryside who had struggled to retain, regain, or redefine their
Jewish identity over against the encroachments of urban Hellenistic culture

in surrounding areas. This would be all the more true in a family like Joseph's if—as I think is the case—it claimed to be of Davidic descent.

2. Judaism in Galilee

The Jewish faith that was shared by pious Galileans in the countryside would have been, for all its fervor, fairly simple and straightforward. Like most traditional religion handed down by largely uneducated groups in rural areas, it would have focused on basic practices rather than on theoretical details debated by the religious elite. In the case of Judaism, the basic practices included circumcision of infant males, kosher food laws, the main purity rules, sabbath rest, and, when possible, pilgrimage to the Jerusalem temple on the great feasts to take part in its sacrifices. These were the actions that marked and sanctified the regular cycle of birth and death, of daily life and harvest seasons. While not defined by detailed creeds, this popular, mainstream Judaism held to certain key beliefs. As is often the case in popular religion, these beliefs were articulated in a dramatic story of origins. For Jews, the story was the national myth of God and Israel: the one true God (whose sacred name, Yahweh, was not to be pronounced) had chosen Israel as his special people, freed it from slavery by the exodus from Egypt, given it the covenant and the Torah at Mt. Sinai, and led it into the promised land of Palestine as its perpetual inheritance. Yet Israel had often proven unfaithful to the covenant and disobedient to God's prophets. Though God had justly punished his people with exile, he had mercifully brought them back to their land and given them the hope of a full, glorious renewal at some future date, with the twelve tribes restored to their land. This story of Israel, this salvation history that undergirded Jewish faith, would have been repeated regularly in the study and teaching of the Scriptures conducted on the sabbath in local religious meetings called "synagogues." Actually, we are poorly informed about the institution of the synagogue in pre-70 Galilee. At the very least, we should not think of Galilean synagogues in terms of grand buildings dedicated to public worship with set liturgies, which is what the Jerusalem temple supplied.

The oft-repeated assertion that Galilean Jews were lax in their practice, alienated from the Jerusalem temple, and constantly rebellious does not seem to have held—if it ever held—during the adult life of Jesus. To be sure, there would have been differences and even tensions between the Judaism of rural Galileans and the urban, in some ways more Hellenized Judaism of Jerusalem, especially when it came to the city's aristocracy. Yet which form of Judaism had proven more fractious and prone to causing civil war? After all, it was Jerusalem and Judea, not rural Galilee, that had spawned in the 2d century B.C. the contending parties of Sadducees, Pharisees, and Essenes. And Jerusalem and Judea continued to be the center of these movements in Jesus' day. It is unlikely that Galilean Jews of the countryside had the learning or the leisure necessary to study, debate, and practice the niceties of observance developed in the *hălākâ* of the three rival groups centered in the south. That the adult Galilean Jew named Jesus should wind up opposing various views of the Pharisees and the Sadducees (and perhaps in passing of the Essenes)— all products, in a sense, of Jerusalem scholasticism and politics—and that he should have shown less than punctilious concern about detailed rules of purity and sabbath observance are hardly surprising. The Nazareth apple had not fallen far from the Galilean tree. A Jew from the Galilean countryside who presented himself in Jerusalem during the great feasts as a prophet possessing charismatic authority over Law and temple could be assured of stiff opposition from both the authorities controlling the temple and the learned experts in the Law, whatever their particular stripe. In this sense, Jesus, from the beginning, was marginal vis-à-vis the Jerusalem establishment. In due time, the temple authorities would work hand in hand with the Roman prefect to make that marginalization permanent. Galilean Jews were fine for purposes of tithing and pilgrimage, but they had to be kept in their place.

From A.D. 6 onwards, Galileans coming to Jerusalem on pilgrimage would have been faced with a new, unpleasant reality: Judea (understood in the narrow sense as distinct from Galilee) had become, along with Samaria and Idumea, an imperial province of the Roman empire, governed by a Roman prefect resident at Caesarea Maritima. While in fact the high priest and the aristocracy around him ran a good deal of daily Jewish life in Jerusalem and Judea, direct Roman rule would naturally tend to increase tensions among the volatile crowds at the pilgrim feasts, precisely the time when the prefect and his troops would be present in Jerusalem for crowd control.

3. Growing up Jewish in Galilee

In comparison to Judea, Galilee during the adult life of Jesus was on the whole peaceful. Up until 4 B.C., Galilee had been part of the relatively autonomous kingdom of Herod the Great, a client king dependent on Rome yet enjoying a great deal of independence in internal matters. Upon Herod the Great's death in 4 B.C., Galilee became part of the tetrarchy of Herod's son, Antipas. As a mere tetrarch or minor prince, Antipas was in a more delicate and vulnerable position than his father. Yet, like his father, he retained basic autonomy in internal affairs. Most important, he maintained his own army. Contrary to the absurdities of TV movies, there were no Roman armies stationed in Galilee during Jesus' lifetime. Moreover, Antipas minted his own

money, and he carefully avoided printing on his coins human or animal figures offensive to Jewish sensibilities. Antipas himself collected taxes from his
subjects and turned around to pay tribute to Rome. He thus acted as something of a soothing buffer; his individual Jewish subjects, unlike their coreligionists in the imperial province of Judea to the south, did not have to pay
direct tribute to Rome. In externals, Antipas played the observant Jew, going
up to Jerusalem for the great feasts. Granted, his divorce from his Nabatean
wife and his scandalous marriage to his niece Herodias, the wife of his half-
brother, would have qualified as incest in the eyes of observant Jews.[2] But the
marital relations of both Hasmonean and Herodian monarchs were often
less than ideal. At least Antipas' new marital situation kept him in the legal
sense monogamous—something that was not obligatory for Jews of the time
and something that had certainly not been true of his father, who had had ten
wives.

All in all, then, Jesus grew up in a Jewish Galilee ruled by an ostensibly observant Jewish monarch. The tensions created by direct Roman rule did not
exist. It may not be entirely by accident that, despite apparent antipathy between Jesus and Antipas (see, e.g., Matt 11:7–9 par.; Mark 8:15; Luke
13:31–33; 23:6–12),[3] Jesus the Galilean prophet perished in Roman Judea
and not Antipas' Galilee. To be sure, we moderns, accustomed to democracy,
due process, and standards of social justice would have found Antipas' rule
intolerable. But there is no hard proof that Antipas' rule was any more politically unjust, socially exploitative, or economically burdensome than most of
the other regimes in the ancient Near East before or after him. The ancient
Near East was always a very rough neighborhood. That Antipas was the
second-longest reigning Herodian monarch in ancient history and that his
reign came to an abrupt end not because of internal rebellion but because of
his ill-advised request that the Emperor Caligula make him a king witnesses
to the relatively stable and peaceful nature of his reign. To state that this
peace and stability were the result of an iron fist, as the death of the Baptist
shows, and not of concern for human rights and democracy, is simply to state
the obvious: Antipas ruled in the ancient Near East, where stability and
peace were achieved in only one way.

I emphasize this point of relative peace and stability in Galilee because all
too often Jesus is portrayed as an angry social rebel emerging from a seething
cauldron of intolerable social and economic injustice. Such a portrait, however attractive to modern academics, gives the historical Jesus a type of social
conscience and political concern for which there is precious little proof in the
Gospels. It also paints a dubious picture of the conditions in Galilee and the
sensibilities of the Galileans during the public ministry. Significantly, around

the turn of the era, Jews revolted a number of times against the powerful Syrian and Roman empires, despite the fact that revolt sometimes seemed madness. In contrast, the Jews of Galilee never attempted an insurrection against the much less powerful Antipas.

4. Jesus' Socioeconomic Status

This, then, was the relatively stable setting in which Jesus grew up. Probably as an apprentice to Joseph, he learned the trade of woodworker (*tektōn*, actually a worker and builder in any hard material). Since he was a craftsman plying his trade in Nazareth and perhaps other towns in lower Galilee, he was not, strictly speaking, a "peasant" (i.e., a person who earns his or her living through tilling the soil and raising livestock), despite the number of book titles and sociological surveys that continue to propagate this label. While, in our eyes, Jesus would have ranked among the poor, we have to realize that up to ninety or so percent of his fellow Galileans belonged to that same huge and vague category, so the designation tells us very little. Since he was able to support himself—and perhaps for a time his family (mother, brothers, and sisters)—by his craft, he was not among "the poorest of the poor," a category that would have included day laborers, tenant farmers, beggars, and slaves at the low end of the social pecking order.

If we ask either how Jesus saw himself or how his early followers saw him, it is striking that neither Jesus in the sayings material of the Gospels nor the evangelists in their narrative ever designate Jesus directly as poor. Instead, the poor constitute a group that Jesus addresses and from which he distinguishes himself: "Happy are *you poor*. . . . The poor you have always with you, me you do not always have." While obviously poor by the standards of modern American affluence (though what of modern standards in Haiti or Bangladesh?), Jesus would not have appeared remarkably or extremely poor to the vast majority of his fellow Galilean Jews. His self-support as a craftsman and his pious Jewish family background would have assured him a reasonable degree of honor in the honor/shame society of rural Galilee. At a certain point, Jesus threw over his traditional position of honor, abandoning his occupation, his town, his (probably widowed) mother, and his family to embark on the career of an itinerant charismatic prophet. This radical shift in his existence was guaranteed to win him shame in the eyes of those who rejected his prophetic claims, and high honor in the eyes of those who accepted them.

5. The Sheer Oddness of Jesus

As Jesus embraced his new career as the Elijah-like prophet of the end time, several things would have made him appear unusual or strange to most of his fellow Jews.

(i) At a time when a good deal of the spiritual leadership in Palestinian Judaism, apart from the Jerusalem priesthood,[4] was passing into the hands of learned Jews like the educated leaders of the Pharisaic movement, the writers of apocalypses, or (for a small segment of the population) the Essenes, Jesus had no particular credentials as a highly educated Jew. Although he was to put himself forward as a religious leader who could give his fellow Jews the correct interpretation of the Scriptures, he had never formally studied Torah under some esteemed teacher in Jerusalem, as apparently Saul/Paul had done. Whatever knowledge Jesus had gained of Jewish Scriptures and traditions at Nazareth would have paled before the brilliance of legal experts in Jerusalem. Indeed, we cannot be sure that Jesus was literate, though I think it more likely that he was. We must leave open, however, the possibility that this religious leader had absorbed the Jewish Scriptures simply by hearing them constantly repeated in oral recitation and commented on in homilies.

Jesus' limited education was reflected in his limited knowledge of languages. He regularly spoke Aramaic, the common language of the common Jewish people of Palestine. Indeed, he may have spoken it with a Galilean accent or in a Galilean dialect that the educated people of Jerusalem found off-putting or laughable. From public reading and oral recitation in the synagogues, if not from his own ability to read the scrolls, he would have been able to cite passages of the Jewish Scriptures in Hebrew. As for Greek, the popular idea of Jesus frequenting the Greek theater in the Galilean capital of Sepphoris is highly dubious for a number of reasons, ranging from Jesus' limited economic circumstances and the total silence of our sources on his supposed visits to the large cities of Galilee (Sepphoris, Tiberias) to the fact that many archaeologists date the theater excavated at Sepphoris to a time later than Jesus' day.[5] Jesus may have learned a smattering of Greek for commercial or social purposes, but there is no reason to think that he publicly taught in Greek during his ministry.

(ii) A second aspect that would have made Jesus stand out as unusual was his status as a male celibate. Celibacy was not totally unknown in Palestinian Judaism of the time; certain Essenes, especially at Qumran, as well as some ascetics along the Jordan River like John the Baptist and Josephus' guru Bannus, seem to have been celibate. Why Jesus, who probably did not come under the influence of the Baptist until the woodworker from Nazareth was in his thirties, remained celibate is unknown and unknowable. The one saying that may bear on the issue (the shocking eunuch-saying in Matt 19:12) suggests that Jesus saw celibacy as part of his total dedication to the cause of God's kingdom, whose coming and presence created a crisis in Israel's history, the end of business as usual and life as usual. There may also be an echo here of the celibate prophet, Jeremiah. In any event, the phenomenon of a celibate itinerant prophet who called other men to leave their families to follow him, and who allowed unchaperoned women to join his traveling entourage, would have raised more than a few pious eyebrows—all the more so since Jesus came not as a severe doomsday prophet of the Jeremiah or Baptist type but rather as a "glutton and wine-drinker, a friend of toll collectors and sinners" (Matt 11:19 par.). While harking back in many ways to the model of Elijah (and at times Elisha) in particular and to the oral prophets of Israel in general, the celibate yet convivial Jesus, accompanied by his female adherents as well as by men who had left their families, inevitably struck observant Jews as either strange or scandalous. For all his traditional prophetic coloring, in this at least he was without any clear precedent in Israel's sacred history.

(iii) An uneducated celibate from a hillside town in lower Galilee, Jesus was also unusual amid the common run of Palestinian Jews in a third way. As a prelude to his joyful, upbeat ministry, he paradoxically gave his adherence to—and perhaps for a while became a disciple of—another odd Jewish prophet, the ascetic John the Baptist, who roamed the lower Jordan valley. By accepting John's baptism—unusual in itself in that one Jew plunged another Jew into the water instead of a Jew administering the cleansing ritual to himself—Jesus proclaimed his acceptance of an eschatological message calling all Israel to repentance in the light of God's imminent judgment. For all the changes visible later on in Jesus' more joyous ministry, there is no indication—present-day American embarrassment not withstanding—that Jesus ever abandoned the basic eschatological message that he embraced on Jordan's banks.

II. THE MINISTRY OF JESUS THE ELIJAH-LIKE PROPHET

Around the year A.D. 28, after his baptism, Jesus emerged from the circle of the prophet John and began his own prophetic ministry. Despite the blood-curdling scenes of chaos in Palestine that are customarily served up by TV miniseries, the time of Jesus' ministry was relatively tranquil. All the major political figures were firmly in place, and there was no transition in high office during Jesus' public activity. Tiberius had been emperor since A.D. 14 and would remain so until A.D. 37. He did not like frequent changes, let alone disruptions, in the rule of the imperial provinces. As Tacitus tells us, the empire was basically quiet under Tiberius, and that included Palestine. Herod Antipas had been tetrarch in Galilee from 4 B.C. onwards and would continue in office until deposed by Caligula in A.D. 39. Joseph Caiaphas assumed the high priesthood in A.D. 18 and would hold on to that office, often controlled by the family of his father-in-law Annas, until A.D. 36. Pontius Pilate was the Johnny-come-lately, the new kid on the block, having become prefect of the imperial province of Judea in A.D. 26 and remaining in office (as either the longest or second-longest reigning Roman governor of pre-70 Judea) until A.D. 36. It was probably not by accident that the deposition of Pilate, caused by the complaints of the Samaritans, not the Judeans, brought in its wake the deposition of Caiaphas. The two leaders, civil and religious, survived for so long in what were often revolving-door appointments apparently because they worked well together, despite some contretemps caused by Pilate's insensitivity to Jewish beliefs and practices. Of the two leaders, Caiaphas had the more difficult task; he had to pull off the tricky balancing act of being the representative and buffer of the prefect to the Judean populace and vice versa.

It was within the context of this relatively well-oiled if not wildly popular Palestinian political machine that Jesus suddenly appeared, proclaiming a prophetic message that could hardly be comforting to the politicians in charge: the present order of things was swiftly coming to an end. The one true God would assert his definitive rule over Israel as he regathered the scattered twelve tribes and so restored his chosen people to their original wholeness. It was to prophesy this coming "kingdom" (= rule and reign) of God" and to began its actualization in symbolic signs and healings that Jesus began touring Galilee and Judea. He consciously took upon himself the role of the prophet Elijah, who was expected to return to restore Israel and prepare it for the coming of its God. In imitation of Elijah, Jesus undertook an itinerant ministry, largely (but not entirely) in northern Israel. Echoing a famous incident in the ministry of Elijah (1 Kgs 19:19–21), he peremptorily called disciples to follow him on his itinerant ministry, sometimes at great cost. Reflecting Elijah's supposed mission of regathering the twelve tribes of Israel, Jesus created an inner circle of twelve disciples and sent them out on mission to Israel. Like Elijah (as well as Elisha), Jesus was thought—even in his own lifetime—to have performed a whole series of miracles, including raising the dead.

If the historical record had contained only one of these elements, one might question Jesus' intention of evoking the image of Elijah. But the convergence of so many different carefully chosen, programmatic actions inevitably creates a *Gestalt,* a complex configuration of interrelated elements that clearly bespeaks the intention of Jesus to present himself to his fellow Jews as the Elijah-like prophet of the end time. By "end time" or "eschatology" one should not understand some phantasmagoric destruction of heaven and earth or the complete end of human history in the manner of Jewish apocalypses like 4 Ezra. Rather, Jesus was announcing the end of the present state of things, the end of sacred history as Israel had known it up until now, and the definitive beginning of a new, permanent state of affairs. God would soon rule Israel directly as its king, and his holy will would be done by his repentant and forgiven people, who would experience the full peace and joy that God had intended for them from the beginning.

What this would mean in detail Jesus did not say. He was not a political leader in the sense of someone enunciating a detailed political and social program that was to be implemented by particular practical measures. Rather, the transformation of Israel in the end time was to be the work of God coming as king. As the prophet of this kingdom, it was Jesus' task to prophesy this world-changing advent of God and to begin the preparation of Israel by calling it to repentance, baptism, and a renewed moral life within a loving, compassionate society. By such attention-grabbing public actions as his miracles, his table fellowship with religiously or socially disreputable Jews, and his sending out of the twelve disciples to their fellow Israelites, Jesus intended both to anticipate and to set in motion what God alone would fully accomplish at his coming. All these symbolic-prophetic acts of Jesus were understood by him to unleash the powers of the kingdom that they foreshadowed.

At the same time, though, these acts were *only* symbolic and prophetic. They were not pragmatic programs intended to set up a new political regime in Palestine. Jesus spoke not in terms of practical agendas to be carried out by bureaucratic committees or rebellious troops. He spoke in parables, in allusive, riddle-like speech that meant to evoke, challenge, and change people's perceptions of themselves, their neighbors, and their God, not to describe the way they were to restructure the system of tax collection or reapportion plots of land. To be sure, Jesus spoke in bold and even hyperbolic fashion of greathearted forgiveness (including the remission of debts), selfless almsgiving, and generosity in assisting others in need. None of this—nor all of it together—added up to a clear and detailed political or economic program.

Yet one can see how tension and confrontation would inevitably arise from Jesus' words and actions. On the one hand, what Jesus said and did had ramifications for the present order of things political, social, and economic.

On the other hand, Jesus himself had no detailed plan for setting up some new rival political or economic order. Jesus was not laying out some practical strategy for restoring autonomy to the kingdom of Israel as it had previously existed in its Davidic, Hasmonean, or Herodian form. As the eschatological prophet, Jesus announced and symbolized a totally different order of things, one created by God alone. That Caiaphas or Pilate, immersed in the task of running Judea day to day, did not appreciate the fine eschatological nuances of Jesus' particular understanding of the kingdom of God is hardly surprising. What they saw out of the windows of their Jerusalem palaces was a popular Jewish prophet stirring up an enthusiastic Jewish populace during the great pilgrim feasts. Not only did he harangue the crowds surging around the temple complex with visions of an imminent new kingdom, he backed up his heady message with supposed miracles that anticipated the coming transformation. Rumors that some of Jesus' followers or family members claimed that he was a descendant of King David would only have made things worse.

After all, John the Baptist had made no overt political claims or moves, but Antipas had decided anyway that an ounce of prevention by way of execution was worth a pound of cure by way of military action. A single execution—we hear nothing of subsequent persecution, let alone execution, of John's disciples—forestalled a possible uprising at a later date. At a certain point, after increasing tensions each time Jesus visited Jerusalem during the feasts, and especially after Jesus staged provocative, prophetic acts by his entry into Jerusalem and by his "cleansing" of the temple just before the Passover of A.D. 30, Caiaphas and Pilate adopted the "Antipas solution": cut off the head of the movement with one swift, preemptive blow. The headless movement, so completely centered and dependent on one charismatic prophet who wielded all authority within the group, would quickly dissolve. In the famous last words of many a politician: it seemed like a good idea at the time.

Christian believers, needless to say, hold that Pilate's exercise in Realpolitik failed to disperse the Jesus movement because the crucified Jesus rose from the dead and commissioned his disciples to spread the gospel throughout the world. As has been emphasized repeatedly in *A Marginal Jew,* a historian in his or her capacity as a historian cannot appeal to such theological explanations because they lie outside the framework of what is in theory empirically verifiable by any and every fair-minded observer, believer and nonbeliever alike. Are there instead any historical reasons discernible in Jesus' public ministry that help explain why Pilate's preemptive strike did not have the same destructive impact on Jesus' movement that Antipas' blow had on the Baptist's movement?[6] One possible answer, which has slowly emerged from these three volumes of *A Marginal Jew,* is that Jesus, even more than John, was not so charismatic that he totally neglected the question of how to structure his movement and give it a distinct identity within Palestinian Judaism.

III. EMBRYONIC STRUCTURES AMONG THE JEWISH FOLLOWERS OF JESUS

To some NT critics, the very idea that Jesus the eschatological prophet, consumed as he was by hopes of the imminent coming of God's final kingdom, should have bothered to provide any structure to his motley group of followers is self-contradictory. Still, as we have seen in chapter 30, no Jewish group was more molded by fervent eschatological expectations than the Qumranites. Yet the Qumranites evinced a veritable mania for structure in the present time of their monastic existence, during the future eschatological battle between the sons of light and the sons of darkness, and in the definitive blessed state of the community of the new covenant beyond their final victory. As a matter of fact, throughout the whole of its history as recorded in the Scriptures, Israel, the people of God, had never existed without some structures. There was no reason for Israelites who awaited the final renewal of God's people to expect that all structures would disappear in the end time. Change of structures, yes; total disappearance, no.

1. Identity Badges

We need not be surprised, then, that Jesus the eschatological prophet supplied his movement with a few basic identity badges and structural elements. Some identity badges were taken over, with modification, from Jesus' mentor, the Baptist. Like the Baptist, Jesus continued to practice baptism, which served as an initiation rite into the company of Jews who accepted Jesus' eschatological message and pledged repentance. Like the Baptist, Jesus had some of his followers remain with him as a relatively stable circle of disciples. To these disciples, Jesus, like John, taught specific religious practices, including the proper way to pray and rules about fasting. Here, though, Jesus began to part company with John. Perhaps to mark off his disciples from those of John as well as from other Jewish movements of renewal, Jesus adopted a number of practices quite different from those of John and most other pious Jews. Most striking among these differences was Jesus' prohibition of all voluntary fasting, a prohibition that lay at the antipodes from the

Baptist's ascetic ways—and, indeed, from the practice of devout Jews in general. Connected with this prohibition of fasting was Jesus' well-known—and, to some, notorious—practice of regularly engaging in feasting and wine-drinking, especially with the social and religious lowlife of the day, "the toll collectors and sinners." For Jesus, this feasting instead of fasting prophesied and began to realize the gathering of all Israel—even the lost sheep—into the joyful banquet of the end time. Jesus the bon vivant thus gave his movement a very different stamp than the ascetic Baptist had given his. Another identity badge, antithetical to the practice of lengthy prayers and hymns found, for instance, at Qumran, was Jesus' terse prayer for the coming of the kingdom, known to Christians as the Lord's Prayer or the Our Father. Unlike the total prohibition of fasting, this was one identity badge that definitely stuck.

2. The Three Concentric Circles of Followers

Beyond individual identity badges, Jesus gave specific contours to his movement by effectively creating three concentric circles of followers. To be sure, as I have stressed repeatedly in this volume, to portray all of Jesus' followers as neatly grouped into three concentric circles is to simplify what was no doubt a much more complex and fluid reality. Yet the three-part model I have laid out does capture something important and distinctive about the Jesus movement during the public ministry. Simply as a matter of fact, there were three distinguishable groups of what could be called "followers" in the literal sense of that word.

(i) The outer circle of followers was made up of the *crowds* that, for at least a while, physically followed the itinerant Jesus on his preaching tours in a desire to hear his message and/or receive a cure. This outer circle of the crowds was by its nature the most fluid and transitory of the groups following Jesus. Nameless and usually numberless in our sources, the crowds came and went, perhaps swelling when Jesus would begin one of his pilgrimages up to Jerusalem for the great feasts. Though unstable and perhaps at times fickle, they were nevertheless pivotal to the outcome of the story we are tracing. Without them and their unpredictable volatility in Jerusalem during the feasts, it is doubtful whether Caiaphas or Pilate would have felt that Jesus had become too dangerous to be allowed to continue his ministry. A prophet without followers and a teacher without disciples would hardly have seemed so menacing.[7]

(ii) From these ever-shifting crowds Jesus probably drew at least some of the members of a more stable group: the middle circle of long-term followers and pupils who would absorb his message and praxis. This middle circle of *disciples* stood out as a separate group not by their design but by Jesus' decision. He seized the initiative in calling whomever he wished to discipleship. Unlike later rabbinical students, who usually sought out particular teachers with whom they wished to study Torah, the disciples of Jesus were chosen by him, not vice versa. Moreover, since, as Jesus understood it, discipleship involved not some general adherence to or study of his message but rather an actual, physical following of the master around Galilee, his peremptory call demanded that disciples leave their families, homes, property, and occupations for an indefinite period. This open-ended following of Jesus exposed the disciples to possible danger and hostility, at times from the very families they had suddenly left behind and perhaps in the lurch.

As with the crowds, so with the disciples, we lack precise numbers. No doubt the circle of disciples remained fluid, though less so than that of the crowds. As for names, besides the names of the Twelve (who counted as disciples), we have only a few: e.g., Levi from the Marcan tradition and Nathanael from the Johannine. These individuals serve as useful reminders that not all disciples belonged to the inner circle of the Twelve, though all of the Twelve were also and first of all disciples. One significant aspect of the circle of disciples is that Jesus apparently wished it to reflect his outreach to *all* Israel, not just to the zealous and pious on the one hand and not just to the marginalized and the outcasts on the other. Rubbing elbows in the circle of disciples were such odd couples as Simon the Zealot and Levi the toll collector. They served as living testimonies to the commitment of this strange inclusive prophet to address not just an ascetic or puritanical elite—and not just religious outcasts—but the whole people of God.

(iii) If the ragtag middle circle of disciples reflected Jesus' desire to reach out to all Israel, the symbolism of a restored Israel was even stronger when it came to the inner circle of *the Twelve*. By its very nature as a living numerical prophecy, the Twelve were the most stable group of followers around Jesus. Over the more than two years of the public ministry, only one variation in membership appears: Luke's "Jude of James" versus Mark's "Thaddeus." Considering the vicissitudes and demands of a two-year trek around Galilee and up to Jerusalem, what is remarkable is that there should have been only one replacement in the ranks of the Twelve. Moreover, despite the shattering events surrounding the death of Jesus, the Twelve soon regathered in Jerusalem and functioned as an important leadership group in the early days of the church. This cohesiveness of the Twelve *precisely as the Twelve* amid so many pressures and despite a few individual changes argues that Jesus had expended no little effort to mold them into a stable group. Intent as he was on the regathering of all Israel in preparation for the coming of God as king,

Jesus saw the Twelve as the prophetic sign and nucleus of the twelve tribes of old. That Jesus sent the Twelve out on a brief mission to Israel during his own ministry betokens not so much Jesus' practical missionary strategy as a further symbolic-prophetic act, unleashing the prophetic power contained in the sign of the Twelve. Their short-term mission to Israel not only symbolized but, in Jesus' mind, actually set in motion the drama that would reach conclusion in God's eschatological act of reconstituting the twelve tribes.

The basic cohesion of the Twelve amid so many changes may have also been aided by certain key figures within the circle. Simon Peter seems to have been the leader and/or spokesman of the circle both during the public ministry of Jesus and in the early days of the Jerusalem church. Apart from Jesus himself, Peter was probably the most important personal link between the "Jews for Jesus" of the public ministry and the "Jews for the risen Lord Jesus" in the embryonic church. A fisherman with roots in the towns of Bethsaida and Capernaum at the north end of the Sea of Galilee, Peter was among the first disciples called by Jesus. We have multiple attestation (Matthew and John, in different streams of traditions and in different stories) that Jesus himself gave Simon the second name, nickname, or title *Kēpāʾ* (Aramaic for "rock" or "stone," *Petros* in Greek). Whatever Jesus' precise intention in giving Simon this name, it should probably be interpreted in the light of Jesus' creation of the Twelve and Peter's place as leader of the Twelve. The famous "You are Peter" text of Matt 16:18–19 would be helpful here if it went back to the historical Jesus, but it is more likely a post–Easter saying.

All four Gospels as well as some of Paul's epistles contribute to the overall impression that Peter was a complicated person. On the one hand, he was energetic and fervent in his commitment to Jesus and his cause. Both the Marcan and the Johannine traditions, in very different ways, affirm that it was Peter who made a profession of faith in Jesus at a critical juncture in the public ministry. On the other hand, Peter was quite capable of insubordination, doubt, and panic. In the end, challenged by servants of the high priest afer Jesus' arrest, he denied that he had ever known Jesus. Peter's career in the early church supplies a similar portrait, with light and dark juxtaposed: a zealous and bold leader of the Jerusalem church, suffering persecution and imprisonment, who was nevertheless capable of sudden reversals in church policy that seemed—at least in the eyes of Paul—to be dishonest and hypocritical. Perhaps the very juxtaposition of these strengths and weaknesses— Peter as chiaroscuro figure in a baroque painting—gave him a special appeal to the early Christians he led as well as to later Christian theology and homiletics. If Simon Peter is the member of the Twelve about whom we know the most, the reason is simply that he was the most prominent and influential member of the Twelve both during the public ministry and in the earliest days of the church.

Very little, if anything, can be said about the rest of the Twelve. The sons of Zebedee, James and John, were likewise fishermen from the northern shores of the Sea of Galilee. The one memorable incident involving them during the public ministry is not a flattering one. The two brothers sought the most prominent places beside Jesus when the kingdom arrived in its fullness. Jesus rebuffed them by promising them only a share in his sufferings; the rest was in the hands of his Father. Jesus' prophecy was fulfilled in the case of James, the first of the Twelve to be martyred. We have no reliable information as to whether it was ever fulfilled in the case of John.

The only other member of the Twelve about whom anything significant is known is Judas Iscariot (or, in John's Gospel, Judas the son of Simon Iscariot). For whatever reasons—and his real motives are forever lost to us— Judas cooperated with the Jerusalem authorities in having Jesus arrested on the night of his final meal with his disciples just before Passover. Despite endless theological speculation about Judas and boundless elaboration of his story in Christian imagination, we know nothing further about him. Like a bird flying through the night, he darts for a moment into the lighted hall of Jesus' ministry, only to plunge again into the dark. In sum, then: the circle of the Twelve was memorable not because of great feats performed by its individual members but because of the meaning the circle had precisely as a group of twelve persons. It was the prophetic symbol and nucleus of the restored Israel that Jesus made a main goal of his mission.

3. Groups of Adherents outside the Three Circles

Even as we complete this rapid survey of these three concentric circles of followers, we must bear in mind that not every Jew who believed Jesus' message or supported his movement fell neatly into one of the three circles. Two important groups did not.

(i) Various Jewish *women* who had come to believe in Jesus' mission had— perhaps gradually over the course of time—attached themselves to Jesus' itinerant band of disciples and *followed him* on his preaching tours of Galilee and up to Jerusalem for his final Passover. Prominent in this group was a Mary from the town of Magdala in Galilee. If Luke is to be believed, she and other women of substance, some with connections with the court of Herod Antipas, helped support Jesus' traveling band with their money as well as with their personal service. According to the independent reports of Mark's and John's Passion Narratives, some of these women viewed the crucifixion and death of Jesus and attended his burial. The narratives of both Mark and

John also connect Mary of Magdala with the finding of the empty tomb on Sunday morning.

One curious aspect of the Gospel reports about these dedicated women is that they, unlike the close-but-hardly-faithful male followers, are never explicitly called disciples. Apart from the possible male bias of the evangelists, the reason for this strange omission may be the simple philological fact that neither ancient Hebrew nor ancient Aramaic had a feminine form for the word "disciple." Then, too, because of either the bias or sheer vagaries of the oral tradition, specific narratives relating Jesus' call of these women to discipleship may not have been known to the evangelists. In any case, the absence of the title "disciple" in the case of these female followers is a good reminder that one should not assess the functions, activities, or importance of particular persons within a religious group simply by the presence or absence of certain titles or labels.

(ii) A second group of significant adherents or supporters of Jesus' movement did not belong to any of the three concentric circles of followers for the simple reason that they did not literally, physically follow Jesus. The Gospel narratives regularly apply the verb "to follow" only to those adherents who literally followed Jesus around Galilee. Hence it is not by accident that the hospitable Mary and Martha, the repentant Zacchaeus, and the beloved Lazarus are not called disciples in the Gospels, despite their commitment and service to Jesus. They were among the "stay-at-home" supporters, whose aid to the movement was by no means negligible. By gifts of money, food, and lodging, they supplied Jesus' traveling band of disciples with the necessary support network for a period of over two years. One would like to know whether or to what extent this support system was more than purely accidental and haphazard and may have represented conscious planning on the part of Jesus. In any event, the support system reminds us once again that not all of Jesus' adherents were desperately poor. Providing hospitality for Jesus and his disciples when they came to town would have been no small burden and no small achievement. The last glimpse we get of such a fairly well-off sedentary supporter is at the end of the public ministry, when some anonymous Jew in Jerusalem, who must have had a relatively large house with full dining facilities, hosts Jesus and his disciples at his last meal.

In short, the Jesus movement, far from being an amorphous blob of wild-eyed enthusiasts whose apocalyptic expectations excluded any practical planning, betrays intriguing hints of planning and structure, however embryonic. Major religious movements in the ancient or medieval Western world usually got off the ground, spread, and endured long term because somewhere within all the enthusiasm there was a leader or leaders who knew how to organize, how to formulate oral traditions and pass them on, or how to record these traditions in what were to become sacred books. Clearly, the early church grew under such leaders as Peter, James, Stephen, Barnabas, and Paul. What is perhaps not so clear is that, before the Christian church ever got off the ground, the Jesus movement survived and spread between A.D. 28 and 30 because Jesus himself was fairly adept at creating identity badges, embryonic structures, and support systems for his movement within 1st-century Judaism. As we have seen, it was a movement with both parallels and competitors in the Palestine of his day.

IV. JEWISH COMPETITORS IN THE RELIGIOUS AND POLITICAL MARKETPLACE OF PALESTINE

If Jesus and his movement had competitors, what was the prize for which they were competing? Put briefly, it was the acceptance and adherence of the people of Israel—or, put the other way round, it was the power, authority, or influence needed to lead Israel. Around the turn of the era, most ordinary Palestinian Jews did not belong to any of the four "philosophical schools" or "opinion groups" *(haireseis)* mentioned by Josephus (*Ant.* 18.1.2–6 §11–25; cf. *J.W.* 2.8.1–8 §117–66): the Pharisees, the Sadducees, the Essenes (with whom most modern scholars associate Qumran), and the "fourth philosophy" (Jews who resisted direct Roman rule and taxation of Judea in A.D. 6 because such Jews held that God was the only true sovereign of Israel). Jesus lines up against this list of four schools of thought in strikingly different ways.

1. The Fourth Philosophy[8]

While there was no doubt political discontent and social unrest among Palestinian Jews at the time of Jesus—though more so in Roman-ruled Judea than in Herodian-ruled Galilee—there is no evidence of an organized group of armed revolutionaries active during the public ministry of Jesus. What Josephus explicitly refers to as "the fourth philosophy" was a group of Jews who opposed the Romans when the latter converted Judea into an imperial province in A.D. 6 and imposed a census in preparation for taxation. Despite Josephus' desire to connect this group with the revolutionaries of the First Jewish War, there was probably no direct historical link via an ongoing organized movement. In Josephus, the term "Zealots," when used to describe an organized band of armed revolutionaries fighting against Rome, refers to a movement that emerged in Jerusalem ca. A.D. 68. Hence to talk about Jesus' relationship to or sympathy for either the fourth philosophy or the Zealots makes no historical sense. The idea of Jesus as a Zealot or Zealot-sympathizer regularly resurfaces in popular books, which often read more like novels; such novels have no basis in serious scholarship. Jesus' day was not unacquainted with violence and banditry, but organized armed revolt against Rome is not attested during the public ministry.

2. The Essenes and Qumran

Likewise invisible in the four Gospels—but for a different reason—are the esoteric and stringently Law-abiding Essenes, of whom the Qumranites con-stituted a special subset, a radical offshoot, a scribal school, or perhaps a "motherhouse." The basic difference in attitude and lifestyle between the aloof, ascetic Essenes and the gregarious, banquet-loving Jesus suggests from the start that Jesus himself was not an Essene. The Essenes' obsession with details of legal and cultic observances (sabbath, regular lustrations, purity at community meals, a correct calendar), its fierce sectarian dualism that fos-tered hatred of enemies, and its priestly-hierarchical structures contrast sharply with Jesus' lack of concern with or outright rejection of such matters. The similarities that did exist between Jesus and the Essenes can often be ex-plained quite simply: both Jesus and the Essenes were eschatologically minded Palestinian Jews who were nourished by the Jewish Scriptures read in a prophetic light, Jews who were concerned with the renewal of Israel in the end time, and Jews who stood in varying degrees of tension vis-à-vis the priestly authorities controlling the Jerusalem temple. This common seedbed naturally fostered certain similarities between Jesus and the Essenes on par-ticular questions. But they were marked by enormous dissimilarities as well:

(i) In regard to *eschatology:* both Jesus and the Essenes held eschatological hopes shaped by a dialectical tension between an "already" and a "not yet." For the Qumranites in particular, the present time, for all its trials, already al-lowed participation in the life and worship of the angels. It was perhaps to such an angelic existence that individual Qumranites were thought to pass at death. Future hopes for Israel here on earth involved a final war between good and evil, at the end of which the sons of light (the Qumranites, natu-rally) would triumph and enter into a definitive state of salvation. The idea of a general resurrection of the dead, if present at all among Essene hopes, lies only at the margins.

Quite contrary to the puritanical, stringently observant Essenes, the "al-ready" of Jesus' eschatological proclamation was realized amid banquets welcoming disreputable types like toll collectors and sinners into his com-pany. This "already" dimension was also realized, according to Jesus, in his

miracles. The kind of wonders Jesus lists in Matt 11:5 are strikingly paralleled in one fragmentary document at Qumran (4Q521), which speaks of the
future time of the Messiah, a time which, for Jesus, is already present. Essene
messianic hopes are difficult to summarize since they range over a whole
spectrum of messianic figures and/or eschatological prophets. The expectation of an eschatological prophet like Elijah, which was dim at best among
the Essenes, was pivotal to Jesus' self-conception. However, the model of the
Elijah-like prophet was not the only way in which Jesus understood himself.
As Volume Four of *A Marginal Jew* will argue, toward the end of his life,
Jesus apparently also made symbolic claims to Davidic messiahship, an idea
that some of his disciples may have harbored during the public ministry. At
Qumran, when a royal or Davidic messiah appears, he is at times subordi-
nated to a priestly figure. Needless to say, there is no counterpart to such an
idea in Jesus' expectations.

(ii) In regard to the *Jerusalem temple:* rejecting the present state of the
priesthood, calendar, and cult in the temple, the Qumranites longed for the
restoration of a legitimate Zadokite priesthood (i.e., the priesthood preserved in their community), the reintroduction of the solar calendar (i.e.,
their calendar) to regulate the festal seasons, and the use of the correct
hălākâ (i.e., their *hălākâ*) for temple rituals. In all this, they reflected the
priestly origins and governance of their community. Their hopes for the future may have included both an idealized temple in this present age and an
eschatological temple in a new creation. In the meantime, the Qumranites
avoided the defiled temple in Jerusalem; they substituted for its impure worship both their own worship in the company of the angels and their scrupu-
lous practice of the Mosaic Law.

In contrast, Jesus saw no difficulty in attending the great festivals in the
temple and thereby implicitly acknowledging and accepting the ministrations of the priests in control. He thus accepted the Jerusalem temple *in the
present order of things.* Toward the end of his ministry, though, in both
prophetic sayings and a prophetic-symbolic action (the "cleansing" of the
temple), Jesus foretold the temple's destruction. Hence, while the Qumranites refused to use the present temple as they awaited a purified temple they
could control, Jesus used the present temple even as he prophesied the
temple's destruction. Whether Jesus expected some new and better temple in
the literal sense of a physical building or in the metaphorical sense of a renewed Israelite community is unclear.

(iii) In regard to *rules governing behavior:* to a certain degree, Jesus and
the Essenes shared an ethical radicalism that flowed from their intense eschatological expectations. At times this radicalism led to similar positions on in-

dividual questions of morality. Both Jesus and the Essenes tended toward stringent standards and prohibitions in sexual matters. Jesus and at least some Essenes practiced celibacy and yet affirmed monogamous marriage for most people as part of the present order of creation. However, while the Essenes developed detailed rules about sexual behavior, such minute regulations played no significant role in Jesus' teaching. Jesus' stringency in sexual matters clearly appears in his teaching on marriage and divorce. Jesus demanded that marriage be monogamous and indissoluble; consequently, he equated divorce (with remarriage understood as the natural result) with adultery. The Essenes likewise had a negative view of divorce, but it is not certain that they absolutely prohibited it in the present age.

The one truly ascetic practice of Jesus was his celibacy. However, while Jesus himself was celibate, he did not make celibacy a condition for being one of his close followers (witness Simon Peter with his mother-in-law). As noted above, Jesus probably understood his own celibacy as an expression of his total commitment to his role as eschatological prophet proclaiming and inaugurating the kingdom of God. While not all Essenes practiced celibacy, apparently some groups (especially at Qumran) did. Presumably celibacy was a requirement for joining those special groups of Essenes who practiced that type of life in community. The reasons for celibacy among the Essenes would have been similar to Jesus' motivation only in their ultimate eschatological basis. The Essenes' specific reasons would have been quite different: e.g., stringent concern for ritual—and especially priestly—purity in a community that served as a living temple in the present age, worship in the company of the (celibate) angels, or possibly preparation for the final Holy War.

On the question of oaths, both Jesus and the Essenes disapproved of the multiplication of oaths, their frivolous use, and the devious practice of vowing part of one's property to God in order to avoid helping a needy parent or neighbor. Yet the Essenes used solemn oaths as part of their ritual of entrance into the community, and they may also have allowed oaths in other special juridical circumstances. While the heterogeneous material on oaths in the Gospels, especially Matthew, points at different times in different directions, it is likely that the historical Jesus prohibited all oaths (Matt 5:34).

(iv) In regard to *wealth and property:* full members of the Qumran community surrendered all their property to the common fund of the group. Since this regimen was not feasible for Essenes living in settlements scattered throughout Israel, these Essenes practiced not a strict system of holding all goods in common but rather a strict system of charitable giving to a common fund for the needy. Thus, in different ways and different degrees, both the Qumranites and the larger group of Essenes sought to avoid the vast disparities between rich and poor that created gross social imbalance in most of the ancient Mediterranean world.

For his part, Jesus warned repeatedly against the dangers of wealth, which easily became an obstacle to total commitment to God and to acceptance of Jesus' proclamation of the kingdom. In his own life, Jesus' personal stance toward ownership of wealth and property was one of renunciation. He had freely given up his own livelihood, home, and family to proclaim the kingdom of God to all Israel. Accordingly, he had to depend on the hospitality and contributions of his supporters. Similarly, those whom he called to discipleship had to leave home and family at least for an indefinite time, though only once in the Gospels does Jesus explicitly demand that a person called to discipleship sell all he has and give it to the poor. What Jesus demanded of *all* his supporters was a complete trust in God's loving providence, a trust that frees one from anxiety about or enslavement to the false goods of money and possessions. The correlative of this warning to those with possessions is Jesus' concern for the poor.

Yet, as has just been noted, Jesus did not demand that all his supporters surrender all their possessions and become literally, economically poor. If he had, there would have been no Martha and Mary or Mary Magdalene to aid him and his followers. Thus, Jesus did not follow the lead of the Qumranites, who demanded that all their full members give up all their goods to the community. The Qumranites could quite fittingly and literally refer to themselves as "the poor" (e.g., 1QpHab 12:3,6,10). Curiously, despite his renunciation of his home, job, and any regular means of support, the itinerant Jesus never uses the label "poor" of himself and never makes that term the defining title of his movement. Rather, the poor constitute a group about which he is concerned but to whom he does not, in his own eyes or speech, belong.

3. The Sadducees

If there were some intriguing links between Jesus and the Qumranites or the wider group of Essenes because of their similar eschatological perspectives, the same cannot be said of Jesus and the Sadducees, another group with links to the Jewish priesthood. What Jesus shared with the Sadducees was simply mainstream Judaism, including a willingness to participate in the sacrificial worship conducted in the Jerusalem temple under the control of the aristocratic chief priests. Beyond that, Jesus and the Sadducees stood at opposite ends of the spectrum both theologically and socially.

The Sadducees, the mainly aristocratic and largely priestly party centered in Jerusalem, had seen its power eclipsed during the reign of Herod the Great. Direct Roman rule in Judea revived its fortunes, for the Romans preferred to use the native aristocrats of border provinces as tools to control such regions. Though not all aristocrats, wealthy people, or priests belonged to the Saducean party, many did, and a considerable number of the high priests under direct Roman rule were probably Sadducees. Relatively few in number and lacking popular support among the common people, the Sadducees relied on their wealth, their influence in many of the high priestly families (and hence in the running of the temple), and the support of the Roman overlords to keep them in power or at least near the levers of power.

In questions of legal observance, the Sadducees opposed the Pharisees' "traditions of the fathers," which lay outside the written Mosaic Law. Yet the Sadducees themselves had to develop their own set of traditions not explicitly found in Scripture, notably in questions of cult and purity. While often portrayed as rigid conservatives and literalists, the Sadducees enforced the relatively new lunar calendar for temple feasts as opposed to the older solar calendar preserved and championed by the Qumranites. In their disputes with the Pharisees over concrete legal rules of behavior *(hălākôt)*, the Sadducees sometimes took the less rigorous position, sometimes the more rigorous. This variability extended to civil and criminal law as well. In doctrinal matters, the Sadducees were indeed conservative in the sense that they rejected a number of beliefs that had become popular in Judaism around the turn of the era: resurrection of the dead, reward and punishment beyond the grave, eternal life, and the luxuriant angelology and demonology of apocalyptic thought. On these points, Jesus was closer to the innovative Pharisees, to various streams of apocalyptic Judaism alive in Palestine at the time, and, indeed, to many ordinary Jews, among whom these ideas had gained acceptance.

Granted this portrait of the Sadducees, we need not be surprised that they appear very rarely in the narratives of the public ministry and play a major role only once in a Gospel pericope (Mark 12:18–27 parr.).[9] This stands to reason, since Jesus spent most of his time addressing ordinary Jews throughout Galilee and Judea, not a small group of rich aristocrats in Jerusalem. Fittingly, when for the only time in the Gospels Jesus and the Sadducees do clash, the scene is laid in the Jerusalem temple, and the dispute centers on a doctrinal point on which Jesus and the Sadducees would certainly have disagreed: the general resurrection of the dead and eternal life. Reflecting their emphasis on the authority of the five books of Moses, the part of the Jewish Scriptures that was a clearly defined corpus and that practically all Jews accepted as normative, the Sadducees draw upon the law of levirate (Deut 25:5) as they concoct a purposely laughable case of a woman marrying in succession seven brothers, all of whom die one after the other. The Sadducees imply that the marital situation of the woman and her husbands at the resurrection would be a hopeless mess involving the scandalous situation of polyandry. The Sadducees may also be intimating a further point: the very fact that Moses went to such lengths to guarantee a dead man the "immortality" involved in having progeny that would bear his name and continue his line suggests that Moses did not count on any other sort of immortality.

Jesus replies to this argument first by denying the underlying presupposition of the Sadducees (and likewise of some Jews who did hold to a resurrection), namely, that the resurrection of the dead was a return to something like present earthly conditions, however improved and ideal. Jesus instead understands resurrection to involve a basic transformation of human existence where marriage, sexual activity, and procreation no longer have a role. Then, responding to the Sadducees' preference for arguments from the Pentateuch, Jesus cites Exod 3:6 ("I am the God of Abraham . . .") to show that the doctrine of the resurrection of the dead is implied if not directly taught in the Law of Moses. Thus, from redefining the nature of the risen life, Jesus goes on to redefine a key passage of the Torah, Yahweh's appearance to Moses in the burning bush. Jesus asserts—apparently alone among Jewish teachers around the turn of the era—that Exod 3:6 shows that God gives life to the dead. In effect, Jesus, taking up the affirmation (implied in Exod 3:6) that God had chosen the patriarchs and their descendants to be his special people and the implied promise that he would act as their protector and savior, extends that promise beyond liberation from evil in this world to the definitive liberation from evil that is the resurrection of the dead. To deny the resurrection is to deny the very nature of the God of Israel as the God of the living. Hence Jesus concludes his attack on the Sadducees with a biting indictment of the would-be leaders of Israel: "You are very much in error" (Mark 12:27).

It is telling that only this confrontation with the Sadducees and only this particular question posed by them call forth from Jesus an explicit reflection on the general resurrection. Elsewhere in his teaching (e.g., Matt 8:11 par.; Luke 14:14; Matt 11:21–24 par.; 12:41–42 par.; Mark 9:43–47; 14:25), he simply alludes to or presupposes it. However he understood the relation of the general resurrection to the major focus of his preaching, the coming kingdom of God and the restoration of all Israel, Jesus held that the resurrection of the dead was part of the consummation of God's plan for Israel. While Jesus may appeal to Exod 3:6 in his scriptural duel with the Sadducees, the overall picture of his ministry suggests that ultimately he knows the fact of the resurrection on the same grounds that he knows the fact of the coming kingdom of God: he is the eschatological prophet who has direct, authoritative knowledge of God's will and plan for his people. This claim to charismatic authority and knowledge, which basically dispenses with all the traditional channels of religious power and knowledge, could not help but unnerve the Sadducees, who were determined to keep the reins of institutional religious power in Palestinian Judaism firmly in their hands. And Caiaphas was most likely a Sadducee.

4. The Pharisees

In contrast to the Sadducees, the Pharisees, who had once held the reins of political power under some of the Hasmonean monarchs, no longer did so under direct Roman rule. All the more necessary, then, was their involvement with the common people as they tried to edify and persuade when they could no longer coerce. All the more inevitable, then, were Jesus' encounters and debates with the Pharisees rather than with the aristocratic Sadducees and the sectarian Essenes. Jesus and the Pharisees represented the two major religious movements active among the ordinary Jews of Palestine in the late 20s of the 1st century. To be sure, the naming of Pharisees as interlocutors or opponents of Jesus in some Gospel stories may be a secondary accretion, reflecting Christian polemics later on in the century. But multiple attestation of sources and forms, as well as the dynamics of religious competition in Palestinian Judaism in the early 1st century, makes it highly probable that Jesus and the Pharisees did engage in dialogue and debate during the public ministry. The ironic point here is that Jesus' major debating partners during his career had nothing directly to do with the end of his career. Having no political power, the Pharisees were not involved in Jesus' arrest and execution. Indeed, the earliest strata of the Passion Narratives, for all their Christian theology, apologetics, and polemics, never claim that the Pharisees were involved.

But who exactly were the Pharisees? Given the wide diversity of scholarly views today, the quest for the historical Pharisees makes the quest for the historical Jesus look easy.[10] A few major assertions about their origin and development seem fairly certain. Arising during the sectarian and political struggles of the early Hasmonean period, the Pharisees had held power in the early part of the reign of John Hyrcanus (134–104 B.C.) and then again during the reign of Queen Salome Alexandra (76–69). During the latter reign, the Pharisees not only imposed their laws on the nation but also took violent revenge on their political enemies. Quietists and pacifists they were not, nor did they ever become so. The downfall of the Hasmoneans spelled the downfall of the direct political power of the Pharisees. Herod the Great tolerated no rival political power in his kingdom. The best the Pharisees could do was try to wield indirect influence, sometimes by palace intrigues. Already the Pharisees were probably beginning to realize that any future power would have to be indirect, based primarily on their influence and popularity with the common people.

Direct Roman rule of Judea from A.D. 6 onwards spelled a rise in fortunes for the Sadducees, since, as already noted, the Romans preferred to rule in border provinces through local aristocrats. The Pharisees were thus once again left out in the cold. All the more, then, would they have redoubled their efforts among the common people, among whom they enjoyed a reputation for exact knowledge of the Mosaic Law. The Pharisees' indirect access to power would have been broadened if, as some think, they formed part of the retainer class on which the rulers depended to keep the government bureaucracy running day to day. If this was the case, they were probably able at times to persuade the ruling aristocrats to accept their views, particularly since some priests were also Pharisees. A few Pharisees even rose to the higher echelons of power or influence, notably the lawyer Gamaliel I during the early days of Christianity (Acts 5:34) and his son Simeon I, a key member of the moderate coalition government in the early days of the First Jewish War. There was also a Pharisaic priest in the delegation sent by the revolutionary government to relieve Josephus of his command in Galilee. In rare cases, then, the Pharisaic party had direct access to power through prominent individual Pharisees.

The disaster of the First Jewish War, ending in the capture of Jerusalem and the destruction of the temple, brought about the destruction as well of many of the competing groups in pre-70 Judaism. The Pharisees were the only group to emerge relatively intact, with significant numbers and a tradition of learning, and with the common people's respect. After the capture of Jerusalem, the Pharisees joined with other survivors, including various priests and scribes, at the Judean town of Yavneh (Jamnia) on the Mediterranean coast in an attempt to preserve, develop, and adapt pre-70 Jewish legal traditions to the very different post–70 era. This coalescing of various groups inaugurated the early rabbinic movement. The pre-70 Pharisees cannot be simplistically equated with the post–70 rabbis, but they were a major influence on and contributor to the new form of Judaism emerging at Yavneh.

To move beyond these generalizations to a detailed statement of Pharisaic practice and belief is extremely difficult. Our three major sources of information, the NT, Josephus, and the rabbinic literature, are all fraught with problems. With the exception of Paul's epistles, they all date from the post–70 period. Each body of literature is burdened with its own biases and sometimes anachronistic points of view. The Gospels reflect the struggle between nascent Christianity and nascent rabbinic Judaism. Josephus, whose descriptions of the Pharisees are often cited without further ado as sober history, seems to shift his evaluation of the Pharisees from work to work and may actually be lying when he claims at the end of his career to have been a Pharisee for the whole of his adult life. The earliest part of rabbinic literature, the Mishna, was composed almost 200 years after Jesus' ministry.

Even in the mishnaic passages that speak of *pĕrûšîn,* it is by no means clear when this Hebrew term refers to what we mean by Pharisees, who, in any case, are not to be automatically equated with the rabbinic "sages" or "scribes." If we restrict ourselves to those passages in the Mishna and Tosepta where Pharisees and Sadducees are presented as opposing one another on legal questions, we are left with about seven cases in which the Pharisees debate their adversaries on issues like the purity of Scripture scrolls and liquids, the responsibility in civil law of human agents causing injury, the proper way of writing a bill of divorce, the purity of cult apparatus in the temple, and the ability of a daughter to receive an inheritance from her father.

In face of the difficulties that our three sources (the NT, Josephus, and rabbinic literature) raise, it is advisable to focus on cases where at least two of these sources agree on some aspect of the Pharisees. Using this minimalist method, one can affirm six major points about the historical Pharisees:

(i) The Pharisees were a Jewish group with both political and religious interests, active in Palestine from the middle of the 2d century B.C. up until the First Jewish War (A.D. 66–70).

(ii) The Pharisees enjoyed a reputation for their exact or precise interpretation and practice of the Mosaic Law. On the whole, their care about the Mosaic Law led them to be lenient rather than harsh in passing judgment.

(iii) In their disputes with other Jewish groups over the Law, the Pharisees at times championed legal views and practices that they openly admitted were not to be found as such in the written Law of Moses. The Pharisees considered these additional views and practices to be venerable traditions that had been handed down by the "fathers" or the "elders" and to be God's will for all Israel. (One should not identify this embryonic idea of the Law of Moses *plus* the traditions of the fathers with the much more elaborate doctrine of the dual Torah, found fully developed only in the two Talmuds. According to this later doctrine, God gave Moses on Mt. Sinai the dual Torah, which included both the five books written by Moses and the oral Torah, passed down by a chain of oral tradition to the rabbinic sages.) In marked contrast to the Sadducees' attitude toward the common people, the Pharisees in the 1st century A.D. were actively engaged in trying to convince ordinary

Jews to observe Pharisaic traditions voluntarily in their daily lives. Needless to say, the Pharisees were not entirely successful in this endeavor, but they never considered the common people heinous sinners beyond the pale simply because they did not follow Pharisaic practice.

(iv) By using multiple attestation of sources, we can be fairly sure about the legal concerns characteristic of the Pharisees: purity rules about food and vessels containing food and liquids; concern about what does or does not defile hands; purity rules concerning corpses and tombs; the purity of cult apparatus; the various forms of contributions given to the temple and its priests; proper observances of the sabbath and holy days; and marriage and divorce, including the bill of divorce and the grounds for divorce.

(v) While the Pharisees, like other groups, were characterized by their views about legal practice, they also had some characteristic doctrinal stances: (a) As opposed to the Sadducees, the Pharisees held to some form of life beyond the grave and specifically to the resurrection of the dead. (b) Indirectly, from echoes of what Paul the former Pharisee takes for granted as he develops his theology, we may surmise that at least certain Pharisees awaited some sort of Messiah, whose coming was foretold in the Scriptures, provided they were read in a creative, i.e., eschatological and messianic light. Indeed, at least some Pharisees probably shared an apocalyptic vision of salvation history, reaching from Israel's election and reception of the Law to the fulfillment of all the promises contained in the Law and the prophets, including the Messiah and the resurrection of the dead. Within this overarching history of salvation, the Law played a special salvific role.

(vi) A final element of Pharisaic doctrine concerned the interaction between divine providence and human effort. Both were somehow affirmed, though the exact position of the Pharisees is obscured by Josephus' oscillating expositions of the subject.

One must remember that these six distinguishing characteristics, even when put together to form a *Gestalt,* did not necessarily separate Pharisees from mainstream Judaism (à la Qumran), but rather marked them out as a special group within mainstream Judaism. At the same time, the Pharisees did not *constitute* mainstream Judaism (let alone a mythical monolithic or "normative" Judaism), nor were they thought to do so by the common people.[11]

Only after this overview can one begin to appreciate how difficult the question of Jesus' relationship to the Pharisees is. In addition to the problems already noted, we must take into account the redactional tendencies of each evangelist when we try to use the Gospel pericopes that mention the Pharisees. For example, Matthew and Luke tend to introduce references, especially negative references, to the Pharisees into passages where the Pharisees do not appear in Mark. Granted these redactional tendencies of Matthew and Luke, one must allow for the possibility that Mark acted in a similar fashion vis-à-vis his sources. Indeed, Mark's artistic and theological concerns in arranging the Galilean and Jerusalem dispute stories at the two ends of the public ministry make us wary of taking the few cases of a direct dispute between Jesus and the Pharisees as a historical report. In addition, both Matthew and John evince the tendency to make the Pharisees *the* enemy of Jesus during the public ministry. They thus reflect the struggle of the early church with the embryonic rabbinic movement of the post–70 period, anachronistically identified with the Pharisees of Jesus' day. Complicating matters still further is the possibility that the historical pre-70 Pharisees were concentrated in and around Jerusalem or at least in Judea in general, with only a minimal presence in Galilee. It could be the "sacred geography" of Mark's story that necessitates relocating the Pharisees in Galilee, where Mark makes the bulk of Jesus' ministry take place before his fateful (and sole) journey up to Jerusalem toward the end of the Gospel.

As one grapples with these problems, one is reminded of the problem created by the miracle stories in Volume Two of *A Marginal Jew*. The basic fact that Jesus at times interacted or debated with Pharisees enjoys abundant multiple attestation of sources and forms (like the basic fact that Jesus claimed and was thought to work miracles during the public ministry). Beyond this basic fact, as one moves to individual pericopes involving the Pharisees, things become much more murky (as they do with individual miracle stories). One can say at least that certain types of Gospel pericopes that present Jesus interacting with or speaking about the Pharisees enjoy historical verisimilitude because of what we know about the Pharisees from other sources.

1. It is the Pharisees who are presented as the debating partners with Jesus on the issue of divorce—a picture that coheres with debates over the grounds of divorce between the House of Hillel and the House of Shammai. Jesus is presented as opposing the Pharisaic permission of divorce because of his eschatological mind-set: the end time would restore the institution of marriage as the Creator had intended it to be from the beginning, namely, as monogamous and permanent. Such an argument is similar to what we find in Essene literature—though perhaps more radical than the Essene view—and reflects an approach different from the debates between the House of Hillel and the House of Shammai.

2. If Jesus the eschatological prophet were involved in theological clashes with the Pharisees, it is not surprising that the Pharisees would be the object of some of the prophetic woes Jesus pronounced against those who rejected his message.

3. Jesus was certainly a spinner of parables, which often inculcated the reversal of values that the end time would bring. Hence the parable of the Pharisee and the toll collector, often taken as coming from the historical Jesus by students of the parables, would be a prime example of turning on its head the estimation the common people would have had of the highly regarded Pharisees and the despised toll collectors.

4. Granted the polemic in the Gospels against the Pharisees, the criterion of discontinuity or embarrassment argues for the historicity of the rare pericopes in which Jesus receives a sympathetic hearing from individual Pharisees.

Beyond these arguments, there is the general consideration that Jesus sought to address the whole of Israel, not just some special group. If indeed the Pharisees constituted a significant popular movement in the Israel of Jesus' day, and if, unlike the Qumranites, they had not separated themselves from but rather were active among the common people, how could Jesus not have come into contact with them? On many points concerning Israel's present and future, Jesus and the Pharisees would have agreed or at least had much in common. The points on which they would have disagreed included Jesus' particular eschatological scenario, the special place that he gave himself, his ministry, and his miracles in that scenario, and the unusual halakic teachings that flowed from that scenario (e.g., the prohibition of divorce, celibacy as one way of serving the kingdom, the rejection of voluntary fasting, the neglect or rejection on an ad-hoc basis of family obligations and purity rules). Granted the long tradition of fiery denunciation used by Israelite prophets against their opponents, we need not be surprised if Jesus the prophet spoke in similar fashion against his opponents, including the Pharisees. Such verbal attacks by the historical Jesus must not be read as an attack on Judaism from without, as they so often have been read in later Christian history.

From all we have seen, it becomes clear that we must not naively conflate the particular question of Jesus' relation to the Pharisees with the much broader question of Jesus' relation to the Mosaic Law. Gospel stories that narrate a pronouncement of Jesus about the Law might be basically historical while the presence of the Pharisees as the debating partners in the stories might be a later Christian creation. The Pharisees were hardly the only 1st-century group of Palestinian Jews concerned about the Mosaic Law. Jesus' teaching on such topics as divorce and fasting would interest and possibly upset many Jews who were not Pharisees. Hence in a later chapter, distinct from this present consideration of the historical Pharisees, we will have to focus our attention on Jesus' relation to the Mosaic Law, the sacred canopy under which all his particular interactions with other Jews took place. The problem is that "Jesus and the Mosaic Law" is a weighty and far-ranging topic that contains endless puzzles and enigmas within itself. Accordingly, I have decided to save this extremely difficult problem for the fourth and final volume of *A Marginal Jew*, a volume that will grapple with the greatest enigmas surrounding the historical Jesus. I have purposely kept these enigmas to the end of our quest, with the hope that what we have seen in the first three volumes will aid our solution of the four great enigmas pondered in Volume Four.

V. LOOKING AHEAD TO THE FINAL ENIGMAS

Thus, the theme of the final volume of our quest will be "The Enigmas Jesus Posed and Was." The four great enigmas to be considered are the enigma of Jesus' teaching on the Law, the enigmas or riddle-speech of Jesus' parables, the enigmas or riddle-speech of Jesus' self-designations (a better term than "titles"), and the final enigma or riddle of his death. I intentionally put these four great puzzles together, a nonmusical "Enigma Variations," precisely because their enigmatic quality has at times been underplayed or overlooked.

1. For example, the Jewishness of Jesus has sometimes been facilely taken to mean that his relationship to the Mosaic Law is straightforward and unproblematic: Jesus was a Jew who affirmed and observed the Mosaic Law, and that is the end of the matter. While the first part of that affirmation is correct, the understanding of the Mosaic Law and the various stances vis-à-vis the Law in 1st-century Palestine were not quite so simple, as has already been indicated by our survey of the Essenes, Sadducees, and Pharisees. When we descend from generalities to particulars, Jesus' stance vis-à-vis the Law poses a notable enigma.

2. To many readers who are well acquainted with books about the historical Jesus, my decision to reserve a treatment of Jesus' parables to the final volume must seem enigmatic in itself. Surely, from Adolf Jülicher through C. H. Dodd and Joachim Jeremias to Norman Perrin, John Dominic Crossan, and the Jesus Seminar, the parables have been for scholars of every stripe the royal road, the easiest path, the surest access route to the historical Jesus. I beg to differ. Not only are the parables themselves enigmas posed in riddle-speech, their precise relation to the historical Jesus poses an enigma as well.

Faced with the same strict application of the criteria of historicity used for any other Gospel material, many of the parables may not fare as well as some scholars would like to believe.

3. Instead of talking about the "titles of Jesus" (or worse still, "the christological titles of Jesus"), I think it best to understand the ways in which the historical Jesus may have referred to himself (e.g., Son of Man, Son) as enigmatic riddle-speech not unlike the parables. Like the parables, the strange phrases he used to refer to himself were meant to tease the mind of his audience into active thought, to pose uncomfortable questions instead of supplying pat answers.

4. Finally, the precise reason(s) why Jesus' life ended as it did, namely, by crucifixion at the hands of the Roman prefect on the charge of claiming to be King of the Jews, is the starkest, most disturbing, and most central of all the enigmas Jesus posed and was. Any reconstruction of the historical Jesus must end with this enigma and ultimately must be judged adequate or inadequate by its ability to shed light on this enigma. It is to the massive task of unraveling these four great enigmas surrounding the historical Jesus that we will turn our attention in the fourth and final volume of *A Marginal Jew*.

NOTES TO CONCLUSION

[1] This summary and synthesis cannot repeat all the arguments and references to ancient literature and modern scholarship that were presented throughout the three volumes. The interested reader is referred to the relevant sections of the respective volumes. This holds true of minor groups treated in chapter 30 (e.g., the Samaritans, the Herodians) who had little or no contact with the historical Jesus.

[2] For detailed consideration of the historical and theological problems involved in Antipas' second marriage, see Harold W. Hoehner, *Herod Antipas* (SNTSMS 17; Cambridge: Cambridge University, 1972) 131–46, esp. n. 4 on pp. 137–39.

[3] I am not claiming here that all the texts cited go back to the historical Jesus; I simply point out that there is multiple attestation in three strands of Synoptic tradition (Mark, Q, and L) for such antipathy. For a consideration of the texts and their historical value, see Hoehner, *Herod Antipas,* 184–250. Apart from individual texts, the mere fact that Antipas imprisoned and executed Jesus' mentor, John the Baptist, is more than sufficient reason for positing such antipathy.

[4] By this comment I am not excluding the priesthood from spiritual leadership; the priests were still an important part of that leadership. I am rather pointing to the new wave of learned leaders who did not necessarily enjoy status through inherited priesthood or aristocratic birth but who gained influence or respect through their zealous study and practice of the Law.

⁵ The ethnic makeup, predominant culture, and religious orientation of the population of Sepphoris in the early 1st century A.D. remain focal points of debate between those scholars who hold that Sepphoris was mostly if not entirely a Jewish city around the time of Jesus and those who claim that it was a thriving Greco-Roman city with strong Gentile influence. For a defense of the prior view, with which I basically agree, see Mark Chancey and Eric M. Meyers, "How Jewish Was Sepphoris in Jesus' Time?" *BARev* 26/4 (2000) 18–33; see also Tsvika Tsuk, "Bringing Water to Sepphoris," ibid., 34–41; Hanan Eshel and Eric Meyers, "The Pools of Sepphoris—Ritual Baths or Bathtubs?" ibid., 42–49. It is unfortunate that at times in this debate the categories "Gentile" (in the sense of "pagan") and "Hellenistic" (or "Greco-Roman") are used interchangeably.

⁶ I readily grant that scattered cells of disciples or sympathizers of the Baptist continued to exist into the latter part of the 1st century A.D. Both John's Gospel and Acts indicate that Christians had to compete to some degree with them. Interestingly, these two works suggest that the competition was taking place not in Palestine but rather in Asia Minor, a veritable caldron of syncretistic religions. However, there is no positive proof that a structured, coherent movement of the Baptist's followers survived his death and continued into subsequent centuries, as was the case with the Jesus movement evolving into the Christian church. On this, see *A Marginal Jew*, 2. 116–17.

⁷ To be sure, there is the case (reported by Josephus in *J. W.* 6.5.3 §300–3) of a lone prophet named Jesus ben Ananias, active in the years just before the fall of Jerusalem. He prophesied against the temple, was arrested by the priests, and was presented by them to the procurator, who first scourged and then released him when he realized that he was harmless. But the differences between this Jesus and Jesus of Nazareth are significant: (1) By the time of Jesus ben Ananias, the situation in Judea and Jerusalem had deteriorated greatly; the final crisis and revolt were looming. Hence the tensions were much more severe. (2) Still, in the end, despite the accusations of the priests, the procurator decided not to execute Jesus ben Ananias precisely because the lone prophet, perhaps insane, seemed to pose no real threat to those in authority.

⁸ Here I simply summarize what we have seen at length in the treatment of Simon the Cananean (or Zealot) in chapter 27 and more briefly in the treatment of the Zealots in chapter 30.

⁹ When the chief priests and in particular the high priest return in the Passion Narratives, they are not designated as Sadducees, perhaps because their vital role in the arrest and trial of Jesus is not as members of a specific theological school of thought (which is the role of the Sadducees in the debate over the resurrection of the dead) but rather as a governing body acting in tandem with the Roman prefect.

¹⁰ On this point, see my review essay, "The Quest for the Historical Pharisee," 713–22.

¹¹ Here I differ with a basic thesis of Deines' massive work, *Die Pharisäer*.

PALESTINE IN THE TIME OF JESUS

Political Boundaries
A.D. 6–44
Major Roads
Other Roads
■ Cities of the Decapolis
✕ Fortresses

Sarepta · S Y R I A

Mt. Hermon

P a n e a s

· Caesarea Philippi
(Paneas)

Leontes

Tyre

Phoenicia

Ladder
of Tyre

U l a t h a

Gischala ·

G a u l a n i t i s

GALILEE

B a t a n e a

Ptolemais ·

Chorazin
Capernaum ·
· Bethsaida–Julias

Raphana

Cana · Magdala

*Sea of
Galilee*

Mediterranean

Sepphoris ·
Gabae ·

· Tiberias

Hippos ■

■ Dion?

Sea

*Mt.
Carmel*

Nazareth ·
Plain of
Esdrealon

▲ *Mt.
Tabor*
· Nain

Yarmuk

Gadara ·

Abila

Dora ·
Crocodilion ·

Arbela ·

Agrippina ·
Scythopolis ■

Caesarea ·

Narbata ·

Pella ■

D E C A P O L I S

Salim ·
Aenon ·

Jordan

Gerasa ■

S A M A R I A

Sebaste ·
(Samaria)

▲ *Mt. Ebal*
· Sychar

Amathus ·

Plain of Sharon

Mt. Gerizim ▲

Jabbok

Apollonia ·

· Antipatris

Alexandrium ✕

Gadara ·

· Arimathea?

Phasaelis ·

· Joppa

Gophna ·

Ephraim ·

P E R E A

Philadelphia ■

· Lydda

Archelais ·

Jamnia ·
Emmaus
(Nicopolis) ·

Emmaus? ·

Jericho ·
Cyprus ✕
· Bethany

Betharamphtha
(Livias, Julias)

Jerusalem ·

Esbus ·

Azotus ·

Bethlehem ·

Hyrcania ✕

· Qumran

Medeba ·

Ascalon ·

Marisa ·

J U D E A

Herodium ✕

Bethsura ·

· Hebron

Callirrhoe ·
Machaerus ✕

Agrippias ·
· Gaza

Engaddi ·

*Lake
Asphaltitis
(Dead Sea)*

Arnon

I D U M E A
· Bersabe

Masada ✕
Malatha ·
✕

Areopolis ·

Charachmoba ·

N A B A T E A

0   20 miles
0   20 km

648

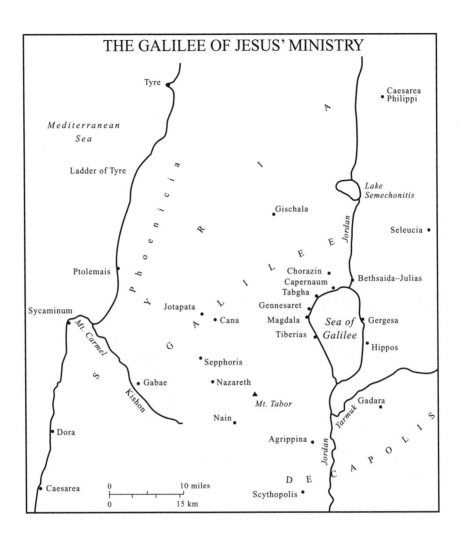

THE GALILEE OF JESUS' MINISTRY

Tyre

Caesarea
Philippi

*Mediterranean
Sea*

P h o e n i c i a

Ladder of Tyre

Lake
Semechonitis

Gischala

Jordan

Seleucia

G A L I L E E

Ptolemais

Chorazin
Capernaum
Tabgha

Bethsaida–Julias

Sycaminum

Jotapata

Gennesaret

Cana

Magdala

Gergesa

Mt. Carmel

Tiberias

*Sea of
Galilee*

Hippos

Kishon

Sepphoris

Gabae

Nazareth

Gadara

▲

Mt. Tabor

Yarmuk

Nain

Dora

Agrippina

Jordan

D E C A P O L I S

Caesarea

0   10 miles

0   15 km

Scythopolis

THE FAMILY OF HEROD THE GREAT

Herod the Great had ten wives. Only the wives and descendants of direct interest to students of the NT are listed here.

b. = born
d. = died
r. = reigned
m. = married
K. = King
E. = Ethnarch
T. = Tetrarch

King Herod the
Great
b. ca. 73 B.C.
d. 4 B.C.

m.

MARIAMME I (Hasmonean) d. 29 B.C.
Aristobulus IV d. 7 B.C.; m. Bernice I

Herod (of Chalcis)
m. Bernice II
r. Chalcis A.D. 41–48 (K.)
d. A.D. 48

Herod Agrippa I
r. tetrarchies of Philip and Lysanias as K.
from A.D. 37—tetrarchy of Antipas
added A.D. 40—Judea and Samaria added
A.D. 41–44
d. A.D. 44

Herodias
m. (1) Herod
(misnamed Philip)*
(2) Herod Antipas

MARIAMME II (misnamed Philip)
Herod (misnamed Philip)
m. Herodias
Salome III
m. Philip

MALTHACE (Samaritan)
Archelaus
r. 4 B.C.–A.D. 6 (E.)

Herod Antipas
m. (1) Daughter of Aretas IV
(Nabatean K.)
(2) Herodias
r. 4 B.C.–A.D. 39 (T.)

CLEOPATRA (of Jerusalem)
Philip
m. Salome III
r. 4 B.C.–A.D. 34 (T.)
d. A.D. 34

*Mark's Gospel confuses Herod, the son of Mariamme II, with Philip; this has led some NT scholars to speak (wrongly) of "Herod Philip" as Herodias' first husband.

THE REGNAL YEARS OF THE ROMAN *PRINCIPES* (EMPERORS)
Compared with the dates of the Prefects/Procurators of Judea, Samaria, and Idumea

OCTAVIAN (AUGUSTUS)	[Prefects]	
31 B.C. (battle of Actium)	Coponius	A.D. 6–9
27 B.C. (assumes title of Augustus)	M. Ambivius	9–12 (?)
A.D. 14 (dies)	Annius Rufus	12–15 (?)
TIBERIUS		
14–37	Valerius Gratus	15–26
	Pontius Pilate	26–36
	Marcellus	36–37
GAIUS (CALIGULA)		
37–41	Marullus	37–41 (?)
CLAUDIUS	[Reign of Agrippa I over the restored	
41–54	kingdom of the Jews, 41–44]	
	[Procurators]	
	C. Cuspius Fadus	44–46
	Tiberius Julius Alexander	46–48
	Ventidius Cumanus	48–52
NERO		
54–68	M. Antonius Felix	52–60 (?)
	Porcius Festus	60–62 (?)
	Lucceius Albinus	62–64
	Gessius Florus	64–66
GALBA, OTHO, VITELLIUS		
(all in 69)		
VESPASIAN	Jewish Revolt	66–70
69–79		

List of Abbreviations

Pss. Sol.   Psalms of Solomon
Sib. Or.   Sibylline Oracles
T. 12 Patr.   Testaments of the Twelve Patriarchs
T. Levi   Testament of Levi
T. Benj.   Testament of Benjamin, etc.
Acts Pil.   Acts of Pilate
Apoc. Pet.   Apocalypse of Peter
Gos. Eb.   Gospel of the Ebionites
Gos. Eg.   Gospel of the Egyptians
Gos. Heb.   Gospel of the Hebrews
Gos. Naass.   Gospel of the Naassenes
Gos. Pet.   Gospel of Peter
Gos. Thom.   Gospel of Thomas
Prot. Jas.   Protevangelium of James
Barn.   Barnabas
1-2 Clem.   1-2 Clement
Did.   Didache
Diogn.   Diognetus
Herm.   Hermas,
    Man.   Mandate
    Sim.   Similitude
    Vis.   Vision
Ign. *Eph.*   Ignatius, Letter to the Ephesians
    Magn.   Ignatius, Letter to the Magnesians
    Phld.   Ignatius, Letter to the Philadelphians
    Pol.   Ignatius, Letter to Polycarp
    Rom.   Ignatius, Letter to the Romans
    Smyrn.   Ignatius, Letter to the Smyrneans
    Trall.   Ignatius, Letter to the Trallians
Mart. Pol.   Martyrdom of Polycarp
Pol. *Phil.*   Polycarp to the Philippians
Bib. Ant.   Ps.-Philo, Biblical Antiquities

3. Abbreviations of Names of Dead Sea Scrolls and Related Texts

CD   Cairo (Genizah text of the) Damascus (Document)
Ḥev   Naḥal Ḥever texts
Mas   Masada texts
Mird   Khirbet Mird texts
Mur   Wadi Murabbaʿat texts
p   Pesher (commentary)
Q   Qumran
1Q, 2Q, 3Q, etc.   Numbered caves of Qumran, yielding written material; followed
      by abbreviation of biblical or apocryphal book
QL   Qumran literature

1QapGen   *Genesis Apocryphon* of Qumran Cave 1

1QH   *Hôdāyôt (Thanksgiving Hymns)* from Qumran Cave 1

1QIsa[a, b]   First or second copy of Isaiah from Qumran Cave 1

1QpHab   *Pesher on Habakkuk* from Qumran Cave 1

1QM   *Milḥāmāh (War Scroll)*

1QS   *Serek hayyaḥad (Rule of the Community, Manual of Discipline)*

1QSa   Appendix A *(Rule of the Congregation)* to 1QS

1QSb   Appendix B *(Blessings)* to 1QS

3Q15   *Copper Scroll* from Qumran Cave 3

4QEn   fragments of *1 Enoch*

4QFlor   *Florilegium* (or *Eschatological Midrashim*) from Qumran Cave 4

4QMess ar   Aramaic "Messianic" text from Qumran Cave 4

4QMMT   fragments of the so-called Halakic Letter

4QpNah   *Pesher on Nahum* from Qumran Cave 4

4QpPs   fragments of a Pesher on various Psalms

4QPrNab   *Prayer of Nabonidus* from Qumran Cave 4

4QTestim   *Testimonia* text from Qumran Cave 4

4QTLev ar[a]   fragments of the so-called Aramaic *Testament of Levi*

4QPhyl   Phylacteries from Qumran Cave 4

11QMelch   *Melchizedek* text from Qumran Cave 11

4QVisSam   *The Vision of Samuel*

4Q246   *Aramaic Apocalypse*

4Q521   *Messianic Apocalpyse*

11QTemple   *The Temple Scroll*

11QtgJob   *Targum of Job* from Qumran Cave 11

4. Targums

Tg. Onq.   *Targum Onqelos*

Tg. Neb.   *Targum of the Prophets*

Tg. Ket.   *Targum of the Writings*

Frg. Tg.   *Fragmentary Targum*

Sam. Tg.   *Samaritan Targum*

Tg. Isa.   *Targum of Isaiah*

Pal. Tgs.   *Palestinian Targums*

Tg. Neof.   *Targum Neofiti*

Tg. Ps.-J.   *Targum Pseudo-Jonathan*

Tg. Yer. I   *Targum Yerušalmi I* *

Tg. Yer. II   *Targum Yerušalmi II* *

Yem. Tg.   *Yemenite Targum*

Tg. Esth. I, II   *First or Second Targum of Esther*

* optional title

5. Abbreviations of Orders and Tractates in Mishnaic and Related Literature

To distinguish the same-named tractates in the Mishna, Tosepta, Babylonian Talmud, and Jerusalem Talmud, we use italicized *m.*, *t.*, *b.*, or *y.* before the title of the tractate. Thus *m. Pe'a* 8:2; *b. Šabb.* 31a; *y. Mak.* 2.31d; *t. Pe'a* 1.4 (Zuck. 18 [= page number of Zuckermandel's edition of the Tosepta]).

'Abot   'Abot
'Arak.   'Arakin
'Abod. Zar.   'Aboda Zara
B. Bat.   Baba Batra
Bek.   Bekorot
Ber.   Berakot
Beṣa   Beṣa (= Yom Ṭob)
Bik.   Bikkurim
B. Meṣ.   Baba Meṣi'a
B. Qam.   Baba Qamma
Dem.   Demai
'Erub.   'Erubin
'Ed.   'Eduyyot
Giṭ.   Giṭṭin
Ḥag.   Ḥagiga
Ḥal.   Ḥalla
Hor.   Horayot
Ḥul.   Ḥullin
Kelim   Kelim
Ker.   Keritot
Ketub.   Ketubot
Kil.   Kil'ayim
Ma'aś.   Ma'aśerot
Mak.   Makkot
Makš.   Makširin (= Mašqin)
Meg.   Megilla
Me'il.   Me'ila
Menaḥ.   Menaḥot
Mid.   Middot
Miqw.   Miqwa'ot
Mo'ed   Mo'ed
Mo'ed Qat.   Mo'ed Qatan
Ma'aś. Š.   Ma'aśer Šeni
Našim   Našim
Nazir   Nazir
Ned.   Nedarim
Neg.   Nega'im

Nez.　Neziqin
Nid.　Niddah
Ohol.　Oholot
ʿOr.　ʿOrla
Para　Para
Peʾa　Peʾa
Pesaḥ.　Pesaḥim
Qinnim　Qinnim
Qidd.　Qiddušin
Qod.　Qodašin
Roš. Haš.　Roš Haššana
Sanh.　Sanhedrin
Šabb.　Šabbat
Šeb.　Šebiʿit
Šebu.　Šebuʿot
Šeqal.　Šeqalim
Soṭa　Soṭa
Sukk.　Sukka
Taʿan.　Taʿanit
Tamid　Tamid
Tem.　Temura
Ter.　Terumot
Ṭohar.　Ṭoharot
Ṭ. Yom　Ṭebul Yom
ʿUq.　ʿUqṣin
Yad.　Yadayim
Yebam.　Yebamot
Yoma　Yoma (= Kippurim)
Zabim　Zabim
Zebaḥ　Zebaḥim
Zer.　Zeraʿim

6. ABBREVIATIONS OF OTHER RABBINIC WORKS

ʾAbot R. Nat.　ʾAbot de Rabbi Nathan
ʾAg. Ber.　ʾAggadat Berešit
Bab.　Babylonian
Bar.　Baraita
Der. Er. Rab.　Derek Ereṣ Rabba
Der. Er. Zuṭ.　Derek Ereṣ Zuṭa
Gem.　Gemara
Kalla　Kalla
Mek.　Mekilta
Midr.　Midraš; cited with usual abbreviation for biblical book; but *Midr. Qoh.*
　　　= *Midraš Qohelet*

Pal. Palestinian
Pesiq. R. Pesiqta Rabbati
Pesiq. Rab. Kah. Pesiqta de Rab Kahana
Pirqe R. El. Pirqe Rabbi Eliezer
Rab. Rabbah (following abbreviation for biblical book: Gen. Rab. [with periods]
        = Genesis Rabbah)
Ṣem. Ṣemaḥot
Sipra Sipra
Sipre Sipre
Sop. Soperim
S. 'Olam Rab. Seder 'Olam Rabbah
Talm. Talmud
Yal. Yalquṭ

7. Abbreviations of Nag Hammadi Tractates

Acts Pet. 12 Apost. Acts of Peter and the Twelve Apostles
Allogenes Allogenes
Ap. Jas. Apocryphon of James
Ap. John Apocryphon of John
Apoc. Adam Apocalypse of Adam
1 Apoc. Jas. First Apocalypse of James
2 Apoc. Jas. Second Apocalypse of James
Apoc. Paul Apocalypse of Paul
Apoc. Pet. Apocalypse of Peter
Asclepius Asclepius 21–29
Auth. Teach. Authoritative Teaching
Dial. Sav. Dialogue of the Savior
Disc. 8–9 Discourse on the Eighth and Ninth
Ep. Pet. Phil. Letter of Peter to Philip
Eugnostos Eugnostos the Blessed
Exeg. Soul Exegesis on the Soul
Gos. Eg. Gospel of the Egyptians
Gos. Phil. Gospel of Philip
Gos. Thom. Gospel of Thomas
Gos. Truth Gospel of Truth
Great Pow. Concept of our Great Power
Hyp. Arch. Hypostasis of the Archons
Hypsiph. Hypsiphrone
Interp. Know. Interpretation of Knowledge
Marsanes Marsanes
Melch. Melchizedek
Norea Thought of Norea
On Bap. A On Baptism A
On Bap. B On Baptism B

On Bap. C On Baptism C
On Euch. A On the Eucharist A
On Euch. B On the Eucharist B
Orig. World On the Origin of the World
Paraph. Shem Paraphrase of Shem
Pr. Paul Prayer of the Apostle Paul
Pr. Thanks. Prayer of Thanksgiving
Sent. Sextus Sentences of Sextus
Soph. Jes. Chr. Sophia of Jesus Christ
Steles Seth Three Steles of Seth
Teach. Silv. Teachings of Silvanus
Testim. Truth Testimony of Truth
Thom. Cont. Book of Thomas the Contender
Thund. Thunder, Perfect Mind
Treat. Res. Treatise on Resurrection
Treat. Seth Second Treatise of the Great Seth
Tri. Trac. Tripartite Tractate
Trim. Prot. Trimorphic Protennoia
Val. Exp. A Valentinian Exposition
Zost. Zostrianos

8. Works of Josephus

Ag. Ap. Against Apion
Ant. Jewish Antiquities
J.W. The Jewish War

9. Abbreviations of Commonly Used Periodicals, Reference Works, and Serials

(Titles not found in this list are written out in full. Titles of periodicals and books are italicized, but titles of series are set in roman characters, as are acronyms of authors' names when they are used as sigla.) Short, one-word titles not on this list are not abbreviated.

AAS Acta apostolicae sedis
AASOR Annual of the American Schools of Oriental Research
AB Anchor Bible
AcOr Acta orientalia
ACW Ancient Christian Writers
AfO Archiv für Orientforschung
AGJU Arbeiten zur Geschichte des antiken Judentums und des Urchistentums
AH F. Rosenthal, *An Aramaic Handbook*
AJA American Journal of Archaeology
AJBA Australian Journal of Biblical Archaeology
AJP American Journal of Philology

AJSL   *American Journal of Semitic Languages and Literature*
AJT   *American Journal of Theology*
ALBO   Analecta lovaniensia biblica et orientalia
ALGHJ   Arbeiten zur Literatur und Geschichte des hellenistischen Judentums
AnBib   Analecta biblica
ANEP   J. B. Pritchard (ed.), *Ancient Near East in Pictures*
ANESTP   J. B. Pritchard (ed.), *Ancient Near East Supplementary Texts and Pictures*
ANET   J. B. Pritchard (ed.), *Ancient Near Eastern Texts*
Ang   *Angelicum*
AnOr   Analecta orientalia
ANQ   *Andover Newton Quarterly*
ANTF   Arbeiten zur neutestamentlichen Textforschung
ANRW   *Aufstieg und Niedergang der römischen Welt*
AOAT   Alter Orient und Altes Testament
AOS   American Oriental Series
AP   J. Marouzeau (ed.)., *L'Année philologique*
APOT   R. H. Charles (ed.), *Apocrypha and Pseudepigrapha of the Old Testament*
Arch   *Archaeology*
ARW   *Archiv für Religionswissenschaft*
ASNU   Acta seminarii neotestamentici upsaliensis
ASOR   American Schools of Oriental Research
ASS   *Acta sanctae sedis*
AsSeign   *Assemblées du Seigneur*
ASSR   *Archives des sciences sociales des religions*
ASTI   *Annual of the Swedish Theological Institute*
ATAbh   Alttestamentliche Abhandlungen
ATANT   Abhandlungen zur Theologie des Alten und Neuen Testaments
AtBib   H. Grollenberg, *Atlas of the Bible*
ATD   Das Alte Testament Deutsch
ATR   *Anglican Theological Review*
Aug   *Augustinianum*
AusBR   *Australian Biblical Review*
AUSS   *Andrews University Seminary Studies*
BA   *Biblical Archaeologist*
BAC   Biblioteca de autores cristianos
BAGD   W. Bauer, W. F. Arndt, F. W. Gingrich, and F. W. Danker, *Greek-English Lexicon of the NT*
BAR   *Biblical Archaelogist Reader*
BARev   *Biblical Archaeology Review*
BASOR   *Bulletin of the American Schools of Oriental Research*
BBB   Bonner biblische Beiträge
BBET   Beiträge zur biblischen Exegese und Theologie
BCSR   *Bulletin of the Council on the Study of Religion*
BDB   F. Brown, S. R. Driver, and C. A. Briggs, *Hebrew and English Lexicon of the Old Testament*

BDF   F. Blass, A. Debrunner, and R. W. Funk, *A Greek Grammar of the NT*
BDR   F. Blass, A. Debrunner, and F. Rehkopf, *Grammatik des neutestamentlichen Griechisch*
BeO   Bibbia e oriente
BETL   Bibliotheca ephemeridum theologicarum lovaniensium
BEvT   Beiträge zur evangelischen Theologie
BFCT   Beiträge zur Förderung christlicher Theologie
BGBE   Beiträge zur Geschichte der biblischen Exegese
BHEAT   Bulletin d'histoire et d'exégèse de l'Ancien Testament
BHH   B. Reicke and L. Rost (eds.), Biblisch-Historisches Handwörterbuch
BHK   R. Kittel, Biblia hebraica
BHS   Biblia hebraica stuttgartensia
BHT   Beiträge zur historischen Theologie
Bib   Biblica
BibB   Biblische Beiträge
BibBh   Bible bhashyam
BibLeb   Bibel und Leben
BibOr   Biblica et orientalia
BibS(F)   Biblische Studien (Freiburg, 1895–)
BibS(N)   Biblische Studien (Neukirchen, 1951–)
BIES   Bulletin of the Israel Exploratory Society (= Yediot)
BIFAO   Bulletin de l'institut français d'archéologie orientale
Bijdr   Bijdragen
BIOSCS   Bulletin of the International Organization for Septuagint and Cognate Studies
BJPES   Bulletin of the Jewish Palestine Exploration Society
BJRL   Bulletin of the John Rylands University Library of Manchester
BK   Bibel und Kirche
BKAT   Biblischer Kommentar: Altes Testament
BLit   Bibel und Liturgie
BN   Biblische Notizen
BO   Bibliotheca orientalis
BR   Biblical Research
BSac   Bibliotheca Sacra
BSOAS   Bulletin of the School of Oriental (and African) Studies
BT   The Bible Translator
BTB   Biblical Theology Bulletin
BTS   Bible et terre sainte
BurH   Buried History
BVC   Bible et vie chrétienne
BWANT   Beiträge zur Wissenschaft vom Alten und Neuen Testament
ByF   Biblia y Fe
BZ   Biblische Zeitschrift
BZAW   Beihefte zur *ZAW*
BZNW   Beihefte zur *ZNW*
BZRGG   Beihefte zur *ZRGG*

CAH   Cambridge Ancient History
CahEv   Cahiers évangile
CahRB   Cahiers de la Revue biblique
Cah Théol   Cahiers théologiques
CAT   Commentaire de l'Ancien Testament
CB   Cultura bíblica
CBQ   Catholic Biblical Quarterly
CBQMS   Catholic Biblical Quarterly—Monograph Series
CC   Corpus christianorum
CCath   Corpus catholicorum
CH   Church History
CHR   Catholic Historical Review
CIG   Corpus inscriptionum graecarum
CII   Corpus inscriptionum iudai carum
CIL   Corpus inscriptionum latinarum
CIS   Corpus inscriptionum semiticarum
CJ   Classical Journal
CJT   Canadian Journal of Theology
CNT   Commentaire du Nouveau Testament
ConB   Coniectanea biblica
ConBNT   Coniectanea biblica, New Testament
ConBOT   Coniectanea biblica, Old Testament
ConNT   Coniectanea neotestamentica
CP   Classical Philology
CQ   Church Quarterly
CQR   Church Quarterly Review
CRAIBL   Comptes rendus de l'académie des inscriptions et belles-lettres
CRINT   Compendia rerum iudaicarum ad Novum Testamentum
CSCO   Corpus scriptorum christianorum
CSEL   Corpus scriptorum ecclesiasticorum latinorum
CTJ   Calvin Theological Journal
CTM   Concordia Theological Monthly (or CTM)
CTQ   Concordia Theological Quarterly
CurTM   Currents in Theology and Mission
DACL   Dictionnaire d'archéologie chrétienne et de liturgie
DBSup   Dictionnaire de la Bible, Supplément
DJD   Discoveries in the Judaean Desert
DRev   Downside Review
DS   Denzinger-Schönmetzer, *Enchiridion symbolorum*
DTC   Dictionnaire de théologie catholique
EBib   Études bibliques
EDB   L. F. Hartman (ed.), Encyclopedic Dictionary of the Bible
EHAT   Exegetisches Handbuch zum Alten Testament
EKKNT   Evangelisch-katholischer Kommentar zum Neuen Testament
EKL   Evangelisches Kirchenlexikon
EncJud   Encyclopedia Judaica (1971)

EnchBib   *Enchiridion biblicum*
ErIsr   Eretz Israel
ErJb   *Eranos Jahrbuch*
EstBib   *Estudios bíblicos*
EstEcl   *Estudios eclesiásticos*
EstTeol   *Estudios teológicos*
ETL   *Ephemerides theologicae lovanienses*
ETR   *Études théologiques et religieuses*
EvK   *Evangelische Kommentare*
EvQ   *Evangelical Quarterly*
EvT   *Evangelische Theologie*
EWNT   H. Balz and G. Schneider (eds.), *Exegetisches Wörterbuch zum Neuen Testament*
ExpTim   *Expository Times*
FB   Forschung zur Bibel
FBBS   Facet Books, Biblical Series
FC   Fathers of the Church
FRLANT   Forschungen zur Religion und Literatur des Alten und Neuen Testaments
GAT   Grundrisse zum Alten Testament
GCS   Griechische christliche Schriftsteller
GKB   Gesenius-Kautzsch-Bergsträsser, *Hebräische Grammatik*
GKC   *Gesenius' Hebrew Grammar*, ed. E. Kautzsch, tr. A. E. Cowley
GNT   Grundrisse zum Neuen Testament
GRBS   *Greek, Roman, and Byzantine Studies*
Greg   *Gregorianum*
GTA   Göttinger theologische Arbeiten
GTJ   *Grace Theological Journal*
HALAT   W. Baumgartner et al., *Hebräisches und aramäisches Lexikon zum Alten Testament*
HAT   Handbuch zum Alten Testament
HDR   Harvard Dissertations in Religion
HeyJ   *Heythrop Journal*
HibJ   *Hibbert Journal*
HKAT   Handkommentar zum Alten Testament
HKNT   Handkommentar zum Neuen Testament
HNT   Handbuch zum Neuen Testament
HNTC   Harper's NT Commentaries
HR   *History of Religions*
HSM   Harvard Semitic Monographs
HSS   Harvard Semitic Studies
HTKNT   Herders theologischer Kommentar zum Neuen Testament
HTR   *Harvard Theological Review*
HTS   Harvard Theological Studies
HUCA   *Hebrew Union College Annual*
HUT   Hermeneutische Untersuchungen zur Theologie

IB   Interpreter's Bible
IBS   Irish Biblical Studies
ICC   International Critical Commentary
IDB   G. A. Buttrick (ed.), Interpreter's Dictionary of the Bible
IDBSup   Supplementary volume to *IDB*
IEJ   Israel Exploration Journal
Int   Interpretation
IOS   Israel Oriental Studies
ITQ   Irish Theological Quarterly
JA   Journal asiatique
JAAR   Journal of the American Academy of Religion
JAC   Jahrbuch für Antike und Christentum
JAL   Jewish Apocryphal Literature
JANESCU   Journal of the Ancient Near Eastern Society of Columbia University
JAOS   Journal of the American Oriental Society
JAS   Journal of Asian Studies
JB   A. Jones (ed.), Jerusalem Bible
JBC   R. E. Brown et al. (eds.), The Jerome Biblical Commentary
JBL   Journal of Biblical Literature
JBR   Journal of Bible and Religion
JDS   Judean Desert Studies
JEH   Journal of Ecclesiastical History
JEOL   Jaarbericht . . . ex oriente lux
JES   Journal of Ecumenical Studies
JETS   Journal of the Evangelical Theological Society
JHNES   Johns Hopkins Near Eastern Studies
JHS   Journal of Hellenic Studies
JJS   Journal of Jewish Studies
JMES   Journal of Middle Eastern Studies
JNES   Journal of Near Eastern Studies
JPOS   Journal of the Palestine Oriental Society
JPSV   Jewish Publication Society Version
JQR   Jewish Quarterly Review
JQRMS   Jewish Quarterly Review Monograph Series
JR   Journal of Religion
JRelS   Journal of Religious Studies
JRH   Journal of Religious History
JRS   Journal of Roman Studies
JRT   Journal of Religious Thought
JSHRZ   Jüdische Schriften aus hellenistisch-römischer Zeit
JSJ   Journal for the Study of Judaism in the Persian, Hellenistic and Roman Periods
JSNT   Journal for the Study of the New Testament
JSNTSup   Journal for the Study of the New Testament—Supplement Series
JSOT   Journal for the Study of the Old Testament
JSOTSup   Journal for the Study of the Old Testament—Supplement Series

JSS *Journal of Semitic Studies*
JSSR *Journal for the Scientific Study of Religion*
JTC *Journal for Theology and the Church*
JTS *Journal of Theological Studies*
Judaica *Judaica: Beiträge zum Verständnis . . .*
KAT E. Sellin (ed.), Kommentar zum A. T.
KB L. Koehler and W. Baumgartner, *Lexicon in Veteris Testamenti libros*
KD *Kerygma und Dogma*
KJV *King James Version*
KlT Kleine Texte
LB *Linguistica biblica*
LCC Library of Christian Classics
LCL Loeb Classical Library
LCQ *Lutheran Church Quarterly*
LD Lectio divina
LLAVT E. Vogt, *Lexicon linguae aramaicae Veteris Testamenti*
LPGL G. W. H. Lampe, *Patristic Greek Lexicon*
LQ *Lutheran Quarterly*
LR *Lutherische Rundschau*
LS *Louvain Studies*
LSJ Liddell-Scott-Jones, *Greek-English Lexicon*
LTK *Lexikon für Theologie und Kirche*
LTP *Laval théologique et philosophique*
LumVie *Lumière et vie*
LW *Lutheran World*
McCQ *McCormick Quarterly*
MDB *Le monde de la Bible*
MDOG Mitteilungen der deutschen Orient-Gesellschaft
MeyerK H. A. W. Meyer, Kritisch-exegetischer Kommentar über das Neue
        Testament
MGWJ *Monatsschrift für Geschichte und Wissenschaft des Judentums*
MM J. H. Moulton and G. Milligan, *The Vocabulary of the Greek Testament*
MNTC Moffatt NT Commentary
MPAIBL Mémoires présentés à l'académie des inscriptions et belles-lettres
MScRel *Mélanges de science religieuse*
MTZ *Münchener theologische Zeitschrift*
Mus *Muséon*
MUSJ *Mélanges de l'université Saint-Joseph*
NAB *New American Bible*
NCB New Century Bible
NCCHS R. D. Fuller et al. (eds.), *New Catholic Commentary on Holy Scripture*
NCE M. R. P. McGuire et al. (eds.), *New Catholic Encyclopedia*
NEB *New English Bible*
Neot *Neotestamentica*
NFT New Frontiers in Theology

NHS   Nag Hammadi Studies
NICNT   New International Commentary on the New Testament
NICOT   New International Commentary on the Old Testament
NIV   New International Version
NJBC   New Jerome Biblical Commentary
NJV   New Jewish Version
NKZ   Neue kirchliche Zeitschrift
NovT   Novum Testamentum
NovTSup   Novum Testamentum, Supplements
NRT   La nouvelle revue théologique
NTA   New Testament Abstracts
NTAbh   Neutestamentliche Abhandlungen
NTD   Das Neue Testament Deutsch
NTF   Neutestamentliche Forschungen
NTS   New Testament Studies
NTTS   New Testament Tools and Studies
Numen   Numen: International Review for the History of Religions
OBO   Orbis biblicus et orientalis
OIP   Oriental Institute Publications
OLP   Orientalia lovaniensia periodica
OLZ   Orientalistische Literaturzeitung
Or   Orientalia (Rome)
OrAnt   Oriens antiquus
OrChr   Oriens christianus
OrSyr   L'Orient syrien
OTA   Old Testament Abstracts
OTL   Old Testament Library
PAAJR   Proceedings of the American Academy for Jewish Research
PCB   M. Black and H. H. Rowley (eds.), *Peake's Commentary on the Bible*
PEFQS   Palestine Exploration Fund, Quarterly Statement
PEQ   Palestine Exploration Quarterly
PG   J. Migne, Patrologia graeca
PGM   K. Preisendanz (ed.), Papyri graecae magicae
Phil   Philologus
PJ   Palästina-Jahrbuch
PL   J. Migne, Patrologia latina
PO   Patrologia orientalis
PSB   Princeton Seminary Bulletin
PSTJ   Perkins School of Theology Journal
PTMS   Pittsburgh Theological Monograph Series
PVTG   Pseudepigrapha Veteris Testamenti graece
PW   Pauly-Wissowa, *Real-Encyclopädie der klassichen Altertumswissenschaft*
PWSup   Supplements to PW
QD   Quaestiones disputatae
QDAP   Quarterly of the Department of Antiquities in Palestine

RAC   Reallexikon für Antike und Christentum
RANE   Records of the Ancient Near East
RArch   Revue archéologique
RB   Revue biblique
RCB   Revista de cultura bíblica
RE   Realencyclopädie für protestantische Theologie und Kirche
REA   Revue des études anciennes
RechBib   Recherches bibliques
REJ   Revue des études juives
RelS   Religious Studies
RelSoc   Religion and Society
RelSRev   Religious Studies Review
RES   Répertoire d'épigraphie sémitique
ResQ   Restoration Quarterly
RevExp   Review and Expositor
RevistB   Revista bíblica
RevQ   Revue de Qumran
RevScRel   Revue des sciences religieuses
RevSem   Revue sémitique
RGG   Religion in Geschichte und Gegenwart
RHE   Revue d'histoire ecclésiastique
RHPR   Revue d'historie et de philosophie religieuses
RHR   Revue de l'histoire des religions
RIDA   Revue internationale des droits de l'antiquité
RivB   Rivista biblica
RNT   Regensburger Neues Testament
RQ   Römische Quartalschrift für christliche Altertumskunde und Kirchenge-
       schichte
RR   Review of Religion
RRef   La revue reformée
RSO   Rivista degli studi orientali
RSPT   Revue des sciences philosophiques et théologiques
RSR   Recherches de science religieuse
RSV   Revised Standard Version
RTL   Revue théologique de Louvain
RTP   Revue de théologie et de philosophie
RUO   Revue de l'université d'Ottawa
RV   Revised Version
SacEr   Sacris erudiri
SANT   Studien zum Alten und Neuen Testament
SB   Sources bibliques
SBA   Studies in Biblical Archaeology
SBAW   Sitzungsberichte der bayerischen Akademie der Wissenschaften
SBB   Stuttgarter biblische Beiträge
SBFLA   Studii biblici franciscani liber annuus

SBJ   *La sainte bible de Jérusalem*
SBLASP   Society of Biblical Literature Abstracts and Seminar Papers
SBLDS   SBL Dissertation Series
SBLMasS   SBL Masoretic Studies
SBLMS   SBL Monograph Series
SBLSBS   SBL Sources for Biblical Study
SBLSCS   SBL Septuagint and Cognate Studies
SBLTT   SBL Texts and Translations
SBM   Stuttgarter biblische Monographien
SBS   Stuttgarter Bibelstudien
SBT   Studies in Biblical Theology
SC   Sources chrétiennes
ScEccl   *Sciences ecclésiastiques*
ScEs   *Science et esprit*
SCHNT   Studia ad corpus hellenisticum Novi Testamenti
SCR   *Studies in Comparative Religion*
Scr   *Scripture*
ScrB   *Scripture Bulletin*
ScrHier   Scripta hierosolymitana
SD   Studies and Documents
SE   Studia Evangelica I, II, III, etc. (= TU 73 [1959], 87 [1964], 88 [1964], 102
         [1968], 103 [1968], 112 [1973])
Sem   *Semitica*
SHT   Studies in Historical Theology
SJ   Studia judaica
SJLA   Studies in Judaism in Late Antiquity
SJT   *Scottish Journal of Theology*
SMSR   *Studi e materiali di storia delle religioni*
SNT   Studien zum Neuen Testament
SNTSMS   Society for New Testament Studies Monograph Series
SO   Symbolae osloenses
SOTSMS   Society for Old Testament Study Monograph Series
SP   J. Coppens et al. (eds.), *Sacra pagina*
SPap   *Studia papyrologica*
SPAW   Sitzungsberichte der preussischen Akademie der Wissenschaften
SPB   Studia postbiblica
SPC   *Studiorum paulinorum congressus internationalis catholicus 1961* (2 vols.)
SR   *Studies in Religion/Sciences religieuses*
SSS   Semitic Study Series
ST   *Studia theologica*
STANT   Studien zum Alten und Neuen Testament
STDJ   Studies on the Texts of the Desert of Judah
Str-B   [H. Strack and] P. Billerbeck, *Kommentar zum Neuen Testament*
StudNeot   Studia neotestamentica
StudOr   Studia orientalia

SUNT   Studien zur Umwelt des Neuen Testaments
SVTP   Studia in Veteris Testamenti pseudepigrapha
SymBU   Symbolae biblicae upsalienses
TAPA   *Transactions of the American Philological Association*
TBei   *Theologische Beiträge*
TBl   *Theologische Blätter*
TBü   Theologische Bücherei
TBT   *The Bible Today*
TCGNT   B. M. Metzger, *A Textual Commentary on the Greek New Testament*
TD   *Theology Digest*
TDNT   G. Kittel and G. Friedrich (eds.), *Theological Dictionary of the New Testament*
TDOT   G. J. Botterweck and H. Ringgren (eds.), *Theological Dictionary of the Old Testament*
TextsS   Texts and Studies
TF   *Theologische Forschung*
TGl   *Theologie und Glaube*
THKNT   Theologischer Handkommentar zum Neuen Testament
ThStud   *Theologische Studien*
TLZ   *Theologische Literaturzeitung*
TP   *Theologie und Philosophie*
TPQ   *Theologisch-Praktische Quartalschrift*
TQ   *Theologische Quartalschrift*
TRE   *Theologische Realenzyklopädie*
TRev   *Theologische Revue*
TRu   *Theologische Rundschau*
TS   *Theological Studies*
TSK   *Theologische Studien und Kritiken*
TToday   *Theology Today*
TTZ   *Trierer theologische Zeitschrift*
TU   Texte und Untersuchungen
TWAT   G. J. Botterweck and H. Ringgren (eds.), *Theologisches Wörterbuch zum Alten Testament*
TWNT   G. Kittel and G. Friedrich (eds.), *Theologisches Wörterbuch zum Neuen Testament*
TynBul   *Tyndale Bulletin*
TZ   *Theologische Zeitschrift*
UBSGNT   United Bible Societies *Greek New Testament*
UNT   Untersuchungen zum Neuen Testament
USQR   *Union Seminary Quarterly Review*
VC   *Vigiliae christianae*
VCaro   *Verbum caro*
VD   *Verbum domini*
VE   *Vox evangelica*
VF   *Verkündigung und Forschung*

VKGNT   K. Aland (ed.), *Vollständige Konkordanz zum griechischen Neuen Testament*

VP   *Vivre et penser* (= *RB* 1941–44)

VS   Verbum salutis

VSpir   *Vie spirituelle*

VT   *Vetus Testamentum*

VTSup   Vetus Testamentum, Supplements

WDB   *Westminster Dictionary of the Bible*

WHAB   *Westminster Historical Atlas of the Bible*

WHJP   World History of the Jewish People

WMANT   Wissenschaftliche Monographien zum Alten und Neuen Testament

WO   *Die Welt des Orients*

WTJ   *Westminster Theological Journal*

WUNT   Wissenschaftliche Untersuchungen zum Neuen Testament

WVDOG   Wissenschaftliche Veröffentlichungen der deutschen Orientgesellschaft

WZKM   *Wiener Zeitschrift für die Kunde des Morgenlandes*

WZKSO   *Wiener Zeitschrift für die Kunde Süd- und Ostasiens*

ZAW   *Zeitschrift für die alttestamentliche Wissenschaft*

ZDMG   *Zeitschrift der deutschen morgenländischen Gesellschaft*

ZDPV   *Zeitschrift des deutschen Palästina-Vereins*

ZHT   *Zeitschrift für historische Theologie*

ZKG   *Zeitschrift für Kirchengeschichte*

ZKT   *Zeitschrift für katholische Theologie*

ZMR   *Zeitschrift für Missionskunde und Religionswissenschaft*

ZNW   *Zeitschrift für die neutestamentliche Wissenschaft*

ZRGG   *Zeitschrift für Religions- und Geistesgeschichte*

ZTK   *Zeitschrift für Theologie und Kirche*

ZWT   *Zeitschrift für wissenschaftliche Theologie*

10. MISCELLANEOUS ABBREVIATIONS

LXX   The Septuagint

MT   Masoretic Text

NT   New Testament

OT   Old Testament

par(r).   parallel(s) in the Gospels

Vg   The Vulgate

VL   Vetus Latina (Old Latin)

‖   two pericopes (often in the Q document) that are basically parallel, though possibly with some differences in wording

Scripture Index

671

Author Index

Abegg, Martin G., 574
Abogunrin, S. O., 268
Abrahams, L., 344
Achtemeier, Paul J., 270, 444
Agnew, Francis H., 164, 192, 196
Agua, A. del, 272
Aland, Barbara, 101
Aland, Kurt, 101
Albright, William Foxwell, 350
Allegro, John Mark, 490, 571
Allison, Dale C., xiv, 3, 13, 102, 172, 253, 272, 486, 589
Alt, Albrecht, 478
Ammassari, Antonio, 468
Anderson, Robert T., 594, 599
Arav, Rami, 254
Arbeitman, Yoël, 259
Archer, Léonie J., 119
Attridge, Harold W., 364, 383
Augsten, Monica, 123
Aune, David E., 487
Aus, Roger D., 265
Avery-Peck, Alan J., 344, 345, 377, 594

Backhaus, Knut, 341
Bacon, B. W., 260, 610, 611
Baeck, Leo, 344, 366, 371, 382
Baker, Aelred, 123
Baker, William R., 582

Balz, Horst, 184
Bammel, Ernst, 256, 444
Baron, S. W., 444, 462
Barrera, Julio Trebolle, 578, 580, 592
Barrett, C. K., 191, 260, 265, 356, 456, 474, 603
Barth, Gerhard, 359
Bartina, Sebastián, 468
Barton, Stephen C., 83
Basser, Herbert W., 272
Bauer, Johannes B., 100
Bauer, Walter, 101, 102, 166, 465
Baumbach, Günther, 352, 354, 355, 444, 468, 487
Baumgarten, Albert I., 343, 347, 348, 351, 353, 358, 359, 366, 370, 382, 570, 578, 582, 583, 584
Baumgarten, Joseph M., 95, 578, 586, 592
Beare, F. W., 184, 185, 186
Beattie, D. R. G., 261
Becker, Jürgen, 3, 13, 258, 382, 463
Beckwith, Roger T., 343, 444
Beilner, Wolfgang, 385
Belle, Gilbert van, 112
Bennett, W. J., 610, 612
Berger, Klaus, 571
Bernard, J. H., 265
Bernstein, Moshe, 578, 591, 592, 593
Besch, Bernt, 592

684

Subject Index